Principles of Computer Hardware

D1354811

226 271

I dedicate this edition to all those who have helped me run the IEEE Computer Society's International Design Competition since 2001. In particular, I express my gratitude to the following who have become my friends and mentors.

Andy Bernat
Simon Ellis
Jerry Engle
Robert Graham
David Hennage
Ivan Joseph
Anne Marie Kelly
Kathy Land
Mike Lutz
Fernando Maymi
Stacy Saul
Deborah Scherrer
Janie Schwark
Steve Seidman

PRINCIPLES OF
COMPUTER
HARDWARE

Alan Clements

School of Computing
University of Teesside

Fourth Edition

NORWICH CITY COLLEGE LIBRARY

Stock No. 226271

G21. 39 CLE

Anx2. 3WL

OXFORD
UNIVERSITY PRESS

OXFORD
UNIVERSITY PRESS

Great Clarendon Street, Oxford OX2 6DP

Oxford University Press is a department of the University of Oxford.
It furthers the University's objective of excellence in research, scholarship,
and education by publishing worldwide in

Oxford New York

Auckland Cape Town Dar es Salaam Hong Kong Karachi
Kuala Lumpur Madrid Melbourne Mexico City Nairobi
New Delhi Shanghai Taipei Toronto

With offices in

Argentina Austria Brazil Chile Czech Republic France Greece
Guatemala Hungary Italy Japan Poland Portugal Singapore
South Korea Switzerland Thailand Turkey Ukraine Vietnam

Oxford is a registered trade mark of Oxford University Press
in the UK and certain other countries

Published in the United States
by Oxford University Press Inc., New York

© Alan Clements, 2006

The moral rights of the author have been asserted
Database right Oxford University Press (maker)

First published 1985
Second edition 1991
Third edition 2000
Fourth edition 2006

All rights reserved. No part of this publication may be reproduced,
stored in a retrieval system, or transmitted, in any form or by any means,
without the prior permission in writing of Oxford University Press,
or as expressly permitted by law, or under terms agreed with the appropriate
reprographics rights organization. Enquiries concerning reproduction
outside the scope of the above should be sent to the Rights Department,
Oxford University Press, at the address above

You must not circulate this book in any other binding or cover
and you must impose the same condition on any acquirer

British Library Cataloguing in Publication Data

Data available

Library of Congress Cataloging in Publication Data

Data available

Typeset by Newgen Imaging Systems (P) Ltd., Chennai, India.
Printed in Great Britain
on acid-free paper by
Bath Press Ltd, Bath

ISBN 0–19–927313–8   978–0–19–927313–3

10 9 8 7 6 5 4 3 2 1

PREFACE

Principle of Computer Hardware is aimed at students taking an introductory course in electronics, computer science, or information technology. The approach is one of *breadth before depth* and we cover a wide range of topics under the general umbrella of *computer hardware*.

I have written *Principles of Computer Hardware* to achieve two goals. The first is to teach students the basic concepts on which the stored-program digital computer is founded. These include the representation and manipulation of information in binary form, the structure or *architecture* of a computer, the flow of information within a computer, and the exchange of information between its various peripherals. We answer the questions, 'How does a computer work', and 'How is it organized?' The second goal is to provide students with a foundation for further study. In particular, the elementary treatment of gates and Boolean algebra provides a basis for a second-level course in digital design, and the introduction to the CPU and assembly-language programming provides a basis for advanced courses on computer architecture/organization or microprocessor systems design.

This book is written for those with no previous knowledge of computer architecture. The only background information needed by the reader is an understanding of elementary algebra. Because students following a course in computer science or computer technology will also be studying a high-level language, we assume that the reader is familiar with the concepts underlying a high-level language.

When writing this book, I set myself three objectives. By adopting an informal style, I hope to increase the enthusiasm of students who may be put off by the formal approach of more traditional books. I have also tried to give students an insight into computer hardware by explaining why things are as they are, instead of presenting them with information to be learned and accepted without question. I have included subjects that would seem out of place in an elementary first-level course. Topics like advanced computer arithmetic, timing diagrams, and reliability have been included to show how the computer hardware of the real world often differs from that of the first-level course in which only the basics are taught. I've also broadened the range of topics normally found in first-level courses in computer hardware and provided sections introducing operating systems and local area networks, as these two topics are so intimately related to the hardware of the computer. Finally, I have discovered that stating a formula or a theory is not enough—many students like to see an actual application of the formula. Wherever possible I have provided examples.

Like most introductory books on computer architecture, I have chosen a specific microprocessor as a vehicle to illustrate some of the important concepts in computer architecture. The ideal computer architecture is rich in features and yet easy to understand without exposing the student to a steep learning curve. Some microprocessors have very complicated architectures that confront the students with too much fine detail early in their course. We use Motorola's 68K microprocessor because it is easy to understand and incorporates many of the most important features of a high-performance architecture. This book isn't designed to provide a practical assembly language programming course. It is intended only to illustrate the operation of a central processing unit by means of a typical assembly language. We also take a brief look at other microprocessors to show the range of computer architectures available.

You will see the words *computer*, CPU, *processor*, *microprocessor*, and *microcomputer* in this and other texts. The part of a computer that actually executes a program is called a CPU (central processing unit) or more simply a *processor*. A *microprocessor* is a CPU fabricated on a single chip of silicon. A computer that is constructed around a *microprocessor* can be called a *microcomputer*. To a certain extent, these terms are frequently used interchangeably.

READING GUIDE

We've already said that this book provides a traditional introductory course in computer architecture plus additional material to broaden its scope and fill in some of the gaps left in such courses. To help students distinguish between foreground and background material, the following guide will help to indicate the more fundamental components of the course.

Chapter 2 introduces the logic of computers and deals with essential topics such as gates, Boolean algebra, and Karnaugh maps. Therefore this chapter is essential reading.

Chapter 3 introduces *sequential circuits* such as the counter that steps through the instructions of a program and demonstrates how sequential circuits are designed. We first introduce the *bistable* (flip-flop) used to construct *sequential circuits* such as registers and counters. We don't provide a comprehensive introduction to the design of sequential circuits; we show how gates and flip-flops can be used to create a computer.

Chapter 4 deals with the representation of numbers and shows how arithmetic operations are implemented. Apart from some of the coding theory and details of multiplication and division, almost all this chapter is essential reading. Multiplication and division can be omitted if the student is not interested in how these operations are implemented.

Chapter 5 is the heart of the book and is concerned with the structure and operation of the computer itself. We examine the instruction set of a processor with a sophisticated architecture.

Chapter 6 provides an overview of assembly language programming and the design of simple 68K assembly language programs. This chapter relies heavily on the 68K cross-assembler and simulator provided with the book. You can use this software to investigate the behavior of the 68K on a PC.

Chapter 7 begins with a description of the functional units that make up a computer and the flow of data during the execution of an instruction. We then describe the operation of the computer's control unit, which decodes and executes instructions. The control unit may be omitted on a first reading. Although the control unit is normally encountered in a second- or third-level course, we've included it here for the purpose of completeness and to show how the computer turns a binary-coded instruction into the sequence of events that carry out the instruction.

Chapter 8 is concerned with the quest for performance. We look at how performance is measured and describe three techniques used to accelerate processors. All students should read about the first two acceleration techniques, pipelining and cache memory, but may omit parallel processing.

Chapter 9 describes two contrasting computer architectures. Introductory texts on computer architecture are forced to concentrate on one processor because students do not have the time to plow through several different instruction sets. However, if we don't cover other architectures, students can end the course with a rather unbalanced view of processors. In this chapter we provide a very brief overview of several contrasting processors. We do not expect students to learn the fine details of these processors. The purpose of this chapter is to expose students to the range of processors that are available to the designer.

Chapter 10 deals with input/output techniques. We are interested in the way in which information is transferred between a computer and peripherals. We also examine the buses, or data highways, along which data flows. This chapter is essential reading.

Chapter 11 introduces some of the basic peripherals you'd find in a typical PC such as the keyboard, display, printer, and mouse, as well as some of the more unusual peripherals that, for example, can measure how fast a body is rotating. Although these topics are often omitted from courses in computer hardware, students should scan this chapter to get some insight into how computers control the outside world.

Chapter 12 looks at the memory devices used to store data in a computer. Information isn't stored in a computer in just one type of storage device. It's stored in DRAM and on disk, CD-ROM, DVD, and tape. This chapter examines the operating principles and characteristics of the storage devices found in a computer. There's a lot of detail in this chapter. Some readers may wish to omit the design of memory systems (for example, address decoding and interfacing) and just concentrate on the reasons why computers have so many different types of memory.

Chapter 13 deals with hardware topics that are closely related to the computer's operating system. The two most important elements of a computer's hardware that concern the operating system are *multiprogramming* and *memory management*. These topics are intimately connected with interrupt handling and data storage techniques and serve as practical examples of the use of the hardware described elsewhere. Those who require a basic introduction to computer hardware may omit this chapter, although it best illustrates how hardware and software come together in the operating system.

Chapter 14 describes how computers can communicate with each other. The techniques used to link computers to create computer networks are not always covered by first-level texts on computer architecture. However, the growth of both local area networks and the Internet have propelled computer communications to the forefront of computing. For this reason we would expect students to read this chapter even if some of it falls outside the scope of their syllabus.

THE HISTORY OF THIS BOOK

Like people, books are born. *Principles of Computer Hardware* was conceived in December 1980. At the end of their first semester our freshmen were given tests to monitor their progress. The results of the test in my 'Principles of computer hardware' course were not as good as I'd hoped, so I decided to do something about it. I thought that detailed lecture notes written in a style accessible to the students would be the most effective solution.

Having volunteered to give a course on computer communications to the staff of the Computer Center during the Christmas vacation, I didn't have enough free time to produce the notes. By accident I found that the week before Christmas was the cheapest time of the year for vacations. So I went to one of the Canary Islands for a week, sat down by the pool, surrounded by folders full of reference material, with a bottle of Southern Comfort, and wrote the core of this book—number bases, gates, Boolean algebra, and binary arithmetic. Shortly afterwards I added the section on the structure of the CPU.

These notes produced the desired improvement in the end-of-semester exam results and were well received by the students. In the next academic year my notes were transferred from paper to a mainframe computer and edited to include new material and to clean up the existing text.

I decided to convert the notes into a book. The conversion process involved adding topics, not covered by our syllabus, to produce a more rounded text. While editing my notes, I discovered what might best be called the *inkblot effect*. Text stored in a computer tends to expand in all directions because it's so easy to add new material at any point; for example, you might write a section on disk drives. When you next edit the section on disks, you can add more depth or breadth.

The final form of this book took a *breadth before depth* approach. That is, I covered a large number of topics rather than treating fewer topics in greater depth. It was my intention to give students taking our introductory hardware/architecture course a reasonably complete picture of the computer *system*.

The first edition of *Principles of Computer Hardware* proved successful and I was asked to write a second edition, which was published in 1990. The major change between the first and second editions was the adoption of the 68K microprocessors as a vehicle to teach computer architecture. I have retained this processor in the current edition. Although members of the Intel family have become the standard processors in the PC world, Motorola's 68K family of microprocessors is much better suited to teaching computer architecture. In short, it supports most of the features that computer scientists wish to teach students, and just as importantly, it's much easier to understand. The 68K family and its derivatives are widely used in embedded systems.

By the mid-1990s the second edition was showing its age. The basic computer science and the underlying principles were still fine, but the actual hardware had changed dramatically over a very short time. The most spectacular progress was in the capacity of hard disks—by the late 1990s disk capacity was increasing by 60% per year.

This third edition included a 68K cross-assembler and simulator allowing students to create and run 68K programs on any PC. It also added details of interesting microprocessor architecture, the ARM, which provides an interesting contrast to the 68K.

When I used the second edition to teach logic design to my students, they built simple circuits using *logic trainers*—boxes with power supplies and connectors that allow you to wire a handful of simple chips together. Dave Barker, one of my former students, has constructed a logic simulator program as part of his senior year project called Digital Works, which runs under Windows on a PC. Digital Works allows you to place logic elements anywhere within a window and to wire the gates together. Inputs to the gates can be provided manually (via the mouse) or from clocks and sequence generators. You can observe the outputs of the gates on synthesized LEDs or as a waveform or table. Moreover, Digital Works permits you to encapsulate a circuit in a macro and then use this macro in other circuits. In other words, you can take gates and build simple circuits, and take the simple circuits and build complex circuits, and so on.

I began writing a fourth edition of this text in late 2003. The fundamental principles have changed little since the third edition, but processors had become faster by a factor of 10 and the capacity of hard disks has grown enormously. This new edition is necessary to incorporate some of the advances. After consultation with those who adopt this book, we have decided to continue to use the 68K family to introduce the computer instruction set because this processor still has one of the most sophisticated of all instruction set architectures.

ACKNOWLEDGEMENTS

Few books are entirely the result of one person's unaided efforts and this is no exception. I would like to thank all those who wrote the books about computers on which my own understanding is founded. Some of these writers conveyed the sheer fascination of computer architecture that was to change the direction of my own academic career. It really is amazing how a large number of gates (a circuit element whose operation is so simple as to be trivial) can be arranged in such a way as to perform all the feats we associate computers with today.

I am grateful for all the comments and feedback I've received from my wife, colleagues, students, and reviewers over the years. Their feedback has helped me to improve the text and eliminate some of the errors I'd missed in editing. More importantly, their help and enthusiasm has made the whole project worthwhile.

Although I owe a debt of gratitude to a lot of people, I would like to mention four people who have had a considerable impact. Alan Knowles of Manchester University read drafts of both the second and third editions with a precision well beyond that of the average reviewer. Paul Lambert, one of my colleagues at The University of Teesside, wrote the 68K cross-assembler and simulator that I use in my teaching. In this edition we have used a Windows-based graphical 68K simulator kindly provided by Charles Kelly.

Dave Barker, one of my former students and an excellent programmer, wrote the logic simulator called Digital Works that accompanies this book. I would particularly like to thank Dave for providing a tool that enables students to construct circuits and test them without having to connect wires together.

One of the major changes to the third edition was the chapter on the ARM processor. I would like to thank Steve Furber of Manchester University (one of the ARM's designers) for encouraging me to use this very interesting device.

CONTENTS

Introduction to computer hardware

1

INTRODUCTION

In this chapter we set the scene for the rest of the book. We define what we mean by computer hardware, explain just why we teach computer hardware to computer science students, provide a very brief history of computing, and look at the role of the computer.

1.1 What is computer hardware?

To begin with I feel we ought to define the terms *hardware* and *software*. I could give a deeply philosophical definition, but perhaps an empirical one is more helpful. If any part of a computer system clatters on the floor when dropped, it's hardware. If it doesn't, it's software. This is a good working definition, but it's incomplete because it implies that hardware and software are unrelated entities. As we will discover, software and hardware are often intimately related. Moreover, the operation of much of today's hardware is controlled by *firmware* (software embedded in the structure of the hardware).

A computer's hardware includes all the physical components that make up the computer system. These components range from the CPU to the memory and input/output devices. The programs that control the operation of the computer are its *software*. When a program is inside a computer its physical existence lies in the state of electronic switches, the magnetization of tiny particles on magnetic disk, or bumps on the surface of a CD or DVD. We can't point to a program in a computer any more than we can point to a thought in the brain.

Two terms closely related to hardware are *architecture* and *organization*. A computer's architecture is an abstract view of the computer, which describes what it can do. A computer's architecture is the assembly language programmer's view of the machine. You could say that architecture has a similar meaning to *functional specification*. The architecture is an

---

HARDWARE, ARCHITECTURE, AND ORGANIZATION

Hardware means *all the parts of the computer that are not software*. It includes the processor, its memory, the buses that connect devices together, and the peripherals.

Architecture describes the internal organization of a computer in an abstract way; that is, it defines the *capabilities* of the computer and its programming model. You can have

two computers that have been constructed in different ways with *different* technologies but with the same architecture.

Organization describes how a computer is implemented. Organization is concerned with a computer's functional components and their interrelationship. Organization is about buses, timing, and circuits.

abstraction of the computer. A computer's *organization* describes how the architecture is implemented; that is, it defines the hardware used to implement the architecture. Let's look at a simple example that distinguishes between architecture and organization. A computer with a 32-bit architecture performs operations on numbers that are 32 bits wide. You could build two versions of this computer. One is a high-performance device that adds two 32-bit numbers in a single operation. The other is a low-cost processor that gets a 32-bit number by bringing two 16-bit numbers from memory one after the other. Both computers end up with the same result, but one takes longer to get there. They have the same architecture but different organizations.

Although hardware and software are different entities, there is often a trade-off between them. Some operations can be carried out either by a special-purpose hardware system or by means of a program stored in the memory of a general-purpose computer. The fastest way to execute a given task is to build a circuit dedicated exclusively to the task. Writing a program to perform the same task on an existing computer may be much cheaper, but the task will take longer, as the computer's hardware wasn't optimized to suit the task.

Developments in computer technology in the late 1990s further blurred the distinction between hardware and software. Digital circuits are composed of gates that are wired together. From the mid-1980s onward manufacturers were producing large arrays of gates that could be interconnected electronically to create a particular circuit. As technology progressed it became possible to reconfigure the connections between gates while the circuit was operating. We now have the technology to create computers that can repair errors, restructure themselves as the state of the art advances, or even evolve.

1.2 Why do we teach computer hardware?

A generation ago, school children in the UK had to learn Latin in order to enter a university. Clearly, at some point it was thought that Latin was a vital prerequisite for everyone going to university. When did they realize that students could still benefit from a university education without a prior knowledge of Latin? Three decades ago students taking a degree in electronics had to study *electrodynamics*, the dance of electrons in magnetic fields, a subject so frightening that older students passed on its horrors to the younger ones in hushed tones. Today, electrodynamics is taught only to students on specialist courses.

We can watch a television program without understanding how a cathode ray tube operates, or fly in a Jumbo jet without ever knowing the meaning of thermodynamics. Why then should the lives of computer scientists and programmers be made miserable by forcing them to learn what goes on inside a computer?

If topics in the past have fallen out of the curriculum with no obviously devastating effect on the education of students, what about today's curriculum? Do we still need to teach computer science students about the internal operation of the computer?

Computer architecture is the oldest component of the computer curriculum. The very first courses on computer science were concerned with the design and construction of computers. At that time programming was in its infancy and compilers, operating systems, and databases did not exist. In the 1940s, working with computers meant building computers. By the 1960s computer science had emerged as a discipline. With the introduction of courses in programming, numerical methods, operating systems, compilers, and databases, the then curriculum reflected the world of the mainframe.

In the 1970s computer architecture was still, to a considerable extent, an offshoot of electronics. Texts were more concerned with the circuits in a computer than with the fundamental principles of computer architecture as now encapsulated by the expression *instruction set architecture* (ISA).

Computer architecture experienced a renaissance in the 1980s. The advent of the low-cost microprocessor-based systems and the single-board computer meant that computer science students could study and even get hands-on experience of microprocessors. They could build simple systems, test them, interface them to peripherals such as LEDs and switches, and write programs in machine code. Bill Gates himself is a product of this era.

Assembly language programming courses once mirrored high-level language programming courses—students were taught algorithms such as sorting and searching in assembly language, as if assembly language were no more than the poor person's C. Such an approach to computer architecture is now untenable. If assembly language is taught at all today, it is used as a vehicle to illustrate instruction sets, addressing modes, and other aspects of a processor's architecture.

In the late 1980s and early 1990s computer architecture underwent another change. The rise of the RISC microprocessor turned the focus of attention from complex instruction set computers to the new high-performance, highly pipelined, 32-bit processors. Moreover, the increase in the performance of microprocessors made it harder and harder for classes to give students the hands-on experience they had a few years earlier. In the 1970s a student could construct a computer with readily available components and simple electronic construction techniques. By the 1990s clock rates rose to well over 100 MHz and buses were 32 bits wide making it difficult for students to construct microprocessor-based systems as they did in the 1980s. High clock rates require special construction techniques and complex chips have hundreds of connections rather than the 40- or 64-pin packages of the 8086/68K era.

In the 1990s computer architecture was largely concerned with the instruction set architecture, pipelining, hazards, superscalar processors, and cache memories. Topics such as microprocessor systems design at the chip level and microprocessor interfacing had largely vanished from the CS curriculum. These topics belonged to the CEng and EE curricula.

In the 1990s a lot was happening in computer science; for example, the introduction of new subject areas such as object-oriented programming, communications and networks, and the Internet/WWW. The growth of the computer market, particularly for those versed in the new Internet-based skills, caused students to look at their computing curricula in a rather pragmatic way. Many CS students will join companies using the new technologies, but very few of them indeed will ever design chips or become involved with cutting-edge work in computer architecture. At my own university, the demand for courses in Internet-based computing has risen and fewer students have elected to take computer architecture when it is offered as an elective.

1.2.1 Should computer architecture remain in the CS curriculum?

Developments in computer science have put pressure on course designers to remove old material to make room for the new. The fraction of students that will ever be directly involved in computer design is declining. Universities provide programs in multimedia-based computing and visualization at both undergraduate and postgraduate levels. Students on such programs do not see the point of studying computer architecture.

Some have suggested that computer architecture is a prime candidate for pruning. It is easy to argue that computer architecture is as irrelevant to computer science as, say, Latin is to the study of contemporary English literature. If a student never writes an assembly language program or designs an instruction set, or interfaces a memory to a processor, why should we burden them with a course in computer architecture? Does the surgeon study metallurgy in order to understand how a scalpel operates?

It's easy to say that an automobile driver does not have to understand the internal combustion engine to drive an automobile. However, it is patently obvious that a driver who understands mechanics can drive in such a way as to enhance the life of the engine and to improve its performance. The same is true of computer architecture; understanding computer systems can improve the performance of software if the software is written to exploit the underlying hardware.

The digital computer lies at the heart of computer science. Without it, computer science would be little more than a branch of theoretical mathematics. The very idea of a computer science

program that did not provide students with an insight into the computer would be strange in a university that purports to educate students rather than to merely train them.

Those supporting the continued teaching of computer architecture employ several traditional arguments. First, education is not the same as training and CS students are not simply being shown how to use commercial computer packages. A course leading to a degree in computer science should also cover the history and the theoretical basis for the subject. Without an appreciation of computer architecture, the computer scientist cannot understand how computers have developed and what they are capable of.

However, there are concrete reasons why computer architecture is still relevant in today's world. Indeed, I would maintain that computer architecture is as relevant to the needs of the average CS student today as it was in the past. Suppose a graduate enters the industry and is asked to select the most cost-effective computer for use throughout a large organization. Understanding how the elements of a computer contribute to its overall performance is vital—is it better to spend $50 on doubling the size of the cache or $100 on increasing the clock speed by 500 MHz?

Computer architecture cannot be divorced entirely from software. The majority of processors are found not in PCs or workstations but in *embedded*[1] applications. Those designing multiprocessors and real-time systems have to understand fundamental architectural concepts and limitations of commercially available processors. Someone developing an automobile electronic ignition system may write their code in C, but might have to debug the system using a logic analyzer that displays the relationship between interrupt requests from engine sensors and the machine-level code.

There are two other important reasons for teaching computer architecture. The first reason is that computer architecture incorporates a wealth of important concepts that appear in other areas of the CS curriculum. This point is probably least appreciated by computer scientists who took a course in architecture a long time ago and did little more than learn about bytes, gates, and assembly language. The second reason is that computer architecture covers more than the CPU; it is concerned with the entire computer system. Because so many computer users now have to work with the whole system (e.g. by configuring hard disks, by specifying graphics cards, by selecting a SCSI or FireWire interface), a course covering the architecture of computer systems is more a necessity than a luxury.

Some computer architecture courses cover the architecture and organization of the processor but make relatively little

---

[1] An embedded computer is part of a product (digital camera, cell phone, washing machine) that is not normally regarded as a computing device. The end user does not know about the computer and does not have to program it.

reference to buses, memory systems, and high-performance peripherals such as graphics processors. Yet, if you scan the pages of journals devoted to personal/workstation computing, you will rapidly discover that much attention is focused on aspects of the computer system other than the CPU itself. Computer technology was once driven by the paperless-office revolution with its demand for low-cost mass storage, sufficient processing power to rapidly recompose large documents, and low-cost printers. Today, computer technology is being driven by the multimedia revolution with its insatiable demand for pure processing power, high bandwidths, low latencies, and massive storage capacities.

These trends have led to important developments in computer architecture such as special hardware support for multimedia applications. The demands of multimedia are being felt in areas other than computer architecture. Hard disks must provide a continuous stream of data because people can tolerate a degraded picture much better than a picture with even the shortest discontinuities. Such demands require efficient track-seeking algorithms, data buffering, and high-speed, real-time error correction and detection algorithms. Similarly, today's high data densities require frequent recalibration of tracking mechanisms due to thermal effects. Disk drives now include SMART technologies from the AI world that are able to predict disk failure before it occurs. These developments have as much right to be included in the architecture curriculum as developments in the CPU.

1.2.2 Supporting the CS curriculum

It is in the realm of software that you can most easily build a case for the teaching of assembly language. During a student's career, they will encounter abstract concepts in areas ranging from programming languages to operating systems to real-time programming to AI. The foundation of many of these concepts lies in assembly language programming and computer architecture. Computer architecture provides bottom-up support for the top-down methodology taught in high-level languages. Consider some of the areas where computer architecture can add value to the CS curriculum.

The operating system Computer architecture provides a firm basis for students taking operating system courses. In computer architecture students learn about the hardware that the operating system controls and the interaction between hardware and software; for example, in cache systems. Consider the following two examples of the way in which the underlying architecture provides support for operating system facilities.

Some processors operate in either a privileged or a user mode. The operating system runs in the privileged or protected mode and all applications run in the user mode. This mechanism creates a secure environment in which the effects of an error in an application program can be prevented from crashing the operating system or other applications. Covering these topics in an architecture course makes the student aware of the support the processor provides for the operating system and enables those teaching operating system courses to concentrate more on operating system facilities than on the mechanics of the hardware.

High-level languages make it difficult to access peripherals directly. By using an assembly language we can teach students how to write *device drivers* that directly control interfaces. Many real interfaces are still programmed at machine level by accessing registers within them. Understanding computer architecture and assembly language can facilitate the design of high-performance interfaces.

Programming and data structures Students encounter the notion of data types and the effect of strong and weak data typing when they study high-level languages. Because computer architecture deals with information in its most primitive form, students rapidly become familiar with the advantages and disadvantages of weak typing. They learn the power that you have over the hardware by being able to apply almost any operations to binary data. Equally, they learn the pitfalls of weak typing as they discover the dangers of inappropriate operations on data.

Computer architecture is concerned with both the type of operations that act on data and the various ways in which the location of an operand can be accessed in memory. Computer addressing modes and the various means of accessing data naturally lead on to the notion of pointers. Students learn about how pointers function at machine level and the support offered for pointers by various architectures. This aspect is particularly important if the student is to become a C programmer.

An understanding of procedure call and parameter passing mechanisms is vital to anyone studying processor performance. Programming in assembly language readily demonstrates the passing of parameters by value and by reference. Similarly, assembly language programming helps you to understand concepts such as the use of local variables and re-entrant programming.

Students sometimes find the concept of recursion difficult. You can use an assembly language to demonstrate how recursion operates by tracing through the execution of a program. The student can actually observe how the stack grows as procedures are called.

Computer science fundamentals Computer architecture is awash with concepts that are fundamental to computer science generally and which do not appear in other parts of the undergraduate curriculum. A course in computer architecture can provide a suitable forum for incorporating fundamental principles in the CS curriculum. For example, a first course in computer architecture introduces the student to bits and binary encoding techniques. A few years ago much time would have been spent on special-purpose codes for BCD arithmetic. Today, the professor is more likely to introduce error-correcting codes (important in data communications systems and secure storage mechanisms) and data-compression codes (used by everyone who has ever zipped a file or used a JPEG-encoded image).

1.3 An overview of the book

It's difficult to know just what should be included in an introductory course on computer architecture, organization, and hardware—and what should be excluded. Any topic can be expanded to an arbitrary extent; if we begin with gates and Boolean algebra, do we go on to semiconductor devices and then semiconductor physics? In this book, we cover the material specified by typical computer curricula. However, I have included a wider range of material because the area of influence encompassed by the digital computer has expanded greatly in recent years. The major subject areas dealt with in this book are outlined below.

Computer arithmetic Our system of arithmetic using the base 10 has evolved over thousands of years. The computer carries out its internal operations on numbers represented in the base two. This anomaly isn't due to some magic power inherent in binary arithmetic but simply because it would be uneconomic to design a computer to operate in denary (base 10) arithmetic. At this point I must make a comment. Time and time again, I read in the popular press that the behavior of digital computers and their characteristics are due to the fact that they operate on bits using binary arithmetic whereas we humans operate on digits using decimal arithmetic. That idea is nonsense. Because there is a simple relationship between binary and decimal numbers, the fact that computers represent information in binary form is a mere detail of engineering. It's the architecture and organization of a computer that makes it behave in such a different way to the brain.

Basic logic elements and Boolean algebra Today's technology determines what a computer can do. We introduce the basic logic elements, or *gates*, from which a computer is made up and show how these can be put together to create more complex units such as arithmetic units. The behavior of these gates determines both the way in which the computer carries out arithmetic operations and the way in which the functional parts of a computer interact to execute a program. We need to understand gates in order to appreciate why the computer has developed in the way it has. The operation of circuits containing gates can be described in terms of a formal notation called *Boolean algebra*. An introduction to Boolean algebra is provided because it enables designers to build circuits with the least number of gates.

As well as gates, computers require devices called *flip-flops*, which can store a single binary digit. The flip-flop is the basic component of many memory units. We provide an introduction to flip-flops and their application to *sequential circuits* such as counters, timers, and sequencers.

Computer architecture and assembly language The primitive instructions that directly control the operation of a computer are called *machine-code* instructions and are composed of sequences of binary values stored in memory. As programming in machine code is exceedingly tedious, an aid to machine code programming called *assembly language* has been devised. Assembly language is shorthand permitting the programmer to write machine-code instructions in a simple abbreviated form of plain language. High-level languages (Java, C, Pascal, BASIC) are sometimes translated into a series of assembly-language instructions by a compiler as an intermediate step on the way to pure machine code. This intermediate step serves as a debugging tool for programmers who wish to examine the operation of the compiler and the output it produces. Computer architecture is the assembly language programmer's view of a computer.

Programmers writing in assembly language require a detailed knowledge of the architecture of their machines, unlike the corresponding programmers operating in high-level languages. At this point I must say that we introduce assembly language to explain the operation of the central processing unit. Apart from certain special exceptions, programs should be written in a high-level language whenever possible.

Computer organization This topic is concerned with how a computer is arranged in terms of its building blocks (i.e. the logic and sequential circuits made from gates and flip-flops). We introduce the architecture of a simple hypothetical computer and show how it can be organized in terms of functional units. That is, we show how the computer goes about reading an instruction from memory, decoding it, and then executing it.

Input/output It's no good having a computer unless it can take in new information (programs and data) and output the results of its calculations. In this section we show how information is moved into and out of the computer. The operation of three basic input/output devices is described: the keyboard, the display, and the printer.

We also examine the way in which analog signals can be converted into digital form, processed digitally by a computer, and then converted back into analog form. Until the mid-1990s it was uneconomical to process rapidly changing analog signals (e.g. speech, music, video) digitally. The advent of high-speed low-cost digital systems has opened up a new field of computing called *digital signal processing* (DSP). We introduce DSP and outline some of the basic principles.

Memory devices A computer needs memory to hold programs, data, and any other information it may require at some point in the future. We look at the immediate access store and the secondary store (sometimes called backing store). An immediate access store provides a computer with the data it requires in approximately the same time as it takes the computer to execute one of its machine-level operations. The secondary store is very much slower and it takes thousands of times longer to access data from a secondary store than from an immediate access store. However, secondary storage is used because it is immensely cheaper than an immediate access store and it is also non-volatile (i.e. the data isn't lost when you switch the computer off). The most popular form of secondary store is the disk drive, which relies on magnetizing a moving magnetic material to store data. Optical storage technology in the form of the CD and DVD became popular in the 1990s because it combines the relatively fast access time of the disk with the large capacity and low cost of the tape drive.

Operating systems and the computer An operating system coordinates all the functional parts of the computer and provides an interface for the user. We can't cover the operating system in detail here. However, because the operating system is intimately bound up with the computer's hardware, we do cover two of its aspects—*multiprogramming* and *memory management*. Multiprogramming is the ability of a computer to appear to run two or more programs simultaneously. Memory management permits several programs to operate as though each alone occupied the computer's memory and enables a computer with a small, high-speed random access memory and a large, low-speed serial access memory (i.e. hard disk) to appear as if it had a single large high-speed random access memory.

Computer communications Computers are *networked* when they are connected together. Networking computers has many advantages, not least of which is the ability to share peripherals such as printers and scanners. Today we have two types of network—the local area network (LAN), which interconnects computers within a building, and the wide area network, which interconnects computers over much greater distances (e.g. the Internet). Consequently, we have devoted a section to showing how computers communicate with each other. Three aspects of computer communications are examined. The first is the *protocols* or rules that govern the way in which information is exchanged between systems in an orderly fashion. The second is the way in which digital information in a computer is encoded in a form suitable for transmission over a serial channel, the various types of channel, the characteristics of the physical channel, and how data is reconstituted at the receiver. The third provides a brief overview of both local area and wide area networks.

1.4 History of computing

The computer may be a marvel of our age, but it has had a long and rich history. Writing a short introduction to computer history is difficult because there is so much to cover. Here we provide some of the milestones in the computer's development.

1.4.1 Navigation and mathematics

The development of navigation in the eighteenth century was probably the most important driving force behind automated computation. It's easy to tell how far north or south of the equator you are—you measure the height of the sun above the horizon at midday and then use the elevation to work out your latitude. Unfortunately, calculating your longitude relative to the prime meridian through Greenwich in England is very much more difficult. Longitude is determined by comparing your local time (obtained by observing the angle of the sun) with the time at Greenwich.

The mathematics of navigation uses trigonometry, which is concerned with the relationship between the sides and angles of a triangle. In turn, trigonometry requires an accurate knowledge of the sine, cosine, and tangent of an angle. Those who originally devised tables of sines and other mathematical functions (e.g. square roots and logarithms) had to do a lot of calculation by hand. If x is expressed in radians (where 2π radians = 360°) and $x < 1$, the expression for $\sin(x)$ can be written as an infinite series of the form

$$\sin(x) = x - \frac{x^3}{3!} + \frac{x^5}{5!} - \frac{x^7}{7!} + \cdots + (-1)^n \frac{x^{2n+1}}{(2n+1)!}$$

Although the calculation of $\sin(x)$ requires the summation of an infinite number of terms, we can obtain a reasonably accurate approximation to $\sin(x)$ by adding just a handful of terms together because x^n tends towards zero as n increases for $x \ll 1$.

An important feature of the formula for $\sin(x)$ is that it involves nothing more than the repetition of fundamental arithmetic operations (addition, subtraction, multiplication, and division). The first term in the series is x itself. The second term is $-x^3/3!$, which is derived from the first term by multiplying it by $-x^2$ and dividing it by $1 \times 2 \times 3$. Each new term is formed by multiplying the previous term by $-x^2$ and dividing it by $2n(2n+1)$, where n is number of the term. It would eventually occur to people that this process could be mechanized.

1.4.2 The era of mechanical computers

During the seventeenth century major advances were made in watch making; for example, in 1656 Christiaan Huygens designed the first pendulum clock. The art of watch making helped develop the gear wheels required by the first mechanical calculators. In 1642 the French scientist Blaise Pascal designed a simple mechanical adder and subtracter using gear wheels with 10 positions marked on them. One complete rotation of a gear wheel caused the next wheel on its left to move one position (a bit like the odometer used to record an automobile's mileage). Pascal's most significant contribution was the use of a ratchet device that detected a carry (i.e. a rotation of a wheel from 9 to 0) and nudged the next wheel on the left one digit. In other words, if two wheels show 58 and the right-hand wheel is rotated two positions forward, it moves to the 0 position and advances the 5 to 6 to get 60. Pascal's calculator, the Pascaline, could perform addition only.

In fact, Wilhelm Schickard, rather than Pascal, is now generally credited with the invention of the first mechanical calculator. His device, created in 1623, was more advanced than Pascal's because it could also perform partial multiplication. Schickard died in a plague and his invention didn't receive the recognition it merited. Such near simultaneous developments in computer hardware have been a significant feature of the history of computer hardware.

Within a few decades, mechanical computing devices advanced to the stage where they could perform addition, subtraction, multiplication, and division—all the operations required by armies of clerks to calculate the trigonometric functions we mentioned earlier.

The industrial revolution and early control mechanisms

If navigation provided a requirement for mechanized computing, other developments provided important steps along the path to the computer. By about 1800 the industrial revolution in Europe was well under way. Weaving was one of the first industrial processes to be mechanized. A weaving loom passes a shuttle pulling a horizontal thread to and fro between vertical threads held in a frame. By changing the color of the thread pulled by the shuttle and selecting whether the shuttle passes in front of or behind the vertical threads, you can weave a particular pattern. Controlling the loom manually is tedious and time consuming. In 1801 Joseph Jacquard designed a loom that could automatically weave a predetermined pattern. The information necessary to control the loom was stored in the form of holes cut in cards—the presence or absence of a hole at a certain point controlled the behavior of the loom. Information was read by rods that pressed against the card and either went through a hole or were stopped by the card. Some complex patterns required as many as 10 000 cards strung together in the form of a tape.

Babbage and the computer

Two of the most significant advances in computing were made by Charles Babbage, a UK mathematician born in 1792: his *difference engine* and his *analytical engine*. Like other mathematicians of his time, Babbage had to perform all calculations by hand and sometimes he had to laboriously correct errors in published mathematical tables. Living in the age of steam, it was quite natural that Babbage asked himself whether mechanical means could be applied to arithmetic calculations.

The difference engine was a complex array of interconnected gears and linkages that performed addition and

Number	Number squared	First difference	Second difference
1	1		
2	4	3	
3	9	5	2
4	16	7	2
5	25	9	2
6	36	11	2
7	49	13	2

Table 1.1 The use of finite differences to calculate squares.

subtraction rather like Pascal's mechanical adder. Its purpose was to mechanize the calculation of polynomial functions and automatically print the result. It was a *calculator* rather than a *computer* because it could carry out only a set of predetermined operations.

Babbage's difference engine employed *finite differences* to calculate polynomial functions. Trigonometric functions can be expressed as polynomials in the form $a_0x + a_1x^1 + a_2x^2 + \cdots$ The difference engine can evaluate such expressions automatically. Table 1.1 demonstrates how you can use the method of *finite differences* to create a table of squares without having to use multiplication. The first column contains the natural integers 1, 2, 3, . . . The second column contains the squares of these integers (i.e. 1, 4, 9, . . .). Column 3 contains the first difference between successive pairs of numbers in column 2; for example, the first value is $4 - 1 = 3$, the second value is $9 - 4 = 5$, and so on. The final column is the second difference between successive pairs of first differences. As you can see, the second difference is always 2.

Suppose we want to calculate the value of 8^2 using finite differences. We simply use Table 1.1 in reverse by starting with the second difference and working back to the result. If the second difference is 2, the next first difference (after 7^2) is $13 + 2 = 15$. Therefore, the value of 8^2 is the value of 7^2 plus the first difference; that is, $49 + 15 = 64$. We have generated 8^2 without using multiplication. This technique can be extended to evaluate many other mathematical functions.

Babbage's difference engine project was cancelled in 1842 because of increasing costs. He did design a simpler difference engine using 31-digit numbers to handle seventh-order differences, but no one was interested in financing it. In 1853 George Scheutz in Sweden constructed a working difference engine using 15-digit arithmetic and fourth-order differences. Incidentally, in 1991 a team at the Science Museum in London used modern construction techniques to build Babbage's difference engine. It worked.

Charles Babbage went on to design the *analytical engine*, which was to be capable of performing any mathematical operation automatically. This truly remarkable and entirely mechanical device was nothing less than a general-purpose computer that could be programmed. The analytical engine included many of the elements associated with a modern electronic computer—an arithmetic processing unit that carries out all the calculations, a memory that stores data, and input and output devices. Unfortunately, the sheer scale of the analytical engine rendered its construction, at that time, impossible. However, it is not unreasonable to call Babbage the father of the computer because his machine incorporated many of the intellectual concepts at the heart of the computer.

Babbage envisaged that his analytical engine would be controlled by punched cards similar to those used to control the operation of the Jacquard loom. Two types of punched card were required. Operation cards specified the sequence of operations to be carried out by the analytical engine and variable cards specified the locations in the store of inputs and outputs.

One of Babbage's collaborators was Ada Gordon[2], a mathematician who became interested in the analytical engine when she translated a paper on it from French to English. When Babbage discovered the paper he asked her to expand the paper. She added about 40 pages of notes about the machine and provided examples of how the proposed analytical engine could be used to solve mathematical problems. Gordon worked closely with Babbage and it's been reported that she even suggested the use of the binary system to store data. She noticed that certain groups of operations are carried out over and over again during the course of a calculation and proposed that a conditional instruction be used to force the analytical engine to perform the same sequence of operations many times. This action is the same as the repeat or loop function found in most of today's high-level languages.

Gordon devised algorithms to perform the calculation of Bernoulli numbers, making her one of the founders of numerical computation. Some regard Gordon as the world's first computer programmer, who was constructing algorithms a century before programming became a recognized discipline—and long before any real computers were constructed.

Mechanical computing devices continued to be used in compiling mathematical tables and performing the arithmetic operations used by everyone from engineers to accountants until about the 1960s. The practical high-speed computer had to await the development of the electronics industry.

1.4.3 Enabling technology— the telegraph

Many of the technological developments required to construct a practical computer took place at the end of the nineteenth century. The most important of these events was the invention of the *telegraph*. We now provide a short history of the development of telecommunications.

One of the first effective communication systems was the optical semaphore, which passed visual signals from tower to tower across Europe. Claude Chappe in France developed a system with two arms, each of which could be in one of seven positions. The Chappe telegraph could send a message across France in about half an hour (good weather permitting). The telegraph was used for commercial purposes, but it also helped Napoleon to control his army.

King Maximilian had seen how the French visual semaphore system had helped Napoleon's military campaigns and in 1809 he asked the Bavarian Academy of Sciences to devise a scheme for high-speed communication over long distances. Samuil T. von Sömmering suggested a crude telegraph using 35 conductors, one for each character. Sömmering's telegraph transmits electricity from a battery down one of these 35 wires where, at the receiver, the current is passed through a tube of acidified water. Passing a current through the water breaks it down into oxygen and hydrogen. To use the Sömmering telegraph you detected the bubbles that appeared in one of the 35 glass tubes and then wrote down the corresponding character. Sömmering's telegraph was ingenious but too slow to be practical.

In 1819 Hans C. Oersted made one of the greatest discoveries of all time when he found that an electric current creates a magnetic field round a conductor. This breakthrough allowed you to create a magnetic field at will. In 1828 Cooke exploited Oersted's discovery when he invented a telegraph that used the magnetic field round a wire to deflect a compass needle.

The growth of the railway networks in the early nineteenth century spurred the development of the telegraph because you had to warn stations down the line that a train was arriving. By 1840 a 40-mile stretch between Slough and Paddington in London had been linked using the telegraph of Charles Wheatstone and William Cooke. The Wheatstone and Cooke telegraph used five compass needles that normally hung in a vertical position. The needles could be deflected by coils to point to the appropriate letter. You could transmit one of 20 letters (J, C, Q, U, X, and Z were omitted).

The first long-distance data links

We take wires and cables for granted. In the early nineteenth century, plastics hadn't been invented and the only material available for insulation waterproofing was a type of pitch called asphaltum. In 1843 a form of rubber called gutta percha was discovered. The Atlantic Telegraph Company created an insulated cable for underwater use containing a single copper conductor made of seven twisted strands, surrounded by gutta percha insulation and protected by a ring of 18 iron wires coated with hemp and tar.

---

[2] Ada Gordon married William King in 1835. King inherited the title Earl of Lovelace and Gordon became Countess of Lovelace. Gordon is often considered the founder of scientific computing.

Submarine cable telegraphy began with a cable crossing the English Channel to France in 1850. The cable failed after only a few messages had been exchanged and a more successful attempt was made the following year. Transatlantic cable laying from Ireland began in 1857 but was abandoned when the strain of the cable descending to the ocean bottom caused it to snap under its own weight. The Atlantic Telegraph Company tried again in 1858. Again, the cable broke after only 3 miles but the two cable-laying ships managed to splice the two ends. The cable eventually reached Newfoundland in August 1858 after suffering several more breaks and storm damage.

It soon became clear that this cable wasn't going to be a commercial success. The receiver used the magnetic field from the current in the cable to deflect a magnetized needle. Unfortunately, after crossing the Atlantic the signal was too weak to be detected reliably. The original voltage used to drive a current down the cable was approximately 600 V. So, they raised the voltage to about 2000 V to drive more current along the cable and improve the detection process. Unfortunately, such a high voltage burned through the primitive insulation, shorted the cable, and destroyed the first transatlantic telegraph link after about 700 messages had been transmitted in 3 months.

In England, the Telegraph Construction and Maintenance Company developed a new 2300-mile-long cable weighing 9000 tons, which was three times the diameter of the failed 1858 cable. Laying this cable required the largest ship in the world, the Great Eastern. After a failed attempt in 1865 a transatlantic link was finally established in 1866. It cost $100 in gold to transmit 20 words across the first transatlantic cable at a time when a laborer earned $20/month.

Telegraph distortion and the theory of transmission lines

The telegraph hadn't been in use for very long before people discovered that it suffered from a problem called *telegraph distortion*. As the length of cables increased it became apparent that a sharply rising pulse at the transmitter end of a cable was received at the far end as a highly distorted pulse with long rise and fall times. This distortion meant that the 1866 transatlantic telegraph cable could transmit only eight words per minute. The problem was eventually handed to William Thomson at the University of Glasgow.

Thomson, who later became Lord Kelvin, was one of the nineteenth century's greatest scientists. He published more than 600 papers, developed the second law of thermodynamics, and created the absolute temperature scale. In 1855 Thomson presented a paper to the Royal Society analyzing the effect of pulse distortion, which became the cornerstone of what is now called *transmission line theory*. The transmission line effect reduces the speed at which signals can change state. The cause of the problems investigated by Thomson

lies in the physical properties of electrical conductors and insulators. Thomson's theories enabled engineers to construct data links with much lower levels of distortion.

Thomson contributed to computing by providing the theory that describes the flow of pulses in circuits, which enabled the development of the telegraph and telephone networks. In turn, the switching circuits used to route messages through networks were used to construct the first electromechanical computers.

Developments in communications networks

Although the first telegraph systems operated from point to point, the introduction of the telephone led to the development of switching centers. First-generation switching centers employed a telephone operator who manually plugged a subscriber's line into a line connected to the next switching center in the link. By the end of the nineteenth century, the infrastructure of computer networks was already in place.

In 1897 an undertaker called Almon Strowger was annoyed to find that he was not getting the trade he expected because the local telephone operator was connecting prospective clients to Strowger's competitor. So, Strowger cut out the human factor by inventing the automatic telephone exchange that used electromechanical devices to route calls between exchanges. When you dial a number using a rotary dial, a series of pulses are sent down the line to a rotary switch. If you dial, for example, '5', the five pulses move a switch five steps clockwise to connect you to line number five, which routes your call to the next switching center. Consequently, when you phoned someone using Strowger's technology the number you dialed determined the route your call took though the system.

By the time the telegraph was well established, radio was being developed. James Clerk Maxwell predicted radio waves in 1864 following his study of light and electromagnetic waves. Heinrich Hertz demonstrated the existence of radio waves in 1887 and Guglielmo Marconi is credited with being the first to use radio to span the Atlantic in 1901.

The light bulb was invented by Thomas A. Edison in 1879. Investigations into its properties led Ambrose Fleming to discover the diode in 1904. A diode is a light bulb surrounded by a wire mesh that allows electricity to flow only one way between the filament (the cathode) and the mesh (the anode). The flow of electrons from the cathode gave us the term 'cathode ray tube'. In 1906 Lee de Forest modified Fleming's diode by placing a wire mesh between the cathode and anode. By changing the voltage on this mesh, it was possible to change the flow of current between the cathode and anode. This device, called a triode, could amplify signals. Without the vacuum tube to amplify weak signals, modern electronics would have been impossible. The term *electronics* refers to circuits with amplifying or active devices such as tubes or transistors. The first primitive computers using electromechanical devices did not use vacuum tubes and, therefore, these computers were not electronic computers.

The telegraph, telephone, and vacuum tube were all steps on the path to the development of the computer and, later, computer networks. As each of these practical steps was taken, there was a corresponding development in the accompanying theory (in the case of radio, the theory came before the discovery).

Typewriters, punched cards, and tabulators

Another important part of computer history is the humble keyboard, which is still the prime input device of most personal computers. As early as 1711 Henry Mill, an Englishman, described a mechanical means of printing text on paper a character at a time. In 1829 the American William Burt was granted the first US patent for a typewriter, although his machine was not practical. It wasn't until 1867 that three Americans, Christopher Sholes, Carlos Glidden, and Samuel Soule, invented their Type-Writer, the forerunner of the modern typewriter. One of the problems encountered by Sholes was the tendency of his machine to jam when digraphs such as 'th' and 'er' were typed. Hitting the 't' and 'h' keys at almost the same time caused the letters 't' and 'h' to strike the paper simultaneously and jam. His solution was to arrange the letters on the keyboard to avoid the letters of digraphs being located side by side. This layout has continued until today and is now described by the sequence of the first six letters on the left of the top row—QWERTY. Because the same digraphs do not occur in different languages, the layout of a French keyboard is different to that of an English keyboard. It is reported that Sholes made it easy to type 'Type-Writer' by putting all these characters on the same row.

Another enabling technology that played a key role in the development of the computer was the tabulating machine, a development of the mechanical calculator that processes data on punched cards. One of the largest data processing operations carried out in the USA during the nineteenth century was the US census. A census involves taking the original data, sorting and collating it, and tabulating the results.

In 1879 Herman Hollerith became involved in the evaluation of the 1880 US Census data. He devised an electric tabulating system that could process data stored on cards punched by clerks from the raw census data. Hollerith's electric tabulating machine could read cards, process the information on the cards, and then sort them. The tabulator helped lay the foundations of the data processing industry.

Three threads converged to make the computer possible: Babbage's calculating machines, which performed arithmetic calculations; communications technology, which laid the foundations for electronics and even networking; and the tabulator because it and the punched card media provided a means of controlling machines, inputting data into them, and storing information.

1.4.4 The first electromechanical computers

The forerunner of today's digital computers used electromechanical components called relays, rather than electronic circuits such as vacuum tubes and transistors. A relay is constructed from a coil of wire wound round an iron cylinder. When a current flows through the coil, it generates a magnetic field that causes the iron to act like a magnet. A flat springy strip of iron is located close to the iron cylinder. When the cylinder is magnetized, the iron strip is attracted, which, in turn, opens or closes a switch. Relays can perform any operation that can be carried out by the logic gates making up today's computers. You cannot construct fast computers from relays because they are far too slow, bulky, and unreliable. However, the relay did provide a technology that bridged the gap between the mechanical calculator and the modern electronic digital computer.

One of the first electromechanical computers was built by Konrad Zuse in Germany. Zuse's Z2 and Z3 computers were used in the early 1940s to design aircraft in Germany. The heavy bombing at the end of the Second World War destroyed Zuse's computers and his contribution to the development of the computer was ignored for many years. He is mentioned here to demonstrate that the notion of a practical computer occurred to different people in different places. The Z3 was completed in 1941 and was the World's first functioning programmable mechanical computer. Zuse's Z4 computer was finished in 1945, was later taken to Switzerland, and was used at the Federal Polytechnical Institute in Zurich until 1955.

As Zuse was working on his computer in Germany, Howard Aiken at Harvard University constructed his Harvard Mark I computer in 1944 with both financial and practical support from IBM. Aiken was familiar with Babbage's work and his electromechanical computer, which he first envisaged in 1937, operated in a similar way to Babbage's proposed analytical engine. The original name for the Mark I was the Automatic Sequence Controlled Calculator, which, perhaps, better describes its nature.

Aiken's machine was a programmable calculator that was used by the US Navy until the end of the Second World War. Just like Babbage's machine, the Mark I used decimal counter wheels to implement its main memory consisting of 72 words of 23 digits plus a sign. The program was stored on a paper tape (similar to Babbage's punched cards), although operations and addresses (i.e. data) were stored on the same tape. Input and output operations used punched cards or an electric typewriter. Because the Harvard Mark I treated data and instructions separately, the term *Harvard architecture* is now applied to any computer with separate paths for data and instructions. The Harvard Mark I didn't support conditional operations and therefore is not strictly a computer.

However, it was later modified to permit multiple paper tape readers with a conditional transfer of control between the readers.

1.4.5 The first mainframes

Relays have moving parts and can't operate at very high speeds. It took the invention of the vacuum tube by John A. Fleming and Lee de Forest to make possible the design of high-speed electronic computers. John V. Atanasoff is now credited with the partial construction of the first completely electronic computer. Atanasoff worked with Clifford Berry at Iowa State College on their computer from 1937 to 1942. Their machine used a 50-bit binary representation of numbers and was called the ABC (Atanasoff–Berry Computer). It was designed to solve linear equations and wasn't a general purpose computer. Atanasoff and Berry abandoned their computer when they were assigned to other duties because of the war.

ENIAC

The first electronic *general purpose* digital computer was John W. Mauchly's ENIAC (Electronic Numerical Integrator and Calculator), completed in 1945 at the University of Pennsylvania. ENIAC was intended for use at the Army Ordnance Department to create firing tables that relate the range of a field gun to its angle of elevation, wind conditions, and so on. For many years, ENIAC was regarded as the first electronic computer, although credit was later given to Atanasoff and Berry because Mauchly had visited Atanasoff and read his report on the ABC machine.

ENIAC used 17 480 vacuum tubes and weighed about 30 t. ENIAC was a decimal machine capable of storing 20 10-digit decimal numbers. IBM card readers and punches implemented input and output operations. ENIAC was programmed by means of a plug board that looked like an old pre-automatic telephone switchboard; that is, a program was set up manually by means of wires. In addition to these wires, the ENIAC operator had to manually set up to 6000 muti-position mechanical switches. Programming ENIAC was very time consuming and tedious.

ENIAC did not support dynamic conditional operations (e.g. IF . . . THEN). An operation could be repeated a fixed number of times by hard wiring the loop counter to an appropriate value. Because the ability to make a decision depending on the value of a data element is vital to the operation of all computers, ENIAC was not a computer in today's sense of the word. It was an electronic calculator.

John von Neumann, EDVAC and IAS

The first US computer to use the *stored program* concept was EDVAC (Electronic Discrete Variable Automatic Computer). EDVAC was designed by some of the same team that designed the ENIAC at the Moore School of Engineering at the University of Pennsylvania.

John von Neumann, one of the leading mathematicians of his age, participated in EDVAC's design. He wrote a document entitled '*First draft of a report on the EDVAC*', which compiled the results of various design meetings. Before von Neumann, computer programs were stored either mechanically or in separate memories from the data used by the program. Von Neumann introduced the concept of the stored program—an idea so commonplace today that we take it for granted. In a stored program *von Neumann machine* both the program that specifies what operations are to be carried out and the data used by the program are stored in the same memory. The stored program computer consists of a memory containing instructions coded in binary form. The control part of the computer reads an instruction from memory, carries it out, then reads the next instruction, and so on. Although EDVAC is generally regarded as the first stored program computer, this is not strictly true because data and instructions did not have a common format and were not interchangeable.

EDVAC promoted the design of memory systems. The capacity of EDVAC's *mercury delay line* memory was 1024 words of 44 bits. A mercury delay line operates by converting data into pulses of ultrasonic sound that continuously reticulate in a long column of mercury in a tube.

EDVAC was not a great commercial success. Its construction was largely completed by April 1949, but it didn't run its first applications program until October 1951. Because of its adoption of the stored program concept, EDVAC became a topic in the first lecture course given on computers. These lectures took place before EDVAC was actually constructed.

Another important early computer was IAS constructed by von Neumann and his colleagues at the Institute for Advanced Studies in Princeton. IAS is remarkably similar to modern computers. Main memory was 1K words and a magnetic drum was used to provide 16K words of secondary storage. The magnetic drum was the forerunner of today's disk drive. Instead of recording data on the flat platter found in a hard drive, data was stored on the surface of a rotating drum.

In the late 1940s the Whirlwind computer was produced at MIT for the US Air Force. This was the first computer intended for real-time information processing. It employed *ferrite-core* memory (the standard form of mainframe memory until the semiconductor integrated circuit came along in the late 1960s). A ferrite core is a tiny bead of a magnetic martial that can be magnetized clockwise or counterclockwise to store a one or a zero. Ferrite core memory is no longer widely used today, although the term remains in expressions such as *core dump*, which means a printout of the contents of a region of memory.

One of the most important centers of early computer development in the 1940s was Manchester University in

England. In 1948 Tom Kilburn created a prototype computer called the Manchester Baby. This was a demonstration machine that tested the concept of the stored program computer and the Williams store, which stored data on the surface of a cathode ray tube. Some regard the Manchester Baby as the world's first true stored program computer.

IBM's place in computer history

No history of the computer can neglect the giant of the computer world, IBM, which has had such an impact on the computer industry. Although IBM grew out of the Computing–Tabulating–Recording (C–T–R) Company founded in 1911, its origin dates back to the 1880s. The C–T–R Company was the result of a merger between the International Time Recording (ITR) Company, the Computing Scale Company of America, and Herman Hollerith's Tabulating Machine Company (founded in 1896). In 1914 Thomas J. Watson, Senior, left the National Cash Register Company to join the C–T–R company and soon became President. In 1917, a Canadian unit of the C–T–R company called International Business Machines Co. Ltd was set up. Because this name was so well suited to the C–T–R company's role, they adopted it for the whole organization in 1924. IBM bought Electromatic Typewriters in 1933 and the first IBM electric typewriter was marketed 2 years later.

IBM's first contact with computers was via its relationship with Aiken at Harvard University. In 1948 Watson Senior at IBM gave the order to construct the Selective Sequence Control Computer. Although this was not a stored program computer, it was IBM's first step from the punched card tabulator to the computer.

Thomas. J. Watson, Junior, was responsible for building the Type 701 EDPM (Electronic Data Processing Machine) in 1953 to convince his father that computers were not a threat to IBM's conventional business. The 700 series was successful and dominated the mainframe market for a decade. In 1956 IBM launched a successor, the 704, which was the world's first supercomputer. The 704 was largely designed by Gene Amdahl who later founded his own supercomputer company in the 1990s.

IBM's most important mainframe was the System/360, which was first delivered in 1965. The importance of the 32-bit System/360 is that it was a member of a series of computers, each with the same architecture (i.e. programming model) but with different performance; for example, the System/360 model 91 was 300 times faster than the model 20. IBM developed a common operating system, OS/360, for their series. Other manufactures built their own computers that were compatible with System/360 and thereby began the slow process towards standardization in the computer industry.

In 1960 the Series/360 model 85 became the first computer to implement cache memory. Cache memory keeps a copy of frequently used data in very high-speed memory to reduce the number of accesses to the slower main store. Cache memory has become one of the most important features of today's high performance systems.

In August 1980 IBM became the first major manufacturer to market a PC. IBM had been working on a PC since about 1979 when it was becoming obvious that IBM's market would eventually start to come under threat from the PC manufacturers such as Apple and Commodore. IBM not only sold mainframes and personal computers—by the end of 1970s IBM had introduced the floppy disk, computerized supermarket checkouts, and the first automatic teller machines.

1.4.6 The birth of transistors, ICs, and microprocessors

Since the 1940s computer hardware has become smaller and faster. The power-hungry and unreliable vacuum tube was replaced by the smaller, reliable transistor in the 1950s. The transistor plays the same role as a thermionic tube; the only real difference is that a transistor switches a current flowing through a crystal rather than a beam of electrons flowing through a vacuum. The transistor was invented by William Shockley, John Bardeen, and Walter Brattain at AT&T's Bell Lab in 1948.

If you can put one transistor on a slice of silicon, you can put two or more transistors on the same piece of silicon. The idea occurred to Jack St Clair Kilby at Texas Instruments in 1958. Kilby built a working model and filed a patent early in 1959. In January of 1959, Robert Noyce at Fairchild Semiconductor was also thinking of the integrated circuit. He too applied for a patent and it was granted in 1961. Today, both Noyce and Kilby are regarded as the joint inventors of the IC.

The minicomputer era

The microprocessor was not directly derived from the mainframe computer. Between the mainframe and the microprocessor lies the *minicomputer*, a cut-down version of the mainframe, which appeared in the 1960s. By the 1960s many departments of computer science could afford their own minicomputers and a whole generation of students learned computer science from PDP-11s and NOVAs in the 1960s and 1970s. Some of these minicomputers were used in real-time applications (i.e. applications in which the computer has to respond to changes in its inputs within a specified time).

One of the first minicomputers was Digital Equipment Corporation's PDP-5, introduced in 1964. This was followed by the PDP-8, in 1966 and the very successful PDP-11, in 1969. Even the PDP-11 would be regarded as a very basic machine by today's standards. Digital Equipment built on their success with the PDP-11 series and introduced their VAX architecture in 1978 with the VAX-11/780, which dominated the minicomputer world in the 1980s. The VAX

EARLY MICROPROCESSOR SPINOFFS

The first two major microprocessors were the 8080 and the 6800 from Intel and Motorola, respectively. Other microprocessor manufacturers emerged when engineers left Intel and Motorola to start their own companies. Federico Faggin, one of the founders of Intel, left the company and founded Zilog in 1974. Zilog made the Z80, which was compatible with Intel's 8080 at the machine-code level. The Z80 has a superset of the 8080's instructions.

A group of engineers left Motorola to form MOS Technologies in 1975. They created the 6502 microprocessor, which was similar to the 6800 but not software compatible with it. The 6502 was the first low-cost microprocessor and was adopted by Apple and several other early PCs.

range was replaced by the 64-bit Alpha architecture (a high-performance microprocessor) in 1991. The Digital Equipment Corporation, renamed Digital, was taken over by Compaq in 1998.

Microprocessor and the PC

Credit for creating the world's first microprocessor, the 4040, goes to Ted Hoff and Fagin at Intel. Three engineers from Japan worked with Hoff to implement a calculator's digital logic circuits in silicon. Hoff developed a general purpose computer that could be programmed to carry out calculator functions. Towards the end of 1969 the structure of a programmable calculator had emerged. The 4004 used about 2300 transistors and is considered the first general purpose programmable microprocessor, even though it was only a 4-bit device.

The 4004 was rapidly followed by the 8-bit 8008 microprocessor, which was originally intended for a CRT application. By using some of the production techniques developed for the 4004, Intel was able to manufacture the 8008 as early as March 1972. The 8008 was soon replaced by a better version, the first really popular general purpose 8-bit microprocessor, the 8080 (in production in early 1974). Shortly after the 8080 went into production, Motorola created its own competitor, the 8-bit 6800.

Six months after the 8008 was introduced, the first ready-made computer based on the 8008, the Micral, was designed and built in France. The term *microcomputer* was coined to refer to the Micral, although the Micral was not successful in the USA. In January 1975 *Popular Electronics* magazine published an article on microcomputer design by Ed Roberts who had a small company called MITS. Roberts' computer was called Altair and was constructed from a kit.

Although the Altair was intended for hobbyists, it had a significant impact and sold 2000 kits in its first year. In March 1976, Steve Wozniak and Steve Jobs designed a 6502-based computer, which they called the Apple 1. A year later in 1977 they created the Apple II with 16 kbytes of ROM, 4 kbytes of RAM, and a color display and keyboard. Although unsophisticated, this was the first practical PC.

As microprocessor technology improved, it became possible to put more and more transistors on larger and larger chips of silicon. Microprocessors of the early 1980s were not only more powerful than their predecessors in terms of the speed at which they could execute instructions, they were also more sophisticated in terms of the facilities they offered. Intel took the core of their 8080 microprocessor and converted it from an 8-bit into a 16-bit machine, the 8086. Motorola did not extend their 8-bit 6800 to create a 16-bit processor. Instead, they started again and did not attempt to achieve either object or source code compatibility with earlier processors. By beginning with a clean slate, Motorola was able to create a 32-bit microprocessor with an exceptionally clean architecture in 1979.

Several PC manufacturers adopted the 68K; Apple used it in the Macintosh and it was incorporated in the Atari and Amiga computers. All three of these computers were regarded as technically competent and had many very enthusiastic followers. The Macintosh was sold as a relatively high-priced black box with the computer, software, and peripherals from a single source. This approach could not compete with the IBM PC, launched in 1981, with an open system architecture that allowed the user to purchase hardware and software from the supplier with the best price. The Atari and Amiga computers suffered because they had the air of the games machine. Although the Commodore Amiga in 1985 had many of the hallmarks of a modern multimedia machine, it was derided as a games machine because few then grasped the importance of advanced graphics and high-quality sound.

The 68K developed into the 68020, 68030, 68040, and 68060. Versions were developed for the embedded processor market and Motorola played no further role in the PC market until Apple adopted Motorola's PowerPC processor. The PowerPC came from IBM and was not a descendent of the 68K family.

Many fell in love with the Apple Mac. It was a sophisticated and powerful PC, but not a great commercial success. Apple's commercial failure demonstrates that those in the semiconductor industry must realize that commercial factors are every bit as important as architectural excellence and performance. Apple failed because their processor, from hardware to operating system, was proprietary. Apple didn't publish detailed hardware specifications or license their BIOS and operating system. IBM adopted open standards and anyone could build a copy of the IBM PC. Hundreds of manufacturers started producing parts of PCs and an entire industry sprang up. You could buy a basic system from one place, a hard disk from another, and a graphics card from yet another supplier. By publishing standards for the PC's bus, anyone could create a peripheral for the PC. What IBM lost in the form of increased competition, they more than made up for in the rapidly expanding market. IBM's open standard provided an incentive for software writers to generate software for the PC market.

The sheer volume of PCs and their interfaces (plus the software base) pushed PC prices down and down. The Apple was perceived as over-priced. Even though Apple adopted the PowerPC, it was too late and Apple's role in the PC world was marginalized. However by 2005, cut-throat competition from PC manufacturers was forcing IBM to abandon its PC business, whereas Apple was flourishing in a niche market that rewarded *style*.

A major change in direction in computer architecture took place in the 1980s when the RISC or Reduced Instruction Set Computer first appeared. Some observers expected the RISC to sweep away all CISC processors like the 8086 and 68K families.

It was the work carried out by David Paterson at the University of Berkley in the early 1980s that brought the RISC philosophy to a wider audience. Paterson was also responsible for coining the term 'RISC' in 1980. The Berkeley RISC was constructed at a university (like many of the first mainframes such as EDSAC) and required only a very tiny fraction of the resources consumed by these early mainframes. Indeed, the Berkeley RISC is hardly more than an extended graduate project. It took about a year to design and fabricate the RISC I in silicon. By 1983 the Berkeley RISC II had been produced and that proved to be both a testing ground for RISC ideas and the start of a new industry. Many of the principles of RISC design were later incorporated in Intel's processors.

1.4.7 Mass computing and the rise of the Internet

The Internet and digital multimedia have driven the evolution of the PC. The Internet provides interconnectivity and the digital revolution has extended into sound and vision. The cassette-based personal stereo system has been displaced by the minidisk and the MP3 players with solid state memory. The DVD with its ability to store an entire movie on a single disk first became available in 1996 and by 1998 over one million DVD players had been sold in the USA. The digital video camera that once belonged to the world of the professional filmmaker is now available to anyone with a modest income.

All these applications have had a profound effect on the computer world. Digital video requires vast amounts of storage. Within 5 years, low-cost hard disk capacities grew from about 1 Gbyte to 400 Gbytes or more. The DVD uses very sophisticated signal processing techniques that require very

high-performance hardware to process the signals in real-time. The MP3 player requires a high-speed data link to download music from the Internet.

The demand for increasing reality in video games and real-time image processing has spurred development in special-purpose video subsystems. Video processing requires the ability to render images, which means drawing vast numbers of polygons on the screen and filling them with a uniform color. The more polygons used to compose an image, the more accurate the rendition of the image.

The effect of the multimedia revolution had led to the *commoditization* of the PC, which is now just another commodity like a television or a stereo player. Equally, the growth of multimedia has forced the development of higher speed processors, low-cost high-density memory systems, multimedia-aware operating systems, data communications, and new processor architectures.

The Internet revolution

Just as the computer itself was the result of a number of independent developments (the need for automated calculation, the theoretical development of computer science, the enabling technologies of communications and electronics, the keyboard and data processing industries), the Internet was the fruit of a number of separate developments.

The principal ingredients of the Internet are communications, protocols, and hypertext. Communications systems have been developed throughout human history as we have already pointed out when discussing the enabling technology behind the computer. The USA's Department of Defense created a scientific organization, ARPA (Advanced Research Projects Agency) in 1958 at the height of the Cold War. ARPA had some of the characteristics of the Manhattan project, which had preceded it during the Second World War. A large group of talented scientists was assembled to work on a project of national importance. From its early days ARPA concentrated on computer technology and communications systems; moreover, ARPA was moved into the academic area which meant that it had a rather different ethos from that of the commercial world because academics cooperate and share information.

One of the reasons why ARPA concentrated on networking was the fear that a future war involving nuclear weapons would begin with an attack on communications centers limiting the capacity to respond in a coordinated manner. By networking computers and ensuring that a message can take many paths through the network to get from its source to its destination, the network can be made robust and able to cope with the loss of some of its links of switching centers.

In 1969 ARPA began to construct a testbed for networking, a system that linked four nodes: University of California at Los Angeles, SRI (in Stanford), University of California at Santa Barbara, and University of Utah. Data was sent in the form of individual packets or frames rather than as complete end-to-end messages. In 1972 ARPA was renamed DARPA (Defense Advances Research Projects Agency).

In 1973 the TCP/IP (transmission control protocol/Internet protocol) was developed at Stanford; this is the set of rules that govern the routing of a packet through a computer network. Another important step on the way to the Internet was Robert Metcalfe's development of the Ethernet, which enabled computers to communicate with each other over a local area network based on a low-cost cable. The Ethernet made it possible to link computers in a university together and the ARPANET allowed the universities to be linked together. Ethernet was, however, based on techniques developed during the construction of the University of Hawaii's radio-based packet-switching ALOHAnet, another ARPA-funded project.

Up to 1983 ARPANET users had to use a numeric IP address to access other users on the Internet. In 1983 the University of Wisconsin created the Domain Name System (DNS), which routed packets to a domain name rather than an IP address.

The World's largest community of physicists is at CERN in Geneva. In 1990 Tim Berners-Lee implemented a hypertext-based system to provide information to other the members of the high-energy physics community. This system was released by CERN in 1993 as the World-Wide Web (WWW). In the same year, Marc Andreessen at the University of Illinois developed a graphical user interface to the WWW, a browser called *Mosaic*. All that the Internet and the WWW had to do now was to grow.

1.5 The digital computer

Before beginning the discussion of computer hardware proper, we need to say what a computer is and to define a few terms. If ever an award were to be given to those guilty of misinformation in the field of computer science, it would go to the creators of HAL in *2001*, R2D2 in *Star Wars*, K9 in *Doctor Who*, and Data in *Star Trek*. These fictional machines have generated the popular myth that a computer is a reasonably close approximation to a human brain, which stores an infinite volume of data.

The reality is a little more mundane. A computer is a machine that takes in information from the outside world, processes it according to some predetermined set of operations, and delivers the processed information. This definition of a computer is remarkably unhelpful, because it attempts to define the word *computer* in terms of the equally complex words *information, operation,* and *process*. Perhaps a better approach is to provide examples of what computers do by looking at the role of computers in data processing, numerical computation (popularly called *number crunching*), workstations, automatic control systems, and electronic systems.

1.5.1 The PC and workstation

The 1980s witnessed two significant changes in computing—the introduction of the PC and the workstation. PCs bring computing power to people in offices and in their own homes. Although primitive PCs have been around since the mid 1970s, the IBM PC and Apple Macintosh transformed the PC from an enthusiast's toy into a useful tool. Software such as word processors, databases, and spreadsheets revolutionized the office environment, just as computer-aided design packages revolutionized the industrial design environment. Today's engineer can design a circuit and simulate its behavior using one software package and then create a layout for a printed circuit board (PCB) with another package. Indeed, the output from the PCB design package may be suitable for feeding directly into the machine that actually makes the PCBs.

In the third edition of this book in 1999 I said

Probably the most important application of the personal computer is in word processing... Today's personal computers have immensely sophisticated word processing packages that create a professional-looking result and even include spelling and grammar checkers to remove embarrassing mistakes. When powerful personal computers are coupled to laser printers, anyone can use desktop publishing packages capable of creating manuscripts that were once the province of the professional publisher.

Now, all that's taken for granted. Today's PCs can take video from your camcorder, edit it, add special effects, and then burn it to a DVD that can be played on any home entertainment system.

Although everyone is familiar with the PC, the concept of the *workstation* is less widely understood. A workstation can be best thought of as a high-performance PC that employs state-of-the-art technology and is normally used in industry. Workstations have been produced by manufacturers such as Apollo, Sun, HP, Digital, Silicon Graphics, and Xerox. They share many of the characteristics of PCs and are used by engineers or designers. When writing the third edition, I stated that the biggest difference between workstations and PCs was in graphics and displays. This difference has all but vanished with the introduction of high-speed graphics cards and large LCD displays into the PC world.

1.5.2 The computer as a data processor

The early years of computing were dominated by the mainframe, which was largely used as a data processor. Figure 1.1 describes a computer designed to deal with the payroll of a large factory. We will call the whole thing a computer, in contrast with those who would say that the CPU (central processing unit) is the computer and all the other devices are peripherals. Inside the computer's immediate access memory is a program, a collection of primitive machine-code

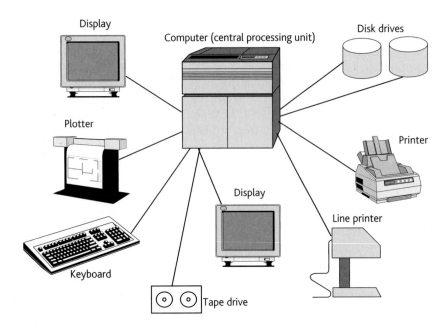

Figure 1.1 The computer as a data processor.

operations, whose purpose is to calculate an employee's pay based on the number of hours worked, the basic rate of pay, and the overtime rate. Of course, this program would also deal with tax and any other deductions.

Because the computer's immediate access memory is relatively expensive, only enough is provided to hold the program and the data it is currently processing. The mass of information on the employees is normally held in secondary store as a disk file. Whenever the CPU requires information about a particular employee, the appropriate data is copied from the disk and placed in the immediate access store. The time taken to perform this operation is a small fraction of a second but is many times slower than reading from the immediate access store. However, the cost of storing information on disk is very low indeed and this compensates for its relative slowness.

The tape transport stores data more cheaply than the disk (tape is called *tertiary* storage). Data on the disks is copied onto tape periodically and the tapes stored in the basement for security reasons. Every so often the system is said to crash and everything grinds to a halt. The last tape dump can be reloaded and the system assumes the state it was in a short time before the crash. Incidentally, the term *crash* had the original meaning of a failure resulting from a read/write head in a disk drive crashing into the rotating surface of a disk and physically damaging the magnetic coating on its surface.

The terminals (i.e. keyboard and display) allow operators to enter data directly into the system. This information could be the number of hours an employee has worked in the current week. The terminal can also be used to ask specific questions, such as 'How much tax did Mr XYZ pay in November?' To be a little more precise, the keyboard doesn't actually ask questions but it allows the programmer to execute a program containing the relevant question. The keyboard can be used to modify the program itself so that new facilities may be added as the system grows. Computers found in data processing are often characterized by their large secondary stores and their extensive use of printers and terminals.

1.5.3 The computer as a numeric processor

Numeric processing or *number crunching* refers to computer applications involving a very large volume of mathematical operations—sometimes billions of operations per job. Computers used in numeric processing applications are frequently characterized by powerful and very expensive CPUs, very high-speed memories, and relatively modest quantities of input/output devices and secondary storage. Some supercomputers are constructed from large arrays of microprocessors operating in parallel.

Most of the applications of numeric processing are best described as *scientific*. For example, consider the application of computers to the modeling of the processes governing the weather. The atmosphere is a continuous, three-dimensional medium composed of molecules of different gases. The scientist can't easily deal with a continuous medium, but can make the problem more tractable by considering the atmosphere to be composed of a very large number of cubes. Each of these cubes is considered to have a uniform temperature, density, and pressure. That is, the gas making up a cube shows no variation whatsoever in its physical properties. Variations exist only between adjacent cubes. A cube has six faces and the scientist can create a model of how the cube interacts with each of its six immediate neighbors.

The scientist may start by assuming that all cubes are identical (there is no initial interaction between cubes) and then consider what happens when a source of energy, the sun, is applied to the model. The effect of each cube on its neighbor is calculated and the whole process is repeated cyclically (iteration). In order to get accurate results, the size of the cubes should be small, otherwise the assumption that the properties of the air in the cube are uniform will not be valid. Moreover, the number of iterations needed to get the results to converge to a steady-state value is often very large. Consequently, this type of problem often requires very long runs on immensely powerful computers, or *supercomputers* as they are sometimes called. The pressure to solve complex scientific problems has been one of the major driving forces behind the development of computer architecture.

Numeric processing also pops up in some *real-time* applications of computers. Here, the term *real-time* indicates that the results of a computation are required within a given time. Consider the application of computers to air-traffic control. A rotating radar antenna sends out a radio signal that is echoed back from a target. Because radio waves travel at a fixed speed (the speed of light), radar can be used to measure the bearing and distance (*range*) of each aircraft. At time t, target i at position $P_{i,t}$ returns an echo giving its range $r_{i,t}$, and bearing $b_{i,t}$. Unfortunately, because of the nature of radar receivers, a random error is added to the value of each echo from a target.

The computer obtains data from the radar receiver for n targets, updated p times a minute. From this raw data that is corrupted by noise, the computer computes the position of each aircraft and its track and warns air traffic control of possible conflicts. All this requires considerable high-speed numerical computation.

Supercomputers are also used by the security services to crack codes and to monitor telecommunications traffic for certain words and phrases.

1.5.4 The computer in automatic control

The majority of computers are found neither in data processing nor in numeric processing activities. The advent of the microprocessor put the computer at the heart of many automatic control systems. When used as a control element, the computer is *embedded* in a larger system and is invisible to the observer. By invisible we mean that you may not be aware of the existence of the computer. Consider a computer in a pump in a gas station that receives cash in a slot and delivers a measured amount of fuel. The user doesn't care whether the pump is controlled by a microprocessor or by a clockwork mechanism, as long as it functions correctly.

A good example of a computer in automatic control is an aircraft's automatic landing system, illustrated in Fig. 1.2. The aircraft's *position* (height, distance from touch down, and

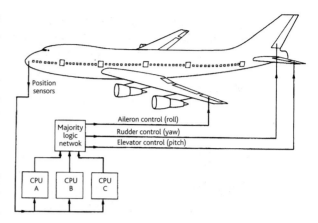

Figure 1.2 The computer as a control element in a flight control system.

distance off the runway centerline) and *speed* are determined by radio techniques in conjunction with a ground-based instrument-landing system. Information about the aircraft's position is fed to the three computers, which, individually, determine the error in the aircraft's course. The error is the difference between the aircraft's measured position and the position it should be in. The output from the computer is the signals required to move the aircraft's control surfaces (ailerons, elevator, and rudder) and adjust the engine's thrust. In this case the computer's program is held in ROM, a memory that can be read from but not written to. Once the program to land the aircraft has been developed, it requires only occasional modification.

The automatic-landing system requires three computers, each working on the same calculation with the same inputs. The outputs of the computers are fed to a majority logic circuit called a *voting network*. If all three inputs to the majority logic circuit are the same, its output is identical to its inputs. If one computer fails, the circuit selects its output to be the same as that produced by the two good computers. This arrangement is called *triple modular redundancy* and makes the system highly reliable.

Another example of the computer as a controller can be found in the automobile. Car manufacturers want to increase the efficiency and performance of the internal combustion engine and reduce the emission of harmful combustion products. Figure 1.3 illustrates the structure of a computerized fuel injection system that improves the performance of an engine. The temperature and pressure of the air, the angle of the crankshaft, and several other variables have to be measured thousands of times a second. These input parameters are used to calculate how much fuel should be injected into each cylinder.

The *glass cockpit* provides another example of the computer as a controller. Until the mid 1980s the flight instrumentation of commercial aircraft was almost entirely electromechanical.

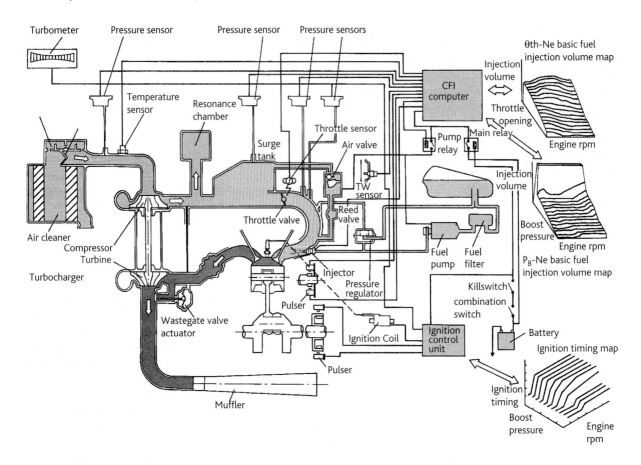

Figure 1.3 The computerized fuel injection system.

Today the mechanical devices that display height, speed, engine performance, and the altitude of the aircraft are being replaced by electronic displays controlled by microcomputers. These displays are based on the cathode ray tube or LED, hence the expression 'glass cockpit'. Electronic displays are easier to read and more reliable than their mechanical counterparts, but they provide only the information required by the flight crew at any instant.

Figure 1.4 illustrates an aircraft display that combines a radar image of clouds together with navigational information. In this example the pilot can see that the aircraft is routed from radio beacon WCO to BKP to BED and will miss the area of storm activity. Interestingly enough, this type of indicator has been accused of *deskilling* pilots, because they no longer have to create their own mental image of the position of their aircraft with respect to the World from much cruder instruments.

In the 1970s the USA planned a military navigation system based on satellite technology called GPS (*global positioning system*), which became fully operational in the 1990s. The civilian use of this military technology turned out to be one of the most important and unexpected growth areas in the late 1990s. GPS provides another interesting application of the computer as a component in an electronic system. The principles governing GPS are very simple. A satellite in medium Earth orbit at 20 200 km contains a very accurate atomic clock and it broadcasts both the time and its position.

Suppose you pick up the radio signal from one of these Navstar satellites, decode it, and compare the reported time with your watch. You may notice that the time from the satellite is inaccurate. That doesn't mean that the US military has wasted its tax dollars on faulty atomic clocks, but that the signal has been traveling through space before it reaches you. Because the speed of light is 300 000 km/s, you know that the satellite must 20 000 km away. Every point that is 20 000 km from the satellite falls on the surface of a sphere whose center is the satellite.

If you perform the same operation with a second satellite, you know that you are on the surface of another sphere. These two spheres must intersect. Three-dimensional geometry tells us that the points at which two spheres merge is a ring. If you receive signals from three satellites, the three spheres intersect at just two points. One of these points is normally located under the surface of the Earth and can be

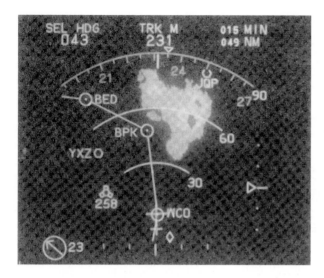

Figure 1.4 Computer-controlled displays in the glass cockpit. This figure illustrates the primary navigation display (or horizontal situation indicator) that the pilot uses to determine the direction in which the aircraft is traveling (in this case 231°—approximately south-west). In addition to the heading, the display indicates the position and density of cloud and the location of radio beacons. The three arcs indicate range from the aircraft (30, 60, 90 nautical miles).

disregarded. You can therefore work out your exact position on the surface of the Earth. This scheme relies on you having access to the exact time (i.e. your own atomic clock). However, by receiving signals from a fourth satellite you can calculate the time as well as your position.

Several companies produce small low-cost GPS receivers that receive signals from the 24 Navstar satellites, decode the timing signals and the ephemeris (i.e. satellite position), and calculate the position in terms of latitude and longitude. By embedding a microprocessor in the system, you can process the position data in any way you want. For example, by comparing successive positions you can work out your speed and direction. If you enter the coordinates of a place you wish to go to, the processor can continually give you a bearing to head, a distance to your destination, and an estimated time of arrival.

By adding a liquid crystal display and a map stored in a read-only memory to a GPS receiver, you can make a hand-held device that shows where you are with respect to towns, roads, and rivers. By 2000 you could buy a device for about $100 that showed exactly where you were on the surface of the Earth to an accuracy of a few meters.

The combination of a GPS unit plus a microprocessor plus a display system became a major growth area from about 2000 because there are so many applications. Apart from its obvious applications to sailing and aviation, GPS can be included in automobiles (the road maps are stored on CD

ROMs). GPS can even be integrated into expensive systems that aren't intended to move—unless they are stolen. If the system moves, the GPS detects the new position and reports it to the police.

1.6 The stored program computer—an overview

Before discussing the *stored program computer*, consider first the human being. It's natural to compare today's wonder, the computer, with the human just as the Victorians did with their technology. They coined expressions like, 'He has a screw loose', or 'He's run out of steam', in an endeavor to describe humans in terms of their mechanical technology.

Figure 1.5 shows how a human can be viewed as a system with inputs, a processing device, and outputs. The inputs are sight (eyes), smell (nose), taste (tongue), touch (skin), sound (ear), and position (muscle tension). The brain processes information from its sensors and stores new information. The storage aspect of the brain is important because it modifies the brain's operation by a process we call *learning*. Because the brain learns from new stimuli, it doesn't always exhibit the same response to a given stimulus. Once a child has been burned by a flame the child reacts differently the next time they encounter fire.

The brain's ability to both store and process information is shared by the digital computer. Computers can't yet mimic the operation of the brain and simplistic comparisons between the computer and the brain are misleading at best and mischievous at worst. A branch of computer science is devoted to the study of computers that do indeed share some of the brain's properties and attempt to mimic the human brain. Such computers are called *neural nets*.

The output from the brain is used to generate speech or to control the muscles needed to move the body.

Figure 1.6 shows how a computer can be compared with a human. A computer can have all the inputs a human has plus inputs for things we can't detect. By means of photoelectric devices and radio receivers, a computer can sense ultraviolet light, infrared, X-rays, and radio waves. The computer's output is also more versatile than that of humans. Computers can produce mechanical movement (by means of motors) and generate light (TV displays), sound (loudspeakers), or even heat (by passing a current through a resistor).

The computer's counterpart of the brain is its *central processing unit* plus its storage unit (memory). Like the brain, the computer processes its various inputs and produces an output.

We don't intend to write a treatise on the differences between the brain and the computer, but we should make a comment here to avoid some of the misconceptions about digital computers. It is probable that the brain's processing

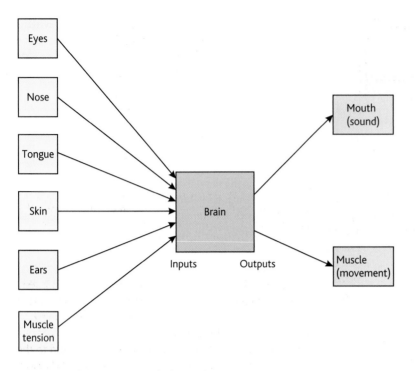

Figure 1.5 The organization of a human being.

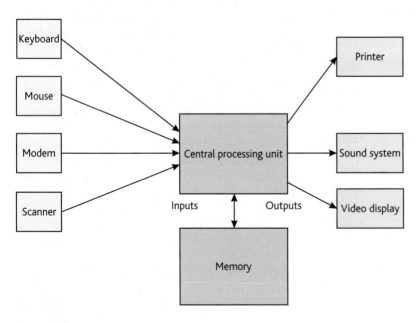

Figure 1.6 The organization of a computer.

brain. In particular, the digital computer is serially organized and performs a single instruction at a time, whereas the brain has a highly parallel organization and is able to carry out many activities at the same time.

Somewhere in every computer's memory is a block of information that we call a *program*. The word *program* has the same meaning as it does in the expression *program of studies*, or *program of music*. A computer program is a collection of instructions defining the actions to be carried out by the computer sequentially. The classic analogy with a computer program is a recipe in a cookery book. The recipe is a sequence of commands that must be obeyed one by one in the correct order. Our analogy between the computer program and the recipe is particularly appropriate because the cookery instructions involve operations on ingredients, just as the computer carries out operations on data stored in memory.

Figure 1.7 describes how a digital computer can be divided into two parts: a *central processing unit* (CPU) and a *memory* system. The CPU reads the program from memory and *executes* the operations specified by the program. The word *execute* means carry out; for example, the instruction *add A to B* causes the addition of a quantity called *A* to a quantity called *B* to be carried out. The actual nature of these instructions does not matter here. What is important is that the most complex actions carried out by a computer can be broken down into a number of more primitive operations. But then again, the most sublime thoughts of Einstein or Beethoven can be reduced to a large number of impulses transmitted across the synapses of the cells in their brains.

The memory system stores two types of information; the program and the data acted on or created by the program. It isn't necessary to store both the program and data in the *same* memory. Most computers store programs and data in a single memory system and are called *von Neumann machines*.

A computer is little more than a black box that moves *information* from one point to another and processes the

and memory functions are closely interrelated, whereas in the computer they are distinct. Some scientists believe that a major breakthrough in computing will come only when computer architecture takes on more of the features of the

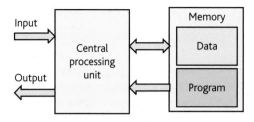

Figure 1.7 Structure of the general purpose digital computer.

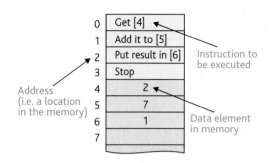

Figure 1.8 The program and data in memory. Throughout this book square brackets denote 'the contents of' so that in this figure, [4] is read as *the contents of memory location number 4* and is equal to 2.

information as it goes along. When we say *information* we mean the data and the instructions held inside the computer. Figure 1.7 shows two *information-carrying* paths connecting the CPU to its memory. The lower path with the single arrowhead from the memory to the CPU (heavily shaded in Fig. 1.7) indicates the route taken by the computer's *program*. The CPU reads the sequence of commands that make up a program one by one from its memory.

The upper path (lightly shaded in Fig. 1.7) with arrows at *both* its ends transfers data between the CPU and memory. The program controls the flow of information along the data path. This data path is *bidirectional*, because data can flow in two directions. During a *write cycle* data generated by the program flows from the CPU to the memory where it is stored for later use. During a *read cycle* the CPU requests the retrieval of a data item from memory, which is transferred from the memory to the CPU.

Suppose the instruction $x = y + z$ is stored in memory. The CPU must first fetch the instruction from memory and bring it to the CPU. Once the CPU has analyzed or *decoded* the instruction it has to get the values of y and z from memory. The CPU adds these values and sends the result, x, back to memory for storage.

Figure 1.8 demonstrates how the instructions making up a program and data coexist in the same memory. In this case the memory has seven locations, numbered from 0 to 7. Memory is normally regarded as an array of storage locations (boxes or pigeonholes). Each of these boxes has a unique location or *address* containing data. For example, in the simple memory of Fig. 1.8, address 5 contains the number 7. One difference between computers and people is that we number m items from 1 to m, whereas the computer numbers them from 0 to $m - 1$. This is because the computer regards 0 (zero) as a valid identifier. Unfortunately, people often confuse 0 the identifier with 0 meaning *nothing*.

Information in a computer's memory is accessed by providing the memory with the address (i.e. location) of the desired data. Only one memory location is addressed at a time. If we wish to search through memory for a particular item because we don't know its address, we have to read the items one at a time until we find the desired item. It appears that the human memory works in a very different way.

Information is accessed from our memories by applying a *key* to all locations within the memory (brain). This key is related to the data being accessed (in some way) and is not related to its location within the brain. Any memory locations containing information that associates with the key respond to the access. In other words, the brain carries out a parallel search of its memory for the information it requires.

Accessing many memory locations in parallel permits more than one location to respond to the access and is therefore very efficient. Suppose someone says 'chip' to you. The word *chip* is the key that is fed to all parts of your memory for matching. Your brain might produce responses of *chip (silicon)*, *chip (potato)*, *chip (on shoulder)*, and *chip (gambling)*.

The program in Fig. 1.8 occupies consecutive memory locations 0–3 and the data locations 4–6. The first instruction, *get [4]*, means *fetch the contents of memory location number 4 from the memory*. We employ square brackets to denote the contents of the address they enclose, so that in this case [4] = 2. The next instruction, at address 1, is *add it to [5]* and means *add the number brought by the previous instruction to the contents of location 5*. Thus, the computer adds 2 and 7 to get 9. The third instruction, *put result in [6]*, tells the computer to put the result (i.e. 9) in location 6. The 1 that was in location 6 before this instruction was obeyed is replaced by 9. The final instruction in location 3 tells the computer to stop.

We can summarize the operation of a digital computer by means of a little piece of *pseudocode* (pseudocode is a method of writing down an algorithm in a language that is a cross between a computer language such as C, Pascal, or Java and plain English). We shall meet pseudocode again.

```
DO
  BEGIN
    Read an instruction from memory
    Execute the instruction
  END
REPEAT FOREVER
```

Figure 1.9 The microcontroller SBC.

1.7 The PC—a naming of parts

The final part of this chapter looks at the computer with which most readers will be familiar, the PC. As we have not yet covered many of the elements of a computer, all we can do here is provide an overview and to name some of the parts of a typical computer system to help provide a context for following chapters.

Figure 1.9 shows a typical *single-board computer* (SBC). As its name suggests, the SBC consists of one printed circuit board containing the microprocessor, memory, peripherals, and everything

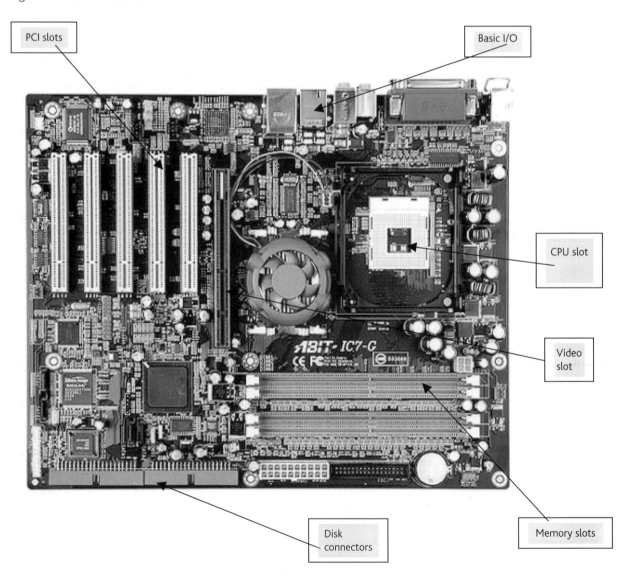

Figure 1.10 The PC motherboard.

else it needs to function. Such a board can be embedded in systems ranging from automobile engines to cell phones. The principal characteristic of the SBC is its lack of expandability or flexibility. Once you've made it, the system can't be expanded.

The PC is very different from the single-board computer because each user has their own requirements; some need lots of memory and fast video processing and some need several peripherals such as printers and scanners.

One way of providing flexibility is to design a system with slots into which you can plug accessories. This allows you to buy a basic system with functionality that is common to all computers with that board and then you can add specific enhancements such as a video card or a sound card.

Figure 1.10 shows a PC *motherboard*. The motherboard contains the CPU and all the electronics necessary to connect the CPU to memory and to provide basic input/output such as a keyboard and mouse interface and an interface to floppy and hard disk drives (including CD and DVD drives).

The motherboard in Fig. 1.10 has four areas of expandability. Program and data memory can be plugged into slots allowing the user to implement enough memory for their application (and their purse). You can also plug a video card into a special graphics slot, allowing you to use a basic system for applications such as data processing or an expensive state-of-the-art graphics card for a high-performance games machine with fast 3D graphics.

The CPU itself fits into a rectangular slot and is not permanently installed on the motherboard. If you want a faster processor, you can buy one and plug it in your motherboard. This strategy helps prevent the computer becoming out of date too soon.

The motherboard has built-in interfaces that are common to nearly all systems. A typical motherboard has interfaces to a keyboard and mouse, a floppy disk drive, and up to four hard disks or CD ROMs. Over the last few years, special-purpose functions have migrated from plug-in cards to the motherboard. For example, the USB serial interface, the local area network, and the audio system have been integrated on some of the high-performance motherboards.

The motherboard in Fig. 1.10 has five PCI connectors. These connectors allow you to plug cards into the motherboard. Each connector is wired to a *bus*, a set of parallel conductors that carry information between the cards and the CPU and memory. One of the advantages of a PC is its expandability because you can plug such a wide variety of cards into its bus. There are modems and cards that capture and process images from camcorders. There are cards that contain TV receivers. There are cards that interface a PC to industrial machines in a factory.

In this book we will be looking at all these aspects of a computer.

■ SUMMARY

We began this chapter with a discussion of the role of computer architecture in computer science education. Computer architecture provides the foundation of computing; it helps you to get the best out of computers and it aids in an understanding of a wide range of topics throughout computing.

We provided a brief history of computing. We can't do justice to this topic in a few pages. What we have attempted to do is to demonstrate that computing has had a long history and is the result of the merging of the telegraph industry, the card-based data processing industry, and the calculator industry.

In this chapter we have considered how the computer can be looked at as a component or, more traditionally, as part of a large system. Besides acting in the obvious role as a *computer system*, computers are now built into a wide range of everyday items from toys to automobile ignition systems. In particular, we have introduced some of the topics that make up a first-level course in computer architecture or computer organization.

We have introduced the notion of the von Neumann computer, which stored instructions and data in the *same* memory. The von Neumann computer reads instructions from memory, one by one and then executes them in turn.

The final part of this chapter provided an overview of the computer system with which most students will be familiar—the PC. This computer has a motherboard into which you can plug a Pentium microprocessor, memory, and peripherals. You can create a computer that suits your own price–performance ratio.

As we progress through this book, we are going to examine how the computer is organized and how it is able to step through instructions in memory and execute them. We will also show how the computer communicates with the world outside the CPU and its memory.

■ PROBLEMS

Unlike the problems at the end of other chapters, these problems are more philosophical and require further background reading if they are to be answered well.

1.1 I have always claimed you cannot name the inventor of the computer because what we now call a computer emerged after a long series of incremental steps. Am I correct?

1.2 If you have to name one person as inventor of the computer, who would you choose? And why?

1.3 What is the difference between computer architecture and computer organization?

1.4 A Rolls–Royce is not a Volkswagen Beetle. Is the difference a matter of architecture or organization?

1.5 List 10 applications of microprocessors you can think of and classify them into the groups we described (e.g. computer as a component). Your examples should cover as wide a range of applications as possible.

1.6   Do you think that a *digital* computer could ever be capable of feelings, free will, original thought, and self-awareness in a similar fashion to humans? If not, why not?

1.7   Some of the current high-performance civil aircraft such as the A320 AirBus have *fly-by-wire* control systems. In a conventional aircraft, the pilot moves a yoke that provides control inputs that are fed to the flying control surfaces and engines by mechanical linkages or hydraulic means. In the A320 the pilot moves the type of joystick normally associated with computer games. The pilot's commands from the joystick (called a *sidestick*) are fed to a computer and the computer interprets them and carries them out in the fashion it determines is most appropriate. For example, if the pilot tries to increase the speed to a level at which the airframe might be overstressed, the computer will refuse to obey the command. Some pilots and some members of the public are unhappy about this arrangement. Are their fears rational?

1.8   The computer has often been referred to as a *high-speed moron*. Is this statement fair?

1.9   Computers use binary arithmetic (i.e. all numbers are composed of 1s and 0s) to carry out their operations. Humans normally use decimal arithmetic (0–9) and have symbolic means of representing information (e.g. the Latin alphabet or the Chinese characters). Does this imply a fundamental difference between people and computers?

1.10   Shortly after the introduction of the computer, someone said that two computers could undertake all the computing in the World. At that time the best computers were no more powerful than today's pocket calculators. The commentator assumed that computers would be used to solve a few scientific problems and little else. As the cost and size of computers has been reduced, the role of computers has increased. Is there a limit to the applications of computers? Do you anticipate any radically new applications of computers?

1.11   A microprocessor manufacturer, at the release of their new super chip, was asked the question, 'What can your microprocessor do?' He said it was now possible to put it in washing machines so that the user could tell the machine what to do verbally, rather than by adjusting the settings manually.

At the same time we live in a world in which many of its inhabitants go short of the very basic necessities of life: water, food, shelter, and elementary health care. Does the computer make a positive contribution to the future well-being of the World's inhabitants? Is the answer the same if we ask about the computer's short-term effects or its long-term effects?

1.12   The workstation makes it possible to design and to test (by simulation) everything from other computers to large mechanical structures. Coupled with computer communications networks and computer-aided manufacturing, it could be argued that many people in technologically advanced societies will be able to work entirely from home. Indeed, all their shopping and banking activities can also be performed from home. Do you think that this step will be advantageous or disadvantageous? What will be the effects on society of a population that can, largely, work from home?

1.13   In a von Neumann machine, programs and data share the same memory. The operation 'get [4]' reads the contents of memory location number 4 and you can then operate on the number you've just read from this location. However, the contents of this location may not be a number. It may be an *instruction* itself. Consequently, a program in a von Neumann machine can modify itself. Can you think of any implications this statement has for computing?

1.14   When discussing the performance of computers we introduced the *benchmark*, a synthetic program whose execution time provides a figure of merit for the performance of a computer. If you glance at any popular computer magazine, you'll find computers compared in terms of benchmarks. Furthermore, there are several different benchmarks. A computer that performs better than others when executing one benchmark might not do so well when executing a different benchmark. What are the flaws in benchmarks as a test of performance and why do you think that some benchmarks favor one computer more than another?

1.15   The von Neumann digital computer offers just one computing paradigm. Other paradigms are provided by analog computers and neural networks. What are the differences between these paradigms and are there others?

Gates, circuits, and combinational logic

2

INTRODUCTION

We begin our study of the digital computer by investigating the elements from which it is constructed. These circuit elements are *gates* and *flip-flops* and are also known as *combinational* and *sequential* logic elements, respectively. A combinational logic element is a circuit whose output depends only on its current inputs, whereas the output from a sequential element depends on its past history (i.e. a sequential element remembers its previous inputs) as well as its current input. We describe combinational logic in this chapter and devote the next chapter to sequential logic.

Before we introduce the gate, we highlight the difference between digital and analog systems and explain why computers are constructed from digital logic circuits. After describing the properties of several basic gates we demonstrate how a few gates can be connected together to carry out useful functions in the same way that bricks can be put together to build a house or a school. We include a Windows-based simulator that lets you construct complex circuits and then examine their behavior on a PC.

The behavior of digital circuits can be described in terms of a formal notation called *Boolean algebra*. We include an introduction to Boolean algebra because it allows you to analyze circuits containing gates and sometimes enables circuits to be constructed in a simpler form. Boolean algebra leads on to *Karnaugh maps*, a graphical technique for the simplification and manipulation of Boolean equations.

The last circuit element we introduce is the *tri-state* gate, which allows you to connect lots of separate digital circuits together by means of a common highway called a *bus*. A digital computer is composed of nothing more than digital circuits, buses, and sequential logic elements.

By the end of this chapter, you should be able to design a wide range of circuits that can perform operations as diverse as selecting between one of several signals to implementing simple arithmetic operations.

Real circuits can fail. The final part of this chapter takes a brief look at how you test digital circuits.

2.1 Analog and digital systems

Before we can appreciate the meaning and implications of digital systems, it's necessary to look at the nature of analog systems. The term *analog* is derived from the noun *analogy* and means a quantity that is related to, or resembles, or corresponds to, another quantity; for example, the length of a column of mercury in a thermometer is an analog of the temperature because the length of the mercury is proportional to the temperature. Analog electronic circuits represent physical quantities in terms of voltages or currents.

An analog variable can have any value between its maximum and minimum limits. If a variable X is represented by a voltage in the range -10 V to $+10$ V, X may assume any one of an infinite number of values within this range. We can say that X is *continuous* in value and can change its value by an arbitrarily small amount. Fig. 2.1 plots a variable X as a continuous function of time; that is, X doesn't jump instantaneously from one value to another. In Fig. 2.1, a fragment of the graph of X is magnified to reveal fluctuations that you can't see on the main graph. No matter how much you magnify this graph, the line will remain continuous and unbroken.

The design of analog circuits such as audio amplifiers is a demanding process, because analog signals must be processed without changing their shape. Changing the shape of an analog signal results in its degradation or *distortion*.

Information inside a computer is represented in *digital* form. A digital variable is *discrete* in both value and in time, as Fig. 2.2 demonstrates. The digital variable Y must take one of four possible values. Moreover, Y changes from one discrete value to another *instantaneously*. In practice, no physical (i.e. real) variable can change instantaneously and a real signal must pass through intermediate values as it changes from one discrete state to another.

All variables and constants in a digital system must take a value chosen from a set of values called an *alphabet*. In decimal arithmetic the alphabet is composed of the symbols 0, 1, 2, . . . 9 and in Morse code the alphabet is composed of the four symbols dot, dash, short space, and long space. Other digital systems are Braille, semaphore, and the days of the week.

A major advantage of representing information in digital form is that digital systems are resistant to error. A digital symbol can be distorted, but as long as the level of distortion is not sufficient for the symbol to be confused with a different symbol, the original symbol can always be recognized and reconstituted. For example, if you write the letter K by hand, most readers will be able to recognize it as a K unless it is so badly formed that it looks like another letter such as an R or C.

Digital computers use an alphabet composed of two symbols called 0 and 1 (sometimes called *false* and *true*, or low and high, or off and on). A digital system with two symbols is called a *binary* system. The physical representation of these symbols can be made as unlike each other as possible to give the maximum discrimination between the two digital values. Computers once stored binary information on paper tape—a hole represented one binary value and no hole represented the other. When reading paper tape the computer has only to distinguish between a hole and no-hole. Suppose we decided to replace this binary computer by a decimal computer. Imagine that paper tape were to be used to store the 10 digits 0–9. A number on the tape would consist of no-hole or a hole in one of nine sizes (10 symbols in all). How does this computer distinguish between a size six hole and a size five or a size seven

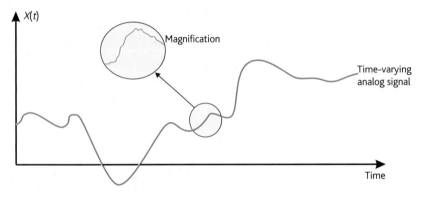

Figure 2.1 Characteristics of an analog variable.

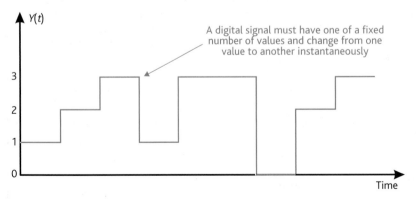

Figure 2.2 Characteristics of an ideal digital variable.

NOTES ON LOGIC VALUES

1. Every logic input or output must assume one of two discrete states. You cannot have a state that is neither 1 nor 0.

2. Each logic input or output can exist in only one state at any one time.

3. Each logic state has an inverse or complement that is the opposite of its current state. The complement of a true or one state is a false or zero state, and vice versa.

4. A logic value can be a constant or a variable. If it is a constant, it always remains in that state. If it is a variable, it may be switched between the states 0 and 1. A Boolean variable is also called a *literal*.

5. A variable is often named by the action it causes to take place. The following logical variables are all self-evident: START, STOP, RESET, COUNT, and ADD.

6. The signal level (i.e. high or low) that causes a variable to carry out a function is arbitrary. If a high voltage causes the action, the variable is called active-high. If a low voltage causes the action, the variable is called active-low. Thus, if an active-high signal is labeled START, a high level will initiate the action. If the signal is active-low and labeled START, a low level will trigger the action.

7. By convention, a system of logic that treats a low level as a 0 or false state and a high-level as a 1 or true state is called positive logic. Most of this chapter uses positive logic.

8. The term asserted is used to indicate that a signal is placed in the level that causes its activity to take place. If we say that START is asserted, we mean that it is placed in a high state to cause the action determined by START. Similarly, if we say that LOAD is asserted, we mean that it is placed in a low state to trigger the action.

LOGIC VALUES AND SIGNAL LEVELS

In a system using a 5 V power supply you might think that a bit is represented by exactly 0 V or 5 V. Unfortunately, we can't construct such precise electronic devices cheaply. We can construct devices that use two ranges of voltage to represent the binary values 0 and 1. For example, one logic family represents a 0 state by a signal in the range 0–0.4 V and a 1 state by a signal in the range 2.8–5 V.

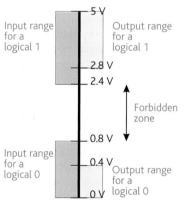

This diagram illustrates the ranges of voltage used to represent 0 and 1 states. Digital component manufacturers make several promises to users. First, they guarantee that the output of a gate in a logical 0 state shall be in the range 0–0.4V and that the output of a gate in a logical 1 state shall be in the range 2.8–5.0V. Similarly, they guarantee that the input circuit of a gate shall recognize a voltage in the range 0–0.8V as a logical 0 and a voltage in the range 2.4–5.0 V as a logical 1.

Here, two gates are wired together so that the output of gate 1 becomes the input of gate 2. The signal at the output of gate 1 is written V_{out} and the input to gate 2 is written V_{in}.

An *adder* (represented by the circle with a '+') is placed between the two gates so that the input voltage to the second gate is given by $V_{in} = V_{out} + V_{noise}$; that is, a voltage called V_{noise} is added to the output from gate 1. In a real circuit there is, of course, no such adder. The adder is fictitious and demonstrates how the output voltage may be modified by the addition of noise or interference. All electronic circuits are subject to such interference; for example, the effect of noise on a weak TV signal is to create *snow* on the screen.

Note that the range of input signals that are recognized as representing a 1 state (i.e. 2.4–5 V) is greater than the range of output signals produced by a gate in a 1 state (i.e. 2.8–5 V). By making the input range greater than the output range, the designer compensates for the effect of noise or unwanted signals. Suppose a noise spike of −0.2 V is added to a logical 1 output of 2.8 V to give a total input signal of 2.6 V. This signal, when presented to the input circuit of a gate, is greater than 2.4 V and is still guaranteed to be recognized as a logical 1. The difference between the input and output ranges for a given logic value known as the gate's *guaranteed noise immunity*.

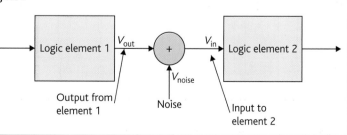

hole? Such a system would require extremely precise electronics.

A single binary digit is known as a bit (BInary digiT) and is the smallest unit of information possible; that is, a bit can't be subdivided into smaller units. Ideally, if a computer runs off, say, 3 V, a low level would be represented by 0.0 V and a high level by 3.0 V.

2.2 Fundamental gates

The digital computer consists of nothing more than the interconnection of three types of primitive elements called AND, OR, and NOT gates. Other gates called NAND, NOR, and EOR gates can be derived from these gates. We shall see that all digital circuits, may be designed from the appropriate interconnection of NAND (or NOR) gates alone. In other words, the most complex digital computer can be reduced to a mass of NAND gates. This statement doesn't devalue the computer any more than saying that the human brain is just a lot of neurons joined in a particularly complex way devalues the brain.

We don't use gates to build computers because we like them or because Boolean algebra is great fun. We use gates because they provide a way of mass producing cheap and reliable digital computers.

2.2.1 The AND gate

The AND gate is a circuit with two or more inputs and a single output. The output of an AND gate is true if and only if each of its inputs is also in a true state. Conversely, if one or more of the inputs to the AND gate is false, the output will also be false. Figure 2.3 provides the circuit symbol for both a two-input AND gate and a three-input AND gate. Note that the shape of the gate indicates its AND function (this will become clearer when we introduce the OR gate).

An AND gate is visualized in terms of an electric circuit or a highway as illustrated in Fig. 2.4. Electric current (or traffic) flows along the circuit (road) only if switches (bridges) A and B are closed. The logical symbol for the AND operator is a dot, so that A AND B can be written $A \cdot B$. As in normal algebra, the dot is often omitted and $A \cdot B$ can be written AB. The logical AND operator behaves like the multiplier operator in conventional algebra; for example, the expression $(A + B) \cdot (C + D) = A \cdot C + A \cdot D + B \cdot C + B \cdot D$ in both Boolean and conventional algebra.

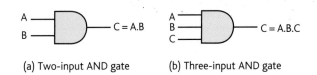

(a) Two-input AND gate   (b) Three-input AND gate

Figure 2.3 The AND gate.

WHAT IS A GATE?

The word gate conveys the idea of a two-state device—open or shut. A gate may be thought of as a black box with one or more input terminals and an output terminal. The gate processes the digital signals at its input terminals to produce a digital signal at its output terminal. The particular type of the gate determines the actual processing involved. The output C of a gate with two input terminals A and B can be expressed in conventional algebra as $C = F(A,B)$, where A, B, and C are two-valued variables and F is a logical function.

The output of a gate is a function only of its inputs. When we introduce the sequential circuit, we will discover that the sequential circuit's output depends on its previous output as well as its current inputs. We can demonstrate the concept of

a gate by means of an example from the analog world. Consider the algebraic expression $y = F(x) = 2x^2 + x + 1$. If we think of x as the input to a black box and y its output, the block diagram demonstrates how y is generated by a sequence of operations on x. The operations performed on the input are those of addition, multiplication, and squaring. Variable x enters the 'squarer' and comes out as x^2. The output from the squarer enters a multiplier (along with the constant 2) and comes out as $2x^2$, and so on. By applying all the operations to input x, we end up with output $2x^2 + x + 1$. The boxes carrying out these operations are entirely analogous to gates in the digital world—except that gates don't do anything as complicated as addition or multiplication.

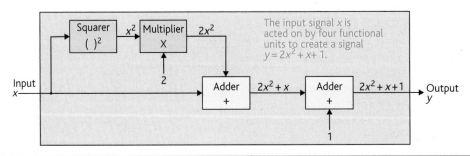

CIRCUIT CONVENTIONS

Because we write from left to right, many logic circuits are also read from left to right; that is, information flows from left to right with the inputs of gates on the left and the outputs on the right.

Because a circuit often contains many signal paths, some of these paths may have to cross over each other when the diagram is drawn on two-dimensional paper. We need a means of distinguishing between wires that join and wires that simply cross each other (rather like highways that merge and highways that fly over each other). The standard procedure is to regard two lines that simply cross as not being connected as the diagram illustrates. The connection of two lines is denoted by a dot at their intersection.

The voltage at any point along a conductor is constant and therefore the logical state is the same everywhere on the line. If a line is connected to the input of several gates, the input to each gate is the same. In this diagram, the value of X and P must be the same because the two lines are connected.

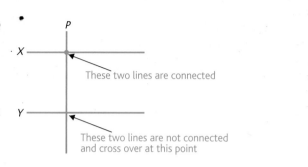

A corollary of the statement that the same logic state exists everywhere on a conductor is that a line must not be connected to the output of more than one circuit—otherwise the state of the line will be undefined if the outputs differ. At the end of this chapter we will introduce gates with special tri-state outputs that can be connected together without causing havoc.

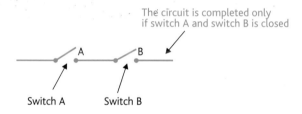

Figure 2.4 The representation of an AND gate.

A useful way of describing the relationship between the inputs of a gate and its output is the truth table. In a truth table the value of each output is tabulated for every possible combination of the inputs. Because the inputs are two valued (i.e. binary with states 0 and 1), a circuit with n inputs has 2^n lines in its truth table. The order in which the 2^n possible inputs are taken is not important but by convention the order corresponds to the natural binary sequence (we discuss binary numbers in Chapter 4). Table 2.1 describes the natural binary sequences for values of n from 1 to 4.

Table 2.2 illustrates the truth table for a two-input AND gate, although there's no reason why we can't have any number of inputs to an AND gate. Some real gates have three or four inputs and some have 10 or more inputs. However, it doesn't matter how many inputs an AND gate has. Only one line in the truth table will contain a 1 entry because all inputs must be true for the output to be true.

When we introduce computer arithmetic, computer architecture, and assembly language programming, we will see that computers don't operate on bits in isolation. Computers process entire groups of bits at a time. These groups are called words and are typically 8, 16, 32, or 64 bits wide. The AND

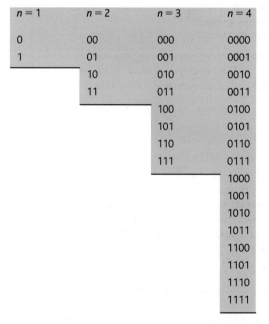

$n = 1$	$n = 2$	$n = 3$	$n = 4$
0	00	000	0000
1	01	001	0001
	10	010	0010
	11	011	0011
		100	0100
		101	0101
		110	0110
		111	0111
			1000
			1001
			1010
			1011
			1100
			1101
			1110
			1111

Table 2.1 The 2^n possible values of an n-bit variable for $n = 1$ to 4.

Inputs		Output
A	B	F = A · B
0	0	0
0	1	0
1	0	0
1	1	1

Table 2.2 Truth table for the AND gate.

operation, when applied to words, is called a logical operation to distinguish it from an arithmetic operation such as addition, subtraction, or multiplication. When two words take part in a logical operation such as an AND, the operation takes place between the individual pairs of bits; for example bit a_i of word A is ANDed with bit b_i of word B to produce bit c_i of word C. Consider the effect of ANDing of the following two 8-bit words A = 11011100 and B = 01100101.x

```
1 1 0 1 1 1 0 0 ◄─ word A
0 1 1 0 0 1 0 1 ◄─ word B
0 1 0 0 0 1 0 0 ◄─ C = A·B
```

In this example the result $C = A \cdot B$ is given by 01000100. Why should anyone want to AND together two words? If you AND bit x with 1, the result is x (because Table 2.2 demonstrates that $1.0 = 0$ and $1.1 = 1$). If you AND bit x with 0 the result is 0 (because the output of an AND gate is true only if both inputs are true). Consequently, a logical AND is used to mask certain bits in a word by forcing them to zero. For example, if we wish to clear the leftmost four bits of an 8-bit word to zero, ANDing the word with 00001111 will do the trick. The following example demonstrates the effect of an AND operation with a 00001111 mask.

```
1 1 0 1 1 0 1 1 ◄─ source word
0 0 0 0 1 1 1 1 ◄─ mask
0 0 0 0 1 0 1 1 ◄─ result
```

2.2.2 The OR gate

The output of an OR gate is true if any one (or more than one) of its inputs is true. Notice the difference between AND and OR operations. The output of an AND is true only if *all* inputs are true whereas the output of an OR is true if at least one input is true. The circuit symbol for a two-input and a three-input OR gate is given in Fig. 2.5. The logical symbol for an OR operation is an addition sign, so that the logical operation A OR B is written as A + B. The logical OR operator is the same as the conventional addition symbol because the OR operator behaves like the addition operator in algebra (the reasons for this will become clear when we introduce Boolean algebra). Table 2.3 provides the truth table for a two-input OR gate.

The behavior of an OR gate can be represented by the switching circuit of Fig. 2.6. A path exists from input to output if either of the two switches is closed.

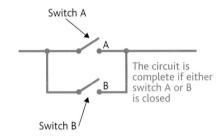

(a) Two-input OR gate.   (b) Three-input OR gate.

Figure 2.5 The OR gate.

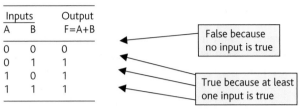

| Inputs | | Output |
A	B	F=A+B
0	0	0
0	1	1
1	0	1
1	1	1

False because no input is true

True because at least one input is true

Table 2.3 Truth table for the OR gate.

Switch A

A

The circuit is complete if either switch A or B is closed

B

Switch B

Figure 2.6 The representation of an OR gate.

The use of the term *OR* here is rather different from the English usage of *or*. The Boolean OR means (either A or B) or (both A and B), whereas the English usage often means A or B but not (A and B). For example, consider the contrasting use of the word *or* in the two phrases: 'Would you like tea or coffee?' and 'Reduced fees are charged to members who are registered students or under 25'. We shall see that the more common English use of the word *or* corresponds to the Boolean function known as the EXCLUSIVE OR, an important function that is frequently abbreviated to EOR or XOR.

A computer can also perform a logical OR on words as the following example illustrates.

```
1 0 0 1 1 1 0 0 ◄─ word A
0 0 1 0 0 1 0 1 ◄─ word B
1 0 1 1 1 1 0 1 ◄─ C = A + B
```

The logical OR operation is used to set one or more bits in a word to a logical 1. The term *set* means make a logical one, just as *clear* means reset to a logical zero. For example, the least-significant bit of a word is set by ORing it with 00 . . . 01. By applying both AND and OR operations to a word we can selectively clear or set its bits. Suppose we have an 8-bit binary word and we wish to clear bits 6 and 7 and set bits 4 and 5. If the bits of the word are d_0 to d_7, we can write:

d_7	d_6	d_5	d_4	d_3	d_2	d_1	d_0	
0	0	1	1	1	1	1	1	Source word
								AND mask
0	0	d_5	d_4	d_3	d_2	d_1	d_0	First result
0	0	1	1	0	0	0	0	OR mask
0	0	1	1	d_3	d_2	d_1	d_0	Final result

2.2.3 The NOT gate

The NOT gate is also called an inverter or a complementer and is a two-terminal device with a single input and a single output. If the input of an inverter is X, its output is NOT X which is written $\overline{X}$ or X^*. Figure 2.7 illustrates the symbol for an inverter and Table 2.4 provides its truth table. Some teachers vocalize $\overline{X}$ as 'not X' and others as 'X not'. The inverter is the simplest of gates because the output is the opposite of the input. If the input is 1 the output is 0 and vice versa. By the way, the triangle in Fig. 2.7 doesn't represent an inverter. The small circle at the output of the inverter indicates the inversion operation. We shall see that this circle indicates logical inversion wherever it appears in a circuit.

We can visualize the operation of the NOT gate in terms of the relay illustrated in Fig. 2.8. A relay is an electromechanical switch (i.e. a device that is partially electronic and partially mechanical) consisting of an iron core around which a coil of wire is wrapped. When a current flows through a coil, it generates a magnetic field that causes the iron core to act as a magnet. Situated close to the iron core is a pair of contacts, the lower of which is mounted on a springy strip of iron. If switch A is open, no current flows through the coil and the iron core remains unmagnetized. The relay's contacts are

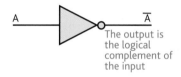

Figure 2.7 The NOT gate or inverter.

Input A	Output F=$\overline{A}$
0	1
1	0

Table 2.4 Truth table for the inverter.

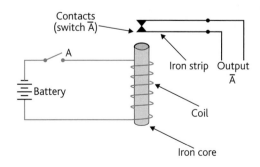

Figure 2.8 The operation of a relay.

normally closed so that they form a switch that is closed when switch A is open.

If switch A is closed, a current flows through the coil to generate a magnetic field that magnetizes the iron core. The contact on the iron strip is pulled toward the core, opening the contacts and breaking the circuit. In other words, closing switch A opens the relay's switch and vice versa. The system in Fig. 2.8 behaves like a NOT gate. The relay is used by a computer to control external devices and is described further when we deal with input and output devices.

Like both the AND and OR operations, the NOT function can also be applied to words:

$$\underline{1\ \ 1\ \ 0\ \ 1\ \ 1\ \ 1\ \ 0\ \ 0} \leftarrow \text{word A}$$
$$\underline{0\ \ 0\ \ 1\ \ 0\ \ 0\ \ 0\ \ 1\ \ 1} \leftarrow \text{B} = \overline{A}$$

2.2.4 The NAND and NOR gates

The two most widely used gates in real circuits are the NAND and NOR gates. These aren't fundamental gates because the NAND gate is derived from an AND gate followed by an inverter (Not AND) and the NOR gate is derived from an OR gate followed by an inverter (Not OR), respectively. The circuit symbols for the NAND and NOR gates are given in Fig. 2.9. The little circle at the output of a NAND gate represents the symbol for inversion or complementation. It is this circle that converts the AND gate to a NAND gate and an OR gate to a NOR gate. Later, when we introduce the concept of mixed logic, we will discover that this circle can be applied to the inputs of gates as well as to their outputs.

Table 2.5 gives the truth table for the NAND and the NOR gates. As you can see, the output columns in the NAND and NOR tables are just the complements of the outputs in the corresponding AND and OR tables.

We can get a better feeling for the effect that different gates have on two inputs, A and B, by putting all the gates together in a single table (Table 2.6). We have also included the EXCLUSIVE OR (i.e. EOR) and its complement the EXCLUSIVE NOR (i.e. EXNOR) in Table 2.6 for reference. The EOR gate is derived from AND, OR, and NOT gates and is described in more detail later in this chapter. It should be noted here that $\overline{A \cdot B}$ is not the same as $\overline{A} \cdot \overline{B}$, just as $\overline{A+B}$ is not the same as $\overline{A} + \overline{B}$.

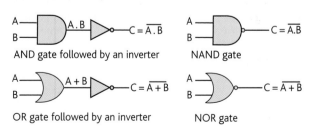

Figure 2.9 Circuit symbols for the NAND and NOR gates.

2.2.5 Positive, negative, and mixed logic

At this point we introduce the concepts of positive logic, negative logic, and mixed logic. Some readers may find that this section interrupts their progress toward a better understanding of the gate and may therefore skip ahead to the next section.

Up to now we have blurred the distinction between two unconnected concepts. The first concept is the relationship between low/high voltages in a digital circuit, 0 and 1 logical levels, and true/false logic values. The second concept is the logic function; for example, AND, OR, and NOT. So far, we have used positive *logic* in which a high-level signal represents a logical one state and this state is called true.

Table 2.7 provides three views of the AND function. The leftmost column provides the logical truth table in which the output is true only if all inputs are true (we have used T and F to avoid reference to signal levels). The middle column describes the AND function in positive logic form in which the output is true (i.e. 1) only if all inputs are true (i.e. 1).

The right hand column in Table 2.7 uses negative logic in which 0 is true and 1 is false. The output A · B is true (i.e. 0) only when both inputs are true (i.e. 0).

As far as digital circuits are concerned, there's no fundamental difference between logical 1s and 0s and it's as sensible to choose a logical 0 level as the true state as it is to choose a logical 1 state. Indeed, many of the signals in real digital systems are active-low which means that their function is carried out by a low-level signal.

Suppose we regard the low level as true and use negative logic, Table 2.7 shows that we have an AND gate whose output is low if and only if each input is low. It should also be apparent that an AND gate in negative logic functions as an OR gate in positive logic. Similarly, a negative logic OR gate functions as an AND gate in positive logic. In other words, the same gate is an AND gate in negative logic and an OR gate in positive logic. Figure 2.10 demonstrates the relationship between positive and negative logic gates.

For years engineers used the symbol for a positive logic AND gate in circuits using active-low signals with the result that the reader was confused and could only understand the

Logical form		Positive logic		Negative logic	
A B	A·B	A B	A·B	A B	A·B
F F	F	0 0	0	1 1	1
F T	F	0 1	0	1 0	1
T F	F	1 0	0	0 1	1
T T	T	1 1	1	0 0	0

Table 2.7 Truth table for AND gate in positive and negative logic forms.

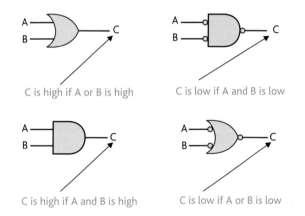

C is high if A or B is high   C is low if A and B is low

C is high if A and B is high   C is low if A or B is low

Figure 2.10 Positive and negative logic.

A	B	NAND C = $\overline{A \cdot B}$	A	B	NOR C = $\overline{A + B}$
0	0	1	0	0	1
0	1	1	0	1	0
1	0	1	1	0	0
1	1	0	1	1	0

Table 2.5 Truth table for the NAND and NOR gates.

Inputs		Output					
A	B	AND A·B	OR A+B	NAND A.B	NOR A + B	EOR A ⊕ B	EXNOR A ⊕ B
0	0	0	0	1	1	0	1
0	1	0	1	1	0	1	0
1	0	0	1	1	0	1	0
1	1	1	1	0	0	0	1

Table 2.6 Truth table for six gates.

GATES AS TRANSMISSION ELEMENTS

We can provide more of an insight into what gates do by treating them as transmission elements *that* control the flow of information within a computer.

We are going to take three two-input gates (i.e. AND, OR, EOR) and see what happens when we apply a variable to one input and a control signal to the other input. The figure illustrates three pairs of gates. Each pair demonstrates the situation in which the control input C is set to a logical 0 and a logical 1 state. The other input is a variable X and we wish to determine the effect the gate has on the transmission of X through it.

Figures (a) and (b) demonstrate the behavior of an AND gate. When C = 0, an AND gate is disabled and its output is forced into a logical zero state. When C = 1, the AND gate is enabled and its X input is transmitted to the output unchanged. We can think of an AND gate as a simple switch that allows or inhibits the passage of a logical signal. Similarly, in Fig (c) and (d) an OR gate is enabled by C = 0 and disabled by C = 1. However, when the OR gate is disabled, its output is forced into a logical one state.

The EOR gate in Fig (e) and (f) is a more interesting device. When its control input is 0, it transmits the other input unchanged. But when C = 1, it transmits the complement of X. The EOR gate can best be regarded as a programmable inverter. Later we shall make good use of this property of an EOR gate.

The reason we've introduced the concept of a gate as a transmission element is that digital computers can be viewed as a complex network through which information flows and this information is operated on by gates as it flows round the system.

(a) AND gate Control input C=0	(a) AND gate Control input C=1
X, C=0 → AND → 0	X, C=1 → AND → X
Gate disabled (output low)	Gate enabled (output=X)
(c) OR gate Control input C=0	(d) OR gate Control input C=1
X, C=0 → OR → X	X, C=1 → OR → 1
Gate enabled (output=X)	Gate disabled (output high)
(e) EOR gate Control input C=0	(f) EOR gate Control input C=1
X, C=0 → EOR → X	X, C=1 → EOR → $\overline{X}$
Gate acts as pass-through element (output=X)	Gate acts as inverter (output=$\overline{X}$)

---

circuit by mentally transforming the positive logic gate into its negative logic equivalent. In mixed logic both positive logic and negative logic gates are used together in the same circuit. The choice of whether to use positive or negative logic is determined only by the desire to improve the clarity of a diagram or explanation.

Why do we have to worry about positive and negative logic? If we stick to positive logic, life would be much simpler. True, but life is never that simple. Many real electronic systems are activated by low-level signals and that makes it sensible to adopt negative logic conventions. Let's look at an example. Consider a circuit that is activated by a low-level signal only when input A is a low level and input B is a low level. Figure 2.11 demonstrates the circuit required to implement this function. Note that the bubble at the input to the circuit indicates that it is activated by a low level.

In Fig. 2.11(a) we employ positive logic and draw an OR gate because the output of an OR gate is 0 only when both its inputs are 0. There's nothing wrong with this circuit, but it's

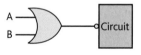

(a) Positive logic system
The circuit is activated when A is low and B is low

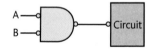

(b) Negative logic system
The circuit is activated when A is low and B is low

Figure 2.11 Mixed logic.

confusing. When you see a gate with an *OR* shape you think of an OR function. However, in this case, the gate is actually performing an AND operation on low-level signals.

What we need is a means of preserving the AND shape and indicating we are using negative logic signals. Figure 2.11(b) does just that. By placing inverter circles at the AND gate's inputs and output we immediately see that the output of the gate is low if and only if both of its inputs are low.

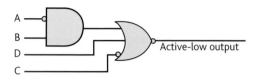

Figure 2.12 Using mixed logic.

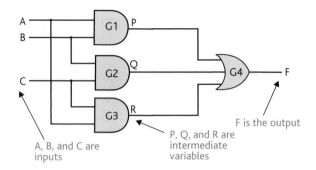

Figure 2.13 The use of gates—Example 1.

There is no physical difference between the circuits of Figs. 2.11(a) and 2.11(b). They are both ways of representing the same thing. However, the meaning of the circuit in Fig. 2.11(b) is clearer.

Consider another example of mixed logic in which we use both negative and positive logic concepts. Suppose a circuit is activated by a low-level signal if input A is low and input B high, or input D is high, or input C is low. Figure 2.12 shows how we might draw such a circuit. For most of this book we will continue to use positive logic.

2.3 Applications of gates

We now look at four simple circuits to demonstrate that a few gates can be connected together in such a way as to create a circuit whose function and importance may readily be appreciated by the reader. Following this informal introduction to circuits we introduce *Digital Works*, a Windows-based program that lets you construct and simulate circuits containing gates on a PC. We then return to gates and provide a more formal section on the analysis of logic circuits by means of Boolean algebra.

Circuits are constructed by connecting gates together. The output from one gate can be connected (i.e. wired) to the input of one or more other gates. However, two outputs cannot be connected together.

Example 1 Consider the circuit of Fig. 2.13 that uses three two-input AND gates labeled G1, G2, and G3, and a three-input OR gate labeled G4. This circuit has three inputs A, B, and C, and an output F. What does it do?

We can tackle this problem in several ways. One approach is to create a truth table that tabulates the output F for all the eight possible combinations of the three inputs A, B, and C. Table 2.8 corresponds to the circuit of Fig. 2.13 and includes columns for the outputs of the three AND gates as well as the output of the OR gate, F.

The three intermediate signals P, Q, and R are defined by $P = A \cdot B$, $Q = B \cdot C$, and $R = A \cdot C$. Figure 2.13 tells us that we can write down the output function, F, as the logical OR of the three intermediate signals P, Q, and R; that is, $F = P + Q + R$.

We can substitute the expressions for P, Q, and R to get $F = A \cdot B + B \cdot C + A \cdot C$. This is a Boolean equation, but it

Inputs			Intermediate values			Output
A	B	C	$P = A \cdot B$	$Q = B \cdot C$	$R = A \cdot C$	$F = P + Q + R$
0	0	0	0	0	0	0
0	0	1	0	0	0	0
0	1	0	0	0	0	0
0	1	1	0	1	0	1
1	0	0	0	0	0	0
1	0	1	0	0	1	1
1	1	0	1	0	0	1
1	1	1	1	1	1	1

Table 2.8 Truth table for Fig. 2.13.

doesn't help us a lot at this point. However, by visually inspecting the truth table for F we can see that the output is true if two or more of the inputs A, B, and C, are true. That is, this circuit implements a majority logic function whose output takes the same value as the majority of inputs. We have already seen how such a circuit is used in an automatic landing system in an aircraft by choosing the output from three independent computers to be the best (i.e. majority) of three inputs. Using just four basic gates, we've constructed a circuit that does something useful.

Example 2 The circuit of Fig. 2.14 has three inputs, one output, and three intermediate values (we've also included a mixed logic version of this circuit on the right hand side of Fig. 2.14). By inspecting the truth table for this circuit (Table 2.9) we can see that when the input X is 0, the output, F, is equal to Y. Similarly, when X is 1, the output is equal to Z. The circuit of Fig. 2.14 behaves like an electronic switch, connecting the output to one of two inputs, Y or Z, depending on the state of a control input X.

The circuit of Fig. 2.14 is a two-input multiplexer that can be represented by the arrangement of Fig. 2.15. Because the word multiplexer appears so often in electronics, it is frequently abbreviated to MUX.

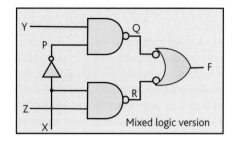

Figure 2.14 The use of gates— Example 2.

Inputs			Intermediate values			Output
X	Y	Z	$P = \overline{X}$	$Q = \overline{P \cdot Y}$	$R = \overline{X \cdot Z}$	$F = \overline{Q \cdot R}$
0	0	0	1	1	1	0
0	0	1	1	1	1	0
0	1	0	1	0	1	1
0	1	1	1	0	1	1
1	0	0	0	1	1	0
1	0	1	0	1	0	1
1	1	0	0	1	1	0
1	1	1	0	1	0	1

Table 2.9 Truth table for Fig. 2.14.

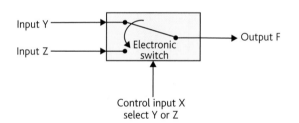

Figure 2.15 The logical representation of Figure 2.14.

We can derive an expression for F in terms of inputs X, Y, and Z in two ways. From the circuit diagram of Fig. 2.14, we can get an equation for F by writing the output of each gate in terms of its inputs.

$$F = \overline{Q \cdot R}$$

$$Q = \overline{Y \cdot P}$$

$$P = \overline{X}$$

Therefore $Q = \overline{Y \cdot \overline{X}}$ by substituting for P

$$R = \overline{X \cdot Z}$$

Therefore $F = \overline{\overline{Y \cdot \overline{X}} \cdot \overline{X \cdot Z}}$

When we introduce Boolean algebra we will see how this type of expression can be simplified. Another way of obtaining a Boolean expression is to use the truth table. Each time a logical one appears in the output column, we can write down

the set of inputs that cause the output to be true. In Table 2.9 the output is true when

(1) X = 0, Y = 1, Z = 0 $(\overline{X} \cdot Y \cdot \overline{Z})$

(2) X = 0, Y = 1, Z = 1 $(\overline{X} \cdot Y \cdot Z)$

(3) X = 1, Y = 0, Z = 1 $(X \cdot \overline{Y} \cdot Z)$

(4) X = 1, Y = 1, Z = 1 $(X \cdot Y \cdot Z)$

There are four possible combinations of inputs that make the output true. Therefore, the output can be expressed as the logical sum of the four cases (1)–(4) above; that is,

$$F = \overline{X} \cdot Y \cdot \overline{Z} + \overline{X} \cdot Y \cdot Z + X \cdot \overline{Y} \cdot Z + X \cdot Y \cdot Z$$

This function is true if any of the conditions (1)–(4) are true. A function represented in this way is called a sum-of-products (S-of-P) expression because it is the logical OR (i.e. sum) of a group of terms each composed of several of variables ANDed together (i.e. products). A sum-of-products expression represents one of the two standard ways of writing down a Boolean expression.

An alternative way of writing a Boolean equation is called a product-of-sums (P-of-S) expression and consists of several terms ANDed together. The terms are made up of variables ORed together. A typical product-of-sums expression has the form

$$F = (A + \overline{B} + C) \cdot (\overline{A} + B + C) \cdot (\overline{A} + \overline{B} + \overline{C})$$

Later we shall examine ways of converting sum-of-products expressions into product-of sums expressions and vice versa.

Each of the terms (1)–(4) in Example 2, is called a minterm. A minterm is an AND (product) term that includes each of the variables in either its true or complemented form. For example, in the case above $X \cdot \overline{Y} \cdot Z$ is a minterm, but if we had had the term $X \cdot \overline{Y}$ that would not be a minterm, because $X \cdot \overline{Y}$ includes only two of the three variables. When an equation is expressed as a sum of minterms, it is said to be in its canonical form. Canonical is just a fancy word that means standard.

As the output of the circuit in Fig. 2.14 must be the same whether it is derived from the truth table or from the logic diagram, the two equations we have derived for *F* must be equivalent, with the result that

$$\overline{\overline{Y \cdot \overline{X}} \cdot \overline{X \cdot Z}} = \overline{X} \cdot Y \cdot \overline{Z} + \overline{X} \cdot Y \cdot Z + X \cdot \overline{Y} \cdot Z + X \cdot Y \cdot Z$$

This equation demonstrates that a given Boolean function can be expressed in more than one way.

The multiplexer of Fig. 2.14 may seem a very long way from computers and programming. However, multiplexers are found somewhere in every computer because computers operate by modifying the flow of data within a system. A multiplexer allows one of two data streams to flow through a switch that is electronically controlled. Let's look at a highly simplified example. The power of a digital computer (or a human brain) lies in its ability to make decisions. Decision taking in a computer corresponds to the conditional branch; for example,

```
IF Day = Weekday
  THEN update stock
  ELSE print stock list
```

We can't go into the details of how such a construct is implemented here. What we would like to do is to demonstrate that something as simple as a multiplexer can implement something as sophisticated as a conditional branch. Consider the system of Fig. 2.16. Two numbers P and Q are fed to a comparator where they are compared. If they are the same, the output of the comparator is 1 (otherwise it's 0). The same output is used as the control input to a multiplexer that selects between two values X and Y. In practice, such a system would be rather more complex (because P, Q, X, and Y are all multi-bit values), but the basic principles are the same.

Example 3 Figure 2.17 describes a simple circuit with three gates: an OR gate, an AND gate, and a NAND gate. This circuit

has two inputs, two intermediate values, and one output. Table 2.10 provides its truth table.

The circuit of Fig. 2.17 represents one of the most important circuits in digital electronics, the exclusive or (also called EOR or XOR). The exclusive or corresponds to the normal English use of the word or (i.e. one or the other but not both). The output of an EOR gate output is true if one of the inputs is true but not if both the inputs are true.

An EOR circuit always has two inputs (remember that AND and OR gates can have any number of inputs). Because the EOR function is so widely used, the EOR gate has its own special circuit symbol (Fig. 2.18) and the EOR operator its own special logical symbol '$\oplus$'; for example, we can write

$$F = A\,EOR\,B = A \oplus B$$

The EOR is not a fundamental gate because it is constructed from basic gates.

Because the EOR gate is so important, we will discuss it a little further. Table 2.10 demonstrates that F is true when $A = 0$ and $B = 1$, or when $A = 1$ and $B = 0$. Consequently, the output $F = \overline{A}\cdot B + A\cdot\overline{B}$. From the circuit in Fig. 2.17 we can write

$$F = P\cdot Q$$

$$P = A + B$$

$$Q = \overline{A\cdot B}$$

Therefore $F = (A + B)\cdot\overline{A\cdot B}$

As these two equations (i.e. $F = \overline{A}\cdot B + A\cdot\overline{B}$ and $F = (A + B)\cdot\overline{A\cdot B}$ are equivalent, we can therefore also build an EOR function in the manner depicted in Fig. 2.19.

It's perfectly possible to build an EOR with four NAND gates (Fig. 2.20). We leave it as an exercise for the reader to verify that Fig. 2.20 does indeed represent an EOR gate. To demonstrate that two different circuits have the same function, all you need do is to construct a truth table for each circuit. If the outputs are the same for each and every possible input, the circuits are equivalent.

Figure 2.16 Application of the multiplexer.

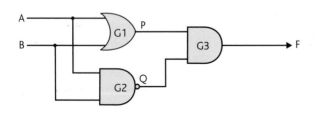

Figure 2.17 The use of gates—Example 3.

Inputs		Intermediate values		Output
A	B	$P = A + B$	$Q = \overline{A\cdot B}$	$F = P\cdot Q$
0	0	0	1	0
0	1	1	1	1
1	0	1	1	1
1	1	1	0	0

Table 2.10 Truth table for the circuit of Fig. 2.17.

The EOR is a remarkably versatile logic element that pops up in many places in digital electronics. The output of an EOR is true if its inputs are different and false if they are the same. As we've already stated, unlike the AND, OR, NAND and NOR gates the EOR gate can have only two inputs. The EOR gate's ability to detect whether its inputs are the same

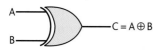

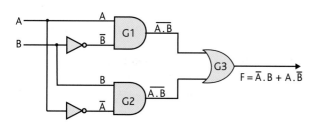

Figure 2.18 Circuit symbol for an EOR gate.

Figure 2.19 An alternative circuit for an EOR gate.

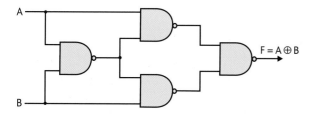

Figure 2.20 An EOR circuit constructed with NAND gates only.

allows us to build an equality tester that indicates whether or not two words are identical (Fig. 2.21).

In Fig. 2.21 two m-bit words (Word 1 and Word 2) are fed to a bank of m EOR gates. Bit i from Word 1 is compared with bit i from Word 2 in the ith EOR gate. If these two bits are the same, the output of this EOR gate is zero.

If the two words in Fig. 2.21 are equal, the outputs of all EORs are zero and we need to detect this condition in order to declare that Word 1 and Word 2 are identical. An AND gate will give a 1 output when all its inputs are 1. However, in this case, we have to detect the situation in which all inputs are 0. We can therefore connect all m outputs from the m EOR gates to an m-input NOR gate (because the output of a NOR gate is 1 if all inputs are 0).

If you look at Fig. 2.21 you can see that the outputs from the EOR gates aren't connected to a NOR gate but to an m-input AND gate with inverting inputs. The little bubbles at the AND gate's inputs indicate inversion and are equivalent to NOT gates. When all inputs to the AND gate are active-low, the AND gate's output will go active-high (exactly what we want). In mixed logic we can regard an AND gate with active-low inputs and an active-high output as a NOR gate.

Remember that we required an equality detector (i.e. comparator) in Fig. 2.21 (Example 2) to control a multiplexer. We've just built one.

Example 4 The next example of *an* important circuit constructed from a few gates is the *prioritizer* whose circuit is given in Fig. 2.22. As this is a rather more complex circuit than the previous three examples, we'll explain what it does first. A prioritizer deals with *competing* requests for attention and grants service to just one of those requesting attention. The prioritizer is a device with n inputs and n outputs. Each of the inputs is assigned a priority from 0 to $n-1$ (assume that the highest priority is input $n-1$, and the lowest is 0).

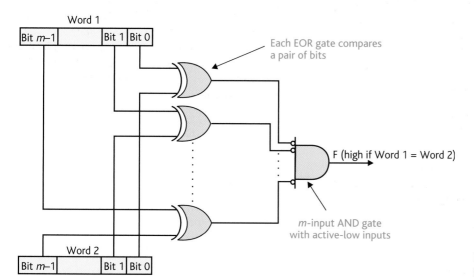

Figure 2.21 The application of EOR gates in an equality tester.

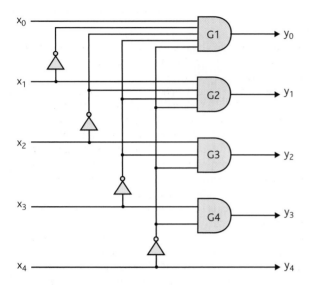

Figure 2.22 Example 4—the priority circuit.

If two or more inputs are asserted simultaneously, only the output corresponding to the input with the highest priority is asserted. Computers use this type of circuit to deal with simultaneous requests for service from several peripherals (e.g. disk drives, the keyboard, the mouse, and the modem).

Consider the five-input prioritizer circuit in Fig. 2.22. The prioritizer's five inputs x_0 to x_4 are connected to the outputs of five devices that can make a request for attention (input x_4 has the highest priority). That is, device i can put a logical 1 on input x_i to request attention at priority level i. If several inputs are set to 1 at the same time, the prioritizer sets only one of its outputs to 1, all the other outputs remain at 0. For example, if the input is $x_4,x_3,x_2,x_1,x_0 = 00110$, the output $y_4,y_3,y_2,y_1,y_0 = 00100$, because the highest level of input is x_2. Table 2.11 provides a truth table for this prioritizer.

If you examine the circuit of Fig. 2.22, you can see that output y_4 is equal to input x_4 because there is a direct connection. If x_4 is 0, then y_4 is 0; and if x_4 is 1 then y_4 is 1. The value of x_4 is fed to the *input* of the AND gates G3, G2, and G1 in the lower priority stages via an inverter. If x_4 is 1, the logical level at the inputs of the AND gates is 0, which disables them and forces their outputs to 0. If x_4 is 0, the value fed back to the AND gates is 1 and therefore they are not disabled by x_4. Similarly, when x_3 is 1, gates G3, G2 and G1 are disabled, and so on.

Example 5 Our final example looks at two different circuits that do the same thing. This is a typical exam question.

(a) *Using AND, OR, and NOT gates only, draw circuits to generate P and Q from inputs X, Y, and Z, where $P = (X + \overline{Y})(Y \oplus Z)$ and $Q = \overline{Y} \cdot Z + X \cdot Y \cdot \overline{Z}$.*

(b) *By means of a truth table establish a relationship between P and Q.*

(c) *Compare the circuit diagrams of P and Q in terms of speed and cost of implementation.*

(a) The circuit diagram for $P = (X + \overline{Y})(Y \oplus Z)$ is given by Fig. 2.23 and the circuit diagram for $Q = \overline{Y} \cdot Z + X \cdot Y \cdot \overline{Z}$ is give by Fig. 2.24.

(b) The truth table for functions P and Q is given in Table 2.12 from which it can be seen that P = Q.

(c) We can compare the two circuits in terms of speed and cost.

Inputs					Outputs				
X_4	X_3	X_2	X_1	X_0	y_4	y_3	y_2	y_1	y_0
0	0	0	0	0	0	0	0	0	0
0	0	0	0	1	0	0	0	0	1
0	0	0	1	0	0	0	0	1	0
0	0	0	1	1	0	0	0	1	0
0	0	1	0	0	0	0	1	0	0
0	0	1	0	1	0	0	1	0	0
0	0	1	1	0	0	0	1	0	0
0	0	1	1	1	0	0	1	0	0
0	1	0	0	0	0	1	0	0	0
0	1	0	0	1	0	1	0	0	0
0	1	0	1	0	0	1	0	0	0
0	1	0	1	1	0	1	0	0	0
0	1	1	0	0	0	1	0	0	0
0	1	1	0	1	0	1	0	0	0
0	1	1	1	0	0	1	0	0	0
0	1	1	1	1	0	1	0	0	0
1	0	0	0	0	1	0	0	0	0
1	0	0	0	1	1	0	0	0	0
1	0	0	1	0	1	0	0	0	0
1	0	0	1	1	1	0	0	0	0
1	0	1	0	0	1	0	0	0	0
1	0	1	0	1	1	0	0	0	0
1	0	1	1	0	1	0	0	0	0
1	0	1	1	1	1	0	0	0	0
1	1	0	0	0	1	0	0	0	0
1	1	0	0	1	1	0	0	0	0
1	1	0	1	0	1	0	0	0	0
1	1	0	1	1	1	0	0	0	0
1	1	1	0	0	1	0	0	0	0
1	1	1	0	1	1	0	0	0	0
1	1	1	1	0	1	0	0	0	0
1	1	1	1	1	1	0	0	0	0

Table 2.11 Truth table for the priority circuit of Fig. 2.22.

COMPARING DIFFERENT DIGITAL CIRCUITS WITH THE SAME FUNCTION

Different combinations of gates may be used to implement the same function. This isn't the place to go into the detailed design of logic circuits, but it is interesting to see how the designer might go about selecting one particular implementation in preference to another. Some of the basic criteria by which circuits are judged are listed below. In general, the design of logic circuits is often affected by other factors than those described here.

Speed The speed of a circuit (i.e. how long it takes the output to respond to a change at an input) is approximately governed by the maximum number of gates through which a change of state must propagate (i.e. pass). The output of a typical gate might take 5 ns to change following a logic change at its input (5 ns = 5×10^{-9} s). Figs 2.17 and 2.19 both implement an EOR function. In Fig. 2.17 there are only two gates in series, whereas in Fig. 2.19 there are three gates in series. Therefore the implementation of an EOR function in Fig. 2.17 is 50% faster. All real gates don't have the same propagation delay, because some gates respond more rapidly than others.

Number of interconnections It costs money to wire gates together. Even if a printed circuit is used, somebody has to design it and the more interconnections used the more it will cost. Increasing the number of interconnections in a circuit also increases the probability of failure due to a faulty connection. One parameter of circuit design that takes account of the number of interconnections is the total number of inputs to gates. In Fig. 2.17 there are six inputs, whereas in Fig. 2.19 there are eight inputs.

Number of packages Simple gates of the types we describe here are available in 14-pin packages (two pins of which are needed for the power supply). As it costs virtually nothing to add extra gates to the silicon chip, only the number of pins (i.e. external connections to the chip) limits the total number of gates in a physical package. Thus, an inverter requires two pins, so that six inverters are provided on the chip. Similarly, a two-input AND/NAND/OR/NOR gate needs three pins, so four of these gates are put on the chip. Because each of these circuits uses three different types of gate, both circuits require three 14 pin integrated circuits. Even so, the circuit of Fig. 2.17 is better than that of Fig. 2.19 because there are more unused gates left in the ICs, freeing them for use by other parts of the computer system. Note that the circuit of Fig. 2.20 uses only one package because all gates are the same type.

You should appreciate that this is an introductory text and what we have said is appropriate only to logic circuits constructed from basic logic elements. Computer-aided design techniques are used to handle more complex systems with hundreds of gates. Indeed, complex circuits are largely constructed from programmable digital elements.

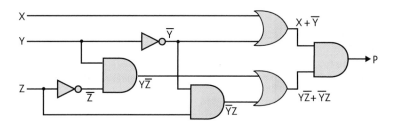

Figure 2.23 Circuit diagram for P.

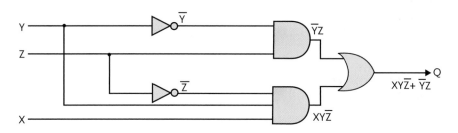

Figure 2.24 Circuit diagram for Q.

Propagation delay The maximum delay in the circuit for P is four gates in series in the Y path (i.e. NOT gate, AND gate, OR gate, AND gate). The maximum delay in the circuit for Q is three gates in series in both Y and Z paths (i.e. NOT gate, AND gate, OR gate). Therefore the circuit for Q is 33% faster than that for P.

Cost Total number of gates needed to implement P is 7. Total number of gates needed to implement Q is 5. Total inputs in the circuit for P is 12. Total inputs in the circuit for Q is 9. Clearly, the circuit for Q is better than that for P both in terms of the number of gates and the number of inputs to the gates.

X	Y	Z	X + $\bar{Y}$	Y $\oplus$ Z	P = (X + $\bar{Y}$)(Y $\oplus$ Z)	$\bar{Y}$·Z	X·Y·$\bar{Z}$	Q = $\bar{Y}$·Z + X·Y·$\bar{Z}$
0	0	0	1	0	0	0	0	0
0	0	1	1	1	1	1	0	1
0	1	0	0	1	0	0	0	0
0	1	1	0	0	0	0	0	0
1	0	0	1	0	0	0	0	0
1	0	1	1	1	1	1	0	1
1	1	0	1	1	1	0	1	1
1	1	1	1	0	0	0	0	0

Table 2.12 Truth table for Figs 2.23 and 2.24.

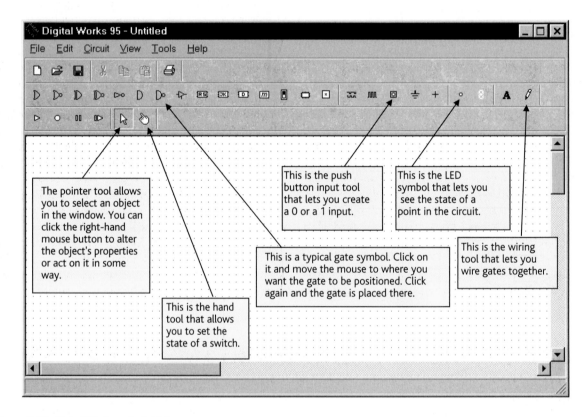

Figure 2.25 Digital Works—the initial screen.

2.4 Introduction to Digital Works

We now introduce a Windows-based logic simulator called Digital Works that enables you to construct a logic circuit from simple gates (AND, OR, NOT, NAND, NOR, EOR, XNOR) and to analyze the circuit's behavior. Digital Works also supports the tri-state logic gate that enables you to construct systems with buses. In the next chapter we will discover that Digital Works simulates both simple 1-bit storage elements called flip-flops and larger memory components such as ROM and RAM.

After installing Digital Works on your system, you can run it to get the initial screen shown in Fig. 2.25. We have annotated six of the most important icons on the toolbars. A circuit is constructed by using the mouse to place gates on the screen or workspace and a wiring tool to connect the gates together. The input to your circuit may come from a clock generator (a continuous series of alternating 1s and 0s), a sequence generator (a user-defined sequence of 1s and 0s), or a manual input (from a switch that you can push by means of the mouse). You can observe the output of a gate by connecting it to a display, LED. You can also send the output of the LED to a window that displays either a waveform or a sequence of binary digits.

Digital Works has been designed to be consistent with the Windows philosophy and has a help function that provides further information about its facilities and commands. The File command in the top toolbar provides the options you would expect (e.g. load, save, save as).

2.4.1 Creating a circuit

We are going to design and test an EOR circuit that has the logic function $A \cdot \overline{B} + \overline{A} \cdot B$. This function can be implemented with two inverters, two AND gates, and an OR gate. Figure 2.26 shows three of the icons we are going to use to create this circuit. The first icon is the new circuit icon that creates a fresh circuit (which Digital Works calls a macro). The second icon is the pointer *tool* used to select a gate (or other element) from the toolbars. The third icon is a gate that can be planted in the work area.

Let's start by planting some gates on the work area. The EOR requires two AND gates, an OR gate, and two inverters. First click on the pointer tool on the bottom row of icons. If it hasn't already been selected, it will become depressed when you select it. The pointer tool remains selected until another tool is selected.

You select a gate from the list on the second row of icons by first left clicking on the gate with the pointer tool and then left

clicking at a suitable point in the workspace as Fig. 2.27 demonstrates. If you hold the control key down when placing a gate, you can place multiple copies of the gate in the workspace. The OR gate is shown in broken outline because we've just placed it (i.e. it is currently selected). Once a gate has been placed, you can select it with the mouse by clicking the left button and drag it wherever you want. You can click the right button to modify the gate's attributes (e.g. the number of inputs).

You can tidy up the circuit by moving the gates within the work area by left clicking a gate and dragging it to where you want it. Figure 2.28 shows the work area after we've moved the gates to create a symmetrical layout. You can even drag gates around the work area after they've been wired up and reposition wires by left clicking and dragging any node (a node is a point on a wire that consists of multiple sections or links).

Digital Works displays a grid to help you position the gates. The grid can be turned on or off and the spacing of the grid lines changed. Objects can be made to snap to the grid. These functions are accessed via the View command in the top line.

Before continuing, we need to save the circuit. Figure 2.29 demonstrates how we use the conventional File function in the toolbar to save a circuit. We have called this circuit OUP_EOR1 and Digital Works inserts the extension .dwm.

The next step is to wire up the gates to create a circuit. First select the wiring tool from the tool bars by left clicking on it (Fig. 2.30). Then position the cursor over the point at which you wish to connect a wire and left click. The cursor changes to wire when it's over a point that can legally be connected to. Left click to attach a wire and move the cursor to the point you wish to connect. Left click to create a connection. Instead of making a direct connection between two points, you can

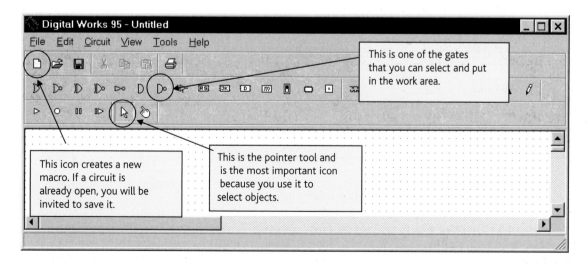

Figure 2.26 Beginning a session with Digital Works.

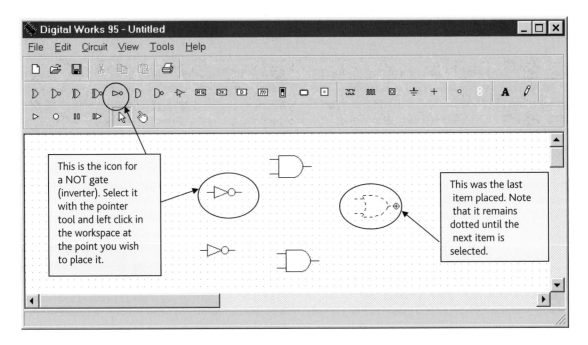

Figure 2.27 Placing gates in the work area.

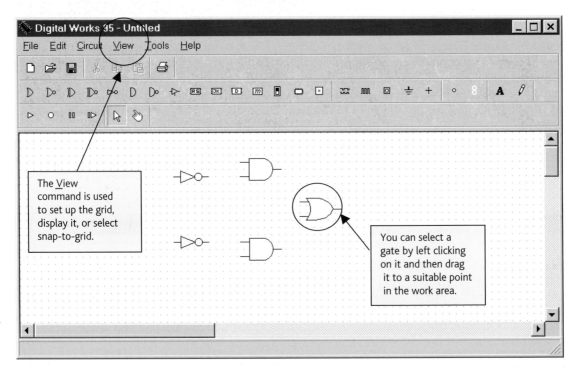

Figure 2.28 Tidying up the circuit.

click on the workspace to create a node (i.e. the connection is series if straight lines.)

You can make the wiring look neat by clicking on intermediate points to create a signal path made up of a series of straight-line segments. If you select the pointer tool and left click on a wire, you can drag any of its nodes (i.e. the points between segments on a line). If you right click on a wire you can delete it or change its color. Once a wire has been

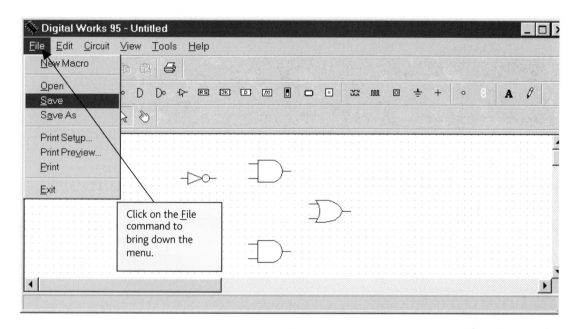

Figure 2.29 Saving the circuit.

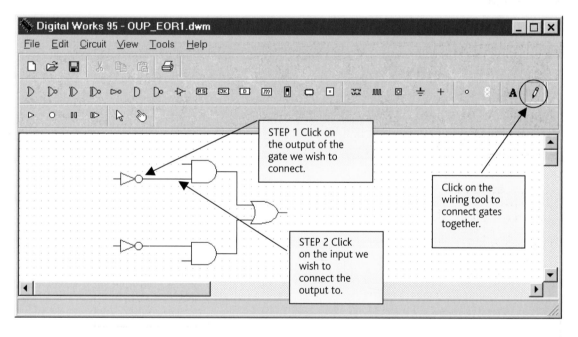

Figure 2.30 Wiring gates together.

connected to another wire (or an input or output), the connection point can't be moved. To move a connection you have to delete the wire and connect a new one.

Digital Works permits a wire to be connected only between two legal connections. In Fig. 2.30 the inputs to the two inverters and the circuit's outputs aren't connected anywhere. This is because each wire must be connected between two points—it can't just be left hanging. In order to wire up the inputs and output we need points we can connect the wire to. In this case we are going to use the interactive input device to provide an input signal from a push button and the LED to show the state of the output.

In Fig. 2.31 we've added two interactive inputs and an LED to the circuit. When we run the simulator, we can set the states of the inputs to provide a 0 or a 1 and we can observe the state of the output on the LED.

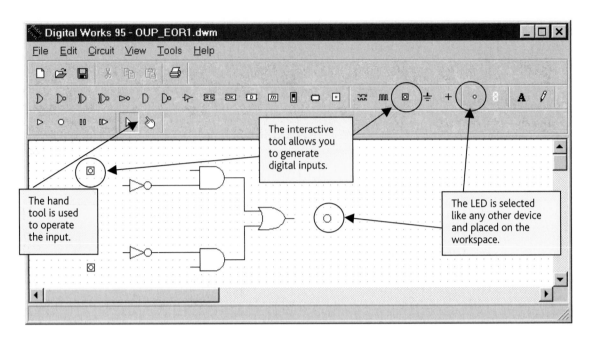

Figure 2.31 Adding inputs and outputs to the circuit.

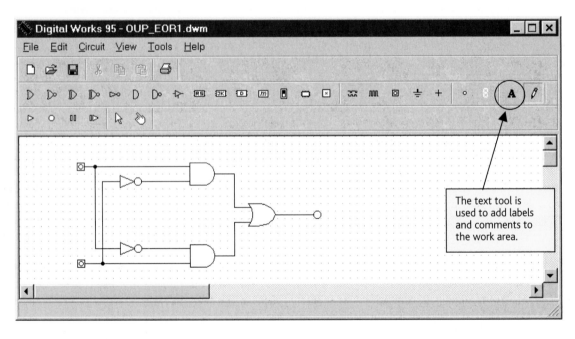

Figure 2.32 Completing the circuit.

We can now wire up the inputs and the output and complete the rest of the wiring as shown in Fig. 2.32. At this stage we could run the circuit if we wanted. However, we will use the text tool (indicated by the letter **A** on the middle toolbar) to give the circuit a title. Click on the **A** and then click on the place at which you wish to add the text to open the text

window. This brings down a text box. Enter the text and click ok to place it on the screen.

We also wish to label the circuit's inputs and outputs. Although you can use the text tool to add text at any point, input and output devices (e.g. clocks, switches, LEDs) can be given names. We will use this latter technique because the

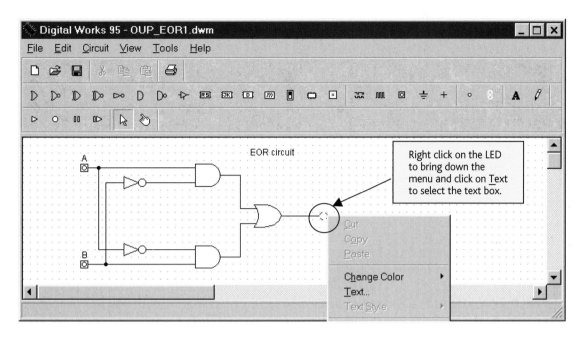

Figure 2.33 Labeling the circuit and inputs and outputs.

names attached to input and output devices are automatically used to label the timing diagrams we will introduce later.

Figure 2.33 shows the circuit with annotation. The label EOR circuit has been added by the text tool, and inputs A and B have been labeled by right clicking on the input devices. In Fig. 2.33 we have right clicked on the LED to bring down a menu and then selected Text to invoke the text box (not shown). You enter the name of the output (in this case Sum) into the text box and click ok. This label is then appended to the LED on the screen. You can change the location of the label by right clicking on its name, selecting Text Style from the menu, and then selecting the required position (Left, Right, Top, Bottom).

2.4.2 Running a simulation

We are now ready to begin simulation. The bottom row of icons is concerned with running the simulation. The leftmost icon (ringed in Fig. 2.34) is left clicked to begin the simulation. The next step is to change the state of the interactive input devices. If you click on the hand tool icon, the cursor changes to a hand when positioned anywhere over the work area.

By putting the hand cursor over one of the input devices, you can left click the mouse to change the status of the input (i.e. input 0 or input 1). When the input device is supplying a 1, it becomes red. Figure 2.34 shows the situation input A = 1, B = 0, and the Sum = 1 (the output LED becomes red when it is connected to a 1 state). You can change the states of the input devices to generate all the possible input

values 0,0, 0,1, 1,0, and 1,1 to verify that the circuit is an EOR (the output LED should display the sequence 0, 1, 1, 0).

Just observing the outputs of the LEDs is not always enough to get a picture of the circuit's behavior. We need a record of the states of the inputs and outputs. Digital Works provides a Logic History function that records and displays inputs and outputs during a simulator run. Any input or output device can be added to Logic History. If you select input A with the pointer tool and then right click, you get a pull down menu from which you can activate the Add to Logic History function to record the value of input A. When this function is selected (denoted by a tick on the menu), all input is copied to a buffer (i.e. store). As we have two inputs, A and B, we will have to assign them to the Logic History function independently.

To record the output of the LED, you carry out the same procedure you did with the two inputs A and B (i.e. right click on the LED and select Add to Logic History) (see Fig. 2.35).

In order to use the Logic History function, you have to activate it from the Tools function on the toolbar. Selecting Tools pulls down a menu and you have to select the Logic History window. Figure 2.36 shows the logic history window after a simulation run. Note that the inputs and outputs have the labels you gave them (i.e. A, B, and Sum).

We now need to say something about the way the simulator operates. The simulator uses an internal clock and a record of the state of inputs and outputs is taken at each clock pulse. Figure 2.37 shows how you can change the clock speed from

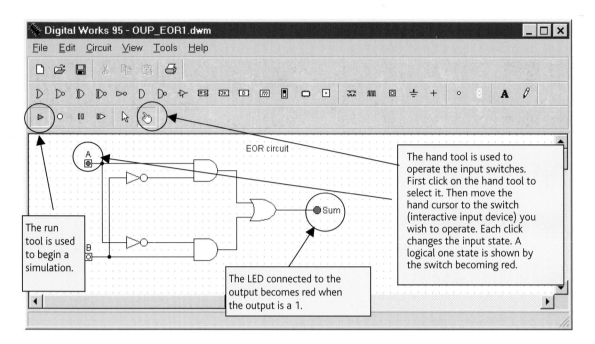

Figure 2.34 Running the simulator.

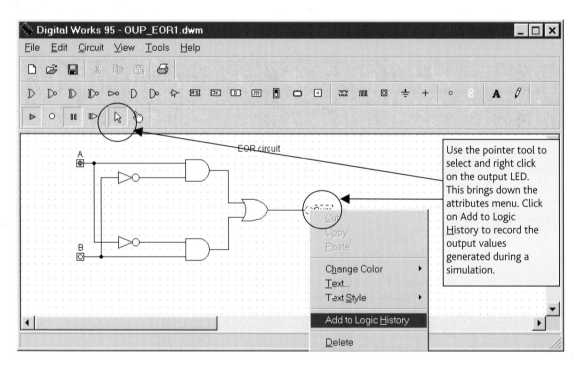

Figure 2.35 Recording inputs and output.

the toolbar by pulling down the <u>C</u>ircuit menu and selecting <u>C</u>lock Speed.

We're not interested in clocks at this stage because we are looking at a circuit that doesn't have a clock. However, because the signals are read and recorded at each clock pulse, the entire simulation is over in a second or so. Blink and you miss it.

We need to stop the clock to perform a manual simulation. The **Logic History** window contains a copy of the run, stop,

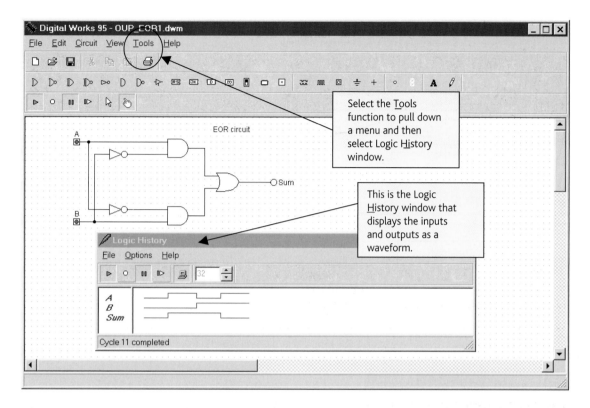

Figure 2.36 The logic history window.

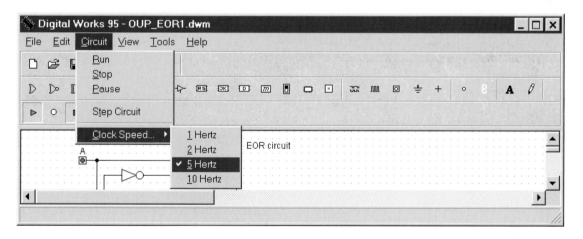

Figure 2.37 Changing the clock rate.

pause, and single-step icons to allow you to step through the simulation. Fig. 2.38 provides details of the **Logic History** window. The waveform in Fig. 2.38 was created by putting the simulator in the pause mode and executing a single cycle at a time by clicking on the single-step button. Between each cycle we have used the hand tool to change the inputs to the EOR gate. We can use the hand tool to both change the state of the inputs and to single step (you don't have to use the pointer tool to perform a single step).

The logic history can be displayed either as a waveform as in Fig. 2.38 or as a binary sequence as in Fig. 2.39 by clicking on the display mode icon in the **Logic History** window. You can also select the number of states to be displayed in this window.

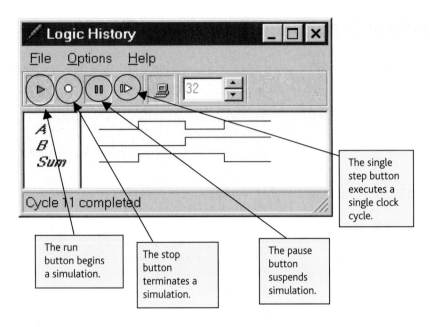

Figure 2.38 Controlling the simulation.

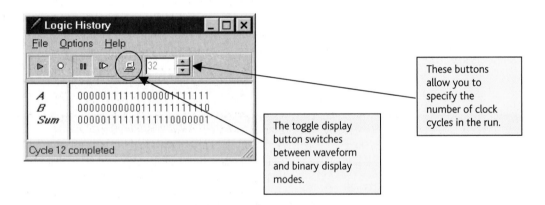

Figure 2.39 Viewing the simulation as a binary sequence.

2.4.3 The clock and sequence generator

Inputting data into a digital circuit by using the hand tool to manipulate push buttons and switches is suitable for simple circuits, but not for more complex systems. Digital Works provides two means of generating signals automatically. One is a simple clock generator, which produces a constant stream of alternating 1s and 0s and the other is a sequence generator, which produces a user-defined stream of 1s and 0s. The sequence generator is controlled by Digital Works' own clock and a new 1 or 0 is output at each clock pulse. Figure 2.40 shows the icons for the clock and pulse generator and demonstrates how they appear when placed in the work area.

Figure 2.41 demonstrates how you can define a sequence of pulses you wish to apply to one of the inputs of a circuit

(in this example, a single AND gate). One of the inputs to the AND gate comes from the clock generator and the other from the sequence generator. We've added LEDs to the gate's inputs and output to make it easy to observe the state of all signals.

Let's go through the operations required to place and set up a sequence generator (called a bit generator by Digital Works). First left click on the sequencer icon on the toolbar and then move the cursor to the point at which you wish to locate this device in the workspace. Then right click to both place it in the workspace and bring down the menu that controls the bit generator. From the pull-down menu, select **Edit Sequence** and the window shown in Fig. 2.41 appears. You can enter a sequence either from the computer's keyboard or by using the mouse on the simulated keyboard in the **Edit Sequence** window. You can either enter the sequence in

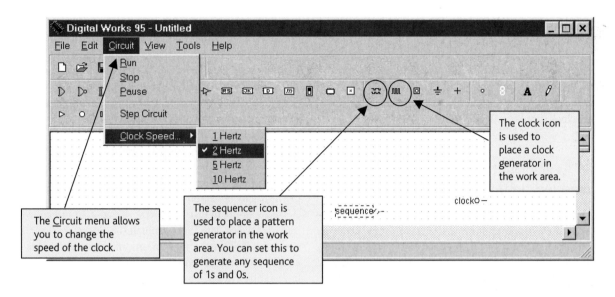

Figure 2.40 The clock generator and sequencer.

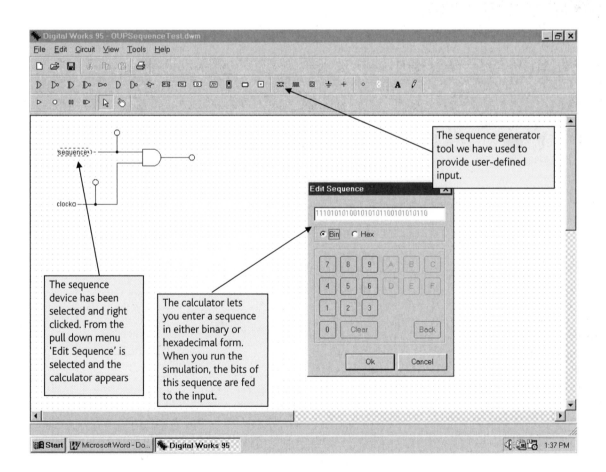

Figure 2.41 Setting up the sequence generator.

binary or hexadecimal form (see Chapter 4 for a discussion of hexadecimal numbers).

We can run the simple circuit by clicking on the run icon. When the system runs you will see the LEDs turn on and off. The speed of the clock pulses can be altered by clicking on Circuit in the toolbar to pull down a menu that allows you to set the clock speed.

2.4.4 Using Digital Works to create embedded circuits

Up to now, we have used Digital Works to create simple circuits composed from fundamental gates. You could create an entire microprocessor in this manner, but it would rapidly become too complex to use in any meaningful way. Digital Works allows you to convert a simple circuit into a logic element itself. The new logic element can be used as a building block in the construction of more complex circuits. These complex circuits can be converted into new logic elements, and so on. Turning circuits into re-usable black boxes is analogous to the use of subroutines in a high-level language.

Let's take the simple two-input multiplexer described in Fig. 2.42 and convert it into a black box with four terminals: two inputs A and B, a control input C whose state selects one of the inputs, and an output. When we constructed this circuit with Digital Works, we used the macro tag icon to place macro tags at the circuit's inputs and outputs. A macro tag can

be wired up to the rest of the circuit exactly like an input or output device. You left-click on the macro tag icon to select it and then move the cursor to the place on the workspace you wish to insert the macro tag (i.e. the input or output port). Then you wire the macro tag to the appropriate input or output point of the circuit. Note that you can't apply a macro tag to the input or output of a gate directly—you have to connect it to an input or output by a wire.

You can also place a macro tag anywhere within the workspace by right clicking the mouse when using the wiring tool. Right clicking terminates the wiring process, inserts a macro tag, and activates a pull-down menu.

We are going to take the circuit of Fig. 2.42 and convert it into a black box with four terminals (i.e. the macro tags). This new circuit is just a new means of representing the old circuit—it is not a different entity. Indeed, this circuit doesn't have a different file name and is saved in the same file as the original circuit.

The first step is to create the macro (i.e. black box) itself. This is a slightly involved and repetitive process because you have to repeat the procedure once for each of the macro tags. Place the cursor over one of the macro tags in Fig. 2.43 and right click to pull down the menu. Select Template Editor from the menu with a left click. A new window called Template Editor appears (Fig. 2.43). You create a black box representation of the circuit in this window. Digital Works allows you to draw a new symbol to represent the circuit (in Fig. 2.43 we've used a special shape for the multiplexer).

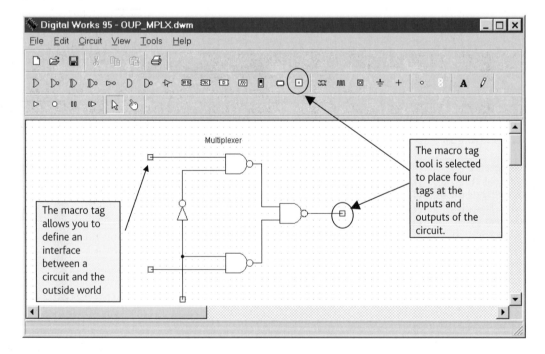

Figure 2.42 Converting the two-input multiplexer circuit into a black box.

Figure 2.43 shows the Template Editor window. We have used the simple polyline drawing tool provided by Digital Works to create a suitable shape for the representation of the multiplexer. You just click on this tool in the Template Editor window and draw the circuit by clicking in the workspace at the points you wish to draw a line. You exit the drawing mode by double clicking. You can also add text to the drawing by using the text tool. Figure 2.43 shows the shape we've drawn

for the multiplexer and the label we've given it. To add a label or text to the circuit, select the text tool and click on the point you wish to insert the text. This action will pull down the Edit Text box.

The next step is to add pins to the black box in the Template Editor window and associate them with the macro tags in the original circuit of Fig. 2.42. Once this has been done, you can use the black box representation of the multiplexer in other circuits. The pins you have added to the black box are the connections to the circuit at the macro tags.

Click on the pin icon in the Template Editor and then left click in the workspace at the point you wish to locate this pin—see Fig. 2.44. You then right click on this new pin and select Associate with Tag. This operation associates the pin you have just placed with a macro tag in the circuit diagram. Each new pin placed on the circuit in the Template Editor window is automatically numbered in sequence.

We add additional pins to the black box by closing the Template Editor, going back to the circuit, clicking on one of the unassigned pins, and selecting Associate with Tag again. Remember that Digital Works automatically numbers the pins in the circuit diagram as you associate them with tags. We can finish the process by using the text tool to add labels to the four pins see Fig. 2.45. We have now created a new element that behaves exactly like the circuit from which it was constructed and which can be used itself as a circuit element.

Figure 2.46 shows the original or expanded version of the circuit. Note how the pins have been numbered automatically.

To summarize, you create a black box representation of a circuit by carrying out the following sequence of operations.

- In Digital Works add and connect (i.e. wire up) a macro tag to your circuit.

- Right click the macro tag to enter the template editor.

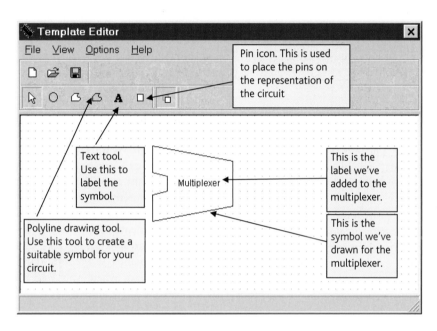

Figure 2.43 Drawing a symbol for the new circuit.

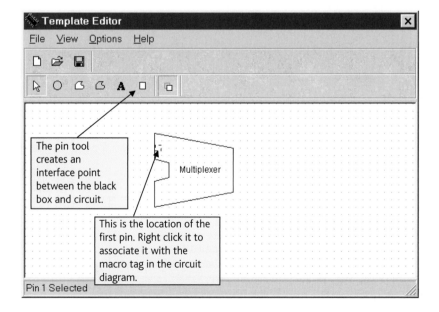

Figure 2.44 Creating an interface point in the black box.

- Use the Template Editor to add a pin to the circuit representation
- In the Template Editor, select this pin and right click to associate it with the macro tag in the circuit diagram.

- Close the Template Editor.
- Repeat these operations, once for each macro tag.

When you exit Digital Works, saving your circuit also saves its black box representation. You can regard these two circuits as being bound together—with one representing a short-hand version of the other. Note that the Template Editor also has a save function. Using this save function simply saves the drawing you've created but not the pins, the circuit, or its logic.

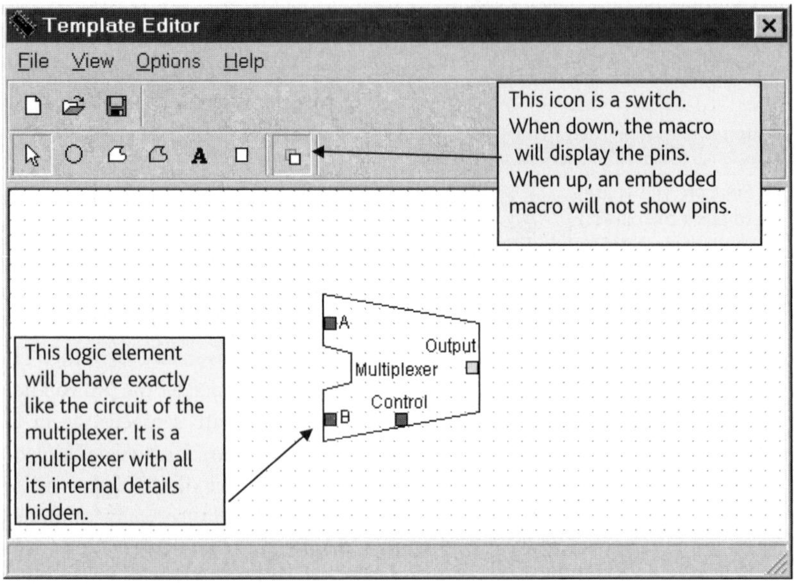

2.4.5 Using a macro

Having created a black box circuit (i.e. a macro), we can now use it as a building block just like any other logic element. We will start a new circuit in Digital Works and begin with an empty work area. The macro for a two-input multiplexer we have just created and saved is used like other circuit elements. You click on the embed macro icon (see Fig. 2.47) and move the pointer to the location in the workspace where you wish to

Figure 2.45 The completed black box representation.

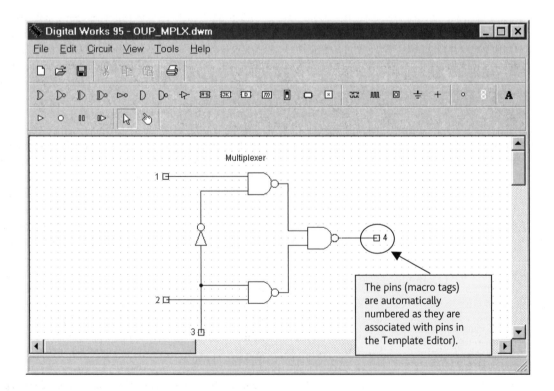

Figure 2.46 The original circuit with the macro tags numbered.

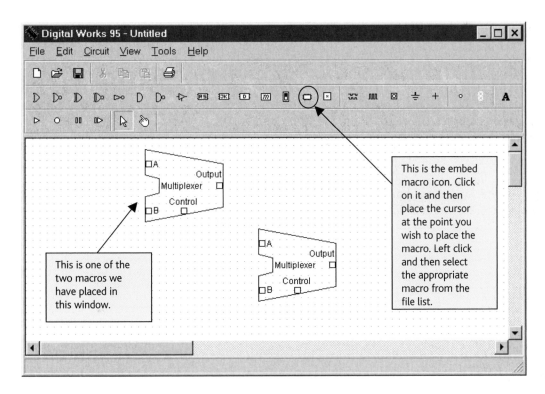

Figure 2.47 Embedding a macro in a circuit.

place the macro. Then you left click and select the appropriate macro from the pull-down menu that appears.

The macro is automatically placed at the point you clicked on and can be used exactly like a circuit element placed from one of the circuit icons. Remember that the macro is the same as the circuit—the only difference is its on-screen representation.

In Fig. 2.47 we have placed two of the multiplexers in the workspace prior to wiring them together. Figure 2.48 demonstrates how we can wire these two macros together, add a gate, and provide inputs and LED displays.

Modifying a circuit

Suppose you build a circuit that contains one or more macros (e.g. Fig. 2.48) and wish to modify it. A circuit can be modified in the usual way by opening its file in Digital Works and making any necessary changes. Digital Works even allows you to edit (i.e. modify) a circuit while it's running.

In order to modify a macro itself, you have to return to the macro's expanded form (i.e. the circuit that the macro represents). A macro is expanded by right clicking on the macro's symbol and selecting the Edit Macro function from the pull-down menu that appears. Figure. 2.49 shows the system of Fig. 2.48 in which the macro representation of the multiplexer in the upper left-hand side of the workspace has been right clicked on.

Selecting the Edit Macro function converts the black box macro representation into the original circuit as Fig. 2.50 demonstrates. You can now edit this circuit in the normal way. When editing has been completed, you select the Close Macro icon that appears on the lower toolbar. Closing this window returns to the normal circuit view, which contains the macro that has now been changed.

There are two macros in the circuit diagram of Fig. 2.48. If we edit one of them what happens to the other and what happens to the original circuit? Digital Works employs object embedding rather than object linking. When a macro is embedded in a circuit, a copy of the macro is embedded in the circuit. If you modify a macro only that copy is changed. The original macro is not altered. Moreover, if you have embedded several copies of a macro in a circuit, only the macro that you edit is changed.

Figure 2.51 demonstrates the effect of editing the macro version of a two-input multiplexer. Figure 2.51(a) shows the modified expanded macro. An OR gate has been wired to the A and B inputs on pins 1 and 2 and a macro tag added to the output of the OR gate. By clicking on the macro tag, the Template Editor window is invoked. You can add a pin and assign it to the macro tag. When you exit the Template Editor and close the macro, the final circuit of Fig. 2.51(b) appears (we have added an LED to the output of the new macro).

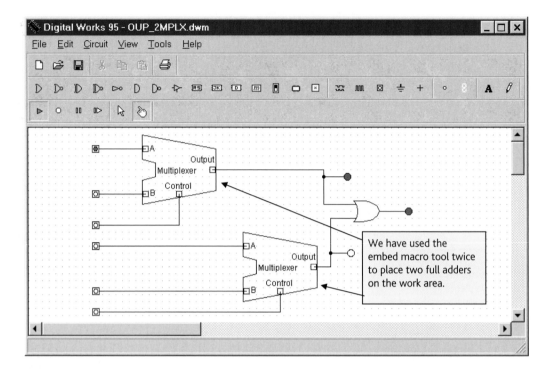

Figure 2.48 Embedding two macros, wiring them, and creating a new macro.

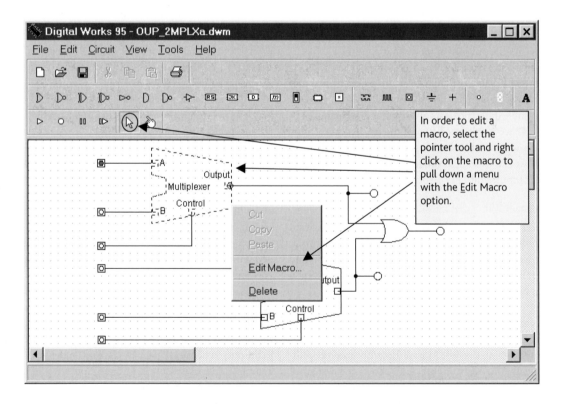

Figure 2.49 Editing a macro in a circuit.

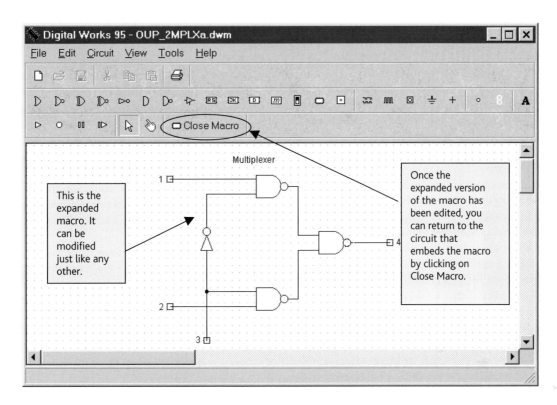

Figure 2.50 Editing the expanded form of the macro.

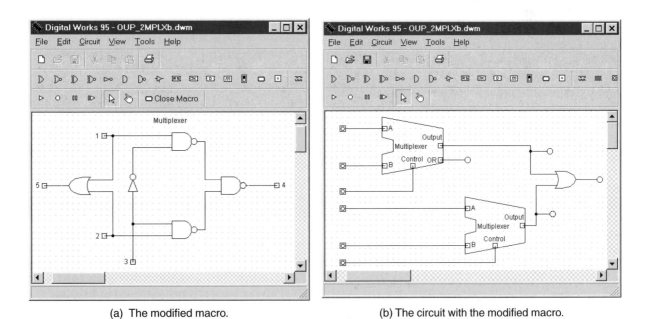

(a) The modified macro.   (b) The circuit with the modified macro.

Figure 2.51 Example of editing a macro.

2.5 An introduction to Boolean algebra

We've already seen that you can describe circuits containing gates in terms of variables and AND, OR, and NOT operators. Consider an AND gate with input variables A and B, and an output C. We can write the Boolean equation C = A · B which uses variables A, B, and C and the AND operator. In this section we introduce Boolean algebra[1], show how equations are manipulated, and demonstrate how logic circuits can be constructed with only one type of gate. Students requiring only a very basic knowledge of Boolean algebra can omit some of the fine detail that appears later in this section.

George Boole was an English mathematician (1815–1864) who developed a mathematical analysis of logic and published it in his book *An Investigation of the Laws of Thought* in 1854. Boole's algebra of logic would probably have remained a tool of the philosopher, had it not been for the development of electronics in the Twentieth Century.

In 1938 Claude Shannon published a paper entitled 'A symbolic analysis of relays and switching circuits', which applied Boolean algebra to switching circuits using relays. Such circuits were widely used in telephone exchanges and later in digital computers. Today, Boolean algebra is used to design digital circuits and to analyze their behavior.

Digital design is concerned with the conversion of ideas or specifications into hardware and Boolean algebra is a tool that facilitates this process. In particular, Boolean algebra permits an idea to be expressed in a mathematical form and the resulting expression to be simplified and then translated into the real hardware of gates and other logic elements.

Let's begin with a formal definition just in case this book falls into the hands of a mathematician. Boolean algebra (or any other algebra) consists of a set of elements E, a set of functions F that operate on members of E, and a set of basic laws called axioms that define the properties of E and F. The set of elements making up a Boolean algebra are variables and constants that have fixed values of 0 or 1. A Boolean algebra with n variables has a set of 2^n possible permutations of these variables.

Only three functions or operations are permitted in Boolean algebra. The first two are the logical OR represented by a plus (e.g. A + B) and the logical AND represented by a dot (e.g. A·B). Some texts use a ∪ (cup) or a ∨ to denote the logical OR operator and a ∩ (cap) or a ∧ to denote a logical AND operator.

The use of the plus and dot symbols is rather confusing because the same symbols are used for addition and multiplication in everyday life. One reason that these particular symbols have been chosen is that they behave rather like conventional addition and multiplication. Another possible reason Boole chose + and · to represent the logical OR and AND functions is that Boole's background was in probability theory. The chance of throwing a 1 or a 2 with two throws of a single die is 1/6 + 1/6, whereas the chance of throwing a 1 and a 2 is 1/6 × 1/6; that is, the or and and in probability theory also behave like addition and multiplication, respectively.

The third operation permitted in Boolean algebra is that of negation or complementation and is denoted by a bar over a constant or a variable. The complement of 0 (i.e. $\overline{0}$) is 1 and vice versa. The equation $X + Y \cdot \overline{Z} = A$ is read as 'X or Y and not Z equals A'. The priority of an AND operator is higher than that of an OR operator so that the expression means A = X + (Y·Z) and not A = (X + Y)$\overline{Z}$. Some texts use an asterisk to denote negation and some use a stroke. Thus, we can write NOT(X) as $\overline{X}$ or X* or /X.

The arithmetic operations of subtraction and division do not exist in Boolean algebra. For example, the Boolean expression X + Y = X + Z, cannot be rearranged in the form (X + Y) − X = (X + Z) − X, which would lead to Y = Z. If you don't believe this, then consider the case X = 1, Y = 1, and Z = 0. The left-hand side of the equation yields X + Y = 1 + 1 = 1, and the right-hand side yields X + Z = 1 + 0 = 1. That is, the equation is valid even though Y is not equal to Z.

2.5.1 Axioms and theorems of Boolean algebra

An axiom or postulate is a fundamental rule that has to be taken for granted (i.e. the axioms of Boolean algebra define the framework of Boolean algebra from which everything else can be derived). The first axiom is called the closure property, which states that Boolean operations on Boolean variables or constants always yield Boolean results. If variables A and B belong to a set of Boolean elements, the operations A · B, A + B, and NOT A and NOT B also belong to the set of Boolean elements.

Boolean variables obey the same commutative, distributive, and associative laws as the variables of conventional algebra. We take these laws for granted when we do everyday arithmetic; for example, the commutative law states that 6 × 3 = 3 × 6. Table 2.13 describes the commutative, distributive, and associative laws of Boolean algebra.

We approach Boolean algebra by first looking at the action of NOT, OR, and AND operations on constants. The effect of these three operations is best illustrated by means of the truth table given in Table 2.14. These rules may be extended to any number of variables.

We can extend Table 2.14, which defines the relationship between the Boolean operators and the constants 0 and 1, to

---

[1] There are, in fact, an infinite number of Boolean algebras. We are interested only in the Boolean algebra whose variables have binary two-state values.

$A + B = B + A$ $A \cdot B = B \cdot A$	The AND and OR operators are **commutative** so that the order of the variables in a sum or product group does not matter.
$A \cdot (B \cdot C) = (A \cdot B) \cdot C$ $A + (B + C) = (A + B) + C$	The AND and OR operators are **associative** so that the order in which sub-expressions are evaluated does not matter.
$A \cdot (B + C) = A \cdot B + A \cdot C$ $A + B \cdot C = (A + B)(A + C)$	The AND operator behaves like multiplication and the OR operator like addition. The first **distributive** property states that in an expression containing both AND and OR operators the AND operator takes precedence over the OR. The second distributive law, $A + B \cdot C = (A + B)(A + C)$, is not valid in conventional algebra.

Table 2.13 Commutative, distributive, and associative laws of Boolean algebra.

NOT	AND	OR
$\overline{0} = 1$	$0 \cdot 0 = 0$	$0 + 0 = 0$
$\overline{1} = 0$	$0 \cdot 1 = 0$	$0 + 1 = 0$
	$1 \cdot 0 = 0$	$1 + 0 = 1$
	$1 \cdot 1 = 1$	$1 + 1 = 1$

Table 2.14 Basic axioms of Boolean algebra.

AND	OR	NOT
$0 \cdot X = 0$	$0 + X = X$	$\overline{\overline{X}} = X$
$1 \cdot X = X$	$1 + X = 1$	
$X \cdot X = X$	$X + X = X$	
$X \cdot \overline{X} = 0$	$X + \overline{X} = 1$	

Table 2.15 Boolean operations on a constant and a variable.

the relationship between a Boolean operator, a variable, and a literal (see Table 2.15).

We can prove the validity of the equations in Table 2.15 by substituting all the possible values for X (i.e. 0 or 1). For example, consider the axiom $0 \cdot X = 0$. If $X = 1$ we have $0.1 = 0$, which is correct because by definition the output of an AND gate is true if and only if all its inputs are true. Similarly, if $X = 0$ we have $0 \cdot 0 = 0$, which is also correct. Therefore, the expression $0 \cdot X = 0$ is correct for all possible

values of X. A proof in which we test a theorem by examining all possibilities is called proof by perfect induction.

The axioms of Boolean algebra could be used to simplify equations, but it would be too tedious to keep going back to first principles. Instead, we can apply the axioms of Boolean algebra to derive some *theorems* to help in the simplification of expressions. Once we have proved a theorem by using the basic axioms, we can apply the theorem to equations.

Theorem 1 $X + X \cdot Y = X$

Proof	$X + X \cdot Y = X \cdot 1 + X \cdot Y$	Using $1 \cdot X = X$ and commutativity
	$= X(1 + Y)$	Using distributivity
	$= X(1)$	Because $1 + Y = 1$
	$= X$	

Theorem 2 $X + \overline{X} \cdot Y = X + Y$

Proof	$X + \overline{X} \cdot Y = (X + X \cdot Y) + \overline{X} \cdot Y$	By Theorem 1 $X = X + X \cdot Y$
	$= X + X \cdot Y + \overline{X} \cdot Y$	
	$= X + Y(X + \overline{X})$	Remember that $X + \overline{X} = 1$
	$= X + Y(1)$	
	$= X + Y$	

Theorem 3 $X \cdot Y + \overline{X} \cdot Z + Y \cdot Z = X \cdot Y + \overline{X} \cdot Z$

Proof	$X \cdot Y + \overline{X} \cdot Z + Y \cdot Z = X \cdot Y + \overline{X} \cdot Z + Y \cdot Z(X + \overline{X})$	Remember that $(X + \overline{X}) = 1$
	$= X \cdot Y + \overline{X} \cdot Z + X \cdot Y \cdot Z + \overline{X} \cdot Y \cdot Z$	Multiply bracketed terms
	$= X \cdot Y(1 + Z) + \overline{X} \cdot Z(1 + Y)$	Apply distributive rule
	$= X \cdot Y(1) + \overline{X} \cdot Z(1)$	Because $(1 + Y) = 1$
	$= X \cdot Y + \overline{X} \cdot Z$	

Inputs			$\overline{X}$	$X \cdot Y$	$\overline{X} \cdot Z$	$Y \cdot Z$	$X \cdot Y + \overline{X} \cdot Z$	$X \cdot Y + \overline{X} \cdot Z + Y \cdot Z$
X	Y	Z						
0	0	0	1	0	0	0	0	0
0	0	1	1	0	1	0	1	1
0	1	0	1	0	0	0	0	0
0	1	1	1	0	1	1	1	1
1	0	0	0	0	0	0	0	0
1	0	1	0	0	0	0	0	0
1	1	0	0	1	0	0	1	1
1	1	1	0	1	0	1	1	1

← — same — →

Table 2.16　Proof of Theorem 3 by perfect induction.

We can also prove Theorem 3 by the method of perfect induction. To do this, we set up a truth table and demonstrate that the theorem holds for all possible values of X, Y, and Z (Table 2.16). Because the columns labeled $X \cdot Y + \overline{X} \cdot Z$ and $X \cdot Y + \overline{X} \cdot Z + Y \cdot Z$ in Table 2.16 are identical for all possible inputs, these two expressions must be equivalent.

Theorem 4	$X(X + Y) = X$	
Proof	$X(X + Y) = X \cdot X + X \cdot Y$	Multiply by X
	$= X + X \cdot Y$	Because $X \cdot X = X$
	$= X$	By Theorem 1
Theorem 5	$X(\overline{X} + Y) = X \cdot Y$	
Proof	$X(\overline{X} + Y) = X \cdot \overline{X} + X \cdot Y$	
	$= 0 + X \cdot Y$	Because $X \cdot \overline{X} = 0$
	$= X \cdot Y$	
Theorem 6	$(X + Y)(X + \overline{Y}) = X$	
Proof	$(X + Y)(X + \overline{Y}) = X \cdot X + X \cdot \overline{Y} + X \cdot Y + \overline{Y} \cdot Y$	
	$= X + X \cdot \overline{Y} + X \cdot Y$	Because $X \cdot X = X, Y \cdot \overline{Y} = 0$
	$= X(1 + \overline{Y} + Y)$	
	$= X$	
Theorem 7	$(X + Y)(\overline{X} + Z) = X \cdot Z + \overline{X} \cdot Y$	
Proof	$(X + Y)(\overline{X} + Z) = X \cdot \overline{X} + X \cdot Z + \overline{X} \cdot Y + Y \cdot Z$	Multiply brackets
	$= X \cdot Z + \overline{X} \cdot Y + Y \cdot Z$	Because $X \cdot \overline{X} = 0$
	$= X \cdot Z + \overline{X} \cdot Y$	By Theorem 3
Theorem 8	$(X + Y)(\overline{X} + Z)(Y + Z) = (X + Y)(\overline{X} + Z)$	
Proof	$(X + Y)(\overline{X} + Z)(Y + Z) = (X \cdot Z + \overline{X} \cdot Y)(Y + Z)$	By Theorem 7
	$= X \cdot Y \cdot Z + X \cdot Z \cdot Z + \overline{X} \cdot Y \cdot Y + \overline{X} \cdot Y \cdot Z$	
	$= X \cdot Y \cdot Z + X \cdot Z + \overline{X} \cdot Y + \overline{X} \cdot Y \cdot Z$	Because $X \cdot X = 1$
	$= X \cdot Z(Y + 1) + \overline{X} \cdot Y(1 + Z)$	
	$= X \cdot Z + \overline{X} \cdot Y$	
	$= (X + Y)(\overline{X} + Z)$	By Theorem 7

We provide an alternative proof for Theorem 8 when we look at de Morgan's theorem later in this chapter.

Theorem 9 $\overline{X \cdot Y \cdot Z} = \overline{X} + \overline{Y} + \overline{Z}$

Proof   To prove that $\overline{X \cdot Y \cdot Z} = \overline{X} + \overline{Y} + \overline{Z}$, we assume that the expression is true and test its consequences.

If $\overline{X} + \overline{Y} + \overline{Z}$ is the complement of $X \cdot Y \cdot Z$, then from the basic axioms of Boolean algebra, we have

$(\overline{X} + \overline{Y} + \overline{Z}) \cdot (X \cdot Y \cdot Z) = 0$ and $(\overline{X} + \overline{Y} + \overline{Z}) + (X \cdot Y \cdot Z) = 1$

Subproof 1 $(\overline{X} + \overline{Y} + \overline{Z}) \cdot X \cdot Y \cdot Z = \overline{X} \cdot X \cdot Y \cdot Z + \overline{Y} \cdot X \cdot Y \cdot Z + \overline{Z} \cdot X \cdot Y \cdot Z$

$= \overline{X} \cdot X \cdot (Y \cdot Z) + \overline{Y} \cdot Y \cdot (Y \cdot Z) + \overline{Z} \cdot Z (X \cdot Y)$

$= 0$

Subproof 2 $(\overline{X} + \overline{Y} + \overline{Z}) + X \cdot Y \cdot Z = Y \cdot Z \cdot (X) + \overline{X} + \overline{Y} + \overline{Z}$ Re-arrange equation

$= Y \cdot Z + \overline{X} + \overline{Y} + \overline{Z}$ Use $A \cdot B + \overline{B} = A + \overline{B}$

$= (\overline{Y} + Y \cdot Z) + \overline{X} + \overline{Z}$ Re-arrange equation

$= \overline{Y} + Z + \overline{Z} + \overline{X}$

$= \overline{Y} + 1 + \overline{X} = 1$ Use $Z + \overline{Z} = 1$

As we have demonstrated that
$(\overline{X} + \overline{Y} + \overline{Z}) \cdot X \cdot Y \cdot Z = 0$ and that
$(\overline{X} + \overline{Y} + \overline{Z}) + X \cdot Y \cdot Z = 1$, it follows that $\overline{X} + \overline{Y} + \overline{Z}$ is the complement of $X \cdot Y \cdot Z$.

Theorem 10 $\overline{X \cdot Y \cdot Z} = \overline{X} + \overline{Y} + \overline{Z}$

Proof   One possible way of proving Theorem 10 is to use the method we used to prove Theorem 9. For the sake of variety, we will prove Theorem 10 by perfect induction (see Table 2.17).

Inputs								
X	Y	Z	X + Y + Z	$\overline{X + Y + Z}$	$\overline{X}$	$\overline{Y}$	$\overline{Z}$	$\overline{X} \cdot \overline{Y} \cdot \overline{Z}$
0	0	0	0	1	1	1	1	1
0	0	1	1	0	1	1	0	0
0	1	0	1	0	1	0	1	0
0	1	1	1	0	1	0	0	0
1	0	0	1	0	0	1	1	0
1	0	1	1	0	0	1	0	0
1	1	0	1	0	0	0	1	0
1	1	1	1	0	0	0	0	0

$\longleftarrow$ same $\longrightarrow$

Table 2.17 Proof of Theorem 10 by perfect induction.

Theorems 9 and 10 are collectively called de Morgan's theorem. This theorem can be stated as an entire function is complemented by replacing AND operators by OR operators, replacing OR operators by AND operators, and complementing variables and literals. We make extensive use of de Morgan's theorem later.

An important rule in Boolean algebra is called the *principle of duality*. Any expression that is true is also true if AND is replaced by OR (and vice versa) and 1 replaced by 0 (and vice versa). Consider the following examples of duals.

Expression	Dual	
X = X + X	X = X · X	(replace + by ·)
1 = X + 1	0 = X · 0	(replace + by · and replace 1 by 0)
X = X(X + Y)	X = X + X · Y	(replace · by + and replace + by ·)

As you can see, the dual of each expression is also true.

OBSERVATIONS

When novices first encounter Boolean algebra, it is not uncommon for them to invent new theorems that are incorrect (because they superficially look like existing theorems). We include the following observations because they represent the most frequently encountered misconceptions.

Observation 1 $\overline{X} \cdot \overline{Y} + X \cdot Y$ is not equal to 1
$\overline{X} \cdot \overline{Y} + X \cdot Y$ cannot be simplified

Observation 2 $\overline{X} \cdot Y + X \cdot \overline{Y}$ is not equal to 1
$\overline{X} \cdot Y + X \cdot \overline{Y}$ cannot be simplified

Observation 3 $\overline{X \cdot Y}$ is not equal to $\overline{X} \cdot \overline{Y}$

Observation 4 $\overline{X + Y}$ is not equal to $\overline{X} + \overline{Y}$

ALL FUNCTIONS OF TWO VARIABLES—ALL POSSIBLE GATES

This table provides all possible functions of two variables A and B. These two variables have $2^2 = 4$ possible different combinations. We can associate a different function with each of these $4^2 = 16$ values to create all possible functions of two variables; that is, there are only 16 possible types of two-input gate. Some of the functions correspond to functions we've already met. Some functions are meaningless.

Inputs		Functions															
A	B	F_0	F_1	F_2	F_3	F_4	F_5	F_6	F_7	F_8	F_9	F_{10}	F_{11}	F_{12}	F_{13}	F_{14}	F_{15}
0	0	0	1	0	1	0	1	0	1	0	1	0	1	0	1	0	1
0	1	0	0	1	1	0	0	1	1	0	0	1	1	0	0	1	1
1	0	0	0	0	0	1	1	1	1	0	0	0	0	1	1	1	1
1	1	0	0	0	0	0	0	0	0	1	1	1	1	1	1	1	1

Function	Expression	Name
F_0	0	
F_1	$\overline{A + B}$	NOR
F_2	$\overline{A} \cdot B$	
F_3	$\overline{A}$	NOT
F_4	$A \cdot \overline{B}$	
F_5	$\overline{B}$	NOT
F_6	$A \oplus B$	EOR
F_7	$\overline{A \cdot B}$	NAND
F_8	$A \cdot B$	AND
F_9	$\overline{A \oplus B}$	ENOR
F_{10}	B	
F_{11}	$\overline{A} \cdot \overline{B} + A \cdot \overline{B} + A \cdot B = \overline{A \cdot \overline{B}} = \overline{A} + B$	
F_{12}	A	
F_{13}	$\overline{A} \cdot \overline{B} + A \cdot \overline{B} + A \cdot B = \overline{\overline{A} \cdot B} = A + \overline{B}$	
F_{14}	$A + B$	OR
F_{15}	1	

Examples of the use of Boolean algebra in simplifying equations

Having presented the basic rules of Boolean algebra, the next step is to show how it's used to simplify Boolean expressions. By simplifying these equations you can sometimes produce a cheaper version of the logic circuit. The following equations are generally random functions chosen to demonstrate the rules of Boolean algebra.

(a) $X + \overline{Y} + \overline{X} \cdot Y + (X + \overline{Y}) \cdot \overline{X} \cdot Y$

(b) $\overline{X} \cdot Y \cdot \overline{Z} + \overline{X} \cdot Y \cdot Z + X \cdot \overline{Y} \cdot Z + X \cdot Y \cdot Z$

(c) $\overline{\overline{\overline{X \cdot Y \cdot X \cdot Z}}}$

(d) $(X + \overline{Y})(\overline{X} + Z)(Y + \overline{Z})$

(e) $(W + X + Y \cdot Z)(\overline{W} + X)(\overline{X} + Y)$

(f) $W \cdot X \cdot \overline{Z} + \overline{X} \cdot Y \cdot Z + W \cdot X \cdot \overline{Y} + X \cdot Y \cdot Z + \overline{W} \cdot Y \cdot Z$

(g) $\overline{W} \cdot X \cdot Z + W \cdot Z + X \cdot Y \cdot \overline{Z} + \overline{W} \cdot X \cdot Y$

(h) $(X + Y + Z)(\overline{X} + Y + Z)(\overline{X} + Y + \overline{Z})$

Solutions

When I simplify Boolean expressions, I try to keep the order of the variables alphabetical, making it easier to pick out logical groupings.

(a) $X + \overline{Y} + \overline{X} \cdot Y + (X + \overline{Y}) \cdot \overline{X} \cdot Y = X + \overline{Y} + \overline{X} \cdot Y + X \cdot \overline{X} \cdot Y + \overline{X} \cdot \overline{Y} \cdot Y$

$\qquad\qquad\qquad = X + \overline{Y} + \overline{X} \cdot Y$ $\qquad\qquad$ As $\overline{A} \cdot A = 0$

$\qquad\qquad\qquad = X + Y + \overline{Y}$ $\qquad\qquad$ as $A + \overline{A} \cdot B = A + B$

$\qquad\qquad\qquad = 1$ $\qquad\qquad\qquad\quad$ as $A + \overline{A} = 1$

Note: When a Boolean expression can be reduced to the constant 1, the expression is always true and is independent of the variables.

(b) $\overline{X} \cdot Y \cdot \overline{Z} + \overline{X} \cdot Y \cdot Z + X \cdot \overline{Y} \cdot Z + X \cdot Y \cdot Z = \overline{X} \cdot Y \cdot (\overline{Z} + Z) + X \cdot Z \cdot (\overline{Y} + Y)$

$\qquad\qquad\qquad\qquad\qquad\qquad\qquad = \overline{X} \cdot Y \cdot (1) + X \cdot Z \cdot (1)$

$\qquad\qquad\qquad\qquad\qquad\qquad\qquad = \overline{X} \cdot Y + X \cdot Z$

(c) $\overline{\overline{\overline{X \cdot Y \cdot X \cdot Z}}} = \overline{\overline{\overline{X} \cdot Y}} + \overline{\overline{X \cdot Z}}$ $\qquad\qquad\qquad\qquad$ By Theorem 9

$\qquad = \overline{X} \cdot Y + X \cdot Z$ $\qquad\qquad\qquad\qquad\quad$ As $\overline{\overline{F}} = F$

Note: Both expressions in examples (b) and (c) simplify to $X \cdot \overline{Y} + X \cdot Z$, demonstrating that these two expressions are equivalent. These equations are those of the multiplexer with (b) derived from the truth table (Table 2.9) and (c) from the circuit diagram of Fig. 2.14.

(d) $(X + \overline{Y})(\overline{X} + Z)(Y + \overline{Z}) = (X \cdot \overline{X} + X \cdot Z + \overline{X} \cdot \overline{Y} + \overline{Y} \cdot Z) \cdot (Y + \overline{Z})$

$\qquad\qquad\qquad\qquad\qquad\quad = (X \cdot Z + \overline{X} \cdot \overline{Y} + \overline{Y} \cdot Z) \cdot (Y + \overline{Z})$ $\qquad$ As $X \cdot \overline{X} = 0$

$\qquad\qquad\qquad\qquad\qquad\quad = (X \cdot Z + \overline{X} \cdot \overline{Y}) \cdot (Y + \overline{Z})$ $\qquad\qquad\quad$ By Theorem 3

$\qquad\qquad\qquad\qquad\qquad\quad = X \cdot Y \cdot Z + X \cdot \overline{Z} \cdot Z + \overline{X} \cdot \overline{Y} \cdot Y + \overline{X} \cdot \overline{Y} \cdot \overline{Z}$

$\qquad\qquad\qquad\qquad\qquad\quad = X \cdot Y \cdot Z + \overline{X} \cdot \overline{Y} \cdot \overline{Z}$

(e) $(W + X + Y \cdot Z)(\overline{W} + X)(\overline{X} + Y) = (W \cdot \overline{W} + \overline{W} \cdot X + \overline{W} \cdot Y \cdot Z + W \cdot X + X \cdot X + X \cdot Y \cdot Z)(\overline{X} + Y)$

$\qquad\qquad\qquad\qquad\qquad\qquad\qquad = (\overline{W} \cdot X + \overline{W} \cdot Y \cdot Z + W \cdot X + X + X \cdot Y \cdot Z)(\overline{X} + Y)$

$\qquad\qquad\qquad\qquad\qquad\qquad\qquad = (X + \overline{W} \cdot Y \cdot Z)(\overline{X} + Y)$

$\qquad\qquad\qquad\qquad\qquad\qquad\qquad = X \cdot \overline{X} + X \cdot Y + \overline{W} \cdot \overline{X} \cdot Y \cdot Z + \overline{W} \cdot Y \cdot Y \cdot Z$

$\qquad\qquad\qquad\qquad\qquad\qquad\qquad = X \cdot Y + \overline{W} \cdot \overline{X} \cdot Y \cdot Z + \overline{W} \cdot Y \cdot Z$

$\qquad\qquad\qquad\qquad\qquad\qquad\qquad = X \cdot Y + \overline{W} \cdot Y \cdot Z(\overline{X} + 1)$

$\qquad\qquad\qquad\qquad\qquad\qquad\qquad = X \cdot Y + \overline{W} \cdot Y \cdot Z$

(f) $W X \overline{Z} + \overline{X} Y Z + W X \overline{Y} + X Y Z + \overline{W} Y Z = W X \overline{Z} + Y Z(\overline{X} + X + \overline{W}) + W X \overline{Y}$

$\qquad\qquad\qquad\qquad\qquad\qquad\qquad\qquad = W X \overline{Z} + Y Z + W X \overline{Y}$

$\qquad\qquad\qquad\qquad\qquad\qquad\qquad\qquad = W X (\overline{Y} + \overline{Z}) + Y Z$

Note that $\overline{Y Z} = \overline{Y} + \overline{Z}$ so we can write

$\qquad\qquad\qquad\qquad\qquad\qquad\qquad = W \cdot X(Y + Z) + \overline{\overline{Y} + \overline{Z}}$

$\qquad\qquad\qquad\qquad\qquad\qquad\qquad = W \cdot X + Y \cdot Z$ $\qquad\qquad\qquad$ Because $A + \overline{A} \cdot B = A + B$

(g) $\overline{W}XZ + WZ + XY\overline{Z} + \overline{W}XY = Z(\overline{W}X + W) + XY\overline{Z} + \overline{W}XY$

$$= Z(X + W) + XY\overline{Z} + \overline{W}XY$$

$$= XZ + WZ + XY\overline{Z} + \overline{W}XY$$

$$= X(Z + Y\overline{Z}) + WZ + \overline{W}XY$$

$$= X(Z + Y) + WZ + \overline{W}XY$$

$$= XZ + XY + WZ + \overline{W}XY$$

$$= XZ + XY(1 + \overline{W}) + WZ$$

$$= XZ + XY + WZ$$

(h) $(X + Y + Z)(\overline{X} + Y + Z)(\overline{X} + Y + \overline{Z}) = (Y + Z)(\overline{X} + Y + \overline{Z})$ as $(A + B)(A + \overline{B}) = A$

$$= Z(\overline{X} + Y) + Y \cdot \overline{Z}$$ as $(A + B)(\overline{A} + C) = A \cdot C + \overline{A} \cdot B$

$$= \overline{X} \cdot Z + Y \cdot Z + Y \cdot \overline{Z}$$

$$= \overline{X} \cdot Z + Y(Z + \overline{Z})$$

$$= \overline{X} \cdot Z + Y$$

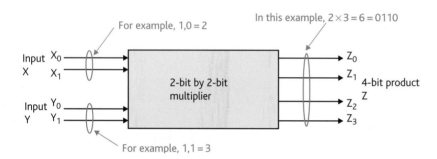

Figure 2.52 A 2-bit multiplier

X x Y = Z	Inputs				Output			
	X		Y		Z			
	X_1	X_0	Y_1	Y_0	Z_3	Z_2	Z_1	Z_0
$0 \times 0 = 0$	0	0	0	0	0	0	0	0
$0 \times 1 = 0$	0	0	0	1	0	0	0	0
$0 \times 2 = 0$	0	0	1	0	0	0	0	0
$0 \times 3 = 0$	0	0	1	1	0	0	0	0
$1 \times 0 = 0$	0	1	0	0	0	0	0	0
$1 \times 1 = 1$	0	1	0	1	0	0	0	1
$1 \times 2 = 2$	0	1	1	0	0	0	1	0
$1 \times 3 = 3$	0	1	1	1	0	0	1	1
$2 \times 0 = 0$	1	0	0	0	0	0	0	0
$2 \times 1 = 2$	1	0	0	1	0	0	1	0
$2 \times 2 = 4$	1	0	1	0	0	1	0	0
$2 \times 3 = 6$	1	0	1	1	0	1	1	0
$3 \times 0 = 0$	1	1	0	0	0	0	0	0
$3 \times 1 = 3$	1	1	0	1	0	0	1	1
$3 \times 2 = 6$	1	1	1	0	0	1	1	0
$3 \times 3 = 9$	1	1	1	1	1	0	0	1

Table 2.18 Truth table for a 2-bit by 2-bit multiplier.

These examples illustrate the art of manipulating Boolean expressions. It's difficult to be sure we have reached an optimal solution. Later we study Karnaugh maps, which provide an approach that gives us confidence that we've reached an optimal solution.

The Design of a 2-bit Multiplier

The following example illustrates how Boolean algebra is applied to a practical problem. A designer wishes to produce a 2-bit by 2-bit binary multiplier. The two 2-bit inputs are X_1, X_0 and Y_1, Y_0 and the four-bit product at the output terminals is Z_3, Z_2, Z_1, Z_0. We have not yet introduced binary arithmetic (see Chapter 4), but nothing difficult is involved here. We begin by considering the block diagram of the system (Fig. 2.52) and constructing its truth table.

The multiplier has four inputs, X_1, X_0, Y_1, Y_0, (indicating a 16-line truth table) and four outputs. Table 2.18 provides a truth table for the binary multiplier. Each 4-bit input represents the product of two 2-bit numbers so that, for example, an input of $X_1, X_0, Y_1, Y_0 = 1011$ represents the product $10_2 \times 11_2$ or 2×3. The corresponding output is a 4-bit product, which, in this case, is 6 or 0110 in binary form.

From Table 2.18, we can derive expressions for the four outputs, Z_0 to Z_3. Whenever a truth table has m output columns, a set of m Boolean equations must be derived. One equation is associated with each of the m columns. To derive an expression for Z_0, the four *minterms* in the Z_0 column are ORed logically.

$$Z_0 = \overline{X}_1 \cdot X_0 \cdot \overline{Y}_1 \cdot Y_0 + \overline{X}_1 \cdot X_0 \cdot Y_1 \cdot Y_0 + X_1 \cdot X_0 \cdot \overline{Y}_1 \cdot Y_0 + X_1 \cdot X_0 \cdot Y_1 \cdot Y_0$$
$$= \overline{X}_1 \cdot X_0 \cdot Y_0 (\overline{Y}_1 + Y_1) + X_1 \cdot X_0 \cdot Y_0 (\overline{Y}_1 + Y_1)$$
$$= \overline{X}_1 \cdot X_0 \cdot Y_0 + X_1 \cdot X_0 \cdot Y_0$$
$$= X_0 \cdot Y_0 (\overline{X}_1 + X_1)$$
$$= X_0 \cdot Y_0$$

$$Z_1 = \overline{X}_1 \cdot X_0 \cdot Y_1 \cdot \overline{Y}_0 + \overline{X}_1 \cdot X_0 \cdot Y_1 \cdot Y_0 + X_1 \cdot \overline{X}_0 \cdot \overline{Y}_1 \cdot Y_0 + X_1 \cdot \overline{X}_0 \cdot Y_1 \cdot Y_0 + X_1 \cdot X_0 \cdot \overline{Y}_1 \cdot Y_0 + X_1 \cdot X_0 \cdot Y_1 \cdot \overline{Y}_0$$
$$= \overline{X}_1 \cdot X_0 \cdot Y_1 (\overline{Y}_0 + Y_0) + X_1 \cdot \overline{X}_0 \cdot Y_0 (Y_1 + \overline{Y}_1) + X_1 \cdot X_0 \cdot \overline{Y}_1 \cdot Y_0 + X_1 \cdot X_0 \cdot Y_1 \cdot \overline{Y}_0$$
$$= \overline{X}_1 \cdot X_0 \cdot Y_1 + X_1 \cdot \overline{X}_0 \cdot Y_0 + X_1 \cdot X_0 \cdot \overline{Y}_1 \cdot Y_0 + X_1 \cdot X_0 \cdot Y_1 \cdot \overline{Y}_0$$
$$= X_0 \cdot Y_1 (\overline{X}_1 + X_1 \cdot \overline{Y}_0) + X_1 \cdot Y_0 (\overline{X}_0 + X_0 \cdot \overline{Y}_1)$$
$$= X_0 \cdot Y_1 (\overline{X}_1 + \overline{Y}_0) + X_1 \cdot Y_0 (\overline{X}_0 + \overline{Y}_1)$$
$$= \overline{X}_1 \cdot X_0 \cdot Y_1 + X_0 \cdot Y_1 \cdot \overline{Y}_0 + X_1 \cdot \overline{X}_0 \cdot Y_0 + X_1 \cdot \overline{Y}_1 \cdot Y_0$$

$$Z_2 = X_1 \cdot \overline{X}_0 \cdot Y_1 \cdot \overline{Y}_0 + X_1 \cdot \overline{X}_0 \cdot Y_1 \cdot Y_0 + X_1 \cdot X_0 \cdot Y_1 \cdot \overline{Y}_0$$
$$= X_1 \cdot \overline{X}_0 \cdot Y_1 (\overline{Y}_0 + Y_0) + X_1 \cdot X_0 \cdot Y_1 \cdot \overline{Y}_0$$
$$= X_1 \cdot \overline{X}_0 \cdot Y_1 + X_1 \cdot X_0 \cdot Y_1 \cdot \overline{Y}_0$$
$$= X_1 \cdot Y_1 (\overline{X}_0 + X_0 \overline{Y}_0)$$
$$= X_1 \cdot Y_1 (\overline{X}_0 + \overline{Y}_0)$$
$$= X_1 \cdot \overline{X}_0 \cdot Y_1 + X_1 \cdot Y_1 \cdot \overline{Y}_0$$

$$Z_3 = X_1 \cdot X_0 \cdot Y_1 \cdot Y_0$$

We have now obtained four simplified sum of products expressions for Z_0 to Z_3; that is,

$$Z_0 = X_0 \cdot Y_0$$
$$Z_1 = \overline{X}_1 \cdot X_0 \cdot Y_1 + X_0 \cdot Y_1 \cdot \overline{Y}_0 + X_1 \cdot \overline{X}_0 \cdot Y_0 + X_1 \cdot \overline{Y}_1 \cdot Y_0$$
$$Z_2 = X_1 \cdot \overline{X}_0 \cdot Y_1 + X_1 \cdot Y_1 \cdot \overline{Y}_0$$
$$Z_3 = X_1 \cdot X_0 \cdot Y_1 \cdot Y_0$$

It's interesting to note that each of the above expressions is *symmetric* in X and Y. This is to be expected—if the problem

itself is symmetric in X and Y (i.e. $3 \times 1 = 1 \times 3$), then the result should also demonstrate this symmetry. There are many ways of realizing the expressions for Z_0 to Z_3. The circuit of Fig. 2.53 illustrates one possible way.

2.5.2 De Morgan's theorem

Theorems 9 and 10 provide the designer with a powerful tool because they enable an AND function to be implemented by

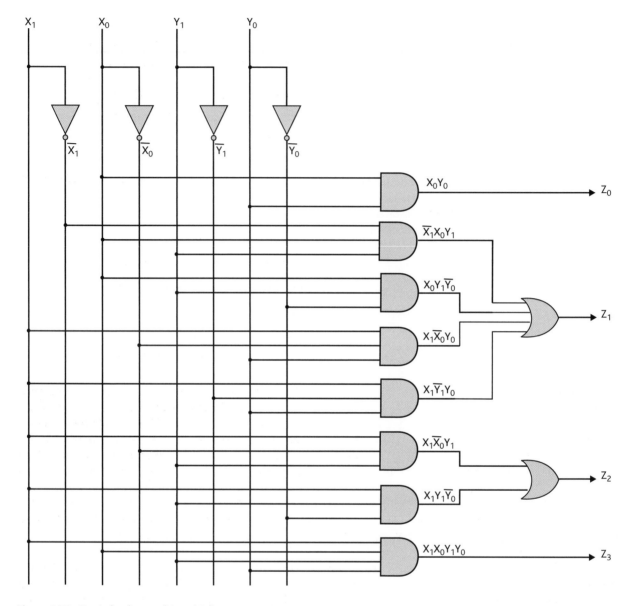

Figure 2.53 Circuit for the two-bit multiplier.

an OR gate and inverter. Similarly, these theorems enable an OR gate to be implemented by an AND gate and inverter. We first demonstrate how de Morgan's theorem is applied to Boolean expressions and then show how circuits can be converted to NAND-only or NOR-only forms. You may wonder why anyone should wish to implement circuits in NAND (or NOR) logic only. There are several reasons for this, but, in general, NAND gates operate at a higher speed than AND gates and NAND gates can be built with fewer components (at the chip level). Later we shall examine in more detail how a circuit can be designed entirely with NAND gates only.

To apply de Morgan's theorem to a function the ANDs are changed into ORs, ORs and the into ANDs and variables (and literals) are complemented. The following examples illustrate the application of de Morgan's theorem.

1. $F = \overline{X \cdot Y + X \cdot Z}$ We wish to apply de Morgan's theorem to the right-hand side

$\quad = \overline{X \cdot Y} \cdot \overline{X \cdot Z}$ The $+$ becomes $\cdot$ and variables 'X $\cdot$ Y' and 'X $\cdot$ Z' complemented

$\quad = (\overline{X} + \overline{Y})(\overline{X} + \overline{Z})$ Variables $\overline{X \cdot Y}$ and $\overline{X \cdot Y}$ are themselves complemented

As you can see, the first step is to replace the OR by an AND operator. The compound variables $X \cdot Y$ and $X \cdot Z$ are complemented to get $\overline{X \cdot Y}$ and $\overline{X \cdot Z}$. The process is continued by applying de Morgan to the two complemented groups (i.e. $\overline{X \cdot Y}$ becomes $\overline{X} + \overline{Y}$ and $\overline{X \cdot Z}$ becomes $\overline{X} + \overline{Z}$).

2. $F = \overline{A{\cdot}B + C{\cdot}D + A{\cdot}D}$

   $= \overline{A{\cdot}B}{\cdot}\overline{C{\cdot}D}{\cdot}\overline{A{\cdot}D}$ Replace $+$ by $\cdot$ and complement the product terms

   $= (\overline{A} + \overline{B})(\overline{C} + \overline{D})(\overline{A} + \overline{D})$ Expand the complemented product terms

3. $F = \overline{A{\cdot}B{\cdot}(C + E{\cdot}D)}$ This is a product term with three elements.

   $= \overline{A} + \overline{B} + \overline{C + E{\cdot}D}$ Replace $\cdot$ by $+$ and complement variables

   $= \overline{A} + \overline{B} + \overline{C}{\cdot}\overline{E{\cdot}D}$ Evaluate the complemented expression (change $+$ to $\cdot$)

   $= \overline{A} + \overline{B} + \overline{C}{\cdot}\,(\overline{E} + \overline{D})$ Final step, evaluate $\overline{E{\cdot}D}$

This example demonstrates how you have to keep applying de Morgan's theorem until there are no complemented terms left to evaluate.

4. A proof of Theorem 8 by de Morgan's theorem

$(X + Y){\cdot}(\overline{X} + Y){\cdot}(Y + Z) = \overline{\overline{(X + Y){\cdot}(\overline{X} + Z){\cdot}(Y + Z)}}$ Complement twice because $X = \overline{\overline{X}}$.

$= \overline{\overline{X + Y} + \overline{\overline{X} + Z} + \overline{Y + Z}}$ Remove inner bar by applying de Morgan

$= \overline{\overline{X}{\cdot}\overline{Y} + X{\cdot}\overline{Z} + \overline{Y}{\cdot}\overline{Z}}$ Complement the three two-variable groups

$= \overline{\overline{X}{\cdot}\overline{Y} + X{\cdot}\overline{Z}}$ Use Theorem 3 to simplify

$= \overline{\overline{X}{\cdot}\overline{Y}}{\cdot}\overline{X{\cdot}\overline{Z}}$ Remove outer bar, change $+$ to $\cdot$

$= (X + Y)(\overline{X} + Z)$ Remove bars over two-variable groups

2.5.3 Implementing logic functions in NAND or NOR two logic only

Some gates are *better* than others; for example, the NAND gate is both faster and cheaper than the corresponding AND gate. Consequently, it's often necessary to realize a circuit using one type of gate only. Engineers sometimes implement a digital circuit with one particular type of gate because there is not a uniform range of gates available. For obvious economic reasons manufacturers don't sell a comprehensive range of gates (e.g. two-input AND, three-input AND, . . . , 10-input AND, two-input OR, . . .). For example, there are many types of NAND gate, from the quad two-input NAND to the 13-input NAND, but there are few types of AND gates.

NAND logic We first look at the way in which circuits can be constructed from nothing but NAND gates and then demonstrate that we can also fabricate circuits with NOR gates only. To construct a circuit solely in terms of NAND gates, de Morgan's theorem must be invoked to get rid of all OR operators in the expression. For example, suppose we wish to generate the expression $F = A + B + C$ using NAND gates only. We begin by applying a double negation to the expression, as this does not alter the expression's value but it does give us the opportunity to apply de Morgan's theorem.

$F = A + B + C$ The original expression using OR logic

$F = \overline{\overline{F}} = \overline{\overline{A + B + C}}$ Double negation has no effect on the value of a function

$F = \overline{\overline{A}{\cdot}\overline{B}{\cdot}\overline{C}}$ Apply de Morgan's theorem

We've now converted the OR function into a NAND function. The three NOT functions that generate $\overline{A}$, $\overline{B}$, and $\overline{C}$ can be implemented in terms of NOT gates, or by means of two-input NAND gates with their inputs connected together.

Figure 2.54 shows how the function $F = A + B + C$ can be implemented in NAND logic only. If the inputs of a NAND gate are A and B, and the output is C, then $C = \overline{A{\cdot}B}$. But if $A = B$, then $C = \overline{A{\cdot}A}$ or $C = \overline{A}$. You can better understand this by looking at the truth table for the NAND gate, and imagining the effect of removing the lines $A, B = 0, 1$ and $A, B = 1, 0$.

It's important to note that we are not using de Morgan's theorem here to simplify Boolean expressions. We are using de Morgan's theorem to convert an expression into a form suitable for realization in terms of NAND (or NOR) gates.

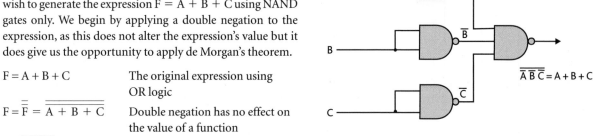

Figure 2.54 Implementing $F = A + B + C$ with NAND logic only.

By applying the same techniques to the 2-bit by 2-bit multiplier we designed earlier we can convert the expressions for the four outputs into NAND-only logic.

$$Z_0 = X_0 \cdot Y_0 = \overline{\overline{X_0 Y_0}} \quad \text{(i.e. NAND gate followed by NOT gate = AND gate)}$$

$$Z_1 = \overline{X_1} X_0 Y_1 + X_0 Y_1 \overline{Y_0} + X_1 \overline{X_0} Y_0 + X_1 \overline{Y_1} Y_0$$
$$= \overline{\overline{\overline{X_1} X_1 Y_0 + X_0 Y_1 \overline{Y_0} + X_1 \overline{X_0} Y_0 + X_1 \overline{Y_1} Y_0}}$$
$$= \overline{\overline{X_1 X_0 Y_1} \cdot \overline{X_0 Y_1 \overline{Y_0}} \cdot \overline{X_1 \overline{X_0} Y_0} \cdot \overline{X_1 \overline{Y_1} Y_0}}$$

$$Z_2 = X_1 \overline{X_0} Y_1 + X_1 Y_1 \overline{Y_0}$$
$$= \overline{\overline{X_1 \overline{X_0} Y_1 + X_1 Y_1 \overline{Y_0}}}$$
$$= \overline{\overline{X_1 \overline{X_0} Y_1} \cdot \overline{X_1 Y_1 \overline{Y_0}}}$$

$$Z_3 = X_1 X_0 Y_1 Y_0$$
$$= \overline{\overline{X_1 X_0 Y_1 Y_0}}$$

Figure 2.55 shows the implementation of the multiplier in terms of NAND logic only. Note that this circuit performs exactly the same function as the circuit of Fig. 2.53.

NOR logic The procedures we've just used may equally be applied to the implementation of circuits using NOR gates

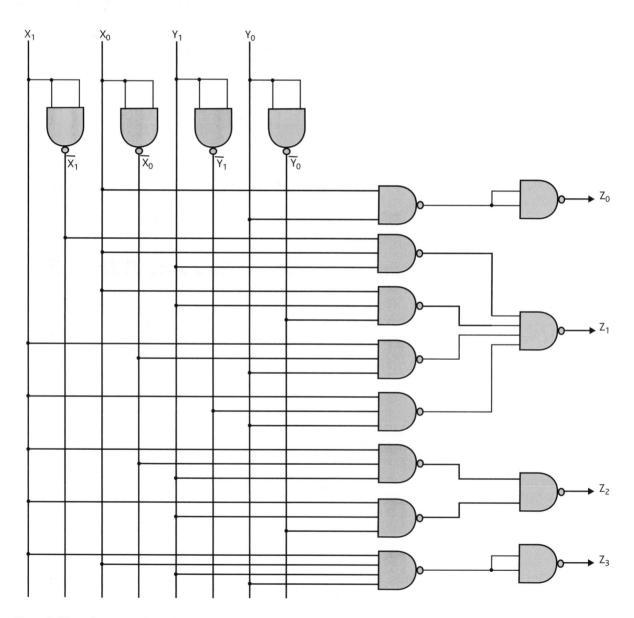

Figure 2.55 Implementing the multiplier circuit in NAND logic only.

only. By way of illustration, the value of Z_3 in the 2-bit multiplier can be converted to NOR logic form in the following way

$$Z_3 = X_1 \cdot X_0 \cdot Y_1 \cdot Y_0$$
$$= \overline{\overline{X_1 \cdot X_0 \cdot Y_1 \cdot Y_0}}$$
$$= \overline{\overline{X}_1 + \overline{X}_0 + \overline{Y}_1 + \overline{Y}_0}$$

Note that negation may be implemented by an inverter or by a NOR gate with its inputs connected together.

As a final example of NAND logic consider Fig. 2.56. A Boolean expression can be expressed in sum-of-products form as $A \cdot B + C \cdot D$. This expression can be converted to NAND logic as

$$\overline{\overline{A \cdot B} \cdot \overline{C \cdot D}}$$

Note how the three-gate circuit in Fig. 2.56(a) can be converted into the three-gate NAND circuit of Fig. 2.56(b).

Fig. 2.57 shows the construction of the two versions of AB + CD in Digital Works. We have provided an LED at each output and manually selectable inputs to enable you to investigate the circuits.

2.5.4 Karnaugh maps

When you use algebraic techniques to simplify a Boolean expression you sometimes reach a point at which you can't proceed, because you're unable to find further simplifications. The *Karnaugh map*, or more simply the *K-map*, is a graphical technique for the representation and simplification of a Boolean expression that shows unambiguously when a Boolean expression has been reduced to its most simple form.

Although the Karnaugh map can simplify Boolean equations with five or six variables, we will use it to solve problems

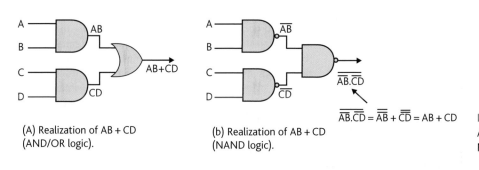

(A) Realization of AB + CD (AND/OR logic).

(b) Realization of AB + CD (NAND logic).

$\overline{\overline{AB} \cdot \overline{CD}} = \overline{\overline{AB}} + \overline{\overline{CD}} = AB + CD$

Figure 2.56 Implementing $A \cdot B + C \cdot D$ in AND/OR and NAND logic.

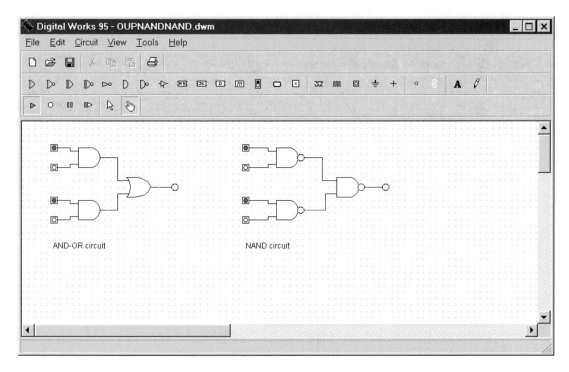

Figure 2.57 Using Digital Works to investigate two circuits.

EXAMPLE

Show that the exclusive or, EOR, operator is associative, so that $A \oplus (B \oplus C) = (A \oplus B) \oplus C$.

$$A \oplus (B \oplus C) = A \oplus (\overline{B} \cdot C + B \cdot \overline{C})$$
$$= A(\overline{\overline{B} \cdot C + B \cdot \overline{C}}) + \overline{A}(\overline{B} \cdot C + B \cdot \overline{C})$$
$$= A(B + \overline{C})(\overline{B} + C) + \overline{A} \cdot \overline{B} \cdot C + \overline{A} \cdot B \cdot \overline{C}$$
$$= A(B \cdot C + \overline{B} \cdot \overline{C}) + \overline{A} \cdot \overline{B} \cdot C + \overline{A} \cdot B \cdot \overline{C}$$
$$= A \cdot B \cdot C + A \cdot \overline{B} \cdot \overline{C} + \overline{A} \cdot \overline{B} \cdot C + \overline{A} \cdot B \cdot \overline{C}$$

$$(A \oplus B) \oplus C = (\overline{A} \cdot B + A \cdot \overline{B}) \oplus C$$
$$= (\overline{A} \cdot B + A \cdot \overline{B})\overline{C} + \overline{(\overline{A} \cdot B + A \cdot \overline{B})}C$$
$$= \overline{A} \cdot B \cdot \overline{C} + A \cdot \overline{B} \cdot \overline{C} + (\overline{\overline{A} \cdot B} \cdot \overline{A \cdot \overline{B}})C$$
$$= \overline{A} \cdot B \cdot \overline{C} + A \cdot \overline{B} \cdot \overline{C} + (A + \overline{B}) \cdot (\overline{A} + B)C$$
$$= \overline{A} \cdot B \cdot \overline{C} + A \cdot \overline{B} \cdot \overline{C} + (A \cdot B + \overline{A} \cdot \overline{B})C$$

Both these expressions are equal and therefore the $\oplus$ operator is associative.

EFFECT OF FINITE PROPAGATION DELAYS ON LOGIC ELEMENTS

We have assumed that if signals are applied to the input terminals of a circuit, the correct output will appear instantaneously at the output of the circuit. In practice, this is not so. Real gates suffer from an effect called propagation delay and it takes about 1 ns for a change in an input signal to affect the output. One nanosecond is an unbelievably short period of time in human terms—but not in electronic terms. The speed of light is 300×10^8 cm/s and electrical signals in computers travel at about 70% of the speed of light. In 1 ns a signal travels about 20 cm.

The propagation delay introduced by logic elements is one of the greatest problems designers have to contend with. The diagram illustrates the effect of propagation delay on a single inverter where a pulse with sharp (i.e. vertical) rising and falling edges is applied to the input of an inverter. An inverted pulse is produced at its output and is delayed with respect to the input pulse. Moreover, the edges of the output pulse are no longer vertical. The time tHL represents the time delay between the rising edge of the input pulse and the point at which the output of the gate has reached V_{OL}. Similarly, t_{LH} represents the time between the falling edge of the input and the time at which the output reaches V_{OH}.

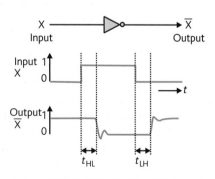

You might think that the effect of time delays on the passage of signals through gates simply reduces the speed at which a digital system may operate. Unfortunately, propagation delays have more sinister effects as demonstrated by the diagram. By the rules of Boolean algebra the output of the AND gate is $X \cdot X$ and should be permanently 0. Now examine its timing diagram.

At point A the input, X, rises from 0 to 1. However, the $\overline{X}$ input to the AND gate does not fall to 0 for a time equal to the propagation delay of the inverter. Consequently, for a short time the inputs of the AND gate are both true, and its output rises to a logical 1 from points B to C (after its own internal delay). The short pulse at the output of the AND gate is called a *glitch*, and can be very troublesome in digital systems. There are two solutions to this problem. One is to apply special design techniques to the Boolean logic to remove the glitch. The other is to connect the output to a flip-flop, and to clock the flip-flop after any glitches have died away.

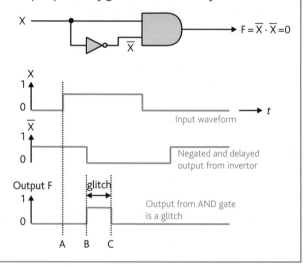

---

with only three or four variables. Other techniques such as the *Quine–McCluskey* method can be applied to the simplification of Boolean expressions in more than six variables. However, these techniques are beyond the scope of this book.

The Karnaugh map is just a two-dimensional form of the truth table, drawn in such a way that the simplification of

a Boolean expression can immediately be seen from the location of 1s on the map. A system with n variables has 2^n lines in its truth table and 2^n squares on its Karnaugh map. Each square on the Karnaugh map is associated with a line (i.e. *minterm*) in the truth table. Figure 2.58 shows Karnaugh maps for one to four variables.

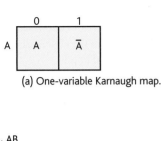

(a) One-variable Karnaugh map.

(b) Two-variable Karnaugh map.

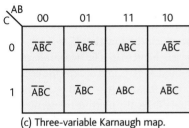

(c) Three-variable Karnaugh map.

(b) Four-variable Karnaugh map.

Figure 2.58 The Karnaugh map.

(a) The region for which A is true.

(b) The region for which B is true.

(c) The region for which C is true.

(d) The region for which D is true.

Figure 2.59 Regions of a Karnaugh map.

As you can see from Fig. 2.58, each line in a truth table is mapped onto a Karnaugh map; for example, in four variables each logical combination from $A \cdot B \cdot C \cdot D$ to $\overline{A} \cdot \overline{B} \cdot \overline{C} \cdot \overline{D}$ has a unique location. However, the key to the Karnaugh map is the *layout* of the squares. Adjacent squares differ by only one variable. By *adjacent* we mean horizontally and vertically adjacent, but not diagonally adjacent. For example, if you look the three-variable map of Fig. 2.58(c) you will see that the left-most two terms on the top line are $\overline{A} \cdot \overline{B} \cdot \overline{C}$ and $\overline{A} \cdot B \cdot \overline{C}$. The only difference between these terms is B and $\overline{B}$.

Figure 2.59 demonstrates the structure of a four-variable Karnaugh map with variables A, B, C, and D. This map has been repeated four times and, in each case, the region in which the selected variable is true has been shaded. The unshaded portion of each map represents the region in which the chosen variable is false.

We will soon see that you need to develop three skills to use a Karnaugh map. The first is to plot terms on the map (i.e. transfer a truth table or a Boolean expression onto the map). The second skill is the ability to group the 1s you've plotted on the map. The third skill is to read the groups of 1s on the map and express each group as a product term.

We now use a simple three-variable map to demonstrate how a truth table is mapped onto a Karnaugh map. One-and two-variable maps represent trivial cases and aren't considered further. Figure 2.60 shows the truth table for a three-variable function and the corresponding Karnaugh map. Each of the three 1s in the truth table is mapped onto its appropriate square on the Karnaugh map.

A three-variable Karnaugh map has four vertical columns, one for each of the four possible values of two out of the three variables. For example, if the three variables are A, B, and C, the four columns represent all the combinations of A and B. The leftmost column is labeled 00 and represents the region for which $A = 0, B = 0$. The next column is labeled 01, and represents the region for which $A = 0, B = 1$. The next column is labeled 11 (not 10), and represents the region for which $A = 1$, $B = 1$. Remember that adjacent columns differ by only one variable at a time. The fourth column, 10, represents the region for which $A = 1, B = 0$. In fact, a Karnaugh map is made up of all possible 2^n *minterms* for a system with n variables.

The three-variable Karnaugh map in Fig. 2.60 has two horizontal rows, the upper row corresponding to $C = 0$ and the lower to $C = 1$. Any square on this Karnaugh map represents a unique combination of the three variables, from $A \cdot B \cdot C$ to $\overline{A} \cdot \overline{B} \cdot \overline{C}$.

Figure 2.60 demonstrates how a function of three variables, $F = \overline{A} \cdot \overline{B} \cdot \overline{C} + \overline{A} \cdot B \cdot C + A \cdot \overline{B} \cdot C$ is plotted on a Karnaugh

map. If it isn't clear how the entries in the table are plotted on the Karnaugh map, examine Fig. 2.60 and work out which cell on the map is associated with each line in the table. A square containing a logical 1 is said to be covered by a 1.

At this point it's worth noting that no two 1s plotted on the Karnaugh map of Fig. 2.60 are adjacent to each other, and that the function $F = \overline{A} \cdot \overline{B} \cdot \overline{C} + \overline{A} \cdot B \cdot C + A \cdot \overline{B} \cdot C$ cannot be simplified. To keep the Karnaugh maps as clear and uncluttered as possible, squares that do not contain a 1 are left unmarked even though they must, of course, contain a 0.

Consider Fig. 2.61 in which the function $F_1 = A \cdot B \cdot \overline{C} + A \cdot B \cdot C$ is plotted on the left-hand map. The two minterms in this function are $A \cdot B \cdot \overline{C}$ and $A \cdot B \cdot C$ and occupy the cells for which $A = 1$, $B = 1$, $C = 0$, and $A = 1$, $B = 1$, $C = 1$, respectively. If you still have difficulty plotting minterms, just think of them as coordinates of squares; for example, $A \cdot B \cdot \overline{C}$ has the coordinates 1,1,0 and corresponds to the square $ABC = 110$.

In the Karnaugh map for F_1 two separate adjacent squares are covered. Now look at the Karnaugh map for $F_2 = A \cdot B$ at the right-hand side of Fig. 2.61. In this case a *group* of two squares is covered, corresponding to the column $A = 1$, $B = 1$. As the function for F_2 does not involve the variable C, a 1 is entered in the squares for which $A = B = 1$ and $C = 0$, and $A = B = 1$ and $C = 1$; that is, a 1 is entered for all values of C for which $AB = 11$. When plotting a product term like $A \cdot B$ on the Karnaugh map, all you have to do is to locate the region for which $AB = 11$.

It is immediately obvious that both Karnaugh maps in Fig. 2.61 are identical, so that $F_1 = F_2$ and $A \cdot B \cdot C + A \cdot B \cdot \overline{C} = A \cdot B$. From the rules of Boolean algebra $A \cdot B \cdot C + A \cdot B \cdot \overline{C} = A \cdot B (C + \overline{C}) = A \cdot B(1) = A \cdot B$. It should be apparent that two adjacent squares in a Karnaugh map can be grouped together to form a single simpler term. It is this property that the Karnaugh map exploits to simplify expressions.

Simplifying Sum-of-Product expressions with a Karnaugh map

The first step in simplifying a Boolean expression by means of a Karnaugh map is to plot all the 1s (i.e. minterms) in the function's truth table on the Karnaugh map. The next step is to combine adjacent 1s into groups of one, two, four, eight, or

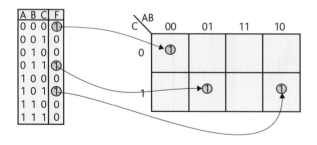

Figure 2.60 Relationship between a Karnaugh map and truth table.

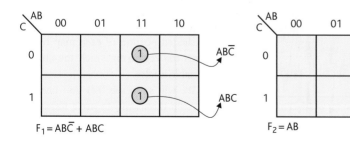

$F_1 = AB\overline{C} + ABC$

$F_2 = AB$

Figure 2.61 Plotting two functions on Karnaugh maps.

16. The groups of minterms should be as large as possible—a single group of four minterms yields a simpler expression than two groups of two minterms. The final stage in simplifying an expression is reached when each of the groups of minterms (i.e. the product terms) are ORed together to form the simplified sum-of-products expression. This process is best demonstrated by means of examples. In what follows, a four-variable map is chosen to illustrate the examples.

Transferring a truth table to a Karnaugh map is easy because each 1 in the truth table is placed in a unique square on the map. We now have to demonstrate how the product terms of a general Boolean expression are plotted on the map. Figures 2.62–2.67 present six functions plotted on Karnaugh maps. In these diagrams various *sum-of-products* expressions have been plotted directly from the equations themselves, rather than from the minterms of the truth table. The following notes should help in understanding these diagrams.

1. For a four-variable Karnaugh map

   one-variable product term covers 8 squares
   two-variable product terms cover 4 squares
   three-variable product terms cover 2 squares
   four-variable product terms cover 1 square.

2. A square covered by a 1 may belong to more than one term in the sum-of-products expression. For example, in Fig. 2.63 the minterm $\overline{A} \cdot \overline{B} \cdot C \cdot D$ belongs to two groups, $\overline{A} \cdot \overline{B}$ and $C \cdot D$. If a 1 on the Karnaugh map appears in two groups, it is equivalent to adding the corresponding minterm to the overall expression for the function plotted on the map *twice*. Repeating a term in a Boolean expression does not alter the value of the expression, because one of the axioms of Boolean algebra is $X + X = X$.

3. The Karnaugh map is not a square or a rectangle as it appears in these diagrams. A Karnaugh map is a *torus* or *doughnut* shape. That is, the top edge is adjacent to the bottom edge and, the left-hand edge is adjacent to the right-hand edge. For example, in Figure 2.65 the term $\overline{A} \cdot \overline{D}$ covers the two minterms $\overline{A} \cdot \overline{B} \cdot \overline{C} \cdot \overline{D}$ and $\overline{A} \cdot \overline{B} \cdot C \cdot \overline{D}$ at the top, and the two minterms $\overline{A} \cdot B \cdot \overline{C} \cdot \overline{D}$ and $\overline{A} \cdot B \cdot C \cdot \overline{D}$ at the bottom of the map. Similarly, in Fig. 2.66 the term $\overline{B} \cdot \overline{D}$ covers all four corners of the map. Whenever a group

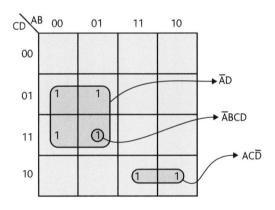

Figure 2.62 Plotting $F = \overline{A}D + AC\overline{D} + \overline{A}BCD$ on a Karnaugh map.

The two-variable term $\overline{A} \cdot D$ covers four squares (the region A = 0 and D = 1). The term $\overline{A} \cdot B \cdot C \cdot D$ covers one square and is part of the same group as $\overline{A} \cdot D$.

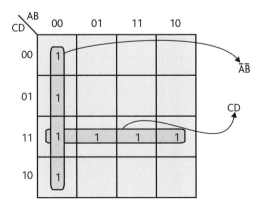

Figure 2.63 Plotting $F = AB + CD$ on a Karnaugh map.

The two-variable term $\overline{A} \cdot \overline{B}$ covers four squares (the region A = 0 and B = 0). The two-variable term $C \cdot D$ covers four squares (the region C = 1 and D = 1). The term $\overline{A} \cdot \overline{B} \cdot C \cdot D$ is common to both groups.

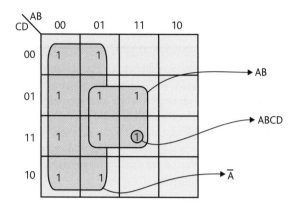

Figure 2.64 Plotting $F = \overline{A} + BD + ABCD$ on a Karnaugh map.

The one-variable term $\overline{A}$ covers four squares (the region A = 0).

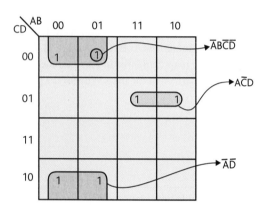

Figure 2.65 Plotting $F = \overline{A}\ \overline{D} + A\overline{C}D + \overline{A}BC\overline{D}$ on a Karnaugh map.

The four-variable term $\overline{A} \cdot \overline{D}$ covers four squares (the region A = 0, D = 0). Note that two squares are at the top (A = 0, C = 0, D = 0) and two are at the bottom (A = 0, C = 1, D = 0).

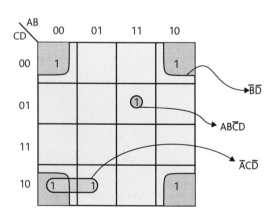

Figure 2.66 Plotting $F = \overline{B}\,\overline{D} + AB\overline{C}D + \overline{A}C\overline{D}$ on a Karnaugh map.

The four-variable term $\overline{B} \cdot \overline{D}$ covers four squares (the region B = 0, D = 0). In this case the adjacent squares are the corner squares. If you examine any pair of horizontally or vertically adjacent corners, you will find that they differ in one variable only.

of terms extends across the edge of a Karnaugh map, we have shaded it to emphasize the wraparound nature of the map.

4. In order either to read a product term from the map, or to plot a product term on the map, it is necessary to ask the question, 'what minterms (squares) are covered by this term?' Consider the term $\overline{A} \cdot D$ in Fig. 2.62. This term covers all squares for which A = 0 and D = 1 (a group of 4).

Having shown how terms are plotted on the Karnaugh map, the next step is to apply the map to the simplification of

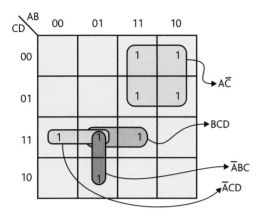

Three two-variable groups overlap. In this example, the square (i.e. minterm) $\overline{A} \cdot B \cdot C \cdot D$ belongs to groups $B \cdot C \cdot D$, $\overline{A} \cdot B \cdot C$, and $\overline{A} \cdot C \cdot D$.

Figure 2.67 Plotting $F = \overline{A}CD + \overline{A}BC + BCD + A\overline{C}$ on a Karnaugh map.

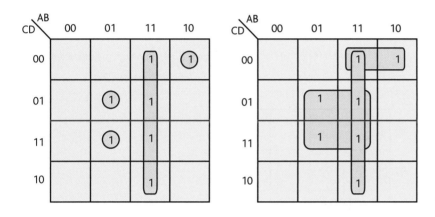

Figure 2.68 Karnaugh map for Example 1.

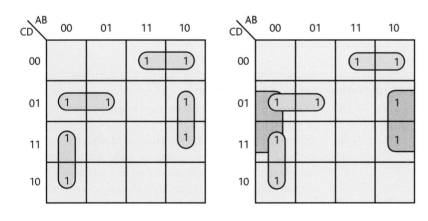

Figure 2.69 Karnaugh map for Example 2.

the expressions. Once again, we demonstrate this process by means of examples. In each case, the original function is plotted on the left-hand side of the figure and the regrouped ones (i.e. minterms) are plotted on the right-hand side.

Example 1 Figure 2.68 gives a Karnaugh map for the expression $F = A \cdot B + \overline{A} \cdot B \cdot \overline{C} \cdot D + \overline{A} \cdot B \cdot C \cdot D + A \cdot \overline{B} \cdot \overline{C} \cdot D$. The simplified function is $F = A \cdot B + B \cdot D + A \cdot \overline{C} \cdot \overline{D}$.

Example 2 $F = A \cdot \overline{C} \cdot \overline{D} + \overline{A} \cdot \overline{B} \cdot C + \overline{A} \cdot \overline{C} \cdot D + A \cdot \overline{B} \cdot D$ (Fig. 2.69). In this case only one regrouping is possible. The simplified function is $F = \overline{B} \cdot D + A \cdot \overline{C} \cdot \overline{D} + \overline{A} \cdot \overline{C} \cdot D + \overline{A} \cdot \overline{B} \cdot C$.

Example 3 $F = \overline{A} \cdot \overline{B} \cdot \overline{C} \cdot \overline{D} + A \cdot \overline{B} \cdot \overline{C} \cdot \overline{D} + \overline{A} \cdot B \cdot \overline{C} \cdot D + A \cdot B \cdot \overline{C} \cdot D + \overline{A} \cdot B \cdot C \cdot D + A \cdot B \cdot C \cdot D + \overline{A} \cdot \overline{B} \cdot C \cdot \overline{D} + A \cdot \overline{B} \cdot C \cdot \overline{D}$ (Fig. 2.70). This function can be simplified to two product terms with $F = \overline{B} \cdot \overline{D} + B \cdot D$.

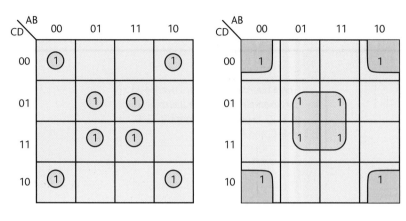

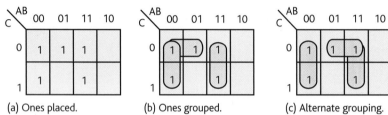

Figure 2.70 Karnaugh map for Example 3.

(a) Ones placed.   (b) Ones grouped.   (c) Alternate grouping.

Figure 2.71 Karnaugh map for Example 4.

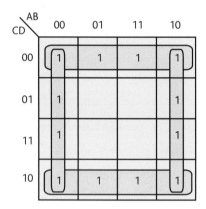

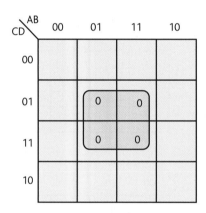

Figure 2.72 Example 5—using a Karnaugh map to obtain the complement of a function.

Example 4 $F = \overline{A} \cdot \overline{B} \cdot \overline{C} + \overline{A} \cdot \overline{B} \cdot C + \overline{A} \cdot B \cdot \overline{C} + A \cdot B \cdot \overline{C} + A \cdot B \cdot C$ (Fig. 2.71). We can group the minterms together in two ways, both of which are equally valid; that is, there are two equally correct simplifications of this expression. We can write either $F = \overline{A} \cdot \overline{B} + \overline{A} \cdot \overline{C} + A \cdot B$ or $F = \overline{A} \cdot \overline{B} + B \cdot \overline{C} + A \cdot B$.

Applications of Karnaugh maps

Karnaugh maps can also be used to convert *sum-of-products* expressions to the corresponding *product-of-sums* form. The first step in this process involves the generation of the complement of the sum-of-products expression.

Example 5 The Karnaugh map in Fig. 2.72 demonstrates how we can obtain the complement of a sum-of-products expression. Consider the expression $F = \overline{C} \cdot \overline{D} + \overline{A} \cdot B + A \cdot \overline{B} + C \cdot \overline{D}$ (left-hand side of Fig. 2.72). If the squares on a Karnaugh map covered by 1s represent the function F, then the remaining squares covered by 0s must represent $\overline{F}$, the complement of F. In the right-hand side of Fig. 2.72, we have plotted the

complement of this function. The group of four 0s corresponds to the expression $\overline{F} = B \cdot D$.

Example 6 We can use a Karnaugh map to convert of sum-of-products expression into a product-of-sums expression. In Example 5, we used the Karnaugh map to get the complement of a function in a product-of-sums form. If we then complement the complement, we get the function but in a sum-of-products form (because de Morgan's theorem allows us to step between SoP and PoS forms). Let's convert $F = A \cdot B \cdot C + \overline{C} \cdot D + \overline{A} \cdot B \cdot D$ into product of sums form (Fig. 2.73).

The complement of F is defined by the zeros on the map and may be read from the right-hand map as

$$\overline{F} = \overline{C} \cdot \overline{D} + \overline{B} \cdot C + \overline{A} \cdot D$$
$$F = \overline{\overline{C} \cdot \overline{D} + \overline{B} \cdot C + \overline{A} \cdot D}$$
$$= (C + D)(B + \overline{C})(A + D)$$

We now have an expression for F in product-of-sums form.

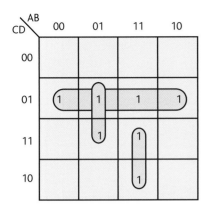

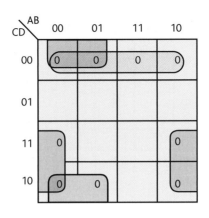

Figure 2.73 Example 6—using a Karnaugh map to convert an expression from SoP to PoS form.

Using the Karnaugh map to design a circuit with NAND logic

Now that we've demonstrated how Karnaugh maps are used to simplify and transform Boolean expressions, we're going to apply the Karnaugh map to the design of a simple logic circuit using NAND logic only.

A fire detection system protects a room against fire by means of four sensors. These sensors comprise a flame detector, a smoke detector, and two high-temperature detectors located at the opposite ends of the room. Because such sensors are prone to errors (i.e. false alarms or the failure to register a fire), the fire alarm is triggered only when two or more of the sensors indicate the presence of a fire simultaneously. The output of a sensor is a logical 1 if a fire is detected, otherwise a logical 0.

The output of the fire alarm circuit is a logical 1 whenever two or more of its inputs are a logical one. Table 2.19 gives the truth table for the fire detector circuit. The inputs from the four sensors are labeled A, B, C, and D. Because it is necessary only to detect two or more logical 1s on any of the lines, the actual order of A, B, C, and D columns doesn't matter. The circuit is to be constructed from two-input and three-input NAND gates only.

The output of the circuit, F, can be written down directly from Table 2.19 by ORing the 11 minterms to get the expression

$$F = \overline{A}\cdot\overline{B}\cdot C\cdot D + \overline{A}\cdot B\cdot\overline{C}\cdot D + \overline{A}\cdot B\cdot C\cdot\overline{D} + \overline{A}\cdot B\cdot C\cdot D$$
$$+ A\cdot\overline{B}\cdot\overline{C}\cdot D + A\cdot\overline{B}\cdot C\cdot\overline{D} + A\cdot\overline{B}\cdot C\cdot D + A\cdot B\cdot\overline{C}\cdot\overline{D}$$
$$+ A\cdot B\cdot\overline{C}\cdot D + A\cdot B\cdot C\cdot\overline{D} + A\cdot B\cdot C\cdot D$$

Plotting these 11 minterms terms on a Karnaugh map we get Fig. 2.74(a). The next step is to group these terms together into six groups of four minterms (Fig. 2.74(b)). Note that the minterm $A\cdot B\cdot C\cdot D$ belongs to all six groups.

Therefore, the simplified sum-of-products form of F is given by

$$F = A\cdot B + A\cdot C + A\cdot D + B\cdot C + B\cdot D + C\cdot D$$

This expression is (as you might expect) the sum of all possible two-variable combinations.

	Inputs			Output
A	B	C	D	F
0	0	0	0	0
0	0	0	1	0
0	0	1	0	0
0	0	1	1	1
0	1	0	0	0
0	1	0	1	1
0	1	1	0	1
0	1	1	1	1
1	0	0	0	0
1	0	0	1	1
1	0	1	0	1
1	0	1	1	1
1	1	0	0	1
1	1	0	1	1
1	1	1	0	1
1	1	1	1	1

Table 2.19 Truth table for a fire detector.

In order to convert the expression into NAND logic only form, we have to eliminate the five logical OR operators. We do that by complementing F twice and then using de Morgan's theorem.

$$F = \overline{\overline{F}} = \overline{\overline{A\cdot B + A\cdot C + A\cdot D + B\cdot C + B\cdot D + C\cdot D}}$$
$$= \overline{\overline{A\cdot B}\cdot\overline{A\cdot C}\cdot\overline{A\cdot D}\cdot\overline{B\cdot C}\cdot\overline{B\cdot D}\cdot\overline{C\cdot D}}$$

Although we have realized the expression in NAND logic as required, it calls for a six-input NAND gate. If the expression for F is examined, it can be seen that six terms are NANDed together, which is the same as ANDing them and then inverting the result. Because of the associative property

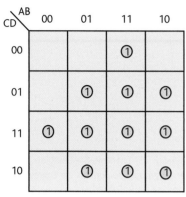

(a) Location of the 1s.

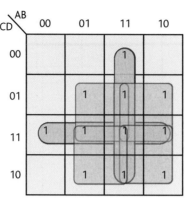

(b) After grouping the 1s.

Figure 2.74 Karnaugh map corresponding to Table 2.19.

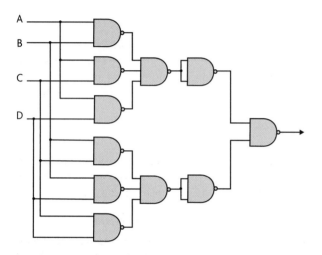

Figure 2.75 NAND-only circuit for fire detector.

of Boolean variables, we can write $X(Y \cdot Z) = (X \cdot Y)Z$ and hence extending this to our equation we get

$$F = \overline{\overline{\overline{\overline{A \cdot B} \cdot \overline{A \cdot C} \cdot \overline{A \cdot D}} \cdot \overline{\overline{B \cdot C} \cdot \overline{B \cdot D} \cdot \overline{C \cdot D}}}}$$

Figure 2.75 shows how this expression can be implemented in terms of two- and three-input NAND gates.

Using Karnaugh Maps—an example

A circuit has four inputs, A, B, C, and D, representing the 16 natural binary integers from 0000 to 1111 (i.e. 0 to 15). The output of the circuit, F, is true if the input is divisible by a multiple of 4, 5, 6, or 7, with the exception of 15, in which case the output is false. Zero is not divisible by 4, 5, 6, or 7. Suppose we wish to design a logic circuit to implement F using NAND gates only.

We can obtain a sum-of-products expression for F from Table 2.20 by writing down the sum of the minterms (i.e. the lines with a 1).

$$F = \overline{A} \cdot B \cdot \overline{C} \cdot \overline{D} + \overline{A} \cdot B \cdot \overline{C} \cdot D + \overline{A} \cdot B \cdot C \cdot \overline{D} + \overline{A} \cdot B \cdot C \cdot D$$
$$+ A \cdot \overline{B} \cdot \overline{C} \cdot \overline{D} + A \cdot \overline{B} \cdot C \cdot \overline{D} + A \cdot B \cdot \overline{C} \cdot \overline{D} + A \cdot B \cdot C \cdot \overline{D}$$

	Inputs			Number	F	
A	B	C	D			
0	0	0	0	0	0	
0	0	0	1	1	0	
0	0	1	0	2	0	
0	0	1	1	3	0	
0	1	0	0	4	1	Divisible by 4
0	1	0	1	5	1	Divisible by 5
0	1	1	0	6	1	Divisible by 6
0	1	1	1	7	1	Divisible by 7
1	0	0	0	8	1	Divisible by 4
1	0	0	1	9	0	
1	0	1	0	10	1	Divisible by 5
1	0	1	1	11	0	
1	1	0	0	12	1	Divisible by 6
1	1	0	1	13	0	
1	1	1	0	14	1	Divisible by 7
1	1	1	1	15	0	False by definition

Table 2.20 Truth table for example.

By means of Boolean algebra the expression can be simplified to

$$F = \overline{A} \cdot B \cdot \overline{C}(D + \overline{D}) + \overline{A} \cdot B \cdot C(D + \overline{D}) + A \cdot \overline{B} \cdot \overline{D}(\overline{C} + C)$$
$$+ A \cdot B \cdot \overline{D}(\overline{C} + C)$$
$$= \overline{A} \cdot B \cdot \overline{C} + \overline{A} \cdot B \cdot C + A \cdot \overline{B} \cdot \overline{D} + A \cdot B \cdot \overline{D}$$
$$= \overline{A} \cdot B(C + \overline{C}) + A \cdot \overline{D}(\overline{B} + B)$$
$$= \overline{A} \cdot B + A \cdot \overline{D}$$

Figure 2.76 gives the Karnaugh map for F. In Fig. 2.77 the squares covered by 1s are formed into two groups of four. This gives $F = \overline{A} \cdot B + A \cdot \overline{D}$, which is reassuringly the same as the result obtained above.

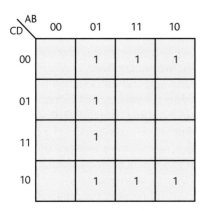

Figure 2.76 Karnaugh map for F.

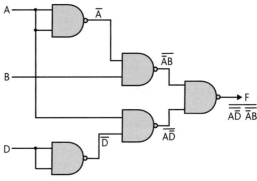

Figure 2.78 NAND-only circuit.

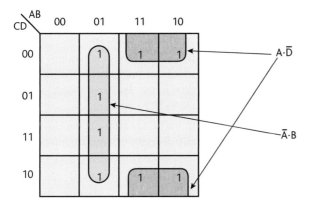

Figure 2.77 Karnaugh map after regrouping the minterms.

To obtain a product-of-sums expression, it's necessary to generate the complement of F in a sum-of-products form and then complement it.

$F = \overline{A} \cdot B + A \cdot \overline{D}$

$\overline{F} = \overline{\overline{A} \cdot B + A \cdot \overline{D}}$	Get the complement of F
$= (A + \overline{B})(\overline{A} + D)$	Complement of F in product-of-sums form
$= A \cdot \overline{A} + A \cdot D + \overline{A} \cdot \overline{B} + \overline{B} \cdot D$	Multiply out sum terms
$= A \cdot D + \overline{A} \cdot \overline{B} + \overline{B} \cdot D$	Complement of F in sum-of-products form
$= A \cdot D + \overline{A} \cdot \overline{B}$	Complement in simplified sum-of-products form
$F = \overline{A \cdot D + \overline{A} \cdot \overline{B}}$	Complement the complement to get F
$= (\overline{A} + \overline{D})(A + B)$	Function in required product-of-sums form

Note that the complement of F in sum-of-products form could have been obtained directly from the Karnaugh map of F by considering the squares covered by zeros.

To convert the expression $F = \overline{A} \cdot B + A \cdot \overline{D}$ into NAND logic form, the '+' must be eliminated.

$$F = \overline{\overline{F}} = \overline{\overline{\overline{A} \cdot B + A \cdot \overline{D}}} = \overline{\overline{\overline{A} \cdot B} \cdot \overline{A \cdot \overline{D}}}$$

The inverse functions $\overline{A}$ and $\overline{D}$ can be generated by two-input NAND gates with their inputs connected together. Figure 2.78 implements F in NAND logic only.

Karnaugh maps and don't care conditions

We now demonstrate how Karnaugh maps can be applied to problems in which the truth table isn't fully specified; that is, for certain input conditions the output is undefined. Occasionally, a system exists in which a certain combination of inputs can't happen; or, if it does, we don't care what the output is. In such cases, the output may be defined as either true or false.

Consider the Karnaugh map of Fig. 2.79 for $F = \overline{A} \cdot B \cdot D + A \cdot B \cdot C \cdot D$. Now suppose that the input conditions $A \cdot B \cdot \overline{C} \cdot D$ and $A \cdot \overline{B} \cdot \overline{C} \cdot D$ cannot occur. We have marked these two inputs on the map with an X. The value of X is undefined (if the input can't occur then the value of the output is undefined).

If an input can't occur and the output is undefined, we can cover that square with either a 0 or a 1. In Fig. 2.79(b) we have made one of the Xs a 1 and one of the Xs a zero. We can express the output function as $F = B \cdot D$, which is simpler than the function in Fig. 2.79(a).

A don't care condition is set to a 0 or a 1 in order to simplify the solution. There is an important exception. Although an impossible input can't occur in normal circumstances, it could under fault conditions (e.g. when an input circuit fails). No designer would assign an output to an impossible input condition that might lead to an unsafe or dangerous situation. However, the ultimate aim is to cover all the 1s in the map and to incorporate them in the smallest number of large groups.

The following example demonstrates the concept of *impossible* input conditions. An air conditioning system has two temperature control inputs. One input, C, from a cold-sensing thermostat is true if the temperature is below 15°C and false otherwise. The other input, H, from a hot-sensing thermostat is true if the temperature is above 22°C and false otherwise. Table 2.21 lists the four possible logical conditions for the two inputs.

The input condition $C = 1, H = 1$ in Table 2.20 has no real meaning, because it's impossible to be too hot and too cold simultaneously. Such an input condition could arise only if at least one of the thermostats failed. Consider now the example of an air conditioning unit with four inputs and four outputs. Table 2.22 defines the meaning of the inputs to the controller.

The controller has four outputs P, Q, R, and S. When $P = 1$ a heater is switched on and when $Q = 1$ a cooler is switched on. Similarly, a humidifier is switched on by $R = 1$ and a dehumidifier by $S = 1$. In each case a logical 0 switches off the appropriate device. The relationship between the inputs and outputs is as follows.

- If the temperature and humidity are both within limits, switch off the heater and the cooler. The humidifier and dehumidifier are both switched off unless stated otherwise.

- If the humidity is within limits, switch on the heater if the temperature is too low and switch on the cooler if the temperature is too high.

- If the temperature is within limits, switch on the heater if the humidity is too low and the cooler if the humidity is too high.

- If the humidity is high and the temperature low, switch on the heater. If the humidity is low and the temperature high, switch on the cooler.

- If both the temperature and humidity are high switch on the cooler and dehumidifier.

- If both the temperature and humidity are too low switch on the heater and humidifier.

The relationship between the inputs and outputs can now be expressed in terms of a truth table (Table 2.23). We can draw Karnaugh maps for P to S, plotting a 0 for a zero state, a 1 for a one state, and an X for an impossible state. Remember that an X on the Karnaugh map corresponds to a state that cannot exist and therefore its value is known as a *don't care* condition.

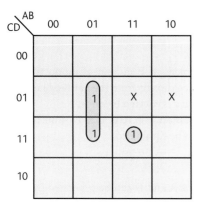
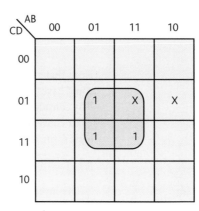

(a) The function $F = \overline{A}BD + ABCD$.
Note that the inputs $AB\overline{C}D$ and $A\overline{B}CD$ cannot occur

(b) The function $F = BD$.
Minterm $AB\overline{C}D$ is included to simplify the expression

Figure 2.79 The effect of don't care conditions.

Inputs		Meaning
C	H	
0	0	Temperature OK
0	1	Too hot
1	0	Too cold
1	1	Impossible condition

Table 2.21 Truth table for a pair of temperature sensors.

Input	Name	Meaning when input = 0	Meaning when input = 1
H	Hot	Temperature < upper limit	Temperature > upper limit
C	Cold	Temperature > lower limit	Temperature < lower limit
W	Wet	Humidity < upper limit	Humidity > upper limit
D	Dry	Humidity > lower limit	Humidity < lower limit

Table 2.22 Truth table for a climate controller.

Inputs				Condition	Outputs			
H	C	W	D		P	Q	R	S
					heater	cooler	humidifier	dehumidifier
0	0	0	0	OK	0	0	0	0
0	0	0	1	Dry	1	0	0	0
0	0	1	0	Wet	0	1	0	0
0	0	1	1	Impossible	X	X	X	X
0	1	0	0	Cold	1	0	0	0
0	1	0	1	Cold and dry	1	0	1	0
0	1	1	0	Cold and wet	1	0	0	0
0	1	1	1	Impossible	X	X	X	X
1	0	0	0	Hot	0	1	0	0
1	0	0	1	Hot and dry	0	1	0	0
1	0	1	0	Hot and wet	0	1	0	1
1	0	1	1	Impossible	X	X	X	X
1	1	0	0	Impossible	X	X	X	X
1	1	0	1	Impossible	X	X	X	X
1	1	1	0	Impossible	X	X	X	X
1	1	1	1	Impossible	X	X	X	X

Table 2.23 Truth table for a climate controller.

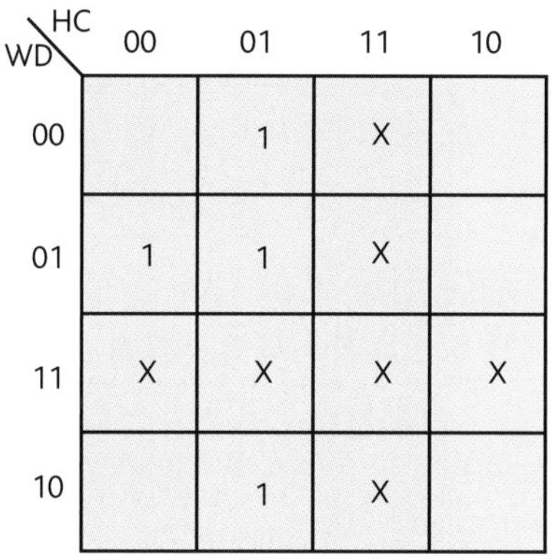

Figure 2.80 Karnaugh map for P (the heater).

Figure 2.80 provides a Karnaugh map corresponding to output P, the heater. We have marked all the don't care conditions with an X. We could replace the Xs by 1s or 0s. However, by forcing some of the don't care outputs to be a 1, we can convert a group of 1s into a larger group.

Figure 2.81 provides Karnaugh maps for outputs P, Q, R, and S. In each case we have chosen the don't care conditions to simplify the output function. For example, the Karnaugh map of Fig. 2.81(a) corresponds to output P where we have included six of the don't care conditions within the groupings to get $P = C + H \cdot D$.

You should appreciate that by taking this approach we have designed a circuit that sets the output 1 for some don't care inputs and 0 for other don't care inputs. You cannot avoid this. The output of any digital circuit must always be in a 0 or a 1 state. As we said at the beginning of this chapter, there is no such state as an indeterminate state. It is up to the designer to choose what outputs are to be assigned to don't care inputs.

Exploiting don't care conditions—constructing a seven-segment decoder

We now design a BCD-to-seven-segment decoder (BCD means binary-coded decimal). The decoder has a 4-bit natural binary BCD input represented by D, C, B, A, where A is the least-significant bit. Assume that the BCD input can never be greater than 9 (Chapter 4 describes BCD codes). The seven-segment decoder illustrated by Fig. 2.82 has seven outputs (a to g), which are used to illuminate any combination of bars a to g of a seven-segment display; for example, if the code for 2 (i.e. 0010) is sent to the decoder, segments a, b, d, e, and g are illuminated to form a '2'.

The truth table for this problem is given in Table 2.24. This table has four inputs and seven outputs (one for each of the segments).

We can now solve the equation for segments a to g. By using Karnaugh maps the don't care conditions can be catered for.

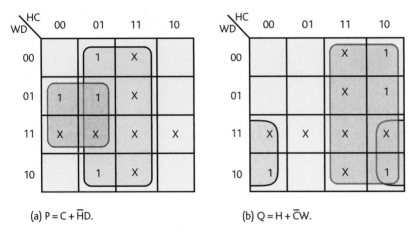

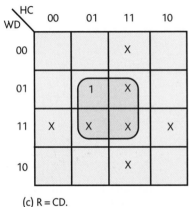

(a) $P = C + \overline{H}D$.

(b) $Q = H + \overline{C}W$.

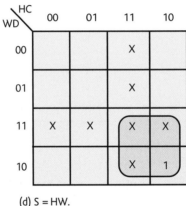

(c) $R = CD$.

(d) $S = HW$.

Figure 2.81 Karnaugh maps for outputs P, Q, R, and S.

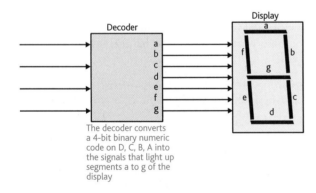

Figure 2.82 The seven-segment display.

The decoder converts a 4-bit binary numeric code on D, C, B, A into the signals that light up segments a to g of the display

Figure 2.83 gives the Karnaugh map for segment a. From the Karnaugh map we can write down the expression for $a = D + B + C{\cdot}A + \overline{C}{\cdot}\overline{A}$.

An alternative approach is to obtain a by considering the zeros on the map to get the complement of a. From the Karnaugh map in Fig. 2.84 we can write $a = \overline{D{\cdot}\overline{C}{\cdot}\overline{B}{\cdot}A + C{\cdot}\overline{B}{\cdot}\overline{A}}$. Therefore,

$$a = \overline{\overline{D}{\cdot}\overline{C}{\cdot}\overline{B}{\cdot}A + C{\cdot}\overline{B}{\cdot}\overline{A}}$$
$$= (D + C + B + \overline{A})\,(\overline{C} + B + A)$$
$$= D{\cdot}\overline{C} + D{\cdot}B + D{\cdot}A + C{\cdot}\overline{C} + C{\cdot}B + C{\cdot}A + \overline{C}{\cdot}B$$
$$\quad + B{\cdot}B + B{\cdot}A + \overline{C}{\cdot}\overline{A} + B{\cdot}\overline{A} + A{\cdot}\overline{A}$$
$$= D{\cdot}\overline{C} + D{\cdot}B + D{\cdot}A + C{\cdot}B + C{\cdot}A + \overline{C}{\cdot}B + B$$
$$\quad + B{\cdot}A + \overline{C}{\cdot}\overline{A} + B{\cdot}\overline{A}$$
$$= D{\cdot}\overline{C} + D{\cdot}A + C{\cdot}A + B + \overline{C}{\cdot}\overline{A}$$
$$= D{\cdot}\overline{C} + C{\cdot}A + B + \overline{C}{\cdot}\overline{A}$$

This expression offers no improvement over the first realization of a.

Figure 2.85 provides the Karnaugh map for segment b, which gives $b = \overline{C} + \overline{B}{\cdot}\overline{A} + B{\cdot}A$. We can proceed as we did for segment a and see what happens if we use $\overline{b}$. Plotting zeros on the Karnaugh map for $\overline{b}$ we get $\overline{b} = C + \overline{B}{\cdot}A{\cdot}C{\cdot}B{\cdot}\overline{A}$ Fig. 2.86. Therefore,

$$b = \overline{C{\cdot}\overline{B}{\cdot}A + C{\cdot}B{\cdot}\overline{A}}$$
$$= (\overline{C} + B + \overline{A})(\overline{C} + \overline{B} + A)$$
$$= \overline{C} + B{\cdot}A + \overline{B}{\cdot}\overline{A}$$

Inputs	Character	Outputs						
D C B A		a	b	c	d	e	f	g
0 0 0 0	[character]	1	1	1	1	1	1	0
0 0 0 1	[character]	0	1	1	0	0	0	0
0 0 1 0	[character]	1	1	0	1	1	0	1
0 0 1 1	[character]	1	1	1	1	0	0	1
0 1 0 0	[character]	0	1	1	0	0	1	1
0 1 0 1	[character]	1	0	1	1	0	1	1
0 1 1 0	[character]	1	0	1	1	1	1	1
0 1 1 1	[character]	1	1	1	0	0	0	0
1 0 0 0	[character]	1	1	1	1	1	1	1
1 0 0 1	[character]	1	1	1	0	0	1	1
1 0 1 0	Forbidden code	X	X	X	X	X	X	X
1 0 1 1		X	X	X	X	X	X	X
1 1 0 0		X	X	X	X	X	X	X
1 1 0 1		X	X	X	X	X	X	X
1 1 1 0		X	X	X	X	X	X	X
1 1 1 1		X	X	X	X	X	X	X

Table 2.24 Truth table for a seven—segment display.

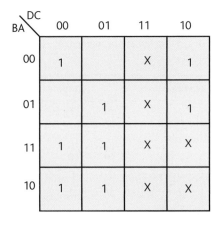

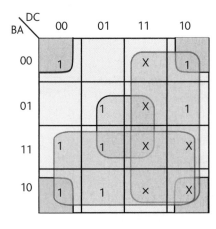

Figure 2.83 Karnaugh map for the segment a control signal.

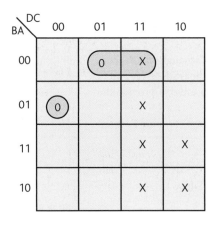

Figure 2.84 Karnaugh map for the complement of segment a.

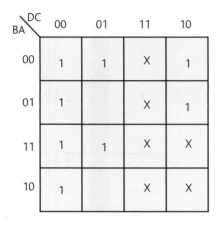

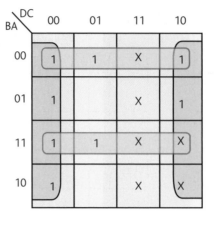

Figure 2.85 Karnaugh map for segment b.

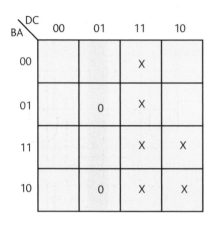

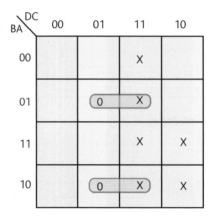

Figure 2.86 Karnaugh map for the complement of segment b.

This expression yields the same result as that obtained directly by considering the 1s on the Karnaugh map. The equations for the remaining five segments can be considered in a similar way.

Example of the use of Karnaugh maps to implement a circuit

A logic circuit has four inputs D, C, B, A, which represent two pairs of bits (D,C) and (B,A). Bits (B,A) are subtracted from bits (D,C) to give a result F_1, F_0 and an n-bit that indicates a negative result. Table 2.25 provides a truth table for this problem.

We first construct three Karnaugh maps for the outputs and use them to obtain simplified sum-of-product expressions (Table 2.25).

Figure 2.87 provides the three Karnaugh maps corresponding to outputs n, F_1, and F_0 in the truth table. The 1s have been regrouped under each truth table to provide the minimum number of large groups.

We can write down expressions for n, F_1, and F_0 from Fig. 2.87 as

$$n = \overline{D}{\cdot}B + \overline{C}{\cdot}B{\cdot}A + \overline{D}{\cdot}\overline{C}{\cdot}A$$

$$F_1 = \overline{D}{\cdot}\overline{C}{\cdot}B + D{\cdot}C{\cdot}\overline{B} + D{\cdot}\overline{B}{\cdot}\overline{A} + \overline{D}{\cdot}B{\cdot}A$$

$$F_0 = \overline{C}{\cdot}A + C{\cdot}\overline{A}$$

Inputs				Number	Outputs		
					n	F_1	F_0
D	C	B	A				
0	0	0	0	$0 - 0 = 0$	0	0	0
0	0	0	1	$0 - 1 = -1$	1	0	1
0	0	1	0	$0 - 2 = -2$	1	1	0
0	0	1	1	$0 - 3 = -3$	1	1	1
0	1	0	0	$1 - 0 = 1$	0	0	1
0	1	0	1	$1 - 1 = 0$	0	0	0
0	1	1	0	$1 - 2 = -1$	1	0	1
0	1	1	1	$1 - 3 = -2$	1	1	0
1	0	0	0	$2 - 0 = 2$	0	1	0
1	0	0	1	$2 - 1 = 1$	0	0	1
1	0	1	0	$2 - 2 = 0$	0	0	0
1	0	1	1	$2 - 3 = -1$	1	0	1
1	1	0	0	$3 - 0 = 3$	0	1	1
1	1	0	1	$3 - 1 = 2$	0	1	0
1	1	1	0	$3 - 2 = 1$	0	0	1
1	1	1	1	$3 - 3 = 0$	0	0	0

Table 2.25 Truth table for a two-bit subtractor.

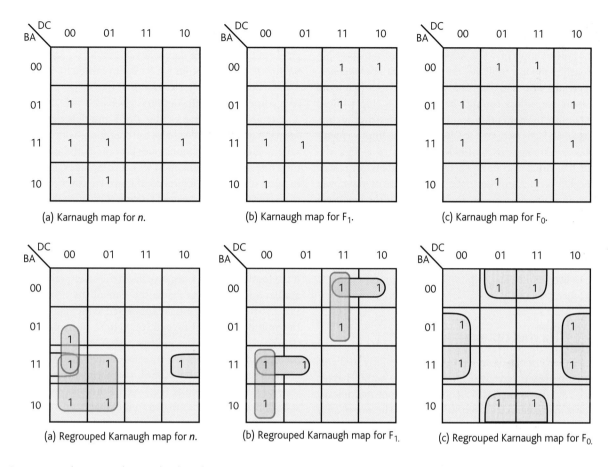

(a) Karnaugh map for *n*.   (b) Karnaugh map for F_1.   (c) Karnaugh map for F_0.

(a) Regrouped Karnaugh map for *n*.   (b) Regrouped Karnaugh map for F_1.   (c) Regrouped Karnaugh map for F_0.

Figure 2.87 The Karnaugh maps for the subtractor.

2.6 Special-purpose logic elements

So far, we've looked at the primitive logic elements from which all digital systems can be constructed. As technology progressed, more and more components were fabricated on single chips of silicon to produce increasingly complex circuits. Today, you can buy chips with tens of millions of gates that can be interconnected electronically (i.e. the chip provides a digital system whose structure can be modified electronically by the user). Indeed, by combining microprocessor technology, electronically programmable with arrays of gates, we can now construct self-modifying (self-adaptive) digital systems.

Let's briefly review the development of digital circuits. The first digital circuits contained a few basic NAND, NOR, AND gates, and were called *small-scale integration* (SSI). Basic SSI gates were available in 14-pin *dual-in-line* (DIL) packages. Dual-in-line simply means that there are two parallel rows of pins (i.e. contacts) forming the interface between the chip and the outside world. The rows are 0.3 inches apart and the

pins are spaced by 0.1 inch. Two pins are used for the power supply (V_{cc} = +5.0 V and ground = 0 V). These devices are often called *74-series* logic elements because the part number of each chip begins with 74; for example, a 7400 chip contains four NAND gates. Today, the packaging of such gates has shrunk to the point where the packages are very tiny and are attached to circuit boards by automatic machines.

It soon became possible to put tens of gates on a chip and manufacturers connected gates together to create logic functions such as a 4-bit adder, a multiplexer, and a decoder. Such circuits are called *medium-scale integration* (MSI). By the 1970s entire systems began to appear on a single silicon chip, of which the microprocessor is the most spectacular example. The technology used to make such complex systems is called *large-scale integration* (LSI). In the late l980s LSI gave way to *very-large-scale integration* (VLSI), which allowed designers to fabricate millions of transistors on a chip. Initially, VLSI technology was applied to the design of memories rather than microprocessors. Memory systems are much easier to design because they have a regular structure (i.e. a simple memory cell is replicated millions of times).

A major change in digital technology occurred in the mid 1990s. From the 1970s to the 1990s, digital logic had largely used a power supply of +5 V. As the number of gates per chip approached the low millions, the problem of *heat management* created a limit to complexity. It was obvious that more and more transistors couldn't be added to a chip without limit because the power they required would destroy the chip. Radiators and fans were used to keep chips cool. Improvements in silicon technology in the 1990s provided digital logic elements that could operate at 3 V or less and, therefore, create less heat. A further impetus to the development of low-power systems was provided by the growth of the laptop computer market.

We now look at the characteristics of some of the simple digital circuits that are still widely available—even though VLSI systems dominate the digital world, designers often have to use simple gates to interface these complex chips to each other.

2.6.1 The multiplexer

A particularly common function arising regularly in digital design is the *multiplexer*, which we met earlier in this chapter. Figure 2.88 shows the 74157, a quad two-input multiplexer, which is available in a 16-pin MSI circuit. The prefix *quad* simply means that there are four multiplexers in one package.

Each of the four Y outputs is connected to the corresponding A input pin when SELECT = 0 and to the B input when SELECT = 1. The multiplexer's $\overline{\text{STROBE}}$ input forces all Y outputs into logical 0 states whenever $\overline{\text{STROBE}}$ = 1. We have already described one use of the multiplexer when we looked at some simple circuits.

Figure 2.89 illustrates the structure of a 1-of-8 data multiplexer, which has eight data inputs, $D_0, D_1, D_2, \ldots, D_7$, an output Y, and three data select inputs, S_0, S_1, S_2. When $S_0, S_1, S_2 = 0, 0, 0$ the output is Y = D_0, and when $S_0, S_1, S_2 = 1, 0, 0$ the output Y = D_1, etc. That is, if the binary value at the data select input is *i*, the output is given by Y = D_i.

A typical application of the 1-of-8 multiplexer is in the selection of one out of eight logical conditions within a digital system. Figure 2.90 demonstrates how the 1-of-8 multiplexer might be used in conjunction with a computer's *flag* register to select one of eight logical conditions. We cover registers in the next chapter—all we need know at this points that a register is a storage unit that holds the value of 1 or more bits.

The flag register in Fig. 2.90 stores the value of up to eight so-called *flags* or marker bits. When a computer performs an operation (such as addition or subtraction) it sets a zero flag if the result was zero, a negative flag if the result was negative, and so on. These flags define the *state* of the computer. In Fig. 2.90 the eight flag bits are connected to the eight inputs of the multiplexer. The 3-bit code on S_0 to S_2 determines which flag bit is routed to the multiplexer's Y output. This code might be derived from the instruction that the computer is currently executing. That is, the bits of the instruction can be used to select a particular flag (via the multiplexer) and the state of this flag bit used to determine what happens next.

Suppose a computer instruction has the form IF x = 0 THEN do something. The computer compares *x* with 0, which sets the zero flag if *x* is equal to zero. The bits that encode this instruction provide the code on S_0 to S_2 that routes the Z flag to the Y output. Finally, the computer uses the value of the Y output to 'do something' or not to 'do something'. Later we shall see how alternative courses of action are implemented by a computer.

2.6.2 The demultiplexer

The inverse function of the multiplexer is the *demultiplexer*, which converts a binary code on *n* inputs into an asserted

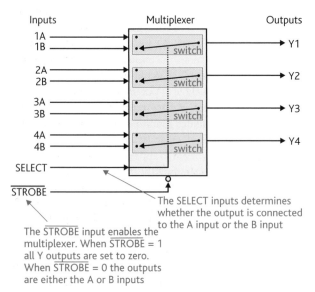

The SELECT inputs determines whether the output is connected to the A input or the B input

The $\overline{\text{STROBE}}$ input enables the multiplexer. When $\overline{\text{STROBE}}$ = 1 all Y outputs are set to zero. When $\overline{\text{STROBE}}$ = 0 the outputs are either the A or B inputs

Figure 2.88 The 74157 quad two-input multiplexer.

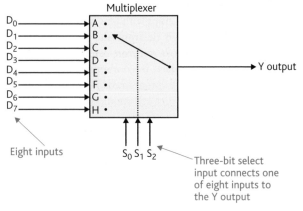

Three-bit select input connects one of eight inputs to the Y output

Figure 2.89 The 1-of-8 multiplexer.

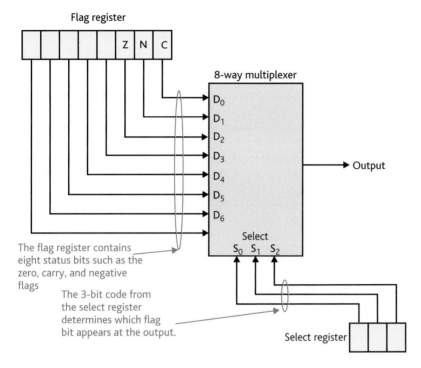

Flag register

8-way multiplexer

D_0
D_1
D_2
D_3
D_4
D_5
D_6

Output

Select
S_0 S_1 S_2

The flag register contains eight status bits such as the zero, carry, and negative flags

The 3-bit code from the select register determines which flag bit appears at the output.

Select register

Figure 2.90 The 1-of-8 multiplexer.

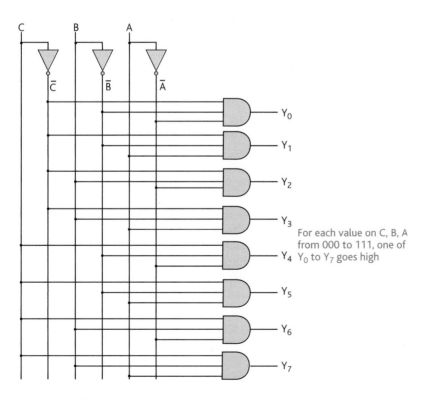

Figure 2.91 The demultiplexer (3-line to 8-line decoder).

For each value on C, B, A from 000 to 111, one of Y_0 to Y_7 goes high

level on one of 2^n outputs. The demultiplexer circuit of Fig. 2.91 has three inputs A, B, and C and eight outputs Y_0 to Y_7. The three inverters generate the complements of the inputs A, B, and C. Each of the eight AND gates is connected to three of the six lines $A, \overline{A}, B, \overline{B}, C, \overline{C}$ (each of the three variables must appear in either its true or complemented forms).

The output of first gate, Y_0, is $\overline{A} \cdot \overline{B} \cdot \overline{C}$ and is 1 if all inputs to the AND gates are 1 (i.e. $\overline{A} = 1, \overline{B} = 1, \overline{C} = 1$). Therefore, Y_0 is 1 when A = 0, B = 0, C = 0. If you examine the other AND gates, you will see that each gate is enabled by one of the eight possible combinations of A, B, C.

This circuit is called a *3-line to 8-line demultiplexer*, because it converts a 3-bit binary value, A, B, C, into one of $2^3 = 8$ outputs. Table 2.26 provides a truth table for this circuit, which is also called a *decoder* because it can take, for example, the bits that define a computer instruction and decode it into individual instructions as Fig. 2.92 demonstrates.

Let's look at an actual demultiplexer, the 74138 3-line to 8-line demultiplexer (Fig. 2.93). The 74138's eight outputs, $\overline{Y}_0$ to $\overline{Y}_7$, are active-low and remain in a high state unless the corresponding input is selected. The device has three enable inputs, $\overline{E1}, \overline{E2}, E3$, which must be 0, 0, 1 respectively, for the chip to be selected. When the chip is selected, one (and only one) of the eight outputs is forced into a 0 state by the 3-bit code at the select inputs, A, B, C. Remember that the 74138's outputs are *active-low*.

One application of this circuit is as a *device selector*. Suppose that a system has eight devices and only one can be active (in use) at any instant. If each device is enabled by a 0 at its input, the binary code applied to the 74138's C, B, A inputs will determine which device is selected (assuming that the 74138 is enabled by 0, 0, 1 at its $\overline{E1}, \overline{E2}, E3$ enable inputs).

The demultiplexer generates the 2^n minterms of an n-bit function. Why? Because a three-variable function has eight minterms and the demultiplexer converts a 3-bit code into one of eight values. For example, if you present a

Inputs			Outputs							
A	B	C	Y_0	Y_1	Y_2	Y_3	Y_4	Y_5	Y_6	Y_7
0	0	0	1	0	0	0	0	0	0	0
0	0	1	0	1	0	0	0	0	0	0
0	1	0	0	0	1	0	0	0	0	0
0	1	1	0	0	0	1	0	0	0	0
1	0	0	0	0	0	0	1	0	0	0
1	0	1	0	0	0	0	0	1	0	0
1	1	0	0	0	0	0	0	0	1	0
1	1	1	0	0	0	0	0	0	0	1

Table 2.26 Truth table for a 3-line demultiplexer.

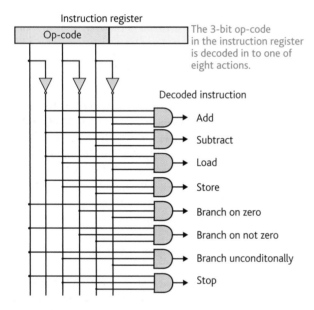

The 3-bit op-code in the instruction register is decoded in to one of eight actions.

Figure 2.92 Application of a demultiplexer as an instruction decoder.

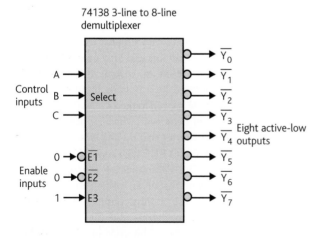

Figure 2.93 The 74138 3-line to 8-line decoder.

74138 with the code 101 (representing $C \cdot \overline{B} \cdot A$), output $\overline{Y}_5$ will be asserted low.

By ORing together the appropriate minterms we can generate an arbitrary sum of products expression in n variables. In other words, any function can be implemented by a demultiplexer and OR gate.

Figure 2.94 demonstrates how a 3-line to 8-line decoder can be used to implement a full-adder that adds three bits to generate a sum and a carry. Chapter 4 discusses binary arithmetic and adders—all we need say here is that the sum of bits A, B, and C_{in} is given by the Boolean expression $\overline{C}_{in} \cdot \overline{A} \cdot B + \overline{C}_{in} \cdot A \cdot \overline{B} + \overline{C_{in} \cdot A} \cdot \overline{B} + C_{in} \cdot A \cdot B$ and the carry by $\overline{C}_{in} \cdot B \cdot A + C_{in} \cdot \overline{B} \cdot A + C_{in} \cdot \overline{A} \cdot B + C_{in} \cdot A \cdot B$.

Note that the outputs of the 74LS138 are active-low and therefore it is necessary to employ a NAND gate to generate the required sum-of-products expression.

Another application of the demultiplexer is in decoding binary characters. Consider the ISO/ASCII character code (to be described in Chapter 4) which represents the alphanumeric characters (A–Z, 0–9, and symbols such as !, @, #, $, % . . .) together with certain non-printing symbols such as the back space and carriage return. The ASCII codes for some of these non-printing control codes are given in Table 2.27.

Suppose we receive an ASCII code from a keyboard and wish to decode its function in hardware. First note that all the codes of interest start with 00001. We can use the most-significant five bits to enable a 74LS138 3-line to 8-line decoder and then decode the three least-significant bits of the word $00001d_2d_1d_0$ to distinguish between the control codes. Figure 2.95 demonstrates how this is achieved. Each output from the decoder can be fed to a circuit to perform the appropriate action (e.g. carriage return).

Medium-scale logic devices like the 74138 make it easy to design circuits with just a handful of chips. However, many

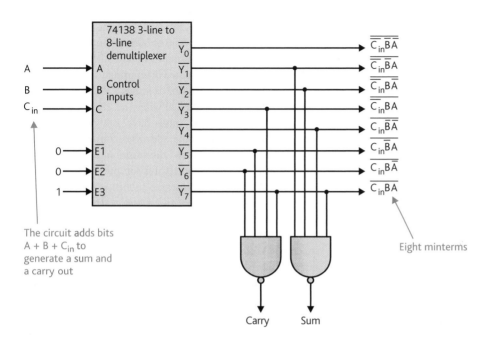

The circuit adds bits A + B + C_{in} to generate a sum and a carry out

Eight minterms

Carry   Sum

Figure 2.94 Generating a logic function with a demultiplexer.

circuits are now constructed from special-purpose user-programmable logic elements. Indeed, today's very low cost single-chip microprocessors sometimes make it feasible to program the microprocessor to carry out the required logic function. These microprocessors are called *microcontrollers* to distinguish them from their more powerful relatives in PCs and workstations.

Mnemonic	Name	Value
BS	Back space	00001000
LF	Line feed	00001010
CR	Carriage return	00001101
HT	Horizontal tabulate	00001001
VT	Vertical tabulate	00001011

Table 2.27 ASCII control characters.

2.7 Tri-state logic

The logic elements we introduced at the beginning of this chapter are used to create functional units in which one or more logical outputs are generated from several inputs. A computer is composed of the interconnection of such functional units together with the storage elements (registers) to be described in Chapter 3. We now examine a special type of gate that enables the various functional units of a computer to be interconnected. This new gate can be any of the gates we've already described—it's not the gate's logical function that's different, it's the behavior of its output. A logic element with a *tri-state* output has the special property that the output can be in a 0 state, a 1 state, or an *unconnected* state (hence the term *tri*-state). Before we can explain the operation of tri-state gates, we have to introduce the reason for their existence—the *bus*.

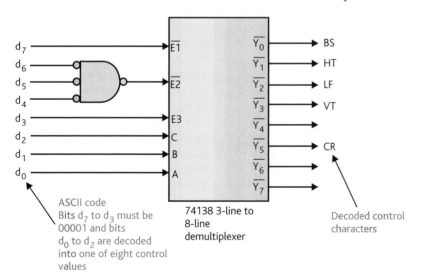

ASCII code
Bits d_7 to d_3 must be 00001 and bits d_0 to d_2 are decoded into one of eight control values

Decoded control characters

Figure 2.95 Decoding ASCII control characters with a demultiplexer.

2.7.1 **Buses**

A computer is like a city. Just as *roads* link homes, shops, and factories, *buses* link processing units, storage devices, and interfaces. Figure 2.96 shows a digital system composed of five functional units, *A*, *B*, *C*, *D*, and *E*. These units are linked together by means of two data highways (or buses), *P* and *Q*, permitting data to be moved from one unit to another. Data can flow onto the bus from a device connected to it and off

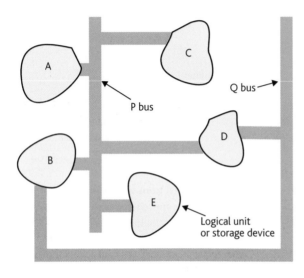

Figure 2.96 Functional units and buses.

the bus to any other device. Buses may be unidirectional (i.e. data always flows the same way) or bidirectional (i.e. data can flow in two directions—but not simultaneously).

A bus is normally represented diagrammatically by a single thick line or a wide shaded line as in Fig. 2.96. Real buses are composed of several individual wires (i.e. electrical connections). Modern computer buses have 100 or more lines, because a bus has to carry data, addresses, control signals, and even the power supply. Indeed the nature of a bus can be an important factor in the choice of a computer (consider the PC with its USB, and PCI buses).

Figure 2.97 demonstrates how a bus is arranged. Logical units A and B are connected to an *m*-bit data bus and can transmit data to the bus or receive data from it. We are not concerned with the nature of the processes A and B here, but simply wish to show how they communicate with each other via the bus. For clarity, the connections to only one line of the bus are shown. Similar arrangements exist for bits d_1 to d_{m-1}.

Suppose unit A wishes to send data to unit B. The system in unit A puts data on the bus via gate A_{out} and B receives the data from the bus via gate B_{in}. These two gates look like inverters but they aren't because they don't have *bubbles* at their output. Such a gate is called a *buffer* and it just copies the signal at its input terminal to its output terminal (i.e. the gate doesn't change the state of the data passing through it). We will soon see why such a gate is needed.

Such an arrangement is, in fact, unworkable and a glance at Fig. 2.98 shows why. In Fig. 2.98(a) the outputs of two AND gates are connected together. Figure 2.98(b) shows the same circuit as Fig. 2.98(a) except that we've included the internal organization of the two gates. Essentially, a gate's output circuit consists of two electronic switches that can connect the output to the +5 V power supply or to the 0 V (i.e. ground) power supply. These switches are transistors that are either conducting or non-conducting. Because only one switch is closed at a time, the output of a gate is always connected either to +5 V or to ground.

In Figure 2.98(b) the output from gate G1 is in a logical 1 state and is pulled up towards +5 V by a switch inside the gate. Similarly, the output from G2 is a logical 0 state and is pulled down towards 0 V. Because the two outputs are wired together and yet their states differ, two problems exist. The first is philosophical. The logical level at all points along a conductor is constant, because the voltage along the conductor is constant. Because the two ends of

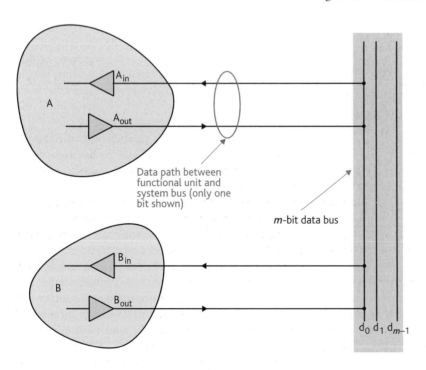

Figure 2.97 Connecting systems to the bus.

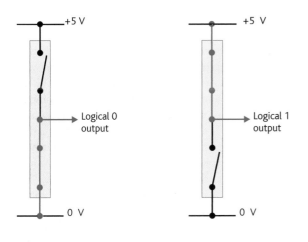

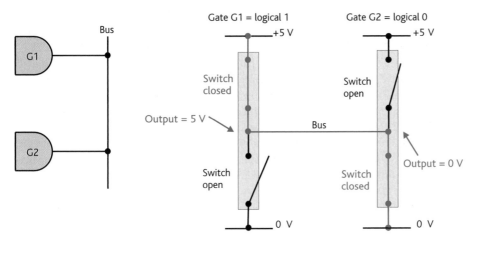

(a) Logical arrangement
Two outputs connected together

(b) Physical arrangement
Two outputs connected together

Figure 2.98 Connecting two outputs together.

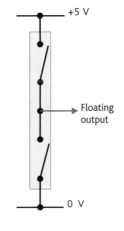

(a) Lower switch closed.
Output connected to ground

(b) Upper switch closed.
Output connected to +5V

(c) Both switches open.
Output disconnected

Figure 2.99 The operation of the tri-state output.

the bus in Fig. 2.98(b) are connected to *different* voltages, the logical level on the conductor is undefined and breaks one of the rules of Boolean algebra. We have stated that in a Boolean system there is no such thing as a valid indeterminate state lying between a logical 1 and a logical 0. Secondly, and more practically, a direct physical path exists between the +5 V power supply and ground (0 V). This path represents is a *short circuit* and the current flowing through the two output circuits could even destroy the gates.

The *tri-state gate* lets you connect outputs together. Tri-state logic is not, as its name might suggest, an extension of Boolean algebra into ternary or three-valued logic. It is a method of resolving the conflict that arises when two outputs are connected as in Fig. 2.98. Tri-state logic disconnects from the bus all those gates not actively engaged in transmitting data. In other words, a lot of tri-state outputs may be wired to

a bus, but only one of them may be actively connected to the bus internally. We shouldn't speak of tri-state logic or tri-state gates, we should speak of (conventional) gates with *tri-state outputs*.

Figure 2.99 illustrates the operation of a gate with a tri-state enable output. In fact, any type of gate can have a tri-state output. All tri-state gates have a special ENABLE input. When ENABLE = 1. the gate behaves normally and its output is either a logical 1 or a logical 0 depending on its input (Fig. 2.99(a) shows a 0 state and Fig. 2.99(b) a 1 state).

When ENABLE = 0, *both* switches in the output circuit of the gate are open and the output is physically disconnected from the gate's internal circuitry (Fig. 2.99(c)). If I were to ask what state the output is in when ENABLE = 0, the answer should be that the question is meaningless. In fact, because the output of an un-enabled tri-state gate is normally connected to a bus, the logic level at the output terminal is the same as that on the bus to which it is connected. For this reason, the output of a tri-state gate in its third state is said to be *floating*. It floats up and down with the bus traffic.

Most practical tri-state gates do, in fact, have active-low enable inputs rather than active-high enable inputs. Figure 2.100 provides the circuit symbols for four tri-state buffers, two of which are inverting buffers (i.e., NOT gates) and two of which are non-inverting buffers. Two of these gates have active-low enable inputs and two have active-high enable inputs. The truth table of an inverter with a tri-state output is given in Table 2.28.

Figure 2.101 demonstrates how tri-state buffers implement a bused structure. The buffers connect or disconnect the three networks A, B, and C, to the bus. The outputs of networks A, B, and C are placed on the bus by three tri-state buffers Ao, Bo, and Co, which are enabled by signals E_{Ao}, E_{Bo}, and E_{Co}, respectively. If any network wishes to put data on to the bus it sets its enable signal (e.g. E_{Bo}) to a 1. It is vital that no more than one of E_{Ao}, E_{Bo}, and E_{Co} be at a 1 level at any instant.

Each of the networks receives data from the bus via its own input buffers (Ai, Bi, and Ci). If a network wishes to receive data, it enables its input buffer by asserting one of E_{Ai}, E_{Bi}, or E_{Ci}, as appropriate. For example, if network C wishes to transmit data to network A, all that is necessary is for E_{CO} and E_{AI} to be set to a logical 1 simultaneously. All other enable signals remain in a logical 0 state for the duration of the information transfer.

Input buffers (Ai, Bi, Ci) are not always necessary. If the data flowing from the bus into a network goes only into the input of one or more gates, a buffer is not needed. If however, the input data is placed on an internal bus (local to the network) on which other gates may put their output, the buffer is necessary to avoid conflict between the various other outputs that may drive the local bus.

The bus in Fig. 2.101 is bidirectional; that is, data can flow onto the bus or off the bus. The pairs of buffers are arranged back to back (e.g. Ai and Ao) so that one buffer reads data from the bus and the other puts data on the bus—but not at the same time.

In the description of the bused system in Fig. 2.101 the names of the gates and their control signals have been carefully chosen. Ao stands for A_{out}, and Ai for A_{in}. This labels the gate and the *direction* in which it transfers data with respect to the network it is serving. Similarly, E_{Ao} stands for *enable gate A out*, and E_{Ai} for *enable gate A in*. By choosing consistent and meaningful names, the reading of circuit diagrams and their associated text is made easier.

Further details of a bused system will be elaborated on in Chapter 3, and Chapter 7 on the structure of the CPU makes extensive use of buses in its description of how the CPU actually carries out basic computer operations.

Digital Works supports tri-state buffers. The device palette provides a simple non-inverting tristate buffer with an active-high enable input. Figure 2.102 shows a system with a single bus to which three tri-state buffers are connected. One end of the bus is connected to an LED to show the state of the bus.

Digital Works requires you to connect a wire between two points so we've added a macro tag to the bottom of the bus to provide an anchor point (we don't use the macro tag for its normal purpose in this example).

The input of each tri-state gate in Fig. 2.102 is connected to the interactive input tool that can be set to a 0 or a 1 by the hand tool. Similarly, the enable input of each gate is connected to an interactive input tool.

By clicking on the run icon and then using the hand tool to set the input and enable switches, we can investigate the operation of the tristate buffer. In Fig. 2.102 inputs 1 and 3 are set

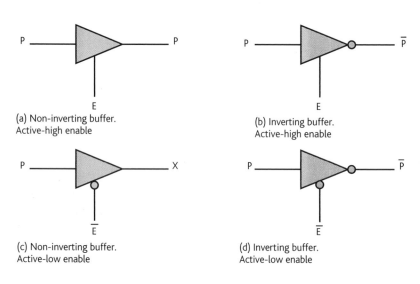

(a) Non-inverting buffer. Active-high enable

(b) Inverting buffer. Active-high enable

(c) Non-inverting buffer. Active-low enable

(d) Inverting buffer. Active-low enable

Figure 2.100 Logic symbol for the tri-state buffer.

ENABLE	Input	Output	
0	0	X	Output floating
0	1	X	Output floating
1	0	0	Output same as input
1	1	1	Output same as input

Table 2.28 Truth table for the non-inverting tri-state buffer with an active-high enable input.

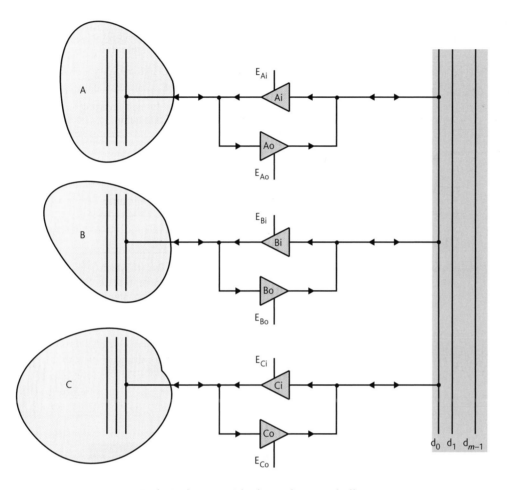

Figure 2.101 Interconnecting logic elements with a bus and tri-state buffers.

to 1 and only buffer 3 is enabled. Consequently, the output of buffer 3 is placed on the bus and the bus LED is illuminated.

We have stated that you shouldn't enable two or more of the tri-state gates at the same time. If you did, that would create bus contention as two devices attempted to put data on the bus simultaneously. In Fig. 2.103 we have done just that and used the hand tool to enable buffer 2 as well as buffer 3. As you can see, the simulation has stopped (the run button is in the off state) and an error message has been generated at the buffer we've attempted to enable.

2.8 Programmable logic

In this short section we introduce some of the single-chip *programmable logic elements* that can be configured by the user to perform any function they require. In the earlier days of logic design, systems were constructed with lots of basic logic elements; for example, the two-input OR gate, the five-input NAND gate, and so on. The introduction of medium

scale integration by the major semiconductor manufacturers generated a range of basic building blocks from multiplexers to digital multiplier circuits and allowed the economic design of more complex systems. We now introduce the next step in the history of digital systems—*programmable logic* that can be configured by the user.

2.8.1 The read-only memory as a logic element

Semiconductor manufactures find it easier to design regular circuits with repeated circuit elements than special-purpose highly complex systems. A typical regular circuit is the *read only memory* or ROM. We deal with memory in a later chapter. All we need say here is that a ROM is a device with n address input lines specifying 2^n unique locations within it. Each location, when accessed, produces an m-bit value on its m output lines. It is called *read only* because the output corresponding to a given input cannot be modified (i.e. written into) by the user. A ROM is specified by its *number of locations*

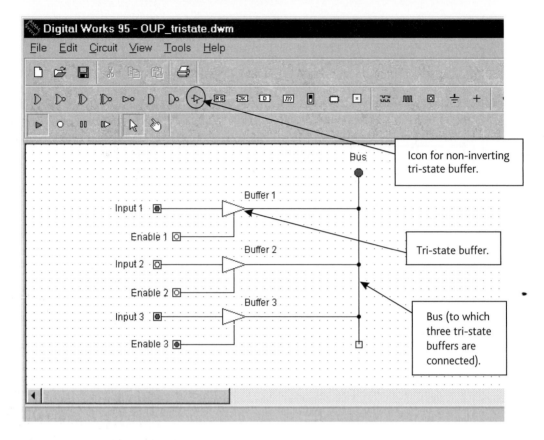

Figure 2.102 Using tri-state buffers in Digital Works.

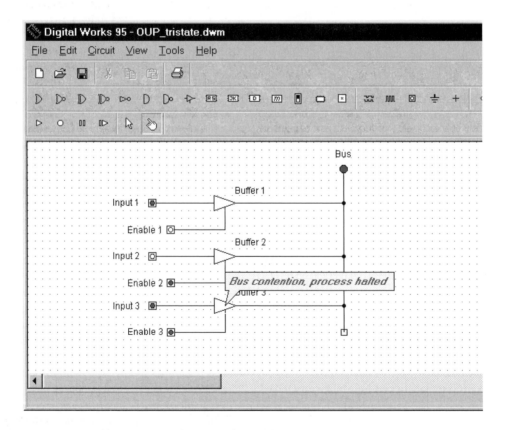

Figure 2.103 Attempting to enable two tri-state drivers simultaneously.

x width of each location; for example, a 16×4 ROM has 16 locations each containing 4 bits.

An alternative approach to the design of digital systems with basic gates or MSI elements is to use ROMs to implement the required function as a *look-up table*. Figure 2.104 shows how a 16×4 ROM implements the 4-bit multiplier we designed earlier in this chapter using AND, OR, and NOT gates. The binary code, X_1, X_0, Y_1, Y_0, at the four address inputs selects one of the 16 possible locations, each containing a 4-bit word corresponding to the desired result. The manufacturer or user of the ROM writes the appropriate output into each of these 16 locations; for example, the location 1011, corresponding to 10×11 (i.e. 2×3), has 0110 (i.e. 6) written into it.

The ROM directly implements not the circuit but the truth table. The value of the output is stored for each of the possible inputs. The ROM look-up table doesn't even require Boolean algebra to simplify the sum-of-products expression derived from the truth table. Not only does a ROM look-up table save a large number of logic elements, but the ROMs themselves can be readily replaced to permit the logic functions to be modified (to correct errors or to add improved facilities). Unfortunately, the ROM look-up table is limited to about 20 inputs and eight outputs (i.e. $2^{20} \times 8 = 8$ Mbits). The ROM can be programmed during its manufacture or a PROM (*programmable* ROM) can be programmed by means of a special device.

2.8.2 Programmable logic families

Because ROM requires a very large number of bits to implement moderately complex digital circuits, semiconductor manufacturers have created much simpler logic elements than ROMs containing a regular structure of AND and OR gates that can be interconnected by the user to generate the required logical function.

Figure 2.105 provides a simplified picture of how programmable logic devices operate. The three inputs on the left-hand side of the diagram are connected to six vertical lines (three lines for the inputs and three for their complements). On the right of the diagram are three two-input AND gates whose inputs run horizontally. The key to programmable logic is the *programmable link* between each horizontal and vertical conductor.

Fusible links between gates are broken by passing a sufficiently large current through the link to melt it. By leaving a link intact or by blowing it, the outputs of the AND gates can be determined by the designer. Modern programmable logic devices have electrically programmed links that can be made and un-made many times.

A real programmable device has many more inputs variables than in Fig. 2.105 and the AND gates can have an input for each of the variables and their complements. The digital designer selects the appropriate programmable device from a manufacturer's catalogue and adapts the Boolean equations to fit the type of gates on the chip. The engineer then plugs the chip into a special programming machine that interconnects the gates in the desired way.

Programmable logic elements enable complex systems to be designed and implemented without requiring large numbers of chips. Without the present generation of programmable logic elements, many of the low-cost microcomputers would be much more bulky, consume more power, and cost considerably more.

Today's designers have several types of programmable logic element at their disposal; for example, the PAL (programmable

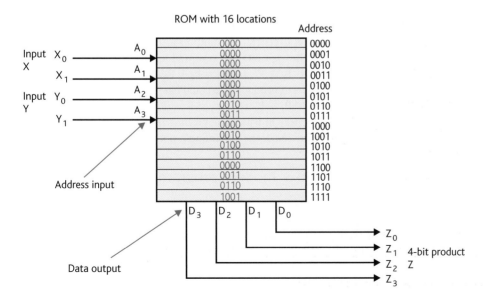

Figure 2.104 Using a ROM to implement a multiplier.

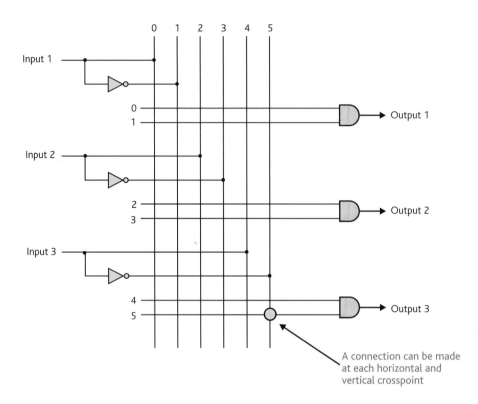

A connection can be made at each horizontal and vertical crosspoint

Figure 2.105 Conceptual structure of a programmable logic device.

array logic), the PLA (programmable logic array), and the PROM (programmable read-only memory). The PROM and the PAL are special cases of the PLA. The difference between the various types of programmable logic element depends on whether one or both of the AND and OR arrays are programmable.

Programmable Logic Array

The *programmable logic array* (PLA) was one of the first field programmable logic elements to become widely available. It has an AND–OR gate structure with a *programmable* array of AND gates whose inputs may be variables, their complements, or don't care states. The OR gates are also programmable, which means that you can define each output as the sum of any of the product terms. A typical PLA has 48 AND gates (i.e. 48 *product terms*) for 16 input variables, compared with the 65 536 required by a 16-input PROM. Figure 2.106 provides a simple example of a PLA that has been programmed to generate three outputs (no real PLA is this simple). Because the PLA has a programmable address decoder implemented by the AND gates, you can create product terms containing between one and *n* variables.

Programmable array logic

A more recent programmable logic element is the *programmable array logic* (PAL), which is not to be confused with the PLA we discussed earlier. The PAL falls between the simple gate array that contains only programmable AND gates and

the more complex programmed logic array. The PLA has both programmable AND and OR arrays, whereas the PAL has a programmable AND array but a *fixed* OR array. In short, the PAL is an AND gate array whose outputs are ORed together in a way determined by the device's programming.

Consider a hypothetical PAL with three inputs x_0 to x_2 and three outputs y_0 to y_2. Assume that inputs x_0 to x_2, generate six product terms P_0 to P_5. These product terms are, of course, *user programmable* and may include an input variable in a true, complement, or don't care form. In other words, you can generate any six product terms you want.

The six product terms are applied to three two-input OR gates to generate the outputs y_0 to y_2 (Fig. 2.107). Each output is the logical OR of two product terms. Thus, $y_0 = P_0 + P_1$, $y_1 = P_2 + P_3$, and $y_2 = P_4 + P_5$. We have chosen to OR three *pairs* of products. We could have chosen three *triplets* so that $y_0 = P_1 + P_2 + P_3$, $y_1 = P_4 + P_5 + P_6$, etc. In other words, the way in which the product terms are ORed together is a function of the device and is not programmable by the user.

2.8.3 Modern programmable logic

Over the years, logic systems have evolved. Once the designer was stuck with basic gates and MSI building blocks. The 1980s were the era of the programmable logic element with PROMs, PALs, PLAs, and so on. Today's programmable logic elements are constructed on a much grander scale. Typical programmable logic devices extend the principles of the PLA

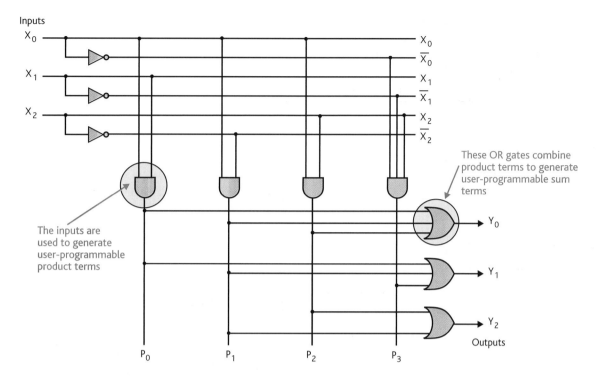

Figure 2.106 Example of a circuit built with a PLA.

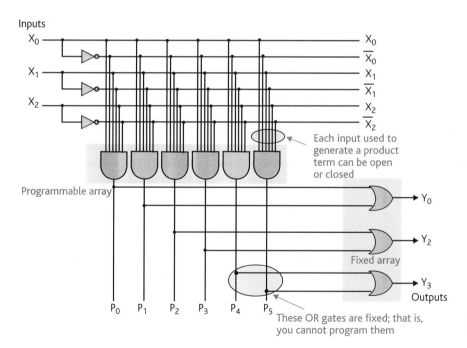

Figure 2.107 Structure of the PAL.

and employ *macro cells* that implement more complex building blocks containing storage elements as well as AND, OR, and EOR gates.

A more recent innovation in programmable logic is the *electrically programmable and erasable logic element*

which can be programmed, erased, and reprogrammed. Reprogrammable logic elements represent a considerable saving at the design stage. Moreover, they can be used to construct systems that can be reconfigured by downloading data from disk.

Design techniques for modern logic

There's little point in developing massively complex programmable logic elements if they can't easily be used. Although the Boolean algebra and logic construction methods we've described earlier in this chapter are perfectly good for simple circuits, more efficient design techniques and tools are needed for complex circuits.

Device manufacturers have developed logic languages that run on PCs and make it possible to configure these programmable logic elements. You can express the required functions in Boolean form and the software will generate the data necessary to program the device.

Just as high-level languages have replaced assembly language in computer programming, circuit designers use high-level design languages. One such language is called VHDL (VHSIC hardware description language, where VHSIC is an acronym for *very-high-speed integrated circuit*), which permits you to specify a digital circuit in a high-level abstract language. VHDL started out as a US Department of Defense project to specify complex circuits and evolved into a general-purpose design tool. VHDL became an IEEE standard in 1987 with the number IEEE 1076.

A designer armed with VHDL can specify a circuit in VHDL code and then simulate the circuit's behavior on a PC (or a workstation under Unix). The software can even cope with the problems of delays in the circuit. Because the device can be simulated, the engineer is reasonably certain that the final circuit will work when it is constructed. This software can even drive the devices that program these logic elements.

About three decades ago, the engineer built digital circuits on *breadboards* with hundreds of small-scale and medium-scale integrated circuits—and then spent weeks debugging the circuit. Today, the engineer can express complex logical operations in a high-level notation, design a circuit, simulate its behavior, and then program a real device knowing that it will probably work first time.

The following fragment of VHDL code is taken from *VHDL of Programmable Logic* by Kevin Skahill (Addison Wesley, 1996) and demonstrates how a quad 4-bit multiplexer can be specified. This device has four 4-bit inputs *a* to *d* and a 4-bit output *x*. A 2-bit input *s* determines which of the four inputs is connected to the output.

Readers who have programmed in almost any high-level language would probably be able to follow this fragment of VHDL. It consists of a declaration block that defines the inputs and outputs and a process block that defines what the circuit is to do.

2.8.4 **Testing digital circuits**

A significant part of the cost of a digital system is its *testing*. Why should testing be so expensive? After all, a system either works or it doesn't. If it doesn't work it can often be scrapped and replaced more economically than repairing it.

Although it's easy to test a light bulb by plugging it into a socket, it's much more difficult to test all but the most primitive of digital systems. Consider a small memory element with 10 address lines and eight data outputs (i.e. 1 kbyte). How many tests do we need to perform to verify that the memory is working correctly? Obviously the memory can be tested by writing a pattern into each of its $2^{10} = 1024$ locations and then reading the pattern back. That is, the test requires a total of 1024 read and 1024 write cycles.

But wait a moment. How do we know that the memory will store every possible data pattern in each possible word location? The test must be extended by writing all possible data values into a location before testing the next location. In this case there are $2^8 = 256$ tests per location, or $2^8 \times 2^{10} = 2^{18}$ tests altogether.

At last we have now thoroughly tested the memory component. No we have not! Some memories display a fault called *pattern sensitivity* in which writing data to one location affects the contents of another location. You can test for pattern sensitivity by writing a data pattern to the location we wish to test and then filling all other locations with a different data pattern. We then reread the data in the location under test to see whether it has changed. So for each of our 2^{18} tests, we must write a different pattern in all the other $2^{10}-1$ word cells. This gives us a total of $2^{18} \times 2^{10}$ or 2^{28} tests. If we were to consider a 64 Mbyte memory, it would require $2^8 \times 2^{26} \times 2^{26} = 2^{52}$ tests (a gigantic number).

This example demonstrates that it's effectively impossible to test any reasonably complex digital system with external inputs and internal states. Even if tests could be carried out at a rate of over 100 million/s, most complex digital systems

```
library ieee;
use ieee.std_logic_1164.all;
entity mux is port(
        a, b, c, d:    in   std_logic_vector(3 downto 0);
        s:             in   std_logic_vector(1 downto 0);
        x:             out  std_logic_vector(3 downto 0));
end mux;


architecture archmux of mux is
begin
with s select
   x <= a when "00",
        b when "01",
        c when "10",
        d when others;
end archmux;
```

(e.g. a microprocessor chip) would take longer to test than the anticipated life of the entire universe. A way out of this dilemma is to perform a test that provides a reasonable level of confidence in its ability to detect a large fraction of possible faults without requiring an excessive amount of time.

The first step in devising such a test is to distinguish between the idea of a *defect* and a *fault*. A real system fails because of a *defect* in its manufacture. For example, a digital system may fail because of a defect at the component level (a crystal defect in a silicon chip), or at the system level (a solder splash joining together two adjacent tracks on a printed circuit board). The observed failure is termed a *fault*.

Although there are an infinite number of possible *defects* that might cause a system to fail, their effects (i.e. faults) are relatively few. In simpler terms, an automobile may suffer from many defects, but many of these defects result in a single observable *fault*—the car doesn't move. That is, a fault is the observable effect due to a defect. A digital system can be described in terms of a fault model (i.e. the list of observable effects of defects). Typical faults are given below.

Stuck-at-one The input or output of a circuit remains in a logical 1 state independently of all other circuit conditions. This is usually written s_a_1.

Stuck-at-zero In this case the input or output is permanently stuck in a 0 state (i.e. s_a_0).

Bridging faults Two inputs or outputs of a circuit are effectively connected together and cannot assume independent logic levels. That is, they must both be 0s or 1.

It is possible to devise a longer list of fault models, but the stuck-at fault model is able to detect a surprisingly large number of defects. In other words, if we test a system by considering all possible stuck-at-1 and stuck-at-0 faults, we are likely to detect almost all of the probable defects.

The sensitive path test

A *sensitive path* between an input and an output is constructed to make the output a function of the input being tested (i.e. the output is sensitive to a *change* in the input). Figure 2.108(a) illustrates a circuit with three gates and six inputs A, B, C, F, I and J. The sensitive path to be tested is between input A and output K.

Figure 2.108(b) demonstrates how we have chosen the sensitive path by ensuring that a change in input A is propagated through the circuit. By setting AND gate 1's B and C inputs high, input A is propagated through this gate to the E input of AND gate 2. The second input of AND gate 2, F, must be set high to propagate E through gate 2. Output G of AND gate 2 is connected to input H of the three-input OR gate 3. In this case, inputs I and J must be set low to propagate input H (i.e. A) through OR gate 3.

By setting inputs B, C, F, I, and J to 1, 1, 1, 0, and 0, the output becomes $K = A$ and, therefore, by setting A to 0 and then to 1, we can test the sensitive path between A and K and determine whether any A_stuck_at fault exists.

A *fault-list* can be prepared for the circuit, which, in this case, might consist of A s_a_0, A s_a_1, B s_a_0, B s_a_1, ... A convenient notation for the fault list is A/0, A/1, B/0, B/1, ... etc. The '/' is read as 'stuck at'.

To test for A s_a_0 (i.e. A/0), the other inputs are set to the values necessary to create a sensitive path and A is switched from 0 to 1. If the output changes state, A is not stuck at zero. The same test also detects A/1.

Fault tests are designed by engineers (possibly using CAD techniques) and can be implemented either manually or by means of computer-controlled *automatic test equipment* (ATE). This equipment sets up the appropriate input signals and tests the output against the expected value. We can specify the sensitive path for A in the circuit of Fig. 2.108(b) as $B \cdot C \cdot F \cdot \bar{I} \cdot \bar{J}$.

It's not always possible to test digital circuits by this sensitive path analysis because of the *topological* properties of some digital circuits. For example, a digital signal may take more than one route through a circuit and certain faults may lead to a situation in which an error is cancelled at a particular node. Similarly, it's possible to construct logic circuits that have an undetectable fault. Figure 2.109 provides an example of such a circuit. This type of undetectable

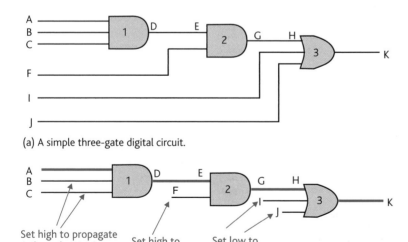

(a) A simple three-gate digital circuit.

(b) Establishing a sensitive path between input A and output K.

Figure 2.108 Using sensitive path analysis to test digital circuits.

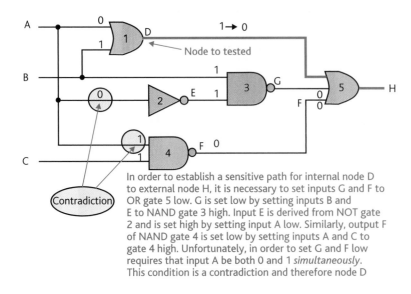

In order to establish a sensitive path for internal node D to external node H, it is necessary to set inputs G and F to OR gate 5 low. G is set low by setting inputs B and E to NAND gate 3 high. Input E is derived from NOT gate 2 and is set high by setting input A low. Similarly, output F of NAND gate 4 is set low by setting inputs A and C to gate 4 high. Unfortunately, in order to set G and F low requires that input A be both 0 and 1 *simultaneously*. This condition is a contradiction and therefore node D

Figure 2.109 Circuit with an undetectable fault.

fault is due to *redundancy* in the circuit and can be eliminated by redesigning the circuit. Alternatively, a circuit can be made easier to test by connecting some of its internal nodes to pins so that they can be directly examined.

■ SUMMARY

In this chapter we have looked at the basic set of logic elements used to create any digital system—the AND, OR, and NOT gates. We have demonstrated how simple functions can be generated from gates by first converting a problem in words into a truth table and then using either graphical or algebraic methods to convert the truth table into a logical expression and finally into a circuit made up of gates. At the end of this chapter we briefly mentioned the new families of programmable logic elements and their design tools that have revolutionized the creation of today's complex digital systems.

We have introduced Digital Works, a design tool that enables you to create digital circuits and to observe their behavior. We also introduced the tri-state buffer, a device that enables you to connect logic subsystems to each other via a common data highway called a bus.

In the next chapter we look at sequential circuits built from flip-flops. As the term *sequential* suggests, these circuits involve the time factor, because the logical state of a sequential device is determined by its current inputs and its past history (or behavior). Sequential circuits form the basis of counters and data storage devices. Once we have covered sequential circuits, we will have covered all the basic building blocks necessary to design a digital system of any complexity (e.g. the digital computer).

■ PROBLEMS

2.1 Explain the meaning of the following terms.

(a) Sum-of-products
(b) Product of sums

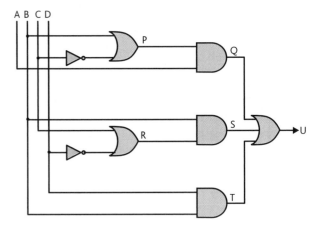

Figure 2.110 Circuit for Question 2.2.

(c) Minterm
(d) Truth table
(e) Literal
(f) Constant
(g) Variable

2.2 Tabulate the values of the variables P, Q, R, S, T, and U in the circuit of Fig. 2.110 for all possible input variables A, B, C, and D. The truth table for this question should be expressed in the form of Table 2.29.

2.3 For the circuit of Fig. 2.110 in Question 2.2 obtain a Boolean expression for the output U, in terms of the inputs A, B, C, and D. You should obtain an expression for the output U by considering the logic function of each gate.

2.4 For the truth table in Question 2.2 (Table 2.29) obtain a sum-of-minterms expression for U and use Boolean algebra to obtain a simplified sum-of-products expression for U.

Inputs				Output					
A	B	C	D	$P = B + \bar{C}$	$Q = P \cdot A$	$R = C + \bar{D}$	$S = B \cdot R$	$T = B \cdot D$	$U = Q + S + T$
0	0	0	0	1	0	1	0	0	0
0	0	0	1	.	.	.	.	.	.
0	0	1	0	.	.	.	.	.	.
0	0	1	1	.	.	.	.	.	.
0	1	0	0	.	.	.	.	.	.
0	1	0	1	.	.	.	.	.	.
.	.	.	.						
.	.	.	.						
1	1	1	1	1	1	1	1	1	1

Table 2.29 Truth table for Question 2.2.

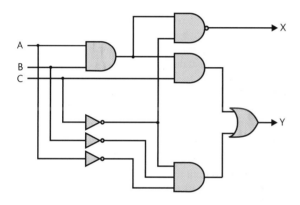

Figure 2.111 Circuit for Question 2.5.

2.5 Use a truth table to obtain the relationship between outputs X and Y and the input variables A, B, and C for the circuit in Fig. 2.111. From the truth table write down Boolean expressions for X and Y. Derive expressions for X and Y by considering the Boolean equations of the gates.

Demonstrate that the two results (i.e. those derived from the truth table and those derived from the Boolean equations) are equivalent by substituting literals (000, 001, etc.) for A, B, and C in the Boolean equations.

2.6 Draw logic diagrams, using AND, OR, and NOT gates only, to implement the following Boolean expressions. In each case draw the diagrams directly from the equations and do not attempt to simplify the expressions.

(a) $F = \bar{A} \cdot B + \overline{A \cdot \bar{B}}$

(b) $F = (A + B + C)(A \cdot B + A \cdot C)$

(c) $F = (A + \bar{C})(A + B \cdot \bar{D})$

(d) $F = \overline{\bar{A} + \bar{C} \cdot A} + B \cdot \bar{D}$

(e) $F = (A \cdot \bar{B} + \bar{A} \cdot B + A \cdot \bar{C})\overline{(\bar{A} \cdot \bar{B} + A \cdot \bar{B} + A \cdot \bar{C})}$

2.7 Plot the following functions on a Karnaugh map.

(a) $F = A \cdot B \cdot C + \bar{A} \cdot \bar{B} \cdot \bar{C}$

(b) $F = \bar{A} \cdot \bar{B} \cdot C + A \cdot \bar{B} \cdot \bar{C} + \bar{A} \cdot B \cdot C$

(c) $F = \bar{A} + A \cdot B + A \cdot C + A \cdot B \cdot C$

(d) $F = A + B \cdot \bar{A} \cdot C + D$

(e) $F = A \cdot B \cdot C \cdot D + A \cdot B \cdot C \cdot D + B \cdot D$

2.8 How would you plot the following expressions on a Karnaugh map?

(a) $(\bar{A} + B + C)(\bar{D} + B)(\bar{A} + C)$

(b) $(\bar{A} \cdot \bar{B} + A \cdot B + \bar{A} \cdot \bar{C})(\bar{A} \cdot D + A \cdot \bar{B} + A \cdot C)$

2.9 Simplify the following expressions by means of Boolean algebra. That is, do not use Karnaugh maps.

(a) $A \cdot \bar{B} \cdot \bar{C} + \bar{A} \cdot \bar{B} \cdot \bar{C} + \bar{A} \cdot B \cdot \bar{C} + \bar{A} \cdot \bar{B} \cdot C$

(b) $A \cdot B \cdot C + \bar{A} \cdot B \cdot C + A \cdot \bar{B} \cdot C + A \cdot \bar{B} \cdot \bar{C} + \bar{A} \cdot B \cdot \bar{C}$
$+ \bar{A} \cdot B \cdot C$

(c) $A \cdot B \cdot C + A \cdot \bar{B} \cdot \bar{C} + \bar{A} \cdot \bar{B} \cdot C + \bar{A} \cdot B \cdot \bar{C} + A \cdot \bar{B} \cdot C$
$+ A \cdot B \cdot \bar{C} + \bar{A} \cdot \bar{B} \cdot \bar{C} + \bar{A} \cdot B \cdot C$

2.10 Simplify the following expressions.

(a) $(A + B + C)(\bar{A} + B + \bar{C})$

(b) $(A \cdot \bar{B} + \bar{A} \cdot B + \bar{A} \cdot C)(\bar{A} \cdot \bar{B} + A \cdot \bar{B} + A \cdot C)$

(c) $A + \bar{B} + (A + C \cdot D)(A + \bar{B} \cdot \bar{C})$

(d) $A \cdot \bar{B} + B \cdot \bar{C} + A \cdot \bar{B} \cdot \bar{C} + A \cdot B \cdot C \cdot \bar{D}$

(e) $(\bar{A} + B)(A + \bar{B} + \bar{C})(A + B + \bar{C})(\bar{A} + \bar{B} + C)$

2.11 Use de Morgan's theorem to complement the following expressions. Do not simplify the expressions either before or after you complement them.

(a) $\overline{\bar{B} \cdot \bar{C}} + B \cdot C$

(b) $\overline{B \cdot C \cdot D + \bar{B} \cdot \bar{C}}$

(c) $\overline{B (C + D) + \bar{B} \cdot \bar{C}}$

(d) $\overline{A \cdot B(\bar{C} \cdot D + C \cdot D)}$

(e) $\overline{A \cdot B(A \cdot \bar{D} + \bar{C} \cdot D)}$

(f) $\overline{B \cdot C + \bar{B} \cdot \bar{C} (A \cdot D + \bar{A} \cdot D)}$

2.12 Convert the following expressions to sum-of-products form.

(a) $(A + B) (\overline{B} + C) (\overline{A} + C)$

(b) $(C + D) (A \cdot \overline{B} + A \cdot C) (\overline{A} \cdot \overline{C} + B)$

(c) $(A + B + C) (A + C \cdot D) (D + F)$

2.13 Simplify

(a) $A \oplus B \oplus C$

(b) $A \cdot \overline{B(C \oplus A)}$

2.14 Convert the following expressions to product-of-sums form.

(a) $A \cdot B + \overline{A} \cdot \overline{B} + B \cdot C$

(b) $\overline{A} \cdot \overline{B} + B \cdot C + \overline{B} \cdot \overline{C} \cdot D$

(c) $A \cdot B + \overline{A} \cdot C + B \cdot \overline{C}$

(d) $A \cdot \overline{B} \cdot \overline{C} + \overline{A} \cdot \overline{B} \cdot \overline{C} + \overline{A} \cdot B \cdot \overline{C} + \overline{A} \cdot \overline{B} \cdot C$

2.15 A circuit has four inputs, P, Q, R, and S, representing the natural binary numbers 0000 = 0, to 1111 = 15. P is the most-significant bit. The circuit has one output, X, which is true if the number represented by the input is divisible by three (regard zero as being indivisible by three.) Design a truth table for this circuit and hence obtain an expression for X in terms of P, Q, R, and S. Give the circuit diagram of an arrangement of AND, OR, and NOT gates to implement this circuit. Design a second circuit to implement this function using NAND gates only.

2.16 A device accepts natural binary numbers in the range 0000 to 1111 which represent 0 to 15. The output of the circuit is true if the input to the circuit represents a prime number and is false otherwise. Design a circuit using AND, OR, and NOT gates to carry out this function. A prime number is an integer that is greater than 1 and is divisible only by itself and 1. Zero and 1 are not prime numbers.

2.17 Demonstrate how you would use a 4-line to 16-line demultiplexer to implement the system in Question 2.16.

2.18 A logic circuit accepts a natural binary number DCBA in the range 0 to 15 (the least-significant bit is bit A). The output is the square of the input; for example, if DCBA = 0101_2 = 5_{10}, the output is 00010101_2 = 25_{10}. Design a circuit to implement this function.

2.19 A logic circuit has three inputs C, B, and A, where A is the least-significant bit. The circuit has three outputs R, Q, and P. For any binary code applied to the input terminals (A, B, and C) the output is given by the input plus 1; for example, if C, B, A = 0, 1, 1, the output R, Q, P is 1, 0, 0. Note that 111 + 1 = 000 (i.e. there is no carry out). Design a circuit to implement this system.

2.20 A 4-bit binary number is applied to a circuit on four lines D, C, B, and A. The circuit has a single output, F, which is true if the number is in the range 3 to 12, inclusive. Draw a truth table for this problem and obtain a simplified expression for F in terms of the inputs. Implement the circuit

(a) in terms of NAND gates only
(b) in terms of NOR gates only

2.21 A circuit has four inputs D, C, B, and A encoded in 8421 natural binary form. The inputs in the range 0000_2 = 0 to 1011_2 = 11 represent the months of the year from January (0) to December (11). Inputs in the range 1100 to 1111 (i.e. 12 to 15) cannot occur. The output of the circuit is a logical one if the month represented by the input has 31 days. Otherwise the output is false. The output for inputs in the range 1100 to 1111 is undefined.

(a) Draw a truth table to represent the problem and use it to construct a Karnaugh map.
(b) Use the Karnaugh map to obtain a simplified expression for the function.
(c) Construct a circuit to implement the function using AND, OR, and NOT gates.
(d) Construct a circuit to implement the function using NAND gates only.

2.22 A multiplexer has eight inputs Y_0 to Y_7 and a single output Z. A further three inputs A, B, and C (A = least-significant bit) determine which output the single input X is connected to. For example, if A, B, C = 110, the output Y_6 = X and all other outputs are low. Design a circuit to implement this function.

2.23 What is tri-state logic and why is it used in digital systems?

2.24 Use Digital Works to construct a circuit that realizes the expression

$$\overline{A} \cdot B \cdot C + \overline{A} \cdot \overline{B} \cdot C + \overline{A} \cdot \overline{B} \cdot \overline{C} + A \cdot B \cdot C$$

Simplify the above expression and use Digital Works to construct a new circuit. Demonstrate that the two circuits are equivalent (by comparing their outputs for all inputs).

2.25 Use Digital Works to construct the system of Question 2.20 and demonstrate that your system works.

Sequential Logic

CHAPTER MAP

2 Logic elements and Boolean algebra

We begin our introduction to the computer with the basic building block from which we construct all computers, the gate. A combinational digital circuit such as an adder is composed of gates and its output is a Boolean (logical) function of its inputs only.

3 Sequential logic

The output of a sequential circuit is a function of both its current inputs and its past inputs; that is, a sequential circuit has memory. The building blocks used to construct devices that store data are called flip-flops. In this chapter we look at basic sequential elements and the counters, registers, and shifters that are constructed from flip-flops.

4 Computer arithmetic

Computer arithmetic concerns the representation of numbers in a computer and the arithmetic used by digital computers. We look at how decimal numbers are converted into binary form and the properties of binary numbers and we demonstrate how operations like addition and subtraction are carried out. We also look at how computers deal with negative numbers and fractional numbers.

5 The instruction set architecture

In this chapter we introduce the computer's instruction set architecture (ISA), which describes the low-level programmer's view of the computer. The ISA describe the type of operations a computer carries out. We are interested in three aspects of the ISA: the nature of the instructions, the resources used by the instructions (registers and memory), and the ways in which the instructions access data (addressing modes). The 68K microprocessor is used to illustrate the operation of a real device.

INTRODUCTION

We now introduce a new type of circuit that is constructed from devices that *remember* their previous inputs. The logic circuits in Chapter 2 were all built with *combinational elements* whose outputs are functions of their inputs *only*. Given a knowledge of a combinational circuit's inputs and its Boolean function, we can always calculate the state of its outputs. The output of a *sequential circuit* depends not only on its current inputs, but also on its *previous* inputs. Even if we know a sequential circuit's Boolean equations, we can't determine its output state without knowing its past history (i.e. its previous internal states). The basic building blocks of sequential circuits are the *flip-flop, bistable*, and *latch* just as the basic building block of the combinational circuit is the gate.

It's not our intention to deal with sequential circuits at anything other than an introductory level, as their full treatment forms an entire branch of digital engineering. Sequential circuits can't be omitted from introductory texts on computer hardware because they are needed to implement registers, counters, and shifters, all of which are fundamental to the operation of the central processing unit.

Figure 3.1 describes the conceptual organization of a sequential circuit. An input is applied to a combinational circuit using AND, OR, and NOT gates to generate an output that is fed to a memory circuit that holds the value of the output. The information held in this memory is called the *internal state* of the circuit. The sequential circuit uses its previous output together with its current input to generate the *next* output. This statement contains a very important implicit concept, the idea of a *next state*. Sequential circuits have a clock input, which triggers the transition from the *current* state to the *next* state. The *counter* is a good example of a sequential machine because it stores the current count that is updated to become the next count. We ourselves are state machines because our future behavior depends on our past

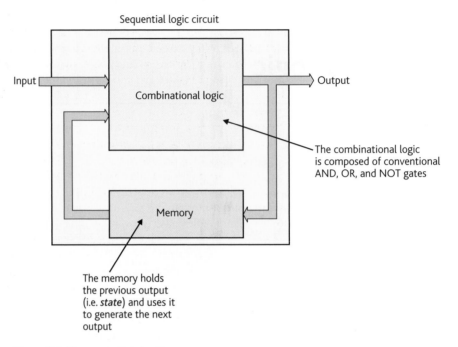

Figure 3.1 The sequential circuit.

WHAT IS SEQUENTIAL LOGIC?

Sequential logic elements perform as many different functions as combinational logic elements; however, they do carry out certain well-defined functions, which have been given names.

Latch A latch is a 1-bit memory element. You can capture a single bit in a latch at one instant and then use it later; for example, when adding numbers you can capture the carry-out in a latch and use it as a carry-in in the next calculation.

Register The register is just m latches in a row and is able to store an m-bit word; that is, the register is a device that stores one memory word. A computer's memory is just a very large array of registers.

Shift register A shift register is a special-purpose register that can move the bits of the word it holds left or right; for example the 8-bit word 00101001 can be shifted left to give 01010010.

Counter A counter is another special-purpose register that holds an m-bit word. However, when a counter is triggered (i.e. clocked) its contents increase by 1; for example, if a counter holding the binary equivalent of 42 is clocked, it will hold the value 43. Counters can count up or down, by 1 or any other number, or they can count through any arbitrary sequence.

State machines A state machine is a digital system that moves from one state to another each time it is triggered. You can regard a washing machine controller as a state machine that steps though all the processes involved in washing (at a rate depending on the load, the temperature, and its preselected functions). Ultimately, the computer itself is a nothing more than a state machine controlled by a program and its data.

---

inputs—if you burn yourself getting something out of the oven, you approach the oven with more care next time.

We begin our discussion of sequential circuits with the *bistable* or *flip-flop*. A bistable is so called because its output can remain in one of two stable states indefinitely, even if the input changes. For a particular input, the bistable's output may be high or low, the actual value depending on the previous inputs. Such a circuit remembers what has happened to it in the past and is therefore a form of memory element. A more detailed discussion of memory elements is given in Chapter 8. A bistable is the smallest possible memory cell and stores only a single bit of information. The term *flip-flop,* which is synonymous with bistable, gives the impression of the circuit going *flip* into one state and then *flop* into its complement. Bistables were constructed from electromagnetic relays that really did make a flip-flop sound as they jumped from one state into another.

The term *latch* is also used to describe certain types of flip-flop. A latch is a flip-flop that is unclocked (i.e. its operation isn't synchronized with a timing signal called a *clock*). The RS flip-flop that we describe first can also be called a latch.

Sequential systems can be divided into two classes: *synchronous* and *asynchronous.* Synchronous systems use a master clock to update the state of all flip-flops periodically. The speed of a synchronous system is determined by its slowest device and all signals must have settled to steady-state values by the time the system is clocked. In an asynchronous system a change in an input signal triggers a change in another circuit and this change ripples through the system (an asynchronous system is rather like a line of closely spaced dominoes on edge—when one falls it knocks its neighbor over and so on). Reliable asynchronous systems are harder to design than synchronous systems, although they are faster and consume less power. We will return to some of these topics later.

We can approach flip-flops in two ways. One is to demonstrate what they do by defining their characteristics as an abstract model and then show how they are constructed. That is, we say this is a flip-flop and this is how it behaves—now let's see what it can do. The other way of approaching flip-flops is to demonstrate how they can be implemented with just two gates and then show how their special properties are put to work. We intend to follow the latter path. Some readers may prefer to skip ahead to the summary of flip-flops at the end of this section and then return when they have a global picture of the flip-flop.

3.1 The RS flip-flop

We begin our discussion of the flip-flop with the simplest member of the family, the RS flip-flop. Consider the circuit of Fig. 3.2. What differentiates this circuit from the combinational circuits of Chapter 2 is that the gates are *cross-coupled* and the output of a gate is fed back to its input. Although Fig. 3.2 uses no more than two two-input NOR gates, its operation is not immediately apparent.

The circuit has two inputs, A and B, and two outputs, X and Y. A truth table for the NOR gate is provided alongside Fig. 3.2 for reference. From the Boolean equations governing the NOR gates we can readily write down expressions for outputs X and Y in terms of inputs A and B.

1. $X = \overline{A + Y}$

2. $Y = \overline{B + X}$

If we substitute the value for Y from equation (2) in equation (1), we get

3. $X = \overline{A + \overline{B + X}}$

$\quad = \overline{A} \cdot \overline{\overline{B + X}}$ By de Morgan's theorem

$\quad = \overline{A} \cdot (B + X)$ Two negations cancel

$\quad = \overline{A} \cdot B + \overline{A} \cdot X$ Expand the expression

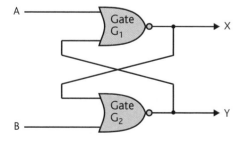

A	B	$\overline{A + B}$
0	0	1
0	1	0
1	0	0
1	1	0

Figure 3.2 Two cross-coupled NOR gates.

Because Boolean algebra doesn't define the operations of division or subtraction we can't simplify this equation any further and are left with an expression in which the *output* is a function of the *output*; that is, the value of X depends on X. Equation (3) is correct but its meaning isn't obvious. We have to look for another way of analyzing the behavior of cross-coupled gates. Perhaps a better approach to understanding this circuit is to assume a value for output X and for the inputs A and B and then see where it leads us.

3.1.1 Analyzing a sequential circuit by assuming initial conditions

Figure 3.3(a) shows the cross-coupled NOR gate circuit with the initial condition X = 1 and A = B = 0 and Fig. 3.3(b) shows the same circuit redrawn to emphasize the way in which data flows between the gates.

Because the inputs to gate G_2 are X = 1, B = 0, its output, $Y = \overline{X + B}$, must be 0. The inputs to gate G_1 are Y = 0 and A = 0, so that its output, X, is $\overline{Y + A}$, which is 1. Note that this situation is *self-consistent*. The output of gate G_1 is X = 1, which is fed back to the input of gate G_1 to keep X in a logical 1 state. That is, the output actually maintains itself. It should now be a little clearer why equation (3) has X on *both* sides (i.e. $X = \overline{A} \cdot B + \overline{A} \cdot X$).

Had we assumed the initial state of X to be 0 and inputs A = B = 0, we could have proceeded as follows. The inputs to G_2 are X = 0, B = 0 and therefore its output is $Y = \overline{X + B} = \overline{0 + 0} = 1$. The inputs to G_1 are Y = 1 and A = 0, and its output is $X = \overline{Y + A} = \overline{1 + 0} = 0$. Once more we can see that the circuit is self-consistent. The output can remain indefinitely in either a 0 or a 1 state for the inputs A = B = 0.

The next step in the analysis of the circuit's behavior is to consider what happens if we change inputs A or B. Assume that the X output is initially in a logical 1 state. If input B to gate G_2 goes high while input A remains low, the output of gate G_2 (i.e. Y) is unaffected, because the output of a NOR gate is low if either of its inputs are high. As X is already high, the state of B has no effect on the state of Y.

If now input A goes high while B remains low, the output, X, of gate G_1 must fall to a logical 0 state. The inputs to gate G_2 are now both in logical 0 states and its output Y rises to a logical 1. However, because Y is fed back to the input of gate G_1, the output X is *maintained* at a logical 0 even if A returns to a 0 state.

The effect of setting A to a 1 causes output X to flip over from a 1 to a 0 and to *remain* in that state when A returns to a 0. We call an RS flip-flop a *latch* because of its ability to capture a signal. Table 3.1 provides a truth table for the circuit of Fig. 3.2. Two tables are presented—one appropriate to the circuit we have described and one with its inputs and outputs relabeled.

Table 3.1(a) corresponds exactly to the two-NOR gate circuit of Fig. 3.2 and Table 3.1(b) to the idealized form of this circuit that's called an RS *flip-flop*. There are two differences between Tables 3.1(a) and 3.1(b). Table 3.1(b) uses the conventional labeling of an RS flip-flop with inputs R and S and an output Q. The other difference is in the entry for the case in which A = B = 1 and R = S = 1. The effect of these differences will be dealt with later.

We've already stated that Fig. 3.2 defines its output in terms of itself (i.e. $X = \overline{A} \cdot B + \overline{A} \cdot X$). The truth table gets round this problem by creating a new variable, X^+ (or Q^+), where X^+ is the *new* output generated by the *old* output X and the current inputs A and B. We can write $X^+ = \overline{A} \cdot B + \overline{A} \cdot X$. The input and output columns of the truth table are now not only separated in space (e.g. input on the left and output on the right) but also in *time*. The *current* output X is combined with inputs A and B to generate a *new* output X^+. The value of X that produced X^+ no longer exists and belongs only to the past.

Labels R and S in the Table 3.1(b) correspond to *reset* and *set*, respectively. The word *reset* means *make 0* (*clear* has the same meaning) and *set* means *make 1*. The output of all flip-flops is called Q by a historical convention. Examining the truth table reveals that whenever R = 1, the output Q is reset to 0. Similarly, when S = 1 the output is set to 1.

(a)

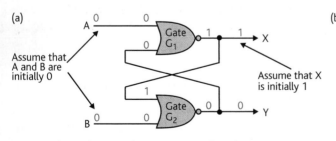

Analyzing the circuit by assuming initial conditions.

(b)

Note that the gates are cross-coupled with the output of one gate connected to the input of the other gate

An alternative view of the circuit.

Figure 3.3 Analyzing the behavior of cross-coupled NOR gates.

(a) Truth table for Fig. 3.2.

Inputs			Output
A	B	X	X^+
0	0	0	0
0	0	1	1
0	1	0	1
0	1	1	1
1	0	0	0
1	0	1	0
1	1	0	0
1	1	1	0
		↑	↑
		Old X	New X

(b) Truth table for relabeled Fig. 3.2.

Inputs			Output	
R	S	Q	Q^+	
0	0	0	0	No change
0	0	1	1	No change
0	1	0	1	Set
0	1	1	1	Set
1	0	0	0	Clear
1	0	1	0	Clear
1	1	0	?	Undefined
1	1	1	?	undefined
		↑	↑	
		Old Q	New Q	

The truth table is interpreted as follows. The output of the circuit is currently X (or Q) and the new inputs to be applied to the input terminals are A, B (or R, S). When these new inputs are applied to the circuit, its output is given by X^+ (or Q^+). For example, if the current output X is 1 and the new values of A and B are A = 1, B = 0, then the new output, X^+, will be 0. This value of X^+ then becomes the next value of X when new inputs A and B are applied to the circuit.

Table 3.1 Truth table for the circuit in Fig. 3.2.

When R and S are both 0, the output does not change; that is, $Q^+ = Q$.

If both R and S are simultaneously 1, the output is conceptually undefined (hence the question marks in Table 3.1(b), because the output can't be set and reset at the same time. In the case of the RS flip-flop implemented by two NOR gates, the output X does, in fact, go low when A = B = 1. In practice, the user of an RS flip-flop should avoid the condition R = S = 1.

The two-NOR gate flip-flop of Fig. 3.2 has two outputs X and Y. An examination of the circuit for all inputs except A = B = 1 reveals that X and Y are *complements*. Because of the symmetric nature of flip-flops, almost all flip-flops have two outputs, Q and its complement $\overline{Q}$. The complement of Q may not always be available to the user of the flip-flop because many commercial devices leave $\overline{Q}$ buried on the chip and not brought out to a pin. Figure 3.4 gives the circuit representation of an RS flip-flop.

We can draw the truth table of the RS or any other flip-flop in two ways. Up to now we've presented truth tables with two output lines for each possible input, one line for Q = 0 and one for Q = 1. An alternative approach is to employ the algebraic value of Q and is illustrated by Table 3.2.

When R = S = 0 the new output Q^+ is simply the old output Q. In other words, the output doesn't change state and remains in its previous state as long as R and S are both 0. The inputs R = S = 1 result in the output $Q^+ = X$. The symbol X is used in truth tables to indicate an *indeterminate* or *undefined* condition. In Chapter 2 we used the same symbol

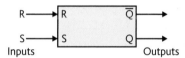

Figure 3.4 Circuit representation of the RS flip-flop as a black box.

Inputs		Output	Description
R	S	Q^+	
0	0	Q	No change
0	1	1	Set output to 1
1	0	0	Reset output to 0
1	1	X	Forbidden

Table 3.2 An alternative truth table for the RS flip-flop.

to indicate a *don't care* condition. An indeterminate condition is one whose outcome can't be calculated, whereas a don't care condition is one whose outcome does not matter to the designer.

3.1.2 Characteristic equation of an RS flip-flop

We have already demonstrated that you can derive an equation for a flip-flop by analyzing its circuit. Such an equation is called the flip-flop's characteristic equation. Instead of using an actual circuit, we can derive a characteristic equation from

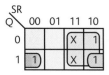

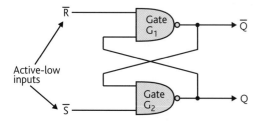

Figure 3.5 Karnaugh map for the characteristic equation of an RS flip-flop.

Inputs		Output	Comment
R	S	Q$^+$	
0	0	X	Forbidden
0	1	1	Reset output to 0
1	0	0	Set output to 1
1	1	Q	No change

Table 3.3 Truth table for an RS flip-flop constructed from NAND gates.

Figure 3.6 RS flip-flop constructed from two cross-coupled NAND gates.

the flip-flop's truth table. Figure 3.5 plots Table 3.1(b) on a Karnaugh map. We have indicated the condition R = S = 1 by X because it is a forbidden condition. From this truth table we can write $Q^+ = S + Q \cdot \overline{R}$.

Note that this equation is slightly different from the one we derived earlier because it treats R = S = 1 as a don't care condition.

3.1.3 Building an RS flip-flop from NAND gates

An RS flip-flop can be constructed from two cross-coupled NAND gates just as easily as from two NOR gates. Figure 3.6 illustrates a two-NAND gate flip-flop whose truth table is given in Table 3.3.

The only significant difference between the NOR gate flip-flop of Fig. 3.2 and the NAND gate flip-flop of Fig. 3.6 is that the inputs to the NAND gate flip-flop are active-low. If we were to place inverters at the R and S inputs to the NAND gate flip-flop, it would then be logically equivalent to the NOR gate flip-flop of Fig. 3.2.

The *no change* input to the NAND gate flip-flop is R, S = 1, 1; the output is cleared by forcing R = 0 and set by forcing S = 0; the forbidden input state is R, S = 0, 0. Suppose that we did set the inputs of a NAND gate RS flip-flop to 0, 0 and then released the inputs to 1,1 to enter the no change state. What would happen? The answer is that we can't predict the final outcome. Initially, when both inputs are 0s, *both* outputs of the RS flip-flop must be 1s (because the output of a NAND gate is a 1 if either of its inputs are a 0). The real problem arises when the inputs change state from 0, 0 to 1, 1. Due to tiny imperfections, either one or the other input would go high before its neighbor and cause the flip-flop to be set or reset.

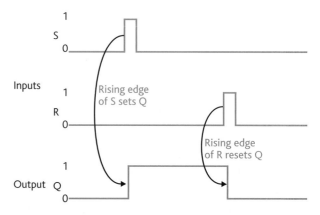

Figure 3.7 Timing diagram of the effect of pulses on an RS flip-flop's inputs.

Real applications of RS flip-flops may employ either two NAND or two NOR gates depending only on which gates provide the simpler solution. In practice, the majority of RS flip-flops are often constructed from NAND gates because most circuits use active-low signals. We began our discussion of RS flip-flops with the NOR gate circuit (unlike other texts that introduce first the more common NAND gate flip-flop) because we have discovered that many students find it hard to come to terms with negative logic (i.e. logic in which the low state is the active state).

3.1.4 Applications of the RS flip-flop

An important application of RS flip-flops is in the recording of short-lived events. If the Q output of a flip-flop is in a zero state, a logical 1 pulse at its S input (assuming the R input is 0) will cause Q to be set to a 1, and to remain at a 1, until the R input resets Q. The effect of a pulse at the S input followed by a pulse at the R input of an RS flip-flop is illustrated in Fig. 3.7.

Consider the following application of RS flip-flops to an indicator circuit. If an aircraft is flown outside its performance envelope no immediate damage may be apparent, but its structure might be permanently weakened. To keep things

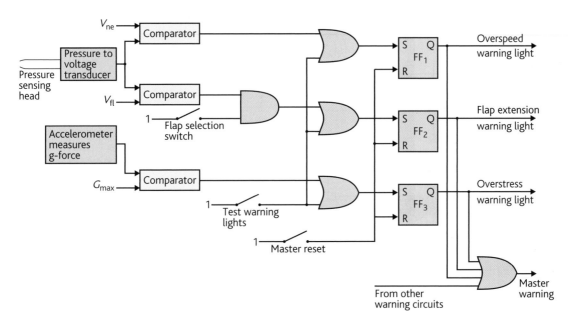

Figure 3.8 Application of RS flip-flops in a warning system.

simple, we will consider three possible events that are considered harmful and might endanger the aircraft.

1. Exceeding the maximum permissible speed V_{ne}.
2. Extending the flaps above the flap-limiting speed V_{fl}. That is, the flaps must not be lowered if the aircraft is going faster than V_{fl}.
3. Exceeding the maximum acceleration (g-force) G_{max}.

If any of the above parameters are exceeded (even for only an instant), a lasting record of the event must be made.

Figure 3.8 shows the arrangement of warning lights used to indicate that one of these conditions has been violated. Transducers that convert acceleration or velocity into a voltage measure the acceleration and speed of the aircraft. The voltages from the transducers are compared with the three threshold values (V_{ne}, V_{fl}, G_{max}) in comparators, whose outputs are true if the threshold is exceeded, otherwise false. In order to detect the extension of flaps above the flap-limiting speed, the output of the comparator is ANDed with a signal from the flap actuator circuit that is true when the flaps are down.

The three signals from the comparators are fed, via OR gates, to the S inputs of three RS flip-flops. Initially, on switching on the system, the flip-flops are automatically reset by applying a logical 1 pulse to all R inputs simultaneously. If at any time one of the S inputs becomes true, the output of that flip-flop is set to a logical 1 and triggers an alarm. All outputs are ORed together to illuminate a master warning light. A master alarm signal makes it unnecessary for the pilot to have to scan all the warning lights periodically. An additional feature of the circuit is a test facility. When the warning

test button is pushed, all warning lights should be illuminated and remain so until the reset button is pressed. A test facility verifies the correct operation of the flip-flops and the warning lights.

A pulse-train generator

Figure 3.9 gives the circuit of a pulse-train generator that generates a sequence of N pulses each time it is triggered by a positive transition at its START input. The value of N is user supplied and is fed to the circuit by three switches to select the values of C_c, C_b, C_a. This circuit uses the counter that we will meet later in this chapter.

The key to this circuit is the RS flip-flop, G_6, used to start and stop the pulse generator. Assume that initially the R and S inputs to the flip-flop are R = 0 and S = 0 and that its output Q is a logical 0. Because one of the inputs to AND gate G_1 is low, the pulse train output is also low.

When a logical 1 pulse is applied to the flip-flop's START input, its Q output rises to a logical 1 and enables AND gate G_1. A train of clock pulses at the second input of G_1 now appears at the output of the AND gate. This gated pulse train is applied to the input of a counter (to be described later), which counts pulses and generates a three-bit output on Q_a, Q_b, Q_c, corresponding to the number of pulses counted in the range 0 to 7. The outputs of the counter are fed to an equality detector composed of three EOR gates, G_2 to G_4, plus NOR gate G_5. A second input to the equality detector is the user-supplied count value C_a, C_b, C_c. The outputs of the EOR gates are combined in NOR gate G_5 (notice that it's drawn in negative logic form to emphasize that the output is 1 if all its inputs are 0).

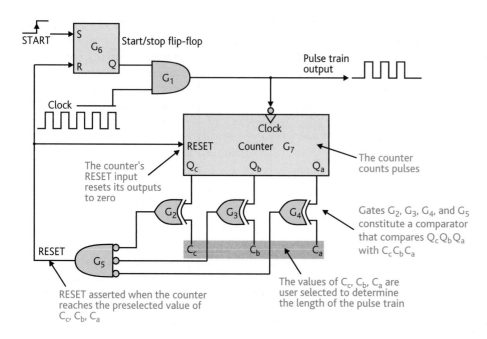

Figure 3.9 Pulse train generator.

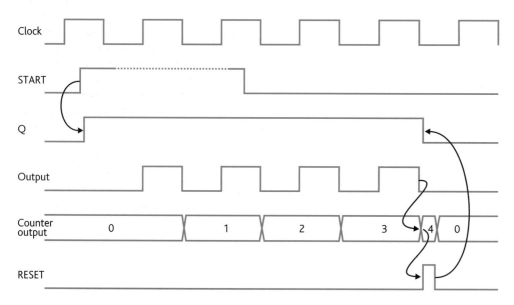

Figure 3.10 Timing diagram of pulse train generator.

Figure 3.10 gives a timing diagram for the pulse generator. Initially the counter is held in a reset state ($Q_a = Q_b = Q_c = 0$). When the counter is clocked, its output is incremented by 1 on the falling edge of each clock pulse. The counter counts upward from 0 and the equality detector compares the current count on Q_a, Q_b, Q_c output with the user-supplied inputs C_a, C_b, C_c. When the output of the counter is equal to the user-supplied input, the output of gate G_5 goes high and resets both the counter and the RS flip-flop. Resetting the counter forces the counter output to 0.

Resetting the RS flip-flop disables AND gate G_1 and no further clock pulses appear at the output of G_1. In this application of the RS flip-flop, its S input is triggered to start an action and its R input is triggered to terminate the action.

3.1.5 The clocked RS flip-flop

The RS flip-flop of Fig. 3.2 responds to signals applied to its inputs according to its truth table. There are situations when we want the RS flip-flop to ignore its inputs until a particular time. The circuit of Fig. 3.11 demonstrates how this is accomplished by turning the RS flip-flop into a clocked RS flip-flop.

A normal, unmodified, RS flip-flop lies in the inner box in Fig. 3.11. Its inputs, R′ and S′, are derived from the external inputs R and S by ANDing them with a clock input C—some texts call these two AND gates '*steering gates*'. As long as C = 0, the inputs to the RS flip-flop, R′ and S′, are forced to remain at 0, no matter what is happening to the external

R and S inputs. The output of the RS flip-flop remains constant as long as these R′ and S′ inputs are both 0.

Whenever C = 1, the external R and S inputs to the circuit are transferred to the flip-flop so that R′ = R and S = S, and the flip-flop responds accordingly. The clock input may be thought of as an *inhibitor*, restraining the flip-flop from acting until the right time. Figure 3.12 demonstrates how we can build a clocked RS flip-flop from NAND gates. Clocked flip-flops are dealt with in more detail later in this chapter.

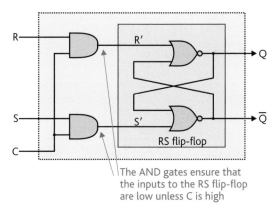

The AND gates ensure that the inputs to the RS flip-flop are low unless C is high

Figure 3.11 The clocked RS flip-flop.

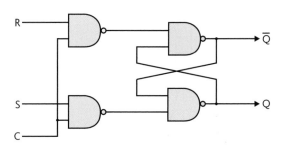

Figure 3.12 Building a clocked RS flip-flop with NAND gates.

3.2 The D flip-flop

Like the RS flip-flop, the D flip-flop has two inputs, one called D and the other C. The D input is referred to as the *data* input and C as the clock input. The D flip-flop is, by its nature, a clocked flip-flop and we will call the act of pulsing the C input high and then low clocking the D flip-flop.

When a D flip-flop is clocked, the value at its D input is transferred to its Q output and the output remains constant until the next time it is clocked. The D flip-flop is a staticizer because it records the state of the D input and holds it constant until it's clocked. Others call it a delay element because, if the D input changes state at time T but the flip-flop is clocked t seconds later, the output Q doesn't change state until t seconds after the input. I think of the D flip-flop as a *census taker* because it takes a census of the input and remembers it until the next census is taken. The truth table for a D flip-flop is given in Table 3.4.

The circuit of a D flip-flop is provided in Fig. 3.13 and consists of an RS flip-flop plus a few gates. The two AND gates turn the RS flip-flop into a clocked RS flip-flop. As long as the C input to the AND gates is low, the R and S inputs are clamped at 0 and Q cannot change.

Full form						Algebraic form		
Inputs			Output Q^+			Inputs		Output Q^+
C	D	Q				C	D	
0	0	0	0	$Q^+ \leftarrow Q$	No change	0	0	Q
0	0	1	1	$Q^+ \leftarrow Q$	No change	0	1	Q
0	1	0	0	$Q^+ \leftarrow Q$	No change	1	0	0
0	1	1	1	$Q^+ \leftarrow Q$	No change	1	1	1
1	0	0	0	$Q^+ \leftarrow D$				
1	0	1	0	$Q^+ \leftarrow D$				
1	1	0	1	$Q^+ \leftarrow D$				
1	1	1	1	$Q^+ \leftarrow D$				

Table 3.4 Truth table for a D flip-flop.

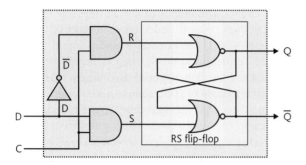

Figure 3.13 Circuit of a D flip-flop.

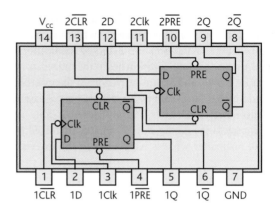

Figure 3.14 The 74LS74 D flip-flop.

When C goes high, the S input is connected to D and the R input to $\overline{D}$. Consequently, (R, S) must either be (0, 1) if D = 1, or (1, 0) if D = 0. Therefore, D = 1 sets the RS flip-flop, and D = 0 clears it.

3.2.1 Practical sequential logic elements

Just as semiconductor manufacturers have provided combinational logic elements in single packages, they have done the same with sequential logic elements. Indeed, there are more special-purpose sequential logic elements than combinational logic elements. Practical flip-flops are more complex than those presented hitherto in this chapter. Real circuits have to cater for real-world problems. We have already said that the output of a flip-flop is a function of its current inputs and its previous output. What happens when a flip-flop is first switched on? The answer is quite simple. The Q output takes on a random state, assuming no input is being applied that will force Q into a 0 or 1 state.

Random states may be fine at the gaming tables in Las Vegas; they're less helpful when the control systems of a nuclear reactor are first energized. Many flip-flops are provided with special control inputs that are used to place them in a known state. Figure 3.14 illustrates the 74LS74, a dual positive-edge triggered D flip-flop that has two active-low control inputs called *preset* and *clear* (abbreviated $\overline{\text{PRE}}$ and $\overline{\text{CLR}}$). In normal operation both $\overline{\text{PRE}}$ and $\overline{\text{CLR}}$ remain in logical 1 states. If $\overline{\text{PRE}}$ = 0 the Q output is set to a logical 1 and if $\overline{\text{CLR}}$ = 0 the Q output is cleared to a logical 0. As in the case of the RS flip-flop, the condition $\overline{\text{PRE}} = \overline{\text{CLR}} = 0$ should not be allowed to occur.

These preset and clear inputs are *unconditional* in the sense that they override all activity at the other inputs of this flip-flop. For example, asserting $\overline{\text{PRE}}$ sets Q to 1 irrespective of the state of the flip-flop's C and D inputs. When a digital system is made up from many flip-flops that must be set or cleared at the application of power, their $\overline{\text{PRE}}$ or $\overline{\text{CLR}}$ lines are connected to a common $\overline{\text{RESET}}$ line and this line is

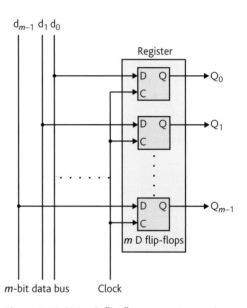

Figure 3.15 Using D flip-flops to create a register.

momentarily asserted active-low by a single pulse shortly after the power is switched on.

3.2.2 Using D flip-flops to create a register

Later we shall discover that a computer is composed of little more than combinational logic elements, buses, and groups of flip-flops called registers that transmit data to and receive data from buses. A typical example of the application of D flip-flops is provided by Fig. 3.15 in which an m-bit wide data bus transfers data from one part of a digital system to another. Data on the bus is constantly changing as different devices use it to transmit their data from one register to another.

The D inputs of a group of m D flip-flops are connected to the m lines of the bus. The clock inputs of all flip-flops are connected together, allowing them to be clocked simultaneously. As long as C = 0, the flip-flops ignore data on the bus and their Q outputs remain unchanged. Suppose some device wishes to transfer its data to the flip-flops. It first puts its data on the bus and then the flip-flops are clocked, latching the data into them. When the clock has returned to zero, the data remains frozen in the flip-flops.

3.2.3 Using Digital Works to create a register

We are now going to use Digital Works to create a simple bused system using D flip-flops. Although Digital Works implements both RS and D flip-flops, we'll construct a D flip-flop from basic gates. Figure 3.16 shows a single 1-bit cell in a register (we can construct an m-bit register by using m identical elements in parallel).

If you examine Fig. 3.16 you will find that the flip-flop is more complex than the simple D flip-flop of Fig. 3.13. We have added a tri-state gate to the Q output to allow the flip-flop to drive a bus or to be disconnected from the bus. Furthermore, we've added an input multiplexer to allow the D input to be connected to one of two sources A and B. The inputs and output of Fig. 3.16 are

- A input
- B input
- A/B select input

- Clock input
- Enable output
- Q output.

In Fig. 3.17 we've used Digital Work's macro facility to convert the circuit in Fig. 3.16 into a black box macro that can be used as a circuit element to build more complex systems.

Figure 3.18 provides a test bed for three of the register slices. We have provided one bit of three registers and three buses (input bus A, input bus B, and output bus C). Each register slice is connected to all three buses. We've added input devices to all the control inputs to enable us to experiment with this circuit.

The system in Fig. 3.18 can't do a lot, but what it can do is very important. Because we've added input devices to buses A and B, we can force our own data on bus A and B. We can select whether each register slice gets its input from bus A or bus B by setting the value of the *Input select* input to 1 (bus A) or 0 (bus B). Data is clocked into any of the register slices by clocking it (i.e. setting its clock input to 1 to capture the data and then setting the clock input to 0 to latch and retain the data). Finally, data from any of the three register slices can be put on bus C by asserting the appropriate output.

This circuit is important because it forms the heart of a computer. All we need to create an ALU (arithmetic and logic unit) are the circuits that take data from bus C, process it, and copy the result to the A or B bus.

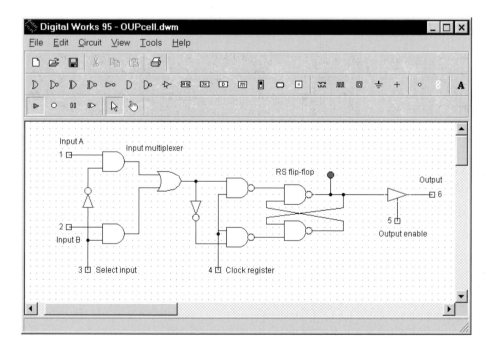

Figure 3.16 Using D flip-flops to create one cell of a register.

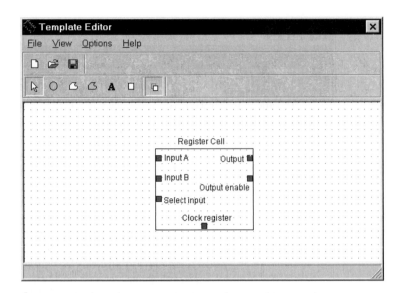

Figure 3.17 Converting the circuit of Fig. 3.16 into a macro (i.e. black box representation).

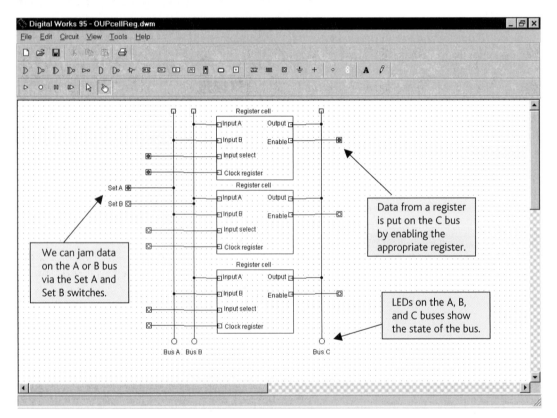

Figure 3.18 Using D flip-flops to create a register in Digital Works.

3.2.4 A typical register chip

You can obtain a single package containing the flip-flops that implement a register. Figure 3.19 illustrates the 74LS373, an octal register composed of D flip-flops that is available in a 20-pin package with eight inputs, eight outputs, two power supply pins, and two control inputs. The clock input, G, is a level-sensitive clock, which, when high, causes the value at D_i to be transferred to Q_i. All eight clock inputs are connected together internally so that the G input clocks each flip-flop simultaneously.

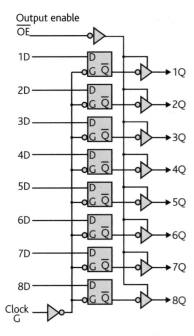

Figure 3.19 The 74LS373 octal register.

The 74LS373's other control input is active-low $\overline{OE}$ (output enable), which controls the output of all flip-flops. When $\overline{OE} = 0$, the flip-flop behaves exactly as we would expect. When $\overline{OE} = 1$, the eight Q outputs are internally disconnected from the output pins of the device; that is, the 74LS373 has tri-state outputs and $\overline{OE}$ is used to turn off the chip's output circuits when it is not driving a bus.

Figure 3.20 demonstrates the 74LS373 octal register in a digital system where four registers are connected to a common data bus. Each register is arranged with *both* its outputs and its inputs connected to the same bus allowing it to transmit data onto the bus or to receive data from it.

Each register has tri-state outputs controlled by an output enable pin. When $\overline{OE}$ is asserted low, the corresponding register drives the bus. Registers are clocked by an active-high clock input labeled G.

IC5a is a 2-line to 4-line decoder; that is, a demultiplexer of the type we described in Chapter 2. When this device is enabled, the 2-bit binary *source code* at the input of IC5a causes one of its output lines, $\overline{Y}_0$ to $\overline{Y}_3$, to go low. These outputs are connected to the respective $\overline{OE}$ inputs of the four registers. Each of the four possible source codes enables one of the registers; for example, if the source code at the input to IC5a is 01, the output of register 1 is enabled and the contents of register 1 are placed on the bus. The outputs of all other registers remain internally disconnected from the bus.

The 74LS139 contains two complete 2-line to 4-line decoders in a single 16-pin package. The second half of this package acts as a destination decoder. Each of the four outputs from IC5b is connected to one of the clock inputs, G, of

the four registers. Because the clock inputs are active-high and the outputs of the decoder are active-low, it's necessary to invert these outputs. Four inverters, IC6, perform this function. When IC5b is enabled, one of its outputs is asserted and the corresponding register clocked. Clocking a register latches data from the data bus.

Suppose the contents of register 1 are to be copied into register 3. The source code at IC5a is set to 01 and the destination code at IC5b is set to 11. This puts the data from register 1 on the bus and latches the data into register 3. We can easily relate the example of Fig. 3.20 to the digital computer. One of the most fundamental operations in computing is the assignment that can be represented in a high-level language as B = A and in a low-level language as MOVE A, **B**. The action MOVE A, **B** (i.e. transfer the contents of A to B) is implemented by specifying A as the source and B as the destination. Note that throughout this text we put the destination of a data transfer in bold font to stress the direction of data transfer.

3.3 Clocked flip-flops

Before we introduce the JK flip-flop we look more closely at the idea of *clocking* sequential circuits. Clocked circuits allow logic elements to respond to their inputs only when the inputs are valid. Some writers use the term *trigger* rather than clock, because *triggering a flip-flop* gives the impression of causing an event to take place at a discrete instant. We begin by examining the effect of delays on the passage of signals through systems.

Figure 3.21 demonstrates the effect of circuit delays on a system with two inputs, A and B, that are acted upon by *processes* A, B, and C to produce an output. The nature of the processes is not important because we're interested only in the way in which they delay signals passing through them. Imagine that at time $t = 0$, the inputs to processes A and B become valid (i.e. these are the correct inputs to be operated on by the processes). Assume that process A in Fig. 3.21 introduces a two-unit delay, process B a one-unit delay, and process C a two-unit delay.

Although the output from process B becomes valid at $t = 1$, it's not until $t = 2$ that the output of process A has become valid. The outputs of processes A and B are fed to process C, which has a two-unit delay. Clearly, the desired output from C due to inputs A and B is not valid until at least *four* time units after $t = 0$. The output from process C changes at least once before it settles down to its final value (Why? Because of the different delays through processes A and B). This poses a problem. How does an observer at the output of process C know when to act upon the data from C?

What we need is some means of capturing data only when we know that it's valid—see Fig. 3.22. If a D flip-flop is placed

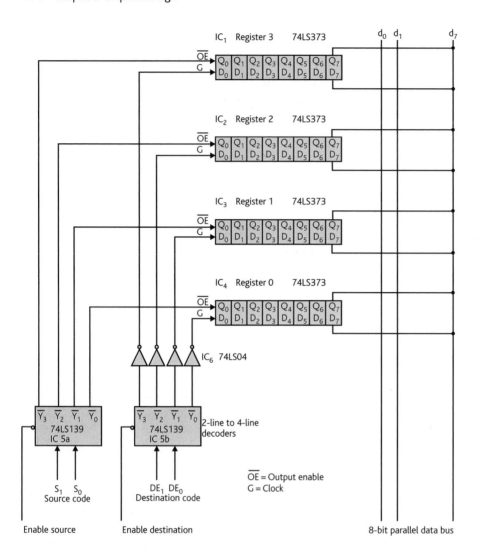

Figure 3.20 Using the 74LS373 octal register in a bused system.

at the output of process C and is clocked four units of time after $t = 0$, the desired data will be latched into the flip-flop and held constant until the next clock pulse. Clocked systems hold digital information constant in flip-flops while the information is operated on by groups of logic elements, analogous to the processes of Fig. 3.21. Between clock pulses, the outputs of the flip-flops are processed by the logic elements and the new data values are presented to the inputs of flip-flops.

After a suitable time delay (longer than the time taken for the slowest process to be completed), the flip-flops are clocked. The outputs of the processes are held constant until the next time the flip-flops are clocked. A clocked system is often called *synchronous*, as all processes are started simultaneously on each new clock pulse. An *asynchronous* system is one in which the end of one process signals (i.e. triggers) the start of the next. Obviously, an asynchronous system must be faster than the corresponding synchronous system. Asynchronous systems are more complex and difficult to design than synchronous

systems and popular wisdom says that they are best avoided because they are inherently less reliable than synchronous circuits. The 1990s saw a renewed interest in asynchronous systems because of their speed and lower power consumption.

3.3.1 Pipelining

Now consider the effect of placing D flip-flops at the *outputs* of processes A, B, and C in the system of Fig. 3.23. Figure 3.23 shows the logical state at several points in a system as a function of time. The diagram is read from left to right (the direction of time flow). Signals are represented by parallel lines to demonstrate that the signal values may be 1s or 0s (we don't care). What matters is the time at which signals change. Changes are shown by the parallel lines crossing over. Lines with arrowheads are drawn between points to demonstrate cause and effect; for example, the line from *Input* A to *Output* A shows that a change in *Input* A leads to a change in *Output* A.

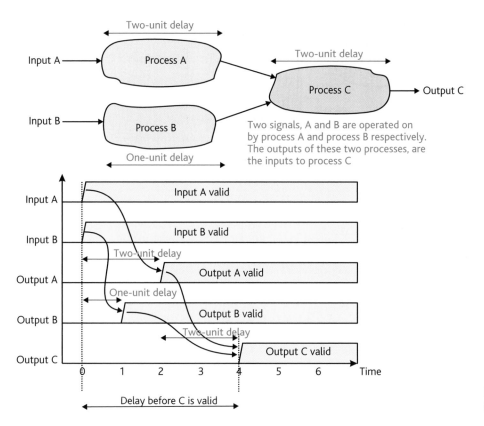

Figure 3.21 Processes and delays.

In this example we assume that each of the processes introduces a single unit of delay and the flip-flops are clocked simultaneously every unit of time. Figure 3.23 gives the timing diagram for this system. Note how a new input can be accepted every unit of time, rather than every two units of time as you might expect. The secret of our increase in throughput is called *pipelining* because we are operating on different data at different stages in the pipeline. For example, when process A and process B are operating on data *i*, process C is operating on data $i - 1$ and the latched output from process C corresponds to data $i - 2$.

When we introduce the RISC processor we will discover that pipelining is a technique used to speed up the operation of a computer by overlapping consecutive operations.

3.3.2 Ways of clocking flip-flops

A clocked flip-flop captures a digital value and holds it constant. There are, however, three ways of clocking a flip-flop.

1. Whenever the clock is asserted (i.e. a level-sensitive flip-flop).
2. Whenever the clock is changing state (i.e. an edge-sensitive flip-flop).
3. Capture data on one edge of the clock and transfer it to the output on the following edge (i.e. a master–slave flip-flop).

A *level-sensitive* clock triggers a flip-flop whenever the clock is in a particular logical state (some flip-flops are clocked by a logical 1 and some by a logical 0). The clocked RS flip-flop of Fig. 3.11 is level sensitive because the RS flip-flop responds to its R and S inputs whenever the clock input is high. A level-sensitive clock is unsuitable for certain applications. Consider the system of Fig. 3.24 in which the output of a D flip-flop is fed through a logic network and then back to the flip-flop's D input. If we call the output of the flip-flop the *current* Q, then the current Q is fed through the logic network to generate a *new* input D. When the flip-flop is clocked, the value of D is transferred to the output to generate Q^+.

If the clock is level sensitive, the new Q^+ can rush through the logic network and change D and hence the output. This chain of events continues in an oscillatory fashion with the *dog chasing its tail*. To avoid such unstable or unpredictable behavior, we need an infinitesimally short clock pulse to capture the output and hold it constant. As such a short pulse can't easily be created, the edge-sensitive clock has been introduced to solve the feedback problem. Level-sensitive clocked D flip-flops are often perfectly satisfactory in applications such as registers connected to data buses, because the duration of the clock is usually small compared to the time for which the data is valid.

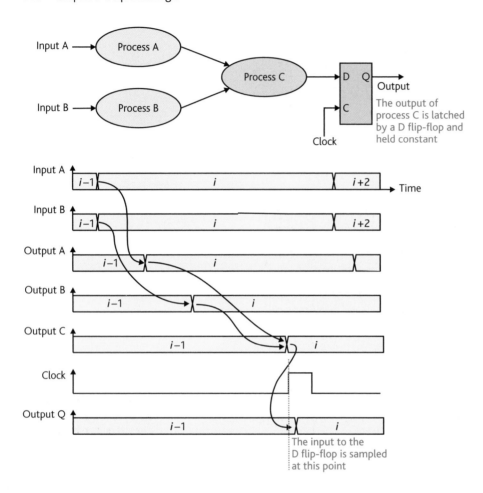

Figure 3.22 Latching the output of a system.

3.3.3 Edge-triggered flip-flops

An edge-triggered flip-flop is clocked not by the level or *state* of the clock (i.e. high or low), but by the *transition* of the clock signal from zero to one, or one to zero. The former case is called a positive or rising-edge sensitive clock and the latter is called a negative or falling-edge sensitive clock. As the rising or falling edge of a pulse may have a duration of less than 1 ns, an edge-triggered clock can be regarded as a level-sensitive clock triggered by a pulse of an infinitesimally short duration. A nanosecond (ns) is a thousand millionth (10^{-9}) of a second. The feedback problem described by Fig. 3.24 ceases to exist if you use an edge-sensitive flip-flop because there's insufficient time for the new output to race back to the input within the duration of a single rising edge.

There are circumstances when edge-triggered flip-flops are unsatisfactory because of a phenomenon called clock *skew*. If, in a digital system, several edge-triggered flip-flops are clocked by the same edge of a pulse, the exact times at which the individual flip-flops are clocked vary. Variation in the arrival time of pulses at each clock input is called *clock skew* and is caused by the different paths by which clock pulses

reach each flip-flop. Electrical impulses move through circuits at somewhat less than the speed of light, which is 30 cm/ns. Unless each flip-flop is located at the same distance from the source of the clock pulse and unless any additional delays in each path due to other logic elements are identical, the clock pulse will arrive at the flip-flops at different instants. Moreover, the delay a signal experiences going through a gate changes with temperature and even the age of the gate. Suppose that the output of flip-flop A is connected to the input of flip-flop B and they are clocked together. Ideally, at the moment of clocking, the old output of A is clocked into B. If, by bad design or bad luck, flip-flop A is triggered a few nanoseconds before flip-flop B, B sees the new output from A, not the old (i.e. previous) output—it's as if A were clocked by a separate and earlier clock.

Figure 3.25 gives the circuit diagram of a positive edge-triggered D flip-flop that also has unconditional preset and clear inputs. Edge triggering is implemented by using the active transition of the clock to clock latches 1 and 2 and then feeding the output of latch 2 back to latch 1 to cut off the clock in the NAND gate. That is, once the clock has been detected, the clock input path is removed.

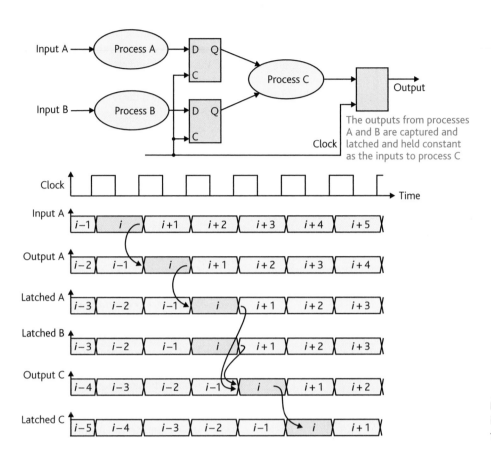

Figure 3.23 Latching the input and output of processes to implement pipelining.

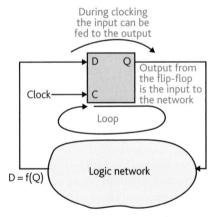

Figure 3.24 Feedback and the level-sensitive clock.

3.3.4 The master–slave flip-flop

The master–slave (MS) flip-flop has the external appearance of a single flip-flop, but internally is arranged as two flip-flops operating in series. One of these flip-flops is called the *master* and the other the *slave*. The term *slave* is used because the slave flip-flop follows the *master*. Figure 3.26 describes a

simple RS master–slave flip-flop composed of two RS flip-flops in series. Note that the master flip-flop is enabled when the clock is high and the slave flip-flop is enabled when the clock is low.

When the clock pulse goes high, the input data at the R and S input terminals of the master flip-flop is copied into the master flip-flop. At this point, the output terminals of the master–slave flip-flop aren't affected and don't change state because the output comes from the slave flip-flop that is in a hold state because its clock is low.

Because the master flip-flop of Fig. 3.26 uses a level-sensitive RS flip-flop, the master responds to data at its RS inputs as long as the clock is asserted high. The data at the RS inputs of the master is latched by the master at the instant the clock input goes low. On the falling edge of the clock, the slave's clock input goes high and data from the master flip-flop's outputs is copied into the save flip-flop. Only now may the output terminals change state. Figure 3.27 provides a timing diagram for the master–slave RS flip-flop.

Master–slave flip-flops totally isolate their input terminals from their output terminals simply because the output of the slave flip-flop does not change until *after* the input conditions have been sampled and latched internally in the master. Conceptually, the master–slave flip-flop behaves like an air

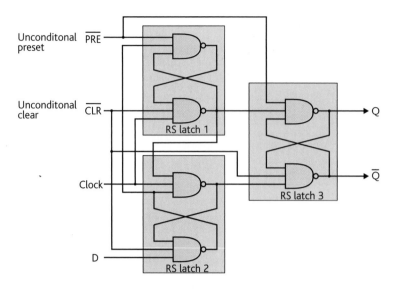

Unconditonal preset $\overline{PRE}$

Unconditonal clear $\overline{CLR}$

RS latch 1

Clock

D

RS latch 2

RS latch 3

Q

$\overline{Q}$

Figure 3.25 Circuit of an edge-triggered flip-flop.

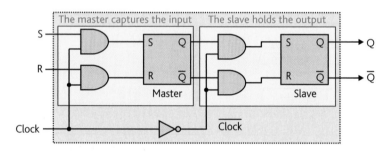

The master captures the input   The slave holds the output

S

R

S   Q

R $\overline{Q}$

Master

S   Q

R $\overline{Q}$

Slave

Q

$\overline{Q}$

Clock

$\overline{Clock}$

Figure 3.26 The master–slave RS flip-flop.

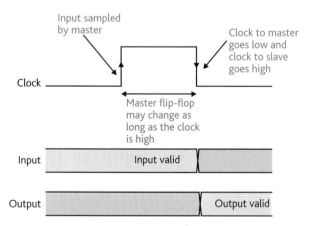

Input sampled by master

Clock to master goes low and clock to slave goes high

Clock

Master flip-flop may change as long as the clock is high

Input   Input valid

Output   Output valid

Figure 3.27 Timing diagram of a master–slave RS flip-flop.

lock in a submarine or spacecraft. An air lock exists to transfer people between regions of different pressure (air-to-vacuum or air-to-water) without ever permitting a direct path between the two pressure regions. A flip-flop is analogous to an air lock because its output must not be fed directly back to its input. To operate an air lock in a submarine, divers in the water open the air lock, enter, and close the door behind them. The divers are now isolated from both the water outside and the air inside. When the divers open the door into the submarine, they step inside and close the air lock door behind them.

In order to demonstrate how the different types of clocked flip-flop behave, Fig. 3.28 presents the output waveforms for four clocked D flip-flops when presented with the same input.

3.3.5 Bus arbitration—an example

We now look at a more advanced application of flip-flops in a *bus arbitration circuit* that decides which of two processors get to access a block of common memory, called dual-ported RAM, when both processors want the memory at the same time. Students may omit this section on a first reading.

Let's look at a system with two processors that communicate via a common block of RAM called DPRAM (dual-ported RAM). Figure 3.29 describes such an arrangement. You could regard the DPRAM as a bridge between two buses.

Because both processors 1 and 2 operate independently, either processor may access the common memory at any time. We need a means of requesting control of the common memory and getting access to the memory even if both processors make near-simultaneous requests.

Figure 3.30 describes an arbiter with a clock input, two request inputs, and two grant outputs. The request and grant inputs and outputs are all active-low. The memory-request inputs, $\overline{Request1}$ and $\overline{Request2}$, are sampled by two positive-edge triggered latches. The arbiter clocks latch 1a on the rising edge of the clock and latch 2a on the falling edge of the clock. This arrangement ensures that the two request inputs are not sampled simultaneously.

Figure 3.31 provides a timing diagram for the case in which both processors request the bus simultaneously. As we can see, processor 2 wins the request and processor 1 must wait until processor 2 has relinquished the bus. That is, processor 1 does not have to try again—it simply waits for the memory to become free. Processor 1 determines that the bus is once more free.

Initially, the arbiter is in an idle state with both request inputs inactive-high. Therefore, both D inputs to latches 1a and 2a are high and in a steady-state condition. Outputs AA, BB, Grant1, and Grant2 are all high.

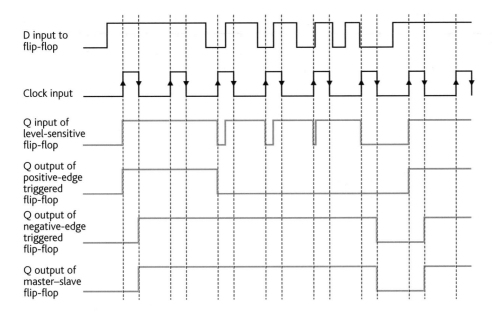

Figure 3.28 Comparison of flip-flop clocking modes.

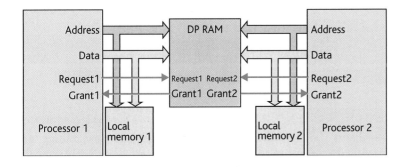

Figure 3.29 Two processors communicating via dual-ported RAM.

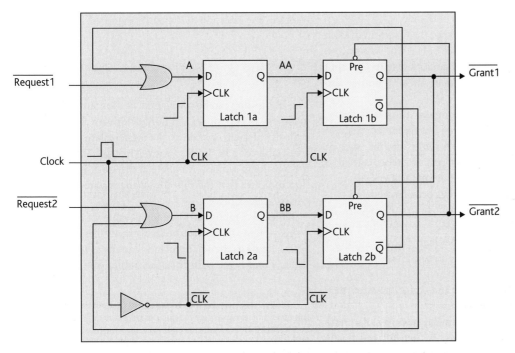

Figure 3.30 An arbiter circuit.

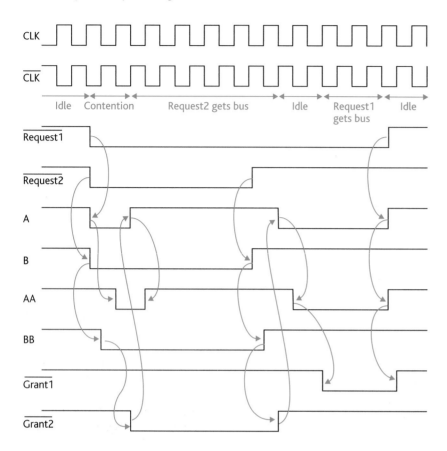

Figure 3.31 Timing diagram for Fig. 3.30.

Suppose that $\overline{\text{Request1}}$ and $\overline{\text{Request2}}$ are asserted almost simultaneously when the clock is in a high state. This results in the outputs of both OR gates (A and B) going low simultaneously. The cross-coupled feedback inputs to the OR gates (Grant1 and Grant2) are currently both low.

On the next rising edge of the clock, the Q output of latch 1a (i.e. AA) and the Q output of latch 2a (i.e. BB) both go low. However, as latch 2a sees a rising edge clock first, its Q output goes low one half a clock cycle before latch 1's output also goes low.

When a latch is clocked at the moment its input is changing, it may enter a metastable[1] state lasting for up to about 75 ns before the output of the latch settles into one state or the other. For this reason a second pair of latches is used to sample the input latches after a period of 80 ns.

One clock cycle after $\overline{\text{Request2}}$ has been latched and output BB forced low, the output of latch 2b, $\overline{\text{Grant2}}$ goes low. Its complement, Grant2 is fed back to OR gate 1, forcing input A high. After a clock cycle AA also goes high. Because $\overline{\text{Grant2}}$ is connected to latch 1b's active-low preset input, latch 1b is held in a high state.

At this point, $\overline{\text{Grant1}}$ is negated and $\overline{\text{Grant2}}$ asserted, permitting processor 2 to access the bus.

When processor 1 relinquishes the memory, $\overline{\text{Request2}}$ becomes inactive-high, causing first B, then BB and finally $\overline{\text{Grant2}}$ to be negated as the change ripples through the arbiter. Once $\overline{\text{Grant2}}$ is high, Grant2 goes low, causing the output of OR gate 1 (i.e. A) to go low. This is clocked through latches 1a and 1b to force $\overline{\text{Grant1}}$ low and therefore permit processor 1 to access the memory. Of course, once $\overline{\text{Grant1}}$ is asserted, any assertion of Request2 is ignored.

3.4 The JK flip-flop

The JK flip-flop can be configured, or programmed, to operate in one of two modes. All JK flip-flops are clocked and the majority of them operate on the master–slave principle. The truth table for a JK flip-flop is given in Table 3.5 and Fig. 3.32 gives its logic symbol. A bubble at the clock input to a flip-flop indicates that the flip-flop changes state on the *falling* edge of a clock pulse.

Table 3.5 demonstrates that for all values of J and K, except $J = K = 1$, the JK flip-flop behaves exactly like an RS flip-flop with J acting as the set input and K acting as the reset input. When J and K are both true, the output of the JK flip-flop

---

[1] If a latch is clocked at the exact moment its input is changing state, it can enter a metastable state in which its output is undefined and it may even oscillate for a few nanoseconds. You can avoid the effects of metastability by latching a signal, waiting for it to settle, and then capturing it in a second latch.

Full form					Algebraic form		
Inputs			Output		Inputs		Output
J	K	Q	Q^+		J	K	Q^+
0	0	0	0	No change	0	0	Q	No change
0	0	1	1	No change	0	1	0	Clear
0	1	0	0	Reset Q	1	0	1	Set
0	1	1	0	Reset Q	1	1	$\overline{Q}$	Toggle
1	0	0	1	Set Q				
1	0	1	1	Set Q				
1	1	0	1	$Q^+ \leftarrow \overline{Q}$				
1	1	1	0	$Q^+ \leftarrow \overline{Q}$				

Table 3.5 Truth table for a JK flip-flop.

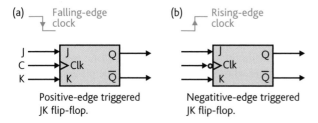

Figure 3.32 Representation of the JK flip-flop.

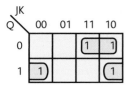

Figure 3.33 Deriving the characteristic equation of a JK flip-flop.

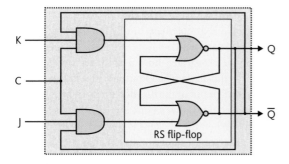

Figure 3.34 Construction of a basic JK flip-flop.

toggles, or changes state, each time the flip-flop is clocked. That is, if Q was a 0 it becomes a 1 and vice versa. It is this property that puts the JK flip-flop at the heart of many counter circuits, the operation of which is dealt with in the

next section. Note that the *T flip-flop* is a JK flip-flop with J = K = 1, which changes state on each clock pulse (we don't deal with T flip-flops further in this text).

We can derive the characteristic equation for a JK flip-flop by plotting Table 3.5 on a Karnaugh map, Fig. 3.33. This gives $Q^+ = J \cdot \overline{Q} + \overline{K} \cdot Q$.

Figure 3.34 demonstrates how a JK flip-flop can be constructed from NAND gates and Fig. 3.35 describes a master–slave JK flip-flop.

3.5 Summary of flip-flop types

To understand flip-flops, it's necessary to appreciate that, unlike combinational circuits, they have internal states as well as external inputs; that is, the output of a flip-flop depends on the previous inputs of the flip-flop. Flip-flops are therefore *memory elements*. The most common forms of flip-flop are the D flip-flop, the RS flip-flop, and the JK flip-flop. Each flip-flop has two outputs, $\overline{Q}$ and its complement Q, although the complementary output is not always connected to a pin in an integrated circuit. Most flip-flops are clocked and have a clock input that is used to trigger the flip-flop. Flip-flops often have unconditional preset and clear inputs that can be used the set or clear the output, respectively. The term unconditional means that these inputs override any clock input.

The D flip-flop D flip-flops have two inputs, a D (data) input and a C (clock) input. The output of a D flip-flop remains in its previous state until its C input is clocked. When its C input is clocked, the Q output becomes equal to D *until the next time it is clocked.*

The RS flip-flop An RS flip-flop has two inputs, R (reset) and S (set). As long as both R and S are 0, the Q output of the RS flip-flop is constant and remains in its previous state. When R = 1 and S = 0, the Q output is forced to 0 (and

The master stage captures the input and holds it constant

The slave stage copies the previous captured input to the output terminals and holds it constant while the next input is being captured

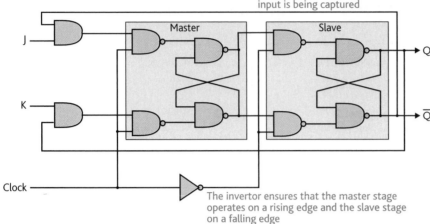

The invertor ensures that the master stage operates on a rising edge and the slave stage on a falling edge

Figure 3.35 Circuit diagram of a master–slave JK flip-flop.

remains at zero when R returns to 0). When S = 1 and R = 0, the Q output is forced to one (and remains at one when S returns to 0). The input conditions R = S = 1 produce an *indeterminate state* and should be avoided. Clocked RS flip-flops behave as we have described, except that their R and S inputs are treated as zero until the flip-flop is clocked. When the RS flip-flop is clocked, its Q output behaves as we have just described.

The JK flip-flop The JK flip-flop always has three inputs, J, K, and a clock input C. As long as a JK flip-flop is not clocked, its output remains in the previous state. When a JK flip-flop is clocked, it behaves like an RS flip-flop (where J = S, K = R) for all input conditions except J = K = 1. If J = K = 0, the output does not change state. If K = 1 and J = 0, the Q output is reset to zero. If J = 1 and K = 0, the Q output is set to 1. If both J and K are 1, the output changes state (or *toggles*) each time it is clocked.

The T flip-flop The T flip-flop has a single clock input. Each time it is clocked, its output *toggles* or changes state. A T flip-flop is functionally equivalent to a JK flip-flop with J = K = 1.

3.6 Applications of sequential elements

Just as the logic gate is combined with other gates to form combinational circuits such as adders and multiplexers, flip-flops can be combined together to create a class of circuits called *sequential circuits*. Here, we are concerned with two particular types of sequential circuit: the *shift register*, which moves a group of bits left or right and the *counter*, which steps through a sequence of values.

3.6.1 **Shift register**

By slightly modifying the circuit of the register we can build a *shift register* whose bits can be moved one place right every time the register is clocked. For example, the binary pattern

	01110101
becomes	00111010 after the shift register is clocked once
and	00011101 after it is clocked twice
and	00001110 after it is clocked three times, and so on.

Note that after the first shift, a 0 has been shifted in from the left-hand end and the 1 at the right-hand end has been lost. We used the expression *binary pattern* because, as we shall see later, the byte 01110101 can represent many things. However, when the pattern represents a binary number, shifting it one place right has the effect of dividing the number by two (just as shifting a decimal number one place right divides it by 10). Similarly, shifting a number one place *left* multiplies it by 2. Later we will see that special care has to be taken when shifting signed two's complement binary numbers right (the sign-bit has to be dealt with).

Figure 3.36 demonstrates how a shift register is constructed from D flip-flops. The Q output of each flip-flop is connected to the D input of the flip-flop on its right. All clock inputs are connected together so that each flip-flop is clocked simultaneously. When the ith stage is clocked, its output, Q_i, takes on the value from the stage on its left, that is, $Q_i \leftarrow Q_{i+1}$. Data presented at the input of the left-hand flip-flop, D_{in}, is shifted into the $(m-1)$th stage at each clock pulse. Figure 3.36 describes a *right*-shift register—we will look at registers that shift the data sequence left shortly.

The flip-flops in a shift register must either be edge-triggered or master-slave flip-flops, otherwise if a level-sensitive flip-flop were used, the value at the input to the left-hand

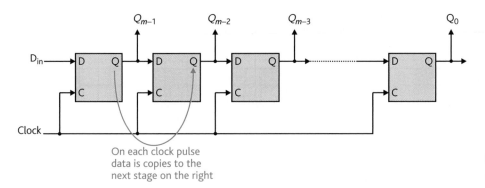

On each clock pulse data is copies to the next stage on the right

Figure 3.36 The right-shift register.

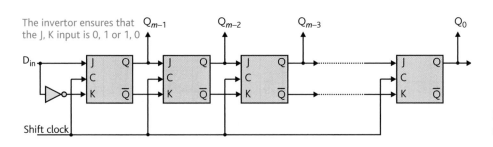

The invertor ensures that the J, K input is 0, 1 or 1, 0

Figure 3.37 Shift register composed of JK flip-flops.

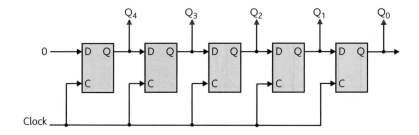

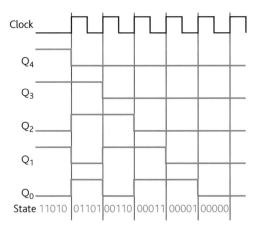

Figure 3.38 Example of a five-stage shift-right register.

stage would ripple through all stages as soon as the clock went high. We can construct a shift register from JK flip-flops just as easily as from RS flip-flops as Fig. 3.37 demonstrates.

Figure 3.38 shows a five-stage shift register that contains the initial value 01101. At each clock pulse the bits are shifted right and a 0 enters the most-significant bit stage. This figure also provides a timing diagram for each of the five Q outputs. The output of the right-hand stage, Q_0, consists of a series of five sequential pulses, corresponding to the five bits of the word in the shift register (i.e. 11010).

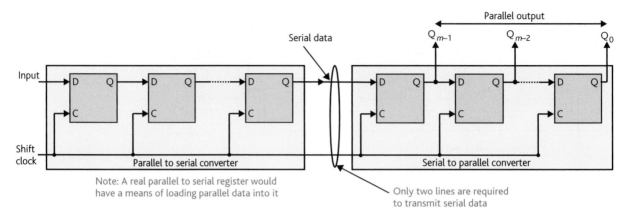

Figure 3.39 Serial to parallel converter.

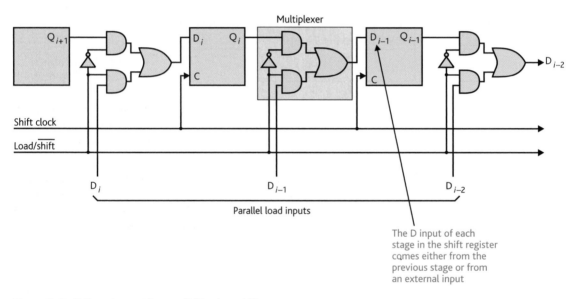

Figure 3.40 Shift register with a parallel load capability.

A shift register can be used to convert a parallel word of m bits into a serial word of m consecutive bits. Such a circuit is called a *parallel to serial converter*. If the output of an m-bit parallel to serial converter is connected to the D_{in} input of an m-bit shift register, after m clock pulses the information in the parallel to serial converter has been transferred to the second (right-hand) shift register. Such a shift register is called a *serial to parallel converter* and Fig. 3.39 describes a simplified version. In practice, a means of loading parallel data into the parallel-to-serial converter is necessary (see Fig. 3.40). There is almost no difference between a parallel to serial converter and a serial to parallel converter.

A flaw in our shift register (when operating as a parallel to serial converter) is the lack of any facilities for loading it with m bits of data at one go, rather than by shifting in m bits through D_{in}. Figure 3.40 shows a right-shift register with a parallel load capacity. A two-input multiplexer, composed of two AND gates, an OR gate, and an inverter switches a flip-flop's D input between the output of the previous stage to the left (*shift* mode) and the load input (*load* mode). The control inputs of all multiplexers are connected together to provide the mode control, labeled load/$\overline{shift}$. When we label a variable name1/$\overline{name2}$, we mean that when the variable is high it carries out action *name1* and when it is low it carries out action *name2*. If load/$\overline{shift}$ = 0 the operation performed is a shift and if load/$\overline{shift}$ = 1 the operation performed is a load.

Constructing a left-shift register with JK flip-flops

Although we've considered the right-shift register, a left-shift register is easy to design. The input of the ith stage, D_i, is

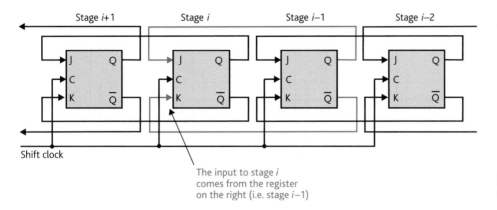

Shift clock

The input to stage *i* comes from the register on the right (i.e. stage *i*−1)

Figure 3.41 The left-shift register.

Shift type	Shift left	Shift right
Original bit pattern before shift	11010111	11010111
Logical shift	10101110	01101011
Arithmetic shift	10101110	11101011
Circular shift	10101111	11101011

Table 3.6 The effect of logical, arithmetic, and circular shifts.

connected to the output of the $(i − 1)$th stage so that, at each clock pulse, $Q_i \leftarrow D_{i-1}$. In terms of the previous example

        01110101
becomes   11101010 after one shift left
and   11212100 after two shifts left

The structure of a left-shift register composed of JK flip-flops is described in Fig. 3.41.

When we introduce the instruction set of a typical computer we'll see that there are several types of shift (logical, arithmetic, circular). These operations all shift bits left or right—the only difference between them concerns what happens to the bit shifted in. So far we've described the *logical* shift where a 0 is shifted in and the bit shifted out at the other end is lost. In an *arithmetic* shift the sign of 2's complement number is preserved when it is shifted right (this will become clear when we introduce the representation of negative numbers in the next chapter). In a *circular* shift the bit shifted out of one end becomes the bit shifted in at the other end. Table 3.6 describes what happens when the 8-bit value 11010111 undergoes three types of shift.

A typical shift register

Figure 3.42 gives the internal structure of a 74LS95 parallel-access bidirectional shift register chip. You access the shift register through its pins and cannot make connections to the internal parts of its circuit. Indeed, its actual internal implementation may differ from the published circuit. As long as it behaves like its published circuit, the precise implementation of

its logic function doesn't matter to the end user. The 74LS95 is a versatile shift register and has the following functions.

Parallel load The four bits of data to be loaded into the shift register are applied to its parallel inputs, the mode control input is set to a logical one, and a clock pulse applied to the clock 2 input. The data is loaded on the falling edge of the clock 2 pulse.

Right-shift A shift right is accomplished by setting the mode control input to a logical zero and applying a pulse to the clock 1 input. The shift takes place on the falling edge of the clock pulse.

Left-shift A shift left is accomplished by setting the mode control input to a logical one and applying a pulse to the clock 2 input. The shift takes place on the falling edge of the clock pulse. A left shift requires that the output of each flip-flop be connected to the parallel input of the previous flip-flop and serial data entered at the D input.

Table 3.7 provides a function table for this shift register (taken from the manufacturer's literature). This table describes the behavior of the shift register for all combinations of its inputs. Note that the table includes don't care values of inputs and the effects of input *transitions* (indicated by ↓ and ↑).

Designing a versatile shift register—an example

Let's design an 8-bit shift register to perform the following operations.

(a) Load each stage from an 8-bit data bus	(parallel load)
(b) Logical shift left	(0 in, MSB lost)
(c) Logical shift right	(0 in, LSB lost)
(d) Arithmetic shift left	(same as logical shift left)
(e) Arithmetic shift right	(MSB replicated, LSB lost)
(f) Circular shift left	(MSB moves to LSB position)
(g) Circular shift right	(LSB moves to MSB position)

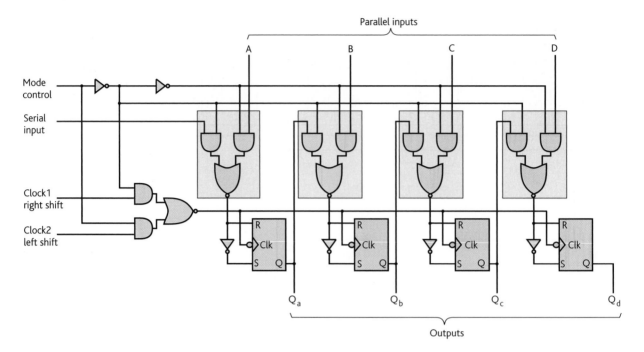

Figure 3.42 The left-shift register.

Inputs								Outputs			
Mode control	Clocks		Serial	Parallel inputs				Q_a	Q_b	Q_c	Q_d
	2 (L)	1(R)		A	B	C	D				
1	1	x	x	x	x	x	x	Q_{a0}	Q_{b0}	Q_{c0}	Q_{d0}
1	↓	x	x	A	B	C	D	A	B	C	D
1	↓	x	x	Q_b	Q_c	Q_d	D	Q_{bn}	Q_{cn}	Q_{dn}	D
0	0	1	x	x	x	x	x	Q_{a0}	Q_{b0}	Q_{c0}	Q_{d0}
0	x	↓	1	x	x	x	x	1	Q_{an}	Q_{bn}	Q_{cn}
0	x	↓	0	x	x	x	x	0	Q_{an}	Q_{bn}	Q_{cn}
↑	0	0	x	x	x	x	x	Q_{a0}	Q_{b0}	Q_{c0}	Q_{d0}
↓	0	0	x	x	x	x	x	Q_{a0}	Q_{b0}	Q_{c0}	Q_{d0}
↓	0	1	x	x	x	x	x	Q_{a0}	Q_{b0}	Q_{c0}	Q_{d0}
↑	1	0	x	x	x	x	x	Q_{a0}	Q_{b0}	Q_{c0}	Q_{d0}
↑	1	1	x	x	x	x	x	Q_{a0}	Q_{b0}	Q_{c0}	Q_{d0}

Notes   1. Left-shift operations assume that Q_b is connected to A, Q_c to B, and Q_d to C.
        2. x = don't care.
        3. ↓ and ↑ indicate high-to-low and low-to-high transitions, respectively.
        4. Q_{a0} indicates the level at Q_a before the indicated inputs were established.
        5. Q_{an} indicates the level of Q_a before the ↓ transition of the clock.

Table 3.7 Function table for a 74LS95 shift register.

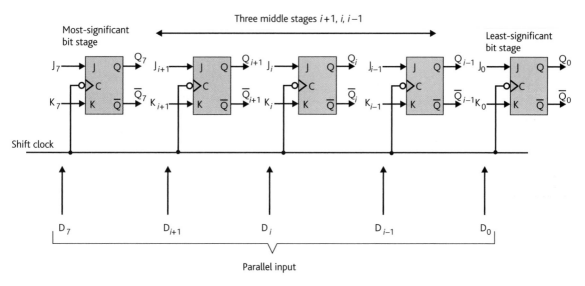

Figure 3.43 End and middle stages of a shift register.

The circuit is composed of eight master–slave JK flip-flops and has a clock input that causes operations (a)–(g) above to be carried out on its falling edge. The circuit has five control inputs:

R   When R = 1 shift right, when R = 0 shift left.
S   When S = 1 perform a shift operation, when S = 0 a parallel load.
L   When L = 1 perform a logical shift (if S = 1).
A   When A = 1 perform an arithmetic shift (if S = 1).
C   When C = 1 perform a circular shift (if S = 1).

Assume that illegal combinations of L, A, and C cannot occur because only one type of shift can be performed at a time. Therefore, more than one of L, A, and C, will never be true simultaneously.

For all eight stages of the shift register obtain algebraic expressions for J and K in terms of control inputs R, S, L, A, and C and the outputs of the flip-flops.

Figure 3.43 illustrates five stages of the shift register. These are the end stages Q_7 and Q_0, the most-significant and least-significant bit stages, respectively. A non-end stage Q_i, together with its left-hand neighbor Q_{i+1} and its right-hand neighbor Q_{i-1}, must also be considered.

All stages except 0 and 7 perform the same functions: parallel load, shift right, and shift left. As the JK flip-flops always load from an external input or another stage, only the inputs J = 1, K = 0, or J = 0, K = 1 have to be considered. Consequently, $J = \overline{K}$ and we need only derive expressions for J, as the corresponding values for K can be obtained from an inverter.

Stage i

Parallel load	$J_i = D_i$	S = 0
Shift right	$J_i = Q_{i+1}$	S = 1, R = 1
Shift left	$J_i = Q_{i-1}$	S = 1, R = 0

Therefore, $J_i = \overline{S} \cdot D_i + S(R \cdot Q_{i+1} + \overline{R} \cdot Q_{i-1})$

Stage 0 (LSB)

Parallel load		$J_0 = D_0$	S = 0
Shift right	logical	$J_0 = Q_1$	S = 1, R = 1, L = 1
	arithmetic	$J_0 = Q_1$	S = 1, R = 1, A = 1
	circular	$J_0 = Q_1$	S = 1, R = 1, C = 1
Shift left	logical	$J_0 = 0$	S = 1, R = 0, L = 1
	arithmetic	$J_0 = 0$	S = 1, R = 0, A = 1
	circular	$J_0 = Q_7$	S = 1, R = 0, C = 1

Therefore,
$$\begin{aligned}
J_0 &= \overline{S} \cdot D_0 + S(R \cdot L \cdot Q_1 + R \cdot A \cdot Q_1 + R \cdot C \cdot Q_1 \\
&\quad + \overline{R} \cdot L \cdot 0 + \overline{R} \cdot A \cdot 0 + \overline{R} \cdot C \cdot Q_7) \\
&= \overline{S} \cdot D_0 + S(R \cdot L \cdot Q_1 + R \cdot A \cdot Q_1 + R \cdot C \cdot Q_1 \\
&\quad + \overline{R} \cdot C \cdot Q_7) \\
&= \overline{S} \cdot D_0 + S(R \cdot Q_1(L + A + C) + \overline{R} \cdot C \cdot Q_7) \\
&\quad \text{Note: } L + A + C = 1 \\
&= \overline{S} \cdot D_0 + S(R \cdot Q_1 + \overline{R} \cdot C \cdot Q_7).
\end{aligned}$$

Stage 7 (MSB)

Parallel load		$J_7 = D_7$	S = 0
Shift right	logical	$J_7 = 0$	S = 1, R = 1, L = 1
	arithmetic	$J_7 = Q_7$	S = 1, R = 1, A = 1
	circular	$J_7 = Q_0$	S = 1, R = 1, C = 1
Shift left	logical	$J_7 = Q_6$	S = 1, R = 0, L = 1
	arithmetic	$J_7 = Q_6$	S = 1, R = 0, A = 1
	circular	$J_7 = Q_6$	S = 1, R = 0, C = 1

Therefore, $J_7 = \bar{S}{\cdot}D_7 + S(R{\cdot}\bar{L}{\cdot}0 + R{\cdot}A{\cdot}Q_7 + R{\cdot}C{\cdot}Q_0$
$\qquad + \bar{R}{\cdot}L{\cdot}Q_6 + \bar{R}{\cdot}A{\cdot}Q_6 + \bar{R}{\cdot}C{\cdot}Q_6)$
$\quad = \bar{S}{\cdot}D_7 + S(R{\cdot}A{\cdot}Q_7 + R{\cdot}C{\cdot}Q_0$
$\qquad + \bar{R}{\cdot}Q_6\,(L + A + C))$
$\quad = \bar{S}{\cdot}D_7 + S(R\,(A{\cdot}Q_7 + C{\cdot}Q_0) + \bar{R}{\cdot}Q_6)$

3.6.2 Asynchronous counters

A counter is a sequential circuit with a clock input and m outputs. Each time the counter is clocked, one or more of its outputs change state. These outputs form a sequence with N unique values. After the Nth value has been observed at the counter's output terminals, the next clock pulse causes the counter to assume the same output as it had at the start of the sequence; that is, the sequence is *cyclic*. For example, a counter may display the sequence 01234501234501 . . . or the sequence 9731097310973 . . .

A counter composed of m flip-flops can generate an arbitrary sequence with a length of not greater than 2^m cycles before the sequence begins to repeat itself.

One of the tools frequently employed to illustrate the operation of sequential circuits is the *state diagram*. Any system with internal memory and external inputs such as the flip-flop can be said to be in a state that is a function of its internal and external inputs. A state diagram shows some (or all) of the possible states of a given system. A labeled circle represents each of the states and the states are linked by unidirectional lines showing the paths by which one state becomes another state.

Figure 3.44 gives the state diagram of a JK flip-flop that has just two states, S_0 and S_1. S_0 represents the state $Q = 0$ and S_1 represents the state $Q = 1$. The transitions between states S_0 and S_1 are determined by the values of the JK inputs at the time the flip-flop is clocked. In Fig. 3.44 we have labeled the flip-flop's input states C_1 to C_4. Table 3.8 defines the four possible input conditions, C_1, C_2, C_3, and C_4, in terms of J and K.

From Fig. 3.44 it can be seen that conditions C_3 or C_4 cause a transition from state S_0 to state S_1. Similarly, conditions C_2 or C_4 cause a transition from state S_1 to state S_0. Condition C_4 causes a change of state from S_0 to S_1 and also from S_1 to S_0. This is, of course, the condition $J = K = 1$, which causes the JK flip-flop to toggle its output. Some conditions cause a state to change to *itself*; that is, there is no overall change. Thus, conditions C_1 or C_2, when applied to the system in state S_0, have the effect of leaving the system in state S_0.

The binary up-counter

The state diagram of a simple 3-bit binary up-counter is given in Fig. 3.45 (an up-counter counts upward 0, 1, 2, 3, . . . in contrast with a down-counter, which counts downward . . . , 3, 2, 1, 0). In this state diagram, there is only a single path from each state to its next higher neighbor. As the system is clocked, it cycles through the states S_0 to S_7 representing the natural binary numbers 0 to 7. The actual design of counters in general can be quite involved, although the basic principle is to ask 'What input conditions are required by the flip-flops to cause them to change from state S_i to state S_{i+1}?'

The design of an *asynchronous* natural binary up-counter is rather simpler than the design of a counter for an arbitrary sequence. Figure 3.46 gives the circuit diagram of a 3-bit binary counter composed of JK flip-flops and Fig. 3.47 provides its timing diagram. The J and K inputs to each flip-flop

J	K	Condition
0	0	C_1
0	1	C_2
1	0	C_3
1	1	C_4

Table 3.8 Relationship between JK inputs and conditions C_1 to C_4.

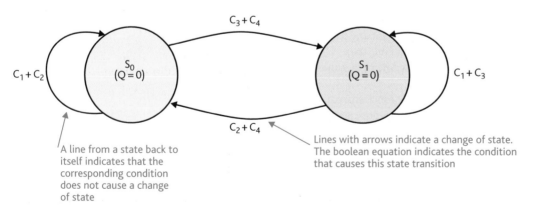

Figure 3.44 The state diagram of a JK flip-flop.

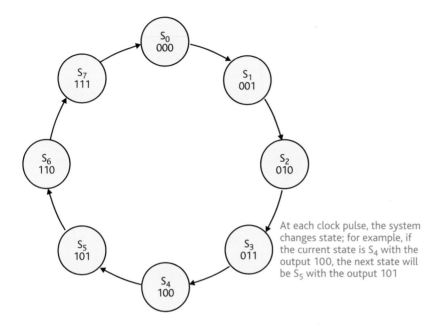

At each clock pulse, the system changes state; for example, if the current state is S_4 with the output 100, the next state will be S_5 with the output 101

Figure 3.45 The state diagram of a binary 3-bit up-counter.

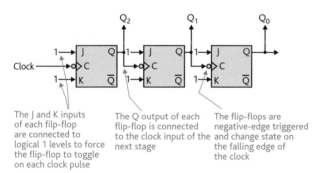

The J and K inputs of each filp-flop are connected to logical 1 levels to force the flip-flop to toggle on each clock pulse

The Q output of each flip-flop is connected to the clock input of the next stage

The flip-flops are negative-edge triggered and change state on the falling edge of the clock

Figure 3.46 Circuit of an asynchronous binary up-counter.

are connected to constant logical 1 levels. Consequently, whenever a flip-flop is clocked, its output changes state. The flip-flops are arranged so that the Q output of one stage triggers the clock input of the next higher stage (i.e. the output Q_i of stage i triggers the clock input of stage $i+1$). The flip-flops in Fig. 3.46 are master–slave clocked and their outputs change on the negative edge of the clock pulse.

Consider the first stage of this counter. When the clock input makes a complete cycle (0 to 1 to 0), the Q output changes state on the falling edge of the clock. It takes two clock cycles to make the Q output execute one cycle; that is, the flip-flop divides the clock input by 2.

The asynchronous binary counter of Fig. 3.46 is called a *ripple counter* because the output of the first stage triggers the input of the second stage, the output of the second stage triggers the input of the third stage, and so on. Consequently, a change of state at the output of the first stage ripples through

the counter until it clocks the final stage. The propagation delay through each stage of the counter determines its maximum speed of operation. The timing diagram of Fig. 3.47 doesn't show the ripple effect—when one stage changes state, there's a short delay before stages to its right change state.

Figure 3.48 demonstrates the construction of a four-stage binary up-counter in Digital Works. We have wired all J and K inputs together and connected them to V_{cc} (the positive power supply that provides a logical 1 to cause the JK flip-flops to toggle when clocked). We have labeled each of the Q outputs and used the **Logic History** function to capture the output waveform. Digital Works clears all flip-flops at the start of each run. However, the flip-flops have two unlabeled set and clear inputs that can be used to preset outputs to 1 or 0, respectively (these are not used in this application).

The binary down-counter

We can also create a binary down-counter that counts backwards from 7 to 0. Figure 3.49 demonstrates the effect of connecting the $\overline{Q}$ output of each stage in a ripple counter to the clock input of the next stage. You can also create a binary down-counter by using JK flip-flops that are clocked on the *positive* or rising edge of the clock pulse by connecting Q_i to Clk_{i+1}.

Designing an asynchronous decimal counter

Let's design a 4-bit asynchronous ripple-through decimal counter to count from 0 to 9 cyclically. We use JK master–slave flip-flops with an unconditional active-low clear input. A decimal counter can be derived from a binary counter by resetting the counter to zero at the appropriate point. A four-stage binary counter counts from 0000 to 1111

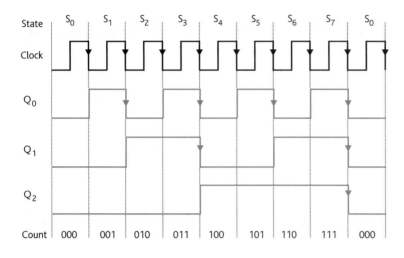

Figure 3.47 Timing diagram of an asynchronous 3-bit binary up-counter.

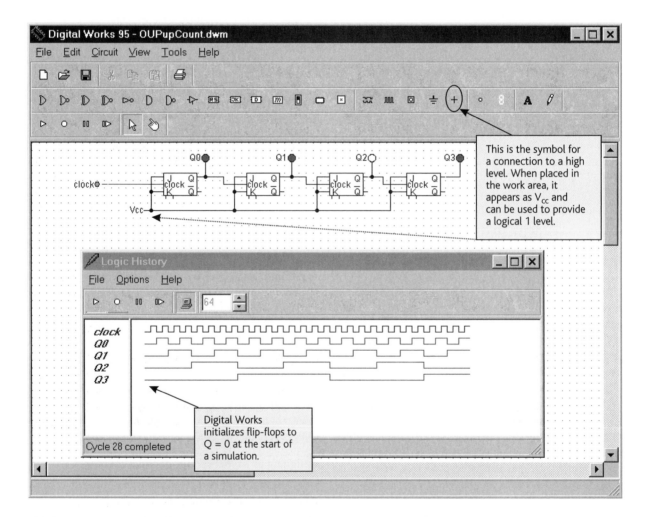

Figure 3.48 Using Digital Works to create a binary up-counter.

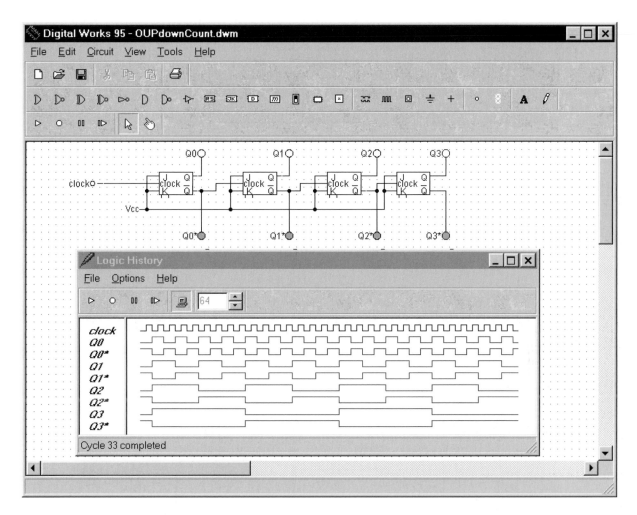

Figure 3.49 Using Digital Works to create a binary down-counter.

(i.e. 0 to 15). To create a decade counter the state 10 (1010) must be detected and used to reset the flip-flops. Fig. 3.50 provides a possible circuit.

The binary counter counts normally from 0 to 9. On the tenth count $Q_3 = 1$ and $Q_1 = 1$. This condition is detected by the NAND gate whose output goes low, resetting the flip-flops. The count of 10 exists momentarily as Fig. 3.51 demonstrates. We could have detected the state 10 with Q_3, Q_2, Q_1, $Q_0 = 1010$. However, that would have required a four-input gate and is not strictly necessary. Although $Q_3 = 1$ and $Q_1 = 1$ corresponds to counts 10, 11, 14, and 15, the counter never gets beyond 10.

The reset pulse must be long enough to reset all flip-flops to zero. If the reset pulse were too short and, say, Q_1 was reset before Q_3, the output might be reset to 1000. The counting sequence would now be: 0, 1, 2, 3, 4, 5, 6, 7, 8, 9, (10), 8, 9, 8, 9, ... However, such a problem is unlikely to occur in this case, because the reset pulse is not removed until at least the output of one flip-flop and the NAND gate has changed state.

The combined duration of flip-flop reset time plus a gate delay will normally provide sufficient time to ensure that all flip-flops are reset.

It is possible to imagine situations in which the circuit would not function correctly. Suppose that the minimum reset pulse required to guarantee the reset of a flip-flop were 50 ns. Suppose also that the minimum time between the application of a reset pulse and the transition $Q \leftarrow 0$ were 10 ns and that the propagation delay of a NAND gate were 10 ns. It would indeed be possible for the above error to occur. This example demonstrates the dangers of designing asynchronous circuits!

The pulse generator revisited

When we introduced the RS flip-flop we used it to start and stop a simple pulse generator that created a train of n pulses. Figure 3.52 shows a pulse generator in Digital Works. This system is essentially the same as that in Fig. 3.9, except that we've built the counter using JK flip-flops and we've added

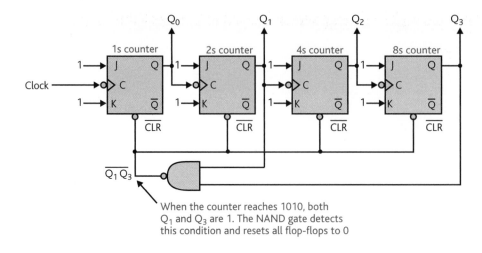

When the counter reaches 1010, both Q_1 and Q_3 are 1. The NAND gate detects this condition and resets all flop-flops to 0

Figure 3.50 Circuit of a decimal counter.

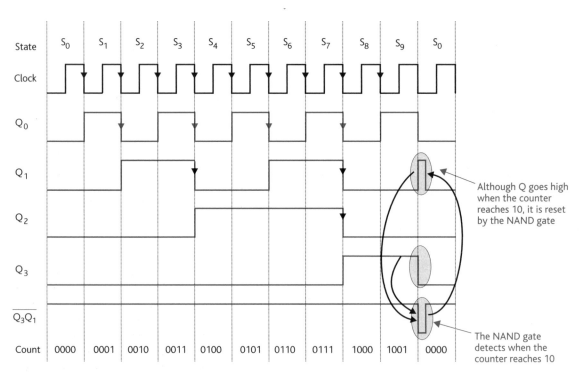

Although Q goes high when the counter reaches 10, it is reset by the NAND gate

The NAND gate detects when the counter reaches 10

Figure 3.51 Timing diagram of a decimal counter.

LEDs to examine the signals produced when the system runs. Note also that the RS flip-flop can be set only when the flip-flop is in the reset mode.

3.6.3 Synchronous counters

Synchronous counters are composed of flip-flops that are all clocked at the same time. The outputs of *all* stages of a synchronous counter become valid at the same time and the ripple-through effect associated with asynchronous counters is entirely absent. Synchronous counters can be easily designed to count through any arbitrary sequence just as well as the natural sequence 0, 1, 2, 3, ...

We design a synchronous counter by means of a state diagram and the *excitation table* for the appropriate flip-flop (either RS or JK). An excitation table is a version of a flip-flop's truth table arranged to display the input states required to force a given output transition. Table 3.9 illustrates the excitation table of a JK flip-flop. Suppose we wish to force the Q output of a JK flip-flop to make the transition from 0 to 1 the next time it is clocked. Table 3.9 tells us that the J, K input should be 1, d (where d = don't care).

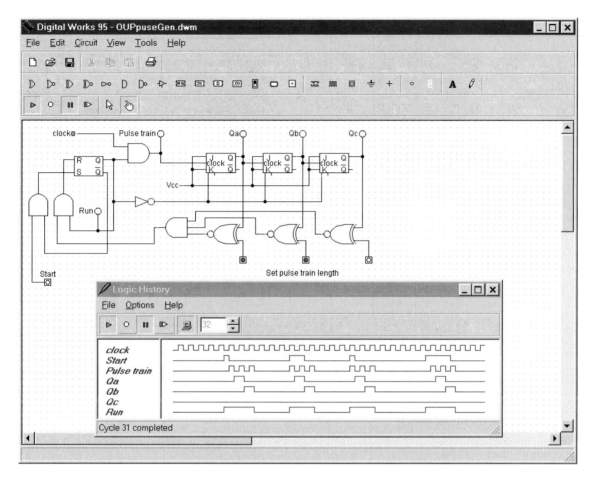

Figure 3.52 Using Digital Works to design a pulse generator.

Inputs		Transition
J	K	$Q \rightarrow Q^+$
0	d	$0 \rightarrow 0$
1	d	$0 \rightarrow 1$
d	1	$1 \rightarrow 0$
d	0	$1 \rightarrow 1$

Table 3.9 Excitation table of a JK flip-flop.

Why is the K input a *don't care condition* when we want a $0 \rightarrow 1$ transition? If we set J = 1 and K = 0, the flip-flop is set when it's clocked and Q^+ becomes 1. If we set J = 1 and K = 1, the flip-flop is toggled when it's clocked and the output Q = 0 is toggled to Q = 1. Clearly, the state of the K input doesn't matter when we wish to set Q^+ to 1 given that Q = 0 and J = 1. It should now be clear why all the transitions in the JK's excitation table have a don't care input—a given state can be reached from more than one starting point.

The next step in designing a synchronous counter is to construct a truth table for the system to determine the JK inputs required to force a transition to the required next state for each of the possible states in the table. It is much easier to explain this step by example rather than by algorithm.

Let's design a synchronous *binary-coded decimal* or modulo-10 counter to count through the natural sequence 0, 1, 2, 3, 4, 5, 6, 7, 8, 9, 0, ... As there are 10 states, we require four JK flip-flops because $2^3 < 10 < 2^4$. Table 3.10 provides a truth table for this counter.

To understand Table 3.10 it's necessary to look along a line and to say, 'Given this state, what must the inputs of the flip-flops be to force the transition to the next state?' For example, in the first line the current state is 0, 0, 0, 0 and the next state is 0, 0, 0, 1. The values for the four pairs of J, K inputs are obtained from the excitation table in Table 3.9. Three of these outputs cause the transition $0 \rightarrow 0$ and one causes the transition $0 \rightarrow 1$. The J, K inputs required are 0, d for the 0 to 0 transitions and 1, d for the 0 to 1 transition.

From the truth table of the synchronous counter we can write down eight Karnaugh maps for the Js and Ks.

Count	Output				Next state				J, K inputs required to force transition							
	Q_d	Q_c	Q_b	Q_a	Q_d	Q_c	Q_b	Q_a	J_d	K_d	J_c	K_c	J_b	K_b	J_a	K_a
0	0	0	0	0	0	0	0	1	0	d	0	d	0	d	1	d
1	0	0	0	1	0	0	1	0	0	d	0	d	1	d	d	1
2	0	0	1	0	0	0	1	1	0	d	0	d	d	0	1	d
3	0	0	1	1	0	1	0	0	0	d	1	d	d	1	d	1
4	0	1	0	0	0	1	0	1	0	d	d	0	0	d	1	d
5	0	1	0	1	0	1	1	0	0	d	d	0	1	d	d	1
6	0	1	1	0	0	1	1	1	0	d	d	0	d	0	1	d
7	0	1	1	1	1	0	0	0	1	d	d	1	d	1	d	1
8	1	0	0	0	1	0	0	1	d	0	0	d	0	d	1	d
9	1	0	0	1	0	0	0	0	d	1	0	d	0	d	d	1
10	1	0	1	0	x	X	x	x	x	x	x	x	x	x	X	x
11	1	0	1	1	x	x	x	x	x	x	x	x	x	x	x	x
12	1	1	0	0	x	x	x	x	x	x	x	x	x	x	x	x
13	1	1	0	1	x	x	x	x	x	x	x	x	x	x	x	x
14	1	1	1	0	x	x	x	x	x	x	x	x	x	x	x	x
15	1	1	1	1	x	x	x	x	x	x	x	x	x	x	x	x

The *d*s in the table correspond to *don't care* conditions in the excitation table of the JK flip-flop. The x's correspond to don't care conditions due to unused states; for example, the counter never enters states 1010 to 1111. There is, of course, no fundamental difference between x and d. We've chosen different symbols in order to distinguish between the origins of the don't care states.

Table 3.10　Truth table for a synchronous counter.

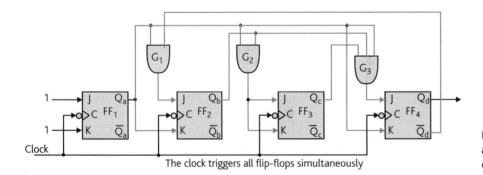

The clock triggers all flip-flops simultaneously

Figure 3.54　Circuit diagram for a 4-bit synchronous BCD counter.

Figure 3.53 gives the Karnaugh maps for this counter. These maps can be simplified to give

$$J_d = Q_c \cdot Q_b \cdot Q_a \qquad K_d = Q_a$$
$$J_c = Q_b \cdot Q_a \qquad K_c = Q_b \cdot Q_a$$
$$J_b = \overline{Q_d} \cdot Q_a \qquad K_b = Q_a$$
$$J_a = 1 \qquad K_a = 1$$

We can now write down the circuit diagram of the synchronous counter (Fig. 3.54). Remember that d denotes a don't care condition and indicates that the variable marked by a d may be a 0 or a 1 state. The same technique can be employed to construct a counter that will step through any arbitrary sequence. We will revisit this technique when we look at state machines.

3.7 Introduction to state machines

No discussion of sequential circuits would be complete without at least a mention of state machines. The state machine offers the designer a formal way of specifying, designing, testing, and analyzing sequential systems. Because the detailed study of state machines is beyond the scope of this introductory text, we shall simply introduce some of the basic concepts here.

It would be impossible to find a text on state machines without encountering the general state machines called Mealy machines and Moore machines (after G. H. Mealy and E. Moore). Figure 3.55 illustrates the structure of a Mealy

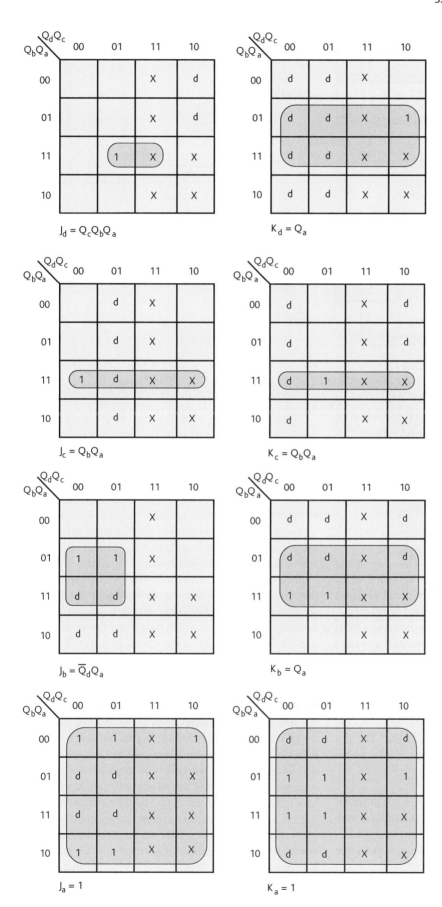

Figure 3.53 Karnaugh maps for a synchronous counter.

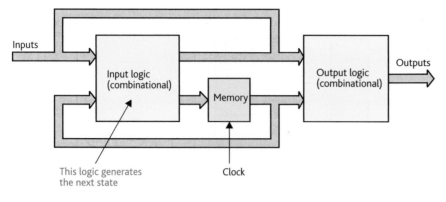

Figure 3.55 The Mealy state machine.

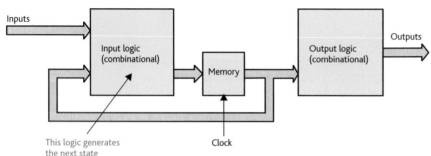

Figure 3.56 The Moore state machine.

state machine and Fig. 3.56 the structure of a Moore state machine. Both machines have a combinational network that operates on the machine's inputs and on its internal states to produce a new internal state. The output of the Mealy machine is a function of the current inputs and the internal state of the machine, whereas the output of a Moore machine is a function of the internal state of the machine only.

3.7.1 Example of a state machine

As we have already said, the state machine approach to the design of sequential circuits is by no means trivial. Here, we will design a simple state machine by means of an example.

Suppose we require a sequence detector that has a serial input X and an output Y. If a certain sequence of bits appears at the input of the detector, the output goes true. Sequence detectors are widely used in digital systems to split a stream of bits into units or *frames* by providing special bit patterns between adjacent frames and then using a sequence detector to identify the start of a frame.

In the following example we design a sequence detector that produces a true output Y whenever it detects the sequence 010 at its X input.

For example, if the input sequence is   00011001 1010110001011,
the output sequence will be   00000000000 0100000010

(the output generates a 1 in the state following the detection of the pattern).

Figure 3.57 shows a black box state machine that detects the sequence 010 in a bit stream. We have provided input and output sequences to demonstrate the machine's action.

We solve the problem by constructing a state diagram as illustrated in Fig. 3.58. Each circle represents a particular state of the system and transitions between states are determined by the current input to the system at the next clock pulse.

A state is marked name/value, where *name* is the label we use to describe the state (e.g. states A, B, C, and D in Fig. 3.58) and *value* is the output corresponding to that state. The transition between states is labeled *a/b*, where *a* is the input condition and *b* the output value after the next clock. For example, the transition from state A to state B is labeled 0/0 and indicates that if the system is in state A and the input is 0, the next clock pulse will force the system into state B and set the output to 0.

Figure 3.59 provides a partial state diagram for this sequence detector with details of the actions that take place during state transitions. State A is the initial state in Fig. 3.59. Suppose we receive an input while in state A. If input X is a 0 we may be on our way to detecting the sequence 010 and therefore we move to state B along the line marked 0/0 (the output is 0 because we have not detected the required sequence yet). If the input is 1, we return to state A because we have not even begun to detect the start of the sequence.

From state B there are two possible transitions. If we detect a 0 we remain in state B because we are still at the start of the desired sequence. If we detect a 1, we move on to state C (we have now detected 01). From state C a further 1 input takes us

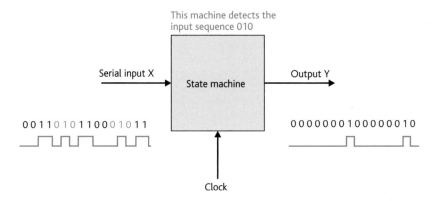

Figure 3.57 State machine to detect the sequence 010.

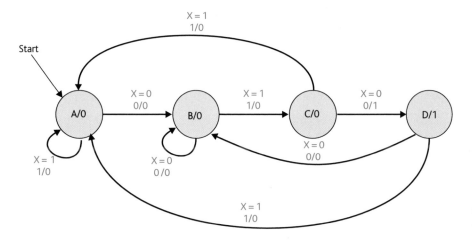

Figure 3.58 State diagram for a 010 sequence detector (X is the current input).

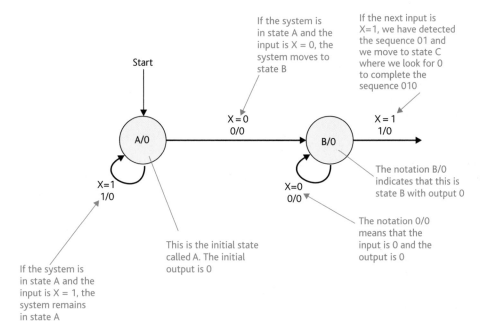

Figure 3.59 Details of the state counter diagram of Fig. 3.58.

Current state	Output	Next state	
		X = 0	X = 1
A	0	B	A
B	0	B	C
C	0	D	A
D	1	B	A

Table 3.11 State table for a 010 sequence detector.

Current state	Flip-flop outputs		Output	Next state	
	Q_1	Q_2		X = 0	X = 1
A	0	0	0	0,1	0,0
B	0	1	0	0,1	1,0
C	1	0	0	1,1	0,0
D	1	1	1	0,1	0,0

Table 3.12 Modified state table for a sequence detector.

Current state			Next state		Output			
Q_1	Q_2	X	Q_1	Q_2	J_1	K_1	J_2	K_2
0	0	0	0	1	0	d	1	d
0	0	1	0	0	0	d	0	d
0	1	0	0	1	0	d	d	0
0	1	1	1	0	1	d	d	1
1	0	0	1	1	d	0	1	d
1	0	1	0	0	d	1	0	d
1	1	0	0	1	d	1	d	0
1	1	1	0	0	d	1	d	1

$J_1 = Q_1 + Q_2 \cdot X$
$J_2 = \overline{X}$
$K_1 = Q_2 + X$
$K_2 = X$

Table 3.13 Determining the JK outputs of the sequence detector.

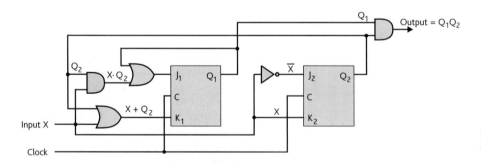

Figure 3.60 Circuit to detect the sequence 010.

right back to state A (because we have received 011). However, if we detect a 0 we move to state D and set the output to 1 to indicate that the sequence has been detected. From state D we move back to state A if the next input is a 1 and back to state B if it is a 0. From the state diagram we can construct a state table that defines the output and the next state corresponding to each current state and input. Table 3.11 provides a state table for Fig. 3.58.

3.7.2 Constructing a circuit to implement the state table

The next step is to go about constructing the circuit itself. If a system can exist in one of several *states*, what then defines the *current* state? In a sequential system flip-flops are used to hold state information—in this example there are four states, which requires two flip-flops.

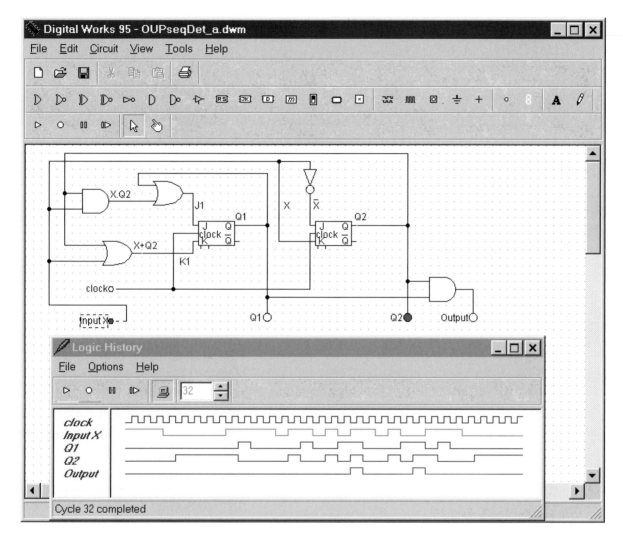

Figure 3.61 Using Digital Works to implement the sequence detector.

Table 3.12 expands Table 3.11 to represent internal states A to D by flip-flop outputs Q_1, $Q_2 = 0$, 0 to 1, 1. We next construct Table 3.13 to determine the JK input of each JK flip-flop that will force the appropriate state transition, given the next input X. Table 3.13 is derived by using the excitation table of the JK flip-flop (see Table 3.9). The final step is to create a circuit diagram from Table 3.13 (i.e. Fig. 3.60).

Figure 3.61 demonstrates the construction of the sequence detector in Digital Works. We've added LEDs to show the state of the flip-flop outputs and control signals and have provided an example of a run. Note the output pulse after the sequence 010. We used the programmable sequence generator to provide a binary pattern for the test.

▓ SUMMARY

In this chapter we've looked at the flip-flop, which provides data storage facilities in a computer and which can be used to create counters and shift registers as well as more general forms of state machine. We have introduced the RS, D, and JK flip-flops. All these flip-flops can capture data and the JK flip-flop is able to operate in a *toggle* mode in which its output changes state each time it is clocked. Any of these flip-flops can be converted into the other two flip-flops by the addition of a few gates.

We have also introduced the idea of clocking or triggering flip-flops. A flip-flop can be triggered by a clock at a given level or by the change in state of a clock. The master–slave flip-flop latches data at its input when the clock is high (or low) and transfers data to the output (slave) when the clock changes state.

We have looked at the counter and shift register. The counter counts through a predetermined sequence such as the natural integers 0, 1, 2, 3, ... A shift register holds a word of data and is able to shift the bits one or more places left or right. Shift registers are used to divide and multiply by two and to manipulate data in both arithmetic and logical operations. Counters and shift registers can be combined with the type of combinational logic we introduced in the previous chapter to create a digital computer.

Sequential machines fall into two categories. Asynchronous sequential machines don't have a master clock and the output from one flip-flop triggers the flip-flop it's connected to. In a synchronous sequential machine all the flip-flops are triggered at the same time by means of a common master clock. Synchronous machines are more reliable. In this chapter we have briefly demonstrated how you can construct a synchronous counter and a machine that can detect a specific binary pattern in a stream of serial data.

■ PROBLEMS

3.1 What is a *sequential circuit* and in what way does it differ from a combinational circuit?

3.2 Explain why it is necessary to employ *clocked* flip-flops in sequential circuits (as opposed to unclocked flip-flops)?

3.3 What are the three basic flip-flop clocking modes and why is it necessary to provide so many clocking modes?

3.4 The behavior of an RS flip-flop is not clearly defined when R = 1 and S = 1. Design an RS flip-flop that does not suffer from this restriction. (Note: What assumptions do you have to make?)

3.5 For the waveforms in Fig. 3.62 draw the Q and $\overline{Q}$ outputs of an RS flip-flop constructed from two NOR gates (as in Fig. 3.2).

3.6 For the input and clock signals of Fig. 3.63, provide a timing diagram for the Q output of a D flip-flop. Assume that the flip-flop is

(a) Level sensitive
(b) positive edge triggered
(c) negative-edge triggered
(d) a master–slave flip-flop

3.7 What additional logic is required to convert a JK flip-flop into a D flip-flop?

3.8 Assuming that the initial state of the circuit of Fig. 3.64 is given by C = 1, D = 1, P = 1, and Q = 0, complete the table. This question should be attempted by calculating the effect of the new C and D on the inputs to both cross-coupled pairs of NOR gates and therefore on the outputs P and Q. As P and Q are also inputs to the NOR gates, the change in P and Q should be taken into account when calculating the effect of the next inputs C and D. Remember that the output of a NOR is 1 if both its inputs are 0, and is 0 otherwise.

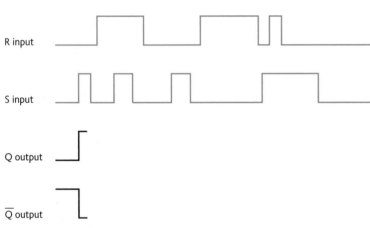

Figure 3.62 R and S inputs to an RS flip-flop.

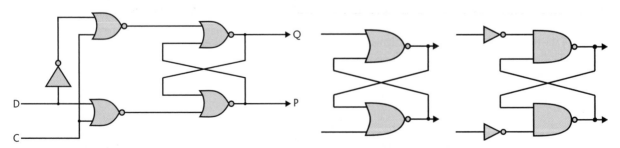

Figure 3.63 Timing diagram of a clock and data signal.

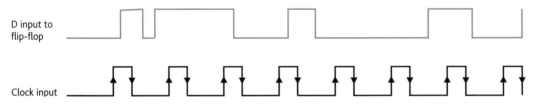

Figure 3.64 Circuit for Question 3.8.

Figure 3.65 Circuit for Question 3.9.

C	D	P	Q
1	1	1	0
1	0		
0	0		
1	1		
0	1		
1	1		
0	1		
0	0		
1	0		

Modify the circuit to provide a new input S which, when 1, will at any time set P to 1 and Q to 0. Provide another input R that will similarly set P to 0 and Q to 1. Note that R and S cannot both be a 1 at the same time and therefore the condition R = S = 1 need not be considered.

3.9 Demonstrate that the flip-flops in Fig. 3.65 are equivalent. Are they exactly equivalent?

3.10 Many flip-flops have unconditional *preset* and *clear* inputs. What do these inputs do and why are they needed in sequential circuits?

3.11 A T flip-flop has a single clock input and outputs Q and $\bar{Q}$. Its Q output toggles (changes state) each time it is clocked. The T flip-flop behaves exactly like a JK flip-flop with its J and K inputs connected permanently to a logical one. Design a T flip-flop using a D flip-flop.

3.12 Why haven't D and RS flip-flops been replaced by the JK flip-flop, because the JK flip-flop can, apparently, do everything a D flip-flop or an RS flip-flop can do?

3.13 What is a *shift register* and why is it so important in digital systems?

3.14 Design a shift register that has two inputs, a clock input and a shift input. Whenever this register receives a pulse at its shift input, it shifts its contents *two* places right.

3.15 Analyze the operation of the circuit of Fig. 3.66 by constructing a timing diagram (assume that Q_0 and Q_1 are initially 0). Construct the circuit using Digital Works and observe its behavior.

3.16 Analyze the operation of the circuit of Fig. 3.67 by constructing a timing diagram (assume any initial value for Q_0 to Q_3). Construct the circuit using Digital Works and observe its behavior. This type of circuit is an important circuit in digital systems because it can be used to generate a pseudo random sequence; that is, the sequence of bits at its Q_0 output look (to an

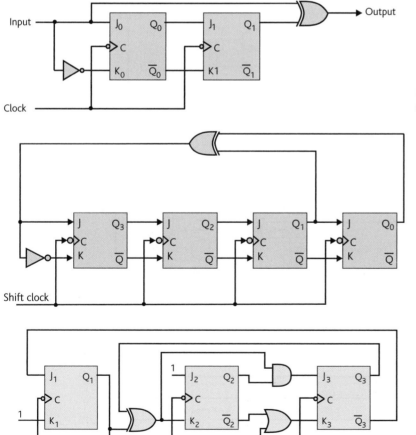

Figure 3.66 Circuit diagram for Question 3.15.

Figure 3.67 Circuit diagram for Question 3.16.

Figure 3.68 Circuit diagram for Question 3.17.

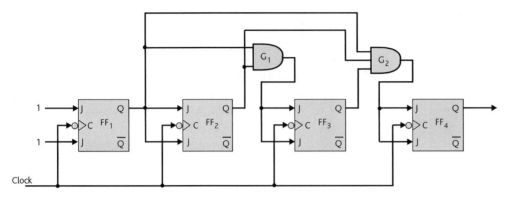

Figure 3.69 Circuit diagram for Question 3.18.

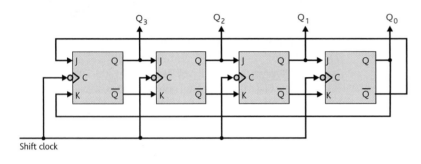

Figure 3.70 Circuit diagram of a Johnson counter.

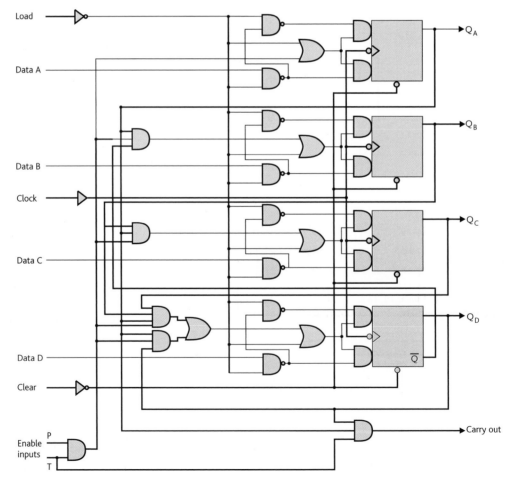

Figure 3.71 Organization of a 74162 synchronous decade counter.

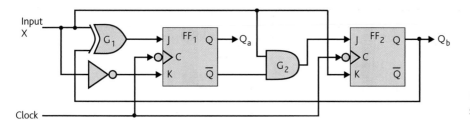

Figure 3.72 Circuit diagram of a sequence processor.

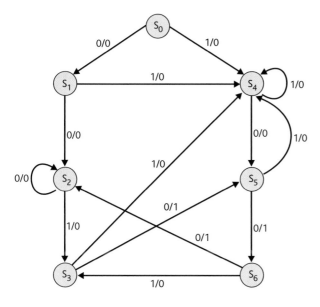

Figure 3.73 Circuit diagram of a sequence processor.

observer) as if they constitute a random series of 1s and 0s. Longer sequences of random numbers are generated by increasing the number of stages in the shift register. The input is the exclusive OR of two or more outputs.

3.17 Use Digital Works to construct the circuit of Fig. 3.68 and then investigate its behavior.

3.18 Investigate the behavior of the circuit in Fig. 3.69.

3.19 Explain the meaning of the terms *asynchronous* and *synchronous* in the context of sequential logic systems. What is the significance of these terms?

3.20 Design an asynchronous base 13 counter that counts through the natural binary sequence from 0 (0000) to 12 (1100) and then returns to zero on the next count.

3.21 Design a synchronous binary duodecimal (i.e. base 12) counter that counts through the natural binary sequence from 0 (0000) to 11 (1011) and then returns to zero on the next count. The counter is to be built from four JK flip-flops.

3.22 Design a synchronous modulo 9 counter using

(a) JK flip-flops
(b) RS flip-flops (with a master–slave clock).

3.23 Design a *programmable* modulo 10/modulo 12 synchronous counter using JK flip-flops. The counter has a control input, TEN/TWELVE, which when high, causes the counter to count modulo 10. When low, TEN/TWELVE causes the counter to count modulo 12.

3.24 How would you determine the maximum rate at which a synchronous counter could be clocked?

3.25 The circuit in Fig. 3.70 represents a *Johnson counter*. This is also called a *twisted ring* counter because feedback from the last (rightmost) stage is fed back to the first stage by crossing over the Q and $\overline{Q}$ connections. Investigate the operation of this circuit.

3.26 Design a simple digital time of day clock that can display the time from 00:00:00 to 23:59:59. Assume that you have a clock pulse input derived from the public electricity supply of 50 Hz (Europe) or 60 Hz (USA).

3.27 Figure 3.71 gives the internal organization of a 74162 synchronous decade (i.e. modulo 10) counter. Investigate its operation. Explain the function of the various control inputs. Note that the flip-flops are master–slave JKs with asynchronous (i.e. unconditional) clear inputs.

3.28 Design a modulo 8 counter with a clock and a control input UP. When UP = 1, the counter counts 0, 1, 2, . . . , 7. When UP = 0, the counter counts down 7, 6, 5, . . . 0. This circuit is a programmable up-/down-counter.

3.29 Design a counter using JK flip-flops to count through the following sequence.

Q_2	Q_1	Q_0	
0	0	1	
0	1	0	
0	1	1	
1	1	0	
1	1	1	
0	0	1	sequence repeats

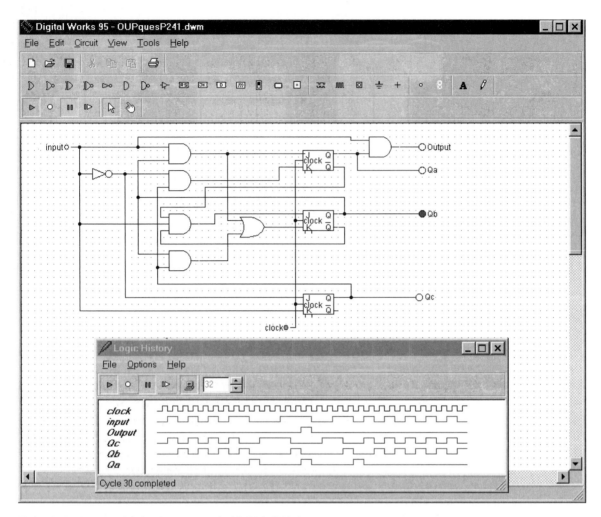

Figure 3.74 A sequential circuit constructed with Digital Works.

3.30 Investigate the action of the circuit in Fig. 3.72 when it is presented with the input sequence 111000001011111, where the first bit is the rightmost bit. Assume that all flip-flops are reset to Q = 0 before the first bit is received.

3.31 Design a state machine to implement the state diagram defined in Fig. 3.73.

3.32 Figure 3.74 provides a screen shot of a session using Digital Works. Examine the behavior of the circuit both by constructing it and by analyzing it.

Computer arithmetic

4

INTRODUCTION

Because of the ease with which binary logic elements are manufactured and because of their remarkably low price, it was inevitable that the binary number system was chosen to represent numerical data within a digital computer. This chapter examines how numbers are represented in digital form, how they are converted from one *base* to another, and how they are manipulated within the computer. We begin with an examination of binary codes in general and demonstrate how patterns of ones and zeros can represent a range of different quantities.

We demonstrate how computers use binary digits to implement codes that detect errors in stored or transmitted data and how some codes can even correct bits that have been corrupted. Similarly, we show how codes can be devised that reduce the number of bits used to encode information (e.g. the type of codes used to *zip* files).

The main theme of this chapter is the class of binary codes used to represent numbers in digital computers. We look at how numbers are converted from our familiar decimal (or *denary*) form to binary form and vice versa. Binary arithmetic is useless without the hardware needed to implement it, so we examine some of the circuits of adders and subtractors. We also introduce error-detecting codes, which enable the computer to determine whether data has been corrupted (i.e. inadvertently modified). Other topics included here are ways in which we represent and handle *negative* as well as positive numbers. We look at the way in which the computer deals with very large and very small numbers by means of a system called *floating point* arithmetic. Finally, we describe how computers carry out multiplication and division—operations that are much more complex than addition or subtraction.

We should stress that error-detecting codes, data compressing codes, and computer arithmetic are not special properties of the binary representation of data used by computers. All these applications are valid for any number base. The significance of binary arithmetic is its elegance and simplicity.

ACCURACY AND WORD LENGTH

If I ask students what the advantages of a 32-bit wordlength over an 8-bit wordlength are, some will say that computers with long wordlengths are more *accurate* than computers with short wordlengths.

This answer is incorrect. All computers are completely accurate unless they have failed. The answer confuses *precision* with *accuracy*. A computer with an 8-bit wordlength can represent one of 256 values, whereas a computer with a 32-bit wordlength can represent one of 4, 294, 967, 296 values. The number of bits in a word indicates how precisely a value can be represented.

An 8-bit computer can deal with any arbitrary wordlength. If you wish to represent integers to a precision of 1 in 32 bits on an 8-bit machine, you have to take four 8-bit words and concatenate them to form a 32-bit entity. When you add two 32-bit values, you have to add each of the two pairs of four bytes. An *m*-bit computer can simulate an *n*-bit computer for any values of *m* and *n* and achieve exactly the same results as the *n*-bit machine. However, simulating, say, a 32-bit computer on a real 8-bit machine may seriously reduce performance (i.e. speed). A real 32-bit machine is faster than a simulated 32-bit machine. The trend toward longer wordlengths is about performance and not accuracy.

4.1 Bits, bytes, words, and characters

The smallest quantity of information that can be stored and manipulated inside a computer is the *bit*, which can take the value 0 or 1. Digital computers store information in the form of groups of bits called *words*. The number of bits per word varies from computer to computer. A computer with a 4-bit word is not less accurate than a computer with a 64-bit word; the difference is one of performance and economics. Computers with small words are cheaper to construct than computers with long words. Typical word lengths of computer both old and new are

Cray-1 supercomputer	64 bits
ICL 1900 series mainframe	24 bits
UNIVAC 1100 mainframe	36 bits
PDP-11 minicomputer	16 bits
VAX minicomputer	32 bits
The first microprocessor (4004)	4 bits
First-generation microprocessors	8 bits
8086 microprocessor	16 bits
Third-generation microprocessors	32 bits
Fourth-generation microprocessors	64 bits
Special-purpose graphics processors	128 bits

A group of 8 bits has come to be known as a *byte*. Today's microprocessors and minicomputers are byte oriented with word lengths that are integer multiples of 8 bits (i.e. their data elements and addresses are 8, 16, 32, or 64 bits). A word is spoken of as being 2, 4, or 8 bytes long, because its bits can be formed into two, four, or eight groups of 8 bits, respectively.[1]

An *n*-bit word can be arranged into 2^n unique bit patterns as Table 4.1 demonstrates for $n = 1, 2, 3,$ and 4. So, what do the *n* bits of a word represent? The simple and correct answer is *nothing*, because there is no intrinsic meaning associated with a pattern of 1s and 0s. The meaning of a particular pattern of bits is the meaning given to it by the programmer.

As Humpty Dumpty said to Alice in *Through the Looking Glass*, 'When I use a word,' Humpty Dumpty said, 'in a rather scornful tone, 'it means just what I choose it to mean—neither more nor less.'

The following are some of the entities that a word may represent.

An instruction An *instruction* or operation to be performed by the CPU is represented by a binary pattern such as 00111010111111111110000010100011. The relationship between the instruction's bit pattern and what it does is *arbitrary* and is determined by the computer's designer. A particular sequence of bits that means add A to B on one computer might have an entirely different meaning on another computer. Instructions vary in length from 8 to about 80 bits.

A numeric quantity A word, either alone or as part of a sequence of words, may represent a numerical quantity.

Bits (*n*)	Patterns 2^n	Values
1	2	0, 1
2	4	00, 01, 10, 11
3	8	000, 001, 010, 011, 100, 101, 110, 111
4	16	0000, 0001, 0010, 0011, 0100, 0101, 0110, 0111, 1000, 1001, 1010, 1011, 1100, 1101, 1110, 1111

Table 4.1 The relationship between the number of bits in a word and the number of patterns.

---

[1] Some early computers grouped bits into *sixes* and called them bytes. Computer science uses *flexible jargon* where a term sometimes has different meanings in different contexts; for example, some employ the term *word* to mean a 16-bit value and *longword* to mean a 32-bit value. Others use the term *word* to refer to a 32-bit value and *halfword* to refer to a 16-bit value. Throughout this text we will use *word* to mean the basic unit of information operated on by a computer except when we are describing the 68K microprocessor.

Numbers can be represented in one of many formats: BCD integer, unsigned binary integer, signed binary integer, BCD floating point, binary floating point, complex integer, complex floating point, double precision integer, etc. The meaning of these terms and the way in which the computer carries out its operations in the number system represented by the term is examined later. Once again we stress that the byte 10001001 may represent the value -119 in one system, 137 in another system, and 89 in yet another system. We can think of a more human analogy. What is *GIFT*? To a Bulgarian it might be their login password; to an American it might be something to look forward to on their birthday; to a German it is something to avoid because it means *poison*. Only the *context* in which GIFT is used determines its meaning.

A character The *alphanumeric* characters (A to Z, a to z, 0 to 9) and the symbols *, −, +, !, ?, etc. are assigned binary patterns so that they can be stored and manipulated within the computer. The *ASCII code* (American Standard Code for Information Interchange) is widely used throughout the computer industry to encode alphanumeric characters. Table 4.2 defines the relationship between the bits of the ASCII code and the character it represents. This is also called the ISO 7-bit character code.

The ASCII code represents a character by 7 bits, allowing a maximum of $2^7 = 128$ different characters. 96 characters are the normal *printing characters*. The remaining 32 characters are non-printing characters that carry out special functions, such as carriage return, backspace, line feed, etc.

To convert an ASCII character into its 7-bit binary code, you read the upper-order three bits of the code from the column in which the character falls and the lower-order four bits of code from the row. Table 4.2 numbers the rows and columns in both binary and hexadecimal forms (we'll introduce hexadecimal numbers shortly); for example, the ASCII representation of the letter 'Z' is given by $5A_{16}$ or 1011010_2. Because most computers use 8-bit bytes, the ASCII code for 'Z' would be 01011010. If you wish to print the letter 'Z' on a printer, you send the ASCII code for Z, 01011010, to the printer.

The ASCII codes for the decimal digits 0, 1, 2, 3, 4, 5, 6, 7, 8, and 9, are 30_{16}, 31_{16}, 32_{16}, 33_{16}, 34_{16}, 35_{16}, 36_{16}, 37_{16}, 38_{16}, and 39_{16}, respectively. For example, the *symbol* for the number 4 is represented by the ASCII code 00110100_2, whereas the *binary value* for 4 is represented by 00000100_2. When you hit the key '4' on a keyboard, the computer receives the input 00110100 and *not* 00000100. Input from a keyboard or output to a display must be converted between the *codes* for the numbers and the *values* of the numbers. In high-level language this translation takes place automatically.

The two left-hand columns of Table 4.2, representing ASCII codes 0000000 to 0011111, don't contain letters, numbers, or symbols. These columns are *non-printing codes* that are used either to control printers and display devices or to control data transmission links. Data link control characters such as ACK (acknowledge) and SYN (synchronous idle) are associated with communications systems that mix the text

	0 000	1 001	2 010	3 011	4 100	5 101	6 110	7 111
0 0000	NULL	DCL	SP	0	@	P	`	p
1 0001	SOH	DC1	!	1	A	Q	a	q
2 0010	STX	DC2	"	2	B	R	b	r
3 0011	ETX	DC3	#	3	C	S	c	s
4 0100	EOT	DC4	$	4	D	T	d	t
5 0101	ENQ	NAK	%	5	E	U	e	u
6 0110	ACK	SYN	&	6	F	V	f	v
7 0111	BEL	ETB	'	7	G	W	g	w
8 1000	BS	CAN	(	8	H	X	h	x
9 1001	HT	EM	)	9	I	Y	i	y
A 1010	LF	SUB	*	:	J	Z	j	z
B 1011	VT	ESC	+	;	K	[	k	}
C 1100	FF	FS	,	<	L	\	l	|
D 1101	CR	GS	-	=	M	]	m	}
E 1110	SO	RS	.	>	N	^	n	~
F 1111	SI	US	/	?	O	_	o	DEL

Table 4.2 The ASCII code.

being transmitted with the special codes used to regulate the flow of the information.

The 7-bit ASCII code has been extended to the 8-bit ISO 8859-1 Latin code to add accented characters such as Å, ö, and é. Although suited to Europe and the USA, ISO 8859-1 can't deal with many of the World's languages. A 16-bit code, called *Unicode*, has been designed to represent the characters of most of the World's written languages such as Chinese and Japanese. The first 256 characters of Unicode map onto the ASCII character set, making ASCII to Unicode conversion easy. The programming language Java has adopted Unicode as the standard means of character representation.

A picture element One of the many entities that have to be digitally encoded is the picture or graphical display. Pictures vary widely in their complexity and there are a correspondingly large number of ways of representing pictorial information. For example, pictures can be parameterized and stored as a set of instructions that can be used to recreate the image (i.e. the picture is specified in terms of lines, arcs, and polygons and their positions within the picture). When the picture is to be displayed or printed, it is recreated from its parameters.

A simple way of storing pictorial information is to employ symbols that can be put together to make a picture. Such an approach was popular with the low-cost microprocessor systems associated with computer games where the symbols were called *sprites*.

Complex pictures can be stored as a *bit-map* (an array of *pixels* or picture elements). By analogy with the bit, a *pixel* is the smallest unit of information of which a picture is composed. Unlike a bit, the pixel can have attributes such as color. If we wish to store a 10 in × 8 in image at a reasonably high resolution of 300 pixels/in in both the horizontal and vertical axes, we require $(10 \times 300) \times (8 \times 300) = 7\,200\,000$ pixels. If the picture is in color and each pixel has one of 256 different colors, the total storage requirement is $8 \times 7\,200\,000$ bits,

or approximately 8 Mbytes. Typical high-quality color video displays have a resolution of 1600 by 1 200 (i.e. 2^{21} pixels) per frame. These values explain why high-quality computer graphics requires such expensive hardware to store and manipulate images in real time. There are techniques for compressing the amount of storage required by a picture. Some techniques operate by locating areas of a constant color and intensity and storing the shape and location of the area and its color. Other techniques such as JPEG work by performing a mathematical transformation on an image and deleting data that contributes little to the quality of the image.

4.2 Number bases

Our modern number system, which includes a symbol to represent zero, was introduced into Europe from the Hindu–Arabic world in about 1400. This system uses a *positional notation* to represent decimal numbers. By *positional* we mean that the value or *weight* of a digit depends on its location within a number. In our system, when each digit moves one place left, it is multiplied by 10 (the base or radix). Thus, the 9 in 95 is worth 10 times the 9 in 49. Similarly, a digit is divided by 10 when moved one place right (e.g. consider 0.90 and 0.09).

If the concept of *positional notation* seems obvious and not worthy of mention consider the Romans. They conquered most of the known world, invented Latin grammar, wrote the screenplays of many Hollywood epics, and yet their mathematics was terribly cumbersome. Because the Roman World did not use a positional system to represent numbers, each new large number had to have its own special symbol. Their number system was one of *give and take* so that if X = 10 and I = 1, then XI = 11 (i.e. 10 + 1) and IX = 9 (i.e. 10 − 1). The decimal number 1970 is represented in Roman numerals by MCMLXX (i.e. 1000 + (1000−100) + (50 + 10 + 10)). The Romans did not have a symbol for zero.

WHAT ARE NUMBERS?

Before we introduce binary numbers, we need to say what we mean by *numbers*. The numbers we use to count things (i.e. 1, 2, 3, 4, . . .) are called *natural numbers* and are whole numbers or *integers*. Natural numbers are so called because they don't depend on our mathematics (there are three stars in Orion's belt whether or not there are humans on the Earth to count them). The way in which we count is defined by the *number system*, which uses 10 special *symbols* to represent numbers.

Not all numbers are natural. For example, we have invented *negative* numbers to handle certain concepts. We have *real* numbers, which describe non-integer values including

fractions. Real numbers themselves are divided into *rational* and *irrational* numbers. A rational number can be expressed as a *fraction* (e.g. 7/12), whereas an irrational number can't be expressed as one integer divided by another. Paradoxically we can draw a line that has a finite length but we can't write down the length as a real number. If a square measures one inch by one inch, its diagonal is $\sqrt{2}$ inches long. You can draw the diagonal, but the irrational value of $\sqrt{2}$ cannot be expressed by a finite number of digits in our number system.

We have introduced these basic concepts because they have implications for the way in which computers process numeric information.

The number *base* lies at the heart of both conventional and computer arithmetic. Humans use base 10 and computers use base 2. We sometimes use other bases even in our everyday lives; for example, we get base 60 from the Babylonians (60 seconds = 1 minute and 60 minutes = 1 hour). We can express the time 1:2:3 (1 hour 2 minutes 3 seconds) as $1 \times 60 \times 60 + 2 \times 60 + 3$ seconds. Similarly, we occasionally use the base 12 (12 = 1 dozen, $12 \times 12 = 1$ gross). Indeed, the Docenal Society of America exists to promote the base 12 (also called duodecimal).

We now examine how a number is represented in a general base using positional notation. Integer N, which is made up of *n* digits can be written in the form

$$a_{n-1}a_{n-2}...a_1a_0$$

The a_is that make up the number are called *digits* and can take one of *b* values (where *b* is the base in which the number is expressed). Consider the decimal number 821 686, where the six digits are $a_0 = 6$, $a_1 = 8$, $a_2 = 6$, $a_3 = 1$, $a_4 = 2$, and $a_5 = 8$, and these digits are taken from a set of 10 symbols {0 to 9}.

The same notation can be used to express real values by using a *radix point* (e.g. decimal point in base 10 arithmetic or binary point in binary arithmetic) to separate the integer and fractional parts of the number. The following real number uses *n* digits to the left of the radix point and *m* digits to the right.

$$a_{n-1}\, a_{n-2} ...a_1\, a_0.a_{-1}a_{-2}a_{-m}$$

The value of this number, expressed in positional notation in the base *b* is written, is defined as

$$N = a_{n-1}b^{n-1}... + a_1b^1 + a_0b^0 + a_{-1}b^{-1}$$
$$+ a_{-2}b^{-2}... + a_{-m}b^{-m}$$
$$i = n-1$$
$$= \sum a_i b^i$$
$$i = -m$$

The value of a number is equal to the sum of its digits, each of which is multiplied by a *weight* according to its position in the number. Let's look at some examples of how this formula works. The decimal number 1982 is equal to $1 \times 10^3 + 9 \times 10^2 + 8 \times 10^1 + 2 \times 10^0$ (i.e. one thousand + nine hundreds + eight tens + two). Similarly, 12.34 is equal to $1 \times 10^1 + 2 \times 10^0 + 3 \times 10^{-1} + 4 \times 0^{-2}$. The value of the binary number 10110.11 is given by $1 \times 2^4 + 0 \times 2^3 + 1 \times 2^2 + 1 \times 2^1 + 0 \times 2^0 + 1 \times 2^{-1} + 1 \times 2^{-2}$, or, in decimal, 16 + 4 + 2 + 0.5 + 0.25 = 22.75. Remember that the value of r^0 is 1 (i.e. any number to the power zero is 1).

In base *seven* arithmetic, the number 123 is equal to the decimal number $1 \times 7^2 + 2 \times 7^1 + 3 \times 7^0 = 49 + 14 + 3 = 66$. Because we are talking about different bases in this chapter, we will sometimes use a *subscript* to indicate the base; for example, $123_7 = 66_{10}$.

We should make it clear that we're talking about *natural positional numbers* with positional *weights* of 1, 10, 100, 1000, ... (decimal) or 1, 2, 4, 8, 16, 32, ... (binary). The *weight* of a number is the value by which it is multiplied by virtue of its position in the number. It's perfectly possible to have weightings that are not successive powers of an integer; for example, we can choose a binary weighting of 2, 4, 4, 2 which means that the number 1010 is interpreted as $1 \times 2 + 0 \times 4 + 1 \times 4 + 0 \times 2 = 6$.

We are interested in three bases: decimal, binary, and hexadecimal (the term *hexadecimal* is often abbreviated to *hex*). Although some texts use base-8 octal arithmetic, this base is ill-fitted to the representation of 8- or 16- bit binary values. Octal numbers were popular when people used 12-, 24- or 36-bit computers. We do not discuss octal numbers further. Table 4.3 shows the digits used by each of these bases. Because the hexadecimal base has 16 digits, we use the letters A to F to indicate decimal values between 10 and 15.

People work in decimal and computers in binary. We use base 10 because we have 10 fingers and thumbs. The hexadecimal system is used by people to handle computer arithmetic. By converting binary numbers to hexadecimal form (a very easy task), the shorter hexadecimal numbers can be more readily remembered. For example, the 8-bit binary number 10001001 is equivalent to the hexadecimal number 89 which is easier to remember than 10001001. Because hexadecimal numbers are more compact than binary numbers (1 hexadecimal digit = 4 binary digits), they are used in computer texts and *core-dumps*. The latter term refers to a printout of part of the computer's memory, an operation normally performed as a diagnostic aid.

There are occasions where binary numbers offer people advantages over other forms of representation. Suppose a computer-controlled chemical plant has three heaters, three valves, and two pumps, which are designated H1, H2, H3, V1, V2, V3, P1, P2, respectively. An 8-bit word from the computer is fed to an interface unit that converts the binary ones and zeros into electrical signals to switch on (logical one) or switch off (logical zero) the corresponding device. For example, the binary word 01010011 has the effect described in Table 4.4 when presented to the control unit:

Decimal	$b = 10$	$a = \{0, 1, 2, 3, 4, 5, 6, 7, 8, 9\}$
Binary	$b = 2$	$a = \{0, 1\}$
Hexadecimal	$b = 16$	$a = \{0, 1, 2, 3, 4, 5, 6, 7, 8, 9, A, B, C, D, E, F\}$

Table 4.3 Three number bases.

Bit	Value	Component	Action
7	0	Heater 1	off
6	1	Heater 2	on
5	0	Heater 3	off
4	1	Valve 1	on
3	0	Valve 2	off
2	0	Valve 3	off
1	1	Pump 1	on
0	1	Pump 2	on

Table 4.4 Decoding the binary sequence 01010011.

By inspecting the binary value of the control word, the status of all devices is immediately apparent. If the output had been represented in decimal (83) or hexadecimal (53) the relationship between the number and its intended action would not have been so obvious.

Now that we've looked at the structure of binary and decimal numbers, the next step is to consider how we convert a number in one base into its equivalent value in another base.

4.3 Number base conversion

It's sometimes necessary to convert numbers from one base to another by means of a pencil-and-paper method. This statement is particularly true when working with micro-processors at the assembly language or machine code level. Computer users don't concern themselves with conversion between number bases, as the computer will have software to convert a decimal input into the computer's own internal binary representation of the input. Once the computer has done its job, it converts the binary results into decimal form before printing them.

A knowledge of the effect of number bases on arithmetic operations is sometimes quite vital, as, for example, even the simplest of decimal fractions (say $1/10 = 0.1$) has no exact binary equivalent. That is, a rational number expressed in a finite number of digits in one base may require an infinite number of digits in another base. Suppose the computer were asked to add the decimal value 0.110 to itself and stop when the result reaches 1. The computer may never stop because the decimal value 0.110 cannot be exactly represented by a binary number, with the result that the sum of 10 binary representations of 0.1 is never exactly 1. The sum may be 1.0000000000001 or 0.99999999999, which is almost as good as 1, but it is not the same as 1, and a test for equality with 1 will always fail.

4.3.1 Conversion of integers

In this section we are going to demonstrate how integers are converted from one base to another.

Decimal to binary To convert a decimal integer to binary, divide the number successively by 2, and after each division record the remainder, which is either 1 or 0. The process is terminated only when the result of the division is 0 remainder 1. In all the following conversions R represents the remainder after a division.

RULES OF ARITHMETIC

If there's one point that we would like to emphasize here, it's that the rules of arithmetic are the same in base x as they are in base y. All the rules we learned for base 10 arithmetic can be applied to base 2, base 16, or even base 5-arithmetic. For example, the base 5 numbers 123_5 and 221_5 represent, in decimal, $1 \times 5^2 + 2 \times 5^1 + 3 \times 5^0 = 38_{10}$ and $2 \times 5^2 + 2 \times 5^1 + 1 \times 5^0 = 61_{10}$, respectively. Let's add both pairs of numbers together using the conventional rules of arithmetic in base 5 and base 10.

Base 5	Base 10
123	38
+221	+61
344	99

If we add 123_5 to 221_5 we get 344_5, which is equal to the decimal number $3 \times 5^2 + 4 \times 5^1 + 4 \times 5^0 = 99_{10}$. Adding the decimal numbers 38_{10} and 61_{10} also gives us 99_{10}.

HOW MANY BITS DOES IT REQUIRE TO REPRESENT A DECIMAL NUMBER?

If we represent decimal numbers in binary form, we need to know how many binary digits are required to express an n-digit decimal number in binary form. For example, how many bits does it take to represent numbers up to 90 000 000? The following explanation requires an understanding of *logarithms*.

Suppose we require m bits to represent the largest n-digit decimal number, which is, of course, 99 . . . 999 or $10^n - 1$. We require the largest binary number in m bits (i.e. 11 . . . 111) to be equal to or greater than the largest decimal number in n bits (i.e. 99 . . . 999) that is,

$10^n - 1 \leqslant 2^m - 1$,
that is, $10^n \leqslant 2^m$

Taking logarithms to base 10 we get

$\log_{10} 10^n \leqslant \log_{10} 2^m$
    Note: $\log_{10} 10^n = n\log_{10} 10$ and $\log_{10} 10 = 1$
$n\log 10_{10} \leqslant m\log_{10} 2$
$n \leqslant m\log_{10} 2$
$m \leqslant 3.322_n$

In other words, it takes approximately 3.3n bits to represent an n-bit decimal number. For example, if we wish to represent decimal numbers up to 1 000 000 in binary, we must use at least 6 × 3.3 bits, which indicates a 20-bit word length.

For example, 245_{10} becomes

```
245 ÷ 2 = 122    R = 1
122 ÷ 2 =  61    R = 0
 61 ÷ 2 =  30    R = 1
 30 ÷ 2 =  15    R = 0
 15 ÷ 2 =   7    R = 1
  7 ÷ 2 =   3    R = 1
  3 ÷ 2 =   1    R = 1
  1 ÷ 2 =   0    R = 1
```
                        Most-significant bit

The result is read from the most-significant bit (the last remainder) upwards to give $245_{10} = 11110101_2$.

Decimal to hexadecimal Decimal numbers are converted from decimal into hexadecimal form in exactly the same way that decimal numbers are converted into binary form. However, in this case the remainder lies in the decimal range 0 to 15, corresponding to the hexadecimal range 0 to F. For example, 53241_{10} becomes

```
53241 ÷ 16 = 3327    R =    9
 3327 ÷ 16 =  207    R = 15₁₀ = F₁₆
  207 ÷ 16 =   12    R = 15₁₀ = F₁₆
   12 ÷ 16 =    0    R = 12₁₀ = C₁₆
```

Therefore, $53241_{10} = \text{CFF9}_{16}$.

Binary to decimal It is possible to convert a binary number to decimal by adding together the requisite powers of two. This technique is suitable for relatively small binary numbers up to about 7 or 8 bits.

For example, 11000111_2 is represented by

```
128 64 32 16  8  4  2  1       128
  1  1  0  0  0  1  1  1  =      64
                                 4
                                 2
                             +   1
                               199
```

A more methodical technique is based on a recursive algorithm as follows. Take the leftmost non-zero bit, double it, and add it to the bit on its right. Now take this result, double it, and add it to the next bit on the right. Continue in this way until the least-significant bit has been added in. The recursive procedure may be expressed mathematically as

$$(a_0 + 2(a_1 + 2(a_2 + \cdots)))$$

where the least-significant bit of the binary number is a_0.

For example, 1010111_2 becomes

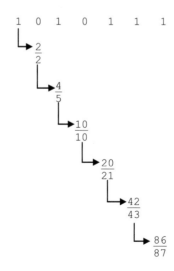

Therefore, $1010111_2 = 87_{10}$.

Hexadecimal to decimal The method is identical to the procedure for binary except that 16 is used as a multiplier.

For example, $24E_{16}$ becomes

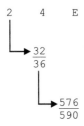

Therefore, $24E_{16} = 590_{10}$.

Binary to hexadecimal The binary number is formed into groups of 4 bits starting at the binary point. Each group is replaced by a hexadecimal digit from 0 to 9, A, B, C, D, E, F. For example, 11001011101 becomes

```
110    0101    1101
 6       5       D
```

Therefore, $11001011101_2 = 65D_{16}$.

Hexadecimal to binary Each hexadecimal digit is replaced by its four bit binary equivalent. For example, $1234AF0C_{16}$ becomes

```
   1    2    3    4    A    F    0    C
0001 0010 0011 0100 1010 1111 0000 1100
```

Therefore,
$1234AF0C_{16} = 00010010001101001010111100001100_2$.

4.3.2 Conversion of fractions

The conversion of fractions from one base to another is carried out in a similar way to the conversion of integers, although it's rather more tedious to manipulate fractions manually. Fortunately, it's rare to have to perform actual pencil and paper conversion of fractions outside the classroom. One way of effectively abolishing fractions is to treat all fractions as integers scaled by an appropriate factor. For example, the binary fraction 0.10101 is equal to the binary integer 10101_2 divided by 2^5 (i.e. 32), so that, for example, 0.10101_2 is the same as $10101_2/2^5 = 21/32 = 0.65625$.

Converting binary fractions to decimal fractions

The algorithm for converting binary fractions to their decimal equivalent is based on the fact that a bit in one column is worth half the value of a bit in the column on its left. Starting at the rightmost non-zero bit, take that bit and halve it. Now add the result to the next bit on its left. Halve this result and add it to the next bit on the left. Continue until the binary point is reached.

For example, consider the conversion of 0.01101_2 into decimal form.

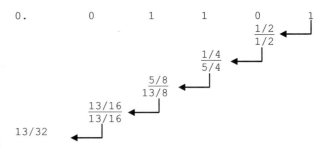

Therefore, $0.01101_2 = 13/32$.

Converting decimal fractions to binary fractions

The decimal fraction is multiplied by 2 and the integer part noted. The integer, which will be either 1 or 0, is then stripped from the number to leave a fractional part. The new fraction is multiplied by two and the integer part noted. We continue in this way until the process ends or a sufficient degree of precision has been achieved. The binary fraction is formed by reading the integer parts from the top to the bottom as illustrated below.

For example, 0.6875_{10} becomes

```
0.6875  x  2  →  1.3750
0.3750  x  2  →  0.7500
0.7500  x  2  →  1.5000
0.5000  x  2  →  1.0000
0.0000  x  2      ends the process
```

Therefore, $0.6875_{10} = 0.1011_2$.
Now consider the conversion of 0.1_{10} into binary form.

```
0.1000  x  2  →  0.2000
0.2000  x  2  →  0.4000
0.4000  x  2  →  0.8000
0.8000  x  2  →  1.6000
0.6000  x  2  →  1.2000
0.2000  x  2  →  0.4000
0.4000  x  2  →  0.8000
0.8000  x  2  →  1.6000
0.6000  x  2  →  1.2000
0.2000  x  2  →  0.4000
0.4000  x  2  →  0.8000
```
etc.

Therefore, $0.1_{10} = 0.00011001100\ldots_2$ etc. As we pointed out before 0.1_{10} cannot be expressed exactly in binary form with a finite number of bits.

Converting between hexadecimal fractions and decimal fractions

We can convert between hexadecimal fractions and decimal fractions using the same algorithms we used for binary conversions. All we have to change is the base (i.e., 2 to 16).

Consider the following example where we convert 0.123_{16} into a decimal fraction.

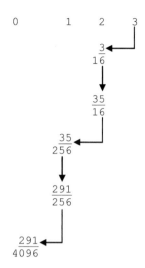

Binary to hexadecimal fraction conversion and vice versa

The conversion of binary fractions to hexadecimal bases is as easy as the corresponding integer conversions. The only point worth mentioning is that when binary digits are split into groups of four, we start grouping bits at the binary point and move to the right. Any group of digits remaining on the right containing fewer than 4 bits must be made up to 4 bits by the addition of zeros to the right of the least-significant bit. The following examples illustrate this point.

Binary to hexadecimal
$0.10101100_2 \rightarrow 0.1010\ 1100_2 \rightarrow 0.AC_{16}$
Binary to hexadecimal
$0.101011001 \rightarrow 0.1010\ 1100\ 1(000) \rightarrow 0.AC8_{16}$
Hexadecimal to binary
$0.ABC_{16} \rightarrow 0.1010\ 1011\ 1100 \rightarrow 0.101010111100_2$

Numbers containing an integer part and a fraction part (e.g. 110101.11010 in base 2 or 123.125 in decimal) are converted from one base to another in two stages. The integer part is converted and then the fractional part.

4.4 Special-purpose codes

Throughout this book a group of binary digits generally represents one of three things: a numerical quantity, an instruction, or a character. However, many different codes exist in the world of computing and digital systems, each of which is best suited to the particular job for which it was designed.

4.4.1 BCD codes

A common alternative to natural binary arithmetic is called BCD or *binary-coded decimal*. In theory BCD is a case of having your cake and eating it. We have already stated that computer designers use two-state logic elements on purely economic grounds. This, in turn, leads to the world of binary arithmetic and the consequent problems of converting between binary and decimal representations of numeric quantities. Binary-coded decimal numbers accept the inevitability of two-state logic by coding the individual decimal digits into groups of four bits. Table 4.5 shows how the 10 digits, 0 to 9, are represented in BCD, and how a decimal number is converted to a BCD form.

BCD arithmetic is identical to decimal arithmetic and differs only in the way the 10 digits are represented. The following example demonstrates how a BCD addition is carried out.

Decimal	BCD
2634	0010 0110 0011 0100
+3825	+0011 1000 0010 0101
6459	0110 0100 0101 1001

As you can see, the arithmetic is decimal with the digits 0 to 9 represented by 4-bit codes. When 6 is added to 8 (i.e. 0110 to 1000), the result is not the binary value 1110, but the decimal $6 + 8 = 14 = 0100_2$ (i.e. 4) carry 1.

Binary code	BCD value
0000	0
0001	1
0010	2
0011	3
0100	4
0101	5
0110	6
0111	7
1000	8
1001	9
1010	Forbidden code
1011	Forbidden code
1100	Forbidden code
1101	Forbidden code
1110	Forbidden code
1111	Forbidden code

Table 4.5 Binary-coded decimal.

Although BCD makes decimal to binary conversion easy, it suffers from two disadvantages. The first is that BCD arithmetic is more complex than binary arithmetic simply because the binary tables (i.e. addition, subtraction, multiplication, and division) can be implemented in hardware by a few gates. The decimal tables involve all combinations of the digits 0 to 9 and are more complex. Today's digital technology makes these disadvantages less evident than in the early days of computer technology where each gate was an expensive item.

BCD uses storage inefficiently. A BCD digit requires 4 bits of storage but only 10 symbols are mapped onto 10 of the 16 possible binary codes making the binary codes 1010 to 1111 (10 to 15) redundant and wasting storage. As we demonstrated earlier, natural binary numbers require an average of approximately 3.3 bits per decimal digit. In spite of its disadvantages, BCD arithmetic can be found in applications such as pocket calculators or digital watches. Some microprocessors have special instructions to aid BCD operations.

There are other ways of representing BCD numbers in addition to the BCD code presented above. Each of these codes has desirable properties making it suitable for a particular application (e.g. the representation of negative numbers). These BCD codes are not relevant to this text.

4.4.2 Unweighted codes

The binary codes we've just described are called *pure* binary, *natural* binary, or *8421 weighted* binary because the 8, 4, 2, and 1 represent the weightings of each of the columns in the positional code. These are not the only types of code available. Some positional codes don't have a natural binary weighting, other codes are called *unweighted* because the value of a bit doesn't depend on its position within a number. Each of the many special-purpose codes has properties that make it suitable for a specific application. One such unweighted code is called a *unit distance code*.

In a *unit* distance code, the Hamming distance between *consecutive* code words is equal to one, and no two consecutive code words differ in more than one bit position. Natural binary numbers are not unit distance codes; for example, the sequential values $0111_2 = 7$ and $1000_2 = 8$ differ by a Hamming distance of *four*. The most widely encountered unit distance code is the *Gray* code, the first 16 values of which are given in Table 4.6. Figure 4.1 illustrates the timing diagrams of 4-bit binary and 4-bit Gray counters. As you can see, only one bit makes a change at each new count of the Gray counter.

Decimal value	Natural binary value	Gray code
	DCBA	DCBA
0	0000	0000
1	0001	0001
2	0010	0011
3	0011	0010
4	0100	0110
5	0101	0111
6	0110	0101
7	0111	0100
8	1000	1100
9	1001	1101
10	1010	1111
11	1011	1110
12	1100	1010
13	1101	1011
14	1110	1001
15	1111	1000

Table 4.6 The 4-bit Gray code (an unweighted unit distance code).

HAMMING DISTANCE

The *Hamming distance* between two words is the number of places (i.e. positions) in which their bits differ. Consider the following five pairs of words.

Word 1	00101101	00101101	00101101	00101101	00101101
Word 2	00101100	11101100	11101101	00100101	11010010
Places different	✓	✓✓	✓	✓✓	✓	✓✓✓✓✓✓✓✓
Hamming distance	1	3	2	1	8

Two *m*-bit words have a zero Hamming distance if they are the same and an *m*-bit distance if they are logical complements.

(a) Binary code

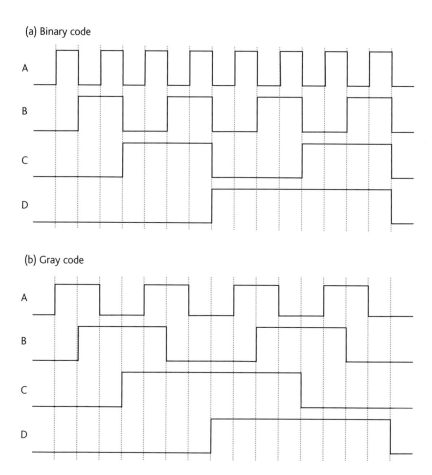

(b) Gray code

Figure 4.1 Sequencing though a 4-bit binary and a 4-bit Gray code.

The Gray code is used by the *optical encoder*, a mechanism for converting the angle of a shaft or spindle into a binary value. An optical encoder allows you to measure the angular position of a shaft electronically without any physical connection between the shaft and the measuring equipment. A typical example of an optical encoder is found in an automated weather reporting system. The direction from which the wind is blowing is measured by one of the World's oldest instruments, the weather vane. The weather vane is mounted on a shaft connected to an optical encoder, which provides the angle of rotation (i.e. wind direction) as a digital signal.

Figure 4.2 shows an optical encoder using a natural binary code and Figure 4.3 shows the same arrangement but with a Gray-encoded disk. A transparent glass or plastic disk is attached to the shaft whose angular position is to be measured. As you can see, the disk is covered with concentric tracks, one for each of the bits in the code representing the position of the shaft. A 4-bit code might be suitable for a wind direction indicator, whereas a 10-bit code may be required to indicate the position of a shaft in a machine. Each of these tracks is divided into sectors that are either opaque or transparent.

A light source is located on one side of the disk over each track. A photoelectric sensor is located on the other side

directly opposite each light source. For any position of the disk, a particular combination of the photoelectric cells detects a light beam, depending on whether or not there is a transparent sector between the light source and detector.

A natural binary code can create problems when more than one bit of the output code changes as the shaft rotates from one code to the next. The photoelectric cells may not be perfectly aligned; the light source isn't a point source; and the edges of the sectors don't have perfectly straight edges. When the disk rotates from one sector to the next and two or three bits change state, one bit may change slightly before the other. For example, the change from the natural binary code 001 to 010 might be observed as the sequence 001, 000, 010. Because the least-significant bit changes *before* the middle bit, the spurious code 000 is generated momentarily. In some applications this can be very troublesome. Figure 4.3 demonstrates that a Gray-encoded disk has the property that only one bit at a time changes, solving the problems inherent in the natural binary system. Once the Gray code has been read into a digital system it may be converted into a natural binary code for processing in the normal way. The EOR gate logic of Fig. 4.4 converts between Gray codes and natural binary codes.

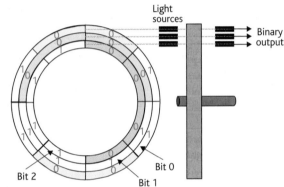

Sector	Angle	Binary code
0	0 – 45	0 0 0
1	45 – 90	0 0 1
2	90 – 135	0 1 0
3	135 – 180	0 1 1
4	180 – 225	1 0 0
5	225 – 270	1 0 1
6	270 – 315	1 1 0
7	315 – 360	1 1 1

Figure 4.2 A natural binary-encoded optical encoder.

Sector	Angle	Binary code
0	0 – 45	0 0 0
1	45 – 90	0 0 1
2	90 – 135	0 1 1
3	135 – 180	0 1 0
4	180 – 225	1 1 0
5	225 – 270	1 1 1
6	270 – 315	1 0 1
7	315 – 360	1 0 0

Figure 4.3 A Gray-encoded optical encoder.

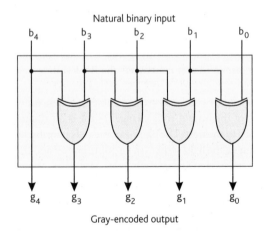

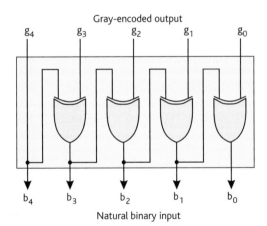

Figure 4.4 Converting binary codes to Gray codes and vice versa.

4.5 Error-detecting codes

In an ideal world, errors don't occur. In reality a bit that should be a 1 sometimes gets changed into a 0, and a bit that should be a 0 sometimes gets changed into a 1. In any electronic system there are always unwanted random signals, collectively called *noise* which may interfere with the correct operation of the system. These random signals arise from a variety of causes, ranging from the thermal motion of electrons in a digital system, to electromagnetic radiation from nearby lightning strikes and power line transients caused by the switching of inductive loads (e.g. starting motors in vacuum cleaners or elevators). The magnitude of these unwanted signals is generally tiny compared with digital signals inside the computer. The two electrical signal levels representing the zero and one binary states are so well separated that one level is almost never spontaneously converted into the other level inside a digital computer under normal operating conditions.

We can use some of the properties of binary numbers to *detect* errors, or even to *correct* errors. Suppose we take the binary pattern 01101011 and ask whether there is an error in it. We can't answer this question, because one binary pattern is just as good as another. Now consider the word '*Jamuary*'. You will immediately realize that it should be spelt *January*, because there is no word '*Jamuary*' in the English language. You can *correct* this spelling error because the *closest* valid word to '*Jamuary*' is January. It's exactly the same with binary codes.

Error-detecting codes, (EDCs), can detect that a word has been corrupted (i.e. changed). The subject of error-detecting codes is large enough to fill several textbooks. Here we look at

threes codes. We also introduce the *error-correcting code* (ECC), which can correct one or more errors in a corrupted word. Of course the ECC is also an EDC whereas the EDC is not necessarily an ECC.

Before we can discuss EDCs and ECCs we must introduce two terms: *source word* and *code word*. A source word is an unencoded string of bits and a code word is a source word that has been encoded. For example, the source code 10110 might be transformed into the code word 111000111111000 by triplicating each bit.

In order to create an *error-detecting* code, we have to construct a code in such a way that an error always leaves a noticeable trace or marker. An error-correcting code increases the length of the source code by adding one (or more) *redundant* bits, so called because they carry no new information. Figure 4.5 demonstrates how r redundant bits are added to an m-bit source word to create an $(m + r)$-bit code word. The redundant bits are also called *check bits* because they are used to check whether the code word is valid or not. Note that the check bits can be interleaved throughout the word and don't have to be located together as Fig. 4.5 shows.

WHERE DO WE FIND ECCs AND EDCs?

Whenever digital signals are transmitted over a long distance by cables, their magnitude is diminished, making it possible for external noise signals to exceed the level of the digital signals and thus corrupt them. The effect of electrical noise is familiar to anyone who has tuned a radio or television to a distant station—the sound or picture is of a lower quality than when a local station is received. Whenever an error occurs in the reception of digital signals, it is important for the event to be detected so that a request for retransmission of the corrupted data can be made.

ECCs and EDCs are also required by data storage technology. Some of the techniques used to store digital data are prone to errors (albeit with a very low probability); for example, DRAM chips are susceptible to errors caused by alpha particles due to radioactivity. ECCs and EDCs can determine whether data has been corrupted during the process of storage and retrieval.

Error detection can be implemented by transmitting the desired digital information (i.e. the source word) plus one or more *check* bits whose value is a function of the information bits. Because check bits convey no new information, they are called *redundant bits*.

At the receiving end of a data link the information bits are used to recalculate the check bits. If the received check bits are the same as those locally generated, error-free transmission is assumed—otherwise the receiver sends a message back to the transmitter asking it to repeat the lost data.

If an error is detected in a word stored in memory, the error can't be corrected by asking the computer what the stored word should have been, because there is no other copy of the word. Consequently the operating system must be informed of the error and then left to take appropriate action (usually by aborting the current task). Memories that use error-correcting codes are able to repair the damage done by an error before the word is passed to the computer.

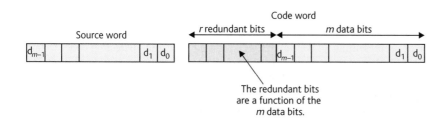

Code word

Source word   ← r redundant bits → ← m data bits →

The redundant bits are a function of the m data bits.

Figure 4.5 Encoding a source word.

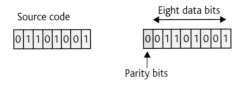

Figure 4.6 Creating a code word with even parity.

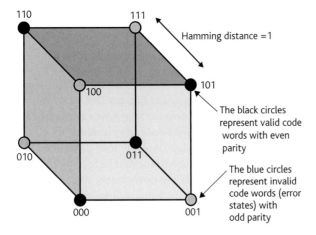

Figure 4.7 A 3-bit error detecting code

4.5.1 **Parity EDCs**

The simplest error-detecting code is called a *parity check code*. We take an *m*-bit *source word* and append a *parity* bit to the source word to produce an (*m* +1)-bit *codeword*. The *parity bit* is chosen to make the total number of 1s in the code word even (an even parity bit) or odd (an odd parity bit). We will assume an even parity bit here.

Figure 4.6 shows an 8-bit source word, 01101001, which is converted into a 9-bit code with even parity. This binary string has a total of four 1s, so the parity bit must be selected as 0 to keep the total number of 1s even. Assuming that the parity bit is appended to the left-hand end of the string, the 9-bit code word is 001101001. If, when this value is stored in memory or transmitted over a data link, any one of the bits is changed, the resulting parity will no longer be even. Imagine that bit 2 is changed from 0 to 1 and the code word becomes 001101101. This word now contains five 1s, which indicates an error, because the parity is odd.

Figure 4.7 provides a graphical representation of a 2-bit source word with an *even* parity bit. Although 3 bits provide eight possible binary values, only four of them are *valid code words* with an even parity (i.e. the black circles representing codes 000, 101, 110, 011). As you can see, a valid code word is separated from another nearest valid code word by two *unit lengths*. In Fig. 4.7 a unit length corresponds to an edge of the cube. If one of the valid codewords suffers a *single* error (i.e.

Message	Code word (even parity)		Code word (odd parity)	
000	0	000	1	000
001	1	001	0	001
010	1	010	0	010
011	0	011	1	011
100	1	100	0	100
101	0	101	1	101
110	0	110	1	110
111	1	111	0	111
	Even parity bit		Odd parity bit	

Table 4.7 Odd and even parity codes.

only one bit changes), the codeword changes from one of the black circles to one of the white circles one unit length away. Because these code words all have an odd parity, you can always detect a single error. Two errors (or any even number of errors) cannot be detected because you move from one valid code word to another valid codeword. Fortunately, if one error is a rare event, two errors are correspondingly rarer (unless the nature of the error-inducing mechanism affects more than one bit at a time).

If you detect an error, you must ask for the correct data to be retransmitted (if the corruption occurred over a data link). If the data was stored in memory, there's little you can do other than to tell the operating system that something has gone wrong.

Table 4.7 gives the eight valid code words for a three-bit source word, for both even and odd parities. In each case the parity bit is the most-significant bit.

As an example of the application of check bits consider a simple two-digit decimal code with a single decimal check digit. The check digit is calculated by adding up the two source digits modulo 10 (modulo 10 simply means that we ignore any carry when we add the digits; for example, the modulo 10 value of 6 + 7 is 3). If the two source digits are 4 and 9, the code word is 493 (the check digit is 3). Suppose that during transmission or storage the code word is corrupted and becomes 463. If we re-evaluate the check digit we get 4 + 6 = 10 = 0 (modulo 10). As the recorded check digit is 3, we know that an error must have occurred.

4.5.2 **Error-correcting codes**

We can design error-detecting and-correcting codes to both locate and fix errors. Figure 4.8 illustrates the simplest 3-bit error detecting and correcting code where only code words 000 and 111 are valid. The Hamming distance between these two valid code words is 3. Suppose that the valid code word

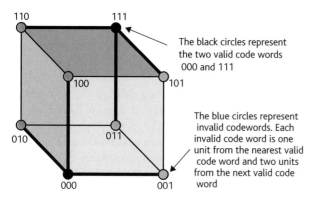

Figure 4.8 A 3-bit error-correcting code.

The black circles represent the two valid code words 000 and 111

The blue circles represent invalid codewords. Each invalid code word is one unit from the nearest valid code word and two units from the next valid code word

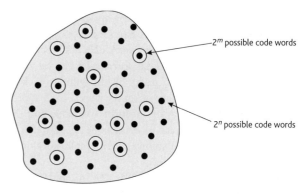

2^m possible code words

2^n possible code words

Figure 4.9 The principle of the EDC.

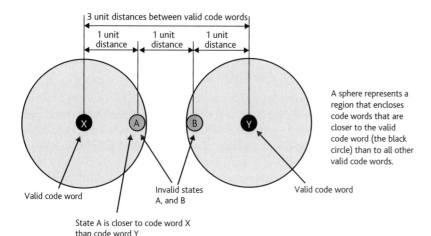

3 unit distances between valid code words

1 unit distance

1 unit distance

1 unit distance

Valid code word

Invalid states A, and B

Valid code word

State A is closer to code word X than code word Y

A sphere represents a region that encloses code words that are closer to the valid code word (the black circle) than to all other valid code words.

Figure 4.10 Minimum condition required to correct a single bit error.

111 is stored in memory and later read back as 110. This code word is clearly invalid, because it is neither 000 nor 111. If you examine Fig. 4.8, you can see that the invalid code word 110 has a Hamming distance of 1 from the valid code word 111 and a Hamming distance 2 from the valid code word 000. An error correcting code selects the correct code as the nearest valid code word to the invalid code word. We assume that the valid code word was 111—we have now both *detected* an error and *corrected* it.

How error-detecting codes work

The idea behind EDCs is simple, as Fig. 4.9 demonstrates. An incorrect code word has to be made to reveal itself. Assume we transmit n-bit messages, where m bits are data bits and $r = n - m$ bits are redundant check bits. Imagine an n-*dimensional space* in which each point is represented by the value of an n-bit signal. This n-dimensional space contains 2^n possible elements (i.e. all the possible combinations of n bits). However, an m-bit source code can convey 2^m unique messages. In other words, only 2^m signals are valid out of the 2^n

possible signals. Should a code word be received that is not one of these 2^m values, an error may be assumed.

If r check bits are added to the m message digits to create an n-bit code word, there are $2^n = 2^{m+r}$ possible code words. The n-dimensional space will contain 2^m *valid* code words, 2^n *possible* code words and $2^n - 2^m = 2^m(2^{n-m} - 1) = 2^m(2^r - 1)$ *error states*.

If we read a word from memory or from a communication system, we can check its location within the n-dimensional space. If the word is located at one of the 2^m valid points we assume that it's error free. If it falls in one of the $2^n - 2^m$ error states, we can reject it.

Error-correcting codes require that all valid code words be separated from each other by a Hamming distance of at least 3. An error-correcting code tries to correct an error by selecting the nearest valid code to the code word in error. Because valid codes are separated by a minimum of three units from each other, a single error moves a code word one unit from its correct value, but it remains two units from any other valid code word. Figure 4.10 illustrates this concept.

Block parity error-correcting codes

The single parity-bit, error-detecting code can be extended to create a *block EDC* (also called a *matrix EDC*). A block EDC uses two types of parity check bit: a *vertical* parity bit and a *horizontal* (or longitudinal) parity bit. Imagine a block of data composed of a sequence of source words. Each source word can be written vertically to form a column and the sequence of source words can be written one after another to create a block. Figure 4.11 demonstrates a simple block of six 3-bit source words.

The source words are 110, 101, 001, 110, 101, and 010 and have been written down as a block or matrix. We can generate a parity bit for each source word (i.e. column) and append it to the bottom of each column to create a new row. Each of these parity bits is called a vertical parity bit. Since a block of source words is made up of a number of columns, a parity word can be formed by calculating the parity across the bits. Each code word (i.e. column) in Fig. 4.12 is composed of four bits: D_0, D_1, D_2, and D_3 (where D_3 is the vertical parity bit). We can now derive a horizontal parity bit by calculating the parity across the columns. That is, we create a parity bit across all the D_0s. Horizontal parity bits for D_1, D_2, and the vertical parity bits, D_3, can be generated in a similar way. Figure 4.12 shows how the source words of Fig. 4.11 are transformed into a block error-detecting code.

A vertical even parity bit has been appended to each column to create a new row labeled D_3. Similarly, a horizontal parity bit has been added to each row to create a new column labeled word 7.

Figure 4.13 demonstrates the action of a block error-detecting code in the presence of a single error. A tick marks each row or column where the parity is correct and a cross marks where it is not. In this example, the bit in error is detected by the intersection of the row and column in which it creates a parity violation. Thus, although the word 1001 is received incorrectly as 1101 it can be corrected. Although the block parity code can detect and correct single errors, it can detect (but not correct) certain combinations of multiple error. Block EDCs/ECCs are sometimes found in data transmission systems and in the storage of serial data on magnetic tape.

By detecting a parity error in a row, we can detect the position of the bit in error (i.e. in this case bit D_1). By detecting a parity error in a column, we can detect the word in error (i.e. in this case word 3). Now we can locate the error, which is bit D_1 of word 3. The error can be corrected by inverting this bit.

4.5.3 Hamming codes

Hamming codes are the simplest class of error-detecting and-correcting codes that can be applied to a single code word (in contrast with a block error-correcting code that is applied to a group of words). A Hamming code takes an *m*-bit source word and generates *r* parity check bits to create an *n*-bit code word. The *r* parity check bits are selected so that a single error in the code word can be detected, located, and therefore corrected.

Bit	Word 1	Word 2	Word 3	Word 4	Word 5	Word 6
D_0	0	1	1	0	1	0
D_1	1	0	0	1	0	1
D_2	1	1	0	1	1	0

Figure 4.11 Six 3-bit words.

Bit	Word 1	Word 2	Word 3	Word 4	Word 5	Word 6	Word 7
D_0	0	1	1	0	1	0	1
D_1	1	0	0	1	0	1	1
D_2	1	1	0	1	1	0	0
D_3	0	0	1	0	0	1	0

Figure 4.12 Creating a block error-detecting code.

Bit	Word 1	Word 2	Word 3	Word 4	Word 5	Word 6	Word 7	
D_0	0	1	1	0	1	0	1	✓
D_1	1	0	1	1	0	1	1	✗
D_2	1	1	0	1	1	0	0	✓
D_3	0	0	1	0	0	1	0	✓
	✓	✓	✗	✓	✓	✓	✓	

Figure 4.13 Detecting and correcting an error in a block code.

Hamming codes are designated $H_{n,m}$ where, for example, $H_{7,4}$ represents a Hamming code with a code word of 7 bits and a source word of 4 bits. The following sequence of bits represents a $H_{7,4}$ code word:

```
Bit position   7     6     5     4     3     2     1
Code bit       I₄    I₃    I₂    C₃    I₁    C₂    C₁
```

I_i = source bit i, C_j = check bit j.

The information (i.e. source word) bits are numbered I_1, I_2, I_3, and I_4, and the check bits are numbered C_1, C_2, and C_3. Similarly, the bit positions in the code word are numbered from 1 to 7. The check bits are located in binary positions 2^i in the code word (i.e. positions 1, 2, and 4). Note how the check bits are interleaved with the source code bits.

The three check bits are generated from the source word according to the following *parity equations*.

$$C_3 = I_2 \oplus I_3 \oplus I_4$$
$$C_2 = I_1 \oplus I_3 \oplus I_4$$
$$C_1 = I_1 \oplus I_2 \oplus I_4$$

For example, C_3 is the parity bit generated by information bits I_2, I_3, and I_4, etc. Suppose we have a source word equal to $I_4, I_3, I_2, I_1 = 1, 1, 0, 1$. The check bits are calculated as

$$C_3 = 0 \oplus 1 \oplus 1 = 0$$
$$C_2 = 1 \oplus 1 \oplus 1 = 1$$
$$C_1 = 1 \oplus 0 \oplus 1 = 0$$

The code word is therefore

```
I₄, I₃, I₂, C₃, I₁, C₂, C₁ = 1, 1, 0, 0, 1, 1, 0
```

Suppose now that the code word is corrupted during storage (or transmission). Assume that the value of I_3 is switched from 1 to 0. The resulting code word is now 1000110. Using the new code word we can recalculate the check bits to give

$$C_3 = 0 \oplus 0 \oplus 1 = 1$$
$$C_2 = 1 \oplus 0 \oplus 1 = 0$$
$$C_1 = 1 \oplus 0 \oplus 1 = 0$$

The new check bits are 1, 0, 0 and the stored check bits are 0, 1, 0. If we take the exclusive OR of the old and new check bits we get $1 \oplus 0, 0 \oplus 1, 0 \oplus 0 = 1, 1, 0$. The binary value 110 expressed in decimal form is 6 and points to bit position 6 in the code word. It is this bit that is in error. How does a Hamming code perform this apparent magic trick? The answer can be found in the equations for the parity check bits. The check bits are calculated in such a way that any single bit error will change the particular combination of check bits that points to its location.

The Hamming code described above can detect and correct a single error. By adding a further check bit we can create a Hamming code that can detect two errors and correct one error.

4.5.4 Hadamard codes

Computer and communication systems designers employ a wide range of error-correcting codes and each code has its own particular characteristics. As the mathematics of error-correcting codes is not trivial, we will demonstrate the construction of an error-correcting code that can be appreciated without any math.

A *Hadamard* matrix of order n is written $[\mathbf{H}]_n$ and has some very interesting properties. All elements in a Hadamard matrix are either 1 or -1 (this is still a *binary* or two-state system because we can write -1 and 1 instead of 0 and 1 without loss of generality). The simplest Hadamard matrix is written $[\mathbf{H}]_2$ and has the following value:

```
+1   +1
+1   -1
```

An interesting property of the Hadamard matrix is that a $2n \times 2n$ Hadamard matrix $[\mathbf{H}]_{2n}$ can be derived from the $n \times n$ Hadamard matrix $[\mathbf{H}]_n$ by means of the expansion

```
+[H]ₙ   +[H]ₙ

+[H]ₙ   -[H]ₙ
```

That is, you just write down the matrix $[\mathbf{H}]_n$ four times, with the appropriate signs in front of each matrix. Let's use this relationship to construct the Hadamard matrix of the order four, $[\mathbf{H}]_4$, from $[\mathbf{H}]_2$. All we have to do is write down $[\mathbf{H}]_2$ four times. Each time a $+[\mathbf{H}]_n$ appears in the expression for $[\mathbf{H}]_{2n}$, we write the value of $[\mathbf{H}]_2$ and each time a $-[\mathbf{H}]_n$ appears in the expression we write the value of $-[\mathbf{H}]_2$ (i.e. $[\mathbf{H}]_2$ with all elements reversed).

```
+1   +1     +1   +1
+1   -1     +1   -1

+1   +1     -1   -1
+1   -1     -1   +1
```

Can you see any pattern in the matrix emerging? Let's construct a Hadamard matrix of the order eight, $[\mathbf{H}]_8$, by taking the value of $[\mathbf{H}]_4$ and using the expansion to generate $[\mathbf{H}]_8$.

```
+1   +1   +1   +1     +1   +1   +1   +1
+1   -1   +1   -1     +1   -1   +1   -1
+1   +1   -1   -1     +1   +1   -1   -1
+1   -1   -1   +1     +1   -1   -1   +1

+1   +1   +1   +1     -1   -1   -1   -1
+1   -1   +1   -1     -1   +1   -1   +1
+1   +1   -1   -1     -1   -1   +1   +1
+1   -1   -1   +1     -1   +1   +1   -1
```

Source code	Row	8-bit code word							
000	0	+1	+1	+1	+1	+1	+1	+1	+1
001	1	+1	−1	+1	−1	+1	−1	+1	−1
010	2	+1	+1	−1	−1	+1	+1	−1	−1
011	3	+1	−1	−1	+1	+1	−1	−1	+1
100	4	+1	+1	+1	+1	−1	−1	−1	−1
101	5	+1	−1	+1	−1	−1	+1	−1	+1
110	6	+1	+1	−1	−1	−1	−1	+1	+1
111	7	+1	−1	−1	+1	−1	+1	+1	−1

Table 4.8 Using a Hadamard matrix to generate an 8-bit codeword from a 3-bit source code.

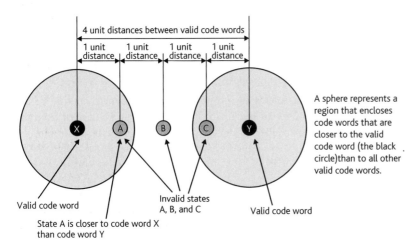

A sphere represents a region that encloses code words that are closer to the valid code word (the black circle) than to all other valid code words.

Figure 4.14 Adjacent code words in a 4-unit code.

If you inspect the rows of this Hadamard matrix of the order eight, you find that each row has a Hamming distance of 4 from each of the other seven rows. The Hamming distance between any row and all other rows of a Hadamard matrix of the order n is $n/2$.

Let's now use the Hadamard matrix of the order eight to transform a 3-bit source code into an 8-bit code word. The matrix for $[\mathbf{H}]_8$ has eight rows, so that a 3-bit source code can be used to select one of the eight possible rows. Table 4.8 is a simple copy of an $[\mathbf{H}]_8$ matrix in which the rows of the matrix are numbered 0 to 7 to represent source codes 000 to 111.

Suppose you want to encode the 3-bit source code 011 using $[\mathbf{H}]_8$. The source word is 011, which corresponds to the 8-bit code word +1 −1 −1 +1 +1 −1 −1 +1 (or 10011001 expressed in conventional binary form) on row 3 of Table 4.8. This code word has *three* information bits and *five* redundant bits. These five redundant bits enable us to both detect and correct an error in the code word.

The most important property of the Hadamard matrix of the order n is that each row differs from all other rows in exactly $n/2$ bit positions. The rows of an $[\mathbf{H}]_8$ matrix differ from each other in four bit positions; that is, the minimum Hamming distance between code words is 4. We have already demonstrated that a code with a minimum Hamming distance of 3 can both detect and correct errors. Consider, for example, the valid code words +1 −1 −1 +1 +1 −1 −1 +1

and +1 +1 +1 +1 −1 −1 −1 −1. The first code word has a unit distance of 4 from the second code word. If the first code word were converted into the second code word, it might go through the intermediate error states +1 +1 −1 +1 +1 −1 −1 +1 , +1 +1 +1 +1 +1 −1 −1 +1, +1 +1 +1 +1 −1 −1 −1 +1, and +1 +1 +1 +1 −1 −1 −1 −1.

Let's look at this code in more detail. Figure 4.14 illustrates two adjacent valid codewords, X and Y, generated by a $[\mathbf{H}]_8$ matrix, which are, of course, separated by a Hamming distance of 4. The intermediate error states between X and Y (i.e. the invalid codewords) are labeled A, B, and C. Each state is separated by 1 unit distance from its immediate neighbors. As you can see, error state A is closer to valid code word X than to the next nearest code word, Y. Similarly, error state C is closer to valid code word Y than to any other valid code word. Error state B is equidistant from the two valid code words and cannot be used to perform error correction. Two errors in a code word are therefore detectable *but not correctable*, because the resulting error state has a Hamming distance of 2 from the correct state and 2 from at least one other valid state.

Suppose that the code word 011 is transformed into the 8-bit Hadamard code 10011001 and an error occurs in storage (or transmission) to give a new incorrect value 10011101 (we have made an error in bit 2). We detect and correct the error by matching the new code word against all the valid code words.

Code	Code word	
000	1 1 1 1 1 1 1 1	
	1 0 0 1 1 1 0 1	Distance 3
001	1 0 1 0 1 0 1 0	
	1 0 0 1 1 1 0 1	Distance 5
010	1 1 0 0 1 1 0 0	
	1 0 0 1 1 1 0 1	Distance 3
011	1 0 0 1 1 0 0 1	
	1 0 0 1 1 1 0 1	Distance 1
100	1 1 1 1 0 0 0 0	
	1 0 0 1 1 1 0 1	Distance 5
101	1 0 1 0 0 1 0 1	
	1 0 0 1 1 1 0 1	Distance 3
110	1 1 0 0 0 0 1 1	
	1 0 0 1 1 1 0 1	Distance 5
111	1 0 0 1 0 1 1 0	
	1 0 0 1 1 1 0 1	Distance 3

> The word 10011101 has a Hamming distance of 1 from the valid code 10011001. Therefore, we assume that the code was 011.

Table 4.9 Correcting an error in a Hadamard code.

Table 4.9 gives the Hamming distance between the code word 10011101 and each row of the Hamming matrix. The smallest Hamming distance is 1, which corresponds to a source code of 011 (i.e. the correct source code). All other Hamming distances are either 3 or 5; that is, the new error state is closer to some of the valid states and further away from some of the valid states.

Having looked at $[\mathbf{H}]_8$ let's continue and construct a Hadamard matrix $[\mathbf{H}]_{16}$, which is even more interesting. The 16×16 Hadamard matrix $[\mathbf{H}]_{16}$ is given by

```
+1 +1 +1 +1 +1 +1 +1 +1   +1 +1 +1 +1 +1 +1 +1 +1
+1 -1 +1 -1 +1 -1 +1 -1   +1 -1 +1 -1 +1 -1 +1 -1
+1 +1 -1 -1 +1 +1 -1 -1   +1 +1 -1 -1 +1 +1 -1 -1
+1 -1 -1 +1 +1 -1 -1 +1   +1 -1 -1 +1 +1 -1 -1 +1
+1 +1 +1 +1 -1 -1 -1 -1   +1 +1 +1 +1 -1 -1 -1 -1
+1 -1 +1 -1 -1 +1 -1 +1   +1 -1 +1 -1 -1 +1 -1 +1
+1 +1 -1 -1 -1 -1 +1 +1   +1 +1 -1 -1 -1 -1 +1 +1
+1 -1 -1 +1 -1 +1 +1 -1   +1 -1 -1 +1 -1 +1 +1 -1

+1 +1 +1 +1 +1 +1 +1 +1   -1 -1 -1 +1 -1 -1 -1 -1
+1 +1 +1 +1 +1 +1 +1 +1   -1 -1 +1 -1 -1 -1 +1 +1
+1 +1 -1 -1 +1 +1 -1 -1   -1 -1 +1 +1 -1 -1 +1 +1
+1 -1 -1 +1 +1 -1 -1 +1   -1 +1 +1 -1 -1 +1 +1 -1
+1 +1 +1 +1 -1 -1 -1 -1   -1 -1 -1 -1 +1 +1 +1 +1
+1 -1 +1 -1 -1 +1 -1 +1   -1 +1 -1 +1 +1 -1 +1 -1
+1 +1 -1 -1 -1 -1 +1 +1   -1 -1 +1 +1 +1 +1 -1 -1
+1 -1 -1 +1 -1 +1 +1 -1   -1 +1 +1 +1 +1 -1 -1 +1
```

In this case there are 16 rows and each row has a minimum Hamming distance of 8 from all other rows. If a 4-bit source word is used to select one of the 16 rows, the resulting 16-bit code word will differ from all other valid code words in eight bit positions. Figure 4.15 illustrates two adjacent valid code words. Up to *three* errors in a code word can still be corrected because a code word with three errors is 3 Hamming units away from the correct code word and 5 Hamming units away from the next nearest valid code word.

Because this 16-bit Hadamard code can correct up to three errors in a code word, it is used in applications in which errors occur relatively frequently (e.g. when transmitting digital data between spacecraft and receiving stations on Earth). Error-correcting codes are widely used to minimize the error rate in digital storage systems (e.g. hard disk and CD-ROM).

4.6 Data-compressing codes

Whoever said 'the best things in life are free' was wrong—very little in life is free. Encoding information into binary form costs *time* and *money*; time because data takes time to process and money because both random access memory and secondary storage systems are not free. Consequently, computer scientists have attempted to squeeze as much information into as few bits as possible.

Most computer users will have heard of *data compression*. Data compression operates by encoding data in such a way that the encoded version occupies fewer bits than the original version. Although you can't compress *random* numbers, you can compress data that contains *redundancy*. Consider the sentence 'I am going to Washington in January 2007'. If you were taking this down in note form, you might write 'I'm gng to W'shtn Jan 07'. You have now compressed 40 ASCII characters into 24 ASCII characters. Digital data can also be compressed if it contains *redundant* information that can later be restored when the data is decompressed—e.g. English text, diagrams, and pictures.

Let's look at how you might go about compressing data. Figure 4.16 shows a radar screen with three targets. Suppose that the radar image is converted into a 16×16 block of pixels, and a 1 is used to represent a target and a 0 no target—see Table. 4.10. The three targets are represented by 1s in this block of 16×16 elements.

The information in Table 4.10 can be stored as a string of $16 \times 16 = 256$ bits. Or, we could just store the *locations* of the three targets as conventional *x, y* coordinates: 4,6 10,10 13,3 (the data block begins at location 0, 0 at the top left hand position and the location is given as row, column). These three coordinates can be stored as the string of six values 4,6, 10,10, 13,3 or 010001101010101011010011 in binary form (each coordinate is a 4-bit value). We have just compressed a 256-bit table into 24 bits. As you can imagine, this type of data compression is effective only if the table is *sparse* and contains relatively few targets.

We can approach the coding in another way. If you look at the data, you can regard it as strings of 0s and 1s (even though there are no multiple 1s in this example). If we regard the start of the string as the top left-hand bit, it can be expressed as 70 zeros, 1 one, 99 zeros, 1 one, 40 zeros, 1 one, 44 zeros. The information needed to store this block of data is 70, 1, 99, 1, 40, 1, 44; i.e. 7 bytes (i.e. 56 bits).

These two examples demonstrate that some data can be greatly compressed, although the type of data found in real

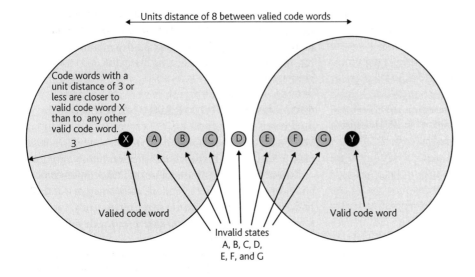

Figure 4.15 Adjacent code words in an 8-unit code.

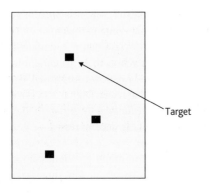

Figure 4.16 A radar image.

```
0000000000000000
0000000000000000
0000000000000000
0000000000000000
0000000000000000
0000001000000000
0000000000000000
0000000000000000
0000000000000000
0000000000000000
0000000000100000
0000000000000000
0000000000000000
0001000000000000
0000000000000000
0000000000000000
```

Table 4.10 Radar data (0 = no target, 1 = target).

computers can't be compressed to such an extent. The figure of merit of a data compression system is its compression ratio, which is defined as *uncompressed size:compressed size*. The compression ratio for a typical mixture of code, text, and images found in a PC is approximately 2:1.

Item	Code
Potatoes	00
Onions	01
Beans	10
Avocado pears	11

Table 4.11 Coding four items with a 2-bit code.

4.6.1 Huffman codes

Huffman codes employ a *variable-length* code word. The idea of a Huffman code isn't new. When Samuel Morse devised his famous code he sent his assistant to a printer to count the number of letters in each storage bin. Morse argued that the printer's storage bins would provide a crude estimate of how much each letter was used on average. The letter E appears so frequently in English language text that there were many Es, whereas there were relatively few Qs. Morse constructed a code that assigned frequently used letters short codes, and infrequently used letters longer codes.

A similar arrangement can be extended to binary codes. Huffman codes are applied only to information in which some elements appear more frequently than others. Plain text (e.g. written English) is such a case. To keep things simple, we provide a simple example before looking at Huffman codes in more depth. A grocer sells only four items (we did say we were keeping things simple), potatoes, onions, beans, and avocado pears. Being a thoroughly modern trader and a computer scientist the grocer has a computerized business. Every time an item is bought, it is encoded in binary form and stored on disk. The grocer wishes to code transactions in such a way as to use the least possible storage. Initially the grocer tried the 2-bit binary code described in Table 4.11.

If there are n transactions, the total storage required to record them is $2n$ bits. At first sight it would seem that there's no way the grocer can get away with less than two bits to encode each transaction. However, after a little thought, the grocer realizes that most customers buy potatoes and therefore devises the encoding scheme of Table 4.12.

Table 4.12 uses codes of different lengths. One code has a 1-bit length, one has a 2-bit length, and two have 3-bit lengths. After a week's trading, the total storage space occupied will be the number of transactions for each item multiplied by the length of its code. The average code length will be:

$$1 \times \tfrac{3}{4} + 2 \times \tfrac{1}{8} + 3 \times \tfrac{1}{16} + 3 \times \tfrac{1}{16} = 1.375$$

By adopting this code, a Huffman code, the average storage has been reduced from 2 bits per transaction to 1.375 bits per transaction, a saving of 31.25%. A Huffman code is often represented in the form of a binary tree, the tree in Fig. 4.17 corresponding to the grocer's example.

The diagram in Fig. 4.17 is sometimes called a *trellis* and is read from left to right. From the left, each of the four *terminal nodes* (labeled node 0, node 10, node 110, and node 111) can be reached by following the marked paths. These paths are indicated by a 1 or a 0 depending on the bit to be decoded. Let's look at how a Huffman code is interpreted. Suppose that the grocer's disk contains the following string of bits, 001100101110. What codes does this string correspond to?

The first (leftmost) bit of the string is 0. From the trellis we can see that a first bit 0 leads immediately to the terminal node 0. Thus, the first code is 0. Similarly, the second code is also 0. The third code begins with a 1, which takes us to a junction rather than to a terminal. We must examine another bit to continue. This is also a 1, and yet another bit must be read. The third bit is a 0 leading to a terminal node 110. This process can be continued until the string is broken down into the sequence: 0 0 110 0 10 111 0 = potatoes, potatoes, beans, potatoes, beans, avocados, potatoes.

Variations of this type code are used in data and program compression algorithms to reduce the size of files (e.g. the widely used *ZIP* program).

Statistical encoding

The type of encoding performed by Samuel Morse employs a *probabilistic model* of the source words to generate code words. Frequently occurring source words are assigned short code words, and infrequently used source words are assigned long code words. We can easily calculate the *average length* of a message that has been Huffman encoded. Suppose that a source word s_i has a probability p_i of appearing as the next element in the information to be encoded. The average length of a Huffman-encoded message is therefore given by the sum of the probability of each source word in the message multiplied by the length of its code word, that is

$$n\Sigma p_i s_i \quad \text{for } i = 1 \text{ to } n \text{ symbols.}$$

If a system employs four code words with the lengths 1, 2, 4, and 5 and the probability of each code word is 0.4, 0.3, 0.2, and 0.1, respectively, the average length of a message with n code words is $1 \times 0.4 + 2 \times 0.3 + 4 \times 0.2 + 5 \times 0.1 = 2.3n$.

Let's look at a simple example of Huffman encoding. Consider an alphabet of five characters A, B, C, D, and E. Table 4.13 provides the relative frequency of the occurrence

Item	Percent of transactions	Code
Potatoes	75	0
Onions	12.5	10
Beans	6.25	110
Avocado pears	6.25	111

Table 4.12 A Huffman code for four items.

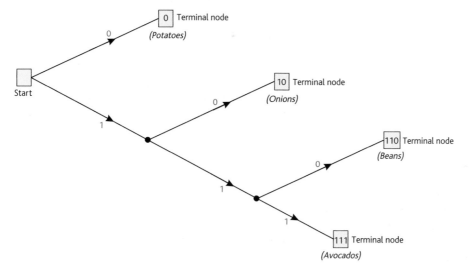

Figure 4.17 The Huffman code corresponding to Table 4.12.

of these letters in a long message. Such a table can be derived by obtaining the statistics from many messages. The values in this table are hypothetical and have been chosen to provide a simple example.

Symbol A is the most common symbol (it occurs eight times more frequently than symbol D) and we will give it the shortest possible code—a single bit. It doesn't matter whether we choose a 1 or a 0. We'll represent A by 0. If symbol A is represented by a single-bit code 0, what is represented by a 1? The answer is, *all* the remaining symbols. We therefore have to qualify the code 1 by other bits in order to distinguish between the remaining four symbols.

We will represent the next most common symbol B by the code 10, leaving the code 11 to be shared among symbols C, D, and E. Continuing in this manner, the code for symbol C is 110, for symbol D is 1110, and for symbol E is 1111. Figure 4.18 provides a *trellis* to illustrate how the symbols are encoded. As you can see, we have now constructed a code in which symbol A is represented by a single bit, whereas symbol E is represented by four bits.

Consider encoding the string BAEAABDA. We begin at the point labeled *start* in Fig. 4.18 and follow the tree until we get to the *terminal symbol* (i.e. A, B, C, D, or E); for example, the bit 0 takes us immediately to the terminal symbol *A*, whereas you have to take the path 1, 1, 1, 0 to reach the terminal symbol D. The encoding of the sequence BAEAABDA is therefore B = 10, A = 0, E = 1111, A = 0, A = 0, B = 10, D = 1110, A = 0, to give the string 1001111001011100.

In this example there are five symbols and the average length of a message is $1 \times 0.5 + 2 \times 0.25 + 3 \times 0.125 +$

$4 \times 0.0625 + 4 \times 0.0625 = 1.875$ bits per symbol. If the same five symbols had been coded conventionally, 3 bits would have been required to represent $000 = A$ to $E = 100$. Huffman encoding has reduced the average storage requirement from 3 to less than 2 bits per symbol.

Now let's look at a more complex example of Huffman encoding. In this case we will use a wider range of symbols and avoid the easy numbers of the previous example (did you notice that all the probabilities were binary fractions?). In this case, we take 16 letters, A to P, and produce a table of relative frequencies, (Table. 4.14). We have not used all 26 letters, to keep the example reasonably simple. The relative frequencies are made up.

Figure 4.19 shows how we can construct a Huffman tree for this code. The letters (i.e. symbols) are laid out along the top with the relative frequencies underneath. The task is to draw a tree whose branches always fork left (a 1 path) or right (a 0 path). The two paths are between branches of equal (or as nearly equal as possible) relative frequency. At each node in the tree, a shaded box shows the cumulative relative frequency of all the symbols above that node. The node at the bottom of the tree has a relative frequency equal to the sum of all the symbols.

Consider the right-hand end of the tree. The symbols G and J each have a relative frequency 1 and are joined at a node whose combined relative frequency is 2. This node is combined with a path to symbol K that has a frequency 2 (i.e. G and J are as relatively frequent as I). You derive the

Symbol	A	B	C	D	E	F	G	H	I	J	K	L	M	N	O	P
Relative frequency	10	3	4	4	12	2	1	3	3	1	2	6	4	5	5	3

Table 4.14 The relative probability of symbols in a 16-symbol alphabet.

Symbol	A	B	C	D	E
Relative frequency	8	4	2	1	1
Relative probability	0.5	0.25	0.125	0.0625	0.0625

Table 4.13 The relative frequency of symbols in an alphabet.

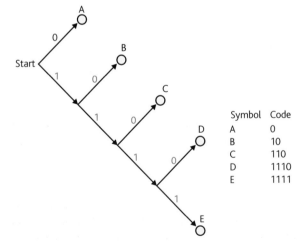

Figure 4.18 A Huffman encoding tree.

Symbol	Code
A	0
B	10
C	110
D	1110
E	1111

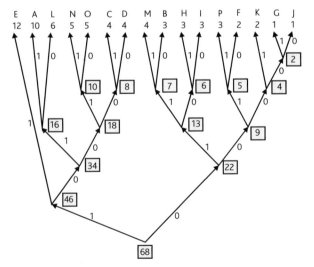

Figure 4.19 A Huffman encoding tree for a 16-symbol code.

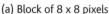

Symbol	A	B	C	D	E	F	G	H	I	J	K	L	M	N	O	P
Code	1011	0110	10001	10000	11	0010	00001	0101	0100	00000	0001	1010	0111	10011	10010	0011

Table 4.15 The Huffman encoding of a 16-symbol alphabet.

(a) Block of 8 x 8 pixels

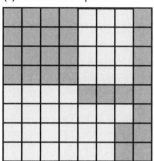

(b) Dividing the block into four quadrants

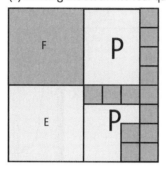

2	3
0	1

Quadrant
numbering

F = full (all elements 1)
E = empty (all elements 0)
P = partially filled

(c) The top right-hand quadrant of (b)
is divided into four quadrants

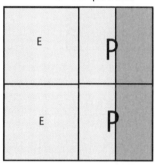

(d) The top right-hand quadrant of (c)
is divided into four quadrants

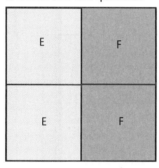

(e) Bottom right-hand quadrant of (a)
is divided into four quadrants

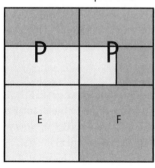

(f) Top right-hand quadrant of (e)
is divided into four quadrants

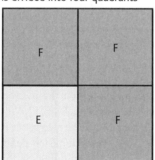

Figure 4.20 The quadtree.

codes for the letters by starting at the bottom-most node and working back to the symbol (see Table. 4.15).

4.6.2 Quadtrees

An interesting data compression technique employs a data structure called the *quadtree*, which is used to encode two-dimensional images. Figure 4.20 illustrates an 8×8 pixel image. This image can be divided into *four* quadrants, as

Fig. 4.20(b) demonstrates (hence the term *quad*tree). As you can see from Fig. 4.20(b), the four quadrants have different properties.

In the top left-hand quadrant, all the pixels are black and are marked 'F' for full. In the bottom left-hand quadrant, all the pixels are white and are marked 'E' for empty. Each of the two right-hand quadrants contains a mixture of black and white pixels—these quadrants are marked 'P' for *partially occupied*.

E, (E, F, (E, E, F, F), (E, F, F, F)), F, (E, (E, F, E, F), E, (E, F, E, F))

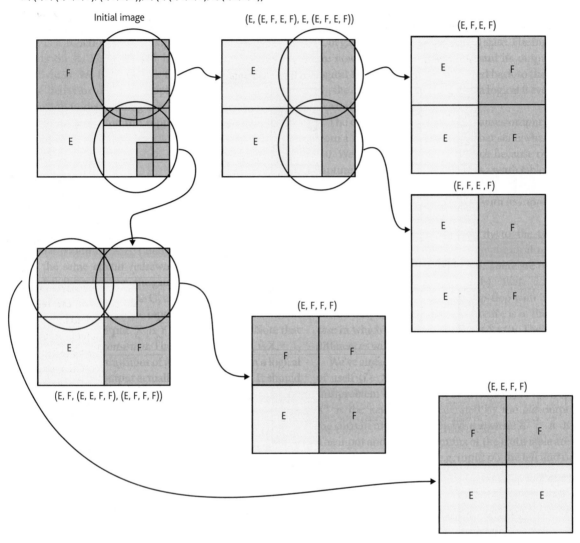

Figure 4.21 The complete quadtree expansion of Fig. 4.20.

The picture of Fig. 4.20(b) can be represented by its four quadrants 0, 1, 2, 3 as E, P, F, P (see figure 4.20 for the quadrant numbering scheme). We can partially regenerate the image because we know that one quadrant is all black and another is all white. However, we don't know anything about the two quadrants marked 'P'.

We can, however, subdivide partially filled quadrants 1 and 3 into further quadrants. Consider the upper right-hand quadrant of Fig. 4.20(b) (i.e. quadrant 3). This can be divided into four quadrants as Fig. 4.20(c) demonstrates. We can describe the structure of Fig. 4.20(c) by E, P, E, P. If we substitute this expansion of quadrant 3 in the original expression for the image, we get: E, P, F, (E, P, E, P).

We haven't yet completely defined quadrant 3 of the image because there are still subdivisions marked 'P'. Figure 4.20(d) demonstrates how the top right-hand quadrant for Fig. 4.20(c) can be subdivided into the quadrants E, F, E, F. If we now substitute this in the expression for the image we get E, P, F, (E, (E, F, E, F), E, P). We can do the same thing to quadrant 1 of Fig. 4.20(c) to get: E, P, F, (E, (E, F, E, F), E, (E, F, E, F)). Now we have completely defined quadrant 3 of the original image.

Continuing in this way and expanding quadrant 1 of the original image, we get the expression E, (E, F, (E, E, F, F), (E, F, F, F)), F, (E, (E, F, E, F), E, (E, F, E, F)). All we have done is to divide an image into four quadrants and successively divided a quadrant into four quadrants until we reach that point at which each quadrant contains only one color. Because many areas of an image contain the same color, the quadtree structure can compress the image. In the case of Fig. 4.20 we have compressed a 64-element block into a string of 29 elements (the elements may be E, F, left bracket, or right bracket).

Figure 4.21 demonstrate the complete quadtree expansion of Fig. 4.20.

The quad tree and the other compression techniques we've described are *lossless* encoding techniques because a file can be compressed and restored with no loss of information (i.e. compress and decompress yields the original source). Some compressing techniques are lossy because information is lost during compression and the original information can't be restored. Lossy compression technology is used to compress images and sound because humans can lose a lot of detail in an image (or piece of music) without noticing missing it. Typical lossy compression techniques are MP3 (sound), JPEG (still images), and MPEG (video).

0	1	2	3	4	5	6	7	8	9
1	2	3	4	5	6	7	8	9	10
2	3	4	5	6	7	8	9	10	11
3	4	5	6	7	8	9	10	11	12
4	5	6	7	8	9	10	11	12	13
5	6	7	8	9	10	11	12	13	14
6	7	8	9	10	11	12	13	14	15
7	8	9	10	11	12	13	14	15	16
8	9	10	11	12	13	14	15	16	17
9	10	11	12	13	14	15	16	17	18

Table 4.16 The decimal addition tables.

0	1	2	3	4	5	6	7	8	9
1	1	2	3	4	5	6	7	8	9
2	2	4	6	8	10	12	14	16	18
3	3	6	9	12	15	18	21	24	27
4	4	8	12	16	20	24	28	32	36
5	5	10	15	20	25	30	35	40	45
6	6	12	18	24	30	36	42	48	54
7	7	14	21	28	35	42	49	56	63
8	8	16	24	32	40	48	56	64	72
9	9	18	27	36	45	54	63	72	81

Table 4.17 The decimal multiplication tables.

4.7 Binary arithmetic

Now that we've introduced binary numbers and demonstrated how it's possible to convert between binary and decimal formats, the next step is to look at how binary numbers are manipulated. Binary arithmetic follows exactly the same rules as decimal arithmetic and all that we have to do to work with binary numbers is to learn the binary tables. Table 4.16 gives the decimal addition tables and Table 4.17 gives the decimal multiplication table. Table 4.18 gives the hexadecimal multiplication table. Table 4.19 gives the binary addition, subtraction, and multiplication tables. As you can see, these are much simpler than their decimal equivalents.

A remarkable fact about binary arithmetic revealed by Table 4.19 is that if we didn't worry about the carry in addition and the borrow in subtraction, then the operations of addition and subtraction would be identical. Such an arithmetic in which addition and subtraction are equivalent does exist and has some important applications; this is called *modulo-2 arithmetic*.

Table 4.19 tells us how to add two single digits. We need to add longer words. The addition of *n*-bit numbers is entirely straightforward, except that when adding the two bits in each column, a carry bit from the previous stage must also be added in. Each carry bit results from a carry-out from the column on its right. In the following example, we present the

0	01	02	03	04	05	06	07	08	9	0A	0B	0C	0D	0E	0F
1	01	02	03	04	05	06	07	08	09	0A	0B	0C	0D	0E	0F
2	02	04	06	08	0A	0C	E	10	12	14	16	18	1A	1C	1E
3	03	06	09	0C	0F	12	15	18	1B	1E	21	24	27	2A	2D
4	04	08	0C	10	14	18	1C	20	24	28	2C	30	34	38	3C
5	05	0A	0F	14	19	1E	23	28	2D	32	37	3C	41	46	4B
6	06	0C	12	18	1E	24	2A	30	36	3C	42	48	4E	54	5A
7	07	0E	15	1C	23	2A	31	38	40	46	4D	54	5B	62	69
8	08	10	18	20	28	30	38	40	48	50	58	60	68	70	78
9	09	12	1B	24	2D	36	3F	48	51	5A	63	6C	75	7E	87
A	0A	14	1E	28	32	3C	46	50	5A	64	6E	78	82	8C	96
B	0B	16	21	2C	37	42	4D	58	63	6E	79	84	8F	9A	A5
C	0C	18	24	30	3C	48	54	60	6C	78	84	90	9C	A8	B4
D	0D	1A	27	34	41	4E	5B	68	75	82	8F	9C	A9	B6	C3
E	0E	1C	2A	38	46	54	62	70	7E	8C	9A	A8	B6	C4	D2
F	0F	1E	2D	3C	4B	5A	69	78	87	96	A5	B4	C3	D2	E1

Table 4.18 The hexadecimal multiplication tables.

numbers to be added on the left, and on the right we include the carry bits that must be added in.

```
 00110111    →        00110111
+01010110    →        01010110
                      111 11     ← carries
 10001101    →        10001101
```

We can carry out hexadecimal addition in the same way that we carry out binary addition. All we have to remember is that if we add together two digits whose sum is greater than 15, we must convert the result into a carry digit whose value is 16 plus the remainder, which is the sum less 16. For example, if we add E and 7 in hexadecimal arithmetic, we get 15_{16} which is 5 carry 1 (i.e. 5 plus 16).

Consider the addition $EA348_{16} + 67019_{16}$.

```
EA348  →        EA348
67019  →        67019
                11   1   ← carries
151361 →        151361
```

Subtraction can also be carried out in a conventional fashion, although we shall see later that a computer does not subtract numbers in the way we do because negative numbers are not usually represented in a *sign plus magnitude* form but by means of their complements.

```
 01010110           86
-00101010          -42
  1 1      ← borrows 44
 0101100
```

The multiplication of binary numbers can be done by the *pencil and paper* method of shifting and adding, although in practice the computer uses a somewhat modified technique.

```
   01101              13
×  01010            × 10
   00000             130
   01101
  00000
  01101
 00000
0010000010
```

4.7.1 The Half adder

We now design circuits to add binary numbers. The most primitive circuit is called the *half adder* or HA which adds together two bits to give a sum, S, and a carry, C as described in Table 4.20. The sum, S, is given by their exclusive OR; that is, $S = \overline{A} \cdot B + A \cdot \overline{A}$. The carry is given by $C = A \cdot B$.

From the chapter on gates we know that this circuit may be realized in at least three different ways as Fig. 4.22 demonstrate. This circuit, whatever its implementation, is often represented in many texts by the symbol in Figure 4.23.

We can use Digital Works to construct a half adder and to simulate its behavior. Figure 4.24 shows a screen in which we've constructed a half adder and used the push-button (i.e. input device) to provide inputs A and B. We have connected the adder's sum and carry outputs to LEDs and have linked all inputs and outputs to the *Logic History* function.

As you can see from fig. 4.24, we've run the simulation in the single step mode, applied all possible inputs to the circuit, and observed the output waveforms.

Addition	Subtraction	Multiplication
0+0 = 0	0−0 = 0	0 × 0 = 0
0+1 = 1	0−1 = 1 borrow 1	0 × 1 = 0
1+0 = 1	1−0 = 1	1 × 0 = 0
1+1 = 0 carry 1	1−1 = 0	1 × 1 = 1

Table 4.19 Binary tables.

A	B	S (sum)	C (carry)
0	0	0	0
0	1	1	0
1	0	1	0
1	1	0	1

Table 4.20 Truth table for a half adder.

PERFORMING ADDITION

The following sequence demonstrates binary addition. Each step shows the current carry in (light blue) and the carry out generated in the next column to the right (bold blue). Only seven stages are shown in order to fit on the page.

Step 1	Step 2	Step 3	Step 4	Step 5	Step 6	Step 7
00110111	00110111	00110111	00110111	00110111	00110111	00110111
+01010110	+01010110	+01010110	+01010110	+01010110	+01010110	+01010110
⓪	⓪	1	1	0	1	1
0	1	1	0	1	1	1
10001101	10001101	10001101	10001101	10001101	10001101	10001101

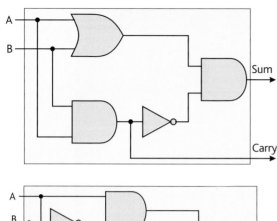

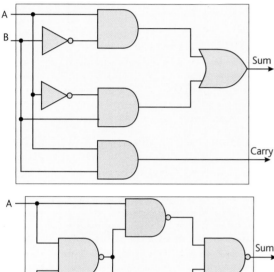

Figure 4.22 Three ways of implementing a half adder.

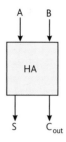

Figure 4.23 The circuit representation of a half adder.

A	B	C_{in}		S (sum)	C_{out} (carry-out)
0	0	0		0	0
0	1	0		1	0
1	0	0		1	0
1	1	0		0	1
0	0	1		1	0
0	1	1		0	1
1	0	1		0	1
1	1	1		1	1

Table 4.21 Truth table for full adder.

4.7.2 The Full Adder

Unfortunately, the half adder is of little use as it stands. When two *n*-bit numbers are added together we have to take account of any *carry bits*. Adding bits a_i of A and b_i of B together must include provision for adding in the carry bit c_{i-1} from the results of the addition in the column to the right of a_i and b_i. This is represented diagrammatically as

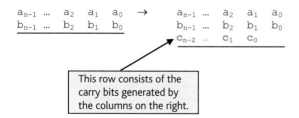

When people perform an addition they deal with the carry automatically, without thinking about it. More specifically they say, 'If a carry is generated we add it to the next column, if it is not we do nothing.' In human terms doing nothing and adding zero are equivalent. As far as the logic necessary to carry out the addition is concerned, we always add in the carry from the previous stage, where the carry bit has the value 0 or 1.

The *full adder*, represented by the circuit symbol of Fig. 4.25, adds together two bits *A* and *B*, plus a carry-in C_{in} from the previous stage, to generate a sum *S* and a carry-out C_{out}. In other words, the full adder is a 3-bit adder. Table 4.21 provides the truth table for a full adder.

You can realize the circuit for a full adder by connecting two half adders in tandem. Conceptually, a full adder requires that the two bits of A and B be added together and then the carry-in is added to the result. Figure 4.26 shows a possible representation of the full adder in terms of two half adders.

The sum output of the full adder is provided by the sum output of the second half adder, HA2. The carry-out from the full adder, C_{out}, is given by ORing the carries from both half adders. To demonstrate that the circuit of Fig. 4.26 does indeed perform the process of full addition a truth table may be used. Table 4.22 provides a truth table for the circuit of Fig. 4.26.

As the contents of the S_2 and C_{out} columns are identical to those of the corresponding columns of the truth table for the full adder (Table 4.22), we must conclude that the circuit of Fig. 4.26 is indeed that of a full adder. Figure 4.27 demonstrates

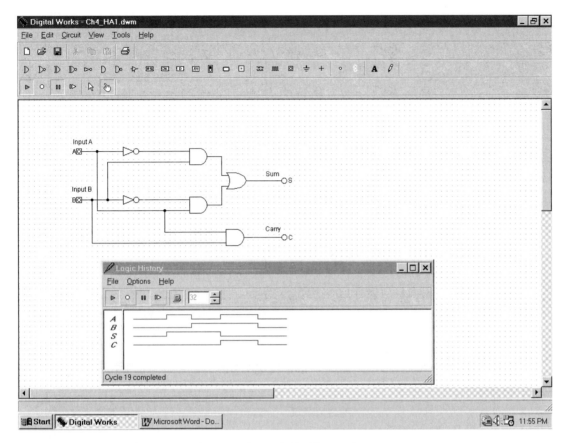

Figure 4.24 Using Digital Works to implement and test a half adder circuit.

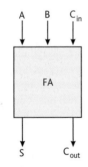

Figure 4.25 The circuit representation of a full adder.

C_{in}	A	B	S_1	C_1	S_2	C_2	C_{out}
0	0	0	0	0	0	0	0
0	0	1	1	0	1	0	0
0	1	0	1	0	1	0	0
0	1	1	0	1	0	0	1
1	0	0	0	0	1	0	0
1	0	1	1	0	0	1	1
1	1	0	1	0	0	1	1
1	1	1	0	1	1	0	1

Table 4.22 Truth table for a full adder implemented by two half adders.

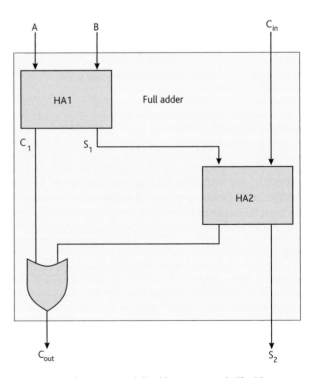

Fig. 4.26 Implementing a full adder using two half adders.

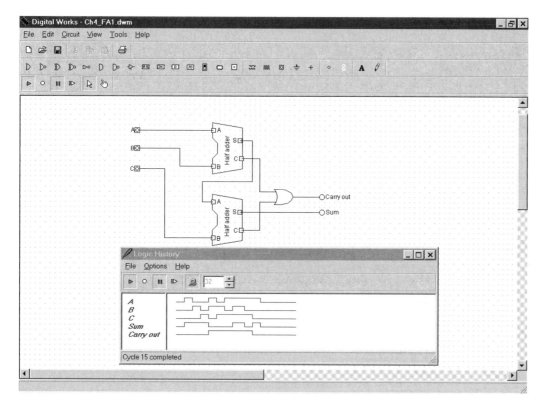

Figure 4.27 Using Digital Works to implement and test a full adder built from two half adders.

the use of Digital Words to construct and simulate a full adder built from two half adders.

In practice the full adder is not implemented in this way because the propagation path through the two half adders involves six units of delay. An alternative full adder circuit may be derived directly from the equations for the sum and the carry from the truth table. Let the sum be S, the carry-out C_o, and the carry-in C.

$$
\begin{aligned}
S &= C\cdot\overline{A}\cdot\overline{B} + \overline{C}\cdot\overline{A}\cdot B + \overline{C}\cdot A\cdot\overline{B} + C\cdot A\cdot B \\
\text{and } C_o &= \overline{C}\cdot A\cdot B + C\cdot\overline{A}\cdot B + C\cdot A\cdot\overline{B} + C\cdot A\cdot B \\
&= \overline{C}\cdot A\cdot B + C\cdot\overline{A}\cdot B + C\cdot A\,(\overline{B} + B) \\
&= \overline{C}\cdot A\cdot B + C\cdot\overline{A}\cdot B + C\cdot A \\
&= \overline{C}\cdot A\cdot B + C\,(\overline{A}\cdot B + A) = \overline{C}\cdot A\cdot B + C\cdot B + C\cdot A \\
&= A\,(\overline{C}\cdot B + C) + C\cdot B = A\,(B + C) + C\cdot B \\
&= C\cdot A + C\cdot B + A\cdot B
\end{aligned}
$$

The carry-out represents a *majority logic* function that is true if two or more of the tree inputs are true. The circuit diagram of the full adder corresponding to the above equations is given in Fig. 4.28. This circuit contains more gates than the equivalent realization in terms of half adders (12 against 9) but it is faster. The maximum propagation delay is three gates in series.

4.7.3 **The addition of words**

Even a full adder on its own is not a great deal of help, as we normally wish to add two *n*-bit numbers together. We now

look at ways in which two *n*-bit numbers can be added together. We begin with the *serial* full adder and then describe the *parallel* full adder.

It is perfectly possible to add two *n*-bit numbers, A and B, together, *serially*, a bit at a time by means of the scheme given in Fig. 4.29. The contents of the shift registers containing the *n*-bit words A and B are shifted into the full adder a bit at a time. The result of each addition is shifted into a result (i.e. sum) register. A single flip-flop holds the carry bit so that the old carry-out becomes the next carry-in. After *n* clock pulses, the sum register, S, contains the sum of A and B. Serial adders aren't used today because parallel adders are much faster.

Parallel adders

A *parallel adder* adds the *n* bits of word A to the *n* bits of word B in one simultaneous operation. Figure 4.30 describes a parallel adder constructed from *n* full adders. The carry-out from each full adder provides the carry-in to the stage on its left. The term *parallel* implies that all *n* additions take place at the same time and it's tempting to think that the parallel adder is *n* times faster than the corresponding serial adder. In practice a real parallel adder is slowed down by the effect of the carry-bit propagation through the stages of the full adder.

Several points are worth noting in Fig. 4.30. You might think that a half adder could replace the least-significant bit stage because this stage doesn't have a carry-in. However,

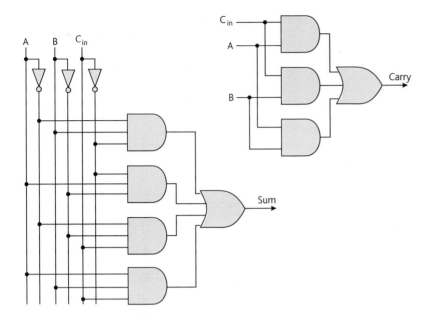

Figure 4.28 A possible circuit for the full adder.

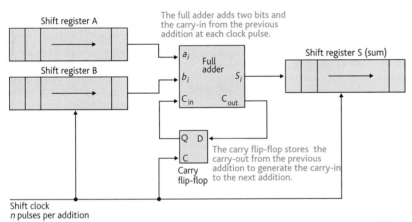

Figure 4.29 The serial adder.

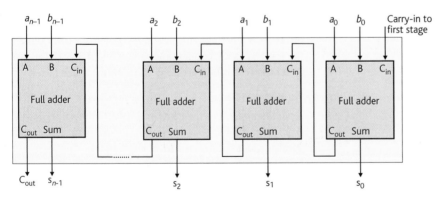

Figure 4.30 The parallel adder.

by using a full adder for this stage, the carry-in may be set to zero for normal addition, or it may be set to 1 to generate $A + B + 1$. If input B is set to zero, $A + 1$ is generated and the circuit functions as an incrementer. A facility to add in 1 to the sum of A plus B will prove very useful when we come to complementary arithmetic.

Another feature of this circuit concerns the carry-out from the most-significant bit stage. If two n-bit words are added and the result is greater than $111\ldots1$, then a carry-out is generated. As the computer cannot store words longer than n bits, the sum cannot be stored in the memory as a single entity. The carry-out of the most-significant stage may be latched into a flip-flop (normally forming part of the computer's condition code register). When addition is performed by software as part of a program, it is usual for the programmer to test the carry bit to check whether the result has gone out of range.

A final point about the parallel adder concerns the meaning of the term parallel. The first stage can add a_0 to b_0 to get S_0 as soon as A and B are presented to the input terminals of the full adder. However, the second stage must wait for the first stage's carry-out to be added in to a_1 plus b_1 before it can be sure that its own output is valid. In the worst case inputs of $111 \ldots 1 + 1$, the carry must ripple through all the stages. This type of adder is referred to as a *ripple-carry adder*.

The full adder we have described here is parallel in the sense that all the bits of A are added to all the bits of B in a single operation without the need for a number of separate clock cycles. Once the values of A and B have been presented to the inputs of the full adders, the system must wait until the circuit has had time to settle down and for all carries to propagate before the next operation is started. Figure 4.31 shows a ripple adder in more detail using the circuits we've developed before. As you can see, the carry in has to ripple through successive stages until it reaches the most-significant bit position.

Real full adders in computers are much more complicated than those we have shown here. The fundamental principles are the same, but the effect of the ripple-through carry from first to last stage cannot be tolerated. A mechanism called

carry look ahead circuits can be used to anticipate a carry over a group of say four full adders. That is, the carry out to stage $i + 5$ is calculated by examining the inputs to stages $i + 4$, $i + 3$, $i + 2$, and $i + 1$, and the carry in to stage $i + 1$, by means of a special high-speed circuit. This anticipated carry is fed to the fifth stage to avoid the delay that would be incurred if a ripple-through carry were used. The exact nature of these circuits is beyond the scope of this book.

4.8 Signed numbers

Any real computer must be able to deal with *negative numbers* as well as positive numbers. Before we examine how the computer handles negative numbers, we should consider how we deal with them. I believe that people don't, in fact, actually use negative numbers. They use positive numbers (the 5 in -5 is the same as in $+5$), and place a negative sign in front of a number to remind them that it must be treated in a special way when it takes part in arithmetic operations. In other words, we treat all numbers as positive and use a sign (i.e. $+$ or $-$) to determine what we have to do with the numbers. For example, consider the following two operations.

$$\begin{array}{r} 8 \\ +5 \\ \hline 13 \end{array} \quad \text{and} \quad \begin{array}{r} 8 \\ -5 \\ \hline 3 \end{array}$$

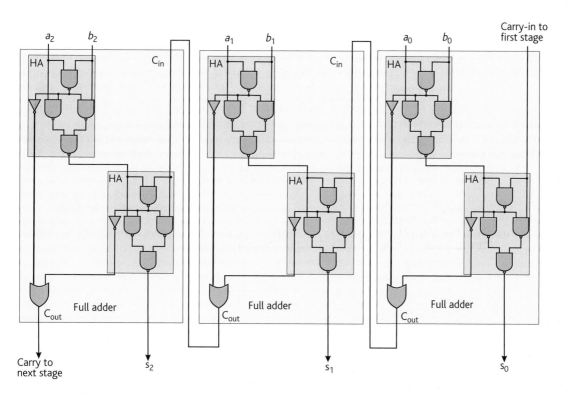

Figure 4.31 Ripple carry.

In both these examples the numbers are the same, but the operations we performed on them were different; in the first case we added them together and in the second case we subtracted them. This technique can be extended to computer arithmetic to give the *sign and magnitude* representation of a negative number.

4.8.1 Sign and magnitude representation

An n-bit word can have 2^n possible different values from 0 to $2^n - 1$; for example, an 8-bit word can represent $0, 1, \ldots, 254, 255$. One way of indicating a negative number is to take the most-significant bit and reserve it to indicate the sign of the number. The usual convention is to choose the sign bit as 0 to represent positive numbers and 1 to represent negative numbers. We can express the value of a sign and magnitude number mathematically in the form $(-1)^S \times M$, where S is the sign bit of the number and M is its magnitude. If $S = 0$, $(-1)^0 = +1$ and the number is positive. If $S = 1$, $(-1)^1 = -1$ and the number is negative. For example, in 8 bits we can interpret the two numbers 00001101 and 10001101 as

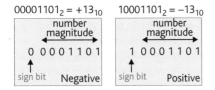

Using a *sign bit* to represent signed numbers is not widely used in integer arithmetic. The range of a sign and magnitude number in n bits is given by $-(2^{n-1} - 1)$ to $+(2^{n-1} - 1)$.

All we've done is to take an n bit number, use 1 bit to represent the sign, and let the remaining $n - 1$ bits represent the number. Thus, an 8-bit number can represent from -127 (11111111) to $+127$ (01111111). One of the objections to this system is that it has two values for zero:

$$00000000 = +0 \quad \text{and} \quad 10000000 = -0$$

Another reason for rejecting this system is that it requires separate adders and subtractors. The are other ways of representing negative numbers that remove the need for subtractor circuits.

Examples of addition and subtraction in sign and magnitude arithmetic are given below. Remember that the most-significant bit is a sign bit and does not take part in the calculation itself. This is in contrast with two's complement arithmetic (see later) in which the sign bit forms an integral part of the number when it is used in calculations. In each of the four examples below, we perform the calculation by first converting the sign bit to a positive or to a negative sign. Then we perform the calculation and, finally, convert the sign of the result into a sign bit.

Sign and magnitude value		Number with sign bit converted into sign		Result with sign converted into sign bit
1.	001011 +001110		+01011 +01110 +11001	011001
2.	001011 +100110		+01011 −00110 +00101	000101
3.	001011 +110110		+01011 −10110 −01011	101011
4.	001011 −001001		+01011 −01001 +00010	000010

4.8.2 Complementary arithmetic

In complementary arithmetic the *negativeness* of a number is contained within the number itself. Because of this, the concept of signs ($+$ and $-$) may, effectively, be dispensed with. If we add X to Y the operation is that of addition if X is positive and Y is positive, but if Y is negative the end result is that of subtraction (assuming that Y is represented by its negative form). It is important to point out here that complementary arithmetic is used to represent and to manipulate both positive and negative numbers. To demonstrate that there is nothing magical about complementary arithmetic, let's examine decimal complements.

Ten's complement arithmetic

The ten's complement of an n-digit decimal number, N, is defined as $10^n - N$. The ten's complement may also be calculated by subtracting each of the digits of N from 9 and adding 1 to the result; for example, if $n = 1$, the value of -1 is represented in ten's complement by 9. Consider the four-digit decimal number 1234. Its ten's complement is:

(a) $10^4 - 1234 = 8766$ or (b) $\begin{array}{r} 9999 \\ -1234 \\ \hline 8765 + 1 = 8766 \end{array}$

Suppose we were to add this complement to another number (say) 8576. We get

$$\begin{array}{r} 8576 \\ +8766 \\ \hline 17342 \end{array}$$

Now let's examine the effect of subtracting 1234 from 8576 by conventional means.

$$\begin{array}{r} 8576 \\ -1234 \\ \hline 7342 \end{array}$$

Notice that the results of the two operations are similar in the least-significant four digits, but differ in the fifth digit by 10^4. The reason for this is not hard to find. Consider the subtraction of Y from X. We wish to calculate $Z = X - Y$, which we do by *adding* the ten's complement of Y to X. The ten's complement of Y is defined as $10^4 - Y$. Therefore we get

$$Z = X + (10^4 - Y) = 10^4 + (X - Y).$$

In other words, we get the desired result, $X - Y$, together with an *unwanted* digit in the leftmost position. This digit may be discarded.

Complementing a number twice results in the original number; for example, -1234 is $10^4 - 1234 = 8876$. Complementing twice, we get $-(-1234) = -8876 = 10^4 - 8876 = 1234$.

4.8.3 Two's complement representation

The equivalent of ten's complement in binary arithmetic is *two's complement*. To form the two's complement of an n-bit binary number, N, we evaluate $2^n - N$. For example, in 5 bits, if $N = 5 = 00101$ then the two's complement of N is given by $2^5 - 00101 = 100000 - 00101 = 11011$. It is important to note here that 11011 represents -00101 (-5) or $+27$ depending only on whether we interpret the bit pattern 11011 as a two's complement integer or as an unsigned integer.

If we add the two's complement of N (i.e. 11011) to another binary number, we should execute the operation of subtraction. In the following demonstration we add 11011 to 01100 (i.e. 12).

```
  01100        12
+ 11011      + −5
 ───────     ─────
 100111        7
```

As in the case of ten's complement arithmetic, we get the correct answer together with the $2^n = 2^5$ term, which is

Let $X = 9 = 01001$ and $Y = 6 = 00110$

$-X = 100000 - 01001 = 10111$
$-Y = 100000 - 00110 = 11010$

```
1. + X   + 9    01001      2. + X   + 9    01001
   + Y   + 6  + 00110         − Y   − 6  + 11010
              ────────                   ─────────
               01111 = 15                .100011  = +3

3. − X   − 9    10111      4. − X   − 9    10111
   + Y   + 6  + 00110         − Y   − 6  + 11010
              ────────                   ─────────
               11101 = −3                110001  = −15
```

discarded. Before continuing further, it is worthwhile examining the effect of adding all the combinations of positive and negative values for a pair of numbers.

All four examples give the result we'd expect when the result is interpreted as a two's complement number. However, examples 3 and 4 give negative results that require a little further explanation. Example 3 calculates $-9 + 6$ by adding the two's complement of 9 to 6 to get -3 expressed in two's complement form. The two's complement representation of -3 is given by $100000 - 00011 = 11101$.

Example 4 evaluates $-X + -Y$ to get a result of -15 but with the addition of a 2^n term. The two's complement representation of -15 is given by $100000 - 01111 = 10001$. In example 4, where both numbers are negative, we have $(2^n - X) + (2^n - Y) = 2^n + (2^n - X - Y)$. The first part of this expression is the redundant 2^n and the second part is the two's complement representation of $-X - Y$. The two's complement system works for all possible combinations of positive and negative numbers.

Calculating two's complement values

The two's complement system would not be so attractive if it weren't for the ease with which two's complements can be formed. Consider the two's complement of N, which is defined as: $2^n - N$.

Suppose we re-arranged the equation by subtracting 1 from the 2^n and adding it to the result.

$$2^n - 1 - N + 1 = \underset{n \text{ places}}{\underleftrightarrow{111 \ldots 1}} - N + 1$$

For example, in 8 bits ($n = 8$) we have

$2^8 - N = 100000000 - N = 100000000 - 1 - N + 1$
(after rearranging) $= 11111111 - N + 1$

In practice, it's easy to evaluate the two's complement of N. All you have to do is invert the bits and add 1. Why? Because the previous expression demonstrates that $1 - N_i = \overline{N_i}$. If bit i of N is 0, subtracting bit i from 1 gives 1, and if the bit is 1, subtracting bit i from 1 gives 0. For example, in 5 bits we have

$7 = 00111$
$-7 = 00111 \ \overline{0}\overline{0}\overline{1}\overline{1}\overline{1} + 1 = 11000 + 1 = 11001$

Evaluating two's complement numbers in this fashion is attractive because it's easy to perform with hardware. Figure 4.32 demonstrate how an adder/subtractor is implemented. All you need is a little extra logic to convert a parallel binary adder into an adder/subtractor for two's complement numbers. Each of the EOR gates has two inputs b_i (where $i = 0$ to $n - 1$) and C, a control signal. The output of the EOR gate is $b_i \cdot \overline{C} + \overline{b_i} \cdot C$. If C is 0 then $\overline{C} = 1$ and the output is b_i. If C is 1 then $\overline{C} = 0$ and the output is b_i. The n EORs form a chain of programmable invertors, complementing the input if C = 1 and passing the input unchanged if C = 0. The carry-in input to the first full adder is C. When addition is being performed, C = 0 and the carry-in is 0. However, when we perform subtraction, C = 1 so that 1 is added to the result of the addition. We have already inverted B's bits so that

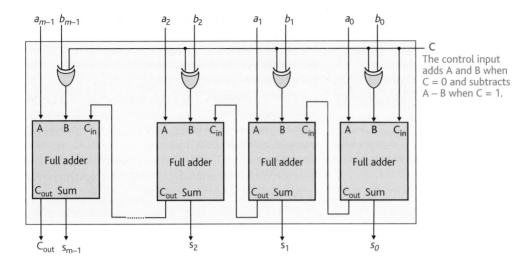

The control input adds A and B when C = 0 and subtracts A − B when C = 1.

Fig. 4.32 The binary adder/subtractor.

adding this 1 forms the two's complement of B enabling the subtraction of B from A to take place.

Properties of two's complement numbers

1. The two's complement system is a true complement system in that $+X + (-X) = 0$. For example, in 5 bits $+13_{10} = 01101_{10}$ and $-13_2 = 10011_2$. The sum of $+13$ and -13 is

    01101
    +10011
    ‾‾‾‾‾‾
    100000 = 0

2. There is one unique zero $00 \ldots 0$.

3. If the number is positive the most-significant bit is 0, and if it is negative the most-significant bit is 1. Thus, the most-significant bit is a sign bit.

4. The range of two's complement numbers in n bits is from -2^{n-1} to $+2^{n-1} - 1$. For $n = 5$, this range is from -16 to $+15$. Note that the total number of different numbers is 32 (16 negative, zero and 15 positive). What this demonstrates is that a 5-bit number can uniquely describe 32 items, and it is up to us whether we choose to call these items the natural binary integers 0 to 31, or the signed two's complement numbers -16 to $+15$.

5. The complement of the complement of X is X (i.e. $-(-X) = X$). In 5 bits $+12 = 01100$ and $-12 = \overline{10011} + 1 = 10100$. If we form the two's complement of -12 (i.e. 10100) in the usual fashion by inverting the bits and adding 1, we get $\overline{10100} + 1 = 01011 + 1 = 01100$, which is the same as the number we started with.

Let's now see what happens if we violate the range of two's complement numbers. That is, we will carry out an operation whose result falls outside the range of values that can be represents by two's complement numbers.

If we choose a 5-bit representation, we know that the range of valid signed numbers is -16 to $+15$. Suppose we first add 5 and 6 and then try 12 and 13.

Case 1
        5 = 00101
      +6 = 00110
    ‾‾‾‾‾‾‾‾‾‾‾‾‾
    11   01011 = 11_{10}

Case 2
        12 = 01100
      +13 = 01101
    ‾‾‾‾‾‾‾‾‾‾‾‾‾
    25   11001 = −7_{10} (as a
          two's complement number)

In case 1 we get the expected answer of $+11_{10}$, but in case 2 we get a *negative* result because the sign bit is '1'. If the answer were regarded as an unsigned binary number it would be $+25$, which is, of course, the correct answer. However, once the two's complement system has been chosen to represent signed numbers, all answers must be interpreted in this light.

Similarly, if we add together two negative numbers whose total is less than -16, we also go out of range. For example, if we add $-9 = 10111_2$ and $-12 = 10100_2$, we get

    − 9   10111
    −12   +10100
    ‾‾‾‾   ‾‾‾‾‾‾
    −27   101011   gives a positive result $01011_{12} = +11_{10}$

Both these cases represent an out-of-range condition called *arithmetic overflow*. Arithmetic overflow occurs during a two's complement addition if the result of adding two positive numbers yields a negative result, or if adding two negative numbers yields a positive result.[2] If the sign bits of A and B are the same but the sign bit of the result is different, arithmetic overflow has occurred. If a_{n-1} is the sign bit of A,

[2] Some define overflow more generally as 'A condition that occurs when the result of an operation does not fit the number representation in use'.

b_{n-1} is the sign bit of B, and s_{n-1} is the sign bit of the sum of A and B, then overflow is defined by

$$V = a_{n-1} \cdot b_{n-1} \cdot \overline{s_{n-1}} + \overline{a_{n-1}} \cdot \overline{b_{n-1}} \cdot s_{n-1}$$

Arithmetic overflow is a consequence of two's complement arithmetic and shouldn't be confused with carry-out, which is the carry bit generated by the addition of the two most-significant bits of the numbers.

In practice, real systems detect overflow from $C_{in} \neq C_{out}$ to the last stage. That is, we detect overflow from

$$V = c_n \cdot \overline{c_{n-1}} + \overline{c_n} \cdot c_{n-1}$$

We now demonstrate that this expression is correct. This proof has been included to improve your understanding of the nature of two's complement arithmetic.

Figure 4.33 illustrates the most-significant stage of a parallel adder that adds together bits a_{n-1}, b_{n-1}, and c_{n-1} to generate a sum bit, s_{n-1}, and a carry-out, c_n. There are four possible combinations of A and B that can be added together

$$+A + +B$$
$$+A + -B$$
$$-A + +B$$
$$-A + -B$$

As adding two numbers of *differing* sign cannot result in arithmetic overflow, we need consider only the cases where A and B are both positive, or both negative.

Case 1 A and B positive $a_{n-1} = 0, b_{n-1} = 0$

The final stage adds $a_{n-1} + b_{n-1} + c_{n-1}$ to get c_{n-1}, because a_{n-1} and b_{n-1} are both 0 (by definition if the numbers are positive). That is, the carry-out, c_n, is 0 and $s_{n-1} = c_{n-1}$.

We know overflow occurs if $s_{n-1} = 1$, therefore overflow occurs if the sum is negative and $\overline{c_n} \cdot c_{n-1} = 1$.

Case 2 A and B negative $a_{n-1} = 1, b_{n-1} = 1$.

The final stage adds $a_{n-1} + b_{n-1} + c_{n-1} = 1 + 1 + c_{n-1}$, to get a sum, $s_{n-1} = c_{n-1}$ and a carry-out $c_n = 1$. Overflow occurs if the sum is positive and $s_{n-1} = 0$. That is, if $c_{n-1} = 0$, or if $c_n \cdot \overline{c_{n-1}} = 1$.

Considering both cases, overflow occurs if $\overline{c_n} \cdot c_{n-1} + c_n \cdot \overline{c_{n-1}} = 1$.

Alternative view of two's complement numbers

We have seen that a binary integer, N, lying in the range $0 \leq N < 2^n - 1$, is represented in a negative form in n bits by the expression $2^n - N$. We have also seen that this expression can be readily evaluated by inverting the bits of N and adding 1 to the result.

Another way of looking at a two's complement number is to regard it as a conventional binary number represented in the positional notation *but with the sign of the most-significant bit negative*. That is,

$$-N = -d_{n-1}2^{n-1} + d_{n-2}2^{n-2} + \ldots + d_0 2^0$$

where $d_{n-1}, d_{n-2}, \ldots d_0$ are the bits of the two's complement number D. Consider the binary representation of 14_{10} and the two's complement form of -14, in 5 bits.

$$+14_{10} = 01110_2$$

$$-14 = 2^n - N = 2^5 - 14 = 32 - 14 = 18 = 10010$$
$$\text{or} -14 = \overline{0\,1\,1\,1\,0} + 1 = 10001 + 1 = 10010_2.$$

We can regard the two's complement representation of -14 (i.e. 10010) as

$-1 \times 2^4 + 0 \times 2^3 + 0 \times 2^2 + 1 \times 2^1 + 0 \times 2^0$ (this is a conventional 8421-coded binary number with a negative weight for the most-significant bit)

$$= -16 + (0 + 0 + 2 + 0)$$
$$= -16 + 2 = -14$$

We can demonstrate that a two's complement number is indeed represented in this way. In what follows N represents a positive integer, and D the two's complement form of $-N$. We wish to prove that $-N = D$.

That is, $-N = -2^{n-1} + \sum_{i=1}^{n-2} d_i 2^i$ (1)

In terms of the bits of N and D we have

$$-(N_{n-1}N_{n-2} \ldots N_1 N_0) = d_{n-1}d_{n-2} \ldots d_1 d_0 = D \quad (2)$$

The bits of D are formed from the bits of N by inverting and adding 1.

$$\overline{N_{n-1}}\,\overline{N_{n-2}} \ldots \overline{N_1}\,\overline{N_0} + 1 = d_{n-1}d_{n-2} \ldots d_1 d_0 \quad (3)$$

Substituting equation 3 in equation 1 to eliminate D we get

$$-N = -2^{n-1} + \sum_{i=0}^{n-2} \overline{N_i} 2^i + 1$$

But $\overline{N_i} = 1 - N_i$, so that

$$-\overline{N} = -2^{n-1} + \sum_{i=0}^{n-2} (1 - N_i)2^i + 1$$

$$= -2^{n-1} + \sum_{i=0}^{n-2} 2^i - \sum_{i=0}^{n-2} N_i 2^i + 1$$

$$= 2^{n-1} + (2^{n-1} - 1) - \sum_{i=0}^{n-2} N_i 2^i + 1$$

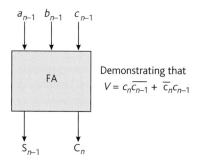

a_{n-1} b_{n-1} c_{n-1}

FA

Demonstrating that
$V = c_n \overline{c_{n-1}} + \overline{c_n} c_{n-1}$

s_{n-1} c_n

Fig. 4.33 Most-significant stage of a full adder.

$$= -2^{n-1} + (2^{n-1} - 1) + 1 - N \text{ (because}$$

$$\sum_{i=0}^{n-2} N_i 2^i = N \text{ as the most-significant bit of } N \text{ is zero}$$

for N to be within its stated range)

$$= -2^{n-1} + 2^{n-1} - N$$

$$= -N$$

Representing two's complement numbers graphically

We can visualize numbers in the two's complement system by arranging numbers around a circle. Figure 4.34 demonstrates such an arrangement for 4-bit numbers in which a circle has been divided up by 16 radials numbered from 0000 to 1111. Suppose we number the radials according to their two's complement values, so that radials 0000 to 0111 are numbered 0 to 7 and radials 1000 to 1111 are numbered -8 to -1. Notice how stepping one place clockwise increases a number and stepping one place counterclockwise decreases a number. We can now see how adding numbers to a negative value causes the result to move in the direction toward zero. For example, if we add 0011 ($+3$) to 1100 (-4) we get 1111 which is -1. If we had added 0101 ($+5$) to 1100, we would have got (1)0001 which is $+1$ and lies to the right of zero.

4.8.4 One's complement representation

An alternative to two's complement arithmetic is *one's complement arithmetic* in which the representation of a negative number, N, in n bits is given by $2^n - N - 1$. The one's complement representation of a number is one less than the corresponding two's complement representation and is formed more simply by inverting the bits of N. For example, for $n = 5$ consider the subtraction of 4 from 9. The binary value of 4 is 00100 and its one's complement is 11011.

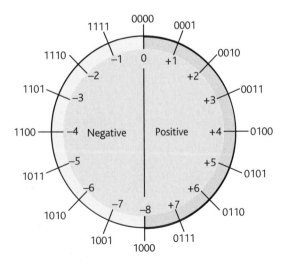

Fig. 4.34 Visualizing two's complement numbers.

```
+9 = +01001  ⟶    01001
-4 = -00100  ⟶  + 11011
                 100100  ⟵ result after addition
                 └─⟶ 1
                  00101  ⟵ result after adding
                           in the end-
                           around-carry
```

After the addition has been completed, the leftmost bit of the result is added to the least-significant bit of the result in an arrangement called *end-around-carry*. This provides us with the final and correct result. Note that if the result of the initial addition yields a carry-out of zero, the result is negative and adding in the carry-out (i.e. zero) also gives the correct answer. Consider the following example.

```
-9 = -01001  ⟶    10110
+4 = +00100  ⟶  + 00100
                 011010  ⟵ result after addition
                 └─⟶ 0
                  11010  ⟵ result after adding
                           in the end-
                           around-carry
```

In one's complement 11010 represents the value -00101 (i.e. -5).

We can demonstrate that end-around-carry works in one's complement arithmetic as follows. Suppose we wish to compute $X - Y$. We add the one's complement of Y to X to get $X + (2^n - Y - 1) = 2^n + (X - Y) - 1$. By transferring the carry-out, 2^n, to the least-significant bit, we correct the result $(X - Y) - 1$ to $(X - Y)$ by canceling the -1 term.

If we add together two one's complement negative numbers we get $-X + -Y = (2^n - X - 1) + (2^n - Y - 1) = 2^n - 1 + 2^n - 1 - (X + Y)$. If we apply end-around-carry to this result, the first 2^n term cancels the first -1 term to leave $2^n - 1 - (X + Y)$. This is, of course, the correct result in one's complement form.

The one's complement system is not a true complement as the value of $X + (-X)$ is not zero. Furthermore, there are two representations for zero: 00...0 and 11...1. Today, the one's complement system is rarely used to represent signed numbers.

It's instructive to compare the various ways of representing numbers we have encountered so far. Table 4.23 shows the sequence of 5-bit binary numbers for $n = 5$ for pure binary numbers, sign and magnitude, one's complement, and two's complement representations. The rightmost column includes the *biased* representation of signed numbers—a system that we will use when we describe floating point numbers. In this case the biased representation of a number

Binary code	Natural binary	Sign and magnitude	One's complement	Two's complement	Biased form
00000	0	0	0	0	−15
00001	1	1	1	1	−14
00010	2	2	2	2	−13
00011	3	3	3	3	−12
00100	4	4	4	4	−11
00101	5	5	5	5	−10
00110	6	6	6	6	−9
00111	7	7	7	7	−8
01000	8	8	8	8	−7
01001	9	9	9	9	−6
01010	10	10	10	10	−5
01011	11	11	11	11	−4
01100	12	12	12	12	−3
01101	13	13	13	13	−2
01110	14	14	14	14	−1
01111	15	15	15	15	0
10000	16	−0	−15	−16	1
10001	17	−1	−14	−15	2
10010	18	−2	−13	−14	3
10011	19	−3	−12	−13	4
10100	20	−4	−11	−12	5
10101	21	−5	−10	−11	6
10110	22	−6	−9	−10	7
10111	23	−7	−8	−9	8
11000	24	−8	−7	−8	9
11001	25	−9	−6	−7	10
11010	26	−10	−5	−6	11
11011	27	−11	−4	−5	12
11100	28	−12	−3	−4	13
11101	29	−13	−2	−3	14
11110	30	−14	−1	−2	15
11111	31	−15	−0	−1	16

Table 4.23 The representation of negative numbers.

is 15 greater than the actual number; for example, 7 is represented by $7 + 15 = 22 = 10110_2$.

4.9 Floating point numbers

So far, we've largely dealt with *integer* values. Let's look at a simple way of handling numbers with both integer and fractional parts (e.g. 13.75_{10} or 1101.11_2). Fortunately, a binary (or decimal) fraction presents no problems. Consider the following two calculations in decimal arithmetic.

Case 1 Integer arithmetic   Case 2 Fixed point arithmetic

```
  7632135              763.2135
+ 1794821            + 179.4821
  9426956              942.6956
```

Although case 1 uses *integer* arithmetic and case 2 uses *fractional* arithmetic, the calculations are entirely identical. The only difference is in the location of the decimal point. We can extend this principle to computer arithmetic. All the computer programmer has to do is to remember where the binary point is assumed to lie. Input to the computer is scaled to match this convention and the output is similarly scaled. The internal operations themselves are carried out as if the numbers were in integer form. This arrangement is called *fixed point arithmetic*, because the binary point is assumed to remain in the same position. That is, there is always the same number of digits before and after the binary point. The advantage of the fixed point representation of numbers is that no complex software or hardware is needed to implement it.

A simple example should make the idea of fixed point arithmetic clearer. Consider an 8-bit fixed point number with the four most-significant bits representing the integer part and the four least-significant bits representing the fractional part.

Let's see what happens if we wish to add the two numbers 3.625 and 6.5 and print the result. An input program first converts these numbers to binary form.

$$3.625 \rightarrow 11.101 \rightarrow 0011.1010 \quad \text{(in 8 bits)}$$

$$6.5 \rightarrow 110.1 \rightarrow 0110.1000 \quad \text{(in 8 bits)}$$

The computer now regards these numbers as 00111010 and 01101000, respectively. Remember that the binary point is only imaginary. These numbers are added in the normal way to give

```
 00111010
+01101000
 10100010
```

This result would be equal to 162_{10} if we were to regard it as an unsigned natural binary integer. But it isn't. We must regard it as a fixed point value. The output program now takes the result and splits it into an integer part 1010 and a fractional part 0010. The integer part is equal to 10_{10} and the fractional part is 0.125_{10}. The result would be printed as 10.125.

In practice, a fixed point number may be spread over several words to achieve a greater range of values than allowed by a single word. The fixed point representation of fractional numbers is very useful in some circumstances, particularly for financial calculations. For example, the smallest fractional part may be (say) 0.1 of a cent or 0.001 of a dollar. The largest integer part may be $1 000 000. To represent such a quantity in BCD a total of $6 \times 4 + 3 \times 4 = 36$ bits are required. A byte-oriented computer would require 5 bytes for each number.

Fixed point numbers have their limitations. Consider the astrophysicist who is examining the sun's behavior. They are confronted with numbers ranging from the mass of the sun (199000000000000000000000000000000 grams) to the mass of an electron (0.000000000000000000000000000910956 grams).

If astrophysicists were to resort to fixed point arithmetic, they would require an extravagantly large number of bits to represent the range of numbers used in their trade. A single byte represents numbers in the range 0 to 255. If the physicist wanted to work with astronomically large and microscopically small numbers, roughly 14 bytes would be required for

the integer part of the number and 12 bytes for the fractional part; that is, they would need a 26-byte (208 bit) number. A clue to a way out of our dilemma is to note that both figures contain a large number of zeros but few significant digits.

4.9.1 Representation of floating point numbers

We can express a decimal number such as 1234.56 in the form 0.123456×10^4 which is called the *floating point format* or *scientific notation*. The computer handles large and small binary values in a similar way; for example, 1101101.1101101 may be represented internally as $0.11011011101101 \times 2^7$ (the 7 is, of course, also stored in a binary format). Before looking at floating point numbers in more detail we should to consider the ideas of *range*, *precision*, and *accuracy*, which are closely related to the way numbers are represented in floating point format.

Range   A number's range tells us how big or how small it can be; for example, the astrophysicist was dealing with numbers as large as 2×10^{33} and those as small as 9×10^{-28}, representing a range of approximately 10^{61}, or 61 decades. The range of numbers capable of representation by a computer must be sufficient for the calculations that are likely to be performed. If the computer is employed in a dedicated application where the range of data to be handled is known to be quite small, then the range of valid numbers may be restricted, simplifying the hardware/software requirements.

Precision   The precision of a number is a measure of its exactness and corresponds to the number of significant figures used to represent it. For example, the constant π may be written as 3.142 or 3.141592. The latter value is more *precise* than the former because it represents π to one part in 10^7 whereas the former value represents π to one part in 10^4.

Accuracy   Accuracy has been included here largely to contrast it with precision, a term often incorrectly thought to mean the same as accuracy. Accuracy is the measure of the correctness of a quantity. For example, we can say $\pi = 3.141$ or $\pi = 3.241592$. The first value is a low-precision number but is more accurate than the higher precision value, which has an error in the second digit. In an ideal world accuracy and precision would go hand in hand. It's the job of the computer programmer to design algorithms that preserve the accuracy that the available precision allows. One of the potential hazards of computation is calculations that take the form

$$\frac{A + B}{A - B}$$

For example,
$$\frac{1234.5687 + 1234.5678 = 2469.1365}{1234.5687 - 1234.5678 = 0.0009}$$

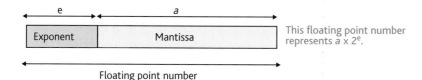

This floating point number represents $a \times 2^e$.

Floating point number

Fig. 4.35 Storing a floating-point number.

When the denominator is evaluated we are left with 0.0009, a number with only one decimal place of precision. Although the result might show eight figures of precision, it may be very inaccurate indeed.

A floating point number can be represented in the form $a \times r^e$ where a is the *mantissa* (also called the *argument*), r is the *radix* or *base*, and e is the *exponent* or *characteristic*. The computer stores a floating point number by splitting the binary sequence representing the number into the two fields illustrated in Fig. 4.35. The radix r is not stored explicitly by the computer.

Throughout the remainder of this section the value of the radix in all floating point numbers is assumed to be two. Before the IEEE format became popular, some computers used an octal or hexadecimal exponent, so that the mantissa is multiplied by 8^e or 16^e, respectively. For example, if a floating-point number has a mantissa 0.101011 and an octal exponent of 4 (i.e. 0100 in 4 bits), the number is equal to 0.101011×8^4 or 0.101011×2^{12}, which is 101011000000_2.

It's not necessary for a floating point number to occupy a single storage location. Indeed with an 8-bit word, such a representation would be useless. Several words are grouped to form a floating point number (the number of words required is bits-in-floating-point-representation/computer-word-length). The split between exponent and mantissa need not fall at a word boundary. That is, a mantissa might occupy 3 bytes and the exponent 1 byte of a two 16-bit word floating-point number.

When constructing a floating point representation for numbers, the programmer must select the following.

1. The total number of bits.
2. The representation of the mantissa (two's complement etc.).
3. The representation of the exponent (biased etc.).
4. The number of bits allocated to the mantissa and exponent.
5. The location of the mantissa (exponent first or mantissa first).

Point 4 is worthy of elaboration. Once you've decided on the total number of bits in the floating point representation, the number must be split into a mantissa and exponent. Dedicating a large number of bits to the exponent lets you represent numbers with a large range. Gaining exponent bits at the expense of the mantissa reduces the precision of the floating point number. Conversely, increasing the bits available for the mantissa improves the precision at the expense of the range.

Once, almost no two machines used the same format. Things improved with the introduction of microprocessors.

Today, the IEEE standard for floating-point numbers dominates the computer industry. Accordingly, we concentrate on this standard.

4.9.2 Normalization of floating point numbers

By convention a floating point mantissa is always *normalized* unless it is equal to zero and is expressed in the form 1.F where F is the *fractional* part.[3] Because a normalized IEEE floating pint mantissa always begins with a 1, this is called 'the leading 1'. A normalized mantissa is therefore in the range $1.00\ldots00$ to $1.11\ldots11$; that is

$$-2 < x \le -1, \text{ or } x = 0, \text{ or } 1 \le x < 2.$$

If the result of a calculation were to yield $11.010\ldots \times 2^e$, the result would be normalized to give $1.1010\ldots \times 2^{e+1}$. Similarly, the result $0.1001\ldots \times 2^e$ would be normalized to $1.001\ldots \times 2^{e-1}$.

By normalizing a mantissa, the greatest possible advantage is taken of the available precision. For example, the unnormalized 8-bit mantissa 0.00001010 has only four significant bits, whereas the normalized 8-bit mantissa 1.0100011 has eight significant bits. It is worth noting here that there is a slight difference between normalized decimal numbers as used by engineers and scientists, and normalized binary numbers. By convention, a decimal floating point number is normalized so that its mantissa lies in the range $1.00\ldots0$ to $9.99\ldots9$.

A special exception has to be made in the case of zero, as this number cannot, of course, be normalized.

Because the IEEE floating-point format uses a *sign and magnitude* format, a sign-bit indicates the sign of a mantissa. A negative floating point mantissa is stored in the form

$$x = -1.11\ldots1 \text{ to } -1.00\ldots0$$

A floating point number is limited to one of the three ranges $-2 < x \le -1$, or $x = 0$, or $1 \le x < 2$ described by Fig. 4.36.

Biased exponents

A floating-point representation of numbers must make provision for both positive and negative numbers, and

---

[3] Before the advent of the IEEE standard, floating point numbers were often normalized in the form $0.1\ldots x\ 2^e$ and constrained to the range $\frac{1}{2} \le x < 1$ or $-\frac{1}{2} > x \ge -1$.

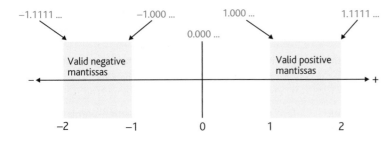

Figure 4.36 Range of valid normalized two's complement mantissas.

Binary value	True exponent	Biased form
0000	−8	0
0001	−7	1
0010	−6	2
0011	−5	3
0100	−4	4
0101	−3	5
0110	−2	6
0111	−1	7
1000	0	8
1001	1	9
1010	2	10
1011	3	11
1100	4	12
1101	5	13
1110	6	14
1111	7	15

For example, if $n = 1010.1111$, we normalize it to $+1.0101111 \times 2^3$. The true exponent is $+3$, which is stored as a biased exponent of $3 + 8$, which is 11_{10} or 1011 in binary form.

Table 4.24 Relationship between true and biased exponents.

Fig. 4.37 Representing zero in floating point arithmetic.

positive and negative exponents. The following example in decimal notation demonstrates this concept.

$$+0.123 \times 10^{12}, \quad -0.756 \times 10^9, \quad +0.176 \times 10^{-3},$$
$$-0.459 \times 10^{-7}$$

The mantissa of an IEEE format floating point number is represented in *sign and magnitude* form. The exponent, however, is represented in a *biased* form. An m-bit exponent provides 2^m unsigned integer exponents from $00 \ldots 0$ to $11 \ldots 1$. Suppose that we relabel these 2^m values from -2^{m-1}

to $+2^{m-1} -1$ by subtracting a constant value (or bias) of $B = 2^{m-1}$ from each of the numbers. We get a continuous natural binary series from 0 to N representing exponents from $-B$ to $N - B$.

If we use a 3-bit decimal biased exponent with $B = 4$, the biased exponents are 0, 1, 2, 3, 4, 5, 6, 7 and represent the actual exponents -4, -3, -2, -1, 0, 1, 2, 3. We've invented a way of representing negative numbers by adding a constant to the most negative number to make it equal to zero. In this example, we've added 4 to each true number so that -4 is represented by the biased values 0, and $- 3$ by $+1$, etc.

We create a biased exponent by adding a constant to the true exponent so that the biased exponent is given by $b' = b + B$, where b' is the biased exponent, b the true exponent, and B a weighting. The weighting B is frequently either 2^{m-1} or $2^{m-1} - 1$. Consider what happens for the case where $m = 4$ and $B = 2^3 = 8$. (See Table 4.24).

The true exponent ranges from -8 to $+7$, allowing us to represent powers of 2 from 2^{-8} to 2^{+7}, while the biased exponent ranges from 0 to $+15$. The advantage of the biased representation of exponents is that the most negative exponent is represented by zero. Conveniently, the floating-point value of zero is represented by $0.0 \ldots 0 \times 2^{\text{most negative exponent}}$ (see Figure 4.37). By choosing the biased exponent system we arrange that zero is represented by a zero mantissa and a zero exponent as Figure 4.36 demonstrates.

The biased exponent representation of exponents is also called *excess n*, where n is typically 2^{m-1}. For example, a 6-bit exponent is called excess 32 because the stored exponent exceeds the true exponent by 32. In this case, the smallest true exponent that can be represented is -32 and is stored as an excess 32 value of 0. The maximum true exponent that can be represented is 31 and this is stored as 63.

A second advantage of the biased exponent representation is that the stored (i.e. biased) exponents form a natural binary sequence. This sequence is *monotonic* so that increasing the exponent by 1 involves adding 1 to the binary exponent, and decreasing the exponent by 1 involves subtracting one from the binary exponent. In both cases the binary biased exponent can be considered as behaving like an unsigned binary number. Consequently, you can use relatively simple logic to compare two exponents. Remember that in 4-bit *signed* arithmetic the number 0110 is larger than 1110 because the second number is negative. If these were biased exponents, 1110 would be larger than 0110.

IEEE floating point format

The Institute of Electronics and Electrical Engineers (IEEE) has defined a standard floating point format for arithmetic operations called ANSI/IEEE standard 754-1985. To cater for different applications, the standard specifies three basic formats, called *single*, *double*, and *quad*. Table 4.25 defines the principal features of these three floating point formats.

An IEEE format floating point number X is formally defined as

$$X = -1^S \times 2^{E-B} \times 1.F,$$

where S = sign bit, 0 = positive mantissa, 1 = negative mantissa, E = exponent biased by B, F = fractional mantissa (note that the mantissa is $1.F$ and has an implicit leading 1).

A single-format 32-bit floating-point number has a bias of 127 and a 23-bit fractional mantissa. A sign and magnitude representation has been adopted for the mantissa; if $S = 1$ the mantissa is negative and if $S = 0$ it is positive.

The mantissa is always normalized and lies in the range $1.000\ldots00$ to $1.111\ldots11$. If the mantissa is always normalized, it follows that the leading 1, the integer part, is redundant when the IEEE format floating point number is stored in memory. If we know that a 1 must be located to the left of the fractional mantissa, there is no need to store it. In this way 1 bit of storage is saved, permitting the precision of the mantissa to be extended by 1 bit. The format of the number when stored in memory is given in Fig. 4.38.

As an example of the use of the IEEE 32-bit format, consider the representation of the decimal number -2345.125.
$-2345.125_{10} = -100100101001.001_2$ (as an equivalent binary number)

$$= -1.00100101001001 \times 2^{11} \quad \text{(as a normalized binary number)}$$

The mantissa is negative so the sign bit S is 1. The biased exponent is given by $+11 + 127 = 138 = 10001010_2$. The fractional part of the mantissa is $.00100101001001000000000$ (in 23 bits). Therefore, the IEEE single format representation of -2345.125 is:

11000101000100101001001000000000

In order to minimize storage space in computers where the memory width is less than that of the floating point number, floating point numbers are *packed* so that the sign bit, exponent and mantissa share part of two or more machine words. When floating point operations are carried out, the numbers are first *unpacked* and the mantissa separated from the exponent. For example, the basic single precision format specifies a 23-bit fractional mantissa, giving a 24-bit mantissa when unpacked and the leading 1 reinserted. If the processor on which the floating point numbers are being processed has a 16-bit word length, the unpacked mantissa will occupy 24 bits out of the 32 bits taken up by two words.

If, when a number is unpacked, the number of bits in its exponent and mantissa is allowed to increase to fill the available space, the format is said to be *extended*. By extending the format in this way, the range and precision of the floating

	Single precision	Double precision	Quad precision
Field width in bits			
S = sign	1	1	1
E = exponent	8	11	15
L = leading bit	1	1	1
F = fraction	23	52	111
Total width	32	64	128
Exponent			
Maximum E	255	2047	32 767
Minimum E	0	0	0
Bias	127	1023	16 383

Notes
S = sign bit (0 for a negative number, 1 for a positive number).
L = leading bit (always 1 in a normalized, non-zero mantissa).
F = fractional part of the mantissa.
The range of exponents is from Min E + 1 to Max E − 1
The number is represented by $-1^S \times 2^{E-\text{exponent}} \times L \cdot F$.
A signed zero is represented by the minimum exponent, $L = 0$, and $F = 0$, for all three formats.
The maximum exponent has a special function that represents signed infinity for all three formats.

Table 4.25 Basic IEEE floating point formats.

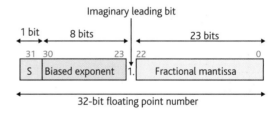

Figure 4.38 Format of the IEEE 32-bit floating point format.

IEEE SPECIAL NUMBERS

When we said that floating point numbers are always normalized, we were being economical with the truth. The IEEE floating point standard does allow for denormalized numbers called denormals. A denormal can be used to represent a value that is less than $1.000\ldots00 \times 2^{E_{min}}$. The denormal permits the representation of numbers below the minimum at the cost of a reduced precision; for example, you can have $0.000001011101\ldots \times 2^{E_{min}}$, where we have lost six places of precision.

The not-a-number (NaN) can be used to speed the processing of chained calculations. For example, if we have $Z = A \cdot B \cdot C$ and C is a NaN, the computer can immediately say that Z is also a NaN.

The special exponent $E_{max} + 1$ is used to represent infinity if the fractional part is zero or a NaN if the fractional part is non-zero.

point number are considerably increased. For example, a single format number is stored as a 32-bit quantity. When it is unpacked the 23-bit fractional mantissa is increased to 24 bits by including the leading 1 and then the mantissa is extended to 32 bits (either as a single 32-bit word or as two 16-bit words). All calculations are then performed using the 32-bit extended precision mantissa. This is particularly helpful when trigonometric functions (e.g., sin x, cos x) are evaluated. After a sequence of floating operations have been carried out in the extended format, the floating point number is repacked and stored in memory in its basic form.

In 32-bit single IEEE format, the maximum exponent E_{max} is $+127$ and the minimum exponent E_{min} is -126 rather than $+128$ to $+127$ as we might expect. The special value $E_{min}-1$ (i.e. -127) is used to encode zero and $E_{max} + 1$ is used to encode plus or minus infinity or a NaN. A NaN is a special entity catered for in the IEEE format and is *not a number*. The use of NaNs is covered by the IEEE standard and they permit the manipulation of formats outside the IEEE standard.

4.9.3 Floating point arithmetic

Unlike integer and fixed point number representations, floating point numbers can't be added in one simple operation. A moment's thought should demonstrate why this is so. Consider an example in decimal arithmetic. Let $A = 12345$ and $B = 567.89$. In decimal floating point form these numbers can be represented by

$A = 0.12345 \times 10^5$ and $B = 0.56789 \times 10^3$

If these numbers were to be added by hand, no problems would arise.

```
12345
 +567.89
12912.89
```

However, as these numbers are held in a normalized floating point format we have the following problem.

```
 0.12345 x 10⁵
+0.56789 x 10³
```

Addition can't take place as long as the exponents are different. To perform a floating-point addition (or subtraction) the following steps must be carried out.

1. Identify the number with the smaller exponent.
2. Make the smaller exponent equal to the larger exponent by dividing the mantissa of the smaller number by the same factor by which its exponent was increased.
3. Add (or subtract) the mantissas.
4. If necessary, normalize the result (post-normalization).

In the above example we have $A = 0.12345 \times 10^5$ and $B = 0.56789 \times 10^3$.

The exponent of B is smaller than that of A which results an increase of 2 in B's exponent and a corresponding division of B's mantissa by 10^2 to give 0.0056789×10^5. We can now add A to the denormalized B.

```
 A  =  0.1234500 × 10⁵
+B  =  0.0056789 × 10⁵
       0.1291289 × 10⁵
```

The result is already in a normalized form and doesn't need post-normalizing. Note that the answer is expressed to a precision of seven significant figures whereas A and B are each expressed to a precision of five significant figures. If the result were stored in a computer, its mantissa would have to be reduced to five figures after the decimal point (because we were working with five-digit mantissas).

When people do arithmetic they often resort to what may best be called floating precision. If they want greater precision they simply use more digits. Computers use a fixed representation for floating point numbers so that the precision may not increase as a result of calculation. Consider the following binary example of floating point addition.

```
A  =  0.11001 × 2⁴
B  =  0.10001 × 2³
```

The exponent of B must be increased by 1 and the mantissa of B divided by 2 (i.e. shifted one place right) to make both exponents equal to 4.

```
A  =  0.11001  × 2⁴
B  =  0.010001 × 2⁴
      1.000011 × 2⁴
```

Because the result is no longer normalized, we have to shift its mantissa one place right (i.e. divide it by 2) and add 1 to the exponent to compensate; that is, the result becomes 0.1000011×2^5. We've gained two extra places of precision. We can simply truncate the number to get

$A + B = 0.10000 \times 2^5$

A more formal procedure for the addition of floating point numbers is given in Fig. 4.39 as a flowchart. A few points to note about this flowchart are given below.

1. Because the exponent shares part of a word with the mantissa, it's necessary to separate them before the process of addition can begin. As we pointed out before, this is called *unpacking*.
2. If the two exponents differ by more than $p + 1$, where p is the number of significant bits in the mantissa, the smaller number is too small to affect the larger and the result is effectively equal to the larger number. For example, there's no point in adding 0.1234×10^{20} to 0.4567×10^2, because adding 0.4567×10^2 to 0.1234×10^{20} has no effect on a four-digit mantissa.
3. During the post-normalization phase the exponent is checked to see if it is less than its minimum possible value or

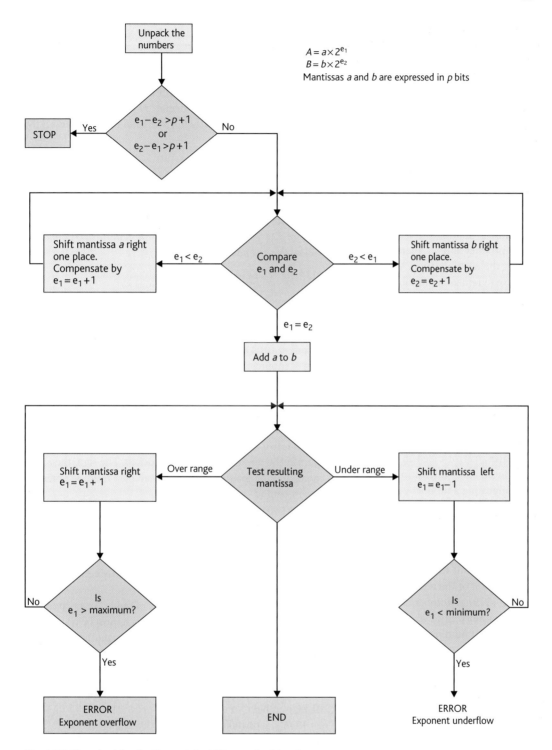

$A = a \times 2^{e_1}$
$B = b \times 2^{e_2}$
Mantissas a and b are expressed in p bits

Unpack the numbers

$e_1 - e_2 > p + 1$ or $e_2 - e_1 > p + 1$

Yes

STOP

No

Shift mantissa a right one place. Compensate by $e_1 = e_1 + 1$

$e_1 < e_2$

Compare e_1 and e_2

$e_2 < e_1$

Shift mantissa b right one place. Compensate by $e_2 = e_2 + 1$

$e_1 = e_2$

Add a to b

Shift mantissa right $e_1 = e_1 + 1$

Over range

Test resulting mantissa

Under range

Shift mantissa left $e_1 = e_1 - 1$

No

Is $e_1 > $ maximum?

Yes

No

Is $e_1 < $ minimum?

Yes

ERROR Exponent overflow

END

ERROR Exponent underflow

Fig. 4.39 Flowchart for floating point addition and subtraction.

greater than its maximum possible value. This corresponds to testing for *exponent underflow* and *overflow*, respectively. Each of these cases represents conditions in which the number is outside the range of numbers that the computer can handle. Exponent underflow would generally lead to the number being made equal to zero, whereas exponent overflow would result in an error condition and may require the intervention of the operating system.

Floating point multiplication is easier than addition or subtraction because we simply multiply mantissas and add exponents. For example if $x = s_1 \times 2^{e_1}$ and $y = s_2 \times 2^{e_2}$ then $x \cdot y = s_1 \cdot s_2 \times 2^{(e_1 + e_2)}$. The multiplication can be done with an integer multiplier (we don't even have to worry about signed numbers). Of course, multiplication of two p-bit numbers yields a $2p$-bit product and we therefore have to round down the result of the multiplication. When we add the two exponents, we have to remember to subtract the bias because each exponent is $E_{\text{true}} + b$.

Rounding and truncation

We have seen that some of the operations involved in floating point arithmetic lead to an increase in the number of bits in the mantissa and that some technique must be invoked to keep the number of bits in the mantissa constant. The simplest technique is called *truncation* and involves nothing more than dropping unwanted bits. For example, if we truncate 0.1101101 to four significant bits we get 0.1101. Truncating a number creates an error called an *induced error* (i.e. an error has been induced in the calculation by an operation on the number). Truncating a number causes a *biased* error because the number after truncation is always smaller than the number that was truncated.

A much better technique for reducing the number of bits in a word is *rounding*. If the value of the lost digits is greater than half the least-significant bit of the retained digits, 1 is added to the least-significant bit of the remaining digits. We have been doing this with decimal numbers for years—the decimal number 12.234 is rounded to 12.23, whereas 13.146 is rounded to 13.15. Consider rounding to four significant bits the following numbers.

$0.1101011 \rightarrow 0.1101$ The three bits removed are 011, so do nothing

$0.1101101 \rightarrow 0.1101 + 1 = 0.1110$ The three bits removed are 101, so add 1

Rounding is always preferred to truncation partially because it is more accurate and partially because it gives rise to an *unbiased error*. Truncation always undervalues the result leading to a systematic error whereas rounding sometimes reduces the result and sometimes increases it. The major disadvantage of rounding is that it requires a further arithmetic operation to be performed on the result.

4.9.4 Examples of floating point calculations

Because handling floating point numbers can be tricky, we provide several examples. An IEEE standard 32-bit floating-point number has the format $N = -1^S \times 1.F \times 2^{E-127}$, where S is the *sign* bit, F is the *fractional* mantissa, and E the *biased* exponent.

EXAMPLE 1

Convert the decimal numbers 123.5 and 100.25 into the IEEE format for floating point numbers. Then carry out the subtraction of 123.5 − 100.25 and express the result as a normalized 32-bit floating point value.

$$123.5_{10} = 1111011.1$$
$$= 1.1110111 \times 2^6$$

The mantissa is positive, so $S = 0$. The exponent is $+6$, which is stored in biased form as $6 + 127 = 133_{10} = 10000101_2$. The mantissa is 1.1110111, which is stored as 23 bits with the leading 1 suppressed. The number is stored in IEEE format as 01000101 10010001000000000000000.

We can immediately write down the IEEE value for 100.25 because it is so close to the 123.5 we have just calculated; that is, 0 10000101 10010001000000000000000.

The two IEEE-format floating point numbers taking part in the operation are first unpacked. The sign, the exponent, and the mantissa (with the leading 1 restored) must be reconstituted.

The two exponents are compared. If they are the same, the mantissas are added. If they are not, the number with the smaller exponent is denormalized by shifting its mantissa right (i.e. dividing by 2) and incrementing its exponent (i.e. multiplying by 2) until the two exponents are equal. Then the numbers are added.

If the mantissa of the result is out of range (i.e. greater than 1.11111 . . . 1 or less than 1.0000 . . . 0) it must be re-normalized. If the exponent goes out of range (bigger than its largest value or smaller than its smallest value) exponent overflow occurs and an error is flagged. The result is then repacked and the leading 1 in front of the normalized mantissa removed.

IEEE number
$123.5_{10} = 00100010111101110000000000000000$
IEEE number
$100.25_{10} = 0\ 01000101100100010000000000000000$

These floating-point numbers have the same exponent, so we can subtract their mantissas (after inserting the leading 1).

$$\begin{array}{r} 1.11101110000000000000000 \\ -\ 1.10010001000000000000000 \\ \hline 0.01011101000000000000000 \end{array}$$

The result is not normalized and must be shifted left twice to get 1.0111010000000000000000. The exponent must be decreased by 2 to get 01000011. The result expressed in floating point format is

0 0100011 01110100000000000000000

EXAMPLE 2

Carry out the operation 42.6875 − 0.09375 by first converting these numbers to the IEEE 32-bit format. Use these floating point numbers to perform the subtraction and then calculate the new floating point value.

$$42.6875_{10} = 101010.1011_2$$
$$= 1.010101011 \times 2^5$$

This number is positive and $S = 0$. The true exponent is 5 and, therefore, the biased exponent is $5 + 127$ (i.e. actual exponent + bias) $= 132 = 10000100_2$ in 8 bits. The fractional exponent is 010101011(00000000000). Therefore 42.6875 is represented as an IEEE floating point value by 01000010001010101100000000000000.

Similarly, $-0.09375_{10} = -0.00011_2 = -1.1 \times 2^{-4}$. The sign-bit $S = 1$ because the number is negative and the biased exponent $E = -4 + 127 = 123 = 01111011_2$. The fractional mantissa is $F = 10000000000000000000000$. The representation of -0.09375 is therefore 1011110111 000000000000000000000. These two numbers are stored as

01000010001010101100000000000000 and
10111101110000000000000000000000, respectively.

In order to perform the addition we have to unpack these numbers to sign + biased exponent + mantissa.

First number   0 10000100 01010101100000000000000
Second number 1 01111011 10000000000000000000000

We must insert the leading 1 into the fractional mantissa to get the true mantissa.

First number   0 10000100 **1**01010101100000000000000
Second number 1 01111011 **1**10000000000000000000000

In order to add or subtract the numbers, the exponents must be the same (we can work with biased exponents). The second number's exponent is smaller by $10000100 - 0111011 = 00001001_2 = 9_{10}$. We increase the second exponent by 9 and shift the mantissa right 9 times to get

First number   0 10000100 **1**01010101100000000000000
Second number 1 10000100 0000000001**1**0000000000000000000000000

We can now subtract mantissas to get 101010100011000000000000. The result is positive with a biased exponent of 10000100 and a mantissa of 1.010101000110000000000000. This number would be stored as 0 10000100 01010100011000000000000 (we've dropped the leading 1 mantissa).

This number is equal to $+ 2^5 \times 1.0101010011 = 101010.10011 = 42.59375$.

EXAMPLE 3

Let's perform a floating point multiplication. We'll use two decimal floating point numbers that can be converted into binary form without a calculator. Assume we wish to calculate $X = 256.5 \times 4.652$.

We can immediately write $256.5 = 100000000.1_2 = 1.000000001 \times 2^8$ and $4.625 = 100.101_2 = 1.00101 \times 2^2$.

In IEEE 32-bit format, these two numbers are represented by

0 10000111 00000000100000000000000   and
0 10000001 00101000000000000000000

To multiply the numbers, we unpack the fractional mantissas, insert the leading 1s, and multiply them. Then we add the two biased exponents and subtract one bias. The new mantissa is

$1.000000001 \times 1.00101 = 1.00101000100101_2$

If we add the biased mantissas and subtract one bias we get $10000111 + 10000001 - 01111111 = 10001001_2$. The final IEEE format result is

0 10001001 00101000100101000000000 = $44944A0_{16}$.

The decimal result is $+1.00101000100101000000000 \times 2^{10001001 - 1111111} = 1.00101000100101 \times 2^{10} = 10010100010.0101_2 = 1186.3125_{10}$.

4.10 Multiplication and division

We've looked at addition and subtraction—now we consider multiplication and division. Other mathematical functions can be derived from multiplication. Division itself will later be defined as an iterative process involving multiplication.

4.10.1 Multiplication

Binary multiplication is no more complex than decimal multiplication. In many ways it's easier as the whole binary multiplication table can be reduced to

$0 \times 0 = 0$
$0 \times 1 = 0$
$1 \times 0 = 0$
$1 \times 1 = 1$

The multiplication of two bits is identical to their logical AND. When we consider the multiplication of strings of bits, things become more complex and the way in which multiplication is carried out, or mechanized, varies from machine to machine. The faster and more expensive the computer, the more complex the hardware used to implement multiplication. Some high-speed computers perform multiplication in a single operation by means of a very large logic array involving hundreds of gates.

Unsigned binary multiplication

The so-called *pencil and paper algorithm* used by people to calculate the product of two multidigit numbers, involves the multiplication of an n-digit number by a single digit followed by shifting and adding. We can apply the same approach to unsigned binary numbers in the following way. The multiplier bits are examined, one at a time, starting with the least-significant bit. If the current multiplier bit is one the multiplicand is written down, if it is zero then n zeros are written down instead. Then the next bit of the multiplier is examined, but this time we write the multiplicand (or zero) one place to the left of the last digits we wrote down. Each of these groups of n digits is called a *partial product*. When all partial products have been formed, they are added up to give the result of the multiplication. An example should make this clear.

10×13 Multiplier $= 1101_2$
Multiplicand $= 1010_2$

```
      1010
    ×1101
      1010        Step 1  first  multiplier bit = 1, write down multiplicand
      0000        Step 2  second multiplier bit = 0, write down zeros shifted left
    1010          Step 3  third  multiplier bit = 1, write down multiplicand shifted left
  1010            Step 4  fourth multiplier bit = 1, write down multiplicand shifted left
10000010          Step 5  add together four partial products
```

The result, $10000010_2 = 130_{10}$, is 8 bits long. The multiplication of two n-bit numbers yields a $2n$-bit product.

Digital computers don't implement the pencil and paper algorithm in the above way, as this would require the storing of n partial products, followed by the simultaneous addition of n words. A better technique is to add up the partial products as they are formed. An algorithm for the multiplication of two n-bit unsigned binary numbers is given in Table 4.26. We will consider the previous example of 1101×1010 using the algorithm of Table 4.26. The mechanization of the product of 1101×1010 is presented in Table 4.27.

Signed multiplication

The multiplication algorithm we've just discussed is valid only for unsigned integers or unsigned fixed point numbers. As computers represent signed numbers by means of two's complement notation, it is necessary to find some way of forming the product of two's complement numbers. It is, of course, possible to convert negative numbers into a modulus-only form, calculate the product, and then convert it into a two's complement form if it is negative. That approach wastes time.

We first demonstrate that the two's complement representation of negative numbers can't be used with the basic shifting and adding algorithm. That is, two's complement arithmetic works for addition and subtraction, but not for multiplication or division (without using special algorithms). Consider the product of X and $-Y$. The two's complement representation of $-Y$ is $2^n - Y$.

If we use two's complement arithmetic, the product $X(-Y)$ is given by $X(2^n - Y) = 2^n X - XY$.

The expected result, $-XY$, is represented in two's complement form by $2^{2n} - XY$. The most-significant bit is 2^{2n} (rather than 2^n) because multiplication automatically yields a

---

(a) Set a counter to n.

(b) Clear the $2n$-bit partial product register.

(c) Examine the rightmost bit of the multiplier (initially the least-significant bit). If it is one add the multiplicand to the n most-significant bits of the partial product.

(d) Shift the partial product one place to the right.

(e) Shift the multiplier one place to the right (the rightmost bit is, of course, lost).

(f) Decrement the counter. If the result is not zero repeat from step c. If the result is zero read the product from the partial product register.

Table 4.26 An algorithm for multiplication.

Multiplier $= 1101_2$		Multiplicand $= 1010_2$		
Step	Counter	Multiplier	Partial product	Cycle
a and b	4	1101	00000000	
c	4	110**1**	10100000	1
d and e	4	0110	01010000	1
f	3	0110	01010000	1
c	3	011**0**	01010000	2
d and e	3	0011	00101000	2
f	2	0011	00101000	2
c	2	001**1**	11001000	3
d and e	2	0001	01100100	3
f	1	0001	01100100	3
c	1	000**1**	100000100	4
d and e	1	0000	10000010	4
f	0	0000	10000010	4

Table 4.27 Mechanizing unsigned multiplication.

```
X =   15 = 01111
Y =  -13 = 10011
```

9 2^9	8 2^8	7 2^7	6 2^6	5 2^5	4 2^4	3 2^3	2 2^2	1 2^1	0 2^0	
					0	1	1	1	1	X
					1	0	0	1	1	Y (Two's complement form)
					0	1	1	1	1	First partial product
				0	1	1	1	1		Second partial product
			0	0	0	0	0			Third partial product
		0	0	0	0	0				Fourth partial product
	0	1	1	1	1					Fifth partial product
0	1	0	0	0	1	1	1	0	1	Uncorrected result
1	0	0	0	1						Correction factor
1	1	0	0	1	1	1	1	0	1	Corrected result

double-length product. In order to get the correct two's complement result we have to add a correction factor of

$$2^{2n} - 2^n X = 2^n(2^n - X)$$

This correction factor is the two's complement of X scaled by 2^n. As a further illustration consider the product of $X = 15$ and $Y = -13$ in 5 bits.

The final result in 10 bits, $1100111101_2 = -195_{10}$, is correct. Similarly, when X is negative and Y is positive, a correction factor of $2^n(2^n - Y)$ must be added to the result.

When both multiplier and multiplicand are negative the following situation exists.

$$(2^n - X)(2^n - Y) = 2^{2n} - 2^n X - 2^n Y + XY$$

In this case correction factors of $2^n X$ and $2^n Y$ must be added to the result. The 2^{2n} term represents a carry-out bit from the most-significant position and can be neglected.

Booth's algorithm

One approach to the multiplication of signed numbers in two's complement form is provided by *Booth's algorithm*. This algorithm works for two positive numbers, one negative and one positive, or both negative. Booth's algorithm is broadly similar to conventional unsigned multiplication but with the following differences. In Booth's algorithm two bits of the multiplier are examined together, to determine which of three courses of action is to take place next. The algorithm is defined below.

1. If the current multiplier bit is 1 and the next lower order multiplier bit is 0, *subtract* the multiplicand from the partial product.

2. If the current multiplier bit is 0 and the next lower order multiplier bit is 1, *add* the multiplicand to the partial product.

3. If the current multiplier bit is the same as the next lower order multiplier bit, do nothing.

Note 1. When adding in the multiplicand to the partial product, discard any carry bit generated by the addition.

Note 2. When the partial product is shifted, an arithmetic shift is used and the sign bit propagated.

Note 3. Initially, when the current bit of the multiplier is its least-significant bit, the next lower-order bit of the multiplier is assumed to be zero.

The flowchart for Booth's algorithm is given in Fig. 4.40. In order to illustrate the operation of Booth's algorithm, consider the three products 13×15, -13×15, and $-13 \times (-15)$. Table 4.28 demonstrates how Booth's algorithm mechanizes these three multiplications.

High-speed multiplication

We don't intend to delve deeply into the subject of high-speed multiplication as large portions of advanced textbooks are devoted to this topic alone. Here two alternative ways of forming products to the method of shifting and adding are explained.

We have seen in Chapter 2 that you can construct a 2-bit by 2-bit multiplier by means of logic gates. This process can be extended to larger numbers of bits. Figure 4.41 illustrates the type of logic array used to directly multiply two numbers.

An alternative approach is to use a *look-up table* in which all the possible results of the product of two numbers are stored in a ROM read-only-memory. Table 4.29 shows how two four-bit numbers may be multiplied by storing all $2^8 = 256$ possible results in a ROM.

The 4-bit multiplier and 4-bit multiplicand together form an 8-bit address that selects one of 256 locations within the ROM. In each of these locations the product of the multiplier (most-significant four address bits) and the multiplicand

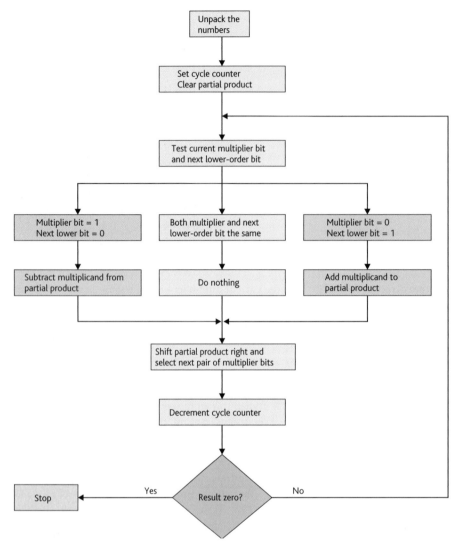

Figure 4.40 Flowchart for Booth's algorithm.

(least-significant four address bits) are stored. For example, the product of 2 and 3 is given by the contents of location 0010 0011, which contains 00000110.

The disadvantage of this technique is the rapid increase in the size of the ROM as the number of bits in the multiplier and multiplicand increases. Table 4.30 provides the relationship between the size of a multiplier and the number of bits a ROM requires to hold the appropriate multiplication table.

The multiplication of two 8-bit numbers requires a memory capacity of 1 048 576 bits. Forming the product of large numbers directly by look-up table is impracticable. Fortunately, it's possible to calculate the product of two $2n$-bit numbers by using an n-bit multiplier.

Before showing how we proceed with binary numbers, let's take a look at the product of two 2-digit decimal numbers, and then extend the technique to binary arithmetic.

$$
\begin{aligned}
34 \times 27 &= (3 \times 10 + 4)(2 \times 10 + 7)\\
&= 3 \times 2 \times 10^2 + 3 \times 7 \times 10 + 4 \times 2 \times 10 + 4 \times 7\\
&= 6 \times 10^2 + 21 \times 10 + 8 \times 10 + 28\\
&= 6 \times 10^2 + 29 \times 10 + 28\\
&= 600 + 290 + 28\\
&= 918
\end{aligned}
$$

Now consider the generation of the product of two 8-bit numbers by means of 4-bit multipliers. Let the two 8-bit numbers A and B be represented by the structure in Fig. 4.42.

A_u represents the four most-significant bits of A, and A_l the four least-significant bits. We have already encountered the idea of splitting up numbers when we performed 64-bit addition on a 32-bit microprocessor. Eight-bit numbers A and B can be represented algebraically as follows

$A = A_u \times 16 + A_l$ and $B = B_u \times 16 + B_l$

Consequently, $A \times B = (A_u \times 16 + A_l)(B_u \times 16 + B_l)$
$$= 256A_uB_u + 16A_uB_l + 16A_lB_u + A_lB_l$$

1. Multiplicand = 01111 = +15
   Multiplier   = 01101 = +13

Step	Multiplier bits	Partial product
		0000000000
Subtract multiplicand	011010	1000100000
Shift partial product right		1100010000
Add multiplicand	01101	10011110000
Shift partial product right		0001111000
Subtract multiplicand	01101	1010011000
Shift partial product right		1101001100
Do nothing	01101	1101001100
Shift partial product right		1110100110
Add multiplicand	01101	10110000110
Shift partial product right		0011000011

The final result is 0011000011_2, which is equal to +195. Note that the underlined numbers represent the bits to be examined at each stage.

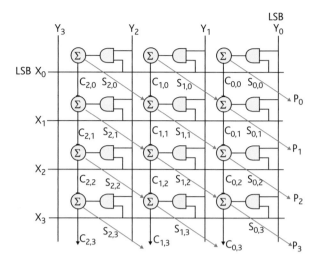

Figure 4.41 The multiplier array.

2. Multiplicand = 01111 = +15
   Multiplier   = 10011 = −13

Step	Multiplier bits	Partial product
		0000000000
Subtract multiplicand	100110	1000100000
Shift partial product right		1100010000
Do nothing	10011	1100010000
Shift partial product right		1110001000
Add multiplicand	10011	10101101000
Shift partial product right		0010110100
Do nothing	10011	0010110100
Shift partial product right		0001011010
Subtract multiplicand	10011	1001111010
Shift partial product right		1100111101

The result is 1100111101_2, which corresponds to −195.

3. Multiplicand = 10001 = ×15
   Multiplier   = 10011 = ×13

Step	Multiplier bits	Partial product
		0000000000
Subtract multiplicand	100110	0111100000
Shift partial product right		0011110000
Do nothing	10011	0011110000
Shift partial product right		0001111000
Add multiplicand	10011	1010011000
Shift partial product right		1101001100
Do nothing	10011	1101001100
Shift partial product right		1110100110
Subtract multiplicand	10011	10110000110
Shift partial product right		0011000011

The result is 0011000011_2, which corresponds to +195.

Table 4.28 Three examples of mechanizing Booth's algorithm.

Address		Data
Multiplier	Multiplicand	Result
0000	0000	00000000
0000	0001	00000000
:	:	:
:	:	:
0000	1111	00000000
0001	0000	00000000
0001	0001	00000001
:	:	:
:	:	:
0001	1111	00001111
0010	0000	00000000
0010	0001	00000010
:	:	:
:	:	:
0010	1111	00011110
:	:	:
:	:	:
1111	0000	00000000
1111	0001	00001111
:	:	:
:	:	:
1111	1111	11100001

Table 4.29 Multiplication by means of a look-up table.

This expression requires the evaluation of four 4-bit products (A_uB_u, A_uB_l, A_lB_u, A_lB_l), the shifting of the products by eight or four positions (i.e. multiplication by 256 or 16), and the addition of four partial products. Figure 4.43 shows how this may be achieved.

Multiplier bits (n)	Address bits (2n)	Lines in table (2^{2n})	Total of bits in ROM ($2n \times 2^{2n}$)
2	4	16	64
3	6	64	384
4	8	256	1024
5	10	1024	10240
6	12	4096	49152
7	14	16384	229376
8	16	65536	1048576

Table 4.30 Relationship between multiplier size and array size.

4.10.2 Division

Division is the inverse of multiplication and is performed by repeatedly subtracting the *divisor* from the *dividend* until the result is either zero or less than the divisor. The number of times the divisor is subtracted is called the *quotient*, and the number left after the final subtraction is the remainder. That is

dividend/divisor = quotient + remainder/ divisor

Alternatively, we can write

dividend = quotient × divisor + remainder

Before we consider binary division let's examine decimal division using the traditional pencil and paper technique. The following example illustrates the division of 575 by 25.

$$\overset{\text{quotient}}{\text{divisor)dividend}}\quad 25\overline{)575}$$

The first step is to compare the two digits of the divisor with the most-significant two digits of the dividend and ask how many times the divisor goes into these two digits. The answer is 2 (i.e. $2 \times 25 = 50$), and 2×25 is subtracted from 57. The number 2 is entered as the most-significant digit of the quotient to produce the situation below.

$$\begin{array}{r} 2 \\ 25\overline{)575} \\ 50 \\ \hline 7 \end{array}$$

The next digit of the dividend is brought down, and the divisor is compared with 75. As 75 is an exact multiple of 25, a three can be entered in the next position of the quotient to give the following result.

$$\begin{array}{r} 23 \\ 25\overline{)575} \\ 50 \\ \hline 75 \\ 75 \\ \hline 00 \end{array}$$

As we have examined the least-significant bit of the dividend and the divisor was an exact multiple of 75, the

division is complete, and the quotient is 23 with a zero remainder.

A difficulty associated with division lies in estimating how many times the divisor goes into the partial dividend (i.e. 57 was divided by 25 to produce 2 remainder 7). Although people do this mentally, some way has to be found to mechanize it for application to computers. Luckily this process is easier in binary arithmetic. Consider, the above example using unsigned binary arithmetic.

$$25 = 11001_2 \quad 575 = 1000111111_2$$

$$\begin{array}{r} 11001\overline{)1000111111} \\ 11001 \end{array}$$

The 5 bits of the divisor do not go into the first 5 bits of the dividend, so a zero is entered into the quotient and the divisor is compared with the first 6 bits of the dividend.

$$\begin{array}{r} 01 \\ 11001\overline{)1000111111} \\ 11001 \\ \hline 001010 \end{array}$$

The divisor goes into the first 6 bits of the dividend once, to leave a partial dividend 001010(1111).

The next bit of the dividend is brought down to give

$$\begin{array}{r} 010 \\ 11001\overline{)1000111111} \\ 11001 \\ \hline 010101 \\ 11001 \end{array}$$

The partial dividend is less than the divisor, and a zero is entered into the next bit of the quotient. The process continues as follows.

$$\begin{array}{r} 010111 \\ 11001\overline{)1000111111} \\ 11001 \\ \hline 00101011 \\ 11001 \\ \hline 000100101 \\ 11001 \\ \hline 000011001 \\ 11001 \\ \hline 0000000000 \end{array}$$

In this case the partial quotient is zero, so that the final result is 10111, remainder 0.

Restoring division

The traditional pencil and paper algorithm we've just discussed can be implemented in digital form with little modification. The only real change is to the way in which the divisor is compared with the partial dividend. People do the comparison mentally whereas computers must perform a subtraction and test the sign of the result. If the subtraction yields a positive result, a one is entered into the quotient, but if the

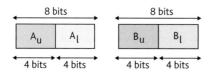

Fig. 4.42 High-speed multiplication.

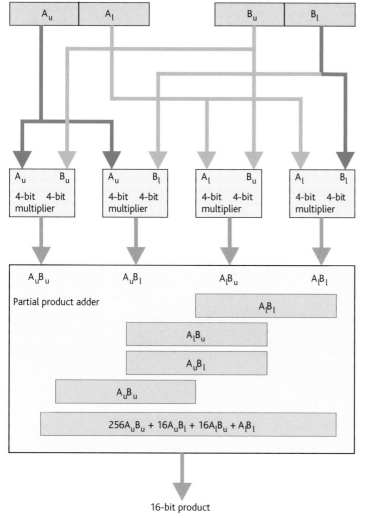

Fig. 4.43 High-speed multiplication.

4. If the resulting partial dividend is positive, place a one in the quotient.

5. Perform a test to determine end of division. If the divisor is aligned so that its least-significant bit corresponds to the least-significant bit of the partial dividend, stop. The final partial product is the remainder. Otherwise, continue with step 6.

6. Shift the divisor one place right. Repeat from step 2.

The flowchart corresponding to this algorithm is given in Fig. 4.44. Consider the division of 01100111_2 by 1001_2, which corresponds to 103 divided by 9 and should yield a quotient 11 and a remainder 4. Figure 4.45 illustrates the division process, step by step.

Non-restoring division

It's possible to modify the restoring division algorithm of Fig. 4.44 to achieve a reduction in the time taken to execute the division process. The *non-restoring* division algorithm is almost identical to the restoring algorithm. The only difference is that the so-called *restoring* operation is eliminated. From the flowchart for restoring division, it can be seen that after a partial dividend has been restored by adding back the divisor, one-half the divisor is subtracted in the next cycle. This is because each cycle includes a shift-divisor-right operation, which is equivalent to dividing the divisor by two. The *restore divisor* operation in the current cycle followed by the subtract half the divisor in the following cycle is equivalent to a single operation of add half the divisor to the partial dividend. That is, $D - D/2 = +D/2$, where D is the divisor.

Figure 4.46 gives the flowchart for non-restoring division. After the divisor has been subtracted from the partial dividend, the new partial dividend is tested. If it is negative, zero is shifted into the least-significant position of the quotient and half the divisor is added back to the partial dividend. If it is positive, one is shifted into the least-significant position of the quotient and half the divisor is subtracted from the partial dividend. Figure 4.47 repeats the example of Fig. 4.4 using non-restoring division.

Division by multiplication

Because both computers and microprocessors perform division less frequently than multiplication, some processors implement multiplication but not division. It is, however, possible to perform division by means of multiplication, addition, and shifting.

result is negative a zero is entered in the quotient and the divisor added back to the partial dividend to restore it to its previous value.

A suitable algorithm for restoring division is as follows.

1. Align the divisor with the most-significant bit of the dividend.

2. Subtract the divisor from the partial dividend.

3. If the resulting partial dividend is negative, place a zero in the quotient and add back the divisor to restore the partial dividend.

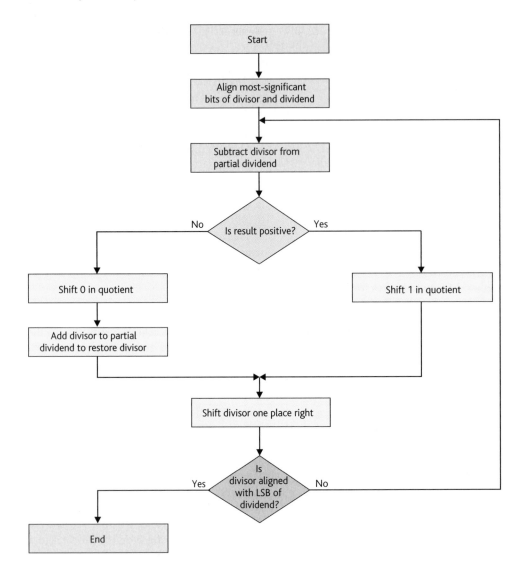

Fig. 4.44 The flowchart for restoring division.

Suppose we wish to divide a dividend N by a divisor D to obtain a quotient Q, so that $Q = N/D$. The first step is to scale D so that it lies in the range

$$1/2 \leq D < 1$$

This operation is carried out by shifting D left or right and recording the number of shifts—rather like normalization in floating point arithmetic. We define a new number, Z, in terms of D as $Z = 1 - D$. Because D lies between ½ and unity, it follows that Z lies between zero and ½. That is, $0 < Z \leq$ ½.

An elementary rule of arithmetic states that the value of the fraction remains unaltered if the top and bottom of a fraction are multiplied by the same number.

Thus, $Q = N/D = KN/KD$. Suppose that $K = 1 + Z$, then

$$Q = \frac{N}{D} = \frac{N(1 + Z)}{D(1 + Z)} = \frac{N(1 + Z)}{(1 - Z)(1 + Z)} = \frac{N(1 + Z)}{1 - Z^2}$$

If we now repeat the process with $K = (1 + Z^2)$, we get

$$Q = \frac{N(1 + Z)}{1 - Z^2} \cdot \frac{1 + Z^2}{1 + Z^2} = \frac{N(1 + Z)(1 + Z^2)}{1 - Z^4}$$

This process may be repeated n times with the result that

$$Q = \frac{N}{D} = \frac{N(1 + Z)(1 + Z^2)(1 + Z^4) \cdots (1 + Z^{2^{n-1}})}{1 - Z^{2^{n-1}}}$$

Because Z is less than unity, the value of $Z^{2^{n-1}}$ rapidly approaches zero as n is increased. Consequently, the approximate value of Q is given by

$$Q = N(1 + Z)(1 + X^2)(1 + Z^4) \cdots (1 + Z^{2^{n-1}})$$

For 8-bit precision n need be only 3, and if $n = 5$ the quotient yields a precision of 32 bits. As the divisor was scaled to lie between ½ and unity, the corresponding quotient, Q,

Step	Description	Partial dividend	Divisor	Quotient
		01100111	00001001	00000000
1	Align	01100111	01001000	00000000
2	Subtract divisor from partial dividend	00011111	01001000	00000000
4	Result positive— shift in 1 in quotient	00011111	01001000	00000001
5	Test for end			
6	Shift divisor one place right	00011111	00100100	00000001
2	Subtract divisor from partial dividend	-00000101	00100100	00000001
3	Restore divisor, shift in 0 in quotient	00011111	00100100	00000010
5	Test for end			
6	Shift divisor one place right	00011111	00010010	00000010
2	Subtract divisor from partial dividend	00001101	00010010	00000010
4	Result positive—shift in 1 in quotient	00001101	00010010	00000101
5	Test for end			
6	Shift divisor one place right	00001101	00001001	00000101
2	Subtract divisor from partial dividend	00000100	00001001	00000101
4	Result positive—shift in 1 in quotient	00000100	00001001	00001011
5	Test for end			

Figure 4.45 Example of restoring division for $1001\overline{)01100111}$.

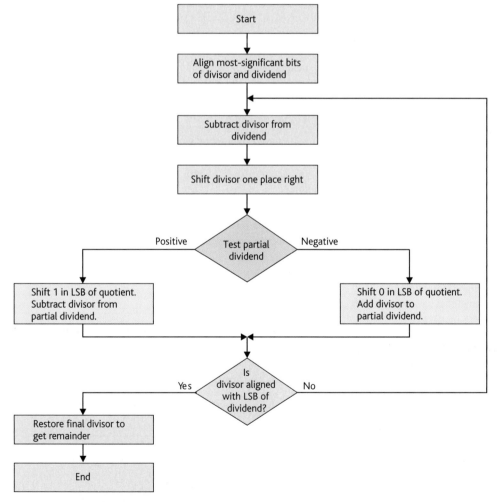

Figure 4.46 Flowchart for non-restoring division.

Step	Description	Partial dividend	Divisor	Quotient
		01100111	00001001	00000000
1	Align divisor	01100111	01001000	00000000
2	Subtract divisor from partial dividend	00011111	01001000	00000000
3	Shift divisor right	00011111	00100100	00000000
4	Test partial dividend—enter 1 in quotient and subtract divisor from partial dividend	-00000101	00100100	00000001
6	Test for end of process	-00000101	00100100	00000001
3	Shift divisor right	-00000101	00010010	00000001
5	Test partial dividend—enter 0 in quotient and add divisor to partial dividend	00001101	00010010	00000010
6	Test for end of process	00001101	00010010	00000010
3	Shift divisor right	00001101	00001001	00000010
4	Test partial dividend enter—1 in quotient and subtract divisor from partial dividend	00000100	00001001	00000101
6	Test for end of process	00000100	00001001	00000101
3	Shift divisor right	00000100	0000100.1	00000101
4	Test partial dividend—enter 1 in quotient and subtract divisor from partial dividend	−00000000.1	0000100.1	00001011
6	Test for end of process	−00000000.1	0000100.1	00001011
7	Restore last divisor	00000100	0000100.1	00001011

Fig. 4.47 An example of non-restoring division for $1001\overline{)0110011}$.

calculated from the above formula must be scaled by the same factor to produce the desired result.

multiplication because the two's complement system cannot be used for signs and unsigned multiplication.

▪ SUMMARY

In this chapter we have looked at how numerical information is represented inside a digital computer. We have concentrated on the binary representation of numbers, because digital computers handle binary information efficiently. Because both positive and negative numbers must be stored and manipulated by a computer, we have looked at some of the ways in which digital computers represent negative numbers. The two's complement system is used to represent negative integers, whereas a biased representation is used to represent negative exponents in floating point arithmetic and a floating point mantissa uses a sign and magnitude representation.

Because digital computers sometimes have to work with very large and very small numbers, we have covered some of the ways in which the so-called *scientific notation* is used to encode both large and small numbers. These numbers are stored in the form of a mantissa and a magnitude (i.e. the number of zeros before/after the binary point) and are called floating point numbers. Until recently, almost every computer used its own representation of floating point numbers. Today, the IEEE standard for the format of floating point numbers has replaced most of these *ad hoc* floating point formats.

At the end of this chapter we have briefly introduced the operations of multiplication and division and have demonstrated how they are mechanized in digital computers. Special hardware has to be used to implement signed

▪ PROBLEMS

4.1 Convert the following decimal integers to their natural binary equivalents.

(a) 12
(b) 42
(c) 255
(d) 4090
(e) 40900
(f) 65530

4.2 Convert the following natural binary integers to their decimal equivalents.

(a) 110
(b) 1110110
(c) 110111
(d) 11111110111

4.3 Complete the table below.

Decimal	Binary	Hexadecimal	Base 7
37			
99			
	10101010 11011011101		
		256 CAB	
			12 666

4.4 Convert the following base 5 numbers into base 9 equivalents. For example, $23_5 = 14_9$.

(a) 14   (b) 144   (c) 444   (d) 431

4.5 Convert the following decimal numbers to their binary equivalents. Calculate the answer to *five binary places* and round the result up or down as necessary.

(a) 1.5   (d) 1024.0625
(b) 1.1   (e) 3.141592
(c) 1/3   (f) $1/\sqrt{2}$

4.6 Convert the following binary numbers to their decimal equivalents.

(a) 1.1   (d) 11011.111010
(b) 0.0001   (e) 111.111111
(c) 111.101   (f) 10.1111101

4.7 Complete the following table. Calculate all values to four places after the radix point.

Decimal	Binary	Hexadecimal	Base 7
0.25			
0.35			
	11011.0111		
	111.1011		
		2.08	
		AB.C	
			1.2
			66.6

4.8 Calculate the error (both absolute and as a percentage) if the following decimal fractions are converted to binary fractions, correct to 5 binary places. Convert the decimal number to six binary digits and then round up the fifth bit if the sixth bit is a 1.

(a) 0.675
(b) 0.42
(c) 0.1975

4.9 An electronics engineer has invented a new logic device that has three states: $-1, 0$, and $+1$. These states are represented by $\bar{1}$, 0, and 1, respectively. This arrangement may be used to form a balanced ternary system with a radix 3, but where the *trits* represent -1, 0, +1 instead of 0, 1, 2. The following examples illustrate how this system works.

Ternary	Balanced ternary	Decimal
11	11	4 (3 + 1)
12	1$\bar{1}$$\bar{1}$	5 (9 − 3 − 1)
22	10$\bar{1}$	8 (9 − 1)
1012	11$\bar{1}$$\bar{1}$	32 (27 + 9 − 3 − 1)

Write down the first 15 decimal numbers in the balanced ternary base.

4.10 The results of an experiment fall in the range -4 to $+9$. A scientist reads the results into a computer and then processes them. The scientist decides to use a 4-bit binary code to represent each of the possible inputs. Devise a 4-bit code capable of representing numbers in the range -4 to $+9$.

4.11 Convert the following decimal numbers into BCD form.

(a) 1237   (b) 4632   (c) −9417

4.12 Perform the following additions on the BCD numbers using BCD arithmetic.

(a) 0010100010010001   (b) 1001100101111000
    0110100001100100   1001100110000010

4.13 The 16-bit hexadecimal value $C123_{16}$ can represent many things. What does this number represent, assuming that it is the following:

(a) an unsigned binary integer
(b) a signed two's complement binary integer
(c) a sign and magnitude binary integer
(d) an unsigned binary fraction

4.14 Convert the following 8-bit natural binary values into their Gray code equivalents.

(a) 10101010
(b) 11110000
(c) 00111011

4.15 Convert the following 8-bit Gray code values into their natural binary equivalents.

(a) 01010000
(b) 11110101
(c) 01001010

4.16 What are the Hamming distances between the following pairs of binary values?

(a) 00101111   (b) 11100111
    01011101   01110101
(c) 01010011   (d) 11111111
    00011011   00000111
(e) 11011101   (f) 0011111
    11011110   0000110

4.17 Decode the Huffman code below, assuming that the valid codes are $P = 0$, $Q = 10$, $R = 110$, and $S = 111$. How many bits would be required if P, Q, R, and S had been encoded as 00, 01, 10, and 11, respectively?

00000111011100000010111111110101000111110 0010

4.18 The hexadecimal dump from part of a microcomputer's memory is as follows.

```
0000   4265 6769 6EFA 47FE BB87 0086 3253 7A29
0010   698F E000
```

The dump is made up of a series of strings of characters, each string being composed of nine groups of four hexadecimal characters. The first four characters in each string provide the starting address of the following 16 bytes. For example, the first byte in the second string (i.e. $C9) is at address $0010 and the second byte (i.e. $8F) is at address $0011.

The 20 bytes of data in the two strings represent the following sequence of items (starting at location 0000):

(a) five consecutive ASCII-encoded characters
(b) one unsigned 16-bit integer
(c) one two's complement 16-bit integer

(d) one unsigned 16-bit fraction

(e) one six-digit natural BCD integer

(f) one 16-bit unsigned fixed-point number with a 12-bit integer part and a 4-bit fraction

(g) One 4-byte floating point number with a sign bit and true fraction plus an exponent biased by 64

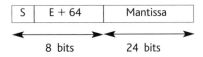

Decode the hexadecimal data, assuming that it is interpreted as above.

4.19 A message can be coded to protect it from unauthorized readers by EORing it with a binary sequence of the same length to produce an encoded message. The encoded message is decoded by EORing it with the same sequence that was used to decode it. If the ASCII-encoded message used to generate the code is ALANCLEMENTS, what does the following encoded message (expressed in hexadecimal form) mean?

09 09 0D 02 0C 6C 12 02 17 02 10 73

4.20 A single-bit error-detecting code appends a parity bit to a source word to produce a code word. An even parity bit is chosen to make the total number of ones in the code word even (this includes the parity bit itself). For example the source words 0110111 and 1100110 would be coded as 01101111 and 1100110, respectively. In these cases the parity bit has been located in the LSB position. Indicate which of the following hexadecimal numbers have parity errors.

$00, $07, $FF, $A5, $5A, $71, $FE.

4.21 A checksum digit is the least-significant digit formed when a series of numbers are added together. For example, the decimal checksum of the sequence 98731 is 8 because $9 + 8 + 7 + 3 + 1 = 28$ and 8 is the least-significant digit. Similarly, the checksum of the hexadecimal sequence A3, 02, 49, FF is ED because $A3 + 02 + 49 + FF = 1ED$.

The purpose of a checksum is to detect errors in a sequence of digits after they have been transmitted or stored in memory or on tape. The following hexadecimal sequences are terminated by a checksum. Which, if any, are in error?

(a) 0001020304050F

(b) 11223344556675

(c) FFA32415751464

The position of the checksum in the above three strings is the right-most byte. Does it matter where the checksum is located? What happens if there is an error in the checksum itself?

4.22 What is the meaning of Hamming distance?

4.23 The $H_{7,4}$ Hamming code is written $I_4 I_3 I_2 C_3 I_1 C_2 C_1$, where I_i = source bit i, and C_i = check bit i. The three Hamming check bits are calculated from the parity equations.

$$C_3 = I_2 \oplus I_3 \otimes I_4$$
$$C_2 = I_1 \oplus I_3 \otimes I_4$$
$$C_1 = I_1 \oplus I_2 \otimes I_4$$

Show that no two valid code words differ by less than 3 bits. Demonstrate that an error in any single bit can be used to locate the position of the error and, therefore, to correct it.

4.24 Examine the following $H_{7,4}$ Hamming code words and determine whether the word is a valid code word. If it isn't valid, what should the correct code word have been (assuming that only 1 error is present)?

(a) 0000000

(b) 1100101

(c) 0010111

4.25 Convert the following image into a quadtree.

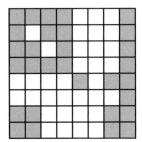

F = full (all elements1)
E = empty (all elements0)
P = partially filled

Quadrant numbering

4.26 Convert the following image into a quadtree.

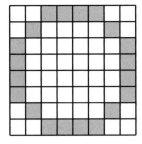

4.27 Almost all computer hardware courses include a section on number bases and the conversion of numbers between bases. Does the base in which a computer represents numbers really matter to the computer user or even to the student of computer science?

4.28 Perform the following binary additions:

(a)
```
  10110
+   101
```

(b)
```
  100111
  111001
+ 101101
```

(c)
```
  11011011
  10111011
  00101011
+ 01111111
```

4.29 Perform the following octal additions. We have not covered octal arithmetic (base 8). You must determine the rules of addition,

(a)
```
  42
+ 53
```

(b)
```
   3357
+ 2741
```

(c)
```
  777
  543
+ 420
```

(d)
```
  437
  426
  772
+ 747
```

4.30 Perform the following hexadecimal additions:

(a)
```
  42
+ 53
```

(b)
```
   3357
+ 2741
```

(c)
```
  777
  543
+ 420
```

(d)
```
  ABCD
  FE10
+ 123A
```

4.31 Using 8-bit arithmetic throughout, express the following decimal numbers in two's complement binary form:

(a) −4   (d) −25   (g) −127
(b) −5   (e) −42   (h) −111
(c) 0   (f) −128

4.32 Perform the following decimal subtractions in 8-bit two's complement arithmetic. Note that some of the answers will result in arithmetic overflow. Indicate where overflow has occurred.

(a) 20   (b) 127   (c) 127   (d) 5
    −5   −126   −128   −20

(e) 69   (f) −20   (g) −127   (h) −42
    −42   −111   −2   +69
                                                        +120

4.33 Using two's complement binary arithmetic with a 12-bit word, write down the range of numbers capable of being represented (both in decimal and binary formats) by giving the smallest and largest numbers. What happens when the smallest and largest numbers are

(a) incremented?   (b) decremented?

4.34 Distinguish between *overflow* and *carry* when these terms are applied to two's complement arithmetic on n-bit words.

4.35 Write down an algebraic expression giving the value of the n-bit integer $N = a_{n-1}, a_{n-2}, \ldots, a_1, a_0$ for the case where N represents a two's complement number.

Hence prove that (in two's complement notation) the representation of a signed binary number in $n + 1$ bits may be derived from its representation in n bits by repeating the leftmost bit. For example, if $n = -12 = 10100$ in 5 bits, $n = -12 = 110100$ in 6 bits.

4.36 Perform the additions below on 4-bit binary numbers.

(a) 0011   (b) 1111   (c) 0110   (d) 1100
    +1100   +0001   +0111   +1010

In each case, regard the numbers as being (i) unsigned integer, (ii) two's complement integer, and (iii) sign and magnitude integer. Calculate the answer and comment on it where necessary.

4.37 Add together the following pairs of numbers. Each number is represented in a 6-bit sign-and-magnitude format. Your answer should also be in sign-and-magnitude format. Convert each pair of numbers (and result) into decimal form in order to check your answer.

(a) 000111   (b) 100111
     010101   010101

(c) 010101   (d) 111111
     000111   000001

(e) 110111   (f) 011111
     110111   000110

4.38 Write down the largest base 5 positive integer in n digits and the largest base 7 number in m digits. It is necessary to represent n-digit base 5 numbers in base 7. What is the minimum number m of digits needed to represent all possible n-digit base 5 numbers? Hint—the largest m-digit base-7 number should be greater than, or equal to, the largest n-digit base 5 number.

4.39 A 4-bit binary adder adds together two 4-bit numbers, A and B, to produce a 4-bit sum, S, and a single-bit carry-out C. What is the range of outputs (i.e. largest and smallest values) that the adder is capable of producing? Give your answer in both binary and decimal forms.

An adder is designed to add together two binary coded decimal (BCD) digits to produce a single digit sum and a 1-bit carry-out. What is the range of valid outputs that this circuit may produce?

The designer of the BCD adder decides to use a pure binary adder to add together two BCD digits as if they were pure 4-bit binary numbers. Under what circumstances does the binary adder give the correct BCD result? Under what circumstances is the result incorrect (i.e. the 4-bit binary result differs from the required BCD result)?

What algorithm must the designer apply to the 4-bit output of the binary adder to convert it to a BCD adder?

4.40 Design a 4-bit parallel adder to add together two 4-bit natural binary-encoded integers. Assume that the propagation delay of a signal through a gate is t ns. For your adder, calculate the time taken to add

(a) 0000 to 0001
(b) 0001 to 0001
(c) 0001 to 1111

4.41 Design a full subtractor circuit that will subtract bit X together with a borrow-in bit B_i from bit Y to produce a difference bit $D = Y - X - B_i$, and a borrow-out B_o.

4.42 In the *negabinary* system an i-bit binary integer, N, is expressed using positional notation as

$$N = a_0 \times -1^0 \times 2^0 + a_1 \times -1^1 \times 2^1 + \cdots + a_{i-1} \times -1^{i-1} \times 2^{i-1}$$

This is the same as conventional natural 8421 binary weighted numbers, except that alternate positions have the additional weighting $+1$ and -1.

For example, $1101 = (-1 \times 1 \times 8) + (+1 \times 1 \times 4) + (-1 \times 0 \times 2) + (+1 \times 1 \times 1) = -8 + 4 + 1 = -3$

The following 4-bit numbers are represented in negabinary form. Convert them into their decimal equivalents.

(a) 0000
(b) 0101
(c) 1010
(d) 1111

4.43 Perform the following additions on 4-bit negabinary numbers. The result is a 6-bit negabinary value. You must construct your own algorithm.

(a) 0000
  +0001

(b) 1010
  +0101

(c) 1101
  1011

(d) 1111
  1111

4.44 Convert the following signed decimal numbers into their 6-bit negabinary counterparts.

(a) 4　　　(b) −7　　　(c) +7　　　(d) 10

4.45 What is the range of values that can be expressed as an n-bit negabinary value? That is, what is the largest positive decimal number and what is the largest negative decimal number that can be converted into an n-bit negabinary form?

4.46 A computer has a 24-bit word length, which, for the purpose of floating point operations, is divided into an 8-bit biased exponent and a 16-bit two's complement mantissa. Write down the range of numbers capable of being represented in this format and their precision.

4.47 Explain the meaning of the following terms (in the context of floating point arithmetic):

(a) biased exponent
(b) fractional part
(c) packed
(d) unpacked
(e) range
(f) precision
(g) normalization
(h) exponent overflow/underflow

4.48 An IEEE standard 32-bit floating point number has the format $N = -1^S \times 1.F \times 2^{E-127}$, where S is the sign bit, F is the fractional mantissa, and E the biased exponent.

(a) (i) Convert the decimal number 1000.708 into the IEEE format for floating point numbers.

    (ii) Convert the decimal number 100.125 into the IEEE format for floating point numbers.

(b) Describe the steps that take place when two IEEE floating point numbers are added together. You should start with the

two packed floating point numbers and end with the packed sum.

(c) Perform the subtraction of $1000.708 - 100.25$ using the two IEEE-format binary floating point numbers you obtained for 1000.708 and 100.25 in part (a) of this question. You should begin the calculation with the packed floating-point representations of these numbers and end with the packed result.

4.49 Convert the 32-bit IEEE format number $C33BD000_{16}$ into its decimal representation.

4.50 Explain why floating point numbers have normalized mantissas.

4.51 What is the difference between a *truncation* error and a *rounding* error?

4.52 The following numbers are to be represented by three significant digits in the base stated. In each case perform the operation by both truncation and rounding and state the relative error created by the operation.

(a) 0.1100100_2 (b) $0.1A34_{16}$
(c) $b.0.0011011_2$ (d) $d.0.12AA_{16}$

4.53 We can perform *division by multiplication* to calculate $Q = N/D$. The iterative expression for Q is given by

$$Q = N(1 + Z)(1 + Z^2)(1 + Z^4)\cdots(1 + Z^{2^{n-1}})$$

where $Z = 1 - D$.

If $N = 50_{10}$ and $D = 0.74_{10}$, calculate the value of Q. Evaluate Q using 1, 2, 3, and 4 terms in the expression.

4.54 For each of the following calculations (using 4-bit arithmetic) calculate the value of the Z (zero), C (carry), N (negative), and V (overflow) flag bits at the end of the operation.

(a) $1010 - 1010$
(b) $1111 - 0001$
(c) $1111 + 0001$
(d) $0110 + 0110$
(e) $1010 - 1110$
(f) $1110 + 1010$

The instruction set architecture

5

INTRODUCTION

There are two ways of introducing the processor. One is to explain how a computer works at the level of its internal information flow by describing the way in which information is transmitted between registers and internal units and showing how an instruction is decoded and interpreted (i.e. executed). The other approach is to introduce the *native language*, or machine code, of a computer and show what computer instructions can do. In practice no-one writes programs in machine code; instead they use *assembly language* which is a human-readable representation of machine code (see the box 'The assembler').

Both approaches to the description of a computer are valid. Beginning with how a computer works by examining its internal operation is intuitive. Once you understand how information flows from place to place through adders and subtractors, you can see how instructions are constructed and then you can examine how sequences of instructions implement programs.

Unfortunately, beginning with the hardware and looking at very primitive operations hides the *big picture*. You don't immediately see where you are going or understand why we need the primitive operations in the first place. This bottom-up approach is rather like studying cellular biochemistry as the first step in a course on sociology. Knowing how a brain cell works doesn't tell you anything about human personality.

Beginning a course with the computer's instruction set gives you a better idea of what a computer does in terms of its capabilities. Once you know what a computer does, you can look inside it and explain how it implements its machine code operations.

In the previous edition of *Principles of Computer Hardware* I began with the internal organization of a computer and explained the steps involved in the execution of an instruction. Later we looked at the nature of instructions. In this edition I've reversed the order and we begin with the instruction set and leave the internal organization of the computer until later. This sequence enables students to take lab classes early in the semester and build up practical experience by writing assembly language programs.

We begin this chapter by introducing the notion of computer architecture, the instruction set, and the structure of a computer. We describe a real processor, the Motorola 68K. This processor is a contemporary of the Intel 8086 but has a more sophisticated architecture and its instruction set is easier for students to understand. This processor has evolved like the corresponding Intel family and its variants are now called the ColdFire family.

THE ASSEMBLER

An assembly language program starts off as a text file written by a programmer (or created by a compiler). An assembler takes the text file together with any library functions required by the program and generates the binary code that the target executes.

The addresses of code and data generated by the assembler are not *absolute* (i.e. actual), but refer to the locations with respect to the start of the program. Another program called a *linker* takes one or more code modules generated by the assembler, puts them together, and creates the actual addresses of data in memory. The output of the linker is the binary that can be executed by the actual computer. This mechanism allows you to write a program in small chunks and to put them together without having to worry about addresses in the different chunks.

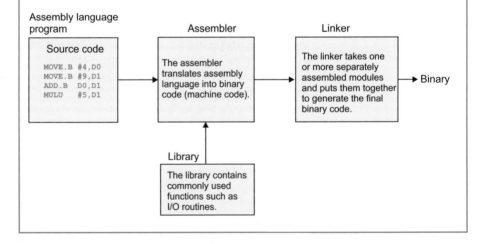

5.1 What is an instruction set architecture?

An *instruction set architecture* (ISA) is an abstract model of a computer that describes *what* it does, rather than *how* it does it. You could say that a computer's architecture is its functional definition. The notion of an architecture dates back to the 1960s and IBM's 360 series mainframes. Each mainframe had the same architecture, but the performance varied from model to model. By adopting a common architecture for all members of the 360 series, users were able to upgrade a model and still use the same software.

An object can be viewed in more than one way. Consider the airline pilot. Passengers see the pilot as an agent responsible for transferring them from one airport to another. The pilot's crew sees them as a colleague with whom they relate at the personal level. The pilot's doctor sees a complex biological mechanism. It's exactly the same with computers—you can view them in different ways.

Suppose you run a spreadsheet on a computer. As far as you're concerned, the machine is a *spreadsheet machine* that behaves exactly as if it were an electronic spreadsheet doing nothing other than spreadsheet calculations. You could construct an electronic device to *directly* handle spreadsheets, but no one does. Instead they construct a computer and run a program to *simulate* a spreadsheet.

ARCHITECTURE AND ORGANIZATION

Architecture describes the functionality of a system, whereas organization describes how it achieves that functionality. Consider the automobile as a good example of the distinction between architecture and organization. The architecture of an automobile covers its steering, acceleration, and braking. An automobile's gearbox is part of its organization rather than its architecture. Why? Because the gearbox is a device that facilitates the operation of an automobile—it is there only because we can't create engines that drive wheels directly.

Figure 5.1 illustrates how a computer can be viewed in different ways. The outer level is the *applications* layer that the end user sees. This level provides a *virtual* spreadsheet or any other user-application because, to all intents and purposes, the machine looks like a spreadsheet machine that does nothing else other than implement spreadsheets.

A spreadsheet, a word processor, or a game is invariably implemented by expressing its behavior in a high-level language such as C or Java. You can view a computer as a machine that directly executes the instructions of a high-level language. In Fig. 5.1 the layer below the application level is the *high-level language* layer.

It's difficult to construct a computer that executes a high-level language like C. Computers execute *machine code*, a primitive language consisting of simple operations such as addition and subtraction, Boolean operations, and data movement. The statements and constructs of a high-level language are translated into sequences of machine code instructions by a *compiler*. The machine code layer in Fig. 5.1 is responsible for executing machine code; it's this layer that defines the computer's architecture.

Figure 5.1 shows two layers between the machine level and high-level language levels. The *assembly language* level sits on

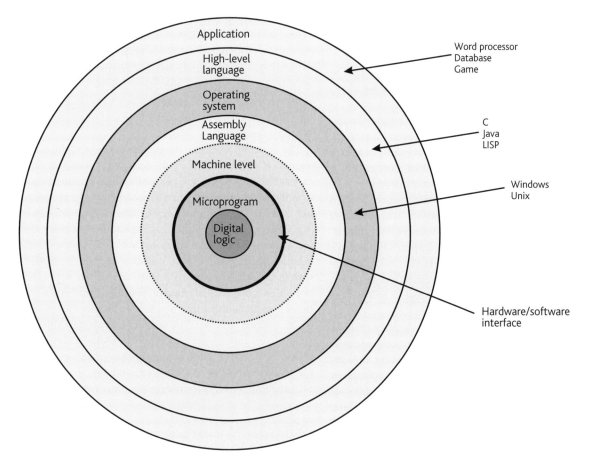

Figure 5.1 Machine levels and virtual architectures.

top of the machine level and represents the human-readable form of the machine code; for example, the binary string 0000001010000001000100000000011 might be the machine code instruction represented in assembly language as MOVE D2,**D1** (move the number in register D2 to the register D1).[1]

To say that assembly language is just a human-readable version of machine code is a little simplistic. An assembly language contains facilities that make it easier for a human to write a program. Moreover, an assembly language allows you to determine where data and code is loaded into memory. We will not use sophisticated assembly language mechanisms and it is reasonably true to say that assembly language instructions are human-readable versions of the strings of 1s and 0s that represent the machine-code binary instructions. The conventions we will adopt in the structure and layout of assembly language programs are, normally, those of the Motorola assembler.

In Fig. 5.1 there is an additional layer between the assembly language layer and the high-level language layer called the *operating system* level. Strictly speaking, this layer isn't like the other layers. The operating system runs on top of the machine code and assembly language layers and provides facilities required by higher-level layers (e.g. memory management and the control of peripherals such as the display and disk drives).

Below the machine-level layer is the *microprogram* layer. A heavy line separates the machine level and microprogram layers because you can access all the layers above this line. The two innermost layers (microprogram and digital logic) are not accessible to the programmer.

The microprogram layer is concerned with the primitive operations that take place inside the computer during the execution of a machine code operation. For example, a MOVE D2,**D1** machine-level instruction might be interpreted by executing a sequence of micro-operations inside the computer. These micro-operations transfer information between functional units such as registers and buses. The sequences of micro-operations that interpret each machine level instruction are stored in *firmware* within the computer. Firmware is the term for read-only memory containing programs or other data that controls the processor's operation. Firmware cannot normally be modified, although modern systems can update their firmware from time to time.

Some modern computers don't have a microprogram layer. If an instruction set is very regular and all instructions involve a simple, single-step operation, there is no need for a microprogram to translate instructions into primitive operations. Where there's a simple relationship between the binary code of an instruction and what it does, the microprogram layer directly translates a machine-level instruction into the control signals required to implement the instruction.

The innermost level of the computer is the *digital logic level* which consists of the gates, flip-flops, and buses. At this level the individual logic elements are hardwired to each other by fixed connections. You can't program or modify the behavior of components at this level. This statement isn't strictly true. Programmable logic elements whose functionality can be modified do exist; for example, it is possible to reconfigure internal connections using the same technology found in flash memory. In the future we may incorporate such components in processors to enable manufacturers to update a processor's instruction set or to fix hardware bugs.

You could, in fact, go even deeper into the hierarchy of Fig. 5.1 because there is a physical layer below the digital logic layer. This physical layer is concerned with the individual transistors and components of the computer that are used to fabricate gates, registers, and buses. Below the physical layer exists the individual atoms of the transistors themselves. We're not interested in the physical layer and the atomic layers, because that's the province of the semiconductor engineer and physicist. In this chapter we are concerned with the machine-level and microprogram layers.

5.2 Introduction to the CPU

Before we look at what a CPU does or how it works, it is important to understand the relationship between the CPU, the memory, and the program. Let's take a simple program to calculate the area of a circle and see how the computer deals with it. In what follows the computer is a hypothetical machine devoid of all the complications associated with reality. Throughout this section we assume that we are operating at the machine level.

The area of a circle, A, can be calculated from the formula $A = \pi r^2$. When people evaluate the area of a circle, they automatically perform many of the calculations at a *subconscious* level. However, when they come to write programs, they must tell the computer exactly what it must do, step by step. To illustrate this point, take a look at the expression πr^2. We write r^2, but we mean a number, which we have given the symbol r, multiplied by itself. We never confuse the *symbol r* with the *value* that we give to r when we evaluate the expression. This may seem an obvious point, but students sometimes have great difficulty when they encounter the concepts of an address and data in assembly language. Although people never confuse the symbol for the radius (i.e. r) and its value, say 4 cm, you must remember that an address (i.e. the place where the value of r is stored) and data (i.e. the value of r) are both binary quantities inside the computer.

---

[1] Throughout this chapter we adopt the convention used by the 68K microprocessor that the rightmost register in an instruction is the destination operand (i.e. where the result goes). To help you remember this, we will use a bold face to indicate the destination operand.

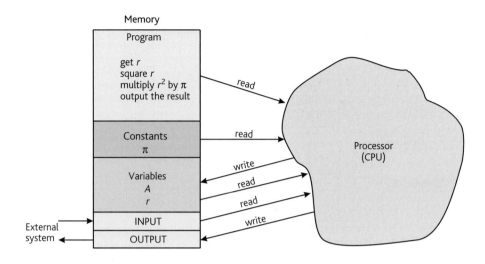

Figure 5.2 The relationship between the memory, processor, and program.

Figure 5.2 illustrates the relationship between the program, memory, and processor. The memory has been divided into five parts: program, constants, variables, input, and output. The program is composed of the sequence of operations to be carried out, or *executed*. The constants (in this case there is only one—π) are numbers used by the program but which do not change during its execution. The variables represent numbers created and modified by the program. When the program squares r, it reads the value of the number in the memory location it has called r, squares it, and puts the result back in the same location. Thus the original value of r is lost. If the programmer wishes to retain the original value of r, rather than by overwriting it with r^2, memory locations must be reserved for both r and r^2.

Although the variables (i.e. the values held in memory locations) are often numerical quantities, there is no reason why this must always be so. For example, the variables used by a word processor are the letters and symbols of the text being manipulated. Indeed, it is perfectly possible for the variable to be another program. That is, one program can operate on, or modify, another program.

A program must be able to communicate with the outside world, otherwise all its efforts are to no effect. We have labeled two memory locations in Fig. 5.2 *input* and *output*. Reading from the input location causes information to be taken from an input device (say a keyboard) and writing to the output location causes information to be moved from the computer to an output device (say a display). Treating input and output as memory locations is not entirely fictional—we'll later discover that many computers really do perform all input/output transactions via the memory by means of a mechanism called memory-mapped I/O.

The processor may either read data from a memory location or write data to a memory location. Of the five regions of memory described above, three are *read-only*, one is *write-only*, and one can be read from or written to.

5.2.1 The memory and registers

We now introduce two important concepts. The first is the notion of a memory that holds programs and data. The second concept is the algebraic notation we use to define operations taking place within a computer.

Figure 5.3 illustrates the so-called *random access memory* system (i.e. RAM). This memory appears as a block of sequential locations, each of which contains a data element. Each location has a unique address that defines the location of the data; for example, in Fig. 5.3 we can say that location number 5 contains the value 7.

The memory in Fig. 5.3 is interfaced to the rest of the computer via three buses (i.e. information paths). The address bus is a one-way path from the computer to the memory, which specifies the location of the memory element being accessed. The data bus is a bidirectional (i.e. two-way) data path along which data flows into memory when it is stored and out of memory when it is retrieved. The control bus includes signals that control the operation of the memory (e.g. read data or write data commands).

Registers

A *register* is a storage device that holds a word exactly like a memory location. In principle, there's no difference between a location in memory and a register because they both do the same thing. The real difference is one of accessibility. Registers are located within the CPU and can be accessed faster than memory locations. Moreover, there are few registers in a computer and millions of address locations, which means that you need far fewer bits to specify a register than a memory location. For example, the 68K has eight data registers and an instruction requires 3 bits to specify which one of the eight registers is to be used by an instruction. If you specify a memory location, you need 32 bits to select one out of 2^{32} possible locations.

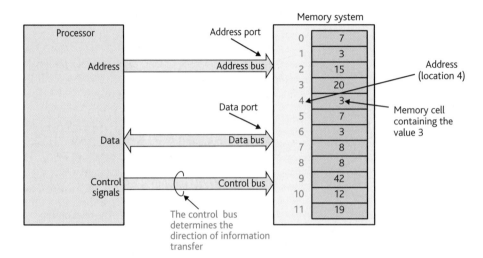

Figure 5.3 The random access memory system.

Registers are not a necessary component of computers—we could use memory to store all variables and temporary data. Registers exist because they are required to construct *practical* computers. We could not build cheap, fast, and effective computers without registers.

Registers are used as temporary storage places to hold frequently used data. Much of a computer's activity is of the form *copy data from a memory location to a register, operate on the data in the register, send the data back to memory.* This sequence involves a lot of moving data from one place to another place.

The size of a register (its width in bits) is normally the same size as memory locations and the size of the arithmetic and logical operations in the CPU. If you have a computer with 32-bit words, they are held in 32-bit memory locations and 32-bit registers and are processed by 32-bit adders, and so on.

Some registers are said to be *visible* and some are invisible to the programmer. In this chapter we are interested only in programmer-visible registers. A register is visible if it can be directly accessed by the programmer though a computer operation. A register is invisible if it is required for internal operations but cannot be directly accessed by the programmer. The 68K's visible register set consists of

- eight 32-bit data registers (D0 to D7)
- eight 32-bit address registers (pointers) (A0 to A7)
- a 16-bit status register (SR)
- a 32-bit program counter (PC).

The address and data registers are used by the programmer to hold temporary data. The status register defines the processor's current operating mode and keeps track of things like the carry-out when you do addition. The program counter contains the location of the next instruction to be executed and, therefore, keeps track of where the computer is up to in a program.

5.2.2 Register transfer language

Throughout this book we adopt shorthand called *register transfer language* (RTL) to help us to explain how the CPU operates. RTL is an algebraic notation that describes how information is accessed from memories and registers and how it is operated on. You should appreciate that RTL is just a *notation* and not a programming language.

RTL uses variables like algebra or computer languages; for example, one or more letters (or letters followed by numbers) to denote registers or storage locations.

It's very important to distinguish between a memory location and its contents. RTL uses square brackets to indicate the *contents* of a memory location; for example, the expression

```
[6] = 3
```

is interpreted as *the contents of memory location 6 contains the value 3*. If we were using symbolic names, we might write

```
[Time] = HoursWorked
```

When dealing with registers, we use their name rather than an address; for example,

```
[D4] = PQR
```

A left or *backward* arrow ($\leftarrow$) indicates the transfer of data. The left-hand side of an expression denotes the *destination* of the data defined by the *source* of the data defined on the right-hand side of the expression. For example, the expression

```
[MAR] ← [PC]
```

indicates that the contents of the program counter (PC) are transferred (i.e. copied) into the memory address register (MAR). The program counter is the register that holds the location (i.e. address) of the next instruction to be executed. The MAR is a register that holds the address of the next item to be read from memory or written to memory. Note that the contents of the PC are not modified by this operation.

The operation

`[3] ← [5]`

means copy the contents of memory location 5 to location 3. In previous editions of this book we used the notation `[M(5)]` to indicate the contents of memory location 5. We have simplified the notation because the meaning of the notation `[5]` is clear and it's easier to read than `[M(5)]`.

If we were writing a program, memory locations 3 and 5 would have been given *symbolic* names, say, *x* and *y*, respectively. A symbolic name is the name given to a number by the programmer—people like to deal with meaningful names rather than, say, the actual numeric addresses of data in memory. The operation `[3] ← [5]` tells us what's happening at the *micro* level—at the high level this operation might be written in the rather more familiar form

`x = y;`

Consider the RTL expression

`[PC] ← [PC] + 4`

which indicates that the number in the PC is increased by 4; that is, the contents of the program counter are read, 4 is added, and the result is copied into the PC.

Suppose the computer executes an operation that stores the contents of the PC in location 2000 in the memory. We can represent this action in RTL as

`[2000] ← [PC]`

Occasionally, we wish to refer to the individual bits of a register or memory location. We will do this by means of the subscript notation $(p:q)$ to mean bits p to q inclusive; for example if we wish to indicate that bits 0 to 7 of a 32-bit register are set to zero, we write[2]

`[R6(0:7)] ← 0`

Numbers are assumed to be decimal, unless indicated otherwise. Computer languages adopt conventions such as 0x12AC or $12AC to indicate hexadecimal values. In RTL we will use a subscript; that is, $12AC_{16}$.

As a final example of RTL notation, consider the following RTL expressions.

```
(a) [20] = 6
(b) [20] ← 6
(c) [20] ← [6]
(d) [20] ← [6] + 3
```

The first example states that memory location 20 contains the value 6. The second example states that the number 6 is *copied* or *loaded* into memory location 20. The third example indicates that the contents of memory location 6 are copied into memory location 20. The last example reads the contents of location 6, adds 3 to it, and stores the result in location 20. The RTL symbol '←' is equivalent to the assignment symbol in high-level languages. Remember that RTL is not a computer language; it is a *notation* used to define computer operations.

Later in this chapter we use the 68K's processor's assembly language. The typographic conventions in an assembly language differ from those of RTL. We use RTL to define the meaning of assembly language instructions. Consider the following examples.

Processor family	Instruction mnemonic		RTL definition
1. 68K	MOVE	D0, **(A5)**	[A5] ← [D0]
2. ARM	ADD	**R1**,R2,R3	[R1] ← [R2] + [R3]
3. IA32	MOV	**ah**,6	[ah] ← 6
3. PowerPC	li	**r25**,10	[r25] ← 10

5.2.3 Structure of the CPU

Figure 5.4 provides a more detailed view of the *central processing unit* and *memory* system. The same memory system stores both the program and the data acted on or created by the program. It isn't necessary to store both the program and data in the *same* memory. However, for largely economic reasons, most computers do store programs and data in a single memory system. Such computers are called *von Neumann machines* in honor of John von Neumann.

A computer is a black box that moves *information* from one point to another and processes the information as it goes along. By *information* we mean the data and the instructions held inside the computer. Figure 5.4 shows two *information-carrying* paths between the CPU and its memory. The lower path (dark blue) with the single arrowhead from the memory to the CPU indicates the route taken by the computer's *program*. The CPU reads the sequence of commands that make up a program one by one from its memory.

The upper path (light blue in Fig. 5.4) with arrows at *both* its ends transfers data between the CPU and memory. The *program* being executed controls the flow of information along the data path. This data path is *bidirectional*, because data can

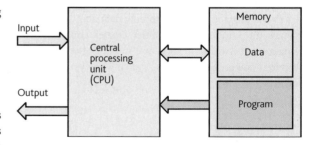

Figure 5.4 The general-purpose digital computer.

---

[2] In the previous editions of this book, we used the notation [R3(0:7)] to indicate bits 0 to 7 of R3. However, by using the subscript [R3 $_{(0:7)}$] we make it easier to indicate a register's subsection.

RISC AND CISC PROCESSORS

Processors fall into two classes: CISC (complex instruction set computer) and RISC (reduced instruction set computer). Intel's Pentium and Motorola's 68K families are CISC processors with large, irregular instruction sets. CSIC processors can perform operations *directly* on the contents of memory locations, whereas RISC processors perform operations only on the contents of registers.

The acronym RISC is misleading. Before the advent of RISC technology, processors had complex and elaborate instruction sets with instruction lengths varying from 16 bits to 80 bits. These processors are retrospectively called CISCs. RISC instructions are the same length with few variations in their formats.

Until the mid-1970s the notation of a RISC processor didn't exist. IBM investigated ways of accelerating computer performance in the 1970s and the computers incorporating IBM's

acceleration techniques later become known as RISCs. The term RISC was coined in the early 1980s by John Hennessey at Stanford University.

RISC processors have lots of on-chip registers and do not allow you to perform operations directly on data in memory. You have to load data into a register, process it, and then store it in memory. For this reason, RISC processors are also called *load/store* processors.

The goal of RISC processor design was to execute an average of one instruction per clock cycle by overlapping the execution of consecutive instructions (i.e. starting executing the next instruction before the current instruction has finished). In order to do this, it is necessary that there is a simple relationship between the bit pattern of an instruction and what the instruction does.

flow in two directions. During a *write cycle* data generated by the program flows from the CPU to the memory where it is stored for later use. During a *read cycle* the CPU requests the retrieval of a data item that is transferred from the memory to the CPU.

Suppose the instruction ADD **X**, Y, Z corresponding to the operation X = Y + Z is stored in memory.[3] The CPU must first fetch this instruction from memory and bring it to the CPU. Once the CPU has analyzed or *decoded* the instruction, the CPU has to get the values of X and Y from memory. The actual values of X and Y are read from the memory and sent to the CPU. The CPU adds these values and sends the result, Z, back to memory for storage. Remember that X, Y, and Z are symbolic names for the locations of data in memory.

Few computers are constructed with two independent information paths between the CPU and its memory as Fig. 5.4 suggests. Most computers have only one path along which information flows between the CPU and its memory—data and instructions have to take turns flowing along this path. Two paths are shown in Fig. 5.4 simply to emphasize that there are two *types* of information stored in the memory (i.e. the *instructions* that make up a program and the *data* used by the program). Indeed, forcing data and instructions to share the same path sometimes creates congestion on the data bus between the CPU and memory that slows the computer down. This effect is called the *von Neumann bottleneck*.

5.3 The 68K family

Anyone introducing computer architecture and the ISA has to make an important choice: should the target architecture used to illustrate the course be a real machine or a hypothetical teaching machine? A hypothetical machine reduces the student's learning curve because you can simplify it. A real

machine is harder to learn, but it does illustrate the real-world constraints faced by its designer.

There's no perfect solution to this dilemma. We've chosen a real machine, the 68K, to introduce an assembly language and machine-level instructions. The 68K is a classic CISC processor and is easier to understand than the Pentium family because the 68K has a more regular instruction set. Another reason for using the 68K processor to illustrate the ISA is its interesting architectural features.

The architecture of a processor is defined by its register set, its instruction set, and its addressing modes (the way in which the location of data in memory is specified). Figure 5.5 describes the 68K's register set. There are eight data registers used to hold temporary variables, eight address registers used to hold pointers to data, a status register, and a program counter, which determines the next instruction to be executed.

Data registers are 32 bits wide and but can be treated as if they were 8 or 16 bits wide. Address registers always hold 32-bit values and are always treated as 32-bit registers that hold two's complement values. However, you can perform an operation on the low-order 16 bits of an address register and the result will be sign-extended to 32 bits automatically.

5.3.1 The instruction

We now look at the instructions executed by the 68K processor. There has been remarkably little progress in instruction set design over the last few decades and computers do today almost exactly what they did in the early days.[4] Much of the

---

[3] Strictly speaking, we should write this operation in RTL as [X] ← [Y] + [Z] to demonstrate that X, Y, and Z refer to memory locations.
[4] An exception to this is *multimedia technology*. Processors such as Intel's Pentium family introduced a special instruction to handle the type of data used in audio and video processing (e.g. the MMX instruction set).

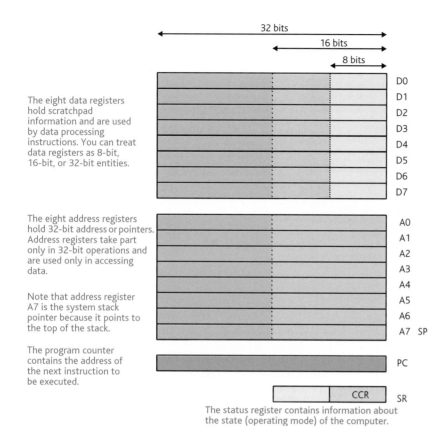

The eight data registers hold scratchpad information and are used by data processing instructions. You can treat data registers as 8-bit, 16-bit, or 32-bit entities.

The eight address registers hold 32-bit address or pointers. Address registers take part only in 32-bit operations and are used only in accessing data.

Note that address register A7 is the system stack pointer because it points to the top of the stack.

The program counter contains the address of the next instruction to be executed.

The status register contains information about the state (operating mode) of the computer.

Figure 5.5 The 68K register set.

progress over the last six decades has been in computer technology, organization, and implementation rather than in computer architecture.

Computer instructions are executed sequentially, one by one in turn, unless a special instruction deliberately changes the *flow of control* or unless an event called an *exception* (interrupt) takes place.

The structure of instructions varies from machine to machine. The format of an instruction running on a Pentium is different to the format of an instruction running on a 68K (even though both instructions might do the same thing). Instructions are classified by type (what they do) and by the number of operands they take. The three basic instruction types are *data movement* which copies data from one location to another, *data processing*, which operates on data, and *flow control*, which modifies the order in which instructions are executed. Instruction formats can take zero, one, two, or three operands. Consider the following examples of instructions with zero to three operands. In these examples operands P, Q, and

R may be memory locations or registers. The two-address instruction is in blue because that is the format used by the 68K.

Let's begin with three operands because it's intuitively easy to understand. A *three-address* computer instruction can be written

`operation source1,source2,`**`destination`**

where `operation` defines the nature of the instruction, `source1` is the location of the first operand, `source2` is the location of the second operand, and **`destination`** is the location of the result. The instruction ADD P,Q,**R** adds P and Q to get R (remember that we really means that the instruction adds the contents of location P to the contents of location Q and puts the sum in location R). Having reminded you that when we mention a variable we mean the contents of the memory location or register specified by that variable, we will not emphasize it again.

Modern microprocessors don't implement three-address instructions exactly like this. It's not the fault of the instruction designer, but it's a limitation imposed by the practicalities of computer technology. Suppose that a computer has a 32-bit address that allows a total of 2^{32} bytes of memory to be accessed. The three address fields, P, Q, and R would each be 32 bits, requiring $3 \times 32 = 96$ bits to specify operands. Assuming a 16-bit operation code (allowing up to $2^{16} = 65\,536$ instructions), the total instruction size would be

Operands	Instruction	Effect
Three	ADD P,Q,**R**	Add P to Q and put the result in R
Two	ADD P,**Q**	Add P to Q and put the result in Q
One	ADD **P**	Add P to an accumulator
Zero	ADD	Add the top two items on the stack

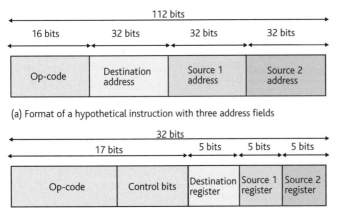

(a) Format of a hypothetical instruction with three address fields

(b) Format of a hypothetical instruction with a register-to-register architecture

Figure 5.6 Possible three-address instruction formats.

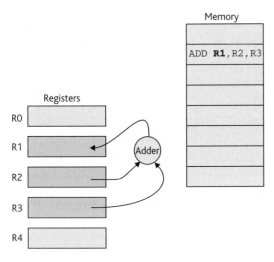

The instruction ADD **R1**,R2,R3 in memory is read by the computer and interpreted.The computer reads registers R2 and R3 to obtain the two source operands, sends these operands to the adder in the ALU, and then writes the sum from the adder to register R1.

Figure 5.7 Implementing a three-address instruction.

$96 + 16 = 112$ bits or 14 bytes. Figure 5.6(a) illustrates a hypothetical three-address instruction.

Computer technology developed when memory was very expensive indeed. Implementing a 14-byte instruction was not cost effective in the 1970s. Even if memory had been cheap, it would have been too expensive to implement 112-bit-wide data buses to move instructions from point to point in the computer. Finally, main memory is intrinsically slower than on-chip registers.

The modern RISC processor allows you to specify three addresses in an instruction by providing three 5-bit operand address fields. This restriction lets you select from one of only 32 different operands that are located in registers within the CPU itself.[5] By using on-chip registers to hold operands, the time taken to access data is minimized because no other storage mechanism can be accessed as rapidly as a register. An instruction with three 32-bit operands requires 3×5 bits to specify the operands, which allows a 32-bit instruction to use

the remaining $32 - 15 = 17$ bits to specify the instruction, as Fig. 5.6(b) demonstrates. Figure 5.7 illustrates the operation of an instruction with three register addresses.

We'll use the ADD instruction to add together four values in registers R2, R3, R4, and R5. In the following fragment of code, the semicolon indicates the start of a comment field, which is not part of the executable code. This code is typical of RISC processors like the ARM.

```
ADD   R1,R2,R3    ;R1 = R2 + R3
ADD   R1,R1,R4    ;R1 = R1 + R4
ADD   R1,R1,R5    ;R1 = R1 + R5
                  = R2 + R3 + R4 + R5
```

[5] I will use RISC very loosely to indicate the class of computers that have a register-to-register architecture such as the ARM, MIPS, PowerPC, and SPARC. The Motorola 68K and the Intel Pentium are not members of this group.

REGISTER-TO-REGISTER ARCHITECTURES

Computers act on data in registers or memory locations. Many data processing operations operate on two operands; for example, X + Y or X − Y or X·Y or Z ⊕ Y. These operations are said to be *dyadic* because they require two operands. The result of such a dyadic operation generates a third operand, called the destination operand; for example, Z = A + B.

First-generation microprocessors of the 1970s and 1980s allowed one source operand to be in memory and one source operand to be in a register in the CPU. A separate destination address was not permitted, forcing you to use one of the source operands as a destination. This restriction means

that one of the source operands is destroyed by the instruction.

A typical two-address instruction is ADD D0,**P**. This adds the contents of memory location P to the contents of register D0 and deposits the result in location P. The original contents of P are destroyed.

Register-to-register architectures permit operations only on the contents of on-chip registers such as ADD **R1**,R2,R3. The source or destination of an operand is never a memory location. Consequently, registers must first be loaded from memory and the results of an operation transferred to memory.

Two-address machines

A CISC machine like the 68K has a two-address instruction format. Clearly, you can't execute P = Q + R with two operands. You can execute Q ← P + Q. One operand appears twice, first as a source and then as a destination. The operation ADD P,**Q** performs the operation [Q] ← [P] + [Q]. The price of a two-operand instruction format is the destruction, by overwriting, of one of the source operands.

Most computer instructions can't directly access two memory locations. Typically, the operands are either two registers or one register and a memory location; for example, the 68K ADD instruction can be written

Instruction	RTL definition	Mode
ADD D0,**D1**	[D1] ← [D1] + [D0]	Register to register
ADD P,**D2**	[D2] ← [D2] + [P]	Memory to register
ADD D7,**P**	[P] ← [P] + [D7]	Register to memory

The 68K has seven general-purpose registers, D0 to D7; there are no restrictions on the way in which you use these registers; that is, if you can use D*i* you can also use D*j* for any *i* or *j* from 0 to 7.

One-address machines

A one-address machine specifies one operand in the instruction. The second operand is a fixed register called an *accumulator*, which doesn't have to be specified. For example, the operation one-address instruction ADD P means [A] ← [A] + [P]. The notation [A] indicates the contents of the accumulator. A simple operation R = P + Q can be implemented by the following fragment of 8-bit code (from a 6800 processor).

```
LDA   P     ;load accumulator with P
ADD   Q     ;add Q to accumulator
STA   R     ;store accumulator in R
```

Eight-bit machines of the Intel 8080 and Motorola 6800 eras have one-address architectures. As you can imagine,

8-bit code is verbose because you have to load data into the accumulator, process it, and then store it to avoid it being overwritten by the next data processing instruction.

One-address machines are still widely used in embedded controllers in low-cost, low-performance systems such as toys. We look at an 8-bit processor in Chapter 9.

Zero-address machines

A zero-address machine doesn't specify the location of an operand because the operand's location is fixed. A zero-address machine uses a stack, which is a data structure in the form of a queue where all items are added and removed from the same end. An ADD instruction would pop the top two items off the stack, add them together, and push the result on the stack. Although stack machines have been implemented to execute languages like FORTH, processors with stack-based architectures have been largely confined to the research lab. There is one exception. The language JAVA is portable because it is complied into bytecode, which runs on a stack machine, which is simulated on the real target machine. We will return to the stack later.

68K instruction format

We will look at 68K instruction in detail when we've covered more of the basics. The 68K has a two-address instruction format. An operand may be a register or a memory location. The following are valid 68K instructions.

Instruction	RTL definition	
ADD D4,**D1**	[D1] ← [D1] + [D4]	
SUB P,**D6**	[D6] ← [D6] − [P]	
AND D7,**P**	[P] ← [P] ∧ [D7]	
MOVE D3,**D1**	[D1] ← [D3]	Register to register
MOVE X,**D1**	[D1] ← [X]	Memory to register
MOVE D2,**Y**	[Y] ← [D2]	Register to memory
MOVE X,**Z**	[Z] ← [X]	The only memory to memory operation
CLR D0	[D0] ← 0	Only one operand required for the clear instruction

Consider the 68K's ADD instruction ADD $00345678, **D2.** This instruction performs the operation $[D2] \leftarrow [D2] + [345678_{16}]$. The two source operands provide the addresses: one address is a memory location and the other a data register. This instruction format is sometimes called '*one-and-a-half address*' because you can specify only a handful of registers.

CISC processors use *variable-length instructions*. The minimum 68K instruction size is 16 bits and instructions can be constructed by chaining together successive 16-bit values in memory. For example, the 68K is one of the few processors to provide a memory-to-memory MOVE instruction that supports absolute 32-bit addressing. You can write MOVE $12345678, **$ABCDDCBA**, which takes 10 consecutive bytes in memory and moves the contents of one memory location to another.

Subword operations

First-generation microprocessors had 8-bit data wordlengths and operations acted on 8-bit values to produce 8-bit results. When 16-bit processors appeared, operations were applied to 16-bit values to create 16-bit results. However, the *byte* did not go away because some types of data such as ASCII-encoded characters map naturally on to 8-bit data elements.

If you wish to access bytes in a 16- or 32-bit processor, you need special instructions. The Motorola 68K family deals with 8-bit, 16-bit, and 32-bit data by permitting most data processing instructions to act on an 8-bit or a 16-bit slice of a register as well as the full 32 bits. RISC processors do not (generally) support 8- or 16-bit operations on 32-bit registers, but they do support 8-bit and 16-bit memory accesses.

Suppose a processor supports operations that act on a subsection of a register. This raises the interesting question, 'What happens to the bits that do not take part in the operation?' Figure 5.8 demonstrates how we can handle operations shorter than 32 bits. Assume that a register is partitioned as Fig. 5.8(a) demonstrates. In this example, we are going to operate on data in the least-significant byte.

We can do three things, as Fig. 5.10(b) and (c) demonstrates. In (b) the bits not acted on remain unchanged—this is the option implemented by the 68K when it operates on data registers. In (c) the bits that do not take part in the operation are cleared to zero. In (d) the bits that do not take part in the operation are set to the value of the most-significant bit (the sign bit) of the bits being operated on. This option preserves the sign of two's complement values. Most processors implement options (c) or (d).

RISC processors like the ARM do not allow general data processing operations on fever than 32 bits. However, they do support 8-bit and 16-bit load instructions with a zero or sign extension.

The 68K calls 32-bit values *longwords*, 16-bit values *words*, and 8-bit values *bytes*. Motorola's terminology is not universal. Others use the term word to mean 32 bits and *halfword* to means 16 bits. The 68K is an unusual processor because it allows variable size operations on most of its data processing instructions. By appending .B after an instruction, you perform an operation on a byte. Appending .W performs the operation on a 16-bit word and appending .L performs the operation on a 32-bit longword. Omitting a size suffix selects a 16-bit default. Consider the following.

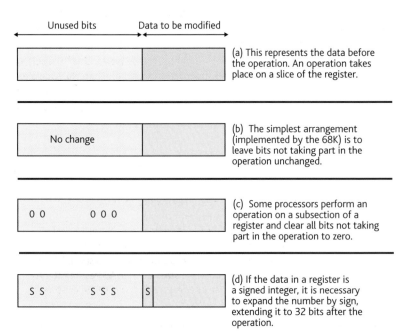

Unused bits   Data to be modified

(a) This represents the data before the operation. An operation takes place on a slice of the register.

No change

(b) The simplest arrangement (implemented by the 68K) is to leave bits not taking part in the operation unchanged.

0 0   0 0 0

(c) Some processors perform an operation on a subsection of a register and clear all bits not taking part in the operation to zero.

S S   S S S   S

(d) If the data in a register is a signed integer, it is necessary to expand the number by sign, extending it to 32 bits after the operation.

Figure 5.8 Extending data.

Instruction	RTL definition
`ADD.B   D0,`**`D1`**	$[D1_{(0:7)}] \leftarrow [D1_{(0:7)}] + [D4_{(0:7)}]$
`ADD.W   D0,`**`D1`**	$[D1_{(0:15)}] \leftarrow [D1_{(0:15)}] + [D4_{(0:15)}]$
`ADD.L   D0,`**`D1`**	$[D1_{(0:31)}] \leftarrow [D1_{(0:31)}] + [D4_{(0:31)}]$
`ADD     D0,`**`D1`**	$[D1_{(0:15)}] \leftarrow [D1_{(0:15)}] + [D4_{(0:15)}]$ `Same as ADD.W  D0,`**`D1`**

5.3.2 Overview of addressing modes

A key concept in computing in both high- and low-level languages is the *addressing mode*. Computers perform operations on data and you have to specify *where* the data comes from. The various ways of specifying the source or destination of an operand are called *addressing modes*.

We can't discuss instructions, the ISA, or low-level programming until we have introduced three fundamental concepts in addressing:

- Absolute addressing   (the operand specifies the location of the data)
- Immediate addressing   (the operand provides the operand itself)
- Indirect addressing   (the operand provides a pointer to the location of the data).

In *absolute addressing* you specify an operand by providing its location in memory or in a register. For example, `ADD P,`**`D1`** uses absolute addressing because the location of the operand P is specified as a memory location. Another example of absolute addressing is the instruction `CLR 1234`, which means set the contents of memory location 1234 to zero.

When you specify a data register as an operand, that is also an example of absolute addressing, although some call it *register direct addressing*.

In *immediate addressing* the operand is an actual value rather than a reference to a memory location. The 68K assembler indicates immediate addressing by prefixing the operand with the '#' symbol; for example, `ADD #4,`**`D0`** means add the value 4 to the contents of register D0 and put the result in register D0. Immediate addressing lets you specify a *constant*, rather than a *variable*. This addressing mode is called *immediate* because the constant is part of the instruction and is immediately available to the computer. The addressing mode is also called *immediate* because the operand is immediately available from the instruction and you don't have to fetch it from memory or a register. When you specify the absolute address of a source operand, the computer has to get the address from the instruction and then read the data at that location.

Indirect addressing specifies a *pointer* to the actual operand, which is invariably in a register. For example, the instruction, `MOVE (A0),`**`D1`** first reads the contents of register A0 to obtain a pointer that gives you the address of the operand. Then it reads the memory location specified by the pointer in A0 to get the actual data. This addressing mode requires *three* memory accesses; the first is to read the instruction to identify the register containing the pointer, and the second is to read the contents of the register to get the pointer, the third is to get the desired operand at the location specified by the pointer.

You can easily see why this addressing mode is called *indirect* because the address register specifies the operand indirectly by telling you *where* it is, rather than *what* it is. Motorola calls this mode of *address register indirect addressing*, because the pointer to the actual operand is in an address register. Figure 5.9 illustrates the effect of executing the operation `MOVE (A0),`**`D0`**.

In Fig. 5.9 address register A0 points to a memory location; that is, the value it contains is the address of an operand in memory. In this case A0 contains 1234 and is, therefore, pointing at memory location 1234. When the instruction `MOVE (A0),`**`D0`** is executed, the contents of the memory location pointed at by A0 (i.e. location 1234) are copied into data register D0. In this example, D0 will be loaded with 3254.

DATA AND ADDRESS REGISTERS

The 68K has eight data registers, D0 to D7. It also has eight address registers, A0 to A7. Data and address registers are similar. Both types of registers are 32 bits wide. The principal difference between these registers lies in their *function*. A data register holds any data (including addresses). An address register is used only to hold the address of an operand in memory.

All data processing operations can be applied to any data register, but not to all address registers. Address registers take part in operations only of relevance to the processing of addresses.

All data registers are equal in the sense that you can use any one in any way. This is not true of address registers. You can use A0 to A6 in any way you want but A7 is special. A7 has a system function called the *stack pointer*. Address register A7 points to the top of the system stack (the place where subroutine return addresses are stored).

Executing a `MOVE (A0),`**`D0`** instruction

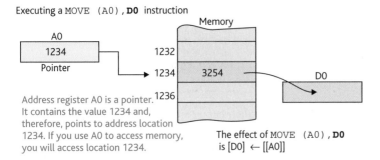

Address register A0 is a pointer. It contains the value 1234 and, therefore, points to address location 1234. If you use A0 to access memory, you will access location 1234.

The effect of `MOVE (A0),`**`D0`** is $[D0] \leftarrow [[A0]]$

Figure 5.9 Address register indirect addressing.

Why do we implement this addressing mode? Consider the following two operations.

```
MOVE  (A0),D0   ;copy the item pointed at by A0 into D0
ADD.L #2,A0     ;increment A0 to point to the next item
```

The first operation loads D0 with the 16-bit element pointed at by address register A0. The second instruction increments A0 by 2 to point to the next element. The increment is 2 because the elements are 2 bytes (i.e. 16 bits) wide and successive elements are 2 bytes apart in memory.

Address register indirect addressing allows you to step though an array or table of values accessing consecutive elements. Suppose we have a table of 20 consecutive bytes that we have to add together. We can write

The first three instructions set up the initial values. We load A0 with the address of the numbers. The location has the symbolic name 'Table'. The # symbol precedes 'Table' because A0 is being loaded with the address table and *not the contents of that address*. Data register D0 is used to hold the sum of the numbers and is cleared prior to its first use. Finally, we put the number 20 into D1 to count the elements as we add them.

The body of the code is in blue. The first instruction fetches the byte pointed at by A0 and adds it to the running total in D0 and the second instruction points to the next byte element in the list. Note that when we increment the pointer we use a longword operation because all pointers are 32 bits.

The last part of the program decrements the element count by one and then branches back to 'Next' if we haven't reached zero. We look at the branching operations in more detail later.

The three addressing modes form a natural progression. Consider their definitions in RTL.

Addressing mode	Assembly form	RTL	Memory accesses
Immediate addressing	`MOVE #4,D1`	$[D1] \leftarrow 4$	1
Absolute addressing	`MOVE P,D1`	$[D1] \leftarrow [P]$	2
Indirect addressing	`MOVE (A1),D1`	$[D1] \leftarrow [[A1]]$	3

```
        MOVE.L  #Table,A0   ;A0 points to the table (A0 has the address of Table)
        CLR.B   D0          ;Use D0 to hold the sum – clear it first
        MOVE.B  #20,D1      ;There are 20 numbers to add

Next    ADD.B   (A0),D0     ;Add a number to the total in D0
        ADD.L   #1,A0       ;Point to the next number in the list

        SUB.B   #1,D1       ;Decrement the counter
        BNE     Next        ;Repeat until all added in
```

IMPORTANT POINTS

The fragment of code to add the 20 numbers is, in principle, very straightforward. However, it contains aspects that many beginners find confusing. Indeed, I would say that probably 90% of the errors made by beginners are illustrated by this fragment of code. Consider the following points.

1. Data register D0 is used to hold the running total. At the machine level, registers and memory locations are not set to zero before they are used. Therefore, the programmer must initialize their contents either by clearing them or by loading a value into them.

2. We are working with byte-wide data elements throughout. Therefore all operations on data in this problem have a `.B` suffix. All operations on pointers have an `.L` suffix. Do not

confuse operations on a pointer with operations on the data elements at which they point!

3. Understand the meaning of the # symbol, which indicates a literal value. `MOVE 1234,`**`D0`** puts the contents of memory location 1234 in register D0. `MOVE #1234,`**`D0`** puts the number 1234 in D0. This is the single most common mistake my students make.

4. An address register used to hold a pointer has to be loaded with the value of the pointer. This value is a memory location where the data lies. If the symbolic name for the address of a table is PQR, then you point to PQR with `MOVE.L #PQR,`**`A0`**. You are putting an actual address in A0 and not the contents of a memory location.

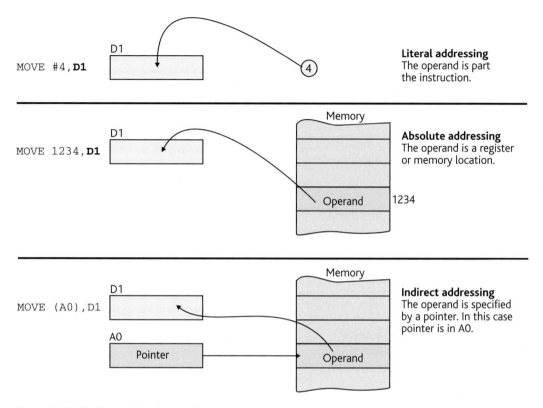

Literal addressing
The operand is part
the instruction.

Absolute addressing
The operand is a register
or memory location.

Indirect addressing
The operand is specified
by a pointer. In this case
pointer is in A0.

Figure 5.10 The three addressing modes.

Figure 5.10 illustrates these three addressing modes graphically.

5.4 Overview of the 68K's instructions

We now look at the type of operations that the 68K and similar processors carry out on data. Here we are interested in general principles. In the next chapter we demonstrate how the instructions can be used. A typical two-operand memory-to-register instruction has the format

```
ADD   P,D0
```

and is interpreted as $[D0] \leftarrow [D0] + [P]$. The source operand appears first (left to right), then the destination operand. Instructions can be divided into various categories. For our current purposes, we will consider the following broad categories.

Data movement These instructions copy data from one place to another; for example, from memory to a register or from one register to another.

Arithmetic Arithmetic instructions perform operations on data in numeric form. In this chapter we assume data is either a signed or an unsigned integer.

Logical A logical operation treats data as a string of bits and performs a Boolean operation on these bits; for example, 11000111 AND 10101010 yields 10000010.

Shift A shift instruction moves the bits in a register one or more places left or right; for example, shifting 00000111 one place left yields 00001110.

Bit A bit instruction acts on an individual bit in a register, rather than the entire contents of a register. Bit instructions allow you to test a single bit in a word (for 1 or 0), to set a bit, to clear a bit, or to flip a bit into its complementary state.

Compare These instructions compare two operands and set the processor's status flags accordingly; for example, a compare operation allows you to carry out the test.

Control Control instructions modify the flow of control; that is, they change the normal sequential execution of instructions and permit instructions to be executed out of order.

5.4.1 Status flags

Before we continue we have to introduce the notion of the *processor status register* because its contents can be modified by the execution of most instructions. The processor status register records the *outcome* of an instruction and it can be used to implement conditional behavior by selecting one of two courses of action. Some processors call this register a *condition code* register.

Conditional behavior is the feature of computer languages that lets us implement high-level language operations such as

```
if (x == 4) then
```

or

```
(i = 0; i < 20; i++).
```

A processor register contains at least four bits, Z, N, C, and V, whose values are set or cleared after an instruction has been executed. These four flags, or status bits, and their interpretations are as follows.

Z-bit Set if the result of the operation is zero.

N-bit Set if the result is negative in a two's complement sense; that is, the leftmost bit is zero.

C-bit Set if the result yields a carry-out.

V-bit Set if the result is out of range in a two's complement sense.

Typical CISC processors update these flags after each operation (see box for more details).

Consider the following example using 8-bit arithmetic. Suppose D0 contains 00110101_2 and D1 contains 01100011_2. The effect of adding these two values together with ADD D0, **D1** would result in

```
  00110101₂
+ 01100011₂
  10011000₂
```

The result is 10011000_2, which is deposited in D1. If we interpret these numbers as two's complement values, we have added two positive values and got a negative result. Consequently, the V-bit is set to indicate arithmetic overflow. The result is not zero, so the Z-bit is cleared. The carry-out is 0. The most-significant bit is 1, so the N-bit is set. Consequently, after this operation $C = 0, Z = 0, N = 1, V = 1$.

5.4.2 Data movement instructions

The most frequently executed computer operation is *data movement*. The data movement instruction is incorrectly named because the one thing it does not do is *move* data. Data movement instructions *copy* data; for example, the instruction MOVE Y, **X** copies the contents of Y to X but does not modify the value of Y. You could say that a data movement instruction is a *data propagate* or *data copy* instruction.

Some processors have a load instruction, a store instruction, and a move instruction. A load copies data from memory to a register, a store copies data from a register to memory, and a move instruction copies data from one register to another. As we already know, the 68K has a single MOVE instruction, which copies data from anywhere to anywhere.

There are other types of move operation; for example, the 68K has an exchange instruction that swaps the contents of two registers; for example,

EXG D1, A2 has the effect [A2]←[D1]; [A1]←[A2]

The purpose of the semicolon in the above RTL indicates that the two operations happen simultaneously.

5.4.3 Arithmetic instructions

Arithmetic operations are those that act on numeric data (i.e. signed and unsigned integers). Table 5.1 lists the 68K's arithmetic instructions. Let's look at these in detail.

Add The basic ADD instruction adds the contents of two operands and deposits the result in the destination operand. One operand may be in memory. There's nothing to stop you using the same source operand twice and writing ADD D0, **D0** to load D0 with the value of $2 \times$ [D0].

All addition and subtraction instructions update the contents of the condition code register unless the destination operand is an address register.

Add with carry The *add with carry* instruction, ADC, is almost the same as the ADD instruction. The only different is that ADC adds the contents of two registers together with the carry bit; that is, ADC D0, **D1** performs [D1]←[D1] + [D0] + C, where C is the carry bit generated by a previous operation.

CONDITION CODE FLAGS

One of the biggest variations between processor families is the treatment of condition code flags . There are three aspects to the way in which these flags are updated.

Update always The condition code flags are updated after each and every instruction has been executed.

Update sometimes The condition code flags are updated after some instructions have been executed but not others. Generally the flags are updated after instructions that might be used in a comparison such as 'is $X < Y$' but not after instructions that perform routine housekeeping tasks.

Update on demand The condition code register is updated only when the programmer requires it. This mode is indicated by appending a suffix to an instruction to indicate an update flags request.

The 68K updates its status bits after most instructions are executed. You simply have to learn which instrucion update the flags and which don't. Instructions that affect the flow of control such as subroutine calls and instructions that act on address registers do not update the conditon code flags.

ADD	D0,**D1**	Add	$[D1] \leftarrow [D1] + [D0]$
ADC	D0,**D1**	Add with carry	$[D1] \leftarrow [D1] + [D0] + C$
SUB	D0,**D1**	Subtract	$[D1] \leftarrow [D1] - [D0]$
SBC	D0,**D1**	Subtract with carry	$[D1] \leftarrow [D1] - [D0] - C$
MULU	D0,**D1**	Multiply (unsigned)	$[D1] \leftarrow [D1] \times [D0]$
MULS	D0,**D1**	Multiply (signed)	$[D1] \leftarrow [D1] \times [D0]$
DIVU	D0,**D1**	Divide (unsigned)	$[D1] \leftarrow [D1] \div [D0]$
DIVS	D0,**D1**	Divide (signed)	$[D1] \leftarrow [D1] \div [D0]$

Table 5.1 The 68K's arithmetic instructions.

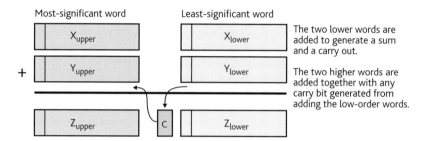

Figure 5.11 Extended addition.

This instruction is used in extended or compound arithmetic. Suppose you wish to add two 64-bit numbers using the 32-bit 68K. Assume that the most-significant 32 bits of X are in D0 and the least-significant 32 bits are in D1, and the most-significant 32 bits of Y are in D2 and the least-significant bits are in D3. We can perform the 64-bit addition X + Y by

```
ADD.L   D0,D2   ;Add the low-order 32 bits, update carry flag
ADC.L   D1,D3   ;Add the high-order 32 bits plus any carry
```

In this example we use ADD.L to add the two low-order 32-bit words. Remember that the .L suffix indicates a 32-bit operation. An addition records any carry bit generated by the addition and moves it to the C-bit. The following instruction ADC adds the high-order longwords together with any carry that was generated by adding the low-order longwords. Figure 5.11 illustrates the addition Z = X + Y where X, Y, and Z are 64-bit values and the addition is to be performed with 32-bit arithmetic. Each of the operands is divided into an upper and lower 32-bit word.

Subtract The subtract instruction subtracts the source operand from the destination operand and puts the result in the destination register; for example, SUB D0,**D1** performs $[D1] \leftarrow [D1] - [D0]$. A special subtraction operation that facilitates multiple length subtraction, SBC D0,**D1**, performs the action $[D1] \leftarrow [D1] - [D0] - C$ (the carry bit is also subtracted from the result).

Multiplication Unfortunately, two's complement arithmetic works only for addition and subtraction; that is, you don't have to use a different addition operation for unsigned and signed integers. The same is not true for multiplication and division. If you are using unsigned integers you have to do multiplication one way and if you are using signed two's complement integers you have to do multiplication in a different way. Consequently, the 68K has two multiplication (and division) instructions and you have to choose the one to reflect the type of numbers you are using. MULU multiplies two unsigned integers and MULS multiplies two signed integers.

The 68K's multiplications do not provide the same flexibility as the 68K's addition instructions. You can multiply only two 16-bit integers to get a 32-bit result (remember that multiplying two n-bit values yields a $2n$-bit product). The operation MULU D0,**D1** performs the operation

$$[D1_{(0:31)}] \leftarrow [D1_{(0:15)}] \times [D0_{(0:15)}]$$

Division The 68K's division instructions are a little more complicated because division results in a quotient plus a remainder; for example, 17 ÷ 3 = 5 remainder 2. The 68K divides a 32-bit value by a 16-bit value to produce a 16-bit quotient and a 16-bit remainder. In order to avoid using an instruction with three operands, the quotient and remainder are packed in the same register. For example, DIVU D0,**D1** divides the 32-bit contents of D1 by the 16-bit lower-order 16-bit word in D0 and puts the 16-bit quotient in the low-order word of D1 and the 16-bit remainder in the high-order word of D1. We can express this as

$$[D1_{(0:15)}] \leftarrow [D1_{(0:31)}] \div [D0_{(0:15)}]$$
$$[D1_{(15:31)}] \leftarrow \text{remainder}$$

If D0 contains 4 and D1 contains 12345_{16}, the operation DIVU D0,**D1** results in D1 = $000148D1_{16}$. Consider the following fragment of code where we divide P by Q and put the quotient in D2 and the remainder in D3.

```
MOVE.L P,D1      ;get P
MOVE.W Q,D0      ;get Q
DIVU    D0,D1    ;divide P by Q
CLR.L   D2       ;clear D2 ready to receive quotient
MOVE.W D1,D2     ;put quotient in D2
CLR.L   D3       ;clear D3 ready to receive remainder (clear = make 0)
SWAP    D1       ;exchange upper and lower words in D1
MOVE.W D1,D3     ;put remainder in D3
```

This code is more complex than you would think and demonstrates the pitfalls of assembly language. First we have to remember that P is a 32-bit value and that Q is a 16-bit value. The divide instruction divides a 32-bit value by a 16-bit value.

Because we get the quotient and remainder in D1, we have to split them and copy them to D2 and D3 respectively. A MOVE instruction always operates on the low-order word in a register, which means that we don't have to worry about the remainder bits in bits 16 to 31 of D1 when we copy the quotient. However, because D2 is a 32-bit register, we should ensure that the upper order bits are zero before we do the transfer. We use CLR.L to set all the bits of D2 to zero before transferring the 16-bit quotient.

We can use the SWAP instruction, which exchanges the upper and lower order words of a register to get the remainder in the low-order 16-bits of D1 before we transfer the remainder to D3.

When writing 68K instructions, you always have to ask yourself '*How? many bits are we operating on?*' and '*What are we going to do about the bits not taking part in the operation*'. Some processors take away that choice; for example, the ARM and similar RISC processors require that all operations be applied to all bits of a register.

5.4.4 Compare instructions

High-level languages provide conditional constructs of the form
if (x == y) {a = b * c};

We examine how these constructs are implemented later. At this stage we are interested in the comparison part of the above construct, (x == y), which tests two variables for equality. We can also test for greater than or less than. The operation that performs the test is called *comparison*.

The 68K provides a compare instruction CMP source, **destination,** which evaluates [Rd] − [Rs] and updates the bits in the condition code register accordingly.

A compare instruction is inevitably followed by a branch instruction that chooses one of two courses of action depending only on the outcome of the comparison. Here we simply demonstrate a (compare, branch) pair because we will soon look at branch instructions in greater detail.

Consider the high-level construct if (x == 5) {x = x + 10}
We can write the following fragment of code:

```
       MOVE X,D0      ;get X in D0
       CMP  #5,D0     ;is X == 5?
       BNE  Exit      ;if not equal then go to "exit"
       ADD  #10,D0    ;else add 10 to X
       MOVE D0,X      ;restore X to memory
Exit ...             ;
```

In this example the branch instruction BNE Exit forces a branch (jump) to the line labeled by Exit if the outcome of the compare operation yields 'not zero'.

5.4.5 Logical instructions

Logical operations allow you to directly manipulate the individual bits of a word. When a logical operation is applied to two 32-bit values, the logical operation is applied (in parallel) to each of the 32 *pairs* of bits; for example, a logical AND between A and B would perform $c_i = a_i \cdot b_i$ for all values of i. Table 5.2 illustrates the 68K's logical operations using an 8-bit example.

The AND operation is *dyadic* and is applied to two source operands. Bit i of the source is ANDed with bit i of the destination and the result is stored in bit i of the destination. If $[D1] = 11001010_2$, the operation

AND #%11110000,**D1**

results in $[D1] = 11000000_2$. Remember that the symbol # indicates a literal or actual operand and the symbol % indicates a binary value. We can represent this operation more conventionally as

```
11001010
11110000
11000000
```

D2	D1	Operation	Processor status flags
10101010	10101010	CMP D1,D2	Z = 1, C = 0, N = 0, V = 0
10101010	00000000	CMP D1,D2	Z = 0, C = 0, N = 1, V = 0
10101010	11000001	CMP D1,D2	Z = 0, C = 1, N = 1, V = 0

Mnemonic	Operation	Definition
AND D0,**D1**	Logical AND	$[D1] \leftarrow [D1] \wedge [D0]$
OR D0,**D1**	Logical OR	$[D1] \leftarrow [D1] \vee [D0]$
EOR D0,**D1**	Exclusive EOR	$[D1] \leftarrow [D1] \oplus [D0]$
NOT **D1**	Logical NOT	$[D1] \leftarrow \overline{[D1]}$

Example
11110000 · 10101010 = 10100000
11110000 + 10101010 = 11111010
11110000 ⊕ 10101010 = 01011010
11110000 = 00001111

Table 5.2 The 68K's logical instructions.

The AND operation is used to *mask* the bits of a word. If you AND bit x with bit y, the result is 0 if $y = 0$, and x if $y = 1$. A typical application of the AND instruction is to strip the parity bit off an ASCII-encoded character. That is,

```
AND   #%01111111,D1
```

clears bit 7 of D1 to zero and leaves bits 0 to 6 unchanged.

The OR operation is used to set one or more bits of a word to 1. ORing a bit with 0 has no effect and ORing the bit with 1 sets it. For example, if $[D1] = 11001010_2$, the operation

```
OR   #%11110000,D1
```

results in $[D1] = 11111010_2$.

The EOR operation is used to toggle (i.e. invert) one or more bits of a word. EORing a bit with 0 has no effect and EORing it with 1 inverts it. For example, if $[D1] = 11001010_2$, the operation

```
EOR #%11110000,D1
```

results in $[D1] = 00111010_2$.

By using the NOT, AND, OR, and EOR instructions, you can perform any logical operations on a word. Suppose you wish to clear bits 0, 1, and 2, set bits 3, 4, and 5, and toggle bits 6 and 7 of the byte in D0. You could write

```
AND   #%11111000,D1   Clear bits 0, 1, and 2
OR    #%00111000,D1   Set bits 3, 4, and 5
EOR   #%11000000,D1   Toggle bits 6 and 7.
```

If $[D1]$ initially contains 01010101_2, its final contents will be 10111000_2. We will look at a more practical application of bit manipulation after we have covered branch operations in a little more detail.

5.4.6 **Bit instructions**

The 68K provides bit instructions that operate on the individual bits of a word. Bit instructions are not strictly necessary, because you can use logical operations to do the same thing.

The 68K's bit instructions can be used to set, clear, or toggle (complement) a single bit in a word. Moreover, the bit instructions also test the state of the bit they have tested and set or clear the Z-bit of the condition control register accordingly. Consider

5.4.7 **Shift instructions**

A shift operation moves a group of bits one or more places left or right; for example, consider the following examples

Source	After shift left	After shift right
00110011	01100110	00011001
11110011	11100110	01111001
10000001	00000010	01000000

Although there are only two shift directions, left and right, there are several variations on the basic shift operation. These variations depend on whether we are treating the value being shifted as an integer or a signed value and whether we include the carry bit in the shifting.

Shift operations are used to multiply or divide by a power of 2, to rearrange the bits of a word, and to access bits in a specific location of a word.

Figure 5.12 illustrates the various types of shift operation. Suppose the 8-bit value 11001010_2 is shifted one place right. What is the new value? A logical shift right operation, LSR introduces a zero into the leftmost bit position vacated by the shift and the new value is 01100101_2.

Arithmetic shifts treat the data shifted as a signed two's complement value. Therefore, the sign bit is propagated by an arithmetic shift right. In this case, the number $11001010_2 = -54$ is negative and, after an arithmetic right shift, ASR, the new result is 11100101_2 (i.e. -27).

When a word is shifted right, the old least-significant bit has been shifted out and 'lost'. Figure 5.12 shows that this bit isn't lost because it's copied into the carry flag bit.

An arithmetic shift left is equivalent to multiplication by 2 and an arithmetic shift right is equivalent to division by 2.

Some computers allow you to shift one bit position at a time. Others let you shift any number of bits. The number of bits to be shifted can be a *constant*; that is, it is defined in the program and the shift instruction always executes the same number of shifts. Some computers let you specify the number of bits to be shifted as the contents of a register. This allows you to implement *dynamic* shifts because you can

```
BTST #4,D0   ;test bit number 4 of D0 and set the Z-bit accordingly
BSET #4,D0   ;test bit 4 of D0, set the Z-bit accordingly, set bit 4
BSET D1,D0   ;test the bit of D0 whose position is in D1
```

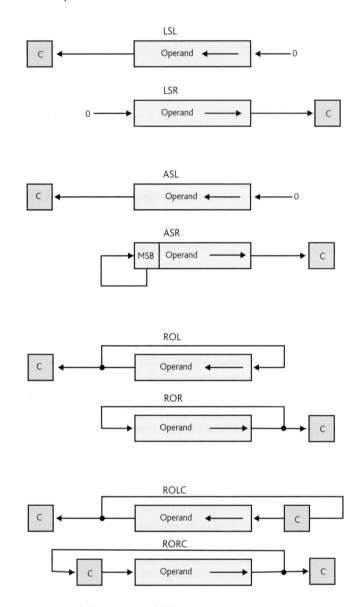

Logical shift left

A zero enters the least-significant bit and the most-significant bit is copied to the carry flag.

Logical shift right

A zero enters the most-significant bit and the least-significant bit is copied to the carry flag.

Arithmetic shift left

A zero enters the least-significant bit and the most-significant bit is copied to the carry flag.

Arithmetic shift right

The old most-significant bit is copied into the new most-significant bit and the least-significant bit is copied to the carry flag.

Rotate left

The most-significant bit is copied into the least-significant bit and the carry flag.

Rotate right

The least-significant bit is copied into the most-significant bit and the carry flag.

Rotate left through carry

The most-significant bit is copied into the carry flag and the old C-bit copied into the least-significant bit.

Rotate right through carry

The least-significant bit is copied into the C flag and the old C-bit copied into the most-significant bit.

Figure 5.12 The four classes of shift instruction.

change the contents of the register that specifies the number of shifts. The 68K lets you write LSL #4, **D0** to shift the contents of data register D0 left by four places or LSL D1, **D0** to shift the contents of D0 left by the number in D1.

Figure 5.12 also describes *circular* shifts or *rotates*. A circular shift operation treats the data being shifted as a ring with the most-significant bit adjacent to the least-significant bit. Circular shifts result in the most-significant bit being shifted into the least-significant bit position (left shift), or vice versa for a right shift. No data is lost during a circular shift. Consider the following examples.

Shift type	Before circular shift	After circular shift
Rotate left, ROL	11001110	10011101
Rotate right, ROR	11001110	01100111

The last pair of shift operations in Fig. 5.12 are called *rotate though carry*. These operations treat the carry bit as part of the shift operation. A circular shift is performed with the old carry bit being shifted into the register and the bit lost from the carry register being shifted into the carry bit. Suppose that the carry bit is currently 1 and that the 8-bit value 11110000_2 is to be shifted one place right through carry. The final result is 11111000$_2$ and the carry bit is 0. A circular shift is a non-destructive shift because no information is lost (bits don't fall off the end).

The 68K's shift instructions are as follows.

LSL The operand is shifted left by 0 to 31 places. The vacated bits at the least-significant end of the operand are filled with zeros.

LSR The operand is shifted right 0 to 31 places. The vacated bits at the most-significant end of the operand are filled with zeros.

ASL The arithmetic shift left is identical to the logical shift left.

ASR The operand is shifted right 0 to 31 places. The vacated bits at the most-significant end of the operand are filled with zeros if the original operand was positive, or with 1s if it was negative (i.e. the sign-bit is replicated). This divides a number by 2 for each place shifted.

ROL The operand is rotated by 0 to 31 places left. The bit shifted out of the most-significant end is copied into the least-significant end of the operand. This shift preserves all bits. No bit is lost by the shifting.

ROR The operand is rotated by 0 to 31 places right. The bit shifted out of the least-significant end is copied into the most-significant end of the operand. This shift preserves all bits. No bit is lost by the shifting.

ROXL The operand is rotated by 0 to 31 places left. The bit shifted out of the most significant end of the operand is shifted into the C-bit. The old value of the C-bit is copied into the least-significant end of the operand; that is, shifting takes place over 33 bits (i.e. the operand plus the C-bit).

ROXR The operand is rotated by 0 to 31 places right. The bit shifted out of the least-significant end of the operand is shifted into the C-bit. The old value of the C-bit is copied into the most-significant end of the operand; that is, shifting takes place over 33 bits (i.e. the operand plus the C-bit).

Shift operations can be used to multiply or divide a number by a power of two. They can be used for several other purposes such as re-arranging binary patterns; for example, suppose register D2 contains the bit pattern 0aaaaxxxbbbb$_2$ and we wish to extract the xxx field (we're using 12-bit arithmetic for simplicity). We could write

```
LSR    #4,D2    ;this will give us  00000aaaaxxx
```

If we want to ensure that we just have the xxx field, we can use a logical AND to clear the other bits by

```
AND  #% 111,D1  ;this will give us 000000000xxx
```

5.4.8 Branch instructions

A *branch instruction* modifies the flow of control and causes the program to continue execution at the *target address* specified by the branch. The simplest branch instruction is the *unconditional* branch instruction, BRA target, which always forces a jump to the instruction at the target address. In the following fragment of code, the BRA Here instruction

```
BRA    Here         ;jump to the line that begins "Here"
       .
       .
       .
Here   ADD    R0,D1
```

forces the 68K to execute next the instruction on the line which is labeled by Here.

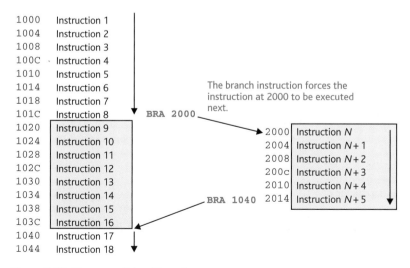

Figure 5.13 The unconditional branch.

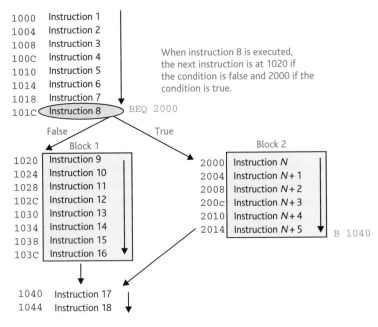

When instruction 8 is executed, the next instruction is at 1020 if the condition is false and 2000 if the condition is true.

Figure 5.14 The conditional branch.

Mnemonic	Condition	Flags
BEQ	equal	$Z = 1$
BNE	not equal	$Z = 0$
BCS/BHS	carry set/higher or same	$C = 1$
BCC/BLO	carry clear/lower	$C = 0$
BMI	negative	$N = 1$
BPL	positive or zero	$N = 0$
BVS	overflow set	$V = 1$
BVC	overflow clear	$V = 0$
BHI	higher than (signed)	$(C = 1) \cdot (Z = 0)$
BLS	lower or same (signed)	$(C = 0) + (Z = 1)$
BGE	greater than or equal (signed)	$N = V$
BLT	less than (signed)	$N \neq V$
BGT	greater than (signed)	$(Z = 0) \cdot (N = V)$
BLE	less than or equal (signed)	$(Z = 1) + (N \neq V)$

Table 5.3 The 68K's conditional branches.

Figure 5.13 demonstrates how an unconditional branch can modify the flow of control. In this example, execution continues sequentially from instruction 1 to instruction 8, which is BRA 2000 (branch to instruction N at location 2000_{16}). The address of the first instruction is 1000_{16} and each instruction takes 4 bytes. Execution then continues with the instruction at location N. Instruction $N + 5$ is BRA 1040 (branch to instruction 17 at location 1040_{16}) and a change of flow takes place again.

The most important feature of any computer is its ability to implement *conditional behavior* by carrying out a test and then branching on the result of the text. Figure 5.14 demonstrates the flow of control with a conditional branch.

Instruction 8 is BEQ 2000 and is interpreted as 'branch to instruction N if the last result was zero, otherwise continue'. Consequently, there is a fork at instruction 8 between the path if the last result was not zero and a path (to instruction N) if the result was zero.

We can imagine that the test for zero leads to the execution of code block 1 or code block 2. At the end of code block 2 a branch back to the main stream of instructions is made.

Let's look at this conditional behavior in high-level language. Consider the following example of the high-level construct

```
if (x == 3) then y = 4
```

We can translate this construct into the following 68K code.

```
CMP    #3,D1      ;(x == 3)?
BNE    exit       ;if x is not 3 then leave
MOVE   #4,D2      ;if x is 3 then y = 4
exit   ...
```

The instruction CMP #3,**D1** compares the contents of register D1 with the literal 3 by evaluating $[D1] - 3$ and setting the status flags. If the result of the operation is zero, the Z-bit is set to 1. If the result is not zero (i.e. D1 does not contain 3), the Z-bit is set to 0.

The key instruction is BNE exit, which means 'branch on not zero to the instruction labeled exit'. The effect of this instruction is to test the Z-bit of the status flags and then branch to the instruction with the label 'exit' if $Z = 0$ (i.e. D1 is not 3). If D1 is 3, $Z = 1$, the branch is not taken, and the MOVE #4,**D2** instruction is executed.

The 68K provides 16 branch instructions of the form B_{CC} where CC defines the branch condition. These 16 conditions, described in Table 5.3, are virtually the same as those provided by many other microprocessors. We will see what the 4 bits in the first column mean later.

Let's look at another application of conditional branching. You can implement a loop construct in the following way

```
       MOVE   #20,D0   ;load the loop counter D0 with 20
Next   .               ;body of loop
       .
       .
       SUB    #1,D0    ;decrement loop counter
       BNE    Next     ;repeat until loop count = zero
```

Let's look at another example of the use of branching. Suppose **A** and **B** are two n-component vectors. As we have already stated, the inner product of **A** and **B** is the scalar value $s = \mathbf{A} \cdot \mathbf{B} = a_1 \cdot b_1 + a_2 \cdot b_2 + a_3 \cdot b_3 \ldots a_n \cdot b_n$. We can now write the code

```
        CLR.L    D6          ;clear initial sum in D6
        MOVE     #24,D5      ;load loop counter with n (assume 24 here)
        MOVE.L   #A,A0       ;A0 points at vector A
        MOVE.L   #B,A1       ;A1 points at vector B

Next    MOVE     (A0),D2     ;Repeat: get A_i and update pointer to A
        ADD.L    #2,A0       ;        point to next element in A
        MOVE     (A1),D3     ;        get B_i and update pointer to B
        ADD.L    #2,A1       ;        point to next element in B
        MULU     D2,D3       ;        A_i x B_i
        ADD.L    D3,D6       ;        s = s + A_i x B_i
        SUB      #1,D5       ;        decrement loop counter
        BNE      Next        ;repeat n times
```

Subroutine calls

A subroutine is a piece of code that is called and executed and a return is made to the calling point. Subroutines are very important because they implement the *function* or *procedure* at the high-level language level. We look at subroutines in more detail in the next chapter. Here we are interested only in the principle of the subroutine call and return.

Figure 5.15 demonstrates the subroutine call. Code is executed sequentially until a subroutine call is encountered. The current place in the code sequence is saved and control is then transferred to the subroutine; that is, the first instruction in the subroutine is executed and the processor continues executing instructions in the subroutine until a *return* instruction is encountered. Then, control is transferred back to the point immediately after the subroutine call by retrieving the saved return address.

Figure 5.16 illustrates this concept with a simple subroutine called ABC that calculates the value of $2x^2$ (where x is a 16-bit value passed in D0). This subroutine is called by the instruction BSR ABC (branch to subroutine), and a return from subroutine is made by an RTS (return from subroutine) instruction.

Figure 5.17 displays the program of Fig. 5.16 in the form of a memory map and demonstrates the flow of control between the calling program and the subroutine ABC.

Figure 5.18 extends the example in Fig. 5.15 by demonstrating a multiple call. We have used the instruction BSR ABC to implement the subroutine call. The main body of the code calls subroutine ABC. At the end of the subroutine, a return instruction makes a return to the instruction following the calling point. As you can see, the subroutine is called from two different places and yet a return is made to the correct point in each case.

In chapter 6 we look at how assembly language programs are constructed. We will also look at a data structure called the *stack*, which is used to hold subroutine return addresses.

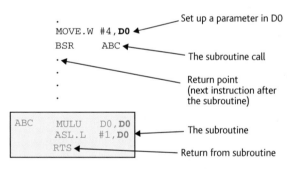

Figure 5.15 The subroutine call.

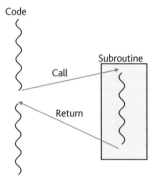

Figure 5.16 The subroutine.

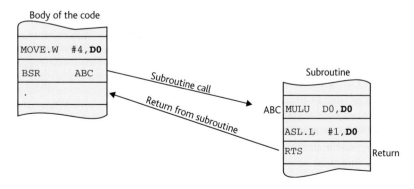

Figure 5.17 Memory map of a subroutine call and flow of control.

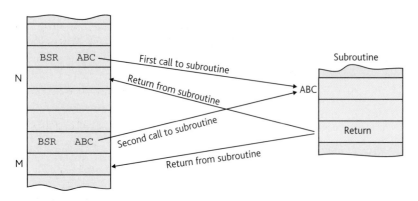

Figure 5.18 Multiple subroutine calls.

■ SUMMARY

We have introduced the CPU and its native language, the assembly language, which is a human-readable representation of machine code. Unfortunately, assembly languages are not portable; each family of microprocessors has its own unique assembly language that is incompatible with any other processor. You can run a C program on most computers with a C compiler. A program written in Pentium assembly language will run only on machines with a Pentium at their core.

We introduced the concept of an architecture, the assembly language programmer's view of the computer in terms of its functionality rather than performance or implementation. To illustrate the characteristics of an architecture we selected the elegant 68K processor, which is, paradoxically, simpler than many of its contemporaries while, at the same time, incorporating a number of sophisticated facilities such as the ability to shift an operand as part of a data processing instruction and the ability to execute an instruction only if certain conditions are met (predication).

An architecture consists of a set of instructions, a set of resources (the registers), and the addressing modes used to access data.

In this chapter we have laid the foundations for the next chapter where we look at how programs can be constructed to run on the instruction set architecture we introduced here.

■ PROBLEMS

5.1 What's the difference between an assembly language and machine code? In order to answer this question fully, you should use the Internet to find out more about assemblers.

5.2 Books and articles on the computer make a clear distinction between *architecture* and *organization*. Do you think that this is a useful distinction? Can you think of other areas (i.e. non-computer example) where such a distinction would be appropriate?

5.3 What are the advantages and disadvantages of dividing a computer's registers into data and address registers like the 68K?

5.4 What are the relative advantages and disadvantages of one-address, two-address, and three-address instruction formats?

5.5 What's a *register-to-register architecture* and why is such an architecture also called a *load and store computer*?

5.6 What are the three fundamental addressing modes? Are they all necessary? What is the minimum number of addressing modes required? Can you think of other possible addressing modes?

5.7 The 68K has two add instructions: ADD and ADC. What is the difference between them? If the processor lacked an ADC instruction, how would you synthesize it (i.e. what other instructions would you use to achieve the same effect)?

5.8 The 68K has an *exchange register pair* instruction, EXG. Why would you want such an instruction?

5.9 The SWAP Di instruction swaps the upper- and lower-order words of data register Di. Why would you want such an instruction? If the 68K's instruction set lacked a SWAP, how would you swap the two halves of a data register?

5.10 Why are so many variations on a shift operation provided by the 68K and many other processors?

5.11 What is the largest memory space (i.e. program) that can be addressed by processors with the following number of address bits?
(a) 12 bits
(b) 16 bits
(c) 24 bits
(d) 32 bits
(e) 48 bits
(f) 64 bits

5.12 The von Neumann stored program computer locates program and data in the same memory. What are the advantages and disadvantages of a system with a combined program and data memory?

5.13 The gear lever is part of an automobile's organization rather than its architecture. Are the brakes part of a car's architecture or organization?

5.14 What does the RTL expression $[100] \leftarrow [50]+2$ mean?

5.15 What does the RTL expression $[100] \leftarrow [50+2]+2$ mean?

5.16 What is an operand?

5.17 In the context of an instruction register, what is a *field*?

5.18 What is a literal operand?

5.19 What is the effect on the C-, V-, Z-, and N-bits when the following 8-bit operations are carried out?

(a) 01110001   (b) 11110101   (c) 10100011
    +01111001   +11000111   +01011101

5.20 Some microprocessors have one general-purpose data register, some two, some eight, and so on. What determines the number of such general-purpose data registers in any given computer?

5.21 What is the difference between a dedicated and a general-purpose computer?

5.22 What is a subroutine and how is it used?

5.23 What is the so-called von Neumann bottleneck?

5.24 For the following memory map explain the meaning of the following RTL expressions in plain English.

(a) `[1000] = 120`
(b) `[1003] = [1001] + 1`
(c) `[1004] ← 5`
(d) `[1000] ← [1005]`
(e) `[1001] ← [1002] + [1003]`
(f) `[1000] ← [1003 + 1]`

1000	120
1001	1003
1002	8
1003	1004
1004	0
1005	23

5.25 Suppose a problem in a high-school algebra text says 'Let $x = 5$'. What exactly is x? Answer this question from the point of view of a computer scientist.

5.26 In the context of a CPU, what is the difference between a data path and an address path?

5.27 Why is the program counter a pointer and not a counter?

5.28 What's the difference between a memory location and a data register?

5.29 Does a computer need data registers?

5.30 Some machines have a one-address format, some a two-address format, and some a three-address format; for example,

```
ADD P1
ADD P1,P2
ADD P1,P2,P3
```

What are the relative merits of each of these instruction formats?

5.31 What is the difference between the C, Z, V, and N flags in a computer's status register (or condition code register)?

5.32 What is the difference between machine code and assembly language?

5.33 What is the advantage of a computer with many registers over one with few registers?

5.34 Translate the following algorithm into assembly language.

```
IF X > 12 THEN X = 2*X+4 ELSE X = X + Y
```

5.35 For the memory map below, evaluate the following expressions, where [N] means *the contents of the memory location whose address is N*. All addresses and their contents are *decimal* values.

00	12
01	17
02	7
03	4
04	8
05	4
06	4
07	6
08	0
09	5
10	12
11	7
12	6
13	3
14	2

(a) [7]
(b) [[4]]
(c) [[[0]]]
(d) [2 + 10]
(e) [[9] + 2]

(f) [[9] + [2]]
(g) [[5] + [13] + 2 * [14]]
(h) [0)] * 3 + [1] * 4
(i) [9] * [10]

5.36 The most frequently executed class of instruction is the data move instruction. Why is this?

Assembly language programming

6

CHAPTER MAP

5 The instruction set architecture

Chapter 5 introduces the computer's instruction set architecture, which defines the low-level programmer's view of the computer and describes the type of operations a computer carries out. We are interested in three aspects of the ISA: the nature of the instructions, the resources used by the instructions (registers and memory), and the way in which the instructions access data (addressing modes).

6 Assembly language programming

Having introduced the basic operations that a computer can carry out, the next step is to show how instructions are used to construct entire programs. We introduce the 68K's programming environment via a simulator that runs on a PC and demonstrate how to implement some basic algorithms.

7 Structure of the CPU

Now we know *what* a computer does, the next step is to show *how* it operates. In Chapter 7 we examine the internal organization of a computer and demonstrate how it reads instructions from memory, decodes them, and executes them.

8 Other processors

We have used the 68K to introduce the CPU and assembly language programming. Here we provide a brief overview of some of the features of other processors.

INTRODUCTION

We introduced the processor and its machine-level language via the 68K CISC processor in the previous chapter. Now we demonstrate how 68K assembly language programs are written and debugged.

Because assembly language programming is a practical activity, we provide a 68K cross-assembler and simulator with this book. Previous editions of this book used the DOS-based Teesside simulator. In this edition we use a more modern Windows-based system called Easy68K. We provide a copy of the EASy68K simulator on the CD accompanying this book, as well as a copy of the Teesside simulator and its documentation for those who wish to maintain compatibility with earlier editions.

Both simulators run on a PC and allow you to execute 68K programs. You can execute a program instruction by instruction and observe the effect of each instruction on memory and registers as it is executed.

6.1 Structure of a 68K assembly language program

Figure 6.1 provides the listing of a simple assembly language program written to run on the 68K cross-assembler. This program implements the high-level language operation $R = P + Q$ (where variables $P = 2$ and $Q = 4$). Few rules govern the layout of a 68K assembly language program. The leftmost column is reserved for user-defined labels—in this case, P, Q, and R. If a line begins with an asterisk in the first column, the assembler ignores the rest of the line. You put an asterisk in column 1 to create a comment. Another rule is that

the mnemonic and its operand must be separated by at least one space and that no embedded spaces may be located within either the mnemonic or operand fields.

Recall that numbers prefixed by the $ symbol are *hexadecimal*, whereas numbers prefixed by % indicate that the following number is expressed in binary form; for example, the following three instructions

```
MOVE 25,D0        load D0 with 25₁₀
MOVE $19,D0       load D0 with 25₁₀
MOVE %11001,D0    load D0 with 25₁₀
```

are equivalent. The assembler translates each of these into exactly the same machine code.

THE 68K ARCHITECTURE REVIEW

The 68K has 16 general-purpose 32-bit user accessible registers. D0 to D7 are data registers and A0 to A7 are address registers. An address register holds a pointer and is used in address register indirect addressing. The only instructions that can be applied to the contents of address registers are add, subtract, move, and compare. Operations on the contents of an address register always yield a 32-bit value whereas operations on data registers can be 8, 16, or 32 bits.

Most 68K instructions are register to register, register to memory, or memory to register. The following defines some 68K instructions.

MOVE.B	D0,**D1**	Copy the low-order byte in D0 to D1$_{(0:7)}$.
MOVE.W	ABC,**D1**	Copy the 16-bit word in memory location ABC to D1$_{(0:15)}$.
MOVE.L	D0,**(A0)**	Copy the 32-bit value in D0 to the memory location pointed at by address register A0.
ADD.B	D1,**ABC**	Add the low-order byte in register D1 to the contents of memory location ABC.
SUB.B	#4,**(A3)**	Subtract 4 from the contents of the byte-wide memory location pointed at by A3.
ADD.L	A1,**D5**	Add the 32-bit contents of address register A1 to data register D5.

The # symbol indicates the immediate addressing mode; that is, the operand is a literal value.

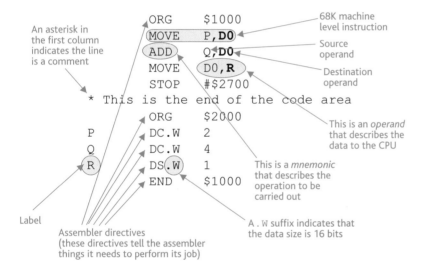

Figure 6.1 Structure of an assembly language program.

Figure 6.2 shows the structure of a typical 68K instruction. Instructions with two operands are always written in the form source, destination, where source is where the operand comes from and destination is where the result goes to.

6.1.1 Assembler directives

Assembly language statements are divided into *executable* instructions and *assembler directives*. An executable instruction is translated into the machine code of the target microprocessor and executed when the program is loaded into memory. In the example in Fig. 6.1, the executable instructions are

```
MOVE  P,D0      Copy contents of P to D0
ADD   Q,D0      Add contents of Q to D0
MOVE  D0,R      Store contents of D0 in memory location R
STOP  #$2700    Stop executing instructions¹
```

We've already encountered the first three instructions. The last instruction, STOP #$2700, terminates the program by halting further instruction execution. This instruction also loads the 68K's status register with the value 2700$_{16}$, a special code that initializes the 68K. We use this STOP instruction to terminate programs running on the simulator.

An *assembler directive* tells the assembler something it needs to know about the program; for example, the assembler directive ORG means *origin* and tells the assembler where instructions or data are to be loaded in memory. The expression ORG $1000 tells the assembler to load instructions in memory

---

[1] Remember that in the instruction STOP #$2700 the operand is #$2700. The '#' indicates a literal operand and the '$' indicates hexadecimal. The literal operand 0010011100000000$_2$ is loaded into the 68K's status register after it stops. The 68K remains stopped until it it receives an interrupt.

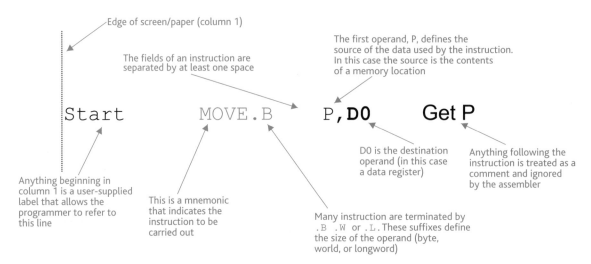

Figure 6.2 Anatomy of an assembly language instruction.

starting at address 1000_{16}. We've used the value 1000_{16} because the 68K reserves memory locations 0 to $3FF_{16}$ for a special purpose and 1000 is an easy number to remember.

The second *origin* assembler directive, ORG $2000, is located after the code and defines the starting point of the data area. We don't need this assembler directive; without it data would immediately follow the code. We've used it because it's easy to remember that the data starts at memory location $2000.

An important role of assembler directives is in reserving memory space for variables, presetting variables to initial values, and binding variables to symbolic names. Languages like C call these operations *declaring variables*. We will be performing assembly level actions similar to the following C declarations.

```
int   time;        /* declare integer "time"                   */
int   x, y;        /* declare two integers x and y             */
int   z3 = 42;     /* declare an integer z3 and assign the value 42  */
char term = '@';   /* declare a character with the initial value '@' */
```

In this fragment of code the operation int z3 = 42; reserves a 16-bit memory location for the variable called z3 and then stores the binary equivalent of 42_{10} in that location. Whenever you use the variable z3 in the program, the compiler will automatically select its appropriate address in memory. All this is invisible to the programmer. The following demonstrates the relationship between 68K assembler directives and the C code.

Figure 6.3 demonstrates what's happening when the 68K program in Fig. 6.1 is assembled by looking at the output produced by EASy68K. This listing has seven columns. The first column is a 32-bit value expressed in hexadecimal form, which contains the current memory address in which instructions or data will be loaded. The next two columns are the hexadecimal values of instructions or data loaded into the current memory location. These are the values produced by the assembler from instructions, addresses, and data in the assembly language program. The fourth column contains the line number that makes it easy to locate a particular line in the program. The remaining right-hand columns in Fig. 6.3 are the instructions or assembler directives themselves followed by any comment field.

As you can see, the instruction MOVE D0,**R** is located on line 12 and is stored in memory location $100C_{16}$. This instruction is translated into the machine code $33C000002004_{16}$, where the operation code is $33C0_{16}$ and the address of operand R is 00002004_{16}.

The symbol table below the program relates symbolic names to their value. This information is useful when you are debugging a program; for example, you can see that variable P has the address 2000.

The assembler maintains a variable called the *location counter*, which keeps track of where the next instruction or data element is to be located in memory. When you write an ORG directive, you preset the value of the location counter to that specified; for example, ORG $1234 means load the following instruction or data into memory at location 1234_{16}. Let's look as some of the other assembler directives in this program.

68K assembler directive			C code equivalent
Time	DS.W	1	int time;
X	DS.W	1	int x, y;
Y	DS.W	1	
Z3	DC.W	42	int z3 = 42;
Term	DC.B	'@'	char term = '@';

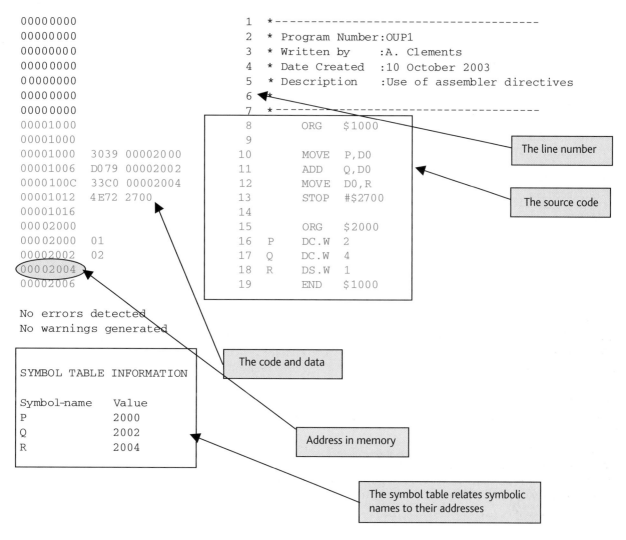

```
00000000                        1   *-----------------------------------------
00000000                        2   * Program Number:OUP1
00000000                        3   * Written by    :A. Clements
00000000                        4   * Date Created  :10 October 2003
00000000                        5   * Description   :Use of assembler directives
00000000                        6   *
00000000                        7   *-----------------------------------------
00001000                        8            ORG    $1000
00001000                        9
00001000    3039 00002000      10            MOVE   P,D0
00001006    D079 00002002      11            ADD    Q,D0
0000100C    33C0 00002004      12            MOVE   D0,R
00001012    4E72 2700          13            STOP   #$2700
00001016                       14
00002000                       15            ORG    $2000
00002000    01                 16    P       DC.W   2
00002002    02                 17    Q       DC.W   4
00002004                       18    R       DS.W   1
00002006                       19            END    $1000
```

No errors detected
No warnings generated

```
SYMBOL TABLE INFORMATION

Symbol-name    Value
P              2000
Q              2002
R              2004
```

The line number

The source code

The code and data

Address in memory

The symbol table relates symbolic
names to their addresses

Figure 6.3 Assembling a program.

The *define constant* assembler directive DC loads a constant in memory *before the program is executed*; that is, it provides a means of presetting memory locations with data before a program runs. This directive is written DC.B to store a byte, DC.W to store a word, and DC.L to store a longword. In the program of Fig. 6.3, the assembler directive P DC.W 2 places the value 2 in memory and labels this location 'P'. Because this directive is located immediately after the ORG $2000 assembler directive, the integer 2 is located at memory location 2000_{16}. This memory location (i.e. 2000_{16}) can be referred to as P. When you wish to read the value of P (i.e. the contents of memory location 2000_{16}), you use P as a source operand; for example, MOVE P,**D0**. Because the size of the operand is a word, the value 0000000000000010_2 is stored in location 2000_{16}. Figure 6.4 demonstrates the effect of this assembler directive.

The next assembler directive, Q DC.W 4, loads the constant 4 in the next available location—2002_{16}. Why 2002_{16} and not 2001_{16}? Because the operands are word sized (i.e. 16

bits) and the 68K's memory is byte addressed. Each word occupies two bytes—P takes up 2000_{16} and 2001_{16}.

The *define storage* directive (DS) tells the assembler to reserve memory space and also takes a .B, .W, or .L qualifier. For example, R DC.W 1 tells the assembler to reserve a word in memory and to equate the name of the word with 'R'. The difference between DC.B N and DS.B N is that the former stores the 8-bit value *N* in memory, whereas the latter reserves *N* bytes of memory by advancing the location counter by *N*.

The final assembler directive, END $1000, tells the assembler that the end of the program has been reached and that there's nothing else left to assemble. The parameter taken by the END directive is the address of the first instruction of the program to be executed. In this case, execution begins with the instruction at address 1000_{16}.

The assembler directive EQU equates a *symbolic name* to a numeric value. If you write Tuesday EQU 3, you can use the symbolic name 'Tuesday' instead of its actual value, 3. For example, ADD #Tuesday,**D0** is identical to ADD #3,**D0**.

We now provide another example of the use of assembler directives.

Half the fun in writing assembly language programs is running and debugging them. In this chapter we will be using the EASy68K simulator, which allows you to cross-assemble a 68K program on a PC and then execute it on a PC. The PC simulates the behavior of a 68K processor and the basic operating system function required to perform simple input and output activities such as reading from the keyboard and writing to the screen. Figure 6.5 gives a screen dump of a session with the simulator.

6.1.2 Using the cross-assembler

The following 68K assembly language program illustrates what an assembler does. This program is designed only to demonstrate the use of assembler directives; it does not perform any useful

(a) `ORG $2000` sets the location counter to 2000.

(b) `P DC.W 2` puts $0002 in the current location and moves the location counter to the next free location.

(c) Location $2000 has the symbolic value P. Using 'P' in the program is the same as using $2000.

Figure 6.4 The effect of a *define constant* assembly directive.

Figure 6.5 Output from the Easy68K simulator.

computation. The source program is followed by its assembled listing file. Examine both the source code and listing file, and try to follow what is happening.

```
        ORG    $400
Test    EQU    6                       Dummy equates
Alan    EQU    7
XXX     DS.W   2                       Save two words of storage
YYY     DC.L   $12345678               Put the longword $12345678 in memory
Name    DC.B   'Clements'              Put an ASCII string in memory
        DC.B   $FF
        DC.L   Test+Name               Store a 32-bit constant
        DC.B   4                       Put 4 in memory
Begin   MOVE.L #Name,A0                Start of code
Next    MOVE.B (A0)+,D0                Pick up a character
        CMP.B  #$FF,D0                 Test for end of string
        BEQ    Exit                    And exit on terminator
        BSR    Print                   Print a character
        BRA    Next                    Repeat
Exit    STOP   #$2700                  Halt the 68K
*
Print   NOP                            Dummy subroutine
        NOP
        RTS                            Return
*
        END    Begin                   END needed ("Begin" is start of code)
```

The following *listing file* was produced by a cross-assembler from the above source code.

```
 1  00000400                    ORG   $400
 2            00000006  TEST:   EQU   6          ;Dummy equates
 3            00000007  ALAN:   EQU   7
 4  00000400 00000004  XXX:    DS.W  2          ;Save two words of storage
 5  00000404 12345678  YYY:    DC.L  $12345678  ;Put the longword $12345678 in memory
 6  00000408 436C656D656E NAME: DC.B 'Clements'  ;Put an ASCII string in memory
             7473
 7  00000410 FF                 DC.B  $FF
 8  00000412 0000040E           DC.L  TEST+NAME  ;Store a 32-bit constant
 9  00000416 04                 DC.B  4          ;Put 4 in memory
10  00000418 207C00000408 BEGIN: MOVE.L #NAME,A0
11  0000041E 1018        NEXT:  MOVE.B (A0)+,D0
12  00000420 0C0000FF           CMP.B  #$FF,D0   ;Test for end of string
13  00000424 67000008           BEQ    EXIT      ;And exit on terminator
14  00000428 61000008           BSR    PRINT     ;Print a character
15  0000042C 60F0               BRA    NEXT      ;Repeat
16  0000042E 4E722700    EXIT:  STOP   #$2700    ;Halt the 68K
17                       *
18  00000432 4E71        PRINT: NOP              ;Dummy subroutine
19  00000434 4E71               NOP
20  00000436 4E75               RTS              ;Return
21                       *
22            00000418           END   BEGIN     ;END needed ("Begin" is start of code)

Lines: 22, Errors: 0, Warnings: 0.
```

The first column provides the line number. The second column defines the location in memory into which data and instructions go. The third column contains the instructions and the constants generated by the assembler. The remainder is the original assembly language program. Consider line 8.

used as a label and refers to the location in memory of the code on this line. This address is $408. Therefore, the constant to be stored is 6 + $0408 = $040E. You can see that this really is the value stored from column 3 in line 8. Note that line 10 has the location $0418 and not $0417 because all

```
8  00000412 0000040E              DC.L  TEST+NAME    ;Store a 32-bit constant
```

The constant stored in memory is TEST+NAME. In line 2 TEST was equated to 6 (i.e. the assembler automatically substitutes 6 for TEST). But what is 'NAME'? On line 6, NAME is

word and longword addresses must be *even*. The following notes will help you understand the assembly process.

The simulator system requires an ORG statement at the beginning of the program to define the point at which code is loaded into the simulated memory.

You can halt a 68K by executing the STOP #data instruction, which stops the 68K and loads the 16-bit value data into its status register. By convention we use the constant $2700 (this puts the processor in the supervisor mode, turns off interrupt requests, and clears the condition code flags).

Operations on address registers always yield longword results because an address register holds a 32-bit pointer. A .W operation is permitted on an address register but the result is treated as a two's complement value and sign-extended to 32 bits.

Because the END address assembler directive terminates the assembly process, no instructions beyond END point are assembled.

6.2 The 68K's registers

The 68K has a *byte-addressable* architecture. Successive bytes are stored at consecutive byte addresses 0, 1, 2, 3 . . . , successive words are stored at consecutive even addresses 0, 2, 4, 6, . . . , and successive 32-bit longwords are stored at addresses

---

BEGINNER'S ERRORS

1. Embedded data

You should not locate data in the middle of a section of code. The microprocessor executes instructions sequentially and will regard embedded data as instructions. Put data between the end of the executable instructions of a program and the END assembler directive as the following demonstrates.

```
         MOVE.B   D3,D4          The last instruction
         STOP     #$2700         This stops the 68K dead in its tracks
Data1    DC.B     'This is data'
Test     DS.B     4              Save 4 bytes of storage
         END      $400           The END directive is that last item in a program
```

The only way that you can locate data in the middle of a program is by jumping past it like this:

```
         MOVE.B   D3,D4          An instruction
         BRA      Continue       Jump past the data
Data1    DC.B     'This is data' Put the string here
Test     DS.B     4              Save 4 bytes of storage
Continue ADD.B    #1,D6          Back to the instructions...
```

Although this code is legal, it is not good practice (for the beginner) to mix code and data.

2. Initialization

I saw a program beginning with the operation MOVE.B (A0),D0 which loads D0 with the byte pointed at by address register A0. It failed because the student had not defined an initial value of A0. You have to set up A0 before you can use it or any other variable by, for example,

```
         LEA      Table,A0       A0 points to  "Table"
           .
         MOVE.B   (A0),D0        Pick up a byte from Table
           .
Table    DC.B     1,2,3,7,2      Here's the table
```

3. Subroutine call

You call a subroutine with a BSR or a JSR instruction. This is the only way you call a subroutine. You cannot call a subroutine with a conditional branch (e.g. BEQ, BNE, BCC, etc.).

4. Misplaced END directives

The END directive indicates the end of the program. No instruction or assembler directive may be placed after the END directive. The END must be followed by the address of the first instruction to be executed.

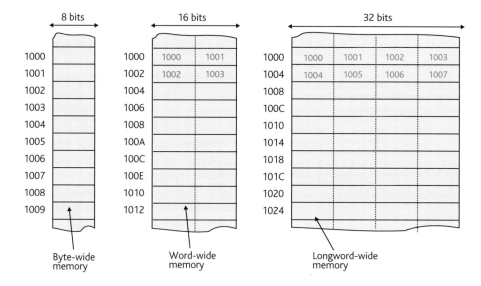

Figure 6.6 The 68K's memory space.

0, 4, 8, ... Figure 6.6 illustrates how the 68K's memory space is organized.

Figure 6.6 poses an interesting question. If you store a 32-bit longword at, say, memory location $1000, where do the 4 bytes go? For example, if the longword is $12345678, does byte $12 go into address $1000 or does byte $78 go into address $1000?

The 68K stores the most-significant byte of an operand at the lowest address (in this case $12 is stored at $1000). This storage order is called *Big Endian* (because the 'big end' of a number goes in first). The term Big Endian has been borrowed from *Gulliver's Travels*. Intel processors are *Little Endian* and store bytes in the reverse order to the 68K family.

The 68K stores the most-significant byte of a word in bits d_{08} to d_{15} at an *even* address and the least-significant byte in bits d_{00} to d_{07} at an *odd* address. Executing MOVE.W D0, **1234**, stores bits d_{00} to d_{07} of D0 at byte address 1235 and bits d_{08} to d_{15} of D0 at byte address 1234. To avoid confusion between registers and bits, we use 'D' to indicate a register and 'd' to indicate a bit. We introduced the 68K's registers in the previous chapter; now we examine some of their features. In Fig. 6.6 we've labeled the individual bytes of the 16-bit and 32-bit memory space in blue to demonstrate that the most-significant byte of a word or longword is at the low address.

6.2.1 Data registers

The 68K has eight general-purpose data registers, numbered D0 to D7. Any operation that can be applied to data register Di can also be applied to Dj. No special-purpose data registers are reserved for certain types of instruction. Some microprocessors do not permit all instructions to be applied to each of their registers. In such cases, learning assembly language is rather like learning to conjugate irregular foreign verbs.

The 68K's data registers are written D0 to D7. To refer to the sequence of consecutive bits i to j in register Dn we write D$n_{i:j}$. For example, we indicate bits 8 to 31, inclusive, of D4 by D4$_{(8:31)}$. This notation is an extension of RTL and is not part of the 68K's assembly language.

When a byte operation is applied to the contents of a data register, only bits d_{00} to d_{07} of the register are affected. Similarly, a word operation affects bits d_{00} to d_{15} of the register. Only the lower-order byte (word) of a register is affected by a byte (word) operation. For example, applying a byte operation to data register D1 affects only bits 0 to 7 and leaves bits 8 to 31 unchanged. CLR.B **D1** forces the contents of D1 to XXXXXXXXXXXXXXXXXXXXXXXX00000000, where the Xs represent the old bits of D1 before the CLR.B D1 was executed. If [D1] = $12345678 before the CLR.B **D1**, then [D1] = $12345600 after it.

Further examples should clarify the action of byte, word, and longword operations. In each case we give the 68K form of the instruction and its definition in RTL. We use slice notation to indicate a range of bits.

Assembly from	RTL definition
ADD.L D0,**D1**	[D1$_{(0:31)}$] ← [D1$_{(0:31)}$] + [D1$_{(0:31)}$]
ADD.W D0,**D1**	[D1$_{(0:16)}$] ← [D1$_{(0:16)}$] + [D0$_{(0:16)}$]
ADD.B D0,**D1**	[D1$_{(0:7)}$] ← [D1$_{(0:7)}$] + [D0$_{(0:7)}$]

If the initial contents of D0 and D1 are $12345678 and $ABCDEF98, respectively, the ADD operation has the following effects on the contents of D1 and the carry bit, C.

ADD.L D0,**D1** results in [D1]	= BE024610	and [C] = 0
ADD.W D0,**D1** results in [D1]	= ABCD4610	and [C] = 1
ADD.B D0,**D1** results in [D1]	= ABCDEF10	and [C] = 1

The state of the carry bit and other bits of the CCR are determined only by the result of operations on bits 0–7 for a byte operation, by the result of operations on bits 0–15 for a word operation, and by the result of operations on bits 0–31 for a longword operation.

One of the most common errors made by 68K programmers is using inconsistent size operations on a data register, as the following example demonstrates.

```
MOVE.B  XYZ,D0   Get the 8-bit contents of memory location XYZ
SUB.B   #5,D0    and subtract 5 to get [XYZ] - 5
CMP.W   #12,D0   Is ([XYZ] - 5) > 12
BGT     Test
```

This example implements the operation IF ([XYZ]-5) > 12 THEN.... But note that the operand XYZ is created as a *byte* value and yet it is compared with a *word* value. This fragment of code might work correctly sometimes if the contents of bits 8 to 15 of D0 are zero. However, if these bits are not zero, this code will not operate correctly.

6.2.2 Address registers

An address register holds the *location* of a variable. Registers A0–A6 are identical in that whatever we can do to Ai, we can also do to Aj. Address register A7 is also used as a stack pointer to keep track of subroutine return addresses. We describe the use of the stack point in detail later in this chapter.

Address registers sometimes behave like data registers. For example, we can move data to or from address registers and we can add data to them. There are important differences between address and data registers; operations on address registers don't affect the status of the condition code register. If you are in the process of adding up a series of numbers, you shouldn't have to worry about modifying the CCR every time you use an address register to calculate the location of the next number in the series.

Because the contents of an address register are considered to be a pointer to an item in memory, the concept of separate independent fields within an address register is quite meaningless. All operations on address registers yield longword values. You can apply a .L operation to an address register but not a .B operation. No instruction may operate on the low-order byte of an address register. However, word operations are permitted on the contents of address registers because the 16-bit result of a .W operation is automatically *sign-extended* to 32 bits. For example, the operation MOVEA.W #$8022,A3 has the effect:

[A3] ← $FFFF8022

The 16-bit value $8022 is sign extended to $FFFF8022. Similarly, MOVEA.W #$7022,A3 has the effect:

[A3] ← $00007022

The concept of a *negative* address may seem strange. If you think of a positive address as meaning *forward* and a negative address as meaning *backward*, everything becomes clear. Suppose address register A1 contains the value 1280. If address register A2 contains the value −40 (stored as the appropriate two's complement value), adding the contents of A1 to the contents of A2 by ADDA.L A1,A2 to create a composite address results in the value 1240, which is 40 locations back from the address pointed at by A1.

We conclude with an example of the use of address registers. Address register A0 points to the beginning of a data structure made up of 50 items numbered from 0 to 49. Each of these 50 items is composed of 12 bytes and data register D0 contains the number of the item we wish

---

MNEMONICS FOR OPERATIONS ON ADDRESS REGISTERS

Although some of the operations that can be applied to the contents of data registers can also be applied to the contents of address registers, the 68K's assembler employs special mnemonics for operations that modify the contents of an address register. The following examples illustrate some of these mnemonics. In each case, the destination operand is an address register

```
ADDA.L   D1,A3  ADDA  = add to address register
MOVEA.L  D1,A2  MOVEA = move to an address register
SUBA.W   D1,A3  SUBA  = subtract from an address register
CMPA.L   A2,A3  SUBA  = compare with an address register
```

Some assemblers for the 68K permit only the use of the ADD mnemonic for both ADD.W A1,D1 and for ADD.W D1,A1. Other assemblers demand that the programmer write ADDA.W D1,A1 and will reject ADD.W D1,A1. The purpose of forcing programmers to write MOVEA, ADDA, and SUBA instead of MOVE, ADD, and SUB when specifying address registers as destinations is to remind them that they are dealing with addresses and that these addresses are treated differently to data values (e.g. because of sign extension). Practical applications of the 68K's address registers are provided when we discuss addressing modes.

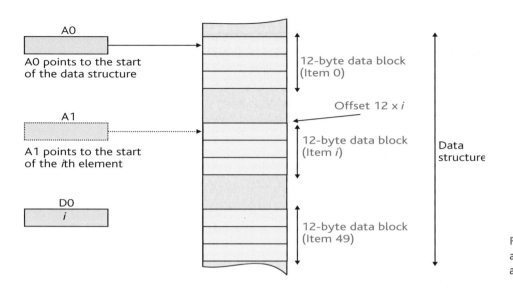

Figure 6.7 Using an address register to access a data element.

to access. Figure 6.7 illustrates this data structure. Suppose we need to put the address of this item in A1. In what follows use the operation MULU #n, **D0**, which multiplies the 16-bit low-order word in D0 by n and puts the 32-bit product in D0.

We need to find where the required item falls within the data structure. In order to do this we multiply the contents of D0 by 12 (because each item takes up 12 bytes). Then we add this offset to the contents of A0 and deposit the result in A1. That is,

processing operations, you can perform any data manipulation you require. However, the 68K provides some special-purpose data movement instructions to generate more compact and efficient code. The following three instructions provide enhanced data movement capabilities.

Name	Assembly form	RTL definition
Exchange	EXG Di,Dj	[Temp] ← [Di], [Di] ← [Dj] [Dj] ← [Temp]
Swap	SWAP Di	$[Di_{(0:15)}]$ ← $[Di_{(16:31)}]$, $[Di_{(16:31)}]$ ← $[Di_{(0:15)}]$
Load effective address	LEA P,**Ai**	[Ai] ← P

The EXG instruction is intrinsically a longword operation that exchanges the contents of two registers (see Fig. 6.8(a)). EXG may be used to transfer the contents of an

```
MULU     #12,D0      Calculate the offset into the data structure
MOVEA.L  A0,A1       Copy A0 to A1
ADDA.L   D0,A1       Add the offset to A1
```

6.3 Features of the 68K's instruction set

We've already described the 68K's basic operations. We now introduce some of the 68K's other instructions and demonstrate how they are used and what happens as they are executed on a simulator.

6.3.1 Data movement instructions

The MOVE instruction is the most common data movement instruction. Indeed, by using a MOVE in conjunction with data

address register into a data register and vice versa. SWAP exchanges the upper- and lower-order words of a given data register. The LEA (load effective address) instruction generates an address and puts it in an address register.

Let's write a program that executes some of these data movement instructions and then use the simulator to observe what happens as we trace through it. This program is just a random selection of data movement instructions—it doesn't actually do anything.

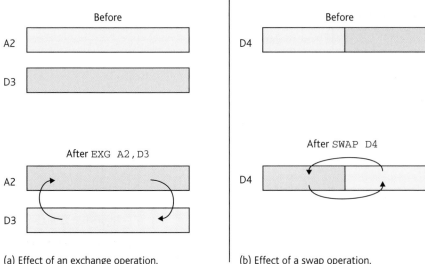

(a) Effect of an exchange operation.

(b) Effect of a swap operation.

Figure 6.8 The EXG and SWAP instructions.

```
        ORG     $400
        MOVE.L  #$12345678,D0   Copy a 32-bit literal to a register
        MOVE.B  D0,D1           Copy a byte from a register to a register
        MOVE.W  D0,D2           Copy a word from a register to a register
        MOVE.L  D0,D3           Copy a longword from a register to a register
        EXG     D0,A0           Exchange the 32-bit contents of two registers
        SWAP    D3              Swap the upper and lower words of a register
        MOVEA.L Data,A1         Copy contents of memory location into an address register
        LEA     Data,A1         Copy the address "Data" into an address register
        STOP    #$2700
Data    DC.L    $ABCDDCBA       Store a longword constant in memory at address "Data"
        END     $400
```

This source file produces the following listing file when assembled.

```
 1    00000400                          ORG       $400
 2    00000400 203C12345678            MOVE.L    #$12345678,D0
 3    00000406 1200                    MOVE.B    D0,D1
 4    00000408 3400                    MOVE.W    D0,D2
 5    0000040A 2600                    MOVE.L    D0,D3
 6    0000040C C188                    EXG       D0,A0
 7    0000040E 4843                    SWAP      D3
 8    00000410 227900000420            MOVEA.L   DATA,A1
 9    00000416 43F900000420            LEA       DATA,A1
10    0000041C 4E722700                STOP      #$2700
11    00000420 ABCDDCBA      DATA:     DC.L      $ABCDDCBA
12             00000400                END       $400
```

We are going to use the simulator to run this program and observe the contents of the simulated 68K's registers as the instructions are executed one by one. Figure 6.9 displays the contents of the simulated computer's registers immediately after the program is loaded.[2] Note that the 68K has two A7 address registers labeled SS and US in all simulator output. SS is the *supervisor state* stack pointer A7 and US is the *user state* stack pointer A7. When the 68K is first powered up, the supervisor stack pointer is selected (we will discuss the difference between these later). Throughout this chapter, all references to the stack pointer refer to the supervisor stack pointer,

----

[2] This is the output from the Teesside simulator, which is a text-based simulator unlike EASy68K which is Windows based. This text uses both simulators. EASy68K is better for running programs in a debug mode, the Teesside simulator is better for creating files that can be used in a book.

The DF command is entered by the user. What follows is the simulator's response

The simulator displays the current contents of the program counter (PC), the status register (SR), the supervisor stack pointer (SS), and the user stack pointer (US)

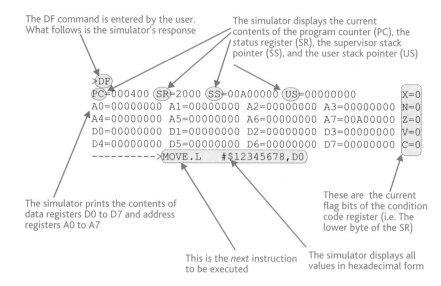

```
>DF
PC=000400  SR=2000  SS=00A00000  US=00000000                X=0
A0=00000000  A1=00000000  A2=00000000  A3=00000000          N=0
A4=00000000  A5=00000000  A6=00000000  A7=00A00000          Z=0
D0=00000000  D1=00000000  D2=00000000  D3=00000000          V=0
D4=00000000  D5=00000000  D6=00000000  D7=00000000          C=0
---------->MOVE.L    #$12345678,D0
```

The simulator prints the contents of data registers D0 to D7 and address registers A0 to A7

These are the current flag bits of the condition code register (i.e. The lower byte of the SR)

This is the *next* instruction to be executed

The simulator displays all values in hexadecimal form

Figure 6.9 Structure of the output from the simulator.

SP (i.e. A7). In Fig. 6.9, PC defines the current value of the program counter, SR the status register containing the 68K's CCR, and X, N, Z, V, and C are the CCR's flag bits.

The last line of the block of data in Fig. 6.9 is the mnemonic of the *next* instruction to be executed. Because the simulator doesn't use *symbolic names*, all addresses, data values, and labels are printed as hexadecimal values. In Fig. 6.9, the program counter is pointing at location 400_{16} and the instruction at this address is MOVE.L #$12345678,**D0**.

We now execute this program, instruction by instruction. The purpose of this exercise is to demonstrate the use of the simulator and to show how each instruction affects the 68K's internal registers as it is executed. To help you appreciate what is happening, registers that have changed are depicted in blue.

```
PC=000406  SR=2000  SS=00A00000  US=00000000                X=0
A0=00000000  A1=00000000  A2=00000000  A3=00000000          N=0
A4=00000000  A5=00000000  A6=00000000  A7=00A00000          Z=0
D0=12345678  D1=00000000  D2=00000000  D3=00000000          V=0
D4=00000000  D5=00000000  D6=00000000  D7=00000000          C=0
---------->MOVE.B    D0,D1
```

The first instruction, MOVE.L #$12345678,**D0**, has been executed. The only registers that have changed are D0 and the program counter. The PC has increased by 6 because the instruction had a 2-byte op-code and a 4-byte immediate value. The shortest 68K instruction is 2 bytes and the longest is 10 bytes. The next instruction to be executed, MOVE.B D0,**D1**, copies the low-order byte of D0 to D1.

```
PC=000408  SR=2000  SS=00A00000  US=00000000                X=0
A0=00000000  A1=00000000  A2=00000000  A3=00000000          N=0
A4=00000000  A5=00000000  A6=00000000  A7=00A00000          Z=0
D0=12345678  D1=00000078  D2=00000000  D3=00000000          V=0
D4=00000000  D5=00000000  D6=00000000  D7=00000000          C=0
---------->MOVE.W    D0,D2
```

As you can see, only the least-significant byte of D0 has been copied to D1. The next two instructions, MOVE.W D0, **D2** and MOVE.L D0, **D3**, demonstrate the transfer of a word and a longword, respectively.

```
PC=00040A SR=2000 SS=00A00000 US=00000000           X=0
A0=00000000 A1=00000000 A2=00000000 A3=00000000 N=0
A4=00000000 A5=00000000 A6=00000000 A7=00A00000 Z=0
D0=12345678 D1=00000078 D2=00005678 D3=00000000 V=0
D4=00000000 D5=00000000 D6=00000000 D7=00000000 C=0
---------->MOVE.L    D0,D3
```

```
PC=00040C SR=2000 SS=00A00000 US=00000000           X=0
A0=00000000 A1=00000000 A2=00000000 A3=00000000 N=0
A4=00000000 A5=00000000 A6=00000000 A7=00A00000 Z=0
D0=12345678 D1=00000078 D2=00005678 D3=12345678 V=0
D4=00000000 D5=00000000 D6=00000000 D7=00000000 C=0
---------->EXG       D0,A0
```

The next instruction, EXG D0, **A0**, exchanges the contents of a pair of registers to give

```
PC=00040E SR=2000 SS=00A00000 US=00000000           X=0
A0=12345678 A1=00000000 A2=00000000 A3=00000000 N=0
A4=00000000 A5=00000000 A6=00000000 A7=00A00000 Z=0
D0=00000000 D1=00000078 D2=00005678 D3=12345678 V=0
D4=00000000 D5=00000000 D6=00000000 D7=00000000 C=0
---------->SWAP      D3
```

The SWAP instruction swaps the upper and lower order words of a data register.

```
PC=000410 SR=2000 SS=00A00000 US=00000000           X=0
A0=12345678 A1=00000000 A2=00000000 A3=00000000 N=0
A4=00000000 A5=00000000 A6=00000000 A7=00A00000 Z=0
D0=00000000 D1=00000078 D2=00005678 D3=56781234 V=0
D4=00000000 D5=00000000 D6=00000000 D7=00000000 C=0
---------->MOVEA.L   $0420,A1
```

The MOVEA.L Data, **A1** and LEA Data, **A1** instructions have the following effects.

```
PC=000416 SR=2000 SS=00A00000 US=00000000           X=0
A0=12345678 A1=ABCDDCBA A2=00000000 A3=00000000 N=0
A4=00000000 A5=00000000 A6=00000000 A7=00A00000 Z=0
D0=00000000 D1=00000078 D2=00005678 D3=56781234 V=0
D4=00000000 D5=00000000 D6=00000000 D7=00000000 C=0
---------->LEA.L     $0420,A1
```

```
PC=00041C SR=2000 SS=00A00000 US=00000000           X=0
A0=12345678 A1=00000420 A2=00000000 A3=00000000 N=0
A4=00000000 A5=00000000 A6=00000000 A7=00A00000 Z=0
D0=00000000 D1=00000078 D2=00005678 D3=56781234 V=0
D4=00000000 D5=00000000 D6=00000000 D7=00000000 C=0
---------->STOP      #$2700
```

A `MOVEA.L Data,`**A1** instruction loads address register A1 with the contents of the operand `Data`, whereas `LEA Data,` **A1** loads A1 with the *address* of the operand (the significance of this will become clear later). We now look at instructions that do more than move data from one place to another.

6.3.2 Using arithmetic operations

We've already encountered arithmetic instructions. Now we demonstrate their use by writing a program to calculate $Z = (X^2 + Y^2)/(X - Y)$ where X and Y are 16-bit unsigned integers. The 68K provides 16-bit x 16-bit multiplication with a 32-bit product. The following program uses unsigned multiplication and division (`MULU` and `DIVU`). We will assume that X and Y are positive values and that $X > Y$.

```
        ORG     $400            Start of the program

        MOVE.W  X,D0            Put the value of X in D0
        MULU    D0,D0           Calculate X² (16-bit operands, 32-bit result)
        MOVE.W  Y,D1            Put the value of Y in D1
        MULU    D1,D1           Calculate Y²
        ADD.L   D0,D1           Add X² to Y² and put the 32-bit result in D1
        MOVE.W  X,D2            Put the value of X in D2
        SUB.W   Y,D2            Subtract Y from D2 to get D2 = X - Y
        DIVU    D2,D1           Divide D1 by D2 to get (X² + Y²)/(X - Y)³
        MOVE.W  D1,Z            Put the result now in D1 into Z
        STOP    #$2700

        ORG     $500            Put the data here

X       DC.W    50              Initial dummy value for variable X
Y       DC.W    12              Initial dummy value for variable Y
Z       DS.W    1               Reserve space for the result

        END     $400            End of program and address of entry point
```

Remember that you can't perform a memory-to-memory subtraction—you have to load one of the operands onto a data register. We assemble this program to create a listing file.

```
1   00000400                      ORG     $400      ;Start of the program
2
3   00000400 303900000500         MOVE.W  X,D0      ;Put the value of X in D0
4   00000406 C0C0                  MULU    D0,D0     ;Calculate X²
5   00000408 323900000502         MOVE.W  Y,D1      ;Put the value of Y in D1
6   0000040E C2C1                  MULU    D1,D1     ;Calculate Y²
7   00000410 D280                  ADD.L   D0,D1     ;Add X² to Y² and put result in D1
8   00000412 343900000500         MOVE.W  X,D2      ;Put the value of X in D2
9   00000418 947900000502         SUB.W   Y,D2      ;Subtract Y from D2 to get X - Y
10  0000041E 82C2                  DIVU    D2,D1     ;Divide D1 by D2 to get (X² + Y²)/(X - Y)
11  00000420 33C100000504         MOVE.W  D1,Z      ;Put the result now in D1 into Z
12  00000426 4E722700             STOP    #$2700

14  00000500                      ORG     $500      ;Put the data here
15
16  00000500 0032         X:      DC.W    50        ;Initial dummy value for X
17  00000502 000C         Y:      DC.W    12        ;Initial dummy value for Y
18  00000504 00000002     Z:      DS.W    1         ;Reserve space for the result
19
20           00000400             END     $400      ;End of program and address of entry point
```

---

[3] The `DIVU D2,`**D1** instruction divides the 32-bit value in D1 by the 16-bit value in D2. The 16-bit quotient is placed in the low-order word of D1 and the 16-bit remainder is placed in the upper-order word of D1.

We can use the simulator to run this program line by line and observe its execution. If we examine memory initially, we get.

```
000500  00 32 00 0C 00 00 00 00 00 00 00 00 00 00 00 00.
```

The first six digits 000500 give the first memory location on the line, and the following 16 pairs of digits give the contents of 16 consecutive bytes starting at the first location. Location 500_{16} contains $32_{16} = 50$, and location 502_{16} contains $0C_{16} = 12$. These values were set up by the two DC.W (define constant) assembler directives.

The state of the system prior to the execution of the first instruction is

```
PC=000400  SR=2000  SS=00A00000  US=00000000          X=0
A0=00000000  A1=00000000  A2=00000000  A3=00000000  N=0
A4=00000000  A5=00000000  A6=00000000  A7=00A00000  Z=0
D0=00000000  D1=00000000  D2=00000000  D3=00000000  V=0
D4=00000000  D5=00000000  D6=00000000  D7=00000000  C=0
---------->MOVE.W    $0500,D0
```

We are going to step through this program a line at a time and display the contents of the registers as we execute each instruction. Values that change are displayed in blue to make the program easier to follow.

```
PC=000406  SR=2000  SS=00A00000  US=00000000          X=0
A0=00000000  A1=00000000  A2=00000000  A3=00000000  N=0
A4=00000000  A5=00000000  A6=00000000  A7=00A00000  Z=0
D0=00000032  D1=00000000  D2=00000000  D3=00000000  V=0
D4=00000000  D5=00000000  D6=00000000  D7=00000000  C=0
---------->MULU.W    D0,D0
```

The instruction MOVE.W $0500,**D0** has been executed and the contents of memory location 500_{16} have been copied into data register D0.

```
PC=000408  SR=2000  SS=00A00000  US=00000000          X=0
A0=00000000  A1=00000000  A2=00000000  A3=00000000  N=0
A4=00000000  A5=00000000  A6=00000000  A7=00A00000  Z=0
D0=000009C4  D1=00000000  D2=00000000  D3=00000000  V=0
D4=00000000  D5=00000000  D6=00000000  D7=00000000  C=0
---------->MOVE.W    $0502,D1
```

We have just executed MULU D0,**D0** and the contents of D0 is $9C4_{16}$. This is $50 \times 50 = 2500 = 9C4_{16}$.

```
PC=00040E  SR=2000  SS=00A00000  US=00000000          X=0
A0=00000000  A1=00000000  A2=00000000  A3=00000000  N=0
A4=00000000  A5=00000000  A6=00000000  A7=00A00000  Z=0
D0=000009C4  D1=0000000C  D2=00000000  D3=00000000  V=0
D4=00000000  D5=00000000  D6=00000000  D7=00000000  C=0
---------->MULU.W    D1,D1
```

```
PC=000410 SR=2000 SS=00A00000 US=00000000          X=0
A0=00000000 A1=00000000 A2=00000000 A3=00000000 N=0
A4=00000000 A5=00000000 A6=00000000 A7=00A00000 Z=0
D0=000009C4 D1=00000090 D2=00000000 D3=00000000 V=0
D4=00000000 D5=00000000 D6=00000000 D7=00000000 C=0
---------->ADD.L    D0,D1
```

At this stage D1 contains $C_{16}^2 = 12 \times 12 = 144 = 90_{16}$.

```
PC=000412 SR=2000 SS=00A00000 US=00000000          X=0
A0=00000000 A1=00000000 A2=00000000 A3=00000000 N=0
A4=00000000 A5=00000000 A6=00000000 A7=00A00000 Z=0
D0=000009C4 D1=00000A54 D2=00000000 D3=00000000 V=0
D4=00000000 D5=00000000 D6=00000000 D7=00000000 C=0
---------->MOVE.W   $0500,D2
```

We have now calculated $X^2 + Y^2$ and deposited the result in data register D1.

```
PC=000418 SR=2000 SS=00A00000 US=00000000          X=0
A0=00000000 A1=00000000 A2=00000000 A3=00000000 N=0
A4=00000000 A5=00000000 A6=00000000 A7=00A00000 Z=0
D0=000009C4 D1=00000A54 D2=00000032 D3=00000000 V=0
D4=00000000 D5=00000000 D6=00000000 D7=00000000 C=0
---------->SUB.W    $0502,D2
```

```
PC=00041E SR=2000 SS=00A00000 US=00000000          X=0
A0=00000000 A1=00000000 A2=00000000 A3=00000000 N=0
A4=00000000 A5=00000000 A6=00000000 A7=00A00000 Z=0
D0=000009C4 D1=00000A54 D2=00000026 D3=00000000 V=0
D4=00000000 D5=00000000 D6=00000000 D7=00000000 C=0
---------->DIVU.W   D2,D1
```

```
PC=000420 SR=2000 SS=00A00000 US=00000000          X=0
A0=00000000 A1=00000000 A2=00000000 A3=00000000 N=0
A4=00000000 A5=00000000 A6=00000000 A7=00A00000 Z=0
D0=000009C4 D1=00160045 D2=00000026 D3=00000000 V=0
D4=00000000 D5=00000000 D6=00000000 D7=00000000 C=0
---------->MOVE.W   D1,$0504
```

The 68K instruction DIVU D2, **D1** divides the 32-bit contents of data register D1 by the lower-order 16 bits in data register D2. The result is a 16-bit quotient in the lower-order word of D1 and a 16-bit remainder in the upper-order word of D1. That is, $A54_{16}/9C4_{16} = 45_{16}$ remainder 16_{16}. The contents of D1 are $00160045.

```
PC=000426 SR=2000 SS=00A00000 US=00000000          X=0
A0=00000000 A1=00000000 A2=00000000 A3=00000000 N=0
A4=00000000 A5=00000000 A6=00000000 A7=00A00000 Z=0
D0=000009C4 D1=00160045 D2=00000026 D3=00000000 V=0
D4=00000000 D5=00000000 D6=00000000 D7=00000000 C=0
---------->STOP     #$2700
```

The MOVE.W D1, **$0504** stores the low-order 16-bit result in D1 in memory location 504_{16} (i.e. Z). We've used a *wordlength* operation and have discarded the remainder in the upper-order word of D1. Now we look at the contents of memory location 500 onward.

000500 00 32 00 0C **00 45** 00 00 00 00 00 00 00 00 00 00.

As you can see, memory location 504_{16} now contains the integer result of $(502 + 122)(50 - 12) = 45_{16} = 69$.

6.3.3 Using shift and logical operations

We now demonstrate the use of shift and logical operations. Logical shifts enable you to extract specific bits in a word. Consider an 8-bit byte in D0 with the format xxyyyzzz, where the xs, ys, and zs are three groups of bits that have been packed into a byte. Suppose we wish to extract the three ys from this byte.

```
LSR.B #3,D0         Shift D0 right 3 places to get 000xxyyy in D0
AND.B #%00000111,D0 Clear bits 3 to 7 of D0 to get 00000yyy
```

The first instruction LSR.B #3, **D0** shifts xxyyyzzz right to get 000xxyyy in D0. We remove the xs by means of the

logical operation AND.B #%00000111, **D0** to get 00000yyy in D0.

By using the NOT, AND, OR, and EOR instructions, you can perform any logical operations on a word. Suppose you wish to clear bits 0, 1, and 2, set bits 3, 4, and 5, and toggle bits 6 and 7 of the byte in D0. You could write

```
AND.B   #%11111000,D0   Clear bits 0, 1, and 2
OR.B    #%00111000,D0   Set bits 3, 4, and 5
EOR.B   #%11000000,D0   Toggle bits 6 and 7.
```

If [D0] initially contains 01010101, its final contents will be 10111000. We will look at a more practical application of bit manipulation after we have covered branch operations in a little more detail.

6.3.4 Using conditional branches

You can't write programs without using the conditional branches required to implement loops and other control constructs. We now look at the branch again and demonstrate its use. Consider the following example of an addition followed by a branch on negative (minus).

SHIFT OPERATIONS—A REMINDER

The assembly language forms of the 68K's shift instructions are

```
LSL #n,D0     shift contents of D0 n places left logically
LSR #n,D0     shift contents of D0 n places right logically
ASL #n,D0     shift contents of D0 n places left arithmetically
ASR #n,D0     shift contents of D0 n places right arithmetically
```

The integer *n* indicates the number of places to be shifted. These instructions can be applied to bytes, words, and long-words. If you shift a word by more than one place, the end value of the carry bit is determined by the final shift. Consider the following examples:

Initial contents of D0	Operation	Final contents of D0
11001100	LSL.B #1,**D0**	10011000
11001100	LSR.B #1,**D0**	01100110
11001100	ASL.B #1,**D0**	10011000
11001100	ASR.B #1,**D0**	11100110
1010111100001100	ASR.W #3,**D0**	1111010111100001
0011100001111101	ASR.W #4,**D0**	0000001110000111
11001110	ROL.B #1,**D0**	10011101
11001110	ROR.B #1,**D0**	01100111
11110000	ROL.B #2,**D0**	11000011

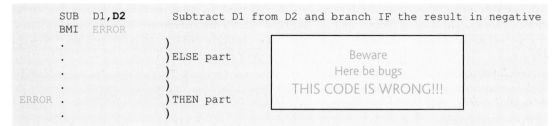

```
        SUB   D1,D2        Subtract D1 from D2 and branch IF the result in negative
        BMI   ERROR
        .            )
        .            ) ELSE part
        .            )
        .            )
ERROR   .            ) THEN part
        .            )
```

Beware
Here be bugs
THIS CODE IS WRONG!!!

The operation SUB D1,**D2** subtracts the contents of D1 from D2, deposits the results in D2, and updates the condition code register accordingly.

When the BMI instruction is executed, the branch is taken (the THEN part) if the N-bit of the CCR is set because the addition gave a negative result. The branch target is the line labeled by ERROR and the intervening code between BMI ERROR and ERROR . . . is not executed.

If the branch is not taken because the result of SUB D1,**D2** was positive, the code immediately following the BMI ERROR is executed. This code corresponds to the ELSE part of the IF THEN ELSE construction.

Unfortunately, there's an error in this example. Suppose that the subtraction yields a positive result and the ELSE part is executed. Once the ELSE code has been executed, we fall through to the THEN part and execute that too, which is not what we want to do. After the ELSE part has been executed, it's necessary to skip round the THEN part by means of an BRA instruction. The unconditional branch instruction, BRA EXIT forces the computer to execute the next instruction at

EXIT and skips past the 'ERROR' clause. Figure 6.10 demonstrates the flow of control for this program.

Remember we said earlier that not all the 68K's instructions affect the CCR. For example, consider the following two examples.

```
ADD   D1,D2   Add the contents of D1 to the contents of D2
BMI   ERROR   If the result is negative, branch to ERROR
```

and

```
ADD   D1,D2   Add the contents of D1 to the contents of D2
EXG   D3,A4   Exchange the contents of D3 and A4
EXG   D5,A6   Exchange the contents of D5 and A6
BMI   ERROR   If the result of the addition was negative,
              branch to ERROR
```

Both these fragments of code have the same effect as far as the BMI ERROR is concerned. However, the second case might prove confusing to the reader of the program who may well imagine that the state of the CCR prior to the BMI ERROR is determined by the EXG D3,DA instruction.

Example 1 Suppose you want to write a subroutine to convert a 4-bit hexadecimal value into its ASCII equivalent.

```
        SUB   D1,D2
        BMI   ERROR
        .            )   ELSE part
        .            )
        BRA   EXIT   Skip past the THEN part
ERROR   .            )
        .            )   THEN part
        .            )
EXIT
```

ASCII character	Hexadecimal value	Binary value
0	30	0000
1	31	0001
2	32	0010
3	33	0011
4	34	0100
5	35	0101
6	36	0110
7	37	0111
8	38	1000
9	39	1001
A	41	1010
B	42	1011
C	43	1100
D	44	1101
E	45	1110
F	46	1111

Table 6.1 Relationship between ISO/ASCII characters and hexadecimal values.

Figure 6.10 Flow of control for an IF . . . THEN . . . ELSE construct.

Table 6.1 illustrates the relationship between the binary value of a number (expressed in hexadecimal form) and its ASCII equivalent (also expressed in hexadecimal form). For example, if the internal binary value in a register is 00001010, its hexadecimal equivalent is A_{16}. In order to print the letter 'A' on a terminal, you have to transmit the ASCII code for the letter 'A' (i.e. \$41) to it. Once again, please note that there is a difference between the internal binary representation of a number within a computer and the code used represent the symbol for that number. The number six is expressed in 8 bits by the binary pattern 00000110 and is stored in the computer's memory in this form. On the other hand, the symbol for a six (i.e. '6') is represented by the binary pattern 00110110 in the ASCII code. If we want a printer to make a mark on paper corresponding to '6', we must send the binary number 00110110 to it. Consequently, numbers held in the computer must be converted to their ASCII forms before they can be printed.

From Table 6.1 we can derive an algorithm to convert a 4-bit internal value into its ASCII form. A hexadecimal value in the range 0 to 9 is converted into ASCII form by adding hexadecimal 30 to the number. A hexadecimal value in the range \$A to \$F is converted to ASCII by adding hexadecimal \$37. If we represent the number to be converted by HEX and the number to be converted by ASCII, we can write down a suitable algorithm in the form

$$\text{IF HEX} \leq 9_{16} \text{ THEN ASCII} = \text{HEX} + 30_{16}$$
$$\text{ELSE ASCII} = \text{HEX} + 37_{16}$$

We can rewrite the algorithm as

```
ASCII = HEX + $30
IF ASCII > $39 THEN ASCII = ASCII + 7
```

This algorithm can be translated into low-level language as

The CMP source, **destination** subtracts the source operand from the destination operand and sets the flag bits of the CCR accordingly; that is, a CMP is the same as a SUB except that the result is not recorded.

Example 2   Consider the following algorithm.

```
*   IF x = y THEN y = 6
*   IF x < y THEN y = y + 1
*
        CMP.B    D1,D0        Assume that x is in D0 and y in D1
        BNE      NotEqu       IF x = y THEN
        MOVE.B   #6,D1            y = 6
        BRA      exit             and leave the algorithm
NotEqu  BGE      exit         IF x ≤ y THEN exit
        ADD.B    #1,D1            ELSE y = y + 1
exit    .                     exit point for the algorithm
```

We perform *two* tests after the comparison CMP.B D0,**D1**. One is a BNE and the other a BGE. We can carry out the two tests in succession because there isn't an intervening instruction that modifies the state of the CCR.

Although conditional tests performed by high-level languages can be complex (e.g. IF X+Y−Z > 3t), the conditional test at the assembly language level is rather more basic as this example demonstrates.

Templates for control structures

We now represent some of the control structures of high-level languages as *templates* in assembly language. A template is a pattern or example that can be modified to suit the actual circumstances. In each of the following examples, the high-level construct is provided as a comment to the assembly language template by means of asterisks in the first column. The condition tested is [D0] = [D1] and the actions to be carried out are Action1 or Action2. The templates can be used by providing the appropriate test instead of CMP D0,**D1** and providing the appropriate sequence of assembly language statements instead of Action1 or Action2.

```
*                Note: D0.B holds HEX value on subroutine entry
*                      D0.B holds the ASCII character code on return
*                      No other register is modified by this subroutine
     ADD.B   #$30,D0     ASCII = HEX + $30
     CMP.B   #$39,D0     IF ASCII ≤ $39 THEN EXIT
     BLE     EXIT
     ADD.B   #7,D0                   ELSE ASCII = ASCII + 7
EXIT RTS
```

```
*           IF [D0] = [D1] THEN Action1
*
            CMP    D0,D1          Perform test
            BNE    EXIT           IF [D0] ≠ [D1] THEN exit
Action1     .                            ELSE execute Action1
            .
EXIT        .                     Exit point for construct
```

```
*           IF [D0] = [D1] THEN Action1 ELSE Action2
*
            CMP    D0,D1          Compare D0 with D1
            BNE    Action2        IF [D0] ≠ [D1] perform Action2
Action1     .                     Fall through to action1 if [D0] = [D1]
            .
            BRA    EXIT           Skip round Action2
Action2     .                     Action2
            .
EXIT        .                     Exit point for construct
```

```
*           FOR K = I TO J
*           .
*           ENDFOR
*
            MOVE   #I,D2          Load loop counter, D2, with I
Action1     .                     Perform Action1
            .
            ADD    #1,D2          Increment loop counter
            CMP    #J+1,D2        Test for end of loop
            BNE    Action1        IF not end THEN go round again
EXIT                                    ELSE exit
```

```
*           WHILE [D0] = [D1] Perform Action1
*
Repeat      CMP    D0,D1          Perform test
            BNE    EXIT           IF [D0] ≠ [D1] THEN exit
Action1     .                            ELSE carry out Action1
            .
            BRA    Repeat         REPEAT loop
EXIT                              Exit from construct
```

```
*           REPEAT Action1 UNTIL [D0] = [D1]
*
Action1     .                     Perform Action1
            .
            CMP    D0,D1          Carry out test
            BNE    Action1        REPEAT as long as [D0] ≠ [D1]
EXIT                              Exit from loop
```

```
*           CASE OF I
*           I = 0 Action0
*           I = 1 Action1
*           I = 2 Action2
*           I = 3 Action3
*           .
*           .
*           I = N ActionN
*           I > N Exception
*
            CMP.B    #N,I         Test for I out of range
            BGT      EXCEPTION    IF I > N THEN exception
            MOVE.W   I,D0         Pick up value of I in D0
            MULU     #4,D0        Each address is a longword
            LEA      Table,A0     A0 points to table of addresses
            LEA      (A0,D0),A0   A0 now points to case I in table
            MOVEA.L  (A0),A0      A0 contains address of case I handler
            JMP      (A0)         Execute case I handler
```

```
*
Table      ORG      <address>       Here is the table of exceptions
Action0    DC.L     <address0>      Address of case 0 handler
Action1    DC.L     <address1>      Address of case 1 handler
Action2    DC.L     <address2)      Address of case 2 handler
  .
  .
  .
ActionN    DC.L     <addressN>      Address of case N handler
*
EXCEPTION           ...             Exception handler here
```

The case number I stored in D0 must be multiplied by 4 before it can be added to the address in A0. This action is necessary because the cases numbers are consecutive integers 0, 1, 2, 3 while the addresses of the case handlers are consecutive longword addresses (i.e. A0 + 0, A0 + 4, A0 + 8, . . .).

Putting it all together

Consider a system with eight single-bit inputs (P, Q, R, S, T, U, V, W) and eight single-bit outputs (A, B, C, D, E, F, G, H). We're not interested in the details of input/output techniques here and assume that reading a memory location whose address is INPUT loads the values of P to W into a data register. Similarly, writing the contents of a data register to memory location OUTPUT sets up the eight output bits A to H. The formats of the input and output control words are defined in Fig. 6.11.

Suppose that a system has to implement the following control operation.

```
IF ((P = 1) AND (Q = 0)) OR ((P = 0) AND (S = 1))
    THEN C = 1; E = 0
    ELSE C = 0; E = 1
ENDIF
```

We have to translate this algorithm into 68K code. The above action involves the testing of three bits of INPUT (P, Q, and S), and then setting or clearing two bits of OUTPUT (C and E). The bits of OUTPUT not involved in the algorithm must not be affected in any way by operations on bits C and E.

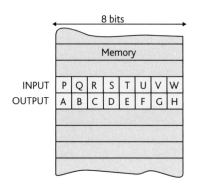

Figure 6.11 The memory map of two input/output ports.

Let's look again at the compare instruction, CMP, that compares two operands and sets the bits of the CCR accordingly. CMP.B #%0001000,**D0** compares the contents of D0 with the value 00010000_2 by evaluating $[D0] - 00010000$. The result is discarded, leaving the contents of D0 unaffected by the CMP operation. Only the bits of the CCR are modified. If D0 contains 00010000, the subtraction yields zero, setting the Z (zero) flag of the CCR. The following operation, BEQ TRUE, results in a branch to the instruction whose address is labeled TRUE. Comparison instructions are of the form CMP source, destination. The difference between CMP Di, **Dj** and SUB Di, **Dj** is that the former evaluates $Di - Dj$

```
         MOVE.B INPUT,D0           Get input status
         AND.B  #%11000000,D0      Mask out all bits but P and Q
         CMP.B  #%10000000,D0      Test for P = 1, Q = 0
         BEQ    TRUE               Goto action on test true
         MOVE.B INPUT,D0           Get input status again
         AND.B  #%10010000,D0      Mask out all bits but P and S
         CMP.B  #%00010000,D0      Test for P = 0, S = 1
         BEQ    TRUE               Goto action on test true
FALSE    MOVE.B OUTPUT,D0          Get the output control word
         AND.B  #%11011111,D0      Clear bit C
         OR.B   #%00001000,D0      Set bit E
         MOVE.B D0,OUTPUT          Set up new output control word
         BRA    EXIT               Branch past actions on test true
TRUE     MOVE.B OUTPUT,D0          Get the output control word
         AND.B  #%11110111,D0      Clear bit E
         OR.B   #%00100000,D0      Set bit C
         MOVE.B D0,OUTPUT          Set up new output control word
EXIT                               Continue
```

POINTS TO REMEMBER

The assembly language symbol % indicates that the following number is interpreted as a binary value and the symbol $ means that the following number is interpreted as a hexadecimal value. AND.B #%11000000,**D0** tells you much more than the hexadecimal and decimal forms of the operand, AND.B #$C0,**D0** and AND.B #192,**D0**, respectively.

The symbol # informs the assembler that the following value is not the address of a memory location containing the operand, but the actual operand itself. AND.B #%11000000,**D0** means calculate the logical AND between the binary value 11000000 and the contents of D0. If we had made a mistake in the program and had written AND.B %11000000,**D0** (rather than AND.B #%11000000,**D0**), the instruction would have ANDed D0 with the contents of memory location %11000000 (i.e. location 192).

---

and throws away the result, whereas the latter evaluates Di − Dj and puts the result in Dj.

The label FALSE is a dummy label and is not in any way used by the assembly program. It merely serves as a reminder to the programmer of the action to be taken as a result of the test being false. At the end of this sequence is an instruction BRA EXIT. A BRA (branch) is equivalent to a GOTO in a high-level language and causes a branch round the action taken if the result of the test is true.

6.4 Addressing modes

Addressing modes include all the ways of specifying the *location* of an operand used by an instruction. We encountered the fundamental addressing modes, absolute, immediate, and address register indirect, in the previous chapter. Now we demonstrate how some of these are used in assembly language programming and introduce a wealth of variations on address register indirect, addressing.

6.4.1 Immediate addressing

Application of immediate addressing
As an arithmetic constant

```
MOVE    NUM,D0        [D0]  ←  [NUM]
ADD     #22,D0        [D0]  ←  [D0] + 22
MOVE    D0,NUM        [NUM] ←  [D0]
```

This sequence of instructions is equivalent to the high-level language construct NUM = NUM + 22 and increases the value in memory location NUM by 22. That is, [NUM] ← [NUM] + 22. The 68K can, in fact, add an immediate operand to a memory location directly without using a data register by

---

REVIEW OF IMMEDIATE ADDRESSING

Immediate addressing allows the programmer to specify a constant as an operand. The value following the op-code in an instruction is not a reference to the address of an operand but is the actual operand itself. The symbol # precedes the operand to indicate immediate addressing. The four instructions below demonstrate how absolute and immediate addressing modes are represented in assembly language and in RTL.

Assembly language form	RTL form	Name
MOVE 1234,**D0**	[D0] ← [1234]	absolute addressing
MOVE #1234,**D0**	[D0] ← 1234	immediate addressing
ADD 1234,**D0**	[D0] ← [D0]+[1234]	absolute addressing
ADD #1234,**D0**	[D0] ← [D0]+1234	immediate addressing

The symbol # is not part of the instruction. It is a message to the assembler telling it to select that code for MOVE that uses the immediate addressing mode. Don't confuse the symbol # with the symbols $ or %. The $ indicates only that the following number is hexadecimal and the % indicates that the following number is binary. The instructions MOVE #25,**D0**, MOVE #$19,**D0**, and MOVE #%00011001,**D0** have identical effects.

Immediate addressing is used when the value of the operand required by an instruction is known at the time the program is written; that is, it is used to handle constants as opposed to variables. Immediate addressing is faster than absolute addressing, because only one memory reference is required to read the instruction during the fetch phase. When the instruction MOVE #5,**D0** is read from memory in a fetch cycle, the operand, 5, is available immediately without a further memory access to location 5, to read the actual operand.

SPECIAL 68K IMMEDIATE OPERATIONS

The 68K provides three instructions with immediate source operands, which allow you to perform an operation directly on the contents of a memory location. These operations can be called data-to-memory and are indicated by appending an I to the instruction mnemonic. The three instructions with this facility are ADDI, SUBI, and CMPI. Consider

```
CMPI.B #42,$1234    Compare the contents of location $1234 with 42
SUB.W  #$F23D,(A0)  Subtract F23D₁₆ from the contents of the
                    memory location pointed at by A0
```

---

means of the special add immediate instruction ADDI. For example, ADDI #22,**NUM** adds the constant value 22 to the contents of the location called NUM.

In a comparison with a constant

Consider the test on a variable, NUM, to determine whether it lies in the range $7 < NUM < 25$.

```
        MOVE   NUM,D0      Get NUM in D0
        CMP    #8,D0       Compare it with 8
        BMI    FALSE       IF negative NUM ≤ 7
        CMP    #25,D0      Compare it with 25
        BPL    FALSE       IF positive NUM > 24
TRUE    ...
          .
          .
FALSE   ...
```

As a method of terminating loop structures.

A typical loop structure in both Java and C is illustrated below.

```
for (i=0; i < N+1; i++)
    {
      ...
      ...  ;
    }
```

The high-level language FOR construct may readily be translated into 68K assembly language. In the following example, the loop counter is stored in data register D0.

such as N+1, the assembler evaluates it and replaces it by the calculated value—in this example #N+1 is replaced by 11. We use the comparison with N + 1, because the counter is incremented before it is tested. On the last time round the loop, the variable I becomes N + 1 after incrementing and the branch to NEXT is not taken, allowing the loop to be exited. This loop construct can be written in a more elegant fashion, but at this point we're interested only in the application of immediate addressing as a means of setting up counters.

6.4.2 Address register indirect addressing

In address register indirect addressing, the operand is specified indirectly via the contents of a pointer register. RISC processors allow any register to act as a pointer, whereas the 68K reserves address registers for this function. The box provides a review of this addressing mode.

Using address register indirect addressing to access a table

Figure 6.12 demonstrates how you'd add up a sequence of numbers using ADD.B (A0), **D0**. The computer reads the contents of address register A0 (i.e. 1000_{16}) and then reads the contents of memory location 1000_{16} (i.e. 25). This operand is then added to the contents of D0.

```
N    EQU   10       Define the loop size - we've used N = 10 here
       .
       .
     MOVE  #1,D0    Load D0 with initial value of the loop counter
NEXT ...            Start of loop
       .
       .
                    Body of loop
       .
       .
     ADD   #1,D0    Increment the loop counter
     CMP   #N+1,D0  Test for the end of the loop
     BNE   NEXT     IF not end THEN repeat loop
```

At the end of the loop, the counter is incremented by ADD #1,**D0**. The counter, D0, is then compared with its terminal value by CMP #N+1,**D0**. If you write an expression

We can add 100 numbers by means of address register indirect addressing in the following way. This isn't efficient code—we'll write a better version later.

REVIEW OF ADDRESS REGISTER INDIRECT ADDRESSING

Register indirect addressing specifies the address of an operand by the contents of an address register. The diagram illustrates the effect of MOVE.B (A0), **D0** when [A0] = 1000_{16}. The computer first reads the contents of address register A0 and then reads the contents of memory pointed at by A0. The contents of A0 are 1000, so the processor reads the contents of memory location 1000 to get the actual operand, 25.

Some texts call this addressing mode *indexed addressing* or *modifier-based addressing*. The manufacturers of the 68K reserve the term *indexed addressing* to indicate a particular variant of address register indirect addressing in which the effective address of an operand is calculated by adding the contents of two registers.

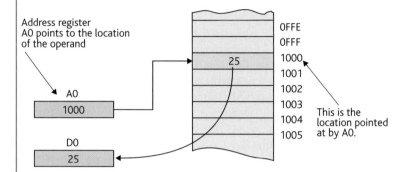

The following instructions illustrate address register indirect addressing and provide RTL definitions for the action to be carried out, together with a plain language description.

Assembly language	RTL definition	Description
MOVE (A0), **D0**	[D0] ← [[A0]]	Move the contents of the memory pointed at by A0 to D0
MOVE D1, **(A2)**	[[A2]] ← [D1]	Move the contents of D1 to the location pointed at by A2
ADD (A1), **D2**	[D2] ← [D2] + [[A1]]	Add the contents of the location pointed at by A1 to the contents of D2
MOVE (A1), **(A2)**	[[A2]] ← [[A1]]	Move the contents of the location pointed at by A1 to the location pointed at by A2

```
        ORG    $001000      Start of the program
        CLR    D0           D0 is the number counter
        MOVEA  #NUM1,A0      A0 points to the first number
        CLR    D1           Clear the total in D1
LOOP    ADD    (A0),D1       Add in the number pointed at by A0
        ADDA   #2,A0         Point to the next number in the list
        ADD    #1,D0         Increment the number counter
        CMP    #100,D0       Have we added the 100 numbers?
        BNE    LOOP          If not then repeat
        STOP   #$2700       Halt the program
        ORG    $2000        Data region
NUM1    DC.W   1,2,3,4,5    Dummy data (only 5 numbers given here)
        END    $1000
```

The pointer in address register A0 is incremented by 2 on each pass round the loop—the increment of 2 is required because the memory elements are words and each word occupies 2 bytes in memory. We can express this program in a more compact way.

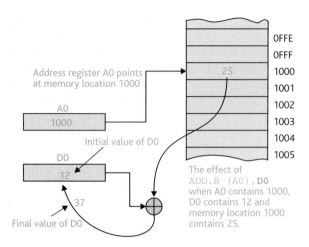

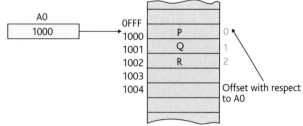

Figure 6.14 Using address register indirect addressing with displacement.

Figure 6.12 Using address register indirect addressing.

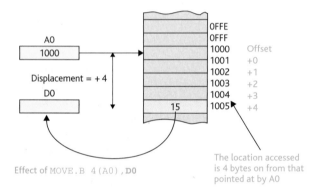

Effect of MOVE.B 4(A0),D0

Figure 6.13 An illustration of address register indirect addressing with displacement.

```
        LEA     NUM1,A0     A0 points at the list of numbers¹
        CLR     D0          Clear the total
        MOVE    #99,D1      Set up the counter for 100 cycles
LOOP    ADD     (A0),D0     Add in a number
        ADDA.L  #2,A0       Point to next number
        DBRA    D1,LOOP     Repeat until all numbers added
```

The 68K's decrement and branch instruction DBRA **D1**, LOOP implements a loop. This instruction subtracts 1 from the contents of D1 and branches back to the line labeled by LOOP. If, however, D1 is decremented and goes from 0 to −1, the loop is not taken and the next instruction in sequence is executed. Because the branch terminates on −1 rather than 0, loading D1 with N causes DBRA **D1**, LOOP to execute N+1 times.

Address register indirect addressing with displacement

A more general form of the 68K's address register indirect addressing mode is called the *address register indirect addressing mode with displacement*. The effective address is written

d16(Ai), where d16 is a 16-bit constant and Ai an address register. The effective address of an operand is calculated by adding the contents of the address register specified by the instruction to the signed two's complement constant that forms part of the instruction. Figure 6.13 illustrates how the effective address is calculated for the instruction MOVE.B 4(A0),**D0**. Some 68K simulators permit you to write either MOVE.B 4(A0),**D0** or MOVE.B (4,A0),**D0**.

We can define MOVE d16(A0),**D0** in RTL as [D0]←[d16 + [A0]], where d16 is a 16-bit two's complement value in the range −32K to 32K. This constant is called a *displacement* or *offset* because it indicates how far the operand is located from the location pointed at by A0. The displacement can be negative; for example; MOVE.B −4(A0), **D0** specifies an operand 4 bytes back from the location pointed at by A0.

Why would you wish to use this addressing mode? Consider the data structure of Fig. 6.14 where three variables P, Q, and R, have consecutive locations on memory. If we load address register A0 with the address of the first variable, P, we can access each variable via the pointer in A0.

In this fragment of code we define the displacements P, Q, and R as 0, 1, and 2, respectively.

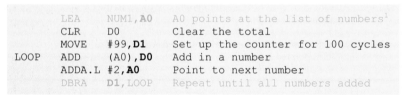

```
P       EQU     0
Q       EQU     1
R       EQU     2
        .
        .
        .
        LEA     Block,A0    A0 points to "Block"
        MOVE.B  P(A0),D0    Evaluate R = P + Q
        ADD.B   Q(A0),D0
        MOVE.B  D0,R(A0)
```

---

⁴ The LEA or *load effective address* instruction loads an address register with an address. The effect of LEA NUM1, **A0** is to load A0 with the address NUM1 (and not the contents of NUM1). This instruction is equivalent to MOVEA.L #NUM1, **A0**. The LEA instruction doesn't require a # symbol to indicate a literal operand because the source operand is always an address.

This code adds two numbers and stores their sum in memory. But where in memory? The location of the three numbers is Block + P, Block + Q, and Block + R, respectively. Because the value of Block can be changed by the programmer, we can locate the variables P, Q, and R in any three consecutive locations anywhere in memory. Why would we want to do that? If we access variables by specifying their location with respect to a pointer, we can move the program about in memory without having to recalculate all addresses.

Using address register indirect addressing with displacement

Let's look at an example of this addressing mode that involves vectors. A vector is composed of a sequence of components; for example, the vector X might be composed of four elements x_0, x_1, x_2, x_3. One of the most common of all mathematical calculations (because it crops up in many different areas—particularly graphics) is the evaluation of the inner or scalar product of two vectors. Suppose **A** and **B** are two n-component vectors; the inner product S, of **A** and **B**, is given by

$$S = \sum a_i \cdot b_i = a_0 \cdot b_0 + a_1 \cdot b_1 + \cdots + a_{n-1} \cdot b_{n-1}$$

If **A** = (1, 3, 6) and **B** = (2, 3, 5), the inner product S is given by $1 \cdot 2 + 3 \cdot 3 + 6 \cdot 5 = 41$. Consider the case in which the components of vectors **A** and **B** are 16-bit integers.

```
N        EQU     $10           16 components (N = 16)
         ORG     $001000       Origin of program
         CLR     D0            [D0] ← 0
         SUBA.L  A0,A0         [A0] ← 0
LOOP     MOVE    VEC1(A0),D1   [D1] ← [[A0] + VEC1]
         MULU    VEC2(A0),D1   [D1] ← [D1] * [[A0] + VEC2]
         ADD     D1,D0         [D0] ← [D0] + [D1]
         ADDA.L  #2,A0         [A0] ← [A0] + 2
         CMPA.L  #2*N,A0       [A0] - 2N ← note N words = 2N bytes
         BNE     LOOP          IF Z = 0 THEN [PC] ← LOOP
         MOVE    D0,S          [S] ← [D0]
*
         ORG     $002000       Origin of data
S        DS      1             Reserve a word for the product
VEC1     DS      $20           Reserve 16 words for Vector1
VEC2     DS      $20           Reserve 16 words for Vector2
```

The instruction MULU <ea>,**Di** multiplies the 16-bit word at the effective address specified by <ea> by the lower-order word in D_i. The 32-bit longword product is loaded into $D_{i(0:31)}$. MULU operates on unsigned values and uses two 16-bit source operands to yield a 32-bit destination operand. As the 68K lacks a *clear address register* instruction, we have to use either MOVEA.L #0,**A0** or the faster SUBA.L A0,**A0** to clear A0.

Note the instruction CMPA.L #2*N,**A0** containing the expression 2*N, which is automatically evaluated by the assembler. The assembler looks up the value of N (equated to $10) and multiples it by 2 to get $20. Consequently, the assembler treats CMPA.L #2*N,**A0** as CMPA.L #$20,**A0**.

Variations on a theme

The 68K supports two variations on address register indirect addressing. One is called address register indirect addressing with *predecrementing* and the other is called address register indirect addressing with *postincrementing*. The former addressing mode is written in assembly language as − (Ai) and the latter (Ai) +. Both these addressing modes use address register indirect addressing to access an operand exactly as we've described. However, the postincrementing mode automatically *increments* the address register *after* it's been used, whereas the predecrementing mode automatically *decrements* the address register *before* it's used. Figure 6.15 demonstrates the operation ADD.B (A0) +,**D0**. This instruction adds the contents of the location pointed at by A0 (i.e. P) to the contents of data register D0. After A0 has been used to access P, the value of A0 is incremented to point at the next element, Q.

Address register indirect addressing is used to access tables. If we access an item by MOVE.B (A0),**D0**, the next item (i.e. byte) in the table can be accessed by first updating the address pointer, A0, by ADDA #1,**A0** and then repeating the MOVE.B (A0),**D0**. The 68K's automatic postincrementing mode increments an address register after it has been used to access an operand. This addressing mode is indicated by (Ai) +. Consider the following examples of address register indirect addressing with post incrementing.

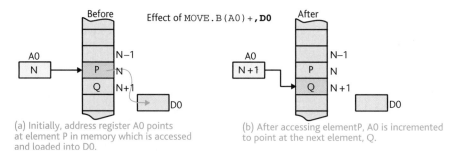

(a) Initially, address register A0 points at element P in memory which is accessed and loaded into D0.

(b) After accessing elementP, A0 is incremented to point at the next element, Q.

Figure 6.15 Address register indirect addressing with postincrementing.

LEGAL AND ILLEGAL ADDRESSING MODES

Because of the real-world constraints imposed by the encoding of instructions and the design of the chips themselves, not all possible variations on addressing modes are supported. Both the predecrementing and postincrementing addressing modes don't support an offset in the calculation of an effective address; that is, only (Ai)+ and −(Ai) are legal. To make this clear, we present several 68K instructions—some of these represent legal and some represent illegal addressing modes.

```
ADD.W    (A2)-,D2        illegal—postdecrementing not allowed
MOVE.W   D0,(12,A1)+     illegal—offset not allowed with postincrementing
MOVE.W   -(A2),(A3)+     legal
SUB.W    D3,+(A4)        illegal—preincrementing not allowed
CMP.W    (A6)+,D3        legal
```

Assembly language form	RTL definition
ADD.B (A2)+,**D2**	[D2] ← [D2] + [[A2]]; [A2] ← [A2] + 1
MOVE.B D0, **(A1)+**	[[A1]] ← [D0]; [A1] ← [A1] + 1
CLR.W **(A0)+**	[[A0]] ← 0; [A0] ← [A0] + 2
MOVE.W (A2)+, **(A3)+**	[[A3]] ← [[A2]]; [A2] ← [A2] + 2; [A3] ← [A3] + 2
CLR.L **(A0)+**	[[A0]] ← 0; [A0] ← [A0] + 4

The pointer register is automatically incremented by 1 for byte operands, 2 for word operands, and 4 for longword operands. Consider the following examples.

```
MOVE.B   (A0)+,D5  ←   [D5(0:7)]  ← [[A0]]; [A0] ← [A0] + 1
MOVE.L   (A0)+,D5  ←   [D5(0:31)] ← [[A0]]; [A0] ← [A0] + 4
```

Examples of register indirect addressing with postincrementing

The 68K provides a predecrementing address register indirect addressing mode with the assembly language form

(A2)+, **D5**. Postincrementing leaves A2 pointing to the new top item on the stack.

Let's revisit the program to add together 100 numbers stored in consecutive locations.

```
       LEA    NUM1,A0      A0 points at list of numbers
       CLR.W  D0           Clear the total
       MOVE.W #99,D1       Set up the counter for 100 cycles
LOOP   ADD.W  (A0)+,D0     Add in a number and move the pointer to next
       DBRA   D1,LOOP      Repeat until all numbers added
```

−(Ai), where the contents of Ai are decremented before they are used to access the operand at the address pointed at by Ai. As above, the predecrement is by 1, 2, or 4, depending on whether the operand is a byte, word, or longword, respectively.

Predecrementing and postincrementing are complementary operations because one undoes the other. Suppose we use MOVE D3,−(A2) to store the contents of D3 on a stack in memory. MOVE D3,−(**A2**) decrements A2 and then copies D3 to the top of the stack pointed at by A2. After this instruction has been executed, A2 is pointing to the top item on the stack. We can remove D3 from the stack and put it in D5 by executing MOVE

The instruction ADD.W (A0)+, **D0** adds the number pointed at by A0 to the contents of D0 and then moves the pointer to point to the next number in the sequence.

Let's look at another example of this postincrementing addressing mode. Suppose we have a table of N unsigned integer bytes and wish to locate the value of the largest. The number of bytes is less than 256. A simple pseudocode algorithm to do this is

```
largest = 0
FOR i = 0 to N-1
    read number_i
    if (number_i > largest) THEN largest = number_i
END_FOR
```

This pseudocode uses the notation number$_i$ to indicate the ith element in a sequence. We can express this in 68K assembly language as

If we use MOVE.B (A0)+, **D0**, the contents of address register A0 incremented to 1001_{16} after the character located at 1000 has been accessed and we are ready to access

```
        ORG      $400
N       EQU      10             Assume a dummy value of N = 10 (number of elements)
        CLR.B    D0             Use D0 as largest and set it to 0
        MOVE.W   #N-1,D1        Use D1 as a counter and preset it to N-1
        LEA      List,A0        Use A0 as a pointer to the list
Next    MOVE.B   (A0)+,D2       Read a number
        CMP.B    D0,D2          Is new number > largest?
        BPL      Last           If it isn't, go and check for end of loop
        MOVE.B   D2,D0          It is, record the new largest number
Last    DBRA     D1,Next        Repeat until count exhausted
        STOP     #$2700
        ORG      $1000          Let's put some test values here
List    DC.B     1,4,8,6,2,3,7,6,9,3
        END      $400
```

Addressing modes and strings

A string is a sequence of consecutive characters. We will assume the characters are 8-bit ASCII-encoded values. It's necessary to indicate a string's size in order to process it. You could store a string as n, char_1, char_2, . . . , char_n, where n is the length of the string. For example, the ASCII-encoded string 'ABC' might be stored in memory as the sequence $03, $41, $42, $43.

You can also use a special terminator or marker to indicate the end of a string. Of course, the terminator must not occur naturally in the string. If the terminator is the null byte, the string 'ABC' would be stored as the sequence $41, $42, $43, $00. Some strings use the terminator $0D because this is the ASCII code for a carriage return.

The address of a string in memory is usually of the first character in the string. Figure 6.16 shows a 10-character string located at location 1000_{16} in memory and terminated by a null byte (i.e. 0).

Most microprocessors don't permit direct operations on strings (e.g. you can't compare two strings using a single instruction). You have to process a string by using byte operations to access individual characters, one by one. The characters of a string can be accessed by means of address register indirect addressing. In Fig. 6.16, address register A0 contains the value 1000_{16}, which is the address or location of the first character in the string.

The operation MOVE.B (A0), **D0** copies the byte pointed at by the contents of address register A0 into data register D0. Applying this instruction to Fig. 6.16 would copy the character 'T' into data register D0 (the actual data loaded into D0 is, of course, the ASCII code for a letter 'T').

the next character in the string. Consider the following example.

Counting characters Suppose we want to count the number of characters in the string pointed at by address register A0 and return the string length in D3. The string is terminated by the null character, which is included in the character count.

```
        MOVE.B   #0,D3         Preset the character counter to 0
Again   MOVE.B   (A0)+,D0      Get a character into D0
        ADD.B    #1,D3         Increment the character counter
        CMP.B    #0,D0         Is the character a null?
        BNE      Again         Repeat until zero found
```

At the end of this code, address register A0 will be pointing at the next location immediately following the string. We can rewrite this fragment of code.

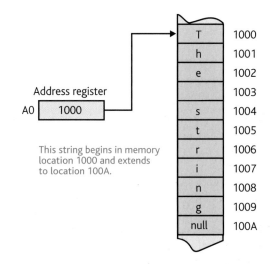

Figure 6.16 Example of a string.

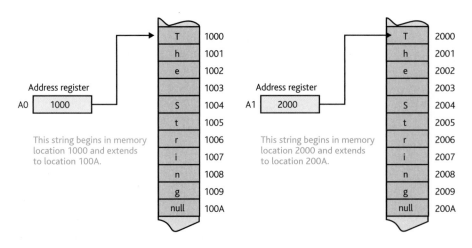

Figure 6.17 Comparing two strings.

```
          CLR.B    D3        Preset the character counter to 0
Again     MOVE.B   (A0)+,D0  Get a character into D0
          ADD.B    #1,D3     Increment the character counter
          TST.B    D0        Is the character a null?
          BNE      Again     Repeat until zero found
```

The new instruction, TST, tests an operand by comparing it with zero and setting the flag bits in the CCR accordingly.

Counting A's Suppose we want to count the number of times 'A' occurs in a string that starts at address Find_A.

```
          LEA      Find_A,A0  A0 points at the start of the string
          CLR.B    D1         Clear the A's counter
Next      MOVE.B   (A0)+,D0   REPEAT Get a character
          CMP.B    #'A',D0            IF 'A'
          BNE      Test
          ADD.B    #1,D1             THEN increment A's counter
          BRA      Next
Test      TST.B    D0         UNTIL terminator found
          BNE      Next
```

The instruction CMP.B #'A',D0 compares the contents of D0 (i.e. the last character read from the string) with the source operand, #'A'. The # symbol means the actual value and the 'A' means the number whose value is the ASCII code for the letter A. If you omit the # symbol, the processor will read the contents of memory location 41_{16} (because 'A' $= 41_{16}$). Because the MOVE instruction sets the CCR, we can test for the terminator as soon as we pick up a character, as the following code demonstrates.

Comparing strings Suppose we wish to test whether two strings are identical. Figure 6.17 shows two strings in memory. One is located at 1000_{16} and the other at 2000_{16}. In this case both strings are identical.

In order to compare the strings we have to read a character at a time from each string. If, at any point, the two characters do not match, the strings are not identical. If we reach two null characters, the strings are the same. A0 points at one string and A1 points at the other. We will set D7 to a zero if the strings are not the same, and one if they are the same.

```
          LEA      Find_A,A0  A0 points at the start of the string
          CLR.B    D1         Clear the A's counter
Next      MOVE.B   (A0)+,D0   REPEAT Get a character
          BEQ      Exit             Exit on null character
          CMP.B    #'A',D0          IF 'A'
          BNE      Next
          ADD.B    #1,D1             THEN increment A's counter
          BRA      Next       END REPEAT
Exit
```

```
         CLR.B    D7              Assume the strings are not the same
Next     MOVE.B   (A0)+,D0        Read a character from the first string
         CMP.B    (A1)+,D0        Compare it with a char from the second string
         BNE      NotSame         IF not the same THEN exit
         TST.B    D0              REPEAT unit terminator found
         BNE      Next
         MOVE.B   #1,D7           IF terminator found then strings are equal
NotSame ....
```

Removing spaces A common string manipulation problem is the removal of multiple spaces in text. If you enter a command into a computer like delete X, Y, Z the various component parts (i.e. fields) of the command are first analyzed. A *command line processor* might remove multiple spaces before processing the command. Figure 6.18 shows how we might go about dealing with this problem. On the left, the string has three spaces. On the right, the same string has been rewritten with only one space.

Because the final string will be the same size or shorter than the original string, we can simply move up characters when we find a multiple space. We can use two pointers, one to point at the original string and one to point at the final string.

We read characters from the string and copy them to their destination until a space is encountered. The first space encountered is copied across. We continue to read characters from the source string but do not copy them across if they are further spaces. This algorithm requires some care. If we are searching for multiple spaces, we will move one character beyond the space because of the autoincrementing addressing mode. Therefore, we have to adjust the pointer before continuing.

Figure 6.19 demonstrates the operation of this algorithm. By the way, there is a flaw in this program. What happens if the end of the string is a space followed by a null? How can you fix the problem?

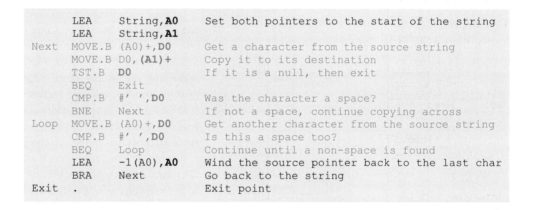

```
         LEA      String,A0       Set both pointers to the start of the string
         LEA      String,A1
Next     MOVE.B   (A0)+,D0        Get a character from the source string
         MOVE.B   D0,(A1)+        Copy it to its destination
         TST.B    D0              If it is a null, then exit
         BEQ      Exit
         CMP.B    #' ',D0         Was the character a space?
         BNE      Next            If not a space, continue copying across
Loop     MOVE.B   (A0)+,D0        Get another character from the source string
         CMP.B    #' ',D0         Is this a space too?
         BEQ      Loop            Continue until a non-space is found
         LEA      -1(A0),A0       Wind the source pointer back to the last char
         BRA      Next            Go back to the string
Exit     .                        Exit point
```

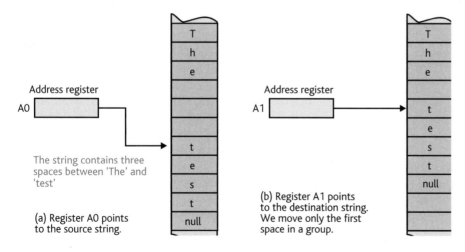

(a) Register A0 points to the source string.

The string contains three spaces between 'The' and 'test'

(b) Register A1 points to the destination string. We move only the first space in a group.

Figure 6.18 Removing spaces from a string.

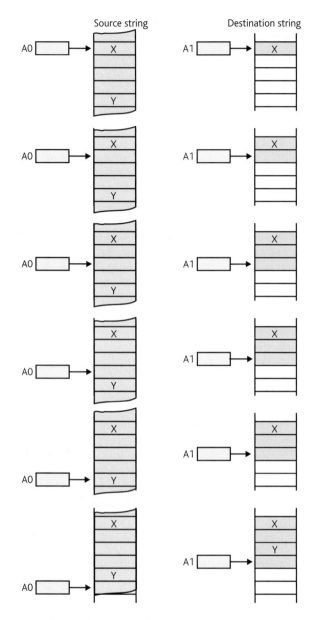

Figure 6.19 Deleting multiple spaces.

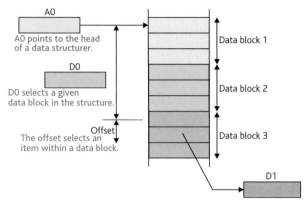

Figure 6.20 Indexed addressing—executing
MOVE.B Offset(A0,D0),**D1**.

Indexed addressing

The 68K provides a variant on the address register indirect addressing mode called *indexed addressing*, which uses two registers to calculate the effective address of an operand. The assembly language form of the effective address is written d8(Ai,Xj), where d8 is an 8-bit signed constant forming part of the instruction, Ai is one of the eight address registers, and Xi is either one of D0–D7 or A0–A7. The effective address is calculated from the expression d8+[Ai]+[Xi]; for example, CLR   28(A3,D6) clears the contents of the location whose effective address is given by the contents of A3

plus the contents of D6 plus 28, that is, [28 + [A3] + [D6]] ← 0. Note that modern 68K assemblers permit you to write either TUESDAY(A0,D0) or (TUESDAY, A0,D0).

Indexed addressing is a variation on address register indirect addressing. Instead of using one pointer register, the effective address is given by the sum of the contents of two registers and a displacement. The displacement in indexed addressing lies in the range −128 to +127, whereas the displacement in address register indirect addressing is −32K to +32K. Indexed addressing can be used to access two-dimensional tables in which the location of an element is specified by its row and its column position.

Figure 6.20 illustrates MOVE.B Offset(A0,D0),**D1**. You can regard A0 as pointing at the beginning of a data structure. In this example, we've shown three blocks of data. By adding the contents of D0 to A0 we can select a specific data block in the structure. In the example of Fig. 6.20, the contents of D0 would be 6 (if each data block occupied 3 bytes).

By adding a constant to the effective address created by adding the two registers, we can access a particular element of one of the data blocks. In Fig. 6.20, the offset is 1.

Consider a data structure representing a diary that consists of several weeks, each of which is divided into 7 days. An item of data is accessed by locating the head of the data structure, counting off the appropriate number of weeks, and then accessing the required day. If the location of the array in memory is called DIARY and we wish to access the location corresponding to Tuesday of week five, we need to access location DIARY + (WEEK-1)*7 + Tuesday. If Tuesday = 2, the location of the required element is DIARY + (5−1) * 7 + 2 = DIARY + 30.

The data structure can be accessed using indexed addressing by loading A0 with DIARY and D0 with the location of the

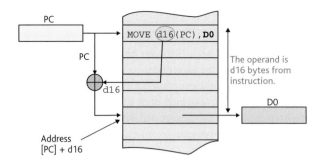

Figure 6.21 Program counter relative addressing—the effect of MOVE d16(PC),**D0**.

d16(PC), for example, the operation 'Load data register D0 relative' is written

MOVE d16(PC),**D0**

and is defined as [D0] ← [[PC] + d16]. As before, d16 is a 16-bit two's complement offset that is normally written in symbolic form and whose value is calculated by the assembler. Figure 6.21 demonstrates the relationship between the PC, the instruction, and the operand address. Figure 6.21 is slightly simplified because the 68K's program counter is automatically incremented by 2 after the instruction fetch phase.

Relative addressing lets you write *position-independent code* (PIC), which avoids absolute addresses. The machine code version of a program written in PIC is independent of the physical location of the program in memory. You can

start of the desired week, and then using the desired day as a constant as demonstrated in the following fragment of code.

```
SUNDAY     EQU   0
MONDAY     EQU   1
TUESDAY    EQU   2
WEDNESDAY  EQU   3
  .
  .
           LEA     DIARY,A0         A0 points to head of structure
           MOVE.L  WEEK,D0          D0 contains week number
           SUB.L   #1,D0            Calculate (Week - 1)*7
           MULU    #7,D0            D0 now contains number of days
           MOVE.B  TUESDAY(A0,D0),D1  Access the required item
```

6.4.3 **Relative addressing**

Before we introduce this addressing mode, we'll pose a problem. Consider the operation MOVE $1234,**D0**, which specifies the absolute address $1234 as a source operand location. If you were to take the program containing this instruction and its data and locate it in a different region of memory, would it work? No. Why not? Because the data accessed by the instruction is no longer in location $1234. The only way to run this program is to change all operand addresses to their new locations. Relative addressing provides a means of relocating programs *without* changing addresses.

Relative addressing is similar to address register indirect addressing because the effective address of an operand is given by the contents of a register plus a displacement. However, relative addressing uses the *program counter* to calculate the effective address rather than an address register; that is, the location of the operand is specified relative to the current instruction. The syntax of a 68K relative address is

move (i.e. relocate) PIC programs in memory without modifying them. MOVE 36(PC),**D0** means load data register D0 with the contents of the memory location 36 locations on from this instruction. It doesn't matter where the operation MOVE 36(PC),**D0** lies in memory, because the data associated with it will always be stored in the 36th location following the instruction.

Calculating the displacement required by an instruction using program counter relative addressing is difficult. Fortunately, you never have to perform this calculation—the assembler does it for you. Consider the following example.

```
        ORG      $400
        MOVE.B   Value1,D0      Put Value1 in D0
        MOVE.B   Value1(PC),D1  Put Value1 in D1
        STOP     #$2700
Value1  DC.B     $23
        END      $400
```

Let's assemble this code and see what happens.

```
1   00000400                        ORG     $400
2   00000400 10390000040E           MOVE.B  Value1,D0      ;Put Value1 in D0
3   00000406 123A0006               MOVE.B  Value1(PC),D1  ;Put Value1 in D1
4   0000040A 4E722700               STOP    #$2700
5   0000040E 23         Value1:     DC.B    $23
6            00000400               END     $400
```

The address of operand `Value1` is $0000040E (as a 32-bit longword). The instruction on line 2, `MOVE.B Value1,D0`, contains an opcode ($1039) and the absolute address of the operand ($0000040E).

Now look at the instruction on line 3, `MOVE.B Value1(PC),D1`. The opcode is $123A and the operand is the 16-bit value $0006. When the 68K reads an instruction, the program counter is automatically incremented by 2. Once `MOVE.B Value1(PC),D1` has been read from memory, the program counter is incremented by 2 from $00000406 to $00000408. If we add the offset $0006 to $00000408, we get $0000040E, which is the address of the operand `Value1`.

You can use relative addressing for *source* operands, but not for *destination* operands. You can specify where an operand comes from but not where it is going to by means of relative addressing (this restriction is a 68K design decision and not a fundamental limitation). The instructions `MOVE 12(PC),D3` and `ADD  8(PC),D2` are legal instructions, whereas `MOVE D3,12 (PC)` and `ADD D2,8 (PC)` are illegal.

We can write completely position-independent code for the 68K by loading the address of the operand into an address register using position-independent code and then using address register indirect addressing to access operands in memory. We use the `LEA` (load effective address) instruction to load an address into an address register. Note that the instructions `MOVEA.L #Temp7,A0` and `LEA Temp7,A0` are equivalent. Consider the following examples of this instruction.

Relative branching

We've already met the branch instructions (e.g. `BEQ`, `BNE`), which can force a branch to the *target* address. What we haven't said is that the target address is expressed relative to the current value of the program counter. Most microprocessors have a relative branching mode in which the destination of a branch instruction is expressed with reference to the current address in the program counter. Figure 6.22 illustrates relative addressing by means of a memory map; Fig. 6.22(a) illustrates the instruction `BRA XYZ`, Fig. 6.22(b) shows how the instruction is encoded, and Fig. 6.22(c) shows a jump instruction that performs the same function with an absolute address.

Figure 6.22(a) illustrates `BRA XYZ`, where `XYZ` is the target address. The machine code form (Fig. 6.22(b)), shows that the offset corresponding to XYZ is stored as 4 because the target address is 4 bytes beyond the end of the branch instruction. Remember that the program counter is automatically incremented by two after the `BRA` instruction is read during an instruction fetch. The programmer doesn't have to worry about short and long branches, or about calculating the branch offset. If you write `BRA ABC`, the assembler computes the offset as `ABC` − `[PC]` − 2. Figure 6.22(c) demonstrates the `JMP XYZ` instruction, which uses an *absolute address*; that is, XYZ is stored as $1006.

The offset used by a relative branch is an 8-bit signed two's complement number in the range −128 to +127. As 2 is

Assembly language form	RTL definition	
LEA $1000,**A0**	[A0] ← 1000$_{16}$	
LEA (A1),**A0**	[A0] ← [A1]	
LEA 10(A1),**A0**	[A0] ← [A1] + 10	
LEA 10(PC),**A0**	[A0] ← [PC] + 10	This lets us generate PIC

The following fragment of code demonstrates how the `LEA` instruction can be used to support position independent code.

```
        LEA    Value1(PC),A0    Calculate the relative address of
        .                       VALUE1 and store it in A0
        .
        .
        MOVE   D2,(A0)          Store D2 at the address pointed at by A0
        .
        MOVE   (A0),D3          Move the word pointed at by A0 to D3
        .
Value1 DS     1                Reserve one word of memory for data
```

When the instruction `LEA Value1(PC),A0` is assembled, the assembler takes the value of `Value1` and subtracts the current value of the program counter from it to evaluate the offset required by the instruction.

We now look at one of the most important applications of program counter relative addressing, relative branching.

automatically added to the PC at the start of an instruction, relative branching is possible within the range −126 to +129 bytes from the start of the current instruction (i.e. the branch). The 68K also supports a *long branch* with a 16-bit offset that provides a range of −32K to +32K bytes.

Figure 6.22 also illustrates the importance of relative branching in the production of position-independent code. The program containing the instruction `BRA XYZ` can be relocated merely by moving it in memory, whereas the

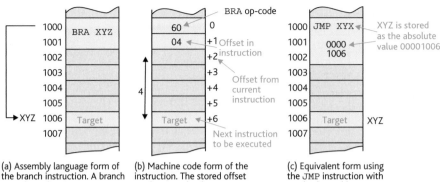

(a) Assembly language form of the branch instruction. A branch is made to the instruction at target address XYZ.

(b) Machine code form of the instruction. The stored offset is 4 because the destination is 4 bytes from the end of the current instruction.

(c) Equivalent form using the JMP instruction with an absolute address.

Figure 6.22 Absolute and relative branching.

program containing JMP XYZ must be modified if it is relocated.

The following program moves a block of data from one region of memory to another and provides examples of both relative branching and relative addressing. The first location of the block to be moved is FROM and the first location of its destination is TO. The number of words to be moved is given by SIZE.

tion is \$00 0410 and the address of the operation MOVE (A0)+, **(A1)** + is \$00 040C. We therefore have to branch four locations from the start of the BNE, or six locations from the end of the BNE. As the CPU always increments the PC by 2 at the start of a branch, the stored offset is −6. In two's complement form this is \$FA (the code is \$66FA).

```
        ORG     $400                Start of program to move a data block
SIZE    EQU     16                  Let's use a 16-byte block
        LEA     FROM(PC),A0         A0 points to the source of the sate
        LEA     TO(PC),A1           A1 points to the destination
        MOVE.B  #SIZE,D0            D0 is the loop counter
REPEAT  MOVE.B  (A0)+,(A1)+         REPEAT Move byte from source to destination
        SUB.B   #1,D0
        BNE     REPEAT              UNTIL all bytes moved
        STOP    #$2700
*
        ORG     $001000
FROM    DS.B    16                  Locate source and destination blocks here
TO      DS.B    16
        END     $400
```

In Fig. 6.23 the instruction BNE REPEAT causes a branch backwards to instruction MOVE (A0)+, **(A1)** + in the event of the zero bit in the CCR not being set. From the memory map of Fig. 6.23, we see that the address of the branch opera-

Note how we use relative addressing to load the address of the source and destination blocks into address registers A0 and A1, respectively. This program can be assembled to give the following.

```
 1 00000400                         ORG     $400        ;Start of program
 2          00000010    SIZE:       EQU     16          ;Let's use a 16-byte block
 3 00000400 41FA0BFE                LEA     FROM(PC),A0 ;A0 points to the source
 4 00000404 43FA0C0A                LEA     TO(PC),A1   ;A1 points to the destination
 5 00000408 103C0010                MOVE.B  #SIZE,D0    ;D0 is the loop counter
 6 0000040C 12D8        REPEAT:     MOVE.B  (A0)+,(A1)+ ;REPEAT move byte from source to destination
 7 0000040E 5300                    SUB.B   #1,D0
 8 00000410 66FA                    BNE     REPEAT      ;UNTIL all bytes moved
 9 00000412 4E722700                STOP    #$2700
10                      *
11 00001000                         ORG     $001000
12 00001000 00000010    FROM:       DS.B    16          ;Locate source and destination blocks here
13 00001010 00000010    TO:         DS.B    16
14          00000400                END     $400
```

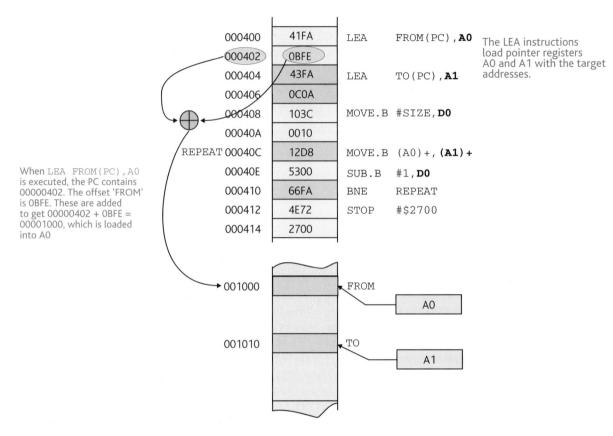

000400	41FA	LEA	FROM(PC),**A0**	The LEA instructions load pointer registers A0 and A1 with the target addresses.
000402	0BFE			
000404	43FA	LEA	TO(PC),**A1**	
000406	0C0A			
000408	103C	MOVE.B	#SIZE,**D0**	
00040A	0010			
REPEAT 00040C	12D8	MOVE.B	(A0)+,**(A1)+**	
00040E	5300	SUB.B	#1,**D0**	
000410	66FA	BNE	REPEAT	
000412	4E72	STOP	#$2700	
000414	2700			

When LEA FROM(PC),A0 is executed, the PC contains 00000402. The offset 'FROM' is 0BFE. These are added to get 00000402 + 0BFE = 00001000, which is loaded into A0

001000 FROM A0

001010 TO A1

Figure 6.23 Moving a block of data in memory.

RELATIVE ADDRESSING—A SUMMARY

Relative addressing is used to specify the location of an operand with respect to the program counter. This addressing mode means that code and its data can be moved in memory without having to recompute operand addresses because the data is the same distance from the code it accesses

irrespective of where the code is located. Relative addressing is also used with branch instructions because the target address is expressed as the number of bytes from the current instruction.

6.5 The stack

We now look at one of the most important data structures in computer science, the *stack*, and describe the facilities provided by the 68K to support the stack (we provided a basic introduction in the previous chapter). A stack is a last-in-first-out *queue* with a *single end*, where items are added or removed. Unlike a conventional first-in-first-out queue (FIFO), the stack has only one end. The stack expands as items are added to it and contracts as they are removed. Items are removed from the stack in the reverse order to which they are entered. The point at which items are added to, or removed from, the stack is called the *top of stack* (TOS). The next position on the stack is referred to as *next on stack* (NOS). When an item is added to the stack it is said to be

pushed on to the stack, and when an item is removed from the stack it is said to be *pulled* (or *popped*) off the stack.

Figure 6.24 presents a series of diagrams illustrating the operation of a stack as items A, B, C, D, and E, are added to it and removed from it.

Before we look at the stack's role in subroutines, we must mention the stack-based architecture that has been implemented by some special-purpose computers and by some experimental machines. Suppose a computer can transfer data between memory and the stack and perform monadic operations on the top item of the stack, or dyadic operations on the top two items of the stack. A dyadic operation (e.g. +, *, AND, OR) removes the top two items on the stack and pushes the result of the operation.

Figure 6.25 shows how an ADD instruction is executed by a stack-based computer. Figure 6.25(a) demonstrates a system

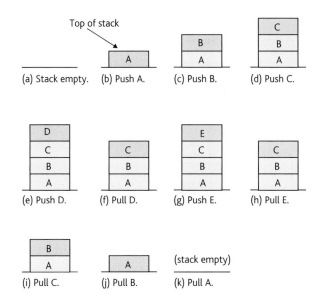

(a) Stack empty.   (b) Push A.   (c) Push B.   (d) Push C.

(e) Push D.   (f) Pull D.   (g) Push E.   (h) Pull E.

(i) Pull C.   (j) Pull B.   (k) Pull A.   (stack empty)

Figure 6.24 The stack.

(a) Initial state of the stack with four items.

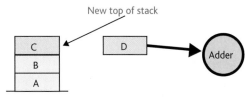

(b) First element pulled off the stack.

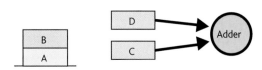

(c) Second element pulled off the stack.

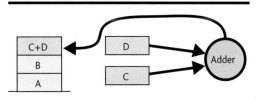

(d) Result pushed on the stack.

Figure 6.25 Executing an ADD operation on a stack machine.

with four data elements on the stack. When the ADD is executed, the element at the top of the stack is pulled (Fig. 6.25(b)) and sent to the adder. The *next* element (i.e. C, the old NOS) is now the new TOS. In Fig. 6.25(c) the element at the top of stack is pulled and sent to the adder. Finally, the output of the adder, D + C, is pushed onto the stack to create a new TOS.

Note how this ADD instruction doesn't have an operand unlike all the instructions we've described so far. A stack-based computer has so-called *addressless* instructions because they act on elements at the top of the stack.

The following example illustrates the evaluation of the expression (A + B)(C − D) on a hypothetical stack-based computer. We assume that the instruction PUSH pushes the contents of D0 onto the stack, ADD, SUB, and MULU all act on the top two items on the stack, and PULL places the top item on the stack in D0.

1. MOVE A,**D0**   Get A in D0
2. PUSH   Push it on the stack
3. MOVE B,**D0**   Get B in D0
4. PUSH   Push it on the stack
5. ADD   Pull the top two items off the stack, add them, and push the result
6. MOVE C,**D0**   Get C in D0
7. PUSH   Push it on the stack
8. MOVE D,**D0**   Get D
9. PUSH   Push it on the stack
10. SUB   Pull the top two items off the stack, subtract them, and push the result
11. MULU   Pull the top two items off the stack, multiply them, and push the result
12. PULL   Pull the result off the stack and put it in D0

Figure 6.26 represents the state of the stack at various stages in the procedure. The number below each diagram corresponds to the line number in the program. Although the 68K and similar microprocessors do not permit operations

on the stack in the way we've just described (e.g. ADD, SUB, MULU), special-purpose microprocessors have been designed to support stack-based languages. The 68K implements instructions enabling it to access a stack, although it's not a stack machine. Pure stack machines do exist, although they have never been developed to the same extent as the two-address machines like the 68K and Pentium.

6.5.1 The 68K stack

A hardware stack can be implemented as a modified shift register. When such a stack is implemented in hardware, the addition of a new item to the top of stack causes all other items on the stack to be pushed down. Similarly, when an item is removed from the stack, the NOS becomes TOS and all items move up.

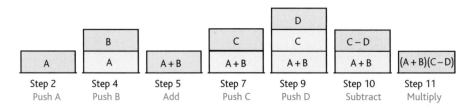

Figure 6.26 Executing a program on a stack machine.

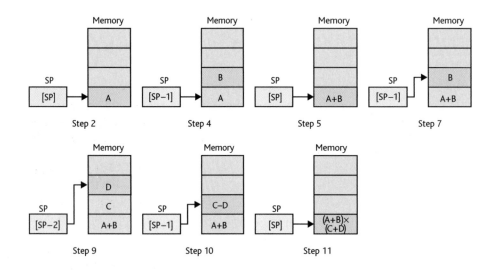

Figure 6.27 Executing the program of Fig. 6.26 on a machine with a stack pointer.

THE TWO 68K STACK POINTERS

The 68K has two A7 registers and, therefore, two *system* stack pointers. One A7 is the *supervisor* stack pointer and is associated with the operating system. The other is the *user* stack pointer and is associated with programs running under the operating system. The operating system controls the allocation of the computer's resources (memory and I/O), and is protected from errors caused by the less reliable user programs. A stack pointer dedicated solely to the operating system prevents user programs accessing and possibly corrupting the operating system's stack. Only one of these two A7s is accessible at a time, because the 68K is either running an operating system or it isn't.

Microprocessors don't implement a stack in this way and the items already on the stack don't move as new items are pushed and old ones pulled. The stack is located in a region of the main store and a *stack pointer* points to the top of the stack. This stack pointer points at the top of stack as the stack grows and contracts. In some microprocessors, the stack pointer points to the next free location on the stack, whereas in others, it points to the current top of stack.

Figure 6.27 demonstrates how the program illustrated in Fig. 6.26 is executed by a computer with a stack in memory and a stack pointer, SP.

The 68K doesn't have a special *system* stack pointer—it uses address register A7. We call A7 the *system* stack pointer because the stack pointed at by A7 stores return addresses during subroutine calls. Assemblers let you write either A7 or SP; for example, MOVE.W D0, (A7) and MOVE.W D0, (SP) are equivalent. The 68K can maintain up to eight stacks

simultaneously, because all its address registers can be used as stack pointers.

In what follows, we use the 68K's stack pointer to illustrate the operation of a stack. You might expect the assembly language instruction that pushes the contents of D0 on the stack to be PUSH D0, and the corresponding instruction to pull an item from the stack and put it in D0 to be PULL D0. Explicit PUSH and PULL instructions are not provided by the 68K. You can use address register indirect with predecrementing addressing mode to push, and address register indirect with postincrementing addressing mode to pull.

Figure 6.28 illustrates the effect of a PUSH D0 instruction, which is implemented by MOVE.W D0,−(SP), and PULL D0, which is implemented by MOVE.W (SP)+,D0. The 68K's stack grows towards lower addresses as data is pushed on it; for example, if the stack pointer contains $80014C and a word is pushed onto the stack, the new value of the stack pointer will be $80014A.

The 68K's push operation MOVE.W D0, − (**SP**) is defined in RTL as

```
[SP] ← [SP] - 2        Predecrement stack pointer to point to next free element
[[SP]] ← [D0]          Copy contents of D0 to the stack
```

and the 68K's pull operation MOVE.W (SP)+,**D0** is defined as

```
[D0] ←  [[SP]]         Copy the element on top of the stack to D0
[SP] ← [SP] + 2        Postincrement the stack pointer to point to the new TOS
```

Push and pull operations use word or longword operands. A longword operand automatically causes the SP to be decremented or incremented by 4. Address registers A0 to A6 may be used to push or pull byte, .B, operands—but not the system stack pointer, A7. The reason for this restriction is that A7 must always point at a word boundary on an even address (this is an operational restriction imposed by the 68K's hardware).

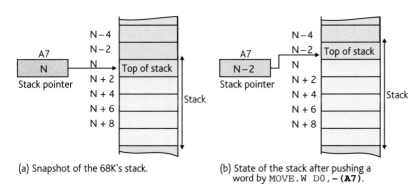

(a) Snapshot of the 68K's stack.

(b) State of the stack after pushing a word by MOVE.W D0, − (**A7**).

Figure 6.28 The 68K's stack.

The 68K's stack pointer is decremented before a push and incremented after a pull. Consequently, the stack pointer always points at the item at the *top* of the stack; for example, MOVE (SP)+, **D3** pulls the top item off the stack and deposits it in D3. Note that MOVE (SP), **D3** copies the TOS into D3 without modifying the stack pointer.

When the stack shrinks after a MOVE.W (SP)+, **D0** operation, items on the stack are not physically deleted; they are still there in the memory until overwritten by, for example, a MOVE.W D0, − (**SP**) operation.

The stack can be used as a temporary data store. Executing a MOVE.W D0, − (SP) saves the contents of D0 on the stack, and executing a MOVE.W (SP)+, **D0** returns the contents of D0. The application of the stack as a temporary storage location avoids storing data in explicitly named memory locations. More importantly, if further data is stored on the stack, it does not overwrite the old data.

The 68K has a special instruction called *move multiple registers* (MOVEM), which saves or retrieves an entire group of registers. For example MOVEM.L D0−D7/A0−A7, − (**A7**) pushes all registers on the stack pointed at by A7. The register list used by MOVEM is written in the form Di−Dj/ Ap−Aq and

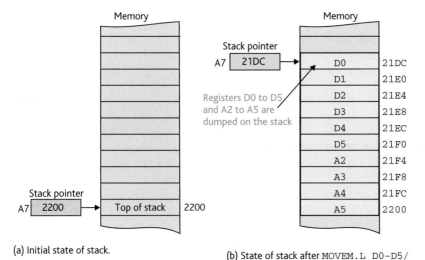

(a) Initial state of stack.

(b) State of stack after MOVEM.L D0−D5/ A2−A5, − (**A7**).

Figure 6.29 The 68K's stack.

SIMULATED INPUT AND OUTPUT

Microprocessors cannot perform input operations from the keyboard or display data on the screen. To do that requires an operating system, peripherals, and their drivers.

In order to allow the assembly language programmer to write programs that do have input or output operations, simulators provide an I/O mechanism. Both EASy68K and the Teesside simulator use the 68K's TRAP #15 instruction. This instruction is a request to the operating system to provide a facility such as input or output. Because there are many

operations that the operating system can perform, you need to tell the operating system what you want. EASy68K and the Teesside simulator use data register D0 to hold a parameter that defined the requested operation; for example, if you load D0 with 5, the request is for input.

This I/O mechanism is specific to EASy68K and the Teesside simulator. It is part of their environment and will not work with any other 68K system.

specifies data registers Di to Dj inclusive and address registers Ap to Aq inclusive. Groups of registers are pulled off the stack by, for example, MOVEM.L (A7)+,**D0−D2/D4/A4−A6**. The most important applications of the stack are in the implementation of subroutines (discussed in the following section) and in the handling of interrupts. When autodecrementing is used, registers are stored in the order A7 to A0 then D7 to D0 with the highest numbered address register being stored at the lowest address. Figure 6.29 illustrates the effect of MOVEM.L D0−D5/A2−A5,−**(A7)**.

6.5.2 The stack and subroutines

A subroutine is called by the instruction BSR <label> or JSR <label>, where BSR means *branch to subroutine* and JSR means *jump to subroutine*. The difference between BSR and JSR is that BSR uses a *relative* address and JSR an *absolute* address. Remember that the programmer simply supplies the label of the subroutine and the assembler automatically calculates the appropriate relative or absolute address. To call a subroutine ABC, all we have to do is write either BSR ABC or JSR ABC. The BSR is preferred to JSR because it permits the use of *position-independent code*. The range of branching with BSR is −32 kbytes to +32 kbytes from the present instruction. JSR

uses an absolute address and cannot therefore be used to generate position-independent code. JSR may use an *address register indirect* address; for example, JSR (A0) calls the subroutine whose address is in A0.

Using subroutines—an example

We now look at an example of how subroutines are used. The following program inputs text from the keyboard and stores successive characters in a buffer in memory until an @ symbol is typed. When an @ is encountered, the text is displayed on the screen. In this simple example, we don't test for buffer overflow.

In this example we use the character input and output mechanisms built into both EASy68K and the Teesside 68K simulators. All I/O is performed by means of a TRAP #15 instruction, which is a *call* to the operating system. We have't yet covered the 68K's TRAP instructions, but all we need say here is that a TRAP calls a function that forms part of the computer's operating system. Before the TRAP is executed, you have to tell the O/S what operation you want by putting a parameter in data register D0. A '5' indicates character input and a '6' indicates character output. When a character is input, it is deposited in D1. Similarly, the character in D1 is displayed by the output routine.

We can express the algorithm is pseudocode as follows.

```
Initialize a pointer to point to the top of the character buffer
REPEAT
      Read a character from the keyboard
      Store it in the buffer at the address given by the pointer
      Update the pointer
UNTIL character = "@"
Reset the pointer to point to the top of the character buffer
REPEAT
      Read a character from the buffer at the address given by the pointer
      IF character = "@" THEN exit
      Display the character on the screen
      Update the pointer
UNTIL exit
```

In the following program, the BUFFER is a region of memory reserved for the data to be stored.

When an RTS instruction is encountered at the end of a subroutine, the longword address on the top of the stack is

```
        ORG     $000400         Define the origin for data
        LEA     BUFFER(PC),A0   Preset A0 as a pointer register
NEXTIN  BSR     GET_CHAR        Get a character
        MOVE.B  D1,(A0)+        Store character and move pointer to next
        CMP.B   #'@',D1         IF character = '@' THEN print
        BNE     NEXTIN          ELSE repeat
PRINT   LEA     BUFFER(PC),A0   Reset pointer to start of buffer
NEXTOUT MOVE.B  (A0)+,D1        Get a character and update pointer
        CMP.B   #'@',D1         IF character = '@' THEN EXIT
        BEQ     DONE
        BSR     PUT_CHAR                       ELSE print character
        BRA     NEXTOUT         Repeat
DONE    STOP    #$2700          Halt the 68K
*
GET_CHAR MOVE.B #5,D0           Input routine (code = 5)
        TRAP    #15             Load input command in D0 and call O/S
        RTS                     Return
*
PUT_CHAR MOVE.B #6,D0           Output routine (code = 6)
        TRAP    #15             Load output command in D0 and call O/S
        RTS                     Return
*
        ORG     $500
BUFFER  DS.B    40              Reserve 40 bytes of storage
        END     $400
```

The instruction CMP.B #'@',D1 compares the contents of the lower-order byte of data register D1 with the byte whose ASCII code corresponds to the symbol @. The instruction LEA BUFFER(PC),A0 generates *position-independent code* because it calculates the address of the *buffer relative to the program counter*. Had we written LEA BUFFER,A0, the code would not have been position independent.

pulled and placed in the program counter in order to force a return to the calling point. The following code is produced by assembling this program. We will need this output when we trace the program (in particular the addresses of the subroutines and the return addresses of subroutine calls).

```
 1  00000400                           ORG     $000400          ;Define the origin for data
 2  00000400 41FA00FE                   LEA     BUFFER(PC),A0    ;Preset A0 as pointer register
 3  00000404 61000022  NEXTIN:          BSR     GET_CHAR        ;Get a character
 4  00000408 10C1                       MOVE.B  D1,(A0)+        ;Store character and move pointer to next
 5  0000040A 0C010040                   CMP.B   #'@',D1         ;IF character = '@' THEN print
 6  0000040E 66F4                       BNE     NEXTIN          ;ELSE repeat
 7  00000410 41FA00EE  PRINT:           LEA     BUFFER(PC),A0   ;Reset pointer to start of buffer
 8  00000414 1218      NEXTOUT:         MOVE.B  (A0)+,D1        ;Get a character and update pointer
 9  00000416 0C010040                   CMP.B   #'@',D1         ;IF character = '@' THEN EXIT
10  0000041A 67000008                   BEQ     DONE
11  0000041E 61000010                   BSR     PUT_CHAR        ;ELSE print character
12  00000422 60F0                       BRA     NEXTOUT         ;Repeat
13  00000424 4E722700  DONE:            STOP    #$2700          ;Halt the 68K
14                     *
15  00000428 103C0005  GET_CHAR:        MOVE.B  #5,D0           ;Input routine
16  0000042C 4E4F                       TRAP    #15             ;Load input command in D0 and call O/S
17  0000042E 4E75                       RTS                     ;Return
18                     *
19  00000430 103C0006  PUT_CHAR:        MOVE.B  #6,D0           ;Output routine
20  00000434 4E4F                       TRAP    #15             ;Load output command in D0 and call O/S
21  00000436 4E75                       RTS                     ;Return
22                     *
23  00000500                            ORG     $500
24  00000500 00000028  BUFFER:          DS.B    40              ;Reserve 40 bytes of storage
25           00000400                   END     $400
```

The following trace output demonstrates the flow of control as subroutine calls and subroutine returns are made—when you read the trace, look at the program counter and the stack pointer (A7 = SS). Remember that the PC is incremented between 2 and 10 bytes after each instruction.

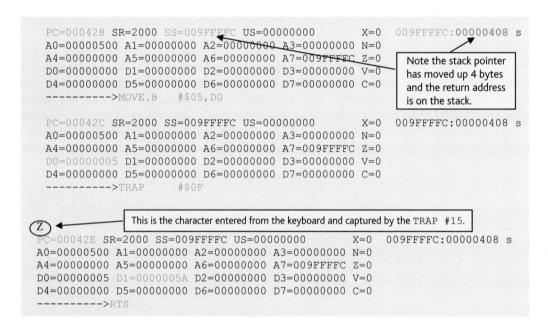

```
PC=000400 SR=2000 SS=00A00000 US=00000000          X=0
A0=00000000 A1=00000000 A2=00000000 A3=00000000 N=0
A4=00000000 A5=00000000 A6=00000000 A7=00A00000 Z=0
D0=00000000 D1=00000000 D2=00000000 D3=00000000 V=0
D4=00000000 D5=00000000 D6=00000000 D7=00000000 C=
---------->LEA.L      $FE(PC),A0
```

Note the position independent code. The value of the PC when LEA $FE(PC),**A0** is executed is 402_{16}. The offset is $00FE_{16}$, so the value loaded into A0 is $402_{16}+FE_{16} = 500_{16}$.

```
PC=000404 SR=2000 SS=00A00000 US=00000000          X=
A0=00000500 A1=00000000 A2=00000000 A3=00000000 N=
A4=00000000 A5=00000000 A6=00000000 A7=00A00000 Z=
D0=00000000 D1=00000000 D2=00000000 D3=00000000 V=0
D4=00000000 D5=00000000 D6=00000000 D7=00000000 C=0
---------->BSR.L      $0428
```

We've set A0 to point to the buffer for input data. The next instruction calls the subroutine to input a character. Note the change in the PC to $428.

```
PC=000428 SR=2000 SS=009FFEFC US=00000000          X=0   009FFFFC:00000408 s
A0=00000500 A1=00000000 A2=00000000 A3=00000000 N=0
A4=00000000 A5=00000000 A6=00000000 A7=009FFFFC Z=0
D0=00000000 D1=00000000 D2=00000000 D3=00000000 V=0
D4=00000000 D5=00000000 D6=00000000 D7=00000000 C=0
---------->MOVE.B     #$05,D0
```

Note the stack pointer has moved up 4 bytes and the return address is on the stack.

```
PC=00042C SR=2000 SS=009FFFFC US=00000000          X=0   009FFFFC:00000408 s
A0=00000500 A1=00000000 A2=00000000 A3=00000000 N=0
A4=00000000 A5=00000000 A6=00000000 A7=009FFFFC Z=0
D0=00000005 D1=00000000 D2=00000000 D3=00000000 V=0
D4=00000000 D5=00000000 D6=00000000 D7=00000000 C=0
---------->TRAP       #$0F
```

This is the character entered from the keyboard and captured by the TRAP #15.

(Z)

```
PC=00042E SR=2000 SS=009FFFFC US=00000000          X=0   009FFFFC:00000408 s
A0=00000500 A1=00000000 A2=00000000 A3=00000000 N=0
A4=00000000 A5=00000000 A6=00000000 A7=009FFFFC Z=0
D0=00000005 D1=0000005A D2=00000000 D3=00000000 V=0
D4=00000000 D5=00000000 D6=00000000 D7=00000000 C=0
---------->RTS
```

Having got the input (in this case Z) in D1, we return from the subroutine. Watch the program counter again. It is currently $42E and will be replaced by $408 (i.e. the address of the instruction after the subroutine call.

```
PC=000408 SR=2000 SS=00A00000 US=00000000          X=0
A0=00000500 A1=00000000 A2=00000000 A3=00000000 N=0
A4=00000000 A5=00000000 A6=00000000 A7=00A00000 Z=0
D0=00000005 D1=0000005A D2=00000000 D3=00000000 V=0
D4=00000000 D5=00000000 D6=00000000 D7=00000000 C=0
---------->MOVE.B     D1,(A0)+
```

We now store the character in D1 in memory and increment the pointer in A0.

```
PC=00040A SR=2000 SS=00A00000 US=00000000          X=0
A0=00000501 A1=00000000 A2=00000000 A3=00000000 N=0
A4=00000000 A5=00000000 A6=00000000 A7=00A00000 Z=0
D0=00000005 D1=0000005A D2=00000000 D3=00000000 V=0
D4=00000000 D5=00000000 D6=00000000 D7=00000000 C=0
---------->CMPI.B   #$40,D1

PC=00040E SR=2000 SS=00A00000 US=00000000          X=0
A0=00000501 A1=00000000 A2=00000000 A3=00000000 N=0
A4=00000000 A5=00000000 A6=00000000 A7=00A00000 Z=0
D0=00000005 D1=0000005A D2=00000000 D3=00000000 V=0
D4=00000000 D5=00000000 D6=00000000 D7=00000000 C=0
---------->BNE.S    $0404
```

We test the character in D1 for equality with '@' = $40 and then branch back to $0404 if we haven't input an '@'.

```
PC=000404 SR=2000 SS=00A00000 US=00000000          X=0
A0=00000501 A1=00000000 A2=00000000 A3=00000000 N=0
A4=00000000 A5=00000000 A6=00000000 A7=00A00000 Z=0
D0=00000005 D1=0000005A D2=00000000 D3=00000000 V=0
D4=00000000 D5=00000000 D6=00000000 D7=00000000 C=0
---------->BSR.L    $0428
```

We haven't, so we continue by reading another character.

```
PC=000428 SR=2000 SS=009FFFFC US=00000000          X=0   009FFFFC:00000408 s
A0=00000501 A1=00000000 A2=00000000 A3=00000000 N=0
A4=00000000 A5=00000000 A6=00000000 A7=009FFFFC Z=0
D0=00000005 D1=0000005A D2=00000000 D3=00000000 V=0
D4=00000000 D5=00000000 D6=00000000 D7=00000000 C=0
---------->MOVE.B   #$05,D0
```

To avoid more tracing, we'll jump ahead to the point at which a '@' has been input in D0.

```
PC=00042C SR=2000 SS=009FFFFC US=00000000          X=0   009FFFFC:00000408 s
A0=00000501 A1=00000000 A2=00000000 A3=00000000 N=0
A4=00000000 A5=00000000 A6=00000000 A7=009FFFFC Z=0
D0=00000005 D1=0000005A D2=00000000 D3=00000000 V=0
D4=00000000 D5=00000000 D6=00000000 D7=00000000 C=0
---------->TRAP     #$0F

@
PC=00042E SR=2000 SS=009FFFFC US=00000000          X=0   009FFFFC:00000408 s
A0=00000502 A1=00000000 A2=00000000 A3=00000000 N=0
A4=00000000 A5=00000000 A6=00000000 A7=009FFFFC Z=0
D0=00000005 D1=00000040 D2=00000000 D3=00000000 V=0
D4=00000000 D5=00000000 D6=00000000 D7=00000000 C=0
---------->RTS
```

Here's the '@' that we entered and its ASCII value in D1.

```
PC=000408 SR=2000 SS=00A00000 US=00000000          X=0
A0=00000502 A1=00000000 A2=00000000 A3=00000000 N=0
A4=00000000 A5=00000000 A6=00000000 A7=00A00000 Z=0
D0=00000005 D1=00000040 D2=00000000 D3=00000000 V=0
D4=00000000 D5=00000000 D6=00000000 D7=00000000 C=0
---------->MOVE.B   D1,(A0)+
```

```
PC=00040A SR=2000 SS=00A00000 US=00000000          X=0
A0=00000503 A1=00000000 A2=00000000 A3=00000000 N=0
A4=00000000 A5=00000000 A6=00000000 A7=00A00000 Z=0
D0=00000005 D1=00000040 D2=00000000 D3=00000000 V=0
D4=00000000 D5=00000000 D6=00000000 D7=00000000 C=0
---------->CMPI.B   #$40,D1

PC=00040E SR=2004 SS=00A00000 US=00000000          X=0
A0=00000503 A1=00000000 A2=00000000 A3=00000000 N=0
A4=00000000 A5=00000000 A6=00000000 A7=00A00000 Z=1
D0=00000005 D1=00000040 D2=00000000 D3=00000000 V=0
D4=00000000 D5=00000000 D6=00000000 D7=00000000 C=0
---------->BNE.S    $0404
```

Because D1 contains the ASCII code for '@', the test for equality will yield true and we will not take the branch back to $0404.

```
PC=000410 SR=2004 SS=00A00000 US=00000000          X=0
A0=00000503 A1=00000000 A2=00000000 A3=00000000 N=0
A4=00000000 A5=00000000 A6=00000000 A7=00A00000 Z=1
D0=00000005 D1=00000040 D2=00000000 D3=00000000 V=0
D4=00000000 D5=00000000 D6=00000000 D7=00000000 C=0
---------->LEA.L    $EE(PC),A0
```

The next instructions reset the pointer to the top of the buffer, read a character, and compare it to '@'.

```
PC=000414 SR=2004 SS=00A00000 US=00000000          X=0
A0=00000500 A1=00000000 A2=00000000 A3=00000000 N=0
A4=00000000 A5=00000000 A6=00000000 A7=00A00000 Z=1
D0=00000005 D1=00000040 D2=00000000 D3=00000000 V=0
D4=00000000 D5=00000000 D6=00000000 D7=00000000 C=0
---------->MOVE.B    (A0)+,D1

PC=000416 SR=2000 SS=00A00000 US=00000000          X=0
A0=00000501 A1=00000000 A2=00000000 A3=00000000 N=0
A4=00000000 A5=00000000 A6=00000000 A7=00A00000 Z=0
D0=00000005 D1=0000005A D2=00000000 D3=00000000 V=0
D4=00000000 D5=00000000 D6=00000000 D7=00000000 C=0
---------->CMPI.B   #$40,D1

PC=00041A SR=2000 SS=00A00000 US=00000000          X=0
A0=00000501 A1=00000000 A2=00000000 A3=00000000 N=0
A4=00000000 A5=00000000 A6=00000000 A7=00A00000 Z=0
D0=00000005 D1=0000005A D2=00000000 D3=00000000 V=0
D4=00000000 D5=00000000 D6=00000000 D7=00000000 C=0
---------->BEQ.L    $0424
```

If it isn't an '@', we will print it by calling the output routine.

```
PC=00041E SR=2000 SS=00A00000 US=00000000          X=0
A0=00000501 A1=00000000 A2=00000000 A3=00000000 N=0
A4=00000000 A5=00000000 A6=00000000 A7=00A00000 Z=0
D0=00000005 D1=0000005A D2=00000000 D3=00000000 V=0
D4=00000000 D5=00000000 D6=00000000 D7=00000000 C=0
---------->BSR.L    $0430
```

```
PC=000430 SR=2000 SS=009FFFFC US=00000000         X=0   009FFFFC:00000422 s
A0=00000501 A1=00000000 A2=00000000 A3=00000000 N=0
A4=00000000 A5=00000000 A6=00000000 A7=009FFFFC Z=0
D0=00000005 D1=0000005A D2=00000000 D3=00000000 V=0
D4=00000000 D5=00000000 D6=00000000 D7=00000000 C=0
---------->MOVE.B    #$06,D0
```

In this case we have branched to address $0430.

```
PC=000434 SR=2000 SS=009FFFFC US=00000000         X=0   009FFFFC:00000422 s
A0=00000501 A1=00000000 A2=00000000 A3=00000000 N=0
A4=00000000 A5=00000000 A6=00000000 A7=009FFFFC Z=0
D0=00000006 D1=0000005A D2=00000000 D3=00000000 V=0
D4=00000000 D5=00000000 D6=00000000 D7=00000000 C=0
---------->TRAP      #$0F
```

We call the operating system with the TRAP. Note that the contents of D1 will be printed as the ASCII character Z. Then we return to the body of the program.

Ⓩ ←————

```
PC=000436 SR=2000 SS=009FFFFC US=00000000         X=0   009FFFFC:00000422 s
A0=00000501 A1=00000000 A2=00000000 A3=00000000 N=0
A4=00000000 A5=00000000 A6=00000000 A7=009FFFFC Z=0
D0=00000006 D1=0000005A D2=00000000 D3=00000000 V=0
D4=00000000 D5=00000000 D6=00000000 D7=00000000 C=0
---------->RTS
```

Note the change in the value of the PC following the RTS.

```
PC=000422 SR=2000 SS=00A00000 US=00000000         X=0
A0=00000501 A1=00000000 A2=00000000 A3=00000000 N=0
A4=00000000 A5=00000000 A6=00000000 A7=00A00000 Z=0
D0=00000006 D1=0000005A D2=00000000 D3=00000000 V=0
D4=00000000 D5=00000000 D6=00000000 D7=00000000 C=0
---------->BRA.S     $0414
```

And so on . . .

6.5.3 Subroutines, the stack, and parameter passing

In order for a subroutine to carry out its function, it is almost always necessary to transfer data between the calling program and the subroutine. Up to now we have passed data to and from the subroutine via data registers. In the previous example, we called the subroutine GET_CHAR to input a character from the keyboard. When this subroutine is invoked by the operation BSR GET_CHAR, a branch is made to the entry point of the sub-routine. This subroutine reads the keyboard until a key is pressed. A return to the calling point is made with the ASCII code of the character in data register D1.

You can even use the C-bit in the CCR to pass informa-tion from a subroutine to its calling program; for example, to indicate an error state. Suppose a subroutine has been called to read data from a terminal and the terminal is faulty or not switched on. By setting the carry bit prior to a return from subroutine, the calling program can be informed that an error exists as the following fragment of a program demonstrates.

```
        BSR     GETDATA  Call subroutine and return with data in D0
        BCS     ERROR    IF carry flag set THEN something went wrong
        .
        .                         ELSE deal with the data
        .
ERROR                    Recover from error condition
```

You can't use registers to transfer large quantities of data to and from subroutines, due to the limited number of registers. You can pass parameters to a subroutine by means of a mailbox in memory. Consider the following.

```
        MOVE.W  Param1,Mbox1   Put first parameter in mail box 1
        MOVE.W  Param2,Mbox2   Put second parameter in mail box 2
        BSR     Sub            Now call the subroutine
        .                      Return here...
        .
        .
Sub     MOVE.W  Mbox1,D0       Retrieve the first parameter
        MOVE.W  Mbox2,D1       Retrieve the second parameter
        .
        .
        .
        RTS                    Return to the calling program
```

Such a solution is poor, because the subroutine can't be interrupted or called by another program. Any data stored in *explicitly named* locations could be corrupted by the interrupting program (see the box on interrupts). Let's look at how data is transferred between a subroutine and its calling program by many high-level languages.

Passing parameters on the stack

An ideal way of passing information between the subroutine and calling program is via the *stack*. Suppose two 16-bit parameters, P1 and P2, are needed by the subroutine ABC(P1,P2). The parameters are pushed on the stack immediately before the subroutine call by the following code:

```
MOVE.W  P1,-(A7)   Push the first parameter on the stack
MOVE.W  P2,-(A7)   Push the second parameter
BSR     ABC        Call ABC(P1,P2)
```

The state of the stack prior to the subroutine call and immediately after it is given in Fig. 6.30. Note that the return address is a longword and takes up two words on the stack.

On entering the subroutine, you can retrieve the parameters from the stack in several ways. However, you must never change the stack pointer in such a way that you move it down the stack. Consider Fig. 6.30(c) where the stack pointer is pointing at the return address. If you add 4 to the stack pointer, it will point to parameter P2 on the stack. You can now get P2 with, say, MOVE.W (A7),D0. However, the return address is no longer on the stack (it's still there in memory

above the top of the stack). If an interrupt occurs or you call a subroutine, the new return address will be pushed on the top of the stack overwriting the old return address. Never move the stack pointer below the top of stack.

You can avoid using the stack pointer by copying it to another address register with LEA (A7),A0. Now you can use A0 to get the parameters; for example, P1 can be loaded into D1 by MOVE.W 6(A0),D1. The offset 6 is required because the parameter P1 is buried under the return address (4 bytes) and P1 (2 bytes). Similarly, P2 can be loaded into D2 by MOVE.W 4(A0),D2.

After returning from the subroutine with RTS, the contents of the stack pointer are [A7] − 4, where A7 is the value of the stack pointer before P1 and P2 were pushed on the stack. The stack pointer can be restored to its original value or *cleaned up* by executing LEA 4(A7),A7 to move the stack pointer down by two words. Note that LEA 4(A7),A7 is the same as ADD.L #4,A7.

P1 and P2 are, of course, still in the same locations in memory but they will be overwritten as new data is pushed on the stack.

By using the stack to pass parameters to a subroutine, the subroutine may be interrupted and then used by the interrupting program without the parameters being corrupted. As the data is stored on the stack, it is not overwritten when the subroutine is interrupted because new data is added at the top of the stack, and then removed after the interrupt has been serviced.

Let's look at another example of parameter passing in detail. In the following program two numbers are loaded into D0 and D1, and then the contents of these registers are pushed on the stack. A subroutine, AddUp, is called to add these two numbers together. In this case the result is pushed on the stack. We've used blue to highlight code that performs the parameter passing.

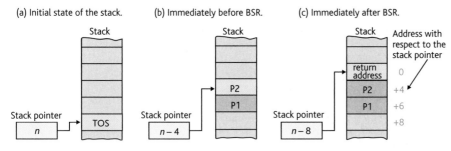

(a) Initial state of the stack.   (b) Immediately before BSR.   (c) Immediately after BSR.

Figure 6.30 Passing parameters on the stack (all values on the stack are words or longwords).

THE INTERRUPT

An *interrupt* is a method of diverting the processor from its intended course of action, and is employed to deal with errors and external events that must be attended to as soon as they occur. Whenever a processor receives an interrupt request from a device, the processor finishes its current instruction and then jumps to the program that deals with the cause of the interrupt. After the interrupt has been serviced, a return is made to the point immediately following the last instruction before the interrupt was dealt with. The return mechanism of the interrupt is almost identical with that of the subroutine— the return address is saved on the stack.

Suppose a subroutine is intrerrupted during the course of its execution. If the interrupt-handling routine also wishes to use the same subroutine (yes, that's possible), any data stored in explicitly named memory locations will be overwritten and corrupted by the re-use of the subroutine. If the data had been stored in registers and the content of the registers pushed on the stack by the interrupt-handling routine, no data in the subroutine would have been lost by its re-use. After the sub-routine has been re-used by the interrupt-handling routine, the contents of the registers stored on the stack are restored and a return from interrupt is made with the state of the registers exactly the same as at the instant the interrupt was serviced.

Interrupts may originate in hardware or software. A hardware interrupt may occur when you move the mouse. A software interrupt may occur when you perform an illegal operation or even when you generate one with a `TRAP #15` instruction.

```
          ORG     $400
          LEA     $1000,A7
          MOVE.W  #1,D0        Set up the stack pointer
          MOVE.W  #2,D1        Set up two parameters in D0 and D1

          MOVE.W  D0,-(A7)     Push parameter 1 on the stack
          MOVE.W  D1,-(A7)     Push parameter 2 on the stack

          BSR     AddUp        Call adder routine
          MOVE.W  (A7)+,D2     Read the result from the stack
          LEA     2(A7),A7     Clean up the stack
          STOP    #$2700       Stop
*
AddUp     MOVE.W  4(A7),D2     Get parameter 2 from the stack
          MOVE.W  6(A7),D3     Get parameter 1 from the stack
          ADD.W   D2,D3        Add them
          MOVE.W  D3,4(A7)     Store the result in the parameter 2 slot
          RTS
```

If we assemble this program, we get the following.

```
1 00000400                        ORG     $400
2 00000400 4FF81000               LEA     $1000,A7    ;Set up the stack pointer
3 00000404 303C0001               MOVE.W  #1,D0       ;Set up two parameters in D0 and D1
4 00000408 323C0002               MOVE.W  #2,D1
5 0000040C 3F00                   MOVE.W  D0,-(A7)    ;Push parameter 1
```

```
 6 0000040E 3F01            MOVE.W    D1,-(A7)     ;Push parameter 2
 7 00000410 6100000C        BSR       ADDUP        ;Call adder routine
 8 00000414 381F            MOVE.W    (A7)+,D4     ;Read the result
 9 00000416 4FEF0002        LEA       2(A7),A7     ;Clean up stack
10 0000041A 4E722700        STOP      #$2700       ;Stop
11                  *
12 0000041E 342F0004 ADDUP: MOVE.W    4(A7),D2     ;Get parameter 2
13 00000422 362F0006        MOVE.W    6(A7),D3     ;Get parameter 1
14 00000426 D642            ADD       D2,D3        ;Add them
15 00000428 3F430004        MOVE.W    D3,4(A7)     ;Store result in the parameter 2 slot
16 0000042C 4E75            RTS
17                  *
18         00000400         END       $400
```

Figure 6.31 shows the state of the stack at various points during the execution of this program. We will now load the program and trace it line by line.

```
PC=000400  SR=2000  SS=00A00000  US=00000000        X=0
A0=00000000 A1=00000000 A2=00000000 A3=00000000 N=0
A4=00000000 A5=00000000 A6=00000000 A7=00A00000 Z=0
D0=00000000 D1=00000000 D2=00000000 D3=00000000 V=0
D4=00000000 D5=00000000 D6=00000000 D7=00000000 C=0
---------->LEA.L    $1000,SP

PC=000404  SR=2000  SS=00001000  US=00000000        X=0  00001000:00000000 s
A0=00000000 A1=00000000 A2=00000000 A3=00000000 N=0  00001004:00000000 s+4
A4=00000000 A5=00000000 A6=00000000 A7=00001000 Z=0  00001008:00000000 s+8
D0=00000000 D1=00000000 D2=00000000 D3=00000000 V=0  0000100C:00000000 s+12
D4=00000000 D5=00000000 D6=00000000 D7=00000000 C=0  00001010:00000000 s+16
---------->MOVE.W    #$01,D0
```

Note the five new entries to the right of the register display. These lines display the five longwords at the top of the stack. Each line contains the stack address, the longword in that address, and the address with respect to the current stack pointer.

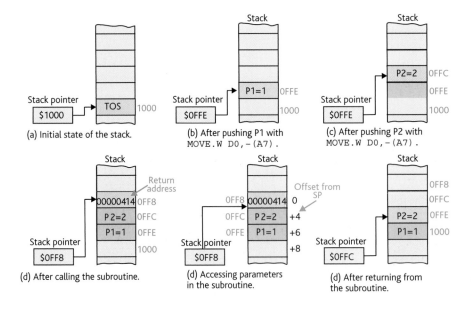

(a) Initial state of the stack.

(b) After pushing P1 with MOVE.W D0,-(A7).

(c) After pushing P2 with MOVE.W D0,-(A7).

(d) After calling the subroutine.

(d) Accessing parameters in the subroutine.

(d) After returning from the subroutine.

Figure 6.31 The state of the stack during the execution of a program.

```
PC=000408 SR=2000 SS=00001000 US=00000000          X=0   00001000:00000000 s
A0=00000000 A1=00000000 A2=00000000 A3=00000000 N=0   00001004:00000000 s+4
A4=00000000 A5=00000000 A6=00000000 A7=00001000 Z=0   00001008:00000000 s+8
D0=00000001 D1=00000000 D2=00000000 D3=00000000 V=0   0000100C:00000000 s+12
D4=00000000 D5=00000000 D6=00000000 D7=00000000 C=0   00001010:00000000 s+16
---------->MOVE.W    #$02,D1

PC=00040C SR=2000 SS=00001000 US=00000000          X=0   00001000:00000000 s
A0=00000000 A1=00000000 A2=00000000 A3=00000000 N=0   00001004:00000000 s+4
A4=00000000 A5=00000000 A6=00000000 A7=00001000 Z=0   00001008:00000000 s+8
D0=00000001 D1=00000002 D2=00000000 D3=00000000 V=0   0000100C:00000000 s+12
D4=00000000 D5=00000000 D6=00000000 D7=00000000 C=0   00001010:00000000 s+16
---------->MOVE.W    D0,-(SP)

PC=00040E SR=2000 SS=00000FFE US=00000000          X=0   00000FFE:00010000 s
A0=00000000 A1=00000000 A2=00000000 A3=00000000 N=0   00001002:00000000 s+4
A4=00000000 A5=00000000 A6=00000000 A7=00000FFE Z=0   00001006:00000000 s+8
D0=00000001 D1=00000002 D2=00000000 D3=00000000 V=0   0000100A:00000000 s+12
D4=00000000 D5=00000000 D6=00000000 D7=00000000 C=0   0000100E:00000000 s+16
---------->MOVE.W    D1,-(SP)
```

Note how the instruction MOVE.W D0, − **(SP)** has modified the stack. The top of the stack is no longer $1000, but $0FFE. You can also see that the contents of D0.W (i.e. 0001) has been pushed on the stack.

```
PC=000410 SR=2000 SS=00000FFC US=00000000          X=0   00000FFC:00020001 s
A0=00000000 A1=00000000 A2=00000000 A3=00000000 N=0   00001000:00000000 s+4
A4=00000000 A5=00000000 A6=00000000 A7=00000FFC Z=0   00001004:00000000 s+8
D0=00000001 D1=00000002 D2=00000000 D3=00000000 V=0   00001008:00000000 s+12
D4=00000000 D5=00000000 D6=00000000 D7=00000000 C=0   0000100C:00000000 s+16
---------->BSR.L     $041E

PC=00041E SR=2000 SS=00000FF8 US=00000000          X=0   00000FF8:00000414 s
A0=00000000 A1=00000000 A2=00000000 A3=00000000 N=0   00000FFC:00020001 s+4
A4=00000000 A5=00000000 A6=00000000 A7=00000FF8 Z=0   00001000:00000000 s+8
D0=00000001 D1=00000002 D2=00000000 D3=00000000 V=0   00001004:00000000 s+12
D4=00000000 D5=00000000 D6=00000000 D7=00000000 C=0   00001008:00000000 s+16
---------->MOVE.W    $04(SP),D2
```

At this point the return address, $00000414, has been pushed on the stack and the stack pointer is now pointing at $00000FF8.

```
PC=000422 SR=2000 SS=00000FF8 US=00000000          X=0   00000FF8:00000414 s
A0=00000000 A1=00000000 A2=00000000 A3=00000000 N=0   00000FFC:00020001 s+4
A4=00000000 A5=00000000 A6=00000000 A7=00000FF8 Z=0   00001000:00000000 s+8
D0=00000001 D1=00000002 D2=00000002 D3=00000000 V=0   00001004:00000000 s+12
D4=00000000 D5=00000000 D6=00000000 D7=00000000 C=0   00001008:00000000 s+16
---------->MOVE.W    $06(SP),D3

PC=000426 SR=2000 SS=00000FF8 US=00000000          X=0   00000FF8:00000414 s
A0=00000000 A1=00000000 A2=00000000 A3=00000000 N=0   00000FFC:00020001 s+4
A4=00000000 A5=00000000 A6=00000000 A7=00000FF8 Z=0   00001000:00000000 s+8
D0=00000001 D1=00000002 D2=00000002 D3=00000001 V=0   00001004:00000000 s+12
D4=00000000 D5=00000000 D6=00000000 D7=00000000 C=0   00001008:00000000 s+16
---------->ADD.W     D2,D3
```

```
PC=000428 SR=2000 SS=00000FF8 US=00000000         X=0   00000FF8:00000414 s
A0=00000000 A1=00000000 A2=00000000 A3=00000000 N=0   00000FFC:00020001 s+4
A4=00000000 A5=00000000 A6=00000000 A7=00000FF8 Z=0   00001000:00000000 s+8
D0=00000001 D1=00000002 D2=00000002 D3=00000003 V=0   00001004:00000000 s+12
D4=00000000 D5=00000000 D6=00000000 D7=00000000 C=0   00001008:00000000 s+16
---------->MOVE.W   D3,$04(SP)

PC=00042C SR=2000 SS=00000FF8 US=00000000         X=0   00000FF8:00000414 s
A0=00000000 A1=00000000 A2=00000000 A3=00000000 N=0   00000FFC:00030001 s+4
A4=00000000 A5=00000000 A6=00000000 A7=00000FF8 Z=0   00001000:00000000 s+8
D0=00000001 D1=00000002 D2=00000002 D3=00000003 V=0   00001004:00000000 s+12
D4=00000000 D5=00000000 D6=00000000 D7=00000000 C=0   00001008:00000000 s+16
---------->RTS

PC=000414 SR=2000 SS=00000FFC US=00000000         X=0   00000FFC:00030001 s
A0=00000000 A1=00000000 A2=00000000 A3=00000000 N=0   00001000:00000000 s+4
A4=00000000 A5=00000000 A6=00000000 A7=00000FFC Z=0   00001004:00000000 s+8
D0=00000001 D1=00000002 D2=00000002 D3=00000003 V=0   00001008:00000000 s+12
D4=00000000 D5=00000000 D6=00000000 D7=00000000 C=0   0000100C:00000000 s+16
---------->MOVE.W   (SP)+,D4

PC=000416 SR=2000 SS=00000FFE US=00000000         X=0   00000FFE:00010000 s
A0=00000000 A1=00000000 A2=00000000 A3=00000000 N=0   00001002:00000000 s+4
A4=00000000 A5=00000000 A6=00000000 A7=00000FFE Z=0   00001006:00000000 s+8
D0=00000001 D1=00000002 D2=00000002 D3=00000003 V=0   0000100A:00000000 s+12
D4=00000003 D5=00000000 D6=00000000 D7=00000000 C=0   0000100E:00000000 s+16
---------->LEA.L    $02(SP),SP

PC=00041A SR=2000 SS=00001000 US=00000000         X=0   00001000:00000000 s
A0=00000000 A1=00000000 A2=00000000 A3=00000000 N=0   00001004:00000000 s+4
A4=00000000 A5=00000000 A6=00000000 A7=00001000 Z=0   00001008:00000000 s+8
D0=00000001 D1=00000002 D2=00000002 D3=00000003 V=0   0000100C:00000000 s+12
D4=00000003 D5=00000000 D6=00000000 D7=00000000 C=0   00001010:00000000 s+16
---------->STOP     #$2700
```

The result $1 + 2 = 3$ is in data register D3, and the stack pointer is the same as its starting value $1000. Passing a parameter to a subroutine by value is easy. Getting a result back from the subroutine is trickier, as we'll soon see.

Passing parameters by reference

We have passed a parameter *by value* to the subroutine by pushing a copy of its *value* on the stack. There are two copies of the parameter, the original in the calling program and its copy on the stack. If a parameter is passed by value, changing it within the subroutine doesn't change its value in the calling program—as the next example demonstrates.

```
*         Program to call a subroutine that swaps two numbers A and B
*
          ORG      $400
          LEA      $1000,A7      Set up the stack pointer
          MOVE.W   A,-(A7)       Push value of parameter A
          MOVE.W   B,-(A7)       Push value of parameter B
          BSR      SWAP          Call subroutine to swap A and B
          LEA      4(A7),A7      Clean up the stack
          STOP     #$2700        Stop
*
SWAP      MOVE.W   4(A7),D1      Get first parameter in D0
          MOVE.W   6(A7),4(A7)   Copy second parameter to first parameter
          MOVE.W   D1,6(A7)      Copy first parameter to second parameter
          RTS
*
A         DC.W     $1234
B         DC.W     $5678
*
          END      $400
```

This program calls a subroutine to swap two numbers, A and B, which are first pushed on the stack in the main program. In subroutine SWAP the two parameters are retrieved from their locations on the stack and swapped over. Once a return from subroutine is made and the stack cleaned up, the parameters on the stack are lost. Parameters A and B in the main program were never swapped.

In this case, there is only one copy of the parameter. We repeat the example in which we added two numbers together, and, this time, pass the parameters to the subroutine by reference.

The following program introduces a new instruction, *push effective address* PEA, which pushes an address in the stack; for example, the operation PEA PQR pushes the address PQR on the stack. The instruction PEA PQR is equivalent to MOVE.L #PQR, −(A7).

```
        ORG     $400
        LEA     $1000,A7    Set up the stack pointer
        PEA     X           Push address of variable X
        PEA     Y           Push address of variable Y
        PEA     Z           Push address of variable Z (the result)
        BSR     AddUp       Call adder routine
        MOVE.W  Z,D2        Read the result (a dummy operation)
        LEA     12(A7),A7   Clean up stack
        STOP    #$2700      Stop
*
AddUp   MOVEA.L 12(A7),A0   Get address of parameter X
        MOVEA.L 8(A7),A1    Get address of parameter Y
        MOVE.W  (A0),D2     Get value of X
        MOVE.W  (A1),D3     Get value of Y
        ADD     D2,D3       Add them
        MOVEA.L 4(A7),A3    Get address of parameter Z
        MOVE.W  D3,(A3)     Put result in variable Z
        RTS
*
        ORG     $500
X       DC.W    1
Y       DC.W    2
Z       DS.W    1
```

You can pass a parameter to a subroutine *by reference* by passing its address on the stack. This is, you don't say 'Here's a parameter'. Instead you say, 'Here's where the parameter is located'.

The following is the assembled version of this program and Fig. 6.32 provides snapshots of memory and registers during the execution of the code.

```
 1  00000400                          ORG     $400
 2  00000400 4FF81000        LEA     $1000,A7    ;Set up the stack pointer
 3  00000404 487900000500    PEA     X           ;Push address of X
 4  0000040A 487900000502    PEA     Y           ;Push address of Y
 5  00000410 487900000504    PEA     Z           ;Push address of Z
 6  00000416 61000010        BSR     ADDUP       ;Call adder routine
 7  0000041A 343900000504    MOVE.W  Z,D2        ;Read the result
 8  00000420 4FEF000C        LEA     12(A7),A7   ;Clean up stack
 9  00000424 4E722700        STOP    #$2700      ;Stop
10                    *
11  00000428 206F000C  ADDUP:  MOVEA.L 12(A7),A0   ;Get address of parameter
12  0000042C 226F0008          MOVEA.L 8(A7),A1    ;Get address of parameter
13  00000430 3410              MOVE.W  (A0),D2     ;Get value of X
14  00000432 3611              MOVE.W  (A1),D3     ;Get value of Y
15  00000434 D642              ADD     D2,D3       ;Add them
16  00000436 266F0004          MOVEA.L 4(A7),A3    ;Get address of parameter
17  0000043A 3683              MOVE.W  D3,(A3)     ;Put result in variable Z
18  0000043C 4E75              RTS
19                    *
20  00000500                  ORG     $500
21  00000500 0001      X:      DC.W    1
22  00000502 0002      Y:      DC.W    2
23  00000504 00000002  Z:      DS.W    1
24                    *
25          00000400          END     $400
```

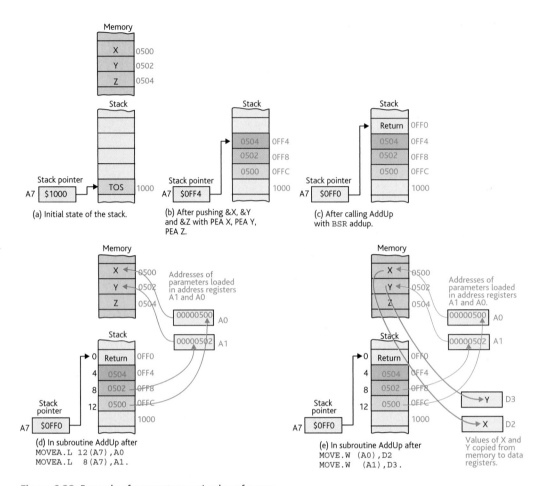

Figure 6.32 Example of parameter passing by reference.

We can now run this program line by line. Note how the addresses of the variables are pushed on the stack and then loaded in address registers in the subroutine.

We will use the simulator command MD 500 to view the data area. Initially it contains the two 16-bit constants 1 and 2.

```
000500   00 01 00 02 00 00 00 00 00 00 00 00 00 00 00 00.

PC=000400 SR=2000 SS=00A00000 US=00000000        X=0
A0=00000000 A1=00000000 A2=00000000 A3=00000000 N=0
A4=00000000 A5=00000000 A6=00000000 A7=00A00000 Z=0
D0=00000000 D1=00000000 D2=00000000 D3=00000000 V=0
D4=00000000 D5=00000000 D6=00000000 D7=00000000 C=0
---------->LEA.L    $1000,SP

PC=000404 SR=2000 SS=00001000 US=00000000        X=0   00001000:00000000 s
A0=00000000 A1=00000000 A2=00000000 A3=00000000 N=0   00001004:00000000 s+4
A4=00000000 A5=00000000 A6=00000000 A7=00001000 Z=0   00001008:00000000 s+8
D0=00000000 D1=00000000 D2=00000000 D3=00000000 V=0   0000100C:00000000 s+12
D4=00000000 D5=00000000 D6=00000000 D7=00000000 C=0   00001010:00000000 s+16
---------->PEA      $0500

PC=00040A SR=2000 SS=00000FFC US=00000000        X=0   00000FFC:00000500 s
A0=00000000 A1=00000000 A2=00000000 A3=00000000 N=0   00001000:00000000 s+4
A4=00000000 A5=00000000 A6=00000000 A7=00000FFC Z=0   00001004:00000000 s+8
D0=00000000 D1=00000000 D2=00000000 D3=00000000 V=0   00001008:00000000 s+12
D4=00000000 D5=00000000 D6=00000000 D7=00000000 C=0   0000100C:00000000 s+16
---------->PEA      $0502
```

The operation **PEA $0500** has pushed the address $00000500 on the stack and moved the stack pointer up by 4.

```
PC=000410  SR=2000  SS=00000FF8  US=00000000         X=0    00000FF8:00000502  s
A0=00000000 A1=00000000 A2=00000000 A3=00000000 N=0   00000FFC:00000500  s+4
A4=00000000 A5=00000000 A6=00000000 A7=00000FF8 Z=0   00001000:00000000  s+8
D0=00000000 D1=00000000 D2=00000000 D3=00000000 V=0   00001004:00000000  s+12
D4=00000000 D5=00000000 D6=00000000 D7=00000000 C=0   00001008:00000000  s+16
---------->PEA       $0504

PC=000416  SR=2000  SS=00000FF4  US=00000000         X=0    00000FF4:00000504  s
A0=00000000 A1=00000000 A2=00000000 A3=00000000 N=0   00000FF8:00000502  s+4
A4=00000000 A5=00000000 A6=00000000 A7=00000FF4 Z=0   00000FFC:00000500  s+8
D0=00000000 D1=00000000 D2=00000000 D3=00000000 V=0   00001000:00000000  s+12
D4=00000000 D5=00000000 D6=00000000 D7=00000000 C=0   00001004:00000000  s+16
---------->BSR.L     $0428

PC=000428  SR=2000  SS=00000FF0  US=00000000         X=0    00000FF0:0000041A  s
A0=00000000 A1=00000000 A2=00000000 A3=00000000 N=0   00000FF4:00000504  s+4
A4=00000000 A5=00000000 A6=00000000 A7=00000FF0 Z=0   00000FF8:00000502  s+8
D0=00000000 D1=00000000 D2=00000000 D3=00000000 V=0   00000FFC:00000500  s+12
D4=00000000 D5=00000000 D6=00000000 D7=00000000 C=0   00001000:00000000  s+16
---------->MOVEA.L   $0C(SP),A0

PC=00042C  SR=2000  SS=00000FF0  US=00000000         X=0    00000FF0:0000041A  s
A0=00000500 A1=00000000 A2=00000000 A3=00000000 N=0   00000FF4:00000504  s+4
A4=00000000 A5=00000000 A6=00000000 A7=00000FF0 Z=0   00000FF8:00000502  s+8
D0=00000000 D1=00000000 D2=00000000 D3=00000000 V=0   00000FFC:00000500  s+12
D4=00000000 D5=00000000 D6=00000000 D7=00000000 C=0   00001000:00000000  s+16
---------->MOVEA.L   $08(SP),A1

PC=000430  SR=2000  SS=00000FF0  US=00000000         X=0    00000FF0:0000041A  s
A0=00000500 A1=00000502 A2=00000000 A3=00000000 N=0   00000FF4:00000504  s+4
A4=00000000 A5=00000000 A6=00000000 A7=00000FF0 Z=0   00000FF8:00000502  s+8
D0=00000000 D1=00000000 D2=00000000 D3=00000000 V=0   00000FFC:00000500  s+12
D4=00000000 D5=00000000 D6=00000000 D7=00000000 C=0   00001000:00000000  s+16
---------->MOVE.W    (A0),D2

PC=000432  SR=2000  SS=00000FF0  US=00000000         X=0    00000FF0:0000041A  s
A0=00000500 A1=00000502 A2=00000000 A3=00000000 N=0   00000FF4:00000504  s+4
A4=00000000 A5=00000000 A6=00000000 A7=00000FF0 Z=0   00000FF8:00000502  s+8
D0=00000000 D1=00000000 D2=00000001 D3=00000000 V=0   00000FFC:00000500  s+12
D4=00000000 D5=00000000 D6=00000000 D7=00000000 C=0   00001000:00000000  s+16
---------->MOVE.W    (A1),D3

PC=000434  SR=2000  SS=00000FF0  US=00000000         X=0    00000FF0:0000041A  s
A0=00000500 A1=00000502 A2=00000000 A3=00000000 N=0   00000FF4:00000504  s+4
A4=00000000 A5=00000000 A6=00000000 A7=00000FF0 Z=0   00000FF8:00000502  s+8
D0=00000000 D1=00000000 D2=00000001 D3=00000002 V=0   00000FFC:00000500  s+12
D4=00000000 D5=00000000 D6=00000000 D7=00000000 C=0   00001000:00000000  s+16
---------->ADD.W     D2,D3

PC=000436  SR=2000  SS=00000FF0  US=00000000         X=0    00000FF0:0000041A  s
A0=00000500 A1=00000502 A2=00000000 A3=00000000 N=0   00000FF4:00000504  s+4
A4=00000000 A5=00000000 A6=00000000 A7=00000FF0 Z=0   00000FF8:00000502  s+8
D0=00000000 D1=00000000 D2=00000001 D3=00000003 V=0   00000FFC:00000500  s+12
D4=00000000 D5=00000000 D6=00000000 D7=00000000 C=0   00001000:00000000  s+16
---------->MOVEA.L   $04(SP),A3

PC=00043A  SR=2000  SS=00000FF0  US=00000000         X=0    00000FF0:0000041A  s
A0=00000500 A1=00000502 A2=00000000 A3=00000504 N=0   00000FF4:00000504  s+4
A4=00000000 A5=00000000 A6=00000000 A7=00000FF0 Z=0   00000FF8:00000502  s+8
D0=00000000 D1=00000000 D2=00000001 D3=00000003 V=0   00000FFC:00000500  s+12
D4=00000000 D5=00000000 D6=00000000 D7=00000000 C=0   00001000:00000000  s+16
---------->MOVE.W    D3,(A3)

PC=00043C  SR=2000  SS=00000FF0  US=00000000         X=0    00000FF0:0000041A  s
A0=00000500 A1=00000502 A2=00000000 A3=00000504 N=0   00000FF4:00000504  s+4
A4=00000000 A5=00000000 A6=00000000 A7=00000FF0 Z=0   00000FF8:00000502  s+8
D0=00000000 D1=00000000 D2=00000001 D3=00000003 V=0   00000FFC:00000500  s+12
D4=00000000 D5=00000000 D6=00000000 D7=00000000 C=0   00001000:00000000  s+16
---------->RTS
```

```
PC=00041A SR=2000 SS=00000FF4 US=00000000        X=0   00000FF4:00000504 s
A0=00000500 A1=00000502 A2=00000000 A3=00000504 N=0   00000FF8:00000502 s+4
A4=00000000 A5=00000000 A6=00000000 A7=00000FF4 Z=0   00000FFC:00000500 s+8
D0=00000000 D1=00000000 D2=00000001 D3=00000003 V=0   00001000:00000000 s+12
D4=00000000 D5=00000000 D6=00000000 D7=00000000 C=0   00001004:00000000 s+16
---------->MOVE.W   $0504,D2


PC=000420 SR=2000 SS=00000FF4 US=00000000        X=0   00000FF4:00000504 s
A0=00000500 A1=00000502 A2=00000000 A3=00000504 N=0   00000FF8:00000502 s+4
A4=00000000 A5=00000000 A6=00000000 A7=00000FF4 Z=0   00000FFC:00000500 s+8
D0=00000000 D1=00000000 D2=00000003 D3=00000003 V=0   00001000:00000000 s+12
D4=00000000 D5=00000000 D6=00000000 D7=00000000 C=0   00001004:00000000 s+16
---------->LEA.L    $0C(SP),SP

PC=000424 SR=2000 SS=00001000 US=00000000        X=0   00001000:00000000 s
A0=00000500 A1=00000502 A2=00000000 A3=00000504 N=0   00001004:00000000 s+4
A4=00000000 A5=00000000 A6=00000000 A7=00001000 Z=0   00001008:00000000 s+8
D0=00000000 D1=00000000 D2=00000003 D3=00000003 V=0   0000100C:00000000 s+12
D4=00000000 D5=00000000 D6=00000000 D7=00000000 C=0   00001010:00000000 s+16
---------->STOP     #$2700
```

If we look at memory again, we will find that the sum of X and Y has been stored in location Z.

```
000500   00 01 00 02  00 03 00 00 00 00 00 00 00 00 00 00
```

We have passed the parameters by reference. In practice, a programmer would pass parameters that aren't changed in the subroutine by value, and only pass parameters that are to be changed by reference.

6.6 Examples of 68K programs

We now put together some of the things we've learned about the 68K's instruction set and write a simple program to implement a text matching algorithm that determines whether a string contains a certain substring. The problem can be solved by sliding the substring along the string until each character of the substring matches with the corresponding character of the string, as illustrated in Fig. 6.33.

The string starts at address $002000 and is terminated by a carriage return (ASCII code $0D). The substring is stored at location $002100 onwards and is also terminated by a carriage return. In what follows, the string of characters is referred to as STRING, and the substring as TEXT.

We will construct a main program that calls a subroutine, MATCH, to scan the string for the first occurrence of the

String	T H I S T H A T T H E N T H E O T H E R	
Substring	T H E N T H E	

Step	Matches	T H I S T H A T T H E N T H E O T H E R
1	5	T H E N T H E
2	0	T H E N T H E
3	0	T H E N T H E
4	1	T H E N T H E
5	0	T H E N T H E
6	6	T H E N T H E
7	0	T H E N T H E
8	0	T H E N T H E
9	1	T H E N T H E
10	0	T H E N T H E
11	8	T H E N T H E
12	0	T H E N T H E
13	0	T H E N T H E

Figure 6.33 Matching a string and a substring.

substring. Because STRING and TEXT are both strings of consecutive characters, we will pass them to MATCH by reference. The subroutine should return the address of the first character in the string matching the first character of the substring. This address is to be returned on the stack. If the match is unsuccessful, the null address, $00000000, is pushed on the stack.

```
CRET      EQU      $0D              ASCII code for carriage return
*
          ORG      $400             Start of the main program
          LEA      $1000,A7         Set up the stack pointer
          PEA      STRING           Push the address of the string
          PEA      TEXT             Push the address of the substring
          LEA      -4(A7),A7        Make room on the stack for the result
          BSR      MATCH            Perform the match
          MOVE.L   (A7)+,D0         Let's have a look at the result
          LEA      8(A7),A7         Clean up the stack (remove the 2 parameters)
          STOP     #$2700
*
*         MATCH matches the substring whose location is pointed at by
*         A0 with the string whose location is pointed at by A1.
*         Both strings are terminated by a carriage return.
*
*         The match is carried out by comparing the first character of
*         the substring with the characters of the string, one by one.
*         If a match is found, the rest of the characters of the
*         substring are matched with the corresponding characters of
*         the string. If they all match up to the substring terminator,
*         the search is successful. As soon as a mismatch is found, we
*         return to matching the first character of the substring with
*         a character from the string. If the terminator of the string
*         is reached, the search has been unsuccessful.
MATCH     MOVEM.L  D0/A0-A3,-(A7)   Save all working registers
          MOVEA.L  32(A7),A0        Get STRING address off the stack
          MOVEA.L  28(A7),A1        Get TEXT (substring) address off the stack
*
NEXT      MOVE.B   (A0)+,D0         Get a character from the string
          CMP.B    #CRET,D0         Is this character a carriage return?
          BEQ      FAIL             If carriage return then no match so exit
          CMP.B    (A1),D0          Match character with char from substring
          BNE      NEXT             If no match then move along the string
*
*         We have found the first match.
*         We have to save the two pointers before performing the
*         submatch in case we have to return to matching the pairs
*         of first characters.
*
          MOVEA.L  A0,A2            Save A0 in A2 in case of no full match
          MOVEA.L  A1,A3            Save A1 in A3
          ADDA.L   #1,A1            Increment pointer to substring
*
LOOP      MOVE.B   (A1)+,D0         Get next character from substring
          CMP.B    #CRET,D0         If terminator found then success
          BEQ      SUCCESS
          CMP.B    (A0)+,D0         Else compare it with next char from string
          BEQ      LOOP             Repeat while they match
*
*         No submatch found so prepare to continue matching pairs
*         of first characters.
*
          MOVEA.L  A2,A0            Restore A0 and A1
          MOVEA.L  A3,A1            to their values before the submatch
          BRA      NEXT             Try again
*
SUCCESS   SUBA.L   #1,A2            Undo work of auto increment
          MOVE.L   A2,24(A7)        Push address of match on stack
          BRA      RETURN
*
FAIL      MOVE.L   #0,24(A7)        Push null address on stack for fail
*
RETURN    MOVEM.L  (A7)+,D0/A0-A3   Restore all working registers
          RTS
*
          ORG      $002000          Location of the string
STRING    DC.B     'THIS THAT THEN',$0D
          ORG      $002100          Location of substring to be matched
TEXT      DC.B     'THEN THE',$0D
*
          END      $400
```

6.6.1 A circular buffer

Many computers can't process data as they receive it; the data is placed in a store until it's ready for use by the computer. This store is a *buffer* and is analogous to a doctor's waiting room. The number of people in the waiting room increases as new patients enter and decreases as patients are treated by the doctor. Consider a 68K-based system with a software module that is employed by both input and output routines, and whose function is to buffer data. When it's called by the input routine, it adds a character to the buffer. When it's called by the output routine, it removes a character from the buffer. Below are the operational parameters of the subroutine.

- Register D0 is to be used for character input and output. The character is an 8-bit value and occupies the lowest-order byte of D0.
- Register D1 contains the code 0, 1, or 2 on entering the subroutine.
- Code 0 means clear the buffer and reset all pointers.
- Code 1 means place the character in D0 into the buffer.
- Code 2 means remove a character from the buffer and place it in D0.
- We assume that a higher-level module ensures that only one of 0, 1, or 2 is passed to the module (i.e. invalid operation codes cannot occur).
- The location of the first entry in the buffer is at $010000 and the buffer size is 1024 bytes. Pointers and storage may be placed after the end of the buffer.
- If the buffer is full, the addition of a new character overwrites the oldest character in the buffer. In this case, bit 31 of D0 is set to indicate overflow and cleared otherwise.

- If the buffer is empty, removing a new character results in the contents of the lower byte of D0 being set to zero and its most-significant bit set.
- Apart from D0, no other registers are to be modified by calling the subroutine.

The first step in solving the problem is to construct a diagram (Fig. 6.34) to help us visualize the buffer. Figure 6.34 shows the memory map corresponding to the buffer. A region of 1024 bytes ($400) is reserved for the buffer together with two 32-bit pointers. IN_ptr points to the location of the next free position into which a new character is to be placed and OUT_ptr points to the location of the next character to be removed from the buffer. At the right-hand side of the diagram is the logical arrangement of the circular buffer. This arrangement provides the programmer with a better mental image of how the process is to operate.

The first level of abstraction in pseudocode is to determine the overall action the module is to perform. This can be written as follows.

```
Module Circular_buffer
      Save working registers
      CASE OF:
              D1 = 0:  Initialize system
              D1 = 1:  Input a character
              D1 = 2:  Output a character
      END_CASE
      Restore working registers
End Circular_buffer
```

At this, the highest level of abstraction, we have provided no indication of how any action is to be carried out and the only control structure is the selection of one of three possible functions. The next step is to elaborate on some of these actions.

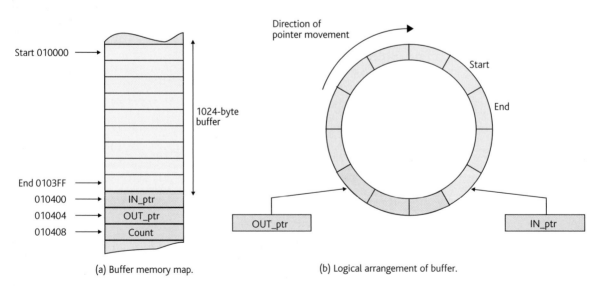

(a) Buffer memory map.   (b) Logical arrangement of buffer.

Figure 6.34 The circular buffer.

```
Module Circular_buffer
      Save working registers
      IF [D1] = 0 THEN Initialize END_IF
      IF [D1] = 1 THEN Input_character END_IF
      IF [D1] = 2 THEN Output_character END_IF
      Restore working registers
End Circular_buffer

Initialize
          Count = 0
          IN_ptr = Start
          OUT_ptr = Start
End Initialize

Input_character
              Store new character
              Deal with any overflow
End Input_character
Output_character
              IF buffer NOT empty THEN Get_character_from_buffer
                                  ELSE return null character
              END_IF
End Output_character
```

The pseudocode is now fairly detailed. Both the module selection and the initialization routines are complete. We still have to work on the input and output routines because of the difficulty in dealing with the effects of overflow and underflow in a circular buffer.

We can determine the state of the buffer by means of a variable, Count, which indicates the number of characters in the buffer. If Count is greater than zero and less than its maximum value, a new character can be added or one removed without any difficulty. If Count is zero, the buffer is empty and we can add a character but not remove one. If Count is equal to its maximum value and therefore the buffer is full, each new character must overwrite the oldest character as specified by the program requirements. This last step is tricky because the next character to be output (the oldest character in the buffer) is overwritten by the latest character. Therefore, the next character to be output will now be the oldest surviving character and the pointer to the output must be moved to reflect this.

Sometimes it is helpful to draw a simplified picture of the system to enable you to walk through the design. Figure 6.35 shows a buffer with four locations. Initially, in state (a), the buffer is empty and both pointers point to the same location. At state (b), a character is entered, the counter incremented, and the input pointer moved to the next free position. States (c) to (e) show the buffer successively filling up to its maximum count of 4. If another character is now input, as in state (f), the oldest character in the buffer is overwritten.

It is not necessary to rewrite the entire module in pseudocode. We will concentrate on the input and output routines and then begin assembly language coding. Because the logical buffer is circular while the physical buffer is not, we must wrap the physical buffer round. That is, when the last location in the physical buffer is filled, we must move back to the start of the buffer.

```
Input_character
    Store new character at IN_ptr
    IN_ptr = IN_ptr + 1
    IF IN_ptr > End THEN IN_ptr = Start END_IF
    IF Count < Max THEN Count = Count + 1
                   ELSE
                        Set overflow flag
                        OUT_ptr = OUT_ptr + 1
                        IF OUT_ptr > End THEN OUT_ptr = Start END_IF
         END_IF
End Input_character

Output_character
    IF Count = 0 THEN return null and set underflow flag
                 ELSE
                      Count = Count - 1
                      Get character pointed at by OUT_ptr
                      OUT_ptr = OUT_ptr + 1
                      IF OUT_ptr > End THEN OUT_ptr = Start END_IF
         END_IF
End Output_character
```

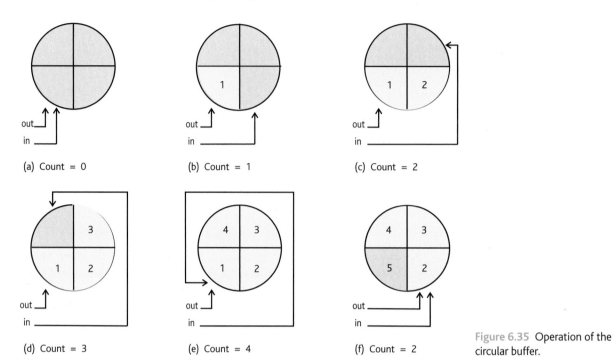

(a) Count = 0   (b) Count = 1   (c) Count = 2

(d) Count = 3   (e) Count = 4   (f) Count = 2

Figure 6.35 Operation of the circular buffer.

The program design language has now done its job and we can translate the routines into the appropriate assembly language.

```
CIRC      EQU       *            This module implements a circular buffer
          MOVEM.L A0-A1,-(SP)    Save working registers
          BCLR.L  #31,D0         Clear bit 31 of D0 (no error)
          CMPI.B  #0,D1          Test for initialize request
          BNE.S   CIRC1          IF not 0 THEN next test
          BSR.S   INITIAL        IF 0 THEN perform initialize
          BRA.S   CIRC3           and exit
CIRC1     CMPI.B  #1,D1          Test for input request
          BNE.S   CIRC2          IF not input THEN must be output
          BSR.S   INPUT          IF 1 THEN INPUT
          BRA.S   CIRC3           and exit
CIRC2     BSR.S   OUTPUT         By default OUTPUT
CIRC3     MOVEM.L (SP)+,A0-A1    Restore working registers
          RTS                    End CIRCULAR
*
INITIAL EQU *     This module sets up the circular buffer
          CLR.W   COUNT          Initialize counter and pointers
          MOVE.L  #BUFFER,IN_PTR Set up IN_ptr
          MOVE.L  #BUFFER,OUT_PTR Set up OUT_ptr
          RTS
*
INPUT     EQU *     This module stores a character in the buffer
          MOVEA.L IN_PTR,A0      Get pointer to input
          MOVE.B  D0,(A0)+       Store char in buffer, update pointer
          CMPA.L  #END+1,A0      Test for wrap-round
          BNE.S   INPUT1         IF not end THEN skip reposition
          MOVEA.L #START,A0      Reposition input pointer
INPUT1    MOVE.L  A0,IN_PTR      Save updated pointer
          CMPI.W  #MAX,COUNT     Is buffer full?
          BEQ.S   INPUT2         IF full THEN deal with overflow
          ADDQ.B  #1,COUNT             ELSE increment character count
          RTS                     and return
INPUT2    BSET.L  #31,D0         Set overflow flag
          MOVEA.L OUT_PTR,A0     Get output pointer
          LEA     1(A0),A0       Increment OUT_ptr
          CMPA.L  #END+1,A0      Test for wrap-round
```

```
              BNE.S    INPUT3                 IF not wrap-round THEN skip fix
              MOVEA.L  #START,A0              ELSE wrap-round OUT_ptr
INPUT3        MOVE.L   A0,OUT_PTR             Update OUT_ptr in memory
              RTS                                 and return
OUTPUT        TST.W    COUNT                  Examine state of buffer
              BNE.S    OUTPUT1                IF buffer not empty output char
              CLR.B    D0                     ELSE return null output
              BSET.L   #31,D0                   set underflow flag
              RTS                                and exit
OUTPUT1       SUBI.W   #1,COUNT               Decrement COUNT for removal
              MOVEA.L  OUT_PTR,A0             Point to next char to be output
              MOVE.B   (A0)+,D0               Get character and update pointer
              CMPA.L   #END+1,A0              Test for wrap-round
              BNE.S    OUTPUT2                IF not wrap-round THEN exit
              MOVEA.L  #START,A0              ELSE wrap-round OUT_ptr
OUTPUT2       MOVE.L   A0,OUT_PTR             Restore OUT_ptr in memory
              RTS
```

Now that we've designed and coded the buffer, the next step is to test it. The following code is the assembled circular buffer program with the necessary driver routines. The program inputs two characters at a time, and implements an 8-byte buffer. The first character of a pair is the control character (i.e. 0 = initialize, 1 = input, and 2 = output). For example, to initialize the buffer you type 0X, where X is any character. If you type 1Y, the character Y is stored in the next free place in the buffer. If you type 2Z, the next character to be output is displayed. After each operation, the contents of the buffer are printed and the current value of the variable count displayed.

```
 1  00000400                          ORG      $400
 2  00000400  4DF900001012            LEA      HEADER,A6       ;Print heading
 3  00000406  6100015E                BSR      PRINT
 4  0000040A  61000104       NEXT:    BSR      GETCHAR         ;REPEAT
 5  0000040E  04010030                SUB.B    #$30,D1         ;Get number (0, 1, or 2)
 6  00000412  1E01                    MOVE.B   D1,D7           ;Save it
 7  00000414  610000FA                BSR      GETCHAR         ;Get character for input routine
 8  00000418  1001                    MOVE.B   D1,D0
 9  0000041A  1207                    MOVE.B   D7,D1           ;Restore number
10  0000041C  6100002A                BSR      CIRC            ;Call the buffer routine
11  00000420  0C010002                CMP.B    #2,D1           ;IF we did output THEN print the char
12  00000424  66000018                BNE      CONT
13  00000428  1C00                    MOVE.B   D0,D6           ;Save character from output
14  0000042A  610000F4                BSR      NEWLINE
15  0000042E  4DF900001023            LEA      OUT,A6          ;Print "output"
16  00000434  61000130                BSR      PRINT
17  00000438  1206                    MOVE.B   D6,D1
18  0000043A  610000DC                BSR      PUTCHAR         ;Now print the character
19  0000043E  610000E0       CONT:    BSR      NEWLINE
20  00000442  610000E8                BSR      DISPLAY         ;Display the buffer contents
21  00000446  60C2                    BRA      NEXT            ;FOREVER
22                           *
23            00000448       CIRC:    EQU      *               ;Implement a circular buffer
24  00000448  48E700C0                MOVEM.L  A0-A1,-(SP)     ;Save working registers
25  0000044C  0880001F                BCLR     #31,D0          ;Clear bit 31 of D0 (no error)
26  00000450  0C010000                CMPI.B   #0,D1           ;Test for initialize request
27  00000454  6604                    BNE.S    CIRC1           ;IF not 0 THEN next test
28  00000456  6114                    BSR.S    INITIAL         ;IF 0 THEN perform initialize
29  00000458  600C                    BRA.S    CIRC3           ;and exit
30  0000045A  0C010001       CIRC1:   CMPI.B   #1,D1           ;Test for input request
31  0000045E  6604                    BNE.S    CIRC2           ;IF not input THEN must be output
32  00000460  6126                    BSR.S    INPUT           ;IF 1 THEN INPUT
33  00000462  6002                    BRA.S    CIRC3           ;and exit
34  00000464  6174           CIRC2:   BSR.S    OUTPUT          ;By default OUTPUT
35  00000466  4CDF0300       CIRC3:   MOVEM.L  (SP)+,A0-A1     ;Restore working registers
36  0000046A  4E75                    RTS                      ;End CIRCULAR
37                           *
38            0000046C       INITIAL: EQU      *               ;Set up the circular buffer
39  0000046C  427900001008            CLR.W    COUNT           ;Initialize counter and pointers
40  00000472  23FC00001000            MOVE.L   #BUFFER,IN_POINT ;Set up IN_ptr
             0000100A
41  0000047C  23FC00001000            MOVE.L   #BUFFER,OUT_POINT ;Set up OUT_ptr
             0000100E
42  00000486  4E75                    RTS
43                           *
44            00000488       INPUT:   EQU      *               ;Store a char in the buffer
45  00000488  20790000100A            MOVEA.L  IN_POINT,A0     ;Get pointer to input
46  0000048E  10C0                    MOVE.B   D0,(A0)+        ;Store char in buffer, update ptr
47  00000490  B1FC00001008            CMPA.L   #LAST+1,A0      ;Test for wrap-round
48  00000496  6606                    BNE.S    INPUT1          ;IF not end THEN skip reposition
```

```
49   00000498 207C00001000          MOVEA.L  #START,A0        ;Reposition input pointer
50   0000049E 23C80000100A INPUT1:  MOVE.L   A0,IN_POINT      ;Save updated pointer
51   000004A4 0C7900080000          CMPI.W   #MAX,COUNT       ;Is buffer full?
              1008
52   000004AC 6708                  BEQ.S    INPUT2           ;IF full THEN deal with overflow
53   000004AE 527900001008          ADDQ.W   #1,COUNT         ;ELSE increment character count
54   000004B4 4E75                  RTS                       ;and return
55   000004B6 08C0001F     INPUT2:  BSET     #31,D0           ;Set overflow flag
56   000004BA 20790000100E          MOVEA.L  OUT_POINT,A0     ;Get output pointer
57   000004C0 41E80001              LEA      1(A0),A0         ;Increment OUT_ptr
58   000004C4 B1FC00001008          CMPA.L   #LAST+1,A0       ;Test for wrap-round
59   000004CA 6606                  BNE.S    INPUT3           ;IF not wrap-round THEN skip fix
60   000004CC 207C00001000          MOVEA.L  #START,A0        ;ELSE wrap-round OUT_ptr
61   000004D2 23C80000100E INPUT3:  MOVE.L   A0,OUT_POINT     ;Update OUT_ptr in memory
62   000004D8 4E75                  RTS                       ;and return
63                         *
64   000004DA 4A7900001008 OUTPUT:  TST.W    COUNT            ;Examine state of buffer
65   000004E0 6608                  BNE.S    OUTPUT1          ;IF buffer not empty output char
66   000004E2 4200                  CLR.B    D0               ;ELSE return null output
67   000004E4 08C0001F              BSET     #31,D0           ;set underflow flag
68   000004E8 4E75                  RTS                       ;and exit
69   000004EA 047900010000 OUTPUT1: SUBI.W   #1,COUNT         ;Decrement COUNT for removal
              1008
70   000004F2 20790000100E          MOVEA.L  OUT_POINT,A0     ;Point to next char to be output
71   000004F8 1018                  MOVE.B   (A0)+,D0         ;Get character and update pointer
72   000004FA B1FC00001008          CMPA.L   #LAST+1,A0       ;Test for wrap-round
73   00000500 6606                  BNE.S    OUTPUT2          ;IF not wrap-round THEN exit
74   00000502 207C00001000          MOVEA.L  #START,A0        ;ELSE wrap-round OUT_ptr
75   00000508 23C80000100E OUTPUT2: MOVE.L   A0,OUT_POINT     ;Restore OUT_ptr in memory
76   0000050E 4E75                  RTS
77                         *
78   00000510 103C0005     GETCHAR: MOVE.B   #5,D0            ;Read an ASCII character into D1
79   00000514 4E4F                  TRAP     #15
80   00000516 4E75                  RTS
81   00000518 103C0006     PUTCHAR: MOVE.B   #6,D0            ;Print the ASCII character in D1
82   0000051C 4E4F                  TRAP     #15
83   0000051E 4E75                  RTS
84   00000520 123C000D     NEWLINE: MOVE.B   #$0D,D1          ;New Line
85   00000524 61F2                  BSR      PUTCHAR
86   00000526 123C000A              MOVE.B   #$0A,D1
87   0000052A 60EC                  BRA      PUTCHAR
88   0000052C 48E7FFFE     DISPLAY: MOVEM.L  A0-A6/D0-D7,-(A7) ;Display the buffer contents
89   00000530 61EE                  BSR      NEWLINE
90   00000532 43F900001000          LEA      BUFFER,A1
91   00000538 3E3C0007              MOVE.W   #7,D7
92   0000053C 1219         DIS1:    MOVE.B   (A1)+,D1
93   0000053E 61D8                  BSR      PUTCHAR          ;Print a character
94   00000540 123C0020              MOVE.B   #$20,D1          ;and a space
95   00000544 51CFFFF6              DBRA     D7,DIS1
96   00000546 4DF900001037          LEA      COUNTER,A6       ;Print header before current count
97   0000054E 61000016              BSR      PRINT
98   00000552 323900001008          MOVE.W   COUNT,D1         ;Display count
99   00000558 06010030              ADD.B    #$30,D1
100  0000055C 61BA                  BSR      PUTCHAR
101  0000055E 61C0                  BSR      NEWLINE
102  00000560 4CDF7FFF              MOVEM.L  (A7)+,A0-A6/D0-D7
103  00000564 4E75                  RTS
104                        *
105  00000566 48E7FFFC     PRINT:   MOVEM.L  A0-A5/D0-D7,-(A7) ;Print the string pointed at by A6
106  0000056A 121E         PRINT1:  MOVE.B   (A6)+,D1
107  0000056C 6700000A              BEQ      PRINT2
108  00000570 103C0006              MOVE.B   #6,D0
109  00000574 4E4F                  TRAP     #15
110  00000576 60F2                  BRA      PRINT1
111  00000578 4CDF3FFF     PRINT2:  MOVEM.L  (A7)+,A0-A5/D0-D7
112  0000057C 4E75                  RTS
113                        *
114  00001000                       ORG      $1000
115           00001000     START:   EQU      *
116           00001007     LAST:    EQU      *+7
117           00000008     MAX:     EQU      8
118  00001000 00000008     BUFFER:  DS.B     8
119  00001008 00000002     COUNT:   DS.W     1
120  0000100A 00000004     IN_POINT: DS.L    1
121  0000100E 00000004     OUT_POINT: DS.L   1
122  00001012 43697263756C HEADER:  DC.B     'Circular Buffer ',0
              617220427566
              6665722000
123  00001023 436861726163 OUT:     DC.B     'Character output = ',0
              746572206F75
              74707574203D
              2000
124  00001037 2020436F756E COUNTER: DC.B     '  Count = ',0
              74203D2000
125           00000400              END      $400
```

This example concludes our overview of 68K assembly language programming. We have only touched the surface of this topic. Real assemblers are far more complex and include facilities to design large programs such as the separate compilation of modules. However, our intention was never to create an assembly language programmer; it was to give you some insight into how machine-level instructions are used to achieve high-level actions.

■ SUMMARY

In this chapter we've looked at how you can use a microprocessor's instruction set to write simple programs.

This is not an assembly language programming text and we cannot delve deeply into assembly language programming. We have, however, demonstrated that the assembly language programmer has to appreciate the programming environment that requires the use of assembly directives to allocate memory space for variables and constants.

We have examined some of the 68K's instructions and demonstrated how to write a program. More importantly, we have looked at the addressing modes supported by the 68K and shown how data structures like lists, tables, and arrays can be accessed.

Finally, we have introduced the stack used by the 68K to keep track of subroutine return addresses and have demonstrated how the stack can be used to pass parameters to and from a subroutine.

■ PROBLEMS

6.1 Describe the action of the following 68K assembly language instructions in RTL (register transfer language). That is, translate the assembly language syntax of the 68K instruction into the RTL notation that defines the action of the instruction.

(a)	MOVE	3000,4000	(g)	MOVE	(A0),D3
(b)	MOVE	D0,D4	(h)	MOVE	#12,(A0)
(c)	MOVE	3000,D0	(i)	MOVE	(A1),(A2)
(d)	MOVE	D0,3000	(j)	ADD	D2,D1
(e)	MOVE	#4000,D4	(k)	ADD	#13,D4
(f)	MOVE	#4000,5000	(l)	ADD	(A3),1234

6.2 Explain why the following assembly language and RTL constructs are incorrect.

(a)	MOVE	D3,#4	(d)	[D3]	← A0 + 3
(b)	MOVE	[D3],D2	(e)	[D3]	← #3
(c)	MOVE	(D3),D2	(f)	3	← [D3]

6.3 Create a simple 68K program called ADDER. Your program should add together the numbers 6, 4, 12, 16, 17, and 50. The program is to be assembled with the 68K cross-assembler and then run on the 68K simulator (either Easy68K or the Teesside assembler/simulator). Run the binary file you have created in the simulation mode.

6.4 Give examples of valid 68K assembly language instructions that use

(a) register-to-register addressing

(b) register-to-memory addressing

(c) memory-to-register addressing

(d) memory-to-memory addressing

6.5 The following 68K assembly language program illustrates what an assembler does and is designed only to illustrate some points. The source program is followed by its assembled listing. Examine both the source code and listing file, and try to follow what is happening.

```
        ORG     $400
Test    EQU     6                       Dummy equates
Alan    EQU     7
XXX     DS.W    2                       Save two words of storage
YYY     DC.L    $12345678               Put the longword $12345678 in memory
Name    DC.B    'Clements'              Put an ASCII string in memory
        DC.B    $FF
        DC.L    Test+Name               Store a 32-bit constant
        DC.B    4                       Put 4 in memory
        MOVE.L  #Name,A0
Next    MOVE.B  (A0)+,D0                Pick up a character
        CMP.B   #$FF,D0                 Test for end of string
        BEQ     Exit                    And exit on terminator
        BSR     Print                   Print a character
        BRA     Next                    Repeat
Exit    STOP    #$2700                  Halt the 68K
*
Print   NOP                             Dummy subroutine
        NOP
        RTS                             Return
*
        END     $400                    END needed ($400 is start address)
```

The following code was produced by a 68K cross-assembler from the above source code.

```
1   00001000                            ORG    $400
2                00000006   TEST:  EQU    6            ;Dummy equates
3                00000007   ALAN:  EQU    7
4   00001000 00000004   XXX:   DS.W   2            ;Save two words of storage
5   00001004 12345678   YYY:   DC.L   $12345678    ;Put longword $12345678 in memory
6   00001008 436C656D656E  NAME: DC.B  'Clements'   ;Put an ASCII string in memory
              7473
7   00001010 FF                 DC.B   $FF
8   00001012 0000100E           DC.L   TEST+NAME    ;Store a 32-bit constant
9   00001016 04                 DC.B   4            ;Put 4 in memory
10  00001018 207C00001008       MOVE.L #NAME,A0
11  0000101E 1018       NEXT:  MOVE.B (A0)+,D0      ;Pick up a character
12  00001020 0C0000FF           CMP.B  #$FF,D0      ;Test for end of string
13  00001024 67000008           BEQ    EXIT         ;And exit on terminator
14  00001028 61000008           BSR    PRINT        ;Print a character
15  0000102C 60F0               BRA    NEXT         ;Repeat
16  0000102E 4E722700   EXIT:  STOP   #$2700       ;Halt the 68K
17                      *
18  00001032 4E71       PRINT: NOP                  ;Dummy subroutine
19  00001034 4E71               NOP
20  00001036 4E75               RTS                  ;Return
21                      *
22                00000400   END    $400         ;END needed
```

6.6 By means of a memory map explain the effect of the following sequence of 68K assembly language directives.

```
        ORG    $600
        DS.L   2
        DC.L   2
        DC.B   '1234'
Time    DC.B   6
Top     DS.B   6
BSc1    EQU    2
IT1     EQU    3
SE1     DS.B   IT1+BSc1
```

6.7 What would the following 68K assembly language fragment store at address $1002?

```
        ORG    $1000
P       EQU    5
Q       DS.B   2
One     DC.W   P+Q
```

6.8 What is wrong with each of the following 68K assembly language operations?

(a) MOVE   Temp,#4
(b) ADD.B   #1,A3
(c) CMP.L   D0,#9
(d) MOVE.B   #500,D5
(e) DS.B   1,2
(f) ADD.W   +(A2),D3
(g) ORG   #400
(h) BEQ.B   Loop_3

(items labeled in image as (a)–(g) with some mis-sequencing)

6.9 Answer the following questions about 68K assembler conventions.

(a) What is the effect of the assembler directive ORG $400?
(b) What is the effect of the assembler directive DS.W 20?

(c) What is the effect of the assembler directive DC.W 1234?
(d) What is the effect of the assembler directive DC.W $1234?

(e) What is the effect of the '+' in the effective address (A0)+?
(f) What is the effect of the '−' in the effective address −(A0)?
(g) Why 'ADDA.L #4, A0', but 'ADD.L #4,D0'?

6.10 What is wrong with the following fragment of 68K assembly language (the error is one of *semantics*)?

```
            CMP.W   #4,Q      IF Q = 4 THEN X = 5 ELSE X = Y
            BNE     ELSE      IF Q ≠ 4 THEN goto 'ELSE'
THEN    MOVE.W  #5,X      IF Q = 4 THEN X = 5
ELSE    MOVE.W  Y,X       ELSE part (i.e. X = Y)
EXIT    ...               Leave the program
```

6.11 Translate the following fragment of high-level language into 68K assembly language.

```
IF T = 5
     THEN X = 4
END_IF
```

Assume that T and X are in memory. Write a program to implement this fragment of code and run it on the 68K simulator. Select your own values for variables T and X. Use the simulator's trace mode to observe the behavior of the program.

6.12 Translate the following fragment of high-level language into 68K assembly language. Use a 68K simulator to test your program.

```
IF T = 5
     THEN X = 4
     ELSE Y = 6
END_IF
```

6.13 The 68K can operate with byte, word, and longword operands. What does this mean? Which type of operand do you use in any particular circumstance?

6.14 Explain what the following 68K program does. Use the 68K simulator to test your observations.

```
         MOVE.B    #20,D0
Again    MOVEA.L   #$1000,A0
         CLR.B     (A0)
         ADDA.L    #1,A0
         SUB.B     #1,D0
         BNE       Again
```

6.15 A sequence, or string of 1-byte ASCII characters is stored at memory location $600 onward. A second sequence of equal length is stored at memory location $700 onward. Each sequence ends with the character $0D (i.e. the ASCII value for a carriage return). Write a 68K assembly language program to determine whether or not these two strings are identical. If they are identical, place the value $00 in data register D0. If they are not, place the value $FF in D0.

Use the 68K cross-assembler and simulator to write the program and test it.

Modify your program to use the simulator's character input routine to input the two strings into memory. The simulator's character input code that puts a byte into D1 is

```
Get_char    MOVE.B    #5,D0
            TRAP      #15
```

6.16 A sequence of ASCII-encoded characters is stored at memory location $600 onwards and is terminated by a $0D. Write a program to reverse the order of the sequence (i.e. the first value at location $600 will now be $0D, which was the old end of the string).

Use the 68K simulator to input a string and print it in reverse order.

The simulator's character output code that prints the byte in D1 is

```
Put_char    MOVE.B    #6,D0
            TRAP      #15
```

6.17 The following program contains both syntax and semantic errors. What is the difference between these two types of error? Locate both types of error.

```
* This is a program to designed locate the smallest number in a table
*
         ORG     #400
Numbers  DS.B    42,3,060,20,8,9,$A,$C,7,2,$F,5AF,8,600,0A,9,40,6,#FF
         MOVE.B  #Numbers,A0       A0 points to table of numbers
         CLR.B   D0                Current smallest number
N_2      MOVE.B  (A0),D1           Get a number
         ADD.B   #1,A1             Point to next number
         CMP.B   D0,D1             Is new number lower?
         BGE     N_1
         MOVE.B  D1,D0             Keep new low number
N_1      CMP.B   D1,#$FF           Check for end
         BNE     N_2
         BRA     Print             Print it
         END     $400
*
Print    MOVE.B  #5,D1
         TRAP    #15
         RTS
         STOP    #$2700
```

6.18 Examine the following fragment of pseudocode and its translation into 68K assembly language. Work through this code and ensure that you understand it. Is the program correct? Can you improve it?

```
*       X = 5
*       Y = 7
*       FOR I= 1 TO 9
*            Y = Y + I
*            IF T(I) = J(I) + X THEN J(I) = T(I) * 4 - Y
*                               ELSE J(I) = J(I) - T(I)
*       END_FOR
*
        ORG      $400
        MOVEA    #T,A0         A0 points at base of array T
        MOVEA    #J,A1         A1 points at base of array J
        MOVE     #1,D0         Use D0 as a counter to hold I
        MOVE     #5,D1         X = 5; D1 is X
        MOVE     #7,D2         Y = 7; D2 is Y
Next    ADD      D0,D2         Y = Y + I
        MOVE     (A0),D3       Read T(I) into D3
        MOVE     (A1),D4       Read J(I) into D4
        MOVE     D4,D5         D5 is a temp copy of J(I)
        ADD      D1,D5         Compute J(I) + X in D5
        CMP      D5,D3         IF T(I) = J(I) + X
        BNE      Else
        MULU     #4,D3         THEN compute T(I) * 4 - Y
        SUB      D2,D3
        MOVE     D3,(A1)       J(I) = T(I) * 4 - Y
        BRA      End_Loop
Else    SUB      D3,D4         J(I) = J(I) - T(I)
        MOVE     D4,(A1)
End_Loop ADDA    #2,A0         Point to next element in T
        ADDA     #2,A1         Point to next element in J
        ADD      #1,D0         Increment the loop counter
        CMP      #10,D0        Repeat until I = 10
        BNE      Next
```

6.19 Write a 68K program to run on the simulator, which

- inputs a single ASCII-encoded numeric character
- converts the character into binary numeric form
- inputs and converts a second character
- adds the two numbers
- converts the numeric result into character form
- prints the result as ASCII characters.

If the input characters are 5 and 7, the displayed result should be 12.

6.20 Write a program to arrange a sequence of eight numbers in descending order. You can store the numbers in memory before the program is executed by means of the DC.B assembler directive. For example

```
List  DC.B 1,2,5,4,8,5,4,2
```

There are many ways of performing this sorting operation. One of the simplest is to search the list for the largest number and put it at the top of the list, then do the same to the remaining numbers, and so on. Use the 68K simulator to test your program.

6.21 Why is it best to pass parameters to and from a subroutine by means of the stack?

6.22 Write a subroutine to carry out the operation X*(Y+Z), where X, Y, and Z are all wordlength (i.e. 16-bit) values. The three parameters, X, Y, and Z, are to be passed on the stack to the procedure. The subroutine is to return the result of the calculation via the stack. Remember that the 68K instruction MULU D0, D1 multiplies the 16-bit unsigned integer in D0 by the 16-bit unsigned integer in D1 and puts the 32-bit product in D1.

Write a subroutine, call it, and pass parameters X, Y, and Z on the stack. Test your program by using the 68K simulator's debugging facilities.

6.23 Write a subroutine ADDABC that performs the operation C = A + B. Variables A, B, and C are all word (i.e. 16-bit) values. Test your program on the 68K simulator.

Your calling code and subroutine should have the following features.

- Parameters A and B should be passed on the stack to the procedure by reference (i.e. by address).

- Because parameters A and B are adjacent in memory, you need pass only the address of parameter A to the subroutine (because the address of parameter B is 2 bytes on from parameter A).

- Parameter C should be passed back to the calling program on the stack by value.

- Before you call the subroutine, make room on the stack for the returned parameter (i.e. parameter C).

- After calling the subroutine, read the parameter off the stack into data register D0 (i.e. D0 should end up containing the value of A+B).

- The subroutine ADDABC must not corrupt any registers. Save all working registers on the stack on entry to the subroutine and restore them before returning from the subroutine.

- When you write your code, preset the stack pointer to a value like $1500 (by using either MOVEA.L #$1500, A7 or LEA $1500, A7). Doing this will make it easier to follow the movement of the stack while your program is running.

- Make certain that you are operating with the correct operand sizes! Use .W for data values and .L for addresses/pointers.

- Some of the important instructions you might need are provided below. Make sure you understand exactly what they do.

```
MOVEM.L   RegList,-(A7)    Push a group of registers on stack
MOVEM.L   (A7)+,RegList    Pull a group of registers off stack
LEA       X(Ai),Aj         Load Aj with the contents of register Ai + X
MOVEA.L   (Ai),Aj          Load Aj with longword pointed at by Ai
```

Your program should be of the general form

```
        ORG   $400
        LEA   $1500,A7    Set up the stack pointer with an easy value
        ...               Pass the parameters
        BSR   ADDABC      Call the subroutine
        ...               Get the result, C, in D0
        ...               Clean up the stack
        STOP #$2700       Halt execution
*
ADDABC ...
        ...
        RTS
*
        ORG   $1200       Put the test data here
A       DC.W $1234        This is the first parameter
B       DC.W $ABAB        This is the second parameter
        END   $400
```

This is not an easy or trivial problem. You will need to draw a map of the stack at every stage and take very great care not to confuse pointers (addresses) and actual parameters.

6.24 Suppose you wish to pre-load memory with the value 1234 before executing a program. Which of the following operations is correct?

(a) `DC.B      #1234`
(b) `DC.W      1234`
(c) `DC.W      #1234`
(d) `DS.B      $1234`
(e) `MOVE.W    #1234,Location`

6.25 Which of the following defines `MOVE.B (A2)+,D3`?

(a) `D3   ← [[A2]]; [A2] ← [A2] + 1`
(b) `[D3] ← [[A2]]; [A2] ← [A2] + 1`
(c) `D3]  ← [[A2]]; [A2] ← [A2] + 1`
(d) `[A2] ← [A2] + 1; [D3] ← [A2];`

6.26 Which of the following statements is true when a parameter is passed to a subroutine by reference (i.e. not by value).

(a) The parameter can be put in an address register.
(b) The address of the parameter can be put in an address register.
(c) The address of the parameter can be pushed on the stack.
(d) The parameter can be pushed on the stack.
(e) Parts (a) and (d) are correct.
(f) Parts (b) and (c) are correct.

6.27 Consider the following code:

```
MOVE.W X,-(A7)    Push X
MOVE.L Y,-(A7)    Push Y
BSR    PQR        Call PQR
Clean_up          Clean up the stack
```

(a) Why do you have to clean up the stack after returning from the subroutine?

(b) What code would you use to clean up the stack?
(c) Draw a memory map of the stack immediately before executing the RTS in the subroutine PQR.

6.28 Write an assembly language program to reverse the bits of a byte.

6.29 Explain why the following assembly language and RTL constructs are incorrect

(a) `MOVE   D4,#$64`
(b) `MOVE   (D3),D2`
(c) `[D3] ← A0 + 3`
(d) `[D3] ← #3`

6.30 The 68K has both *signed* and *unsigned* conditional branches. What does this statement mean?

6.31 You cannot (should not?) exit a subroutine by jumping out of it by means of a branch instruction. You must exit it with an RTS instruction. Why?

6.32 Assume that a string of ASCII characters is located in memory starting at location $2000. The string ends with the character 'Z'. Design and write a 68K assembly language program to count the number of 'E's, if any, in the string.

6.33 Express the following sequence of 68K assembly language instructions in register transfer language and explain in plain English what each instruction does.

(a) `LEA       4(A2),A1`
(b) `MOVEA.L A3,A2`
(c) `MOVE.B   (A1),D3`
(d) `MOVE.B   #5,(A1)`
(e) `BCS       ABC`
(f) `MOVE.B   (A1)+,-(A3)`

6.34 The following fragment of 68K assembly language has several serious errors. Explain what the errors are. Explain how you would correct the errors.

```
         MOVE.B   X,D0              Get X in a data register
         CMP.B    #4,D0             IF X = 4 THEN X = X + 6
         BEQ      Add_6
         MOVE.B   D0,X              Restore X in memory
         PEA      X                 Push X on the stack
         BSR      Sqr               Calculate X2
X        DS.W     1                 Save space for X
         STOP     #$2700
*
ADD_6.   ADD.B    #6,D0             X = X + 6
         RTS                        Return
Sqr      MOVE.L   (A7)+,D2          Get X
         MULU     D2,D2             Square X
         MOVE.L   D2,-(A7)          Put X*X on the stack
         RTS                        Return
```

6.35 Suppose you are given an algorithm and asked to design and test a program written in 68K assembly language. How would you carry out this activity? Your answer should include considerations of program design and testing, and the necessary software tools.

6.36 Suppose that D0 contains $F12C4689 and D1 contains $211D0FF1. What is the result of

(a) ADD.B D0,D1
(b) ADD.W D0,D1
(c) ADD.L D0,D1

In each case, give the contents of D1 after the operation and the values of the C, Z, N, and V flags.

6.37 Suppose that A0 contains $F12CE600. What is the result of

(a) ADDA.L #$1234,A0
(b) ADDA.W #$1234,A0
(c) ADDA.W #$4321,A0

6.38 What is the effect of the following code?

```
         CLR      D0
         MOVE.B   D0,D1
         MOVE.B   #10,D2
XXX      ADD.B    D2,D0
         ADD.B    #1,D1
         ADD.B    D1,D0
         SUB.B    #1,D2
         BNE      XXX
         STOP     #$2700
```

Structure of the CPU

7

INTRODUCTION

In Chapters 2 and 3 we introduced combinational and sequential logic elements and demonstrated how to build functional circuits. In Chapters 5 and 6 we introduced the instruction set architecture and low-level programming. This chapter bridges the gap between digital circuits and the computer by demonstrating how we can construct a computer from simple circuits; that is, we show how a computer instruction is *interpreted* (i.e. executed).

We begin by describing the structure of a simple generic CPU. Once we see how a computer operates in principle, we can look at how it may be implemented. We describe the operation of a very simple *one-and-a-half* address machine whose instructions have two operands; one in memory and one a register. Instructions are written in the form ADD A, **B** that adds A to B and puts the result in B. Either A or B must be a register.

Some readers will read this introduction to the CPU before the previous two chapters on assembly language programming. Consequently, some topics will be re-introduced.

Instead of introducing the computer all at once, we will keep things simple and build up a CPU step by step. This approach helps demonstrate how an instruction is executed because the development of the computer broadly follows the sequence of events taking place during the execution of an instruction. In the next chapter we will find that this computer is highly simplified; real computers don't execute an instruction from start to finish. Today's computers *overlap* the execution of instructions. As soon as one instruction is fetched from memory, the next instruction is fetched before the previous instruction has completed its execution. This mechanism is called *pipelining* and we examine it more closely in the next chapter.

7.1 **The CPU**

A von Neumann stored program digital computer operates by reading instructions from memory and executing them one by one in sequence. If you wish to evaluate $X^2 + 1$ on a 68K processor where X is a memory location, you may write

```
MOVE.W  X,D0    Get X in a register
MULU    D0,D0   Square it
ADD.W   #1,D0   Add 1
MOVE.W  D0,X    Update X in memory
```

We now demonstrate how instructions like MOVE.W X,D0 are read from memory and how the sequence of actions that implement this operation are carried out inside the CPU.

Because the CPU is such a complex device, we have decided to walk through the execution of an instruction, step by step, on a very primitive hypothetical computer. We begin with the address paths that are used to locate the next instruction to be executed.

7.1.1 **The address path**

Figure 7.1 provides the block diagram of part of a CPU. In this diagram only the address paths and the paths needed to read an instruction from memory are shown for clarity. We have omitted most of the data paths required to execute instructions to avoid clutter. Address paths are shown in blue and data paths are in light blue.

The address paths are the highways along which addresses flow from one part of the CPU to another. An address represents the location of a data element within the memory. There are three types of information flow in a computer: address,

---

A HYPOTHETICAL COMPUTER

Anyone describing the internal operation of a computer must select an architecture and an organization for their target machine. We have two choices: *register to memory* or *register to register*. The register-to-memory model fits the architecture of processors like the Pentium and 68K, whereas the register-to-register model corresponds to processors like the ARM, which we introduce later. When describing the internal structure of a computer, we could describe either a system that executes an instruction to completion before beginning the next instruction, or a computer that overlaps or *pipelines* the execution of instructions.

I have decided to begin this chapter with the description of a register-to-memory, non-pipelined processor. A non-pipelined organization is easier to describe than one that overlaps the execution of instructions.

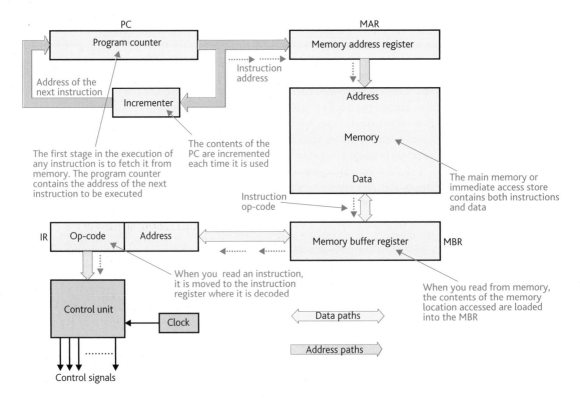

Figure 7.1 The CPU's address paths.

CONSTANTS, VARIABLES, POINTERS—A REMINDER

A *constant* or *literal* is a value that does not change during the execution of a program. Its value is set at compile time or assemble time. Literal addressing is used to handle constants.

A *variable* is a value that changes during the execution of a program.

A *pointer* is a variable that contains the address of a variable; that is, a pointer points to a variable in memory. An address register is a pointer register.

The following code implements the expression $X = 5 + Y + Z_3$ and illustrates the nature of constants, variables, and pointers.

```
MOVE.W  Y,D0        ;load D0 with the variable Y
ADD.W   #5,D0       ;add the constant 5
LEA     Z,A0        ;load A0 with a pointer to Z
ADD.W   3(A0),D0    ;add the variable Z₃
MOVE.W  D0,X        ;store the result in variable X
```

data, and control. Data comprises the instructions, constants, and variables that are stored in memory and registers. Control paths comprise the signals that trigger events, provide clocks, and control the flow of data and addresses throughout the computer.

7.1.2 Reading the instruction

Before the CPU can execute an instruction, the instruction must first be brought to the CPU from the computer's memory. We begin our description of the way in which a program is executed with the CPU's *program counter* (also called *instruction counter* or *location counter*). The expression *program counter* is a misnomer. The program counter contains the address of the next instruction in memory to be executed and it doesn't count programs or anything else.

The program counter *points to* the next instruction to be executed. If, for example, [PC] = 1234 (i.e. the PC contains the number 1234), the next instruction to be executed is to be found in memory location 1234.

Fetching an instruction begins with the contents of the program counter being moved to the memory address register (i.e. [MAR] ← [PC]). Once the contents of the program counter have been transferred to the memory address register, the contents of the program counter are incremented and moved back to the program counter; that is,

[PC] ← [PC] + 4

At the end of this operation, the program counter points to the *next* instruction while the current instruction is being executed. The program counter in incremented by 4 rather than 1 because many of today's high-performance computers have 32-bit instructions. Computers are byte-addressed but have 32-bit architectures; that is, they can address individual bytes in memory, although instructions and data normally fall on 32-bit (i.e. 4-byte) boundaries.[1]

The *memory address register* (MAR), holds the address of the location in the memory into which data is being written in a write cycle, or from which data is being read in a read cycle. At this stage, the MAR contains a copy of the (previous) contents of the PC. When a *memory read cycle* is performed, the contents of the memory location specified by the MAR are read from the memory and transferred to the *memory buffer register* (MBR). We can represent this read operation in RTL terms as

[MBR] ← [[MAR]]

We interpret the expression [[MAR]] as *the contents of the memory whose address is given by the contents of the MAR*. The memory buffer register is a temporary holding place for data received from memory in a read cycle, or for data to be transferred to memory in a write cycle. Some texts refer to the MBR as the *memory data register* (MDR). At this point in the execution of an instruction, the MBR contains the bit pattern of the instruction to be executed.

The instruction is next moved from the MBR to the *instruction register* (IR) where it is divided into two fields. One field in the IR contains the *operation code* (op-code) that tells the CPU what operation is to be carried out. The other field, called the *operand field*, contains the address of the data to be used by the instruction. The operand field can also provide a constant to be employed by the operation code when immediate or literal addressing is used. Note that we are assuming a one-address instruction format.

The control unit (CU) takes the op-code from the instruction register together with a stream of clock pulses and generates signals that control all parts of the CPU. The time between individual clock pulses is in the range 0.3 ns to 100 ns (i.e. 3×10^{-10} to 10^{-7}s). The control unit is responsible for moving the contents of the program counter into the MAR, executing a read cycle, and moving the contents of the MBR to the IR. Later we look at the control unit in more detail and demonstrate how it goes about interpreting an op-code.

---

[1] Remember that the 68K has variable-length instruction and its PC is incremented by 2, 4, 6, 8, or 10; that is instruction fall on 16-bit boundaries For the purpose of this chapter, we assume that instructions are all 4 bytes long.

THE INSTRUCTION REGISTER

A modern RISC processor like the ARM, which we introduce in Chapter 9 has a 32-bit instruction register which is sufficient for an op-code and three register addresses; for example, ADD **R1**, R2, R3. Processors like the Pentium and 68K have very complex *variable-length* instruction

formats and you cannot use a simple fixed-length instruction register. The processor has to fetch the first 16 bits of an instruction from memory, decode it, and execute successive fetches to assemble the rest of the instruction.

```
FETCH  [MAR]  ←  [PC]          Copy contents of the PC to the MAR
       [PC]   ←  [PC] + 4      Increment the contents of the PC
       [MBR]  ←  [[MAR]]       Read the instruction from memory
       [IR]   ←  [MBR]         Move the instruction to the IR
       CU     ←  [IR(op-code)] Transmit the op-code to the control unit
```

Table 7.1   The FETCH phase expressed in register transfer language.

All instructions are executed in a two-phase operation called a *fetch–execute cycle*. During the *fetch phase*, the instruction is read from memory and decoded by the control unit. The fetch phase is followed by an *execute phase* in which the control unit generates all the signals necessary to execute the instruction. Table 7.1 describes the sequence of operations taking place in a fetch phase. In Table 7.1 FETCH is a label that serves to indicate a particular line in the sequence of operations. The notation $IR_{(op-code)}$ means the operation-code field of the instruction register.

7.1.3 The CPU's data paths

Now that we've sorted out the fetch phase, let's see what else we need to actually execute instructions. Figure. 7.2 adds new data paths to the simplified CPU of Fig. 7.1, together with an address path from the address field of the instruction register to the memory address register. Other modifications to Fig. 7.1 included in Fig. 7.2 are the addition of a data register, D0, and an *arithmetic and logical unit*, ALU.

The *data register* called D0 holds temporary results during a calculation. You need a data register in a one-address machine because *dyadic* operations with two operands such as ADD X, **D0** take place on one operand specified by the instruction and the contents of the data register. This instruction adds the contents of memory location X to the contents of the data register and deposits the result of the addition in the data register, destroying one of the original operands.

The arrangement of Fig. 7.2 has only one general-purpose data register, which we've called D0 for compatibility with the 68K we used in the previous chapters. Some first-generation 8-bit microprocessors had only one general-purpose data register, which was called the *accumulator*.

We can represent an ADD X, **D0** instruction[2] by the RTL expression

$$[D0] ← [D0] + [X]$$

The *arithmetic and logic unit* (ALU) is the workhorse of the CPU because it carries out all the calculations. Arithmetic and logical operations are applied either to the contents of the data register or MBR alone, or to the contents of the data register and the contents of the MBR. The output of the ALU is fed back to the data register or to the MBR.

Two types of operation are carried out by the ALU—*arithmetic* and *logical*. The fundamental difference between arithmetic and logical operations is that logical operations don't generate a carry when bit a_i of word A and bit b_i of B are operated upon. Table 7.2 provides examples of typical arithmetic and logical operations. A logical shift treats an operand as a string of bits that are moved left or right. An arithmetic shift treats a number as a signed two's complement value and propagates the sign bit during a right shift. Most of these operations are implemented by computers like the 68K, Pentium, and ARM.

Having developed our computer a little further, we can now execute an elementary program. Consider the high-level language operation P = Q + R. Here the *plus* symbol means arithmetic addition. The assembly language program required to carry out this operation is given below. Remember that P, Q, and R are symbolic names that refer to the *locations* of the variables in memory.

LOAD   Q, **D0**   Load data register D0 with the contents of memory location Q[3]

ADD   R, **D0**   Add the contents of memory location R to data register D0

STORE **D0**, **P**   Store the contents of data register D0 in memory location P

---

[2] A machine with a single accumulator does not need to specify it explicitly; for example, an 8-bit microprocessor may use ADD P to indicate *add the contents of P to the accumulator*. We write ADD P, **D0** and make D0 explicit to be consistent with the notation we used for 68K instructions.

[3] We have defined explicit LOAD and STORE operations to be consistent with the CPU we construct later in this chapter. The 68K uses a single MOVE operation to indicate LOAD and STORE

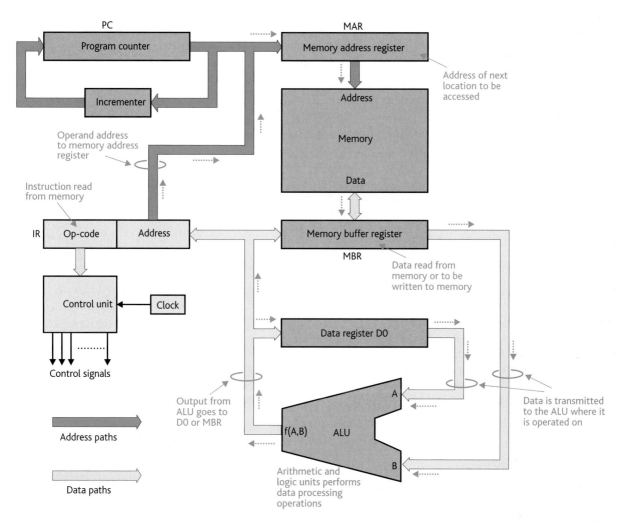

Figure 7.2 The CPU's address and data paths.

Operation	Class	Typical mnemonic
Addition	Arithmetic	ADD
Subtraction	Arithmetic	SUB
Negation	Arithmetic	NEG
Multiplication	Arithmetic	MULU
Division	Arithmetic	DIVU
Divide by 2	Arithmetic	ASR
Multiply by 2	Arithmetic	ASL
AND	Logical	AND
OR	Logical	OR
NOT	Logical	NOT
EOR	Logical	EOR
Shift left	Logical	LSL
Shift right	Logical	LSR

Table 7.2 Typical arithmetic and logical operations.

The one-address machine requires a rather cumbersome sequence of operations just to carry out the simple action of adding two numbers. If we had a computer with a three-address format, we could have written

ADD Q,R,**P**   Add the contents of Q to the contents of R and put the result in P

Three-address machines are *potentially*[A] faster than one-address machines, because they can do in one instruction things that take other machines three operations. However, the power of three-address machines can be achieved only by means of a more complex and expensive CPU and memory system.

We can demonstrate how the CPU operates by examining the execution of ADD R, **D0** in terms of register transfer language. Table 7.3

FETCH	[MAR]	← [PC]	Move the contents of the PC to the MAR
	[PC]	← [PC] + 4	Increment the contents of the PC
	[MBR]	← [[MAR]]	Read the current instruction from the memory
	[IR]	← [MBR]	Move the contents of the MBR to the IR
	CU	← [IR$_{(op\text{-}code)}$]	Move the op-code from the IR to the CU
ADD	[MAR]	← [IR$_{(address)}$]	Move the operand address to the MAR
	[MBR]	← [[MAR]]	Read the data from memory
	ALU	← [MBR], ALU ← [D0]	Perform the addition
	[D0]	← ALU	Move the output of ALU to the data register

Operations sharing the same line are executed simultaneously. ALU ← [MBR] and ALU ← [D0] are executed simultaneously.

Table 7.3 Expressing the FETCH/EXECUTE cycle for an ADD instruction in RTL.

MICROPROGRAMMING

The terms microprogram, microprogramming, microcode, microinstruction, and micro-operation have nothing to do with *microprocessor* or *microcomputer*. A micro-operation is the smallest event that can take place within a computer; typical micro-operations are the clocking of data into a register, a memory read operation, putting data on a bus, or adding two numbers together.

A microprogram consist of a sequence of microinstructions that, when executed, implement a machine-level instruction. For example, the machine-level or *macro-level* operation ADD P, **D0** can be implemented by executing a sequence of micro-operations. The instructions that comprise a microprogram are called *microcode*.

---

gives the sequence of operations carried out during the fetch and execute phases of an ADD R, **D0** instruction. These operations tell us what is actually going on inside the computer.

During the fetch phase the op-code is fed to the control unit by CU ← [IR$_{(op\text{-}code)}$] and used to generate all the internal signals required to perform the addition—this includes programming the ALU to do addition by adding together the data at its two input terminals to produce a sum at its output terminals.

Operations of the form [PC] ← [MAR] or [D0] ← [D0] + [MBR] are often referred to as *microinstructions*. Each assembly level instruction (e.g. LOAD, ADD) is executed as a series of microinstructions. Microinstructions and microprogramming are the province of the computer designer. In the 1970s some machines were user-microprogrammable; that is, you could define your own instruction set. We take a further look at microinstructions later in this chapter.

7.1.4 Executing conditional instructions

So far, we've considered the architecture of the *single-instruction single-data* CPU capable of executing programs in a purely

sequential mode; that is, the computer can execute only a stream of instructions, one by one in strict order. We covered conditional behavior in the previous chapter and we require a means of implementing instructions such as BEQ Target (branch on zero flag set to Target).

The computer in Fig. 7.2 lacks a mechanism for making choices or repeating a group of instructions. To do this, the CPU must be able to execute *conditional branches* or *jumps* such as BEQ XYZ. We've already met the branch that forces the CPU to execute an instruction out of the normal sequence. The block diagram of Fig. 7.3 shows the new address and data paths required by the CPU to execute conditional branches.

Three items have been added to our computer in Fig. 7.3:

- a condition code register, CCR
- a path between the CCR and the control unit
- a path between the address field of the instruction register and the program counter.

---

[4] A three-address machine is faster than a machine with register-to-register instructions only if the access time of memory is comparable to the access time of register. Memory takes much longer to access than internal registers and, therefore, a three-address machine is not currently practical.

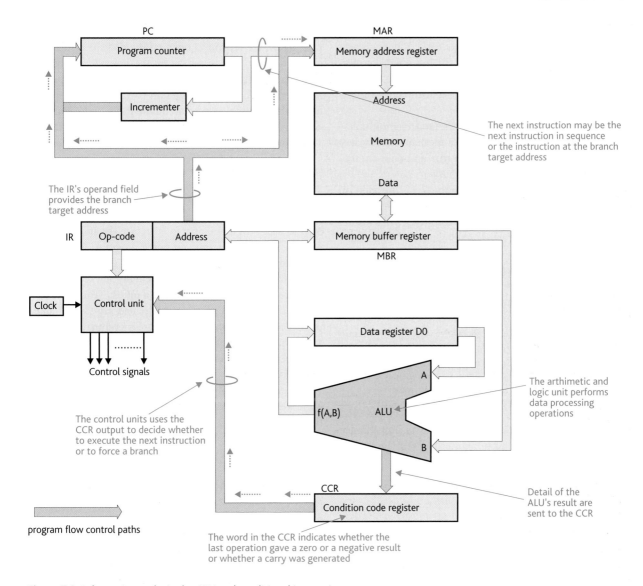

Figure 7.3 Information paths in the CPU and conditional instructions.

The *condition code register* or *processor status register* takes a snapshot of the state of the ALU after each instruction has been executed and records the state of the carry, negative, zero, and overflow flag bits. A conditional branch instruction interrogates the CCR's current state. The control unit then either forces the CPU to execute the next instruction in series or to branch another instruction somewhere in the program. Let's look at the details of the conditional branch.

The CPU updates the bits of its condition code register after it carries out an arithmetic or a logical operation to reflect the nature of the result. The following is a reminder of the operations of the condition code bits.

C = **carry** Set if a carry was generated in the last operation. The C-bit is, of course, the same as the carry bit in the carry flip-flop.

Z = **zero** Set if the last operation generated a zero result.

N = **negative** Set if the last result generated a negative result.

V = **overflow** Set if the last operation resulted in an *arithmetic overflow*; that is, an operation on one or two two's complement values gave a result that was outside its allowable range (an arithmetic overflow occurs during addition if the sign bit of the result is different from the sign bit of both operands).

The condition code register is connected to the control unit, enabling instructions to interrogate the CCR. For example, some instructions test whether the last operation performed by the central processor yielded a positive result, or whether the carry bit was set, or whether arithmetic overflow occurred.

There's no point in carrying out an interrogation unless the results are acted upon. We need a mechanism that does one thing if the result of the test is true and does another thing if the result of the test is false.

The final modification included in Fig. 7.3 is the addition of a path between the operand field (i.e. target address) of the instruction register and the program counter. It's this feature that enables the computer to respond to the result of its interrogation of the CCR.

A *conditional branch* instruction tests a bit of the CCR and, if the bit tested is clear, the next instruction is obtained from memory in the normal way. But if the bit tested is set, the next instruction is obtained from the location whose *target address* is in the instruction register. In the above description we said that a branch is made if a certain bit of the CCR is set; equally a branch can be made if the bit is clear (branches can also be made on the state of several CCR bits).

The precise way in which conditional branches are actually implemented inside the computer is discussed later when we deal with the design of the control unit. Branch operations can be expressed in register transfer language in the form

```
IF condition THEN action
```

Typical machine-level conditional operations expressed in RTL are

1. Branch on carry clear (jump to the target address if the carry bit in the CCR is 0)
   ```
   BCC target: IF [C]=0 THEN [PC]←[IR(address)]
   ```
2. Branch on equal (jump to the target address if the Z-bit in the CCR is 1)
   ```
   BEQ target: IF [Z]=1 THEN [PC]←[IR(address)]
   ```

An example of a conditional branch is as follows.

SUB	X,**D0**	Subtract X from contents of D0
BEQ	Last	If the result was zero then branch to
.		Last, otherwise continue
.		
Last		Target address of branch (if taken)

7.1.5 Dealing with literal operands

The CPU of Fig. 7.2 assumes all instructions (e.g. ADD and BEQ etc.) refer to an operand somewhere within the CPU's

memory. Sometimes we wish to use instructions such as ADD #12,**D0**, where the source operand supplies the *actual value* of the data being referred to by the op-code part of the instruction. Although the symbol '#' appears as part of the operand when this instruction is written in mnemonic form, the assembler uses a different op-code code for ADD #literal,**D0** than it does for ADD address,**D0**.

The instruction ADD.B #12,**D0** is defined in RTL as

```
[D0] ← [D0] + 12.
```

Figure 7.4 shows that an additional data path is required between the operand field of the IR and the data register and ALU to deal with literal operands. In fact, the architecture of Fig. 7.4 can execute any computer program. Any further modifications to this structure improve the CPU's performance without adding any fundamentally new feature.

Figure 7.5 completes the design of the computer. We have added a second general-purpose data register D1 and a pointer register A0. In principle, there is nothing stopping us adding any number of registers. As you can see, three buses, A, B, and C are used to transfer data between the registers and ALU.

The structure of Fig. 7.5 can implement instructions with more complex addressing modes than the simple direct (absolute) addressing we have used so far; for example MOVE (A0),**D1** can be implemented by the following sequence of micro-operations.

[MAR]	← [A0]	Move source operand address to MAR
[MBR]	← [[MAR]]	Read the actual operand from memory
[D0]	← [MBR]	Copy data to D1

This sequence has been simplified because, you will see from Fig. 7.5, that there is no direct path between register A0 and the MBR. You would have to put the contents of A0 onto bus A, pass the contents of bus A through the ALU to bus C, and then copy bus C to the MAR. We will return to this theme when we look at the detailed design of computers.

We have now demonstrated the flow of information that takes place during the execution of a single address computer instruction. In the next section we reinforce some of the things we have covered by showing how you can simulate a computer architecture in C.

7.2 Simulating a CPU

One way of learning how a processor operates is to build one. We present a program in C that simulates a very simple 8-bit CPU. In order to make the simulator as accessible to as many readers as possible, we have written the simulator in C but

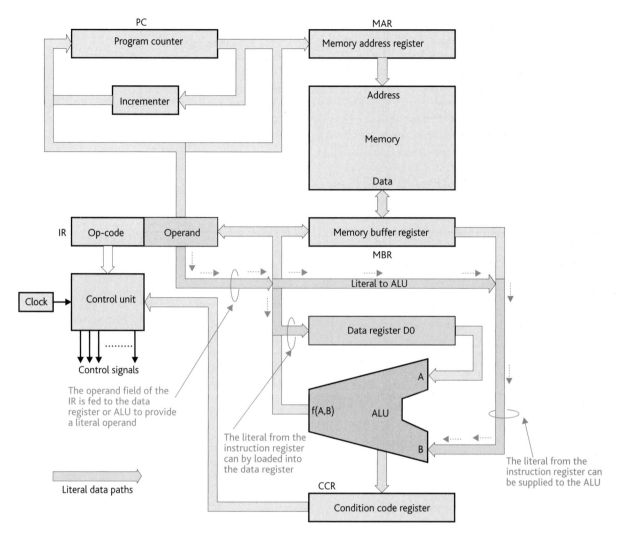

Figure 7.4 Modifying the CPU to deal with literal operands.

have avoided all but C's most basic elements. All data types are 8 bits and the only C constructs we use are the `while`, the `if . . . then . . . else`, and the `switch` constructs, which select one of several courses of action.

We are going to construct two simulators—the first is a very primitive CPU with an 8-bit instruction that simply demonstrates the fetch/execute cycle, and the second is not too dissimilar to typical first-generation 8-bit microprocessors.

7.2.1 CPU with an 8-bit instruction

Our first computer has a single data register (i.e. accumulator) called D0 and all instructions are memory to register apart from the store and the

branch instructions. Only the store instruction performs a write to memory.

Choosing an instruction set requires many compromises; for example, if the number of bits in an instruction is fixed, increasing the number of different instructions reduces the number of bits left for other functions such as addressing modes or register selection.

We can define an instruction set for our primitive 8-bit machine as

Instruction	Mnemonic	RTL definition
Load D0 from memory	LDA N	[D0] ← [N]
Store D0 in memory	STA N	[N] ← [D0]
Add memory to D0	ADD N	[D0] ← [D0] + [N]
Branch to location N	BRA N	[PC] ← N
If [D0] = 0 then branch to N	BEQ N	IF [D0] = 0 THEN [PC] ← N

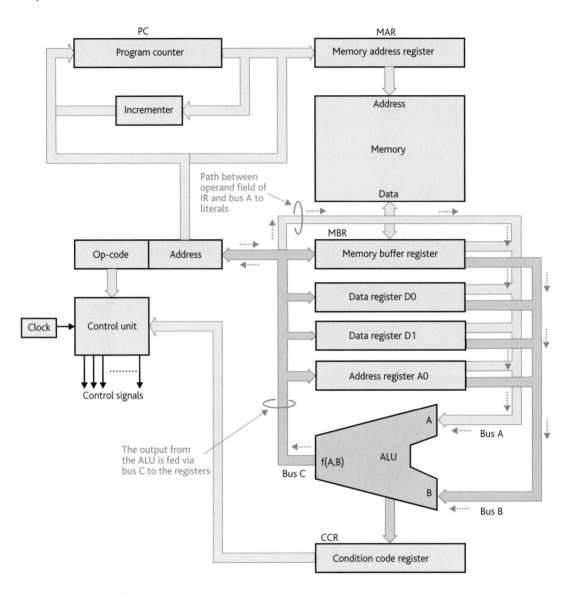

Figure 7.5 Processor with multiple registers.

We have provided only five instructions because these are illustrative of all instructions. This computer has an 8-bit instruction format that includes both the op-code and the operand. If we chose a 3-bit op-code (eight instructions) and a 4-bit operand (a 16-bit memory), the remaining bit can be used to specify the addressing mode (absolute or literal). Real 8-bit microprocessors solve the problem of instruction set design by using 1 byte to provide an operation code and then 0, 1, or 2 succeeding bytes to provide an operand.

Figure 7.6 defines the structure of an 8-bit instruction for our simulated machine.

The first step in constructing a simulator is to describe the action of the computer in pseudocode.

```
PC = 0
REPEAT
  Read the instruction pointed at by the PC
  Increment the program counter
  Split the instruction into
                         1. operation code
                         2. addressing mode
                         3. operand
  IF the addressing mode is direct THEN get the operand from memory
                         ELSE the operand is a literal

  Execute the instruction
FOREVER
```

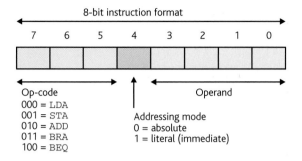

8-bit instruction format

| 7 | 6 | 5 | 4 | 3 | 2 | 1 | 0 |

Op-code
000 = LDA
001 = STA
010 = ADD
011 = BRA
100 = BEQ

Addressing mode
0 = absolute
1 = literal (immediate)

Operand

Figure 7.6 Format of an 8-bit instruction.

C allows you to operate on individual bits of a byte; for example, the operator $>>$ n performs a right shift by n bits. The opcode is obtained from the three most-significant bits of the IR by shifting right five times. A bitwise logical AND can be performed between a variable and a hexadecimal value; for example IR & 0x0F ANDs the IR with 00001111_2 to extract the operand bits in the four least-significant bit positions.

Once we've extracted the addressing mode (bit 4 of the instruction register) with amode = (IR & 0x10) $>>$ 4, we can calculate the source operand for the load and add instruction by

```
if (amode == 0) source = memory[operand]; else source = operand;
```

We can now write a program to implement this algorithm. The following fragment of code is largely self-explanatory.

The instruction in the 8-bit instruction register (IR) is decoded by the three operations

```
opcode  = IR >> 5;             /* get the op-code              */
amode   = (IR & 0x10) >> 4;    /* extract the address mode bit */
operand = IR & 0x0F;           /* extract the operand          */
```

The following listing provides the C code for this CPU simulator.

```
#define LDA    0
#define STA    1
#define ADD    2
#define BRA    3
#define BEQ    4
#define STOP   8

void main(void)
{
  unsigned short int  PC  = 0;     /* program counter               */
  unsigned short int  D0  = 0;     /* data register                 */
  unsigned short int  MAR;         /* memory address register       */
  unsigned short int  MBR;         /* memory buffer register        */
  unsigned short int  IR;          /* instruction register          */
  unsigned short int  operand;     /* the 8-bit operand from the IR */
  unsigned short int  source;      /* source operand                */
  unsigned short int  opcode;      /* the 3-bit op-code from the IR */
  unsigned short int  amode;       /* the 1-bit addressing mode     */
  unsigned short int  memory[16];  /* the memory                    */
  unsigned short int  run = 1;     /* execute program while run is 1 */

/* Instruction format:                                    */
/* 7  6  5  4  3  2  1  0                                  */
/* Bits 3 to 0   4-bit operand                            */
/* Bit  4        1-bit addressing mode                    */
/* Bits 7 to 5   3-bit instruction code                   */

/* main loop */

  while (run)
  {
    MAR = PC;                       /* PC to MAR                     */
```

```
PC  = PC + 1;                    /* increment PC              */
MBR = memory[MAR];               /* get next instruction      */
IR  = MBR;                       /* copy MBR to IR            */

opcode  = IR >> 5;               /* get the op-code           */
amode   = (IR & 0x10) >> 4; /* extract the address mode bit  */
operand = IR & 0x0F;             /* extract the operand       */

if (amode == 0) source = memory[operand]; else source = operand;

switch (opcode) /* now execute the instruction */
   { case LDA:  { D0 = source;                   break;}
     case STA:  { memory[operand] = D0;          break;}
     case ADD:  { D0 = D0 + source;              break;}
     case BRA:  { PC = operand;                   break;}
     case BEQ:  { if (D0 == 0) PC = operand; break;}
     case STOP: { run = 0;                       break;}
   }
  }
}
```

Most of the work done in the simulator takes place in the switch construct at the end of this program where each instruction is interpreted.

7.2.2 CPU with a 16-bit instruction

We now describe a CPU that is much closer to the architecture of typical 8-bit microprocessors. The simulator uses an 8-bit memory with 256 locations. Each instruction occupies two consecutive memory locations—an 8-bit instruction followed by an 8-bit operand. This arrangement provides us with a much richer instruction set than the previous example. However, each fetch cycle requires *two* memory accesses. The first access is to fetch the op-code and the seconds to fetch the operand; that is;

```
FETCH [MAR]   ← [PC]        Copy contents of the PC to the MAR
      [PC]    ← [PC] + 1    Increment contents of the PC
      [MBR]   ← [[MAR]]     Read the instruction from memory
      [IR]    ← [MBR]       Move the instruction to the IR
      opcode  ← [IR]        Save the op-code

      [MAR]   ← [PC]        Copy contents of the PC to the MAR
      [PC]    ← [PC] + 1    Increment contents of the PC
      [MBR]   ← [[MAR]]     Read the operand from memory
      [IR]    ← [MBR]       Move the operand to the IR
      operand ← [IR]        Save the operand
```

This multibyte instruction format is used by 8-bit and 16-bit microprocessors. Indeed, the 68K has one 10-byte instruction.

The architecture of this computer is memory to register or register to memory; for example, it supports both ADD D0, M and ADD M, D0 instructions. In addition to the direct and literal addressing modes, we have provided address register indirect addressing with a single A0 register. We have also

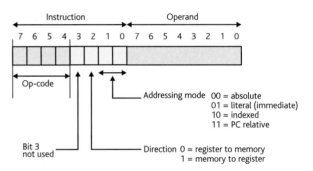

Figure 7.7 Format of the CPU's instruction.

provided program counter relative addressing (discussed in the next chapter) in which the operand is specified with respect to the current value of the program counter; for example, MOVE D0, 12(PC) means store the contents of data register D0 12 bytes on from the location pointed at by the program counter.

The instruction itself is divided into four fields, as Fig. 7.7 demonstrates. A 4-bit op-code in bits 7, 6, 5, 4 provides up to 16 instructions. A 2-bit addressing mode in bits 1, 0 selects the way in which the current operand is treated. When the addressing mode is 00, the operand provides the address of the data to be used by the current instruction. When the addressing mode is 01 the operand provides the actual (i.e. literal) operand. Modes 10 and 11 provide indexed and program counter relative addressing respectively (i.e. the operand is added to the A0 register or the PC, respectively).

Bit 2 of the instruction is a direction bit that determines whether the source operand is in memory or is provided by the data register; for example, the difference between MOVE D0, 123 and MOVE 123, D0 is determined by the value of the direction bit.

We can express the basic fetch cycle and decode instruction phase in C as

```
while (run)

  {                              /* Fetch instruction        */
    MAR = PC;                    /* PC to MAR                */
    PC  = PC + 1;                /* increment PC             */
    MBR = memory[MAR];           /* get next instruction     */
    IR  = MBR;                   /* copy MBR to IR           */
    opcode  = IR;                /* store the op-code bits    */

    MAR = PC;                    /* PC to MAR                 */
    PC  = PC + 1;                /* increment PC              */
    MBR = memory[MAR];           /* get the operand           */
    IR  = MBR;                   /* copy MBR to IR            */
    operand = IR;                /* store the operand bits     */
    amode   = opcode & 0x03;     /* extract the address mode bits */
    direction = (opcode & 0x04) >> 2; /* get data direction 0 = register to memory
                                                             1 = memory to register */
    opcode = opcode >> 4;        /* get the 4-bit instruction code */


  /* use the address mode to get the operand */

    switch (amode)
       { case 0: {source = memory[operand];       break; /* absolute */
                 }

         case 1: {source = operand;               break; /* literal  */
                 }

         case 2: {source = memory[A0 + operand];  break; /* indexed */
                 }
         case 3: {source = memory[PC + operand];  break; /* PC relative */
       }
```

Each instruction is executed by means of the switch construct. Note that the CCR has only a zero flag (it would have been more complex to have provided a C- and V-bit). The following provides the complete code for the processor.

```
#define MOVE  0
#define ADD   1
#define SUB   2
#define BRA   3
#define CMP   4
#define BEQ   5
#define BNE   6
#define EXG   7    / *EXG exchanges the contents of two registers */
#define STOP  15

void main(void)
{
  unsigned short int  PC  = 0;    /* program counter             */
  unsigned short int  D0  = 0;    /* data register               */
  unsigned short int  A0  = 0;    /* address register            */
  unsigned short int  CCR = 0;    /* condition code register     */
  unsigned short int  MAR;        /* memory address register     */
  unsigned short int  MBR;        /* memory buffer register      */
  unsigned short int  IR;         /* instruction register        */
  unsigned short int  operand;    /* the 8-bit operand from the IR */
  unsigned short int  source;     /* source operand              */
```

```
  unsigned short int  destination;  /* the destination value       */
  unsigned short int  opcode;       /* the 4-bit op-code from the IR */
  unsigned short int  amode;        /* the 2-bit addressing mode     */
  unsigned short int  direction;    /* the 1-bit data direction flag */
  unsigned short int  memory[256];  /* the memory */
  unsigned short int  run = 1;      /* execute program while run is 1 */


/* Instruction format:                              */
/* 7  6  5  4  3  2  1  0                            */
/* Bit 1 and 0 2-bit address mode                   */
/*                   00 address mode = absolute      */
/*                   01 address mode = literal       */
/*                   10 address mode = indexed       */
/*                   11 address mode = relative      */
/* Bit 2      1-bit direction (source/operand)       */
/* Bit 3      not used                               */
/* Bit 7 to 4  4-bit instruction code                */


/* main loop */

  while (run)
  {
    MAR = PC;                /* PC to MAR                        */
    PC  = PC + 1;            /* increment PC                     */
    MBR = memory[MAR];       /* get next instruction             */
    IR  = MBR;              /* copy MBR to IR                    */
    opcode  = IR;            /* store the op-code bits            */
    MAR = PC;                /* PC to MAR                        */
    PC  = PC + 1;            /* increment PC                     */
    MBR = memory[MAR];       /* get the operand                  */
    IR  = MBR;              /* copy MBR to IR                    */
    operand = IR;            /* store the operand bits            */
    amode   = opcode & 0x03; /* extract the address mode bits     */
    direction = (opcode & 0x04) >> 2; /* get data direction 0 = register to memory
                                                            1 = memory to register */
    opcode = opcode >> 4;     /* get the 4-bit instruction code */

    /* use the address mode to get the source operand */


    switch (amode)
      { case 0: {source = memory[operand];       break;} /* absolute */
        case 1: {source = operand;               break;} /* literal  */
        case 2: {source = memory[A0 + operand];  break;} /* indexed */
        case 3: {source = memory[PC + operand];  break;} /* PC relative */
      }

  /* now execute the instruction */

  switch (opcode)
   {case MOVE: {if (direction == 0) destination = D0;
                else               D0 = source;
                if (D0 == 0) CCR = 1; else CCR = 0;    /* update CCR */
               break;
               }

    case ADD:   {if (direction == 0)
                    { destination = D0 + source;
                      if (destination == 0) CCR = 1; else CCR = 0;
                    }
                 else
                    { D0 = D0 + source;
                      if (D0 == 0 ) CCR = 1; else CCR = 0;
                    }
                 break;
                }
```

```
        case SUB:   {if (direction == 0)
                        { destination = D0 - source;
                          if (destination == 0) CCR = 1; else CCR = 0;
                        }
                     else
                        { D0 = D0 - source;
                          if (D0 == 0 ) CCR = 1; else CCR = 0;
                        }
                     break;
                    }

        case BRA:   { if (amode == 0) PC = operand;
                      if (amode == 1) PC = PC + operand; break;
                    }

        case CMP:   { MBR = D0 - source;
                      if (MBR == 0) CCR = 1;
                      else CCR = 0; break;
                    }


        case BEQ:   {if (CCR == 1)
                        { if (amode == 0) PC = operand;
                          if (amode == 1) PC = PC + operand;
                        } break;
                    }

        case BNE:   {if (CCR != 1)
                        { if (amode == 0) PC = operand;
                          if (amode == 1) PC = PC + operand;
                        } break;
                    }

        case EXG:   {MBR = D0; D0 = A0; A0 = MBR; break;
                    }

        case STOP:  {run = 0; break;
                    }
        }

    /* save result in memory if register to memory */
    if (direction == 0)
        switch (amode)
        { case 0: { memory[operand] = destination;      break; /* absolute */
                  }

          case 1: {                                     break; /* literal  */
                  }

          case 2: { memory[A0 + operand] = destination; break; /* indexed  */
                  }

          case 3: { memory[PC + operand] = destination; break; /* PC relative */
                  }
        }
    }
}
```

Now that we have examined the sequence of events that take place during the execution of an instruction, the next step is to demonstrate how the binary code of an instruction is translated into the actions that implement the instruction. In the next two sections we describe two different types of control unit; the *micropro-grammed control unit* and the so-called r*andom logic control unit*.

7.3 **The random logic control unit**

We've demonstrated how you can write a program using assembly language instructions. We've shown how an assembly language instruction can be reduced to the flow of information between registers and functional units in a CPU. We've shown how register, counters, and logical units can be created from primitive gates and flip-flops. What's left?

What we have not yet demonstrated is how a binary pattern such as, say, 1101101110101001_2 can be turned into the sequence of operations that causes a machine-level operation like ADD $A9, **D0** to be executed. We now make good this omission and complete the final link in the chain between gate and computer.

There are two ways of transforming an instruction into the operations that *interpret* it. One is to create the logic that directly transforms instructions into control signals. The other is to design a special computer that takes a machine-level instruction as a program and generates control signals as an output. We first describe the *random logic unit*, which uses gates and flip-flops to generate control signals.

When engineers design a *random logic control unit* (RALU) they ask 'What sequence of microinstructions is needed

to execute each machine code instruction and what logic elements do we need to implement them?' In other words, designers resort to the Boolean techniques we described in Chapter 2. The word *random* in the expression *random logic element* is employed in a specific sense and implies that the arrangement of gates from which the control unit is constructed varies widely from computer to computer. The same microprogrammed control unit can readily be adapted to suit many different computers with relatively little modification, whereas the random logic control unit is dedicated to a specific CPU and cannot easily be modified.

7.3.1 **Implementing a primitive CPU**

Before designing a random logic control unit, let's look at the structure of a very simple CPU in order to determine what control signals we need to synthesize. Figure 7.8 illustrates a computer with a single bus that is connected to all registers and the memory. This arrangement reduces the amount of logic required to implement the processor, but it is inefficient because only one word at a time can be copied from a source to a destination. The ALU has two inputs P and Q. The P input comes only from data register D0 and the Q input

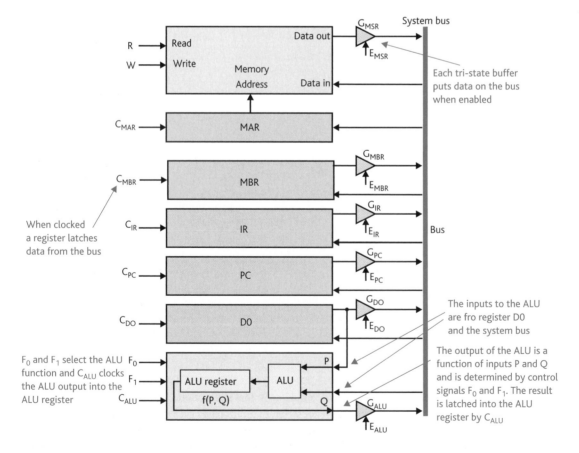

Figure 7.8 Structure of a single-bus CPU.

Signal number	Signal	Type	Operation
1	R	Memory control	Read from memory
2	W	Memory control	Write to memory
3	C_{MAR}	Register clock	Clock data into MAR
4	C_{MBR}	Register clock	Clock data into MBR
5	C_{PC}	Register clock	Clock data into program counter
6	C_{IR}	Register clock	Clock data into instruction register
7	C_{D0}	Register clock	Clock data into data register
8	C_{ALU}	Register clock	Clock data into ALU register
9	E_{MSR}	Bus control	Gate data from the memory onto the bus
10	E_{MBR}	Bus control	Gate data from the MBR onto the bus
11	E_{IR}	Bus control	Gate operand from IR onto the bus
12	E_{PC}	Bus control	Gate program counter onto the bus
13	E_{D0}	Bus control	Gate data register onto the bus
14	E_{ALU}	Bus control	Gate ALU function register onto the bus
15	F_0	ALU control	Select ALU function bit 0
16	F_1	ALU control	Select ALU function bit 1

Table 7.4 The control signals in the CPU of Fig. 7.8.

comes only from the system bus. Note that this structure allows the memory to transfer data directly to or from any register; that is, all data does not have to pass through the MBR.

The memory receives the address of the location to be accessed directly from the MAR, whose output is permanently connected to the memory's address input. A dedicated connection between the MAR and memory is possible because the memory never receives an address input from a source other than the memory address register. A permanent connection removes the need for bus control circuits.

Two data paths link the memory to the system bus. In a read cycle when memory control input R is asserted, data is transferred from the memory to the system bus via tri-state gate G_{MSR}. During a memory write cycle when memory control input W is asserted, data is transferred from the system bus directly to the memory.

The MBR, data register, program counter, and instruction register are each connected to the system bus in the same way. When one of these registers wishes to place data on the bus, its tri-state gate is enabled. Conversely, data is copied into a register from the bus by clocking the register. The instruction register (IR) receives data from the memory directly, without the data having to pass through the MBR.

The ALU receives data from two sources, the system bus and data register D0, and places its own output on the system bus. This arrangement begs the question, 'If the ALU gets data from the system bus how can it put data on the same bus at the same time it is receiving data from this bus?' Figure 7.8 shows that the ALU contains an internal ALU register. When

F_1	F_0	function
0	0	add P to Q
0	1	subtract Q
1	0	increment Q
1	1	decrement Q

Table 7.5 Decoding the ALU control code, F_0, F_1.

this register is clocked by C_{ALU}, the output from the ALU is captured and can be put on the system bus by enabling gate G_{ALU}.

Table 7.4 defines the 16 control signals in Fig. 7.8. Instruction decoding takes an instruction and uses it to create a sequence of 16-bit signals that control the system in Fig. 7.8.

The ALU is controlled by a two-bit code, F_1, F_0, which determines its functions as defined in Table 7.5. These operations are representative of real instructions, although a practical ALU would implement, typically, 16 different functions.

In order to keep the design of a random logic control unit as simple as possible, we will construct a 3-bit operation code giving a total of eight instructions. This instruction set defined in Table 7.6 presents a very primitive instruction set indeed, but it does include the types of instruction found in real first-generation processors. We have defined explicit LOAD and STORE instructions rather than a single MOVE instruction which does the work of both LOAD and STORE.

Having constructed an instruction set, we define each of the instructions in terms of RTL and determine the

Op-code	Mnemonic	Operation
000	LOAD N	[D0] ← [N]
001	STORE N	[N] ← [D0]
010	ADD N	[D0] ← [D0] + [N]
011	SUB N	[D0] ← [D0] - [N]
100	INC N	[N] ← [N] + 1
101	DEC N	[N] ← [N] - 1
110	BRA N	[PC] ← N
111	BEQ N	IF Z = 1 THEN [PC] ← N

sequence of operations necessary to carry them out on the computer in Fig. 7.8. Table 7.7 gives the micro-operations for each instruction including the fetch phase. The symbol Z is the zero-flag bit from the CCR, which is assumed to be part of the ALU.

Note that N is the operand field used by the instruction.

Table 7.6 A primitive instruction set for the CPU of Fig. 7.8.

Instruction	Op-code	Operations (RTL)		Control actions	
Fetch		[MAR]	← [PC]	E_{PC} = 1	C_{MAR}
		[IR]	← [[MAR]]	R = 1, E_{MSR} = 1,	C_{IR}
		[ALU]	← [PC]	E_{PC} = 1, F_1, F_0 = 1,0,	C_{ALU}
		[PC]	← [ALU]	E_{ALU} = 1	C_{PC}
LOAD	000	[MAR]	← [IR]	E_{IR} = 1	C_{MAR}
		[D0]	← [[MAR]]	R = 1, E_{MSR} = 1,	C_{D0}
STORE	001	[MAR]	← [IR]	E_{IR} = 1	C_{MAR}
		[[MAR]]	← [D0]	E_{D0} = 1	W = 1
ADD	010	[MAR]	← [IR]	E_{IR} = 1	C_{MAR}
		[MBR]	← [[MAR]]	R = 1, E_{MSR} = 1,	C_{MBR}
		[ALU]	← [MBR]	E_{MBR} = 1, F_1, F_0 = 0,0,	C_{ALU}
		[D0]	← [ALU]	E_{ALU} = 1	C_{D0}
SUB	011	[MAR]	← [IR]	E_{IR} = 1	C_{MAR}
		[MBR]	← [[MAR]]	R = 1, E_{MSR} = 1,	C_{MBR}
		[ALU]	← [MBR]	E_{MBR} = 1, F_1, F_0 = 0,1,	C_{ALU}
		[D0]	← [ALU]	E_{ALU} = 1	C_{D0}
INC	100	[MAR]	← [IR]	E_{IR} = 1	C_{MAR}
		[MBR]	← [[MAR]]	R = 1, E_{MSR} = 1,	C_{MBR}
		[ALU]	← [MBR]	E_{MBR} = 1, F_1, F_0 = 0,1,	C_{ALU}
		[[MAR]]	← [ALU]	E_{ALU} = 1	W = 1
DEC	101	[MAR]	← [IR]	E_{IR} = 1	C_{MAR}
		[MBR]	← [[MAR]]	R = 1, E_{MSR} = 1,	C_{MBR}
		[ALU]	← [MBR]	E_{MBR} = 1, F_1, F_0 = 1,1,	C_{ALU}
		[[MAR]]	← [ALU]	E_{ALU} = 1	W = 1
BRA	110	[PC]	← [IR]	E_{IR} = 1	C_{PC}
BEQ	111	IF Z = 1 THEN [PC] ← [IR]		E_{IR} = 1	IF Z = 1 THEN C_{PC}

Table 7.7 Interpreting the instruction set of Table 7.6 in RTL and microinstructions.

Consider the *load D0 from memory* operation; this requires the following two steps:

[MAR] ← [IR] E_{IR} = 1 C_{MAR} Copy operand address to MAR
[D0]   ← [[MAR]]   R = 1, E_{MSR} = 1, C_{D0} Read memory and copy to D0

We have to send the operand address in the instruction register to the memory address register by enabling the G_{IR} gate and then clocking the data into the memory address register.

Then we have to put the memory in read mode, put the data from the memory onto the bus by enabling the G_{MSR} gate, and finally capture the data in D0 by clocking register D0.

Table 7.7 tells us what signals have to be asserted to execute the two operations required to interpret LOAD N. Table 7.8

Instruction	Operations (RTL)		R	W	C_{MAR}	C_{MBR}	C_{PC}	C_{IR}	C_{D0}	C_{ALU}	E_{MSR}	E_{MBR}	E_{IR}	E_{PC}	E_{D0}	E_{ALU}	F_1	F_0
Fetch	[MAR]	← [PC]	0	0	1	0	0	0	0	0	0	0	0	1	0	0	0	0
	[IR]	← [[MAR]]	1	0	0	0	0	1	0	0	1	0	0	0	0	0	0	0
	[ALU]	← [PC]	0	0	0	0	0	0	0	1	0	0	0	1	0	0	1	0
	[PC]	← [ALU]	0	0	0	0	1	0	0	0	0	0	0	0	0	1	0	0
LOAD	[MAR]	← [IR]	0	0	1	0	0	0	0	0	0	0	1	0	0	0	0	0
	[D0]	← [[MAR]]	1	0	0	0	0	0	1	0	1	0	0	0	0	0	0	0
STORE	[MAR]	← [IR]	0	0	1	0	0	0	0	0	0	0	1	0	0	0	0	0
	[[MAR]]	← [D0]	0	1	0	0	0	0	0	0	0	0	0	0	1	0	0	0
ADD	[MAR]	← [IR]	0	0	1	0	0	0	0	0	0	0	1	0	0	0	0	0
	[MBR]	← [[MAR]]	1	0	0	0	0	0	0	0	1	1	0	0	0	0	0	0
	[ALU]	← [MBR]	0	0	0	0	0	0	0	1	0	1	0	0	0	0	0	0
	[D0]	← [ALU]	0	0	0	0	0	0	1	0	0	0	0	0	0	1	0	0
SUB	[MAR]	← [IR]	0	0	1	0	0	0	0	0	0	0	1	0	0	0	0	0
	[MBR]	← [[MAR]]	1	0	0	0	0	0	0	0	1	1	0	0	0	0	0	0
	[ALU]	← [MBR]	0	0	0	0	0	0	0	1	0	1	0	0	0	0	0	1
	[D0]	← [ALU]	0	0	0	0	0	0	1	0	0	0	0	0	0	1	0	0
INC	[MAR]	← [IR]	0	0	1	0	0	0	0	0	0	0	1	0	0	0	0	0
	[MBR]	← [[MAR]]	1	0	0	0	0	0	0	0	1	1	0	0	0	0	0	0
	[ALU]	← [MBR]	0	0	0	0	0	0	0	1	0	1	0	0	0	0	1	0
	[[MAR]]	← [ALU]	0	1	0	0	0	0	0	0	0	0	0	0	0	1	0	0
DEC	[MAR]	← [IR]	0	0	1	0	0	0	0	0	0	0	1	0	0	0	0	0
	[MBR]	← [[MAR]]	1	0	0	0	0	0	0	0	1	1	0	0	0	0	0	0
	[ALU]	← [MBR]	0	0	0	0	0	0	0	1	0	1	0	0	0	0	1	1
	[[MAR]]	← [ALU]	0	1	0	0	0	0	0	0	0	0	0	0	0	1	0	0
BRA	[PC]	← [IR]	0	0	0	0	1	0	0	0	0	0	1	0	0	0	0	0
BEQ	IF Z = 1 THEN																	
	[PC]	← [IR]	0	0	0	0	Z	0	0	0	0	0	1	0	0	0	0	0

Table 7.8 Interpreting the micro-operations of Table 7.7 as microinstructions.

gives all the signals in the form of a 16-component vector; that is, the two vectors are

0010000000100000 and
1000000010001000

Figure 7.9 shows the timing of the execution phase of this instruction. We have included only five of the 16 possible control signals because all the other 12 signals remain inactive during these two micro-operations.

7.3.2 From op-code to operation

In order to execute an instruction we have to do two things. The first is to convert the 3-bit op-code into one of eight possible sequences of action and the second is to cause these actions to take place.

Figure 7.10 shows how the instructions are decoded and is similar in operation to the 3-line to 8-line decoder described in Chapter 2. For each of the eight possible three-bit op-codes, one and only one of the eight outputs is placed in an active-high condition. For example, if the op-code corresponding to ADD (i.e. 010) is loaded into the instruction register during a fetch phase, the ADD line 2 from the AND gate array is asserted high while all other AND gate outputs remain low.

It's no good simply detecting and decoding a particular instruction. The control unit has to carry out the sequence of microinstructions that will execute the instruction. To do this we require a source of signals to trigger each of the microinstructions. A circuit that produces a stream of trigger signals is called a *sequencer*. Figure 7.11 provides the logic diagram of a simplified eight-step sequencer.

The outputs of three JK flip-flops arranged as a 3-bit binary up-counter counting 000, 001, 010, . . . ,111, are connected to eight three-input AND gates to generate timing signals T_0 to T_7. Figure 7.12 illustrates the timing pulses created by this circuit. Note that the timing decoder is similar to the instruction decoder of Fig. 7.11. As not all macroinstructions require the same number of microinstructions to interpret them, the sequencer of Fig. 7.11 has a reset input that can be used to reset the sequencer by returning it to state T_0.

The sequencer of Fig. 7.11 is illustrative rather than practical, because, as it stands, the circuit may generate spurious timing pulses at the timing pulse outputs due to the use of an asynchronous counter. All outputs of an asynchronous counter don't change state at the same instant and therefore the bit pattern at its output may pass through several states (if only for a few nanoseconds) before it settles down to its final value. Unfortunately, these transient states or *glitches* may last long enough to create spurious timing signals, which, in turn, may trigger undesired activity within the control unit. A solution to these problems is to disable the output of the timing pulse generator until the counter has settled down (or to use a synchronous counter).

The next step in designing the control unit is to combine the signals from the instruction decoder with the timing signals from the sequencer to generate the actual control signals. Figure 7.13 shows one possible approach.

There are nine vertical lines in the decoder of Fig. 7.13 (only three are shown). One vertical line corresponds to the fetch phase and each of the other eight lines is assigned to one of the eight instructions. At any instant one of the vertical lines from the instruction decoder (or fetch) is in a logical one state, enabling the column of two-input AND gates to which it is connected. The other inputs to the column of AND gates are the timing pulses from the sequencer.

As the timing signals, T_0 to T_7, are generated, the outputs of the AND gates enabled by the current instruction synthesize the control signals required to implement the random logic control unit. The output of each AND gate corresponding to a particular microinstruction (e.g. C_{MAR}) triggers the actual microinstruction (i.e. micro-operation). As we pointed out earlier, not all macroinstructions require eight clock cycles to execute them.

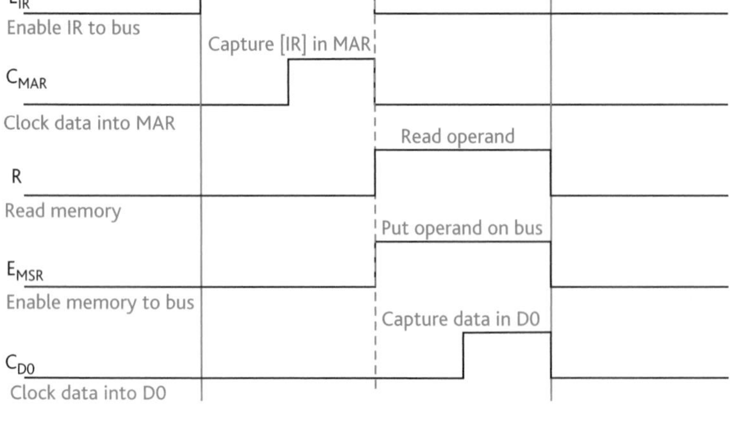

Figure 7.9 Timing of the execute phase of a LOAD N instruction.

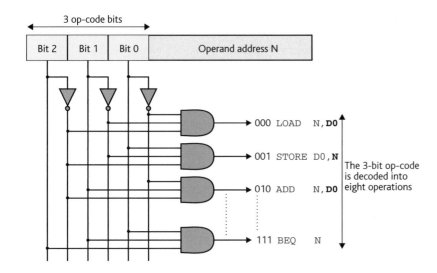

Figure 7.10 The instruction decoder.

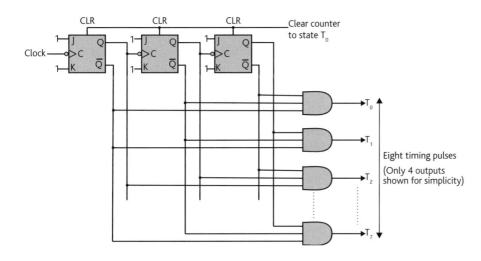

Figure 7.11 The timing pulse generator (sequencer).

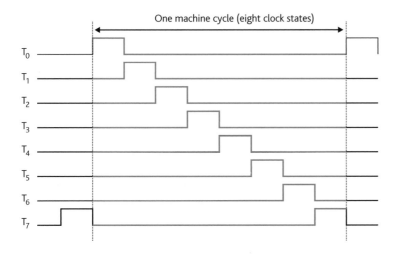

Figure 7.12 The outputs from the timing pulse generator.

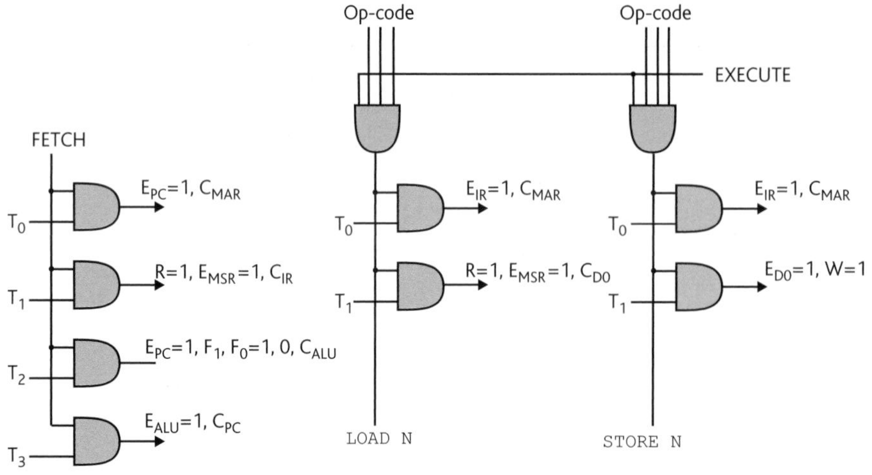

Op-code Op-code

EXECUTE

FETCH

T_0 — $E_{PC}=1, C_{MAR}$ T_0 — $E_{IR}=1, C_{MAR}$ T_0 — $E_{IR}=1, C_{MAR}$

T_1 — $R=1, E_{MSR}=1, C_{IR}$ T_1 — $R=1, E_{MSR}=1, C_{D0}$ T_1 — $E_{D0}=1, W=1$

T_2 — $E_{PC}=1, F_1, F_0=1, 0, C_{ALU}$

T_3 — $E_{ALU}=1, C_{PC}$ LOAD N STORE N

Figure 7.13 Combining control signals.

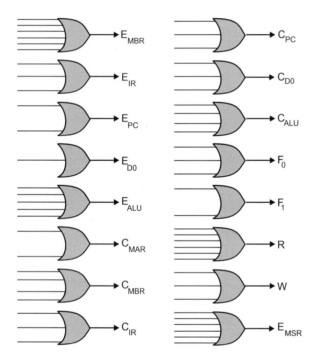

E_{MBR} C_{PC}

E_{IR} C_{D0}

E_{PC} C_{ALU}

E_{D0} F_0

E_{ALU} F_1

C_{MAR} R

C_{MBR} W

C_{IR} E_{MSR}

Figure 7.14 The OR gate array used to generate the actual microinstructions.

Each microinstruction is activated by one or more control signals from the nine columns of AND gates. Figure 7.14 shows the array of OR gates that combine the outputs from the AND gates to generate the control signals. The inputs from these OR gates come from the nine columns of AND gates.

The fetch–execute flip-flop

So far we have devised a mechanism to interpret each macroinstruction but have not looked at how we implement the two-phase fetch–execute cycle. As the control unit is

always in one of two states (fetch or execute), an RS flip-flop provides a convenient way of switching from one state to another. When $Q = 0$ the current operation is a fetch phase, and when $Q = 1$ an execute phase is being performed. Figure 7.15 is an extension of Figure 7.13 and demonstrates how the instruction decoder is enabled by the Q output of the fetch–execute flip-flop, and the fetch decoder by the $\bar{Q}$ output.

At the end of each fetch phase, a clock pulse from the timing generator sets the fetch–execute flip-flop, permitting the current op-code to be decoded and executed. The timing-pulse generator is reset at the end of each fetch. At the end of each execute phase, the fetch–execute flip-flop is cleared and the sequencer reset, enabling the next fetch phase to begin.

Table 7.9 shows how the machine-level instructions can be represented in terms of both timing signals and microinstructions. Note that we've included the micro-operation [MAR] ← [IR] in the fetch phase.

The microinstructions are the enable signals to the bus drivers, the register clocks, the ALU function select bits, the memory controls (R and W), and the reset and set inputs of the fetch–execute flip-flop. For each of the microinstructions we can write down a Boolean expression in terms of the machine-level instruction and the sequence of timing pulses. For example, consider expressions for E_{MBR}, E_{IR}, and C_{MAR}.

$$E_{MBR} = ADD \cdot T_1 + SUB \cdot T_1 + INC \cdot T_1 + DEC \cdot T_1$$

$$E_{IR} = Fetch \cdot T_4 + BRA \cdot T_0 + BEQ \cdot T_0$$

$$C_{MAR} = Fetch \cdot T_0 + Fetch \cdot T_4$$

We should note, of course, that this CPU and its micropro-gram are very highly simplified and illustrate the nature of the random logic CU rather than its exact design.

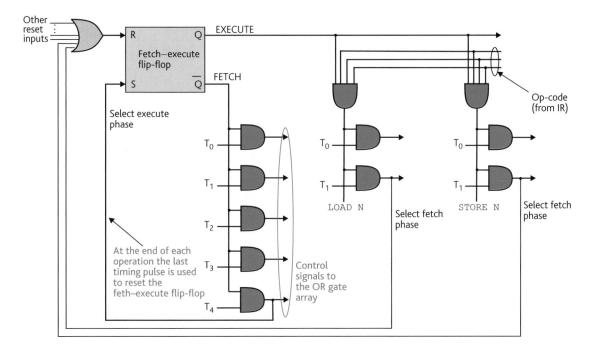

Figure 7.15 The fetch–execute flip-flop.

In the next section we look at how the design of a control unit can be simplified by putting the sequence of micro-operations in a table and then reading them from a table, rather than by synthesizing them in hard logic.

7.4 Microprogrammed control units

Before we describe the microprogrammed control unit, let's remind ourselves of the *macro-level* instruction, *micro-level* instruction, and *interpretation*. The natural or native language of a computer is its machine code whose mnemonic representation is called *assembly language*. Machine-level instructions are also called *macroinstructions*. Each macroinstruction is executed by means of a number of primitive actions called *microinstructions*. The process whereby a macroinstruction is executed by carrying out a series of microinstructions is called *interpretation*.

Let's begin with another simple computer. Consider Fig. 7.16. The internal structure of this primitive CPU differs slightly from that of Fig. 7.8 because there's more than one bus. The CPU in Fig. 7.16 includes the mechanisms by which information is moved within the CPU. Each of the registers (program counter, MAR, data register, etc.) is made up of D flip-flops. When the clock input to a register is pulsed, the

data at the register's D input terminals is transferred to its output terminals and held constant until the register is clocked again. The connections between the registers are by means of *m*-bit wide data highways, which are drawn as a single bold line. The output from each register can be gated onto the bus by enabling the appropriate tri-state buffer. We have used a multiplexer, labeled MPLX, to select the program counter's input from either the incrementer or the operand field of the instruction register. The multiplexer is controlled by the 1-bit signal Mux, where Mux = 0 selects the incre-menter path, and Mux = 1 selects the branch target address from the address/operand field of the instruction register, $IR_{address}$.

Suppose our computer performs a fetch–execute cycle in which the op-code is ADD N, **D0**. This instruction adds the contents of the memory location specified by the operand field N to the contents of the data register (i.e. D0) and deposits the result in D0. We can write down the sequence of operations that take place during the execution of ADD not only in terms of register transfer language, but also in terms of the enabling of gates and the clocking of flip-flops. Table 7.10 illustrates the sequence of microinstructions executed during the fetch–execute cycle of an ADD instruction. It should be emphasized that the fetch phase of all instructions is identical and it is only the execute phase that varies according to the nature of the op-code read during the fetch phase.

Instruction	Time	Memory		Gate enables						Register clocks						ALU		Fetch–execute	
		R	W	MBR	IR	PC	DO	MSR	ALU	MAR	MBR	IR	PC	DO	ALU	F_1	F_0	R	S
Fetch	T_0	0	0	0	0	1	0	0	0	1	0	0	0	0	0	X	X	0	0
	T_1	1	0	0	0	0	0	1	0	0	0	1	0	0	0	X	X	0	0
	T_2	0	0	0	0	1	0	0	0	0	0	0	0	0	1	1	0	0	0
	T_3	0	0	0	0	0	0	0	1	0	0	0	1	0	0	X	X	0	0
	T_4	0	0	0	1	0	0	0	0	1	0	0	0	0	0	X	X	0	1
LOAD	T_0	1	0	0	0	0	0	1	0	0	0	0	0	1	0	X	X	1	0
STORE	T_0	0	1	0	0	0	1	0	0	0	0	0	0	0	0	X	X	1	0
ADD	T_0	1	0	0	0	0	0	1	0	0	1	0	0	0	0	X	X	0	0
	T_1	0	0	1	0	0	0	0	0	0	0	0	0	0	1	0	0	0	0
	T_2	0	0	0	0	0	0	0	1	0	0	0	0	1	0	X	X	1	0
SUB	T_0	1	0	0	0	0	0	1	0	0	1	0	0	0	0	X	X	0	0
	T_1	0	0	1	0	0	0	0	0	0	0	0	0	0	1	0	1	0	0
	T_2	0	0	0	0	0	0	0	1	0	0	0	0	1	0	X	X	1	0
INC	T_0	1	0	0	0	0	0	1	0	0	1	0	0	0	0	X	X	0	0
	T_1	0	0	1	0	0	0	0	0	0	0	0	0	0	1	1	0	0	0
	T_2	0	1	0	0	0	0	0	1	0	0	0	0	0	0	X	X	1	0
DEC	T_0	1	0	0	0	0	0	1	0	0	1	0	0	0	0	X	X	0	0
	T_1	0	0	1	0	0	0	0	0	0	0	0	0	0	1	1	1	0	0
	T_2	0	1	0	0	0	0	0	1	0	0	0	0	0	0	X	X	1	0
BRA	T_0	0	0	0	1	0	0	0	0	0	0	0	1	0	0	X	X	1	0
BEQ	T_0	0	0	0	1	0	0	0	0	0	0	0	Z	0	0	X	X	1	0

Table 7.9 The interpretation of machine code instructions.

7.4.1 The microprogram

Imagine that the output of the control unit in Fig. 7.16 consists of 10 signals that enable gates G_1 to G_{10}, the PC input multiplexer, two signals that control the memory, and five clock signals that pulse the clock inputs of the PC, MAR, MBR, IR, and D0 registers. Table 7.11 presents the 17 outputs of the control unit as a sequence of binary values that are generated during the fetch and execute phases of an ADD instruction. We have not included the ALU function signals in this table.

When the memory is accessed by $E = 1$, a memory read or write cycle may take place. The R/$\overline{W}$ (i.e. read/write) signal determines the nature of the memory access when $E = 1$. When R/$\overline{W} = 0$ the cycle is a write cycle, and when R/$\overline{W} = 1$ the cycle is a read cycle.

If, for each of the seven steps in Table 7.11, the 17 signals are fed to the various parts of the CPU in Fig. 7.16, then the fetch–execute cycle will be carried out. Real microprogrammed computers might use 64 to 200 control signals rather than the 17 in this example. One of the most significant differences between a microinstruction and a macroinstruction is that the former contains many fields and may provide several operands, while the macroinstruction frequently specifies only an op-code and one or two operands.

The seven steps in Table 7.11 represent a *microprogram* that interprets a fetch phase followed by an ADD instruction.

We have demonstrated that a macroinstruction is interpreted by executing a microprogram, which comprises a sequence of microinstructions. Each of the CPU's instructions has its own microprogram. We now look at the

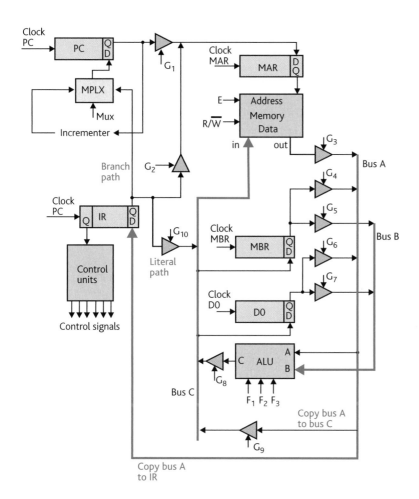

Figure 7.16 Controlling the flow of information in a computer.

Step	Register transfer language	Operations required
1	[MAR] ← [PC]	enable G_1, clock MAR
1a	INC ← [PC]	
2	[PC] ← INC	Mux = 0, clock PC
3	[MBR] ← [[MAR]]	enable memory, R/$\overline{\text{W}}$=1, enable G_3 enable G_9, clock MBR
4	[IR] ← [MBR]	enable G_4, clock IR
4a	CU ← [IR$_{(op-code)}$]	
5	[MAR] ← [IR$_{(address)}$]	enable G_2, clock MAR
6	[MBR] ← [[MAR]]	enable memory, R/$\overline{\text{W}}$=1, enable G_3, enable G_9, clock MBR
7	ALU ← [MBR]	enable G_4, set ALU function to add
7a	ALU ← [D0]	enable G_7
7b	[D0] ← ALU	enable G_8, clock data register D0

Note 1 Where there is no entry in the column labeled 'Operations required', that operation happens automatically. For example, the output of the program counter is always connected to the input of the incrementer and therefore no explicit operation is needed to move the contents of the PC to the incrementer.

Note 2 Any three-state gate not explicitly mentioned is not enabled.

Note 3 Steps 1, 1a are carried out simultaneously, as are 4, 4a and 7, 7a, 7b.

Table 7.10 Interpreting a fetch–execute cycle for an ADD N, D0 instruction in terms of RTL.

Step	Gate control signals and MPLX control											Memory		Register clocks				
	G_1	G_2	G_3	G_4	G_5	G_6	G_7	G_8	G_9	G_{10}	Mux	E	R/W	PC	MAR	MBR	DO	IR
1	1	0	0	0	0	0	0	0	0	0	0	0	0	0	1	0	0	0
2	0	0	0	0	0	0	0	0	0	0	0	0	0	1	0	0	0	0
3	0	0	1	0	0	0	0	0	1	0	0	1	1	0	0	1	0	1
4	0	0	0	1	0	0	0	0	0	0	0	0	0	0	0	0	0	1
5	0	1	0	0	0	0	0	0	0	0	0	0	0	0	1	0	0	0
6	0	0	1	0	0	0	0	0	1	0	0	1	1	0	0	1	0	0
7	0	0	0	1	0	0	1	1	0	0	0	0	0	0	0	0	1	0

Table 7.11 Control signals generated during the fetch and execution phases of an ADD instruction.

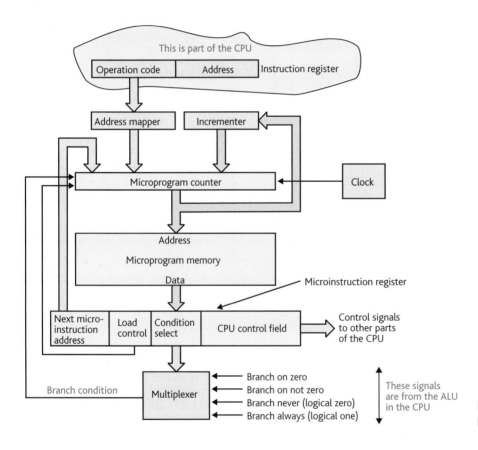

Figure 7.17 The micro-programmed control unit.

microprogram itself and consider the hardware required to execute it. The microprogram is executed by the same type of mechanism used to execute the macroprogram (i.e., machine code) itself. This is a good example of the common expression *wheels within wheels*.

Figure 7.17 describes the basic structure of a micropro-grammed control unit that has a microprogram counter, a microprogram memory, and a microinstruction register (this structure is typical of the 1980s). The microinstruction address from the microprogram counter is applied to the address input of the microprogram memory and the data output of the memory fed to the microinstruction register. As we've said, the structure of the control unit that executes the macroinstruction is very much like the structure of the CPU itself. However, there is one very big difference between the macroinstruction world and the microinstruction world—the microinstruction register is very much longer than the macroinstruction register and the microinstruction's structure is much more complex that of the macro-instruction.

Information in the microinstruction register is divided into four fields: next microinstruction address field, micro-program counter load control field, condition select field, and CPU control field. Most of the bits in the microinstruction register belong to the CPU control field, which controls the flow of information within the CPU by enabling tri-state gates and clocking registers as we've described; for example, all the control signals in Table 7.11 belong to this field. Our next task is to describe one of the principal differences between the micro- and macroinstruction. Each microinstruction is also a conditional branch instruction that determines the location of the next microinstruction to be executed. We will now explain how microinstructions are sequenced.

7.4.2 Microinstruction sequence control

If the microprogram counter were to step through the micro-program memory in the natural sequence, 0, 1, 2, 3, ... etc., a stream of consecutive microinstructions would appear in the microinstruction register, causing the CPU to behave in the way described by Table 7.11. The CPU control bits of each microinstruction determine the flow of information within the CPU. However, just as in the case of the macroprogram control unit, it is often necessary to modify the sequence in which microinstructions are executed. For example, we might wish to repeat a group of microinstructions *n* times, or we may wish to jump from a fetch phase to an execute phase, or we may wish to call a (microinstruction) procedure.

Microinstruction sequence control is determined by the three left-hand fields of the microinstruction register in Fig. 7.17, enabling the microprogram counter to implement both conditional and unconditional branches to locations within the microprogram memory. We shall soon see that this activity is necessary to execute macroinstructions such as BRA, BCC, BCS, BEQ, etc.

In normal operation, the microprogram counter steps through microinstructions sequentially and the next micro-program address is the current address plus one. By loading the contents of the next microinstruction address field of the current microinstruction field into the microprogram counter, a branch can be made to any point in the micropro-gram memory. In other words each microinstruction determines whether the next microinstruction is taken in sequence or whether it is taken from the next address field of the current microinstruction. The obvious question to ask is, 'What determines whether the microprogram counter continues in sequence or is loaded from the next microinstruction address field of the current microinstruction?'

The microprogram *load control* field in the microinstruction register tells the microprogram counter how to get the next microinstruction address. This next address can come from the incrementer and cause the microprogram to continue in sequence. The next address can also be obtained from the *address mapper* (see below) or from the address in the next microinstruction address field of the microinstruction register.

The *condition select field* in the microinstruction register implements conditional branches at the macroinstruction level by executing a conditional branch at the microinstruction level. In the simplified arrangement of Fig. 7.17, the condition select field directly controls a 4-to-1 multiplexer that selects one of four flag bits representing the state of the CPU. These flag bits are obtained from the ALU and are usually the flag bits in the condition code register (e.g. Z, N, C, V). The condition select field selects one of these flag bits for testing (in this example only the Z-bit is used). If the output of the multiplexer is true, a microprogram jump is made to the address specified by the contents of the next microinstruction address field, otherwise the microprogram continues sequentially. In Fig. 7.17 two of the conditions are obtained from the CCR and two bits are permanently true and false. A false condition implies *branch never* (i.e. continue) and a true condition implies *branch always* (i.e. goto).

To emphasize what we've just said, consider the hypothetical microinstruction of Fig. 7.18. This microinstruction is interpreted as:

```
IF Z = 1 THEN [PC] ← ADD3 ELSE [PC] ← [PC] + 1
```

where PC indicates the microprogram counter.

A conditional branch at the macroinstruction level (e.g. BEQ) is interpreted by microinstructions in the following

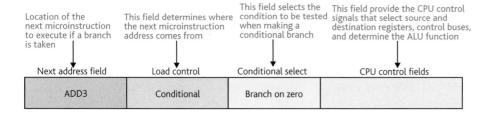

Location of the next microinstruction to execute if a branch is taken

This field determines where the next microinstruction address comes from

This field selects the condition to be tested when making a conditional branch

This field provide the CPU control signals that select source and destination registers, control buses, and determine the ALU function

Next address field	Load control	Conditional select	CPU control fields
ADD3	Conditional	Branch on zero	

Figure 7.18 Structure of a microinstruction.

way. The condition select field of the microinstruction selects the appropriate status bit of the CCR to be tested. For example, if the macroinstruction is BEQ the Z-bit is selected. The microprogram counter *load control* field contains the operation 'branch to the address in the microinstruction register on selected condition true'. Thus, if the selected condition is true (i.e. Z = 1), a jump is made to a point in the microprogram that implements the corresponding jump in the macroprogram. If the selected condition is false (i.e. Z = 0), the current sequence of microinstructions is terminated by the start of a new fetch–execute cycle.

Implementing the fetch–execute cycle

The first part of each microprogram executed by the control unit corresponds to a macroinstruction fetch phase that ends with the macroinstruction op-code being deposited in the instruction register. The op-code from the instruction register is first fed to the *address mapper*, which is a look-up table containing the starting address of the microprogram for each of the possible op-codes. That is, the address mapper translates the arbitrary bit pattern of the op-code into the location of the corresponding microprogram that will execute the op-code. After this microprogram has been executed, an unconditional jump is made to the start of the microprogram that interprets the macroinstruction execute phase, and the process continues.

7.4.3 User-microprogrammed processors

Before the advent of today's powerful microprocessors, engineers in the 1980s requiring high performance sometimes constructed their own microprogrammed computers; that is, the engineer designed a CPU to their own specifications. This was fun because you could create your own architecture and instruction set. On the other hand, you ended up with a computer without an off-the-shelf operating system, compilers, or any of the other tools you take for granted when you use a mainstream CPU.

At the heart of many of these systems was the *bit-slice* component, which provided a middle path between microcomputer and mainframe. Bit-slice components, as their name suggests, are really subsections of a microprocessor that can be put together to create a custom CPU. For example, a 64-bit computer is made by putting together eight 8-bit bit-slice chips.

Bit-slice components are divided into two types corresponding to the functional division within the microprocessor (i.e. the microprogram control and ALU). By using several ALU and microprogram controller bit-slices plus some additional logic and a microprogram in ROM, a CPU with a user-defined instruction set and wordlength may be created. Of course, the designer doesn't have to construct a new CPU out of bit-slice components. You can emulate an existing microprocessor or even add machine-level instructions to enhance it.

Figure 7.19 describes a typical bit-slice arithmetic logic unit that can generate one of eight functions of two inputs R and S. These functions vary from R plus S to the exclusive NOR of R and S. The values of R and S may be selected from a register file of 16 general-purpose data registers, an external input, a Q register, or zero.

The bit-slice ALU is controlled (i.e. programmed) by a 9-bit input, which selects the source of the data taking part in an arithmetic or logical operation, determines the particular operation to be executed, and controls the destination (together with any shifting) of the result. Typical ALU operations are

```
[R7] ← [R7] + [R1]
[R6] ← [R6] – [R5]
[R9] ← [R9]·[R2]
[R7] ← [R7] + 1
```

An arithmetic unit of any length (as long as it is a multiple of 4) is constructed by connecting together bit-slice ALUs. Designers can use the ALU's internal registers in any way they desire. For example, they may choose to implement eight addressable data registers, two stack pointers (described later), two index registers, a program counter, and three scratchpad registers. Flexibility is the most powerful feature of bit-slice microprocessors.

This description of the microprogrammed control unit is highly simplified. In practice the microprogram might include facilities for dealing with interrupts, the memory system, input/output, and so on.

One of the advantages of a microprogrammed control unit is that it is possible to alter the content of the microprogram memory (sometimes called the *control store*) and hence design your own machine-level instructions. In fact it is perfectly possible to choose a set of microprograms that will execute the machine code of an entirely different computer. In this case the computer is said to *emulate* another computer. Such a facility is useful if you are changing your old computer to a new one whose own machine code is incompatible with your old programs. Emulation applies to programs that exist in binary (object) form on tape or disk. By writing microprograms (on the new machine) to interpret the machine code of the old machine, you can use the old software and still get the advantages of the new machine.

One of the greatest problems in the design of a bit-slice computer lies in the construction and testing of the

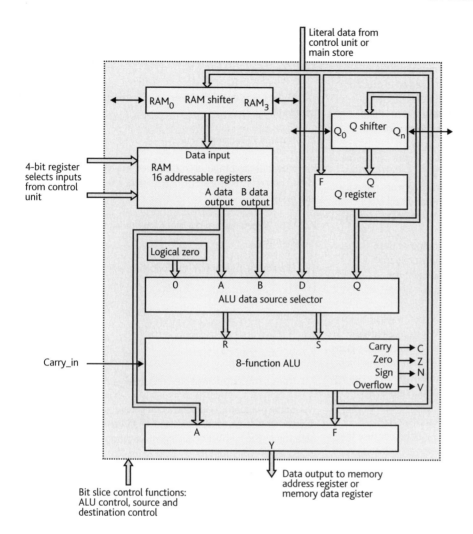

Figure 7.19 The micro-programmed ALU.

microprogram. You can, or course, write a program to emulate the bit-slice processor on another computer. A popular method of developing a microprogram is to replace the microprogram ROM with read/write memory and to access this memory with a conventional microprocessor. That is, the microprogram memory is common to both the bit-slice system and the microprocessor. In this way, the microprocessor can input a microprogram in mnemonic form, edit it, assemble it, and then pass control to the bit-slice system. The microprocessor may even monitor the operation of the bit-slice system.

Such a microprogram memory is called a writable control store and once a writable control store was regarded as a big selling point of microprogrammed minicomputers and mainframes. However, we have already pointed out that a microprogrammable control store is of very little practical use due to the lack of applications software. Even if a computer user has the expertise to design new microprogrammed macroinstructions, it is unlikely that the system software and compilers will be able to make use of these new instructions. Finally, RISC technology (as we shall see) does not use microprogramming and interest in microprogramming is much less than it once was.

In the next chapter we look at how the performance of computers can be enhanced by three very different techniques. We begin with a brief introduction to the RISC revolution of the 1970s and 1980s and show how processors with regular instruction sets lend themselves to pipelining (the overlapping of instruction execution). We also look at cache memory and explain how a small quantity of very-high-speed random access memory can radically improve a computer's performance. Finally, we describe the multiprocessor—a system that uses more than one processing unit to accelerate performance.

■ SUMMARY

We have taken a step back from the complex CPU architecture we described in the previous chapters and have looked at how a simple processor can read an instruction from memory, decode it, and execute it. We did this by considering the sequence of events that takes place when an instruction is executed and the flow of information within the computer.

In principle, the computer is a remarkably simple device. The program counter contains the address of the next instruction to be executed. The computer reads the instruction from memory and decodes it. We have demonstrated that a typical instruction requires a second access to memory to fetch the data used by the instruction.

We have demonstrated how a simple computer that can execute only instructions that load and store data or perform arithmetic operations can implement the conditional behavior required for loop and if . . . then . . . else constructs.

The second part of this chapter looked at two ways of implementing a computer's control unit. We started with a simple computer structure and demonstrated the control signals required to implement several machine-level instructions. Then we showed how you can use relatively simple logic and a timing sequencer to generate the signals required to interpret an instruction.

Random logic control units are faster than their micro-programmed counterparts. This must always be so because the random logic control unit is optimized for its particular application. Moreover, a microprogrammed control unit is slowed by the need to read a microinstruction from the microprogram memory. Memory accesses are generally slower than basic Boolean operations.

Microprogramming offers a flexible design. As the micro-program lives in read-only memory, it can easily be modified at either the design or the production stage. A random logic control unit is strictly special purpose and cannot readily be modified to incorporate new features in the processor (e.g. additional machine-level instructions), and sometimes it is difficult to remove design errors without considerable modification of the hardware.

The highpoint of microprogramming was the early 1970s when main memory had an access time of 1–2 μs and the control store used to hold microprograms had an access time of 50–100 ns. It was then sensible to design complex machine level instructions that were executed very rapidly as microcode. Today, things have changed and memories with access times of below 50 ns are the norm rather than the exception. Faster memory makes microprogramming less attractive because hard-wired random logic control units execute instructions much more rapidly than microcoded control units. Today's generation of RISC (reduced instruction set computers) and post-RISC architectures are not microprogrammed.

■ PROBLEMS

7.1 Within a CPU, what is the difference between an address path and a data path?

7.2 In the context of a machine-level instruction, what is an operand?

7.3 What is a literal operand?

7.4 How does a computer 'know' whether an operand in its instruction register is a literal or a reference to memory (i.e. an address)?

7.5 Why is the program counter a *pointer* and not a *counter*?

7.6 Explain the function of the following registers in a CPU:
(a) PC
(b) MAR
(c) MBR
(d) IR

7.7 What is the CCR?

7.8 Does a computer need data registers?

7.9 Some microprocessors have one general-purpose data register, some two, some eight, and so on. What do you think determines the number of such general-purpose data registers in any given computer?

7.10 What is the significance of the *fetch–execute cycle*?

7.11 What is the so-called von Neumann bottleneck?

7.12 Design a computer (at the register and bus level) to implement a zero address instruction set architecture.

7.13 In the context of CPU design, what is a *random logic control unit*? What is the meaning of the word *random* in this expression?

7.14 What is a microprogrammed control unit?

7.15 Microprogramming has now fallen into disfavor. Why do you think this is so?

7.16 For the computer structure of Fig. 7.20, state the sequence of micro-operations necessary to carry out the following instruction. Assume that the current instruction is in the IR.

```
ADDsquare D0, D1
```

This instruction reads the contents of register D0, squares that value, and then adds it to the contents of register D1. The result

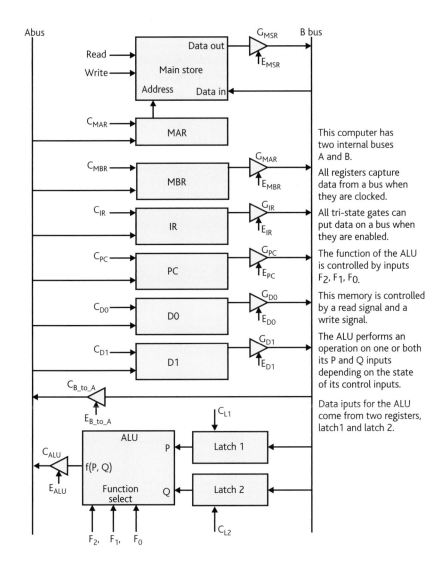

Abus

Read

Write

Main store

Address   Data out G_{MSR} B bus

E_{MSR}

Data in

C_{MAR} MAR

C_{MBR} MBR G_{MAR}

E_{MBR}

C_{IR} IR G_{IR}

E_{IR}

C_{PC} PC G_{PC}

E_{PC}

C_{D0} D0 G_{D0}

E_{D0}

C_{D1} D1 G_{D1}

E_{D1}

$C_{B\_to\_A}$

$E_{B\_to\_A}$

C_{L1}

ALU

C_{ALU} P   Latch 1

f(P, Q)

E_{ALU} Function
select   Q   Latch 2

F_2, F_1, F_0 C_{L2}

This computer has
two internal buses
A and B.

All registers capture
data from a bus when
they are clocked.

All tri-state gates can
put data on a bus when
they are enabled.

The function of the ALU
is controlled by inputs
F_2, F_1, F_0.

This memory is controlled
by a read signal and a
write signal.

The ALU performs an
operation on one or both
its P and Q inputs
depending on the state
of its control inputs.

Data iputs for the ALU
come from two registers,
latch1 and latch 2.

Figure 7.20 A microprogrammed CPU.

is put in register D1. The function codes F_2, F_1, and F_0 are given below.

F_2	F_1	F_0	Operation	
0	0	0	Copy P to F	F = P
0	0	1	Add P to Q	F = P + Q
0	1	0	Subtract Q from P	F = P − Q
0	1	1	Add 1 to P	F = P + 1
1	0	0	Add 1 to Q	F = Q + 1
1	0	1	Multiply P by Q	F = Q x 1

7.17 For the structure of Fig. 7.20 write a microprogram to implement the operation

D1 = [A] + [B] + [C] + 1

Assume that only one operand, A, is required by the instruction and that operands B and C are in the next consecutive two memory locations, respectively.

7.18 For the architecture of the hypothetical two-bus computer of Fig. 7.20, derive a microprogram to carry out the operation

MOVE D0, [D1]

This operation copies the contents of register D0 into the memory location whose address is given by the contents of register D1.

You should describe the actions that occur in plain English (e.g. 'Put data from this register on the B bus') and as a sequence of events (e.g. Read = 1, E_{MSR}). The table in Question 16 defines the effect of the ALU's function code. All data has to pass through the ALU to get from bus B to bus A.

Note that the ALU has two input latches. Data has to be loaded into these latches before an ALU operation takes place.

7.19 For the computer of Fig. 7.20, what is the effect of the following sequence of micro-operations?

E_{D0}	= 1,			C_{L1}
E_{D0}	= 1,			C_{L2}
F_2, F_1, F_0	= 0, 0, 1,		E_{ALU},	C_{MBR}
E_{MBR}	= 1,			C_{L1}
E_{D0}	= 1,			C_{L2}
F_2, F_1, F_0	= 0, 0, 1,		E_{ALU},	C_{D1}

Your answer should explain what each of the micro-operations does individually. You should also state what these actions achieve collectively; that is, what is the effect of the equivalent assembly language operation?

Accelerating performance

INTRODUCTION

We want faster computers. In this chapter we examine three very different ways in which we can take the conventional von Neumann machine described in the last chapter and increase its performance with little or no change in the underlying architecture or its implementation.[1]

The development of the computer comprises three threads: computer architecture, computer organization, and peripheral technology. Advances in each of these threads have contributed to increasing the processing power of computers over the years. The least progress has been made in computer architecture and the programming model of a modern microprocessor would probably not seem too strange to someone who worked with computers in the 1950s. They, would, however, be astonished by developments in internal organization such as pipelining and instruction-level parallelism. Similarly, someone from the 1940s would be utterly amazed by the development of peripherals such as disk and optical storage. In 1940 people were struggling to store hundreds or thousands of bits, whereas some home computers now have storage capacities of about 2^{41} bits.

We look at the way in which three particular techniques have been applied to computer design to improve throughput. We begin with *pipelining*, a technique that increases performance by overlapping the execution of instructions. Pipelining is the electronic equivalent of Henry Ford's production line where multiple units work on a stream of instructions as they flow through a processor. We then look at the way in which the apparent speed of memory has been improved by *cache memory*, which keeps a copy of frequently used data in a small, fast memory. Finally, we provide a short introduction to *multiprocessing* where a problem can be subdivided into several parts and run on an array of computers.

Before discussing how we speed up computers, we need to introduce the notion of *computer performance*. We need to be able to measure how fast a computer is if we are to quantify the effect of enhancements.

---

[1] Although we introduce some of the factors that have made computers so much faster, we can't cover the advances in semiconductor physics and manufacturing technology that have increased the speed of processors, improved the density of electronic devices, and reduced the power consumption per transistor. These topics belong to the realm of electronic engineering.

8.1 **Measuring performance**

How do we measure performance? The answer is quite simple—'With difficulty'. A computer's performance is a measure of its throughput[2] or the time to execute a program. However, because performance depends on the computer's operating system, disk drives, memory, cache memory, bus structure, architecture, internal processor organization, and clock rate, it is very difficult to compare two computer systems. When you do compare systems, just what are you actually comparing?

There are many ways of measuring a computer's performance. A technique widely used in the computer industry is the *benchmark*. A benchmark is a *figure-of-merit*, which is usually the time taken to execute a set of programs. These benchmark programs are chosen to mimic the type of work that will be performed by the computer. A common benchmark is called SPEC and was devised by a vender-independent organization that serves the computer industry. A computer's SPEC benchmark is calculated by running a series of different tasks (i.e. programs) on the computer under test and then dividing the time each task takes by the time the same program takes on a *reference machine*. These figures constitute a set of *normalized* execution times. The geometric mean[3] of the individual normalized times is then taken to provide a single benchmark for the computer: its *SPEC-mark*. The SPEC benchmark tests the entire system including CPU, cache, memory, buses, and system software. Suppose a machine executes programs A, B, and C in 45, 20, and 60 s, respectively. If, say, the times for these targets on the reference machine are 60, 25, and 50 s, the *normalized* times are 0.75, 0.80, and 1.10, respectively, corresponding to a benchmark of 0.87.

Although the speed of a machine is dependent on all its components including the hardware, we are first going to look at the CPU and neglect the contribution to performance made by memory, I/O, and software. Considering only the CPU, we can say that the time taken to execute a program is given by the expression

$$T_{\text{execute}} = N_{\text{inst}} \times 1/W_{\text{inst}} \times \text{CPI} \times T_{\text{cyc}}$$

T_{execute} is the time taken to execute a program, N_{inst}, is the number of instructions in the program, W_{inst} is the work carried out per instruction, CPI is the average number of *clock cycles per instruction*, and T_{cyc} is the clock period. Each of these terms plays a role in the equation and each of them is determined by a different factor in the computer design process.

N_{inst} tells us how many instructions we need to implement the program. The size of a program is dependent on both the architecture of the processor and the algorithm used to solve the problem. This term is also dependent on the efficiency of the compiler because some compilers generate more compact code than others. The N_{inst} term is determined by the programmer and compiler writer.

The W_{inst} term[4] tells us how much computation an instruction performs and is a function of the CPU's architecture. A simple architecture has a low value of W_{inst}, because many instructions are required to perform a certain action. A complex architecture has a high value of W_{inst} because individual instructions perform quite sophisticated operations. Consider the 68020's BFFFO (*bit field find first one*) instruction, which scans an arbitrary sequence of 1 to 32 bits and returns the location of the first bit in the string that is set to 1; for example, the instruction BFFFO (A0){63:23}, **D0** scans the string of 23 bits pointed at by address register A0. This 23-bit-wide string starts at 63 bits from the most-significant bit of the byte pointed at by A0. The position of the first bit in this string set to 1 (plus the string offset 63) is loaded into register D0. Without this instruction you'd need a handful of primitive machine-level instructions to implement it. The value of a processor's W_{inst} term is determined by the computer architect.

The CPI (cycles per instruction) term depends on the internal organization of the computer and expresses how many clock cycles are needed to execute an instruction. First- and second-generation processors had large CPI values. Modern RISC processors are much better with CPIs approaching the ideal value, 1. Some processors, called *superscalars*, have multiple processing units and execute instructions in parallel; these have CPIs less than unity. This term is determined by the chip designer.

All digital operations take an integer number of clock cycles. The T_{cyc} term expresses the processor's clock speed, which is determined both by device physics and the internal organization of the chip.

We derived the expression $T_{\text{execute}} = N_{\text{inst}} \times 1/W_{\text{inst}} \times \text{CPI} \times T_{\text{cyc}}$ to demonstrate that the speed of a CPU is determined by the combined efforts of the programmer, compiler writer, computer architect, chip designer, and semiconductor physicist. It is important to appreciate that a processor's clock speed cannot be used to compare it with a different microprocessor; for example, you cannot directly compare an AMD processor with an Intel processor on the basis of clock speed alone because the internal organizations of these two processor families are radically different.

8.1.1 **Comparing computers**

Before we describe ways of speeding up computers, we need to explain why we have to be able to compare the speeds of

---

[2] The term 'throughput' implies the number of programs that can be executed in a given time.

[3] The geometric mean of *n* numbers is the *n*-th root of their product.

[4] This is a made-up term. It would be very difficult to create a parameter that defines the work done by an instruction. I've included it here to demonstrate that some instructions are more powerful than others.

different computers. Broadly speaking, there are three types of computer user. The first is the home or small business user; the second is the large corporate user such as the bank, hospital, government agency, or university; the third is the specialist such as the aircraft designer, weather forecaster, or nuclear physicist. Members of each of these groups have to select the computers they use; a process that requires an understanding of *performance*.

The domestic or small business user falls into one of two classes: the casual user and the sophisticated user. The casual user is someone who knows little of computing and who is very much at the mercy of advertising and personal advice. Casual users lack the training to understand computer literature and may well select a computer on spurious advertising claims. Fortunately, the increasing performance of computers means that almost anything they buy will be satisfactory for most purposes. The sophisticated user will look at reviews published in popular computing magazines and read the detailed specifications of any computer they are thinking of buying. Reviews in the popular computing press may use suites of programs such as computer games, the type of programs that many users will run.

The corporate buyer of computers is in a different situation. They may be buying thousands of computers for an organization where it's possible to set down criteria by which the competing computers can be judged. For example, suppose two computers are contenders for a large contract but computer A uses an AMD processor and computer B uses an Intel processor. These processors have, essentially, the same architectures but radically different internal organizations. How do you decide which to buy if, say, professor A costs $50 more that processor B and A's manufacture claims it has a better performance?

The situation with high-end personal computers and workstations is more complex. Here, the machine is being used to perform massive amounts of computing and it is very important to specify the best machine. Performance becomes a critical issue.

We begin our discussion of accelerating computer performance with the notion of *pipelining*. Before we do that, we need to say a little about the RISC revolution, which spearheaded the drive toward performance.

8.2 **The RISC revolution**

Microprocessor manufacturers looked anew at processor architectures in the 1980s and started designing simpler, faster machines. Some designers turned their backs on the conventional *complex instruction set computer* (CISC) and started producing *reduced instruction set computers* (RISCs). By the mid-1990s some of these RISC processors were considerably more complex than the CISCs they replaced. This isn't a paradox. The RISC processor is not really a cut-down computer architecture—it represents a new approach to architecture design. In fact, the distinction between CISC and RISC is now so blurred that all modern processors incorporate RISC features even if they are officially CISCs.

From the introduction of the microprocessor in the mid-1970s to the mid 1980s there was an almost unbroken trend towards more and more complex architectures. Some microprocessor architectures developed like a snowball rolling downhill; each advance in the chip fabrication process allowed designers to add more to the microprocessor's central core. Intel's 8086 family illustrates this trend particularly well, because Intel took their original 16-bit processor and added more features in each successive generation. This approach to chip design leads to cumbersome architectures and inefficient instruction sets, but it has the tremendous commercial advantage that the end users don't have to buy new software when they use the latest reincarnation of a microprocessor. Intel's 8086 appeared in the 1970s and yet the Pentium 4 that powers many of today's PCs is a direct descendent of the 8086.

Although processors were advancing in terms architectural sophistication in the late 1970s, a high price was being paid for this progress in terms of efficiency. Complex instructions required complex decoders and a lot of circuitry to implement. There was no guarantee that these instructions would be used in actual programs. An instruction such as ADD **R1**, R2 is relatively easy to decode and interpret. You simply clock R1 and R2 on to buses to the ALU, select the ALU function for addition, and then clock the output from the ALU into R1. Couldn't be simpler.

Consider the implementation of the 68K instruction MOVE (12,A2,D0),**(A1)**+. Although this instruction copies

---

RISC—REDUCED OR REGULAR?

What does the *R* in *R*ISC stand for? The accepted definition of RISC is *reduced instruction set computer*. First-generation experimental RISC processors were much simpler devices than existing CISC processors like the Intel 8086 family or the Motorola 68K family. These RISCs had very simple instruction set architectures with limited addressing modes and no complex special-purpose instructions.

However, as time passed, RISC instruction sets grew in complexity; by the time the PowerPC was introduced, it had more variations on the branching instruction than some CISCs had instructions. However, RISC processors are still characterized by the regularity of their instruction sets; there are very few variations in the format of instructions.

data from A to B, it is not easy to implement. The source operand is in the memory location given by 12 + [A2] + [D0]. The processor has to extract the constant 12 and the register identifiers A2 and D0 from the op-code. Two registers have to be read and their values added to the literal 12 to get the address used to access memory (i.e. there is a memory access cycle to get the source operand). The value at this location is stored at the destination address pointed at by address register A1. Getting the destination address requires more instruction decoding and the reading of register A1. Finally, the destination operand uses autoincrementing, so the contents of register A1 have to be incremented by 2 and restored to A1. All this requires a large amount of work.

A reaction against the trend toward greater complexity began at IBM with their 801 architecture and continued at Berkeley where David Patterson and Divid Ditzel coined the term RISC to describe a new class of architectures that reversed earlier trends in microcomputer design. RISC architectures redeploy to better effect some of the silicon real estate used to implement complex instructions and elaborate addressing modes in conventional microprocessors of the 68K and 8086 generation.

Those who designed first-generation 8-bit architectures in the 1970s were striving to put a computer on a chip, rather than to design an optimum computing engine. The designers of 16-bit machines added sophisticated addressing modes and new instructions and provided more general-purpose registers. The designers of RISC architectures have taken the design process back to fundamentals by studying what many computers actually do and by starting from a blank sheet (as opposed to modifying an existing chip á la Intel).

Two factors that influenced the architecture of first- and second-generation microprocessors were microprogramming and the complex instruction sets created to help programmers. By complex instructions we mean operations like MOVE 12(A3,D0),**D2** and ADD (A6)+,**D3**.

Microprogramming achieved its highpoint in the 1970s when ferrite core memory had a long access time of 1 μs or more and semiconductor high-speed random access memory was very expensive. Quite naturally, computer designers used the slow main store to hold the complex instructions that made up the machine-level program. These machine-level instructions are interpreted by microcode in the much faster microprogram control store within the CPU. Today, main stores use semiconductor memory with an access time of 40 ns or less and cache memory with access times below

5 ns. Most of the advantages of microprogramming have evaporated. The goal of RISC architectures is to execute an instruction in a single machine cycle. A corollary of this statement is that complex instructions cannot be executed by *pure* RISC architectures. Before we look at RISC architectures themselves, we provide an overview of the research that led to the hunt for better architectures.

8.2.1 Instruction usage

Computer scientists carried out extensive research over a decade or more in the late 1970s into the way in which computers execute programs. Their studies demonstrated that the relative frequency with which different classes of instructions are executed is not uniform and that some types of instruction are executed far more frequently than others. Fairclough divided machine-level instructions into eight groups according to type and compiled the statistics described by Table 8.1. The mean value represents the results averaged over both program types and computer architecture.

The eight instruction groups are

- data movement
- program modification (i.e. branch, call, return)
- arithmetic
- compare
- logical
- shift
- bit manipulation
- input/output and miscellaneous.

This data demonstrates that the most common instruction type is the data movement primitive of the form P = Q in a high-level language or MOVE Q,**P** in a low-level language. The *program modification group* which includes conditional and unconditional branches together with subroutine calls and returns, is the second most common group of instructions. The data movement and program modification groups account for 74% of all instructions. A large program may contain only 26% of instructions that are not data movement or program modification primitives. These results apply to measurements taken in the 1970s and those measurements were the driving force behind computer architecture development; more modern results demonstrate similar trends as Table 8.2 shows.

Instruction group	1	2	3	4	5	6	7	8
Mean value	**45.28**	**28.73**	10.75	5.92	3.91	2.93	2.05	0.44

Table 8.1 Frequency of instruction usage (very old data).

Benchmark	Branch	Integer	Load	Store
008.espresso	22.9%	46.8%	21.1%	5.3%
022.li	20.7%	34.2%	25.6%	15.5%
023.eqntott	27.9%	42.8%	27.0%	0.9%
026.compress	19.5%	53.8%	17.6%	9.0%
072.sc	23.5%	40.1%	20.1%	10.7%
085.gcc	21.1%	42.0%	21.7%	11.1%
average	22.1%	39.7%	23.8%	10.7%

Note: The PowerPC is a RISC machine with a load/store architecture. All data processing operations act on internal registers. The only memory accesses are via loads and stores.

Table 8.2 Instruction usage figures for the PowerPC processor.[5]

An inescapable inference from such results is that processor designers might be better employed devoting their time to optimizing the way in which machines handle instructions in groups one and two, than in seeking new *powerful* instructions that are seldom used. In the early days of the microprocessor, chip manufacturers went out of their way to provide special instructions that were unique to their products. These instructions were then heavily promoted by the company's sales force. Today, we can see that their efforts should have been directed towards the goal of optimizing the most frequently used instructions. RISC architectures have been designed to exploit the programming environment in which most instructions are data movement or program control instructions.

Constants, parameters, and local storage

Another aspect of computer architecture that was investigated was the optimum size of literal operands (i.e. constants). Tanenbaum reported the remarkable result that 56% of all constant values lie in the range -15 to $+15$ and that 98% of all constant values lie in the range -511 to $+511$. Consequently, the inclusion of a 5-bit constant field in an instruction would cover over half the occurrences of a literal. RISC architectures have sufficiently long instruction lengths to include a literal field as part of the instruction that caters for the majority of literals.

Programs use subroutines heavily and an effective architecture should optimize the way in which subroutines are called, parameters are passed to and from subroutines, and workspace provided for local variables created by subroutines. Research showed that in 95% of cases 12 words of storage are sufficient for parameter passing and local storage; that is, an architecture with 12 words of on-chip register storage should be able to handle all the operands required by most subroutines without accessing main store. Such an arrangement

reduces the processor-memory bus traffic associated with subroutine calls.

8.2.2 Characteristics of RISC architectures

We begin by summarizing the characteristics of a classic RISC architecture of the 1980s. These characteristics don't define the RISC architecture; they are general attributes of processors that were called RISC.

1. RISC processors have sufficient on-chip memory in the form of registers to overcome the worst effects of the processor–memory bottleneck. On-chip memory can be accessed more rapidly than off-chip main store.

2. RISC processors have *three-address, register-to-register architectures*. Instructions are of the form OPERATION Ra, Rb, Rc, where Ra, Rb, and Rc are general-purpose registers.

3. Because subroutine calls are so frequently executed, RISC architectures facilitate the passing of parameters between subroutines.

4. Instructions that modify the flow of control (e.g. branch instructions) are implemented efficiently because they comprise about 20 to 30% of a typical program.

5. RISC processors don't attempt to implement infrequently used instructions. Complex instructions waste space on a chip. Moreover, the inclusion of complex instructions increases the time taken to design, fabricate, and test a processor.

6. RISC processors aim to execute on average one instruction per clock cycle. This goal imposes a limit on the maximum complexity of instructions.

7. A corollary of point 6 is that an efficient architecture should not be microprogrammed, as microprogramming interprets an instruction by executing microinstructions. In the limit, a RISC processor is close to a microprogrammed architecture in which the distinction between machine cycle and microcycle has vanished.

8. An efficient processor should have a single instruction format. A typical CISC processor has variable-length instructions (e.g. from 2 to 10 bytes). By providing a single instruction format, the decoding of an instruction into its component fields can be performed by a minimum level of decoding logic. A RISC's instruction length should be sufficient to accommodate the operation code field and one or more operand fields. Consequently, a RISC processor may not utilize memory space as efficiently as a conventional CISC microprocessor.

---

[5] From IBM's *Power PC compiler writer's guide Appendix C.*

We now look at two of the fundamental aspects of the RISC architecture—its register set and pipelining. Multiple overlapping register windows have been implemented to reduce the need to transfer parameters between subroutines. Pipelining is a mechanism that permits the overlapping of instruction execution (i.e. internal operations are carried out in parallel). Note that many of the features of RISC processors are not new. They have been employed long before the advent of the microprocessor. The RISC revolution happened when all these performance-enhancing techniques were brought together and applied to microprocessor design.

The Berkeley RISC, SPARC, and MIPS

Although the CISC processors came from the large semiconductor manufacturers, one of the first RISC processors came from the University of California at Berkeley.[6] The Berkeley RISC was not a commercial machine, but it had a tremendous impact on the development of other RISC architectures. Figure 8.1 describes the format of a Berkeley RISC instruction. Each of the 5-bit operand fields permits one of 32 internal registers to be accessed.

The Scc field determines whether the condition code bits are updated after the execution of an instruction; if Scc = 1, the condition code bits are updated after an instruction. The source 2 field uses an IM (immediate mode) bit to select one of two functions. When IM = 0, bits 5 to 12 are zeros and bits 0 to 4 provide the second source operand register. When IM = 1, the second source operand is a literal and bits 0 to 12 provide a 13-bit constant (i.e. immediate value).

Because five bits are allocated to each operand field, it follows that this RISC has $2^5 = 32$ internal registers. This last statement is emphatically not true, because the Berkeley RISC has 138 user-accessible general-purpose internal registers. The reason for the discrepancy between the number of registers directly addressable and the actual number of registers is due to a mechanism called *windowing*, which gives the programmer a view of only a subset of all registers at any instant.

The Berkeley RISC and several other RISC processors hardware register R0 to zero. Although this *loses* a register because you can't change the contents of R0, it *gains* a constant. By specifying register R0 in an instruction, you force the value zero; for example, ADD R1,R1,R2 implements MOVE R1,R2 .

The experimental Berkeley led to the development of the commercial SPARC processor (Scalable Processor ARChitecture) by Sun Microsystems. SPARC is an open architecture and is also manufactured by Fujitsu. Similarly, a RISC project at Stanford led to the design of another classic RISC machine, the MIPS. Figure 8.2 illustrates the format of the MIPS instruction, which has three basic formats, a register-to-register format for all data processing instructions, an immediate format for either data processing instructions with a literal or load/store instructions with an offset, and a branch/jump instruction with a 26-bit literal that is concatenated with the six most-significant bits of the program counter to create a 32-bit address.

Register windows

An important feature of the Berkeley RISC architecture is the way in which it allocates new registers to subroutines; that is, when you call a subroutine, you get some new registers. Suppose you could create 12 registers out of thin air each time you call a subroutine. Each subroutine would have its own workspace for temporary variables, thereby avoiding relatively slow accesses to main store. Although only 12 or so registers are required by each invocation of a subroutine, the successive nesting of subroutines rapidly increases the total number of on-chip registers assigned to subroutines. You might think that any attempt to dedicate a set of registers to each new procedure is impractical, because the repeated calling of nested subroutines will require an unlimited amount of storage.

Although subroutines can be nested to any depth, research has demonstrated that on average subroutines are not nested to any great depth over short periods. Consequently, it is

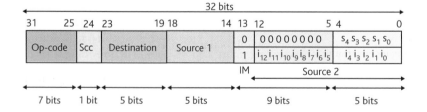

Figure 8.1 Format of the Berkeley RISC instruction.

....

[6] It would be unfair to imply that RISC technology came entirely from academia. As early at 1974 John Cocke was working on RISC-like architectures at IBM's Thomas J. Watson Research Center. The project was called '801' after then number of the building in which the researchers worked. Cocke's work led to IBM's RISC System/6000 and the PowerPC.

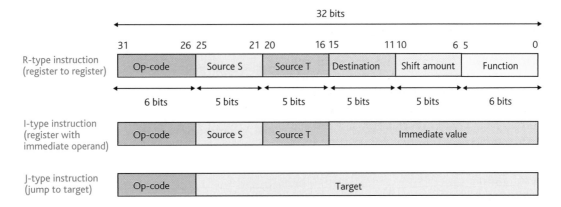

Figure 8.2 Format of the MIPS instruction.

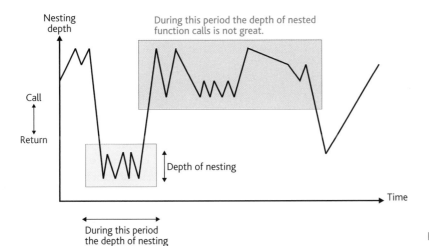

Figure 8.3 Depth of subroutine nesting as a function of time.

feasible to adopt a modest number of local register sets for a sequence of nested subroutines.

Figure 8.3 provides a graphical representation of the execution of a program in terms of the depth of nesting of subroutines as a function of time. The trace goes up each time a subroutine is called and down each time a return is made. Even though subroutines may be nested to considerable depths, there are long runs of subroutine call that do not require a nesting level of greater than about five.

An ingenious mechanism for implementing local variable work space for subroutines was adopted by the Berkeley RISC. Up to eight nested subroutines could be handled using on-chip work space for each subroutine. Any further nesting forces the CPU to dump registers to main memory. Before we demonstrate the Berkeley RISC's windowing mechanism, we describe how the memory used by subroutines can be divided into four types.

Global space is directly accessible by all subroutines that hold constants and data that may be required from any point within the program. Most conventional microprocessors have only global registers.

Local space is private to the subroutine. That is, no other subroutine can access the current subroutine's local address space from outside the subroutine. Local space is employed as temporary working space by the current subroutine.

Imported parameter space holds the parameters imported by the current subroutine from its parent. In RISC terminology these are called the high registers.

Exported parameter space holds the parameters exported by the current subroutine to its child. In RISC terminology these are called the low registers.

Consider the following fragment of C code. Don't worry if you aren't a C programmer—the fine details don't matter. What we are going to do is to demonstrate the way in which memory is allocated to parameters. The main program creates three variables x, y, and z. Copies of x and y are passed to the function (i.e. subroutine) calc. The result is returned to the main program and assigned to z. Figure 8.4 illustrates a possible memory structure for the program.

Parameters x, y, and z are local to function main, and copies of x and y are sent to function calc as imported parameters. We will assume that copies of these parameters are placed on the stack before calc is called. The value returned by function calc is an exported parameter, and sum and diff are local variables in calc.

```
void main (void)
   {
      int x = 204, y = 25, z;
      z = calc (x, y)            /* let's calculate (x + y)/(x - y)  */
   }


int calc (int a, int b)         /* this function calculates (a + b)/(a - b) */
   {
      int sum, diff;
      sum  = a + b;             /* calculate a + b */
      diff = a - b;             /* calculate a - b */
      return (sum/diff)
   }
```

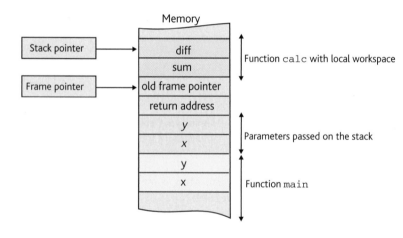

Figure 8.4 Parameter space.

Register name	Register type
R0 to R9	The global register set is always accessible
R10 to R15	Six registers used by the subroutine to receive parameters from its parent and to pass results back to its parent
R16 to R25	10 local registers accessed only by the current subroutine that cannot be accessed directly by any other subroutine
R26 to R31	Six registers used by the subroutine to pass parameters to and from its own child (i.e., a subroutine called by itself).

Table 8.3 Berkeley RISC register types.

Windows and parameter passing

One reason for the high frequency of data movement operations is the need to pass parameters to subroutines and to receive them from subroutines. The Berkeley RISC architecture improves parameter passing by means of *multiple overlapped windows*. A window is the set of registers visible to the current subroutine. Figure 8.5 illustrates the structure of the RISC's overlapping windows.

Suppose that the processor is currently using the ith window set. A special-purpose register, called the *window pointer* (WP), indicates the current active window. In this case the WP contains the value i. Each window is divided into four parts as described by Table 8.3.

All windows consist of 32 addressable registers, R0 to R31. A Berkeley RISC instruction of the form ADD R3,R12,R25 implements [R25] ← [R3] + [R12], where R3 is within the window's global address space, R12 is within its import from (or export to) parent subroutine space, and R25 is within its local address space. RISC arithmetic and logical instructions always involve 32-bit values (there are no 8-bit or 16-bit operations).

Whenever a subroutine is invoked by an instruction of the form CALLR Rd,address, the contents of the window pointer are incremented by 1 and the current value of the program counter saved in register Rd of the new window. The Berkeley RISC does not employ a conventional stack in external main memory to save subroutine return addresses.

Once a new window has been invoked (in Fig. 8.3 this is window i), the new subroutine sees a different set of registers to the previous window. Global registers R0 to R9 are an exception since they are common to all windows. Window R10 of the child subroutine corresponds to (i.e. is the same as) window R26 of the calling (i.e. parent) subroutine. The

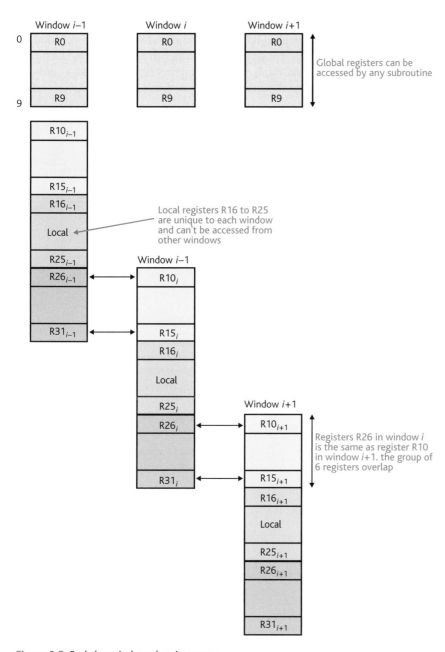

Figure 8.5 Berkeley windowed register sets.

total number of registers required to implement the Berkeley windowed register set are

10 global + 8 × 10 local
+ 8 × 6 parameter transfer registers = 138 registers

Although windowed register sets are a good idea, there are flaws and only one commercial processor implements windowing, the SPARC. The major problem with windows is that the number of registers is finite. If there are more nested calls than register sets, then old register sets have to be moved from windowed registers to main store and later restored. When all windowed registers are in use, a subroutine call results in register overflow and the system software has to intervene. Register sets also increase the size of a task's environment. If the operating system has to switch tasks or deal with an exception, it may be necessary to save a lot of program context to main store.

The Berkeley RISC instruction set

Although the Berkeley RISC is not a commercial computer, we briefly look at its instruction set because it provides a template for later RISC-like processors such as the MIPS, the SPARC, and the ARM. The instruction set is given below. The effect of most instructions is self-explanatory. As you can see, instructions have a three-operand instruction format and the only memory operations are load and store. In the absence of byte, word, and longword operations, this RISC includes several memory reference operations designed to access

Register to register operations

AND	Rs,S2,**Rd**	logical
OR	Rs,S2,**Rd**	logical
XOR	Rs,S2,**Rd**	exclusive
ADD	Rs,S2,**Rd**	add
ADDC	Rs,S2,**Rd**	add with carry
SUB	Rs,S2,**Rd**	subtract $Rd = Rs - S2$
SUBC	Rs,S2,**Rd**	subtract with borrow $Rd = S2 - Rs$
SUBI	Rs,S2,**Rd**	subtract reverse
SUBCI	Rs,S2,**Rd**	subtract reverse with borrow
SLL	Rs,S2,**Rd**	shift left logical
SRA	Rs,S2,**Rd**	shift right arithmetic
SRL	Rs,S2,**Rd**	shift right logical

> This is a very simple instruction processing set of operations covering logical, arithmetic, and shift operations.

Load instructions

LDXW	(Rx)S2,**Rd**	load long
LDXHU	(Rx)S2,**Rd**	load short unsigned
LDXHS	(Rx)S2,**Rd**	load short signed
LDXBU	(Rx)S2,**Rd**	load byte unsigned
LDXBS	(Rx)S2,**Rd**	load byte signed
LDRW	Y,**Rd**	load relative long
LDRHU	Y,**Rd**	load relative short unsigned
LDRHS	Y,**Rd**	load relative short signed
LDRBU	Y,**Rd**	load relative byte unsigned
LDRBS	Y,**Rd**	load relative byte signed

> Load instructions use address relative addressing. There are 32-bit, 16-bit, and 8-bit versions.

Store instructions

STXW	**Rm**,(Rx)S2	store long
STXH	**Rm**,(Rx)S2	store short
STXB	**Rm**,(Rx)S2	store byte
STRW	**Rm**,Y	store relative long
STRH	**Rm**,Y	store relative short
STRB	**Rm**,Y	store relative byte

> Store instructions use address register indirect addressing and are available for 8-, 16-, and 32-bit stores.

Control transfer instructions

JMPX	COND,(Rx)S2	conditional jump
JMPR	COND,Y	conditional relative jump
CALLX	Rd,(Rx)S2	call and change window
CALLR	Rd,Y	call relative and change window
RET	COND,(Rx)S2	return and change window
CALLI	Rd	call an interrupt
RETI	COND,(Rx)S2	return from interrupt

> These are the subroutine call and return instructions. Note that program counter relative adddressing is supported.

Miscellaneous instructions

LDHI	Rd,Y	load immediate high
GETLPC	Rd	load PC into register
GETPSW	Rd	load PSW into register
PUTPSW	Rm	put contents of register Rm in PSW

> These perform special register accesses to the PC and processor status register.

8-, 16-, and 32-bit values (bytes, half words, and words, respectively).

Load and store instructions use *register indirect addressing* with a constant and a pointer; for example, LDXW (Rx)S2,**Rd** loads destination register Rd with the 32-bit value at the address pointed at by register Rx plus offset S2. The value of the second source operand S2 is either a register or a literal. Because register R0 is always zero, we can write LDXW (R0)S2,**R3** to generate LDXW S2,**R3**.

8.3 RISC architecture and pipelining

Historically, the two key attributes of RISC architectures are their uniform instruction sets and the use of *pipelining* to increase throughput by *overlapping* instruction execution. We now look at *pipelining*.

Figure 8.6 illustrates the machine cycle of a hypothetical microprocessor executing an ADD R1,R2,R3 instruction. Imagine that this instruction is executed in the following five phases.

Instruction fetch Read the instruction from the system memory and increment the program counter.

Instruction decode Decode the instruction read from memory during the previous phase. The nature of the instruction decode phase is dependent on the complexity of the instruction encoding. A regularly encoded instruction might be decoded in a few nanoseconds with two levels of gating whereas a complex instruction format might require ROM-based look-up tables to implement the decoding.

Operand fetch The operand specified by the instruction is read from the system memory or an on-chip register and loaded into the CPU. In this example, we have two operands.

Execute The operation specified by the instruction is carried out.

Operand store The result obtained during the execution phase is written into the operand destination. This may be an on-chip register or a location in external memory.

Each of these five phases may take a specific time (although the time taken is an integer multiple of the system's master clock period). Some instructions may require phases; for example, the CMP R1,R2 instruction, which compares R1 and R2 by subtracting R1 from R2, does not need an operand store phase.

The inefficiency in the arrangement of Fig. 8.6 is clear. Consider the execution phase of an instruction. This takes one-fifth of an instruction cycle leaving the instruction execution unit idle for the remaining 80% of the time. The same applies to the other functional units of the processor that also lie idle for 80% of the time. A technique called *pipelining* can be employed to increase the effective speed of the processor by overlapping the various stages in the execution of an instruction. For example, when a pipelined processor is executing one instruction, it is fetching the next instruction.

The way in which a RISC processor implements pipelining is described in Fig. 8.7. Consider the execution of two instructions. At time i instruction 1 begins execution with its instruction fetch phase. At time $i+1$ instruction 1 enters its instruction decode phase and instruction 2 begins its instruction fetch phase. This arrangement makes sense because it ensures that the functional units in a computer are used more efficiently.

Figure 8.8 illustrates the execution of five instructions in a pipelined system. We use a four-stage pipeline for the rest of this section because RISC processors don't need an *instruction decode* phase because their encoding is so simple. As you can see, the total execution time is eight cycles. After instruction 4 has entered the pipeline, the pipeline is said to be full and all stages are active.

Pipelining considerably speeds up a processor. Suppose an unpipelined processor has four stages and each operation takes 10 ns. It takes 4×10 ns $= 40$ ns to execute an instruction. If pipelining is used and a new instruction enters the pipeline every 10 ns, a completed instruction leaves the pipeline every 10 ns. That's a speed up of 400% without improving the underlying semiconductor technology.

Consider the execution of n instructions in a processor with an m-stage pipeline. It will take m clock cycles for the first instruction to be competed. This leaves $n - 1$ instructions to be executed at a rate of one instruction per cycle. The total time to execute the n instructions is, therefore, $m + (n - 1)$ cycles.

If we do not use pipelining, it takes $n \cdot m$ cycles to execute n instructions, assuming that each instruction is

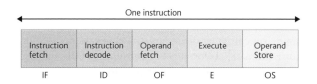

Instruction fetch	Instruction decode	Operand fetch	Execute	Operand Store
IF	ID	OF	E	OS

One instruction

IF   ADD R1,R2,R3   Read this instruction from memory
ID   ADD R1,R2,R3   Decode this instruction into "ADD" and registers 1, 2, 3
OF   ADD R1,**R2,R3**   Read operands R2 and R3 from the register file
E   **ADD** R1,R2,R3   Add the two operands together
OS   ADD **R1**,R2,R3   Store the result in R1

Figure 8.6 Instruction execution.

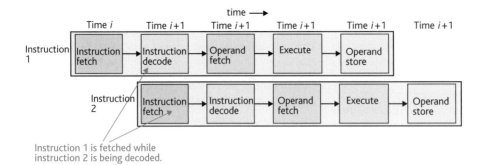

Figure 8.7 Pipelining and instruction overlap.

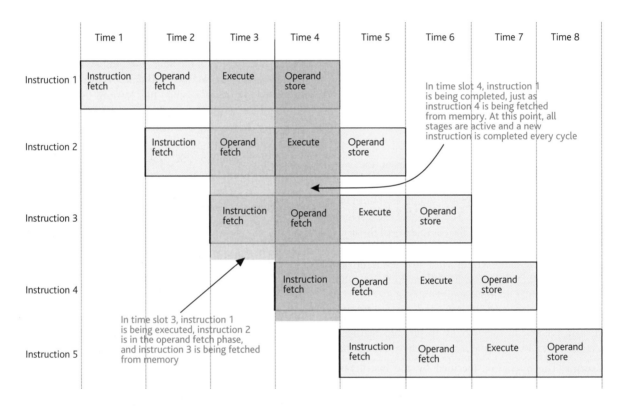

Figure 8.8 Pipelining and instruction overlap.

executed in m phases. The speedup due to pipelining is, therefore,

$$S = \frac{n \cdot m}{m + (n - 1)}$$

Let's put some numbers into this equation and see what happens when we vary the values of n (the code size) and m (the number of stages in the pipeline). Table 8.4 gives the results for $m = 3$, 6, and 12 with instruction blocks ranging from 4 to 1000 instructions.

Table 8.4 demonstrates that pipelining produces a speedup that is the same as the number of stages when the number of instructions in a block is large. Small blocks of instructions

running on computers with large pipelines do not demonstrate a dramatic performance improvement; for example, a 12-stage pipeline with four-instruction blocks has a speedup ratio of 3.2 rather than 12. We will return to the implications of this table when we've introduced the notion of the pipeline *hazard*.

8.3.1 Pipeline hazards

Table 8.4 demonstrates that pipelining can provide a substantial performance acceleration as long at the block of instructions being executed is much longer than the number of

Block size	Three-stage pipeline	Six-stage pipeline	12-stage pipeline
4	2.0000	2.6667	3.2000
8	2.4000	3.6923	5.0526
20	2.7272	4.8000	7.7419
100	2.9411	5.7143	10.810
1000	2.9940	5.9701	11.8694
∞	3.0000	6.0000	12.0000

Table 8.4 Pipelining efficiency as a function of pipeline length and block size.

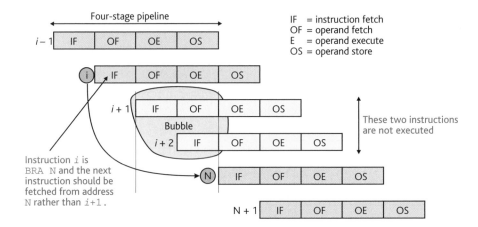

Figure 8.9 The pipeline bubble.

stages in the pipeline. Unfortunately, machine code is divided into blocks with breaks between blocks that have come to be known as *hazards* (hazards possibly a misnomer) or pipeline stalls. We are interested in two types of hazard, the *bubble* created by branch instructions and the *data dependency* caused by certain combinations of instructions.

A pipeline is an ordered structure that thrives on *regularity*. At any stage in the execution of a program, a pipeline contains components of two or more instructions at varying stages in their execution. Consider Fig. 8.9 in which a sequence of instructions is being executed in a pipelined processor. The second instruction, *i*, enters the pipeline and begins execution. Let's assume that this is a simple unconditional branch instruction, BRA N. The branch instruction enters the pipeline during its fetch phase. In the next clock cycle, any operands required by the branch instruction are fetched and the next instruction in sequence is dragged into the pipeline. In the next phase the branch instruction is executed and another instruction brought into the pipeline. However, when the branch instruction is executed, the program counter is reloaded with the *branch target address*, in this case N.

Because the program counter is loaded with a new value when the processor encounters a *branch instruction*, any

instructions loaded into the pipeline immediately following the branch are not executed. All the work performed by the pipeline on these instructions must be thrown away, because the instructions are not executed. When data in a pipeline is rejected or the pipeline is held up by the introduction of idle states, we say that a *bubble* has been introduced. Of course, the longer the pipeline the more instructions that must be rejected once the branch is encountered.

Because program control instructions are so frequent, any realistic processor using pipelining must do something to overcome the problem of bubbles caused by this class of instructions. The Berkeley RISC reduces the effect of bubbles by refusing to throw away the instruction immediately following a branch; that is, the instruction immediately after a branch is always executed. Consider the effect of the following sequence of instructions:

```
ADD R1,R2,R3    [R3] ← [R1] + [R2]
JMPXN           [PC] ← [N]          Goto address N
ADD R2,R4,R5    [R5] ← [R2] + [R4] This is executed
ADD R7,R8,R9    Not executed because of branch taken
```

The processor calculates R5 = R2 + R4 *before* executing the branch. This sequence of instructions is most strange to

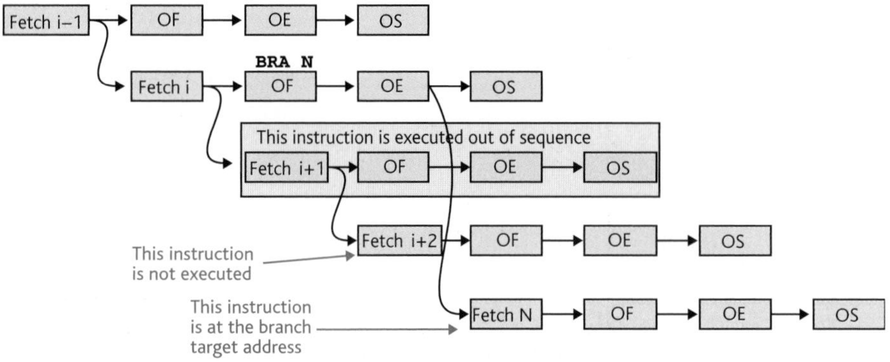

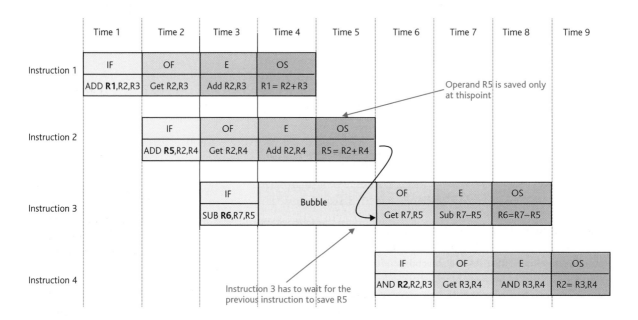

Figure 8.10 Delayed branch.

Figure 8.11 Data dependency.

the eyes of a conventional assembly language programmer, who is not accustomed to seeing an instruction executed after a branch has been taken.

Unfortunately, it's not always possible to arrange a program in such a way as to include a useful instruction immediately after a branch. Whenever this happens, the compiler must introduce a no operation (NOP) instruction after the branch and accept the inevitability of a bubble. This mechanism is called a *delayed jump* or a branch-and-execute technique. Figure 8.10 demonstrates how a RISC processor implements a delayed jump. The branch described in

Figure 8.10 is a computed branch whose target address is calculated during the execute phase of the instruction cycle.

8.3.2 Data dependency

Another problem caused by pipelining is *data dependency* in which an instruction cannot be executed because it requires a result from a previous operation that has not yet left the pipeline. Consider the following sequence of operations.

```
ADD  R1,R2,R3      [R1] ← [R2] + [R3]
ADD  R5,R2,R4      [R5] ← [R2] + [R4]
SUB  R6,R7,R5      [R6] ← [R7] − [R5]    Note: R5 may not have been computed
AND  R2,R3,R4      [R2] ← [R3] . [R4]
```

These instructions are executed sequentially. However, a problem arises when the third instruction, SUB R6, R7, R5,

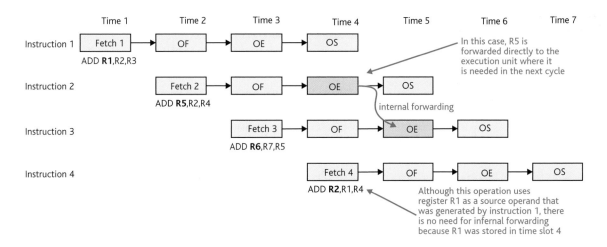

Figure 8.12 Internal forwarding.

is executed on a pipelined machine. This instruction uses R5, which *is calculated by the preceding instruction*, as a source operand. Clearly, the value of R5 will not have been stored by the *previous* instruction by the time it is required by the *current* instruction. Figure 8.11 demonstrates how data dependency occurs.

Figure 8.11 demonstrates that the pipeline is held up or *stalled* after the fetch phase of instruction 3 for two clock cycles. It is not until the end of time slot 5 that operand R5 is ready and execution can continue. Consequently a bubble must be introduced in the pipeline while an instruction waits for its data generated by the previous instruction.

Figure 8.12 demonstrates a technique called *internal forwarding* designed to overcome the effects of data dependency. The example provided corresponds to a three-stage pipeline like the RISC. The following sequence of operations is to be executed.

1.	ADD **R1**,R2,R3	[R1] ← [R2] + [R3]
2.	ADD **R5**,R2,R4	[R5] ← [R2] + [R4]
3.	SUB **R6**,R7,R5	[R6] ← [R7] − [R5]
4.	ADD **R2**,R1,R4	[R2] ← [R1] + [R4]

Instruction 2 generates a destination operand R5 that is required as a source operand by the next instruction. If the processor were to read the source operand requested by instruction 3 directly from the register file, it would see the old value of R5. By means of *internal forwarding* the processor transfers R5 from instruction 2's execution unit directly to the execution unit of instruction 3 (see Fig. 8.12).

In this example, instruction 4 uses an operand generated by an instruction 1 (i.e. the contents of register R1). However, because of the intervening instructions 2 and 3, the destination operand generated by instruction 1 has time to be written into the register file before it is read as a source operand by instruction 4.

8.3.3 Reducing the branch penalty

If we're going to reduce the effect of branches on the performance of RISC processors, we need to determine the effect of branch instructions on the performance of the system. Because we cannot know how many branches a given program will contain, or how likely each branch is to be taken, we have to construct a *probabilistic model* for the system. We will make the following assumptions.

1. Each non-branch instruction is executed in one cycle.
2. The probability that a given instruction is a branch is p_b.
3. The probability that a branch instruction will be taken is p_t.
4. If a branch is taken, the additional penalty is b cycles.
5. If a branch is not taken, there is no penalty.

The average number of cycles executed during the execution of a program is the sum of the cycles taken for non-branch instructions, plus the cycles taken by branch instructions that are taken, plus the cycles taken by branch instructions that are not taken.

If the probability of an instruction being a branch is p_b, the probability that an instruction is not a branch is $1-p_b$ because the two probabilities must add up to 1. Similarly, if p_t is the probability that a branch will be taken, the probability that a branch will not be taken is $1-p_t$.

The total cost (i.e. time) of an instruction is

$$T_{ave} = (1 - p_b)\cdot 1 + p_b\cdot p_t\cdot(1 + b) + p_b\cdot(1 - p_t)\cdot 1$$
$$= 1 + p_b\cdot p_t\cdot b.$$

The expression, $1 + p_b \cdot p_t \cdot b$, tells us that the number of branch instructions, the probability that a branch is taken, and the overhead per branch instruction all contribute to the branch penalty. We are now going to examine some of the ways in which $p_b \cdot p_t \cdot b$ can be reduced.

Branch prediction

If we can predict the outcome of the branch instruction *before* it is executed, we can start filling the pipeline with instructions from the branch target address if the branch is going to be taken. For example, if the instruction is BRA N, the processor can start fetching instructions at locations N, N + 1, N + 2 etc., as soon as the branch instruction is fetched from memory. In this way, the pipeline is always filled with useful instructions.

This prediction mechanism works well with an unconditional branch like BRA N. Unfortunately, *conditional* branches pose a problem. Consider a conditional branch of the form BCC N (branch to N on carry bit clear). Should the RISC processor make the assumption that the branch will not be taken and fetch instructions in sequence, or should it make the assumption that the branch will be taken and fetch instruction at the branch target address N?

Conditional branches are required to implement various types of high-level language construct. Consider the following fragment of high-level language code.

```
IF (J < K) I = I + L;
(FOR T = 1; T <= I; T++)
    {
        .
        .
        .
    }
```

The first conditional operation compares J with K. Only the nature of the problem will tell us whether J is often less than K.

The second conditional in this fragment of code is provided by the FOR construct, which tests a counter at the end of the FOR and then decides whether to jump back to the body of the construct or to terminate the loop. In this case, you could bet that the loop is more likely to be repeated than exited. Some loops are executed thousands of times before they are exited. Therefore, it might be a shrewd move to look at the type of conditional branch and then either fill the pipeline from the branch target if you think that the branch will be taken, or fill the pipeline from the instruction after the branch if you think that it will not be taken.

If we attempt to predict the behavior of a system with two outcomes (branch taken or branch not taken), there are four possibilities.

1. Predict branch taken and branch taken—successful outcome.
2. Predict branch taken and branch not taken—unsuccessful outcome.
3. Predict branch not taken and branch not taken—successful outcome.
4. Predict branch not taken and branch taken—unsuccessful outcome.

Suppose we apply a branch penalty to each of four these possible outcomes. The penalty is the number of cycles taken by that particular outcome, as Table 8.5 demonstrates. For example, if we think that a branch will not be taken and get instructions following the branch and the branch is actually taken (forcing the pipeline to be loaded with instructions at the target address), the branch penalty in Table 8.5 is c cycles.

We now need to calculate the average penalty for a particular system. To do this we need more information about the system. The first thing we need to know is the probability that an instruction will be a branch (as opposed to any other category of instruction). Assume that the probability that an instruction is a branch is p_b. The next thing we need to know is the probability that the branch instruction will be taken, p_t. Finally, we need to know the accuracy of the prediction. Let p_c be the probability that a branch prediction is correct. These values can be obtained by observing the performance of real programs. Figure 8.13 illustrates all the possible outcomes of an instruction. We can immediately write

$(1 - p_b)$ = probability that an instruction is not a branch
$(1 - p_t)$ = probability that a branch will not be taken
$(1 - p_c)$ = probability that a prediction is incorrect

These equations are obtained by using the principle that if one event or another must take place, their probabilities must add up to unity. The average branch penalty per branch instruction, C_{ave}, is therefore

$$C_{ave} = a(p_{branch\_predicted\_taken\_and\_taken})$$
$$+ b(p_{branch\_predicted\_taken\_but\_not\_taken})$$
$$+ c(p_{branch\_predicted\_not\_taken\_but\_taken})$$
$$+ d(p_{branch\_predicted\_not\_taken\_and\_not\_taken})$$

$$C_{ave} = a \cdot (p_t \cdot p_c) + b \cdot (p_t - 1) \cdot (1 - p_c)$$
$$+ c \cdot p_t \cdot (1 - p_c) + d \cdot (1 - p_t) \cdot p_c$$

Prediction	Result	Branch penalty
Branch taken	Branch taken	a
Branch taken	Branch not taken	b
Branch not taken	Branch taken	c
Branch not taken	Branch not taken	d

Table 8.5 The branch penalty.

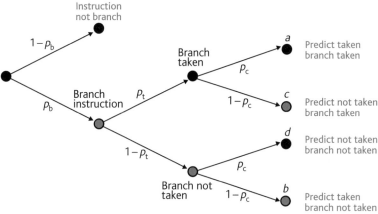

Figure 8.13 Branch prediction.

The average number of cycles taken by a branch instruction is $C_{\text{ave}} \cdot p_b$

$$= p_b \cdot (a \cdot (p_t \cdot p_c) + b \cdot p_t \cdot (1 - p_c)$$
$$+ \; c \cdot (1 - p_t) \cdot (1 - p_c) + d \cdot (1 - p_t) \cdot p_c).$$

We can make two assumptions to help us to simplify the first expression. The first is that $a = d = N$ (i.e. if the prediction is correct the number of cycles is N). The other simplification is that $b = c = B$ (i.e. if the prediction is wrong the number of cycles is B). The average number of cycles per branch instruction is therefore

$$p_b \cdot (N \cdot p_t \cdot p_c + B \cdot p_t \cdot (1 - p_c) + B \cdot (1 - p_t) \cdot (1 - p_c)$$
$$+ \; N \cdot (1 - p_t) \cdot p_c) = p_b \cdot (N \cdot p_c + B \cdot (1 - p_c)).$$

There are several ways of implementing branch prediction (i.e. increasing the value of p_c). Two basic approaches are *static branch prediction* and *dynamic branch prediction*. Static branch prediction makes the assumption that branches are always taken or never taken. Because observations of real code have demonstrated that branches have a greater than 50% chance of being taken, the best static branch prediction mechanism would be to fetch the next instruction from the branch target address as soon as the branch instruction is detected.

A better method of predicting the outcome of a branch is by observing its op-code, because some branch instructions are taken more or less frequently than other branch instructions. Using the branch op-code to predict that the branch will or will not be taken results in a 75% accuracy. An extension of this technique is to devote a bit of the op-code to the static prediction of branches. This bit is set or cleared by the compiler depending on whether the compiler estimates that the branch is most likely to be taken. This technique provides branch prediction accuracy in the range 74 to 94%.

Dynamic branch prediction techniques operate at run-time and use the past behavior of the program to predict its future behavior. Suppose the processor maintains a table of branch instructions. This branch table contains information about the likely behavior of each branch. Each time a branch is executed, its outcome (i.e. taken or not taken) is used to update the entry in the table. The processor uses the table to determine whether to take the next instruction from the branch target address (i.e. branch predicted taken) or from the next address in sequence (branch predicted not taken).

Single-bit branch predictors provide an accuracy of over 80% and 5-bit predictors provide an accuracy up to 98%. A typical branch prediction algorithm uses the last two outcomes of a branch to predict its future. If the last two outcomes are X, the next branch is assumed to lead to outcome X. If the prediction is wrong it remains the same the next time the branch is executed (i.e. two failures are needed to modify the prediction). After two consecutive failures, the prediction is inverted and the other outcome assumed. This algorithm responds to trends and is not affected by the occasional single *different* outcome.

8.3.4 Implementing pipelining

We demonstrated how the fetch–execute cycle operated at the logic level in Chapter 7. Now we show how the basic model is extended to incorporate pipelining.

In principle, pipelining is straightforward. Information is passed though a system (e.g. a logic unit or a memory) and then captured in a latch at the output of the system on the next clock cycle. Once the information has been captured in a latch, it can be held constant and used by the next processing stage.

Consider the highly simplified pipelined processor of Fig. 8.14 (we have omitted all but the basic detail—there is no data memory or facilities for dealing with literal operations and conditional behavior).

We are going to look at the operation of Fig. 8.14 cycle by cycle using the timing diagram of Fig. 8.15. All data is latched on the rising edge of a clock signal. Assume that the first cycle is timeslot T_0 and that the program counter contains the address of instruction i at the start of T_0.

ACCESSING EXTERNAL MEMORY

CISC processors have a wealth of addressing modes that can be used with memory reference instructions. The 68K implements ADD D0, − (A5) which adds the contents of D0 to the top of the stack pointed at by A5 and then pushes the result on to this stack. Designers of the Berkeley RISC restricted the way in which it accesses external memory.

The Berkeley RISC permits only two types of reference to external memory: a *load* and a *store*. Similarly, it provides a limited number of addressing modes with which to access an operand. It's not hard to find the reason for these restrictions on external memory accesses—an external memory reference takes longer than an internal operation.

Consider a LOAD (Rx) S2, **Rd** which implements [Rd] ← [[Rx] + S2]. The diagram demonstrates a possible sequence of actions performed during the execution of this instruction. In the source operand fetch phase, Rx is read from the register file to calculate the effective address of the operand. The processor can't progress beyond the execute phase to the store operand phase, because the operand has not been read from the main store. A bubble is introduced in the pipeline until the operand has been read from memory. Because memory accesses introduce bubbles into the pipeline, they are avoided wherever possible.

The effective address in the program counter relative mode is given by

$$EA = [PC] + S2$$

where PC represents the contents of the program counter and S2 is an offset as above.

These addressing modes provide zero, one, or two pointers, and a constant offset. If you wonder how we can use an addressing mode without a pointer register, recall that R0 contains the constant zero. There is a difference between addressing modes permitted by load and store operations. A *load* instruction permits the second source, S2, to be either an immediate value or a second register, whereas a *store* instruction permits S2 to be a 13-bit immediate value only.

The Berkeley RISC instruction has two formats. The short immediate format provides a 5-bit destination, a 5-bit source 1 operand and a 14-bit short source 2 operand. The short immediate format has two variations: one that specifies a 13-bit literal for source 2 and one that specifies a 5-bit source 2 register address. Bit 13 is used to specify whether the source 2 operand is a 13-bit literal of a 5-bit register pointer.

The long immediate format provides a 19-bit source operand by concatenating the two source operand fields.

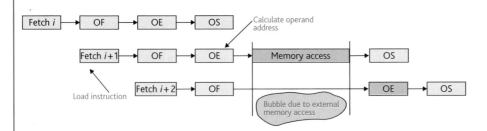

The Berkeley RISC implements two addressing modes: indexed and program counter relative. All other addressing modes must be synthesized from these two primitives. The effective address in the indexed mode is given by

$$EA = [PC] + S2$$

Thirteen-bit and 19-bit immediate fields may sound a little strange at first sight. However, because 13 + 19 = 32, RISC permits a full 32-bit value to be loaded into a window register in two operations. A typical microprocessor might take the same number of instruction bits to perform the same action (i.e. a 32-bit operation code field followed by a 32-bit literal). The following describes some of the addressing modes that can be synthesized from the RISC's basic addressing modes.

1. Absolute addressing	EA = 13-bit offset:	implemented by setting Rx = R0 = 0, S2 = 13-bit constant
2. Register indirect	EA = [Rx];	implemented by setting S2 = R0 = 0
3. Indexed addressing	EA = [Rx] + Offset	implemented by setting S2 = 13-bit constant (i.e. offset)
4. Two-dimensional addressing	EA = [Rx] + [Ry]	implemented by setting S2 = [Ry] (LOAD instructions only)

where Rx is the index register (one of the 32 general purpose registers) and S2 is an offset. The offset can be either a general-purpose register or a 13-bit constant.

Conditional instructions do not require a destination address and therefore the 5 bits, 19 to 23, normally used to specify a destination register are used to specify the condition (one of 16 because bit 23 is not used by conditional instructions).

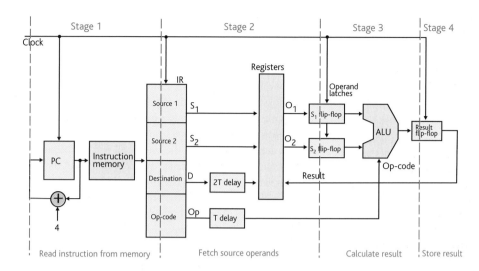

Figure 8.14 Using latches to implement pipelining.

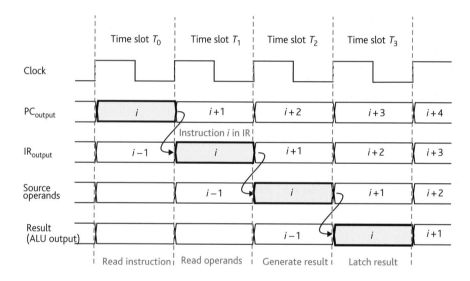

Figure 8.15 Timing diagram for a pipelined computer.

During cycle T_0 the output of the program counter interrogates the program memory and instruction i is read from memory.

When the next clock pulse appears at the beginning of cycle T_1, instruction i is latched in the instruction register and held constant for a clock cycle. The program counter is incremented and instruction $i + 1$ is read from memory. The instruction in the instruction register is decoded and used to read its two source operands during cycle T_1.

At the end of cycle T_1, the two source operands for instruction i appear at the operand latches (just as instruction $i + 1$ appears at the IR).

During cycle T_2, the operands currently in the operand latches are processed by the ALU to produce a result that is captured by the result latch at the beginning of cycle T_3. At this point, instruction i has been executed. Note that in time

slot T_2, the program counter contains the address of instruction $i + 2$ and the instruction register contains the op-code for instruction $i + 1$.

In Fig. 8.14 there is a block marked T *delay* in the path between the op-code field of the IR and the ALU, and a block marked *2T delay* between the destination field of the op-code and the register file. These delays are necessary to ensure that data arrives at the right place at the right time. For example, the operand data that goes to the ALU passes through the operand latches, which create a one-cycle delay. Consequently, the op-code has to be delayed for a cycle to avoid the data for instruction i getting to the ALU at the same time as the op-code for instruction $i + 1$.

During cycle T_3 the result of instruction i from the ALU is latched into the register file. In cycle T_3, instruction $i + 3$ is in the program counter, instruction $i + 2$ is in the instruction register, instruction $i + 1$ is being executed, and the result of instruction i is being written back into the register file. A new instruction is completed (or *retired*) on each further clock pulse.

There is little point in increasing the speed of the processing if memory cannot deliver data and instructions when they are needed. This is a particularly critical issue in computer design because memory speed has not kept up with processor speed. In the next section we look at how the effective speed of main store can be increased.

8.4 Cache memory

We now look at the *cache memory* that can dramatically increase the performance of a computer system at relatively little cost.

Cache memory provides system designers with a way of exploiting high-speed processors without incurring the cost of large high-speed memory systems. The word cache is pronounced 'cash' or 'cash-ay' and is derived from the French word meaning hidden. Cache memory is hidden from the programmer and appears as part of the system's memory space. There's nothing mysterious about cache memory—it's simply a quantity of very-high-speed memory that can be accessed rapidly by the processor. The element of magic stems from the ability of systems with a tiny cache memory (e.g. 512 kbytes of cache memory in a system with 2 Gbytes of DRAM) expecting the processor to make over 95% of its accesses to the cache rather than the slower DRAM.

First-generation microprocessors had truly tiny cache memories; for example, 256 bytes. Up to the mid-1990s, cache sizes of 8 to 32 kbytes were common. By the end of the 1990s, PCs had internal on-chip caches of 128 kbytes and external second-level caches of up to 1 Mbyte and in 2004 on-chip cache memories of 2 Mbytes and up to 4 Gbytes of main store.

Cache memory can be understood in everyday terms by its analogy with a diary or notebook used to jot down telephone numbers. A telephone directory contains hundreds of thousands of telephone numbers and nobody carries a telephone directory around with them. However, lots of people have a notebook with a hundred or so telephone numbers that they keep with them. Although the fraction of all possible telephone numbers in someone's notebook might be less than 0.01%, the probability that their next call will be to a number in the notebook is high because they frequently call the same people. Cache memory operates on exactly the same principle, by locating frequently accessed information in the cache memory rather than in the much slower main memory. Unfortunately, unlike the personal notebook, the computer cannot know, in advance, what data is most likely to be accessed. You could say that computer caches operate on a learning principle. By experience they learn what data is most frequently used and then transfer it to the cache.

The general structure of a cache memory is provided in Fig. 8.16. A block of cache memory sits on the processor's address and data buses in parallel with the much larger main memory. The implication of *parallel* in the previous sentence is that data in the cache is also maintained in the main memory. To return to the analogy with the telephone notebook, writing a friend's number in the notebook does not delete their number in the directory.

Cache memory relies on the same principle as the notebook with telephone numbers. The probability of accessing the next item of data in memory isn't a random function. Because of the nature of programs and their attendant data structures, the data required by a processor is often highly clustered. This aspect of memories is called the locality of reference and makes the use of cache memory possible (it is of course the same principle that underlies virtual memory).

A cache memory requires a cache controller to determine whether the data currently being accessed by the CPU resides in the cache or whether it must be obtained from the main

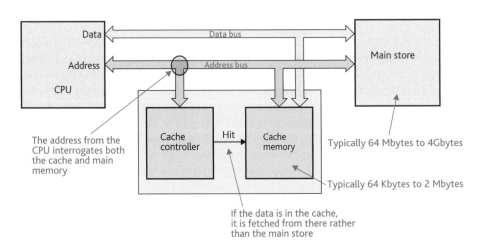

Figure 8.16 Structure of a cache memory.

memory. When the current address is applied to the cache controller, the controller returns a signal called *hit*, which is asserted if the data is currently in the cache. Before we look at how cache memories are organized, we will demonstrate their effect on a system's performance.

8.4.1 Effect of cache memory on computer performance

A key parameter of a cache system is its *hit ratio* (h), which defines the ratio of hits to all accesses. The hit ratio is determined by statistical observations of a real system and cannot readily be calculated. Furthermore, the hit ratio is dependent on the specific nature of the programs being executed. It is possible to have some programs with very high hit ratios and others with very low hit ratios. Fortunately, the effect of *locality of reference* usually means that the hit ratio is very high—often in the region of 95%. Before calculating the effect of a cache memory on a processor's performance, we need to introduce some terms.

Access time of main store	t_m
Access time of cache memory	t_c
Hit ratio	h
Miss ratio	m
Speedup ratio	S

The figure of merit of a computer with cache is called the *speedup ratio,* which indicates how much the cache accelerates the memory's access time. The speedup ratio is defined as the ratio of the memory system's access time without cache to its access time with cache.

N accesses to a system without cache memory requires Nt_m seconds. N accesses to a system with cache requires $N(ht_c + mt_m)$ seconds; that is, the time spent in accessing the cache plus the time spent accessing the main memory multiplied by the total number of memory accesses. We can express m in terms of h as $m = (1 - h)$, because if an access is not a hit it must be a miss. Therefore the total access time for a system with cache is given by $N(ht_c + (1 - h)t_m)$.

The speedup ratio is therefore given by

$$S = \frac{Nt_m}{N(ht_c + (1 - h)t_m)} = \frac{t_m}{ht_c + (1 - h)t_m}$$

We can introduce a new parameter, k, which defines the ratio of the access time of cache memory to main memory. That is, $k = t_c/t_m$. Typical values for t_m and t_c might be 50 ns and 10 ns, respectively, which gives a value for k of 0.2. Therefore,

$$S = \frac{t_m/t_m}{ht_c/t_m + ((1 - h)t_m/t_m)} = \frac{1}{hk + (1 - h)}$$

Figure 8.17 provides a plot of S as a function of the hit ratio (h). As you might expect, when $h = 0$ and all accesses are made to the main memory, the speedup ratio is 1. Similarly, when $h = 1$ and all accesses are made to the cache the speedup ratio is $1/k$. The most important conclusion to be drawn from Fig. 8.17 is that the speedup ratio is a sensitive function of the hit ratio. Only when h approaches about 90% does the effect of the cache memory become really significant. This result is consistent with common sense. If h drops below about 90%, the accesses to main store take a disproportionate amount of time and accesses to the cache have little effect on system performance.

Life isn't as simple as these equations suggest. Computers are clocked devices and run at a speed determined by the clock. Memory accesses take place in one or more whole clock cycles. If a processor accesses main store in one clock cycle, adding cache memory is not going to make the system faster. If we assume that a computer has a clock cycle time t_{cyc}, and accesses cache memory in p clock cycles (i.e. access time $= pt_{cyc}$) and main store in q clock cycles, its speedup ratio is

$$S = \frac{t_m}{ht_c + (1 - h)t_m} = \frac{qt_{cyc}}{pht_{cyc} + (1 - h)t_{cyc}}$$

$$= \frac{q}{ph + (1 - h)}$$

If $q = 4$ and $p = 2$, the speedup ratio is given by $1/(2h/4 + 1 - h) = 2/(2 - h)$.

In practice, we are more concerned with the performance of the entire system. A computer doesn't spend all its time accessing memory. The following expression gives a better picture of the average cycle time of a computer because it takes into account the number of cycles the processor spends performing internal (i.e. non-memory reference) operations.

$$t_{average} = F_{internal} \cdot Nt_{cyc} + F_{Memory} \cdot t_{cyc}(t_{cache} + (1 - h)(t_{cache} + t_{delay}))$$

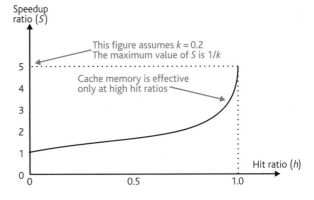

Figure 8.17 Speedup as a function of hit ratio.

where

F_{Internal} = fraction of cycles the processor spends doing internal operations

N = average number of cycles per internal operation

t_{cyc} = processor cycle time

F_{Memory} = fraction of cycles processor spends doing memory accesses

t_{delay} = additional penalty clock cycles required caused by a cache miss

h = hit ratio

t_{cache} = cache memory access time (in clock cycles)

Note that, by convention, the main memory access time is given by the number of cycles to access cache plus the additional number of cycles (i.e. the penalty) to access main store. If we put some figures into this equation, we get

$$t_{\text{average}} = 40\% \times 2 \times 20\,\text{ns} + 60\% \times 20\,\text{ns}$$
$$\times \left(0.9 \times 1 + 0.1(1 + 3) \right)$$
$$= 16\,\text{ns} + 26\,\text{ns}$$
$$= 42\,\text{ns}$$

The effect of cache memory on the performance of a computer depends on many factors including the way in which the cache is organized and the way in which data is written to main memory when a write access takes place. We will return to some of these considerations when we have described how cache systems are organized.

8.4.2 Cache organization

There are at least three ways of organizing a cache memory—direct-mapped, associative-mapped, and set associative-mapped cache. Each of these systems has its own *performance:cost* trade-off.

Direct-mapped cache

The easiest way of organizing a cache memory employs direct mapping, which relies on a simple algorithm to map data block *i* from the main memory into data block *j* in the cache. For the purpose of this section we will regard the smallest unit of data held in a cache as a line that is made up of typically two or four consecutive words. The line is the basic unit of data that is transferred between the cache and main store and varies between 4 and 32 bytes.

Figure 8.18 illustrates the structure of a highly simplified direct-mapped cache. As you can see, the memory space is divided into sets and the sets into lines. This memory is composed of 32 words and is accessed by a 5-bit address bus from

the CPU. For the purpose of this discussion we need only consider the set and line (as it doesn't matter how many words there are in a line). The address in this example has a 2-bit set field, a 2-bit line field, and a 1-bit word field. The cache memory holds $2^2 = 4$ lines of two words. When the processor generates an address, the appropriate line in the cache is accessed. For example, if the processor generates the 5-bit address 10100_2, word 0 of line 2 in set 2 is accessed.

A glance at Fig. 8.18 reveals that there are four possible lines numbered two—a line 2 in set 0, a line 2 in set 1, a line 2 in set 2, and a line 2 in set 3. In this example the processor accessed line 2 in set 2. The obvious question is, 'How does the system know whether the line 2 accessed in the cache is the line 2 from set 2 in the main memory?'

Figure 8.19 shows how a direct-mapped cache resolves the contention between lines. Each line in the cache memory has a *tag* or label, which identifies which set this particular line belongs to. When the processor accesses line 2, the tag belonging to line 2 in the cache is sent to a comparator. At the same time the set field from the processor is also sent to the comparator. If they are the same, the line in the cache is the desired line and a hit occurs.

If they are not the same, a miss occurs and the cache must be updated. The old line 2 from set 1 is either simply discarded or rewritten back to main memory depending on how the updating of main memory is organized.

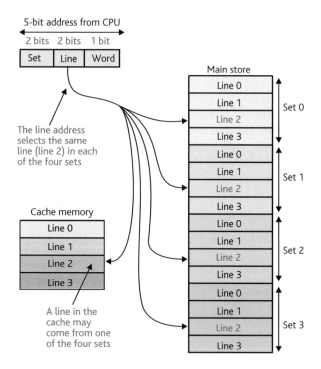

Figure 8.18 The direct-mapped cache.

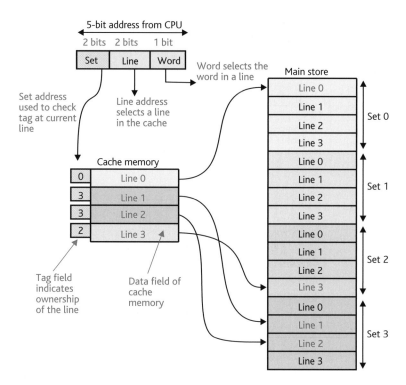

Figure 8.19 Resolving contentions between lines in a direct-mapped cache.

Figure 8.20 provides a skeleton structure of a direct-mapped cache memory system. The cache memory itself is nothing more than a block of very-high-speed random access read/write memory. The cache tag RAM is a fast combined memory and comparator that receives both its address and data inputs from the processor's address bus. The cache tag RAM's address input is the line address from the processor that is used to access a unique location (one for each of the possible lines). The data in the cache tag RAM at this location is the tag associated with that location. The cache tag RAM also has a data input that receives the tag field from the processor's address bus. If the tag field from the processor matches the contents of the tag (i.e. set) field being accessed, the cache tag RAM returns a hit signal.

As Fig. 8.20 demonstrates, the cache tag RAM is nothing more than a high-speed random access memory with a built-in data comparator. Some of the major semiconductor manufacturers have implemented single-chip cache tag RAMs.

The advantage of the directly mapped cache is almost self-evident. Both the cache memory and the cache tag RAM are widely available devices which, apart from their speed, are no more complex than other mainstream devices. Moreover, the direct-mapped cache requires no complex line replacement algorithm. If line x in set y is accessed and a miss takes place, line x from set y in the main store is loaded into the frame for line x in the cache memory and the tag set to y. That is, there is no decision concerning which line has to be rejected when a new line is to be loaded.

Another important advantage of direct-mapped cache is its inherent parallelism. Because the cache memory holding the data and the cache tag RAM are entirely independent, they can both be accessed simultaneously. Once the tag has been matched and a hit has occurred, the data from the cache will also be valid (assuming the two cache data and cache tag memories have approximately equal access times).

The disadvantage of direct-mapped cache is almost a corollary of its advantage. A cache with n lines has one restriction—at any instant it can hold only one line numbered x. What it cannot do is hold a line x from set p and a line x from set q. This restriction exists because there is one page frame in the cache for each of the possible lines. Consider the following fragment of code:

```
REPEAT
      Get_data
      Compare
UNTIL match OR end_of_data
```

This fragment of code reads data and compares it with another string until a match is found. Suppose that the Get_data routine is in set x, line y and that part of the Compare routine is in set z, line y. Because a direct-mapped cache can hold only one line y at a time, the frame corresponding to line y must be reloaded twice for each path through the loop. Consequently, the performance of a direct-mapped cache can sometimes be poor. Statistical measurements on real programs indicate that the very poor

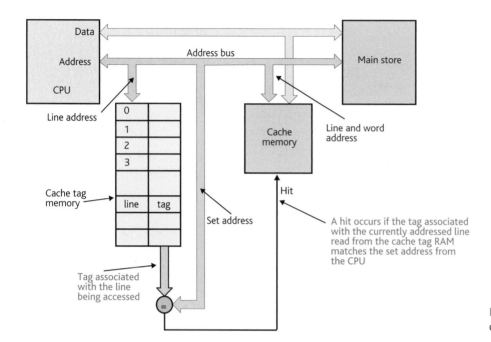

Figure 8.20 Implementation of direct-mapped cache.

worst-case behavior of direct-mapped caches has no significant impact on their average behavior.

Suppose a cache is almost empty and most of its lines have not yet been loaded with active data. Certain lines may have to be swapped out of the cache frequently because *data* in the main store just happens to share the same line numbers. In spite of this objection to direct-mapped cache, it is very popular because of its low cost of implementation and high speed.

Associative-mapped cache

One way of organizing a cache memory that overcomes the limitations of direct-mapped cache is described in Fig. 8.21. Ideally, we would like a cache that places no restrictions on what data it can contain. The *associative cache* is such a memory.

An address from the processor is divided into three fields: the tag, the line, and the word. Like the direct-mapped cache, the smallest unit of data transferred into and out of the cache is the line. Unlike the direct-mapped cache, there's no pre-determined relationship between the location of lines in the cache and lines in the main memory. Line p in the memory *can* be put in line q in the cache with no restrictions on the values of p and q. Consider a system with 1 Mbyte of main store and 64 kbytes of associatively mapped cache. If the size of a line is four 32-bit words (i.e. 16 bytes), the main memory is composed of $2^{20}/16 = 64$K lines and the cache is composed of $2^{16}/16 = 4096$ lines. Because an associative cache permits any line in the main store to be loaded into one of its lines, line i in the associative cache can be loaded with any one of the 64K possible lines in the main store. Therefore, line i

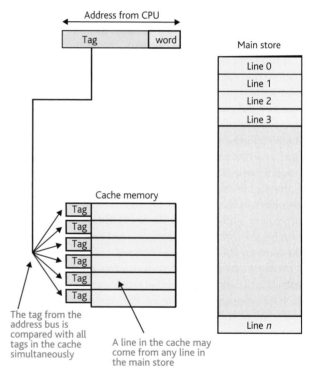

Figure 8.21 Associative-mapped cache.

requires a 16-bit tag to uniquely label it as being associated with line i from the main store.

When the processor generates an address, the word bits select a word location in both the main memory and the cache. Unlike the direct-mapped cache memory, the line address from the processor can't be used to address a line in the associative cache. Why? Because each line in the direct-mapped cache can come only from one of n lines in the main store (where n is the number of sets). The tag resolves which of the lines is actually present. In an associative cache, any of the 64K lines in the main store can be located in any of the lines in the cache. Consequently, the associative cache requires a 16-bit tag to identify one of the 2^{16} lines from the main memory. Because the cache's lines are not ordered, the tags are not ordered and cannot be stored in a simple look-up table like the direct-mapped cache. In other words, when the CPU accesses line i, it may be anywhere in the cache or it may not be in the cache.

Associative cache systems employ a special type of memory called associative memory. An associative memory has an n-bit input but not necessarily 2^n unique internal locations. The n-bit address input is a tag that is compared with a tag field in each of its locations simultaneously. If the input tag matches a stored tag, the data associated with that location is output. Otherwise the associative memory produces a miss output. An associative memory is not addressed in the same way that a computer's main store is addressed. Conventional computer memory requires the explicit address of a location, whereas an associative memory is accessed by asking, 'Do you have this item stored somewhere?'

Associative cache memories are efficient because they place no restriction on the data they hold. In Fig. 8.21 the tag that specifies the line currently being accessed is compared with the tag of each entry in the cache simultaneously. In other words, all locations are accessed at once. Unfortunately, large associative memories are not yet cost effective. Once the associative cache is full, a new line can be brought in only by overwriting an existing line that requires a suitable line replacement policy (as in the case of virtual memories).

Set associative-mapped cache

Most computers employ a compromise between the direct-mapped cache and the fully associative cache called a *set associative cache*. A set associative cache memory is nothing more than multiple direct-mapped caches operated in parallel. The simplest arrangement is called a two-way set associative cache and consists of two direct-mapped cache memories so that each line in the cache system is duplicated. For example, a two-way set associative cache example has two line 5s and it's possible to store one line 5 from set x and one line 5 from set y.

If the cache has n parallel sets, an n-way comparison is performed in parallel against all members of the set. Because n in small (typically 2 to 16), the logic required to perform the comparison is not complex.

Figure 8.22 describes the common four-way set associative cache. When the processor accesses memory, the

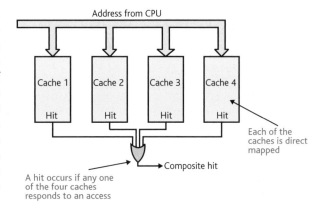

Figure 8.22 Set associative-mapped cache.

appropriate line in each of four direct-mapped caches is accessed simultaneously. Because there are four lines, a simple associative match can be used to determine which (if any) of the lines in cache are to supply the data. In Fig. 8.22 the hit output from each direct-mapped cache is fed to an OR gate, which generates a hit if any of the caches generate a hit.

Level 2 cache

The memory hierarchy can be expanded further by dividing the cache memory into a level 1 and a level 2 cache. A level 1 cache is normally located on the same chip as the CPU itself; that is, it is integrated with the processor. Over the years, level 1 caches have grown in size as semiconductor technology has advanced and more memory devices can be integrated on a chip. A level 2 cache was once invariably located off the processor chip but modern high-performance devices have on-chip level 1 and level 2 caches. By 2005 Intel Pentium processors were available with 2 Mbyte level 2 caches.

When the processor makes a memory access, the level 1 cache is first searched. If the data isn't there, the level 2 cache is searched. If it isn't in the level 2 cache, the main store is accessed. The average access time is given by

$$t_{ave} = h_{L1}t_{c1} + (1 - h_{L1})h_{L2}t_{c2}$$
$$+ (1 - h_{L1})(1 - h_{L2})t_{memory}$$

where h_{L1} and h_{L2} are the hit rates of the level 1 and level 2 caches, and t_{c1} and t_{c2} are the access times of the L1 and L2 caches, respectively.

Consider a system with a hit ratio of 0.90, a single-level cache access time of 4 ns, and a main store access time of 50 ns. The speedup ratio is given by $1/(hk + 1 - h) = 5.81$.

Suppose we add a level 2 cache to this system and that the level 2 cache has a hit ratio of 0.7 and an access time of 8 ns. In this case, the access time is

$$t_{ave} = h_{L1}t_{c1} + (1-h_{L1})h_{L2}t_{c2} + (1-h_{L1})(1-h_{L2})$$
$$t_{memory} = 0.9 \times 4 + 0.1 \times 0.7 \times 8 + 0.1 \times 0.3 \times 50 = 5.66 \text{ ns}$$

The speedup ratio with a level 2 cache is 50 ns/ 5.66 ns = 8.83.

8.4.3 Considerations in cache design

Apart from choosing the structure of a cache system and the line replacement policy, the designer has to consider how write cycles are to be treated. Should write accesses be made only to the cache and then the main store updated when the line is replaced (a *writeback* policy)? Should the main memory also be updated each time a word in the cache is modified (a *writethrough* policy)? The writethrough policy allows the cache to be written to rapidly and the main memory updated over a longer span of time (if there is write buffer to hold the data until the bus becomes free). A writethrough policy can lead to more memory write accesses than are strictly necessary.

When a cache miss occurs, a line of data is fetched from the main store. Consequently, the processor may read a byte from the cache and then the cache requires a line of, say, 8 bytes from the main store. As you can imagine, the cost of a miss on an access to cache carries an additional penalty because an entire line has to be filled from memory. Fortunately, modern memories, CPUs, and cache systems support a burst-fill mode in which a burst of consecutive data elements can be transferred between the main store and cache memory. Let's look at cache access times again.

If data is not in the cache, it must be fetched from memory and loaded in the cache. If t_l is the time taken to reload the cache on a miss, the effective average access time is given by

$$t_{ave} = ht_c + (1-h)t_m + (1-h)t_l$$

The term $(1-h)t_l$ is the additional time required to reload the cache following each miss. This expression can be rewritten as

$$t_{ave} = ht_c + (1-h)(t_l + t_m)$$

The term $(t_l + t_m)$ corresponds to the time taken to access main memory and to load a line in the cache following a miss. However, because both accessing the element that caused the miss and filling the cache take place in parallel, we can note that $t_l > t_m$ and simplify the equation to get

$$t_{ave} = ht_c + (1-h)t_l$$

The performance of cache memory systems is also determined by the relative amounts of read and write accesses and the different ways in which read and write cache accesses are treated. Relatively few memory accesses are write operations

(about 5 to 30% of memory accesses). If we take into account the action taken on a miss during a read access and on a miss during a write access, the average access time for writethough memory is given by

$$t_{ave} = ht_c + (1-h)(1-w)t_l + (1-h)wt_c$$

where w is the fraction of write accesses and t_l is the time taken to reload the cache on a miss. The $(1-h)(1-w)t_l$ term is the time taken to reload the cache on a read access and $(1-h)wt_c$ represents the time taken to access the cache on a write miss. This equation is based on the assumption that writes occur infrequently and therefore the main store has time to store writethrough data between two successive write operations.

Another aspect of cache memories that has to be taken into account in sophisticated systems is *cache coherency*. As we know, data in the cache also lives in the main memory. When the processor modifies data it must modify both the copy in the cache and the copy in the main memory (although not necessarily at the same time). There are circumstances when the existence of two copies (which can differ) of the same item of data causes problems. For example, an I/O controller using DMA might attempt to move an old line of data from the main store to disk without knowing that the processor has just updated the copy of the data in the cache but has not yet updated the copy in the main memory. Cache coherency is also known as data *consistency*.

8.5 Multiprocessor systems

One way of accelerating the performance of a computer without resorting to either new technology or to a new architecture is to use a *multiprocessor system*; that is, you take two or more CPUs and divide the work between them. Here we introduce some basic concepts of multiprocessing hardware and the topology of multiprocessors.

The speedup ratio, S_p, of a multiprocessor system using p processors is defined as $S_p = T_1/T_p$, where T_1 is the time taken to perform the computation on a single processor and T_p is the time taken to perform the same computation on p processors. The value of S_p must fall in the range $1 \leq S_p \leq p$. The lower limit on S_p corresponds to a situation in which the parallel system cannot be exploited and only one processor can be used. The upper limit on S_p corresponds to a problem that can be divided equally between the p processors. The efficiency, E_p, of a multiprocessor system is defined as the ratio between the speedup factor and the number of processors; that is $E_p = S_p/p = T_1/pT_p$. The efficiency, E_p, must fall in the range 1 (all processors used fully) to 1/p (only one processor out of p used).

Whenever I think of multiprocessing I think of air travel. Suppose you want to get from central London to downtown

Manhattan. The time taken is the sum of the time to travel to Heathrow airport, the check-in time, the transatlantic journey, the baggage reclaim time, and the time to travel from JFK to downtown Manhattan. The approximate figures (in hours) are $0.9 + 1.5 + 6.5 + 0.5 + 1 = 10.4$. Suppose you now decide to speed things up and travel across the Atlantic in a supersonic aircraft that takes only 3 hours; the new times are $0.9 + 1.5 + 3 + 0.5 + 1 = 6.9$ hours. The speedup ratio between these two modes of travel is $10.4/6.9 = 1.51$. Increasing the speed of the aircraft by a factor of 2.17 has resulted in a speedup ratio of only 1.51, because all the other delays have not been changed.

The same problem affects multiprocessing—the speedup ratio is profoundly affected by the parts of a problem that cannot be computed in parallel. Consider, for example, the product $(P + Q)(P - Q)$. The operations $P + Q$ and $P-Q$ can be carried out simultaneously in parallel, whereas their product can be carried out serially only after $P + Q$ and $P - Q$ have been evaluated.

Figure 8.23 shows how a task may have components that must be executed serially, P_s, and tasks that can be executed in parallel, P_p. If each task in Fig. 8.23 requires t seconds, the total time required by a serial processor is $8t$. Because three pairs of tasks can be carried out in parallel, the total time taken on a parallel system is $4t$.

Suppose a task consists of a part that must be computed *serially* and a part that can be computed by processors in parallel. Let the fraction of the task executed serially be f and the fraction executed in parallel be $(1 - f)$. The time taken to process the task on a parallel processor is $fT_1 + (1 - f)T_1/p$, where t is the time required to execute the task on a single processor and p is the number of processors. The speedup ratio is $S_p = T_1/(fT_1 + (1 - f)T_1/p) = p/(1 + (p - 1)f)$. This equation is *Amdahl's law* and tells us that increasing the number of processors in a system is futile unless the value of f is very low.

Figure 8.24 demonstrates the relationship between the speedup ratio, $S(f)$, and f (the fraction of serial processing) for a system with 16 processors. The horizontal axis is the fraction of a task that is executed in parallel, $1 - f$. As you can see, the speedup ratio rises very rapidly as $1 - f$ approaches 1.

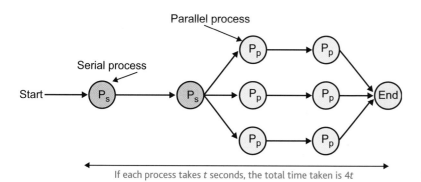

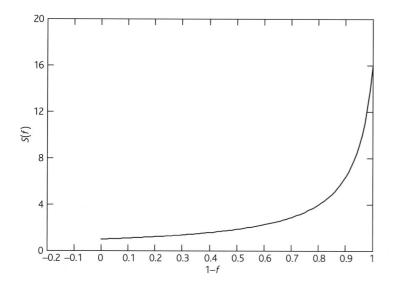

If each process takes t seconds, the total time taken is $4t$

Figure 8.23 Executing a task in serial and parallel.

Figure 8.24 The effect of f on the speedup ratio ($p = 16$).

You can't just plug an extra processor into an existing system to convert it into a multiprocessor. The global implications for the system hardware and its software are not trivial, because the individual processors have to share the available resources (i.e. memory and input/output). An effective multiprocessor system must be able to allocate resources to contending processors without seriously degrading the performance of the system.

Some multiprocessor systems are termed *reconfigurable*, because the structure of the hardware itself can be modified by the operating system. For example, the way in which memory is distributed between the individual processors or the paths between the processors can be changed dynamically under software control. Similarly, interrupt handling can be dynamically partitioned between the various processors to maximize efficiency. We do not discuss reconfigurable architectures further here.

Although the architecture of a stored-program computer (i.e. a von Neumann machine) can be defined quite precisely, there is no similar definition of a multiprocessor system. Multiprocessor systems come in many different flavors and a configuration suitable for one particular application may be useless for another. The only really universal characteristic common to all multiprocessor systems is that they have more than one processor. We shall soon examine the various classes of multiprocessor system.

Multiprocessor systems design is not easy; there are a lot of factors to take into account; for example, the distribution of tasks between processors, the interconnection of the processors (i.e. the topology of the multiprocessor system), the management of the memory resources, the avoidance of *deadlock*, and the control of input/output resources. Deadlock occurs when two or more processors cannot continue because each is blocking the other.

The distribution of tasks between processors is of crucial importance in selecting the architecture of the processor system itself. In turn, the distribution of tasks is strongly determined by the nature of the problem to be solved by the computer. In other words, the architecture of a multiprocessor system can be optimized for a certain type of problem. Conversely, a class of programs that runs well on one multiprocessor system may not run well on another.

A classic problem that can be solved by multiprocessing belongs to the world of air-traffic control. A radar system receives a periodic echo from the targets (i.e. aircraft) being tracked. Each echo E, is a function of the bearing, θ and distance or range, r, of the target. Due to noise and imperfections in the system, there is an uncertainty or error, ε, associated with each echo. A new echo is received every few millisecond. Given this stream of inputs, $E_{r,\theta,\tau} + \varepsilon_{r,\theta,\tau}$, the computer connected to the radar receiver has to calculate the current positions of the targets and then estimate the future track of each target and report any possible conflicts. Such a system requires very large amounts of computer processing power with relatively little I/O activity or disk access. Obviously it is reasonable to try to solve the problem by means of multiprocessing. For example, as one processor is updating a target's current position, another processor can be calculating its future position.

The preceding problem is described as classic, because it is so well suited to multiprocessing. There are several ways of allocating the mathematics involved in the radar calculations to the various processors. It is, unfortunately, much less easy to decompose a general task into a number of subtasks that can be run in parallel. Often it is necessary for the programmer to write programs in such a way that they involve the greatest amount of parallel activity. Other problems well suited to parallel processing are the simulation of complex dynamic systems such as the atmosphere or the motion of liquids.

8.5.1 Topics in multiprocessor systems

A key parameter of a multiprocessor system is its *topology*, which defines how the processors are arranged with respect to each other and how they communicate. A more important parameter of a multiprocessor system is the degree of coupling between the various processors. We will discuss processor coupling first and then look at multiprocessor topologies.

Processors with facilities for exchanging large quantities of data very rapidly are said to be tightly coupled. Such computers share resources like buses or blocks of memory. The advantage of tightly coupled systems is their potential speed, because one processor doesn't have to wait long periods of time while data is transferred from another. Their disadvantage arises from the complexity of the hardware and software necessary to coordinate the processors. If they share a bus or memory, an arbiter is needed to determine which processor is permitted to access the resource at any time.

Although not a problem associated entirely with multiprocessors, the avoidance of *deadlock* must feature in the design of some classes of multiprocessor. Deadlock describes the situation in which two tasks are unable to proceed because each task holds something needed by the other. In a real-time system, the sequential tasks (i.e. the software) require resources (memory, disk drives, I/O devices, etc.), whereas in a multiprocessor system these resources are required by the individual processors.

Every multiprocessor system, like every single-processor system, has facilities for input or output transactions. We therefore have the problem of how I/O transactions are to be treated in a multiprocessor system. Does each processor have its own I/O arrangements? Is the I/O pooled between the processors, with each processor asking for I/O facilities as they are needed? Finally, is it possible to dedicate one or more processors solely to the task of I/O processing?

In a similar vein, the designer of a multiprocessor may need to construct an appropriate interrupt-handling system. When an I/O device interrupts a processor in a single-processor system, there is not a lot to decide. Either the processor services the interrupt or it is deferred. In a multiprocessor system we have to decide which processor will service an interrupt, which in turn begs the question, 'Do we pool interrupts or do we allocate certain types of interrupt to specific processors?' If interrupts are pooled, the interrupt-handling software must also be pooled, as processor A must deal with an interrupt from device X in exactly the same way that processor B would deal with the same interrupt. In addition to interrupts generated by I/O devices, it is possible for one processor to interrupt another processor.

Like any other computer, the multiprocessor requires an operating system. There are two basic approaches to the design of operating systems for multiprocessors. One of the simplest arrangements is the master–slave operating system in which a single operating system runs on the master processor and all other processors receive tasks that are handed down from the master. The master–slave operating system is little more than the type of operating system found in conventional single-processor systems.

The distributed operating system provides each processor with its own copy of the operating system (or at least a processor can access the common operating system via shared memory). Distributed operating systems are more robust than their master–slave counterparts because the failure of a single processor does not necessarily bring about a complete system collapse.

The problems we have just highlighted serve to emphasize that a multiprocessor system cannot easily be built in a vacuum. Whenever we are faced with the design of a multiprocessor system, it is necessary to ask, 'Why do we need the multiprocessor system and what are its objectives?' and then to configure it accordingly. In other words, almost all design aspects of a multiprocessor system are very much problem dependent.

8.5.2 Multiprocessor organization

Although there is an endless variety of multiprocessor architectures, we can identify broad groups whose members have certain features in common. One possible approach to the classification of multiprocessor systems, attributed to Michael J. Flynn, is to consider the type of the parallelism (i.e. architecture or topology) and the nature of the interprocessor communication. Flynn's four basic multiprocessor architectures are referred to by the abbreviations SISD, SIMD, MISD, and MIMD and are described later. However, before continuing, we must point out that Flynn's topological classification of multiprocessor systems is not the only one possible, as multiprocessors may be categorized by a number

of different parameters. One broad classification of multiprocessors depends on the processor's relationship to memory and to other processing elements. Multiprocessors can be classified as processor to memory (P to M) structures or as processing element to processing element (PE to PE) structures. Figure 8.25 describes these two structures. A P to M architecture has n processors, an interconnection network, and n memory elements. The interconnection network allocates processor X to memory Y. The more general PE to PE architecture uses n processors, each with its own memory, and permits processor element X to communicate with PE Y via an interconnection network. The multiprocessors described in this chapter best fit the PE to PE model.

SISD (single instruction single data-stream)

The SISD machine is nothing more than the conventional single-processor system. It is called single instruction because only one instruction is executed at a time, and single data-stream because there is only one task being executed at any instant.

SIMD (single instruction multiple data-stream)

The SIMD architecture executes instructions sequentially, but on data in parallel. The idea of a single instruction operating on parallel data is not as strange as it may sound. Consider vector mathematics. A vector is a multicomponent data structure; for example, the four-component vector **A** might be 0.2, 4.3, 0.2, 0.1. A very frequent operation in most branches of engineering is the calculation of the *inner product* of two n-component vectors, **A** and **B**:

$$s = A \cdot B = a_i b_i$$

For example, if **A** is $(1, 4, 3, 6)$ and **B** is $(4, 6, 2, 3)$, the inner product **A** · **B** is $1 \times 4 + 4 \times 6 + 3 \times 2 + 6 \times 3 = 4 + 24 + 6 + 18 = 52$. The inner product can be expressed as single operation (i.e. $s = (\mathbf{A} \cdot \mathbf{B})$, but involves multiple data elements (i.e. the $\{a_i \cdot b_i\}$. Such calculations are used extensively in computer graphics and image processing. One way of speeding up the calculation of an inner product is to assign a processor to the generation of each of the individual elements, the $\{a_i \cdot b_i\}$. The simultaneous calculation of $a_i \cdot b_i$ for $i = 1$ to n requires n processors, one for each component of the vector.

Such an arrangement consists of a single controller that steps through the program (i.e. the single instruction-stream) and an array of processing elements (PEs) acting on the components of a vector in parallel (i.e. the multiple data-stream). Often, such PEs are number crunchers or high-speed ALUs, rather than the general-purpose microprocessors we have been considering throughout this text.

The SIMD architecture, or array processor, has a high performance/cost ratio and is very efficient, as long as the task running on it can be decomposed largely into vector operations. Consequently, the array processor is best suited to the

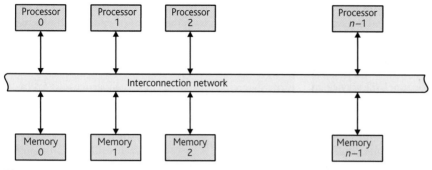

(a) Processor to memory multiprocessor organization (P to M).

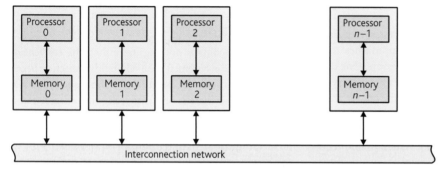

(b) Processing element to processing element multprocessor organization (PE to PE).

Figure 8.25 Processor to memory, and processor to processor structures.

air-traffic control problem discussed earlier, to the processing of weather information (this involves partial differential equations), and to computerized tomography where the output of a body scanner is processed almost entirely by vector arithmetic. As the SIMD architecture is generally built around a central processor controlling an array of special-purpose processors, the SIMD architecture is not discussed in any further detail here. However, we provide an example of a SIMD architecture to illustrate one of its applications.

Figure 8.26 demonstrates the application of a SIMD architecture to image smoothing—an operation performed on images to remove noise (we discuss image processing further when we introduce computer graphics).[7] In this example, an image from a noisy source such as a spacecraft camera is smoothed or filtered to yield a relatively noise-free image. Consider an input array, I, of 512 × 512 pixels, which is to be smoothed to produce an output array S.

A pixel is an 8-bit unsigned integer representing one of 256 gray levels from 0 (white) to 255 (black). Each pixel $S_{i,j}$ in the smoothed array, S, is the average of the gray levels of its eight nearest neighbors. By averaging the pixels in this way, the effects of noise bursts are reduced. The neighbors of $S_{i,j}$ in the input array are $I_{i-1,j-i}, I_{i-1,j}, I_{i-1,j+1}, I_{i,j-1}, I_{i,j+1}, I_{i+1,j-1}, I_{i+1,j}$ and $I_{i+1,j+1}$. The top, bottom, and left- and right-edge pixels of S are set to zero, because their corresponding pixels in I do not have eight adjacent neighbors.

The following example demonstrates how this smoothing algorithm operates. The left-hand array represents the near neighbors of a pixel before it is smoothed. The right-hand array shows the pixel after smoothing. As you can see the value 6 has been reduced to 3.2.

```
2        3        3              2        3        3
2        6        3              2        3.2      3
2        1        2              2        1        2

Before smoothing                    After smoothing
```

If the smoothing algorithm were performed serially, it would be necessary to compute the value for each of the 512 × 512 pixels by looking at its eight nearest neighbors. Parallel processing allows us to process groups of pixels at the same time.

Assume that an SIMD array has 1024 processing elements (PEs), logically arranged as an array of 32 × 32 PEs as shown in Fig. 8.26. Each PE stores a 16 × 16 pixel sub-image block of the 512 × 512 pixel image I. For example, PE_0 stores a 16 × 16 pixel sub-image block composed of columns 0 to 15 and rows 0 to 15; PE_1 stores the pixels in columns 16 to 31 of rows 0 to 15, etc. Each PE smoothes its own subimage, with all

[7] Example from *Large-scale Parallel Processing Systems*, Microprocessors and Microsystems, January 1987, by Howard J. Siegel *et al.* pp. 3–20.

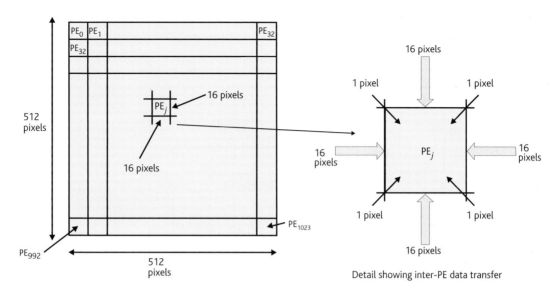

Figure 8.26 Using a SIMD architecture in image processing.

PEs operating on their subimages concurrently. At the edges of each 16×16 subimage, data must be transferred between adjacent PEs in order to calculate the smoothed value. The necessary data transfers for PE_j are shown in Fig. 8.26. Transfers between different PEs can take place simultaneously. For example, when PE_{j-1} sends its upper right corner pixel to PE_j, PE_j can send its own upper right corner pixel to PE_{j+1}, and so on.

To perform a smoothing operation on a 512×512 pixel image by the parallel smoothing of 1024 subimage blocks of 16×16 pixels, 256 parallel smoothing operations are executed. However, the neighbors of each subimage edge pixel must be transferred between adjacent PEs and the total number of parallel data transfers required is $(4 \times 16) + 4 = 68$ (i.e. 16 for each of the top, bottom and left- and right-side edges). The corresponding serial algorithm needs no data transfers between PEs but $512^2 = 264\ 144$ smoothing calculations must be executed. If no data transfers were needed, the parallel algorithm would be faster than the serial algorithm by a factor of $262\ 144/256 = 1024$. If the inter-PE data transfer time is included and it is assumed that each parallel data transfer requires at most as much time as one smoothing operation, then the time factor improvement is $262\ 144/(256 + 68) = 809$.

The last step in the smoothing process is to set the edge pixels of S to zero. This creates an additional (although negligible) overhead, which is to enable only the appropriate PEs when the zero values are stored for these edge pixels (only enabled PEs execute the instructions broadcast to the PEs). Serially, this would require $(4 \times 512) - 4 = 2044$ parallel stores. The SIMD architectures can be implemented by means of arrays of relatively primitive processing elements (e.g. ALUs). It is not usually necessary to make each processing element as complex as a CPU.

MISD (multiple instruction single data-stream)

The MISD architecture performs multiple operations concurrently on a single stream of data and is associated with the pipeline processor. We described the concept of the pipeline when we introduced the RISC processor. The difference between a MISD pipeline and a RISC pipeline is one of scale.

In multiprocessor terms, the various processors are arranged in line and are synchronized so that each processor accepts a new input every t seconds. If there are n processors, the total execution time of a task is $n \cdot t$ seconds. At each epoch, a processor takes a partially completed task from a downstream processor and hands on its own task to the next upstream processor. As a pipeline processor has N processors operating concurrently and each task may be in one of the N stages, it requires a total of $N \cdot t + (K - 1)$ time slots to process K tasks. The MISD architecture is not suited to multiprocessor systems based on general-purpose microprocessors. MISD systems are highly specialized and require special-purpose architectures; they have never been developed to the same extent as SIMD and MIMD architectures.

MIMD (multiple instruction multiple data-stream)

The MIMD architecture is really the most general-purpose form of multiprocessor system and is represented by systems in which each processor has its own set of instructions operating on its own data structures. In other words, the processors are acting in a largely autonomous mode. Each individual processor may be working on part of the main task and does not necessarily need to get in touch with its

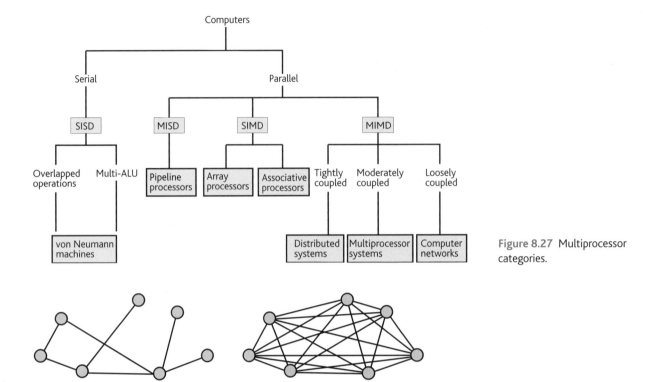

Figure 8.27 Multiprocessor categories.

(a) The unconstrained topology.   (b) The fully connected topology.   **Figure 8.28** The unconstrained topology.

neighbors until it has finished its subtask. The PE to PE architecture described in Fig. 8.25 can be thought of as a generic MIMD machine.

Because of the generality of the MIMD architecture, it can be said to encompass the relatively tightly coupled arrangements to be discussed shortly and the very loosely coupled geographically distributed LANs. Figure 8.27 provides a graphical illustration of the classification of multiprocessor systems according to E. T. Fathi and A. M. Krieger (Multiple Microprocessor Systems: What, Why and When, Computer, March 1983, pp. 23–32).

8.5.3 MIMD architectures

Although the array processor or the pipeline processor is likely to be constructed from very special units, the more general MIMD architecture is much more likely to be built from widely available off-the-shelf microprocessors. Therefore, the major design consideration in the production of such a multiprocessor concerns the topology of the system, which describes the arrangement of the communications paths between the individual processors.

Figures 8.28 to 8.32 depict the five classic MIMD topologies. Multiprocessor structures are described both by their topology and by their *interconnection level*. The level of interconnection is a measure of the number of switching units through which a message must pass when going from

processor X to processor Y. The four basic topologies are the unconstrained topology, the bus, the ring, and the star, although, of course, there are many variants of each of these pure topologies.

The unconstrained topology

The unconstrained topology is so called because it is a random arrangement in which a processor is linked directly to each processor with which it wishes to communicate (Fig. 8.28(a)). The unconstrained topology is not practicable for any but the simplest of systems. As the number of processors grows, the number of buses between processors becomes prohibitive. Figure 8.28(b) shows the limiting case of this topology, called the fully connected topology, because each processor is connected to each other processor. The advantage of the unconstrained topology system is the very high degree of coupling that can be achieved. As all the buses are dedicated to communication between only two processors, there is no conflict between processors waiting to access the same bus.

The bus topology

The bus (Fig. 8.29) is the simplest of topologies because each processor is connected to a single common data highway—the bus. The bus is a simple topology; not least because it avoids the problem of how to route a message from processor X to processor Y. All traffic between processors must use the

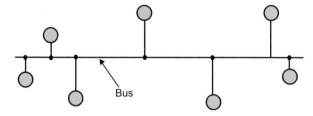

Figure 8.29 The bus topology.

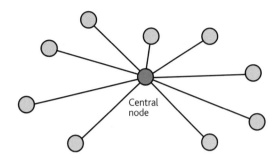

Figure 8.31 The star topology.

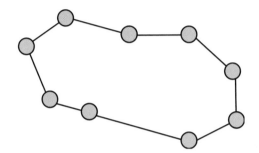

Figure 8.30 The ring topology.

bus. The disadvantage of the bus as a method of implementing a multiprocessor system lies in the problem of controlling access to the bus. As only one processor at a time can use the bus, it is necessary to design an arbiter to determine which processor may access the bus at any time. Arbitration between two or more contending processors slows down the system and leads to bottlenecks. A bus offers a relatively high degree of coupling but is more suitable for schemes in which the quantity of data exchanged between the individual processors is small.

The *symmetric multiprocessor* is a practical realization of a bus-based multiprocessor. In a system with symmetric multiprocessing, all processors are of equal priority and each processor is given access to the common bus in sequence. Symmetric multiprocessing is used on PCs and the Pentium family implements mechanisms to support symmetric multiprocessing. However, it is not a scalable technology and the symmetric multiprocessors are limited to about eight processors.

The ring topology

The ring topology of Fig. 8.30 is arranged so that each processor is connected only to its two nearest neighbors. One neighbor is called the upstream neighbor and the other the downstream neighbor. A processor receives information from its downstream neighbor and passes it on to its upstream neighbor. In this way, information flows round the ring in one direction only and a packet of information passes through each of the processors in the ring. The information

passed to a processor contains a destination address. When a processor receives a packet, it checks the address and, if the packet address corresponds to the processor's own address, the processor reads the packet. Similarly, a processor is able to add packets of its own to the stream of information flowing round the ring.

The ring topology offers certain advantages for some classes of loosely coupled multiprocessor networks and represents one of the most popular forms of local area network. It is less widely used as a method of interconnecting processors in a tightly-coupled MIMD architecture. A ring network is vulnerable to a break in the ring. Some systems employ a double ring that does not fail if one of the rings fails.

The star topology

The star topology of Fig. 8.31 employs a central processor as a switching network, rather like a telephone exchange, between the other processors that are arranged logically (if not physically) around the central node. The advantage of the star is that it reduces bus contention, as there are no shared communication paths, moreover, the star does not require the large number of buses needed by unconstrained topologies.

On the other hand, the star network is only as good as its central node. If this node fails, the entire system fails. Consequently, the star topology does not display any form of graceful degradation. The central network must be faster than the nodes using its switching facilities if the system is to be efficient. In many ways, both the ring and the star topologies is are better suited to local area networks, where the individual signal paths are implemented by serial data channels, rather than by the parallel buses of the tightly-coupled multiprocessor.

The hypercube topology

An *n*-dimensional hypercube multiprocessor connects $N = 2^n$ processors in the form of an *n*-dimensional binary cube. Each corner (vertex or node) of the hypercube consists of a processing element and its associated memory. Because of the topology of a hypercube, each node is directly

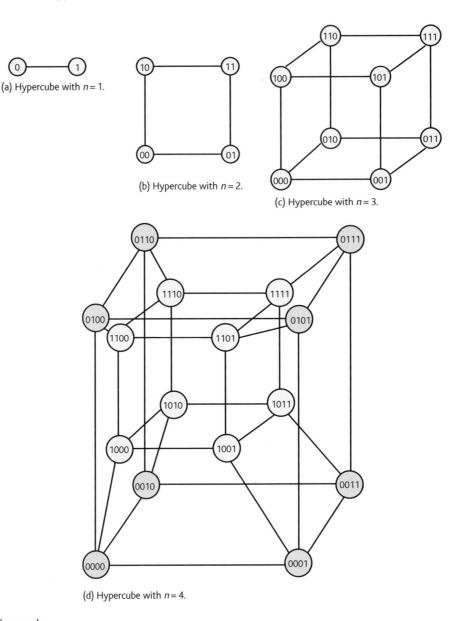

(a) Hypercube with $n = 1$.

(b) Hypercube with $n = 2$.

(c) Hypercube with $n = 3$.

(d) Hypercube with $n = 4$.

Figure 8.32 The hypercube.

connected to exactly n other neighbors. Figure 8.32 illustrates the hypercube for $n = 1, 2, 3$, and 4.

Each processor in a hypercube has an n-bit address in the range $0\ldots00$ to $1\ldots11$ (i.e. 0 to $2^n - 1$) and has n nearest neighbors with an address that differs from the node's address by only 1 bit. If $n = 4$ and a node has an address 0100, its four nearest neighbors have addresses 1100, 0000, 0110, and 0101.

A hypercube of dimension n is constructed recursively by taking a hypercube of dimension $n - 1$, prefixing all its node addresses by 0, and adding to this another hypercube of dimension $n - 1$ whose node addresses are all prefixed by 1. In other words, a hypercube of dimension n can be subdivided

into two hypercubes of dimension $n-1$, and these two subcubes can, in turn, be divided into four subcube of dimension $n-2$ and so on.

The hypercube is of interest because is has a topology that makes it relatively easy to map certain groups of algorithm onto the hypercube. In particular, the hypercube is well suited to problems involving the evaluation of fast Fourier transforms (FFTs)—used in sound and video signal processing. The first practical hypercube multiprocessor was built at Caltech in 1983. This was called the Cosmic Cube and was based on 64 8086 microprocessors plus 8087 floating point coprocessors.

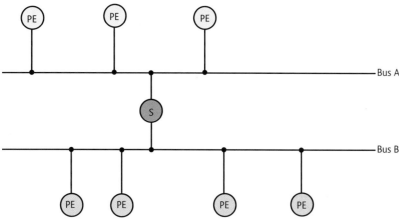

(a) Twin-bus multiprocessor with a switch between buses.

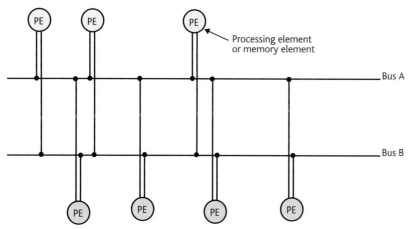

(b) Twin-bus multiprocessor with dual bus access from each processor.

Figure 8.33 The dual-bus multiprocessor.

Hybrid topologies

In addition to the above pure network topologies, there are very many hybrid topologies, some of which are described in Fig. 8.33 to 8.36. Figure 8.33(a) and (b) both illustrate the dual-bus multiprocessor, although this topology may be extended to include any number of buses. In Fig. 8.33(a) the processors are split into two groups, with one group connected to bus A and one connected to bus B. A switching unit connects bus A to bus B and therefore allows a processor on one bus to communicate with a processor on the other. The advantage of the dual-bus topology is that the probability of bus contention is reduced, because both buses can be operated in parallel (i.e. simultaneously). Only when a processor connected to one bus needs to transfer data to a processor on the other does the topology become equal to a single-bus topology.

The arrangement of Fig. 8.33(b) also employs two buses, but here each processor is connected directly to both buses via suitable switches. Two communication paths always exist between any pair of processors, one using bus A and one using bus B. Although the provision of two buses reduces the bottleneck associated with a single bus, it requires more connections between the processors and the two buses and more complex hardware is needed to determine which bus a processor is to use at any time.

The crossbar network

Another possible topology, described in Fig. 8.34, is the so-called *crossbar switching architecture*, which has its origin in the telephone exchange where it is employed to link subscribers to each other.

The processors are arranged as a single column (processors P_{c1} to P_{cm}) and a single row (processors P_{r1} to P_{rn}). That is, there are a total of $m + n$ processors. Note that the processors may be processing elements or just simple memory elements. Each processor in a column is connected to a horizontal bus and each processor in a row is connected to a vertical bus. A switching network, $S_{r,c}$, connects the processor on row r to

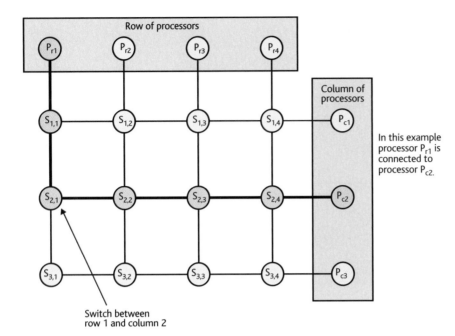

Figure 8.34 The crossbar switching network.

In this example processor P_{r1} is connected to processor P_{c2}.

the processor on column c. This arrangement requires $m + n$ switching networks for the $m + n$ processors.

The advantage of the crossbar matrix is the speed at which the interconnection between two processors can be set up. Furthermore, it can be made highly reliable by providing alternative connections between nodes, should one of the switch points fail. Reliability is guaranteed only if the switches are failsafe and always fail in the off or no-connection position.

If the switches at the crosspoints are made multiway (vertical to vertical, horizontal to horizontal or horizontal, to vertical), we can construct a number of simultaneous pathways through the matrix. The provision of multiple pathways considerably increases the bandwidth of the system.

In practice, the crossbar matrix is not widely found in general-purpose systems, because of its high complexity. Another penalty associated with this arrangement is its limited expandability. If we wish to increase the power of the system by adding an extra processor, we must also add another bus, together with its associated switching units.

The binary tree

An interesting form of multiprocessor topology is illustrated in Fig. 8.35. For obvious reasons this structure is called a *binary tree*, although I am not certain whether it is really a special case of the unconstrained topology of Fig. 8.26, or a trivial case of the star topology (using three processors), repeatedly iterated! Any two processors (nodes) in the tree communicate with each other by traversing the tree right to left until a processor common to both nodes is found, and then traversing the tree left to right. For example, Fig. 8.35

shows how processor P_{0110} communicates with processor P_{0100}, by establishing backward links from P_{0110} to P_{01} and then forward links from P_{01} to P_{010} to P_{0100}.

The topology of the binary tree has the facility to set up multiple simultaneous links (depending on the nature of each of the links), because the whole tree is never needed to link any two points. In practice, a real system would implement additional pathways to relieve potential bottlenecks and to guard against the effects of failure at certain switching points. The failure of a switch in a right-hand column, for example, P_{0010}, causes the loss of a single processor, whereas the failure of a link at the left-hand side, for example, P_0, immediately removes half the available processors from the system.

Cluster topology

Figure 8.36 illustrates the cluster topology, which is a hybrid star–bus structure. The importance of this structure lies in its application in highly reliable systems. Groups of processors and their local memory modules are arranged in the form of a cluster. Figure 8.36 shows three processors per cluster in an arrangement called triple modular redundancy. The output of each of the three processors is compared with the output of the other two processors in a voting network. The output of the voting circuit (or majority logic circuit) is taken as two out of three of its inputs, on the basis that the failure of a single module is more likely than the simultaneous failure of two modules.

The design of a clustered triple modular redundancy system is not as easy as might be first thought. One of the major problems associated with modular redundancy arises

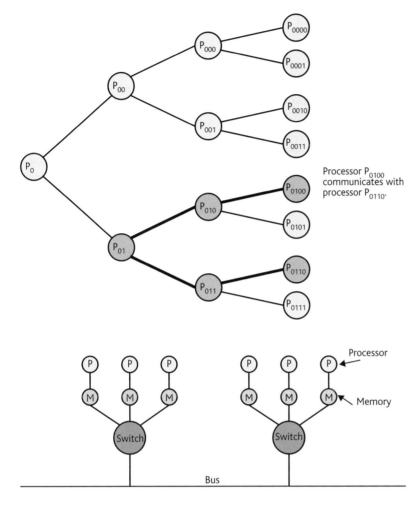

Processor P_{0100} communicates with processor P_{0110}.

Figure 8.35 The binary tree topology

Processor

Memory

Bus

Figure 8.36 The cluster topology.

from a phenomenon called divergence. Suppose that three identical processors have identical hardware and software and that they receive identical inputs and start with the same initial conditions at the same time; therefore, unless one processor fails, their outputs are identical, as all elements of the system are identical.

In actual fact, the above statement is not entirely true. In order to create truly redundant systems, each of the three processors in a cluster must have its own independent clock and I/O channels. Therefore, events taking place externally will not be seen by each processor at exactly the same time. If these events lead to conditional branches, the operation of a processor in the cluster may diverge from that of its neighbors quite considerably after even a short period of operation. In such circumstances, it becomes very difficult to tell whether the processors are suffering from divergence or whether one of them has failed.

The problem of divergence can be eliminated by providing synchronizing mechanisms between the processors and by comparing their outputs only when they all wish to access the system bus for the same purpose. Once more it can be seen

that, although the principles behind the design of multiprocessor systems are relatively straightforward, their detailed practical design is very complex due to a considerable degree of interaction between hardware and software. As we have already pointed out, topologies for multiprocessor systems are legion.

Coupling

Up to now we have been looking at the topology of multiprocessor systems with little or no consideration of the nuts and bolts of the actual connections between the processors. Possibly more than any other factor, the required degree of coupling between processors in a multiprocessor system determines how the processors are to be linked. A tightly coupled multiprocessor system passes data between processors either by means of shared memory or by allowing one processor to access the other processor's data, address, and control buses directly. When shared memory, sometimes called dual-port RAM, is employed to couple processors, a block of read/write memory is arranged to be common to both processors. One processor writes data to the block and the other reads that data. Data can be transferred as fast as each processor can execute a memory access.

The degree of coupling between processors is expressed in terms of two parameters: the transmission *bandwidth* and the *latency* of the interprocessor link. The transmission bandwidth is defined as the rate at which data is moved between processors and is expressed in bits/s. For example, if a microprocessor writes a byte of data to an 8-bit parallel port every 1 μs, the bandwidth of the link is 8 bits/1 μs or 8 Mbits/s. However, if a 32-bit port is used to move words at the same rate, the bandwidth rises to 32 Mbits/s.

The latency of an interprocessor link is defined as the time required to initiate a data transfer. That is, latency is the time that elapses between a processor requesting a data transfer and the time at which the transfer actually takes place. A high degree of coupling is associated with large transmission bandwidths and low latencies. As might be expected, tightly coupled microprocessor systems need more complex hardware than loosely coupled systems.

SUMMARY

It's taken a concerted attempt to make computers run as fast as they do today. This chapter has demonstrated three ways in which the performance of the computer has been enhanced over the years. We have concentrated on three aspects of computer acceleration: pipelining to improve the throughput of the CPU, cache memory to reduce the effective access time of the memory system, and increased parallelism to improve performance without modifying the instruction set architecture.

The movement towards RISC processors in the 1980s was driven by a desire to exploit instruction level parallelism by overlapping, or *pipelining*, the execution of instructions. We have seen how pipelining can be very effective with an *n*-stage pipeline providing an *n*-fold increase in performance—in theory. In practice, the ultimate performance of pipelined architectures is degraded by the branch penalty and data dependency. Instructions that alter the flow of control (branches, subroutine calls, and returns) throw away the instructions that are already in the pipeline.

The second part of this chapter introduced the cache memory, which can radically improve the performance of a computer system for relatively little cost. Cache memory uses a small amount of high-speed memory to hold frequently used data. Cache memory is effective because most programs may have large program or data sets but, for 80% of the time, they access only 20% of the data. We looked at how the performance of cache memory can be calculated and how cache memory is organized. We described the three forms of cache organization: directly mapped, associative, and set associative. Direct-mapped cache is easy to design but is limited by its restriction on what data can be stored. Associative memory provides the optimum performance in theory but is impossible to construct and you have to implement an algorithm to replace old data once the cache is full. Set associative cache is only slightly more complex

than direct-mapped cache and achieves a performance close to associative cache.

The final part of this chapter introduced the multiprocessor, which uses two or more computers operating in parallel to improve performance. The speedup ratio of a parallel processor (i.e. multiprocessor) is the ratio of the time taken by one processor to solve a task to the time taken by *p* processors to solve the same task. Ideally the speedup factor is *p*. However, Amdahl's law states that the speedup ratio in a multiprocessor system with *p* processors is given by $p/(1 + (p - 1)f)$, where *f* is the fraction of the code that is executed serially.

We introduced the topology of multiprocessor systems, which describes the way the individual processors are interconnected. Multiprocessor topologies like the hypercube, the crossbar switching network, and the binary tree are well suited for solving particular classes of problem. However, a class of problem that is well suited to one type of topology may be ill suited to a different type of topology.

PROBLEMS

8.1 The power of computers is often quoted in *MIPS* and *megaflops*. Some computer scientists believe that such figures of merit are, at best, misleading and, at worst, downright dishonest. Why?

Why can't you compare two different processors on the basis of their clock speeds? Surely, a processor with a 4 GHz clock is twice as fast as a processor with a 2 GHz clock.

8.2 What are the characteristics of a CISC processor?

8.3 The most frequently executed class of instruction is the data move instruction. Why is this? What are the implications for computer design?

8.4 The 68020 microprocessor has a BFFFO (bit field find first one) bit-field instruction. This instruction scans a string of up to 32 bits at any point in memory (i.e. the string does not have to start on any 8-bit boundary) and returns the location of the first bit set to 1 in the instruction. For example, BFFFO (A0){D1:D2},D0 takes the byte at the address pointed at by address register A0 and locates the start of the bit string at the number of bits in D1 away from the most-significant bit at this address. The string, whose length is in register D2, is scanned and the location of the first 1 is deposited in D0 (this is a simplified description of the BFFFO instruction).

In order to demonstrate the complexity of a BFFFO instruction, write the equivalent 68K assembly language code to implement BFFFO (A0){D1:D2},D0.

8.5 The Berkeley RISC has a 32-bit architecture and yet provides only a 13-bit literal. Why is this and does it really matter?

8.6 What are the advantages and disadvantages of register windowing?

8.7 Some RISC processors with 32 registers, r0 to r31, force register r0 to contain zero. That is, if you read the contents of r0, the value returned is always 0. Why have the designers wasted a register by making it read-only and permanently setting its content to 0?

8.8 What is *pipelining* and how does it increase the performance of a computer?

8.9 Consider the expression

$(A+1)(A+2)(A+B)(A+B+C)(A+B+C+1)$
$(A+B+C-1)(D+E)(A-B)(A-B-C)$

Assuming a simple three-operand format with instructions ADD, SUB, MULT, and DIV (and that all data is in registers), write the assembly language code to implement this expression with the minimum data dependency (assuming that dependency extends to the next instruction only).

8.10 The code of a computer is examined and it is found that, on average, for 70% of the time the runlength between instructions that change the flow of control is 15 instructions. For the remainder of the time, the runlength is 6 instructions. Other cases can be neglected.
This computer has a five-stage pipeline and no special techniques are used to handle branches.
What is the speedup ratio of this computer?

8.11 A pipeline is defined by its length (i.e. the number of stages that can operate in parallel). A pipeline can be short or long. What do you think are the relative advantages of long and short pipelines?

8.12 What is *data dependency* in a pipelined system and how can its effects be overcome?

8.13 RISC architectures don't permit operations on operands in memory other than load and store operations. Why?

8.14 The average number of cycles required by a RISC to execute an instruction is given by

$$T_{ave} = 1 + p_b p_t b = p_e b$$

where
the probability that a given instruction is a branch is p_b
the probability that a branch instruction will be taken is p_t
if a branch is taken, the additional penalty is b cycles
if a branch is not taken, there is no penalty
p_e is the effective probability of a branch $(p_b.p_t)$
The *efficiency* of a pipelined computer is defined as the average number of cycles per instruction without branches divided by the average number of instructions with branches. This is given by $1/T_{ave}$.
Draw a series of graphs of the average number of cycles per instruction as a function of p_e for $b = 1, 2, 3,$ and 4. The horizontal axis is the effective probability of a branch instruction and ranges from 0 to 1.

8.15 What is *branch prediction* and how can it be used to reduce the so-called branch penalty in a pipelined system?

8.16 A computer has main memory with an access time of 60 ns and cache memory with an access time of 15 ns. If the average hit ratio is 92%, what is the maximum theoretical speedup ratio?

8.17 A computer has main memory with an access time of 60 ns and cache memory with an access time of 15 ns. The computer has a 50 Mhz clock and all operations require at least two clock cycles. If the hit ratio is 92%, what is the theoretical speedup ratio for this system?

8.18 A computer has main memory with an access time of 60 ns and cache memory with an access time of 15 ns. The computer has a 50 Mhz clock and all operations require two clock cycles. On average the computer spends 40% of its time accessing memory and 60% performing internal operations (an internal operation is a non-memory access). If the hit ratio is 92%, what is the speedup ratio for this system?

8.19 What is the fundamental limitation of a direct-mapped cache?

8.20 How can the performance of a direct-mapped cache memory be improved?

8.21 A computer has main memory with an access time of 50 ns and cache memory with an access time of 10 ns. The cache has a line size of 16 bytes and the computer's memory bus is 32 bits wide. The cache controller operates in a burst mode and can transfer 32 bytes between cache and main memory in 80 ns. Whenever a miss occurs the cache must be reloaded with a line. If the average hit ratio is 90%, what is the speedup ratio?

8.22 What is *cache coherency* and why is it important only in sophisticated systems?

8.23 What are the similarities and differences between memory cache and so-called disk cache?

8.24 For the following ideal systems, calculate the hit ratio (*h*) required to achieve the stated speedup ratio *S*.

(a) $t_m = 60$ ns $t_c = 10$ ns $S = 1.1$
(b) $t_m = 60$ ns $t_c = 10$ ns $S = 1.5$
(c) $t_m = 60$ ns $t_c = 10$ ns $S = 3.0$
(d) $t_m = 60$ ns $t_c = 10$ ns $S = 4.0$

8.25 Draw a graph of the speedup ratio for an ideal system for $k = 0.5, k = 0.2, k = 0.1$ (plot the three lines on the same graph). The value of k defines the ratio of cache to main store access times (t_c/t_m).

8.26 What is the meaning of speedup ratio and efficiency in the context of multiprocessor systems?

8.27 In a multiprocessor with p processors, the ideal speedup factor is p and the efficiency is 1. In practice, both of these ideal values are not achieved. Why?

8.28 What is Amdahl's law and why is it so important? Is it the same as 'the law of diminishing returns'?

8.29 If a system has 128 processors and the fraction of code that must be carried out serially is 0.1, what is the speedup ratio of the system?

8.30 A computer system has 32 microprocessors and the fraction of code that is carried out serially is 5%. Suppose you wish to run the same code on a system with 24 processors. What fraction of the code may be executed serially to maintain the same speedup ratio?

8.31 In the context of a multiprocessor system, define the meaning of the following terms.

    (a) Topology

    (b) Deadlock

    (c) Tightly coupled

    (d) Arbitration

    (e) Latency

8.32 What are the relative advantages and disadvantages of the unconstrained topology, the bus, and the ring multiprocessor topologies?

8.33 A *fully connected* multiprocessor topology is one in which each of the p processors is connected directly to each of the other processors. Show that the number of connections between processors is given by $p(p-1)/2$.

Processor architectures

9

CHAPTER MAP

INTRODUCTION

When we introduced the CPU and assembly language programming, we were forced to limit the discussion to one processor to avoid confusing readers by presenting a range of different processor architectures. Because students should at least appreciate some of the differences between architectures, we now look at two variations on the von Neumann architecture. We begin with the *microcontroller,* which is a descendant of the first-generation 8-bit microprocessor. Our aim is only to provide students with an idea of how the instruction set of a microcontroller differs from that of more sophisticated architectures like the 68K.

The second processor to be introduced here is the ARM, a high-performance RISC processor. This device has a 32-bit architecture with the characteristics of traditional RISC processors like MIPS but which has some very interesting architectural facilities. We look at the ARM in greater detail than the microcontroller and provide development tools on the disk accompanying this text.

This chapter is not essential reading in for all computer architecture courses—but it is worth skimming though just to appreciate some of the architectural differences between processors.

9.1 Instruction set architectures and their resources

All mainstream computer architectures have remarkably similar architectures. Differences between families are often a matter of detail rather than substance. Before we look at competing families, we list some of the differences between processors.

9.1.1 Register sets

Microprocessors use registers to hold temporary data. The more registers you have, the less you need to access slower external memory. More registers require more silicon to implement them and more bits to specify them in an instruction. Consequently, early microprocessors had very few registers. Modern processors such as Intel's Itanium have

---

WHY DO WE HAVE DIFFERENT PROCESSOR FAMILIES?

Life would be simpler if there were only one microprocessor. All software would be compatible across all platforms and manufacturers would compete on price and performance rather than the architecture itself.

Different professor families exist for various reasons. First, competing companies working independently of each other developed the microprocessor. Trade secrets and product confidentiality guaranteed that processors from, for example, Intel, Motorola, and TI would be different. Developments in technology also help create diversity. First-generation

processors were 8-bit machines because it was not economically feasible to create 16- and 32-bit processors in the 1970s. Technological progress forced companies to jump from 8-bit processors to 16-bit processors. Some companies moved from register-to-memory architectures to register-to-register architectures to exploit developments in computer organization such as pipelining. Finally, economics required that some processors be cheap and cheerful whereas others could command premium prices because of their power.

---

large register sets (the Itanium has 128 general-purpose 64-bit registers).

Processors with few registers use special instructions to indicate the register such as LDX or LDY to specify load the X or Y register. Processors with many registers number their registers sequentially and implement instructions such as ADD **R1**, R2, R3.

9.1.2 Instruction formats

We have already seen that computer architectures can be specified by the number of operands used by the instruction; for example,

or more of the operands must be a register; that is, memory-to-memory operations are not generally permitted.

The three-address format is used by RISC processors such as MIPS, the PowerPC, and the ARM. Real processors require three register addresses. Typically, the only memory accesses permitted by RISC processors are load and store.

9.1.3 Instruction types

The instruction sets of most computers are very similar. All processors have arithmetic, logical, shift, data transfer, data movement, and program flow control instructions. Some processors have a richer instruction set than others; for

Format	Typical operation	Description
Zero address	ADD	Pull the top two words off the stack, add them, and push the result.
One address	ADD P	Add the contents of memory location P to the accumulator
Two address	ADD **R1**, P	Add the contents of memory location P to register R1
Three address	ADD **R1**, R2, R3	Add the contents of register R2 to register R3 and put the result in register R1

The zero address format doesn't require operand addresses because operations are applied to the element or elements at the top of the stack. This format is used only by some calculators designed for arithmetic operations and some experimental processors; for example, performing the operation $(Y + Z) \cdot X$ might be implemented by the following hypothetical code

example, a processor may not include a multiplication instruction, which means that you have to write a routine to perform multiplication by shifting and adding.

Some processors have instructions that are not necessary; for example, one processor might implement CLR **D0** to load the contents of D0 with 0, whereas another processor may require you to write MOVE #0, **D0** or SUB D0, **D0** to do the same thing.

```
Push X    Save X on the stack
Push Y    Save Y on the stack (stack = Y, X)
Push Z    Save Z on the stack (stack = Z, Y, X)
ADD       Pull top two elements Z and Y, add them, and push the result Y+Z (stack = Y+Z, X)
MUL       Pull top two elements Y+Z and X, multiply them and push the result (Y+Z) · X.
```

The one-address format was adopted by first-generation processors and is still used by microcontrollers.

The two-address instruction format is used by the mainstream CISC processors such as the 68K or the Pentium. This is often called a 'one-and-a-half-address' format because one

The trend to complex instruction sets in the 1980s led to instructions such as the 68020's BFFFO which scans a sequence of bits and returns the location first bit that was set to 1. Such complex instructions appeared to be dying out with the advent of the high-speed, streamlined RISC architectures of the 1980s.

MICROCONTROLLER FAMILIES

High-performance microcomputers are like jet aircraft; their development costs are so high that there are relatively few different varieties. The same is not true of microcontrollers and there are more members of microcontroller families than varieties of salad dressing. Because microcontrollers are a very-low-cost circuit element, they have been optimized for very specific applications. You can select a particular version of a microcontroller family with the RAM, ROM, and I/O you require for your application.

The generic Motorola microcontroller families are as follows.

6800 This was the original 8-bit Motorola microprocessor. The 6800 is not a microcontroller because it lacks internal memory and peripherals.

6805 Motorola's 6805 was their first microcomputer with an architecture very similar to the 6800. It was initially aimed at the automobile market.

68HC11 The 68HC11 is one of the best-selling microcontrollers of all time. It has a 6800-like architecture but includes ROM, RAM, and peripherals.

68HC12 The 68HC12 is an extension of the 68HC11. It has more instructions, enhanced addressing modes and some 16-bit capabilities.

68HC16 The 68HC16 has a 16-bit architecture and is an enhanced 68HC12 rather than a new architecture.

In recent years, the trend towards simplicity has reversed with the advent of the so-called SIMD (single instruction, multiple data) instruction. Such an instruction acts on *multiple* data elements at the same time; for example, a 64-bit register may contain eight 8-bit bytes that can be added in parallel to another eight bytes at the same time. These instructions are used widely in multimedia applications where large numbers of data elements representing sound or video are processed (e.g. Intel's MMX extensions).

9.1.4 Addressing modes

An important element of an instruction set is the addressing mode used to access operands. First-generation microprocessors used absolute addressing, literal addressing, and indexed (register indirect) addressing. The generation of 16- and 32-bit CISC processors widened addressing, modes by providing a richer set of indexed addressing modes; for example, the 68K provided autoincrementing with (A0)+, and double indexing with a literal displacement with 12(A0,D0).

9.1.5 On-chip peripherals

Microprocessor families also differ in terms of the facilities they offer. The processor intended for use in workstations or high-end PCs is optimized for performance. Peripherals such as I/O ports and timers are located on the motherboard.

A microcontroller intended of use in an automobile, cell phone, domestic appliance, or toy is a one-chip device that contains a wealth of peripherals as well as the CPU itself. For example, a microcontroller may contain an 8-bit CPU, random access memory, user-programmable read-only memory, read/write RAM, several timers, parallel and serial I/O devices, and even analog-to-digital converters. The microcontroller can be used to implement a complete computer system costing less than a dollar.

We look at two processors. We begin with the 68HC12 microcontroller to demonstrate what an embedded controller looks like. Then we introduce the ARM, a RISC processor with a simple instruction set and some interesting architectural features.

9.2 The microcontroller

One of the first major competitors to Intel's 8080 8-bit microprocessor was the Motorola 6800, which has a significantly simpler register model than the 8080. The 6800 has a single 8-bit accumulator and 16-bit index register, which limits its performance because you have to load the accumulator, perform a data operation, and then store the result before you can reuse the accumulator.

First-generation microprocessors had 16-bit program counters that supported only 64 kbytes of directly addressable memory. Although 64 kbytes is tiny by today's standard's, in the mid-1970s 64 kbytes was considered as positively gigantic.

Motorola later introduced the 6809, an architecturally advanced 8-bit processor, to overcome the deficiencies of the 6800. Unfortunately, the 6809 appeared just as the 68K was about to enter the market; few wanted a super 8-bit processor when they could have a 16- or 32-bit device.[1]

Motorola created a range of microcontrollers aimed at the low-cost high-volume industrial microcontroller market. We are going to describe the architecture of the popular 8-bit

---

[1] 'Better late than never'. No way! Motorola seems to have been very unlucky. The high-performance 68K with a true 32-bit architecture lost out to Intel's 16-bit 8086 when IBM adopted the Intel architecture because IBM couldn't wait for the 68K. Similarly, the 6809 appeared just as the world of high-performance computing was moving from 8 bits to 16/32 bits.

M68HC12, which is object code compatible with Motorola's 8-bit MC68HC11 but with more sophisticated addressing modes and 16-bit arithmetic capabilities.

Before we look at microcontroller register sets, we will say a few words about one of the differences between the Intel-style processors and Motorola-style processors. The bits of an instruction are precious, because we wish to cram as many different instructions into an 8-bit instruction set as possible. Intel processors reduce the number of bits required to specify a register by using dedicated registers. For example, if arithmetic operations can be applied only to one accumulator, it's not necessary to devote op-code bits to specifying the register. On the other hand, this philosophy makes life difficult for programmers who have to remember what operations can be applied to what registers. Moreover, programmers with limited registers have to spend a lot of time moving data between registers.

Motorola-style processors employed fewer specialized registers than Intel-style processors. This approach reduced the number of different instructions, because more bits have to be devoted to specifying which register is to take part in an operation. Equally, it makes it easier to write assembly language code.

9.2.1 The M68HC12

In this chapter we are interested in the instruction set architecture of microprocessors. The MC68HC12 microcontroller family provides an interesting contrast with the 68K because of its simplicity and its similarity to first-generation 8-bit microprocessors. We are not able to discuss the microprocessor's most important features—its on-chip peripherals that let you implement a complete computer in one single chip. Figure 9.1 provides an indication of the

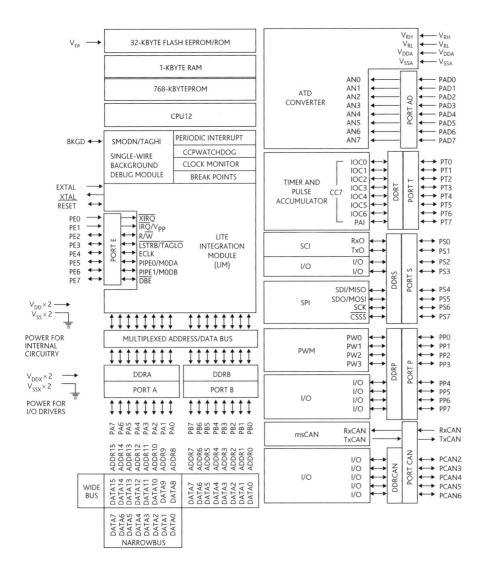

Figure 9.1 The MC68HC12 structure.

WHAT'S IN A NAME? PART I

You access *variable* locations in memory by means of a *pointer-based* addressing mode. The register that supplies the address of an operand was called a *modifier register*. Some microprocessors call these registers *index register*, the term used by Motorola in its microcontroller literature.

The 68K family provides eight 32-bit pointer registers called *address registers*, although their function is identical to that of index registers. The 68k family has an addressing mode that uses the sum of two pointer registers to provide an effective address; for example, MOVE (A0, D2), **D7**. Motorola calls this addressing mode *Indexed addressing*.

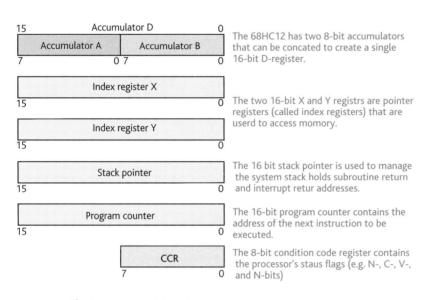

number of accesses the M68HC12 has to make to the main store. The two 8-bit accumulators, A and B, can be concatenated to create a single 16-bit data accumulator D, where $D_{(0:7)} = A$, $D_{(8:15)} = B$. Because the D register can take part in 16-bit operations (albeit to limited extent), it can be used for some of the applications that would normally require a 16-bit pointer register (e.g. X, Y, SP).

We've covered sufficient computer architecture and assembly language to write a simple program in M68HC12 code that you can follow with little difficult. In what follows, A and B are 8-bit registers and X is a 16-bit pointer. The following are some M68HC12 instructions.

Figure 9.2 The M68HC12 register set.

Assembly form	Description in words	RTL description
LDX #P	Load X register with a literal	[X] ← P
STX P	Store X register in P	[P] ← [X]
LDAB P	Load B register	[B] ← [P]
LDAA 0,X	Load A register indexed	[A] ← [[X]]
INX	Increment X register by 1	[X] ←[X] + 1
STAA 0,X	Store A register indexed	[[X]] ← [A]
DECB	Decrement B register	[B] ← [B] − 1
BNE P	Branch on not zero	IF [Z]=1 [PC] ← [PC] + P

MC68HC12's capabilities. The microcontroller contains both read–write memory for scratchpad storage and flash EPROM to hold programs and fixed data. There is a wealth of input and output ports, serial interfaces, and counter timers. Such a chip can be used to control a small system (e.g. a digital camera or a cell phone) with very little additional hardware.

Figure 9.2 illustrates a user register model of the M68HC12 microcomputer family. Unlike the first 8-bit processors, it has two general-purpose 8-bit accumulators A and B. The inclusion of a second accumulator reduces the

Note how the 8-bit mnemonic combines the operation and the operand; for example, INX increments the X register and INCA and INCB increment the A and B accumulators. The M68HC12 uses load and store mnemonics to move data between memory and registers, rather than the 68K's more generic MOVE instruction; for example, LDX and STX load and store data in the X register.

Eight-bit code uses variable-length instructions. Common operations like INCA are encoded as a single byte. The equivalent operation, ADDA #1, takes two bytes—one for the op-code and one for the literal.

WHAT'S IN A NAME? PART II

Modern RISC processors and the 68K family have lots of internal registers that use sequential alpha-numeric names such as D0–D7, A0–A7, and R0–R31.

Microcontrollers have few general-purpose registers and use special names; for example, the A and B accumulators or the X and Y index registers. The operation load accumulator A might be written LDAA and load accumulator B might be written LDAB.

Operations such as increment and decrement are implemented by the 68K as additions and subtractions by ADD #1, **D0** or SUB #4, **A2**. Microcontrollers avoid an explicit literal by using increment and decrement; for example, INX increments the contents of the M68HC12's X index register. Typical M68HC2 mnemonics that apply to a specific register are

INX	increment X register		INY	increment Y register
DEX	decrement X register		DEY	decrement Y register
LDX	load X register		LDY	load Y register
STX	store X register		STY	store Y register
LDS	load stack pointer		STS	store stack pointer
TXS	transfer X register to stack pointer		TSX	transfer stack pointer to X register

---

Assembly language	RTL form	Comment
LDAA #d8	[A] ← d8	Literal addressing
LDAA EA	[A] ← [EA]	Absolute addressing
LDAA d8,X	[A] ← [[X] + d8]	Indexed addressing with an 8-bit offset
LDAA d16,X	[A] ← [[X] + d16]	Indexed addressing with a 16-bit offset
LDAA B,X	[A] ← [[X] + [B]]	Indexed addressing with a variable 8-bit offset
LDAA D,X	[A] ← [[X] + [D]]	Indexed addressing with a variable 16-bit offset
LDAA 1,−X	[X] ← [X]−1; [A] ← [[X]]	Indexed addressing with predecrement
LDAA 1,X−	[A] ← [[X]]; [X] ← [X]−1	Indexed addressing with postdecrement
LDAA 1,+X	[X] ← [X]+1; [A] ← [[X]]]	Indexed addressing with preincrement
LDAA 1,X+	[A] ← [[X]]; [X] ← [X]+1	Indexed addressing with postincrement
LDAA [d16,X]	[A] ← [[d16 + [X]]];	Memory indirect addressing with index register and offset
LDAA [D,X]	[A] ← [[[D] + [X]]];	Memory indirect addressing with two index registers

Table 9.1 The M68HC11's indexed addressing modes (you can replace A by B and X by Y).

Consider the following fragment of M68HC12 code, which uses two pointers, the X and Y registers, to copy a string from its source to its destination.

```
TABLE1    EQU    <address of source>
TABLE2    EQU    <address of destination>
N         EQU    <number of bytes to move>
*
          LDX    #TABLE1   X points to source string [X] ← Table1
          LDY    #TABLE2   Y points to destination string.
LOOP      LDAA   0,X       Read source byte, store it in accumulator A
          STAA   0,Y       Copy accumulator A to destination
          INX              Update X pointer
          INY              Update Y pointer
          CPX    #TABLE1+N Test for end of loop
          BNE    LOOP
```

This fragment of code is not too difficult to understand. All you have to remember is that one of the operands is specified by the mnemonic (e.g. A, B, X, or Y registers).

M68HC12 addressing modes

The M68HC12 has 16-bit pointer registers and can address up to 64 kbytes of memory. Memory addressing modes are absolute (the operand is specified by a 16-bit address), literal (either an 8-bit or a 16-bit offset), and indexed. Table 9.1 illustrates the M68HC12's addressing modes.

The M68HC12's indexed addressing modes are particularly extensive. Like the 68K, indexed addressing with both a literal and a variable offset is supported. Auto-incrementing and -decrementing modes are provided; indeed both pre- and postdecrementing and pre- and postincrementing modes are supported. Note that the increment size is user selectable in the range 1 to 8.

Unusually, the MC68HC12 provides a *memory indirect* addressing mode. The operation LDDA [12, X] adds 12 to the contents of the X register to create a pointer. The memory location at that address is accessed to yield a second 16-bit pointer. This pointer is used to access the target operand. Memory indirect addressing allows you to index into a table of pointers which can be useful when implementing two-dimensional data structures.

The M68HC12 has a full complement of pointer register transfer instructions. Pointer registers can be pushed on the stack or pulled off it. The stack operation uses a 2-byte instruction, the second byte specifying the list of registers to be pulled or pushed. It is also possible to push multiple registers on the stack with one instruction.

M68HC12 instruction set

Table 9.2 lists some of the M68HC12's mnemonics and indicates the actions carried out by the instructions (note that M is a memory location). All we need here is an indication of the types of operation performed by these computers. The M68HC12 microprocessor is reasonably complete in its data movement, arithmetic, logical, shift, and branch instructions. Complex arithmetic operations such as multiply or divide except for the M68HC12's unsigned 8-bit multiply instruction are absent.

Eight-bit microprocessors offer very effective ways of manipulating character-oriented data, implementing input/output operations, and designing embedded

Operation	RTL definition	Mnemonic
Arithmetic group		
Add M to A	$[A] \leftarrow [A] + [EA]$	ADDA
Add M to A	$[B] \leftarrow [B] + [EA]$	ADDB
Add M to D	$[D] \leftarrow [D] + [EA]$	ADDD
Add B to X	$[X] \leftarrow [X] + [B]$	ABX
Add B to Y	$[Y] \leftarrow [Y] + [B]$	ABY
Add B to A	$[A] \leftarrow [A] + [B]$	ABA
Add M to A with carry	$[A] \leftarrow [A] + [EA] + [C]$	ADCA
Add M to B with carry	$[B] \leftarrow [B] + [EA] + [C]$	ADCB
Subtract M from A	$[A] \leftarrow [A] - [EA]$	SUBA
Subtract M from B	$[B] \leftarrow [B] - [EA]$	SUBB
Subtract M from D	$[D] \leftarrow [D] - [EA]$	SUBD
Subtract B from A	$[A] \leftarrow [A] - [B]$	SBA
Subtract M from A with carry	$[A] \leftarrow [A] - [EA] - [C]$	SBCA
Subtract M from B with carry	$[B] \leftarrow [B] - [EA] - [C]$	SBCB
Clear M	$[EA] \leftarrow 0$	CLR
Clear A	$[A] \leftarrow 0$	CLRA
Clear B	$[B] \leftarrow 0$	CLRB
Negate M	$[EA] \leftarrow 0 - [EA]$	NEG
Negate A	$[A] \leftarrow 0 - [A]$	NEGA
Negate B	$[B] \leftarrow 0 - [B]$	NEGB
Multiply A by B	$[D] \leftarrow [A] \times [B]$	MUL
Compare A with M	$[A] - [EA]$	CMPA
Compare B with M	$[B] - [EA]$	CMPB
Compare D with M	$[D] - [EA]$	CMPD
Compare A with B	$[A] - [B]$	CBA
Test M	$[EA] - 0$	TST
Test A	$[A] - 0$	TSTA
Test B	$[B] - 0$	TSTB
Sign extend [B] into [D]	IF $[B_7] = 1$ THEN $[A_{(0:7)}] = 11111111$ ELSE $[A_{(0:7)}] = 0$	SEX

Table 9.2 (*Continues*)

Table 9.2 (*Continued*)

Operation	RTL definition	Mnemonic
Decrement and increment group		
Decrement M	$[EA] \leftarrow [EA] - 1$	DEC
Decrement A	$[A] \leftarrow [A] - 1$	DECA
Decrement B	$[B] \leftarrow [B] - 1$	DECB
Decrement S	$[S] \leftarrow [S] - 1$	DES
Decrement X	$[X] \leftarrow [X] - 1$	DEX
Decrement Y	$[Y] \leftarrow [Y] - 1$	DEY
Increment M	$[EA] \leftarrow [EA] + 1$	INC
Increment A	$[A] \leftarrow [A] + 1$	INCA
Increment B	$[B] \leftarrow [B] + 1$	INCB
Increment S	$[S] \leftarrow [S] + 1$	INS
Increment X	$[X] \leftarrow [X] + 1$	INX
Increment Y	$[Y] \leftarrow [Y] + 1$	INY
Logical group		
Bit A with M	$[A].[EA]$	BITA
Bit B with M	$[B].[EA]$	BITB
AND A with M	$[A] \leftarrow [A].[EA]$	ANDA
AND B with M	$[B] \leftarrow [B].[EA]$	ANDB
Complement M	$[EA] \leftarrow [\overline{EA}]$	COM
Complement A	$[A] \leftarrow [\overline{A}]$	COMA
Complement B	$[B] \leftarrow [\overline{B}]$	COMB
EOR A with M	$[A] \leftarrow [A] \oplus [EA]$	EORA
EOR B with M	$[B] \leftarrow [B] \oplus [EA]$	EORB
OR A with M	$[A] \leftarrow [A] + [EA]$	ORAA
OR B with M	$[B] \leftarrow [B] + [EA]$	ORAB
Shift and rotate group		
Arithmetic shift M left		ASL
Arithmetic shift A left		ASLA
Arithmetic shift B left		ASLB
Arithmetic shift M right		ASR
Arithmetic shift A right		ASRA
Arithmetic shift B right		ASRB
Logical shift M left		LSL
Logical shift A left		LSLA
Logical shift B left		LSLB
Logical shift M right		LSR
Logical shift A right		LSRA
Logical shift B right		LSRB
Rotate M left		ROL
Rotate A left		ROLA
Rotate B left		ROLB
Rotate M right		ROR
Rotate A right		RORA
Rotate B right		RORB

Table 9.2 (*Continued*)

Operation	RTL definition	Mnemonic
Data movement group		
Exchange register pair	`[Ri] ← [Rj]; [Rj] ← [Ri]`	EXG
Load A with M	`[A] ← [EA]`	LDA
Load B with M	`[B] ← [EA]`	LDB
Load D with M	`[D] ← [EA]`	LDD
Store A in M	`[EA] ← [A]`	STA
Store B in M	`[EA] ← [B]`	STB
Store D in M	`[EA] ← [D]`	STD
Transfer reg j to reg i	`[Ri] ← [Rj]`	TFR
Transfer B to A	`[A] ← [B]`	TAB
Transfer A to B	`[B] ← [A]`	TBA
Push A on system stack	`[SP] ← [SP]−1;[[SP]] ← [A]`	PSHSA
Push B on system stack	`[SP] ← [SP]−1;[[SP]] ← [B]`	PSHSB
Push register list on system stack		PSHS
Push register list on user stack		PSHU
Pull A off system stack	`[A] ← [[SP]];[SP] ← [SP]+1`	PULSA
Pull B off system stack	`[B] ← [[SP]];[SP] ← [SP]+1`	PULSB
Pull register list off system stack		PULS
Pull register list off user stack		PULU
Branch group		
Branch on equal	`IF [Z]= 0 THEN [PC]←[PC]+ T`	BEQ
Branch on not equal	`IF [Z]= 1 THEN [PC]←[PC]+ T`	BNE
Branch unconditionally	`[PC] ← [PC] + address`	BRA
Branch to subroutine	`[SP] ← [SP]−2;`	
	`[[SP]] ← [PC];`	
	`[PC] ← [PC]+d8`	BSR
Jump	`[PC] ← address`	JMP
Jump to subroutine	`[SP] ← [SP]−2;`	
	`[[SP]] ← [PC];`	
	`[PC] ← address`	JSR
Return from interrupt		RTI
Return from subroutine	`[PC] ← [[SP]]; [SP] ← [SP]+2`	RTS
Pointer register load, store, and manipulation group		
Add A to X	`[X] ← [X] + [A]`	ABX
Decrement X	`[X] ← [X] − 1`	DEY
Decrement stack pointer	`[S] ← [S] − 1`	DES
Increment Y	`[X] ← [X] + 1`	INX
Increment X	`[Y] ← [Y] + 1`	INY
Increment stack pointer	`[S] ← [S] + 1`	INS
Load X with M	`[X] ← [EA]`	LDX
Load Y with M	`[Y] ← [EA]`	LDY
Load stack pointer with M	`[SP] ← [EA]`	LDS
Load user SP with M	`[U] ← [EA]`	LDU
Store X in M	`[EA] ← [X]`	STX
Store Y in M	`[EA] ← [Y]`	STY

Table 9.2 (*Continued*)

Operation	RTL definition	Mnemonic
Store stack pointer in M	[EA] ← [S]	STS
Store user SP in M	[EA] ← [U]	STU
Transfer SP to M	[X] ← [S]	TSX
Transfer X to SP	[S] ← [X]	TXS
Transfer A to X	[X] ← [A]	TAX
Transfer X to A	[A] ← [X]	TXA
Transfer A to Y	[Y] ← [A]	TAY
Transfer Y to A	[A] ← [Y]	TYA
Load X with EA	[X] ← EA	LEAX
Load Y with EA	[Y] ← EA	LEAY
Load system SP with EA	[S] ← EA	LEAS
Load user SP with EA	[U] ← EA	LEAU
Compare X with M	[X] − [EA]	CMPX
Compare Y with M	[Y] − [EA]	CMPY
Compare system SP with M	[S] − [EA]	CMPS
Compare user SP with M	[U] − [EA]	CMPU
CCR manipulation group		
Clear carry	[C] ← 0	CLC
Set carry	[C] ← 1	SEC
Clear interrupt	[I] ← 0	CLI
Set interrupt	[I] ← 1	SEI
Clear overflow	[V] ← 0	CLV
Set overflow	[V] ← 1	SEV
Set decimal mode		SED
Clear decimal mode		CLD
Transfer A to CCR	[CCR] ← [A]	TAP
Transfer CCR to A	[A] ← [CCR]	TPA
AND CCR with M	[CCR] ← [CCR] AND [EA]	ANDCC
OR CCR with M	[CCR] ← [CCR] OR [EA]	ORCC
Push CCR		PHP
Pull CCR		PLP

Table 9.2 Summary of the MC68HC12 instruction set.

controllers. They are rather less effective when asked to perform numeric operations on floating point data or when they attempt to compile programs in modern high-level languages.

The MC68HC12's instruction set is conventional with just a few special instructions intended to accelerate some applications; for example, instructions are provided to extract the maximum and minimum of two values. Consider the following example, which compares the memory location pointed at by the X register and the *unsigned* contents of the

16-bit D register and puts the larger value in the memory location or D register.

```
EMAXM 0,X    [[X]] ← max([[X]],[D])   maximum value in memory
EMAXD 0,X      [D] ← max([[X]],[D])   maximum value in D register
```

Similarly, EMIND 0, X puts the lower of the memory location and the D register in the D register.

Consider the following fragment of code, which uses the 8-bit *signed* minimum function and indexed addressing with postincrementing to find the minimum value in a four-element vector.

```
LDX  #List ;X register points to List
LDAA #$FF  ;dummy minimum in A register
MINA 1,X+  ;min(A,List1) in A
MINA 1,X+  ;min(A,List2) in A
MINA 1,X+  ;min(A,List3) in A
MINA 1,X+  ;min(A,List4) in A. We now have the smallest element
```

Sample MC68HC12 code

In many ways, MC68HC12 code is not too dissimilar to 68K code; it's just rather more verbose. The lack of on-chip registers means that you have to frequently load one of the two accumulators from memory, perform an operation, and then restore the element to memory. The following example demonstrates a program to find the maximum of a table of 20 values.

```
N       EQU    64             ; size of table

        LDAA   #0             ; clear A
        STAA   Maximum        ; set up dummy maximum value of 0
        LDX    #Table+N-1     ; X points to the end of the table
        LDAB   #N-1           ; register B is the element counter set to count down

Next    LDAA   Maximum        ; get the current largest value
        CMPA   0,X            ; compare maximum with table_i
        BLE    TstLast        ; IF new not bigger then test for end
        LDAA   0,x            ; ELSE update maximum
        STAA   Maximum
TsTLast DEX                   ; Decrement table pointer
        DBNE   B,Next         ; Decrement loop count in B, branch if not zero

Maximum db 0                  ; memory location to hold array max
Table   db  7,2,5,3,...       ; dummy data
```

The following code presents the core of a 68K version of this program. Notice that it is more compact.

```
        CLR      D0           ; D0 contains the maximum - preset to 0
        LEA      Table,A0     ; A0 points to table
        MOVE.B   #N-1,D1      ; D1 is the loop counter (set to size - 1)
Next    CMP.B    D0,(A0)+     ; Test the next element
        BLE      TsTLast      ; If not larger than check for end
        MOVE.B   -1(A0),D0    ; IF bigger then record new largest element
TsTLast DBRA     D1,Next      ; Repeat until all done
```

9.3 The ARM—an elegant RISC processor

One of the strongest arguments made by the supporters of RISC processors in the 1980s was that they were easy to design and fabricate. From 1983 onward Acorn Computers created a series of chips solidly based on RISC principles, which demonstrated the proof of this statement. The same company later set up Advanced RISC Machines, of Cambridge, UK, to develop further generations of RISC processors (called the ARM family). In 1998 the company was floated on the stock market and became ARM Ltd. We are going to use the ARM processor to illustrate the RISC philosophy because it is easy to understand and it incorporates some interesting architectural features.

9.3.1 ARM's registers

Like most mainstream RISC architectures, the ARM is a 32-bit machine with a register-to-register, three-operand instruction set. First-generation ARMs supported 32-bit words and unsigned bytes, whereas later members of the ARM family provide 8-bit signed bytes and 16-bit signed and unsigned half-words. The ARM processor doesn't implement delayed branches and therefore the instruction following a branch is not automatically executed.

SHADOW REGISTERS

When an interrupt occurs, a processor is forced to suspend the current program and to carry out a task defined by the operating system. This means that registers being used by the pre-interrupt program might be overwritten by the interrupting program.

A simple solution is for interrupt handlers to save data in registers, use the registers, and then restore the data before returning from the interrupt. This process takes time.

Some devices like the ARM provide *shadow registers*. These are copies of a register that are associated with an interrupt. When an interrupt occurs and the processor handles it, an old register is 'switched out' and a new one switched in. When the interrupt has completed, the old register is switched in again. In this way, no data has to be moved.

All operands are 32 bits wide, except for some multiplication instructions that generate a 64-bit product in two registers, and byte and halfword accesses (64-bit and halfword accesses are available only on some members of the ARM family). The ARM has 16 user-accessible general-purpose registers called r0 to r15 and a current program status register (CPSR), that's similar to the condition code register we've described earlier.

The ARM doesn't divide registers into address and data registers like the 68K—you can use any register as an address register or a data register. Most 32-bit RISC processors have 32 general-purpose registers, which require a 5-bit operand field in the instruction. By reducing the number of bits in an instruction used to specify a register, the ARM has more bits available to select an op-code. The ARM doesn't provide lots of different instructions like a CISC processor. Instead, it provides flexibility by allowing instructions to do two or more things at once (as we shall soon see). In some ways, the ARM is rather like a microprogrammed CPU.

The ARM's registers are not all general purpose because two serve special purposes. Register r15 contains the program counter and register r14 is used to save subroutine return addresses. In ARM programs you can write pc for r15 and lr (*link register*) for r14.

Because r15 is as accessible to the programmer as any other register, you can easily perform *computed gotos*; that is, MOV **pc**, r10 forces a jump to the address in register r10.

By convention, ARM programmers reserve register r13 as a stack pointer, although that is not mandatory.

The ARM has more than one *program status register* (CPSR—see Fig. 9.3). In normal operation the CPSR contains the current values of the condition code bits (N, Z, C, and V) and eight system status bits. The I and F bits are used to disable interrupt requests and fast interrupt requests, respectively. Status bits M0 to M4 indicate the processor's current operating mode. The T flag is implemented only by the Thumb-compatible versions of the ARM family. Such processors implement *two* instruction sets, the 32-bit ARM instruction set and a compressed 16-bit Thumb instruction set.[2]

When an interrupt occurs, the ARM saves the pre-exception value of the CPSR in a stored program status register (there's one for each of the ARM's five interrupt modes).

The ARM runs in its user mode except when it switches to one of its other five operating modes. These modes correspond to interrupts and exceptions and are not of interest to us in this chapter. Interrupts and exceptions switch in new r13 and r14 registers (the so-called *fast interrupt* switches in new r8 to r14 registers as well as r13 and r14). When a mode switch occurs, registers r0 to r12 are unmodified. For our current purposes we will assume that there are just 16 user-accessible registers r0 to r15. Figure 9.3 describes the ARM's register set.

The *current processor status register* is accessible to the programmer in all modes. However, user-level code can't modify the I, F, and M0 to M4 bits (this restriction is necessary to enable the ARM to support a protected operating system). When a context switch occurs between states, the CPSR is saved in the appropriate SPSR (*saved processor state register*). In this way, a context switch does not lose the old value of the CPSR.

Summary of the ARM's register set

- The ARM has 16 accessible 32-bit registers called r0 to r15.
- Register r15 acts as the program counter, and r14 (called the *link register*) stores the subroutine return address.
- You can write PC for r15 in ARM assembly language, lr for r14, and sp for r13.
- By convention, register r13 is used as a stack pointer. However, there is no hardware support for the stack pointer.
- The ARM has a current program status register (CPSR), which holds condition codes.
- Some registers are not unique because processor exceptions create new instances of r13 and r14.
- Because the return address is not necessarily saved on the stack by a subroutine call, the ARM is very fast at implementing subroutine return calls.

As most readers will have read the chapter on the CISC processor and are now familiar with instruction sets and

---

[2] The ARM's Thumb mode is designed to make the processor look like a 16-bit device in order to simplify memory circuits and bus design in low-cost applications such as cell phones.

User registers	Supervisor registers	Abort registers	Undefined registers	Interrupt registers	Fast interrupt registers
r0	r0	r0	r0	r0	r0
r1	r1	r1	r1	r1	r1
r2	r2	r2	r2	r2	r2
r3	r3	r3	r3	r3	r3
r4	r4	r4	r4	r4	r4
r5	r5	r5	r5	r5	r5
r6	r6	r6	r6	r6	r6
r7	r7	r7	r7	r7	r7
r8	r8	r8	r8	r8	r8_FIQ
r9	r9	r9	r9	r9	r9_FIQ
r19	r19	r19	r19	r19	r19_FIQ
r11	r11	r11	r11	r11	r11_FIQ
r12	r12	r12	r12	r12	r12_FIQ
r13	r13_SCV	r13_abort	r13_undef	r13_IRQ	r13_FIQ
r14	r14_SCV	r14_abort	r14_undef	r14_IRQ	r14_FIQ
r15=PC	r15=PC	r15=PC	r15=PC	r15=PC	r15=PC

Gray registers are banked

Processor status register

31	30	29	28	27	26	25	24	23 ...		9	8	7	6	5	4	3	2	1	0
N	Z	C	V								I	F	T	M4	M3	M2	M0	M1	

Condition flag bits

Interrupt control bits

Figure 9.3 The ARM's register set.

addressing modes, we provide only a short introduction to the ARM's instruction set before introducing some of its development tools and constructing simple ARM programs.

9.3.2 ARM instructions

The basic ARM instruction set is not, at first sight, exciting. A typical three-operand register-to-register instruction has the format

ADD **r1**,r2,r3

and is interpreted as [r1] ← [r2] + [r3]. Note the order of the operands—the destination appears first (left to right), then the first source operand, and finally the second source operand. Table 9.3 describes some of the ARM's data processing instructions.

The ARM has a *reverse* subtract; for example, SUB **r1**,r2, r3 is defined as [r1] ← [r2] − [r3], whereas the reverse subtract operation RSB **r1**, r2, r3 is defined as [r1]← [r3] − [r2]. A reverse subtract operation is useful because you can do things like

SUB **r1**,r2,#5 ; [r1] = [r2] − 5
RSB **r1**,r2,#5 ; [r1] = 5 − [r2]

The *bit clear* instruction BIC performs the operation AND NOT so that BIC **r1**,r2,r3 is defined as [r1] ←[r2]·[r̄3]. Consider the effect of BIC **r1**,r2,r3 on operands [r2] = 11001010 and [r3] = 11110000. The result loaded into r1 is 00001010 because each bit in the second operand set to 1 clears the corresponding bit of the first operand.

The multiply instruction, MUL, has two peculiarities. First, the destination (i.e. result) register must not be the same as the first source operand register; for example, MUL **r0**, r0, r1 is illegal whereas MUL **r0**, r1, r0 is legal. Second, the MUL instruction may not specify an immediate value as the second operand.

The *multiply and accumulate* instruction MLA performs a multiplication and adds the result to a running total. It has the four-operand form MLA **Rd**, Rm, Rs, Rn. The RTL definition of MLA is

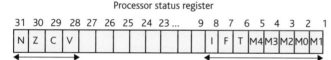

$$[\mathrm{R_d}] \leftarrow [\mathrm{R_m}] \times [\mathrm{R_s}] + [\mathrm{R_n}]$$

The result is truncated to 32 bits.

note how the normal order of the source operands is reversed

Mnemonic	Operation	Definition
ADD	Add	$[Rd] \leftarrow Op1 + Op2$
ADC	Add with carry	$[Rd] \leftarrow Op1 + Op2 + C$
SUB	Subtract	$[Rd] \leftarrow Op1 - Op2$
SBC	Subtract with carry	$[Rd] \leftarrow Op1 - Op2 + C - 1$
RSB	Reverse subtract	$[Rd] \leftarrow Op2 - Op1$
RSC	Reverse subtract with carry	$[Rd] \leftarrow Op2 - Op1 + C - 1$
MUL	Multiply	$[Rd] \leftarrow Op1 \times Op2$
MLA	Multiply and accumulate	$[Rd] \leftarrow Rm \times Rs + Rn$
AND	Logical AND	$[Rd] \leftarrow Op1 \wedge Op2$
ORR	Logical OR	$[Rd] \leftarrow Op1 \vee Op2$
EOR	Exclusive OR	$[Rd] \leftarrow Op1 \oplus Op2$
BIC	Logical AND NOT	$[Rd] \leftarrow Op1 \wedge \overline{Op2}$
CMP	Compare	Set condition codes on $Op1 - Op2$
CMN	Compare negated	Set condition codes on $Op1 + Op2$
TST	Test	Set condition codes on $Op1 \wedge Op2$
TEQ	Test equivalence	Set condition codes on $Op1 \oplus Op2$
MOV	Move	$[Rd] \leftarrow Op2$
MVN	Move negated	$[Rd] \leftarrow \overline{Op2}$
LDR	Load register	$[Rd] \leftarrow [M]$
STR	Store register	$[M] \leftarrow [Rd]$
LDM	Load register multiple	Load a block of registers from memory
STM	Store register multiple	Store a block of registers in memory
SWI	Software interrupt	$[PC] \leftarrow [r14]$, $[PC] \leftarrow 8$, enter supervisor mode

Table 9.3 The ARM data processing and data move instructions.

The ARM has two compare instructions. The conventional CMP Rn, Rs evaluates $[Rn] - [Rd]$ and sets the condition codes in the CPSR register. The *compare negated* instruction, CMN Rn, Rs, also performs a comparison, except that the second operand is negated before the comparison is made.

The ARM has a *test equivalence* instruction, TEQ Rn, Rs, which tests whether two values are equivalent. If the two operands are equivalent, the Z-bit is set to 1. This instruction is very similar to the CMP, except that the V-bit isn't modified by a TEQ.

The test instruction, TST Rn, Rs, tests two operands by ANDing their operands bit by bit and then setting the condition code bits. The TST instruction allows you to mask out bits of the operand you wish to test. For example, if r0 contains $0 \ldots 00011112$, the effect of TST r1, r0 is to mask the contents of r1 to four least-significant bits and then to compare those bits with 0.

The ARM's built-in shift mechanism

ARM data processing instructions can combine an arithmetic or logical operation with a shift operation. The shift is applied to *operand 2* rather than the result. For example, the ARM instruction

```
ADD r1,r2,r3, LSL #4
```

shifts the 32-bit operand in register r3 left by four places before adding it to the contents of register r2 and depositing the result in register r1. In RTL terms, this instruction is defined as

```
[r1] ← [r2] + [r3] × 16
```

Figure 9.4 illustrates the format of a data processing instruction. As you can see, the encoding of an ARM instruction follows the general pattern of other RISC architectures: an opcode, some control bits, and three operands. Operands Rn and Rd specify registers. Operand 2 in bits 0 to 11 of the

---

EXPLICIT CONDITION CODE REGISTER UPDATING

The 68K automatically updates the CCR register after most operations. The ARM and several other RISC processors allow the programmer to update the condition codes only when needed.

If an ARM instruction has the suffix 'S', the CPSR is updated—otherwise it is not; for example, ADDS **r3**, r1, r2

adds r1 to r2, puts the result in r3, and sets the condition code flags accordingly.

However, ADD **r3**, r1, r2 performs exactly the same addition but does not update the condition codes in the CPSR. Bit 20 of an instruction, the S-bit, is used to force an update of the condition code register, CPSR.

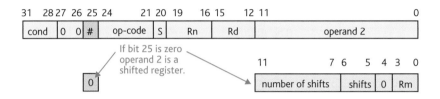

Figure 9.4 Format of the ARM's data processing instructions.

op-code in Fig. 9.4 selects either a third register or a literal. The ARM's designers use this field to provide a shift function on all data processing instructions.

When bit 25 of an op-code is 0, operand 2 both selects a second operand register and a shift operation. Bits 5 to 11 specify one of five types of shift and the number of places to be shifted. The shifts supported by the ARM are LSL (logical shift left), LSR (logical shift right), ASR (arithmetic shift right), ROR (rotate right), and RRX (rotate right extended by one place). The RRX shift is similar to the 68K's ROXL (rotate right extended) in which the bits are rotated and the carry bit is shifted into the vacated position. These shifts are similar to the corresponding 68K shifts and are defined as:

shifts the second operand in r3 three places left to multiply it by 8. This value is added to operand 1 (i.e. r3) to generate $8 \times R3 + R3 = 9 \times R3$. However, instructions such as ADD **r3**, r3, r3, LSL #3 take an extra cycle to complete because the ARM can read only two registers from the register file in a single cycle.

This ability to scale operands is useful when dealing with tables. Suppose that a register contains a pointer to a table of 4-byte elements in memory and we wish to access element number i. What is the address of element i? The address of the ith element is the pointer plus $4 \times i$. If we assume that the pointer is in register r0 and the offset is in r1, the pointer to the required element, r2, is given by

LSL	The operand is shifted left by 0 to 31 places. The vacated bits at the least-significant end of the operand are filled with zeros.
LSR	The operand is shifted right 0 to 31 places. The vacated bits at the most-significant end of the operand are filled with zeros.
ASL	The arithmetic shift left is identical to the logical shift left. This multiplies a number by 2 for each shift.
ASR	The operand is shifted right 0 to 31 places. The vacated bits at the most-significant end of the operand are filled with zeros if the original operand was positive, or with 1s if it was negative (i.e. the sign-bit is replicated). This divides a number by 2 for each place shifted.
ROR	The operand is rotated by 0 to 31 places right. The bit shifted out of the least-significant end is copied into the most-significant end of the operand. This shift preserves all bits. No bit is lost by the shifting.
RRX	The operand is rotated by one place right. The bit shifted out of the least-significant end of the operand is shifted into the C-bit. The old value of the C-bit is copied into the most-significant end of the operand; that is, shifting takes place over 33 bits (i.e. the operand plus the C-bit).

You can use this shifting facility to perform clever short cuts; for example, suppose you want to multiply the contents of r3 by 9. The operation

ADD **r3**, r3, r3, LSL #3

$[r0] + 4 \times [r1]$. In ARM assembly language, we can load this pointer into r2 by

ADD **r2**, r0, r1, LSL #2

We have been able to scale the offset by 4 (because each integer requires 4 bytes) before adding it to r0 in a conventional way. This instruction performs the operation [r2] ← [r0] + [r1] × 4.

The ARM permits *dynamic shifts* in which the number of places shifted is specified by the contents of a register. In this case the instruction format is similar to that of Fig. 9.4, except that bits 8 to 11 specify the register that defines the number of shifts, and bit 4 is 1 to select the dynamic shift mode. If register r4 specifies the number of shifts, we can write

```
ADD r1,r2,r3, LSL r4
```

which has the RTL definition [r1] ← [r2] + [r3] × $2^{[r4]}$

How do you shift an operand itself without using a data processing operation such as an addition? You can apply a shift to the source operand of the move instruction; for example,

```
MOV r0,r1,LSL #2;    ; shift the contents of r1 left twice and copy result to r0
MOV r0,r1,LSL #6;    ; multiply [r1] by 64 and copy result to r0
MOV r0,r1,ASR #2;    ; divide [r1] by 4 and copy result to r0
```

9.3.3 ARM branch instructions

One of the ARM's most interesting features is that each instruction is *conditionally executed*. Bits 28 to 31 of each ARM instruction provide a condition field that defines whether the current instruction is to be executed—see Table 9.4.

The 16 conditions described in Table 9.4 are virtually the same as those provided by many other microprocessors. One condition is the default case *always* and means that the current instruction is to be executed. The special case *never* is reserved by ARM for future expansion and should not be used. In order to indicate the ARM's conditional mode to the assembler, all you have to do is to append the appropriate condition to a mnemonic. Consider the following example in which the suffix EQ is appended to the mnemonic ADD to get

```
ADDEQ r1,r2,r3
```

The addition is now performed only if the Z-bit in the CPSR is set. The RTL form of this operation is

```
IF Z = 1 THEN [r1] ← [r2] + [r3]
```

Consider the high-level expression

```
IF x = y THEN p = q + r
```

If we assume, that x, y, p, q, and r are in registers r0, r1, r2, r3, and r4, respectively, we can express this algorithm as

```
CMP    r0,r1
ADDEQ  r2,r3,r4
```

The ARM's ability to make the execution of each instruction conditional makes it easy to write compact code. Consider the following extension of the previous example

```
CMP    r0,r1       ;compare x and y
ADDEQ  r2,r3,r4    ;IF x = y THEN p = q + r
SUBLS  r2,r3,r4    ;      ELSE IF x < y THEN p = q - r
```

Op-code bits 31-28	Mnemonic prefix	Condition	Flags
0000	EQ	equal	$Z = 1$
0001	NE	not equal	$Z = 0$
0010	CS/HS	carry set/higher or same	$C = 1$
0011	CC/LO	carry clear/lower	$C = 0$
0100	MI	negative	$N = 1$
0101	PL	positive or zero	$N = 0$
0110	VS	overflow set	$V = 1$
0111	VC	overflow clear	$V = 0$
1000	HI	higher than (signed)	$(C = 1) \cdot (Z = 0)$
1001	LS	lower or same (signed)	$(C = 0) + (Z = 1)$
1010	GE	greater than or equal (signed)	$N = V$
1011	LT	less than (signed)	$N \neq V$
1100	GT	greater than (signed)	$(Z = 0) \cdot (N = V)$
1101	LE	less than or equal (signed)	$(Z = 1) + (N\,V)$
1110	AL	always (default)	don't care
1111	NV	never (do not use)	none

Table 9.4 The ARM's condition codes.

There is, of course, nothing to stop you combining conditional execution and shifting because the branch and shift fields of an instruction are independent. You can write

```
ADDCC r1,r2,r3 LSL r4
```

which is interpreted as

IF C = 0 THEN [r1] ← [r2] + [r3] x $2^{[r4]}$

The following example from Steve Furber demonstrates the ARM's ability to generate very effective code for the construct

```
IF (a = b) AND (c = d)
    THEN e ← e + 1;
```

Assume that a is in register r0, b is in register r1, c is in register r2, d is in register r3, and e is in register r4.

```
CMP    r0,r1        Compare a and b
CMPEQ  r2,r3        If a = b THEN compare c and d
ADDEQ  r4,r4,#1     if c = d then increment e by 1
```

In this example, the first instruction, CMP r0, r1, compares a and b. The next instruction, CMPEQ r2,r3, performs a comparison only if the result of the first line was true (i.e. a = b).

8-bit literal is N and the 4-bit alignment is n in the range 0 to 12, the value of the literal is given by $N \times 2^{2n}$. Note that the scale factor is $2n$. This mechanism is, of course, analogous to the way in which floating point numbers are represented. Scaling is performed automatically by the assembler. If you write

```
ADD r1,r2,#65536
```

This assembler deals with the out-of-range literal by scaling it. That is, the assembler converts a literal into an alignment and a literal (when that is possible).

Summary of data processing instructions

The ARM's instruction set is both simple and powerful. It's simple because instructions are regular and the instruction set is very small. The instruction set is powerful because you can apply three attributes to each instruction. You can choose whether to update the condition codes by appending an S to the op-code. You can make the instruction's execution conditional by appending the condition to the instruction. You can specify a register or a literal as operand 2 and then shift the operand before it is used. Consider the following examples:

Op-code		Operation
ADD	r1,r2,r3	[r1] ← [r2] + [r3]
ADDS	r1,r2,r3	[r1] ← [r2] + [r3], update flags
ADDEQ	r1,r2,r3	IF Z = 1 THEN [r1] ← [r2] + [r3]
ADDEQS	r1,r2,r3	IF Z = 1 THEN [r1] ← [r2] + [r3], update flags
ADD	r1,r2,r3, LSL #2	[r1] ← [r2] + [r3] x 4
ADD	r1,r2,r3, LSL r4	[r1] ← [r2] + [r3] x $2^{[r4]}$
ADD	r1,r2, #125	[r1] ← [r2] + 125
ADD	r1,r2, #0xFF00	[r1] ← [r2] + 255 * 2^8
ADDCSS	r1,r2,r3, LSL r4	IF C = 1 THEN [r1] ← [r2] + [r3] x $2^{[r4]}$, update flags

The third line, ADDEQ r4, r4, #1, is evaluated only if the previous line was true (i.e. c = d). The third line adds the literal 1 to r4 to implement the e ← e + 1 part of the expression.

9.3.4 Immediate operands

ARM instructions can specify an *immediate operand* as well as a register. Figure 9.5 demonstrates how an immediate operand is encoded. When bit 25 of an instruction is 0, the ARM specifies a register for use as operand 2. When bit 25 is 1, the 12-bit operand 2 field *could* provide a 12-bit literal. But it doesn't. Those who designed the ARM argued that *range* is more important than *precision* and provided an 8-bit literal in the range 0 to 255 that can be *scaled* to provide a 32-bit value.

In Fig. 9.5 the four most-significant bits of the operand 2 field specify the literal's alignment within a 32-bit frame. If the

9.3.5 Sequence control

The ARM implements a conventional branching mechanism using the conditions described in Table 9.4. For example, the instruction BEN LOOP forces a branch if the Z-bit of the condition code register (i.e. CPSR) is clear. The branch instruction is encoded in 32 bits, which includes an 8-bit op-code and a 24-bit signed offset, which is added to the contents of the program counter. The signed offset is a 26-bit value, which is stored as a word offset in 24 bits because ARM

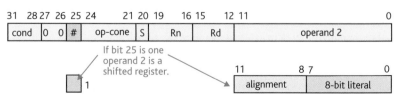

Figure 9.5 Format of the ARM's instructions with immediate operands.

instructions are word aligned on a 32-bit boundary. Consequently, the byte and halfword parts of the offset do not have to be stored as they will always be zero.

The simple unconditional branch has the single-letter mnemonic B, as the following demonstrates

```
B    Next         ;branch to "Next"
```

You can implement a loop construct in the following way

```
      MOV   r0,#20        ;load the loop counter r0 with 20
Next  .                   ;body of loop
      .
      .
      SUBS  r0,r0,#1       ;decrement loop counter
      BNE   Next           ;repeat until loop count = zero
```

This fragment of code is exactly like that of many CISC processors, but note that you have to explicitly update the condition codes when you decrement the loop counter with SUBS r0,r0,#1.

The ARM also implements a so-called *branch with link* instruction, which is similar to the subroutine call. A branch operation can be transformed into a 'branch with link' instruction by appending L to its mnemonic. Consider the following

```
BL    Next         ;branch to "Next" with link
```

The ARM copies the program counter held in register r15 into the link register r14. That is, the branch with link preserves the return address in r14. We can express this instruction in RTL as

```
[r14] ← [PC]       ;copy program counter to link register
[r15] ← Next       ;jump to "Next"
```

The value loaded into r14 is actually [PC] − 4 because the PC actually points to the instruction being fetched into the pipeline, rather than the instruction being currently executed.

A return from subroutine is made by copying the saved value of the program counter to the program counter. You can use the move instruction, MOV, to achieve this:

```
MOV  PC,r14   ;copy r14 to r15 (restore the program counter)
```

Because the subroutine return address is stored in r14 rather than on the stack in external memory, the ARM's subroutine call and return mechanism is very fast indeed. However, you have to be careful not to accidentally overwrite the return address in r14. Moreover, if a subroutine calls another subroutine, you have to save the previous return address in r14 on the stack.

Because the branch with link instruction can be made conditional, the ARM implements a full set of conditional subroutine calls. You can write, for example,

```
CMP  r9,r4    ;if r9 < r4
BLLT ABC      ;then call subroutine ABC
```

The mnemonic BLLT is made up of B (branch unconditionally), L (branch with link), and LT (execute on condition less than).

9.3.6 Data movement and memory reference instructions

ARM processors support register-to-register operations and load and store operations between registers and memory. The ARM implements two instructions that copy data from one register to another (or a literal to a register). MOV ri,rj copies the contents of register r_j into register ri. MVN ri,rj copies the *logical complement* of the contents of register r_j into register r_i. The logical complement is calculated by inverting its bits (i.e. it's the one's complement rather than the arithmetic two's complement).

The MOV instruction can be used conditionally and combined with a shifted literal. Consider the following examples.

```
MOV   r0,#0          ;[r0] ← 0; Clear r0
MOV   r0,r1, LSL #4  ;[r0] ← [r1] * 16
MOVNE r3,r2, ASR #5  ;IF Z = 0 THEN [r3] ← [r2]/32
MOVS  r0,r1, LSL #4  ;[r0] ← [r1] * 16; update condition codes

MVN   r0,#0          ;[r0] ← −1; the 1's complement of 0 is 111...1
MVN   r0,r0          ;[r0] ← [r0]; complement the bits of r0
MVN   r0,#0xF        ;[r0] ← 0xFFFFFFF0
```

The ARM provides a move instruction that lets you examine or modify the contents of the current processor status register (CPSR). The operation MRS Rd,CPSR copies the value of the CPSR into general register Rd. Similarly, MSR_f CPSR, Rm copies general register Rm into the CPSR (note that bits 28, 29, 30, and 31 of the CPSR holds the V, C, Z, and N flags, respectively). This instruction is privileged and can't be executed in the user mode (to prevent users changing to a privileged mode).

Loading an address into a register

Up to now, we have assumed that an address is already in a register. We cannot load a 32-bit literal value into a register because 32-bit literals aren't supported and the ARM doesn't implement multiple-length instructions. However, we can load an 8-bit literal shifted by an even power of 2 into a register.

The ARM *assembly language programmer* can use the ADR (load address into register) instruction to load a register with a 32-bit address; for example,

```
ADR   r0,table
```

loads the contents of register r0 with the 32-bit address 'table'. The ARM assembler treats the ADR as a *pseudo instruction* and then generates the code that causes the appropriate action to be carried out. The ADR instruction attempts to generate a MOV, MVN, ADD, or SUB instruction to load the address into a register.

Figure 9.6 demonstrates how the ARM assembler treats an ADR instruction. We have used ARM's development system to show the source code, the disassembled code, and the registers during the execution of the program (we'll return to this system later). As you can see, the instruction ADR **r5,** table1 has been assembled into the instruction ADD **r5,**pc,0x18, because table1 is 18_{16} bytes onward from the current contents of the program counter in r15. That is, the address table1 has been synthesized from the value of the PC plus the constant 18_{16}.

The ARM assembler also supports a similar pseudo operation. The construct LDR **rd,** = value is used to load value into register rd. The LDR pseudo instruction uses

the MOV or MOV instructions, or it places the constant in memory and uses program counter relative addressing to load the constant.

Accessing memory

The ARM implements two flexible memory-to-register and register-to-memory data transfer operations, LDR and STR. Figure 9.7 illustrates the structure of the ARM's memory reference instructions. Like all ARM instructions, the memory access operations LDR and STR have a conditional field and can, therefore, be executed conditionally.

The ARM's load and store instructions use *address register indirect addressing* to access memory. ARM literature refers to this as *indexed addressing*. Any of the ARM's 16 registers can act as an address (i.e. index) register.

Bit 20 of the op-code determines whether the instruction is a load or a store, and bit 25, the # bit, determines the type of the offset used by indexed addressing. Let's look at some of the various forms of these instructions. Simple versions of the load and store operations that provide indexing can be written

```
LDR  r0,[r1]   ;load r0 with the word pointed at by r1
STR  r2,[r3]   ;store the word in r2 in the location pointed at by r3
```

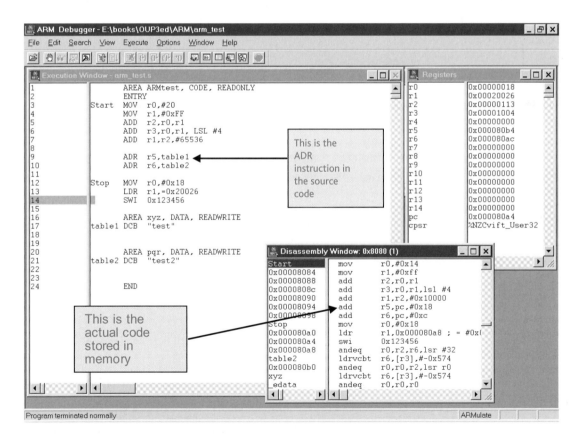

Figure 9.6 Effect of the ADR pseudo instruction.

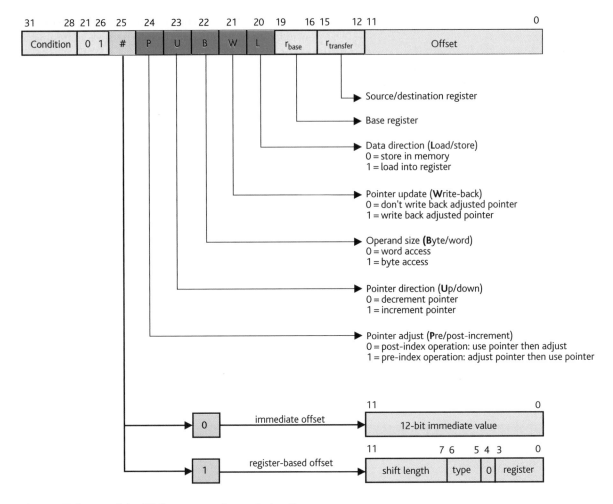

Figure 9.7 Format of the ARM's memory reference instructions.

These addressing modes correspond exactly to the 68k's address register indirect addressing modes MOVE.L (A1),**D0** and MOVE.L D2, **(A3)**, respectively.

The simple indexed addressing mode can be extended by providing an offset to the base register; for example,

```
LDR r0,[r1,#8] ;load r0 with the word pointed at by [r1] + 8
```

The ARM goes further and permits the off-set to be *permanently* added to the base register in a form of auto-indexing (rather like the 68K's predecrementing and postin-crementing addressing modes). This mode is indicated by using the ! suffix as follows:

```
LDR r0,[r1,#8]! ;load r0 with the word pointed at by [r1] + 8
               ;and post-index by adding 8 to r1
```

In this example, the effective address of the operand is given by the contents of register r1 plus the offset 8. However, the pointer register is also incremented by 8. By modifying the above syntax slightly, we can perform post-indexing by accessing the operand at the location pointed at by the base register and then incrementing the base register, as the following demonstrates.

```
LDR r0,[r1],#8  ;load r0 with the word pointed at by r1
                ;and post-index by adding 8 to r1
```

We can summarize these three forms as

```
LDR r0,[r1,#8]  ;effective address = [r1] + 8, r1 is unchanged
LDR r0,[r1,#8]! ;effective address = [r1] + 8, [r1] ← [r1] + 8
LDR r0,[r1],#8  ;effective address = [r1], [r1] ← [r1] + 8
```

Let's look at Fig. 9.7 in greater detail. The base register, r_n, acts as a memory pointer (much like other RISC processors) and the U-bit defines whether the final address should be calculated by adding or subtracting the offset. The B-bit can be set to force a *byte* operation rather than a word. Whenever a byte is loaded into a 32-bit register, bits 8 to 31 are set to zero (i.e. the byte is not sign-extended).

The P- and W-bits control the ARM's auto-indexing modes. When W = 1 and P = 1, pre-indexed addressing is performed. When W = 0, P = 0, post-indexed addressing is performed.

Consider the following example, which calculates the total of a table of bytes terminated by zero.

```
        MOV   r0,#Table      ;r0 points to Table
        MOV   r2,#0          ;clear the running total
Next    LDRB  r1,[r0],#1     ;get a byte and increment the pointer
        ADD   r2,r1,r2       ;calculate the new total
        CMP   r1,#0          ;test for end
        BNE   Next
```

There is no *clear register* instruction so you use SUB **r2**,r2,r2 or MOV **r2**,#0.

EXAMPLE

The example consolidates some of the things we've learned. Let's calculate the inner product of two *n*-component of vectors **A** and **B**; that is, $s = \mathbf{A} \cdot \mathbf{B} = a_1 \cdot b_1 + a_2 \cdot b_2 + a_3 \cdot b_3 + \cdots + a_n \cdot b_n$. The code is as follows.

```
        MOV   r4,#0          ;clear initial sum in r4
        MOV   r5,#24         ;load loop counter with n (assume 24 here)
        ADR   r0,A           ;r0 points at vector A
        ADR   r1,B           ;r1 points at vector B
Next    LDR   r2,[r0],#4     ;Repeat: get Ai and update pointer to A
        LDR   r3,[r1],#4     ;        get Bi and update pointer to B
        MLA   r4,r2,r3,r4    ;        s = s + Ai x Bi
        SUBS  r5,r5,#1       ;        decrement loop counter
        BNE   Next           ;repeat n times
```

This block of ARM *RISC* code is not too dissimilar to the corresponding 68k *CISC* code.

```
        CLR.B   D2           ;clear initial sum in D2
        MOVE.B  #24,D0       ;load loop counter with n (assume 24 here)
        LEA     A,A0         ;A0 points at vector A
        LEA     B,A1         ;A1 points at vector B
Next    MOVE.W  (A0)+,D1     ;Repeat: get Ai and update pointer to A
        MULU    (A1)+,D1     ;        Ai x Bi and update pointer to B
        ADD.L   D1,D2        ;        s = s + Ai x Bi (sum in D2)
        SUB     #1,D0        ;        decrement loop counter
        BNE     Next         ;repeat n times
```

All ARM processors can operate with 32-bit values. The ARMv4 also supports byte and halfword (i.e. 16-bit) operations. A 16-bit unsigned word can be loaded into a register and stored in memory, or a 16-bit or 8-bit value can be loaded and sign-extended. Typical load/store instructions are

LDHR	Load unsigned halfword (i.e., 16 bits)
LDRSB	Load signed byte
LDHSH	Load signed halfword
STHR	Store halfword

9.3.7 Using the ARM

We are now going to look at ARM's development system, which allows you to write programs in assembly language, assemble them, and then run the programs. The software needed to carry out these operations is provided on the CD that accompanies this book. This software consists of three parts: an *assembler*, a *linker* (which generates binary code), and a *simulator* (which lets you execute the binary code on a PC). Let's begin with its assembly language.

The ARM assembler

All assembly languages and their assemblers are roughly similar (there isn't the same difference between the 68K and the

---

MULTIPLE REGISTER MOVEMENT

The ARM supports a powerful set of multiple register movement instructions that allow you to copy any subset of the ARM's 16 registers to or from memory.

Memory can be treated as a stack that can grow up or down. We do not go into the details of these instructions here.

However, the instruction

```
LDMIA   r1!,{r2-r5, r7-r10}
```

copies registers r2 to r5 and r7 to r10 inclusive from memory, using r1 as a pointer with auto-indexing.

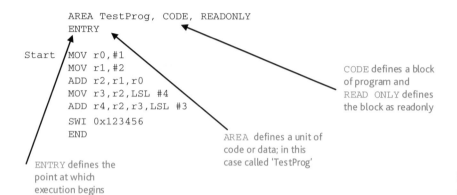

```
        AREA TestProg, CODE, READONLY
        ENTRY
Start   MOV r0,#1
        MOV r1,#2
        ADD r2,r1,r0
        MOV r3,r2,LSL #4
        ADD r4,r2,r3,LSL #3
        SWI 0x123456
        END
```

CODE defines a block of program and READ ONLY defines the block as readonly

AREA defines a unit of code or data; in this case called 'TestProg'

ENTRY defines the point at which execution begins

Figure 9.8 Structure of an ARM assembly language program.

ARM assembly languages as there is between, for example, Pascal and LISP). Most assemblers follow the layout

```
label mnemonic operand comment
```

There are, however, differences in the conventions they employ and in the way in which assembler directives are implemented. Figure 9.8 shows a simple ARM assembly language program (which does nothing other than manipulate a few numbers).

As you can see, the program in Fig. 9.8 begins with the assembler directive

```
AREA TestProg, CODE, READONLY
```

This directive provides the name of the section of code and describes its properties. The ENTRY directive on the next line provides the code's unique entry point. An END directive terminates the code.

We have used the software interrupt, SWI, an operating system call to terminate the program.

Once a program has been written, you can assemble it with the ARM assembler. An ARM assembly language program has the extension .s. If the program is called ARMtest1.s, you enter the command (from the DOS prompt)

```
armasm -g ARMtest1.s
```

Assembling the program produces an object file called ARMtest1.o. The ARM development system requires that a program be *linked* before you can execute its code. *Linking* is performed in both high-level language compilation and low-level language assembly and involves bringing together

separately compiled/assembled units of code. To link the object file generated by the assembler you enter

```
armlink ARMtest1.o -o ARMtest1
```

The command armlink takes the object file ARMtest1.o and creates an executable file ARMtest1.

Now that we've created the binary code, we can run it in the debugger that can be called from DOS or from Windows. We've used the Windows version (see Fig. 9.9).

After invoking the simulator, we've loaded the program ARMtest1 and opened a window that displays the disassembled source code and shows the contents of the registers. In Fig. 9.8 we have stepped through the program line by line by clicking on the single-step icon. The program has ended with an error message caused by the SWI instruction. Note the values of the registers. We are now going to provide a tutorial on the use of the ARM development system. The full development system provides a very powerful set of tools and is available from ARM Ltd. Here we are interested only in writing an assembly language program and observing its execution.

Using the ARM development system

Let's go through the steps necessary to develop and debug a program written in ARM assembly language. We begin by writing a simple program to determine whether a given string is a palindrome or not. A palindrome is a string that reads the same from left to right as from right to left—in this example the string is 'ANNA'. All we have to do is to remove a character from each end of the string and compare this pair of characters. If they are the same the string might be a palindrome; if

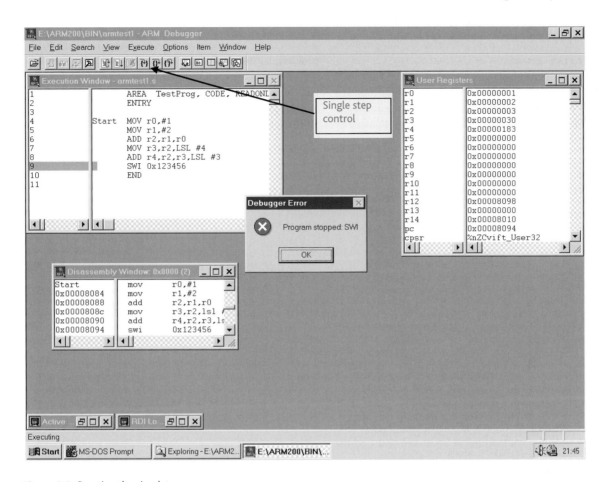

Figure 9.9 Running the simulator.

they differ the string isn't a palindrome. We then repeat the same operation on the remaining string (i.e. substring), and so on. If we reach the middle of the string, the string is a palindrome.

The algorithm to determine whether a string is a palindrome requires at least three variables. We need a pointer to the character at the left-hand end of the string, a pointer to the character at the right-hand end of the string, and a flag that indicates whether the string is a palindrome or not.

The following fragment of pseudocode provides a first-level solution to the problem. The variables `left_pointer` and `right_pointer` point at the characters at the ends of the string currently being examined and Palindrome is true if the string is a `palindrome` and false otherwise. We begin by assuming that the string is a palindrome and set the flag `palindrome` false if ever a pair of characters don't match.

```
Palindrome = true
Set left_pointer to point at leftmost character
Set right_pointer to point at rightmost character
REPEAT
    Get left character at left_pointer position
    Get right character at right_pointer position
    IF left character ≠ right character THEN Palindrome = false
    left_pointer  = left_pointer + 1
    right_pointer = right_pointer - 1
UNTIL middle of string OR Palindrome = false
```

The only tricky part of this problem is determining when we reach the middle. Consider the palindromes ABCCBA and ABCBA. The first palindrome has an even number of letters and the second an odd number of letters. Consider the following:

Step	Even length	Pointers at end of test	Odd length	Pointers at end of test
1	ABCCBA		ABCBA	
2	ABCCBA		ABCBA	
3	ABCCBA	Left_pointer = right_pointer + 1	ABCBA	Left_pointer = right_pointer

The middle of the string is located when either the left pointer is one less than the right pointer or the left pointer is equal to the right pointer.

We can easily write a fragment of code that scans the string. In the following code (written in the form of a subroutine), register r0 points to the left-hand end of the string and register r1 points to the right hand end of the string. Remember

character-fetch operations and therefore we have to take account of this when comparing the pointers). We can fix the problem in three ways: update the pointers only *after* the test for the middle, take copies of the pointers and move them back before comparing them, or perform a new test on the copies for left_ pointer = right_pointer + 2 and left_pointer = right_pointer + 1. We will use the first option to get

```
                                    ;r0 points at left hand end of string
                                    ;r1 points at right hand end of string
pal       MOV    r10,#0x0           ;r10 = success/fail flag
again     LDRB   r3,[r0]            ;get left hand character
          LDRB   r4,[r1]            ;get right hand character
          CMP    r3,r4             ;compare the ends of the string
          BNE    notpal            ;if different then fail
                                    ;test for middle of string
          CMP    r0,r1             ;if r0 = r1 then odd length palindrome
          BEQ    waspal            ;if same then exit with palindrome found
          ADD    r2,r0,#1          ;copy left pointer to r2 and move right
          CMP    r2,r1             ;if r2 = r1 then even length palindrome
          BEQ    waspal            ;if same then exit with palindrome found

          ADD    r0,r0,#1          ;move left pointer right
          SUB    r1,r1,#1          ;move right pointer left
          B      again             ;REPEAT

waspal    MOV    r10,#0x1          ;r10 = 1 = success flag
notpal    MOV    pc,lr             ;return
```

that the ARM instruction LDRB **r3,**[r0],#1 means 'load register r3 with the byte pointed at by r0 and add 1 to the contents of r0'.

```
again     LDRB   r3,[r0],#1        ;get left hand character and update pointer
          LDRB   r4,[r1],#-1       ;get right hand character and update pointer
          CMP    r3,r4             ;compare characters the at ends of the string
          BNE    notpal            ;if characters different then fail
            .
            .                       ;test for middle of string
            .
          BNE    again             ;if middle not found then repeat
waspal                              ;end up here if string is palindrome
notpal    MOV    pc,lr             ;return from subroutine
```

We can test for the middle of a string in the following way:

```
          CMP    r0,r1             ;if r2 = r1 then odd length palindrome
          BEQ    waspal            ;if same then exit with palindrome found
          ADD    r2,r0,#1          ;copy left pointer to r2 and move right
          CMP    r2,r1             ;if r2 = r1 then even length palindrome
          BEQ    waspal            ;if same then exit with palindrome found
```

The code we wrote to scan the palindrome automatically updates the pointers when they are used to fetch characters (e.g. the left pointer is used and updated by LDRB **r3,** [r0],#1 and the right pointer is updated by LDRB **r3,**[r1],#-1) This means that both pointers are updated during the

The following code provides the complete program to test a string. We begin by scanning the string (which is terminated by a 0) to find the location of the right-hand character. The subroutine either returns 0 in r10 (not palindrome) or 1 (is palindrome).

```
        AREA palindrome, CODE, READONLY
        ENTRY
start                                   ;locate the ends of the string
        LDR   r0,=string                ;r0 points to start of string to test
        MOV   r1,r0                     ;copy left pointer to right pointer in r1
loop    LDRB  r2,[r1],#1                ;get char and update right pointer
        CMP   r2,#0                     ;repeat until terminator located
        BNE   loop
        SUB   r1,r1,#2                  ;fix right pointer to point to end of string
        BL    pal                       ;call subroutine to test for palindrome

stop    MOV   r0,#0x18                  ;stop program execution by calling the O/S
        LDR   r1,=0x20026               ;the three lines of "magic" code in this
        SWI   0x123456                  ;block are an operating system call

                                        ;test for palindrome
                                        ;r0 points at left hand end of string
                                        ;r1 points at right hand end of string
pal     MOV   r10,#0x0                  ;r10 =  Palindrome = 0 = set fail flag
again   LDRB  r3,[r0]                   ;get left hand character
        LDRB  r4,[r1]                   ;get right hand character
        CMP   r3,r4                     ;compare the ends of the string
        BNE   notpal                    ;if different then fail
                                        ;test for middle of string
        CMP   r0,r1                     ;if r0 = r1 then odd length palindrome
        BEQ   waspal                    ;if same then exit with palindrome found
        ADD   r2,r0,#1                  ;copy left pointer to r2 and move right
        CMP   r2,r1                     ;if r2 = r1 then even length palindrome
        BEQ   waspal                    ;if same then exit with palindrome found

        ADD   r0,r0,#1                  ;move left pointer right
        SUB   r1,r1,#1                  ;move right pointer left
        B     again                     ;REPEAT

waspal  MOV   r10,#0x1                  ;r10 = 1 = success flag
notpal  MOV   pc,lr                     ;return
```

Note the three lines of code labeled by stop. I copied the code from ARM's literature because it offers a means of halting program execution by calling an operating system function. Other versions of the ARM simulator may require different termination mechanisms. You can always terminate a program by implementing an infinite loop:

```
Finish  B     Finish
```

Having written the program (using an ASCII editor), we assemble it with the command ARMASM. If the program is called PROG1.s, it is assembled by

```
ARMASM -g PROG1.s
```

The assembly process produces a new object file called PROG1.o. The '-g' option generates debugging information for later use. If no errors are found during the assembly phase, the object code must be linked to produce the binary code that can be executed by an ARM processor (or simulated on a PC). The command used to link a program is ARMLINK. In this case we write

```
ARMLINK PROG1.o -o PROG1
```

The linker creates a new file called PROG1, which can be loaded into the ARM simulator.

Once we have created a file to run, we can call the Windows-based ARM debugger by clicking on the ADW icon (assuming you've loaded ARM's package on your system). This loads the development system and creates the window shown in Fig. 9.10. By selecting the **File** item on the top toolbar, you get a pull-down menu whose first item is **Load image** (see Fig. 9.11). Clicking on **Load image** invokes the window used to open a file and lists the available files (see Fig. 9.12). In this case, we select the file called **Prog1**. Figure 9.13 shows the situation after this program has been loaded.

The **Execution** window in Fig. 9.13 shows the code loaded into the debugger. Note that the ARM development system creates a certain amount of header code in addition to your program. We are not interested in this code. Figure 9.13 shows address 0 × 00008008 highlighted—this is the point at which execution is to begin (i.e. the initial value of the program counter). However, you can also start

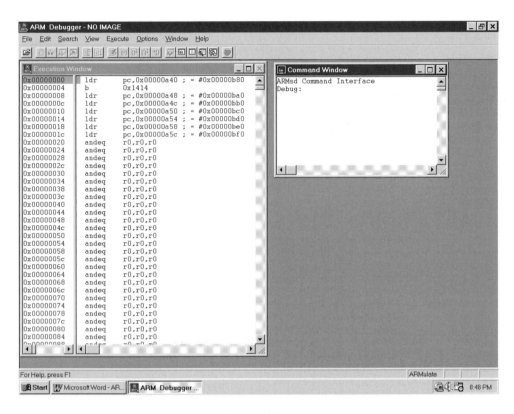

Figure 9.10   The initial window after loading the ARM debugger.

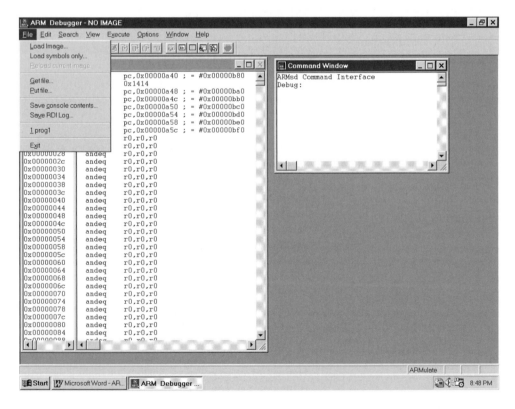

Figure 9.11   The **File** pull-down menu.

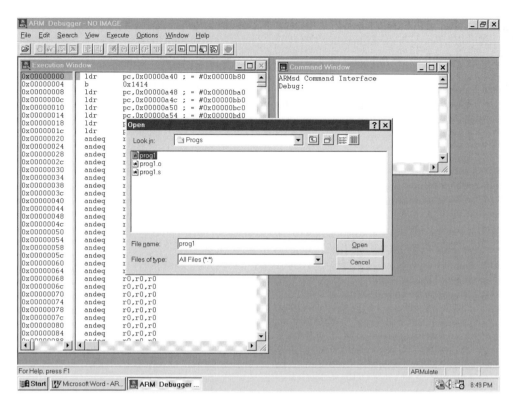

Figure 9.12 Loading a program into the simulator.

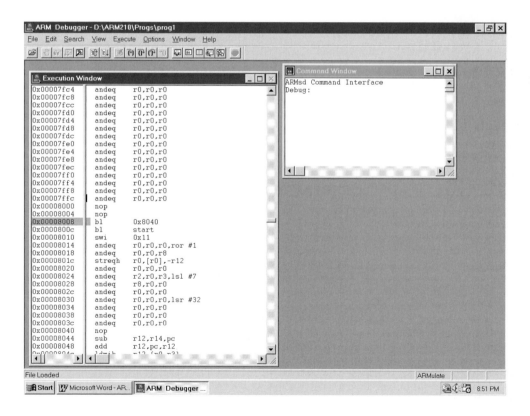

Figure 9.13 The screen after loading prog1.

the program by setting a breakpoint to 0 × 8080 and then running the code to the breakpoint. Doing this executes the start up code and then stops simulation at the appropriate point.

We can view other windows beside the **Execution** window. In Fig. 9.14 we have selected the **View** command on the top toolbar and have chosen **Registers** from the pull-down list to give a second pull-down list of registers.

Figure 9.15 shows the debugger with the register window active. You can modify the contents of any register in this window by double clicking on the appropriate register. Figure 9.16 shows how the current contents of a register appear in a **Modify Item** window. In this diagram the PC contains 0 × 00008008, which we alter to 0 × 00008080 (the address of the start of prog1). This address (i.e. 8080) is a feature of the ARM development system I used.

Figure 9.17 shows the state of the system after the PC has been reloaded. As you can see, the code that we originally entered is now displayed.

In Fig. 9.17 we have resized the windows to make best use of the available space in order to see as much as possible of the

program's comment field (without losing the **Registers** window). The first instruction to be executed is highlighted.

We can now begin to execute the program's instructions to test whether a string is a palindrome. There are several ways of running a program in the ARM debugger; for example, we can run the whole program until it terminates, execute a group of instructions, or execute a single instruction at a time. If you click on the *step-in* icon on the toolbar, a single instruction at a time is executed. The effect of program execution can be observed by monitoring the contents of the registers in the **Registers** window.

In Fig. 9.18 we have begun execution and have reached the second instruction of the subroutine 'pal'. In Fig. 9.19 we have executed some more instructions and have reached line number 25 in the code.

Let's return to the **View** pull-down menu on the tool bar to display more information about the program. In Fig. 9.20 we have pulled down the menu and in Fig. 9.21 we have selected the **Disassembly** mode and have been given the disassembly address window.

Figure 9.22 shows the **Disassembly** window. You can see the contents of the memory locations starting at 0 × 00008080.

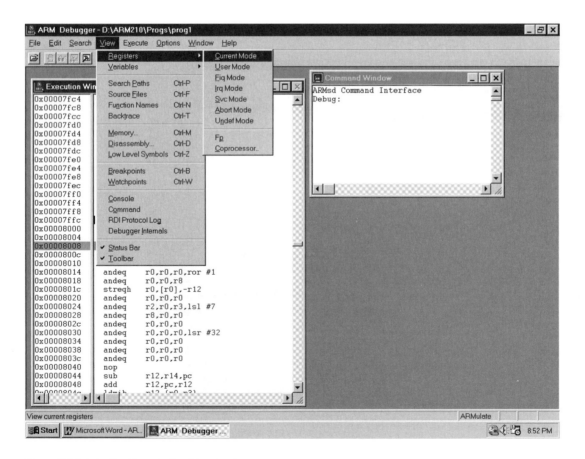

Figure 9.14 Selecting the set of registers to view.

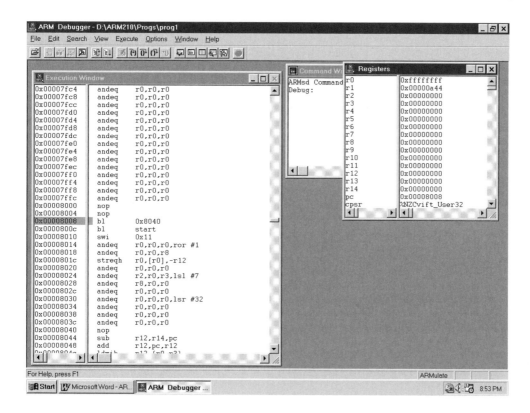

Figure 9.15 Viewing the ARM's registers.

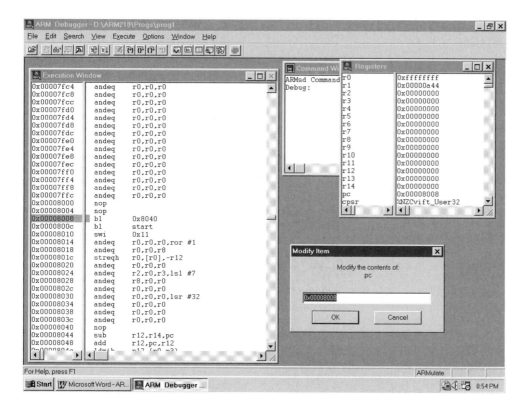

Figure 9.16 Reloading the simulated PC.

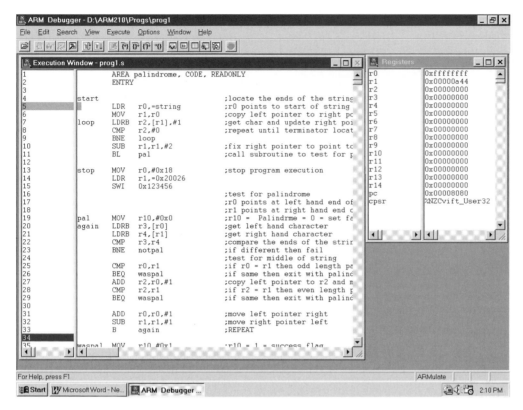

Figure 9.17 The system after resetting the PC.

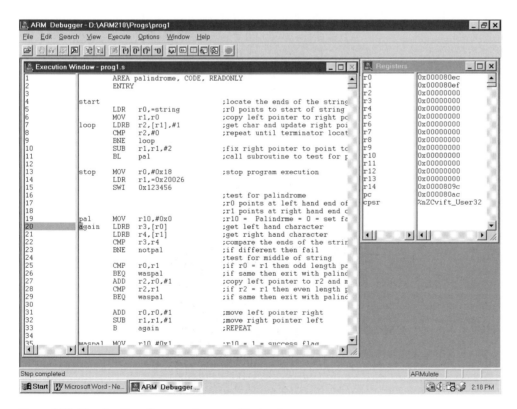

Figure 9.18 The situation after executing several instructions.

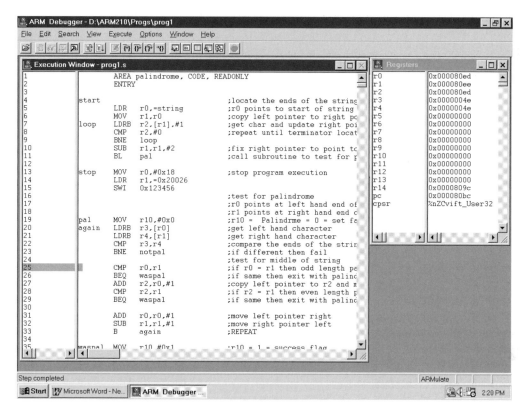

Figure 9.19 The situation after executing part of the subroutine `pal`.

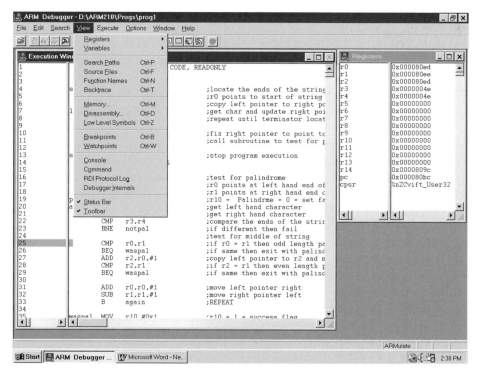

Figure 9.20 Using the **View** function to select the **Disassembly** display

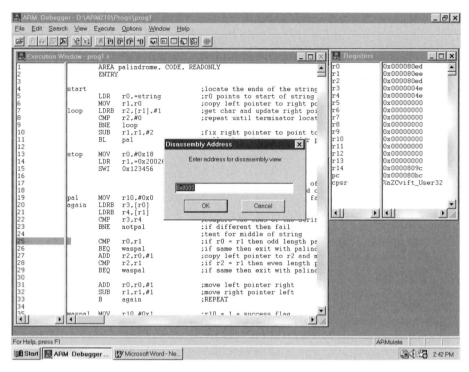

Figure 9.21 Selecting the point at which to start disassembly.

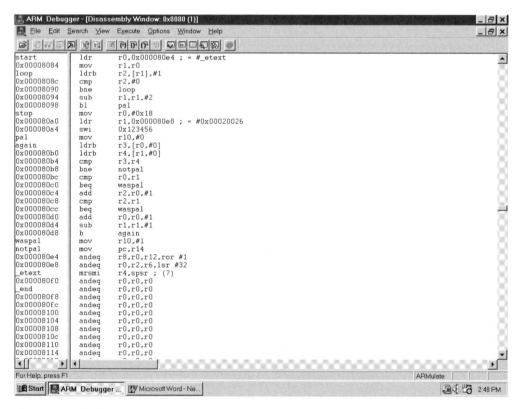

Figure 9.22 The disassembled code.

Note that the symbolic labels are displayed, although the text string is interpreted as instructions.

Simplifying the code

We can simplify the code we've developed to test for a palindrome; that's one of the advantages of writing a program in assembly language. The following provides an improved version (without the header, data, and termination mechanism, which don't change).

```
start    LDR    r0,=string      ;r0 points to start of string to test
         MOV    r1,r0           ;copy left pointer to right pointer in r1
loop     LDRB   r10,[r1],#1     ;get character and update right pointer
         CMP    r10,#0          ;repeat until terminator located
         BNE    loop
         SUB    r1,r1,#2        ;fix right pointer to point to end of string
         BL     pal             ;call subroutine to test for palindrome
stop                            ;stop program execution

pal      LDRB   r3,[r0],#1      ;get left hand character
         LDRB   r4,[r1],#-1     ;get right hand character
         CMP    r3,r4           ;compare the ends of the string
         BNE    notpal          ;if different then fail
         SUBS   r3,r1,r0        ;get difference between pointers
         BEQ    waspal          ;if same then exit with palindrome found
         BMI    waspal          ;if left pointer past right then palindrome
         B      pal             ;REPEAT
waspal   MOV    r10,#0x1        ;r10 = 1 = success flag
notpal   MOV    pc,lr           ;return
```

We've used two improvements. The first is to use r10 (the success/fail flag) to test for the terminator at the end of the string. In this way, we begin the subroutine with [r10] = 0 and save an instruction. The major change is in the test for the middle of the string. If we automatically increment the left pointer and decrement the right pointer when they are used, we will have one of two situations when we reach the middle. If the string is even, the left and the right hand pointers will have swapped over. If the string is odd, the two pointers will be pointing at the same character. The code subtracts the left pointer from the right pointer and stops on zero or negative.

Further simplification

Steve Furber at Manchester University pointed out that the code can be simplified even further. Look at the way I handled a return if the string wasn't a palindrome.

```
         CMP    r3,r4   ;compare the ends of the string
         BNE    notpal  ;if different then fail
         .
         .
notpal   MOV    pc,lr   ;return
```

We test two characters and then branch to notpal if they aren't the same. From notpal, we perform a return by placing the return address in the link register into the pc. Steve uses conditional execution to combine these two instructions; that is,

```
CMP    r3,r4   ;compare the ends of the string
MOVNE  pc,lr   ;if not same then return
```

Steve's final version is

```
pal      LDRB   r3,[r0],#1      ;get left hand character
         LDRB   r4,[r1],#-1     ;get right hand character
         CMP    r3,r4           ;compare the ends of the string
         MOVNE  pc,lr           ;if not same then return
         CMP    r0,r1           ;compare pointers
         BMI    pal             ;not finished
         MOV    r10,#1
         MOV    pc,lr           ;return (success)
```

■ SUMMARY

When we first introduced the computer, we used Motorola's 68K as a teaching vehicle because it is both powerful and easy to understand. In this chapter, we have looked at two contrasting microprocessors; a simple 8-bit device used in devices ranging from toys to cell phones, and a more sophisticated 32-bit RISC processor, the ARM.

The 8-bit M68HC12 looks very much like the first-generation processors that go back to the late 1970s. These processors have relatively few internal registers and you have only two general-purpose accumulators. However, their processors have a wealth of on-chip I/O ports, which means that they provide a single-chip solution to many computing problems.

The ARM processor is a 32-bit machine with a register-to-register (or load/store) architecture with instructions like ADD **r1**, r2, r3. We introduced the ARM because it has some very interesting features. The program counter is one of the processor's general-purpose registers, which means that the programmer can access the PC like any other register. This feature can be exploited in returning from a subroutine because you can transfer the return address to the PC without having to perform a memory access.

Another feature of the ARM is its ability to shift the second operand as part of a normal data processing instruction. This mechanism provides a limited degree of parallel processing because you can execute two instructions at once (provided one is a shift).

One of the most interesting features of the ARM is its conditional execution, where an instruction is executed only if a condition is met. This facility makes it possible to generate very compact code.

■ PROBLEMS

9.1 What are the advantages and disadvantages of microprocessor wordlengths that are not powers of 2 (e.g. 12 bits and 24 bits)?

9.2 We said that all processors permit register-to-memory, memory-to-register, and register-to-register moves, whereas few microprocessors permit direct memory-to-memory moves. What are the advantages and disadvantages of direct memory-to-memory moves?

9.3 Some computers have a wide range of shift operations (e.g. logical, arithmetic, and rotate). Some computers have very few shift operations. Suppose that your computer had only a single logical shift left operation. How would you synthesize all the other shifts using this instruction and other appropriate operations on the data?

9.4 Some microprocessors implement simple unconditional procedure (i.e. subroutine) calls with a BSR (branch to subroutine) instruction. Other microprocessors have a conditional branch to subroutine instruction that let's you call a subroutine conditionally. What are the relative merits and disadvantages of these two approaches to instruction design?

9.5 Some registers in a microprocessor are part of its architecture which is visible to the programmer, whereas other registers belong to the processor's organization and are invisible to the programmer. Explain what this statement means.

9.6 The MC68HC12 instruction set of Table 9.2 has a very large number of instructions. Design a new instruction set that performs the same operations but uses fewer instruction types (e.g. employ a MOVE instruction to replace many of the 6809's existing data transfer instructions).

9.7 What are the relative advantages and disadvantages of variable-length instructions (in contrast with fixed-length instructions).

9.8 In what significant ways does the ARM differ from the 68K?

9.9 Most RISC processors have 32 user-accessible registers, whereas the ARM has only 16. Why is this so?

9.10 Construct an instruction set that has the best features of a CISC processor like the 68K and a RISC processor like the ARM. Write some test programs for your architecture and compare them with the corresponding pure 68K and ARM programs.

9.11 All ARM instructions are conditional, which means that they are executed only if a defined condition is met; for example, ADDEQ means 'add if the last result set the zero flag'.

Explain how this feature can be exploited to produce very compact code. Give examples of the use of this feature to implement complex conditional constructs.

9.12 What is the effect of the following ARM instructions?

(a) MOV   **r1**, #0xFF
(b) MVN   **r1**, #0xFF
(c) MVN   **r1**, #25
(d) MVN   **r1**, #0xF
(e) MOVS **r1**, #0xF
(f) MLA   **r3**, r5, r6, r2
(g) LDR   **r1**, [r3,#8]!
(h) LDR   **r1**, [r3,#8]

9.13 The ARM has a wealth of move multiple register instructions, which copy data between memory and several registers. The load versions of these instructions are

LDMIA, LDMIB, LDMDA, LDMDB, LDMFD, LDMFA, LDMED, LDMEA

What do these instructions do? You will need to look up ARM literature to answer this question.

9.14 How are subroutines handled in ARM processors?

9.15 Implement a jump table in ARM assembly language. A jump table is used to branch to one of a series of addresses stored in a table. For example, if register r3 contains the value *i*, a jump (i.e. branch) will be made to the address of the *i*th entry in the table. Jump tables can be used to implement the case or switch construct in high-level languages.

9.16 Consider the fragment of C-code if (p = = 0) q = q11; else q = q*4;

How can conditional execution be exploited by the compiler for this code?

9.17 A 32-bit IEEE floating point number is packed and contains a sign bit, biased exponent, and fractional mantissa. Write an ARM program that takes a 32-bit IEE floating point number and returns a sign-bit (most significant bit of r1), a true exponent in r3, and a mantissa with a leading 1 in register r3.

Write a program to convert an unsigned 8-digit decimal integer into a 32-bit IEEE floating point number. The 8-digit decimal integer is stored at the memory location pointed at by r1 and the result is to be returned in r2. The decimal number is right justified and leading digits are filled with zeros; for example, 1234 would be stored at 00001234.

Buses and input/output mechanisms

CHAPTER MAP

9 Processor architectures

Chapter 9 provides a brief overview of two contrasting processors; the purpose of this chapter is to expose students to the range of processors that are available to the designer.

10 Buses and input/output mechanisms

This chapter deals with input/output *techniques*. We are interested in how information is transferred between a computer and peripherals, and between the peripherals themselves. We look at internal buses, which link devices within the computer and external buses, which link remote devices such as printers with the computer. We also describe two peripheral interface components that perform I/O operations autonomously by performing many of the activities required to move data between a computer and external peripherals.

11 Computer peripherals

The power of a computer is much a function of its peripherals as its data processing capabilities. We examine several peripherals found in a typical PC such as the keyboard, display, printer, and mouse, as well as some of the more unusual peripherals that, for example, can measure how fast a body is rotating.

12 Computer memory

Information isn't stored in a computer in just one type of storage device; it's stored in DRAM and on disk, CD-ROM, DVD, and tape. This chapter examines the operating principles and characteristics of the storage devices found in a computer.

INTRODUCTION

Computers receive data from a wide variety of sources such as the keyboard and mouse, the modem, the scanner, and the microphone. Similarly, computers transmit data to printers, displays, and modems. Computer peripherals can be discussed under two headings. The first is the *techniques* or *strategies* whereby information is moved into and out of a computer (or even within the computer). The second is the peripherals themselves; their characteristics, operating modes, and functions. We first look at the way in which information is moved into and out of the computer and in the next chapter we describe some important peripherals.

We begin with the *bus*, the device that distributes information within a computer and between a computer and external peripherals. We describe both high-speed parallel buses and slower, low-cost buses such as the USB bus that connects keyboards and similar devices to the computer. We introduce a very unusual bus, the IEEE488 bus, which illustrates many important aspects of I/O technology.

The middle part of this chapter looks at the *strategies* used to implement I/O such as programmed I/O and interrupt-driven I/O.

This chapter concludes with a description of two peripheral chips that automate the transmission of data between a computer and peripheral. One interface chip handles parallel data and the other serial data. The precise details of these chips are not important. Their operating principles are because these chips demonstrate how a lot of the complexity associated with input and output transactions can be moved from the CPU to an interface.

10.1 The bus

We've examined the internal structure and operation of the computer's central processing unit. The next step is to show how the computer communicates with the outside world. In this chapter we look at how information gets into and out of a computer; in the next chapter we turn our attention to devices like the printer and the display that are connected to the computer.

This chapter begins with the *bus* that distributes information both within a computer and between a computer and external devices. We then demonstrate how the CPU implements input and output transactions—the CPU doesn't dirty its hands with the fine details of input/output (I/O) operations. The CPU hands over I/O operations to special-purpose interface chips; for example, the computer sends data to one of these chips and logic within the chip handles the transfer of data between the chip and the external device. We describe the operation of two typical interface chips—one that handles I/O a byte (or a word) at a time and one that handles I/O a bit at a time.

10.1.1 Bus architecture

A bus is used by the processor and peripherals to move data from point to point in a computer. An important feature of some buses is their ability to allow several devices with different characteristics to communicate with each other over a common highway.

Figure 10.1 illustrates a generic computer bus that is composed of several sub-buses; there's a data transfer bus that transfers data between the CPU and memory or peripherals, an arbitration bus that allows one or more CPUs to request access to the bus, and an interrupt bus that deals with requests for attention from peripherals. The data transfer bus is, itself, composed of sub-buses; for example, there's an address bus to communicate the address of the memory location being accessed, a data bus to carry data between memory and CPU, and a control bus, which determines the sequence of operations that take place during a data transfer.

Buses are optimized for their specific application; for example, speed (throughput), functionality, or cost (e.g. the USB bus). A computer such as the PC may have several buses. Figure 10.2 illustrates the structure of a PC with buses that are linked by bridges (i.e. circuits) that control the flow of traffic between buses that might have widely different parameters.

In Fig. 10.2 a system bus links together the processor and its memory. This is the fastest bus in the system because the computer cannot afford to wait for instructions or data from memory. The system bus is connected to a local bus that deals with data transfers between slower devices such as audio subsystems or interfaces to external peripherals. A logic system that may be as complex as a CPU is used to connect the system bus to the local bus.

10.1.2 Key bus concepts

Before we look at buses in greater detail, we need to introduce concepts that are intimately bound up with the way in which both buses and other I/O mechanisms control the flow of data. The most important concept is that of the *open-* and *closed-loop* data transfer.

Irrespective of the strategy by which data is moved between the processor and peripheral, all data transfers fall into one of two classes: *open-ended* or *closed-loop*. In an open-ended I/O transaction the data is sent on its way and its safe

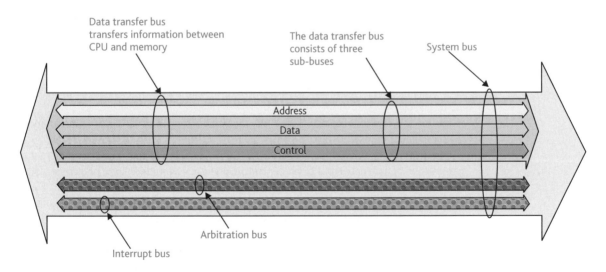

Figure 10.1 Structure of a generic bus.

reception assumed. Open-ended data transfers correspond to the basic level of service offered by the mail system. A letter is written and dropped into a mailbox. The sender believes that after a reasonable delay, the letter will be received. However, the sender doesn't know whether the letter was received.

In many circumstances the open-ended transfer of data is perfectly satisfactory. The probability of data getting lost or corrupted is very small and its loss may be of little importance. If Aunt Mabel doesn't get a birthday card, the world doesn't come to an end. Consider now the following exchange of information between a control tower and an aircraft.

Approach control 'Cherokee Nine Four Six November cleared for straight in approach to runway 25. Wind 270 degrees 10 knots. Altimeter 32 point 13. Report field in sight.'

Aircraft 'Straight in runway 25. 32 point 13. Cherokee Nine Four Six November.'

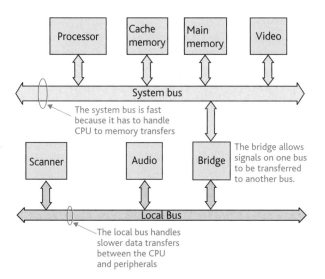

Figure 10.2 A system with multiple buses.

The aircraft acknowledges receipt of the message and reads back any crucial data (i.e. the identification of the runway is 25 and the altimeter pressure setting is 32.13 inches of mercury). This data transfer demonstrates the operation of a closed-loop system. In the computer world, a closed-loop data transfer simply indicates that data has been received (the data itself isn't read back).

Open-loop data transfer

Figure 10.3 illustrates an open-loop data transfer between a computer and a peripheral. Figure 10.3(a) shows a computer and peripheral with a data path and a 1-bit control signal, DAV, Fig. 10.3(b) gives a timing diagram for an open-loop write in which data is sent from the computer to the peripheral, and Fig. 10.3(c) provides a transaction of protocol diagram that presents the sequence of actions in the form of messages.

At point A data from the computer becomes valid (the shading before point A indicates that the data is invalid). At point B the computer asserts the DAV (data valid) control signal to indicate that the data from the computer is valid. The peripheral must read the data before it vanishes at point D. DAV is negated at point C to inform the peripheral that the data is no longer valid. This data transfer is called *open loop* because the peripheral doesn't communicate with the CPU and doesn't indicate that it has received the data.

Closed-loop data transfer

In a *closed-loop* data transfer, the device receiving the data acknowledges its receipt. Figure 10.4 illustrates a closed-loop data transfer between a computer and peripheral. Initially, the computer (i.e. originator of the data) makes the data available and then asserts data DAV at point B to indicate that the data is valid just as in an open-loop data transfer. The peripheral receiving the data sees that DAV has been asserted, indicating that new data is ready. The peripheral asserts its acknowledgement, DAC (data accepted), at point C and reads

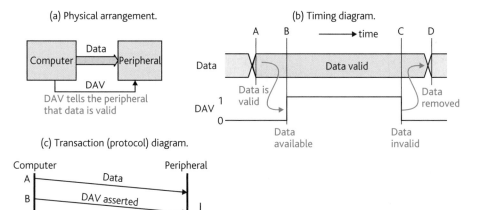

Figure 10.3 Open-loop data transfer between computer and peripheral.

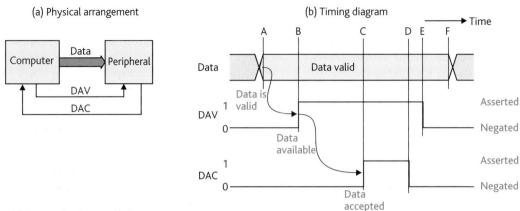

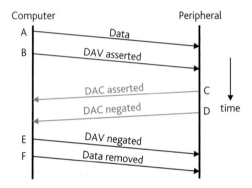

Figure 10.4 Closed-loop data transfer between computer and peripheral

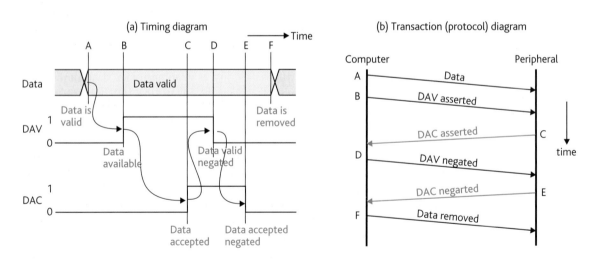

Figure 10.5 Fully interlocked handshaking.

the data. The data accepted signal is a reply to the computer informing it that the data has been accepted. Once the data has been read by the peripheral, the DAV and DAC signals may be negated and the data removed. This sequence of events is known as *handshaking*. Apart from indicating the receipt of data, handshaking also caters to slow peripherals,

because the transfer is held up until the peripheral indicates its readiness by asserting DAC.

Figure 10.5 shows how the handshaking process can be taken a step further in which the acknowledgement is itself acknowledged, to create a *fully interlocked data transfer*. The term fully interlocked means that each stage in the handshaking

---

HANG UPS

In data transfers with handshaking, a problem arises when the transmitter asserts DAV, but DAC isn't asserted by the receiver in turn (because the equipment is faulty or the receiver is not switched on). When the transmitter wishes to send data, it starts a timer concurrently with the assertion of DAV. If the receiver doesn't assert DAC after a given time has passed, the operation is aborted. The period of time between the start of an action and the declaration of a failure state is called a *timeout*.

When a timeout occurs, an interrupt (see Section 10.2.2) is generated, forcing the computer to take action. In a poorly designed system without a timeout mechanism, the non-completion of a handshake causes the transmitter to wait for DAC forever and the system is then said to hang up.

---

procedure can continue only when the previous stage has been acknowledged. At point A in Fig. 10.5 the data becomes valid and at point B the transmitter asserts DAV indicating the availability of data. At C the receiver asserts DAC indicating that DAV has been observed and the data accepted. So far this is the same procedure as in Fig. 10.4.

The transmitter sees that DAC is asserted and de-asserts (i.e. negates) DAV at D, indicating that data is no longer valid and that it is acknowledging that the receiver has accepted the data. Finally, at E the receiver de-asserts (i.e. negates) DAC to complete the cycle, and to indicate that it has seen the transmitter's acknowledgement of its receipt of data.

The difference between the handshaking and fully interlocked handshaking of Figs. 10.4 and 10.5 should be stressed. Handshaking merely involves an acknowledgement of data, which implies that the assertion of DAV is followed by the assertion of DAC. What happens after this is undefined. In fully interlocked handshaking, each action (i.e. the assertion or negation of a signal) takes place in a strict sequence that ends only when all signals have finally been negated. Interlocked handshaking is a two-way process because the receiver acknowledges the assertion of DAV by asserting DAC whereas the transmitter acknowledges the assertion of DAC by negating DAV. Moreover, because fully interlocked handshaking also acknowledges negations, it is said to be *delay insensitive*.

Many real systems employing closed-loop data transfers make the entire handshaking sequence automatic in the sense that it is carried out by special-purpose hardware. The computer itself doesn't get involved in the process. Only if something goes wrong does the processor take part in the handshaking.

How fast should an interface operate? As fast as it can—any faster and it wouldn't be able to keep up with the data—any slower and it would waste time waiting for data. Unfortunately, most real interfaces don't transfer data at anything like an optimum speed. In particular, data can sometimes arrive so fast that it's impossible to process one element before the next is received.

Doctors have a similar problem. If a doctor took exactly *m* minutes to treat a patient and a new patient arrived every *m* minutes, all should be well. However, even if patients arrive on average every *m* minutes and a consultation takes on average *m* minutes, the system wouldn't work because some patients arrive at approximately the same time. Doctors have solved this problem long ago by putting new patients in a waiting room until they can be dealt with. Sometimes the waiting room becomes nearly full when patients enter more rapidly than average.

The solution used by doctors can be applied to any I/O process. Data is loaded into a FIFO (first-in first-out) memory that behaves almost exactly like a waiting room. Data arrives at the memory's input port and is stored in the same sequence in which it arrives. Data leaves the memory's output port when it is required. Like the doctor's waiting room, the FIFO can fill with data during periods in which data arrives faster than it can be processed. It's up to the designer to provide a FIFO with sufficient capacity to deal with the worst case input burst. There is, however, one significant difference between the FIFO and the waiting room. FIFOs aren't littered with piles of battered 10-year-old copies of *National Geographical*. Saving data in a store until it is required is called *buffering* and the FIFO store is often called a *buffer*. Some interfaces incorporate a buffer into their input or output circuits to control the flow of data.

Bus terminology

Bus technology has its own vocabulary. Before we continue it's necessary to introduce some of the concepts and terminology associated with computer buses.

Arbitration Arbitration is a process whereby a device on the bus competes with other devices for control of the bus and is granted access to the bus. A simple bus-based system with only one processor and no other bus master doesn't require bus arbitration because the CPU permanently controls the bus.

Backplane Parallel buses fall into two groups: *passive backplanes* and *motherboards*. A motherboard is a printed circuit board that includes the CPU and its associated circuitry; for example, the motherboard found in the PC. A backplane contains the bus and slots (sockets) into which modules such as memory cards, processors, and peripherals can be plugged. The backplane is *passive* because it provides information paths but not functionality; that is, there is no CPU or other subsystem on the backplane. A backplane is more versatile than a motherboard and is generally found in commercial or professional systems.

Bandwidth The bandwidth of a bus is a measure of its throughput, the rate at which data is transmitted over the bus. Bandwidth is normally expressed in bytes/s and is proportional to the width of the data bus; for example, if an 8-bit data bus can transfer 200 Mbytes/s, increasing the bus's width to 64 bits increases the bandwidth to 1.6 Gbytes/s.

Bus architecture Just as we speak about processor architecture or memory architecture, we can refer to a bus's architecture. The architecture of a bus (by analogy with the CPU) is an expression of its functionality and how it appears to the user. Bus architecture includes a bus's topology, its data exchange protocols, and its functionality such as its arbitration and interrupt-handling capabilities.

Bus contention When two or more devices attempt to access a common bus at the same time, *bus contention* takes place. This situation is resolved by *arbitration*, the process that decides which of the contenders is going to gain access to the bus.

Bus driver Logic systems are wired to bus lines via gates. Special gates called *bus drivers* have been designed to interface the CPU to a bus or other logic. A bus driver is a digital circuit with the added property that its output terminal can provide the necessary voltage swing and current necessary to drive a bus up to a 1 state or down to a 0 state. Bus drivers are required because of the electrical characteristics of bus lines.

Bus master A bus master is a device that can actively take control of a bus and use it to transfer data. CPUs are bus masters. A *bus slave*, on the other hand, is a device that is attached to a bus but which can only be accessed from a bus master. A bus slave cannot initiate a bus access.

Bus protocol A bus is defined by the electrical characteristics of its signals (i.e. what levels are recognized as 1s and 0s) and the sequence of signals on the various lines of the bus used to carry out some transaction. The rules governing the sequencing of signals during the exchange of data are known as a *protocol*.

Bus termination A bus can be quite long and extend the width of a computer system. Signals put on the bus propagate along the bus at close to the speed of light (the actual speed is given by the electrical properties of the bus lines and insulators between them). When a pulse reaches the end of a bus, it may be reflected back towards its source just like a wave that hits the side of a swimming pool. If you place a terminating network across the ends of a bus, it can absorb reflections and stop them bouncing from end to end and triggering spurious events.

Bus topology The *topology* of a bus is a description of the paths that link devices together.

Latency A bus's latency is the time the bus takes to respond to a request for a data transfer. Typically, a device requests the bus for a data transfer (or a burst of data transfers) and then waits until the bus has signaled that it is ready to perform the transfer. This waiting period is the bus's *latency*.

Motherboard A motherboard is similar to a backplane because it contains a bus and sockets that accept modules such as memory and peripherals. The difference between a backplane and motherboard is that the motherboard is *active*; it contains a processor and control logic. Modern PCs have such sophisticated motherboards that they can operate without any cards plugged into the system bus because the motherboard implements I/O, sound, and even the video display.

Multiplexed bus Some data transfer buses have separate address and data sub-buses; that is, the address bus sends the location of the next word to be accessed in memory and the data bus either transmits information to the memory in a write cycle or receives information in a read cycle. Some computer buses use the same lines to carry both addresses and data. This arrangement, called *multiplexing*, reduces the number of lines required by the bus at the expense of circuit complexity. A multiplexed bus works in two or more phases; an address is transmitted on the common address/data lines and then the same lines are used to transfer data.

10.1.3　The PC bus

You might think it would be easier to wire peripherals and memory directly to a PC's own address and data bus. Indeed, some single-board microcontrollers do take this approach. Connecting the processor to memory and peripherals is not viable in sophisticated systems for several reasons. First, a processor chip cannot provide the electrical energy to drive lots of memory or peripheral chips. Second, a bus can be standardized and equipment from different manufacturers plugged into it. Third, if we didn't have buses, all interface circuits would have to be modified whenever a new processor were introduced.

A bus makes a computer system independent of processor, memory, or peripheral characteristics and allows independent development of CPU or processor technology.

The history of the IBM PC and its clones is as much the history of its bus as its central processing unit. Indeed, the PC's bus structure has advanced more radically than its

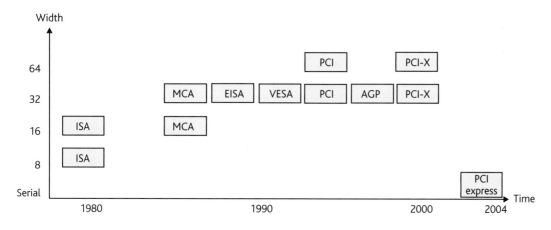

Figure 10.6 PC bus history.

processor architecture. Figure 10.6 describes some of the steps along the path of the PC's bus architecture.

When the PC was first created, its bus was very limited in terms of its speed, width, and functionality. The original XT bus supported the Intel 8088, a processor with a 16-bit internal architecture and an 8-bit external data bus. The XT bus operated with a 4.77 MHz clock and could access 1 Mbytes of memory. The 8088 was soon replaced by the 8086, a processor with an identical architecture but with a true 16-bit data bus. A new version of the PC with a 16-bit bus called ISA (*Industrial Standard Architecture*,) was created.

As performance increased, the ISA bus rapidly became obsolete and was replaced by three competing buses forcing PC users to choose between one of these mutually incompatible systems. IBM produced its high-performance propriety Micro Channel Architecture bus, which was protected by patents. This bus died because it was uncompetitive. Two other PC buses were the VESA and EISA buses.

In 1992 Intel announced the PCI (peripheral interconnect) bus to provide higher performance, to provide a path for future expansion, and to gain control of the bus market. The PCI 2.0 bus was 32 bits wide and had a speed of 33 MHz. The original PCI 2.0 specification was replaced by the PCI 2.1 specification and the PCI bus was so successful that it rapidly replaced all other buses in PCs.[1]

In 2004 the PCI express bus was introduced. This is a major departure from conventional backplane buses because it uses a pair of serial data paths operating at 2.5 Gbytes/s in each direction. Such a pair of buses is called a *lane* and the PCI express may use multiple lanes to increase the overall data rate.

Figure 10.7 illustrates the structure of the PCI bus in a typical PC system. The processor bus is also called the host bus, or in PC terminology, the *front side bus*. The logic system that connects the processor bus to the PCI bus is called a *north bridge*. The circuits that implement inter-bus interfaces in a PC environment have come to be known colloquially as *chipsets*.

Figure 10.8 describes Intel's 875 chipset, which uses an 82875 MCH chip to provide a north bridge interface between the processor and memory and AGP (the advanced graphics card slot that provides a fast dedicated interface to a video card) and an ICH5 chip, which provides an interface to the PCI bus, LAN, and other subsystems. This chipset provides much of the functionality that was once provided on plug-in PCI cards such as an audio interface, a USB bus interface, and a LAN interface.

The PCI bus operates at clock speeds of 33 or 66 MHz and supports both 32- and 64-bit systems. Data can be transferred in an efficient high-speed burst mode by sending an address and then transferring a sequence of data bytes. A 64-bit-wide bus operating at 66 MHz can transfer data at a maximum rate of $66 \times 8 = 528$ Mbytes/s.

The PCI supports arbitration; that is, a PCI card can take control of the PCI bus and access other cards on the PCI bus.

We now look at the IEEE488 bus, which was designed for use in professional systems in commercial environments such

---

[1] Computer buses did not originate in the PC world. Professional systems had long since used standardized computer buses such as Motorola's VMEbus or the Multibus.

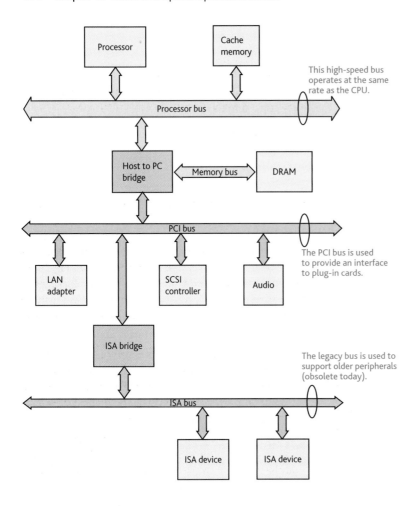

Figure 10.7 The PCI bus in a PC.

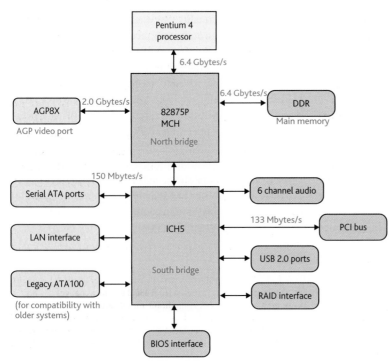

Figure 10.8 The Intel 875 PCI chipset.

LEGACY DEVICES

The term *legacy device* describes facilities that were incorporated in all PCs but which have now become largely obsolete. For example, the ISA bus is obsolete. However, because there are many ISA cards such as modems still in existence, some PCs contain both PCI and ISA buses to enable users to keep their old modem cards. As time passes, fewer and fewer systems have ISA buses.

Similarly, the growth of the high-performance and flexible USB interface has largely rendered the traditional serial and parallel PC interfaces used by modems and printers unnecessary. These interfaces are also called legacy devices and are omitted from many modern high-performance PCs.

as instrumentation and control. Some students may omit this section because the IEEE488 bus is very specialized—we have included it because it illustrates several important aspects of bus design and operation.

10.1.4 The IEEE 488 bus

The IEEE 488 bus dates from 1967 when the Hewlett Packard Company began to look for a standard bus to link together items of control and test instrumentation[2] in automatic test environments in industry. We cover it here because it has two interesting facets. First, it implements an unusual patented three-line data transfer protocol. You have to have a license from the patent holders to use the IEEE 488 bus. Second, it transmits control messages in two ways: via special control signals and via encoded data messages.

Figure 10.9 illustrates the relationship between the IEEE bus, the IEEE interface, and the devices that communicate with each other via the bus. As this diagram demonstrates, the IEEE standard covers only the bus and the interfaces but not the devices connected to the interfaces. This distinction is important because we shall soon discover that the IEEE bus implements different communication methods between devices and between interfaces.

The IEEE bus supports three types of device: the controller, the talker, and the listener. A *talker* (transmitter) can put data on the bus, a *listener* (receiver) can read data from the bus, and a *controller* is a device that manages the bus and determines which device may talk and which may listen. Only one controller may be active at any given time. An active controller can give up control of the bus by permitting another controller to take control. In general, the controller is part of the host computer on which the applications program is being run. Furthermore, this computer invariably has the functions of controller, talker, and listener.

At any instant only one talker can send messages over the IEEE bus, although several listeners may receive the messages from the talker. The ability to support a single talker and multiple listeners simultaneously demonstrates a fundamental difference between typical backplane buses and the IEEE bus. Backplane buses transfer data between a master and a single slave, whereas the IEEE bus is able to transfer data between a

master (talker) and several slaves (listeners) in a broadcast mode of operation.

The IEEE bus uses 16 information lines that are divided into three distinct groups—the data bus, the data bus control lines and the bus management lines (see Fig. 10.9). The data lines, carry two types of information: bus control information and information sent from one bus user to another. The IEEE bus supports the following three data transmission modes.

1. A byte of user data is called a multiline message and is transmitted over the 8-bit data bus. The message doesn't directly affect the operation of the bus itself or the IEEE bus interface and its meaning depends only on the nature of the devices sending and receiving it.

2. A byte of IEEE bus interface control information can be transmitted over the data bus. Control information acts on the interfaces in the devices connected to the bus or affects the operation of the devices in some predetermined fashion defined in the IEEE 488 standard.

3. A single bit of information can be transmitted over one of the five special-purpose bus management lines. Certain bus management lines may be used concurrently with the operations on the data bus.

Information flow on DIO1 to DIO8 is managed by three control lines, NRFD, DAV, and NDAC (i.e. not ready for data, data available, and not data accepted). All data exchanges between a talker and one or more listeners are fully interlocked, and, if a talker is sending information to several listeners, the data is transmitted at a rate determined by the slowest listener. The operation of the three data bus control lines is controlled by the bus interfaces in the devices connected to the bus, and is entirely transparent to the user.

The bus management lines, IFC, ATN, SRQ, REN, and EOI, perform functions needed to enhance the operation of

---

[2] The IEEE standard was introduced in 1976 and revised in 1978. An updated version of the standard IEEE 488.2 includes changes to the software environment but no significant modifications to the underlying physical layer. The IEEE 488 bus is known by several names: the General Purpose Interface Bus (GPIB), the Hewlett Packard Instrument Bus (HPIB) the, IEC 625-1 bus, the ANSI MC1-1 bus, or, more simply, the IEEE bus.

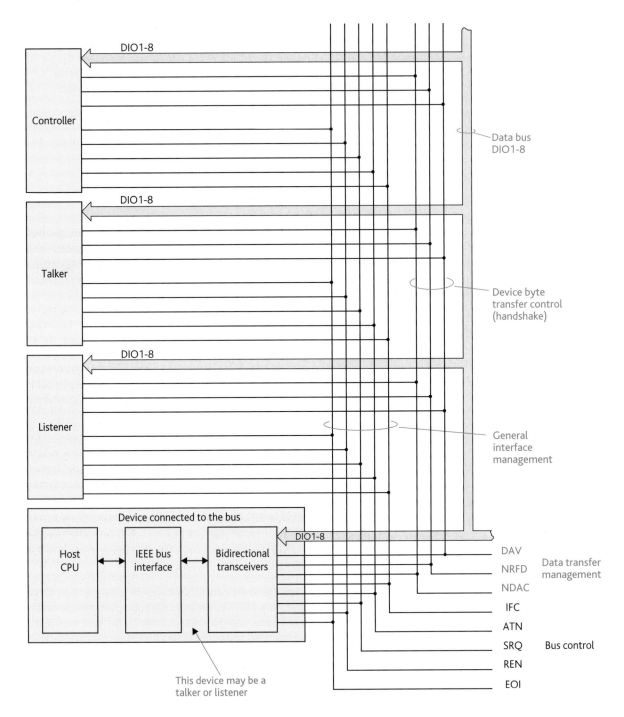

Figure 10.9 The IEEE 488 bus.

the bus. In a minimal implementation of the IEEE 488 bus, only ATN is absolutely necessary. The functions of the bus management lines are summarized as follows.

ATN (attention) The ATN line distinguishes between data and control messages on the eight data lines. When ATN is true (i.e. electrically low), the information on DIO1 to DIO8 is interpreted as a control message. When ATN is false (i.e. electrically high) the message is a device-dependent message from a talker to one or more listeners. The expression *device-dependent data* means that the data is in a format that has a meaning only to the device using the IEEE bus. Only the controller can assert the ATN line (or the IFC or REN lines).

IFC (interface clear) The controller uses the IFC line to place the bus in a known state. Asserting IFC resets the IEEE bus interfaces but not the devices connected to them. After an IFC message has been transmitted by a controller for at least 100 ms, any talker and all listeners are disabled and the serial poll mode (if active) is aborted.

SRQ (service request) The SRQ line performs the same role as an interrupt request and is used by a device to indicate to the controller that it wants attention. The controller must perform a serial poll to identify the device concerned, using a specified protocol.

REN (remote enable) The REN line is used by the controller to select between two alternative sources of device control. When REN is true a device is controlled from the IEEE bus, and when false it is controlled locally. In general, local control implies that the device is operated manually from its front panel. The REN line allows a device to be attached to the IEEE bus, or to be removed from it. In the world of automated testing, the assertion of REN turns a manually controlled instrument into one that is remotely controlled.

EOI (end or identify) The EOI line serves two, mutually exclusive, purposes. Although the mnemonic for this line is EOI, it is frequently written END (end) or IDY (identify), depending on the operation being carried out. When asserted by a talker, END indicates the end of a sequence of device-dependent messages. When a talker is transmitting a string of device-dependent messages on DIO1 to DIO8, the talker asserts EOI concurrently with the last byte to indicate that it has no more information to transmit. When asserted by the controller in conjunction with the ATN line, the EOI line performs the identify (IDY) function and causes a *parallel poll* in which up to eight devices (or groups of devices) may indicate simultaneously whether they require service.

Data transfer

Data transfers on the IEEE data bus, DIO1 to DIO8, are interesting because they involve a patented three-line, fully interlocked handshaking procedure. The signals used by the IEEE bus are all active-low, with an electrically high level representing a negated level and an electrical low level representing an asserted level. Active-low signal levels make it possible to take advantage of the wired-OR property of the open-collector bus driver (i.e. if any open-collector circuit pulls the line down to ground, the state of the line is a logical one). The definitions of the three signals controlling data movement on the IEEE bus are as follows.

DAV (data valid) When true (i.e. electrically low), DAV indicates to a listener or listeners that data is available on the eight data lines.

NRFD (not ready for data) When true, NRFD indicates that one or more listeners are not ready to accept data.

NDAC (Not Data Accepted) When true, NRFD indicates that one or more listeners have not accepted data.

The timing diagram of a data transfer between a talker and several listeners is given in Fig. 10.10. Suppose the bus is initially quiet with no transmitter activity and that three active receivers are busy and have asserted NRFD to inform the transmitter that they are busy. In this state, the NRFD line will be pulled down by open-collector bus drivers into a logical one state (remember that the IEEE bus uses negative logic in which the true or asserted state is the electrically low state).

When one of the listeners becomes free, it releases (i.e. negates) its NRFD output. The negation of NRFD by a listener has no effect on the state of the NRFD line, as other listeners are still holding it down. This situation is shown by dotted lines in Fig. 10.10. When, at last, all listeners have released their NRFD outputs, the NRFD line is negated, signifying that the listeners are all not 'not ready for data'—that is, they are ready for data. Now the talker can go ahead with a data transfer.

The talker places data on DIO1 to DIO8 and asserts DAV. As soon as the listeners detect DAV asserted, they assert NRFD to indicate that they are once more busy.

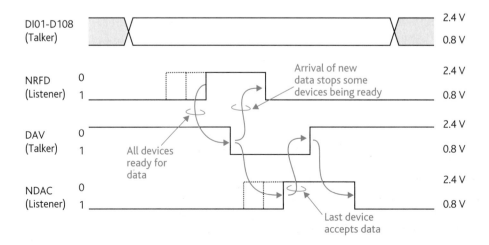

Figure 10.10 The three-wire handshake.

Meanwhile, the listeners assert their NDAC outputs electrically low to indicate that they have not accepted data. When a listener detects that DAV has been asserted, it reads the data off DIO1 to DIO8 and negates its NDAC output. That is, if its 'not data' accepted output is negated, then it must be signifying data accepted.

Because all listeners must negate their NDAC outputs before the NDAC line can rise to an electrical high state, the talker does not receive a composite data-accepted signal until the last listener has released NDAC. The talker terminates the data transfer cycle when it releases DAV and the receivers release NDAC in turn.

Configuring the IEEE bus

Before the IEEE bus can be used by the devices connected to it, the controller must first assign one device as a talker and one or more devices as listeners The controller communicates with all other devices either by uniline messages (asserting one of the bus management lines), or by multiline messages (asserting ATN and transmitting a message via DIO1 to DIO8). Multiline messages can be further subdivided into those intended for all devices (universal commands) and those intended for specific devices (addressed commands). Remember that all messages use only 7 bits of an 8-bit byte, enabling 7-bit ISO characters to be assigned to the control messages.

Three multiline messages are used by the controller to configure talkers and listeners on the bus: MLA (my listen address), MTA (my talk address), and MSA (my secondary address). Consider first the action of the MLA command. Before a device may listen to device-dependent traffic on the bus, it must be addressed to listen by the controller. The 31 my listen address codes from 00100000 to 00111110 select 31 unique listener addresses. Each listener has its own address, determined either at the time of its manufacture or by manually setting switches, generally located on its rear panel.

By sending a sequence of MLAs, a group of devices can be configured as active listeners. The 32nd listener address, 00111111, has a special function called *unlisten* (UNL). Whenever the UNL command is transmitted by the controller, all active listeners are disabled. An unlisten command is issued before a string of MLAs to disable any listeners previously configured for some other purpose.

Having set up the listeners, the next step is to configure a talker, which is done by transmitting an MTA. There are 31 my talk address codes from 01000000 to 01011110. As only one device can be the active talker at any given time, the act of issuing a new MTA has the effect of automatically disabling the old (if any) talker. The special code 01011111 is called UNT (untalk) and deactivates the current talker. Once a talker and one or more listeners have been configured, data can be transmitted from the talker to the listener(s) at the rate of the slowest device taking part in the exchange and without

the aid (or intervention) of the controller. The format and interpretation of this data is outside the scope of the IEEE 488 standard, but, as we have said, is frequently represented by ISO (ASCII) characters. Note that the controller is acting as an intermediary between talkers and listeners, in contrast to other buses in which potential talkers and listeners are usually autonomous.

Serial and parallel polling

Like many other buses, the IEEE 488 bus provides facilities for devices to request service from controllers (i.e. an interrupt mechanism). The IEEE bus supports two forms of supervisor request—the serial poll and the parallel poll, although the parallel poll cannot strictly be classified as an interrupt.

A device connected to the IEEE bus can request attention by asserting the SRQ (service request) bus management line. The controller detects the service request and may respond by initiating a serial poll. A service request, in IEEE bus terminology, corresponds to an interrupt request in conventional computer terminology. As the controller does not know which device initiated the service request, it must poll all devices sequentially. The recommended sequence of actions that should be carried out by the controller in response to a service request is

```
Serial-poll
    Unlisten all active listeners with UNL
    Enable serial poll with SPE
    REPEAT
        Transmit a MTA to a device to be polled
        Read the response from the polled device
    UNTIL all devices polled
    Disable serial poll with SPD
    Untalk all devices with UNT
End serial_poll
```

After entering the serial poll mode the controller transmits successive talk addresses (MTAs) and examines the service messages from each of the devices addressed to talk, until an affirmative response is obtained. The controller ends the polling sequence by an SPD (serial poll disable) command.

A parallel poll is initiated by the controller and involves several devices concurrently. The controller sets up the parallel poll by assigning individual data bus lines to devices (or groups of devices). For example, device 5 may be told to respond to a parallel poll by asserting DIO3. Then, the controller initiates the parallel poll and the configured devices respond.

The controller asserts the ATN and IDY (identify) lines simultaneously to carry out a parallel poll. Whenever the IEEE bus is in this state with ATN and IDY asserted, the predetermined devices place their response outputs on the assigned data lines and the controller then reads the contents of the data bus. A parallel poll can be completed in only a few microseconds unlike the serial poll.

10.1.5 The USB serial bus

First-generation PCs suffered from poor connectivity. PCs had an RS232C serial port for modems and a parallel port for printers. All external systems had to be interfaced to these relatively slow interfaces that had not been designed to be flexible. You could plug a special card into the PC's motherboard to support a particular interface or use the expensive SCSI bus designed for hard-disk interfaces.

Two of the greatest advances in PC technology were the USB interface and the plug-and-play philosophy. The USB, or *universal serial bus*, interface is a low-cost plug and socket arrangement that allows you to connect devices from printers and scanners to digital cameras and flash-card readers to a PC with minimal effort. Moreover, the USB is expandable—you can connect a USB port to a hub and that hub can provide other USB connectors. A processor with a USB port lets you connect up to 127 devices to the computer. Plug-and-play allows the device connected to the USB port to negotiate with the operating system running on the host and to supply the necessary drivers and set-up parameters.

The first-generation USB implementation supported a data rate of 11 Mbps whereas the USB 2.0 replacement that emerged in 2000 supports data transfer rates of 1.5, 12, and 480 Mbps.

A USB connector has four pins. Two provide a 5 V power supply and two transmit the data. The power supply can be used by a USB device as long as its power requirements are modest. This arrangement allows devices like keyboards, mice, flashcard readers, etc. to be connected to a USB port without the need for their own power supply or batteries.

Data on the USB is transmitted *differentially*, that is, the signal on the two data lines is transmitted as the pair (+0.1 V −0.1 V) or (−0.1 V, +0.1 V) so that the information content lies in the potential difference between the data terminals, which is either 0.2 V or −0.2 V. Information encoding is called NRZ1 (non-return to zero 1) where the voltage between the data lines is unchanged to transmit a 1 and it is switched to transmit a 0; that is, information is transmitted by switching polarity whenever there is a 0 in the data stream.

Information is transmitted without a reference clock leaving the receiver to extract data from the incoming stream of pulses. If you transmit a long string of 1s, there are no transitions in the data stream from which you can extract timing information. Consequently, whenever six 1s are transmitted, a 0 is automatically transmitted to force a data transition to help create a synchronizing signal. If you recover six 1s, you know the next bit must be a 0 and you simply drop it. This mechanism is called *bit stuffing*.

The individual bits transmitted across the USB bus are grouped into units called *packets* or *frames*. Figure 10.11 illustrates four of the 10 USB packets. Packets begin with a synchronizing field followed by a *packet identification* field, *Packet identition* (PID) Field, which defines the type of the

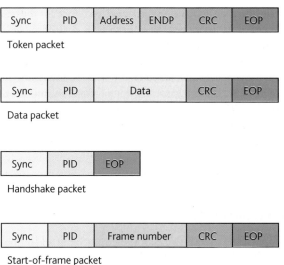

Figure 10.11 USB packets.

current packet. Packets are terminated by an *end-of-packet* (EOP) field.

Other packet fields in Fig. 10.11 are the data field used to transport applications-oriented data between the host computer and USB device, and the CRC field, which is used to detect retransmission errors. The ENDP field defines the packet's *endpoint*, which provides a destination (one of four) for the packet within a USB device. This arrangement allows the USB to treat packets as belonging to four different types of stream or *pipe*. The four pipes supported by the USB are the default or control pipe, the bulk pipe used for raw data transmission, the interrupt pipe, and the isochronous pipe for streaming video or audio. Note that each pipe consists of two pipes in opposite directions for host-to-USB device and USB device-to-host data transfers.

Most data transfers use the bulk data pipe where information is sent in units of up to 64 bytes. *Isochronous* data transfers provide a guaranteed bandwidth that is needed for video or audio links. These data transfers don't use error checking because there's nothing that can be done if an error occurs in a real-time video or audio stream.

Setting up the USB

The universal serial bus is a dynamic system that can adapt to changing circumstances; that is, you can hot-plug devices into the USB bus at any time without powering down and you can remove devices from the bus at any time.

When a device is plugged into the USB, the host detects that a new device has been connected and then waits 100 ms to ensure that the new device has had time to be properly inserted and powered up. The host then issues a reset command to place the new device in its default state and allow it to respond to address zero (the initial default address).

The host then asks the newly connected device for the first 64 bytes of its *device descriptor*. Each USB device is able to supply a device descriptor that defines the device to the host processor; for example, the descriptor includes information about the product and its vendor, its power requirements, the number of interfaces it has, endpoint information, and so on. Once the full device descriptor has been transmitted, the host is able to communicate with the USB device using the appropriate device drivers. The host can now assign an address to the new device.

10.2 I/O fundamentals

Computer I/O covers several topics because input and output transactions involve the host processor, its software, and the peripherals sending or receiving data. We can divide I/O into three areas.

1. The strategy by which data is moved into or out of the computer.

2. The interface circuit that actually moves the data into or out of the computer.

3. The input/output devices themselves that convert data into a form that can be used by an external system or that take data from the outside world and convert it into a form that can be processed digitally. Data may be converted into an almost infinite number of representations, from a close approximation to human speech to a signal that opens or closes a valve in a chemical factory. Input/output devices are frequently called peripherals.

The difference between these three aspects of I/O can be illustrated by two examples. Consider first a computer connected to a keyboard and an LCD display. Data is moved into or out of the computer by a strategy called *programmed*

data transfer. Whenever the computer wants to send data to the display, an instruction in the program writes data into the output port that communicates with the display. Similarly, when the computer requires data, an instruction reads data from the input port connected to the keyboard. The term *port* indicates a gateway between the computer and an external I/O device. Programmed data transfer or programmed I/O represents the strategy by which the information is moved but tells us nothing about how the data is moved—that is handled by the interface between the computer and external peripheral. In this example the keyboard and display are the I/O devices proper (i.e. peripherals).

Consider data that's sent from a computer to a remote display terminal (see Fig. 10.12). When the computer sends data to its output port, the output port transmits that data to the display. The output port is frequently a sophisticated integrated circuit whose complexity may approach that of the CPU itself. Such a semi-intelligent device relieves the computer of the tedious task of communicating with the LCD display directly, and frees it to do useful calculations.

The connection between a computer and a display may consist of a twisted pair (two parallel wires twisted at regular intervals). Because the data written into the output port by the CPU is in parallel form, the output port must serialize the data and transmit it a bit at a time over the twisted pair to the display. Moreover, the output port must supply start and stop bits to enable the display to synchronize itself with the stream of bits from the computer. Chapter 14 deals in more detail with serial data transmission. We can now see that the output port is the device that is responsible for moving the data between the processor and the peripheral.

The display terminal is the output device proper. It accepts serial data from the computer, reconstitutes it into a parallel form, and uses the data to select a character from a table of symbols. The symbols are then displayed on a screen. Sometimes the transmitted character performs a control

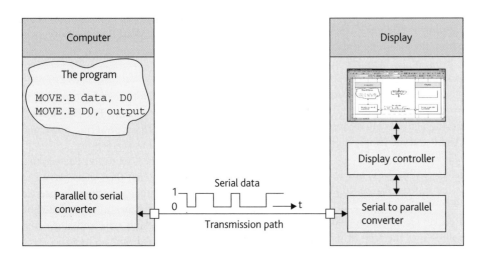

Figure 10.12 Relationship between a computer and a peripheral.

function (e.g. carriage return, line-feed, or backspace) that determines the layout of the display.

Figure 10.13 illustrates the relationship between the CPU, the peripheral interface chip, and the peripheral device itself. As you can see, the peripheral interface chip looks just like a memory location to the CPU (i.e. you read or write data to it). However, this chip contains specialized logic that allows it to communicate with the peripheral.

The way in which a block of data is written to a disk drive provides another example of the relationship between I/O strategy, the I/O interface, and the peripheral. It's impractical to use programmed data transfers for disk I/O because that is too slow. The I/O strategy most frequently used is *direct memory access* (DMA) in which the data is transferred from the computer's memory to a peripheral, or vice versa, without passing through the CPU's registers. The CPU tells the DMA hardware to move a block of data and the DMA hardware gets on with the task, allowing the CPU to continue its main function of information processing. This strategy (i.e. DMA) requires special hardware to implement it.

An interface chip called a *DMA controller* (DMAC) is responsible for moving the data between the memory and the peripheral. The DMAC provides addresses for the source or destination of data in memory, and informs the peripheral that data is needed or is ready. Furthermore, the DMAC must grab the computer's internal data and address buses for the duration of a data transfer. Data transfer by DMA must be performed while avoiding a conflict with the CPU for the possession of the buses. In this example the peripheral is a disk drive—a complex mixture of electronics and high-precision mechanical engineering designed to store data by locally affecting the magnetic properties of the surface of a disk rotating at a high speed.

10.2.1 Programmed I/O

Programmed I/O takes place when an instruction in the program performs the data transfer; for example, a programmer writes MOVE.B Keyboard,**D0** to read a byte of data from the keyboard and puts it in D0. Some microprocessors have special instructions that are used only for I/O; for example,

when a microprocessor executes an OUT 123 operation, the contents of a data register are placed on the data bus. At the same time the number 123 is placed on the eight least-significant bits of the address bus and a pulse is generated on the system's I/O write line. Each of the I/O ports in such a system monitors the address lines. When an I/O interface sees its own address together with a read-port or a write-port signal, the interface acts on that signal and executes an I/O data transfer.

Memory-mapped I/O

Many microprocessors lack explicit I/O instructions like the OUT <port> we've just described and have no special input or output instructions whatsoever. Microprocessors without special I/O instruction must use *memory-mapped I/O* in which the processor treats interface ports as an extension to memory. That is, part of the CPU's normal memory space is dedicated to I/O operations and all I/O ports look exactly like normal memory locations.

Memory-mapped I/O ports are accessed by memory reference instructions like MOVE D0,**IO_PORT** (to output data) and MOVE IO_PORT,**D0** (to input data). A disadvantage of memory-mapped I/O is that memory space available to programs and data is lost to the I/O system.

Figure 10.14 describes the organization and memory map of an I/O port. An output port located at address 8000_{16} is connected to a display device. Data is transmitted to the display by storing it in memory location 8000_{16}. As far as the processor is concerned, it's merely storing data in memory. The program in Table 10.1 sends 128 characters (starting at 2000_{16}) to the display. Note that we've provided both conventional comments and RTL definitions of the instructions.

The numbers in the right-hand column in Table 10.1 give the time to execute each instruction in microseconds, assuming a clock rate of 8 MHz. To output the 128 characters takes approximately $128 + (8 + 8 + 8 + 10)/8 = 544$ μs, which is a little over ½ thousandth of a second. Data is transferred at a rate of one character per 4¼ μs.

Although the program in Table 10.1 looks as if it should work, it's unsuited to almost all real situations involving programmed output. Most peripherals connected to an output

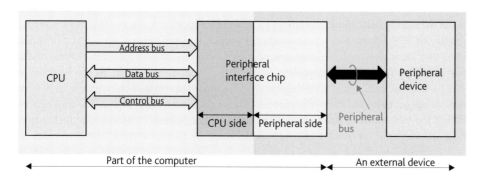

Figure 10.13 Relationship between a computer and a peripheral.

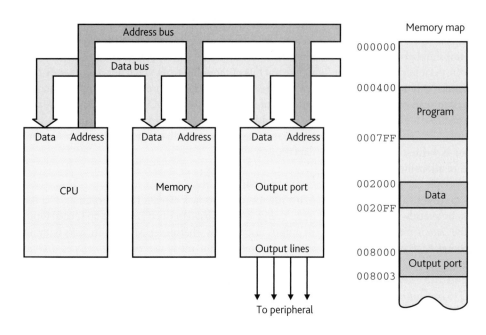

Figure 10.14 Memory mapped I/O.

```
*    FOR i = 1 to 128
*        Move data from Table_i to output_port
*    ENDFOR
*
PORT  EQU    $008000      Location of memory-mapped port
COUNT EQU    128          Size of block to be output
      ORG    $000400      Origin of program
*
      MOVE   #COUNT,D1    [D1]    128           Set up loop counter
      LEA    TABLE,A0     [A0]    TABLE         A0 points to the table
      LEA    PORT,A1      [A1]    Port1         A1 points to the port
*
LOOP  MOVE.B (A0)+,D0     [D0] ← [[A0]]         Get data to be output      8
                         [A0] ← [A0] + 1
      MOVE.B D0,(A1)      [[A1]] ← [D0]         Output the data            8
      SUB    #1,D1        [D1] ← [D1] - 1       Decrement counter          8
      BNE    LOOP         Repeat until counter = 0                        10

      ORG    $002000      Origin for data area
TABLE DS.B   128          Reserve 128 bytes for the table of data
```

Table 10.1 A hypothetical example of a programmed output transfer.

port are slow devices and sending data to them at this rate would simply result in almost all the data being lost. Some interfaces can deal with short bursts of high-speed data because they store data in a buffer; they can't deal with a continuous stream of data at high speeds because the buffer fills up and soon overflows.

You can deal with a mismatch in speed between the computer and a peripheral by asking the peripheral if it's ready to receive data, and not sending data to it until it is ready to receive it. That is, we introduce a *software handshaking procedure* between the peripheral and the interface.

Almost all memory-mapped I/O ports occupy two or more memory locations. One location is reserved for the actual data to be input or output, and one holds a *status byte* associated with the port. For example, let 8000_{16} be the location of the port to which data is sent and let 8002_{16} be the location of the status byte. Suppose that bit 0 of the status byte is a 1 if the port is ready for data and a 0 if it is busy. The fragment of program in Table 10.2 implements memory-mapped output at a rate determined by the peripheral. The comments at the beginning of the program describe the data transfer in pseudocode.

```
*   FOR i = 1 TO 128
*          REPEAT
*              Read Port_status_byte
*          UNTIL Port_not_busy
*          Move data from Table_i to output_port
*   ENDFOR
*
1.  PORTDATA  EQU    $008000       Location of memory-mapped port
2.  PORTSTAT  EQU    $008002       Location of port's status byte
3.  COUNT     EQU    128           Size of block to be output
4.            ORG    $000400       Origin of program
5.            MOVE   #COUNT,D1     Set up character counter in D1
6.            LEA    TABLE,A0      A0 points to table in memory
7.            LEA    PORTDATA,A1   A1 points to data port
8.            LEA    PORTSTAT,A2   A2 points to port status byte
9.  LOOP      MOVE.B (A0)+,D0      Get a byte from the table
10. WAIT      MOVE.B (A2),D2         REPEAT Read the port's status
11.           AND.B  #1,D2            Mask all but lsb of status
12.           BEQ    WAIT             Until port ready
13.           MOVE.B D0,(A1)        Store data in peripheral
14.           SUB    #1,D1         Decrement loop counter
15.           BNE    LOOP          Repeat until COUNT = 0
16. *
17.           ORG    $002000       Start of data area
18. TABLE     DS.B   128           Reserve 128 bytes of data
```

Table 10.2 Using the polling loop to control the flow of data.

The program in Table 10.2 is similar to the previous example in Table 10.1 except for lines 8 to 12 inclusive. In line 8 an address register, A2, is used to point to the status byte of the interface at address 8002_{16}. In line 10 the status byte of the interface is read into D2 and masked down to the least-significant bit (by the action of AND.B #1,D2 in line 11). If the least-significant bit of the status byte is zero, a branch back to line 10 is made by the instruction in line 12. When the interface becomes free, the branch to WAIT is not taken and the program continues exactly as in Table 10.1.

Lines 10, 11, and 12 constitute a *polling loop*, in which the output device is continually polled (questioned) until it indicates it is free, allowing the program to continue. A slow mechanical printer might operate at 30 characters/second, or approximately 1 character per 33 000 μs. Because the polling loop takes about 3 μs, the loop is executed 11 000 times per character.

Operating a computer in a polled input/output mode is grossly inefficient because so much of the computer's time is wasted waiting for the port to become free. If the micro-computer has nothing better to do while it is waiting for a peripheral to become free (i.e. not busy) polled I/O is per-fectly acceptable. Many first-generation PCs, were operated in this way. However, a more powerful computer working in a multiprogramming environment can attend to another task program during the time the I/O port is busy. In this case a better I/O strategy is to ignore the peripheral until it is ready for a data transfer and then let the peripheral ask the CPU for attention. Such a strategy is called *interrupt-driven I/O*.

Note that all the I/O strategies we are describing use memory-mapped I/O.

By the way, if you are designing a computer with memory-mapped I/O and a memory cache,[3] you have to tell the cache controller not to cache the port's status register. If you don't do this, the cache memory would read the status once, cache it, and then return the cached value on successive accesses to the status. Even if the status register in the peripheral changes, the old value in the cache is frozen.

10.2.2 Interrupt-driven I/O

A computer executes instructions sequentially unless a jump or a branch is made. There is, however, an important excep-tion to this rule called an *interrupt*, an event that forces the CPU to modify its sequence of actions. This event may be a signal from a peripheral (i.e. a hardware interrupt) or an internally generated call to the operating system (i.e. a software interrupt). The term *exception* describes both hardware and software interrupts.

Most microprocessors have an active-low interrupt request input, $\overline{\text{IRQ}}$, which is asserted by a peripheral to request attention. The word request implies that the interrupt request may or may not be granted. Figure 10.15 illustrates the organization. of a system with a simple interrupt-driven I/O mechanism.

---

[3] Cache memory is very fast memory that contains a copy of frequently accessed data. We looked at cache memory in Chapter 8.

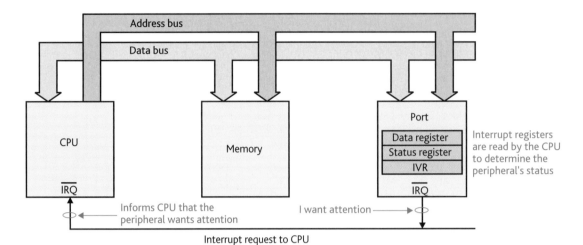

Figure 10.15 Interrupt organization.

In Figure 10.15 an active-low interrupt request line connects all peripherals to the CPU. A peripheral asserts its $\overline{\text{IRQ}}$ output when it requires attention. This system is analogous to the emergency handle in a train. When the handle is pulled in one of the carriages, the driver knows that a problem has arisen but doesn't yet know who pulled the handle. Similarly, the CPU doesn't know which peripheral caused the interrupt or why.

When the CPU detects that its $\overline{\text{IRQ}}$ input has been asserted, the following sequence of events takes place.

- The CPU finishes its current instruction because microprocessors cannot be stopped in mid-instruction. Individual machine code instructions are *indivisible* and must always be executed to completion.[4]
- The contents of the program counter and the processor status word are pushed onto the stack. The processor status must be saved because the interrupt routine will almost certainly modify the condition code bits.
- Further interrupts are disabled to avoid an interrupt being interrupted (we will elaborate on this partially true statement later).
- The CPU deals with the interrupt by executing a program called an *interrupt handler*.
- The CPU executes a return from interrupt instruction at the end of the interrupt handler. Executing this instruction pulls the PC and processor status word off the stack and execution then continues normally—as if the interrupt had never happened.

Figure 10.16 illustrates the sequence of actions taking place when an interrupt occurs. In a 68K system the processor status word consists of the system byte plus the condition code register. The system byte is used by the operating system and interrupt processing mechanism.

Interrupt-driven I/O requires a more complex program than programmed I/O because the information transfer takes place not when the programmer wants or expects it, but when the data is available. The software required to implement interrupt-driven I/O is frequently part of the operating system. A fragment of a hypothetical interrupt-driven output routine in 68K assembly language is provided in Table 10.3. Each time the interrupt handling routine is called, data is obtained from a buffer and passed to the memory-mapped output port at $008000. In a practical system some check would be needed to test for the end of the buffer.

Because the processor executes this code only when a peripheral requests an I/O transaction, interrupt-driven I/O is very much more efficient than the polled I/O we described earlier.

Although the basic idea of interrupts is common to most computers, there are considerable variations in the precise nature of the interrupt-handling structure from computer to computer. We are now going to look at how the 68K deals with interrupts because this microprocessor has a particularly comprehensive interrupt handling facility.

Prioritized interrupts

Computer interrupts are almost exactly analogous to interrupts in everyday life. Suppose two students interrupt me when I'm lecturing—one with a question and the other because they feel unwell. I will respond to the more urgent of the two requests. Once I've dealt with the student who's unwell, I answer the other student's question and then continue my teaching. Computers behave in the same way.

---

[4] This statement is not true of all microprocessors. It is possible to design microprocessors that can save sufficient state information to interrupt an instruction and then continue from the point at which execution had reached.

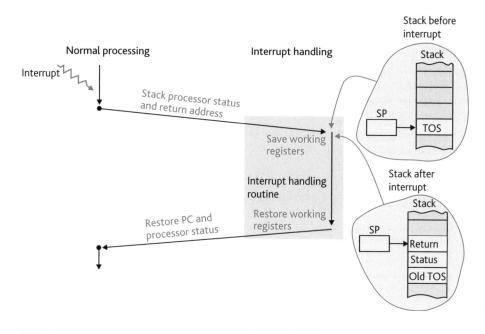

Figure 10.16 Interrupt sequence.

```
*   Pick up pointer to next free entry in the table (buffer)
*   Read a byte from the table and transmit it to the interface
*   Move the pointer to the next entry in the table and save
*   the pointer in memory
*   Return from interrupt
*
OUTPUT   EQU      $008000          Location of memory-mapped output port
         ORG      $000400          Start of the program fragment
*
         LEA      POINTER,A0       Load A0 with the pointer to the buffer
         MOVE.B   (A0)+,OUTPUT     Read character from buffer and output
         MOVE.L   A0,POINTER       Save the updated pointer
         RTE                       Return from interrupt

         ORG      $002000          Data origin
BUFFER   DS.B     1024             Reserve 1024 bytes for the table
POINTER  DS.L     1                Reserve a longword for the pointer
```

Table 10.3 A simple interrupt handler.

Most computers have more than one interrupt request input. Some interrupt request pins are connected to peripherals requiring immediate attention (e.g. a disk drive), whereas others are connected to peripherals requiring less urgent attention (e.g. a keyboard). For the sake of accuracy, we should point out that the processor's interrupt request input is connected to the peripheral's interface, rather than the peripheral itself. If the disk drive is not serviced when its data is available, the data will be lost because it will be replaced by new data. In such circumstances, it is reasonable to assign a priority to each of the interrupt request pins.

The 68K supports seven interrupt request inputs, from $\overline{IRQ7}$, the most important, to $\overline{IRQ1}$, the least important. Suppose an interrupt is caused by the assertion of $\overline{IRQ3}$ and no other interrupts are pending. The interrupt on $\overline{IRQ3}$ will be serviced. If an interrupt at a level higher than $\overline{IRQ3}$ occurs, it will be serviced before the level 3 interrupt service routine is completed. However, interrupts generated by $\overline{IRQ1}$ or $\overline{IRQ2}$ will be stored pending the completion of $\overline{IRQ3}$'s service routine.

The 68K does not have seven explicit $\overline{IRQ1}$ to $\overline{IRQ7}$ interrupt request inputs (simply because such an arrangement would require seven precious pins). Instead, the 68K has a 3-bit encoded interrupt request input, $\overline{IPL0}$ to $\overline{IPL2}$. The 3-bit value on $\overline{IPL0}$ to $\overline{IPL2}$ reflects the current level of interrupt request from 0 (i.e. no interrupt request) to 7 (the highest level corresponding to $\overline{IRQ7}$). Figure 10.17 illustrates some of the elements involved in the 68K's interrupt handling structure. A priority encoder chip is required to convert an interrupt request on $\overline{IRQ1}$ to $\overline{IRQ7}$ into a 3-bit code in $\overline{IPL0}$

to $\overline{IPL2}$. The priority encoder automatically prioritizes interrupt requests and its output reflects the highest interrupt request level asserted.

The 68K doesn't automatically service an interrupt request. The processor status byte in the CPU in Fig. 10.17 controls the way in which the 68K responds to an interrupt. Figure 10.18 describes the status byte in more detail. The 3-bit interrupt mask field in the processor status byte, I_2, I_1, I_0, determines how the 68K responds to an interrupt. The current interrupt request is serviced if its level is greater than that of the interrupt mask; otherwise the request is ignored. For example, if the interrupt mask has a current value of 4, only interrupt requests on $\overline{IRQ5}$ to $\overline{IRQ7}$ will be serviced.

When the 68K services an interrupt, the interrupt mask bits are reset to make them equal to the level of the interrupt currently being serviced. For example, if the interrupt mask bits were set to 2 and an interrupt occurred at level $\overline{IRQ5}$, the mask bits would be set to 5. Consequently, the 68K can now be re-interrupted only by interrupt levels 6 and 7. After the interrupt has been serviced, the old value of the processor status byte saved on the stack, and therefore the interrupt mask bits, are restored to their original level.

Non-maskable interrupts

Microprocessors sometimes have a special interrupt request input called a *non-maskable interrupt request*. The term

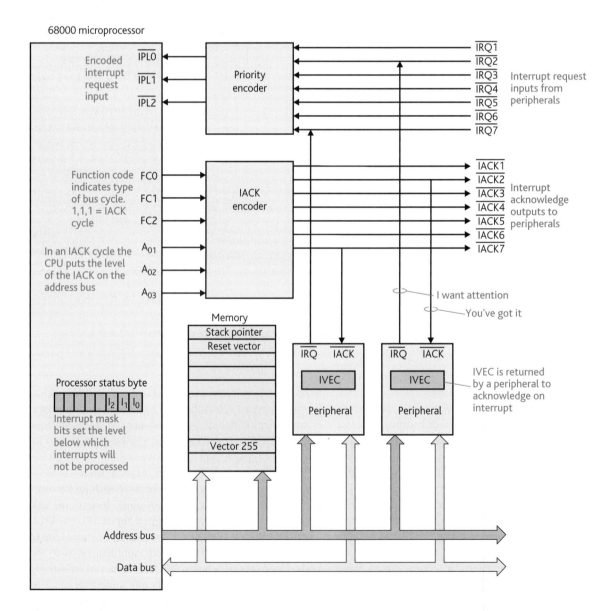

Figure 10.17 The 68K's interrupt structure.

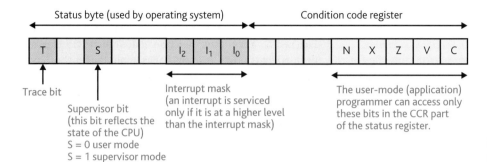

Figure 10.18 The 68K's status word.

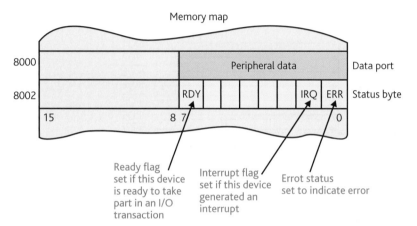

Figure 10.19 A memory-mapped data and status port.

non-maskable means that the interrupt cannot be turned off (i.e. delayed or suspended) and must be serviced immediately. Non-maskable interrupts are necessary when the interrupt is caused by a critical event that must not be missed; for example, an interruption of the power supply. When power is lost, the system still functions for a few milliseconds on energy stored in capacitors (devices found in all power supplies). A non-maskable interrupt generated at the first sign of a power loss is used to shut down the computer in an orderly fashion so that it can be restarted later with little loss of data and no corruption of disk files.

A second application of non-maskable interrupts is in *real-time systems*. Suppose that the temperature and pressure at various points in a chemical process must be measured periodically. If these points aren't polled on a programmed basis, a stream of regularly spaced non-maskable interrupts will do the trick. At each interrupt, the contents of a counter register are updated and, if a suitable span of time has elapsed, the required readings are taken.

The 68K reserves its level 7 interrupt ($\overline{\text{IRQ7}}$) as a non-maskable interrupt, because an interrupt on $\overline{\text{IRQ7}}$ is always serviced by the 68000. If a level 7 interrupt is currently being serviced by the 68K, a further active transition on $\overline{\text{IRQ7}}$ (i.e. a high-to-low edge) results in the 68K servicing the new level 7 interrupt.

Vectored interrupts

Following the detection and acceptance of an interrupt, the appropriate interrupt-handling routine must be executed. You can test each of the possible interrupters, in turn, to determine whether they were responsible for the interrupt. This operation is called *polling* and is the same mechanism used for programmed I/O.

We now look at how the 68K deals with the identification of an interrupt request that came from one of several possible devices. However, before we do this it's instructive to consider how first-generation microprocessors performed the task of isolating the cause of an interrupt request.

Figure 10.19 shows the structure of a memory-mapped I/O port with a data port at address 8000_{16} and a status byte at location 8002_{16}. We have defined 3 bits in the status byte:

- RDY (ready) indicates that the port is ready to take part in a data transaction
- IRQ indicates that the port has generated an interrupt
- ERR indicates that an error has occurred (i.e. the input or output is unreliable).

The RDY bit of a peripheral is tested until it is ready to take part in an I/O transaction. A system with interrupt-driven I/O and device polling waits for an interrupt and then reads the IRQ bit in the status register of each peripheral. This technique is fairly efficient as long as there are few devices capable of generating an interrupt.

Because the programmer chooses the order in which the interfaces are polled following an interrupt, a measure of prioritization is built into the polling process. However, a well-known law of the universe states that when searching through a pile of magazines for a particular copy, the desired issue is always at the opposite end to the point at which the search was started. Likewise, the device that generated the interrupt is the last device to be polled. A system with polled interrupts could lead to the situation in which a device requests service but never gets it. We next demonstrate how some processors allow the peripheral that requested attention to identify itself by means of a mechanism called the *vectored interrupt*.

In a system with *vectored interrupts* the interface itself identifies its interrupt-handling routine, thereby removing the need for interrupt polling. Whenever the 68K detects an interrupt, the 68K acknowledges it by transmitting an *interrupt acknowledge* (called IACK) message to all the interfaces that might have originated the interrupt.

The 68K uses function code outputs, FC0, FC1, FC2, to inform peripherals that it's acknowledging an interrupt (see Fig. 10.17). These three function code outputs tell external devices what the 68K is doing. For example, the function code tells the system whether the 68K is reading an instruction or an operand from memory. The special function code 1,1,1 indicates an interrupt acknowledge.

Because the 68K has seven levels of interrupt request, it's necessary to acknowledge only the appropriate level of

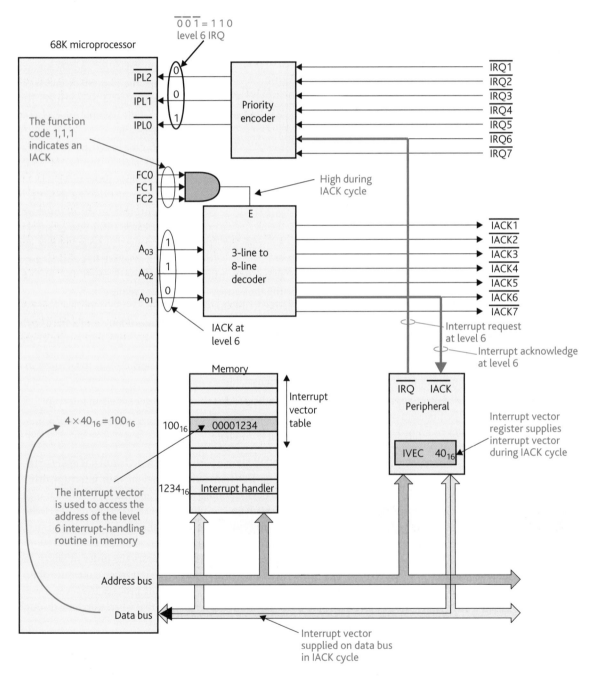

Figure 10.20 Responding to a level 6 vectored interrupt.

interrupt. It would be unfair if a level 2 and a level 6 interrupt occurred nearly simultaneously and the interface requesting a level 2 interrupt thought that its interrupt was about to be serviced. The 68K indicates which level of interrupt it's acknowledging by providing the level on the three least-significant bits of its address bus (A_{01} to A_{03}). External logic detects FC0, FC1, FC2 = 1, 1, 1 and uses A_{01} to A_{03} to generate seven interrupt acknowledge signals IACK0 to IACK7 .

After issuing an interrupt request, the interface waits for an acknowledgement on its $\overline{\text{IACK}}$ input. When the interface detects $\overline{\text{IACK}}$ asserted, it puts out an interrupt vector number on data lines d_{00} to d_{07}. That is, the interface responds with a number ranging from 0 to 255. When the 68K receives this interrupt vector number, it multiplies it by 4 to get an entry into the 68K's *interrupt vector table*; for example, if an interface responds to an IACK cycle with a vector number of 100, the CPU multiplies it by 4 to get 400. In the next step, the 68K reads the contents of memory location 400 to get a pointer to the location of the interrupt-handling routine for the interface that initiated the interrupt. This pointer is loaded into the 68K's program counter to start interrupt processing.

Because an interface can supply one of 256 possible vector numbers, it's theoretically possible to support 256 unique interrupt-handling routines for 256 different interfaces. We say theoretically, because it's unusual for 68K systems to dedicate all 256 vector numbers to interrupt handling. In fact, the 68K itself uses vector numbers 0 to 63 for purposes other than handling hardware interrupts (these vectors are reserved for other types of exception).

The 68K multiplies the vector number by 4 because each vector number is associated with a 4-byte pointer in memory.

The interrupt vector table itself takes up $4 \times 256 = 1024$ bytes of memory. Figure 10.20 illustrates the way in which the 68K responds to a level 6 vectored interrupt.

Daisy-chaining

The vectored interrupt scheme we've just described has a flaw. Although there are 256 interrupt vector numbers, the 68K supports only seven levels of interrupt. A mechanism called *daisy-chaining* provides a means of increasing the number of interrupt levels by linking the peripherals together in a line. When the CPU acknowledges an interrupt, a message is sent to the first peripheral in the daisy chain. If this peripheral doesn't require attention, it passes the IACK down the line to the next peripheral.

Figure 10.21 shows how interrupt requesters at a given priority level are prioritized by daisy chaining. Each peripheral has an $\overline{\text{IACK\_IN}}$ input and an IACK_OUT output. The IACK_OUT pin of a peripheral is wired to the IACK_IN pin of the peripheral on its right. Suppose an interrupt request at level 6 is issued and acknowledged by the 68K. The interface at the left-hand side of the daisy chain closest to the 68K receives the $\overline{\text{IACK}}$ signal first from the CPU. If this interface generated the interrupt, it responds with an interrupt vector. If the interface did not request service, it passes the IACK signal to the device on its right. That is, $\overline{\text{IACK\_IN}}$ is passed out on $\overline{\text{IACK\_OUT}}$. The $\overline{\text{IACK}}$ signal ripples down the daisy chain until a device responds with an interrupt vector.

Daisy-chaining interfaces permit an unlimited number of interfaces to share the same level of interrupt and each interface to have its own interrupt vector number. Individual

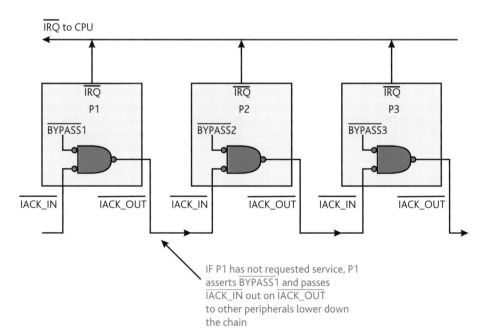

$\overline{\text{IRQ}}$ to CPU

IF P1 has not requested service, P1 asserts $\overline{\text{BYPASS1}}$ and passes $\overline{\text{IACK\_IN}}$ out on $\overline{\text{IACK\_OUT}}$ to other peripherals lower down the chain

Figure 10.21 Daisy-chaining interrupts at the same level of priority.

interfaces are prioritized by their position with respect to the CPU. The closer to the CPU an interface is, the more chance it has of having its interrupt request serviced in the event of multiple interrupt requests at this level.

10.3 Direct memory access

The third I/O strategy, called *direct memory access* (DMA), moves data between a peripheral and the CPU's memory without the direct intervention of the CPU itself. DMA provides the fastest possible means of transferring data between an interface and memory, as it requires no CPU overhead and leaves the CPU free to do useful work. DMA is complex to implement and requires a relatively large amount of hardware. Figure 10.22 illustrates the operation of a system with DMA.

DMA works by grabbing the data and address buses from the CPU and using them to transfer data directly between the peripheral and memory. During normal operation of the computer in Fig. 10.22, bus switch 1 is closed and bus switches 2 and 3 are open. The CPU controls the buses, providing an address on the address bus and reading data from memory or writing data to memory via the data bus.

When a peripheral wishes to take part in an I/O transaction it asserts the TransferRequest input of the DMA controller (DMAC). In turn, the DMA controller asserts DMArequest to request control of the buses from the CPU; that is the CPU is taken offline. When the CPU returns DMAgrant to the DMAC, a DMA transfer takes place. Bus switch 1 is opened and switches 2 and 3 closed. The DMAC provides an address to the address bus and hence to the memory. At the same time, the DMAC provides a TransferGrant signal to the peripheral, which is then able to write to, or read from, the memory directly. When the DMA operation has been completed, the DMAC hands back control of the bus to the CPU.

A real DMA controller is a very complex device. It has several internal registers with at least one to hold the address of the next memory location to access and one to hold the number of words to be transferred. Many DMACs are able to handle several interfaces, which means that their registers must be duplicated. Each interface is referred to as a *channel* and typical single-chip DMA controllers handle up to four channels (i.e. peripherals) simultaneously.

Figure 10.23 provides a protocol flowchart for the sequence of operations taking place during a DMA operation. This figure shows the sequence of events that takes place in the form of a series of transactions between the peripheral, DMAC, and the CPU.

DMA operates in one of two modes: *burst mode* or *cycle stealing*. In the burst mode the DMA controller seizes the system bus for the duration of the data transfer operation (or at least for the transfer of a large number of words). Burst mode DMA allows data to be moved into memory as fast as the weakest link in the chain memory/bus/interface permits. The CPU is effectively halted in the burst mode because it cannot use its data and address buses.

In the cycle steal mode described by Fig. 10.24, DMA operations are interleaved with the computer's normal memory accesses. As the computer does not require access to the system buses for 100% of the time, DMA can take place when they are free. This free time occurs while the CPU is busy generating an address ready for a memory read or write cycle.

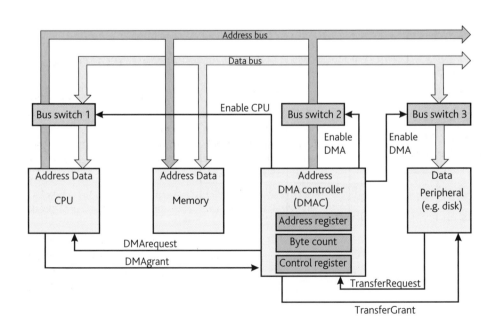

Figure 10.22 Input/Output by means of DMA.

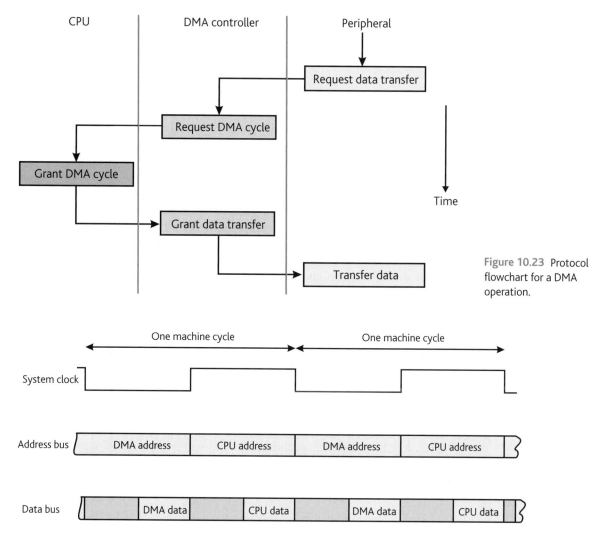

Figure 10.23 Protocol flowchart for a DMA operation.

Figure 10.24 DMA by cycle stealing.

When the system clock is low, the CPU doesn't need the buses, so the DMAC grabs them and carries out a data transfer. When the clock goes high the CPU carries out its normal memory access cycle. DMA by cycle stealing is said to be *transparent* because the transfer is invisible to the computer and no processing time is lost. A DMA operation is initiated by the CPU writing a start address and the number of words to be transferred into the DMAC's registers. When the DMA operation has been completed, the DMAC generates an interrupt, indicating to the CPU that the data transfer is over and that a new one may be initiated or results of the current transfer made use of.

In systems with a cache memory, DMA can take place in parallel with normal CPU activity; that is, the CPU can access data and code that's been cached while the I/O interface is copying data between a peripheral and the main memory.

10.4 Parallel and serial interfaces

Having described how I/O transactions can be programmed, be interrupt driven, or use DMA, we now look at typical interfaces between the CPU and the outside world. These devices look like a block of memory locations to the CPU and implement the protocol required to communicate with the external system. Although we describe two actual devices, the general principles apply to all interface devices. Readers not interested in the fine details of I/O systems may skip this section.

The first interface to be described is the *peripheral interface adapter*, which transfers data between an external system and a processor, and the second interface is the asynchronous communications adapter, which transfers data on a single-bit serial highway. These devices are typical first-generation circuits with 8-bit data interfaces allowing them to be used with 8-bit processors.

10.4.1 The parallel interface

The *peripheral interface adapter* (PIA) is an integrated circuit with two independent 8-bit ports. It contains all the logic needed to control the flow of data between an external peripheral and a computer. A port's eight pins may be programmed *individually* to act as inputs or outputs; for example, an 8-bit port can be configured with two input lines and six output lines. The PIA can automatically perform handshaking with devices connected to its ports.

Figure 10.25 gives a block diagram of the PIA from which it can be seen that the two I/O ports, referred to as the *A side* and the *B side*, appear symmetrical. In general this is true, but small differences in the behavior of these ports are described when necessary. Each port has two control pins that can transform the port from a simple I/O latch into a device capable of performing a handshake or initiating interrupts, as required.

The interface between the PIA and the CPU is conventional; the PIA's CPU-side looks like a block of four locations in RAM to the CPU. CPU-side pins comprise a data bus and its associated control circuits. Two *register-select* pins RS0 and RS1 are connected to the lower-order bits of the CPU's address bus and discriminate between the PIA's internal registers.

The PIA has two independent interrupt request outputs, one for each port. When the PIA is powered up, the contents of all its internal registers are put in a zero state. In this mode the PIA is in a safe state with all its programmable pins configured as inputs. It would be highly dangerous to permit the PIA to assume a random initial configuration, because any random output signals might cause havoc elsewhere.

To appreciate how the PIA operates, we have to understand the function of its six internal registers. The PIA has two *peripheral data registers* (PDRA and PDRB), two *data-direction registers* (DDRA, and DDRB), and two *control registers* (CRA and CRB). The host computer accesses a location within the PIA by putting the appropriate 2-bit address on register select lines RS0 and RS1. Because RS0 and RS1 can directly

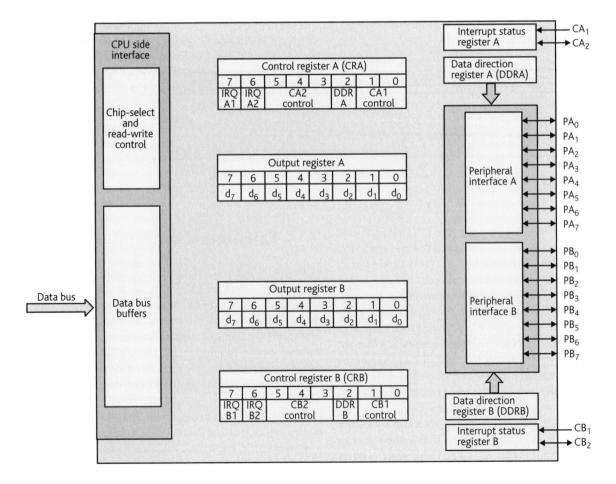

Figure 10.25 Structure of the PIA.

distinguish between only four of the six internal registers, we need a means of accessing the other registers. The PIA uses bit 2 in the control registers (CRA2 or CRB2) as a pointer to either the data register or the data-direction register. Table 10.4 demonstrates how this arrangement works.

Register select input RS1 determines which of the two 8-bit I/O ports of the PIA is selected and RS0 determines whether the control register or *one of the pair of registers formed by the peripheral data register and the data register*, is selected. The control registers can always be unconditionally accessed when RS0 = 1, but to select a peripheral data register or a data-direction register, bit 2 of the appropriate control register must be set or cleared, respectively.

The peripheral data registers provide an interface between the PIA and the outside world. When one of the PIA's 16 I/O pins is programmed as an input, data is moved from that pin through the peripheral data register onto the CPU's data bus during a read cycle. Conversely, when acting as an output, the CPU latches a 1 or 0 into the appropriate bit of the peripheral data register to determine the state of the corresponding output pin.

The *data-direction registers* determine the direction of data transfer at the PIA's I/O pins. Writing a zero into bit i of DDRA configures bit i of the A side peripheral data register as an input. Conversely, writing a one into bit i of DDRA configures bit i of the A side peripheral data register as an output. The pins of the PIA's A side or B side ports may be defined as inputs or outputs by writing an appropriate code into DDRA or DDRB, respectively. The PIA's I/O pins can be configured *dynamically* and the direction of data transfer altered during the course of a program. The DDR's bits are cleared during a power-on-reset to avoid accidentally forcing any pin into an output mode.

Table 10.5 demonstrates how side A of a PIA memory-mapped at address $80 0000 is configured as an input and side B as an output. The registers are accessed at $80 0000, $80 0002, $80 0004, and $80 0006. Consecutive addresses differ by 2 rather than 1 because the 68K's data bus is 16 bits wide (2 bytes) whereas the PIA is 8 bits wide.

Once the PIA has been configured, data can be read from side A of the PIA into data register D0 by a MOVE.B PDRA, **D0** instruction, and data may written into side B by writing to the PIA with a MOVE.B D0, **PDRB** instruction.

RS1	RS0	CRA2	CRB2	Location selected	Address
0	0	1	X	Peripheral data register A	BASE
0	0	0	X	Data direction register A	BASE
0	1	X	X	Control register A	BASE+2
1	0	X	1	Peripheral data register B	BASE+4
1	0	X	0	Data direction register B	BASE+4
1	1	X	X	Control register B	BASE+6

X = don't care
BASE = base address of the memory-mapped PIA
RS0 = register select 0   RS1 = register select 1
CRA2 = bit 2 of control register A   CRB2 = bit 2 of control register B

Table 10.4 The register selection scheme of the PIA.

```
PDRA    EQU    $800000    Base address of PIA (data register side A)
DDRA    EQU    $800000    Data direction register shares PDRA address
CRA     EQU    $800002    Control register address (side A)
PDRB    EQU    $800004    Side B registers
DDRB    EQU    $800004
CRB     EQU    $800006

*       Select side A DDR by setting CRA2 to 0 (we clear all bits)
        CLR.B   CRA

*       Configure side A data register as input by writing 0s into DDRA
        MOVE.B #0,DDRA (this is the same as CLR.B DDRA)

*       Select side B data direction register B by setting CRB2 to 0
        CLR.B   CRB

*       Select side B as an output by writing 1s into DDRB
        MOVE.B #%11111111,DDRB

*       Select PDRA as an input port by setting bit CRA2 to 1
        OR.B    #%00000100,CRA

*       Select PDRB as an output port by setting bit CRB2 to 1
        OR.B    #%00000100,CRB
```

Table 10.5 Configuring a PIA.

Controlling the PIA

The control registers control the special-purpose pins associated with each port of the PIA. Pins CA1 and CA2 control the flow of information between the peripheral's A side and the PIA by providing any required handshaking between the peripheral and PIA. Similarly, side B has control pins CB1 and CB2.

The bits of control register A (CRA) can be divided into four groups according to their function. Bits CRA0 to CRA5 define the PIA's operating mode (Fig. 10.26). Bits CRA6 and CRA7 are interrupt status bits that are set or cleared by the PIA itself. Bit CRA6 is interrupt request flag 1 (IRQA1), which is set by an active transition at the CA1 input pin. Similarly, CRA7 corresponds to the IRQA2 interrupt request flag and is set by an active transition at the CA2 input pin. We now examine the control register in more detail.

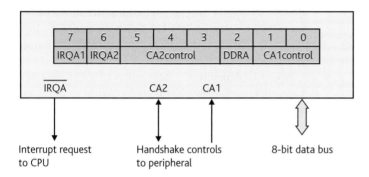

Figure 10.26 Structure of the PIA's side A control register.

CRA1	CRA0	Transition of CA1 control input	IRQA1 interrupt flag status	Status of side A interrupt request
0	0	negative edge	set on negative edge	masked
0	1	negative edge	set on negative edge	enabled
1	0	positive edge	set on positive edge	masked
1	1	positive edge	set on positive edge	enabled (asserted)

Table 10.6 Effect of CA1 control bits.

CRA5	CRA4	CRA3	Transition of CA2 control input	IRQA2 interrupt flag status	Status interrupt request
0	0	0	negative edge	set on negative edge	masked
0	0	1	negative edge	set on negative edge	enabled (asserted)
0	1	0	positive edge	set on positive edge	masked
0	1	1	positive edge	set on positive edge	enabled (goes low)

Table 10.7 Effect of CA2 control bits when CRA5 = 0 (note that E is the PIA's clock).

CA1 control Bits CRA0 and CRA1 determine how the PIA responds to a change of level (0-to-1 or 1-to-0) at the CA1 control input. The relationship between the CA1 control input, CRA0, CRA1, and the interrupt flag IRQA1 is described in Table 10.6. CRA1 determines the sense (i.e. *up* or *down*) of the transition on CA1 that causes the CRA7 interrupt flag (i.e. IRQA1) to be set. CRA0 determines whether an active transition on CA1 generates an interrupt request by asserting the $\overline{\text{IRQA}}$ output. CA1 can be used as an auxiliary input if bit CRA0 is clear, or as an interrupt request input if bit CRA0 is set.

Whenever an interrupt is caused by an active transition on CA1, the interrupt flag in the control register, IRQA1, is set and the $\overline{\text{IRQA}}$ output pin goes low. After the CPU has read the contents of peripheral data register A, interrupt flag IRQA1 is automatically reset. In a typical application of the PIA, CA1 is connected to a peripheral's RDY output so that the peripheral can request attention when it is ready to take part in a data transfer.

For example, if CRA1, CRA0 is set to 0, 1, a negative (falling) edge at the CA1 control input sets the IRQA1 status flag in control register CRA to 1, and the PIA's $\overline{\text{IRQA}}$ interrupt request output is asserted to interrupt the host processor. CRA1 determines the sense of the transition on CA1 that sets the interrupt flag status and CRA0 determines whether the PIA will interrupt the host processor when the interrupt flag is set.

Data direction access control (CRA2) When register select input RS0 is 0, the data-direction access control bit determines whether data-direction register A or peripheral data register A is selected. When the PIA is reset, CRA2 is 0 so that the data-direction register is always available after a reset.

CA2 control (CRA3, CRA4, CRA5) The CA2 control pin may be programmed as an input that generates an interrupt request in a similar way to CA1, or it may be programmed as an output. Bit 5 of the control register determines CA2's function. If bit 5 is 0, CA2 is an interrupt request input (Table 10.7) and if bit 5 is 1, CA2 is an output (Table 10.8). Table 10.7 demonstrates that the behavior of CA2, when acting as an interrupt-request input, is entirely analogous to that of CA1.

When CA2 is programmed as an output with CRA5 = 1 it behaves in the manner defined in Table 10.8.

1. Case 1 (CRA5 = 1, CRA4 = 0, CRA3 = 0). This is the *handshake mode* used when a peripheral is transmitting data to the CPU via the PIA. A timing diagram of the action of the handshake mode of CA2 is given in Fig. 10.27, together with an

Case	CRA5	CRA4	CRA3	Output CA2	
0	1	0	0	Low on the falling edge of the E clock after a CPU read side A data operation	High when interrupt flag bit CRA7 is set by an active transition of CA1 input
1	1	0	1	Low on the falling edge of E after a CPU read side A data operation	High on the negative edge of the first E pulse occurring during a deselect state
2	1	1	0	Low when CRA3 goes low as a result of a CPU write to CRA.	Always low as long as CRA3 is low. Will go high on a CPU write to CRA that changes CRA3 to a 1
3	1	1	1	Always high as long as CRA3 is high. Will be cleared on a CPU write to CRA that clears CRA3	High when CRA23 goes high as a result of a CPU write to CRA

Table 10.8 Effect of CA2 control bits when CRA5 = 1.

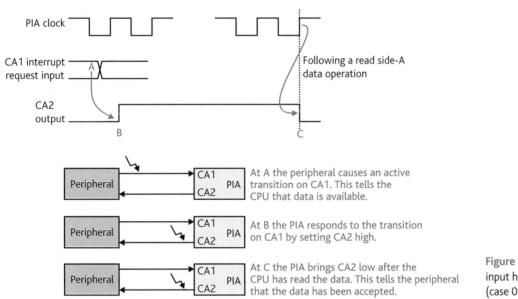

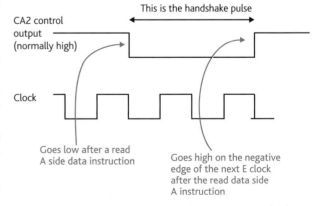

Figure 10.27 The PIA input handshake mode (case 0 in Table 10.8).

explanation of the steps involved. In handshake mode CA2 goes high whenever a peripheral has data ready for reading and remains high until the CPU has read the data from the PIA's data register.

2. Case 2 (CRA5 = 1, CRA4 = 0, CRA3 = 1). This is the *autohandshaking mode* and is illustrated in Fig. 10.28. CA2 automatically produces a single pulse at a low level after the side A peripheral data register has been read by the CPU. Because the peripheral receives a pulse on CA2 after the CPU has read the PIA, the peripheral knows that its data has been received and that the PIA is ready for new data.

3. Case 3 (CRA5 = 1, CRA4 = 1, CRA3 = 0). In this mode CA2 is set low and remains in that state until CRA3 is set. That is, CA2 is cleared under program control.

Figure 10.28 The PIA autohandshake input mode.

4. Case 4 (CRA5 = 1, CRA4 = 1, CRA3 = 1). Now CA2 is set to a high level and remains in that state until CRA3 is cleared. Cases 3 and 4 demonstrate the use of CA2 as an additional output, set or cleared under program control.

10.4.2 The serial interface

We now describe the serial interface device that connects a computer to a modem or a similar device. Although the serial interface was once used to connect PCs to a wide range of external peripherals, the USB and FireWire interfaces have largely rendered the serial interface obsolete in modern PCs.

Serial data transmission is used by data transmission systems that operate over distances greater than a few meters and Chapter 14 will have more to say on the subject of data transmission. Here we're more interested in the *asynchronous communications adapter* (ACIA) interface, which connects a CPU to a serial data link.

The serial interface transfers data into and out of the CPU a bit at a time along a single wire; for example, the 8-bit value 10110001_2 would be sent in the form of eight or more pulses one after the other. Serial data transfer is slower than the parallel data transfer offered by a PIA, but is inexpensive because it requires only a single connection between the serial interface and the external world (apart from a ground-return).

We are not concerned with fine details of the ACIA's internal operation, but rather in what it does and how it is used to transmit and receive serial data. When discussing serial transmission we often use the term *character* to refer to a unit of data rather than byte, because many transmission systems are designed to transmit information in the form of ISO/ASCII-encoded characters.

Figure 10.29 demonstrates how a 7-bit character is transmitted bit by bit asynchronously. During a period in which no data is being transmitted from an ACIA, the serial output is at a high level, which is called the *mark* condition. When a character is to be transmitted, the ACIA's serial output is put in a low state (a *mark-to-space* transition) for a period of one bit time. The bit time is the reciprocal of the rate at which successive serial bits are transmitted and is measured in *Baud*. In the case of a two-level binary signal, the Baud corresponds to bits/s. The initial bit is called the *start bit* and tells the receiver that a stream of bits, representing a character, is about to be received. If data is transmitted at 9600 Baud, each bit period is $1/9600 = 0.1042$ ms.

During the next seven time slots (each of the same duration as the start bit) the output of the ACIA depends on the value of the character being transmitted. The character is transmitted bit by bit. This data format is called *non-return to zero* (NRZ) because the output doesn't go to zero between individual bits. After the character has been transmitted, a further two bits (a parity bit and a stop bit) are appended to the end of the character.

At the receiver, a parity bit is generated locally from the incoming data and then compared with the received parity bit. If the received and locally generated parity bits differ, an error in transmission is assumed to have occurred. A single parity bit can't correct an error once it has occurred, nor detect a pair of errors in a character. Not all serial data transmission systems employ a parity bit error detector.

The stop bit (or optionally two stop bits) indicates the end of the character. Following the reception of the stop bit(s), the transmitter output is once more in its mark state and is ready to send the next character. The character is composed of 10 bits but contains only 7 bits of useful information.

The key to asynchronous data transmission is that once the receiver has detected a start bit, it has to maintain synchronization only for the duration of a single character. The receiver examines successive received bits by sampling the incoming

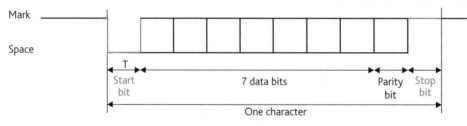

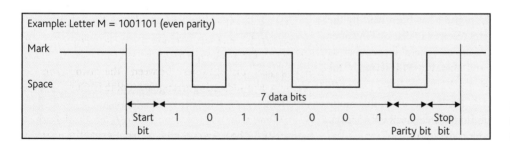

Figure 10.29 Format of an asynchronous serial character.

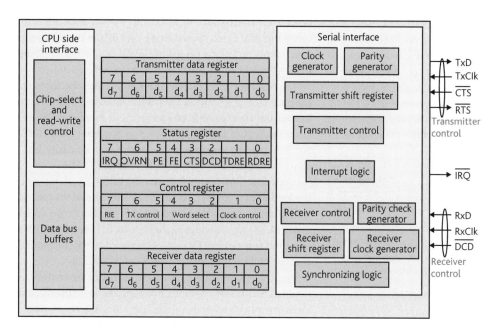

Figure 10.30 Organization of the ACIA.

signal at the center of each pulse. Because the clock at the receiver is not synchronized with the clock at the transmitter, each received data bit will not be sampled exactly at its center.

Figure 10.30 provides the internal arrangement of a typical ACIA, a highly programmable interface whose parameters can be defined under software control. The ACIA has a single receiver input pin and a single transmitter output pin.

The ACIA's Peripheral side pins

The ACIA communicates with a peripheral via seven pins, which may be divided into three groups: receiver, transmitter, and modem control. At this point, all we need say is that the modem is a black box that interfaces a digital system to the public switched telephone network and therefore permits digital signals to be transmitted across the telephone system. A modem converts digital signals into audio (analog) tones. We'll look at the modem in more detail in Chapter 14.

Receiver The receiver part of the ACIA has a clock input and a serial data input. The receiver clock is used to sample the incoming data bits and may be 64, 16, or 1 times that of the bit rate of the received data; for example, an ACIA operating at 9600 bits/s might use a $16\times$ receiver clock of 153 600 Hz. The serial data input receives data from the peripheral to which the ACIA is connected. Most systems require a special interface chip between the ACIA and the serial data link to convert the signal levels at the ACIA to the signal levels found on the data link.

Transmitter The transmitter part of the ACIA has a clock input from which it generates the timing of the transmitted data pulses.

Modem control The ACIA communicates with a modem or similar equipment via three active-low pins (two inputs and

one output). The ACIA's *request to send* ($\overline{\text{RTS}}$) output may be set or cleared under software control and is used by the ACIA to tell the modem that it is ready to transmit data to it.

The two active-low inputs to the ACIA are clear-to-send ($\overline{\text{CTS}}$) and data-carrier-detect ($\overline{\text{DCD}}$). The $\overline{\text{CTS}}$ input is a signal from the modem to the ACIA that inhibits the ACIA from transmitting data if the modem is not ready (because the telephone connection has not been established or has been broken). If the $\overline{\text{CTS}}$ input is high, a bit is set in the ACIA's status register, indicating that the modem (or other terminal equipment) is not ready for data.

The modem uses the ACIA's $\overline{\text{DCD}}$ input to tell the ACIA that the carrier has been lost (i.e. a signal is no longer being received) and that valid data is no longer available at the receiver's input. A low-to-high transition at the $\overline{\text{DCD}}$ input sets a bit in the status register and may also initiate an interrupt if the ACIA is so programmed. In applications of the ACIA that don't use a modem, the $\overline{\text{CTS}}$ and $\overline{\text{DCD}}$ inputs are connected to a low level and not used.

The ACIA's internal registers

The ACIA has four internal registers: a transmitter data register (TDR), a receiver data register (RDR), a control register (CR), and a status register (SR). Because the ACIA has a single register-select input RS, only two internal registers can be directly accessed by the CPU. Because the status and receiver data registers are always read from, and the transmitter data register and control register are always written to, the ACIA's R/$\overline{\text{W}}$ input distinguishes between the two pairs of registers. The addressing arrangement of the ACIA is given in Table 10.9.

The control register is a write-only register that defines the operational properties of the ACIA, particularly the format of the transmitted or received data. Table 10.10 defines the control register's format. The counter division field, CR0 and CR1, determines the relationship between the transmitter and receiver bit rates and their respective clocks (Table 10.11).

When CR1 and CR0 are both set to one, the ACIA is reset and all internal status bits, with the exception of the CTS and DCD flags, are cleared. The CTS and DCD flags are entirely dependent on the signal level at the respective pins. The ACIA

RS	R/$\overline{\text{W}}$	Type of register	ACIA register
0	0	Write only	Control
0	1	Read only	Status
1	0	Write only	Transmitter data
1	1	Read only	Receiver data

Table 10.9 Register selection scheme of the ACIA.

7	6	5	4 3 2	1 0
Receive interrupt enable	Transmitter control		Word select	Counter division

Table 10.10 Format of the ACIA's control register.

CR1	CR0	Division ratio
0	0	÷1
0	1	÷16
1	0	÷64
1	1	Master reset

Table 10.11 Relationship between CR1, CR0, and the division ratio.

CR4	CR3	CR2	Word length	Parity	Stop bits	Total bits
0	0	0	7	Even	2	11
0	0	1	7	Odd	2	11
0	1	0	7	Even	1	10
0	1	1	7	Odd	1	10
1	0	0	8	None	2	11
1	0	1	8	None	1	10
1	1	0	8	Even	1	11
1	1	1	8	Odd	1	11

Table 10.12 The word select bits.

is initialized by first writing ones into bits CR1 and CR0 of the control register, and then writing one of the three division ratio codes into these positions. In the majority of systems CR1 = 0 and CR0 = 1 for a divide by 16 ratio.

The word select field, CR2, CR3, CR4, defines the format of the received or transmitted characters. These three bits allow the selection of eight possible arrangements of number of bits per character, type of parity, and number of stop bits (Table 10.12). For example, if you require a word with 8 bits, no parity, and 1 stop bit, control bits CR4, CR3, CR2 must set to 1, 0, 1.

The transmitter control field, CR5 and CR6, determines the level of the request to send ($\overline{\text{RTS}}$) output, and the generation of an interrupt by the transmitter portion of the ACIA. Table 10.13 gives the relationship between these controls bits and their functions. $\overline{\text{RTS}}$ can be employed to tell the modem that the ACIA has data to transmit.

The transmitter interrupt mechanism can be enabled or disabled depending on whether you are operating the ACIA in an interrupt-driven or in a polled data mode. If the transmitter interrupt is enabled, a transmitter interrupt is generated whenever the transmitter data register (TDR) is empty, signifying the need for new data from the CPU. If the ACIA's clear-to-send input is inactive-high, the TDR empty flag bit in the status register is held low, inhibiting any transmitter interrupt.

The effect of setting both CR6 and CR5 to a logical one requires some explanation. If both these bits are high, a *break* (space level) is transmitted until the bits are altered under software control. A break can be used to generate an interrupt at the receiver because the asynchronous format of the serial data precludes the existence of a space level for more than about 10 bit periods.

The receiver interrupt enable field consists of bit CR7 which, when clear, inhibits the generation of interrupts by the receiver portion of the ACIA. Whenever bit CR7 is set, a receiver interrupt is generated by the receiver data register (RDR) flag of the status byte going high, indicating the presence of a new character ready for the CPU to read. A receiver interrupt can also be generated by a low-to-high transition at the data-carrier-detect ($\overline{\text{DCD}}$) input, signifying the loss of a carrier. CR7 is a composite interrupt enable bit. It is impossible to enable either an interrupt caused by the RDR being empty or an interrupt caused by a positive transition on the DCD pin alone.

CR6	CR5	RTS	Transmitter interrupt
0	0	Low	Disabled
0	1	Low	Enabled
1	0	High	Disabled
1	1	Low	Disabled—a break level is placed on the transmitter output

Table 10.13 Function of transmitter control bits CR5, CR6.

Configuring the ACIA

The following 68000 assembly language listing demonstrates how the ACIA is initialized before it can be used to transmit and receive serial data.

```
* Setting up an ACIA
*
ACIA      EQU    $800000        Location of ACIA in memory
CR        EQU    0              Control register offset
          LEA    ACIA,A0        A0 points to ACIA
*
* Perform a software reset by writing 1,1 to CR1, CR0
          MOVE.B #%00000011,CR(A0)
*
* Select counter division ratio as clk/16 CR1,CR0 = 0,1
* Select character format CR4,CR3,CR2 = 1,0,1
* Select operating mode
*     CR6,CR5 = 0,1 = assert RTS and enable transmitter interrupt
* Select receiver interrupt mode CR7 = 1 to enable Rx interrupt
          MOVE.B #%10110101,CR(A0) Set up ACIA
```

The status register The status register has the same address as the control register, but is distinguished from it by being a read-only register. Table 10.14 gives the format of the status register. Let's look at the function of these bits.

Bit 0—receiver data register full (RDRF) When set the RDRF bit indicates that the receiver data register is full and a character has been received. If the receiver interrupt is enabled, the interrupt request flag, bit 7, is also set whenever RDRF is set. Reading the data in the receiver data register clears the RDRF bit. Whenever the $\overline{DCD}$ input is high, the RDRF bit remains at a logical zero, indicating the absence of any valid input.

The RDRF bit is used to detect the arrival of a character when the ACIA is operated in a polled input mode.

Bit 1—transmitter data register empty (TDRE) This flag is the transmitter counterpart of RDRF. A logical 1 in TDRE indicates that the contents of the transmitter data register (TDR) have been transmitted and the register is now ready for new data. The IRQ bit is also set whenever the TDRE flag is set if the transmitter interrupt is enabled. The TDRE bit is 0 when the TDR is full, or when the $\overline{CTS}$ input is high, indicating that the terminal equipment is not ready for data. The fragment of code below demonstrates how the TDRE flag is used when the ACIA is operated in a polled output mode.

```
    Subroutine to transmit a character
* REPEAT
*    Read ACIA status
* UNTIL TDRE = 1
* Write data to ACIA
*
ACIA      EQU    $800000
TDRE      EQU    1              Transmitter data register empty = bit 1
SR        EQU    2              Offset for status register
DR        EQU    0              Offset for data register
          LEA    ACIA,A0        A0 points to ACIA base
POLL      BTST   #TDRE,SR(A0)   Test transmitter for empty state
          BEQ    POLL           Repeat until transmitter ready
          MOVE.B D0,DR(A0)      Move byte from D0 to ACIA
          RTS
```

Bit 2—data carrier detect (DCD) The DCD bit is set whenever the $\overline{DCD}$ input is high, indicating that a carrier is not present. The $\overline{DCD}$ pin is normally employed only in conjunction with a modem. When the signal at the $\overline{DCD}$ input makes a low-to-high transition, the DCD bit in the status register is set and the IRQ bit is also set if the receiver interrupt is enabled. The DCD bit remains set even if the $\overline{DCD}$ input returns to a low state. To clear the DCD bit, the CPU must read the contents of the ACIA's status register and then the contents of the data register.

Bit 3—clear to send (CTS) The CTS bit directly reflects the status of the ACIA's $\overline{CTS}$ input. A low level on the $\overline{CTS}$ input indicates that the modem is ready for data. If the CTS bit is set, the transmitter data register empty bit is inhibited (clamped at zero) and no data may be transmitted by the ACIA.

```
*   Subroutine to receive a character
*   REPEAT
*     Read ACIA status
*   UNTIL RDRF = 1
*   Read ACIA data
*
ACIA      EQU    $800000
RDRF      EQU    0              Rx data ready = bit 0 of SR
SR        EQU    2              Offset for status register
DR        EQU    0              Offset for data register
          LEA    ACIA,A0        A0 points to ACIA
POLL      BTST   #RDRF,SR(A0)   REPEAT Test Rx status bit
          BEQ    POLL           UNTIL character received
          MOVE.B DR(A0),D0      Move input from ACIA to D0
          RTS
```

7	6	5	4	3	2	1	0
IRQ	PE	OVRN	FE	CTS	DCD	TDRE	RDRF

Table 10.14 Format of the ACIA's control register.

Bit 4—framing error (FE) The FE bit is set whenever a received character is incorrectly framed by a start bit and a stop bit. A FE is detected by the absence of the first stop bit and indicates a synchronization (timing) error, a faulty transmission, or a break condition. The FE flag is set or cleared during receiver data transfer time and is present throughout the time that the associated character is available.

Bit 5—receiver overrun (OVRN) The OVRN flag bit is set when a character is received, but hasn't been read by the CPU before a subsequent character is received. The new character overwrites the previous character, which is now lost. Consequently, the OVRN bit indicates that one or more characters in the data stream have been lost. Synchronization is not affected by an overrun error—the error is caused by the CPU not reading a character, rather than by a fault in the transmission process. The overrun bit is cleared after reading the data from the RDR or by a master reset. Modern ACIAs usually have FIFO buffers to hold several characters to give the CPU more time to read them.

Bit 6—parity error (PE) The PE is set whenever the received parity bit does not agree with the parity bit generated locally at the receiver from the preceding data bits. Odd or even parity may be selected by writing the appropriate code into bits 2, 3, and 4 of the control register. If no parity is selected, then both the transmitter parity generator and the receiver parity checker are disabled. Once a PE has been detected and the PE bit set, it remains set as long as a character with a PE is in the receiver data register.

Bit 7—interrupt request (IRQ) The IRQ bit is a composite interrupt request flag because it is set whenever the ACIA wishes to interrupt the CPU, for whatever reason. The IRQ bit may be set by any of the following:

- receiver data register full (SR bit 0 set)
- transmitter data register empty (SR bit 1 set)
- DCD bit set (SR bit 2).

Whenever IRQ = 1 the ACIA's $\overline{\text{IRQ}}$ pin is forced active-low to request an interrupt from the CPU. The IRQ bit is cleared by a read from the receiver data register or a write to the transmitter data.

Programming the ACIA

We are now going to look at a more complete program that uses some of the ACIA's error-detecting facilities when receiving data.

```
ACIAC   EQU     $800000     Base address of ACIA
ACIAD   EQU     ACIAC+2     Address of data register
RDRF    EQU     0           Receiver data register full
TDRE    EQU     1           Transmitter data register empty
DCD     EQU     2           Data carrier detect
CTS     EQU     3           Clear to send
FE      EQU     4           Framing error
OVRN    EQU     5           Over run
PE      EQU     6           Parity error

INPUT   MOVE.B  ACIAC,D0    Get status from ACIA
        BTST    #RDRF,D0    Test for received character
        BNE     ERR_CK      If character received then test SR
        BTST    #DCD,D0     Else test for loss of signal
        BEQ     INPUT       Repeat loop while DCD clear
        BRA     DCD_ERR     Else deal with loss of signal
ERR_CK  BTST    #FE,D0      Test for framing error
        BNE     FE_ERR      If framing error, deal with it
        BTST    #OVRN,D0    Test for overrun
        BNE     OV_ERR      If overrun, deal with it
        BTST    #PE,D0      Test for parity error
        BNE     PE_ERR      If parity error deal with it
        MOVE.B  ACIAD,D0    Load the input into D0
        BRA     EXIT        Deal with loss of signal
*
DCD_ERR
        BRA     EXIT
*
FE_ERR  Deal with framing error
        BRA     EXIT
*
OV_ERR  Deal with overrun error
        BRA     EXIT
*
PE_ERR  Deal with parity error
*
EXIT    RTS
```

So far we've examined how information in digital form is read by a computer, processed in the way dictated by a program and then output in digital form. We haven't yet considered how information is converted between real-world form and digital form. In the next chapter we describe some of the most frequently used computer interfaces such as the keyboard, the display, and the printer.

■ SUMMARY

A computer is not just a device that executes instructions; it is a complete system with subsystems that process data, store data, and move data between the computer and outside world.

In this chapter we began by examining the bus, the data highway that moves information between a computer's various parts. There is not, in fact, a single bus. Like CPUs, buses have developed over the years and different computers use different buses. Even within a computer there may be a family of buses, each of which is optimized for a specific application.

We have described the characteristics of a computer bus and introduced some of the members of the bus family. As well as the conventional parallel bus, we've looked at the USB serial bus used to provide a low-cost high-performance solution to the interconnection of peripherals ranging from the keyboard to the printer or scanner.

We have also looked at the IEEE488 bus that was designed for use in a computer-controlled automated laboratory environment. This bus incorporates some very interesting principles such as the ability to transfer data between groups of devices with very different characteristics. In particularly, it is able to send data between serial devices simultaneously using a three-wire handshake that ensures the transfer does not continue until each device has completed the data transfer. Moreover, it uses two different methods of sending control messages to devices connected to the bus. One method uses encoded messages on the 8-bit data bus and the other method used single-line control signals on a special control bus.

There are three broad strategies for moving information onto or out of a computer. One is called *programmed I/O* in which the programmer copies data to or from the peripheral directly by means of appropriate instructions in the program. One is called *interrupt driven* I/O in which an external device requests a data transfer when it is ready and then the operating system handles the transfer. The third technique is called *direct memory access* in which a subsystem that is almost as complex as the CPU itself takes over and transfers data directly between the peripheral and memory. We have looked at how all these three I/O strategies are implemented and their advantages and disadvantages.

The final part of this chapter described two special-purpose integrated circuits that are designed to facilitate the transfer of data between a computer and external peripherals such as modems and printers. Both these devices control the flow of information between the computer and peripheral. One, the parallel interface, uses handshaking to sequence the flow of information and the other, the serial device, uses flow control signals between the peripheral and external modem.

■ PROBLEMS

10.1 Why is the bus such an important element of a computer system?

10.2 Why do computers use *families* of buses rather than a single bus?

10.3 In the context of buses, what is the meaning of *arbitration*?

10.4 It takes 1 μs for a computer to take control of a 64-bit bus. Suppose it takes 20 ns to set up a data transfer and 40 ns to terminate a transfer and that a transfer consists of sending eight 64-bit values in 32 ns. What is the average data rate in bytes/s that this bus can support?

10.5 What is the difference between an open-loop and a closed-loop data transfer?

10.6 What is special (different) about the IEEE 488 bus three-wire data handshake?

10.7 What factors determine the ultimate rate at which data can be transported by a bus?

10.8 Although most microprocessors implement memory-mapped I/O, are there any advantages in implementing dedicated I/O mechanisms with dedicated I/O instructions and appropriate control signals?

10.9 What is an input/output *strategy*, as opposed to and input/output *device*?

10.10 What is programmed I/O?

10.11 Define the meaning of the following terms in the context of I/O operations.

(a) Port
(b) Peripheral
(c) FIFO
(d) Handshake
(e) Interlocked handshake
(f) Polling loop

10.12 What is the difference between an unintelligent I/O device (e.g. a flip-flop) and an intelligent I/O device (e.g. a PIA)?

10.13 Why does the CPU have to save the processor status (i.e. status byte and CCR) before responding to an interrupt?

10.14 What is a non-maskable interrupt and how is it used?

10.15 Explain how daisy-chaining can be used to improve the way in which interrupts are handled in a system with many peripherals.

10.16 What is the role of the 68K's interrupt mask in its prioritized interrupt handling system?

10.17 What is a prioritized interrupt?

10.18 What is a vectored interrupt?

10.19 To what extent are interrupts and subroutines the same and to what extent do they differ?

10.20 In a particular computer, the overhead involved in an interrupt call is 5 μs and the overhead involved in a return from interrupt is 6 μs. Suppose that this computer executes

10 instructions/μs. How many instructions can be used in an interrupt handling routine if the overall interrupt handling efficiency is to be greater than 70%?

10.21 What is DMA and why is it so important in high performance systems?

10.22 What are the advantages and disadvantages of memory-mapped I/O in comparison with dedicated I/O that uses special instructions and signals?

10.23 The PIA has six internal registers and two register select lines. How does the PIA manage to select six registers with only two lines?

10.24 Can you think of any other way of implementing a register select scheme (other than the one used by the PIA)?

10.25 In the context of the PIA, what is a data direction register (DDR), and how is it used?

10.26 How does the PIA use its CA1 and CA2 control lines to implement handshaking?

10.27 How are the characters transmitted over a serial data link divided into individual characters and bits?

10.28 What are the functions of the ACIA's $\overline{\text{DCD}}$ and $\overline{\text{CTS}}$ inputs?

10.29 What is the difference between a framing error and an overrun error?

10.30 The 68K's status register (SR) contains the value $2601. How is this interpreted?

Computer peripherals

INTRODUCTION

Humans communicate with each other by auditory and visual stimuli; that is, we speak, gesticulate, write to each other, and use pictures. You would therefore expect humans and computers to communicate in a similar way. Computers are good at communicating visually with people; they can generate sophisticated images, although they are rather less good at synthesizing natural-sounding speech. Unfortunately, computers can't yet *reliably* receive visual or sound input directly from people. Hardware and software capable of reliably understanding speech or recognizing visual input does not yet exist—there are systems that can handle speech input and systems that can recognize handwriting, but the error rate is still too large for general-purpose use.[1] Consequently, people communicate with computers in a different way than they communicate with other people.

The keyboard and video display are the principal input and output devices used by personal computers. The terms *input* and *output* refer here to the device as seen from the CPU; that is, a keyboard provides an output, which, in turn, becomes the CPU's input.

The CRT (cathode ray tube) display is an entirely electronic device that's inexpensive to produce. It is cheap because it relies on semiconductor technology for its electronics and on tried-and-tested television technology for its display. By 2000 the more compact but expensive LCD panel was beginning to replace the CRT display. Less than 4 years later, the trend had accelerated and large, high-quality, high-resolution LCD displays were widely available. By 2005 CRT displays were in decline.

This chapter looks at keyboards, pointers, displays, and printers. We also look at input devices that do more than communicate with people; we show how physical parameters from temperature and pressure to the concentration of glucose in blood can be measured.

The second part of this chapter demonstrates how the digital computer interacts with the analog world by converting analog values into digital representations and vice versa. At the end of this chapter we provide a very brief insight into how a computer can be used to control real-world analog systems with the aid of digital signal processing (DSP).

---

[1] You can buy speech recognition programs but they have to be trained to match a particular voice. Even then, their accuracy is less than perfect. Similarly, hand-held computers provide handwriting recognition provided you write in a rather stylized way.

11.1 Simple input devices

We begin this chapter by introducing some of the simplest computer peripherals, the input devices used by personal computers. We describe both the keyboard and the pointing device.

11.1.1 The keyboard

The keyboard is an efficient interface—especially if you're a professional typist entering text at 60 words/minute. Sometimes the keyboard provides a poor interface; for example, you can't easily use it to control a flight simulator.

Figure 11.1 illustrates the layout of the ubiquitous QWERTY keyboard. The term QWERTY isn't an acronym but the sequence of letters on the back row of characters on a keyboard. When the first mechanical typewriters were constructed, the sequence of letters was chosen to reduce the probability of letters jamming. If 't' and 'h' were next to each other, typing 'the' would sometimes cause the letters 't' and 'h' to collide and jam. The anti-jamming property of the QWERTY keyboard is optimum only for the English language.

Because today's keyboards are electronic with no moving parts except the keys themselves, there's no longer any need for a QWERTY layout. You could devise a much better layout for the keys that would make it easier to type by reducing the distance a typist's fingers have to move. Indeed, a keyboard was developed in the 1920s to make it easier to type English. Studies demonstrate that a typist using a Dvorak keyboard can achieve a 10 to 15% improvement. The Dvorak is biased in favor of right-handed typists. However, so many typists and programmers have been trained on the QWERTY keyboard, that it would be difficult to retrain them to use a new layout. The Dvorak keyboard has therefore failed to topple the QWERTY standard.

Some systems designed for infrequent computer users and non-typists have a simple ABCDE keyboard in which the keys are laid out in alphabetic order—this keyboard makes it easy for users to locate keys, but prevents experienced users entering data rapidly (because they will have been trained on a QWERTY layout).

A radically different form of keyboard is the *chord* keyboard, which has only a few (typically 4 or 5) keys. You enter a letter by hitting a subgroup of keys simultaneously; it's rather like using Morse code or Braille. The chord keyboard is very small indeed and can be used with one hand. Chord keyboards have found a niche market for people who operate in cramped spaces or for those who want a pocket-sized device that they can use to make notes as they move about. Figure 11.2 illustrates the structure of the cord keyboard.

Special purpose keys

In order to provide the total number of keys necessary for efficient computer operation a keyboard would have to be gigantic. In practice, most keys have a multiple function; that is, the meaning of a given key can be modified by pressing another key at the same time. The *shift* key selects lower case characters as the default mode and upper case characters when it's pressed at the same time as a letter. The shift key also selects between pairs of symbols that share the same key (e.g.: and ;, @ and ', + and = , etc.) and between numbers and symbols (e.g. 4 and $, 5 and %, 8 and *, etc.).

Although the layout of the letters and numbers on a QWERTY keyboard is standard throughout the English-speaking world, the layout of other keys (e.g. symbols) is not—in particular, there is a difference between keyboards designed for use in the USA and those designed for use in the

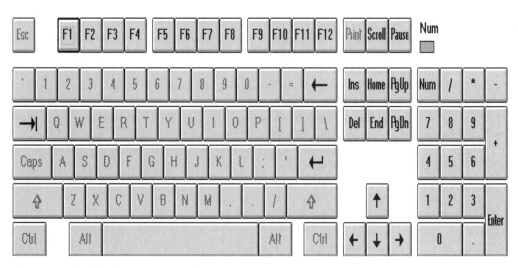

Figure 11.1 Layout of the QWERTY keyboard.

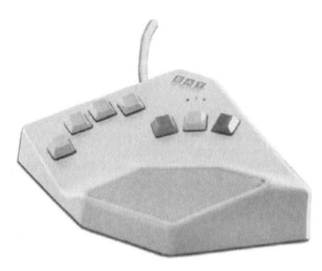

Figure 11.2 Layout of the cord keyboard.

UK. Consequently, software has to be configured for the specific version of the keyboard currently in use.

Computer keyboards also include a *control* (ctrl) key, which behaves like a shift key and gives a key a different meaning when control is pressed at the same time. Computer texts indicate the act of pressing the control key and, say, the letter D at the same time by the notation CTRL-D.

Why do we need all these special keys? When we communicate with a computer we need to provide it with two types of information. One type of information is the data the computer is going to process (e.g. the text entered into a word processor, or a booking entered into an airline's database). The other type of information entered into a computer is the commands that you want it to execute. Suppose that you are entering text into a word processor and wish to save the file. You can't simply type *Save file* because the computer cannot distinguish between the command you want to carry out and the words you are entering into the document. By typing, for example, CTRL-S, you are telling the computer unambiguously that you are entering the command to save a file.[2]

PC keyboards also provide an *alternative* (alt) key to give yet another set of meanings to the keys. Consequently, you can enter a key unshifted, on with shift, control, alternative, or any combination of the three function-modifier keys. In addition to the shift, control, and alternative keys, the PC keyboard contains 12 function keys labeled F1 to F12 that perform special functions; e.g. function key F1 is normally used to invoke a program's 'Help' function. Finally, keyboards have several dedicated keys like home, end, PgDn, PgUp, Del, Ins, and so on.

Computer displays invariably have a cursor—a marker on the screen indicating the currently active position; that is, if you enter a character, it will appear at the position indicated by the cursor. Cursors can be vertical or horizontal lines, small blocks, highlighted text, or even reversed text (i.e. white on black). Modern applications frequently make use of several different types of cursor; for example, a solid line indicates where text can be entered, an arrow points at a command, and a cross indicates the edge of a picture or a table. Cursors sometimes blink because human vision can more easily detect a change in a static picture). Computer keyboards also contain cursor control keys that move the cursor on the screen up, down, left, or right, by one unit—either a character position horizontally or a line position vertically.

Several technologies can be used to detect a keystroke (e.g. mechanical, magnetic, capacitive, etc.). The difference between keyboards is often a matter of cost and personal preference—some typists prefer to hear a satisfying click when they depress a key, others don't. Important keys like enter, shift, control, and space are often made larger than other keys to make it easy to hit them. If you are a real sadist, keyboard design is just for you because you can guarantee a maximum level of user misery by locating a key that has a potentially destructive function (e.g. delete text) next to a normal key such as the space bar. Good practice would ensure that it is difficult to enter a potentially fatal command by accident. Consider the following two examples of *safe operation*: you can't start a VCR recording without pressing two buttons simultaneously, and the master engine switches in some aircraft are under a metal bar that blocks access to the switch to ensure that you can't switch an engine off accidentally.

Character codes

The ASCII code for the upper-case letter[3] we call 'A' is 01000001_2. In order to convert this computer representation of 'A' into the actual letter 'A' on paper we have to use a peripheral called a *printer*. Similarly, we have to strike a key on a keyboard with the symbol 'A' on it in order to get the code 01000001_2 into the computer. We now look at peripherals in typical personal computers that input and output data—beginning with the keyboard. Following the keyboard we describe the video display and printer, respectively. This chapter concludes with some of the interfaces associated with computers used in more general applications.

The switch

A keyboard is composed of two parts, a set of keys that detect the pressure of a finger and an encoder, which converts the output of a key into a unique binary code representing that key.

The *keyswitch*, which detects the pressure of a finger, called a *keystroke*, is often a mechanical device (see Fig. 11.3(a). A typical keyswitch contains a plunger that is moved by a finger

---

[2] The Windows environment has much reduced the need for special-purpose keys because you can use a ponting device to pull down a menu and select the required option.

[3] A character as represented on paper or a screen is called a glyph. A, A, and **A** are all glyphs.

against the pressure of a spring. As it moves down, the plunger forces two wires together to make a circuit—the output of this device is inherently binary (on or off). A small stainless steel *snap-disk* located between the plunger and base of the switch produces an audible click when bowed downwards by the plunger. A similar click is made when the plunger is released. This gives depressing a keyswitch a positive feel because of its tactile feedback.

Figure 11.3(b) describes the *membrane switch*, which provides a very-low-cost mechanical switch for applications such as microwave oven control panels. A thin plastic membrane is coated with a conducting material and spread over a printed circuit board. Either by forming the plastic membrane into slight bubbles or by creating tiny pits in the PCB, it is possible to engineer a tiny gap between contacts on the PCB and the metal-coated surface of the membrane. Pressure on the surface of the membrane due to a finger pushes the membrane against a contact to close a circuit. The membrane switch can be hermetically sealed for ease of cleaning and is well suited to applications in hazardous or dirty environments (e.g. mines). Equally, the membrane switch suffers all the disadvantages of other types of low-cost mechanical switch.

Another form of mechanical switch employs a plunger with a small magnet embedded in one end. As this magnet is pushed downwards, it approaches a *reed relay* composed of two gold-plated iron contacts in a glass tube. These contacts become magnetized by the field from the magnet, attract each other, and close the circuit (Fig. 11.3(c)). Because the contacts are in a sealed tube, the reed relay is one of the most reliable types of mechanical switches.

Non-mechanical switches

Non-mechanical switches have been devised to overcome some of the problems inherent in mechanical switches. Three of the most commonly used non-mechanical switches are the

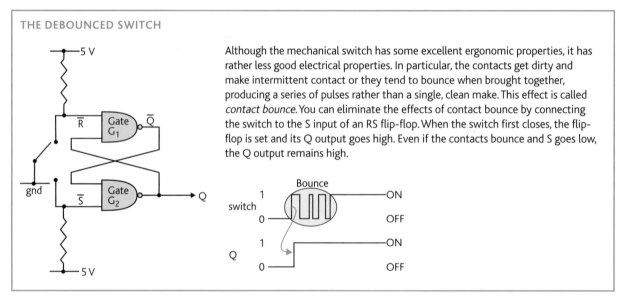

THE DEBOUNCED SWITCH

Although the mechanical switch has some excellent ergonomic properties, it has rather less good electrical properties. In particular, the contacts get dirty and make intermittent contact or they tend to bounce when brought together, producing a series of pulses rather than a single, clean make. This effect is called *contact bounce*. You can eliminate the effects of contact bounce by connecting the switch to the S input of an RS flip-flop. When the switch first closes, the flip-flop is set and its Q output goes high. Even if the contacts bounce and S goes low, the Q output remains high.

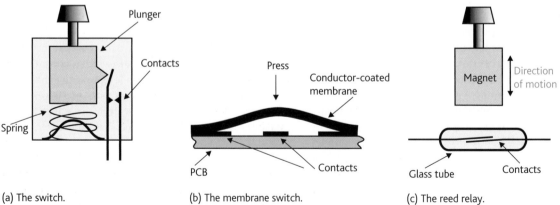

(a) The switch.   (b) The membrane switch.   (c) The reed relay.

Figure 11.3 The mechanical switch: (a) basic switch, (b) membrane switch, (c) reed relay.

Hall-effect switch, the *elastomeric* switch, and the *capacitive* switch. The Hall-effect switch consists of a magnet that is pushed against the force of a spring towards a Hall cell. The Hall cell is a semiconductor device through which a steady current flows. When a magnetic field is applied at right angles to the current, a voltage is produced across the terminals of the cell at right angles to both the magnetic field and the current flow. Figure 11.4 illustrates the operation of such a switch. By detecting the Hall-effect voltage due to the magnetic field you can generate a digital output corresponding to the state 'switch-open' or 'switch-closed'. The Hall-effect switch does not suffer from contact bounce, but is relatively expensive.

The *capacitive switch* relies on the change in capacitive coupling between two metallic contacts when a finger is pressed against them. The great advantage of a capacitive switch keyboard is its extremely low cost and small size because it is often nothing more than a printed-circuit board with contacts etched on the surface. Some capacitive switches use a single contact to sense a keystroke and rely on the capacitive coupling between the contact and ground via the finger.

Unfortunately, the capacitive switch keyboard has no tactile feedback and is rather unpleasant to use. Designers can get round the lack of tactile feedback by providing audio feedback. Each time a keystroke is made, a short audio bleep is sounded from a loudspeaker. The capacitive switch is found in some very-low-cost PCs, in television touch-sensitive tuners, and in professional equipment that must be hermetically sealed for operation in hazardous environments.

Elastomeric switches employ certain types of material that change their electrical resistance when subjected to pressure. When a finger is pressed against the material, the drop in its electrical resistance is detected by a suitable interface. This type of switch lacks any tactile feedback and its feel is said to be *mushy and ill defined*.

The keyboard encoder

The conversion of a keystroke into its ISO/ASCII-encoded equivalent can be performed by a special purpose chip called a *keyboard encoder*. Figure 11.5 illustrates the operation of such a chip, which contains all the circuitry necessary to convert a signal from an array of switches into a binary code together with a *strobe* (i.e. a pulse that indicates a new character).

Figure 11.5 demonstrates how the keyboard encoder operates. Eight horizontal lines are connected to the pins of an 8-bit output port. Similarly, eight vertical lines are connected to an 8-bit input port. A switch is located at each of the $8 \times 8 = 64$ cross-points between horizontal and vertical lines. When a key is pressed, a connection is made between the vertical line and the corresponding horizontal line. As long as no key is pressed, there is no connection between any

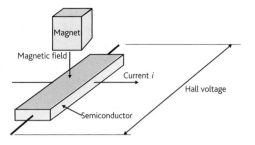

Figure 11.4 The Hall-effect switch.

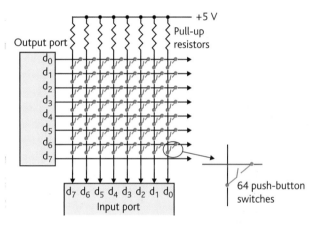

Figure 11.5 Structure of the keyboard encoder.

vertical and any horizontal line. If a switch is pressed we can determine which key it was by determining its row and its column.

The eight vertical input lines are each terminated in a resistor connected to +5 V, so that these lines are pulled up to a high level. That is, if a byte were read from the input port, it would be 11111111. Suppose now the output port puts the binary value 11111110 onto its eight output lines, as illustrated in Fig. 11.6. If the CPU reads from its input port with, say, the top right-hand key pressed, it will see 11111110. If the next key to the left on the same row is pressed it will see 11111101. Pressing a key on the topmost row causes a 0 to be read into the vertical position corresponding to that key. Pressing a key in any other row has no effect on the data read.

The CPU next outputs the byte 11111101 and reads the input lines to interrogate the second row of keys. This process is continued cyclically with the CPU outputting 11111110, 11111101, 11111011, 11110111 ... to 01111111, as the 0 is shifted one place left each time. In this way all eight rows of the switch matrix are interrogated one by one. The assembly language program in Table 11.1 gives an idea of the software necessary to operate the keyboard.

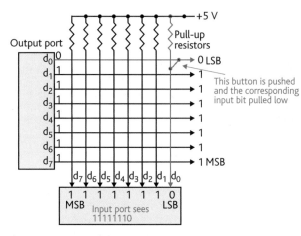

Figure 11.6 State of the keyboard encoder with one key pressed.

11.1.2 Pointing devices

Although the keyboard is excellent for inputting text, it can't be used efficiently as a *pointing device* to select an arbitrary point on the screen. PCs invariably employ one of three pointing devices: the joystick, the mouse, and the trackball (Fig. 11.7). Portable computers normally use either an *eraser pointer* or a trackpad as a pointing device in order to conserve space.

The joystick is so called because it mimics the pilot's joystick. A joystick consists of a vertical rod that can be moved simultaneously in a left–right or front–back direction. The computer reads the position of the stick and uses it to move a cursor on the screen in sympathy. You don't look at the joystick when moving it; you look at the cursor on the

```
* Set X to 11111110
* Set X counter to -1
* REPEAT
*   Rotate X left
*   Output X
*   Read Y
* UNTIL Y ≠ 0 (i.e., a key is pressed)
*
* Compress Y value to to 3-bit code
* Set Y counter to -1

* REPEAT
*   Increment Y counter
*   Compare Y with 11111110
*   Shift Y right
* UNTIL Y = 11111110
* Concatenate X and Y to get 6-bit value key location
*
        ORG     $002000         Subroutine origin
XLINES  EQU     $008000         Output port for horizontal lines
YLINES  EQU     $008002         Input port for vertical lines
*
        MOVE.B  #%01111111,D0   Preset the initial value of X output
        MOVE.B  #-1,D1          Preset X counter to -1
XLOOP   ROL.B   #1,D0           Rotate value of X output one place left
        ADD.B   #1,D1           Increment X counter in step
        AND.B   #%00000111,D1   X counter value is modulo 8
        MOVE.B  D0,XLINES       Send X value to output port
        MOVE.B  YLINES,D2       Read value of Y from input lines
        CMP.B   #%11111111,D2   Has a key been pressed?
        BEQ     XLOOP           Repeat if Y is all ones
*
        CLR.B   D3              Preset Y counter to 0
YLOOP   CMP.B   #%11111110,D2   Test for Y = 0
        BEQ     CONCAT          Exit to concatenate X and Y values
        ROR.B   #1,D2           Rotate value of Y one place right
        ADD.B   #1,D3           Increment Y counter
        BRA     YLOOP           Repeat
*
CONCAT  LSL.B   #3,D2           Shift value of Y counter 3 places left
        OR.B    D2,D1           Add in value of X counter
        RTS                     Return with key value in D1
```

Table 11.1 Reading data by scanning a keyboard.

(a) The mouse.

(b) The joystick.

(c) The Trackball.

Figure 11.7 Pointing devices.

screen. Without this visual feedback between the hand and the eye, people would not be able to use this, or similar, pointing devices. Joysticks and mice have one or more buttons that can be used to enter commands. The joystick is well suited to computer games.

Although the joystick is similar to the mouse and trackball, there is one difference. When the mouse is not being moved, there is no signal from them and the computer unambiguously interprets this as no input. However, the joystick continually transmits a position, which means that it is very difficult to centralize or neutralize its output. Consequently, joysticks often have a *dead zone* around their neutral position. Until you move the joystick out of the dead zone, the cursor on the screen doesn't move.

The mouse

The mouse, invented by Douglas Engelbart in 1964, is the PC's most popular pointing device. A mechanical mouse consists of a housing that fits comfortably in the hand and a ball that rotates in contact with the surface of a desk—you could say that a mouse is a larger version of the ball-point pen. As the mouse is dragged along the desk, the ball rotates. Circuits in the mouse translate the ball's movement into a signal that can be read by the computer.

When the computer receives a signal from the mouse, the signal is processed and used to move a cursor on the screen. The software that controls the mouse may allow you to

modify the mouse's sensitivity; that is, you can determine how much the cursor moves for a given movement of the mouse.

A modern mouse is comfortable to hold and can be used to move the cursor rapidly to any point on the screen. Once the mouse is at the correct point, you depress one of two buttons that fit naturally under your fingers as you move the mouse. Some versions of the mouse have one or three buttons. Pressing a button activates some predefined application-dependent function on the screen. Typical mouse-based systems require you to click the button once to select an application (i.e. highlight it) and twice to launch an application (i.e. run it). Clicking a button twice in this way is called double-clicking and is not always easy to perform because the interval between the clicks must fall within a given range.

Figure 11.8 demonstrates the principle of an opto-mechanical mouse.[4] As the ball rotates due to the friction between itself and the desk, its motion is resolved into two axes by means of the rollers located at right angles to each other. If the mouse is moved upwards or from left to right, only one roller rotates. If the mouse is moved diagonally both rollers rotate and their relative speed is a function of the diagonal angle.

Each roller is connected to a shaft that rotates an optical encoder (i.e. an opaque disc with holes in its surface). The rotation of the encoder interrupts a beam of light between an LED and a detector. Each pulse is fed to the computer and by adding up the number of pulses received, it is possible to determine how far the mouse has moved along that axis. In practice, two beams of light are necessary because a single beam would make it impossible to determine whether the mouse was moving in a positive or a negative direction. A second detector is required to produce a quadrature signal that is out of phase with the main signal. If the ball is rotated one way, the quadrature signal leads the main signal and if the rotation is reversed the quadrature signal lags the main signal.

An entirely optical mouse doesn't rely on a moving ball. First-generation optical mice used a special pad with a fine grid of horizontal and vertical lines. This mouse reflects a

---

[4] It is called opto-mechanical because it has moving parts but uses optical techniques to sense the position of a rotating disk.

MODERN MICE

Nothing stands still in the world of the PC. The humble mouse has developed in three ways. Its sensing mechanism has developed from crude mechanical motion sensors to precise optical sensors. Its functionality has increased with the addition of two buttons (left click and right click) to permit selection followed by a third button and a rotating wheel that let you scroll through menus or documents. Some mice let you move the wheel left or right to provide extra capacities. Finally, the mouse interface has changed from the original PS2 serial interface to the USB serial interface to wireless interfaces that allow cordless mouse operation.

The *gyro mouse* is the most sophisticated of all computer mice and is both cordless and deskless. You can use it in space simply by waving it about (as you might do when giving a presentation to an audience). The gyro mouse employs solid-state gyroscopic sensors to determine the mouse's motion in space. Consequently, you are not restricted to dragging it across a surface.

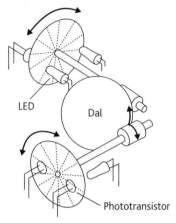

(a) Ball and disk arrangement

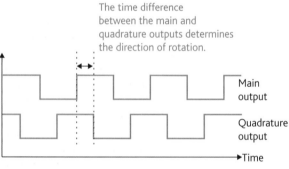

The time difference between the main and quadrature outputs determines the direction of rotation.

Main output

Quadrature output

Time

(b) Detecting the direction of motion

Figure 11.8 Operation of the optical mouse.

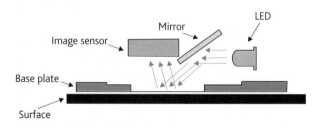

Figure 11.9 The optical mouse.

light beam off the grid and counts the number of horizontal and vertical lines crossed as the mouse moves about the pad.

An optical mouse does not require intimate contact and friction with the surface, although it does require that the surface have an optical texture—you can't use a mirror. The *resolution* of an optical mouse is higher then that of a mechanical mouse.[5]

Second-generation optical mouse technology uses a light-emitting diode to illuminate the surface underneath the mouse. Light reflected back from the surface is picked up and focused on a sensor array (Fig. 11.9). The image from the array consists of a series of pixels. As the mouse moves, the image changes unless the surface beneath the mouse is blank. A special-purpose signal-processing chip in the mouse compares consecutive surface images and uses the difference between them to calculate the movement of the mouse in the x and y planes. A new image is generates once every 1/2000 s. This type of optical mouse has no moving parts to wear out or become clogged with dust. The second-generation optical mouse is a miracle of modern engineering because it has an image sensing system, an image processing system, and a computer interface in a package that sells for a few dollars.

The joystick

The joystick is a low-cost pointing device found largely in games applications. Its principal advantage over the mouse or trackball is that it can provide three motion axes—the conventional left–right and up–down axes, plus a *twist* or rotate axis that you can control by rotating the joystick.

Figure 11.10 illustrates the operation of the joystick, which uses two potentiometers to sense the position of the control column. A potentiometer consists of a thin film of a partially conducting material and a metallic contact (the slider) that can move along the thin film. Mechanical linkages between the joystick and potentiometers move the arms of the two sliders. The potentiometers employ a fixed resistance (i.e. the thin

---

[5] The *resolution* of a mouse is the minimum distance you need to move it for the output to change. The resolution of a typical optical mouse is 800 dpi, which means that the mouse generates 800 steps when you move it one inch and it can detect a movement of 1/800 inch.

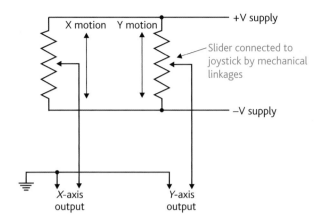

Figure 11.10 Operation of the joystick.

film) that has a constant voltage across its two terminals. If the resistance is linear, the voltage at any point along the resistance is proportional to its distance from its end. Consequently, the slider supplies an analog voltage output that is an approximately linear function of its position. Two analog-to-digital converters are needed to transform the two analog outputs into X and Y digital position inputs required by the computer.

A joystick usually has a dead zone of up to 10% of its full-scale output about its neutral position. The dead zone is a property of a joystick's construction, which means that small movements of the joystick about its central neutral position generate no change in its X and Y outputs. This effect has the advantage that the joystick produces a null output in its 'hands off' neutral position and is unaffected by small movements. However, a dead zone makes it harder to make precise movements when the joystick is near to its neutral position.

Joysticks can be produced using non-contact technology such as optical or even magnetic sensing and it is now possible to obtain high-precision joysticks. Indeed, some commercial aircraft such as the Airbus 320 have removed the conventional control column or *yoke* and have replaced it by a side-mounted joystick that they call a *sidestick*.

Another innovation in joystick design is the addition of *force feedback*. In first-generation aircraft, the control column directly moved the ailerons and elevators by wire links. As the aircraft flew faster, the force needed to move the control column grew and it could be quite difficult to maneuver an aircraft at high speeds unless you were very strong. When hydraulics were used to move control surfaces, the pilot didn't need the same effort at high speeds. Unfortunately, making large control inputs at high speeds can put an aircraft in a maneuver that breaks it up. Hydraulic systems were designed that gave the pilot an artificial feel; as the speed increases and the forces on the aircraft grow, it becomes increasingly harder to move the control column. Replacing the control column with a joystick in a fly-by-wire computer-controlled aircraft removes the natural tactile feedback

between the aircraft and pilot. The force feedback joystick combines a joystick with motors or solenoids that generate a computer-controlled force on the joystick as you move it. Now, the computer can restore the tactile feedback lacking in conventional joysticks.

The trackball

A trackball is an upside-down mouse—it remains stationary on the desk and you rotate a 1″ to 4″ ball to move the cursor on the screen. Unlike the mouse, the trackball requires no desk space and can be fitted on the keyboard of a laptop portable. Trackballs are often built into electronic equipment that requires an operator to select a point on a screen (e.g. a target on a radar screen).

Other input devices

Two other input sensors worth mentioning are the *eraser tip* pointer (or pointing stick) and *trackpad* used by some laptop computers. The eraser tip pointer is a tiny joystick that juts out of a keyboard. It is operated like a joystick except that it doesn't move. It senses pressure and uses a pressure-to-voltage converter to move the cursor. The track pad consists of a small flat region that senses the position of a finger and uses the finger as if it were a mouse. Both these devices are not as precise as the mouse and are used simply because they require no desk space.

Three other pointing devices are the touch screen, the light-pen, and the tablet. The touch screen, found on all PDAs, uses a display coated with transparent conductors to detect the location of a finger on the surface of the screen. Some touch screens sense the finger's position by ultrasonic or infra-red beams. The touch screen can be used as an input device simply by touching the point you want to activate. A typical system displays a menu of commands. Touch-sensitive screens are still relatively expensive and are found only in specialized applications. The finger is a rather course pointer and cannot be used as precisely as a mouse or joystick (PDAs require the use of a pencil-like stylus). Touch screens are useful when the operator has no computer experience whatsoever (e.g. a user-controlled guide in a shopping mall) or when the system must be hermetically sealed (e.g. in potentially explosive atmospheres).

The light-pen uses a stylus with a light-sensitive device in its tip. When placed against the computer's screen, the light-pen sends a signal to the computer when the beam passes under it. The light-pen is just a much more precise form of the touch screen and is cheaper to implement. Sophisticated algorithms can be used to convert the light-pen's movement over the screen (i.e. handwriting) into an ASCII-encoded text format for internal storage and manipulation. Unfortunately, it's not easy to convert the output from a light-pen into text, because the way in which one person writes, say, a letter 'a', is often different from the way another person writes it.

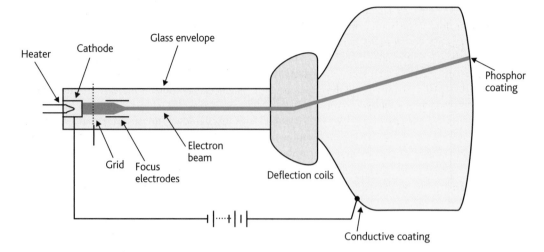

Figure 11.11 Structure of the CRT.

The document scanner was once a very expensive device and has now become a very-low-cost but high-precision input device. A document is placed on a glass sheet that forms the top of a largely empty box. A light source on tracks is moved along the length of the document and photo sensors read light intensity along a scan line. The scanner is able to create a high-resolution color image of the document being scanned (typically 2400 dpi). Indeed, the accuracy of some document scanners is sufficient to give national mints a headache because of the potential for forgery. Some banknotes are designed with color schemes that are difficult to copy precisely by document copiers.

11.2 CRT, LED, and plasma displays

General-purpose computers communicate with people via a screen, which may be a conventional *CRT* or a *liquid crystal display*. We begin by describing the *cathode ray tube* (CRT) display that lies at the heart of many display systems. A CRT is little more than a special type of the vacuum tube that was once used in all radios and TVs before they were replaced by transistors.

The way in which human visual perception operates is important to those designing displays; for example, we can see some colors better than others, we cannot read text if it is too small nor can we read it rapidly if it is too large. Colors themselves are described in terms of three parameters: *hue* is determined by the wavelength of the light, *saturation* is determined by the amount of white light present in the color, and *intensity* is determined by the brightness of the light. Objects on a screen are viewed against background objects—the luminosity of an object in comparison with its background is called its *contrast*. All these factors have to be taken into account when designing an effective display.

Figure 11.11 describes the construction of the *cathode ray tube* (CRT).[6] It is a remarkably simple device that uses a technology discovered early in the twentieth century. The CRT is a glass tube from which all the air has been removed. A wire coil, called a *heater*, is located at one end of the CRT and becomes red-hot when a sufficiently large current flows through it—exactly like the element in an electric fire. The heater raises the temperature of a cylinder, called the *cathode*, which is coated with a substance that gives off electrons when it is hot. The negatively charged electrons leaving the surface of the cathode are launched into space unimpeded by air molecules because of the high vacuum in the CRT.

When the negatively charged electrons from the CRT's cathode boil off into space, they don't get very far because they are pulled back to the positively charged cathode. To overcome the effect of the positive charge on the cathode, the surface and sides of the glass envelope at the front of the CRT are coated with a conducting material connected to a very high positive voltage with respect to the cathode. The high positive voltage (over 20 000 V attracts electrons from the cathode to the screen. As the electrons travel along the length of the CRT, they accelerate and gain kinetic energy. When they hit *phosphors* coating the front of the screen, their energy is dissipated as light. The color and intensity of the light depend on chemical characteristics of the phosphor coating and the speed and quantity of the electrons. For the time being, we will assume that the composition of the phosphor gives out a white light; that is, the display is black and white or *monochrome*.

The beam of electrons from the cathode flows through a series of cylinders and wire meshes located near the cathode. Using the principle that *like charges repel and unlike charges*

---

[6] The cathode ray tube was originally invented in Germany by Karl Braun in 1910 and later developed by Vladimir Zworykin in 1928.

attract, various electrical potentials are applied to these cylinders and meshes to control the flow of the beam from the cathode to the screen and to focus the electrons to a tight spot—the smaller the spot, the better the *resolution* of the display. The cathode and focusing electrodes are called a *gun*.

A wire mesh called a *control grid* is placed in the path of the electron beam and connected to a negative voltage with respect to the cathode. The stronger the negative voltage on the grid, the more the electrons from the cathode are repelled, and the fewer get through to the screen. By changing or *modulating* the voltage on the grid, the number of electrons hitting the screen and, therefore, the brightness of the spot, can be controlled.

11.2.1 Raster-scan displays

Two scanning coils at right angles (called a *yoke*) are placed around the neck of the CRT. Passing a current through one coil creates a magnetic field that deflects the beam along the horizontal axis and passing a current through the other coil causes a deflection along the vertical axis. These coils let you deflect the beam up–down and left–right to strike any point on the screen.

The magnetic field in the coil that deflects the beam in the horizontal axis is increased *linearly* to force the spot to trace out a horizontal line across the face of the CRT. This line is called a *scan line* or a *raster*. When the beam reaches the right-hand side, it is rapidly moved to the left-hand edge, ready for the next horizontal scan.

While the beam is being scanned in the horizontal direction, another linearly increasing current is applied to the vertical deflection coils to move the beam downward. The rate at which the beam moves vertically is a fraction of the rate at which it moves horizontally. During the time it takes the beam to scan from top to bottom, it makes hundreds of scans in the horizontal plane. A scan in the vertical axis is called a *frame*. Figure 11.12(a) shows the combined effects of the fast horizontal and slow vertical scans—eventually, the beam covers or scans the entire surface of the screen.

As the beam scans the surface of the screen, the voltage on the grid is varied to change the brightness of the spot to draw an image. Figure 11.12(b) demonstrates how the letter 'A' can be constructed by switching the beam on and off as it scans the screen. The scanning process is carried so rapidly that the human viewer cannot see the moving spot and perceives a continuous image. Typically, the horizontal scan rate is in the region of 31 000 lines/s and the vertical scan rate is 50 to 100 fields/s. We will return to the scanning process later when we describe the system used to store images.

The simplest CRT screen would be a *hemisphere*, because any point on its surface is a constant distance from the focusing mechanism. Such a screen is unacceptable, and, over the years, the CRT screens have become both flatter and squarer

at the cost of ever more sophisticated focusing mechanisms. The CRT's screen is not square; its width:height or *aspect* ratio is the same as a television, 4:3.

The CRT is an *analog* device employing electrostatic and electromagnetic fields to focus an electron beam to a point on a screen. The engineering problems increase rapidly with the size of the screen and large CRTs are difficult to construct and expensive. The weight of the CRT also increases dramatically with screen size. In the early 1990s the cost of a 17-inch screen was about four times that of a 14-inch screen and a 19-inch screen cost over 10 times as much as a 14-inch screen. The CRT was one of the last components of the computer to experience falling prices. However, by the late 1990s the price of CRTs had dramatically fallen; not least because of competition with LCD displays. By 2003, the LCD was beginning to replace the CRT in domestic TV displays.

11.2.2 Generating a display

The next step is to explain how an image is generated. Figure 11.13 provides a more detailed description of the *raster-scan* display based on the CRT. A *sawtooth* waveform is applied to the vertical scan coils of a CRT to cause the spot to move from the top of the screen to the bottom of the screen at a constant linear rate. When the spot reaches the bottom of the screen, it rapidly flies back to the top again. At the same time, a second sawtooth waveform is applied to the horizontal scanning coils to cause the beam to scan from the left-hand side to the right-hand side before flying back again. A negative pulse is applied to the grid during the flyback period to turn off the beam.

As the beam is scanned across the surface of the screen, passing every point, the voltage on the grid can be changed to modify the spot's brightness. Although at any instant a TV screen consists of a single spot, the viewer perceives a complete image for two reasons. First, the phosphor coating continues to give out light for a short time after the beam has struck it, and, second, a phenomenon called the *persistence of vision* causes the brain to perceive an image for a short time after it has been removed.

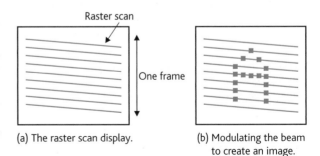

(a) The raster scan display.

(b) Modulating the beam to create an image.

Figure 11.12 The raster scan.

A raster-scan display system can be constructed by mapping the screen onto memory. As the beam scans the physical display screen, the corresponding location in the computer memory is interrogated and the resulting value used to determine the brightness of the spot. Figure 11.14 provides a highly simplified arrangement of a system that generates an n column by m row display.

In Fig. 11.14 a clock called a *dot clock* produces pulses at the dot rate (i.e. it generates a pulse for each dot or pixel on the display). The dot clock is fed into a divide-by-n circuit that produces a single pulse every time n dots along a row are counted. It also produces a dot number in the range 0, 1, 2, ... $n - 1$. The output of the divide-by-n circuit is a pulse at the row (i.e. raster) rate, which is fed to a divide-by-m circuit.

The output of the divide-by-m circuit is a pulse at the *frame rate* (i.e. a pulse for each complete scan of the screen). This pulse is fed to the CRT's control circuits and is used to lock or *synchronize* the scanning circuits in the CRT unit with the dot clock. The divide-by-m circuit produces an output in the range 0, 1, 2, $m - 1$ corresponding to the current row. The *column and row address combiner* takes the current column and row addresses from the two dividers and generates the address of the corresponding pixel in the video memory. The pixel at this address is fed to the CRT to either turn the beam on (a white dot), or to turn the beam off (no dot).

A real display system differs from that of Fig. 11.14 in several ways. Probably the most important component of the display generator is the

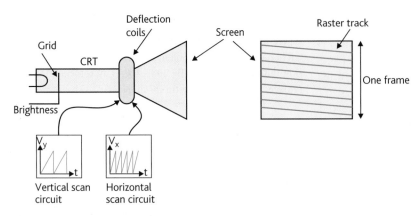

Figure 11.13 Details of the raster-scan display.

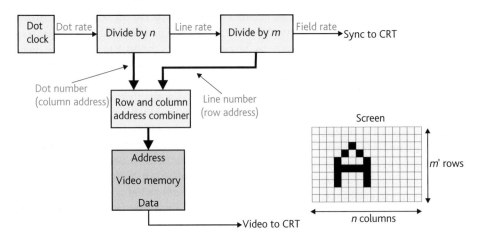

Figure 11.14 The display controller.

TV DISPLAYS

Because the computer display grew out of the television, let's look at some of the details of a TV display. In the USA a TV image uses 60 vertical scans a second and each vertical scan (called a *field*) is composed of $262\frac{1}{2}$ lines. A frame is made up of two consecutive fields containing $262\frac{1}{2}$ odd-numbered lines and $262\frac{1}{2}$ even-numbered lines. The total number of lines per frame is $2 \times 262\frac{1}{2} = 525$. In Europe there are 50 vertical scans a second and each vertical scan is composed

of $312\frac{1}{2}$ lines. The total number of lines per frame is $2 \times 312\frac{1}{2} = 625$.

A display composed of consecutive fields of odd and even lines is called an *interlaced display* and is used to reduce the rate at which lines have to be transmitted. However, interlaced displays are effective only with broadcast TV and generate unacceptable flicker when used to display text in a computing environment.

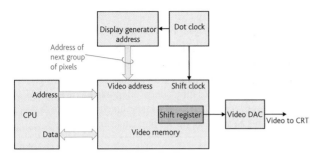

Figure 11.15 The video memory.

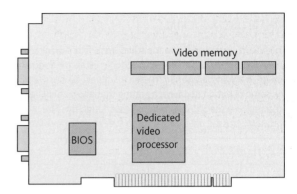

Figure 11.16 The video display card.

video memory (sometimes called *VRAM*), which holds the image to be displayed. Figure 11.15 shows the structure of a *dual-ported* video memory. We call this memory dual ported because it can be accessed by both an external CPU and the display generator *simultaneously*. The CPU needs to access the video memory in order to generate and modify the image being displayed.

One of the problems of video display design is the high rate at which its pixels are accessed. Consider a super VGA display with a resolution of 1024×768 pixels and a refresh rate (frame rate) of 70 Hz. In one second, the system must access $1024 \times 768 \times 70 = 55\,050\,240$ pixels. The time available to access a single pixel is approximately $1/55\,000\,000$ s $= 18$ ns, which is too short for typical video memory. In practice even less time is available to access pixels, because some time is lost to left- and right-hand margins and the flyback.

A practical video display system reads a group of pixels from video memory at a time and then sends them to the CRT one at a time. Figure 11.15 shows how the video memory performs this operation. The address from the display generator selects a row of pixels that are loaded into a *shift register* once per row clock. This arrangement means that the video memory is accessed by the display generator only once per row, rather than once per pixel. Consequently, the memory doesn't require such a low access time. The individual pixels of a row are read out of the shift register at the dot (i.e. pixel) rate. A shift register is capable of much higher speed operation than a memory.

Modern display systems permit more sophisticated images than the simple on/off dot displays of a few years ago. Several video memories (called *planes*) are operated in parallel, with each memory plane contributing one bit of the current pixel. If there are q memory planes, the q bits can be fed to a q-bit digital-to-analog converter to generate one of 2^q levels of brightness (i.e. a gray scale), or they can be used to select one of 2^q different colors (we discuss color later).

PC display systems

You can integrate a PC's display electronics onto the motherboard or you can locate the display subsystem on a plug-in board. High-performance computers use a plug-in display card because a card can be optimized for video applications. Figure 11.16 illustrates the organization of a typical display card. Because it's necessary to transfer large volumes of data between the CPU and the video display, PCs have a special interface slot that provides a very-high-speed data bus between the display card and the CPU; this is called the AGP bus.

It is impossible to cover display cards in any depth in this book. They are very complex devices that contain their own massively powerful special-purpose processors with 128-bit-wide internal buses. These processors free the host processor on the motherboard from display processing.

The video display memory forms part of the display card and is not normally part of the processor's memory space. This means that video and processor memory can be accessed in parallel. Some low-cost computers integrate the video controller on the motherboard and use system memory for display memory.

The original PC display was 640×480 pixels. Over the years, the average size of mainstream PC displays has increased. By the 1990s most PCs had 1024×768 displays and Web applications frequently used 800×600 display formats. Today, displays with resolutions of 1280×1024 are common and some LCD displays have a resolution of 1600×1200.

In practical terms, a 640×480 display can present a page of rather chunky text. A SXGA display with 1600×1200 pixels can display two word-processed pages side by side. Figure 11.17 illustrates the growth in the size (resolution) of displays for the PC.

11.2.3 Liquid crystal and plasma displays

For a long time, the CRT remained the most popular display mechanism. The late 1980s witnessed the rapid growth of a rival to the CRT, the *liquid crystal display* or *LCD*. By the mid-1990s color LCD displays were widely found in laptop

POLARIZING MATERIAL

The polarizing materials we use today were first produced by Edwin Land in 1932. Dr Land embedded crystals of idoquinine sulfate in a transparent film. These crystals are all oriented in the same direction and form a grating that allows only light polarized in a specific direction to pass though the film. If you place two crossed polarizing films in series with one rotated at 90° with respect to the other, no light passes through the pair, because one filter stops the passage of vertically polarized light and the other stops the passage of horizontally polarized light.

Dr Land marketed his filters under the trade name *Polaroid* and later went on to develop the instant picture camera that took pictures and developed the film while in the camera.

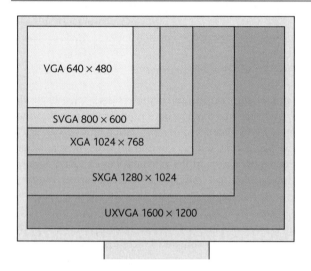

Figure 11.17 Video display formats.

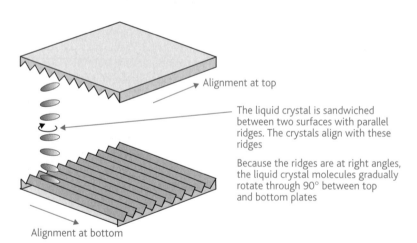

The liquid crystal is sandwiched between two surfaces with parallel ridges. The crystals align with these ridges

Because the ridges are at right angles, the liquid crystal molecules gradually rotate through 90° between top and bottom plates

Alignment at top

Alignment at bottom

Figure 11.18 The LCD cell with no applied field.

to the direction of its propagation. Light from an incandescent bulb is composed of large numbers of individual light waves, all arranged with their axes of vibration at random. Such light is said to be *unpolarized* because the vibrations do not favor a specific axis. If the vibrations are all along the same axis, the light is *polarized*. When light passes through a *polarizing filter*, only light whose axis of vibration has a certain angle is transmitted through the filter. The polarization of light and the polarizing filter can be used as the basis of a display system—all you need is a material that can be polarized on demand.

Unlike the molecules in a solid crystal, which are arranged in a fixed pattern, the molecules of a liquid are arranged at random. *Liquid crystals* are liquid but their molecules have a *preferred* alignment; that is, they are liquids that share some of the properties of solids. The intermolecular forces between molecules in a liquid crystal are not the same in all directions. The molecules are arranged at random in one plane but are organized or structured in another plane. You can imagine a liquid crystal as sheets or layers of molecules where the orientation of molecules within individual layers is random.

Figure 11.18 illustrates a liquid crystal cell where the liquid crystal film is placed between two plates. Each plate has a series of ridges scored on it that cause the long, rod-like molecules of the liquid crystal to align with the ridges. The two plates in Fig. 11.18 are *crossed* so that the molecules gradually rotate through 90° between the top and bottom surfaces. The polarization of light passing though such a structure is rotated by 90°.

A particular group of substances known as *nematic* liquid crystals are affected by an electric field. When an electric field is applied to a nematic liquid crystal, the molecules *twist* or rotate under the influence of the field. Figure 11.19 illustrates the same arrangement in which an electric field has been applied across the plates. This field overcomes the preferred alignment of the molecules.

The polarization of light passing though such a *twisted* liquid crystal is either unmodified or rotated through 90°, depending on whether a field is applied across the liquid crystal.

portables. First-generation LCDs had a resolution of 640 × 480 pixels and they cost much more than CRTs. The 800 × 600 pixel displays were rapidly replaced by the 14-inch 1024 × 768 pixel display. By 2004 top-of-the-range LCDs had 21-inch screens with resolutions of 1600 × 1200 pixels.

In order to understand how LCDs operate, we need to introduce *polarization*. Light is a form of *electromagnetic radiation* that shares some of the properties of *waves*; for example, the vibration of a light wave is at right angles

The liquid crystal display mimics the behavior of the CRT; that is, it creates a pixel that can be switched on or off. All we have to do is to make a sandwich of a polarizing substance and a liquid crystal—light will pass through it if the liquid crystal is polarized in the same plane as the polarizing material. Otherwise, the two polarizing filters block the transmission of light.

We now have all the ingredients of a *flat panel display*: a polarizing filter that transmits light *polarized* in one plane only and a liquid crystal cell that can rotate the polarization of light by 90° (or more) electronically. Figure 11.20 demonstrates the structure and operation of a single-pixel LCD cell.

In Fig. 11.20 light is passed first through a polarizer arranged with its axis of polarization at 0°, then through the liquid crystal, and finally through a second polarizer at 90°. If the liquid crystal does not rotate the plane of polarization of the light, all the light is blocked by the second polarizer. If, however, an electrostatic field is applied to the two electrodes, the liquid crystal rotates the polarization of the light by 90° and the light passes through the second polarizer. Consequently, a light placed behind the cell will be visible or invisible.

An entire LCD display is made by creating rows and columns of cells like those of Fig. 11.20. Each cell is selected or *addressed* by applying a voltage to the row and the column in which it occurs. The voltage is connected to each cell by depositing transparent conductors on the surface of the glass sandwich that holds the liquid crystals.

Because an LCD cell can be only on or off, it's impossible to achieve directly different levels of light transmission (i.e. you can display only black or white). However, because you can rapidly switch a cell on and off, you can generate intermediate light levels by modulating the time for which a cell transmits light. Typical LCDs can achieve 64 gray levels.

LCD displays can be operated in one of two modes. The *reflective* mode relies on the ambient light that falls on the cell, whereas the *transmissive* mode uses light that passes through the cell. Ambient light displays have a very low *contrast ratio* (i.e. there's not a lot of difference between the on state and the off state) and are often difficult to read in poor light, but they do consume very little power indeed.

Reflective LCD displays are found in pocket calculators, low-cost toys, and some personal organizers. Displays operating in a transmissive mode using *back-lighting* are easier to read, but require a light source (often a fluorescent tube) that consumes a considerable amount of power. Ultimately, it's the power taken by this fluorescent tube that limits the life of a laptop computer's battery.

Plasma displays

Plasma technology was invented in the 1960s. The plasma display uses a flat panel that shares many similarities with the LCD display. Both displays consist of an array of pixels that are addressed by *x*, *y* coordinates. The LCD cell uses a liquid crystal *light-gate* to switch a beam

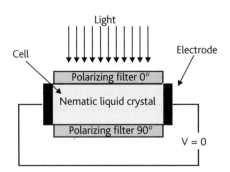

Direction of the field

Alignment of ridges at top

When an electric field is applied between the plates, the liquid crystal molecules change their alignment and line up in the direction of the field

Alignment of ridges at bottom

Figure 11.19 The LCD cell with an applied electric field.

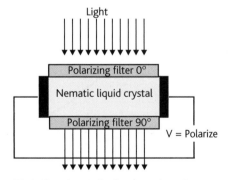

(a) The liquid crystal cell has no effect on the light passing through it. The polarizing filters stop light passing through them.

(b) The liquid crystal cell rotates the polarization of the light by 90°. This allows the light to pass through the lower polarizing filter.

Figure 11.20 Displaying a pixel.

of light on or off, whereas the plasma panel uses a tiny flores-cent light to generate a pixel.

Each pixel in a plasma display is a tiny neon light. A cell (i.e. pixel) contains a gas at a low pressure. Suppose a voltage can be applied to a pair of electrodes across the cell. At low volt-ages, nothing happens. As the voltage increases, electrons are pulled off the atoms of the gas in the cell by the electric field. As the voltage increases further, these electrons collide with other atoms and liberate yet more electrons. At this point an *avalanche* effect occurs and a current passes through the cell.

The passage of a current through the gas in a cell generates light or UV radiation. First-generation plasma display panels used cells containing neon, which glows orange-red when energized. By about 2000 color plasma panels were beginning to appear; these use cells with *phosphors*, which glow red,

green or blue when bombarded by UV light. By 2003 plasma panel production was rapidly increasing and plasma panels offered a realistic alternative to large CRT displays.

Plasma technology offers significant advantages over LCD technology; in particular, plasma displays have a higher con-trast ratio (i.e. the ratio of black to white) and plasma panels are brighter because they operate by generating light rather than by gating it through filters and a liquid crystal.

Figure 11.21 illustrates the structure of a plasma cell. The display is constructed from two sheets of glass separated by a few hundred microns. Ribs are molded on one of the plates to provide the cell structure. The phosphors that define the colors are deposited on the surface of the glass sheet. When the unit is assembled it is filled with xenon at low pressure.

A display is initiated by applying a voltage across two elec-trodes to break down the gas and start the discharge. Once the cell has been activated, a lower voltage is applied to the keep-alive electrode to main-tain the discharge.

Although plasma panels have advantages over LCD displays, they also have disadvan-tages. They consume more power than LCDs, which can cause problems with unwanted heat. The phosphors gradually degrade and the display slowly loses its brightness over a few years. Finally, the individual cells sufferer a *memory effect*. If a cell is continuously ener-gized for a long time, it can lose some inten-sity. This means that a static picture can be burnt onto the screen; you see this effect with plasma displays in airports where the ghostly details of some flights are perma-nently burnt onto the screen.

The *contrast ratio* of a display is the ratio of the lightest and darkest parts of the display. Although many regard the plasma panel as having a better contrast ratio than an LCD, the situation is more complicated. Contrast ratio is affected not only by the transmissivity of an LCD or the on/off light ratio of a plasma cell, but also by ambient light. Figure 11.22 gives the contrast ratios of LCDs and plasma displays as a function of ambient light. This demonstrates that the plasma display is far superior in a dark room but is less good in bright light.

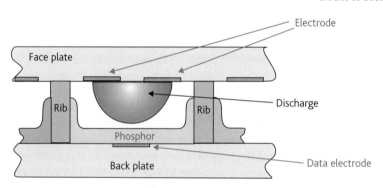

Figure 11.21 The plasma display cell.

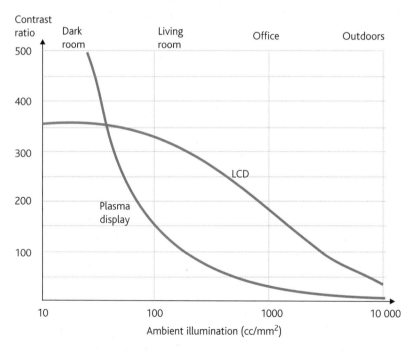

Figure 11.22 Contrast LDC and plasma displays.

11.2.4 **Drawing lines**

Having come so far in describing display systems, we'd just like to demonstrate how dots are transformed into lines by

ORGANIC DISPLAYS

Conventional electronics uses semiconductors fabricated from silicon or compounds such as gallium arsenide. Organic semiconducting materials have been discovered that have many interesting properties. Unfortunately, organic semiconducting materials are often difficult to work with. They suffer from low electron and hole mobility and are limited to low-speed applications. From a manufacturing standpoint, they are sensitive to high temperatures, cannot be soldered into conventional circuits, and degrade when exposed to atmospheric moisture and oxygen.

On the other hand, organic electronics have remarkable commercial potential. They offer the promise of flexible, paper-thin circuits and displays because they can be deposited on flexible plastic foils rather than the heavy and fragile glass surfaces required by LCDs. OLEDs (organic light-emitting diodes) have far lower power consumption than LCDs.

The OLED pioneered by Kodak in the mid-1980s, is already in large-scale production. The first applications of this

technology were in automobile instrument panels, digital watches, and small, low-power displays in mobile phones.

The OLED uses organic materials that have weak intermolecular bonds that give them the properties of both semiconductors and insulators. The organic molecules of an OLED are sandwiched between conductors (anode and cathode). When a current flows through the molecules of the OLED, electron and hole charge carriers recombine to give off light in a process called *fluorescence*.

OLEDs can be constructed in the form of TOLEDs (transparent OLEDs) for use in automobile or aircraft windshields to provide 'head-up' displays, or in the form of FOLEDs (flexible OLEDs), which can be bent or rolled into any shape.

By vertically stacking TOLEDs in layers with each layer having a different color, you can create the SOLED (stacked OLED), which forms the basis of a multicolor display.

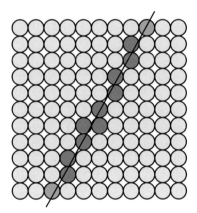

Figure 11.23 Drawing a line.

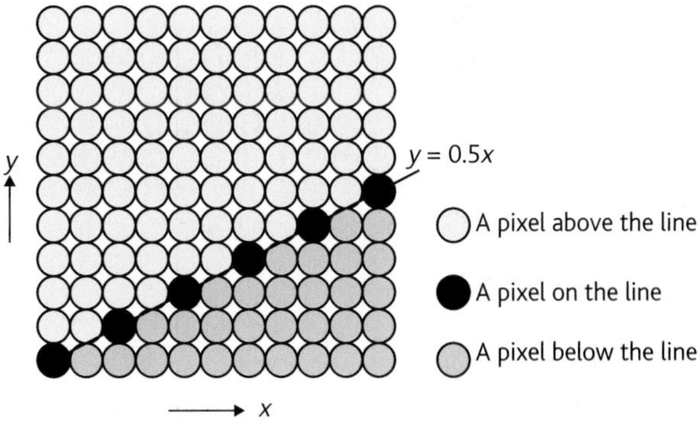

Figure 11.24 The equation of a straight line.

software. There are two types of image: the *bit-mapped* image and the *parameterized* image. All images in the video memory are bit mapped in the sense that each pixel in the display corresponds to a pixel in the video memory (strictly speaking, perhaps we should use the term *pixel mapped*). Photographs and TV pictures are examples of bit-mapped images.

A *parameterized* image is defined in terms of an *algorithm*; for example, you might describe a line as running from point $(-4, 12)$ to point $(30, 45)$, or as the equation $y = 4x + 25$ for $-9 < x < 70$. The graphics software is responsible for taking the parameterized image and converting it into a bit-mapped image in the display's memory. We now look at the parameterized image because it can be specified with relatively few bits and it can easily be manipulated.

Figure 11.23 demonstrates how a line is mapped onto a display by evaluating the *equation* of the line and then select-

ing every pixel that passes through the line. In a practical system, relatively few pixels will lie exactly on the line and it is necessary to select pixels close to the line.

Jack Bresenham invented a classic line-drawing algorithm in 1965. A straight line can be expressed as $ay = bx + c$, where x and y are variables, and a, b, and c constants that define the line. The line's *slope* is given by b/a and the point at which the line goes through the x origin is given by $y = c/a$. For the sake of simplicity, consider a line that goes through the origin, so that $ay = bx$, where $a = 1$ and $b = +0.5$. Figure 11.24 illustrates how the line corresponding to this equation goes through some pixels (shown black in Fig. 11.24). All other pixels are either *above* or *below* the line. If the equation of the line is rearranged in the form $ay - bx = 0$, the pixels above the line (light in Fig. 11.24) satisfy the relation $ay - bx > 0$, and those below the line (dark in Fig. 11.24) satisfy the relation $ay - bx < 0$.

The Bresenham algorithm draws lines with a slope $m = b/a$ in the range 0 to 1. This algorithm evaluates the *sign* of $ay - bx$ at regular intervals. By monitoring the *sign* of the function, you can determine whether you are above or below the line. The line is drawn from its starting point from, say, left to right. Suppose we select a pixel somewhere along this line. Bresenham's algorithm tells us how to go about selecting the next pixel. Figure 11.25 demonstrates that the new pixel is selected to be either the pixel directly to the right of the current pixel or the pixel both above and to the right of the current pixel.

The algorithm evaluates the value of the function at the midpoint between the two candidates for the new pixel along the line. The pixel selected to be the next pixel is the one that lies closest to the line, as Fig. 11.25 demonstrates. The details of the Bresenham algorithm are more complex than we've described. The algorithm must handle lines that don't pass through the origin and lines that don't have slope in the range 0 to 1.

The following fragment of pseudocode implements the Bresenham line-drawing algorithm. Assume that a straight line with a slope between 0 and 1 is to be drawn from x_1, y_1 to x_2, x_2. At each step in drawing the line we increment the value of the x coordinate by x_step. The corresponding change in y is $x\_step * (y2 - y1)/(x2 - x1)$.

The Bresenham algorithm eliminates this calculation by either making or not making a fixed step along the y axis.

```
DrawLine(x1,y1,x2,y2)
int x, y, e, dx, dy;
{
    dx = x2 - x1;
    dy = y2 - y1;
    e = 2*dy - dx;
    y = y1;
    for (x = x1; x1 d"x2; x++)
      {
        plot(x,y);
        while (e e"0)
          {
            e = e - 2*dx;
            y++;
          }
        e = e + 2*dy;
      }
}
```

If the line's slope is greater than 1, we can use the *same* algorithm by simply swapping x and y.

Antialiasing

The Bresenham and similar algorithms generate lines that suffer from a *step-like* appearance due to the nature of the line-following mechanism. These steps are often termed *jaggies* and spoil the line's appearance. The effect of finite pixel size and jaggies is termed *aliasing*, a term taken from the world of signal processing to indicate the error introduced when analog signals are sampled at too low a rate to preserve fidelity. Figure 11.26 demonstrates how we can reduce the effects of aliasing.

The antialiasing technique in Fig. 11.26 uses pixels with gray-scale values to create a line that appears less jagged to the human eye. A pixel that is on the line is made fully black. Pixels that are partially on the line are displayed as less than 100% black. When the human eye sees the line from a distance, the eye–brain combination perceives a line free of jaggies. That is, the brain averages or smoothes the image.

Now that we've looked at how images are created on a screen, we examine how they are printed on paper.

11.3 The printer

The printer produces a hard-copy output from a computer by converting digital information into marks on paper. Because printers rely on precisely machined moving mechanical

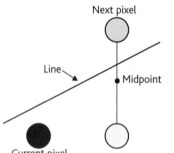
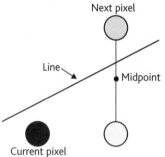

(a) Select next pixel up and right.   (b) Select next pixel right.

Figure 11.25 Searching along a line.

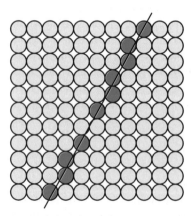

Figure 11.26 Improving a line by antialiasing.

parts, they are less reliable than the purely electronic devices such as CRT and LCD displays.

Like all the other subsystems of a PC, the printer has seen a remarkable drop in its price over the last three decades. In 1976 a slow, unreliable dot matrix printer cost about $800 and by 2005 you could buy a laser printer for $150 and a photo-quality inkjet printer for about $60.

Printers come in a wider range than other display devices because there are more printer technologies. Mechanical printers must perform the following basic functions.

1. Move the paper to a given line.
2. Move the print-head to a given point along a line.
3. Select a character or symbol to be printed.
4. Make a mark on the paper corresponding to that character.

The first and last of these functions are relatively easy to explain and are dealt with first. Depending on the application, paper is available in single sheet, continuous roll, or fan-fold form. Paper can be moved by *friction feed*, in which the paper is trapped between a motor-driven roller and pressure rollers that apply pressure to the surface of the paper. As the roller (or platen) moves, the paper is dragged along with it. An alternative paper feeding mechanism is the tractor or sprocket feed where a ring of conical pins round the ends of the platen engage in perforations along the paper's edge. As the platen rotates, the paper is accurately and precisely pulled through the printer. The rise of the PC has seen the decline of fan-fold paper. Today's printers found in the home or small office use plain paper. Some banks and similar institutions still employ fan-fold paper to print statements (and other pre-printed forms).

11.3.1 Printing a character

Printers are described by the way in which marks on the paper are made; for example, the matrix printer, the inkjet printer, and the laser printer. The earliest method of marking paper used the impact of a hard object against an ink-coated ribbon, to make an imprint in the shape of the object. This is how the mechanical office typewriter operates. The tremendous reduction in the cost of laser and inkjet printers in the early 1990s rendered impact printers obsolete, except in specialized applications.

Non-impact printers form characters without physically striking the paper. The *thermal printer* employs special paper coated with a material that turns black or blue when heated to about 110°C. A character is formed by heating a combination of dots within a matrix of, typically, 7 by 5 points. Thermal printers are very cheap, virtually silent in operation, and are used in applications such as printing receipts in mobile ticket

dispensers. A similar printing mechanism uses black paper coated with a thin film of shiny aluminum. When a needle electrode is applied to the surface and a large current passed through it, the aluminum film is locally vaporized to reveal the dark coating underneath.

Another method of printing involves spraying a fine jet of ink at the paper. As this technique also includes the way in which the character is selected and formed, it will be dealt with in detail later.

The hardware that actually prints the character is called the *print head*. There are two classes of print head: the *single* print head and the *multiple* print head found in line printers. Typewriters employ a fixed print head and the paper and platen move as each new character is printed. A fixed print head is unsuitable for high-speed printing, as the platen and paper have a large mass and hence a high inertia, which means that the energy required to perform a high-speed carriage return would be prohibitive. Because the mass of the print head is very much less than that of the platen, most printers are arranged so that the paper stays where it is and the print head moves along the line.

One way of moving the print head is to attach it to a nut on a threaded rod (the lead screw). At the end of the rod is a stepping motor, which can rotate the rod through a fixed angle at a time. Each time the rod rotates the print head is moved left or right (depending on the direction of rotation). In another arrangement the print head is connected to a belt, moved by the same technique as the paper itself. The belt passes between two rollers, one of which moves freely and one of which is controlled by a stepping motor.

11.3.2 The inkjet printer

Inkjet printers were originally developed for professional applications and the technology migrated to low-cost PC applications. The original continuous inkjet owes more to the CRT for its operation than the impact printer. A fine jet of ink is emitted from a tiny nozzle to create a high-speed stream of ink drops. The nozzle is vibrated ultrasonically so that the ink stream is broken up into individual drops. As each drop leaves the nozzle it is given an electrical charge, so that the stream of drops can be deflected electrostatically, just like the beam of electrons in a CRT. By moving the beam, characters can be written on to the surface of the paper. The paper is arranged to be off the central axis of the beam, so that when the beam is undeflected, the ink drops do not strike the paper and are collected in a reservoir for re-use.

Continuous inkjet printers are high-speed devices, almost silent in operation, and are used in high-volume commercial applications. The original inkjet printer was very expensive and was regarded with suspicion because it had suffered a number of problems during its development. In particular, they were prone to clogging of the nozzle. Many of the early problems have now been overcome.

Drop-on-demand printing

The modern drop-on-demand inkjet printer is much simpler than its continuous jet predecessor. In fact, it's identical to a dot matrix printer apart from the print head itself. The print head that generates the inkjet also includes the ink reservoir. When the ink supply is exhausted the head assembly is thrown away and a new head inserted. Although this looks wasteful, it reduces maintenance requirements and increases reliability. Some inkjet printers do have permanent print heads and just change the ink cartridge.

In the 1980s inkjet printers had maximum resolution of 300 dpi (dots per inch) and by the late 1990s inkjet printers with resolution of over 1400 dpi were available at remarkably low cost. In 2004 you could buy inkjet printers with a resolution of 5700 dpi that could print photographs that were indistinguishable from conventional color photographs. Later we will look at the color inkjet printer, which created the mass market in desktop digital photography.

The drop-on-demand print head uses multiple nozzles, one for each of the dots in a dot matrix array. The head comes into contact with the paper and there's no complex ink delivery and focusing system. The holes or *capillary nozzles* through which the ink flows are too small to permit the ink to leak out.

Ink is forced through the holes by creating a shock wave in the reservoir that expels a drop of ink though the nozzle to the paper.

One means of creating a shock wave is to place a thin film of piezoelectric crystal transducer in the side of the reservoir (see Fig. 11.27(a)). When an electronic field is applied across a piezoelectric crystal, the crystal flexes. By applying an electrical pulse across such a crystal in a print head, it flexes and creates the shock wave that forces a single drop of ink through one of the holes onto the paper (see Fig. 11.27(b)). Note that there is a separate crystal for each of the holes in the print head.

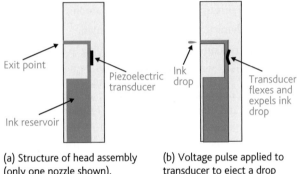

(a) Structure of head assembly (only one nozzle shown).

(b) Voltage pulse applied to transducer to eject a drop of ink.

Figure 11.27 Structure of the ink jet.

OLD PRINTER TECHNOLOGIES

Dot matrix printer A dot matrix printer forms characters from a matrix of dots in much the same way as a CRT. The dots are generated by a needle pressing an inked ribbon onto the paper or the needles may be used with spark erosion techniques or may be replaced by heating elements in a thermal printer. The dot matrix printer was very popular in the 1970s and 1980s when it offered the only low-cost means of printing.

Cylinder, golf-ball and daisy-wheel printers The cylinder print head is a metallic cylinder with symbols embossed around it. The ribbon and paper are positioned immediately in front of the cylinder, and a hammer is located behind it. The cylinder is rotated about its vertical axis and is moved up or down until the desired symbol is positioned next to the ribbon. A hammer, driven by a solenoid, then strikes the back of the cylinder, forcing the symbol at the front onto the paper through the inked ribbon.

The golf-ball head was originally used in IBM electric typewriters. Characters are embossed on the surface of a metallic sphere. The golf-ball rotates in the same way as a cylinder, but is tilted rather than moved up or down to access different rows of characters. The golf-ball is propelled towards the ribbon and the paper by a cam mechanism, rather than by a hammer striking it at the back.

The daisy-wheel printer has a disk with slender petals arranged around its periphery. An embossed character is located at the end of each of these spokes. The wheel is made of plastic or metal and is very lightweight, giving it a low inertia. A typical daisy wheel has 96 spokes, corresponding to the upper and lower case subsets of the ISO/ASCII code.

The daisy wheel rotates in the vertical plane in front of the ribbon. As the wheel rotates, each of the characters passes between a solenoid-driven hammer and the ribbon. When the desired character is at a print position, the hammer forces the spoke against the ribbon to mark the paper.

Line printer A line printer prints a whole line of text at one go. Line printers are expensive, often produce low quality output, and are geared to high-volume, high-speed printing.

A metal drum extends along the entire width of the paper in front of the ribbon. The character set to be printed is embossed along the circumference of the drum. This character set is repeated, once for each of the character positions, along the drum. A typical line printer has 132 character positions and a set of 64 characters. As the drum rotates, the rings of characters pass over each of the 132 print positions, and a complete set of characters passes each printing point once per revolution. A mark is made on the paper by a hammer hitting the paper and driving it into the head through the ribbon. By controlling the instant at which the hammer is energized, any particular character may be printed. As there is one hammer per character position, a whole line may be printed during the course of a single revolution of the drum.

XEROGRAPHY

Xerography has a long history. In 1935 a patent attorney, Carlton Chester, had an idea for a cheap copying process that didn't require the wet and messy chemicals then used in photography. While looking for a dry process that allowed photocopying, Chester turned his attention to the phenomenon of *photoconductivity* (i.e. the relationship between light and the electrical conductivity of materials). He was awarded a patent on *electrophotography* in 1937.

Chester's first experiments used a metal plate covered with sulfur (a photoconductive material). The sulfur was electrically charged by rubbing it, and then a glass plate was placed over it. Chester wrote on the glass. In the next step, a bright light was shone on the assembly for several seconds. The effect of the light was to cause the sulfur to conduct and permit the electrostatic charge to leak away to the metal plate under the sulfur.

The glass was removed and a fine power dusted on the sulfur-coated plate. This powder clung to the regions that retained their charge because they hadn't been illuminated by the light (i.e. the writing). Finally, a sheet of waxed paper was placed on the powder-covered plate and pressed against it. A copy of the writing on the glass plate was now impressed on the wax paper.

It took until 1944 for Chester to find someone who was interested in his invention—the Battelle Memorial Institute. Battelle's scientists rapidly discovered that selenium had far better photoconductive properties than sulfur and that a fine-pigmented resin could easily be fused onto the surface of paper to create the copy.

Battelle develop the process further in conjunction with the Haloid Company. They decided that Chester's electrophotography was too cumbersome a term and asked a professor of Greek to come up with a better name. He suggested 'dry writing' because the process did not involve liquids. The corresponding Greek word was *xerography*. Haloid changed its name to Haloid Xerox in 1958 and then to the Xerox Corporation in 1961.

Some inkjet printers employ a fine wire behind the nozzle to instantaneously heat the ink to 300°C, well above its boiling point, which creates bubble that force out a tiny drop. These printers are called *bubble jet* printers.

Although inkjet printers are capable of high resolution with over 1000 dpi, the ink drops spread out on paper due to the capillary action of fibers on the paper's surface (this effect is called *wicking*). Specially coated paper considerably reduces the effect of wicking, although such paper is expensive. Canon's photo paper has a four-layered structure with a mirror-finished surface. The outer surface provides an ink-absorption layer, consisting of ultrafine inorganic particles. By instantly absorbing the ink, this layer prevents ink from spreading and preserves the round ink dots. The second layer reflects light. The third layer is the same material used in conventional photographic paper. The bottom layer is a back coating, which counteracts the stresses placed on the paper by the upper layers, to prevent curling.

11.3.3 The laser printer

The dot matrix printer brought word processing to the masses because it produced acceptable quality text at a low cost. The laser printer has now brought the ability to produce high-quality text and graphics to those who, only a few years ago, could afford no more than a medium-quality dot matrix printer. In fact, the quality of the laser printer is sufficiently high to enable a small office to create artwork similar to that once produced by the professional typesetter; that is, desktop publishing (DTP).

The laser printer is just a photocopier specially modified to accept input from a host computer. The principle of the photocopier and the laser printer is both elegant and simple. At the heart of a laser printer lies a precisely machined drum, which is as wide as the sheet of paper to be printed. The secret of the drum lies in its *selenium* coating.[7] Selenium is an electrical insulator with an important property—when selenium is illuminated by light, it becomes conductive.

A photocopier works by first charging up the surface of the drum to a very high electrostatic potential (typically 1000 V with respect to ground). By means of a complex arrangement of lenses and mirrors, the original to be copied is scanned by a very bright light and the image projected onto the rotating drum. After one rotation, the drum contains an invisible image of the original document. If the image is invisible we are entitled to ask ourselves, 'What form does this image take?' Black regions of the source document reflect little light and the corresponding regions on the drum receive no light. The selenium coating in these regions is not illuminated, doesn't become conducting, and therefore retains its electrical charge.

Light regions of the document reflect light onto the drum, causing the coating to become conducting and to lose its charge. In other words, the image on the drum is painted with an electrostatic charge, ranging from high voltage (black) to zero voltage (white).

One of the effects of an electrostatic charge is its ability to attract nearby light objects. In the next step the drum is rotated in close proximity to a very fine black powder called the *toner*. Consequently, the toner is attracted to those parts of the drum with a high charge. Now the drum contains a true positive image of the original. The image is a positive image because black areas on the original are highly charged and pick up the black toner.

---

[7] Modern drums don't use selenium; they use complex organic substances that have superior photo-electric properties.

The drum is next rotated in contact with paper that has an even higher electrostatic charge. The charge on the paper causes the toner to transfer itself from the drum to the paper. Finally, the surface of the paper is heat-treated to fix the toner on to it. Unfortunately, not all toner is transferred from the drum to the paper. Residual toner is scraped off the drum by rotating it in contact with a very fine blade. Eventually, the drum becomes scratched or the selenium no longer functions properly and it must be replaced. In contrast with other printers, the laser printer requires the periodic replacement of some of its major components. Low-cost laser printers sometimes combine the drum and the toner, which means that the entire drum assembly is thrown away once the toner has been exhausted. This approach to printer construction reduces the cost of maintenance while increasing the cost of consumables.

Unlike the photocopier, the laser printer has no optical imaging system. The image is written directly onto the drum by means of an electromechanical system. As the drum rotates, an image is written onto it line by line in very much the same way that a television picture is formed in a cathode ray tube.

Figure 11.28(a) illustrates the organization of the laser scanner and Fig. 11.28(b) provides details of the scanning mechanism. A low-power semiconductor laser and optical system produces a very fine spot of laser light. By either varying the intensity of the current to the laser or by passing the beam through a liquid crystal whose opacity is controlled electronically (i.e. modulated), the intensity of the light spot falling on the drum can be varied.

The light beam strikes a multi-sided rotating mirror. As the mirror turret rotates, the side currently in the path of the light beam sweeps the beam across the surface of the selenium-coated drum. By modulating the light as the beam sweeps across the drum, a single line is drawn. This scanning process is rather like a raster-scan mechanism found in a CRT display. After a line has been drawn, the next mirror in the rotating turret is in place and a new line is drawn below the previous line, because the selenium drum has moved by one line.

The combined motions of the rotating mirror turret and the rotating selenium drum allow the laser beam to scan the entire surface of the selenium drum. Of course, the optical circuits required to perform the scanning are very precise indeed. The resolution imposed by the optics and the laser beam size provided low-cost first-generation laser printers with a resolution of about 300 dots per inch. Such a resolution is suitable for moderately high-quality text but is not entirely suitable for high-quality graphics. Second-generation laser printers with resolutions of 600 or 1200 dpi became available in the mid-1990s.

Not all laser printers employ the same optical arrangement, because the rotating mirror turret is complex and requires careful alignment. An alternative technique designed by Epson uses an incandescent light source behind

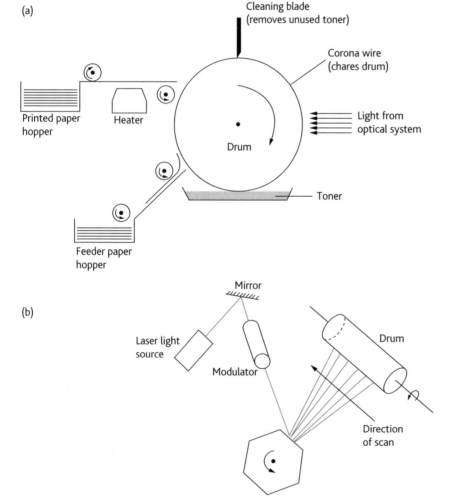

(a)

Cleaning blade
(removes unused toner)

Corona wire
(chares drum)

Printed paper hopper

Heater

Drum

Light from optical system

Toner

Feeder paper hopper

(b)

Mirror

Laser light source

Modulator

Drum

Direction of scan

Rotating mirror drum

Figure 11.28 The laser printer.

a stationary liquid crystal shutter. The liquid crystal shutter has a linear array of 2000 dots, each of which can be turned on and off to build up a single line across the drum. By writing a complete line in one operation, the only major moving part involved in the scanning process is the photosensitive drum itself. Technically, a laser printer without a laser scanner isn't really a laser printer. However, the term *laser printer* is used to describe any printer that generates an image by using an electrostatic charge to deposit a fine powder (the toner) on paper.

Other ways of avoiding the complex rotating drum mirror turret are a linear array of light-emitting diodes (LEDs) in an arrangement similar to the liquid crystal shutter, or a CRT projection technique that uses a CRT to project a line onto the photosensitive drum.

Laser printers can print dot-map pictures; that is, each pixel of the picture is assigned a bit in the printer's memory. A linear resolution of 300 dpi requires $300 \times 300 = 90\,000$ dots/square inch. A sheet of paper measuring 11 inches by 8 inches (i.e. 88 square inches) can hold up to $88 \times 90\,000 = 7\,720\,000$ dots or just under 1 Mbyte of storage.

Having introduced the principles of monochrome displays and printers, we are going to look at how color displays and printers are constructed.

11.4 Color displays and printers

It's been possible to print color images for a long time, although color printers were astronomically expensive until relatively recently. Low-cost printers began to appear in the early 1990s (largely based on inkjet technology) although the quality was suitable only for draft work. By the late 1990s high-quality low-cost color printers were widely available and the new term *photorealistic* was coined to describe that they were almost able to match the quality of color photographs. Before we discuss color printers we need to say a little about the nature of color.

11.4.1 Theory of color

Light is another type of *electromagnetic radiation* just like X-rays and radio waves. The eye is sensitive to electromagnetic radiation in the visible spectrum and light waves of different frequencies are perceived as different colors. This visible spectrum extends from violet to red (i.e. wavelengths from 400 nm to 700 nm). Frequencies lower than red are called *infra-red* and higher than violet are called *ultra-violet*. Both these frequencies are invisible to the human eye, although they play important roles in our life.

A single frequency has a pure color or *hue* and we perceive its intensity in terms of is brightness. In practice, we see few pure colors in everyday life. Most light sources contain visible radiation over a broad spectrum. If a light source contains approximately equal amounts of radiation across the entire visual spectrum we perceive the effect as *white light*. In practice light often consists of a mixture of white light together with light containing a much narrower range of frequencies. The term *saturation* describes the ratio of colored light to white light; for example, pink is unsaturated red at about 700 nm plus white light. An unsaturated color is sometimes referred to as a *pastel* shade.

Most light sources contain a broad range of frequencies (e.g. sunlight and light from an incandescent lamp). Sources that generate a narrow band of visible frequencies are gas discharge lamps and LEDs; for example, the sodium light used to illuminate streets at night emits light with two very closely spaced wavelengths at about 580 nm (i.e. yellow).

COLOR TERMINOLOGY

Hue This describes the color of an object. The hue is largely dependent on the dominant wavelength of light emitted from or reflected by an object.

Saturation This describes the strength of a color. A color may be pure or it may be blended with white light; for example, pink is red blended with white.

Luminance This measures the intensity of light per unit area of its source.

Gamma This expresses the contrast range of an image.

Color space This provides a means of encoding the color. The following color spaces are used to define the color of objects.

    RGB The red, green, blue color space defines a color as the amount of its red, blue, and green components. This color space is based on the additive properties of colors.

CMY The cyan, magenta, yellow color space is used in situations in which color is applied to a white background such as paper. For example, an object appears yellow because it absorbs blue but reflects red and green. Suppose you wanted to create blue using a CMY color space. Blue is white light with red and green subtracted. Because green is absorbed by cyan and red is absorbed by magenta, combining cyan and magenta leads to the absorption of green and red; that is, blue.

HSB The HSB model defines light in the way we perceive it (H = hue or color, S = saturation, B = brightness or intensity).

Pantone matching system This is an entirely arbitrary and a proprietary commercial system. A very large number of colors are defined and given reference numbers. You define a color by matching it against the colors in the Pantone system.

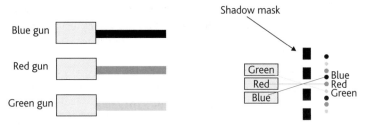

(a) Three independent electron guns produce three electron beams.

(b) Each beam hits only its own phosphors.

Figure 11.29 Generating a color image.

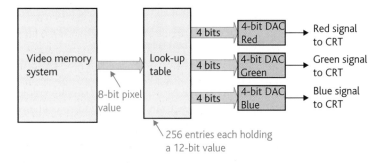

Figure 11.30 The color look-up table.

Whatever jumble of frequencies the eye detects, the brain perceives a single color. Suppose a particular light source contains the colors red and green. We don't see these two colors, we perceive a single color whose frequency is intermediate between red and green; that is, we see yellow. By mixing various quantities of the three primary colors red, green, and blue we can create any other color. Moreover, because we can add red, green, and blue to create white light, we can control the level of saturation.

11.4.2 Color CRTs

The majority of general-purpose computers employ color displays—partially because we see the world in color, and partially because we already have color TV and the cinema. In principle the operation of a color CRT is very simple as Fig. 11.29 demonstrates. The color CRT is similar to a monochrome CRT. Instead of having a *single* gun assembly, the color CRT has *three* gun assemblies, one for each of the primary colors red, green, and blue (Fig. 11.29(a)). The focusing system aims each beam at the same spot on the screen and the three beams are deflected in unison by the scanning coils.

The key to the color CRT is the *shadow mask* located immediately in front of the screen. The *shadow mask* is made of metal and has a very large number of tiny holes punched in it (Fig. 11.29(b)). Millions of tiny dots of phosphor are deposited behind the shadow mask on the surface of the CRT's screen. These phosphors are arranged as triplets. One dot produces a

green light when bombarded by electrons, one a red light, and one a blue light. Because of the geometry of the shadow mask, the phosphor dots on the screen, and the electron guns, the electron beam from the green gun can hit only green phosphors (the red and blue phosphors are shielded by the shadow mask). The same is true for beams from the other two guns. Some CRTs employ a different type of shadow mask; for example, the *trinitron* shadow mask employs vertical stripes rather than dots to generate a brighter image.

By applying three independent control voltages to each of the three guns, you can control the intensities of each of the beams. Consequently, you can control the intensity of each of the three pixels—red, green, and blue. Any color can be generated by adding suitable intensities of green, red, and blue light, and, therefore, the human eye sees each pixel not as three different colors, but as a single color.

Figure 11.30 illustrates the interface between a color CRT and a computer which lets you generate a large number of colors specified by relatively few bits. The output of the video memory specifies the current pixel's attributes. In the example of Fig. 11.30, the pixel is defined by an 8-bit integer that provides one of $2^8 = 256$ possible values. The 8-bit pixel value is sent to a *look-up table* that produces one of 256 12-bit outputs; that is, each of the 256 locations contains a *12-bit* value. Each 12-bit output is divided into three 4-bit fields representing the primary colors red, green, and blue. In turn, each of these 4-bit values is fed to a DAC to generate one of $2^4 = 16$ levels of brightness. This system can select 1 of 16 levels of red, 1 of 16 levels of green, and 1 of 16 levels of blue. The pixel can therefore have any one of $16 \times 16 \times 16 = 4096$ values (i.e. colors).

An 8-bit pixel code from the video memory can perform the apparently impossible act of selecting one of 4096 different pixels. The paradox is resolved by the nature of the look-up table. It has 256 entries, each of which can select one of 4096 colors; that is, at any instant the look-up table allows the display to address 256 colors out of a *palette* of 4096 colors. The look-up table is loaded with the values appropriate to the application being run.

Because the surface of the screen is made up of dots, the resolution of a color CRT is limited—the smallest element that can be displayed on the screen is a single dot. The resolution of color CRTs is often specified in terms of the *pitch* or distance between clusters of the three dots. Typical CRT resolutions lie

Monitor size	Image size	Resolution (pixels)	Dots per inch
15-inch	270 × 200 mm	640 × 480	60
		800 × 600	75
		1024 × 768	96
17-inch	315 × 240 mm	640 × 480	51
		800 × 600	63
		1024 × 768	85
21-inch	385 × 285 mm	640 × 480	42
		800 × 600	52
		1024 × 768	85
		1280 × 1024	84
		1600 × 1200	106

Table 11.2 Monitor size, image size, and resolution.

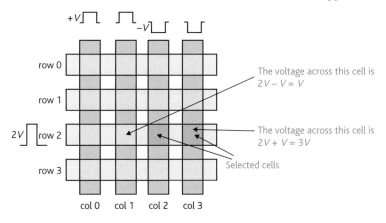

Figure 11.31 The passive matrix.

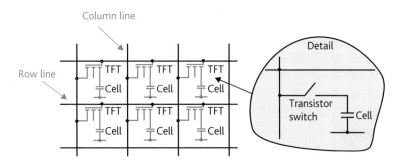

Figure 11.32 The active matrix.

in the range 0.28 to 0.31 mm. Table 11.2 provides relates image size to resolution for some popular configurations.

Color LCDs

Color LCDs operate on a similar principle to the color CRT and generate a color pixel from three cells with three primary colors. The individual cells of a color LCD display include red, green, or blue filters to transmit light of only one color. As in the case of the color CRT, the three primary colors are clustered to enable other colors to be synthesized by combining red, green, or blue. Color LCD displays are divided into two types: *active* and *passive*. Both active and passive displays employ the same types of LCD cells—the difference lies in the ways in which the individual cells of a matrix are selected.

The so-called *passive* liquid crystal matrix of Fig. 11.31 (this arrangement applies to both monochrome and color displays) applies a large pulse to all the cells (i.e. pixels) of a given row. This pulse is marked $2V$ in Fig. 11.31 and is currently applied to row 2. A smaller pulse that may be *either* positive or negative is applied to each of the columns in the array. The voltage from the row and the column pulses are applied across each cell in a row, and are summed to either polarize the cell or to leave it unpolarized. This arrangement displays an entire row of pixels at a time. Once a row has been drawn, a pulse is applied to the next row, and so on.

Each cell is connected to one row line and to one column line. In Fig. 11.32 a pulse of level $2V$ is applied to one terminal of all the cells in row 2 of the matrix. A pulse of level $+V$ or $-V$ is then applied in turn to each of the column cells, 0, 1, 2, and 3. The voltage *across* each cell in the matrix must be either 0 (neither row nor column selected), V (row selected with $+2V$, column selected with $+V$), or $3V$ (row selected with $+2V$, column selected with $-V$). The matrix is designed so that the $3V$ pulse across a cell is sufficient to polarize the liquid crystal and turn the cell on.

The passive matrix suffers from *cross-talk* caused by the pulse on one row leaking into cells on adjacent rows. Furthermore, if the matrix has m rows, each row is driven (i.e. accessed) for only $1/m$ of the available time. These limitations produce a display that has low contrast, suffers from smearing when moving images are displayed, and has a less bright image than the TFT active matrix alternative to be described next. Although passive matrix displays were popular in the 1990s, improvements in active matrix manufacturing technology have rendered them obsolete.

A better arrangement is the *active matrix* of Fig. 11.32; the cell structure is exactly the same as that of a passive display, only the means of addressing a cell is different. A transistor, which is simply an *electronic switch*, is located at the junction of each row and column line; that is, there is one transistor for each cell. The transistor can be turned on or off by applying a pulse to its row and column lines. However, the electrical capacitance of each cell is able to store a charge and maintain the cell in the on or off condition while the matrix is addressing another transistor. That is, a transistor can be accessed and turned on or off, and that transistor will maintain its state until the next time it is accessed. The active matrix array produces a sharper and more vivid picture. The lack of cross-talk between adjacent cells means that the active matrix suffers less smearing than the passive array equivalent.

The transistors that perform the switching are not part of a silicon chip but are laid down in thin films on a substrate— hence the name TFT (*thin film transistor*). It takes $3 \times 1024 \times 768$ thin film transistors to make a XVGA active matrix display, and, if just a few of these transistors are faulty, the entire display has to be rejected. The manufacturing yield of good arrays is not 100%, which means that the cost of a TFT active matrix array is considerably higher than the passive equivalent.

11.4.3 Color printers

Color printers don't employ the same RGB (red, green, blue) principle used by the color CRT. Suppose we look at an object that we call *red*, which is illuminated by white light. The red object absorbs part of the white light and reflects some of the light to the observer. If all the light is reflected we call the object *white* and if all the light is absorbed we call the object *black*. However, if all frequencies are absorbed *except* red, we call if the object *red*. In other words, if we wish to print images we have to consider what light is *absorbed* rather than what light is *generated* (as in a CRT).

The RGB model is called *additive* because a color is created by adding three primary colors. The CMY (cyan, magenta, yellow) color model used in printing is called *subtractive* because a color is generated by subtracting the appropriate components from white light. Cyan (blue–green) is the absence of red, magenta the absence of green, and yellow the absence of blue. Mixing equal amounts of cyan, magenta, and yellow subtracts all colors from white light to leave black. To create a color such as purple the printer generates a pattern of magenta and cyan dots. The saturation can be controlled by leaving some of the underlying white paper showing through.

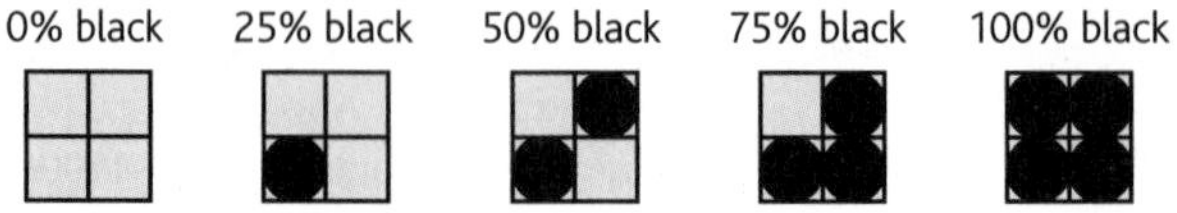

Adding the three subtractive primaries together doesn't produce a satisfactory black; it creates a dark muddy looking color. Although the human eye is not terribly sensitive to slight color shifts, it is very sensitive to any color shift in black (black must be true black). Printers use a four-color model CMYK, where K indicates *black*. Including a pure black as well as the three subtractive primaries considerably improves the image.

Printing color is much more difficult than displaying it on a CRT. Each of the red, green, and blue beams can be modulated to create an infinite range of colors (although, in practice, a digital system is limited to a finite number of discrete colors). When you print an image on paper, you have relatively little control over the size of the dot. Moreover, it's not easy to ensure that the dots created from the different subtractive primaries are correctly lined up (or *registered*). You can generate different levels or *shades* of a color by *dithering* (a technique that can also be applied to black and white printers to create shades of gray).

Dithering operates by dividing the print area into an array of, say, 2-by-2 matrices of 4 dots. Figure 11.33 provides a simple example of dithering in black and white. Because the dots in the matrices are so small, the eye perceives a composite light level and the effect is to create one of five levels of gray from black to white.

Dithering isn't free. If you take a 3×3 matrix to provide 10 levels of intensity, the effective resolution of an image is divided by three; for example, a 300 dpi printer can provide a resolution of 300 dpi or a resolution of 100 dpi with a 10-level gray scale. In other words, there's a trade-off between resolution and the range of tones that can be depicted.

The principle of dithering can be extended to *error diffusion* where dots are placed at random over a much larger area than the 2 by 2 matrix. This technique is suited to printing areas of color that require subtle changes of gradation (e.g. skin tones).

An alternative approach to dithering that provides more tones without reducing resolution is to increase the number of colors. This technique was introduced by some manufacturers to provide the photorealism required to print the output from digital cameras. One enhanced subtractive inkjet printer uses six inks: cyan, magenta, yellow, light magenta, light cyan, and black. The lighter colors make it possible to render skin tones more realistically. Another printer uses cyan, magenta, yellow, two types of black, plus red and blue.

Color inkjet printers

The color inkjet printer is virtually the same as the black and white counterpart. The only difference lies in the multiple heads. Typical color printers use a separate black cartridge and a combined color cartridge. Because the head and ink reservoirs form a combined unit, the cartridge has to be thrown away when the first of the color inks runs out. Some

0% black	25% black	50% black	75% black	100% black

Figure 11.33 Dithering.

printers use separate print heads and reservoirs and only the ink cartridge need be replaced.

Inkjet printer ink can be dye based or pigment based. A *dye* is a soluble color dissolved in a solvent and is used by most printers. A *pigment* is a tiny insoluble particle that is carried in suspension. Pigment-based inks are superior to dyes because pigments are more resistant to fading and can provide more highly saturated colors. Pigment-based inks have less favorable characteristics from the point of view of the designer; for example, the pigments can separate out of the liquid.

Inkjet printers can be prone to *banding*, an effect where horizontal marks appear across the paper due to uneven ink distribution from the print head.

Apart from its cost, the advantage of color inkjet printing is the bright, highly saturated colors. However, good results can be achieved only with suitable paper. The type of plain paper used in laser printers gives poor results. The drops of ink hit the paper and soak into its surface to mix with adjacent drops. This mixing effect reduces the brightness and quality of the colors.

By about 2000, advances in inkjet printing, ink technology, and inkjet papers and the advent of the digital camera had begun to wipe out the large photographic industry based on traditional silver halide photographic paper, the optical camera, and the *developing, enlarging, and printing process*. Moreover, the availability of digital-image processing programs such as Photoshop gave amateurs a level of control over the photographic image that only professionals had a few years ago.

Thermal wax and dye sublimation printers

The *thermal wax* printer is rather like the dot matrix printer with heat-sensitive paper. The print head extends the length of the paper and contains a matrix of thousands of tiny pixel-size heaters. Instead of a ribbon impregnated with ink, a sheet of material coated with colored wax is placed between the head and the paper. When the individual elements are heated to about 80°C, the wax is melted and sticks to the paper. An entire line of dots is printed at a time. The paper must make three or more passes under the print head to print dots in each of the primary (subtractive) colors. The sheet containing the wax consists of a series of bands of color.

Dye sublimation is similar to the thermal wax technique but is more expensive and is capable of a higher quality result. Electrical elements in the print head are heated to 400°C, which vaporizes the wax. These special waxes undergo *sublimation* when heated; that is, they go directly from the solid state to the gaseous state without passing through the liquid state.

By controlling the amount of heating, the quantity of wax transferred to the paper can be modified making it possible to generate precise colors without having to resort to techniques such as dithering. Unlike the thermal wax process, which deposits drops of wax on the paper, dye sublimation impregnates the paper with the wax. Dye sublimation can create very-high-quality images on special paper. The cost of the consumables (waxed sheets and special paper) make sublimation printing much more expensive than inkjet printing.

The phase-change printer

The phase-change printer falls somewhere between the inkjet printer and the thermal wax printer. The basic organization is that of the inkjet printer. The fundamental difference is that the print head contains a wax that is heated to about 90°C to keep it in liquid form. The wax is bought in the form of sticks, which are loaded into the print head.

The print head itself uses a piezo-electric crystal to create a pressure wave that expels a drop of the molten wax onto the paper. The drops freeze on hitting the paper, causing them to adhere well without spreading out. You can print highly saturated colors on plain paper. Because the paper is covered with lumpy drops, some phase-change printers pass the paper through pressure rollers to flatten the drops.

The color laser

Color laser printers are almost identical to monochrome printers. Instead of using a black toner, they use separate toners in each of the subtractive primary colors. The image is scanned onto a drum using a toner with the first primary color and then transferred to paper. The same process is repeated three more times using a different color toner after each scan. Advances in color laser technology have produced color lasers that cost as much today in real terms as monochrome lasers did a decade ago. However, the consumables for color lasers (i.e. three tones plus a block tone) are still expensive.

11.5 Other peripherals

We've looked at several peripherals found in a personal computer. We now describe some of the peripherals that can be connected to a digital computer. Computers are used mainly in *embedded control systems*—the PC is just the tip of a very large iceberg. Embedded controllers take information from the outside world, process it, and control something. We begin by looking at some of the sensors that can measure properties such as temperature and pressure.

11.5.1 Measuring position and movement

The most fundamental measurement is that of *position*; for example, the position of the gas pedals in a car or the position of the arm in a crane. Position is measured either as *rotation* (i.e. the position of a dial or knob) or as a *linear*, position (i.e. the position along a line).

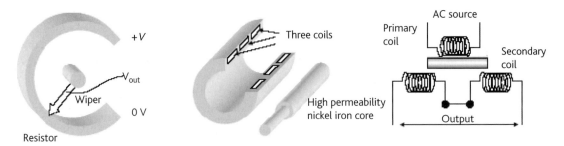

(a) The angle-sensing potentiometer.   (b) The magnetic position sensor.

Figure 11.34 Position transducers.

Figure 11.34(a) describes a simple position transducer called the *potentiometer,* which can measure linear or angular movement. An arm or wiper moves along the surface or a resistor with a voltage of V between its ends. The voltage picked up by the sliding arm is proportional to its position along the resistor, The potentiometer is cheap, gives a large electrical output that is easy to measure, but is unreliable because it wears out due to friction. Another position transducer uses a magnetic field. Figure 11.34(b) demonstrates a transformer where one coil generates a magnetic field and the other coil detects it. The amount of magnetic field picked up is dependent on the position of the magnetic core.

Measuring very small distances requires a device that generates a signal when it moved by even the tiniest amount. The *strain gauge* consists of a zigzag path of wire embedded in a substrate such as plastic. When the strain gauge is deformed by bending, the resistance of the wire increases slightly because it has been stretched. The change in resistance in response to strain is usually very small indeed—the resistance of a 200 Ω strain gauge might change by only a few millionths of an ohm. A strain gauge might be bonded to, say, the wing of an aircraft to measure how much it flexes in flight.

An alternative to the resistive strain gauge employs the *piezo-electric effect*; certain crystals generate a voltage across their faces when they are flexed.

A modern form of the pressure sensor is constructed with semiconductor technology. Four resistors are deposited on a 1 mm diameter wafer of silicon in the form of a bridge. When the silicon flexes due to stress, the voltage across two of the terminals changes. If one side of the wafer is adjacent to a vacuum (created beneath the silicon disk during the manufacturing process), the device measures the absolute pressure on the other side. This type of pressure transducer is very versatile and can measure very tiny pressures or very high pressures. It is used in some electronic engine management systems to measure the manifold pressure, which is required to calculate engine power and to control optimum spark timing.

Velocity can be measured either indirectly by measuring the rate of change of position, or more directly with a

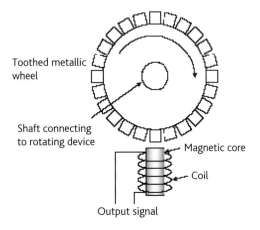

Figure 11.35 The tachometer.

transducer or tachometer. A simple means of measuring velocity is to measure the speed of a magnet traveling down a long coil because the voltage generated is proportional to the velocity of the magnet. A *tachometer* measures speed of rotation (e.g. the speed of a car's wheels) by either an optical disc or a toothed wheel and proximity sensor (see Fig. 11.35).

You can measure the speed of a liquid or a gas by placing a turbine in the path of the liquid and then using a tachometer to measure the speed of the turbine. Figure 11.36 describes an alternative flowmeter that measures the flow rate of a liquid or gas by using the pressure differential between a pipe and a constriction.

An interesting flow rate device is the *thermal anemometer*. If your coffee is too hot, you blow on it because the forced airflow carries heat away from the coffee. The thermal anemometer uses a heater in a tube though which a gas is flowing. If the temperature of the heating element is kept constant, it requires more current to keep the heater at a constant temperature as the gas flow increases. By measuring the current being supplied to the heater, you can determine the gas flow.

Finally, you can measure the rate of flow of a liquid by *ultrasonic techniques*, which are non-invasive and do not require direct contact with the fluid. A beam of ultrasound is

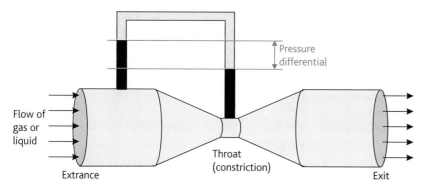

Figure 11.36 The Venturi flowmeter.

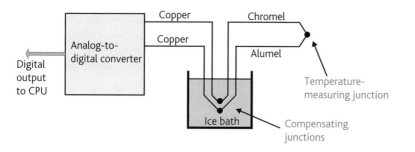

Figure 11.37 Temperature-compensated thermocouple.

although no single thermocouple can cover this whole range.

Figure 11.37 illustrates the structure of a temperature-compensated thermocouple where the potential difference between a junction composed of chromel and alumel alloy wires is measured. Because these two wires must be connected to the measuring system, two further junctions are used and put in an ice bath to provide a reference junction.

The output of a thermocouple is not a *linear* function of temperature. Thermocouple manufacturers publish algorithms and the associated coefficients to convert the output of a thermocouple into an accurate temperature.

Another temperature-measuring technique uses the *resistance* of a metal that changes with temperature. A platinum resistance temperature detector (RTD) has a resistance of 10 Ω that changes by 0.385%/°C. The RTD is more linear than the thermocouple but is unsuited to the measurement of temperatures over about 800°C.

Semiconductor devices, called *thermistors*, have an electrical resistance that varies with temperature. These devices are very sensitive to small changes in temperature. The temperature coefficient is negative so that the thermistor conducts more as the temperature rises. Because of their high sensitivity (e.g. a change of 100 Ω/°C) thermistors can be used to measure temperature precisely over a small range. Unfortunately, the thermistor cannot be used above about 200° C.

Another temperature-measuring element is the *band-gap* device, which employs a *semiconductor junction* (i.e. the region between two differently doped[8] areas of silicon in a transistor). The band-gap detector operates over a relatively narrow range of temperatures but can provide an accuracy of 0.1°C. All the temperature sensors we've just described can be made very small indeed (e.g. 1 mm or less across).

Yet another means of measuring temperature exploits the *radiation* from a body. Any body whose temperature is above absolute zero radiates energy in the infra-red region of the spectrum. Figure 11.38 gives the radiation intensity produced by an ideal object, called a *black body*, as a function of temperature and radiation wavelength. A perfect black body generates

directed through the pipe into the flowing liquid. You can measure the rate of flow either by determining the transit time of the ultrasound beam or by measuring the Doppler frequency shift in the sound reflected by particles and bubbles in the liquid. This is the technique used by ultrasound scanners to measure the flow of blood within the heart.

11.5.2 Measuring temperature

One of the most common sensors is the temperature probe. The everyday temperature transducer is the *thermometer*, which converts the temperature into the length of a column of liquid. Mercury or alcohol in a glass bulb expands with temperature and is driven up a fine transparent tube against a scale calibrated in degrees.

Computers don't measure temperature via the thermal expansion of a liquid. There are several ways of converting temperature into a voltage that can be measured by an analog-to-digital converter. The first is the *thermoelectric* effect in which two wires of dissimilar metals are connected together to form a *thermocouple* (e.g. copper and constantan, or chromel and alumel). If the junction between the wires is heated, a voltage appears across it (about 50 μ V/°C). This technique is used to measure a wide range of temperatures; for example, a platinum/platinum–rhodium alloy thermocouple can measure furnace temperatures up to 1500°C. The thermocouple operating range is about -270°C to 2300°C,

---

[8] Doping a semiconductor refers to the addition of an element in amounts as low as one part in 10^6 to change the semiconductor's electrical properties.

radiation proportional to the fourth power of the body's temperature (Stefan's law) and the wavelength of the radiation with the greatest amplitude falls as the temperature rises (Wein's law). Once the temperature rises sufficiently, the radiation falls into the visible band and we say that the object has become *red hot*.

Real materials don't have ideal black body radiation characteristics. If the *emissivity*[9] of a body is less than that of a black body, it is called a *gray body*. If the emissivity varies with temperature, it is called a *non-gray* body.

The temperature of a body can be measured by examining the radiation it radiates. This temperature measurement technique is *non-contact* because it does not affect or disturb the temperature of the object whose temperature is being recorded. Moreover, you can measure the temperature of moving objects. In recent years this technique has been used to measure human body temperatures by measuring the radiation produced inside the ear.

11.5.3 Measuring light

Light intensity has been measured for hundreds of years. When it was noticed that compounds of silver and iodine darken on exposure to light, the effect was quickly exploited to create photography. In the early 1900s Max Planck suggested that light consists of individual packets containing a discrete amount of energy called *photons*. When a photon hits an atom, an electron may be knocked out of its orbit round the nucleus. If this atom is metallic, the movement of electrons generates a current that flows in the metal. Some light detectors operate by detecting the flow of electrons when light interacts with the atoms of a material.

The *photodiode* is a semiconductor photosensor comprising a junction between two differently doped regions of silicon. The photons of light falling on the junction create a current in the device. These devices are sensitive to light in the region 400 nm to 1000 nm (this includes infra-red as well as visible light). Another means of measuring light intensity exploits the *photovoltaic effect* in silicon and selenium.

Light intensity can also be measured by the *photoresistor*. Certain substances such as cadmium sulfide change their electrical resistance when illuminated.

11.5.4 Measuring pressure

The effect of pressure or *stress* on a material is to deform it by compression or expansion, an effect we call *strain*. Strain is defined as the change in length per unit length. We can measure stress (pressure) from the effect of the strain it causes.

11.5.5 Rotation sensors

If you sometimes feel you're going round in circles, a rotation sensor can at least confirm it. At first sight it's hard to imagine a sensor that can tell you how fast something is turning.

One way of measuring rotation is to exploit the mechanism that creates the World's weather patterns—the *Coriolis* force. Air at the equator is heated by the sun and flows north and south. Figure 11.39 shows the direction of flowing to the north. It doesn't travel due north. Let's consider what happens to the northward-moving stream of air. The Earth rotates on its north–south axis once every 24 hours. Because the circumference of the Earth is 24 000 miles, the Earth is moving at 1000 mph at the equator. And so is the air above the equator because the Earth drags the air around with it.

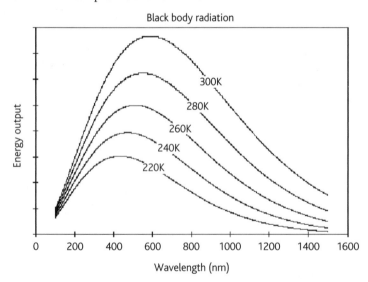

Figure 11.38 Radiation emitted by an ideal black body.

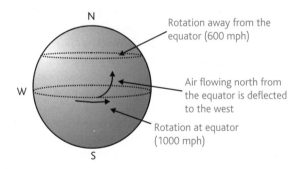

Figure 11.39 The Coriolis force.

---

[9] Emissivity is the ratio of a body's radiation at a given frequency to the radiation given off by a perfect black body at the same temperature. A material-like rock may have an emissivity of 0.9, whereas a metal might have an emissivity of 0.1.

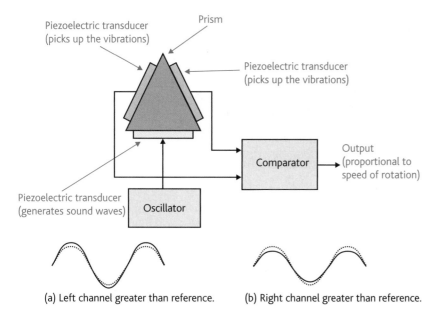

(a) Left channel greater than reference.   (b) Right channel greater than reference.

Figure 11.40 Exploiting the Coriolis effect to measure rotation.

The output from the left transducer (a) is greater than that from right transducer (b).

You might wonder who would want to sense rotation. As in many other areas of electronics, the introduction of a new device often leads to applications that couldn't have been imagined in the past. Low-cost rotation sensors can be used in automatic applications to follow the motion of the car. If you know how far the car has traveled (from the odometer) and the angular velocity (from which you can calculate the angular position), you can work out where the car is (if you know its initial position). This technology can be used to provide in-car navigation systems—especially when coupled with GPS. Another application of a rotation sensor is in stabilizing platforms; for example, the video camera. By detecting the motion of the camera, you can move the image sensor or lens in the opposite direction to obtain a stable image free of camera shake and jitter.

The circumference of the Earth gets less as you move away from the equator and the speed at which the Earth's surface moves reduces. If you live in the USA you're moving at about 600 mph. The stream of air flowing north from the equator it is also moving west to east at 1000 mph (because that's the speed it had at the equator). Because the rotational speed of the Earth drops as you go north, an observer on the ground sees the air deflected toward the east. That is, the air appears to come from the south-west. Because it takes a force to deflect an object, we say that the wind has been deflected by a force called the Coriolis force (this force does not actually exist).

Figure 11.40 demonstrates how the Coriolis force is used to measure the rate of rotation of a body. A triangular prism has three piezoelectric transducers bonded to its sides. A piezoelectric crystal flexes when a voltage is applied across its face; equally a voltage is generated when it is flexed (i.e. the piezoelectric effect is reversible). An alternating voltage is applied to one of the transducers to create a high-frequency sound wave that propagates through the prism. The two facing piezoelectric transducers convert the vibrations into two equal alternating voltages when the prism is stationary.

When the prism rotates the vibrations spread out from the transducer through the medium that is rotating. The motion of the vibrations and the motion of the rotating prism interact and the direction of the vibrations is altered by the Coriolis force. Consequently, the two sensors don't pick up equal amounts of vibration in a rotating prism. The difference between the outputs of the sensors can be used to generate a signal whose amplitude depends on the rate of rotation. Figure 11.40 illustrates the effect of a left rotation.

11.5.6 Biosensors

One of the greatest revolutions in the late twentieth Century was *biotechnology*, which may eventually dwarf the computer revolution. If computers are to be used in biotechnology systems, it's necessary to be able to detect biological parameters electronically. Until relatively recently, the only way of measuring a biological quantity such as the level of glucose or oxygen in blood was to take a sample and send it to a laboratory for chemical analysis. In circumstances where time is critical such as during an operation, a knowledge of a biological parameter like the blood oxygen level is vital.

It's difficult to describe biosensors in a few paragraphs because it requires an understanding of biochemical reactions. Here, we describe only the underlying principles. The first biosensor was developed by Clark in the 1950s to measure the amount of dissolved oxygen in blood.

Suppose you connect two electrodes to a voltage supply and immerse them in a liquid (see Fig. 11.41(a)). A current will flow between the electrodes if there's a means of transporting electrons. Unfortunately, blood contains many molecules capable of carrying a charge and their combined effect would swamp the current carried by oxygen molecules. Clark's solution was to surround the electrodes with a plastic *gas-permeable membrane* (a form of molecular sieve). Now only oxygen is able to pass through the membrane and carry

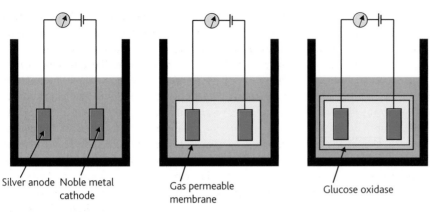

(a) A current flows between two electrodes in a cell.

(b) The electrodes are enclosed by a membrane that is permeable to oxygen.

(c) A second permeable membrane surrounds the inner membrane. Glucose oxidase gel fills the space between the membranes.

Figure 11.41 The biosensor.

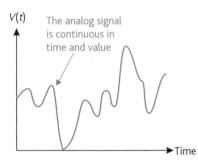

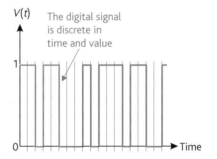

Figure 11.42 Analog and digital signals.

a charge between the electrodes. By measuring the current flow you can determine the oxygen concentration (Fig. 11.41(b)) in the liquid surrounding the cell.

This technique can be extended to detect more exotic molecules such as glucose. A third membrane can be used to surround the membrane containing the electrodes. Between the outer and inner membranes is a gel of glucose oxidase enzyme that reacts with glucose and oxygen to generate gluconic acid. The amount of glucose in the liquid under test is inversely proportional to the amount of oxygen detected (Fig. 11.41(c)).

Because these techniques were developed in the 1960s the number of detectors has vastly increased and the size of the probes reduced to the point at which they can be inserted into veins.

11.6 The analog interface

We now look at *analog* systems and their interface to the digital computer. In an analog world, measurable quantities are not restricted to the binary values 0 and 1; they may take one of an *infinite* number of values within a given range. For example, the temperature of a room changes from one value to another by going through an infinite number of increments on its way. Similarly, air pressure, speed, sound intensity, weight, and time are all analog quantities. When computers start to control their environment, or generate speech or music, or process images, we have to understand the relationship between the analog and digital worlds.

We first examine analog signals and demonstrate how they are captured and processed by a digital computer. Then we look at the hardware that converts analog signals into digital form, and digital values into analog signals.

A full appreciation of the relationship between and analog and digital signals and the transformation between them requires a knowledge of electronics; this is particularly true when we examine analog-to-digital and digital-to-analog converters. Readers without an elementary knowledge of electronics may wish to skip these sections.

11.6.1 Analog signals

In Chapter 2 we said that a signal is said to be *analog* if it falls between two arbitrary levels, V_x and V_y, and can assume any one of an infinite number of values between V_x and V_y. If the analog signal, $V(t)$, is time dependent, it is a continuous function of time, so that its *slope*, dV/dt, is never infinite, which would imply an instantaneous change of value. Figure 11.42 illustrates how both an analog voltage and a digital voltage vary with time.

Analog signals are processed by analog circuits. The principal feature of an analog circuit is its ability to process an analog signal faithfully, without distorting it—hence the expression *hi-fidelity*. A typical analog signal is produced at the output terminals of a microphone as someone speaks into it. The voltage varies continuously over some finite range, depending only on the loudness of the speech and on the physical characteristics of the microphone. An amplifier is used to increase the amplitude of this time-varying signal to a level suitable for driving a loudspeaker. If the voltage gain of the amplifier is A, and the voltage from the microphone $V(t)$, the output of the amplifier is equal to $A \cdot V(t)$. The output signal from the amplifier, like the input, has an infinite range of values, but within a range A times that of the signal from the microphone.

Because digital signals in computers fall into two ranges (e.g. 0 to 0.4 V for logical 0 and 2.4 to 5.0 V for logical 1 levels in LS TTL logic systems), small amounts of *noise* and *crosstalk* have no effect on digital signals as long as the noise is less than about 0.4 V. Life is much more difficult for the analog systems designer. Even small amounts of noise in the millivolt or even microvolt region can seriously affect the accuracy of analog signals. In particular, the analog designer has to worry about power-line noise and digital noise picked up by analog circuits from adjacent digital circuits.

11.6.2 Signal acquisition

At first sight it might appear that the analog and digital worlds are mutually incompatible. Fortunately a gateway exists between the analog and digital worlds called *quantization*. The fact that an analog quantity can have an infinite range of values is irrelevant. If somebody says they will arrive at 9.0 a.m., they are not being literal—9.0 a.m. exists for an infinitesimally short period. Of course, what they really mean is that they will arrive at *approximately* 9.0 a.m. In other words, if we measure an analog quantity and specify it to a precision sufficient for our purposes (i.e. quantization), the error between the actual analog value and its measured value is unimportant. Once the analog value has been measured, it exists in a *numeric* form that can be processed by a computer.

The conversion of an analog quantity into a digital value requires two separate operations; the extraction of a sample value of the signal to be processed and the actual conversion of that sample value into a binary form. Figure 11.43 gives the block diagram of an analog signal acquisition module. As the analog-to-digital converter (ADC) at the heart of this module may be rather expensive, it is not unusual to provide a number of different analog *channels*, all using the same ADC. The cost of an ADC also depends on its speed of conversion.

Each analog channel in Fig. 11.43 begins with a *transducer* that converts an analog quantity into an electrical value. Transducers are almost invariably separate from the signal acquisition module proper. Sometimes the transducer is a *linear* device, so that a change in the physical input produces a proportional change in the electrical output. All too often, the transducer is highly *non-linear* and the relationship between the physical input and the voltage from the transducer is very complex; for example, the output of a transducer that measures temperature might be $V = V_0 e^{t/kT}$. In such cases it is usual to perform the linearization of the input in the digital computer after the signal has been digitized. It is possible to perform the linearization within the signal acquisition module by means of purely analog techniques.

The electrical signal from the transducer is frequently very tiny (sometimes only a few microvolts) and must be *amplified* before further processing in order to bring it to a level well above the noise voltages present in later circuits. Amplification

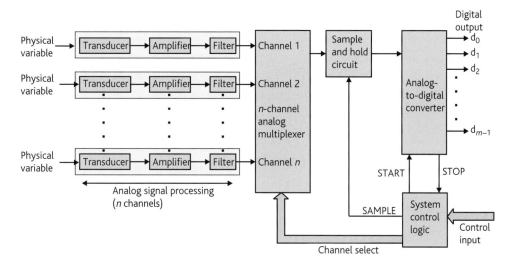

Figure 11.43 An analog signal acquisition module.

is performed by an analog circuit called an op-amp (operational amplifier). Some transducers have an internal amplifier.

After amplification comes *filtering*, a process designed to restrict the passage of certain signals through the circuit. Filtering blocks signals with a frequency above or below a cut-off point; for example, if the signal from the transducer contains useful frequency components only in the range 0 to 20 Hz (as one might expect from, say, an electrocardiogram), it is beneficial to filter out all signals of a higher frequency. These *out of band* signals represent unwanted noise and have no useful effect on the interpretation of the electrocardiogram. Moreover, it is necessary for the filter to cut out all frequencies above one-half the rate at which the analog signal is sampled. The reasons for this are explained later.

The outputs of the filters are fed to an electronic switch called a *multiplexer*, which selects one of the analog input channels for processing. The multiplexer is controlled by the digital system to which the signal acquisition module is connected. The only purpose of the multiplexer is to allow one analog-to-digital converter to be connected to several inputs.

The analog output of the multiplexer is applied to the input of the last analog circuit in the acquisition module, the *sample and hold* (S/H) circuit. The sample and hold circuit takes an almost *instantaneous* sample of the incoming analog signal and holds it constant while the *analog-to-digital converter* (ADC) is busy determining the digital value of the signal.

The *analog-to-digital converter* (ADC) transforms the voltage at its input into an m-bit digital value, where m varies from typically 4 to 16 or more. Several types of analog-to-digital converter are discussed at the end of this section. We now look at the relationship between the analog signal and the analog-to-digital conversion process.

Signal quantization

Two fundamental questions have to be asked when considering any analog-to-digital converter. Into how many levels or values should the input signal be divided and how often should the conversion process be carried out? The precise answer to both these questions requires much mathematics. Fortunately, they both have simple conceptual answers and in many real situations a rule-of-thumb can easily be applied. We look at how analog signals are quantized in value and then how they are quantized or *sampled* in time.

When asked how much sugar you want in a cup of coffee, you might reply: none, half a spoon, one spoon, one-and-a-half spoons, etc. Although a measure of sugar can be quantized right down to the size of a single grain, the practical unit chosen by those who add sugar to coffee is the half-spoon. This unit is both easy to measure out and offers reasonable discrimination between the quanta (i.e. half-spoons). Most drinkers could not discriminate between, say, 13/27 and 14/27 of a spoon of sugar. As it is with sugar, so it is with signals. The level of quantization is chosen to be the minimum interval between successive values that carries meaningful information. You may ask, 'Why doesn't everyone use an ADC with the greatest possible resolution?' The answer is perfectly simple. The cost of an ADC rises steeply with resolution. A 16-bit ADC is very much more expensive than an 8-bit ADC (assuming all other parameters to be equal). Therefore, engineers select the ADC with a resolution compatible with the requirements of the job for which it is intended.

Let's look at an *ideal* 3-bit analog-to-digital converter that converts a voltage into a binary code. As the analog input to this ADC varies in the range 0 V to 7.5 V, its digital output varies from 000 to 111. Figure 11.44 provides a *transfer function* for this ADC.

Consider the application of a linear voltage *ramp* input from 0.0 V to 7.5 V to this ADC (a ramp is a signal that increases at a constant rate). Initially the analog input is 0.0 V and the digital output 000. As the input voltage rises, the output remains at 000 until the input passes 0.5 V, at which point the output code *jumps* from 000 to 001. The output code remains at 001

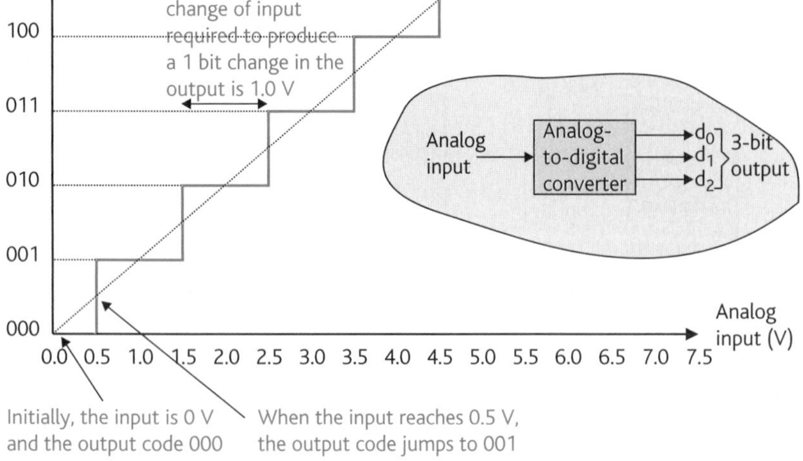

Figure 11.44 The transfer function of an ideal 3-bit A/D converter.

until the input rises above 1.5 V. Clearly, for each 1.0 V change in the input, the output code changes by one unit. Figure 11.44 shows that the input can change in value by up to 1 V without any change taking place in the output code.

The *resolution* of an ADC, Q, is the largest change in its input required to guarantee a change in the output code and is 1.0 V in this example. The resolution of an ADC is expressed indirectly by the number of bits in its output code, where resolution $= V_{maximum}/2^n - 1$. For example, an 8-bit ADC with an input in the range 0 V to $+8.0$ V has a resolution of 8.0 V/255 $= 0.03137$ V $= 31.37$ mV. Table 11.3 gives the basic characteristics of ADCs with digital outputs ranging from 4 to 16 bits. The figures in Table 11.3 represent the optimum values for perfect ADCs. In practice, real ADCs suffer from imperfections such as non-linearity, drift, offset error, and missing codes, which are described later. Some ADCs are *unipolar* and handle a voltage in the range 0 to V and some are *bipolar* and handle a voltage in the range $-V/2$ to $+V/2$.

The column labeled value of Q for 10 V FS in Table 11.3 indicates the size of the step (i.e. Q) if the maximum input of the ADC is 10 V. The abbreviation 'FS' means *full-scale*.

Figure 11.45 provides a graph of the difference or *error* between the analog input of a 3-bit ADC and its digital output. Suppose that the analog input is 5.63 V. The corresponding digital output is 110, which represents 6.0 V; that is, the digital output corresponds to the *quantized* input, rather than the *actual* input. The difference between the actual input and the idealized input corresponds to an error of 0.37 V. Figure 11.45 shows that the maximum error between the input and output is equal to $Q/2$. This error is called the *quantization error*.

The output from a real ADC can be represented by the output from a perfect ADC whose input is equal to the applied signal plus a noise component. The difference between the input and the quantized output (expressed as an analog value) is a time-varying signal between $+Q/2$ and $-Q/2$ and is called the *quantization noise* of the ADC.

Because the quantization noise is a *random* value, engineers characterize it by its RMS (*root mean square*)—the RMS value expresses the *power* of the signal. The RMS value of a signal is obtained by squaring it, taking the average, and then taking the square root of the average. The RMS of the quantization noise of an analog-to-digital converter is equal to $Q/\sqrt{12}$. Increasing the resolution of the converter reduces the amplitude of the quantization noise as Table 11.3 demonstrates.

A figure-of-merit of any analog system is its *signal-to-noise* ratio, which measures the ratio of the wanted signal to the unwanted signal (i.e. *noise*). The signal-to-noise ratio (SNR) of a system is expressed in units called *decibels*, named after Graham Bell, a pioneer of the telephone. The SNR ratio of two signals is defined as $20\log(V_{signal}/V_{noise})$. The signal-to-noise ratio of an ideal *n*-bit ADC is given by

$$\begin{aligned}
\text{SNR (in dB)} &= 20\log(2^n Q)/Q/\sqrt{12} \\
&= 20\log(2^n) + 10\log(12) \\
&= 6.02n + 10.8
\end{aligned}$$

This expression demonstrates that the signal-to-noise ratio of the ADC increases by 6.02 dB for each additional bit of precision. Table 11.3 gives the signal-to-noise ratio of ADCs from 4 to 16 bits. An 8-bit ADC has a signal-to-noise ratio similar to that of some low-quantity audio equipment, whereas a 10-bit ADC approaches the S/N ratio of high-fidelity equipment.

Another figure-of-merit of an analog system is its *dynamic range*. The dynamic range of an ADC is given by the ratio of its full-scale range (FSR) to its resolution, Q, and is expressed in decibels as $20\log(2^n) = 20n\log 2 = 6.02n$. Table 11.3 also gives the dynamic range of the various ADCs. Once again you can see that a 10- to 12-bit ADC is suitable for moderately high-quality audio signal processing. Because of other impairments in the system and the actual behavior of a real ADC, high-quality audio signal processing is normally done with a 16-bit ADC.

Sampling a time-varying signal

What is the minimum *rate* at which a signal should be sampled to produce an accurate digital representation of it?

Resolution (bits)	Discrete states	Binary weight	Value of Q for 10 V FS	SNR (dB)	Dynamic range (dB)
4	16	0.0625	0.625 V	34.9	24.1
6	64	0.0156	0.156 V	46.9	36.1
8	256	0.00391	39.1 mV	58.1	48.2
10	1024	0.000977	9.76 mV	71.0	60.2
12	4096	0.000244	2.44 mV	83.0	72.2
14	16 384	0.0000610	610 μV	95.1	84.3
16	65 536	0.0000153	153 μV	107.1	96.3

Table 11.3 The performance of ideal analog-to-digital converters.

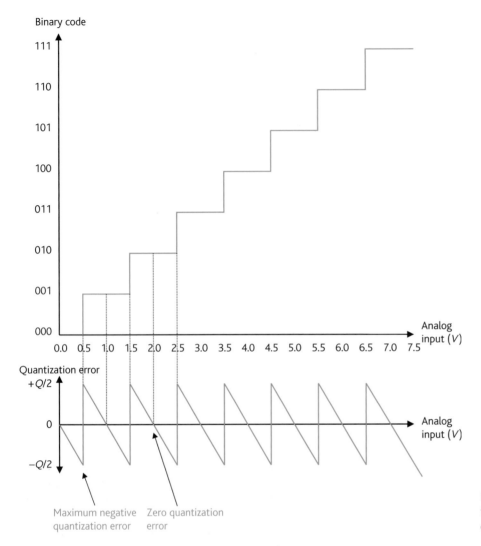

Figure 11.45 The error function of an ideal 3-bit A/D converter.

We need to know the minimum rate at which a signal must be sampled, because we want to use the slowest and cheapest ADC that does the job we require.

Intuitively, we would expect the rate at which a signal must be sampled to be related to the rate at which it is changing; for example, a computer controlling the temperature of a swimming pool might need to sample the temperature of the water once every 10 minutes. The thermal inertia of such a large body of water doesn't permit sudden changes in temperature. Similarly, if a microcomputer is employed to analyze human speech with an upper frequency limit of 3000 Hz, it is reasonable to expect that the input from a microphone must be sampled at a much greater rate than 3000 times a second, simply because in the space of 1/3000 second the signal can execute a complete sine wave.

A simple relationship exists between the rate at which a signal changes and the rate at which it must be sampled if it is to be reconstituted from the samples without any loss of information content. The *Sampling Theorem* states 'If a continuous signal containing no frequency components higher than f_c is sampled at a rate of at least $2f_c$, then the original signal can be completely recovered from the sampled value without distortion'. This minimum sampling rate is called the *Nyquist* rate.

The *highest frequency component in the signal* means just that and includes any noise or unwanted signals present together with the desired signal. For example, if a signal contains speech in the range 300 to 3000 Hz and noise in the range 300 to 5000 Hz, it must be sampled at least 10 000 times a second. One of the purposes of filtering a signal before sampling it is to remove components whose frequencies are higher than the signals of interest, but whose presence would nevertheless determine the lower limit of the sampling rate.

If a signal whose maximum frequency component is f_c, is sampled at less than $2f_c$ times a second, some of the high-frequency components in it are *folded back* into the spectrum of the wanted signal. In other words, sampling a speech signal in the range 300 to 3000 Hz containing noise components up to

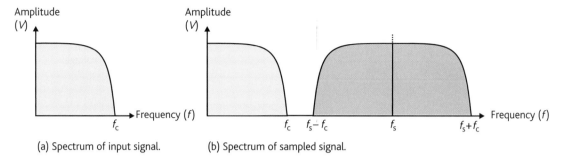

(a) Spectrum of input signal.   (b) Spectrum of sampled signal.

Figure 11.46 Sampling a signal at more than the Nyquist rate.

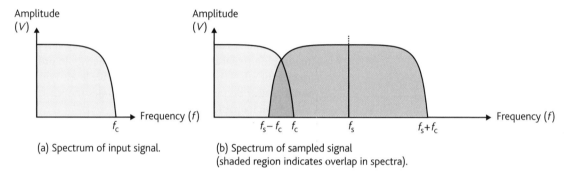

(a) Spectrum of input signal.   (b) Spectrum of sampled signal
                                        (shaded region indicates overlap in spectra).

Figure 11.47 Sampling a signal at slightly less than the Nyquist rate.

5000 Hz at only 6000 times a second would result in some of this noise appearing within the speech band. This effect is called *frequency folding* and, once it has occurred, there is no way in which the original, wanted, signal can be recovered.

Figures 11.46 and 11.47 illustrate the effect of sampling an analog signal at both below and above the Nyquist rate. In Fig. 11.46 the input signal consists of a band of frequencies from zero to f_c, sampled at a rate equal to f_s times a second, where f_s is greater than $2f_c$. The *spectrum* of the sampled signal contains components in the frequency range $f_s - f_c$ to $f_s + f_c$ that do not fall within the range of the input signal. Consequently, you can recover the original signal from the sampled signal.

In Fig. 11.47 the input signal has a maximum frequency component of f_c and is sampled at f_{si}, where $f_s < 2f_c$. Some energy in the region $f_s - f_c$ to f_c falls in the range of the input frequency and is represented by the gray region in Fig. 11.47. This situation results in *frequency folding* and a loss of information; that is, you cannot recover the original information from the sampled signal.

The classic example of sampling at too low a rate is the *wagon wheel effect* seen in movies. A cine film runs at 24 frames/s and each frame samples the image. If the spokes of a rotating wheel are sampled (i.e. photographed) at too low a rate, the wheel appears to move backward. Why? Suppose a wheel rotates 10° clockwise between each frame. The eye

perceives this as a clockwise rotation. Now suppose the wagon is moving rapidly and the wheel rotates 350° between each frame. The eye perceives this as a 10° *counterclockwise* rotation.

It is difficult to appreciate the full implications of the sampling theorem without an understanding of the mathematics of sampling and modulation. However, all we need say here is that the overlap in spectra caused by sampling at too low a frequency results in unwanted noise in the sampled signal.

Another way of looking at the relationship between a signal and its sampling rate is illustrated by Figs 11.48 and 11.49. Figure 11.48(a) gives the continuous input waveform of an analog signal and Fig. 11.48(b) its sampled form. These sampled amplitudes are, of course, stored in a digital computer numerically. Figure 11.48(c) shows the output of a circuit, called a *filter*, fed from the digital inputs of Fig. 11.48(b). The simplest way of describing this circuit is to say that it *joins up the dots* of the sampled signal to produce a smooth output. As you can see, the reconstructed analog signal is virtually a copy of the original analog signal.

Figure 11.49 is similar to Fig. 11.48, except that the input signal is sampled at less than $2f_c$. A glance at the sampled values of Fig. 11.49(b) is enough to show that much of the detail in the input waveform has been lost. When this sampled signal is reconstituted into a continuous signal (Fig. 11.49(c)) its frequency is not the same as the input signal. The erroneous signal

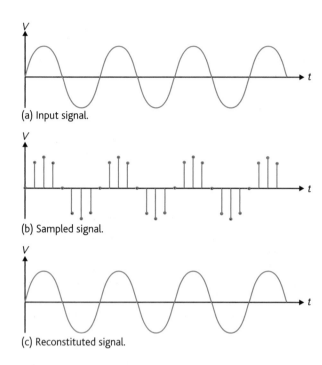

(a) Input signal.

(b) Sampled signal.

(c) Reconstituted signal.

Figure 11.48 Sampling at $f_s > 2f_c$.

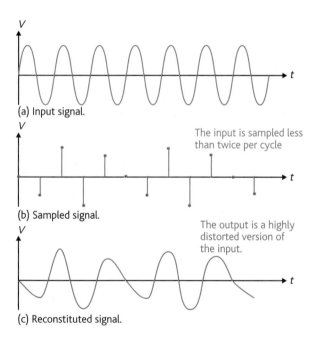

(a) Input signal.

The input is sampled less than twice per cycle

(b) Sampled signal.

The output is a highly distorted version of the input.

(c) Reconstituted signal.

Figure 11.49 The aliasing effect $(f_s < 2f_c)$.

of Fig. 11.49(c) is called an *alias*. Once more, it must be stressed that if frequencies greater than $^1/_2 f_s$ appear in the input signal they can play havoc with the results of sampling.

Most signal acquisition modules have low-pass filters with a sharp cut-off frequency to attenuate signals and noise outside the band of interest. As it is impossible to construct a perfect filter that passes frequencies in the range 0 to f_c and

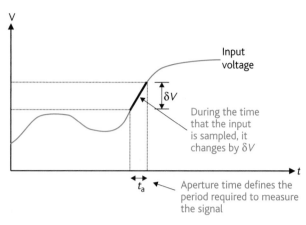

Figure 11.50 The effect of a finite measurement time on the A/D conversion process.

which attenuates all frequencies above f_c infinitely, it is usual to sample a signal at a much greater rate than $2f_c$ in order to reduce the effects of aliasing to an acceptable level. Typically, a signal may be sampled at up to five times the rate of its maximum frequency component.

Aperture time

As well as the sampling frequency, we also have to think about the time taken by the sampling process itself. Signals of interest are time dependent. One question we should ask is, 'What happens if a signal changes while it is being measured?' Figure 11.50 illustrates the problem of trying to measure a dynamic quantity where the quantization process takes t_a seconds, which is called the *aperture time*. The term *aperture time* suggests an analogy with the camera—a image is captured when the camera's aperture (i.e. shutter) is open and any movement of the subject blurs the image. During the aperture time, the input voltage being measured changes by δV, where δV is given by

$$t_a \cdot \frac{dV}{dt}$$

The value of dV/dt is the slope of the graph. The change in the input, δV, is called the *amplitude uncertainty*. A perfect, instantaneous digitizer has a zero aperture time and $\delta V = 0$, resulting in a spot-sample of the input.

Suppose we apply a linearly rising ramp voltage to the input of an analog-to-digital converter that has a full-scale range of 5 V. Let's imagine that the input changes by 5 V in 100 ms, corresponding to a rate-of-change of 5 V in 0.1 s = 50 V/s. If the analog-to-digital converter takes 1 ms to perform a conversion, we can calculate the amount by which the input changes while it's being converted.

$$\delta V = t_a \cdot dV(t)/dt = 1 \text{ ms} \times 50 \text{ V/s}$$
$$= 1 \times 10^{-3} \times 50 \text{ V/s} = 0.05 \text{ V}$$

That is, the input changes by 0.05 V during the period that the A/D conversion is taking place. Consequently, there's little point in using an ADC with a resolution of better than 0.05 V. This resolution corresponds to 1 in 100, and a 7-bit ADC would be suitable for this application.

In order to get a feeling for the importance of aperture time, let's consider a data acquisition system in processing human speech. Suppose a system with an 8-bit analog-to-digital converter is required to digitize an input with an upper frequency limit of 4000 Hz. We need to know the maximum aperture time necessary to yield an accuracy of one least significant bit in the digitized output. Assuming a *sinusoidal* input, $V(t) = V\sin \omega t$, the amplitude uncertainty is given by

$$\delta V = t_a \cdot d(V_{\sin} \omega t)/dt = t_a \cdot \omega \cdot V \cdot \cos \omega t$$

The differential of $\sin \omega t$ is $\omega \cos \omega t$, where ω is defined as $2\pi f$. The maximum rate-of-change of $V(t)$ occurs at the *zero-crossing* of the waveform when $t = 0$ (i.e. the maximum value of $\cos \omega t$ is 1). Therefore, the worst case value of δV is

$$\delta V = t_a \cdot V \cdot \omega$$
and
$$\delta V/V = t_a \cdot \omega = t_a \cdot 2\pi \cdot f$$

We can substitute 1/256 for $\delta V/V$ and 4000 Hz for f in the above equation to calculate the desired aperture time as follows:

$$\delta V/V = 1/256 = t_a 2\pi f = t_a \times 2 \times 3.142 \times 4000$$
$$t_a = 1/(256 \times 2 \times 3.142 \times 4000) \text{ s} = 0.146 \text{ μs}$$

An aperture time of 0.146 μs (i.e. 146 ns) is very small, although not too small to be achieved by the some ADCs. Fortunately, we can use a *sample and hold* circuit to capture a sample of the input and hold it constant while a relatively slow and cheap ADC performs the conversion. Of course, even a sample and hold circuit is itself subject to the effects of aperture uncertainty. Although an aperture time of 1 μs is

relatively small for an analog-to-digital converter, a sample and hold circuit can achieve an aperture time of 50 ns with little effort. We look at the sample and hold circuit in more detail later.

11.6.3 Digital-to-analog conversion

Beginning with digital-to-analog converters (DACs) may seem strange. It's more logical to discuss analog-to-digital (ADC) conversion first and then deal with the inverse process. There are two reasons for disregarding this natural sequence. The first is that the DAC is less complex than the corresponding ADC, and the second is that some analog-to-digital converters, paradoxically, have a digital-to-analog converter at their heart.

Conceptually, the DAC is a simple device. To convert a binary value into analog form, all we have to do is to generate an analog value proportional to each bit of the digital word and then add these values to give a composite analog sum. Figure 11.51 illustrates this process. An m-bit digital signal is latched by m D flip-flops and held constant until the next value is ready for conversion. The flip-flops constitute a digital *sample and hold circuit*. Each of the m bits operates an electronic switch that passes either zero or V_i volts to an analog adder, where V_i is the output of the ith switch. The output of this adder is

$$V = d_0 V_0 + d_1 V_1 + \cdots + d_{m-1} V_{m-1}$$

The $m\{d_i\}$ in this equation represent binary values 0 or 1 and the $\{V_i\}$ represent binary powers of the form $(1, 1/2, 1/4, 1/8, \ldots)$.

Figure 11.52 gives a possible (but not practical) implementation of a digital-to-analog converter. The total current flowing into the inverting terminal of the *operational amplifier* is equal to the linear sum of the currents flowing through the individual resistors (the panel describes how the operational

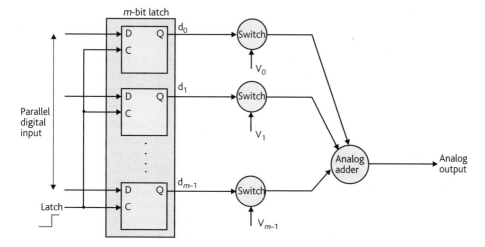

Figure 11.51 The digital-to-analog converter.

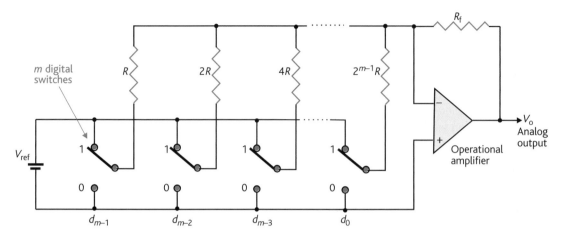

Figure 11.52 A possible implementation of the D/A converter.

THE OPERATIONAL AMPLIFIER

The *operational amplifier* is a simple circuit that is widely used in many applications. In the figure below, an amplifier has two input terminals, one called the *inverting input* marked by '−' and one called the *non-inverting input marked* by '+'. The output of the amplifier is $-AV_i$, where V_i is the voltage difference between the two input terminals and A is its gain (amplification).

To analyze the operational amplifier, all you need know is Ohm's law, which states 'the current i flowing through a resistor R is given by V/R, where V is the voltage across the ends of' the resistor

From the diagram we can immediately write down

$$i_1 = (V_{in} - V_i)/R_1$$

$$i_2 = (V_i - V_{out})/R_2$$

and

$$V_{out} = -AV_i$$

If we assume that the current flowing into the inverting terminal of the amplifier is zero (approximately true in practice), we have $i_1 = i_2$. That is

$$(V_{in} - V_i)/R_1 = (V_i - V_{out})/R_2$$

We can substitute for $V_i = -V_{out}/A$ in this equation to get

$$(V_{in} + V_{out}/A)/R_1 = (-V_{out}/A - V_{out})/R_2$$

Re-arranging this equation gives

$$V_{out}/V_{in} = -R_2/R_1/(1 + (1 + R_2/R_1)/A)$$

In a practical operational amplifier, the gain of the amplifier, $-A$, approaches infinity and $(1 + R_2/R_1)/A$ approaches zero. Therefore we can write the gain of the operational amplifier as

$$V_{out}/V_i = -R_2/R_1$$

This remarkable result shows that the gain is dependent only on the value of the components R_1 and R_2 and not on the amplifier itself (as long as the value of A is very large).

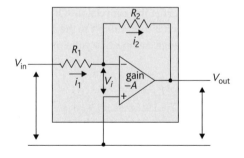

---

amplifier works). As each of the resistors in Fig. 11.52 can be connected to ground or to a precisely maintained reference voltage, V_{ref}, the current flowing through each resistor is either zero or $V_{ref}/2^iR$, where $i = 0, 1, 2, \ldots, m-1$. The total current flowing into the operational amplifier is given by

$$\frac{V_{ref}}{R} \sum_{i=0}^{m-1} \frac{d_{m-i-1}}{2^i}$$

where d_i represents the state of the ith switch. The voltage at the output terminal of the operational amplifier is given by

$$V_o = -2V_{ref} \times R_f/R \times [d_{m-1} \times 2^{-1} + d_{m-2} \times 2^{-2} + \cdots + d_0 \times 2^{-m}]$$

Real digital-to-analog converters implement the m switches, typically, by *field-effect* transistors (a field-effect transistor behaves as a fast electronic switch—the voltage at

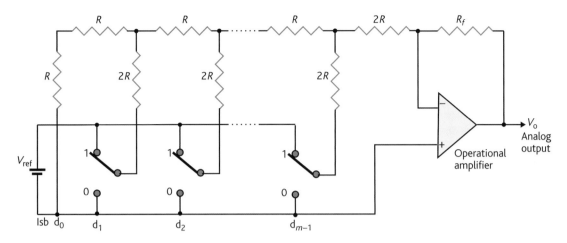

Figure 11.53 The R–$2R$ ladder D/A converter.

its gate determines whether the path between the other two terminals is open or closed). By switching the control gate of these transistors between two logic levels, the resistance between their source and drain terminals is likewise switched between a very high value (the off or open state) and a very low value (the on or closed state). A perfect field-effect transistor switch has off and on values of infinity and zero, respectively. Practical transistor switches have small but finite on-resistances that degrade the accuracy of the DAC.

Although the circuit of Fig. 11.52 is perfectly reasonable for values of m below six, larger values create manufacturing difficulties associated with the resistor chain. Suppose a 10-bit DAC is required. The ratio between the largest and smallest resistor is 2^{10}:1 or 1024:1. If the device is to be accurate to one LSB, the precision of the largest resistor must be at least one-half part in 1024, or approximately 0.05%. Manufacturing resistors to this absolute level of precision is difficult and costly with thin-film technology, and virtually impossible with integrated circuit technology.

The R–$2R$ ladder

An alternative form of digital-to-analog converter is given in Fig. 11.53, where the DAC relies on the R–$2R$ ladder (pronounced R two R). This DAC is so called because all resistors in the ladder have either the value R or $2R$. Although it's difficult to produce highly accurate resistors over a wide range of values, it is much easier to produce *pairs* of resistors with a precise 2:1 ratio in resistance.

As the current from the reference source, V_{ref}, flows down the ladder (from left to right in Fig. 11.53), it is divided at each junction (i.e. the node between the left R, right R, and $2R$ resistors) into two equal parts, one flowing along the ladder to the right and one flowing down the $2R$ shunt resistor. The network forms a linear circuit and we can apply the *Superposition Theorem*. This theorem states that, in a linear system, the effect is the sum of all the causes. Consequently, the total current

flowing into the inverting terminal of the operational amplifier is equal to the sum of all the currents from the shunt (i.e. $2R$) resistors, weighted by the appropriate binary value.

A digital-to-analog converter based on the R–$2R$ ladder has three advantages over the type described in Fig. 11.54.

1. All resistors have a value of either R or $2R$, making it easy to match resistors and to provide a good measure of temperature tracking between resistors. Furthermore, the residual on-resistance of the transistor switches can readily be compensated for.

2. By selecting relatively low values for R in the range 2.5 kΩ to 10 kΩ, it is both easy to manufacture the DAC and to achieve a good response time because of the low impedance of the network.

3. Due to the nature of the R–$2R$ ladder, the operational amplifier always sees a constant impedance at its input, regardless of the state of the switches in the ladder, which improves the accuracy of the operational amplifier circuit.

The R–$2R$ ladder forms the basis of many commercially available DACs. Real circuits are arranged slightly differently to that of Fig. 11.53 to reduce still further the practical problems associated with a DAC.

DACs based on the potentiometric network

Another form of digital-to-analog converter is called the *potentiometric* or *tree network*. Figure 11.54 describes a 3-bit arrangement of such a network where a chain of n resistors is placed in series between the reference supply and ground. The value of n is given by 2^m, where m is the resolution of the DAC. In the example of Fig. 11.54, $m = 3$ and $n = 8$. An 8-bit DAC requires 256 resistors in series. The voltage between ground and the lower end of the ith resistor is given by

$$V = V_{ref}iR/nR = V_{ref}i/n \qquad \text{for } i = 0 \text{ to } n - 1.$$

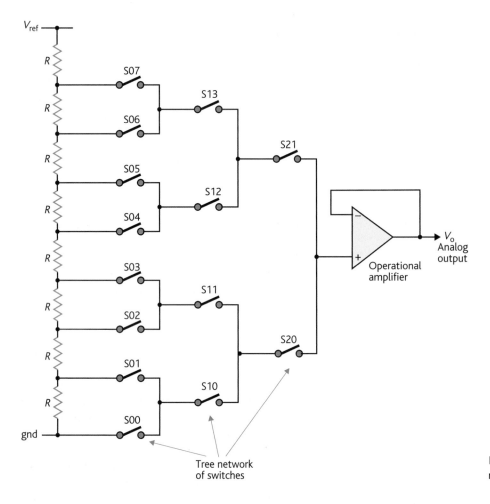

Figure 11.54 The tree-network D/A converter.

The value of the resistors, R, does not appear in this equation. All that matters is that the resistors are of equal value. Because the flow of current through the resistors is constant, the effects of resistor heating found in some forms of R–$2R$ ladder are eliminated.

The switch tree serves only to connect the input terminal of the operational amplifier to the appropriate tap (i.e. node) in the resistor network. In fact, this switching network is nothing but an n:1 demultiplexer. Moreover, because the switches do not switch a current (as in the case of the R–$2R$ network), the values of their on and off resistances are rather less critical.

A DAC based on a switch tree is also inherently *monotonic*. That is, as the digital input increases from $00 \ldots 0$ to $11 \ldots 1$, the analog output always increases for each increment in the input.

Before we look at analog-to-digital converters, we need to say something about errors in digital-to-analog converters.

Errors in DACs

Real DACs differ from the ideal DACs described above. Differences between input code and output voltages are

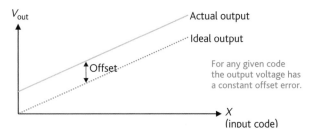

Figure 11.55 The constant offset error.

caused by errors that originate in the DAC's analog circuits. Figures 11.55 to 11.59 give five examples of errors in DACs. We have drawn the outputs of Figs 11.55 to 11.59 as straight lines for convenience—in practice they are composed of steps because the input is a binary code.

In Fig. 11.55, the DAC's output voltage differs from its ideal value by a constant *offset*. If the input is a binary value X, the output is equivalent to that of a *perfect* DAC plus a constant error signal e; that is $V_{out} = KX + e$. A constant error is easy to deal with because it can be *trimmed out* by adding a compensating voltage of equal magnitude but of opposite sign to the error.

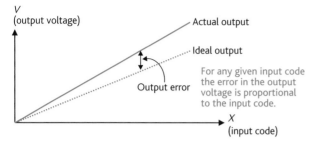

Figure 11.56 The gain error.

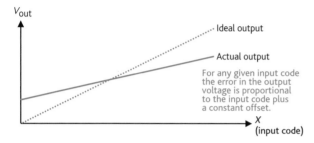

Figure 11.57 The combined effect of offset and gain errors.

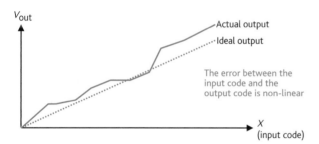

Figure 11.58 The non-linear error.

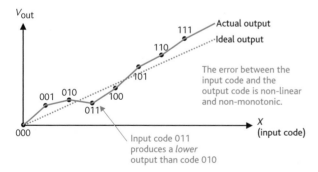

Figure 11.59 Non-monotonicity.

Figure 11.56 illustrates a *gain error* in which the difference between the output of the DAC and its ideal value is a linear function of the digital input. In this case, if the ideal output is $V_{out} = KX$, the actual output is given by $V_{out} = k \cdot KX$, where k is the gain error (ideally $k = 1$). The gain error can be

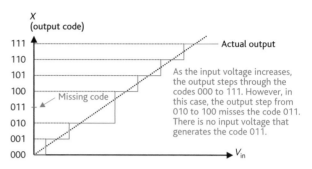

Figure 11.60 The missing code.

corrected by passing the DAC's output through an amplifier with a gain factor of $1/k$.

Real DACs suffer from both offset and gain errors as illustrated in Fig. 11.57. The combined offset and gain errors can both be removed separately by injecting a negative offset and passing the output of the DAC through a compensating amplifier as we've just described.

A more serious error is the *non-linear response* illustrated in Fig. 11.58 where the change in the output, Q, for each step in the input code is not constant. The error between the input code and the output voltage is a random value. Non-linear errors cannot easily be corrected by simple circuitry. Many DACs are guaranteed to have a maximum non-linearity less than one-half Q, the quantization error; i.e. the DAC's output error is always less than $Q/2$ for any input.

Figure 11.59 illustrates a *non-monotonic* response, a form of nonlinearity in which the output voltage does not always increase with increasing input code. In this example, the analog output for the code 011 is less than that for the code 010. Non-monotonic errors can be dangerous in systems using feedback. For example, if an increasing input produces a decreasing output, the computer controlling the DAC may move the input in the wrong direction.

Analog-to-digital converters suffer from similar errors to DACs—only the axes of the graphs in Figs 11.55 to 11.59 are changed. An interesting form of an ADC error is called the *missing code* where the ADC steps from code X to code $X + 2$ *without* going through code $X + 1$. Code $X + 1$ is said to be a *missing code*, because there is no input voltage that will generate this code. Figure 11.60 demonstrates the transfer function of an ADC with a missing code. As the input voltage to the ADC is linearly increased, the output steps through its codes one by one in sequence. In Fig. 11.60 the output jumps from 010 to 100 without passing through 011.

11.6.4 Analog-to-digital conversion

Although converting a digital value into an analog signal is relatively easy, converting an analog quantity into a digital value is rather more difficult. In fact, apart from one special

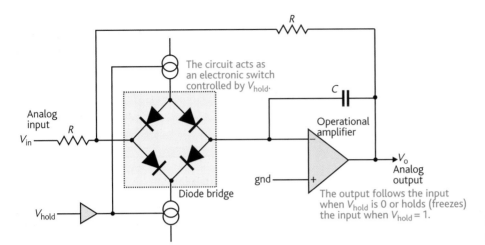

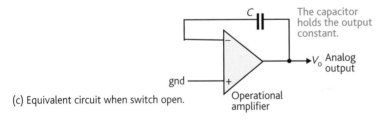

Figure 11.61 The sample and hold circuit.

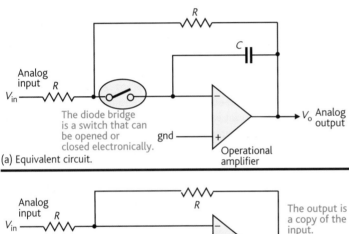

(a) Equivalent circuit.

(b) Equivalent circuit when switch closed.

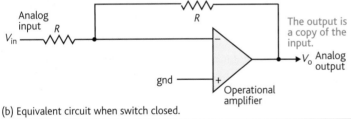

(c) Equivalent circuit when switch open.

Figure 11.62 Operation of the sample and hold circuit.

type of A/D converter, analog-to-digital conversion is performed in a roundabout way. In this section, we describe three types of A/D converter: the *parallel* converter (the only direct A/D converter), the *feedback* converter, and the *integrating* converter.

Before we describe ADCs in detail, we look at the *sample and hold* circuit used to freeze time-varying analog signals prior to their conversion. This circuit is sometimes called a *follow and hold* circuit. We mentioned this circuit when we discussed *aperture time*.

The sample and hold circuit

Like many other analog circuits, the *sample and hold* (S/H) circuit is simple in principle but very complex in practice. The divergence between theory and practice stems from the effect of second-or even third-order non-linearities of analog circuits. Such problems don't affect digital circuits.

Figure 11.61 gives the circuit of a sample and hold amplifier. Readers without a background in electronics may skip the details of this circuit's operation—all it does is to charge a capacitor to the same level as the input signal, and then connect the capacitor to its output terminals. For a short time, the voltage on the capacitor remains constant, allowing the ADC to perform a conversion with a relatively constant input.

If we forget the *diode bridge* and regard the input resistor, R, as being directly connected to the inverting terminal of the operational amplifier, we have a simple inverting buffer with unity gain (see Fig. 11.62(a)). That is, $V_{out} = -V_{in}$. Assume also that the capacitor C has negligible effect on the circuit.

The diode bridge in Fig. 11.61 acts as an on/off switch that either connects the analog input to the inverting terminal of the op-amp via R, or isolates the inverting terminal from the input. When the switch is in the closed position, the S/H

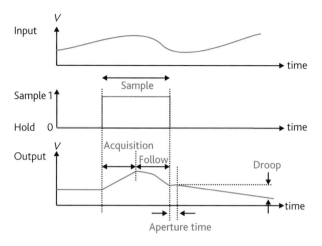

Figure 11.63 Timing details of the sample and hold circuit.

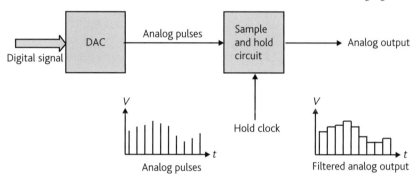

Figure 11.64 The sample and hold circuit as a filter.

uncertainty time. We've already met this parameter, which defines the period during which the input must not change by more than, say, a least-significant bit. Aperture times vary from about 50 ns to 50 ps, or less. One pico second (ps), is 10^{-12} seconds.

In the hold mode, the capacitor discharges and the output begins to *droop.* Droop rates vary, typically, between 5 μV/μs and 0.01 μV/μs. The parameters of the S/H circuit are often interrelated and optimizing one parameter may degrade the values of other parameters.

Sample and hold circuits are vital when analog-to-digital converters with appreciable conversion times are to be connected to time-varying inputs. Sample and hold circuits must sometimes be used with digital-to-analog converters. A sample and hold circuit can be fed from a DAC and used to turn the sequence of analog values from the DAC into a continuous analog signal. In this mode the S/H circuit is called a *zero-order hold filter* and its output consists of steps between the analog values see Fig. 11.64. Another advantage of the S/H circuit is that it *deglitches* the DAC and removes any spikes in its output.

Now that we have described how an analog signal can be captured, the next step is to show how it can be converted into a digital value.

The parallel analog-to-digital converter

The parallel A/D converter is called the *flash* converter because of its great speed of conversion when compared with the two indirect techniques described later. It works by simultaneously comparing the analog input with $2^m - 1$ equally spaced reference voltages. Figure 11.65 illustrates a 3-bit flash A/D converter (real flash ADCs are typically 6- to 8-bit devices). A chain of 2^m equal-valued resistors forms a *tapped potentiometer* between two reference voltages. The voltage between consecutive taps in the chain of resistors differs by $1/2^m$ of the full-scale analog input. Each of the $2^m - 1$ taps is connected to the inverting input of a high-speed differential comparator, whose output depends on the sign of the voltage difference between its two inputs. The non-inverting inputs of the comparators are all wired together and connected to the analog input of the ADC. The output of the *i*th comparator in Fig. 11.65 is given by

$$\text{sign} (V_{in} - V_{ref}i/8).$$

For any given analog input voltage, the outputs of the comparators, whose reference input is below that of the analog input to be converted into digital form, are at a logical 1 level. All other outputs are at a logical 0. The seven outputs are fed

circuit operates in its *sample mode* and $V_{out} = -V_{in}$ (Fig. 11.62(b)); that is, the output *follows* the input. At the same time, the capacitor, C, is charged up to the output voltage because its other terminal is at ground potential (the inverting terminal of the op-amp is a virtual ground).

When the diode bridge switch is opened, the output of the op-amp is held constant by the charge on the capacitor (Fig. 11.62(c)). The charge stored in the capacitor will eventually leak away and the output will fall to zero. However, in the short term the output remains at the level the input was in at the instant the diode bridge switch was opened.

Figure 11.63 illustrates the timing parameters of a sample and hold amplifier. When the diode switch is closed and the circuit goes into its *sample mode,* the capacitor begins to charge up to the level of the input. The period in which the capacitor is charged is called the *acquisition time* and is about 3 μs for a low-cost S/H circuit. The output now tracks the input up to the maximum *slew rate* of the S/H circuit. *Slew rate* defines the fastest rate at which the output of a circuit can change.

When the S/H circuit is switched into its *hold mode* and the diode switch turned off, there's a finite delay during which the capacitor is disconnected from the input called the *aperture*

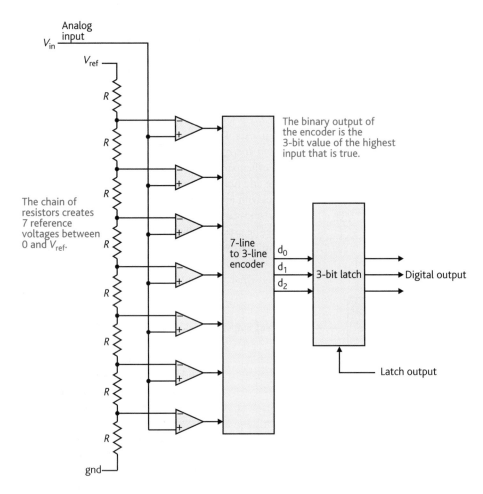

Figure 11.65 The flash AID converter.

to a *priority encoder* that generates a 3-bit output corresponding to the number of logical 1s in the input.

The parallel A/D converter is very fast and can digitize analog signals at over 30 million samples per second. High conversion rates are required in real-time signal processing in applications such as radar data processing and image processing. As an illustration of the speeds involved consider digitizing a television picture. The total number of samples required to digitize a TV signal with 500 pixels/line in real-time is

samples = pixels per line $\times$ lines per field $\times$ fields per second
$$= 500 \times 312\tfrac{1}{2} \times 50 = 7812500 \text{ samples per second (UK)}$$
$$= 500 \times 265\tfrac{1}{2} \times 60 = 7875500 \text{ samples per second (USA)}$$

Because the flash converter requires so many comparators, it is difficult to produce with greater than about 8-bit precision. Even 6-bit flash ADCs are relatively expensive.

The feedback analog-to-digital converter

The *feedback* analog-to-digital converter, paradoxically, uses a digital-to-analog converter to perform the required conversion. Figure 11.66 illustrates the basic principle behind this

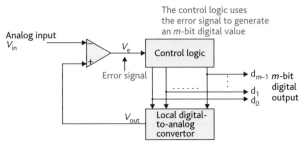

Figure 11.66 The feedback ADC.

class of converter. A local digital-to-analog converter transforms an m-bit digital value, $D = d_0, d_1, \ldots, d_{m-1}$, into an analog voltage, V_{out}. The value of the m-bit digital word D is determined by the block labeled *control logic* in one of the ways to be described later.

V_{out} from the DAC is applied to the inverting input of an operational amplifier and the analog input to be converted is applied to its non-inverting input. The output of the operational amplifier corresponds to an error signal, V_e, and is equal to A times $(V_{out} - V_{in})$, where A is the gain of the amplifier. This error signal is used by the control logic

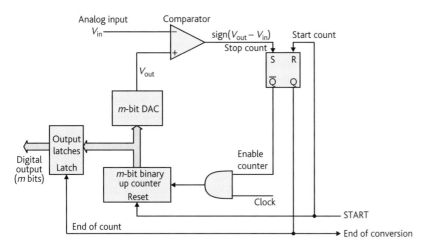

Figure 11.67 The ramp feedback ADC.

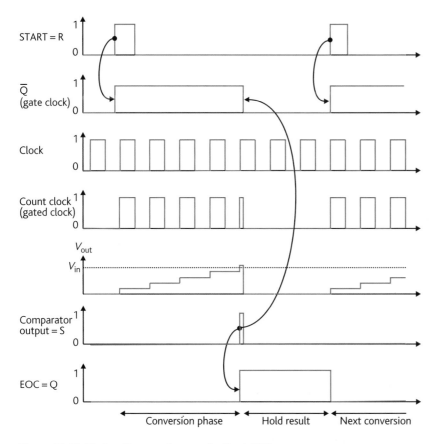

Figure 11.68 Timing diagram of a ramp feedback ADC.

In plain English, the digital signal is varied by trial and error until the locally generated analog voltage is as close to the analog input as it is possible to achieve. The next step is to examine ways of implementing this *trial and error* process.

The ramp converter

The simplest feedback A/D converter is the *ramp converter* of Fig. 11.67, which uses a binary counter to generate the digital output, D. Initially, the binary counter is cleared to 0. A new conversion process starts with the resetting of the RS flip-flop. When $\overline{Q}$ goes high following a reset, the AND gate is enabled and clock pulses are fed to the m-bit binary up-counter. These pulses cause the output of the counter, D, to increase monotonically from zero (i.e. $0, 1, 2, \ldots, 2^{m-1}$).

The output from the counter is applied to both an m-bit output latch and a D/A converter. As the counter is clocked, the output of the local D/A converter ramps upwards in the manner shown in the timing diagram of Fig. 11.68. The locally generated analog signal is compared with the input to be converted in a digital comparator, whose output is the sign of the local analog voltage minus the input; that is, $\text{sign}(V_{out} - V_{in})$. When this value goes positive, the flip-flop is set. At the same time, its $\overline{Q}$ output goes low, cutting off the stream of clock pulses to the counter and its Q output goes high, providing an `End_of_conversion` (EOC) output and latching the contents of the binary counter into the output latches.

The ramp feedback A/D converter has a variable conversion time. If the analog input is close to the maximum (i.e. full-scale) value, approximately 2^m clock pulses are required before the locally generated analog signal reaches the unknown input. The maximum conversion time of an 8-bit ADC is 256 times the DAC's settling time plus associated delays in the comparator and counter. The ramp feedback converter produces a *biased* error in its output, because the counter stops only when the local DAC output is higher

network to modify the digital data, D, to minimize the error signal $A(V_{out} - V_{in})$. When the difference between V_{in} and V_{out} is less than that between two quantized signal levels (i.e. Q), the conversion process is complete.

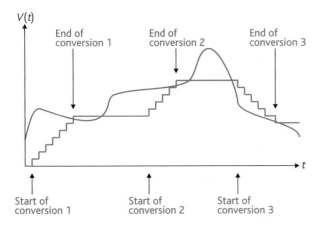

Figure 11.69 The ramp converter using an up/down counter.

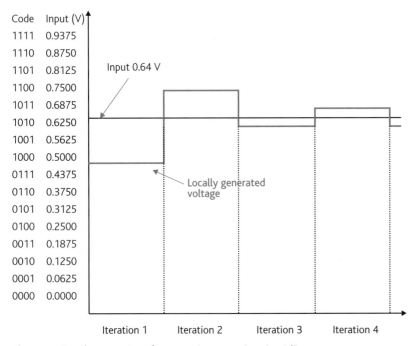

Figure 11.70 The operation of a successive approximation A/D converter.

comparator changes state, at which point the analog input is said to be acquired by the converter. Figure 11.69 demonstrates the operation of this type of convertor by showing how three successive conversions are performed.

If the analog input is constant, the conversion time of the counter is effectively zero once the input has been initially acquired. As long as the input changes slowly with respect to the rate at which the output of the local DAC can ramp upward or downward, the tracking counter faithfully converts the analog input into the appropriate digital output. If the analog input rapidly changes rapidly, the local analog voltage may not be able to track the input and acquisition is lost.

The tracking A/D converter is most useful when the input is changing slowly and is highly auto-correlated. Human speech represents such a signal. If the converter is subject to essentially random inputs (e.g. it is fed from a multiplexer), it offers little or no advantage over a ramp converter.

The successive approximation converter

Intuitively, it would seem reasonable to take very large steps in increasing the analog signal from the local DAC early in the conversion process, and then to reduce the step size as the conversion proceeds and the local analog voltage approaches the analog input. Such an A/D converter is known as a *successive approximation* A/D converter and uses a binary search algorithm to guarantee an m-bit conversion in no more than m iterations (i.e. clock cycles).

The structure of a successive approximation D/A converter is adequately illustrated by the generic feedback converter of Fig. 11.67. Only the strategy used to generate successive steps makes the successive approximation converter different from a ramp converter. At the start of a new conversion process, the digital logic sets the most-significant bit (MSB), of the input of the local D/A converter to a logical 1 level and all other bits to 0 (i.e. D = 1000 . . . 0). In other words, the first guess is equal to one-half the full-scale output of the converter.

If the analog input is greater than half the full-scale output from the local D/A converter, the MSB is retained at a logical 1 level, otherwise it is cleared. On the second iteration, the next most significant bit (i.e. d_{m-2} in an m-bit word) is set to a logical 1 and retained at 1 if the output of the D/A converter is less than the analog input, or cleared if it is not. This process is repeated m times until the LSB of the D/A converter has

than the input to be converted. This local analog value is not necessarily closest to the true digital equivalent of the analog input. The advantage of the ramp A/D converter is its simplicity and low hardware cost.

The *tracking converter* is a ramp converter with the addition of a *bidirectional* (i.e. up/down) counter and slightly more complex control logic. At the start of each new conversion process, the comparator determines whether the analog input is above or below the feedback voltage from the local DAC. If the analog input is greater, the counter is clocked up and if it is lower the counter is clocked down. Thus, the counter ramps upwards or downwards until the output of the

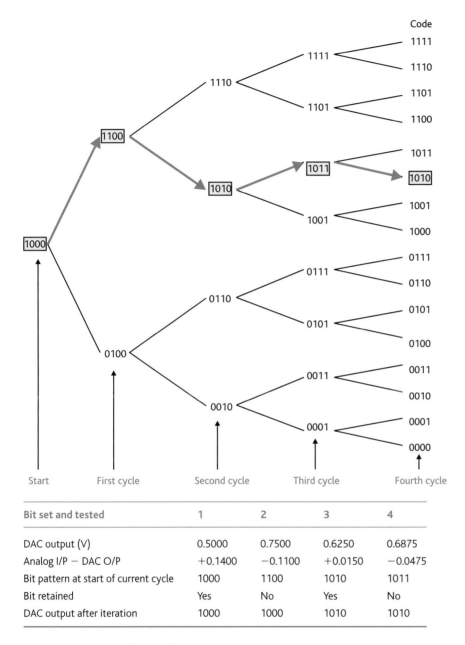

Code

Figure 11.71 The decision tree for a successive approximation ADC.

Bit set and tested	1	2	3	4
DAC output (V)	0.5000	0.7500	0.6250	0.6875
Analog I/P − DAC O/P	+0.1400	−0.1100	+0.0150	−0.0475
Bit pattern at start of current cycle	1000	1100	1010	1011
Bit retained	Yes	No	Yes	No
DAC output after iteration	1000	1000	1010	1010

been set and then retained or cleared. After the LSB has been dealt with in this way, the process is at an end and the final digital output may be read by the host microprocessor.

Figure 11.70 illustrates the operation of a 4-bit successive approximation A/D converter whose full-scale input is nominally 1.000 V. The analog input to be converted into digital form is 0.6400 V. As you can see, a conversion is complete after four cycles.

Figure 11.71 provides another way of looking at the successive approximation process described in Fig. 11.70.

Figure 11.71 takes the form of a *decision tree* that shows every possible sequence of events that can take place when an analog signal is converted into a 4-bit digital value. The path taken through the decision tree when 0.6400 V is converted into digital form is shown by a heavy line.

Figure 11.72 illustrates the structure of a 68K-controlled successive approximation A/D converter. The microprocessor is connected to a memory mapped D/A converter that responds only to a write access to the lower byte of the base address chosen by the address decoder. The analog output of the converter is compared with the unknown analog input in a comparator, whose output is gated onto data line D_{15}, whenever a read access is made to the upper byte of the base address. The software to operate the A/D converter of Fig. 11.72 is

```
Successive_approximation
  DAC_output = 0
   Increment = ½ full-scale output {100...00}
  FOR I = 1 TO Number_of_bits
      DAC_output = DAC_output + Increment
      Error_sign = sign(Vin — DAC_output)
      IF Error_sign negative THEN
                            DAC_output = DAC_output — Increment
      ENDIF
    Increment := Increment/2
  ENDFOR
End successive_approximation


*                     D0 contains the increment
*                     D1 is the DAC output
*                     D2 is the cycle counter
*
        ORG    $00F000      Base address of DAC
DAC_IN  DS.B   1            Reserve byte for sign input from DAC
DAC_OT  DS.B   1            Reserve byte for output to DAC
        ORG    $001000      Program origin
CONV    MOVE.B #$80,D0      Set the half-scale increment
        MOVE.B D0,D1        Setup initial value for the output
        MOVE.W #7,D2        We are going to do 8 cycles
AGAIN   MOVE.B D1,DAC_OT    Transmit output to DAC
        BTST   #7,DAC_IN    Examine output from comparator
        BPL    NEXT         IF positive THEN add next increment
        SUB.B  D0,D1        ELSE remove the increment
NEXT    LSR.B  #1,D0        Increment := increment/2
        ADD.B  D0,D1        Add increment to output
        DBRA   D2,AGAIN     Repeat for 8 cycles END
        RTS                 End of conversion
```

The integrating analog-to-digital converter

The *integrating*, or more specifically, the *dual-slope integrating analog-to-digital converter*, transforms the problem of measuring an analog voltage into the more tractable problem of measuring another analog quantity—*time*. An integrating operational amplifier circuit converts the analog input into a charge stored on a capacitor, and then evaluates the charge by measuring the time it takes to discharge the capacitor. The block diagram of a *dual-slope* integrating A/D converter is given in Fig. 11.73 and its timing diagram in Fig. 11.74.

A typical integrating converter operates in three phases: *auto-zero*, *integrate the unknown analog signal*, and *integrate the reference voltage*. The first phase, auto-zero, is a feature of many commercial dual-slope converters, which reduces any offset error in the system. As it isn't a basic feature of the dual-slope process, we won't deal with it here. During the second phase of the conversion, the unknown analog input linearly charges the integrating capacitor C. In this phase, the input of the electronic switch connects the integrator to the voltage to be converted, V_{in}.

Figure 11.74 shows how the output from the integrator, V_{out}, ramps upward linearly during phase 2 of the conversion process. At the start of phase 2, a counter is triggered that counts upwards from 0 to its maximum value $2^n - 1$. After a fixed period $T_1 = 2^n/f_c$ where f_c is the frequency of the converter's clock, the counter overflows (i.e. passes its maximum count). The electronic switch connected to the integrator then connects the integrator's input to $-V_{ref}$, the negative reference supply. The output of the integrator now ramps downwards to 0, while the counter runs up from 0. Eventually, the output of the integrator reaches zero and the conversion process stops—we'll assume that the counter contains M at the end of this phase.

Readers without a knowledge of basic electronics may skip the following analysis of the dual slope integrating ADC. At the end of phase 2 the capacitor is charged up to a level

$$\frac{1}{CR}\int V_{in}\, dt$$

The voltage rise during the second phase is equal to the fall in the third phase because the output of the integrator begins at zero volts and ends up at zero volts. Therefore, the following equation holds:

$$\frac{1}{CR}\int_{t_1}^{t_2} V_{in}\, dt = \frac{1}{CR}\int_{t_2}^{t_3} V_{ref}\, dt$$

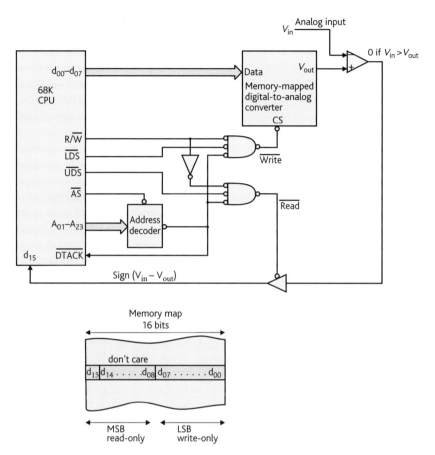

Figure 11.72 The circuit of a successive approximation A/D converter.

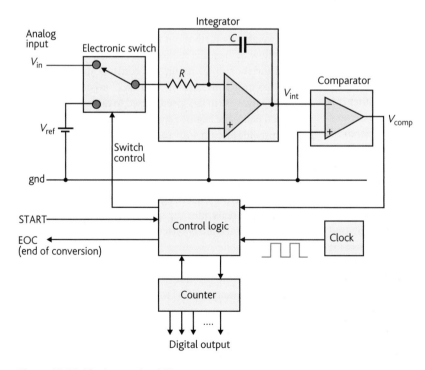

Figure 11.73 The integrating A/D converter.

Assuming that $t_1 = 0$, $t_2 = 2^n/f_c$, $t_3 = t_2 + M/f_c$, we can write

$$\frac{1}{CR}\left[V_{in}t\right]_0^{2^n/f_c} = \frac{1}{CR}\left[V_{ref}t\right]_{2^n/f_c}^{2^n/f_c} + M/f_c$$

or

$$\frac{V_{in}2^n}{f_c} = \frac{V_{ref}M}{f_c}$$

$$V_{in} = \frac{V_{ref}M}{2^n}$$

This remarkable result is dependent only on the reference voltage and two integers, 2^n and M. The values of C and R and the clock frequency, f_c, do not appear in the equation. Implicit in the equation is the condition that f_c is constant throughout the conversion process. Fortunately, this is a reasonable assumption even for the simplest of clock generators.

The dual-slope integrating A/D converter is popular because of its very low cost and inherent simplicity. Moreover, it is exceedingly accurate and can provide 12 or more bits of precision at a cost below that of 8-bit ADCs. Because this converter requires no absolute reference other than V_{ref}, it is easy to fabricate the entire device in a single integrated circuit.

The conversion time is variable and takes $2^n + M$ clock periods in total. A 12-bit converter with a 1 μs clock has a maximum conversion time of $2 \times 2^n/f_c$ seconds, because the maximum value of N is 2^n. Using these figures, the maximum conversion time is equal to $2 \times 4096 \times 1$ μs, or 8.192 ms, which is very much slower than most forms of feedback A/D converter.

Because the analog input is integrated over a period of $2^n/f_c$ seconds, noise on the input is attenuated. Sinusoidal input signals, whose periods are submultiples of the integration period, do not affect the output of the integrator and hence the measured value of the input. Many high-precision converters exploit this property to remove any noise at the power line frequency. Integrating converters are largely used in instrumentation such as digital voltmeters.

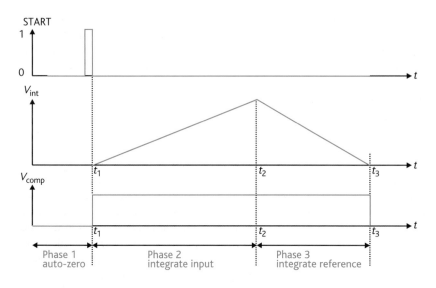

Figure 11.74 Timing diagram of an integrating A/D converter.

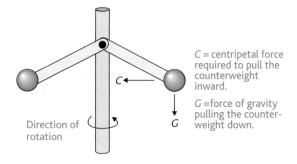

C = centripetal force required to pull the counterweight inward.

G = force of gravity pulling the counterweight down.

Figure 11.75 The mechanical governor.

Now that we've described how analog signals can be captured, processed, and then used to generate an analog output, we provide in insight into some of the things a computer can do with analog signals.

11.7 Introduction to digital signal processing

Digital signal processing (DSP) forms an entire branch of electronics covering electronic circuits, mathematics, and computer science. Here we explain why DSP is so important by looking at just two areas: control systems and audio signal processing. We set the scene by describing an early mechanical analog control system before looking at the principles of digital control systems. The final part of this section describes DSP that is used in control systems and sound and video processing systems.

Control systems have been used for a long time; for example, the *governor* used to keep the speed of stream engines

constant during the nineteenth century. Figure 11.75 shows the shaft of a steam engine driving a vertical spindle. Two arms connected to the spindle by pivots carry counterweights at the ends of the arms. The arms are pivoted and are free to swing outward as the spindle rotates.

As the spindle rotates, the counterweights move outward. In everyday life people use the term *centrifugal force* to describe the tendency of a body following a curved path to fly outward. Centrifugal force doesn't exist. Any moving body tends to continue in a straight line. In order to force a body to follow a curved path (e.g. an orbit), a force is necessary to pull it toward the center. This force is called *centripetal force*.

In Fig. 11.75 the force of gravity on the counterweights provides the centripetal force that pulls the counterweights inward. This situation is analogous to camber in a road bend—tilting the car inward provides the centripetal force required to pull the car round the bend without skidding.

The position of the counterweights in Fig. 11.75 depends on the speed at which the spindle rotates. As the arms connected to the counterweights move in and out, they control a valve that regulates the flow of stream to the engine. Below a certain speed, the valve is open and more steam is fed to the engine to cause it to speed up. As the spindle rotates faster, the counterweights fly further out until the valve begins to close and the flow of steam is reduced. Eventually equilibrium is reached and the spindle rotates at a constant speed.

This control mechanism employs *negative feedback*, because an increase in the speed is used to decrease the flow of steam and hence the engine's speed. Similar mechanisms were used to provide aircraft with autopilots long before the age of the microprocessor. Today, the digital computer has replaced the governor. The speed of a spindle can be read with great precision and fed to a computer. The computer processes the speed according to a suitable algorithm and generates the control signals that determine the spindle's speed.

Modern digital control systems are everywhere; for example, an automobile measures the external air pressure, the manifold pressure, the external air temperature, the speed of the engine, and the position of the gas pedal to determines the optimum amount of fuel to inject into each cylinder.

11.7.1 Control systems

Analog-to-digital and digital-to-analog conversion techniques are found in process control applications. Consider the automatic pilot of an aircraft. At any instant the location and altitude of an aircraft is measured, together with its performance (heading, speed, rate of climb, rate of turn, and engine power). All these values are converted into digital form and fed into a computer that determines the best position for the throttle, elevator, aileron, and rudder controls. The digital output from the computer is applied to digital-to-analog converters, whose analog outputs operate actuators that directly move the appropriate control surfaces.

Figure 11.76 describes a primitive control system. The input is an analog value that is digitized and processed by the computer. Real control systems are often much more sophisticated than that of Fig. 11.76—consider the problem of overshoot. Suppose you apply a new demand input to a system such as banking an aircraft's wings. The aircraft rolls into the bank and attempts to attain the angle requested. However, the mechanical inertia of the aircraft might cause it to roll past (i.e. overshoot) the point it was aiming for. A practical control system should also take account of rapidly changing conditions.

Let's look at how control systems have evolved from the simplest possible mechanisms. The crudest control mechanism is found in central heating systems where the desired temperature or *setpoint* is obtained from a control unit on the wall. The demand input is compared with the actual temperature measured by a sensor. If it is colder than the setpoint, the heater is turned on. Otherwise the heater is turned off.

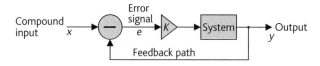

Figure 11.76 The control system.

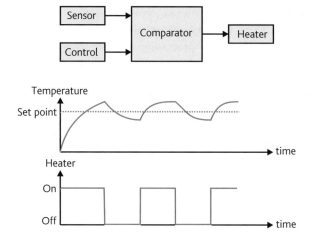

Figure 11.77 The on–off control system.

Figure 11.77 demonstrates the operation of such a system. The temperature of the room rises and eventually the heater is turned off. Because of the heater's thermal inertia the room, the temperature will continue to rise after the current has been cut off. Eventually, the room begins to cool and the heater is turned on and the temperature starts rising again.

This type of on–off control system is also called a bang–bang control system to indicate its crude approach—bang the system goes on and bang it goes off. There is no intermediate point between on and off, and the room is never at the correct temperature because it's either slightly too hot or too cold.

A better method of controlling the temperature of a room is to measure the difference between the desired temperature and the actual temperature and use this value to determine how much power is to be fed to the heater. The colder the room, the more power sent to the heater. If the room is close to its desired temperature, less power if fed to the heater. This is an example of a *proportional control system*. As the room temperature approaches its desired setpoint value, the power fed to the heater is progressively reduced; that is, the current supplied to the heater is $K(t_{setpoint} - t_{room})$.

The proportional control system can be improved further by taking into account changes in the variable you are trying to control. Suppose you're designing a camera with an automatic focusing mechanism for use at sporting events. The camera measures the distance of the subject from the camera using the difference between the current point of focus and the desired point of focus to drive the motor that performs the focusing.

Suppose the subject suddenly changes direction, speeds up, or slows down. A proportional control system can't deal with this situation well. If the subject is in focus and then begins accelerating away, a proportional control signal can't apply a large correction until the target is out of focus. What we need is a control signal that doesn't depend on the magnitude of the error but on the *rate* at which the error is changing.

A *differential* control system uses the rate of change of the error as a control signal; for example, a camera with auto-focusing can use any rapid change in the subject's position to control the focusing motor—even if the subject is approximately in focus and there's no proportional error. A differential control system must also incorporate proportional control because if the subject were out of focus but not moving there would be no differential feedback signal.

If we call the error between the setpoint in a control system and its output e, the control input in a *proportional plus derivative* (i.e. differential) control system is given by

$$y = K_1 e + K_2 de/dt,$$

where K_1 and K_2 are the proportional and derivative control coefficients, respectively.

Even this control algorithm isn't perfect. Suppose you design a radar-controlled docking system for two spacecraft. One craft can track the other by using both proportional

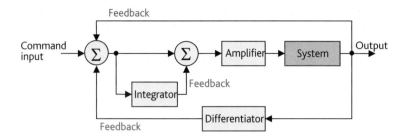

Figure 11.78 The derivative and integral control system.

```
FOR i = 1 TO k DO
    Output = M_i
ENDFOR
```

The digitally stored music is reconverted into analog form by sending it to the output port connected to a DAC. This algorithm does nothing other than retrieve the stored music. In the next example, the samples from the array are amplified by a scalar factor *A*. By changing the value of *A*, the amplitude (i.e. the loudness) of the music can be altered. Now we have a digital volume control with no moving parts that can be programmed to change the sound level at any desired rate.

```
FOR i = 1 TO k DO
    Output = A * M_i
ENDFOR
```

We can average consecutive samples to calculate the loudness of the signal and use it to choose a value for *A*. The following expression shows how we might average the loudness over a period of *k* samples.

$$\text{Loudness} = \frac{1}{k}\sqrt{\sum_{i=0}^{k-1} m_i^2}$$

Suppose we choose the scale factor *A* to make the average power of the signal approximately constant. When the music is soft, is the volume is increased, and when it is loud, the volume is decreased. This process is called *compressing* the music and is particularly useful for listeners with impaired hearing who cannot hear soft passages without turning the volume up so far that loud passages are distorted.

In the next example, the signal fed to the loudspeaker is composed of two parts. M_i represents the current value, and $B \cdot M_{i-j}$ the value of the signal *j* samples earlier, scaled by a factor *B*. Normally the factor *B* is less than unity. Where do we get a signal plus a delayed, attenuated value? These features are found in an *echo* and are of interest to the makers of electronic music. By very simple processing, we are able to generate echoes entirely by digital techniques. Analog signal processing requires complex and inflexible techniques. Synthesizing an echo by analog techniques requires you to first convert the sound into vibration by a transducer. A spring is connected to the transducer and the acoustic signal travels down it to a microphone at the other end. The output of the microphone represents a delayed version of the original signal— the echo. The length of the delay is increased by using a longer spring. In the digital version, simply modifying the value of *j* changes the delay.

```
FOR i = i+1 TO k DO
    Output= M_i + B * M_{i-j}
ENDFOR
```

control and derivative control to minimize the difference between their trajectories. However, once their trajectories are closely (but not exactly) matched, there is neither a proportional error signal nor a derivative error signal to force exact tracking. What we need is a mechanism that takes account of a persistent small error.

An *integral* control system adds up the error signal over a period of time. The integral correction term is $K_3 \int e \, dt$ Even the smallest error eventually generates a control signal to further reduce the error. Integral control ensures that any drift over time is corrected.

A high-performance controller might combine proportional control, rate-of-change control, and integral control as Fig. 11.78 demonstrates. This system is called a PID (*proportional, integral, and derivative*) controller. In Fig. 11.78 the box marked *differentiator* calculates the rate of change of the system output being controlled.

The equation for a PID can be expressed in the form

$$y = K_1 e + K_2 de/dt + K_3 \int e \, dt$$

The control signal *y* now depends and the size of the error between the desired and actual outputs from the controller, the rate at which the error is changing, and the accumulated error over a period.

We can't go into control theory here but we should mention several important points. Designing a PID system is not easy. You have to choose the amounts of proportional, derivative, and integral feedback as well as the time constant of the integrator. If the system is not correctly designed it can become unstable and oscillate.

In the final part of this section we look at how digital signals are processed by the computer.

11.7.2 Digital signal processing

Let's begin with a simple example of signal processing. Suppose music from a microphone is quantized, converted into a sequence of digital values by an ADC, fed into a computer, and stored in an array, *M*. We can read consecutive digital values from the array and use a DAC to convert them into an analog signal that is fed to a loudspeaker. Consider the following algorithm.

The final example of signal processing represents the linear transversal equalizer that implements a general-purpose digital filter. In audio terms, a digital filter acts as tone controls or an equalizer. We are going to look at this topic in a little more detail next.

```
FOR i = 1 TO k DO
        a = K4 * M_i-4
        b = K3 * M_i-3
        c = K2 * M_i-2
        d = K1 * M_i-1
        e = K0 * M_i
        Output = a + b + c + d + e
ENDFOR
```

The output is a fraction of the current sample plus weighted fractions of the previous four samples. Let's look at this operation in a little more detail.

Digital filters

An important application of digital signal processing is the digital filter. A digital filter behaves like an analog filter—it can pass or stop signals whose frequencies fall within certain ranges. Consider an analog signal, X, that has been digitized and its successive values are

$$x_0, x_1, x_2, x_3, \ldots, x_{i-1}, x_i, x_{i+1}, \ldots$$

Now suppose we generate a new sequence of digital values, Y, whose values are $y_0, y_1, y_2, \ldots$, where,

$$y_i = C_0 \cdot x_i + C_1 \cdot x_{i-1}$$

An element in the output series, y_i, is given by a fraction of the *current* element from the input series $C_0 \cdot x_i$ plus a fraction of the *previous* element $C_1 \cdot x_{i-1}$ of the input series. Figure 11.79 illustrates this operation. The symbol Z^{-1} is used to indicate a 1-unit delay (i.e. the time between two successive samples of a signal). In other words the operation $x_i Z^{-1}$ is equivalent to delaying signal x_i by one time unit—similarly Z^{-2} delays x_i by two time units. This notation belongs to a branch of mathematics called Z transforms.

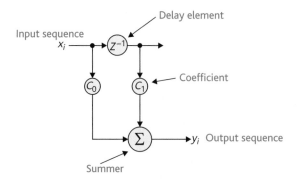

Input sequence x_i — Delay element — Z^{-1} — Coefficient — C_0 — C_1 — Summer — Σ — y_i Output sequence

Figure 11.79 The digital filter.

Let's give see what happens when we give the filter coefficients C_0 the value 0.6 and C_1 the value 0.4, and make the input series $X = 0, 0, 1, 1, 1, 1, \ldots 1$, which corresponds to a *step function*. The output sequence is given by

$$y_0 = 0.6 \cdot x_0 + 0.4 \cdot x_{-1} = 0.6 \cdot 0 + 0.4 \cdot 0.0 = 0.0$$
$$y_1 = 0.6 \cdot x_1 + 0.4 \cdot x_0 \ = 0.6 \cdot 0 + 0.4 \cdot 0.0 = 0.0$$
$$y_2 = 0.6 \cdot x_2 + 0.4 \cdot x_1 \ = 0.6 \cdot 1 + 0.4 \cdot 0.0 = 0.6$$
$$y_3 = 0.6 \cdot x_3 + 0.4 \cdot x_2 \ = 0.6 \cdot 1 + 0.4 \cdot 1.0 = 1.0$$
$$y_4 = 0.6 \cdot x_4 + 0.4 \cdot x_3 \ = 0.6 \cdot 1 + 0.4 \cdot 1.0 = 1.0$$

The output sequence is a rounded or smoothed step function (i.e. when the input goes from 0 to 1 in one step, the output goes 0.0, 0.6, 1.0). This type of circuit is called a *low-pass filter* because sudden changes in the input sequence are diminished by averaging consecutive values. Real digital filters have many more delays and coefficients. Consider the output of a filter with four delay units given by

$$y_i = C_0 \cdot x_i + C_1 \cdot x_{i-1} + C_2 \cdot x_{i-2} + C_3 \cdot x_{i-3} + C_4 \cdot x_{i-4}$$

If we use this filter with coefficients 0.4, 0.3, 0.2, 0.1 and subject it to a step input, we get

$$y_0 = 0.4 \cdot x_0 + 0.3 \cdot x_{-1} + 0.2 \cdot x_{-2} + 0.1 \cdot x_{-3}$$
$$= 0.4 \cdot 0 + 0.3 \cdot 0 + 0.2 \cdot 0 + 0.1 \cdot 0 = 0.0$$
$$y_1 = 0.4 \cdot x_1 + 0.3 \cdot x_0 + 0.2 \cdot x_{-1} + 0.1 \cdot x_{-2}$$
$$= 0.4 \cdot 1 + 0.3 \cdot 0 + 0.2 \cdot 0 + 0.1 \cdot 0 = 0.4$$
$$y_2 = 0.4 \cdot x_2 + 0.3 \cdot x_1 + 0.2 \cdot x_0 + 0.1 \cdot x_{-1}$$
$$= 0.4 \cdot 1 + 0.3 \cdot 1 + 0.2 \cdot 0 + 0.1 \cdot 0 = 0.7$$
$$y_3 = 0.4 \cdot x_3 + 0.3 \cdot x_2 + 0.2 \cdot x_1 + 0.1 \cdot x_0$$
$$= 0.4 \cdot 1 + 0.3 \cdot 1 + 0.2 \cdot 1 + 0.1 \cdot 0 = 0.9$$
$$y_4 = 0.4 \cdot x_4 + 0.3 \cdot x_3 + 0.2 \cdot x_2 + 0.1 \cdot x_1$$
$$= 0.4 \cdot 1 + 0.3 \cdot 1 + 0.2 \cdot 1 + 0.1 \cdot 1 = 1.0$$

In this case, the output is even more rounded (i.e. 0.0, 0.4, 0.7, 0.9, 1.0).

A more interesting type of filter is called a *recursive filter* because the output is expressed as a fraction of the current input and a fraction of the previous output. In this case, the output sequence for a recursive filter with a single delay unit is given by

$$y_i = C_0 \cdot x_i + C_1 \cdot y_{i-1}.$$

Figure 11.80 shows the structure of a recursive filter. Suppose we apply the same step function to this filter that we used in the previous examples. The output sequence is given by

$$y_0 = 0.6 \cdot x_0 + 0.4 \cdot y_{-1} \quad y_0 = 0.6 \cdot 0 + 0.4 \cdot 0 = 0.0$$
$$y_1 = 0.6 \cdot x_1 + 0.4 \cdot y_0 \quad y_1 = 0.6 \cdot 0 + 0.4 \cdot 0 = 0.0$$
$$y_2 = 0.6 \cdot x_2 + 0.4 \cdot y_1 \quad y_2 = 0.6 \cdot 1 + 0.4 \cdot 0 = 0.6$$
$$y_3 = 0.6 \cdot x_3 + 0.4 \cdot y_2 \quad y_3 = 0.6 \cdot 1 + 0.4 \cdot 0.6 = 0.84$$
$$y_4 = 0.6 \cdot x_4 + 0.4 \cdot y_3 \quad y_4 = 0.6 \cdot 1 + 0.4 \cdot 0.84 = 0.936$$
$$y_5 = 0.6 \cdot x_5 + 0.4 \cdot y_4 \quad y_5 = 0.6 \cdot 1 + 0.4 \cdot 0.936 = 0.9744$$
$$y_6 = 0.6 \cdot x_6 + 0.4 \cdot y_5 \quad y_6 = 0.6 \cdot 1 + 0.4 \cdot 0.9744 = 0.98976$$
$$y_7 = 0.6 \cdot x_7 + 0.4 \cdot y_6 \quad y_7 = 0.6 \cdot 1 + 0.4 \cdot 0.98976 = 0.995904$$

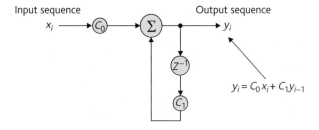

Figure 11.80 The recursive digital filter.

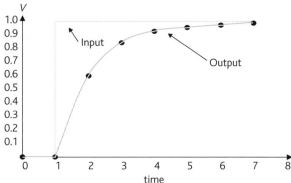

Figure 11.81 Response of the filter of Fig. 11.80 to a step input.

Figure 11.81 plots the input and output series for the recursive filter of Fig. 11.80. As you can see, the output series (i.e. the y_i) rises exponentially to 1. The effect of the operation $C_0 \cdot x_i + C_1 \cdot y_{i-1}$ on a digital sequence is the same as that of a low-pass analog filter on a step signal. You can see that the recursive digital filter is more powerful than a linear digital filter. By changing the constants in the digital equation we can change the characteristics of the digital filter. Digital filters are used to process analog signals and to remove noise.

The opposite of a low-pass filter is a *high-pass filter*, which passes rapid changes in the input sequence and rejects slow changes (or a constant level). Consider the recursive digital filter defined by

$$y_i = C_0 \cdot x_i - C_1 \cdot y_{i-1}.$$

All we have done is change the sign of the constant C_1 and subtracted a fraction of the old output from a fraction of the new input. In this case, a constant or slowly changing signal is subtracted from the output. Consider the previous example with a step input and coefficients $C_0 = 0.6$ and $C_1 = 0.4$:

$$y_0 = 0.6 \cdot x_0 - 0.4 \cdot y_{-1} \quad y_0 = 0.6 \cdot 0 - 0.4 \cdot 0 = 0.0$$
$$y_1 = 0.6 \cdot x_1 - 0.4 \cdot y_0 \quad y_1 = 0.6 \cdot 0 - 0.4 \cdot 0 = 0.0$$
$$y_2 = 0.6 \cdot x_2 - 0.4 \cdot y_1 \quad y_2 = 0.6 \cdot 1 - 0.4 \cdot 0 = 0.60$$
$$y_3 = 0.6 \cdot x_3 - 0.4 \cdot y_2 \quad y_3 = 0.6 \cdot 1 - 0.4 \cdot 0.6 = 0.36$$
$$y_4 = 0.6 \cdot x_4 - 0.4 \cdot y_3 \quad y_4 = 0.6 \cdot 1 - 0.4 \cdot 0.36 = 0.4176$$
$$y_5 = 0.6 \cdot x_5 - 0.4 \cdot y_4 \quad y_5 = 0.6 \cdot 1 - 0.4 \cdot 0.4176 = 0.43296$$
$$y_6 = 0.6 \cdot x_6 - 0.4 \cdot y_5 \quad y_6 = 0.6 \cdot 1 - 0.4 \cdot 0.43296 = 0.426816$$
$$y_7 = 0.6 \cdot x_7 - 0.4 \cdot y_6 \quad y_7 = 0.6 \cdot 1 - 0.4 \cdot 0.426816 = 0.42927$$

In this case the step function dies away as Fig. 11.82 demonstrates.

Correlation

One of the most important applications of digital signal processing is the recovery of very weak signals that have been corrupted by noise. Signals received from satellites and deep space vehicles are often so weak that there is considerably more noise than signal—anyone listening to such a signal on a loudspeaker would hear nothing more than the hiss of white noise. Modern signal processing techniques enable you to extract signals from noise when the signal level is thousands of times weaker than the noise.

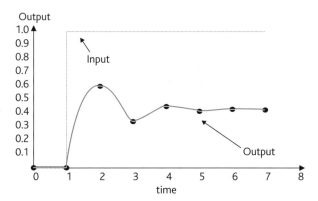

Figure 11.82 Response of a high-pass filter to a step input.

The technique used to recover signals from noise is called *correlation*. We met correlation when we discussed the waveforms used to record data on disks—the more unlike the waveforms used to record 1s and 0s, the better. Correlation is a measure of how similar two waveforms or binary sequences are. Correlation varies from -1 to 0 to $+1$. If the correlation is $+1$, the signals are identical. If the correlation is 0, the two signals are unrelated. If the correlation is -1, one signal is the inverse of the other.

Two signals can be correlated by taking successive samples from each of the series, multiplying the pairs of samples, and then averaging the sum of the product. Consider now the correlation function of two series $X = x_0, x_1, x_2, x_3, x_4$ and $Y = y_0, y_1, y_2, y_3, y_4$.

The correlation between X and Y is given by $1/5(x_0 \cdot y_0, + x_1 \cdot y_1, + x_2 \cdot y_2, + x_3 \cdot y_3)$.

An example of the use of correlation is the effect of rainfall in the mountains on crop growth in the plain. Simply correlating the sequence of rainfall measurements with crop growth doesn't help because there's a delay between rainfall and plant growth. We can generate several correlation functions by correlating one sequence with a

---

THE KALMAN FILTER

The *Kalman* filter, which was introduced in the early 1960s, provides a spectacular application of digital filtering. This filter was proposed by Rudolf Emil Kalman who was born in Budapest but emigrated to the USA from Hungary during the Second World War. A Kalman filter takes a time-varying signal corrupted by noise and *predicts* the future value of the signal; that is, it can eliminate some of the effects of noise. Kalman filters have been applied to a wide range of systems from space vehicles to medical systems.

The mathematics of Kalman filters belongs in advanced courses in control theory. All we can do here is mention some of the underlying concepts. A dynamic system that varies with time can be described by *state variables*. For example, you can write $x_i + 1 = ax_i$, where $x_i + 1$ represents the state of the system at time $I + 1$, x_i represents the system at time I, and a characterizes the behavior of the system. In practice, the state equation is given by $x_i + 1 = ax_i + w_i$, where w_i represents a random noise component.

The Kalman filter lets you predict (i.e. make a best guess) the next state of the system when the system is affected by random noise and the measurements themselves are also affected by noise. Suppose you design an aircraft's autopilot to enable it to follow the ground from a very low level. The height of the aircraft about the ground is measured by radar techniques. However, the successive readings from the radar altimeter are corrupted by random noise, which means that any particular reading can't be relied on. Furthermore, successive altimeter readings can't just be averaged because the terrain itself is undulating.

If the ith estimate of the aircraft's height is h_i, the Kalman filter evaluates:

$$h_i = a_i h_{i-1} + (1 - a_i)x_i$$

The underscore under h_i and $h_i - 1$ indicates that these are estimated values. The current value of h is obtained from the previous estimate, $h_i - 1$, plus the new data, x_i. The coefficient of the filter, a, is a function of i; that is, the coefficient varies with time. The recursive nature of the Kalman filter means that trends in the input are taken into account.

---

delayed version of the other sequence. Now we have a sequence of correlation functions that depend on the delay between the sequences, and we can express the kth correlation value as

$$C_k = \sum x_i \cdot y_{i+k}$$

Suppose that $X = 1, 2, 3, -1, 4, 2, 0, 1$ and $Y = 0, 0, 1, -1, 0, 1, 1, 0, 0, 0$:

$C_0 = 1 \cdot 0 + 2 \cdot 0 + 3 \cdot 1 + -1 \cdot -1 + 4 \cdot 0 + 2 \cdot 1 + 0 \cdot 1 + 1 \cdot 0 = 6$
$C_1 = 1 \cdot 0 + 2 \cdot 1 + 3 \cdot 1 + -1 \cdot 0 + 4 \cdot 1 + 2 \cdot 1 + 0 \cdot 0 + 1 \cdot 0 = 5$
$C_2 = 1 \cdot 1 + 2 \cdot -1 + 3 \cdot 0 + 1 \cdot 1 + 4 \cdot 1 + 2 \cdot 0 + 0 \cdot 0 + 1 \cdot 0 = 4$

These results don't seem very interesting until we apply this technique to a real situation. Suppose a transmitter uses the sequence 0.25, −0.5, 1.0, −0.5, 0.25 to represent a logical 1; that is a 1 is transmitted as the sequence of values 0.25, −0.5, 1.0, −0.5, 0.25. Suppose we receive this signal without noise and correlate it with the sequence representing a 1. That is,

$C_0 = 0.25 \cdot 0.25 + -0.5 \cdot -0.50 + 1 \cdot 1.0$
$\quad + -0.5 \cdot -0.5 + 0.25 \cdot 0.25$
$\quad = 1.625$
$C_1 = 0.25 \cdot 0.00 + -0.5 \cdot 0.25$
$\quad + 1 \cdot -0.5 + -0.5 \cdot 1.0 + 0.25 \cdot -0.5 + 0.0 \cdot 0.25$
$\quad = -1.25$
$C_2 = 0.25 \cdot 0.00 + -0.5 \cdot 0.00 + 1 \cdot 0.25 + -0.5 \cdot -0.5$
$\quad + 0.25 \cdot 1.0 + 0.0 \cdot -0.5 + 0.0 \cdot 0.25$
$\quad = 0.75$

As you can see, the greatest correlation factor occurs when the sequence is correlated with itself. If the sequence is corrupted by. samples of random noise, the noise is not correlated with the sequence and the correlation function is low. Noisy data from, say, a satellite, is correlated with the same sequence used to generate the data. This operation is performed by correlating the incoming data with the appropriate sequence and varying the delay k. A sequence of correlation values are recorded and compared with a threshold value. If the correlation is above the threshold, it is assumed that the sequence is present in the received signal.

Here we have done little more than mention a few examples of digital signal processing. The techniques we have described can be used in both the audio and visual domains. Processing the signals that represent images allows us to, for example, sharpen blurred images or to remove noise from them, or to emphasize their edges.

■ SUMMARY

In this chapter we've looked at some of the many peripherals that can be connected to a computer. We began with the two most important peripherals from the point of view of the average PC user, the input device (keyboard and mouse) and the output device (CRT, LCD, and plasma display).

We have looked at the construction of input/output devices and have described how printers work. In particular, we have demonstrated how computers handle color displays.

Some devices receive or generate analog signals. We have examined how analog signals from sensors are processed by the computer. We have provided a brief discussion of how analog signals can be converted into digital form and vice versa and the problems of sampling a time-varying signal.

We have also briefly introduced some of the devices that enable us to control the World around us: temperature, pressure, and even rotation sensors.

■ PROBLEMS

11.1 Why are mechanical switches unreliable?

11.2 Imagine that keyboards did not exist (i.e. you are free from all conventional design and layout constraints) and you were asked to design a keyboard for today's computers. Describe the layout and functionality of your keyboard.

11.3 Why are optical mice so much better than mechanical mice?

11.4 A visual display has a resolution of 1600×1200 pixels. If the display is updated at 60 frames a second, what is the average rate at which a pixel must be read from memory?

11.5 Most displays are two-dimensional. How do you think three-dimensional displays can be constructed? Use the Internet to carry out your research.

11.6 How do dot printers (for example, the inkjet printer) increase the quality of an image without increasing the number of dots?

11.7 What is the difference between additive and subtractive color models?

11.8 Use the Internet or a current computer magazine to calculate the ratio of the cost of a 17-inch monitor to a basic color printer. What was the value of this ratio 12 months ago?

11.9 Why does an interlaced CRT monitor perform so badly when used as a computer monitor?

11.10 Describe, with the aid of diagrams, how an integrating analog-to-digital converter operates. Explain also why the accuracy of an integrating converter depends only on the reference voltage and the clock.

11.11 What is a tree network (when applied to DACs) and what is its advantage over other types of DAC (e.g. the R–2R ladder)?

11.12 A triangular-wave generator produces a signal with a peak-to-peak amplitude of 5 V and a period of 200 μs. This analog signal is applied to the input of a 14-bit A to D converter.

(a) What is the signal-to-noise ratio that can be achieved by the converter?
(b) What is the minimum input change that can be reliably resolved?

(c) For this signal explain how you would go about calculating the minimum rate at which it must be sampled.

11.13 What is a sample and hold circuit and how is it used in ADC systems?

11.14 One of the most important applications of microprocessors in everyday systems is the controller. Describe the structure of a three-term PID (proportional, integral, derivative) control system and explain how, for example, it can be used in tracking systems.

11.15 Find further examples of the use of digital signal processing.

11.16 What is the meaning of $x_0, x_1, x_2, x_3, x_4, \ldots, x_i, \ldots, x_n$ in the context of digital filter.

11.17 A digital filter is defined by the equation $y_n = 0.2 \cdot x_n + 0.1 \cdot x_{n-1} + 0.4 \cdot y_{n-1} + 0.3 \cdot y_{n-2}$ where y_n is the nth output and x_n is the nth input.

(a) What is the meaning of this equation in plain English?
(b) What is the difference between y_n and y_{n-1}?
(c) How is the above equation represented diagrammatically?
(d) Does the above equation represent a recursive filter?
(e) Describe the circuit elements in the diagram.
(f) If the input sequence $x_0, x_1, x_2, x_3, x_4, \ldots$ is 0.0, 0.1, 0.2, 0.3, 0.4, \ldots, what is the output sequence?
(g) What does this filter do?

11.18 A recursive digital filter is described by the expression

$$y_n = c_0 \cdot x_n + c_1 \cdot x_{n-1} + c_2 \cdot y_{n-1}$$

where the output of the filter is the sequence $y_0, y_1, y_2, \ldots, y_{n-1}, y_n$ and the input is the sequence $x_0, x_1, \ldots, x_{n-1}, x_n$. The terms c_0, c_1, and c_2 are filter coefficients with the values $c_0 = 0.4, c_1 = 0.1$, and $c_2 = 0.3$.

(a) What is the meaning of a recursive filter?
(b) Draw a block diagram of the structure of this filter (note that the delay element is represented by Z^{-1}).
(c) Draw a graph of the output sequence from this filter corresponding to the input sequence given by the step function 0, 0, 1, 1, 1, 1, \ldots 1.
(d) In plain English, what is the effect of this filter on the step input?

11.19 Why is speech not used more widely as a form of computer input?

11.20 Suppose that speech were used as a form of computer input. Do you think that all languages would have the same degree of accuracy (i.e. the number of errors in the input stream) or would some languages work better with speech recognition software than others?

Computer memory

CHAPTER MAP

10 Buses and input/output mechanisms

Chapter 10 deals with input/output techniques and shows how information is transferred between a computer and its peripherals. We look at internal buses that link devices within the computer and external buses that link remote devices such as printers with the computer.

11 Peripherals computer

The power of a computer is as much a function of its peripherals as of its data processing capabilities. Chapter 11 introduces some of the peripherals found in a typical PC such as the keyboard, display, printer, and mouse, as well as some of the more unusual peripherals that, for example, can measure how fast a body is rotating.

12 Computer memory

Having described the structure and operation of the CPU, we now look at how data is stored. Information isn't stored in a computer in just one type of storage device; it's stored in DRAM and on disk, CD-ROM, DVD, and tape. There is such a large range of storage devices and technologies because each storage mechanism is ideal for some tasks but not others. Here we look at both high-speed immediate access semiconductor technology and the much slower magnetic and optical secondary storage systems used to archive data.

13 The operating system

Chapter 13 provides a brief overview of the software that controls the computer's interface and the way in which it accesses memory—the operating system.

INTRODUCTION

Memory systems are divided into two classes: *immediate access memory* and *secondary storage*. We begin with the high-speed immediate access main store based on semiconductor technology and demonstrate how memory components are interfaced to the CPU. Then we look at magnetic and optical secondary stores that hold data not currently being processed by the CPU. Secondary stores have gigantic capacities but are much slower than immediate access stores.

Over the years, memory systems have been subject to three trends, a reduction in their cost, an increase in their capacity, and an increase in their speed. Figure 12.1 (from IBM) demonstrates just how remarkably memory costs have declined over a decade for both semiconductor and magnetic memory. Fifteen years has witnessed a reduction of costs by *three orders of magnitude*.

12.1 Memory hierarchy

Computer memory systems are not *homogeneous*. The various memory devices in a typical PC may use four or more different technologies, each with its own properties. For example, internal registers within the CPU itself are built with semiconductor technology and have access times of the order of one nanosecond, whereas the hard disks that holds programs and data use magnetic technology and are millions of times slower.

A computer may have registers, cache memory, flash memory, a floppy disk, a hard disk, a CD ROM, and a DVD. Some computers even have tape storage systems. If all these devices store data, why do we need so many of them? As in every aspect of life, economics plays a dominant role in memory systems design. The characteristics a computer designer would like to see in a memory device are often mutually exclusive. The ideal memory has the following characteristics.

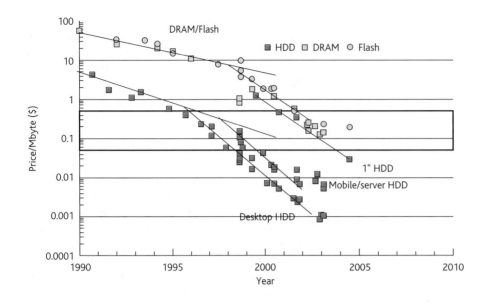

Figure 12.1 The downward trend in memory cost (from IBM).

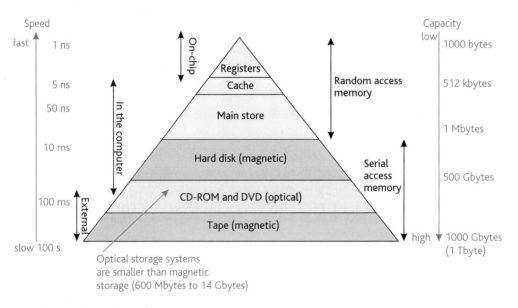

Figure 12.2 Memory hierarchy.

High speed A memory's access time should be very low, preferably 0.1 ns, or less.

Small size Memory should be physically small. Five hundred thousand megabytes (i.e. 500 Gbytes) per cubic centimeter would be nice.

Low power The entire memory system should run off a watch battery for 100 years.

Highly robust The memory should not be prone to errors; a logical one should never spontaneously turn into a logical zero or vice versa. It should also be able to work at temperatures of −60°C to 200°C in dusty environments and tolerate high levels of vibration—the military are very keen on this aspect of systems design.

Low cost Memory should cost nothing and, ideally, should be given away free with software (e.g. buy Windows 2015® and get the 500 Gbytes of RAM needed to run it free).

Figure 12.2 illustrates the memory hierarchy found in many computers. Memory devices at the top of the hierarchy are expensive and fast and have small capacities. Devices at the bottom of the hierarchy are cheap and store vast amounts of data, but are abysmally slow. This diagram isn't exact because, for example, the CD-ROM has a capacity of

600 Mbytes and (from the standpoint of capacity) should appear above hard disks in this figure.

Internal CPU memory lies at the tip of the memory hierarchy in Fig. 12.2. Registers have very low access times and are built with the same technology as the CPU. They are expensive in terms of the silicon resources they take up, limiting the number of internal registers and scratchpad memory within the CPU itself. The number of registers that can be included on a chip has increased dramatically in recent years.

Immediate access store holds programs and data during their execution and is relatively fast (10 ns to 50 ns). Main store is implemented as semiconductor static or dynamic memory. Up to the 1970s ferrite core stores and plated wire memories were found in main stores. Random access magnetic memory systems are now obsolete because they are slow, they are costly, they consume relatively high power, and they are physically bulky. Figure 12.2 shows the two types of random access memory, cache and main store.

The magnetic disk stores large quantities of data in a small space and has a very low cost per bit. Accessing data at a particular point on the surface is a serial process and a disk's access time, although fast in human terms, is orders of magnitude slower than immediate access store. A disk drive can store 400 Gbytes (i.e. $>2^{38}$ bytes) and has an access time of 5 ms. In the late 1990s an explosive growth in disk technology took place and low-cost hard disks became available with greater storage capacities than CD-ROMs and tape systems.

The CD-ROM was developed by the music industry to store sound on thin plastic disks called CDs (compact disks). CD-ROM technology uses a laser beam to read tiny dots embedded on a layer within the disk. Unlike hard disks, CD-ROMs use *interchangeable media*, are inexpensive, and store about 600 Mbytes, but have longer access times than conventional hard disks. The CD-ROM is used to distribute software and data. Writable CD drives and their media are more expensive and are used to back up data or to distribute data. The CD-ROM was developed into the higher capacity DVD in the 1990s.

Magnetic tape provides an exceedingly cheap serial access medium that can store 1000 Gbytes on a tape costing a few dollars. The average access time of tape drives is very long in comparison with other storage technologies and they are used only for archival purposes. Writable CDs and DVDs have now replaced tapes in many applications.

By combining all these types of memory in a single computer system, the computer engineer can get the best of all worlds. You can construct a low-cost memory system with a performance only a few percent lower than that of a memory constructed entirely from expensive high-speed RAM. The key to computer memory design is having the right data in the right place at the right time. A large computer system may have thousands of programs and millions of data files. Fortunately, the CPU requires few programs and files at any one time. By designing an operating system that moves data from disk into the main store so that the CPU always (or nearly always) finds the data it wants in the main store, the system has the speed of a giant high-speed store at a tiny fraction of the cost. Such an arrangement is called a *virtual memory* because the memory appears to the user as, say, a 400 Gbyte main store, when in reality there may be a real main memory of only 512 Mbytes and 400 Gbytes of disk storage. Figure 12.3 summarizes the various types of memory currently available.

Before we begin our discussion of storage devices proper, we define memory and introduce some of the terminology and underlying concepts associated with memory systems.

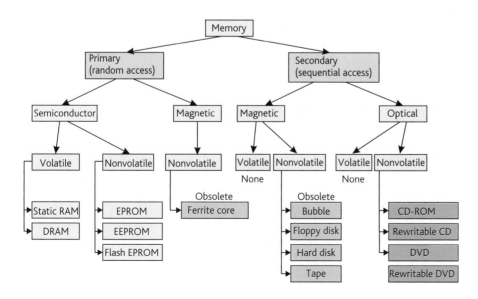

Figure 12.3 Classes of memory.

12.2 What is memory?

Everyone knows what memory is, but it's rather more difficult to say exactly what we mean by memory. We can define memory as the long- or short-term change in the physical properties of matter caused by an event. For example, ice forms on a pond during a spell of cold weather and remains for a short time after the weather gets warmer. The water has changed state from a liquid to a solid under the influence of a low temperature and now remembers that it has been cold, even though the temperature has risen above freezing point. To construct a computer memory, we have to choose a property of matter that can be modified (i.e. written) and later detected (i.e. read).

Without human memory we wouldn't be able to follow a movie, because anything that happened prior to the current point in time would have vanished. As we watch the movie, optical signals from the retina at the back of the eye cause changes within the brain—the event has passed but its effect remains. The movie itself is yet another memory device. The photons of light once generated by a scene alter the chemical structure of a thin coating of silver compounds on a film of plastic.

The von Neumann stored program computer is based on the sequential execution of instructions. Clearly, the program must be stored if the individual instructions are to be carried out one after the other. Furthermore, as computation yields temporary values, memory is needed to hold them. Such memory is called *immediate access memory* because it must be able to access its contents at the same rate the CPU executes instructions.

Programs not currently being executed have to be stored somewhere. Secondary storage devices hold vast amounts of information cheaply but cannot retrieve data at anything like the rate at which a computer executes instructions. Immediate access stores are approximately 1 000 000 times faster than secondary stores.

Because digital logic devices operate on binary signals, it's reasonable to expect computer memories to behave in a similar fashion. Memory systems store information in binary form by exploiting a two-valued property of the storage medium.

The most important requirements of a memory element are that it must be able to assume one of two stable states, and that an energy barrier must separate these states; that is, it must require energy to change the state of the memory. If there were no energy barrier separating the states, it would be possible for a stored binary value to change its state at the least provocation. In the case of a piece of string, it requires a considerable energy input either to tie a knot or to untie it.

12.3 Memory technology

Memory systems employ a wider range of technologies than any other component of a digital computer. Each technology has advantages and disadvantages; for example, cost, speed, density (bits/mm^3), power consumption, physical size, and reliability. We now provide a brief overview of some of these memory technologies.

12.3.1 Structure modification

We can store information by modifying the *structure, shape,* or *dimensions* of an object. Three decades ago this storage technology was found in punched cards and paper tape systems that use the *there/not-there* principle in which holes are made or not made in paper. The gramophone record is a structural memory that stores analog information by deforming the sides of a spiral groove cut into the surface of a plastic disk. At any instant the analog information is a function of the depth of the cut in the side of the groove. The CD-ROM and DVD are structural memories because information is stored as a string of dots on a sheet of plastic.

12.3.2 Delay lines

Superman used a neat trick to view the past—he just zoomed away from Earth at a speed faster than light and then viewed past events from their light, which had been streaming away from the Earth at a constant speed of 300 000 km/s. A stream of photons moving through space represents the memory of the event. We can call this spatial memory because data is stored as a wave traveling through a medium. Early computers converted data into ultrasonic sound pulses traveling down tubes filled with mercury. When the train of pulses representing the stored binary sequence travels from one end of the tube to the other end, it is detected, amplified, and then recirculated. This type of memory is also called a delay-line memory and is no longer found in digital computers.

12.3.3 Feedback

Data can be stored in an electronic device by means of *feedback* like the flip-flop, which is held in a stable logical state by feeding its output back to its input. Modern semiconductor devices based on feedback have a very low access time and are found in cache memory systems. Semiconductor memory based on feedback can be designed to consume very little power. Such memory is used in portable systems.

MEMORY TECHNOLOGY—SOME DEFINITIONS

Memory cell A memory cell is the smallest unit of information storage and holds a single 0 or 1. Memory cells are grouped together to form words. The location of each cell in the memory is specified by its *address*.

Capacity A memory's capacity is expressed as the quantity of data that it can hold. Sometimes the capacity of a memory device is quoted in bits and sometimes in bytes. We use the convention that $1K = 2^{10} = 1024$ and $1M = 2^{20} = 1\,048\,576$. Some manufacturers use the convention that $1K = 1000$ and $1M = 1\,000\,000$. Note that $1G$ (gigabyte) $= 2^{30}$ and $1T$ (terabyte) $= 2^{40}$.

Density The density of a memory system is a measure of how much data can be stored per unit area or per unit volume; that is density = capacity/size.

Access time A memory component's most important parameter is its *access time*, which is the time taken to read data from a given memory location, measured from the start of a read cycle. Access time is the time taken to locate the required memory cell within the memory array plus the time taken for the data to become available from the memory cell. We should refer to read cycle access time and write cycle access time because some devices have quite different read and write access times.

Random access When memory is organized so that the access time of any cell within it is constant and is independent of the actual location of the cell, the memory is said to be *random access memory* (RAM); that is, the access time doesn't depend where the data being accessed is located. This means that the CPU doesn't have to worry about the time taken to read a word from memory because all read cycles have the same duration. If a memory is random access for the purpose of read cycles, it is invariably random access for the purpose of write cycles. The term RAM is often employed to describe read/write memory where data may be read from the memory or written into it (as opposed to read-only memory). This usage is incorrect, because random access indicates only the property of constant access time. The dialed telephone system is a good example of random access system in everyday life. The time taken to access any subscriber is constant and independent of their physical location.

Serial access In a serial or *sequential* access memory, the time taken to access data is dependent on the physical location of the data within the memory and can vary over a wide range for any given system. Examples of serial access memories are magnetic tape transports, disk drives, CD drives, and shift registers. If data is written on a magnetic tape, the time taken to read the data is the time taken for the section of tape containing the data to move to the read head. This data might be 1" or 2400 ft from the beginning of the tape.

Bandwidth The *bandwidth* of a memory system indicates the speed at which data can be transferred between the memory and the host computer and is measured in bytes/second or bits/second. Bandwidth is determined by the access time of the memory, the type of data path between the memory and the CPU, and the interface between the memory and CPU.

Latency Bandwidth indicates how fast you can transfer data once you have the data to transfer. *Latency* refers to the delay between beginning a memory access and the start of the transfer.

Volatile memory Volatile memory loses its stored data when the source of power is removed. Most semiconductor memories are volatile, although devices such as EPROM and flash memory are non-volatile. Memories based on magnetism are non-volatile because their magnetic state doesn't depend on a continuous supply of power.

Read-only memory The contents of a read-only memory (ROM) can be read but not modified under normal operating conditions. Read-only memories are non-volatile and are used to hold system software. Flash memory is a form of *erasable* ROM that can be written to. This is also called *read-mostly memory* and is used in compact flash cards in digital cameras.

Static memory Once data has been written into a *static* memory cell, the data is stored until it is either altered by over-writing it with new data, or by removing the source of power if the memory is volatile.

Dynamic memory Dynamic memories (DRAMs) store data as an electronic charge on the inter-electrode capacitance of a field effect transistor. The charge gradually leaks away and the data is lost after a few milliseconds. Dynamic memories have to restore the charge on the capacitors every 2 to 16 ms in an operation known as memory *refreshing*. DRAMs are much cheaper than static memories of the same capacity.

12.3.4 Charge storage

Dynamic memory devices store data as an electrical charge. If a conductor is electrically insulated from its surroundings, it can be given an electrical charge. Binary information is stored by regarding one state as electrically charged and the other state as not charged. The insulation prevents the charge from rapidly draining away. Such a memory element is known as a *capacitor* and was used in one of the World's first computers. (In 1946, Dr F. C. Williams used a cathode ray tube to store a bit as a charge on the screen. Tom Kilburn worked with Williams at Manchester University to extend the CRT store to 2048 bits in 1947.) The most popular form of immediate memory found in today's PCs and workstations, DRAM, employs charge storage.

12.3.5 Magnetism

The most common low-cost, high-capacity storage mechanism uses magnetism. An atom consists of a nucleus around which electrons orbit. The electrons themselves have a spin that can take one of two values, called *up* and *down*. Electron spin generates a magnetic field and the atom can be in one of two possible magnetic states. Atoms themselves are continually vibrating due to thermal motion. In most substances, the spin axes of the electrons are randomly oriented, because of the stronger thermal vibrations of the atoms and there is no overall magnetic effect. A class of materials exhibit *ferromagnetism*, in which adjacent electrons align their spin axes in parallel. When all the atoms in the bulk material are oriented with their spins in the same direction, the material is magnetized. Because we can magnetize material with its electron spins in one of two states and then detect these states, magnetic materials are used to implement memory. Up to the 1960s, immediate access memories stored data in tiny ferromagnetic rings called ferrite cores (hence the term core stores). Ferrite core stores are virtually obsolete today and the most common magnetic storage device is the hard disk.

12.3.6 Optical

The oldest mechanism used to store data is *optical* technology. Printed text is an optical memory because ink modifies the optical (i.e. reflective) properties of the paper. The same mechanism stores digital information in barcodes. More recently, two technologies have been combined to create high-density optical storage devices.

The laser creates a tiny beam of light that illuminates a correspondingly tiny dot that has been produced by semiconductor fabrication techniques. These dots store information rather like the holes in punched cards and paper tape.

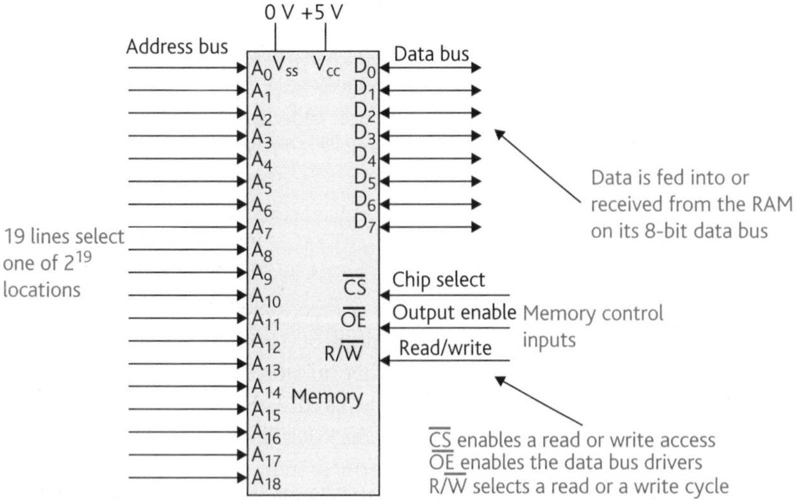

12.4 Semiconductor memory

Semiconductor random access memory is fabricated on silicon chips by the same process used to manufacture microprocessors. Without the availability of low-cost semiconductor memory, the microprocessor revolution would have been delayed had microprocessors used the slow, bulky, and expensive ferrite core memory of 1960s and 1970s mainframes. The principal features of semiconductor memory are its high density and ease of use.

12.4.1 Static semiconductor memory

Static semiconductor memory is created by fabricating an array of latches on a single silicon chip. It has a very low access time, but is about four times more expensive than dynamic memory because it requires four transistors per bit unlike the DRAM's cell, which uses one transistor. Static RAM is easy to use from the engineer's point of view and is found in small memories. Some memory systems use static memory devices because of their greater reliability than dynamic memory. Large memories are constructed with dynamic memory because of its lower cost.

Figure 12.4 illustrates a 4M CMOS semiconductor memory. The acronym CMOS means *complementary metal oxide semiconductor* and indicates the semiconductor technology used to manufacture the chip. The 4M denotes the memory's capacity in bits; that is, 2^{22} bits. Power is fed to the memory via its V_{ss} and V_{cc} pins.

The chip in Fig. 12.4 is interfaced to the computer via its 32 pins, of which 19 are the address inputs needed to select one of $2^{19} = 524\ 288$ (i.e. 512K) unique locations. Eight data lines transfer data from the memory during a read cycle and receive data from the processor during a write cycle. Electrical power is fed to the chip via two pins. The three control

Figure 12.4 The 512K × 8 static RAM.

MEMORY ORGANIZATION

Memory components are *organized* as *n* words by *m* bits (the total capacity is defined as *m* × *n* bits). Bit-organized memory components have a 1-bit width; for example, a bit-organized 256K chip is arranged as 256K locations each of one bit. Some devices are *nibble* organized; for example, a

256K chip can be arranged as 64K locations, each containing 4 bits. The device in Fig. 12.4 is *byte organized* as 512K words of 8 bits and is suited to small memories in microprocessor systems in which one or two chips may be sufficient for all the processor's read/write memory requirements.

---

pins, $\overline{CS}$, $\overline{OE}$, and R/$\overline{W}$ determine the operation of the memory component as follows.

Pin	Name	Function
$\overline{CS}$	Chip select	When low, $\overline{CS}$ selects the chip for a memory access
R/$\overline{W}$	Read/not write	When high R/$\overline{W}$ indicates a read cycle; when low it indicates a write cycle
$\overline{OE}$	Output enable	When low in a read cycle, $\overline{OE}$ allows data to be read from the chip and placed on the data bus

In order for the chip to take part in a read or write operation, its $\overline{CS}$ pin must be in a low state. Whenever $\overline{CS}$ is inactive-high, the memory component ignores all signals at its other pins. Disabling the memory by turning off its internal tri-state bus drivers permits several memories to share the same data bus as long as only one device is enabled at a time. The R/$\overline{W}$ input determines whether the chip is storing the data at its eight data pins (R/$\overline{W}$ = 0), or is transferring data to these pins (R/$\overline{W}$ = 1). The output enable pin, $\overline{OE}$, turns on the memory's tri-state bus drivers during a read cycle and off at all other times. Some chips combine $\overline{OE}$ with $\overline{CS}$ and R/$\overline{W}$ so that the output data buffers are automatically enabled when $\overline{CS}$ = 0 and R/$\overline{W}$ = 1.

Address decoding and read/write electronics is located on the chip, simplifying the design of modern memory systems. Figure 12.5 demonstrates how this device can be connected to a CPU. Because the chip is 8 bits wide (i.e. it provides 8 bits at a time), two chips would be connected in parallel in a system with a 16-bit data bus, and four chips in a system with a 32-bit data bus.

The CPU's data bus is connected to the memory's data pins and the CPU's address bus is connected to the memory's address pins. The memory's $\overline{CS}$, R/$\overline{W}$, and $\overline{OE}$ control inputs are connected to signals from the block labeled 'Control logic'. This block takes control signals from the CPU and generates the signals required to control a read or a write cycle.

Suppose the memory device is connected to a CPU with a 32-bit address bus that can access 2^{32} locations. This RAM has 19 address inputs and provides only a fraction of the address space that the CPU can access (i.e. 512 kbytes out of 4 Gbytes). Extra logic is required to map this block of RAM onto an appropriate part of the processor's address space. The high-order address lines from the CPU (in this case, A_{19} to A_{31}) are connected to a control logic block that uses these address lines to perform the mapping operation. Essentially, there are $4G/512K = 2^{32}/2^{19} = 2^{13}$ slots into which the RAM can be mapped. We'll explain how this is done later.

12.4.2 Accessing memory—timing diagrams

The computer designer is interested in the relationship between the memory and the CPU. In particular, the memory must provide data when the CPU wants it, and the CPU must provide data when the memory wants it. The engineer's most important design tool is the *timing diagram*. A timing diagram is a *cause-and-effect diagram* that illustrates the sequence of actions taking place during a read or write cycle. The designer is concerned with the relationship between information on the address and data buses, and the memory's control inputs. Figure 12.6 shows the simplified timing diagram of a static RAM memory chip during a read cycle.

The timing diagram illustrates the state of the signals involved in a memory access as a function of time. Each signal may be in a 0 or a 1 state and sloping edges indicate a change of signal level. The timing diagram of the address bus appears as two parallel lines crossing over at points A and B. The two parallel lines mean that some of the address lines may be high and some low; it's not the actual logical values of the address lines that interest us, but the time at which the contents of the address bus become stable for the duration of the current memory access cycle. We haven't drawn the R/$\overline{W}$ line because it must be in its electrically high state for the duration of the entire read cycle.

Let's walk through this diagram from left to right. At point A in Figure 12.6, the contents of the address bus have changed from their previous value and are now stable; that is, the old

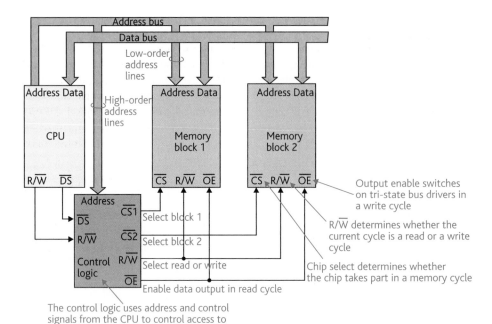

Figure 12.5 Interfacing memory components to a CPU.

Output enable switches on tri-state bus drivers in a write cycle

R/W determines whether the current cycle is a read or a write cycle

Chip select determines whether the chip takes part in a memory cycle

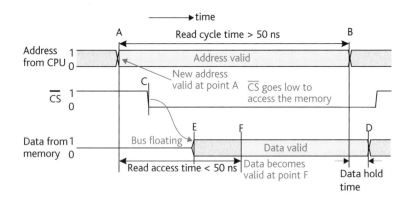

Figure 12.6 Timing diagram of the read cycle of a static RAM.

address from the CPU has been replaced by a new address. Because logic transitions from 0 to 1 or 1 to 0 are never instantaneous, changes of state are depicted by sloping lines. Some timing diagrams use the high-to-low transition of $\overline{CS}$ as the principal reference point.

Between points A and B the address bus contains the address of the memory location currently being read from. During this time the address from the CPU must not change. The time between A and B is the *minimum cycle time* of the memory. If the minimum cycle time is quoted as 50 ns, another memory access cannot begin until at least 50 ns after the start of the current cycle.

Consider the operation of the memory component in a read cycle. The CPU first puts out an address on its address bus. The higher-order address lines from the CPU cause

a chip-select output of the address decoder in the control logic to be asserted and to select a memory component as described in Fig. 12.5. At point C in Figure 12.6 the memory's active-low chip select input, $\overline{CS}$, goes low and turns on the three-state bus driver outputs connected to the data pins. Up to point E the contents of the data bus are represented by a single line mid-way between the two logic levels. This convention indicates that the data bus is floating and is disconnected from the data output circuits of the memory.

When a low level on $\overline{CS}$ turns on the memory's three-state output circuits at point E, the data bus stops floating and data appears at the output terminals. Sufficient time has not yet elapsed for the addressed memory word to be located and its contents retrieved. Consequently, the contents of the data bus between points E and F are not valid and cannot be used. At point F the data is valid and the time between points A and F is called the chip's *read access time*.

At the end of the read cycle at point B, the contents of the address bus change. Because of propagation delays in the chip, the data at its output pins does not change until a guaranteed minimum time has elapsed. This delay is called the *data hold time* and is the duration between points B and D.

The write cycle

A static RAM's write cycle is similar to its read cycle, except that R/W must be in a low state, and data placed on the chip's

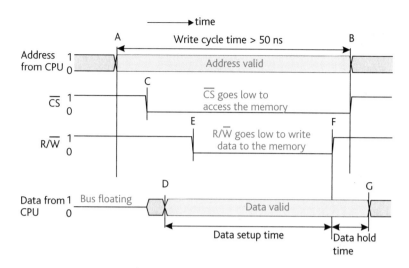

Figure 12.7 Timing diagram of the write cycle of a static RAM.

12.4.3 Dynamic memory

The immediate access store of the typical PC is fabricated with dynamic random access read/write memory (DRAM), which stores 1 bit of information in a single transistor memory cell. In 2000 a typical DRAM had a capacity of 64 Mbits organized as 16M × 4 bits and by 2004 128-Mbit chips were becoming standard.

Data in a dynamic memory cell is stored as an electrical charge on a terminal of a field-effect transistor. This charge generates an electrostatic field that modifies the flow of current between the transistor's other two terminals. A dynamic memory chip contains all the electronics needed to access a given cell, to write a one or a zero to it in a write cycle, and to read its contents in a read cycle.

Figure 12.8 illustrates the internal arrangement of a 16M × 4 dynamic memory chip (i.e. the chip has 16M locations each holding 4 bits). You might think that a 16M × 4-bit DRAM requires 24 address lines, because it takes 24 address lines to access 16M locations (i.e. $2^{24} = 16M$). In order to reduce the size of the DRAM's package, its address bus is *multiplexed*; that is, an address is input in two halves. One half of the address is called the *row* address and the other half is called the *column* address. A DRAM requires two control signals to handle the address: a *row address strobe* ($\overline{RAS}$), which captures the row address and a *column address strobe* ($\overline{CAS}$), which captures the column address.

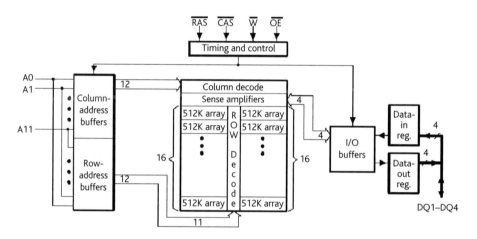

Figure 12.8 The internal organization of a 16M × 4 dynamic RAM.

data input lines by the CPU. Figure 12.7 shows the write-cycle timing diagram of a static RAM. We haven't provided $\overline{OE}$ timing (we'll assume that output enable is inactive-high throughout the write cycle).

During the write cycle described by Fig. 12.7, data from the CPU is presented to the memory at its data inputs, $R/\overline{W}$ is set low for a write access, and $\overline{CS}$ asserted. Data is latched into the memory cell by the rising edge of the $R/\overline{W}$ input. The critical timing parameters in a write cycle are the duration of the write pulse width (i.e. the minimum time for which $R/\overline{W}$ must be low) and the data setup time with respect to the rising edge of $R/\overline{W}$. *Data setup* time is the time for which data must be present at the input terminals of a memory before the data is latched into the memory.

Multiplexing the address bus increases the complexity of the interface between the DRAM and the CPU. As the 16M × 4 memory component contains only 4 bits in each of its 16M addressable locations, 16 of these chips are required to construct a 64-bit wide memory module.

The electrical charge on the transistor in a memory cell gradually leaks away and the cell loses its stored data. A typical dynamic memory cell is guaranteed to retain data for up to 16 ms after it has been written. In order to retain data for longer than 16 ms, data must be *rewritten* into every cell periodically in an operation called *refreshing*. In practice, simply accessing a memory cell refreshes it (and all cells in the same row). The need to refresh dynamic memories periodically increases the complexity of the CPU-DRAM interface.

The DRAM read cycle

We now describe the *generic* DRAM memory component. Although several variations on the standard DRAM have been introduced to improve access time, they all have the same basic memory cell—only the access mechanism and timing have changed. We provide a box at the end of this section that highlights some of the DRAM variations.

Figure 12.9 provides the simplified timing diagram of a DRAM read cycle with 2^{24} addressable locations. Note that there are two address traces. One trace describes the address from the CPU and the other the address at the DRAM's address inputs. A read cycle starts with the row address of the current memory location being applied to the address inputs of the DRAM. An address multiplexer in the memory control system transmits bits A_{00} to A_{11} from the CPU to address inputs A_0 to A_{11} at the DRAM. The chip's row address strobe ($\overline{RAS}$) is then asserted active-low to latch the row address into the chip (point A in Fig. 12.9).

The next step is to switch over the address from row to column (point B) and apply the column address to the chip. In this case, address lines A_{12} to A_{23} from the CPU are connected to address lines A_0 to A_{11} at the DRAM. The column address strobe ($\overline{CAS}$) is asserted at point C to capture the column address. At this point, the entire 24-bit address has been captured by the DRAM and the address bus plays no further role in the read cycle. The data in the cell accessed by the address appears on the data-output line after a delay of typically 30 to 70 ns from the point at which $\overline{RAS}$ went active low (point D). A read cycle ends when the first of either $\overline{RAS}$ or $\overline{CAS}$ returns inactive high.

Figure 12.9 shows the role of the CPU's R/$\overline{W}$ signal, which must go high before $\overline{CAS}$ is asserted and remain high for the rest of the cycle. Note that many DRAM designers write $\overline{W}$ rather than R/$\overline{W}$.

The dynamic RAM's cycle time is longer than its access time because internal operations take place within the DRAM before another access can begin. A DRAM might have an access time of 30 ns and a cycle time of 60 ns. Cycle time is important because it places a limitation on the speed of the system.

Figure 12.10 indicates the organization of dynamic memory control logic. The DRAM control must carry out the address multiplexing and generate the necessary $\overline{RAS}$ and $\overline{CAS}$ signals. You can obtain much of the logic

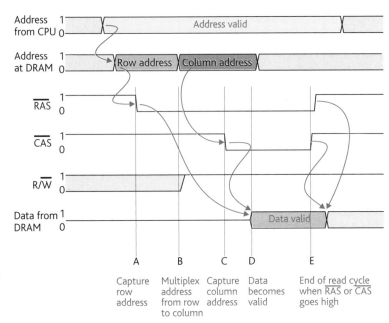

Figure 12.9 Timing diagram of the read cycle of a dynamic RAM.

needed to implement a dynamic memory controller on a single chip.

The DRAM write cycle

A DRAM write cycle, described in Fig. 12.11, is similar to a read cycle except that the DRAM's R/$\overline{W}$ input must go low before $\overline{CAS}$ goes low, and the data to be stored in the addressed cell must be applied to the data-in line.

The timing of the DRAM's address and the $\overline{RAS}$ and $\overline{CAS}$ signals are the same in both read and write cycles. However, in a write cycle the data from the CPU must be available and the R/$\overline{W}$ control signal must be low before the DRAM's $\overline{CAS}$ input is asserted (some DRAMs support other write modes).

Refreshing DRAM

A DRAM memory cell must be periodically rewritten if its data is not to be lost. DRAMs are designed so that you don't have to refresh cells individually. Accessing a row simultaneously refreshes all cells in that row. A typical refresh controller performs all row refresh cycles every 16 ms.

All that needs be done to refresh a DRAM is to assert $\overline{CAS}$ while $\overline{RAS}$ is high. This mode is called $\overline{CAS}$-before-$\overline{RAS}$ refresh to distinguish it from a normal read or write access when $\overline{CAS}$ goes low after $\overline{RAS}$. The DRAM automatically generates row refresh addresses internally. The DRAM refresh logic stops the processor and carries out a burst of refresh cycles at a time.

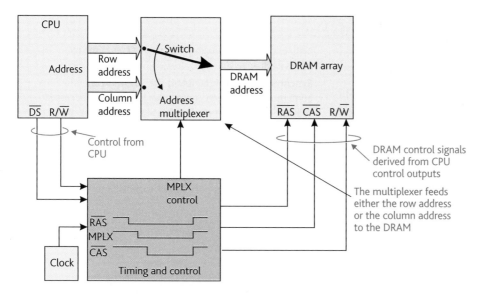

Figure 12.10 Controlling the dynamic memory.

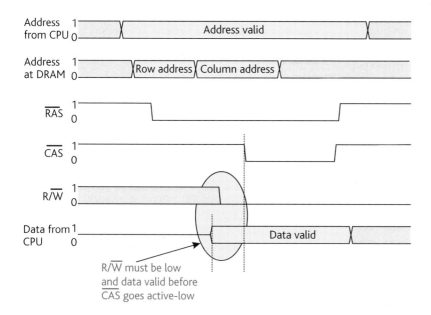

Figure 12.11 The write-cycle timing diagram of a dynamic RAM.

DRAM reliability

Dynamic memory suffers from two peculiar weaknesses. When a memory cell is accessed and the inter-electrode capacitor charged the dynamic memory draws a very heavy current from the power supply causing a voltage drop along the power supply lines. This voltage drop can be reduced by careful layout of the circuit of the memory system. Another weakness of the dynamic memory is its sensitivity to *alpha particles*. Semiconductor chips are encapsulated in plastic or ceramic materials that contain tiny amounts of radioactive material. One of the products of radioactive decay is the alpha particle (helium nucleus), which is highly ionizing and corrupts data in cells through which it passes.

DRAM ORGANIZATION

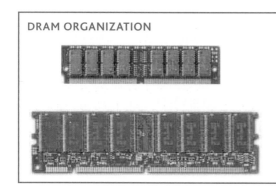

DRAM chips are fabricated by the same technology as CPUs and encapsulated in a ceramic or plastic material. These small packages and then soldered onto printed circuit boards that can be plugged into PCs.

PCs once used SIMMs (single in-line memory modules) with 72 pins that supported 32-bit data buses. Today, the SIMM has been replaced by the 168-pin dual in-line (DIMM) module that supports modern 64-bit data buses. DIMMs are available as 1 Gbyte modules.

DRAM FAMILIES

Over the years, the access time of DRAMs has declined, but their performance has improved less than that of the CPU. Manufacturers have attempted to hide the DRAM's relatively poor access time by introducing enhanced DRAM devices.

Fast page mode DRAM (FPD) This variation lets you provide a row address and then access several data elements in the same row just by changing the column address. Access time is reduced for sequential addresses.

Extended data out DRAM (EDO) An EDO provides a small improvement by starting the next memory access early and thereby reducing the overall access time by about 15%.

Synchronous DRAM (SDRAM) The SDRAM is operated in a burst mode and several consecutive locations are accessed sequentially; for example 5-1-1-1 SDRAM provides the first data element in five clock cycles but the next three elements are provided one clock cycle after each other.

Double data rate synchronous DRAM (DDR DRAM) This is a version of SDRAM where the data is clocked out on both the rising and falling edges of its clock to provide twice the data transfer rate.

LIMITS TO MEMORY DENSITY

Since their introduction in the 1960s, the density of semiconductor memories has steadily grown. Semiconductor memories have grown from a capacity of 16 bytes to 256 Mbytes, a growth of 2^{24} in three decades. Unfortunately, such progress can't continue because there are limits to memory density. Consider the following factors.

Feature size Semiconductor devices are manufactured by a process that involves a step called *photolithography*. Silicon is coated with a photosensitive material and an image projected onto the surface. This image is developed and used to create the transistors that make up the memory. If you can create a smaller image, you can make smaller transistors and therefore build memories with more cells on a silicon chip. The smallest feature that can be etched on the silicon is, of course, governed by the smallest line that can be projected. The minimum width of a line projected onto the silicon is determined by the wavelength of the light used by the projector, because a beam of light spreads out due to an effect called *diffraction*. Even blue light with its short wavelength cannot generate features small enough for modern chips. Today, electron beams are used to draw features on the silicon.

Quantum mechanical effects One of the consequences of quantum mechanics is that an object can spontaneously penetrate a barrier without having the energy to go through it. The probability of penetrating a barrier depends on the barrier's width and the size of the object—the thinner the barrier the more likely the penetration. If the insulators that separate one transistor from another in a memory become too thin, electrons will be able to tunnel spontaneously through the insulators.

Statistical nature of a current An electrical current is composed of a flow of electrons. In normal systems the number of electrons flowing in a circuit is staggeringly large. If memories are made smaller and smaller, the number of electrons flowing will diminish. At some point, the random nature of a current flow will have to be taken into account.

Energy It requires a finite amount of energy to change a memory cell from one state to another. However, the minimum amount of energy that can be used in switching is limited by quantum mechanics (i.e. there is a fixed minimum level of energy that can be used to perform switching).

Power It requires energy to operate a microcircuit. Energy consumption has two problems: *source* (important if the equipment is battery operated) and dissipation. Getting rid of heat is one of the factors limiting the complexity of silicon-based circuits.

When an alpha particle passes through a DRAM cell, a *soft* error occurs. An error is called soft if it is not repeatable (i.e. the cell fails on one occasion but has not been permanently damaged). The quantity of alpha particles can be reduced by careful quality control in selecting the encapsulating material, but never reduced to zero. By the way, all semiconductor memory is prone to alpha-particle errors—it's just that DRAM cells have a low stored energy/bit and are more prone to these errors than other devices.

A random soft error that corrupts a bit once a year in a PC is an irritation. In professional and safety-critical systems the consequences of such errors might be more severe. The practical solution to this problem lies in the type of *error-correcting codes* we met in Chapter 3. For example, five check bits can be appended to a 16-bit data word to create a 21-bit code word. If one of the bits in the code word read back from the DRAM is in error, you can calculate which bit it was and correct the error.

12.4.4 Read-only semiconductor memory devices

As much as any other component, the ROM (read-only memory) was responsible for the growth of low-cost PCs in the 1980s when secondary storage mechanisms such as disk drives were still very expensive. In those days a typical operating system and BASIC interpreter could fit into an 8- to 64-kbyte ROM. Although PCs now have hard disks, ROMs are still found in diskless palm-top computers and personal organizers. All computers require read-only memory to store the so-called *bootstrap program* that loads the operating system from disk when the computer is switched on (called the BIOS (basic input/output system)).

ROMs are used in dedicated microprocessor-based controllers. When a microcomputer is assigned to a specific task, such as the ignition control system in an automobile, the software is fixed for the lifetime of the device. A ROM provides the most cost-effective way of storing this type of software.

Semiconductor technology is well suited to the production of high-density, low-cost, read-only memories. We now describe the characteristics of some of the read-only memories in common use: mask-programmed ROM, PROM, EPROM, flash EPROM, and EEPROM.

Mask-programmed ROM

Mask-programmed ROM is so called because its contents (i.e. data) are permanently written during the manufacturing process. A mask (i.e. stencil) projects the pattern of connections required to define the data contents when the ROM is fabricated. A mask-programmed ROM cannot be altered because the data is built into its physical structure. It is the cheapest type of read-only semiconductor memory when manufactured in bulk. These devices are used only when large numbers of ROMs are required because the cost of setting up the mask is high. The other read-only memories we describe next are all user programmable and some are *reprogrammable*.

PROM

A PROM (*programmable read-only memory*) can be programmed once by the user in a special machine. A transistor is a switch that can pass or block the passage of the current through it. Each memory cell in a PROM contains a transistor that can be turned on or off to store a 1 or a 0. The transistor's state (on or off) is determined by the condition of a tiny metallic link that connects one of the transistor's inputs to a fixed voltage. When you buy a PROM, it is filled with all 1s because each link forces

the corresponding transistor into a 1 state. A PROM is programmed by passing a current pulse to melt it and change the state of the transistor from a 1 to a 0. For obvious reasons, these links are often referred to as *fuses*. A PROM cannot be reprogrammed because if you fuse a link it stays that way. The PROM has a low access time (5 to 50 ns) and is largely used as a logic element rather than as a means of storing programs.

EPROM

The EPROM is an *erasable programmable read-only memory* that is programmed in a special machine. Essentially, an EPROM is a dynamic memory with a refresh period of tens of years. Data is stored in an EPROM memory cell as an electrostatic charge on a highly insulated conductor. The charge can remain for periods in excess of 10 years without leaking away.

We don't cover semiconductor technology, but it's worth looking at how EPROMs operate. All we need state is that semiconductors are constructed from pure silicon and that the addition of tiny amounts of impurities (called *dopants*) changes the electrical characteristics of silicon. Silicon doped with an impurity is called *n*-type or *p*-type silicon depending on how the impurity affects the electrical properties of the silicon.

Figure 12.12 illustrates an EPROM memory cell consisting of a single NMOS field effect transistor. A current flows in the N+ channel between the transistor's positive and negative terminals, V_{dd} and V_{ss}. By applying a negative charge to a gate electrode, the negatively charged electrons flowing through the channel are repelled and the current turned off. The transistor has two states: a state with no charge on the gate and a current flowing through the channel, and a state with a charge on the gate that cuts off the current in the channel.

A special feature of the EPROM is the floating gate that is insulated from any conductor by means of a thin layer of silicon dioxide—an almost perfect insulator. By placing or not placing a charge on the floating gate, the transistor can by turned on or off to store a one or a zero in the memory cell.

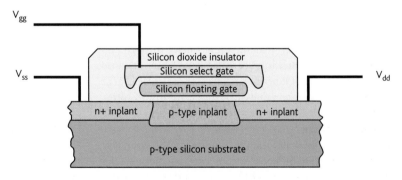

Figure 12.12 The structure of an EPROM memory cell.

If the floating gate is entirely insulated, how do we put a charge on it in order to program the EPROM? The solution is to place a second gate close to the floating gate but insulated from it. By applying typically 12 to 25 V to this second gate, some electrons cross the insulator and travel to the floating gate (in the same way that lightning crosses the normally non-conducting atmosphere).

You can program an EPROM, erase it, and reprogram it many times. Illuminating the silicon chip with ultra-violet light erases the data stored in it. Photons of ultra-violet light hit the floating gate and cause the stored charge to drain away through the insulator. The silicon chip is located under a quartz window that is transparent to ultra-violet light.

EPROMs are suitable for small-scale projects and for development work in laboratories because they can be programmed, erased, and reprogrammed by the user. The disadvantage of EPROMs is that they have to be removed from a computer, placed under a ultra-violet light to erase them, and then placed in a special-purpose programmer to reprogram them. Finally, they have to be re-inserted in the computer. EPROMs have largely been replaced by flash EPROMs.

Flash EPROM

The most popular read-only memory is the *flash EPROM*, which can be erased and reprogrammed electronically. Until recently, typical applications of the flash EPROM were the personal organizers and system software in personal computers (e.g. the BIOS in PCs). Today, the flash EPROM is used to store images in digital cameras and audio in MP3 players. When flash memories first appeared, typical capacities were 8 Mbytes. By 2005 you could buy 12-Gbyte flash memories.

The structure of an EPROM memory cell and a flash EPROM cell are very similar. The difference lies in the thickness of the insulating layer (silicon oxynitride) between the floating gate and the surface of the transistor. The insulating layer of a conventional EPROM is about 300 Å thick, whereas a flash EPROM's insulating layer is only 100 Å thick. Note that $1 \text{ Å} = 1 \times 10^{-10}$ m (or 0.1 nanometers).

When an EPROM is programmed, the charge is transferred to the floating gate by the *avalanche effect*. The voltage difference between the gate and the surface of the transistor causes electrons to burst through the oxynitride insulating layer in the same way that lightning bursts through the atmosphere. These electrons are called *hot electrons* because of their high levels of kinetic energy (i.e. speed). The charge on the floating gate is removed during exposure to ultra-violet light which gives the electrons enough energy to cross the insulating layer.

A flash EPROM is programmed in exactly the same way as an EPROM (i.e. by hot electrons crashing through the insulator). However, the insulating layer in a flash EPROM is so thin that a new mechanism is used to transport electrons across it when the chip is erased. This mechanism is known as

Fowler–Nordheim tunnelling and is a quantum mechanical effect. When a voltage in the range 12 to 20 V is applied across the insulating layer, electrons on the floating gate are able to tunnel through the layer, even though they don't have enough energy to cross the barrier.

A flash EPROM is divided into sectors with a capacity of typically 1024 bytes. Some devices let you erase a sector or the whole memory and others permit only a full chip erase. Flash EPROMs can't be programmed, erased, and reprogrammed without limit. Repeated write and erase cycles eventually damage the thin insulating layer. Some first-generation flash EEPROMs are guaranteed to perform only 100 erase/write cycles, although devices are now available with lifetimes of at least 10 000 cycles.

EEPROM

The *electrically erasable and reprogrammable ROM* (EEPROM or E²PROM) is similar to the flash EPROM and can be programmed and erased electrically. The difference between the EEPROM and the flash EPROM is that the flash EPROM uses Fowler–Nordheim tunneling to erase data and hot electron injection to write data, whereas pure EEPROMs use the tunneling mechanism to both write and erase data. Table 12.1 illustrates the difference between the EPROM, flash EPROM, and EEPROM.

EEPROMs are more expensive than flash EPROMs and generally have smaller capacities. The size of the largest state-of-the-art flash memory is usually four times that of the corresponding EEPROM. Modern EEPROMs operate from single 5 V supplies and are rather more versatile than flash EPROMs. Like the flash memory, they are read-mostly devices, with a lifetime of 10 000 erase/write cycles. EEPROMs have access times as low as 35 ns but still have long write cycle times (e.g. 5 ms).

The differences between a read/write RAM and an EEPROM are subtle. The EEPROM is non-volatile, unlike the typical semiconductor RAM. Second, the EEPROM takes much longer to write data than to read it. Third, the EEPROM can be written to only a finite number of times. Successive erase and write operations put a strain on its internal structure and eventually destroy it. Finally, EEPROM is much more expensive than semiconductor RAM. The EEPROM is found in special applications where data must be retained when the power is off. A typical application is in a radio receiver that can store a number of different frequencies and recall them when the power is re-applied.

12.5 Interfacing memory to a CPU

We now look at how the semiconductor memory components are interfaced to the microprocessor. Readers who are not interested in microprocessor systems design may skip this section.

Device	EPROM	Flash EPROM	EEPROM
Normalized cell size	1.0	1.0 to 1.2	3.0
Programming mechanism	Hot electron injection	Hot electron injection	Tunneling
Erase mechanism	Ultra-violet light	Tunneling	Tunneling
Erase time	20 minutes	1 s	5 ms
Minimum erase	Entire chip	Entire chip (or sector)	Byte
Write time (per cell)	$<100\,\mu s$	$<100\,\mu s$	5 ms
Read access time	200 ns	200 ns	35 ns

Table 12.1 Programmable EPROM differences.

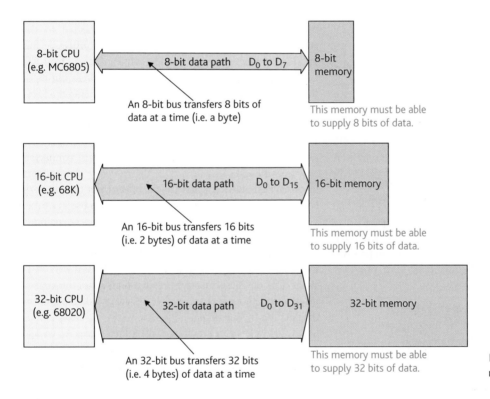

Figure 12.13 CPU, bus, and memory organization.

12.5.1 Memory organization

A microprocessor operates on a word of width w bits and communicates with memory over a bus of width b bits. Memory components of width m bits are connected to the microprocessor via this bus. In the best of all possible worlds, the values of w, b, and m are all the same. This was often true of 8-bit microprocessors, but is rarely true of today's high-performance processors. Consider the 68K microprocessor, which has an internal 32-bit architecture and a 16-bit data bus interface. When you read a 32-bit value in memory, the processor automatically performs two 16-bit read cycles. The programmer doesn't have to worry about this, because

the memory accesses are carried out automatically. Memory components are normally 1, 4, or 8 bits wide. If you use 4-bit-wide memory devices in a 68K system, you have to arrange them in groups of four because a memory block must provide the bus with 16 bits of data. Figure 12.13 shows the organization of 8-bit, 16-bit, and 32-bit systems.

A memory system must be as wide as the data bus. That is, the memory system must be able to provide an 8-bit bus with 8 bits of data, a 16-bit bus with 16 bits of data, and a 32-bit bus with 32 bits of data, etc. Consider the following examples.

Example 1 An 8-bit computer with an 8-bit bus uses memory components that are 4 bits wide. Two of these

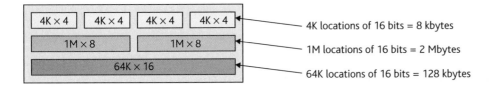

4K locations of 16 bits = 8 kbytes

1M locations of 16 bits = 2 Mbytes

64K locations of 16 bits = 128 kbytes

Figure 12.14 16-bit memory organization.

devices are required to supply 8 bits of data; each chip supplies 4 bits.

Example 2 The amount of data in a block of memory, in bytes, is equal to the width of the data bus (in bytes) multiplied by the number of locations in the block of memory. A 16-bit computer with a 16-bit bus uses memory components that are 1 bit wide. Sixteen of these devices are required to supply 16 bits of data at a time.

Example 3 An 8-bit computer uses memory components organized as 64K × 4 bits; that is, there are 64K = 2^{16} different addressable locations in the chip. Two of these chips are required to provide the CPU with 8 data bits. The total size of the memory is 64 kbytes.

Example 4 A 16-bit computer uses memory components that are 64K × 4 bits. Four of these chips must be used to provide the CPU with 16 bits of data. Therefore, each of the 64K locations provide 16 bits of data or 2 bytes (i.e. each of the 4 chips provides 4 of the 16 bits). The total size of the memory is 2 bytes × 64K = 128 kbytes.

Example 5 A 16-bit computer uses 64K × 16-bit memory components, Only one of these chips is required to provide 16 bits of data (2 bytes). Therefore, each chip provides 2 × 64K = 128 kbytes.

Figure 12.14 demonstrates memory organization by showing how three 16-bit-wide blocks of memory can be constructed from 4-bit-wide, 8-bit-wide, and 16-bit-wide memory components.

12.5.2 Address decoders

If the memory in a microprocessor system were constructed from memory components with the same number of uniquely addressable locations as the processor, the problem of address decoding would not exist. For example, an 8-bit CPU with address lines, A_{00} to A_{31}, would simply be connected to the corresponding address input lines of the memory component. Microprocessor systems often have memory components that are smaller than the addressable memory space. Moreover, there are different types of memory: read/write memory, read-only memory, and memory-mapped peripherals. We now look at some of the ways in which memory components are interfaced to a microprocessor.

In order to simplify the design of address decoders we will assume an 8-bit microcontroller with a 16-bit address bus

spanned by address lines A_0 to A_{15}. We are not going to use the 68K because it has a 23-bit address bus, a 16-bit data bus, and special byte selection logic. These features of the 68K make it more powerful than earlier 8-bit processors, but they do get in the way of illustrating the basic principles. We provide several 68K-based examples later in this chapter.

Consider the situation illustrated by Fig. 12.15, in which two 1K × 8 memory components are connected to the address bus of an 8-bit microprocessor. This processor has 16 address lines, A_0 to A_{15}. Ten address lines, A_0 to A_9, from the CPU are connected to the corresponding address inputs of the two memory components, M1 and M2. Whenever a location (one of 2^{10} = 1K) is addressed in M1, the corresponding location is addressed in M2. The data outputs of M1 and M2 are connected to the system data bus. Because the data outputs of both memory devices M1 and M2 are connected together, the data bus drivers in the memory components must have tri-state outputs. That is, only one of the memory components may put data onto the system data bus at a time.

Both memory devices in Fig. 12.15 have a chip-select input ($\overline{\text{CS1}}$ for block 1 and $\overline{\text{CS2}}$ for block 2). Whenever the chip-select input of a memory is active-low, that device takes part in a memory access and puts data on the data bus if $R/\overline{W} = 1$. When $\overline{\text{CS1}}$ or $\overline{\text{CS2}}$ is inactive (i.e. in a high state) the appropriate data bus drivers are turned off, and no data is put on the data bus by that chip.

Let $\overline{\text{CS1}}$ be made a function of the address lines A_{10} to A_{15}, so that $\overline{\text{CS1}} = f1(A_{15}, A_{14}, A_{13}, A_{12}, A_{11}, A_{10})$. Similarly, let $\overline{\text{CS2}}$ be a function of the same address lines, so that $\overline{\text{CS2}} = f2(A_{15}, A_{14}, A_{13}, A_{12}, A_{11}, A_{10})$. Suppose we choose functions $f1$ and $f2$ subject to the constraint that there are no values of $A_{15}, A_{14}, A_{13}, A_{12}, A_{11}, A_{10}$ that cause both $\overline{\text{CS1}}$ and $\overline{\text{CS2}}$ to be low simultaneously. Under these circumstances, the conflict between M1 and M2 is resolved, and the memory map of the system now contains two disjoint 1K blocks of memory. There are several different strategies for decoding A_{10} to A_{16} (i.e. choosing functions $f1$ and $f2$). These strategies may be divided into three groups: partial address decoding, full address decoding, and block address decoding.

Partial address decoding

Figure 12.16 demonstrates how two 1 kbyte blocks of memory are connected to the address bus in such a way that both blocks of memory are never accessed simultaneously. The conflict between M1 and M2 is resolved by connecting $\overline{\text{CS1}}$

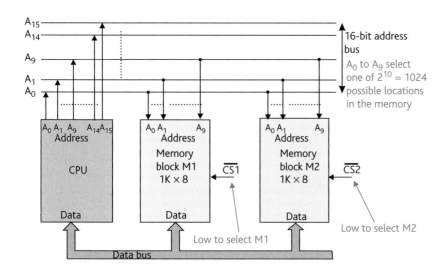

Figure 12.15 Connecting two 1 kbyte memories to a 16-bit address bus.

EXAMPLE 1

An 8-bit microprocessor with a 16-bit address bus accesses addresses in the range $101xxxxxxxxxxxxx_2$ *(where bits* A_{15}, A_{14}, A_{13} *marked 101 are selected by the address decoder and the xs refer to locations within the memory block).*

What range of addresses does this block correspond to?

How big is this block?

The lowest address is 1010000000000000_2 and the highest address is 1011111111111111_2. This corresponds to the range $A000_{16}$ to $BFFF_{16}$.

Three address lines are decoded to divide the address space spanned by A_0 to A_{15} into eight blocks. The size of one block is $64K/8 = 8K$. You could also calculate the size of the block because you know it is spanned by 13 address lines and $2^{13} = 8K$.

EXAMPLE 2

An 8-bit microprocessor with a 16-bit address bus addresses a block of 32 kbytes of ROM.

(a) *How many memory components are required if the memory is composed of 8 kbyte chips?*

(b) *What address lines from the processor select a location in the 32 kbyte ROM?*

(c) *What address lines have to be decoded to select the ROM?*

(d) *What is the range of memory locations provided by each of the chips (assuming that the memory blocks are mapped contiguously in the region of memory space starting at address* 0000_{16})?

(a) The number of chips required is (memory block)/(chip size) = $32K/8K = 4$.

(b) Each chip has $8K = 2^{13}$ locations, which are accessed by the 13 address lines A_0 to A_{12} from the processor.

(c) Address lines A_0 to A_{12} from the CPU select a location in the chip leaving A_{13} to A_{15} to be decoded.

(d) The memory blocks are
0000_{16} to $1FFF_{16}$
2000_{16} to $3FFF_{16}$
4000_{16} to $5FFF_{16}$
6000_{16} to $7FFF_{16}$.

---

directly to A_{15} of the system address bus and by connecting $\overline{CS2}$ to A_{15} via an inverter. M1 is selected whenever $A_{15} = 0$, and M2 is selected whenever $A_{15} = 1$. Although we have distinguished between M1 and M2 for the cost of a single inverter, a heavy price has been paid. Because $A_{15} = 0$ selects M1 and A15 = 1 selects M2, it follows that either M1 or M2 will *always* be selected. Although the system address bus can specify $2^{16} = 64K$ unique addresses, only 2K different

locations can be accessed. Address lines A_{10} to A_{14} take no part in the address-decoding process and consequently have no effect on the selection of a location within either M1 or M2.

Figure 12.17 gives the memory map of the system corresponding to Fig. 12.16. Memory block M1 is repeated 32 times in the lower half of the memory space and M2 is repeated 32 times in the upper half of the memory space

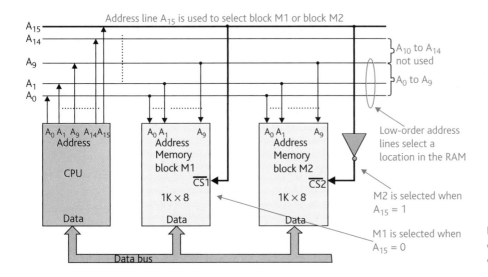

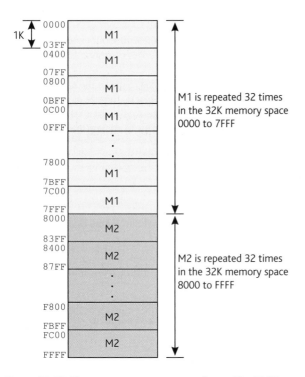

Figure 12.16 Resolving contention by partial address decoding.

Figure 12.17 The memory map corresponding to Fig. 12.16.

accessed by a single address on the system's address bus; that is, all the microprocessor's address lines are used to access each physical memory location, either by specifying a given memory device or by specifying an address within it. Full address decoding represents the ideal but is sometimes impractical because it may require an excessive quantity of hardware to implement it. We will design an address decoder for the pervious example of a system with two 1K blocks of memory. Address lines A_0 to A_9 select a location in one of the memory components, leaving A_{10} to A_{15} to be decoded. Suppose we select M1 when $A_{15}, A_{14}, A_{13}, A_{12}, A_{11}, A_{10} = 0, 0, 0, 0, 0, 0$ and M2 when $A_{15}, A_{14}, A_{13}, A_{12}, A_{11}, A_{10} = 0, 0, 0, 0, 0, 1$. These address values correspond to the 1K address blocks 0000 to 03FF and 0400 to 07FF. Figure 12.18 demonstrates how we might perform the address decoding with random logic.

Block address decoding

Block address decoding is a compromise between partial address decoding and full address decoding. It avoids the inefficient memory usage of partial address decoding, by dividing the memory space into blocks or pages. Block address decoding is implemented by dividing the processor's address space into a number of equal-sized blocks. This operation is easy to perform because you can use commonly available logic devices to carry out this function.

In a typical application of block address decoding, an 8-bit microprocessor's 64K memory space is divided into four blocks of 16K. A 2-line to 4-line decoder logic element converts the two high-order address lines, A_{15} and A_{14}, into four lines. Each of these four lines is associated with one of the binary states of address lines A_{15} and A_{14}. The four outputs of this address decoder are used as the chip-select inputs of memory components. The advantage of block address decoding is that no memory component can occupy a memory space larger than a single block. In practice, real

because the five address lines A_{10} to A_{14} take no part in address decoding. In this section, all addresses will be given in hexadecimal form (we don't need to use a subscript).

The penalty paid when a partial address-decoding scheme is employed is that it prevents full use of the microprocessor's address space and frequently makes it difficult to expand the memory system at a later date.

Full address decoding

A microprocessor system has *full address decoding* when each addressable location within a memory component is

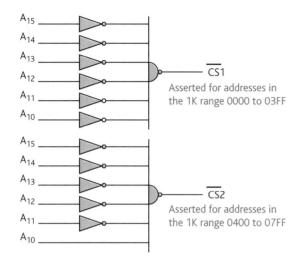

Figure 12.18 A full address decoder for two 1K memory blocks of Fig. 12.16.

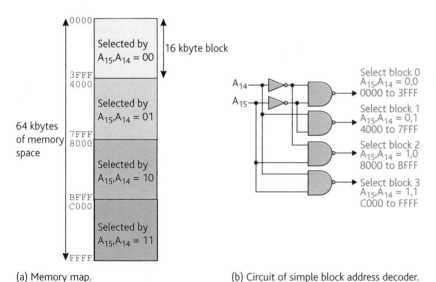

(a) Memory map.   (b) Circuit of simple block address decoder.

Figure 12.19 Dividing 64K memory space into 4 blocks.

microprocessor systems often employ a combination of partial address decoding, full address decoding, and block address decoding. You can further decode these 16K blocks and divide the memory space between several peripheral devices. Figure 12.19 describes how this arrangement might be implemented.

Decoding using *m*-line to *n*-line decoders

The problems of address decoding can be greatly diminished by means of data decoders that decode an *m*-bit binary input into one of *n* outputs, where $n = 2^m$. Table 12.2 gives the truth table of the 74138, a typical 3-line to 8-line decoder. This decoder has active-low outputs, making it especially

suitable for address-decoding applications, because the majority of memory components have active-low chip-select inputs. Because the 74138 has three enable inputs (two active-low and one active-high) it is particularly useful when decoders are to be connected in series, or when the enable inputs are to be connected to address lines in order to reduce the size of the block of memory being decoded.

Consider an example of address decoding in an 8-bit microprocessor system using the 74138 3-line to 8-line decoder. A microprocessor system is to be designed with 16 kbytes of ROM in the range 0000 to 3FFF using 4-kbyte EPROMs and 8 kbytes of read/write memory in the range 4000 to 5FFF using a single 8-kbyte chip. Provision must be made for at least eight memory-mapped peripherals in the 256 byte range 6000 to 60FF.

The first step is to work out what address lines have to be decoded to select each memory block. We can do this in two ways. First, if we know the size of the block we can calculate how many address lines are required to select it out of all possible blocks of the same size. Consider the 8K RAM block. The memory space is 64K, so there are 64K/8K = 8 blocks. Because $8 = 2^3$, the three high-order address lines have to be decoded. Alternatively, we can write down the first and last addresses in the block and note which address values are common to all locations; that is,

$$4000 = 0\,1\,0\,0\,0\,0\,0\,0\,0\,0\,0\,0\,0\,0\,0\,0$$
$$5FFF = 0\,1\,0\,1\,1\,1\,1\,1\,1\,1\,1\,1\,1\,1\,1\,1$$

As you can see, only the three high-order address lines are common to every location within this memory block.

Table 12.3 gives the address table for this system and shows how one 74LS138 divides the memory space into eight 4K blocks. A second decoder subdivides one of these blocks to provide memory space for the peripherals. Figure 12.20 gives a circuit diagram of the address decoder and Figure 12.21 illustrates its memory map. It is easy to see the advantages of block address decoding. First, RAM, ROM, or peripheral devices can be added without further alterations to the address-decoding circuitry by employing the unused outputs of the three decoders. Second, the system is flexible. By modifying the connections between the decoder circuits and the memory components they select, the effective address of those memory components may be altered.

Note how we've selected the 8K block of RAM in Fig. 12.20. Because the RAM is selected if either of the two 4K blocks selected by $\overline{Y}_4$ or $\overline{Y}_5$ is selected, we can OR (in negative logic terms) $\overline{Y}_4$ and $\overline{Y}_5$ to select the RAM. Because the

Enable inputs			Control inputs			Outputs							
$\overline{E1}$	$\overline{E2}$	$\overline{E3}$	C	B	A	$\overline{Y}_0$	$\overline{Y}_1$	$\overline{Y}_2$	$\overline{Y}_3$	$\overline{Y}_4$	$\overline{Y}_5$	$\overline{Y}_6$	$\overline{Y}_7$
1	1	0	X	X	X	1	1	1	1	1	1	1	1
1	1	1	X	X	X	1	1	1	1	1	1	1	1
1	0	0	X	X	X	1	1	1	1	1	1	1	1
1	0	1	X	X	X	1	1	1	1	1	1	1	1
0	1	0	X	X	X	1	1	1	1	1	1	1	1
0	1	1	X	X	X	1	1	1	1	1	1	1	1
0	0	0	X	X	X	1	1	1	1	1	1	1	1
0	0	1	0	0	0	0	1	1	1	1	1	1	1
0	0	1	0	0	1	1	0	1	1	1	1	1	1
0	0	1	0	1	0	1	1	0	1	1	1	1	1
0	0	1	0	1	1	1	1	1	0	1	1	1	1
0	0	1	1	0	0	1	1	1	1	0	1	1	1
0	0	1	1	0	1	1	1	1	1	1	0	1	1
0	0	1	1	1	0	1	1	1	1	1	1	0	1
0	0	1	1	1	1	1	1	1	1	1	1	1	0

Table 12.2 Truth table of a 74138 3-line to 8-line decoder.

Device	Size	Address Range	A_{15}	A_{14}	A_{13}	A_{12}	A_{11}	A_{10}	A_9	A_8	A_7	A_6	A_5	A_4	A_3	A_2	A_1	A_0
ROM1	4K	0000–0FFF	0	0	0	0	x	x	x	x	x	x	x	x	x	x	x	x
ROM2	4K	1000–1FFF	0	0	0	1	x	x	x	x	x	x	x	x	x	x	x	x
ROM3	4K	2000–2FFF	0	0	1	0	x	x	x	x	x	x	x	x	x	x	x	x
ROM4	4K	3000–3FFF	0	0	1	1	x	x	x	x	x	x	x	x	x	x	x	x
RAM	8K	4000–5FFF	0	1	0	x	x	x	x	x	x	x	x	x	x	x	x	x
P1	32	6000–601F	0	1	1	0	0	0	0	0	0	0	0	x	x	x	x	x
P2	32	6020–603F	0	1	1	0	0	0	0	0	0	0	1	x	x	x	x	x
.	.	.	.	.	.	.	.	.	.	.	.	.	.				
P8	32	60E0–60FF	0	1	1	0	0	0	0	0	1	1	1	x	x	x	x	x

Table 12.3 Address table of a microprocessor system.

peripherals don't occupy a 4K block, we have used address lines A_8 to A_{11} to select a second 3-line to 8-line decoder that decodes the peripheral address space.

Address decoding with the PROM

Address decoding is the art of generating a memory component's chip-select signal from the high-order address lines. An alternative to logic synthesis techniques is the *programmable read-only memory* (PROM) look-up table. Instead of calculating whether the current address selects this or that device, you just read the result from a table. The PROM was a popular address decoder because of its low access time and its ability to perform most of the address decoding with a single chip. The PROM address decoder saves valuable space on the microprocessor board and makes the debugging or modification of the system easier. Because PROMs consume more power than modern devices, they've largely been replaced by CMOS programmable array logic devices.

The PROM's n address inputs select one of 2^n unique locations. When accessed, each of these locations puts a word on the PROM's m data outputs. This word is the value of the various chip-select signals themselves; that is, the processor's higher-order address lines directly look up a location in the PROM containing the values of the chip selects.

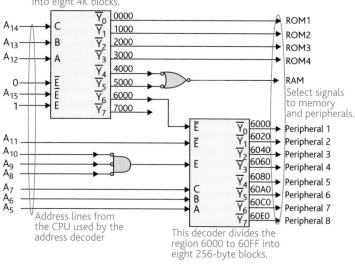

This decoder divides the lower 32 kbytes of memory into eight 4K blocks.

Address lines from the CPU used by the address decoder

Select signals to memory and peripherals.

This decoder divides the region 6000 to 60FF into eight 256-byte blocks.

Figure 12.20 Circuit of an address decoder for Table 12.3.

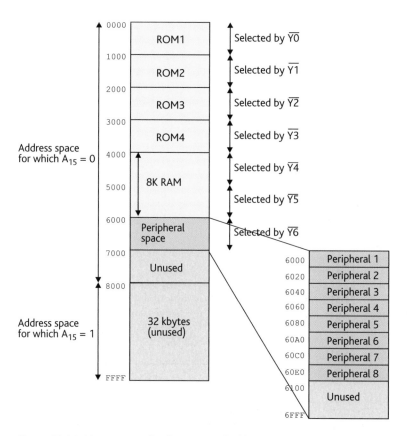

Figure 12.21 Memory map for the system of Table 12.3 and Fig. 12.20.

Let's look at a very simple example of a PROM-based address decoder. Table 12.4 describes a 16-location PROM that decodes address lines A_{12} to A_{15} in an 8-bit microcomputer. Address lines A_{12} to A_{15} are connected to the PROM's A_0 to A_3 address inputs. Whenever the CPU accesses its 64K memory space, the contents of one (and only one) of the locations in the PROM are read. Suppose that the processor reads the contents of memory location E124. The binary address of this location is 1110000100100100_2 whose four higher-order bits are 1110. Memory location 1110 in the PROM is accessed and its contents applied to the PROM's data pins D0 to D7 to give the values of the eight chip selects $\overline{CS0}$ to $\overline{CS7}$. In this case, the device connected to D5 (i.e. $\overline{CS5}$) is selected. Figure 12.22 demonstrates how the PROM-based address decoder is used. This is a simplified diagram-in practice we would have to ensure that the PROM was enabled only during a valid memory access (for example, by using the processor's data strobe to enable the decoder).

Table 12.4 divides the CPU's memory space into 16 equal-sized blocks. Because the processor has a 64 kbyte memory space, each of these blocks is 64K/16 = 4 kbytes. Consequently, this address decoder can select 4-kbyte devices. If we wanted to select devices as small as 1 kbyte, we would require a PROM with 64 locations (and six address inputs). If you examine the D4 ($\overline{CS4}$) output column, you find that there are two adjacent 0s in this column. If the processor accesses either the 4K range 6000 to 6FFF or 7000 to 7FFF, $\overline{CS4}$ goes low. We have selected an 8K block by putting a 0 in two adjacent entries. Similarly, there are four 0s in the $\overline{CS5}$ column to select a $4 \times 4K = 16K$ block.

As we have just observed, the PROM can select blocks of memory of differing size. In a system with a 16-bit address bus, a PROM with n address inputs (i.e. 2^n bytes) can fully decode a block of memory with a minimum size of $2^{16}/2^n = 2^{16-n}$ bytes. Larger blocks of memory can be decoded by increasing the number of active entries (in our case, 0s) in the data column of the PROM's address/ data table. The size of the block of memory decoded by a data output is equal to the minimum block size multiplied by the number of active entries in the appropriate data column.

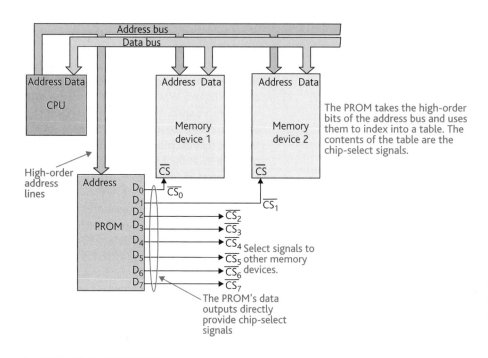

The PROM takes the high-order bits of the address bus and uses them to index into a table. The contents of the table are the chip-select signals.

Select signals to other memory devices.

The PROM's data outputs directly provide chip-select signals

Figure 12.22 Simplified circuit of a PROM-based decoder corresponding to Table 12.4.

Inputs				Outputs								
A_{15}	A_{14}	A_{13}	A_{12}	CPU name	$\overline{CS0}$	$\overline{CS1}$	$\overline{CS2}$	$\overline{CS3}$	$\overline{CS4}$	$\overline{CS5}$	$\overline{CS6}$	$\overline{CS7}$
A_3	A_2	A_1	A_0	PROM name	D_0	D_1	D_2	D_3	D_4	D_5	D_6	D_7
				Range								
0	0	0	0	0000 to 0FFF	0	1	1	1	1	1	1	1
0	0	0	1	1000 to 1FFF	1	0	1	1	1	1	1	1
0	0	1	0	2000 to 2FFF	1	1	0	1	1	1	1	1
0	0	1	1	3000 to 3FFF	1	1	1	0	1	1	1	1
0	1	0	0	4000 to 4FFF	1	1	1	1	1	1	1	1
0	1	0	1	5000 to 5FFF	1	1	1	1	1	1	1	1
0	1	1	0	6000 to 6FFF	1	1	1	1	0	1	1	1
0	1	1	1	7000 to 7FFF	1	1	1	1	0	1	1	1
1	0	0	0	8000 to 8FFF	1	1	1	1	1	1	1	1
1	0	0	1	9000 to 9FFF	1	1	1	1	1	1	1	1
1	0	1	0	A000 to AFFF	1	1	1	1	1	1	1	1
1	0	1	1	B000 to BFFF	1	1	1	1	1	1	1	1
1	1	0	0	C000 to CFFF	1	1	1	1	1	0	1	1
1	1	0	1	D000 to DFFF	1	1	1	1	1	0	1	1
1	1	1	0	E000 to EFFF	1	1	1	1	1	0	1	1
1	1	1	1	F000 to FFFF	1	1	1	1	1	0	1	1

Table 12.4 Address decoding with a PROM.

Today, the systems designer can also use programmable logic elements such as PALs and PLAs to implement address decoders. Moreover, modern microprocessors now include sufficient RAM, flash EPROM, and peripherals on-chip to make address decoding unnecessary.

The structure of 68K-based memory systems

To conclude this section on memory organization, we look at how memory components are connected to a 68K microprocessor with its 16-Mbyte memory space and 16-bit data bus. Because the 68K has 16 data lines d_{00} to d_{15}, memory

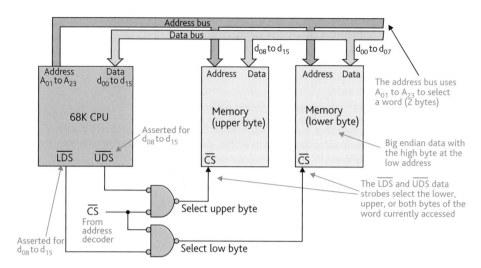

Figure 12.23 Dealing with byte and word accesses in a 68K-based system.

EXAMPLE 3

Draw an address decoding table to satisfy the following 68K memory map

    RAM1   00 0000 to 00 FFFF
    RAM2   01 0000 to 01 FFFF
    I/O_1   E0 0000 to E0 001F
    I/O_2   E0 0020 to E0 003F

		Address lines																						
Device	Range	23	22	21	20	19	18	17	16	15	14	13	12	11	10	9	8	7	6	5	4	3	2	1	0
RAM1	00 0000 to 00 FFFF	0	0	0	0	0	0	0	0	x	x	x	x	x	x	x	x	x	x	x	x	x	x	x	x
RAM2	01 0000 to 01 FFFF	0	0	0	0	0	0	0	1	x	x	x	x	x	x	x	x	x	x	x	x	x	x	x	x
I/O_1	E0 0000 to E0 001F	1	1	1	0	0	0	0	0	0	0	0	0	0	0	0	0	0	0	0	x	x	x	x	x
I/O_2	E0 0020 to E0 003F	1	1	1	0	0	0	0	0	0	0	0	0	0	0	0	0	0	0	1	x	x	x	x	x

---

blocks must be 16 bits wide in order to support both word and byte accesses. The address bus is not composed of *24* address lines A_{23} to A_{00}, but *23* address lines A_{23} to A_{01}. These address lines select a 16-bit word (i.e. 2 bytes), rather than a single byte. Two control signals, $\overline{UDS}$ (upper data strobe) and $\overline{LDS}$ (lower data strobe), distinguish between the upper and lower bytes of a 16-bit word, respectively.

Figure 12.23 shows the arrangement of a 68K-based system. If the 68K accesses a byte on data lines d_{00} to d_{07}, it asserts data strobe $\overline{LDS}$. If the 68K accesses a byte on data lines d_{08} to d_{15}, it asserts data strobe $\overline{UDS}$. If the 68K accesses a word on d_{00} to d_{15}, it asserts both $\overline{LDS}$ and $\overline{UDS}$ simultaneously. This mechanism provides a *pseudo* A_{00} (i.e. $\overline{LDS}$ asserted, $\overline{UDS}$ negated $= A_{00} = 1$, and $\overline{LDS}$ negated, $\overline{UDS}$ asserted $= A_{00} = 0$). By means of its two data strobes and 23-bit address bus, the 68K can address a word and then access either of the bytes at the word address or both bytes at this address. The byte on data lines d_{00} to d_{07} is at the odd address and the byte on data lines d_{08} to d_{15} is at the even address.

12.6 Secondary storage

Secondary storage describes storage with a relatively large access time that is used to hold large quantities of data. The term *secondary store* is synonymous with disk drives, tape transports, and optical storage.

In the last few years, storage capacities have increased at up to 100% a year. Figure 12.24 illustrates the growth in disk capacity for three disk form factors (i.e. physical disk size).

12.6.1 Magnetic surface recording

We first examine the nature of the *ferromagnetic* materials used to store data. The origin of magnetism lies in the motion of electrons in their orbits—an electron orbiting a nucleus generates a magnetic field and the atom behaves like a tiny

EXAMPLE 4

A 68K microprocessor system implements the following memory blocks:

(a) 1 Mbyte of ROM using 256K x 16-bit chips

(b) 8 Mbytes of DRAM using 2M x 4-bit chips

Construct a suitable address-decoding table and design an address decoder for this system.

A 16-bit-wide chip provides 2 bytes of data per location. Therefore, a single 256K x 16-bit ROM provides 512 kbytes of data. We need two of these chips to provide 1-Mbyte. A 1-Mbyte block of data contains 2^{20} bytes and is spanned by address lines A_{00} to A_{19}. In a 68K-based system address lines A_{20} to A_{23} must be decoded to select this block. Assume that the block of ROM is located at address 00 0000 and that $A_{23}, A_{22}, A_{21}, A_{20} = 0, 0, 0, 0$. This 1-Mbyte block is composed of two 512-kbyte sub-blocks. Therefore one of these sub-blocks is selected when $A_{19} = 0$ and the other when $A_{19} = 1$.

The 8 Mbytes of DRAM are spanned by A_{00} to A_{22} (i.e. 2^{23} bytes). This block of memory must be on an 8-Mbyte boundary (i.e. 00 0000 or 80 0000 in a 68K-based system). Because 00 0000 is occupied by ROM, we'll put the DRAM at 80 0000 for which $A_{23} = 1$. This block is composed of 2M-location by 4-bit-wide devices. Four 4-bit-wide chips are required to provide 16 bits (2 bytes) of data. The amount of data provided by these four chips per location is 2M locations $\times$ 2 bytes = 4M. We need two of these sub-blocks to get 8 Mbytes. The first sub-block is selected by $A_{22} = 0$ and the second by $A_{22} = 1$.

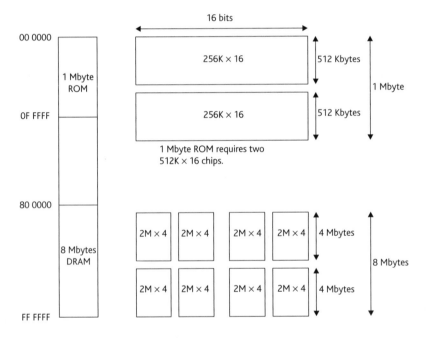

The next step is to construct an address-decoding table. A memory block must be on a boundary equal to its own size. The following address decoding table shows address lines A_{23} to A_{00}. Although the 68K lacks an A_{00} line, it's easier to add an A_{00} line to the table so that we can operate in bytes.

Device	Range	A_{23}	A_{22}	A_{21}	A_{20}	A_{19}	A_{18}	. . .	A_{00}
ROM 1	00 0000 to 07 FFFF	0	0	0	0	0	x	. . .	x
ROM 2	08 0000 to 0F FFFF	0	0	0	0	1	x	. . .	x
DRAM 1	80 0000 to BF FFFF	1	0	x	x	x	x	. . .	x
DRAM 2	C0 0000 to FF FFFF	1	1	x	x	x	x	. . .	x

If you didn't treat the 8-Mbyte block of DRAM as a single block, but as two separate 4 Mbyte blocks, you could put each of these 4-Mbyte sub-block on any 4 Mbyte boundary. The following address decoding table is also a legal solution.

Device	Range	A_{23}	A_{22}	A_{21}	A_{20}	A_{19}	A_{18}	. . .	A_{00}
ROM 1	00 000 to 07 FFFF	0	0	0	0	0	x	. . .	x
ROM 2	00 000 to 0F FFFF	0	0	0	0	1	x	. . .	x
DRAM 1	40 000 to 07 FFFF	0	1	x	x	x	x	. . .	x
DRAM 2	80 000 to BF FFFF	1	0	x	x	x	x	. . .	x

EXAMPLE 5

Design an address decoder using a PROM to implement the following 68K memory map.

(a) 4 Mbytes ofROM at address 00 0000 using 1M × 8-bit chips

(b) 8 Mbytes of RAM at address 80 0000 using 4M × 4-bit chips

(c) 1 Mbyte of RAM at address 60 0000 using 512K × 8-bit chips

We begin by working out the sub-blocks of memory required from the size of the specified memory components.

(a) A pair of 1M × 8-bit chips gives 2 Mbytes. We need two sub-blocks to get 4 Mbytes.

(b) Four 4M × 4-bit chips gives 8 Mbytes. This provides all our needs.

(c) A pair of 512K × 8-bit chips gives 1 Mbyte. This provides all our needs.

Address decoding table

Device	Range	A_{23}	A_{22}	A_{21}	A_{20}	A_{19}	A_{18}	...	A_{00}	Size
ROM 1	00 0000 to 1F FFFF	0	0	0	x	x	x	...	x	2 Mbytes
ROM 2	20 0000 to 3F FFFF	0	0	1	x	x	x	...	x	2 Mbytes
RAM 1	80 0000 to FF FFFF	1	x	x	x	x	x	...	x	8 Mbytes
RAM 2	60 0000 to 6F FFFF	0	1	1	0	x	x	...	x	1 Mbyte

Each line in the PROM must select a block equal to the smallest block to be decoded; that is, 1 Mbyte. The PROM must decode A_{23} to A_{20}. In the following table, D_0 from the PROM selects ROM$_1$, D_1 selects ROM2, D_2 selects RAM2, and D_3 selects RAM1.

Device	Range	A_{23}	A_{22}	A_{21}	A_{20}	D_0 ROM1	D_1 ROM2	D_2 RAM2	D_3 RAM1
ROM 1	00 0000 to 0F FFFF	0	0	0	0	0	1	1	1
ROM 1	10 0000 to 1F FFFF	0	0	0	1	0	1	1	1
ROM 2	20 0000 to 2F FFFF	0	0	1	0	1	0	1	1
ROM 2	30 0000 to 3F FFFF	0	0	1	1	1	0	1	1
unused	40 0000 to 4F FFFF	0	1	0	0	1	1	1	1
unused	50 0000 to 5F FFFF	0	1	0	1	1	1	1	1
RAM2	60 0000 to 6F FFFF	0	1	1	0	1	1	0	1
unused	70 0000 to 7F FFFF	0	1	1	1	1	1	1	1
RAM 1	80 0000 to 8F FFFF	1	0	0	0	1	1	1	0
RAM 1	90 0000 to 9F FFFF	1	0	0	1	1	1	1	0
RAM 1	A0 0000 to AF FFFF	1	0	1	0	1	1	1	0
RAM 1	B0 0000 to BF FFFF	1	0	1	1	1	1	1	0
RAM 1	C0 0000 to CF FFFF	1	1	0	0	1	1	1	0
RAM 1	D0 0000 to DF FFFF	1	1	0	1	1	1	1	0
RAM 1	E0 0000 to EF FFFF	1	1	1	0	1	1	1	0
RAM 1	F0 0000 to FF FFFF	1	1	1	1	1	1	1	0

---

magnet. In most matter the magnetic effects of electron spin are overcome by the stronger force generated by the thermal vibration of the atoms that prevents magnetic interaction between adjacent atoms.

In ferromagnetic materials such as iron there is a stronger interaction between electron spins, which results in the alignment of electrons over a region called a *domain*. Domains range from 1 μm to several centimeters in size. Because the electron spins are aligned within a domain, the domain exhibits a strong spontaneous magnetization and behaves like a tiny magnet with a North Pole at one end and a South Pole at the other end. Within a large piece of ferromagnetic material, the magnetic axes of individual domains are arranged at random and there is no overall magnetic field in the bulk material.

Suppose we thread a wire through a hole in a ring (called a *toroid*) of a ferromagnetic material and pass a current, *i*, through the wire. The current generates a vector magnetic

EXAMPLE 6

A memory board in a 68K-based system with a 16-bit data bus has 1 Mbyte of RAM composed of 128K × 8 RAM chips located at address C0 0000 onward. The board also has a block of 256 kbytes of ROM composed of 128K × 8 chips located at address D8 0000. Design an address decoder for this board.

Two byte-wide RAM chips span the 16-bit data bus. The minimum block of memory is $2 \times 128K = 256$ kbytes accessed by address lines A_{17} to A_{00}. We require 1 Mbyte of RAM, or four 256 kbyte blocks. Address lines A_{19} to A_{18} select a block and A_{23} to A_{20} select a Mbyte block out of the 16 possible 1 Mbyte blocks (A_{23} to $A_{20} = 1100$). The ROM is implemented as a single 256-kbyte block using two 128-kbyte chips. The following table can be used to construct a suitable decoder.

Device	A_{23}	A_{22}	A_{21}	A_{20}	A_{19}	A_{18}	$A_{17}\ldots$	A_{01}	A_{00}	Address range
RAM1	1	1	0	0	0	0	x...	x	x	C0 0000 to C3 FFFF
RAM2	1	1	0	0	0	1	x...	x	x	C4 0000 to C7 FFFF
RAM3	1	1	0	0	1	0	x...	x	x	C8 0000 to CB FFFF
RAM4	1	1	0	0	1	1	x...	x	x	CC 0000 to CF FFFF
ROM	1	1	0	1	1	0	x...	x	x	D8 0000 to DB FFFF

EXAMPLE 7

Design an address decoder that locates three block of memory in the following ranges: 00 0000 to 7F FFFF, A0 8000 to A0 8FFF, and F0 0000 to FF FFFF.

Address range		A_{23} to A_{20}	A_{19} to A_{16}	A_{15} to A_{12}	A_{11} to A_8	A_7 to A_4	A_3 to A_0	Block size
000000 to 7FFFFF	First location	0000	0000	0000	0000	0000	0000	8 Mbytes
	Last location	0111	1111	1111	1111	1111	1111	spanned by 22 lines
A08000 to A08FFF	First location	1010	0000	1000	0000	0000	0000	4 kbytes
	Last location	1010	0000	1000	1111	1111	1111	spanned by 12 lines
F00000 to FFFFFF	First location	1111	0000	0000	0000	0000	0000	1 Mbyte
	Last location	1111	1111	1111	1111	1111	1111	spanned by 20 lines

From the table, you can see that the first block is selected by address line A_{23}, the second block by address lines A_{23} to A_{12}, and the third block by address lines A_{23} to A_{20}.

EXAMPLE 8

The following address decoding PROM selects three blocks of memory in a 68K-based system. How large is each block and what address range does it occupy?

CPU address line	A_{23}	A_{22}	A_{21}	CS_2	CS_1	CS_0
PROM address line	A_2	A_1	A_0	D_2	D_1	D_0
	0	0	0	0	1	1
	0	0	1	1	1	1
	0	1	0	1	0	1
	0	1	1	1	0	1
	1	0	0	1	1	0
	1	0	1	1	1	0
	1	1	0	1	1	0
	1	1	1	1	1	0

The PROM decodes the 68K's three highest-order address lines A_{23} to A_{21}. These address lines partition the 68K's 16-Mbyte address space into eight 2-Mbyte blocks. CS_2 selects the 2-Mbyte block for which $A_{23}, A_{22}, A_{21} = 0, 0, 0$. This is the address space 00 0000 to 1F FFFF. CS_1 selects two 2-Mbyte blocks for which $A_{23}, A_{22} = 0, 1$. This is the 4-Mbyte address space 40 0000 to 7F FFFF. CS_0 selects the four 2-Mbyte blocks for which $A_{23} = 1$. This is the 8-Mbyte address space 80 0000 to FF FFFF.

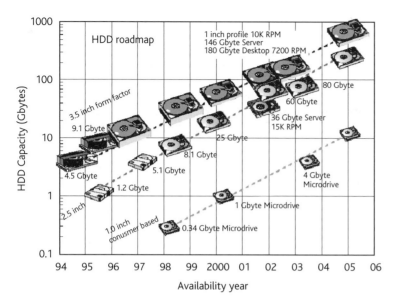

Figure 12.24 The increase in disk capacity (from Hitachi Global Storage Technologies, San Jose Research Centre).

this magnetic material has two stable states and can remain in either of the states indefinitely. Unlike the flip-flop, the ferromagnetic material is a non-volatile store and requires no power source to retain data.

Assume that initially the ferromagnetic material is magnetized in a logical zero state and has an internal field $-B_r$. If a negative external field is applied (i.e. negative i, therefore negative H), the value of the internal magnetization B goes slightly more negative than $-B_r$ and we move towards point P in Fig. 12.25. If H is now reduced to zero, the remnant magnetization returns to $-B_r$. In other words, there is no net change in the state of the ferromagnetic material.

Now consider applying a small positive internal field H. The internal magnetization is slightly increased from $-B_r$ and we move along the curve towards point Q. If the external magnetization is reduced we move back to $-B_r$. However, if H is increased beyond the value $+H_m$, the magnetization of the material flips over at Q, and we end up at point R. When we reduce the external field H to zero, we return to $+B_r$ and not to $-B_r$. If the material is initially in a negative state, increasing the external magnetization beyond H_m causes it to assume a positive state. A magnetic field of less than H_m is insufficient to change the material's state.

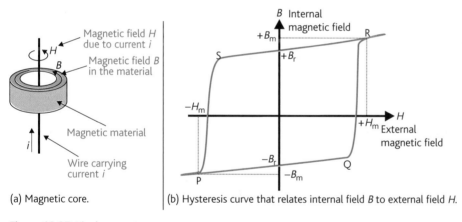

(a) Magnetic core.

(b) Hysteresis curve that relates internal field B to external field H.

Figure 12.25 The hysteresis curve.

field, H, in the surrounding space, where H is proportional to i. A magnetic field, B, is produced inside the ring by the combined effects of the external field, H and the internal magnetization of the core material. A graph of the relationship between the internal magnetic field B and the external magnetic field H for a ferromagnetic material is given in Figure 12.25. This curve is called a *hysteresis loop*.

Suppose that the external field round the wire is initially zero; that is, $H = 0$ because the current flowing through the wire, i, is zero. Figure 12.25 demonstrates that there are two possible values of B when $H = 0$: $+B_i$ and $-B_r$. These two states represent a logical one and a logical zero. The suffix r in B_r stands for remnant and refers to the magnetism remaining in the ring when the external field is zero. Like the flip-flop,

Similarly, if the ferromagnetic material is in a one state $(+B_r)$, a positive value of H has little effect, but a more negative value of H than $-H_m$ will switch the material to a zero state $(-B_r)$.

The switching of a ferromagnetic material from one state to another is done by applying a pulse with a magnitude greater than I_m to the wire. A pulse of $+I_m$ always forces the material into a logical one state, and a pulse of $-I_m$ forces it into a logical zero state.

The hysteresis curve can readily be explained in terms of the behavior of domains. Figure 12.26 shows a region of a ferromagnetic material at three stages. At stage (a) the magnetic material is said to be in its virgin state with the domains oriented at random and has no net magnetization. This corresponds to the origin of the hysteresis curve, where $H = 0$ and $B = 0$.

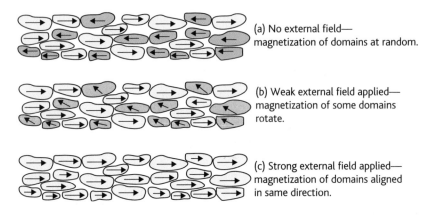

(a) No external field—
magnetization of domains at random.

(b) Weak external field applied—
magnetization of some domains
rotate.

(c) Strong external field applied—
magnetization of domains aligned
in same direction.

Figure 12.26 The behavior of domains.

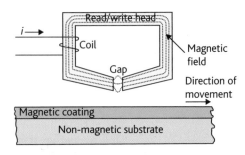

Figure 12.27 Surface recording.

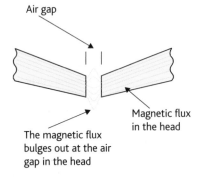

Figure 12.28 The air gap.

At stage (b) an external magnetic field has been applied and some of the domains have rotated their magnetic axes to line up with the external field. As the external field is increased, more and more domains flip over, and there comes a point where the domains already aligned with the external field reinforce it, causing yet more domains to flip over. This process soon develops into an avalanche as the internal field rapidly builds up, and all domains are aligned with the external field. At this point, stage (c), the bulk material is fully magnetized and is said to be saturated.

The precise form of the hysteresis or *B–H* curve of Fig. 12.25 differs from one magnetic material to another. The best *B–H* curve for the purpose of storing data is square, so that the transition from one state to another (i.e. from $-B_r$ to $+B_r$) takes place for an infinitesimally small change in *H*. Such a magnetic material is said to have a *square-loop B–H characteristic*. Magnetic materials displaying strong hysteresis effects are called *hard*, whereas those displaying little are called *soft*. Now that we've described the basic principles of magnetization, we look at how it is applied in practice.

Magnetizing a flat surface

The operating principles of disk drives, tape transports, and VCRs are the same: the former records data on a flat platter coated with a magnetic material, whereas the latter records data on a thin band of flexible plastic coated with magnetic material. Figure 12.27 illustrates the generic recording process—the same model serves both disk and tape systems.

The write head used to store data consists of a ring of *high-permeability* soft magnetic material with a coil wound round it. High permeability means that the material offers a low resistance to a magnetic field. The material of the write head is *magnetically soft* and doesn't have a square-loop hysteresis; that is, it doesn't exhibit residual magnetization.

The most important feature of the write head is a tiny air gap in the ring. When a current flows in the coil a magnetic flux is created within the ring. This flux flows round the core, but when it encounters the air gap, it spreads out into the surrounding air as illustrated in Fig. 12.28; this external field is called a *fringing field*.

Because the head is close to the recording medium, the magnetic field round the air gap passes through the magnetic material coating the backing. If this field is strong enough, it causes the domains within the coating to become aligned with the field from the head. Because the magnetic surface is moving, a continuous strip of surface is magnetized as it passes under the write head. If the direction of the current in the coil is changed the field reverses and the magnetic particles in the coating are magnetized in the opposite direction. Figure 12.29 shows how the domains in the surface material might be magnetized (north–south or south–north) after passing under the write head. We have also plotted the current in the write head on the same figure.

As time has passed, engineers have produced greater and greater packing densities (about 10 Gbits per square inch in 1995 and 100 Gbits per square inch by 2004). One of the improvements is due to the composition of the magnetic

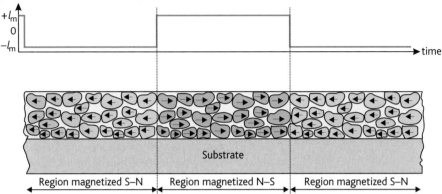

Figure 12.29 The magnetized layer.

medium used to store data. The size of the particles has been reduced and their magnetic properties improved. Some tapes employ a thin metallic film, rather than individual particles. Metal oxide coatings are about 800 μm thick with oxide particles approximately 25 μm by 600 μm with an ellipsoidal shape. A thin film coating is typically only 100 μm thick.

Reading data

A first-generation read head was essentially the same as a write head (sometimes a single head serves as a both a read and a write head). When the magnetized material moves past the gap in the read head, a magnetic flux is induced in the head. The flux, in turn, induces a voltage across the terminals of the coil that is proportional to the rate of change of the flux, rather than the absolute value of the magnetic flux itself. Figure 12.30 shows the waveforms associated with writing and reading data on a magnetic surface. The voltage from the read head is given by

$$v(t) = K\,d\Phi/dt$$

K is a constant depending on the physical parameters of the system and Φ is the flux produced by the moving magnetic medium. Because the differential of a constant is zero, only transitions of magnetic flux can be detected. The output from a region of the surface with a constant magnetization is zero, making it difficult to record digital data directly on tape or disk.

12.6.2 Data encoding techniques

Now that we've described the basic process by which information is recorded on a magnetic medium, we are going to look at some of the ways in which digital data is encoded before it is recorded. Magnetic secondary stores record data serially, a bit at a time, along the path described by the motion of the magnetic medium under the write head. Tape transports have multiple parallel read/write heads and record several parallel tracks simultaneously across the width of the tape.

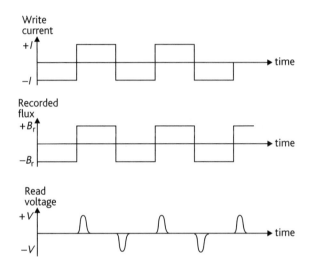

Figure 12.30 Read/write waveforms.

You can't transmit the sequence of logical 1s and 0s to be recorded directly to the write head. If you were to record a long string of 0s or 1s by simply saturating the surface at $-B_r$ or $+B_r$, no signal would be received during playback. Why? Because only a *change* in flux creates an output signal. A process of *encoding* or *modulation* must first be used to transform the data pattern into a suitable code so that the recorded data is always changing even if the source is all 1s or 0s. Similarly, when the information is read back from the tape it must be decoded or demodulated to extract the original digital data. The actual encoding/decoding process chosen is a compromise between the desire to pack as many bits of data as possible into a given surface area while preserving the reliability of the system and keeping its complexity within reasonable bounds.

Let's look as some of the possible recording codes (beginning with a code that illustrates the problem of recording long strings of 1s and 0s). However, before we can compare

ENCODING CRITERIA

Efficiency A code's storage efficiency is defined as *the number of stored bits per flux reversal* and is expressed in percent. A 100% efficiency corresponds to 1 bit per flux reversal.

Self-clocking The encoded data must be separated into individual bits. A code that provides a method of splitting the bits off from one another is called *self-clocking* and is highly desirable. A non-self-clocking code provides no timing information and makes it difficult to separate the data stream into individual bits.

Noise immunity An ideal code should have the largest immunity to noise and extraneous signals. Noise is caused by imperfections in the magnetic coating leading to drop-outs and drop-ins. A drop-out is a loss of signal *caused* by missing magnetic material and a drop-in is a noise pulse. Another source of noise is *cross-talk*, which is the signal picked up by the head from adjacent tracks. Cross-talk is introduced because the read/write head might not be perfectly aligned with the track on the surface of the recording medium. Noise can also be caused by imperfect erasure. Suppose a track is recorded and later erased. If the erase head didn't pass exactly over the center of the track, it's possible that the edge of the track might not have been fully erased. When the track is rerecorded and later played back, a spurious signal from the unerased portion of the track will be added to the wanted signal.

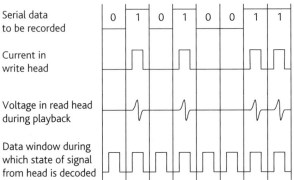

Figure 12.31 Return-to-bias recording.

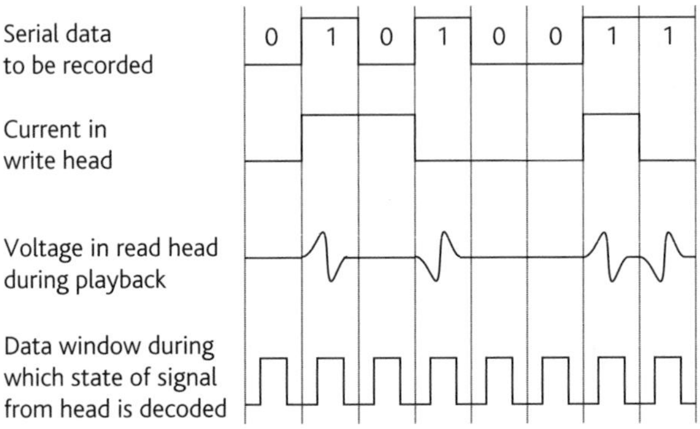

Figure 12.32 Non-return to zero one recording (NRZ1).

various encoding techniques we need to describe some of the parameters or properties of a code. In what follows the term *flux reversal* indicates a change of state in the recorded magnetic field in the coating of the tape or disk. Simply reversing the direction of the current in the write head causes a flux reversal. Some of the criteria by which a recording code may be judged are described in the box.

Return-to-zero encoding

Return-to-zero (RZ) recording requires that the surface be unmagnetized to store a zero and magnetized by a short pulse to store a 1. Because no signal is applied to the write head when recording a 0, any 1s already written on the tape or disk are not erased or overwritten. *Return-to-bias recording* (RB) is a modification of RZ recording in which a 0 is recorded by saturating the magnetic coating in one direction and a 1 by saturating it in the opposite direction by a short pulse of the opposite polarity.

Figure 12.31 illustrates the principles of return-to-bias recording and playback. A negative current in the write head saturates the surface to $-B_r$. A positive pulse saturates the surface to $+B_r$ to write a 1. The pulse width used depends on

the characteristics of the head and the magnetic medium. A wide pulse reduces the maximum packing density of the recorded data and is wasteful of tape or disk surface but is easy to detect, whereas a very narrow pulse is harder to detect.

Data is read from the disk/tape by first generating a *data window*, which is a time slot during which the signal from the read head is to be sampled. The signal from the read head is sampled at the center of this window. A sequence of 0s generates no output from the read head and there is no simple way of making sure that the data window falls exactly in the middle of a data cell. For this reason return-to-bias is said to be *non-self-clocking*. The worst-case efficiency of RB recording is 50% (when the data is a string of 1s) and its noise sensitivity is poor. RB recording is not used in magnetic recording.

Non-return to zero encoding

One of the first widely used data encoding techniques was *modified non-return to zero* or NRZ1. Each time a 1 is to be recorded, the current flowing in the head is reversed. When reading data each change in flux is interpreted as a 1. Figure 12.32 illustrates NRZ1 recording which requires a maximum of one flux transition per bit of stored data giving

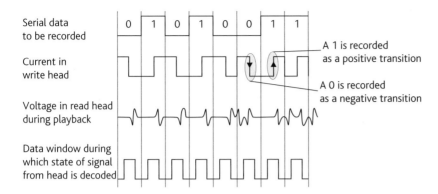

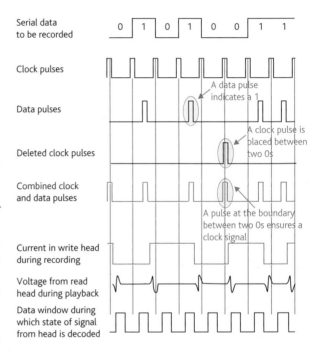

Figure 12.33 Phase encoded recording (PE).

it an optimum packing density of 100%. NRZ1 isn't self-clocking and it's impossible to reliably retrieve a long string of 0s.

Phase encoding

Several codes are based on *phase* or *Manchester* encoding, which was once widely used by magnetic tape transports. A flux transition is located at the center of each bit cell: a low-to-high transition indicates a 1 and a high-to-low transition a 0. Because there's always a flux transition at the center of each data cell, a clock signal can be derived from the recorded data and therefore this encoding technique is self-clocking. A stream of alternate 1s and 0s requires one flux transition per bit, whereas a stream of 1s or 0s requires two flux changes per bit.

Fig. 12.33 illustrates how the sequence 01010011 is phase encoded. Phase encoding has a low efficiency of 50% because up to two transitions per bit is required. Because up to two flux transitions are required per bit, the maximum recorded frequency is twice that of NRZ1 at an equivalent bit density. Phase encoding has a good immunity to noise. Phase encoding is widely used in digital data transmission systems as well as magnetic recording systems.

Modified frequency modulation

Modified frequency modulation, (MFM) (also called *Miller* encoding and *double density recording*) became a standard for the recording of data on floppy disks. MFM is 100% efficient and needs only one flux transition per bit.

Figure 12.34 demonstrates how a data stream may be divided conceptually into two separate signals: a timing signal consisting of a pulse at each cell boundary, and a data signal consisting of a pulse at the center of each data cell containing a 1.

A data pulse is placed at the center of each cell containing a 1. The clock pulses at the boundary of the cells are deleted, but with one exception. Whenever two 0s are to be recorded in succession, a clock pulse is placed between them (see Fig. 12.34). Because the maximum gap between flux transitions is no more than $2T$, where T is the width of a data cell, MFM is self-clocking.

Figure 12.34 Modified frequency modulation (MFM).

Group codes and RLL codes

An encoding technique found in both magnetic disk and tape stores is the *group code*, which gained popularity in the early 1970s when IBM first adopted it for their tape systems. Simple coding schemes assign a particular waveform to each bit to be recorded, which proves incompatible with some of the requirements of an optimum code. A *group code* takes n bits to represent an m-bit source word, where $n > m$. Although there are 2^n possible code words, only 2^m of these 2^n values are used to create 2^m different waveforms for recording on the tape or disk. Waveforms with poor characteristics can be removed from the code words to be stored on the tape or disk; that is, only the best waveforms are used to store data. The 4/5 group code in Table 12.5 uses 5 bits to encode 4 bits

Input code	Output code
0000	11001
0001	11011
0010	10010
0011	10011
0100	11101
0101	10101
0110	10110
0111	10111
1000	11010
1001	01001
1010	01010
1011	01011
1100	11110
1101	01101
1110	01110
1111	01111

Table 12.5 ANSI X3.54 4/5 group code.

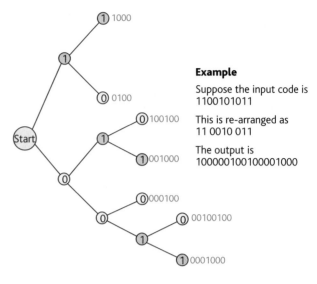

Example

Suppose the input code is
1100101011

This is re-arranged as
11 0010 011

The output is
1000001001000001000

Figure 12.35 RLL 2,7 encoding algorithm.

of data. The algorithm that maps the 4 bits of data onto the 5-bit group code to be recorded avoids the occurrence of more than two 0s in succession. This group code and a self-clocking modification of NRZ1 guarantees at least one flux transition per three recorded bits.

Another class of recording codes are the RLL or *run-length limited codes*. Instead of inserting clock pulses to provide timing information as in MFM recording, RLL codes limit the longest sequence of 0s that can be recorded in a burst. Because the maximum number of 0s in succession is fixed, timing circuits can be designed to reliably locate the center of each bit cell. A run-length limited code is expressed as $R_{m,n}$, where m defines the minimum number of 0s and n the maximum number of 0s between two 1s.

A typical RLL code is RLL 2,7 which means that each 1 is separated from the next 1 by two to seven 0s. In RLL a maximum of four 0s may precede a 1 and three 0s may follow a 1. Because RLL records only certain bit patterns, the source data must be encoded before it can be passed to the RLL coder; for example, the source pattern 0011 would be converted to 00001000.

Figure 12.35 illustrates the RLL 2,7 encoding algorithm. You take the source code and use its bits to locate a terminal node on the tree. Suppose the source string is 0010110 . . . The first bit is zero and we move down the zero branch from *Start*. The second bit is 0 and we move down the 0 branch to the next junction. The third bit is 1 and we move to the next junction. The fourth bit is 0 and we move along the 0 branch. This is a terminal node with the value 00100100; that is, the encoded value of the input sequence 00100.

The next bit in the input sequence is 1 and we move from *Start* along the 1 branch. The second bit is 1 and that leads us to a terminal node whose output code is 1000. This process continues until we reach the end of the input code and each group of 2, 3, or 4 input bits have been replaced by a terminal value.

12.7 Disk drive principles

We now look at the construction and characteristics of the disk drive. The hard disk stores data on the surface of a flat, circular, rigid *platter* of aluminum coated with a thin layer of magnetic material.[1] Hard disks vary in size from 8 inches (obsolete) to 3½ and 5¼ inches (PCs) to 1.3 to 2½ inches (laptops and portable devices). The platter rotates continually about its central axis in much the same way as a black vinyl disk on the turntable of a gramophone (for readers old enough to remember the days before the CD). The rotational speed of disks in PCs was 3600 rpm, although 7200 rpm is now common and some disks rotate at 15 000 rpm.

The read/write head is positioned at the end of an arm above the surface of the disk. As the disk rotates, the read/write head traces a circular path called a *track* around the disk. Digital information is stored along the concentric tracks (Fig. 12.36). Data is written in blocks called *sectors* along the track. Track spacing is of the order of 120 000 tracks/inch. As time passes, track spacing will continue to improve, whereas the speed of rotation will not grow at anything like the same rate.

Figure 12.37 illustrates the structure of a disk drive. A significant difference between the vinyl record and the magnetic

---

[1] Some modern platters are made of glass because of its superior mechanical properties such as a low coefficient of thermal expansion.

HISTORY OF DISK DRIVES

The first high-speed magnetic storage devices were *magnetic drums* where data was recorded on the surface of a rotating cylinder. Magnetic drums were used in Manchester University's Mark 1 computer in 1948. In 1950 ERA built the world's first commercially produced computer for the USA navy, the ERA 1101, which used a magnetic drum to store over 1 million bits.

In 1956 IBM introduced its 305 RAMAC (Random Access Method of Accounting and Control) computer, which incorporated the first disk drive. The RAMAC's disk drive stored 5 million 7-bit characters on 50 24-inch rotating disks.

In the 1960s IBM invented the first disk drive with removable storage media and in 1973 IBM shipped their first *Winchester* disk drive. The Winchester disk drive is the forerunner of all today's hard disk drives.

In 1980 Seagate Technology introduced the ST506, the first disk drive for PCs. This was a 5¼ inches disk drive with a capacity of 5 Mbytes.

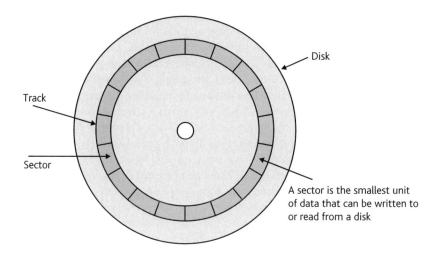

Track

Sector

Disk

A sector is the smallest unit of data that can be written to or read from a disk

Figure 12.36 Structure of a disk.

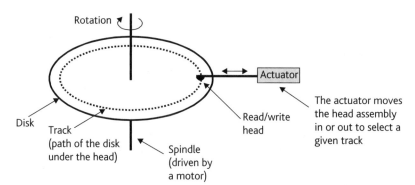

Rotation

Disk

Track (path of the disk under the head)

Spindle (driven by a motor)

Read/write head

Actuator

The actuator moves the head assembly in or out to select a given track

Figure 12.37 Principle of the disk drive.

disk is that the groove on the audio disk is physically cut into its surface, whereas the tracks on a magnetic disk are simply the circular paths traced out by the motion of the disk under the read/write head. Passing a current through the head magnetizes the moving surface of the disk and writes data along the track. Similarly, when reading data, the head is moved to the required track and the motion of the magnetized surface induces a tiny voltage in the coil of the read head.

A precision servomechanism called an *actuator* moves or *steps* the arm holding the head horizontally along a radius from track to track. An actuator is an electromechanical device that converts an electronic signal into mechanical motion. Remember the difference between the magnetic disk and the gramophone record. In the former the tracks are concentric and the head steps from track to track, whereas in the latter a continuous spiral groove is cut into the surface of the disk and the stylus gradually moves towards the center as the disk rotates. The actuator in Fig. 12.37 is a *linear actuator* and is no longer used in hard disks.

Modem disk drives use a *rotary head positioner* to move the read/write heads rather than the linear (in and out) positioners found on earlier hard disk drives. Figure 12.38 shows how a rotary head positioner called a *voice coil actuator* rotates an arm about a pivot, causing the head assembly to track over the surface of the disks. A voice coil is so called because it works like a loudspeaker. A current is passed through a coil

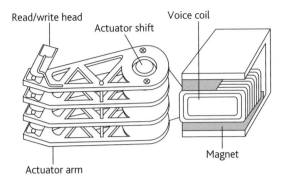

Read/write head   Voice coil

Actuator shift

Actuator arm

Magnet

When a current flows through the *voice coil*, it is either attracted to the magnet or repelled (depending on the direction of the current). One end of an arm is connected to the voice coil and the other end of the arm carries the read/write heads. The arm is pivoted on a shaft so that the heads move across the disk and the voice coil moves in or out.

Figure 12.38 A head assembly positioning mechanism.

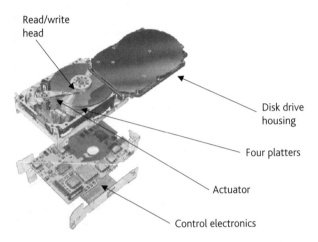

Read/write head

Disk drive housing

Four platters

Actuator

Control electronics

Figure 12.39 Structure of a the disk drive.

positioned within a strong magnetic field provided by a permanent magnet. The current in the coil generates a magnetic field, causing the coil to be attracted to, or repelled by, the fixed magnet, moving the pivoted arm. The multiple head arrangement of Fig. 12.38 means that the hard disk can access the same track on several surfaces simultaneously. These tracks form a *cylinder*.

The characteristics of disk drives vary from manufacturer to manufacturer and are being improved on at an immense rate. A high-performance disk drive of the late 1990s had a rotational speed of 5400 rpm (i.e. 90 revolutions per second), a capacity of 9 Gbytes (approximately 10^{36} bits), and an average seek time of 8 ms (seek time is the time taken to locate a given track) and could transfer data to the computer at over 10 Mbytes per second. A decade earlier, a typical hard disk in a PC had a capacity of 20 Mbytes and an access time of over 70 ms. During the 1990s, average disk storage densities were increasing at a phenomenal rate of about 70% per year compounded. The improvement in access time and data rate over the same period grew at a more modest 7% per year. By 2005 disk drives with a capacity of 500 Gbytes were available and the standard drive speed was 7200 rpm.

Prior to the mid-1990s, disk drives were expensive items that often cost more than the CPU and main memory. Even today, a high-capacity, fast, state-of-the-art hard disk is one of the most expensive components in a computer. The cost of a disk drive lies in its complex and precise mechanical structure. Manufacturers have reduced the effective cost per megabyte of disk drives by stacking two or more disks on a common spindle and using multiple heads as described by Fig. 12.39. A drive might have three disks with six surfaces and six heads that move together when driven by the common actuator. The motion of the heads over the corresponding tracks on each of the surfaces describes a *cylinder*.

The parameters of a rigid disk are impressive. The magnetic layer is about 2000 atoms deep and the read/write head is positioned 0.01 μm above the surface of the platter. On top of the magnetic layer is a lubricating layer of a fluorocarbon that is about one molecule thick. The structure of the heads themselves is quite complex. They must not only have the correct electrical and magnetic properties, but also the correct mechanical properties. If the head were actually in physical contact with the disk surface, the abrasive magnetic coating would soon wear it out because its velocity over the surface of the disk is of the order of 140 mph at 15 000 rpm.

The head is mounted in a holder called a *slipper* positioned above the disk at about 0.01 μm from the surface. We cannot directly achieve such a level of precision with current engineering technology. However, by exploiting the head's aerodynamic properties it can be made to fly in the moving layer of air just above the surface of the disk.

When an object moves, the air near its surface, called the *boundary layer*, moves with it. At some distance above the surface the air is still. Consequently a velocity gradient exists between the surface and the still air. At a certain point above the disk's surface, the velocity of the air flowing over the head generates enough lift to match the pressure of the spring pushing the head towards the disk. At this point, the head is in equilibrium and floats above the disk. Modern slippers fly below 10×10^{-9} m (i.e. 0.01 μm) and have longitudinal grooves cut in them to dump some of the lift. The precision of a modern slipper is so great that the acid in a fingerprint caused by careless handling can destroy its aerodynamic contour.

WINCHESTER DISK DRIVES

Hard disk drives in the early 1980s found in compact, low-cost minicomputers and high-performance microprocessor systems were often called *Winchester* disks. The generic term Winchester describes a wide range of small disk drives and there appears to be no single feature that makes a drive a Winchester. The term is associated with IBM and some say it's related to the town of Winchester. Most say it's a reference to the 30–30 Winchester rifle because the original drive had two spindles, each holding 30 Mbytes. Winchester technology was originally applied to 14-inch disks and then extended to 8-5$\frac{1}{4}$-3$\frac{1}{2}$-and the 2$\frac{1}{2}$-inch drives found in laptop computers. Although modern drives incorporate the features of the original Winchester drives, the term Winchester is seldom used today.

As the recording density increased and inter-track spacing reduced, it became increasingly necessary to ensure that the head flies exactly over the track it is accessing. This led to increasingly complex head-positioning mechanisms and their associated electronics. Winchester technology solved the problem of head tracking by making the disks, read/write heads, and positioner, an integral unit. Earlier large hard drives

had replaceable disk packs. Winchester disks cannot be changed so the problem of trying to follow a track on a disk written by another unit doesn't arise. Because the head disk assembly requires no head alignment, the track spacing can be reduced and the storage density increased. The Winchester disk drive is a sealed chassis that stops the entry of dirt and dust. Most drives have a small hole in the unit protected by an air filter to equalize internal and external air pressures. As the disk rotates in a clean environment, the flying height of the head can be reduced, and the recording density increased.

Unlike earlier hard disk drives, it is not necessary to retract the heads beyond the outer rim of the disks when the unit is not in use. Because the heads fly only when the disks are rotating and aren't retracted when the disk is stationary, it's necessary to allocate a portion of the disk's surface as a landing area. That is, the heads are permitted to come into contact with (i.e. land on) a part of the disk where data is not stored. In order to make this possible it is necessary to lubricate the surface of the disk. Such disks must be brought up to speed (and stopped) as quickly as possible to reduce the time for which the heads are in contact with the disks.

The height at which the head flies above the surface of the disk is related to the surface finish or roughness of the magnetic coating. If the magnetic material is polished, the surface to head gap can be reduced by 50% in comparison with an unpolished surface.

Occasionally, the head hits the surface and is said to *crash*. A crash can damage part of the track and this track must be labeled bad and the lost data rewritten from a back-up copy of the file.

The disk controller (i.e. the electronic system that controls the operation of a disk drive) specifies a track and sector and either reads its contents into a buffer (i.e. temporary store) or writes the contents of the buffer to the disk. Some call a disk drive a random access device because you can step to a given track without first having to read the contents of each track. Disk drives are sequential access devices because it is necessary to wait until the desired sector moves under the head before it can be read.

12.7.1 Disk drive operational parameters

Disk drive users are interested in three parameters: the total capacity of the system, the rate at which data is written to or read from the disk, and its average access time. In the late 1990s typical storage capacities were 14 Gbytes, data rates were several Mbytes/s and average access times from 8 ms to 12 ms. By the end of the century, data densities had reached 10 Gbits/in^2 and track widths of the order of 1 μm. In 2004

data densities had reached 100 Gbits/in^2 and it was thought that densities would increase by a factor of 10 to yield 1 Tbits/in^2 within a decade.

Access time

A disk drive's average access time is composed of the time required to step to the desired track (*seek time*), the time taken for the disk to rotate so that the sector to be read is under the head (*latency*), the time for the head to stop vibrating when it reaches a track (*settle time*), and the time taken to read the data from a sector (*read time*). We can represent access time as

$$t_{access} = t_{seek} + t_{latency} + t_{settle} + t_{read}$$

The average time to step from track to track is difficult to determine because the modern voice coil actuated head doesn't move at constant velocity and considerations such as head settling time need to be taken into account. Each seek consists of four distinct phases:

- acceleration (the arm is accelerated until it reaches approximately half way to its destination track)
- coasting (after acceleration on long seeks the arm moves at its maximum velocity)
- deceleration (the head must slow down and stop at its destination)
- settling (the head has to be exactly positioned over the desired track and any vibrations die out).

Designing head-positioning mechanisms isn't easy. If you make the arm on which the head is mounted very light to

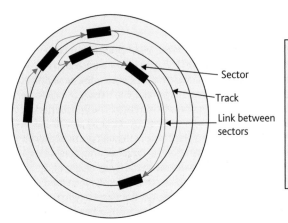

In a random access file, each sector in the file has a pointer to the next sector. This means that sectors can be read one-after-another without having to read all sectors. However, it is necessary to perform a new seek between each read.

Modern disk systems read sectors before they are needed and store them in a buffer.

Figure 12.40 The arrangement of the sectors of a file.

improve the head assembly's acceleration, the arm will be too flimsy and twist. If you make the arm stiffer and heavier, it will require more power to accelerate it.

The average number of steps per access depends on the arrangement of the data on the disk and on what happens to the head between successive accesses. If the head is parked at the periphery of the disk, it must move further on average than if it is parked at the center of the tracks. Figure 12.40 shows a file composed of six sectors arranged at random over the surface of the disk. Consequently, the head must move from track to track at random when the file is read sector by sector.

A crude estimate of the average stepping time is one-third the number of tracks multiplied by the time taken to step from one track to the adjacent track. This figure is based on the assumption that the head moves a random distance from its current track to its next track each time a seek operation is carried out. If the head were to be retracted to track 0 after each seek, the average access time would be half the total number of tracks multiplied by the track-to-track stepping time. If the head were to be parked in the middle of the tracks after each seek, the average access time would be 1/4 of the number of tracks multiplied by the track-to-track stepping time. These figures are valid only for older forms of actuators.

Very short seeks (1 to 4 tracks) are dominated by *head settling time*. Seeks in the range 200 to 400 tracks are dominated by the constant acceleration phase and the seek time is proportional to the square root of the number of tracks to step plus the settle time. Long seeks are dominated by the constant velocity or coasting phase and the seek time is proportional to the number of tracks.

A hard disk manufacturer specifies seek times as minimum (e.g. 1.5 ms to step one track), average (8.2 ms averaged over all possible seeks), and maximum (17.7 ms for a full stroke end-to-end seek). These figures are for a 250 Gbyte Hitachi Deskstar.

The access time of a disk is made up of its seek time and the time to access a given sector once a track has been reached

(the latency). The latency is easy to calculate. If you assume that the head has just stepped to a given track, the minimum latency is zero (the sector is just arriving under the head). The worst case latency is one revolution (the head has just missed the sector and has to wait for it to go round). On average, the latency is $1/2\ t_{rev}$, where t_{rev} is the time for a single revolution of the platter. If a disk rotates at 7200 rpm, its latency is given by

$$\frac{1}{2} \times 1/(7200 \div 60) = 0.00417\,\text{s} = 4.17\,\text{ms}$$

An important parameter is the rate at which data is transferred to and from the disk. If a disk rotates at R revolutions per minute and has s sectors per track, and each sector contains B bits, the capacity of a track is $B \cdot s$ bits. These $B \cdot s$ bits are read in $60/R$ seconds giving a data rate of $B \cdot s/(60/R) = B \cdot sR/60$ bits/s. This is, of course, the actual rate at which data is read from the disk. Buffering the data in the drive's electronics allows it to be transmitted to the host computer at a different rate.

The length of a track close to the center of a disk is less than that of a track near to the outer edge of the disk. In order to maximize the storage capacity, some systems use *zoning* in which the outer tracks have more sectors than the inner tracks.

Modern disk drives must be tolerant to shock (i.e. acceleration caused by movement such as a knock or jolt). This requirement is particularly important for disk drives in portable equipment such as laptop computers. Two shock parameters are normally quoted. One refers to the tolerance to shock when the disk is inoperative and the other to shock while the disk is running. Shock can cause two problems. One is physical damage to the surface of the disk if the head crashes into it (this is called *head slap*). The other is damage to data structures if the head is moved to another track during a write operation. Shock sensors can be incorporated in the disk drive to detect the beginning of a shock event and disable any write operation in progress.

THE DISK ELECTRICAL INTERFACE

A disk drive's electrical interface defines the way in which it communicates with the host computer. When hard disk drives first appeared, data was transferred between the computer and drive in the form it was to be written or read (i.e. the raw digital pulses). Disk drives were unintelligent and lacked sophisticated control systems. The signal processing electronics was located on an interface card in the computer. All signal processing is now carried out by circuits located inside the disk drive housing.

Disk drives are described in terms of the interface between drive and the computer; for example, IDE (integrated drive electronics), serial ATA (AT attachment), or SCSI (small computer system interface).

The first interface for disks in PC systems was the ST-506 from Seagate technologies, which used two ribbon cables to connect an *unintelligent* disk to a controller card in the PC. This bus was replaced by the ESDI interface (an improved version of ST-506) in the mid-1980s.

The IDE (integrated drive electronics) interface was the first high-performance PC disk interface introduced in 1986 to support disks up to 528 Mbytes at rates up to 3 Mbytes/s. In the late 1990s the E-IDE (enhanced IDE) interface was designed to handle disks up to 9.4 Gbytes and data rates up to 20 Mbytes/s. Over the years, the IDE interface has been developed and some of its variants are called ATA, ATA/ATAPI, EIDE, ATA-2, Fast ATA, ATA-3, Ultra ATA, and Ultra DMA.

IDE is little more than a parallel data highway that copies data between the PC's AT bus and the disk drive. The drive control electronics is now located where it belongs, in the disk drive.

The general-purpose *small computer systems interface* (SCSI) connects up to eight independent disk drives or similar peripherals to a computer. SCSI interfaces are associated with high-performance computers and a special controller is required to operate the SCSI bus. The SCSI-1 standard, adopted in 1986, defines how data is transferred over the SCSI bus. As in the case of the IDE interface, the SCSI standard has been amended to provide a higher level of performance. The original SCSI interface had an 8-bit data path and operated at 2 Mbps (2 million bits/s). A new standard, SCSI-2, was introduced in 1990 to provide synchronous data transfers at 10 Mbps. A SCSI-2 option called *wide* SCSI provides a 16-bit data path and a maximum transfer rate of 20 Mbps. The SCSI-3 standard now supports data rates up to 80 Mbps.

In 2002 the Serial ATA interface was introduced into PCs. This interface is a serial version of the IDE interface which very much simplifies the integration of hard drives into a PC because a serial connector is less bulky than an IDE's bulky ribbon connector. In 2004 a second-generation serial interface with a data rate of 300 Mbps was introduced.

AUDIO VISUAL DRIVES

In the mid-1990s three things happened to PCs; their speed increased to the point at which they could process audio and video signals, the capacity of hard disks became sufficient to store over an hour of video, and computing entered an audio-visual age. Conventional drives suffer from *data discontinuity* when there is a short gap during a stream of data. Data processing applications require a low average access time and it doesn't matter if there are infrequent short gaps in the data stream. When data represents sound or moving images, the ear or the eye can detect even tiny interruptions.

Because data elements are very small, tiny imperfections in the magnetic media cause errors in the data stream when data is read from a disk. Powerful error-correcting codes are used to protect the stored data. On readback, the data from the disk is processed and errors automatically corrected. A conventional disk might take 800 ms to recover from an error.

Disk manufacturers created the so-called *audio-visual* (A/V) drive which employs the same storage technology as conventional drives, but uses high-speed error-correction hardware and algorithms.

As the density of bits on platters has increased, the thermal characteristics (i.e. expansion or contraction with temperature changes) of the disk and read/write mechanism have become more important. Temperature changes affect the head's ability to follow a track. Some disk drives include *thermal calibration* that periodically compensates for temperature changes. This calibration takes place every few minutes and is invisible to the user. However, it does cause an interruption of about 0.1 s in the data flow. A/V disks perform thermal calibration intelligently and delay calibration if a data request is pending. If thermal calibration is taking place and data is requested, the drive reschedules the recalibration process and immediately begins to access the data.

An important parameter of the disk drive is its *mean time between failure* (MTBF), which is the average time between failures. The MTBF ranges from over 1 000 000 hours for large drives to 100 000 hours for smaller and older drives. A 100 000-hour MTBF indicates that the drive can be expected to operate for about 11½ years continually without failure—a value that is longer than the average working life of a PC.

A disk with a MTBF of 1 000 000 hours can be expected to run for over 100 years.

12.7.2 High-performance drives

Several technologies have been used to dramatically increase the performance of disk drives. Here we discuss two of them:

PROGRESS

In 1980 IBM introduced the world's first 1 Gbyte disk drive, the IBM 3380, which was the size of a refrigerator, weighed 550 pounds, and cost $40 000. In 2000 IBM introduced a 1-Gbyte microdrive, the world's smallest hard disk drive with a platter that's about the size of an American quarter.

In 2002 IBM dropped out of the disk drive market and merged its disk drive division with Hitachi to create HGST (Hitachi Global Storage Technologies).

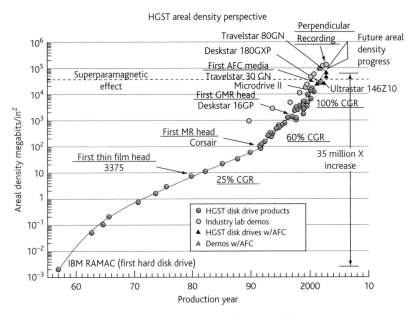

Figure 12.41   Data density as a function of time (from HGST).

magnetoresistive head technology and *partial response maximum likelihood data demodulation* (PRML).[2] Figure 12.41 shows the increase in areal densities for IBM disk drives since 1980 and the recent growth rate made possible largely through the use of magnetoresistive heads.

The magnetoresistive head

The ultimate performance of a disk drive using the traditional read head we described earlier is limited because the recording head has to perform the conflicting tasks of writing data on the disk and retrieving previously written data. As the bit patterns recorded on the surface of disks have grown smaller, the amplitude of the signal from the read head has been reduced making it difficult for the drive's electronics to identify the recorded bit patterns. You can increases the read signal enough to determine the magnetic pattern recorded on the disk by adding turns around the magnetic core of the head because the read signal is proportional to the number of turns. However, increasing turns also increases the head's inductance—the resistance of a circuit to a change in the

current flowing through it. A high inductance limits the frequency with which the current reversals can occur during write operations.

Magnetoresistive head technology uses separate read and write heads. An inductive head, optimized for writing information, is integrated with a magnetoresistive structure optimized for reading. Each of the two elements can be optimized to perform its particular function— reading or writing data

A magnetoresistive head operates in a different way to conventional read heads. In a conventional head, a change in magnetic flux from the disk induces a voltage in a coil. In a magnetoresistive head, the flux modifies the electrical resistance of a conductor (i.e. more current flows through the conductor when you apply a voltage across it). Lord Kelvin discovered this phenomenon, called *anisotropic magnetoresistance*, in 1857. The read element of an MR head consists of a minute stripe of a permalloy material (a nickel-iron compound, NiFe) placed next to one of the write element's magnetic pole pieces. The electrical resistance of the permalloy changes by a few percent when it is placed in a magnetic field. This change in the material's resistance allows the MR head to detect the magnetic flux transitions associated with recorded bit patterns. During a read operation, a small current is passed through the stripe of resistive material. As the MR stripe is exposed to the magnetic field from the disk, an amplifier measures the resulting voltage drop across the stripe.

In the 1980s a phenomenon called the *giant magnetoresistive effect* was discovered which provided a much greater sensitivity than the conventional magnetoresistivity. By 1991

---

[2] A description of PRML is beyond the scope of this book. PRML encoding places pulses so close together that the data from one pulse contains interference from adjacent pulses. Digital signal processing algorithms are used to reconstruct the original digital data.

SUPERPARAMAGNETISM

Recording density increased by several orders of magnitude over a few years. However, such increases cannot continue because of the physical limitations of magnetic materials. Suppose we decide to scale magnetic media down and make the magnetic particles half their previous size. Halving the size of particles increases the areal density by 4 because you halve both length and width. Halving the size reduces the *volume* of a particle by 8; in turn this reduces the magnetic energy per particle by a factor of 8.

In a magnetic material, particles are aligned with the internal field. However, thermal vibrations cause the magnetic orientation of the particles to oscillate and some particles can spontaneously reverse direction. Reducing a particle's size can dramatically increase its tendency to spontaneously change state. According to an IBM paper, halving the size of particles can change the average spontaneous flux reversal time form 100 years to 100 ns! When particle sizes are so small that they spontaneously lose their magnetization almost instantaneously, the effect is called superparamagnetism. The limit imposed by superparamagnetism is of the order of 100 Gbits/in^2. Fortunately, techniques involving the use of complex magnetic structures have been devised to delay the onset of superparamagnetism by at least an order of magnitude of areal density.

IBM was exploiting the effect in their drives. This technology became known as GMR and the GMR head is now the standard in high-performance disk drives.

12.7.3 **RAID systems**

RAID (redundant array of inexpensive disks) technology combines separate disk drives into a single system. In the 1980s and 1990s low-capacity disks were relatively cheaper than their high-capacity counterparts—due to the low cost of mass-produced disk drives targeted at the PC market. It was more cost effective to create a large memory system by using several low-capacity drives than by using a single high-capacity drive.

In 1987 Garth Gibson, Randy H. Katz, and David A. Patterson at the University of California in Berkeley devised RAID technology using low-cost disk drives to create a large and reliable disk store. There are several variations of the RAID technologies called RAID 0, RAID 1, RAID 2, . . . , RAID 5. We discuss only RAID 1, RAID 3, and RAID 5 systems here.

RAID 0 systems provide performance enhancement rather than increasing fault tolerance. The data stream is split into blocks and distributed between the drives in a RAID array.

RAID 1 systems connect two hard drives to a single disk controller to provide *disk mirroring*. Two copies are made of all files and each copy can be read independently of the other. Read access time is improved because the controller can obtain data from the first drive that has it ready. RAID 1 systems improve reliability because there are two copies of each file. If the probability of one drive failing is p (where $p \ll 1$), the probability of both drives failing is p^2, which greatly enhances reliability. RAID 1 technology is inefficient because the amount of disk space required is doubled.

RAID 3 technology transfers data in parallel to multiple disks. RAID 3 systems have n data disks and a separate parity disk (n is typically 4). Data in a RAID 3 system is said to be

Stripe	Disk 1 bit 1	Disk 2 bit 2	Disk 3 bit 3	Disk 4 bit 4	Disk 5 P
1	0	1	0	0	1
2	1	1	0	0	0
3	0	1	1	1	1
4	1	0	1	0	0

Table 12.6 Principle of the RAID 3 array.

striped so that a stripe is sent in parallel to each of the n drives. A parity byte (generated across the n stripes) is stored on the parity disk. If an error occurs in any of the stripes, the missing data can be regenerated from the parity information. An error in a data block of one of the disks can be detected by the error-detecting code used whenever data is stored on disk.

Let's illustrate the RAID 3 system with a simple example, where P represents a parity bit across bits (i.e. disks) 1 to 4. Table 12.6 shows four stripes across the five disks. The value of stripe 1 is 0100 and its even parity bit is 1, which is stored on the parity disk number 5.

Suppose disk drive 3 in the array fails to give the situation in Table 12.7. The error-detecting codes on disk 3 indicate that the data has been corrupted but cannot tell you what the data should have been. However, because we still have the data on disks 1, 2, and 4 and the parity disk, we can reconstruct the missing data. For example, stripe 2 is 11?00. In order to maintain correct parity the missing bit must be 0 and the corrected stripe is 11000. RAID 3 systems require that the heads of the disk be synchronized.

Another popular implementation of RAID technology is the RAID 5 array, which is similar to a RAID 3 array because n drives are used to store stripes of data and one is used to store a parity stripe. However, the stripes in a RAID 5 system are sectors rather than bytes and the parity stripes are distributed

Stripe	Disk 1 bit 1	Disk 2 bit 2	Disk 3 bit 3	Disk 4 bit 4	Disk 5 P
1	0	1	?	0	1
2	1	1	?	0	0
3	0	1	?	1	1
4	1	0	?	0	0

Table 12.7 Correcting an error in a RAID 3 array.

across the array rather than stored on a specific drive. RAID 5 systems are more suited to smaller blocks of data (e.g. in network systems) and are simpler because they don't require the read/write heads of each of the drives to be synchronized.

Both RAID 3 and RAID 5 systems can tolerate the complete failure of one of the disks in the array. When that happens, their error-correcting property vanishes although the array can operate (assuming no further errors) until a new drive is swapped in. The operator can pull out the failed drive and plug in a spare drive to keep the system running smoothly.

By the way, the mean time between failures of an array of disks is less than that of a single disk. If you have five drives, it's five times more likely that one of them will fail over a given period than if you had just one drive. However, the use of redundancy (i.e. the ability to tolerate a single failure) in a RAID system more than compensates for the increased probability of a single disk failure because two disks have to fail to bring the system down.

Parameters of a disk drive

Table 12.8 describes the characteristics of a disk drive that represented the state of the art in 2004. We can be fairly confident that within 1 or 2 years its capacity will become commonplace and within 5 years its capacity will be well below that of newer drives. Equally, we can be confident that its access time and many of its other characteristics will not change much over a 5-year time span.

12.7.4 The floppy disk drive

The floppy disk is a removable secondary storage medium that can be transported between systems. Floppy disks have long access times and low capacities and are almost obsolete. Better removable magnetic media such as the Zip drive, writable optical storage, and the flash EPROM USB pen drive have replaced the floppy disk. We cover the floppy disk drive partially for historical reasons and partially because it demonstrates magnetic recording principles well.

The floppy disk drive is an IBM invention dating back to the 1960s, when it was first used to load microcode into

Configuration Interface	Parallel-ATA (Serial-ATA) Ultra ATA/133 (SATA 2 3 Gbytes/s)
Capacity	500 Gbytes/s
Platters	5
Heads	10
Data buffer	16 Mbytes (SATA 2 version)
Rotational speed	7200 rpm
Maximum media transfer rate	817 Mbytes/s
Interface data transfer rate	133 Mbytes/s (3 GBytes/s SATA2)
Sustained data rate	61.8 to 31 Mbytes/s (depends on zone)
Average read seek time	8.5 ms
Non-recoverable hard error rate	1 in 10^{14}
Operating shock (duration 2 ms)	55 G

Table 12.8 Parameters of the Deskstar 7K500.

IBM's 370 computers and later to store information in the IBM 3740 Data Entry System. The original floppy disk was made of plastic coated with a magnetic material enclosed in an 8-inch square protective envelope. The 8-inch floppy disk was replaced by the 5¼-inch minifloppy disk, which was replaced by the 3½-inch floppy disk, which comes in a more robust rigid plastic case. The capacity of an 8-inch floppy disk was 300 kbytes and the capacity of a first-generation 5½-inch floppy disk was 80 Kbytes; 3½-inch floppies store 1.44 Mbytes (some have capacities of 2.88 Mbytes). Such tiny capacities mean that the floppy disk drive can be used only to copy small files such as text and emails or device drivers. Many modern PCs no longer provide floppy disk drives.

Floppy disks rotate at 360 rpm, about 5% the speed of a hard disk drive, to reduce the frictional heating of the disk in its envelope. This gives a rotational latency of 166 ms.

A 3½-inch floppy disk's read/write head is moved to the desired track by a stepping mechanism. The head positioned over the disk accesses its surface through a sliding metal window in a 3½-inch disk. Floppy drives use two heads to record data on both sides of the disk. The head in a floppy disk comes into contact with the surface. In order to prevent undue wear on the head and the disk's surface, the drive motor may be stopped after a period of disk inactivity.

The 3½-inch 1.44 Mbyte floppy disk has 80 0.115 mm wide tracks of 18 sectors spaced at 135 tracks per inch. Data is recorded at an average density of about 17000 bits/in. The capacity is expressed as formatted capacity and represents the data available to users. It does not include data that performs housekeeping tasks such as labeling the track and sector number of each sector stored on the disk. In hard disk terms this capacity is tiny indeed.

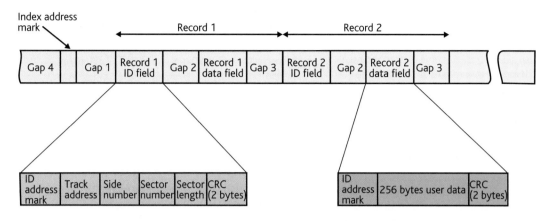

Figure 12.42 Structure of a track.

12.7.5 Organization of data on disks

Having described the principles of magnetic recording systems we now briefly explain how data is can be arranged on a disk. This section provides an overview but doesn't describe a complete system in detail. Although there is an almost infinite number of ways in which digital data may be organized or formatted on a disk, two systems developed by IBM have become standard: the IBM 3740-compatible single-density recording and the IBM System 34-compatible double-density recording.

A disk must be *formatted* before it can be used by writing sectors along the tracks in order to let the controller know when to start reading or writing information. Formatting involves writing a series of sector headers followed by empty data fields that can later be filled with data as required.

Figure 12.42 describes the structure of a track formatted according to the IBM 34 format double-density system. Gaps are required between data structures to allow for variations in the disk's speed and time to switch between read and write operations. The disk drive is a mechanical device and doesn't rotate at an exactly constant speed. Consequently, the exact size of a sector will be slightly different each time you write it. Second, the drive electronics needs a means of locating the beginning of each sector.

A track consists of an index gap followed by a sequence of sectors. The number and size of sectors varies from operating system to operating system. Each sector includes an *identity field* (ID field) and a data field. The various information units on the disk are separated by gaps. A string of null bytes is written at the start of the track followed by an index address mark to denote the start of the current track. The address mark is a special byte, unlike any other. We've already seen that the MFM recording process uses a particular algorithm to encode data. That is, only certain recorded bit patterns are valid. By deliberately violating the recording algorithm and recording a bit pattern that does not conform to the set of

valid patterns, uniquely identifiable bit patterns can be created to act as special markers. Such special bit patterns are created by omitting certain clock pulses.

The sectors following the index gap are made up of an ID (identification) address mark, an ID field, a gap, a data field, and a further gap. The ID field is 7 bytes long including the ID address mark. The other 6 bytes of the address field are the track number, the side number (0 or 1), the sector address, the sector length code, and a 2-byte cyclic redundancy check (CRC) code. The 16-bit CRC provides a powerful method of detecting an error in the sector's ID field and is the 16-bit remainder obtained by dividing the polynomial representing the field to be protected by a standard generator polynomial.

The beginning of the data field itself is denoted by one of two special markers: a data address mark or a deleted data address mark (these distinguish between data that is active and data that is no longer required). Following the data address mark comes a block of user data (typically 128 to 1024 bytes) terminated by a 16-bit CRC to protect the data field from error. The data field is bracketed by two gaps to provide time for the write circuits in the disk to turn on to write a new data field and then turn off before the next sector is encountered. Gap 2 must have an exact size for correct operation with a floppy disk controller, whereas gaps 1, 3, and 4 are simply delimiters and must only be greater than some specified minimum.

Disk data structures

The large-scale structure of information on disks belongs to the realm of operating systems. However, now that we've come so far we should say something about files. Conceptually, we can imagine that a filing system might require three data structures: a list of sectors available to the filing system (i.e. the free sectors), a directory of files, and the files themselves.

PROBLEM

A 3½-inch floppy disk drive uses two-sided disks and records data on 80 tracks per side. A track has nine sectors and each holds 512 bytes of data. The disk rotates at 360 rpm, the seek time is 10 ms track to track, and the head settling time is 10 ms. From the above information calculate the following.

(a) The total capacity of the floppy disk in bytes.

(b) The average rotational latency.

(c) The average time to locate a given sector assuming that the head is initially parked at track 0.

(d) The time taken to read a single sector once it has been located.

(e) The average rate at which data is moved from the disk to the processor during the reading of a sector. This should be expressed in bits per second.

(f) The packing density of the disk in terms of bits per inch around a track located at 3 inches from the center.

(a) Total capacity = sides × tracks × sectors × bytes/sector = 2 × 80 × 9 × 512 = 737 280 bytes (called 720 Kbyts).

(b) Average rotational latency = ½ period of revolution 360 rpm corresponds to 360/60 = 6 revolutions per second one revolution = 1/6 second average latency is therefore 1/12 second = 83.3 ms.

(c) Average time to locate sector = latency + head settling time + seek time = 83.3 ms + 10 ms + 80/2 × 10 ms

(d) In one revolution (1/6 second), nine sectors pass under the head. Therefore, time to read one sector is 1/6 × 1/9 = 18.52 ms.

(e) During the reading of a sector, 512 bytes are read in 18.52 ms. The average data rate is the number of bits read divided by the time taken = (512 × 8)/0.01852 = 221 166 bits/s.

(f) Packing density = total number of bits divided by track length = 9 × 512 × 8/(2 × 3.142 × 1.5) = 1955.4 bits/in.

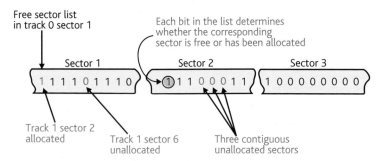

Figure 12.43 Free sector list.

The free sector list

A simple method of dealing with the allocation of sectors to files is to provide a bit-map (usually in track 0, sector 1). Each bit in the bit-map represents one of the sectors on the disk and is clear to indicate a free sector and set to indicate an allocated sector. *Free* means that the sector can be given to a new file and *allocated* means that the sector already belongs to a file. If all bits of the bit-map are set, there are no more free sectors and the disk is full. Figure 12.43 illustrates the free sector list.

Suppose the disk file manager creates a file. It first searches the bit-map for free sectors, and then allocates the appropriate number of free sectors to the new file. When a file is deleted, the disk file manager returns the file's sectors to the pool of free sectors simply by clearing the corresponding bits in the bit-map. The sectors comprising the deleted file are not overwritten when the file is deleted by the operating system.

You can recover so-called deleted files as long as they haven't been overwritten since they were removed from the directory and their sectors returned to the pool of free sectors.

There's little point in storing data on a disk unless it can be easily accessed. To achieve this objective, a data structure called a *directory* holds information about the nature of each file and where the file can be found. Information in directories varies from the file name plus the location of the first sector of the file to an extensive description of the file including attributes such as file ownership, access rights, date of creation, and date of last access.

The sectors of a file can be arranged as a linked list in which each sector contains a pointer to the next sector in the list as Fig. 12.44 demonstrates. The final sector contains a null pointer because it has no next sector to point to. Two bytes are required for each pointer; one for the track number and one for the sector number. The advantage of a linked list is that the sectors can be randomly organized on the disk (randomization occurs because new files are continually being created and old files deleted).

Linked lists create sequential access files rather than random access files. The only way of accessing a particular sector in the file is by reading all sectors of the list until the desired sector is located. Such a sequential access is, of course, highly inefficient. Sequential access files are easy to set up and a sequential file system is much easier to design than one that caters for random access files.

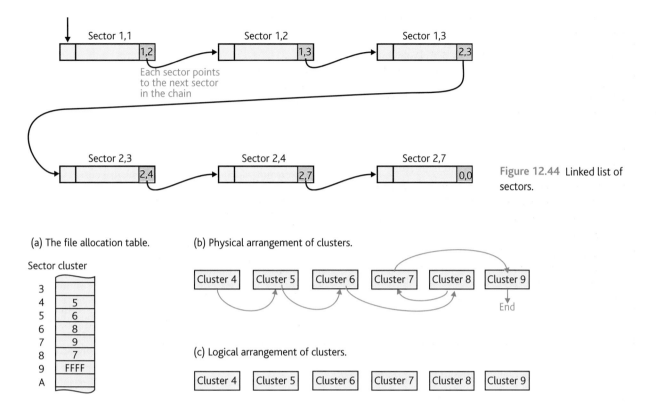

Figure 12.44 Linked list of sectors.

Figure 12.45 The file allocation table.

As time passes and files are created, modified, and deleted, files on a disk may become very fragmented (i.e. the locations of their sectors are, effectively, random). Once the sectors of a file are located at almost entirely random points on the disk, disk accesses become very long because of the amount of head movement required. Defragmentation programs are used to clean up the disk by reorganizing files to make consecutive logical sectors have consecutive addresses. We now briefly describe the structure of the filing system used by MS-DOS.

The MS-DOS file structure

MS-DOS extends the simple bit-map of Fig. 12.43 to a linked list of *clusters*, where each cluster represents a group of sectors. DOS associates each entry in a *file allocation table* (FAT), with a cluster of two to eight sectors (the size of the clusters is related to the size of the disk drive). Using a cluster-map rather than a bit-map reduces both the size of the map and the number of times that the operating system has to search the map for new sectors. However, the cluster-map increases the granularity of files because files are forced to grow in minimum increments of a whole cluster. If sectors hold 1024 bytes, four-sector clusters mean that the minimum increment for a file is 4×1024 bytes = 4 Kbytes. If the disk holds many files, the total wasted space can be quite large.

Each entry in the FAT corresponds to an actual cluster of sectors on the disk. Figure 12.45 illustrates the structure of a FAT with entries 4 to 9 corresponding to clusters 4 to 9. Assume that a file starts with cluster number 4 and each cluster points to the next cluster in a file. The FAT entry corresponding to the first cluster contains the value 5, which indicates that the next cluster is 5. Note how entry 6 contains the value 8 indicating that the cluster after 6 is 8. Clusters aren't allocated sequentially, which leads to the fragmentation we described earlier. Figure 12.45(b) shows the physical sequence of clusters on the disk corresponding to this FAT. We have used lines with arrows to show how clusters are connected to each other. Figure 12.45(c) shows how the operating system sees the file as a logical sequence of clusters.

Cluster 9 in the FAT belonging to this file contains the value $FFFF_{16}$, which indicates that this is the last cluster in a file. Another special code used by DOS, $FFF7_{16}$, indicates that the corresponding cluster is unavailable because it is damaged (i.e. the magnetic media is defective). The FAT is set up when the disk is formatted and defective sectors are noted. The first two entries in a file allocation table provide a media descriptor that describes the characteristics of the disk.

When MS-DOS was designed, 12-bit FAT entries were sufficient for disks up to 10 Mbytes. A 16-bit FAT, called FAT16, can handle entries for disks above 10 Mbytes. The maximum size disk that can be supported is the number of clusters multiplied by the number of sectors per cluster multiplied by the number of bytes per sector. Because the FAT16 system supports only 65 525 clusters, the maximum disk size is limited (assuming a limit on the size of sectors and clusters). These figures demonstrate how rapidly the face of computing changed in the 1990s—a 10 Mbyte hard disk was once considered large, whereas today it's difficult to find a disk less than about 80 Gbytes (apart from in some portable systems). The rapid growth in disk capacity forced Microsoft to adopt a 32-bit FAT with Windows NT and later releases of Windows 95. FAT32 allows the operating system to handle disks up to 2 terabytes.

DOS storage media hold four types of data element. The first element is called the boot record and identifies the operating system, and structure of the disk (number of sectors and clusters, size of clusters) and can provide a boot program used when the system is first powered up). Following the boot sector are two FATs (one is a copy of the other provided for security). After the FATs a root directory provides the details of the files. These details include the file name, the file characteristics (when created etc.) and the address of the file's first cluster in the FAT. The remainder of the disk is allocated to the files themselves.

12.8 Optical memory technology

Optical storage is the oldest method of storing information known to humanity. Early systems employed indentations in stone or pottery that were eventually rendered obsolete by flexible optical storage media such as papyrus and later paper.

Up to the 1980s, general-purpose digital computers used magnetic devices to store information. Optical storage systems were not widely used until the 1990s, because it was difficult to perform all the actions required to store and to retrieve data economically until improvements had been made in a wide range of technologies.

The optical disk or CD-ROM dramatically changed secondary storage technology and made it possible to store large quantities of information on a transportable medium at a low cost. A CD-ROM can store over 500 Mbytes of user data on one side of a single 120 mm (4.72 in) disk which is equivalent to around 200 000 pages of text. The optical disk is a rigid plastic disk, (Fig. 12.46), whose surface contains a long spiral track. The track is laid down on a clear polycarbonate plastic substrate inside the disk and is covered with a transparent plastic protective layer. Like the magnetic disk, information is stored along a track in binary form. Unlike the

---

THE RISE OF OPTICAL TECHNOLOGY

- 1980—James T. Russell develops the principle of optical storage in 1980.

- 1982—Philips and Sony release the first CD designed to store about 650 Mbytes of audio information (74 minutes).

- 1988—The CD-R format that defines writable CDs is defined.

- 1996—DVD emerges. DVD is almost identical to the CD but stores information more efficiently.

- 1997—A consortium of manufacturers release CD-RW, a re-writable CD.

- 2002—Release of high-speed DVD recording standards 4 × DVD-R and 4 × DVD-RW.

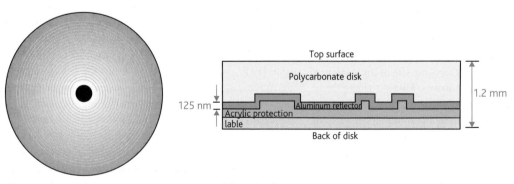

(a) View of CD. (b) Cross-section of CD.

Figure 12.46 The optical disk system.

magnetic disk, the track in an optical disk is a continuous spiral (like that of a gramophone record). The spiral on a CD begins at the innermost track and spirals outward, whereas the track on a gramophone record begins at the edge and spirals inward.

Although the principles of the optical disk are almost trivial, the details of its operation are very complex. The fundamental problems of optical storage are reliability, detecting the presence of tiny dents called *pits* on the surface of the disk, optically tracking the reflective elements, and encoding/decoding the data.

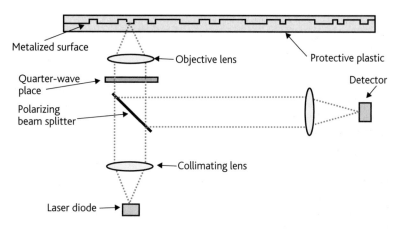

Figure 12.47 Structure of CD optics.

12.8.1 Storing and reading information

An optical disk stores information by means of dots along a track. Figure 12.47 shows how a beam of light produced by a semiconductor laser is focused onto the surface of the track and a photosensitive transistor detects the light reflected back from the surface.

To give you an idea of the precision involved, the objective lens is positioned about 1 mm above the surface of the disk and the depth of focus of the spot is 2 μm. The lens must be positioned to an accuracy of about one millionth of a meter above the disk.

The amount of light reflected back from a laser depends on the height of the reflecting surface on the disk. The base of this reflecting surface is called the *land* and indentations in it are known as *pits* (when viewed from above the disk).

Data is recorded as a series of variable length pits along a spiral track at a 1.6 μm constant pitch. A CD has 20 000 tracks and a track is 30 times narrower than a single human hair. The pits and land are coated onto a substrate and covered with a protective transparent layer. The disk is produced by stamping from a master disk that is, itself, produced by the same type of technology employed to fabricate microprocessors. It's expensive to make one CD-ROM, but very cheap to make thousands. Indeed, by the late 1990s CD-ROMs were used to distribute advertising material and software from Internet service providers so freely that computer magazines were full of readers' letters asking what they should do with all these unwanted CDs.

Light from the laser is focused first through an objective lens and then by the air-disk interface onto the pits and land as Fig. 12.48 demonstrates. This arrangement means that the spot of light on the surface is very much larger (by three orders of magnitude) than the pits. Consequently, surface imperfections and dust particles don't interfere with the read-back process. In other words, you can tolerate a speck of dust on the surface of a CD that's over 100 times larger than

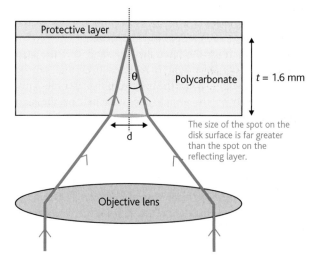

Fig. 12.48 Focusing on the pits and land.

the pit on which the beam is focused without getting a read error. By the way, many CD users put a CD down with the clear side up because they think the clear side must be protected. That's not so. The side with the pits and lands is covered with a thin 0.02 mm protective coating and is more vulnerable to scratches than the clear side.

In order to understand how data from a CD is read, you have to know something about the nature of laser light. The individual light waves in light from the sun or from a lamp are *incoherent* or random; that is, the light source is composed of a very large number of random waves. Light from a laser is *coherent* and all the waves are synchronized—they go up and down together. If you take two laser beams with identical frequencies and shine them on the same spot the beams add up. If the beams are in phase (i.e. the light waves go up and down at the same time) the resulting spot will be four times

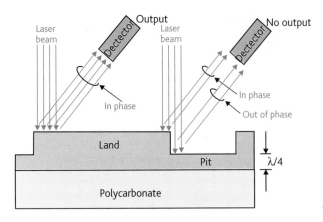

Figure 12.49 Light reflected from a CD.

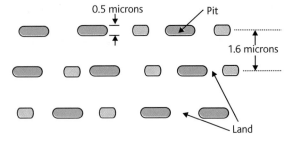

Figure 12.50 Organization of the track with land/pits.

as bright (not twice as bright because the beam's energy is the square of its amplitude). However, if the beams are 180° out of phase with one wave going up as the other goes down, the waves will cancel and the spot will disappear.

When light from the laser hits the land (i.e. the area between the pits), the light is reflected back and can be detected by a sensor. When the light from the laser hits a pit, about half falls on the pit and the other half on the land around the pit (see Fig. 12.49). The height of the pit is approximately 0.13 μm above the surrounding land so that light that hits the land has to travel an extra 2 × 0.13 μm further to get to the detector. However, 0.13 μm corresponds to 1/4 of the wavelength of the light in the plastic medium and the light reflected back from around a pit travels 1/2 wavelength further than the light reflected from the top of a pit. The light from the pit and light reflected from the surrounding land destructively interfere and the light waves cancel each other out. A change in the level of light intensity reflected from the surface of the disk represents a change from land to pit or from pit to land. Figure 12.50 shows the structure of the pits and land in more detail.

The spot of laser light that follows a track should be as small as possible in order to pack as many pits and therefore data onto the disk as possible. The minimum size of the spot is determined by a number of practical engineering considerations. The resolution (i.e. the smallest element that can be seen) of the optical system is determined by the wavelength of the laser light (780 nm) and the *numerical aperture* of the objective lens (0.45). Numerical aperture (NA) is defined as lens diameter divided by the focal length and is a measure of a lens's light-gathering power. The value of 0.45 is a compromise between resolution and depth of focus. Increasing the resolution and hence storage capacity makes it harder to focus the beam on the disk. These values of wavelength and NA provide a minimum resolution of 1 μm. Note that there is sometimes confusion about the wavelength of the laser light. The wavelength is 780 nm in air, but when the laser

beam travels through the plastic material of the disk its wavelength is reduced to 500 nm.

The sizes of the pits are such that half the energy of the spot falls on a pit and half falls onto the land. The reflected energy is ideally zero if the light from the pits and land interfere destructively. The optimum separation of the pits is determined by the wavelength of the light used by the laser.

The data stored on the CD-ROM has to be encoded to achieve both maximum storage density and freedom from errors. Moreover, the encoding technique must be self-clocking to simplify the data recovery circuits. Figure 12.51 illustrates the basic encoding scheme chosen by the designers of the CD-ROM. The length of the pits themselves is modulated and the transition of a pit to land (or from land to pit) represents a one bit.

The source data is encoded so that each 8-bit byte is transformed into a 14-bit code. Although there are $2^{14} = 16\,384$ possible 14-bit patterns, only $2^8 = 256$ of these patterns are actually used. The encoding algorithm chooses 14-bit code words that do not have two consecutive 1s separated by less than two 0s. Moreover, the longest permitted run of 0s is 10. These two restrictions mean that the 14-bit code has 267 legal values, of which 256 are actually used. The 14-bit codes corresponding to the first 10 8-bit codes are given in Table 12.9.

The groups of 14-bit code words are not simply joined end to end, but are separated by three so-called *merging bits*. The function of the merging bits is to ensure that the encoding rules are not violated when the end of one group is taken in conjunction with the start of the next. These merging bits carry no useful data and are simply separators. The following example demonstrates the need for merging bits.

Source data: 0010   1000 . . . . . .

These two patterns generate the sequence ..00101000 . . . Note how the end of the first group and the start of the second group create the forbidden pattern 101 that has a 1 separated from another 1 by less than two 0s. We can solve the problem by inserting the separator 000 between the groups to get

Encoded data: . . . . 00100001000 . . . .

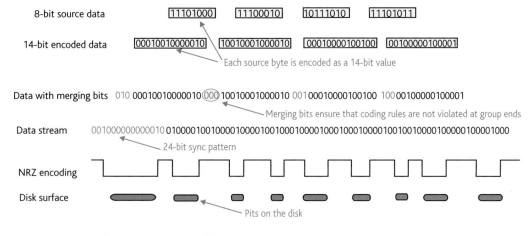

Figure 12.51 Encoding data on an optical disk.

	Source data bits	Encoded bits
0	00000000	01001000100000
1	00000001	10000100000000
2	00000010	10010000100000
3	00000011	10001000100000
4	00000100	01000100000000
5	00000101	00000100010000
6	00000110	00010000100000
7	00000111	00100100000000
8	00001000	01001001000000
9	00001001	10000001000000
10	00001010	10010001000000

Table 12.9 Converting 8-bit values to a 14-bit code.

Three 0s (i.e. merging bits) have been inserted between the two code words to eliminate the possibility of a forbidden sequence of bits.

Another factor in the choice of the pattern of bits to be used as the merging bits is the need to keep the average lengths of the track and land along the surface of the tracks equal. This restriction is necessary because the CD drive's focusing and tracking mechanism uses the average energy reflected from the surface and, therefore, it is necessary to avoid changes in average energy due to data dependency.

The channel clock derived from the signal recovered from the pits and land is 4.3218 MHz because this is the maximum rate of change of signal from the pits and land at the standard CD scanning speed of 1.3 m/s. The bit density is 1.66 bits/μm or 42 kbits/inch. At a track pitch of 1.6 μm this corresponds to 6×10^8 bits/in^2 or 10^6 bit/mm^2.

Because of the way in which pits are laid down to the very high mechanical precision required by the system, it's impossible to avoid large numbers of errors. We therefore have to employ powerful error-correcting codes to nullify the effect of the errors. Due to the complexity of these codes, all we can do here is to describe their characteristics. Note that the encoding mechanism for data is different to that for audio information because data requires more protection. Consequently, a CD stores fewer bytes of used digital data than audio data.

The Cross Interleaved Reed–Solomon code (CIRC) takes groups of 24 bytes of data and encodes them into groups of 32 bytes. Information is interleaved (spread out over the surface of a track) so that a burst of errors at one physical location affects several code groups. The following hypothetical example should clarify this concept. Suppose data is recorded in groups of 4 bytes $a_1a_2a_3a_4$ $b_1b_2b_3b_4$ $c_1c_2c_3c_4$ $d_1d_2d_3d_4$ and that a group is not corrupted unless 2 bytes are lost in a group (because of some form of error-correcting mechanism). Because errors tend to occur in groups (because of, say, a scratch), large amounts of data will be lost. If we interleave the bytes, we might get $a_1b_1c_1d_1$ $a_2b_2c_2d_2$ $a_3b_3c_3d_3$ $a_4b_4c_4d_4$. In this case, if we lose 2 consecutive bytes, we will be able to correct the error because the bytes are from different groups.

One of the differences between the CD used to store audio information and the CD-ROM used by computers is that the latter employs an extra layer of encoding to reduce further the undetected error rate to one in 10^{13} bits. Moreover, the sophisticated CIRC encoding makes it possible to correct an error burst of up to 450 bytes (which would take up 2 mm of track length). The capacity of a CD-ROM is 553 Mbytes of user data (an audio CD can store 640 Mbytes of sound).

The spiral track of the CD-ROM is divided into individually addressable sectors. The address of a sector is expressed absolutely with respect to the start of the track and is in the

CD SPEED

The speed at which a CD rotates was determined by the conflicting requirements of the technology at the time the CD was first manufactured and the desire to store as much data as possible. Because the CD was originally devised to store audio information, its duration was set as 74 minutes to allow von Karajan's Beethoven's Ninth Symphony to go on a single CD.

First-generation CDs operated in real time; if it took 74 minutes to play a symphony, the disk took 74 minutes to read. When CDs began to be used to store data, it was not convenient to wait up to about 74 minutes to load a program.

Advances in technology allowed the disks to spin faster to read data in less time. A CD reader described as 8X can read data eight times faster than a standard drive. Modern CDs have read speeds of over 50 that of an audio disk, although such a sustained increase in speed is rarely achieved in practice.

Write speeds and rewrite speeds have also increased; for example, in 2004 a writable and re-writable CD drive might be described as $52 \times 32 \times 52$; that is, it has a 52X read speed, a 52x write speed, and a 32x rewrite speed.

form of minutes, seconds, and blocks from the start (this format is the same as that of the audio CD). A sector or block is composed of 12 synchronizing bytes (for clock recovery), a 4-byte header that identifies the sector, a block of 2048 bytes of user data and 288 auxiliary bytes largely made up of the error-correcting code.

Because the size of the pits is constant and they are recorded along a spiral on a disk, the number of pits per revolution must vary between the inner and outer tracks. Contrast this with the magnetic disk, in which the bit density changes between inner and outer tracks because the bits must be smaller on inner tracks if there are to be the same number as in outer tracks.

A consequence of constant-size pits is that the speed of the disk depends on the location of the sector being read (i.e. the disk moves with a constant linear velocity, rather than a constant angular velocity). If the pits have a constant length, there are more pits around an outer track and therefore the disk must rotate slowly to read them at a constant rate. As the read head moves in towards the center, the disk must speed up because there are fewer pits around the circumference. First-generation CD-ROMs (and audio CDs) spin at between about 200 and 500 rpm. As you might imagine, this arrangement severely restricts the access time of the system. Moreover, the relatively heavy read head assembly also reduces the maximum track-to-track stepping time. These factors together limit the average access time of a CD-ROM to in the region of 100 to 200 ms (an order of magnitude worse than hard disks). We used the expression track-to-track stepping, even through the track is really a continuous spiral. When in the seek mode, the head steps across the spiral and reads an address block to determine whether it has reached the correct part of the spiral. As the technology used to manufacture CD drives improved through the 1990s, drive speeds were increased. Speeds went up from twice to 32 times the nominal CD rotation speed by the end of the 1990s and average access times dropped to 80 ms.

12.8.2 Writable CDs

When the CD drive first appeared, it was a read-only mechanism. Today, CD drives are available that can write data to a CD once only (CD-R), or write to CDs that can be erased and rewritten (CD-RW).

Some CD write mechanisms simply ablate (i.e. blast away) the surface of a non-reflecting layer of material above a reflecting background to create a pit. Others employ a powerful laser to melt a region of a coating of tellurium to create a pit. Another writable disk uses an organic dye within a layer in the disk. When the dye is hit by a laser during the write operation, the dye's optical properties are modified. The write laser has a power of 30 mW, which is about six times more powerful than the laser used to read data from a CD.

You can create true read/write optical storage systems that write data onto the disk, read it, and then erase it in order to write over it again. Clearly, any laser technology that burns or ablates a surface cannot be used in an erasable system. Erasable CDs exploit two fundamental properties of matter, its optical properties and its magnetic properties.

Figure 12.52 illustrates the principle of an erasable CD. The CD substrate is prestamped with the track structure and the track or groove coated with a number of layers (some are for the protection of the active layer). The active layer uses a material like *terbium iron cobalt* (TeFeCo), which changes the polarization of the reflected laser light. The magnetization of the TeFeCo film determines the direction of the reflected light's polarization.

Initially the film in Fig. 12.52(a) is subjected to a uniform magnetic field to align the TeFeCo molecules and therefore provide a base direction for the polarization of the reflected light. This base can be thought of as a continuous stream of zero bits. During the write phase (Fig. 12.52(b)) a short pulse of laser light hits the surface and heats the film

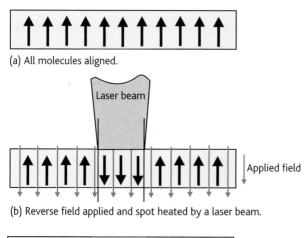

(a) All molecules aligned.

Laser beam

Applied field

(b) Reverse field applied and spot heated by a laser beam.

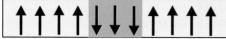

(c) Laser removed. Direction of magnetization of spot reversed.

Laser beam   Laser beam

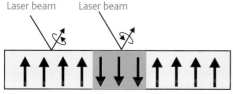

(d) Magnetization changes optical properties of surface.

Figure 12.52 Principle of the rewritable optical disk.

Transfer rate	
Burst transfer rate	3.0 Mbytes/s (async., max.)
	10.0 Mbytes/s (sync., max.)
Sustained transfer rate	6.14 Mbytes/s to 3.07 Mbytes/s (9.1 Gbyte/media)
	5.84 Mbytes/s to 2.87 Mbytes/s (8.6 Gbyte/media)
Speed	
Access Time	25 ms (avg.)
Latency	8.3 ms (avg.)
Rotational speed	3600 rpm
Buffer memory	8 Mbytes
Reliability	
MTBF	100 000 POH
MSBF	750 000 Cycles
MTTR	30 minutes
Bit error rate	10^{-17} bits

Table 12.10 Characteristics of a magneto-optical disk drive.

describes the characteristics of a typical magneto-optical disk drive.

The greatest physical difference between optical disks is the reflectivity of the surface; CD-ROMs are 70% reflective, CD-R 65%, and CD-RW about 20%.

High-capacity optical storage and the DVD

Not very long ago, the 600 Mbyte 5¼ inch CD-ROM was the state of the art. Progress in everything from laser technology to head-positioning to optical technology soon meant that the CD-ROM was no longer at the cutting edge of technology. Like all the other parts of the computer, the CD-ROM has evolved. In the late 1990s a new technology called the DVD-ROM (digital versatile disk) appeared. The DVD-ROM has a minimum capacity six times that of a CD-ROM and a potential capacity much more than that. Part of the driving force behind the development of the DVD-ROM was to put feature-length movies in digital video form on disk.

The DVD-ROM looks like a conventional CR-ROM and the underlying technology is exactly the same. Only the parameters have changed. Improvements in optical tracking have allowed the track spacing to be reduced and hence the length of the track to be considerably increased. DVD tracks are 0.74 µm apart (conventional CD-ROMs use 1.6 µm spacing). Lasers with shorter wavelengths (635 nm) have permitted the use of smaller pits.

changing its magnetic properties. When the surface is heated up to 300°C, the surface reaches its *Curie point* and loses the magnetization. By simultaneously activating an electromagnet under the surface of the disk, the direction of the film's magnetization can be reversed with respect to the base direction when the laser is switched off and the material cools. This action creates a 1 state. As the spot cools down (Fig. 12.52(c)), the drop in temperature fixes the new direction of magnetization.

The disk is read by focusing a weaker polarized beam on the disk and then detecting whether the reflected beam was rotated clockwise or counterclockwise (Fig. 12.52(d)). The same laser can be used for both reading and writing; the read power is much less than the write power.

To erase a bit, the area that was written to is pulsed once again with the high power laser and the direction of the magnetic field from the electromagnet reversed to write a zero.

High-capacity magneto-optical disks use a rugged polycarbonate disk platter mounted inside an enclosed cartridge that can store over 9 Gbytes of data. Table 12.10

Feature	DVD	CD
Disc diameter	120 mm	120 mm
Disc thickness	1.2 mm	1.2 mm
Track pitch	0.74 μm	1.6 μm
Track density	34 ktracks/in	16 ktracks /in
Bit density	96 kbits/in	43 kbits/in
Data rate	11 Mbits/s	1.2 to 4.8 Mbits/s
Data density	3.28 Gbits/in^2	0.68 Gbits/in^2
Minimum pit length	0.40 μm	0.834 μm
Laser wavelength	635 to 650 nm (red)	780 nm (infrared)
Numerical aperture of	0.60	0.45
Single layer data capacity	4.7 Gbytes	0.68 Gbytes
Reference speed	4.0 m/s	1.2 m/s
Reference user data rate	1108 kbytes/s	Mode 1: 153.6 kbytes/s
Signal modulation method	8/16 modulation	8/14 modulation

Table 12.11 Comparison of CD and DVD.

Parameter	CD	DVD	Improvement factor
Bit length	0.277 μm	0.13 μm	2.1
Track pitch	1.6 μm	0.74 μm	2.16
Data area	8605 mm^2	8759 mm^2	1.02
Modulation efficiency	17/8	16/8	1.06
Error correction loss	34%	13%	1.32
Sector overhead	8.2%	2.6%	1.07
Total increase			7

Table 12.12 Improvements in the efficiency of DVD in terms of data density.

The DVD-ROM can be double-sided, which instantly doubles its data capacity. Moreover, by using semitransparent layers, it is possible to have several optical layers within the disk. Focusing the laser on a particular layer accesses data in that layer. Other layers are out of focus.

Just as writable CDs have been developed, it is possible to buy writable DVDs. Unfortunately, several mutually incompatible technologies were developed nearly simultaneously forcing consumers to select a particular system (a similar situation existed in the early days of the VCR until the VHS format swept away its competitors). By 2004 DVD manufacturers were selling drives that were compatible with most of the available formats. Table 12.11 describes the differences between CDs and DVDs and Table 12.12 highlights the improvements in DVD technology.

Writable DVDs

In principal, writable DVDs are implemented in the same way as writable CDs. You modify the pit/land structure by a laser beam that either modifies the disk's magnetic or optical properties. Unfortunately, the DVD industry has not settled on a single writable disk standard due to competing economic, technical, and political (industrial) pressures. There are five basic standards for recordable DVDs: DVD-R, DVD-RW, DVD+R, DVD+RW, and DVD-RAM.

The write-once standards are DVD-R and DVD+R. These use a laser to change the optical properties of a material by burning pits on a dye layer within the disk. The rewritable standards, DVD-RW and DVD+RW, use a laser to reversibly change the optical properties of a material by changing, for example, its state between crystalline (reflective) and amorphous (dull).

The DVD-R and DVD+R formats compete against each other; the differences between them lie principally in the structure of the data on the disk. The most widely compatible format is DVD-R (in particular, it's compatible with the DVD players and with old DVD drives in PCs). In recent years, many DVD drives are able to handle a range of different formats by changing the laser properties to suit the actual media and the read/write software to suit the required data structures.

Another rewritable DVD is DVD-RAM, which uses DVDs with a pattern pressed onto the surface. DVD-RAM was originally designed for random access data storage by computers.

Sector address information is molded into the side of the track. DVD-RAM is the most incompatible of the DVD recordable formats (i.e. fewer drives read DVD-RAM than other recordable formats).

All types of DVD reserve a control area at the inside edge of the track that contains the disk's identification. This mechanism allows the drive to identify the type of medium currently loaded.

▧ SUMMARY

The von Neumann machine needs memory to store programs and data. Lots of memory. As computer technology has advanced, the size of user programs and operating systems has more than kept up. In the early 1980s a PC with a 10 Mbyte hard disk was state of the art. Today, even a modest utility might require over 10 Mbytes and a high-resolution digital camera is quite happy to create 5 Mbyte files when operating in it RAW (uncompressed) mode.

In this chapter we have looked at the computer's memory system. We began with a description of the characteristics of fast semiconductor memory and then moved on to characteristics of slower but much cheaper secondary storage. Today, there is a bewildering number of memory technologies. We have briefly covered some of them: from semiconductor dynamic memory to devices based on magnetism to optical storage technology. Memory technology is important because, to a great extent, it determines the way in which we use computers. Faster CPUs make it possible to process data rapidly, enabling us to tackle problems like high-speed, real-time graphics. Faster, denser, and cheaper memories make it possible to store and process large volumes of data. For example, the optical disk makes it possible to implement very large on-line databases. Low-cost high-capacity hard disks now enable people to carry more than 80 Gbytes of data in a portable computer or over 400 Gbytes in a desktop machine. In just two decades the capacity of hard disks in personal PCs has increased by a factor of 40 000.

▧ PROBLEMS

12.1 Why is memory required in a computer system?

12.2 Briefly define the meaning of the following terms associated with memory technology:
(a) random access
(b) non-volatile
(c) dynamic memory
(d) access time
(e) EPROM
(f) serial access

12.3 What properties of matter are used to store data?

12.4 A computer has a 64-bit data bus and 64-bit-wide memory blocks. If a memory access takes 10 ns, what is the bandwidth of the memory system?

12.5 A computer has a 64-bit data bus and 64-bit-wide memory blocks. The memory devices have an access time of 35 ns. A clock running at 200 MHz controls the computer and all operations take an integral (i.e. whole number) of clock cycles. What is the effective bandwidth of the memory system?

12.6 What is the purpose of a semiconductor memory's $\overline{CS}$ (chip select) input?

12.7 A dynamic RAM chip is organized as 64M × 4 bits. A memory composed of 1024 Mbytes is to be built with these chips. If each word of the memory is 64 bits wide, how many chips are required?

12.8 What are the principal characteristics of random access and serial access memory?

12.9 Why is all semiconductor ROM RAM but not all semiconductor RAM ROM?

12.10 If *content addressable memory* (CAM) could be manufactured as cheaply as current semiconductor memories, what impact do you think it would have on computers? We haven't covered CAM in this text—you'll have to look it up.

12.11 What is *flash memory* and why is it widely used to store a PC's BIOS (basic input/output system)?

12.12 Use a copy of a current magazine devoted to personal computing to work out the cost of memory today (price per megabyte for RAM, hard disk, flash memory, CD ROM, and DVD).

12.13 Give the size (i.e. the number of addressable locations) of each of the following memory blocks as a power of 2. The blocks are measured in bytes.
(a) 4K   (b) 16K
(c) 2M   (d) 64K
(e) 16M   (f) 256K

12.14 What address lines are required to span (i.e. address) each of the memory blocks in the previous problem? Assume that the processor is byte addressable and has 24 address lines A_{00} to A_{23}. What address lines must be decoded to select each of these blocks?

12.15 What is an *address decoder* and what role does it carry out in a computer?

12.16 A computer's memory can be constructed from memory components of various capacities (i.e. total number of bits) and organizations (i.e. locations x width of each location). For each of the following memory blocks, calculate how many of the specified memory chips are required to implement it.

Memory block	Chip organization
(a) 64 kbytes	8K × 8
(b) 1 Mbyte	32K × 4
(c) 16 Mbytes	256K × 8

12.17 What is *partial address decoding* and what are its advantages and disadvantages over full address decoding?

12.18 An address decoder in an 8-bit microprocessor with 16 address lines selects a memory device when address lines $A_{15}, A_{14}, A_{13}, A_{11} = 1, 1, 0, 1$. What is the size of the memory block decoded and what range of addresses does it span (i.e. what are the first and last addresses in this block)?

12.19 An address decoder in a 68K-based microprocessor selects a memory device when address lines $A_{23}, A_{22}, A_{21}, A_{20} = 1, 1, 0, 1$. What is the size of the memory block decoded and what range of addresses does it span (i.e. what are the first and last addresses in this block)?

12.20 Design address decoders to implement each of the following 68K address maps. In each case, the blocks of memory are to start from address $00 0000.

(a) 4 blocks of 64 kbytes using 32K $\times$ 8-bit chips
(b) 8 blocks of 1 Mbyte using 512K $\times$ 8-bit chips
(c) 4 blocks of 128 kbytes using 64K $\times$ 8-bit chips

12.21 A memory system in a 68K-based computer includes blocks of ROM, static RAM, and DRAM. The sizes of these three blocks are

ROM: 4 Mbytes
SRAM: 2 Mbytes
DRAM: 8 Mbytes

These memory blocks are implemented with the following memory components:

ROM: 1M $\times$ 16-bit chips
SRAM: 512K $\times$ 8-bit chips
DRAM: 4M $\times$ 4-bit chips

(a) Show how the blocks of memory are organized in terms of the memory devices used to implement them.
(b) Draw a memory map for this system and indicate the start and end addresses of all blocks.
(c) Draw an address decoding table for this arrangement.
(d) Design an address decoder for this system using simple logic gates logic.
(e) Construct an address decoder using a PROM for this system and design a decoding table to show its contents.

12.22 A computer's memory system is invariably non-homogeneous. That is, it is made up of various types of storage mechanism, each with its own characteristics. Collectively, these storage mechanisms are said to form a memory hierarchy. Explain why such a memory hierarchy is necessary, and discuss the characteristics of the memory mechanisms that you would find in a modern high-performance PC.

12.23 In the context of memory systems, what is the meaning of hysteresis?

12.24 Can you think of any examples of the effects of hysteresis in everyday life?

12.25 Why does data have to be encoded before it can be recorded on a magnetic medium?

12.26 Explain how data is recorded using PE encoding and draw a graph of the current in the write head generated by the data stream 10101110.

12.27 A disk is a serial (sequential) access device that can implement random access files. Explain this apparent contradiction of terminology.

12.28 How do the following elements of a track-seek time affect the optimum arrangement of data on a disk: acceleration, coasting, deceleration, and settling?

12.29 What is an audio-visual drive and how does it differ from a conventional hard drive?

12.30 What are the advantages of the SCSI interface over the IDE interface?

12.31 What are the limits on ultimate performance of the following.

(a) The hard disk.
(b) The floppy disk.
(c) The CD-ROM.

12.32 What are the operational characteristics of the serial access devices found in a PC? Use one or more of the magazines devoted to the PC to answer this question.

12.33 An image consists of 64 columns by 64 rows of pixels. Each pixel is a 4-bit 16-level gray-scale value. A sequence of these images is stored on a hard disk. This hard disk rotates at 7200 rpm and has 64 1024-byte sectors per track.

(a) Assuming that the images are stored sequentially, how fast can they be transferred from disk to screen?
(b) If the images are stored randomly throughout the disk, what is the longest delay between two consecutive images if the disk has 1500 tracks and the head can step in or out at a rate of one track per millisecond.

12.34 A hard disk drive has 10 disks and 18 surfaces available for recording. Each surface is composed of 200 concentric tracks and the disks rotate at 7200 rpm. Each track is divided into 8 blocks of 256 32-bit words. There is one read/write head per surface and it is possible to read the 18 tracks of a given cylinder simultaneously. The time to step from track to track is 1 ms (10^{-3} s). Between data transfers the head is parked at the outermost track of the disk.

Calculate the following.

(a) The total capacity in bits of the disk drive.
(b) The maximum data rate in bits/second.
(c) The average access time in milliseconds.
(d) The average transfer rate when reading 256 word blocks located randomly on the disk.
(e) If the disk has a 3-inch diameter and the outermost track comes to 1 inch from the edge of the disk calculate the recording density (bits/in) of the

innermost and the outermost tracks. The track density is 200 tracks/in.

12.35 Derive an expression for the average distance moved by a head from one cylinder to another (in terms of the number of head movements). Movements are made at random and the disk has N concentric cylinders numbered from 0 to $N-1$ with the innermost cylinder numbered 0. Assume that when seeking the next cylinder, all cylinders have an equal probability of being selected. Show that the average movement approaches $N/3$ for large values of N. Hint: Consider the Kth cylinder and calculate the number of steps needed to move to the Jth cylinder where J varies from 0 to $(N-1)$.

12.36 A floppy disk drive has the following parameters:

sides: 2

tracks: 80
sectors/track: 9
bytes/sector: 1024
rotational speed: 360 rpm
track-to-track step time: 1 ms

Using the above data, calculate the following.

(a) total capacity of the disk.
(b) average time to locate a sector.
(c) time to read a sector once it has been located.
(d) data transfer rate during the reading of a sector.

12.37 Why does a floppy disk have to be formatted before data can be written to it? How do you think that sector size affects the performance of a disk system?

12.38 What is a CRC?

12.39 Several books state that if you get the interleave factor of a disk wrong, the operating system's performance will be dramatically degraded. Why?

12.40 What are the advantages of MS-DOS's file allocation table (FAT) over the free-sector bit-map and linked list of sectors.

12.41 Interpret the meaning of the following extract from a FAT.

1	2
2	4
3	7
4	FFFF
5	6
6	8
7	5
8	FFFF
9	FFF7

12.42 Why are gaps required when a data structure is set up on a floppy disk during formatting?

12.43 Why are error-detecting systems so important in secondary storage systems (in comparison with primary storage systems)?

12.44 What are the advantages of a magnetoresistive head over a thin-film head?

12.45 Use the Internet to find the properties of today's large hard disk drives.

12.46 SMART technology is used to predict the failure of a hard disk. To what extent can this technology be applied to other components and subsystems in a computer?

12.47 The speed (access time) of semicouductor devices has increased dramatically over the past few decades. However, the access time of hard discs has failed to improve at the same rate. Why is this so?

12.48 A magnetic tape has a packing density of 800 characters per inch and an interblock gap of ½ inch and is filled with records. Each contains 400 characters. Calculate the fraction of the tape containing useful data if the records are written as

(a) single record blocks
(b) blocks containing four records

12.49 Data is recorded on magnetic tape at 9600 bpi along each track of nine-track tape. Information is organized as blocks of 20 000 bytes and an interblock gap of 0.75 in is left between blocks. No information is recorded in the interblock gaps. What is the efficiency of the storage system?

12.50 An engineer proposes to use a video recorder (VCR) to store digital data. Assume that the useful portion of each line can be used to store 256 bits. What is the storage capacity of a 1-hour tape (in bits), and at what rate is data transferred? A TV picture is transmitted as 525 lines, repeated 30 times per second in the USA and 625 lines, repeated 25 times per second in the UK.

12.51 Do standards in memory technology help or hinder progress?

12.52 Does magnetic tape have a future as a secondary storage medium?

12.53 What are the relative advantages and disadvantages of magnetic and optical storage systems?

12.54 Why is a laser needed to read the data on a CD-ROM?

12.55 Why is it relatively harder to write data on a CD than to read it?

12.56 Discuss the ethics of this argument: *Copying software ultimately benefits the manufacturer of the copied software, because it creates a larger user base for the software and, in turn, creates new users that do pay for the software.*

12.57 Data is recorded along a continuous spiral on a CD-ROM. Data is read from a CD-ROM at a constant bit rate (i.e. the number of bits/s read from the CD-ROM is constant). What implications do you think that this statement has for both the designer and the user of a CD-ROM?

12.57 A disk platter has bit density of 1000 bits/mm². Its innermost track is at a radius of 2 cm, its outermost track at a radius of 5 cm. What is the total capacity of the disk if we assume a uniform bit density and no data overhead?

12.59 How fast does a hard disk have to rotate in order for its stored energy to be equivalent to its own weight in TNT? Assume a 3½-inch aluminum platter. Note: the energy density of TNT is 2175 J/g and the energy of rotation of a disk is $\frac{1}{2}I\omega^2$ and $I = mr^2$ where m is the disk's mass, r its radius, and ω its rotational velocity in radians per second.

12.60 When a '1' is recorded on a disk drive and the analog signal read back from the read head, the resulting sampled signal is 0.0, 0.4, 1.0, 0.4, 0.0, where the signal is sampled every T seconds. If a '0' is recorded, the sampled signal is 0.0, -0.4, -1.0, -0.4, 0.0. Suppose the binary string 011010 is written to the disk and each bit is transmitted at T-second intervals. What signal would be read back from the disk corresponding to 011010 if the signal were sampled every T seconds?

The operating system

CHAPTER MAP

INTRODUCTION

We now look at one of the most important components of a modern computer, the *operating system*. Operating systems can be very large programs indeed (e.g. 100 Mbytes). Some might argue that a section on operating systems is out of place in an introductory course on computer hardware. We include this topic here for two reasons. First, the operating system is intimately connected with the hardware that it controls and allocates to user programs. Second, some students may not encounter the formal treatment of operating systems until later in their studies.

We begin with an overview of operating systems and then concentrate on three areas in which hardware and software overlap: multitasking, exception handling, and memory management.

Multitasking permits a computer to run several programs at the same time. *Exception handling* is concerned with the way in which the operating system communicates with user applications and external hardware. *Memory management* translates addresses from the computer into the actual addresses of data within the CPU's memory system.

Before continuing, we need to make a comment about terminology. The terms *program* and *job* are used synonymously in texts on operating systems and mean the same thing. Similarly, the terms *task* and *process* are also equivalent. A process (i.e. task) is an instance of a program that includes the code, data, and volatile data values in registers. The ability of a computer to execute several processes concurrently is called multitasking or multiprogramming. However, the term *multiprocessing* describes a system with several processors (CPUs) that run parts of a process in parallel.

13.1 The operating system

The relationship between an operating system and a computer is similar to the relationship between a conductor and an orchestra. The great conductor is a celebrity who gets invited to take part in talk shows on television and is showered with society's highest awards. And yet the conductor doesn't add a single note to a concert. The importance of conductors is well known—they co-ordinate the players. A good conductor knows the individual strengths and weaknesses of players and can apply them in such a way as to optimize their collective performance.

An operating system is the most important piece of software in a computer system. Its role is to co-ordinate the functional parts of the computer to maximize the efficiency of the system. We can define efficiency as the fraction of time for which the CPU is executing user programs. It would be more accurate if we were to say that the operating system is designed to remove inefficiency from the system. Suppose a program prints a document. While the printer is busy printing the document, the CPU is idling with nothing to do. The operating system would normally intervene to give the CPU something else to do while it's waiting for the printer to finish.

A second and equally important role of the operating system is to act as the interface between the user and the computer. Programmers communicated with first-generation operating systems via a *job control language* (JCL), which looked rather like any other conventional computer language. Today's operating systems such as Microsoft's Windows provide an interface that makes use of a WIMP (windows, icons, mouse, and pointer) and GUI (graphical user interface) environment.

From the user's point of view an operating system should behave like the perfect bureaucrat; it should be efficient, helpful, and, like all the best bureaucrats, should remain in the background. A poorly designed operating system, when asked to edit a file, might reply 'ERROR 53'. A really good operating system would have replied, 'Hi. Sorry, but my disk is full. I've noticed you've got a lot of backup copies, so if you delete a couple I think we'll be able to find room for your file. Have a nice day'. Raphael A. Finkel, in his book *An Operating System's Vade Mecum*' (Prentice-Hall, 1988) calls this aspect of an operating system *the beautification principle*, which he sums up by '. . . an operating system is a collection of algorithms that hides the details of the hardware and provides a more pleasant environment'.

Figure 13.1 shows how the components of the operating system relate to each other and to the other programs that run under the operating system's supervision. The diagram is depicted as a series of concentric circles for a good reason—programs in the outer rings use facilities provided by programs in the inner rings. At the center of the circle lies the *scheduler*, which switches from one task to another in a multitasking environment. The scheduler is smaller than programs in the outer ring such as database managers and word processors. A scheduler is often said to be *tightly coded* because it uses a small amount of code optimized for speed.

Sophisticated operating systems employ hardware and software mechanisms to protect the important inner rings from accidental or illegal access by other components. If a user task corrupts part of the kernel, the operating system may crash and the system halts.

Not all computers have an operating system. A computer used as a controller in, for example, a digital camera may not need an operating system (although complex embedded controllers do have operating systems). Whenever functions normally performed by an operating system are required, they are incorporated into the program itself.

13.1.1 Types of operating system

Operating systems can be divided into categories: single-user, batch mode, demand mode, real-time, and client–server. The distinction between operating system classes can be vague and a real operating system may have attributes common to several classes. We now briefly describe the various types of operating system (although the modern high-performance PC and the local area network have rendered some of them obsolete).

The *single-user* operating system (e.g. MS-DOS) allows only one user or process to access the system at a time. First-generation mainframe operating systems worked in a batch-mode. Jobs to be executed were fed into the computer, originally in the form of punched cards. Each user's program began with job control cards telling the operating system which of its facilities were required. The operating system scheduled the jobs according to the resources they required and their priority, and eventually generated an output.

Batch mode operation is analogous to a dry cleaning service. Clothes are handed in and are picked up when they've been cleaned. Batch-mode operating systems accepted jobs on punched card (or magnetic tape). The disadvantage of batch mode systems is their lengthy turn around time. It was frustrating in the 1970s to wait 5 hours for a printout only to discover that the job didn't run because of a simple mistake in one of the cards.

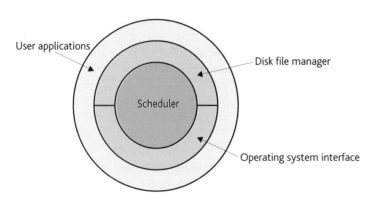

Figure 13.1 Hierarchical model of an operating system.

MODERN OPERATING SYSTEMS

It is unfair to imply that an operating system only coordinates the hardware and provides a user interface. Modern operating systems include components that could be regarded as applications programs; for example, Windows incorporates a web browser called Internet Explorer. Web browsers can be obtained from more than one supplier and installed as user applications.

By incorporating a function such as a web browser, an operating system like Windows can provide a consistent user interface across applications. Moreover, Windows achieves a constant look and feel across the operating system, Microsoft's web browser, and Microsoft's applications.

MS-DOS

When IBM was creating the PC in 1890, Bill Gates was approached to supply a simple operating system. Bill Gates came up with MS-DOS (Microsoft Disk Operating System), which was loosely based on a first-generation microprocessor operating system called CP/M. MS-DOS allowed you to create, list, delete, and manipulate files on disk.

MS-DOS was released as MS-DOS 1.0 in 1981 and developed by stages to become MS-DOS 6.22 in 1994. Future developments were not necessary because the market for a command line operating system dried up when graphical operating systems like Windows became available.

The final version of DOS, 7.0, was released in 1995 when it was incorporated in Windows 95.

LINUX AND WINDOWS

There are three major operating systems in the PC world. The vast majority of PCs use Microsoft's Windows or Linux (a public domain version of UNIX). The Apple Mac uses OS X (which is a variation of Linux).

Microsoft's Windows has been developed since it first appeared in 1995. It is easy to use and has been responsible for bringing computing to the non-computer-specialist masses. Windows is relatively expensive, costing about 20% of the PC's hardware.

Linux is an open-source, public domain operating system developed by Linus Tovalds. Tovalds created Linux by extending Andy Tannenbaum's mini operating system Minix.

Modern versions of Linux now have a Windows-style front end.

Demand mode operating systems allow you to access the computer from a terminal, which was a great improvement over batch mode operation because you can complete each step before going on to the next one. Such an arrangement is also called interactive because the operating system and the user are engaged in a dialogue. Each time the user correctly completes an operation, they are informed of its success and invited to continue by some form of prompt message. If a particular command results in an error, the user is informed of this by the operating system and can therefore take the necessary corrective action.

Real-time operating systems belong to the world of industrial process control. The primary characteristic of a real-time operating system is that it must respond to an event within a well-defined time. Consider a computer-controlled petrochemical plant. The conditions at many parts of the plant are measured and reported to the computer on a regular basis. Control actions must be taken as conditions in the plant change; for example, sudden build-up of pressure in a reaction vessel cannot be ignored. The computer running the plant invariably has a real-time operating

system that responds to interrupts generated by external events.

Real-time operating systems are found wherever the response time of the computer must closely match that of the system it is controlling. Real-time operating systems are so called because the computer is synchronized with what people call clock time. Other operating systems operate in computer time. A job is submitted and its results delivered after some elapsed time. There is no particular relationship between the elapsed time and the time of day. The actual elapsed time is a function of the loading of the computer and the particular mix of jobs it is running. In a real-time system the response time of the computer to any stimulus is guaranteed.

Modern multimedia systems using sound and video are also real-time systems—not least because a pause in a video clip while the computer is carrying out another process is most disconcerting. Real-time operating system technology has had a strong influence on the way in which processors have developed; for example, Intel's multimedia extensions (MMX) added special-purpose instructions to the Pentium's instruction set to handle video and sound applications.

Some modern operating systems are called *client–server* and run on distributed systems. A client–server system may be found in a university where each user has their own computer with a CPU, memory, and a hard disk drive, linked to a server by a local area network. Processes running on one of the terminals are called client processes and are able to make requests to the server. The operating system is distributed between the client and the server. A client on one host can use the resources of a server on another host.

13.2 Multitasking

Multitasking is the ability of a computer to give the impression that it can handle more than one job at once. A computer cannot really execute two or more programs simultaneously, but it can give the impression that it is running several programs concurrently. The following example demonstrates how such an illusion is possible.

Consider a game of simultaneous chess where a first-class player is pitted against several weaker opponents by stepping from board to board making a move at a time. As the master player is so much better than their opponents, one of the master's moves takes but a fraction of the time they take. The players share the illusion that they have a single opponent of their own.

The organization of a game of simultaneous chess can readily be applied to the digital computer. All we need is a periodic signal to force the CPU to switch from one job to another and a mechanism to tell the computer where it was up to when it last executed a particular job. The jobs are referred to as *tasks* or *processes* and the concept of executing several processes together is called *multiprogramming* or *multitasking*. A *process* is a program together with its associated program counter, stack, registers, and any resources it's using.

Before we look at how multitasking is implemented we discuss some of its advantages. If each process required only CPU time, multitasking would have little advantage over running processes consecutively (at least in terms of the efficient use of resources). If we re-examine simultaneous chess, we find that its success is based on the great speed of the master player when compared with that of their opponents. While each player is laboriously pondering their next move, the master player is busy making many moves.

A similar situation exists in the case of computers. While one task is busy reading information from a disk drive and loading it into memory or is busy printing text on a printer, another task can take control of the CPU. A further advantage

---

HISTORY OF WINDOWS

Microsoft's first version of Windows, version 1.0, was released in 1985. This was a graphical version of Microsoft's command-line MS-DOS operating system. Version 2.0 appeared in 1987 and provided better windows management facilities.

Windows 3.0 was released in 1990 and was Microsoft's first really successful GUI-based operating system. This version made better use of the processor's memory management mechanisms.

Windows 95 and 98 (released in 1995 and 1998 respectively) continued the development of Microsoft's GUI technology. Changes were incremental rather than revolutionary; for example, Windows 95 provided support for long file names (rather than the old '6.3' DOS format, which restricted names to six characters). Windows 98 provided a better integration of operating system and Internet browser as well as the beginning of support for peripherals such as the universal serial bus, USB.

Microsoft released Windows ME (Millennium Edition) in 2000. This was the end of the line for Microsoft's operating systems that began with Windows 3.0. ME provided further modest improvements to Windows 98 such as the incorporation of a media player and a system restore mechanism. ME was regarded as unstable and bug ridden and was not a significant success.

Microsoft launched a separate range of graphical operating systems; first NT in 1993 (*New Technology*) and then Windows 2000. These were regarded as professional operating systems, targeted at corporate users. NT (and later Windows

2000) used underlying 32-bit binary code rather than the 16-bit code of DOS and earlier versions of Windows. Windows NT also introduced the *NTFS* file system that was far more sophisticated and reliable than the *FAT* system used by MS-DOS and early versions of Windows.

Windows XP was launched in 2001 and brought together Microsoft's previous two lines (Windows 98 aimed at the PC user and Windows 2000 aimed at the corporate user). Windows XP may be thought of as a mature version of Windows in the sense that it used true 32-bit code, supported the NTFS file management mechanism, and provided extensive support for multimedia applications, new high-speed interfaces, and local area networks. There are two versions of XP. The standard version, XP home, is intended for the small-scale user and XP professional is aimed at the corporate and high-performance user. XP professional supports remote processing (using the system via an Internet connection) and symmetrical multiprocessing (systems with more than one CPU).

The Windows operating system became the target of many malware writers (malware includes computer viruses, worms, Trojan horses, and spyware). Microsoft has had to keep up with malware writers by continually releasing updates to close the loopholes exploited by, for example, virus writers. In late 2004 Microsoft released its Service pack 2 to update XP. This service pack included a firewall to prevent illegal access from the Internet.

of multiprogramming is that it enables several users to gain access to a computer at the same time.

Consider two processes, A and B, each of which requires a several different activities to be performed during the course of its execution (e.g. video display controller, code execution, disk access, etc.). The sequence of activities carried out by each of these two processes as they are executed is given in Fig. 13.2. Note that VDT1 and VDT2 are two displays.

If process A were allowed to run to completion before process B were started, valuable processing time would be wasted while activities not involving the CPU were carried out. Figure 13.3 shows how the processes may be scheduled to make more efficient use of resources. The boxes indicate the period of time for which a given resource is allocated to a particular process. For example, after process A has first used the CPU, it accesses the disk. While the disk is being accessed by process A, process B can use the processor.

The fine details of multiprogramming operating systems are beyond the scope of an introductory book. However, the following principles are involved.

1. The operating system *schedules* a process in the most efficient way and makes best use of the facilities available. The algorithm may adapt to the type of jobs that are running, or the operator may feed system parameters into the computer to maximize efficiency.

2. Operating systems perform *memory management*. If several processes run concurrently, the operating system must allocate memory space to each of them. Moreover, the operating system should locate the processes in memory in such a way as to make best possible use of the memory. The operating system must also protect one task from unauthorized access to another.

3. If the CPU is to be available to one process while another is accessing a disk or using a printer, these devices must be capable of autonomous operation. That is, they must either be able to take part in DMA (i.e. direct memory access) operations without the active intervention of the CPU, or they must be able to receive a chunk of high-speed data from the CPU and process it at their leisure.

One of the principal problems a complex multitasking operating system has to overcome is that of *deadlock*. Suppose process A and process B both require CPU time and a printer to complete their activity. If process A has been allocated the CPU and the printer by the operating system, all is well and process B can proceed once process A has been completed. Now imagine the situation that occurs when process A requests both CPU time and the printer but receives only the CPU, and process B makes a similar request and receives the printer but not the CPU. In this situation both processes have one resource and await the other. As neither process will give up its resource, the system is deadlocked and hangs up indefinitely. Much work has been done on operating system resource allocation algorithms to deal with this problem.

13.2.1 What is a process?

A task or process is a piece of executable code. Each process runs in an environment made up of the contents of the processor's registers, its program counter, its status register (SR), and the state of the memory allocated to this process. The environment defines the current state of the process and tells the computer where it's up to in the execution of a process.

At any instant a process is in one of three states: *running*, *runnable*, or *blocked*. Figure 13.4 provides a state diagram for a process in a multitasking system. When a process is created, it is in a *runnable* state waiting its turn for execution. When the scheduler passes control to the process, it is *running* (i.e. being executed). If the process has to wait for a system resource such as a printer before it can continue, it enters the *blocked state*. The difference between runnable and blocked is simple—a runnable process can be executed when its turn comes; a blocked process cannot enter the runnable state until the resources it requires become free.

13.2.2 Switching processes

We now outline the way in which process switching uses two mechanisms described earlier—the *interrupt* and the *stack*. A clock connected to the CPU's interrupt request input generates a pulse, say, every 0.01 seconds. At the moment the interrupt occurs, the information that defines the process is in the CPU (i.e. processor status word, program counter, and registers in use). This information is called the *process's context* or *volatile portion*. An interrupt saves the program counter and machine status on the stack, and makes a jump to the interrupt handling routine.

Process A					Process B			
VDT1	CPU	Disk	CPU	VDT1	VDT2	CPU	Disk	VDT2	CPU

→ *time*

Figure 13.2 Example of computing without multitasking.

Resource	Activity					
	Slot 1	Slot 2	Slot 3	Slot 4	Slot 5	Slot 6
VDT1	Process A				Process A	
VDT2	Process B				Process B	
Disk			Process A	Process B		
CPU		Process A	Process B	Process A		Process A

→ *time*

Figure 13.3 Applying multitasking to the system of Fig. 13.2.

At the end of the interrupt handling routine an RTE (return from exception) instruction is executed and the program then continues from the point at which it was interrupted.

The 68K's RTE instruction is similar to its RTS (return from subroutine) instruction. When a subroutine is called, the return address is pushed on the stack. When an exception (i.e. interrupt) is generated, both the return address and the current value of the processor status word (containing the CCR) are pushed on the stack. The RTE instruction restores both the program counter and the status word. Consequently, an exception doesn't affect the status of the processor.

Suppose now that the interrupt handling routine modifies the stack pointer before the return from exception is executed. That is, the stack pointer is changed to point at another process's volatile portion. When the RTE is executed, the value of the program counter retrieved from the stack isn't that belonging to the program being executed just before the interrupt. The value of the PC loaded by the return from exception belongs to a different process that was saved earlier when another program was interrupted—that process will now be executed.

Figure 13.5 demonstrates the sequence of events taking place during process switching. Initially process A at the top of Fig. 13.5 is running. At time T, the program is interrupted by a real-time clock and control passed to the scheduler in the operating system. The arrow from the program to the scheduler shows the flow of control from process A to the operating system. The scheduler stores process A's registers, program counter, and status in memory. Process switching is also called *context switching* because it involves switching

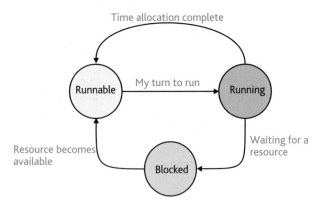

Figure 13.4 State diagram of a process in a multitasking system.

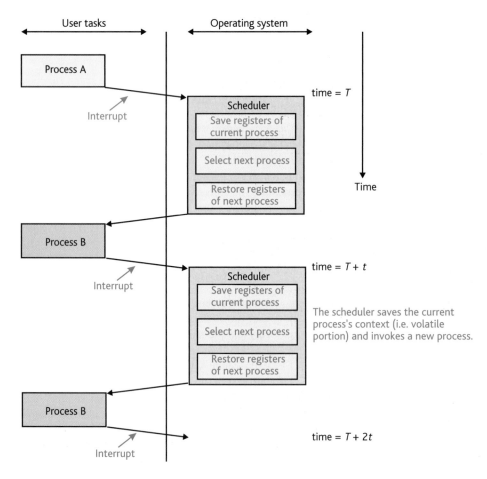

Figure 13.5 Switching processes.

from the volatile portion of one process to the volatile portion of another process. The scheduler component of the operating system responsible for switching processes is called the *first-level interrupt handler*.

In Fig. 13.5 an interrupt occurs at $T, T + t, T + 2t, \ldots$, and every t seconds switching takes place between processes A and B. We have ignored the time required to process the interrupt. In some real-time systems, the process-switching overhead is very important.

Figure 13.6 demonstrates how process switching works. Two processes, A and B, are located in memory. To keep things simple, we will assume that the regions of memory allocated to these processes do not change during the course of their execution. Each process has its own stack, and at any instant the stack pointer may be pointing to either A's stack or B's stack.

In Fig. 13.6(a) process A is running and process A's stack pointer SP_A is pointing at the top of the stack. In Fig. 13.6(b)

a process-switching interrupt has occurred and the contents of the program counter and machine status have been pushed onto the stack (i.e. A's stack). For the sake of simplicity Fig. 13.6 assumes that all items on the stack occupy a single location.

In Fig. 13.6(c) the operating system has changed the contents of the system stack pointer so that it is now pointing at process B's stack (i.e. the stack pointer is SP_B). Finally, in Fig. 13.6(d) the operating system executes an RTE and process B's program counter is loaded from its stack, which causes process B to be executed. Thus, at each interrupt, the operating system swaps the stack pointer before executing an RTE and a new process is run.

A more realistic operating system maintains a table of processes to be executed. Each entry in the table is a *task control block* (TCB), which contains all the information the operating system needs to know about the process. The TCB

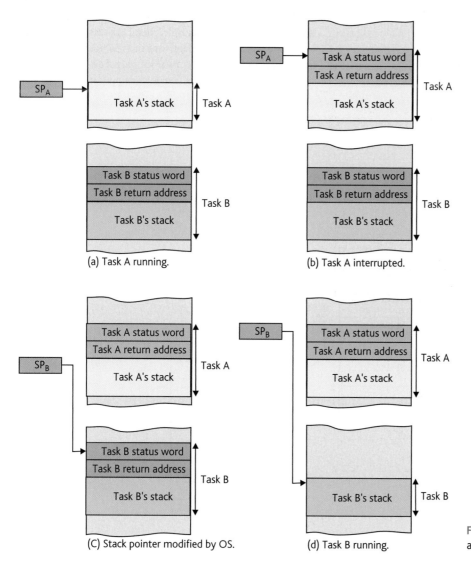

(a) Task A running.

(b) Task A interrupted.

(C) Stack pointer modified by OS.

(d) Task B running.

Figure 13.6 Process switching and the stack.

includes details about the process's priority, its maximum run time, and whether or not it is currently runnable (as well as its registers).

Figure 13.7 illustrates the structure of a possible task control block. In addition to the process's environment, the TCB contains a *pointer* to the next TCB in the chain of TCBs; that is, the TCBs are arranged as a linked list. A new process is created by inserting its TCB into the linked list.

Some operating systems allow processes to be prioritized so that a process with a high priority will always be executed in preference to a process with a lower priority. A runnable process is executed when its turn arrives

(subject to the limitations of priority). If the process is not runnable (i.e. blocked), it remains in the computer but is bypassed each time its turn comes. When the process is to be run, its run flag is set and it will be executed next time round.

13.3 Operating system support from the CPU

We now describe how a processor supports operating system functions. It's possible to design processors that are protected from certain types of error or that provide hardware support for multitasking. First-generation 8-bit microprocessors didn't provide the operating systems designer with any special help. Here, we concentrate on the 68K family because it provides particularly strong support to operating systems.

At any instant a processor can be in one of several states or levels of privilege; for example, members of the 68K family provide two levels of privilege. One of the 68K's states is called the supervisor state and the other the user state. The operating system runs in the supervisor state and applications programs

---

> **PRE-EMPTIVE MULTITASKING**
>
> There are two versions of multitasking. The simplest version is called *non-pre-emptive* multitasking or co-operative multitasking. When a task runs, it executes code until it decides to pass control to another task. Co-operative multitasking can lead to system crashes when a task does not relinquish control.
>
> In *pre-emptive* multitasking, the operating system forces a task to relinquish control after a given period.

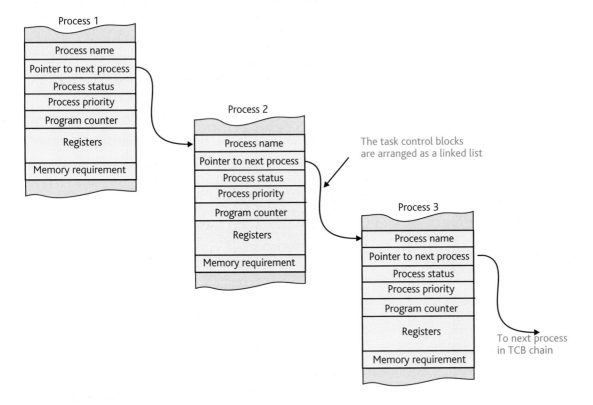

Fig. 13.7 The task control block.

running under the control of the operating system run in the user state. We will soon see that separating the operating system from user applications makes the system very robust and difficult to crash. When an applications program crashes (e.g. due to a bug), the crash doesn't affect the operating system running in its protected supervisor environment.

13.3.1 Switching states

Let's start from the assumption that the supervisor state used by the operating system confers first-class privileges on the operating system—we'll find out what these privileges are shortly. When the processor is running in its user state, any interrupt or exception forces it into its supervisor state. That is, an exception causes a transition to the supervisor state and, therefore, calls the operating system.

Figure 13.8 illustrates two possible courses of action that may take place in a 68K system when an exception is generated. Both these diagrams are read from the top down. In each case, the left-hand side represents user or applications programs running in the user state and the right-hand side represents the operating system running in the supervisor state.

In Fig. 13.8(a) a user program is running and an exception occurs (e.g. a disk drive may request a data transfer). A jump is made to the exception handler that forms part of the operating system. The exception handler deals with the request and a return is made to the user program. However, the exception might have been generated by a *fatal error* condition that arises during the execution of a program. Figure 13.8(b) shows the situation in which an exception caused by a fatal error occurs. In this case, the operating system terminates the *faulted* user program and then runs another user program.

Figure 13.8(a) and (b) show user programs and the operating system existing in separate compartments or environments. We now explain why user programs and the operating system sometimes really do live in different universes. In simple 68K-based systems, the processor's supervisor and user state mechanisms aren't exploited, and all code is executed in the supervisor state. More sophisticated systems with an operating system do make good use of the 68K's user and supervisor state mechanisms.

When power is first applied to the 68K, it automatically enters its supervisor state. This action makes sense, because you would expect the operating system to initially take control of the computer while it sets everything up and loads the user processes that it's going to run.

The three questions we've now got to answer are the following.

- How does the 68K know which state it's in?
- How is a transition made from one state to another?
- What does it matter anyway?

The answer to the first question is easy—the 68K uses a flag bit, called an S-bit, in its status register to indicate what state it's currently operating in. If $S = 1$, the processor is in its supervisor state and if $S = 0$, the processor is in its user state. The S-bit is located in bit 13 of the 16-bit status register (SR). The lower-order byte of the status register is the condition code register (CCR). The upper byte of the status register containing the S-bit is called the *system byte* and defines the operating state of the processor.

The second question we asked was 'How is a transition made from one state to another?' The state diagram in Fig. 13.9 describes the relationship between the 68K's user

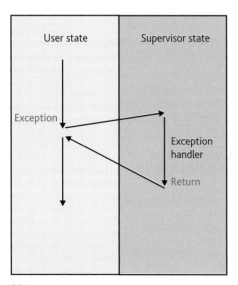

(a) Program execution continues after an exception.

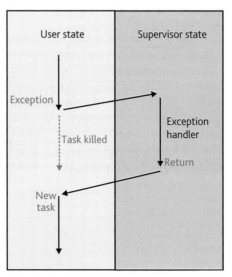

(b) The operating system kills the current task and starts another.

Figure 13.8 Taking action after an exception.

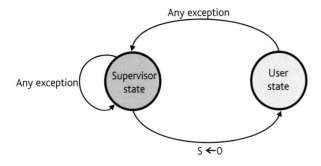

Figure 13.9 Switching between user and supervisor states.

and supervisor states. Lines with arrows indicate transitions between states (text against a line explains the action that causes the transition). Figure 13.9 shows that a transition from the supervisor state to the user state is made by clearing the S-bit in the status register. Executing a MOVE #0, **SR** instruction clears the S-bit (and the other bits) of the status byte and puts the 68K in the user state. You could clear only the S-bit with the instruction ANDI #$DFFF, **SR**.

When the operating system wishes to execute an applications program in the user state, it clears the S-bit and executes a jump to the appropriate program; that is, the operating system invokes the less privileged user state by executing an instruction that clears the S-bit to 0.

Figure 13.9 demonstrates that once the 68K is running in its user state, the only way in which a transition can be made to the supervisor state is by means of an exception—any exception. A return can't be made to the supervisor state by using an instruction to set the S-bit to 1. If you could do this, anyone would be able to access the supervisor state's privileged features and the security mechanism it provides would be worthless. Let's say that again—a program running in the user state cannot deliberately invoke the supervisor state directly.

Suppose a user program running in the user state tries to enter the privileged supervisor state by executing MOVE $2000, **SR** to set the S-bit. Any attempt by the user state programmer to modify the S-bit results in a privilege violation exception. This exception forces the 68K into its supervisor state, where the exception handler deals with the problem.

We can now answer the third question—what's the benefit of the 68K's two-state mechanism? Some instructions such as STOP and RESET can be executed only in the supervisor state

and are said to be privileged. The STOP instruction brings the processor to a halt and the RESET acts on external hardware such as disk drives. You might not want the applications programmer to employ these powerful instructions that may cause the entire system to crash if used inappropriately. Other privileged instructions are those that operate on the system byte (including the S-bit) in the status register. If the applications programmer were permitted to access the S-bit, they could change it from 0 (user state) to 1 (supervisor state) and bypass the processor's security mechanism.

If the 68K's user/supervisor mode mechanism were limited to preventing the user-state programmer executing certain instructions, it would be a nice feature of the processor, but of no earth-shattering importance. The user/supervisor state mechanism has two important benefits; the provision of dual stack pointers and the support for memory protection. These two features protect the operating system's memory from either accidental or deliberate modification by a user application. We now describe how the 68K's supervisor state protects its most vital region of memory—the stack.

13.3.2 The 68K's two stacks

Most computers manage subroutine return addresses by means of a stack. The processor's stack pointer points to the top of the stack and the stack pointer is automatically updated as items are pushed onto the stack or are pulled off it. When a subroutine is called by an instruction like BSR XYZ, the address immediately after the subroutine call (i.e. the return address) is pushed on the stack. The final instruction of the subroutine, RTS (return from subroutine), pulls the return address off the stack and loads it in the program counter.

If you corrupt the contents of the stack by overwriting the return address or if you corrupt the stack pointer itself, the RTS will load an undefined address into the program counter. Instead of making a return to a subroutine's calling point, the processor will jump to a random point in memory and start executing code at that point. The result might lead to an illegal instruction error or to an attempt to access non-existent memory. Whatever happens, the program will crash.

Consider the following fragment of very badly written code that contains a serious error. Don't worry about the fine details—it's the underlying principles that matter. Remember that the 68K's stack pointer is address register A7.

```
        MOVE.W  D3,-(A7)  Push the parameter in register D3 onto the stack
        BSR     Sub_X     Call a subroutine
        .                 Return here
        .
Sub_X   ADDA.L  #4,A7     Step over the return address on the top of the stack
        MOVE.L  (A7)+,D0  Read the parameter from the stack
        SUBA.L  #6,A7     Restore the stack pointer
        .                 The body of the subroutine goes here....
        RTS               Return from subroutine
```

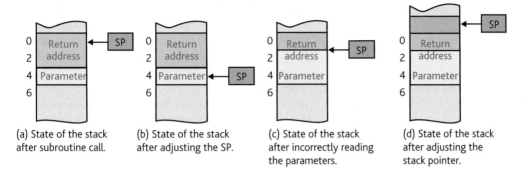

(a) State of the stack after subroutine call.

(b) State of the stack after adjusting the SP.

(c) State of the stack after incorrectly reading the parameters.

(d) State of the stack after adjusting the stack pointer.

Figure 13.10 The effect of an error on the stack.

The programmer first pushes the 16-bit parameter in data register D3 onto the stack by means of MOVE.W D3, (A7), and then calls a subroutine at location Sub_X. Figure 13.10(a) illustrates the state of the stack at this point. As you can see, the stack contains the 16-bit parameter (one word) and the 32-bit return address (two words) on top of the buried parameter.

When the subroutine is executed, the programmer attempts to retrieve the parameter from the stack by first stepping past the 4-byte return address on the top of the stack. The instruction ADDA.L #4,A7 adds 4 to the stack pointer to leave it pointing at the required parameter (Figure 13.10(b)). This is a terrible way of accessing the parameter because you should never move the stack pointer down the stack when there are valid items on the stack above the stack pointer—do remember that we're providing an example of how not to do things.

The programmer then reads the parameter from the stack by means of the operation MOVE.L (A7)+, D0. This instruction pulls a longword off the stack and increments the stack pointer by the size of the operand (four for a longword) (Fig. 13.10(c)). Because the stack pointer has been moved down by first stepping past the return address and then pulling the parameter off the stack, it must be adjusted by six to point to the subroutine's return address once more (i.e. a 4-byte return address plus a 2-byte parameter) (Fig. 13.10(d)). Finally, the return from subroutine instruction RTS) pulls the 32-bit return address off the stack and loads it in the program counter.

This fragment of code fails because it contains a serious error. The parameter initially pushed on the stack was a *16-bit* value, but the parameter read from the stack in the subroutine was a *32-bit* value. The programmer really intended to write the instruction MOVE.W (A7)+, D0 rather than MOVE.L (A7)+, D0; the error in the code is just a single letter. The effect of this error is to leave the stack pointer pointing at the second word of the 32-bit return address, rather than the first word. The SUBA.L #6,A7 instruction was intended to restore the stack pointer to its original value. However, because the stack pointer is pointing 2 bytes above the correct return address, the RTS instruction loads the program counter with

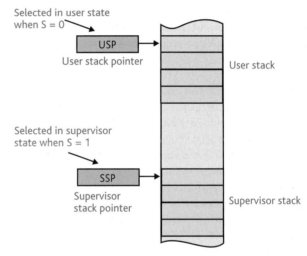

Figure 13.11 The 68K's two stack pointers.

an erroneous return address resulting in a jump to a random region of memory. We have demonstrated that this blunder not only gives the wrong result, but also generates a fatal error. We now demonstrate how the user/supervisor mechanism helps us to deal with such a situation.

The 68K's user and supervisor stack pointers

There's very little the computer designer can do to prevent programming errors that corrupt either the stack or the stack pointer. What the computer designer can do is to limit the effects of possible errors. Members of the 68K family approach the problem of stack security by providing two identical stack pointers—each of which is called address register A7 (see Fig. 13.11). However, both stack pointers can't be active at the same time because either one or the other is in use (it's a bit like Clark Kent and Superman—you never see them together).

One of the 68K's two stack pointers is called the *supervisor stack pointer* (SSP) and is active whenever the processor is in the supervisor state. The other stack pointer, the *user stack pointer*

(USP) is active when the processor is in the user state. Because the 68K is always in either the user state or the supervisor state, only one stack pointer is available at any instant. The supervisor stack pointer is invisible to the user programmer—there's no way in which the user programmer can access the supervisor stack pointer. However, the operating system in the supervisor state can use privileged instruction MOVE USP,**Ai** and MOVE Ai,**USP** to access the user stack pointer.

Let's summarize what we've just said. When the 68K is operating in its supervisor state, its S-bit is 1 and the supervisor stack pointer is active. The supervisor stack pointer points at the stack used by the operating system to handle its subroutine and exception return addresses. Because an exception sets the S-bit to 1, the return address is always pushed on the supervisor stack even if the 68K was running in the user mode at the time of the exception. When the 68K is operating in its user state, its S-bit is 0 and the user stack pointer is active. The user stack pointer points at the stack used by the current applications program to store subroutine return addresses.

Consider the previous example of the faulty applications program running in the user state (see Fig. 13.11). When the return from subroutine instruction is executed, an incorrect return address is pulled off the stack and a jump to a random location made. An illegal instruction exception will eventually occur when the processor tries to execute a data pattern that doesn't correspond to a legal op-code. An illegal instruction exception forces a change of state from user to supervisor mode. The illegal instruction exception handler runs in the supervisor state, whose own stack pointer has not been corrupted. That is, the applications programmer can corrupt their own stack pointer and crash their program, but the operating system's own stack pointer will not be affected by the error. When a user program crashes, the operating system mounts a rescue attempt.

You may wonder what protects the supervisor stack pointer. Nothing. It is assumed that a well constructed and debugged operating system rarely corrupts its stack and crashes (at least in comparison with user programs and programs under development).

The 68K's two-stack architecture doesn't directly prevent the user programmer from corrupting the contents of the operating system's stack. Instead, it separates the stack used by the operating system and all exception-processing software from the stack used by the applications programmer by implementing two stack pointers. Whatever the user does in their own *environment* cannot prevent the supervisor stepping in and dealing with the problem.

Use of two stacks in process switching

Earlier in this chapter we described the notion of multitasking. The 68K's two stack pointer mechanism is particularly useful in implementing multitasking. Each user program has its own private stack. When the process is running, it uses the USP to point to its stack. When the process is waiting or blocked, its own stack pointer is saved alongside the other elements of its volatile portion (i.e. environment) in its task control block.

The supervisor stack pointer is used by the operating system to manage process switching and other operating system functions. In this way, each application can have its own user stack pointer and the operating system's stack can be separated from the user processes.

Suppose an applications program (i.e. process) is running and a process-switching interrupt occurs. A jump is made to the scheduler, the S-bit is set, the supervisor stack pointer becomes active, and the return address and status word are saved on the supervisor stack.

The CPU's address and data registers plus its PC and status register hold information required by the interrupted process. These registers constitute the process's *volatile portion*. The scheduler saves these registers on the supervisor stack. You can use MOVEM.L D0-D7/A0-A6,-(**A7**) to push registers D0 to D7 and A0 to A6 onto the stack pointed at by A7.[1] We don't save A7 because that's the supervisor stack pointer. We do need to save the user stack pointer because that belongs to the process. We can access the USP by MOVE USP,**A0** and then save A0 on the supervisor stack with the other 15 registers (PC and SR).

Having saved the last process's volatile portion, the scheduler can go about its job of switching processes. The next step would be to copy these registers from the stack to the process's entry in its task control block. Typically, the scheduler might remove the process's volatile environment from the top of the supervisor stack and copy these registers to the process's task control block.

The scheduler can now locate the next process to run according to an appropriate algorithm (e.g. first-come-first-served, highest priority first, smallest process first, etc.). Once the next process has been located it can be restarted by copying the process's registers from the TCB to the supervisor stack and then pulling the registers off the stack immediately before executing an RTE instruction. Note that restoring a process's volatile environment is the mirror image of saving a process's volatile environment.

The behavior of the task-switching mechanism can be expressed as pseudocode.

---

[1] The 68K instruction MOVEM.L A0-A3/D2-D4-(**A7**) pushes registers A0 to A3 and D2 to D4 on the stack pointed at by A7. The mnemonic MOVEM means *move multiple* and lets you copy a group of registers onto the stack in one operation. MOVEM.L (A7)+,**A0-A3/D2-D4** performs the inverse operation and pulls seven registers off the stack and restores them to A0 to A3 and D2 to D4.

```
Module TaskSwitch
      Disable all further interrupts
      Push registers D0 to D7 and A0 to A6 on the supervisor stack
      Get the process's stack pointer from the USP and put it on the stack
      Transfer all registers, PC, and SR from the stack to TaskControlBlockᵢ
      Locate Processⱼ the next process to run
      Copy registers of next process from TaskControlBlockⱼ to the stack
      Copy process j's stack pointer from TCB to USP
      Pull registers D0 to D7 and A0 to A6 from the stack
      Enable interrupts
      Return from exception (i.e., restore SR, and PC)
End module
```

We represent this algorithm in the following 68K program. In order to test the task-switching mechanism, we've created a dummy environment with two processes. Process 1 prints the number 1 on the screen whenever it is executed. Process 2 prints the sequence 2, 3, 4, . . . , 9, 2, 3, . . . when it is called. If we allow each process to complete one print cycle before the next process is called, the output should be 12131415 . . . . 18191213 . . .

In a real system, a real-time clock might be used to periodically switch tasks. In our system we use a TRAP #0 instruction to call the task switcher. This instruction acts like a hardware interrupt that is generated internally by an instruction in the program (i.e. the program counter and status registers are pushed on the supervisor stack and a jump is made to the TRAP #0 exception handling routine whose address is in memory location $00 0080.

The program is entered at $400 where the supervisor stack pointer is initialized and dummy values loaded into A6 and A0 for testing purposes (because much of the program involves transferring data between registers, the stack, and task control blocks, it's nice to have visible markers when you are debugging a program by single-stepping it).

We have highlighted the body of the task switcher. The subroutine NEW selects the next process to run. In this case, there are only two processes and the code is as follows.

```
IF task 1 running THEN next task = task 2
                  ELSE next task = task 1

              ORG     $80               TRAP  #0 vector
              DC.L    TRAP0             Address of trap 0 handler

              ORG     $400              Entry point of program
              LEA     $4000,A7          Preset the SSP
              LEA     $A6A6A6A6,A6      Dummy value in A6 to help in tracing
              MOVEA.L #$12121212,A0     Dummy value for USP
              MOVE.L  A0,USP
              BRA     TASK1             Jump into task 1

*             The task switcher is entered from TRAP #0

TRAP0         MOVEM.L A0-A7/D0-D7,-(SP)  Dump all registers on the stack
              MOVEA.L CURRENT,A0         Get pointer to current TCB

              MOVE.W  #34,D0             Copy SR, PC, and registers to TCB
SAVE          MOVE.W  (SP)+,(A0)+        This is 35 words (SR + PC + 16 registers)
              DBRA    D0,SAVE

              MOVE.L  USP,A1             Get task's A7 = USP
              MOVE.L  A1,-10(A0)         Save USP in A7 slot in TCB

*             All the current task's environment is now saved in its TCB

              BSR     NEW                Switch tasks

*             Now restore the new task

              MOVEA.L  CURRENT,A0        Get pointer to the new TCB
              LEA      70(A0),A0         Point to past end of TCB

              MOVE.W  #34,D0             Copy SR, PC, registers from TCB
```

```
RESTORE    MOVE.W    -(A0),-(SP)      This is 35 words (1 + 2 + 16 x 2)
           DBRA      D0,RESTORE
           MOVEA.L   $0(A0),A1        Get USP from TCB
           MOVE.L    A1,USP           Restore USP
           MOVEM.L   (SP)+,A0-A6/D0-D7 Restore registers from stack
           LEA       4(SP),SP         Skip past A7 on stack
           RTE                        Load SR and PC to return from exception

*          Switch tasks (simple routine goes 1,2,1,2,...)
NEW        MOVEA.L   CURRENT,A0       Get current task pointer
           CMPA.L    #TCB1,A0         If it's 1 then make it 2
           BNE       NOT1
           MOVE.L    #TCB2,CURRENT
           BRA       FINISH
NOT1       MOVE.L    #TCB1,CURRENT    If it's 2 then make it 1
FINISH     RTS
TASK1      MOVE.B    #'1',D1          A dummy task that prints 1 and ends
           MOVE.B    #6,D0            Call OS to print
           TRAP      #15
           TRAP      #0               Switch tasks
           BRA       TASK1            Repeat

TASK2      ADD.B     #1,D1            A dummy task that prints a number and ends
           MOVE.B    #6,D0            Call OS to print
           TRAP      #15
           TRAP      #0               Switch tasks
           CMP.B     #'9',D1
           BNE       TASK2
           MOVE.B    #'1',D1          Reset sequence
           BRA       TASK2            Repeat

           ORG       $1000
CURRENT    DC.L      TCB1             Pointer to current TCB

           ORG       $2000
TCB1       DS.W      35               Space for task 1 TCB

           ORG       $2080            Task 2 TCB (preset)
TCB2       DC.L      $D0D0D0D0        Dummy D0
           DC.L      $00000031        Initial D1 (ASCII "1")
           DS.L      6
           DC.L      $A0A0A0A0        Dummy A0
           DS.L      6
           DC.L      $77777770        Dummy A7 = USP
           DC.W      $00FF            Dummy SR
           DC.L      TASK2            Address of TASK2 for PC

           END       $400
```

Let's look at how task switching takes place. When an exception takes place (in this case a TRACE #0 exception), the program counter (return address) and status register are pushed on the supervisor stack to give the situation of Fig. 13.12(a).

The first instruction in the process switcher, MOVEM.L A0-A7/D0-D7,-(SP) pushes all the 68K's address and data registers on the supervisor stack. Together with the PC and SR, we now have the process's entire volatile environment on the stack. Well, not entirely. Remember that the 68K has a user stack pointer. So, we copy it into A1 and then put it in the 'A7' slot on the stack (thereby overwriting the copy of the supervisor stack pointer in that slot).

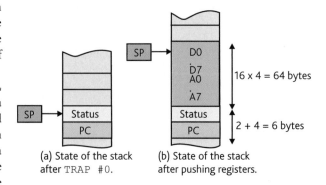

(a) State of the stack after TRAP #0.

(b) State of the stack after pushing registers.

Figure 13.12 Use of the stack during process switching.

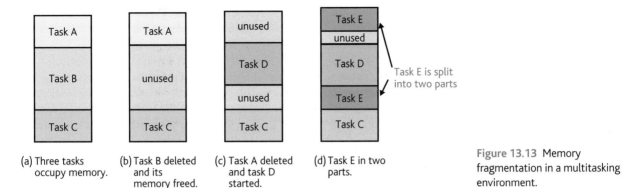

(a) Three tasks occupy memory.

(b) Task B deleted and its memory freed.

(c) Task A deleted and task D started.

(d) Task E in two parts.

Figure 13.13 Memory fragmentation in a multitasking environment.

The next step is to copy all these registers to the task control block pointed at by CURRENT (the variable that points to the active TCB). This operation saves the current task's volatile portion.

The task control block is changed by calling NEW to find the next task. The registers saved in the TCB are then copied to the stack and then restored from the stack to invoke the new process.

Now that we've described the 68K's user and supervisor modes and the role of exceptions in process switching, we can introduce one of the most important aspects of an operating system, memory management.

13.4 Memory management

We've assumed that the computer's central processing unit generates the address of an instruction or data and that this address corresponds to the actual location of the data in memory. For example, if a computer executes MOVE $1234,D0, the source operand is found in location number 1234_{16} in the computer's random access memory. Although this statement is true of simple microprocessor systems, it's not true of computers with operating systems such as UNIX and Windows. An address generated by the CPU doesn't necessarily correspond to the actual location of the data in memory. Why this is so is the subject of this section.

Memory management is a general term that covers all the various techniques by which an address generated by a CPU is translated into the actual address of the data in memory. Memory management plays several roles in a computer system. First, memory management permits computers with small main stores to execute programs that are far larger than the main store.[2] Second, memory management is used in multitasking operating systems to make it look as if each process has sole control of the CPU. Third, memory management can be employed to protect one process from being corrupted by another process. Finally, memory management, in

conjunction with the operating system, deals with the allocation of memory to variables.

If all computers had an infinite amount of random access memory, life would be much easier for the operating system designer. When a new program is loaded from disk, you can place it immediately after the last program you loaded into memory. Moreover, with an infinitely large memory you never have to worry about loading programs that are too large for the available memory. In practice, real computers may have too little memory. In this section we are going to look at how the operating system manages the available memory.

Figure 13.13(a) demonstrates multitasking where three processes, A, B, and C are initially in memory. This diagram shows the location of programs in the main store. In Fig. 13.13(b) process B has been executed to completion and deleted from memory to leave a hole in the memory. In Fig. 13.13(c) a new process, process D, is loaded in part of the unused memory and process A deleted. Finally, in Fig. 13.13(d) a new process, process E, is loaded in memory in two parts because it can't fit in any single free block of memory space.

A multitasking system rapidly runs into the memory allocation and memory fragmentation problems described by Fig. 13.13. Operating systems use memory management to map the computer's programs onto the available memory space. Memory management is carried out by means of special-purpose hardware called a *memory management unit* (MMU) (see Fig. 13.14). Today's sophisticated microprocessors like the Pentium include an MMU on the same chip as the CPU. Earlier microprocessors often used external MMUs.

The CPU generates the address of an operand or an instruction and places it on its address bus. This address is called a *logical address*—it's the address that the programmer sees. The MMU translates the logical address into the location or *physical address* of the operand in memory. Figure 13.14 shows how

---

[2] Running programs larger than the actual immediate access memory was once very important when memory cost a fortune and computers had tiny memory systems.

the logical address 12345678_{16} address from the CPU gets *mapped* onto the physical address $ABC678_{16}$.

The logical address consists of two parts, a *page* address and a *word* address. In the previous example, page 12345_{16} gets translated into page ABC_{16} and the word address 678_{16} remains unchanged. Figure 13.15 illustrates the relationship between word address and page address for a very simple computer system with four pages of eight words (i.e. $4 \times 8 = 32$ locations).

The logical address from the CPU in Fig. 13.15 consists of a 2-bit page address that selects one of $2^2 = 4$ pages, and a 3-bit word address that provides an offset (or index) into the currently selected page. A 3-bit offset can access $2^3 = 8$ words

within a page. If, for example, the CPU generates the address 10110_2, location 6 on logical page 2 is accessed.

In a system with memory management the 3-bit word address from the CPU goes directly to the memory, but the 2-bit page address is sent to the memory management unit (see Fig. 13.16). The logical page address from the CPU selects an entry in a table of pages in the MMU as Fig. 13.16 demonstrates. Suppose the processor accesses logical page 2 and the corresponding page table entry contains the value 3. This value (i.e. 3) corresponds to the physical page address of the location being accessed in memory; that is, the MMU has translated logical page 2 into physical page 3. The physical

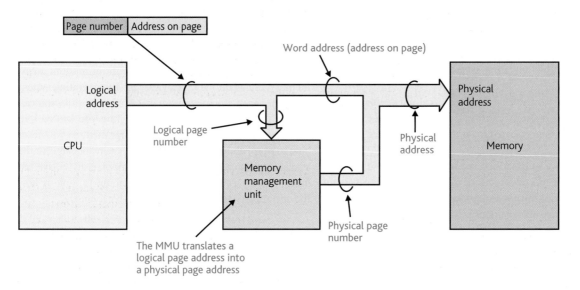

Figure 13.14　The memory management unit.

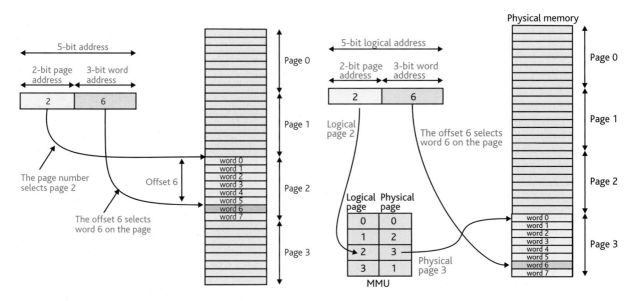

Figure 13.15　The structure of paged memory.

Figure 13.16　Mapping logical onto physical pages.

address corresponds to the location of the actual operand in memory. If you compare Figs 13.15 and 13.16 you can see that the same logical address has been used to access two different physical addresses.

Why should the operating system take an address from the processor and convert it into a new address to access physical memory? To answer this question we have to look at how programs are arranged in memory. Figure 13.17 shows the structure of both logical memory and physical memory during the execution of processes A, B, C, and D. As far as the processor is concerned, the processes all occupy single blocks of address space that are located consecutively in logical memory (Fig. 13.17(a)).

If you examine the physical memory (Fig. 13.17(b)), the actual processes are distributed in real memory in an almost random fashion. Processes B and C are split into non-consecutive regions and two regions of physical memory are unallocated. The logical address space seen by the processor is larger than the physical address space—process D is currently located on the hard disk and is not in the computer's RAM. This mechanism is called *virtual memory*.

A processor's *logical address space* is composed of all the addresses that the processor can specify. If the processor has a 32-bit address, its logical address space consists of 2^{32} bytes. The physical address space is the memory and its size depends on how much memory the computer user can afford. We will soon see how the operating system deals with situations in which the processor wishes to run programs that are larger than the available physical address space. The function of the MMU is to map the addresses generated by the CPU onto the actual memory and to keep track of where data is stored as new processes are created and old ones removed. With an MMU, the CPU doesn't have to worry about where programs and data are actually located.

Consider a system with 4-kbyte logical and physical pages and suppose the processor generates the logical address 881234_{16}. This 24-bit address is made up of a 12-bit logical page address 881_{16} and a 12-bit word address 234_{16}. The 12 low-order bits (234_{16}) define the same relative location within both logical and physical address pages. The logical page address is sent to the MMU, which looks up the corresponding physical page address in entry number 881 in the page table. The physical page address found in this location is passed to memory.

Let's look at the way in which the MMU performs mapping. Figure 13.18 demonstrates how the *pages* or *frames* of logical address space are mapped onto the frames of physical address space. The corresponding address mapping table is described in Table 13.1. Notice that logical page 3 and logical page 8 are both mapped onto physical page 6. This situation might arise when two programs share a common resource (e.g. a compiler or an editor). Each program thinks that it has a unique copy of the resource, although both programs access a shared copy of the resource.

13.4.1 Virtual memory

We've already said that a computer can execute programs larger than its physical memory. In a virtual memory system the programmer sees a large array of physical memory (the virtual memory), which appears to be entirely composed of high-speed main store. In reality, the physical memory is composed of a relatively small high-speed RAM and a much larger but slower disk store. Virtual memory has two advantages. It allows the execution of programs larger than the physical memory would normally permit and frees the programmer from worrying about choosing logical addresses falling within the range of available physical addresses. Programmers may choose any logical address they desire for their program and its variables. The actual addresses selected by a programmer don't matter, because the logical addresses are automatically mapped into the available physical memory space as the operating system sees fit.

The means of accomplishing such an apparently impossible task is called *virtual memory* and was first used in the Atlas computer at the University of Manchester, England in 1960. Figure 13.19 illustrates a system with 10 logical address pages but only five physical address pages. Consequently, only 50% of the logical address space can be mapped onto physical address space at any instant. Table 13.2 provides a logical page to physical page mapping table for this situation. Each entry in the logical address page table has two entries: one is the *present bit*, which indicates whether the corresponding page is available in physical memory and the other is the logical page to physical page mapping.

Part of a program that's not being used resides on disk. When this code is to be executed, it is copied from disk to the

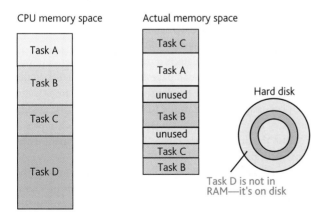

(a) Logical address space.   (b) Physical address space.

Figure 13.17 Logical and physical address space.

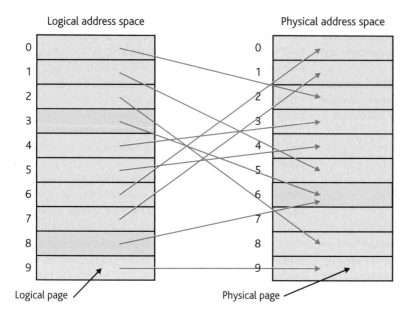

Figure 13.18 Mapping logical address space onto physical address space.

Logical page	Physical page
0	2
1	5
2	8
3	6
4	3
5	4
6	0
7	1
8	6
9	9

Table 13.1 Logical to physical address mapping table corresponding to Fig. 13.18.

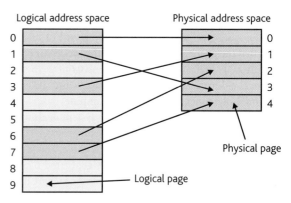

Figure 13.19 A system where physical address space < logical address space.

computer's immediate access memory. Sometimes it's impossible to fit all the program (and the data required by the program) in main memory. Consequently, only part of the program can be loaded into random access memory. The operating system divides the program into pages and loads some of these pages into its random access memory. As pages are loaded, the operating system updates the page table in the MMU so that each logical page can be mapped onto the corresponding physical page in RAM.

Consider what happens when a program that resides partially in memory and partially on disk is executed. When the processor generates a logical address, the memory management unit reads the mapping table to look up the corresponding physical page address. If the page is present in RAM, a logical to physical address translation takes place and

the information is accessed. However, if the logical page is currently not in RAM, an address translation cannot take place. In this case, the MMU sends a special type of interrupt to the processor called a *page fault*.

When the processor detects a page fault, the operating system intervenes and copies a page of data from the disk to the random access memory. Finally, the operating system updates the page-mapping table in the MMU and reruns the faulted memory access. This arrangement is called *virtual memory* because the processor appears to have a physical memory as large as its logical address space.

Virtual memory works effectively only if, for most of the time, the data being accessed is in physical memory. Fortunately, accesses to programs and their data are highly clustered. Operating systems designers speak of the *80:20 rule*—for 80% of the time the processor accesses only 20% of a program. Note that the principles governing the operation of virtual memory are, essentially, the same as those governing the operation of cache memory (described later).

When a page fault is detected, the operating system transfers a new page from disk to physical memory and overwrites a page in physical memory. If physical memory is full, it's necessary to discard an existing page. The most sensible way of selecting an old page for removal is to take the page that is not going to be required in the near future. Unfortunately, this scheme is impossible to implement. A simple page replacement algorithm is called the *not-recently-used* algorithm, which is not optimum but it is very easy to implement.

When a new page replaces an old page, any data in the old page frame that has been modified since it was created must be written back to disk. A typical virtual memory system clears a *dirty bit* in the page table when the page is first created. Whenever the processor performs a write operation to an operand on this page, the dirty bit is set. When this page is swapped out (i.e. overwritten by a new page), the operating

system looks at its dirty bit. If this bit is clear, nothing need be done; if it is set, the page must be copied to disk.

Virtual memory allows the programmer to write programs without having to know anything about the characteristics of real memory and where the program is to be located.

13.4.2 Virtual memory and the 68K family

Members of Motorola's 68K family are well suited to virtual memory technology. We've already stated that the 68K's architecture provides mechanisms to support operating systems. The 68K's protected state when S = 1 separates operating system and application level programs (aided by the dual stack pointer mechanism). 68K processors have a *function control output* that tells an external system such as a memory management unit whether the CPU is executing an instruction in the user or the supervisor state.

Figure 13.20 illustrates the dialogue that takes place between the CPU, the memory management unit (MMU), and the memory system during a read or a write cycle. The MMU is configured by the operating system when the computer is first powered up. The operating system sets up logical address to physical address translation tables and defines the type of access that each page may take part in (we'll see the reason for this shortly).

At the start of a memory access the CPU generates a logical address and sends it to the MMU together with the control signals that define the type of the access (i.e. read or write, program or data, user or supervisor mode). If the location being accessed is not currently in the main store or is an illegal access, the MMU sends an error message to the CPU to abort the current access and to begin exception processing and error recovery. An illegal access occurs when a process attempts to write to a page that has been designated read-only, or when a user program is attempting to access a page assigned to supervisor space and the operating system.

Logical page	Present bit	Physical page
0	1	0
1	1	3
2	0	
3	1	1
4	0	
5	0	
6	1	2
7	1	4
8	0	
9	0	

Table 13.2 Logical to physical address mapping table corresponding to Fig. 13.19.

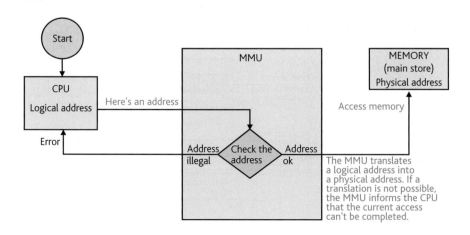

Figure 13.20 Dialogue between the CPU, MMU, and memory.

By dividing memory space into regions of different characteristics, you can provide a considerable measure of security. A user program cannot access memory space belonging to the operating system, because an attempt to access this memory space would result in the MMU generating an interrupt. Not only does the processor protect the supervisor stack pointer from illegal access by a user program, the 68K and MMU combination protects the supervisor stack (and any other address space allocated to the supervisor) from illegal access.

Figure 13.21 illustrates the structure of a memory management system in a 68K-based computer that checks whether the address space currently being accessed is legal. Each entry in the MMU's page translation table contains the details about the page's access rights. Whenever the 68K performs a memory access, it indicates the type of access on its function code output pins (e.g. user/supervisor, code/data). For example, the 68020 may say 'I'm operating in the user state performing a read access to data with a logical address 12345678_{16}'. The MMU compares the CPU's function code and the read/write signal with the information in the currently accessed page in its mapping table. If the access is legal, a memory access takes place. If either the corresponding physical page is not in memory or the access is illegal, a page fault is generated and a signal returned to the 68K's *bus error* input. In terms of the previous example, the logical address 12345678_{16} might generate a page address 12345_{16}. If this page is in the MMU and it can be accessed by a user-mode write, a logical-to-physical page translation can take place.

A *bus error* is a special type of exception and the 68K calls the appropriate handler in the operating system to deal with it. A missing physical page results in the operating system copying a page from disk to main store and then updating the MMU. An illegal access would probably result in the offending process being suspended.

The 68K's user/supervisor modes, exception-handling facilities, and memory management make it a very robust processor. Errors in a user program that would otherwise bring the system to a halt force a switch to the 68K's supervisor state and allow the operating system to either repair the damage or to terminate the faulty program. The memory management mechanism protects the operating system from illegal access by applications programs and even protects one user program from access by another.

Memory management in real systems

In reality, memory management is a very complex mechanism, even though the underlying concepts are very simple. The picture we have just presented is very simplified because we've omitted the detail.

A real memory management system does not normally have a single page table; it would be a too big. If we have a 32-bit virtual address and an 8 kbyte page, the number of bits used to specify a logical page is $32 - 13 = 19$. This arrangement would require a page table with 2^{19} entries.

Figure 13.22 demonstrates how a real system solves the page table problem by means of a *hierarchical table search*. The 10 most-significant bits of the virtual address access a first-level table. The output of the first-level table is a pointer to a second-level table that is indexed into by 9 bits from the virtual address. This table provides that actual physical page number. A multilevel table scheme allows us to use the first-level table to point to, for example, different processes, and the second-level table to point to the pages that make up each

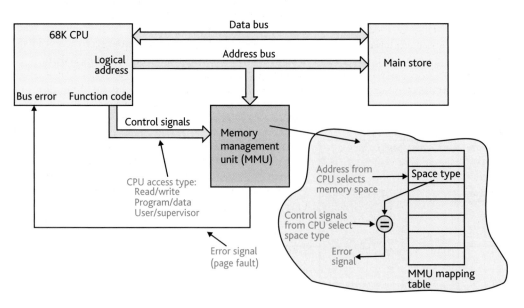

Figure 13.21 Memory space matching hardware.

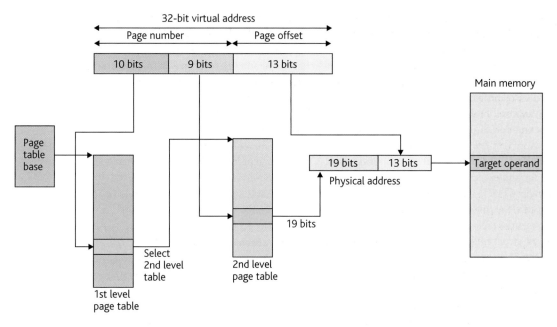

Figure 13.22 Multiple levels of page tables.

MALWARE

Memory management is an important line of defense against errors that occur when an application accesses memory space not allocated to it. Some programs deliberately perform operations that are unintended by the computer user; these are collectively called *malware* and include viruses, worms, Trojan horses, and spyware.

People who would never dream of going into the street and assaulting a passer-by will quite cheerfully release programs via the Internet that create havoc on people's computers; they will destroy a child's homework, modify patient records in a hospital, or delete a photographer's images. They use the excuse that they are testing people's computer security (even Bonnie and Clyde never claimed that they were testing bank security) or they say that they are leading an attack on Microsoft's evil empire.

A virus is a program that has strong analogies with biological viruses because it replicates itself, spreads autonomously, mutates, and can damage its host. A virus is introduced into a host via the Internet or via an infected program on a floppy disk, flash memory, or CD/DVD.

A virus must be an executable program in order for it to run and to replicate itself. In the PC world, a virus may have the extension .exe or .pif. However, one of the strengths of modern computer applications is the use of *scripting languages* and *macros* that allow a user program to respond to its environment. These facilities are employed by virus writers to embed viruses in data used by applications programs such as e-mails.

Viruses can be injected by ingenious techniques such as *buffer overflow*. A buffer is a region of memory used to store data. Buffer overflow occurs when the data takes more space than that allocated by the buffer. By exploiting buffer overflow you can fill a region of memory with code (rather than data) and then transfer control to that code to activate the virus. Some processors now contain hardware mechanisms to prevent the execution of such code.

Commercially available antivirus programs are widely available to scan memories for the *signature* of a virus (a signature is the binary sequence left behind when the code of a virus is compressed rather like a cyclic redundancy code). Some viruses are *polymorphic* and mutate as they spread, making it difficult to detect their signature.

A Trojan horse is a program that appears harmless but which carries out a task unknown to the user. A worm is a program that exploits the Internet and spreads from computer to computer generating so much traffic that the Internet can be dramatically slowed.

Spyware is a class of program that may spread like a virus or may be introduced as part of another program. Spyware monitors your surfing habits (or even accesses to personal data) and sends this information to a third party.

process. Performing a logical-to-physical address translation to locate a physical page address is called a *table walk*.

The arrangement of Fig. 13.22 requires 2^{10} level-one pages and 2^9 level-two pages; that is, 3×2^9 pages. A single-level page table would require 2^{19} pages.

The price paid for a memory management system (especially one with multilevel tables) is the time it takes to perform an address translation. Practical memory mapping is possible only because very few table accesses take place. Once a sequence of logical-to-physical address mappings have been performed the address translation is cached in a *translation look aside buffer* (TLB). The next time the same logical page address appears, the corresponding page address is read from the TLB to avoid a table walk. Because of the way data and programs are structured, address translations mainly take place using the TLB.

■ SUMMARY

The operating system is a unique topic in computer science because nowhere else does hardware and software so closely meet. Although most computers today see the operating system as the GUI and the file manager, there is another part of the operating system that lies hidden from the user. This is the kernel that performs process switching in a multitasking system and allocates logical address space to the available memory.

In this chapter we have shown how the multitasking can be implemented by saving one process's *volatile portion* and then restoring another task by loading its volatile portion in the processor's registers.

One of the most important functions carried out by operating systems is the management of the memory. We have shown how logical addresses in the program can be mapped onto locations in the immediate access memory. We have also looked at the 68K's user/supervisor mode facility and described how it can be used to create secure operating systems.

■ PROBLEMS

13.1 What is an operating system?

13.2 What is the difference between a modern operating system and a typical operating system from the 1970s?

13.3 What is the difference between operating systems on large and small computers?

13.4 WIMP-based operating systems have largely replaced JCL-based operating systems on PCs. Do JCL-based operating systems such as Microsoft's DOS 6 and UNIX have any advantages over WIMP-based systems?

13.5 Is it necessary for a CPU to support interrupts in order to construct an operating system?

13.6 A process in a multitasking system can be in one of three states: running, runnable, or blocked. What does this statement mean and what are the differences between the three states?

13.7 What is a *process control block* and what is the minimum amount of information that it must store?

13.8 What are the 68K's user and supervisor states and why have they been implemented?

13.9 Explain why the stack is such an important data structure and how stack errors can cause the system to crash.

13.10 The 68K provides a greater degree of protection from user (applications) errors by implementing two stack pointers. Explain how this protection mechanism works.

13.11 If two stack pointers are a good thing (i.e. the 68K's user and supervisor stack pointers), can you see advantages in having two PCs or two sets of data registers, and so on?

13.12 What is the difference between a *physical* address and a *logical* address?

13.13 When a new physical page is swapped into memory, one of the existing pages has to be rejected. How is the decision to reject an existing page made?

13.14 What is the difference between virtual memory and cache memory?

13.15 Write a program in 68K assembly language that periodically switches between two processes (assume these are fixed processes permanently stored in memory).

13.16 What is the difference between pre-emptive and non-pre-emptive operating systems? Are the various Windows operating systems pre-emptive?

13.17 What is malware? How has it developed over the last few years?

13.18 What hardware facilities in a computer can be used to defeat the spread of malware?

Computer communications

14

CHAPTER MAP

INTRODUCTION

Two of the greatest technologies of our age are *telecommunications* and *computer engineering*. Telecommunications is concerned with moving information from one point to another. We take the telecommunications industry for granted. If you were to ask someone what the greatest technological feat of 1969 was, they might reply, 'The first manned landing on the moon.' You could say that a more magnificent achievement was the ability of millions of people half a million kilometers away to watch events on the moon in their own homes.

It's not surprising that *telecommunications* and *computer engineering* merged to allow computers to communicate and share resources. Until the 1990s developments in telecommunications didn't greatly affect the average person in the same way that computer technology had revolutionized every facet of life. Better communications meant lower telephone bills and the cell phone.

Computer networks began as part of a trend towards distributed computing with multicomputer systems and distributed databases. From the 1970s onward computer networks were implemented to allow organizations such as the military, the business world, and the academic communities to share data. Easy access to the Internet and the invention of the browser created a revolution almost as big as the microprocessor revolution of the 1970s. The success of the Internet drove developments in communications equipment.

This chapter examines the way in which computers communicate with each other, concentrating more on the hardware-related aspects of computer communication than the software.

We begin with a short history of communications, concentrating on the development of long-distance signaling systems. We then introduce the idea of protocols and standards, which play a vital role in any communications system. Simply moving data from one point to another isn't the whole story. Protocols are the mutually agreed rules or procedures enabling computers to exchange data in an orderly fashion. By implementing a suitable protocol we ensure that the data gets to its correct destination and deal with the problems of lost or corrupted data.

The next step is to examine how digital data in serial form is physically moved from one point to another. We look at two types of data path, the telephone network and the RS232C interface that links together computers and peripherals. Two protocols for the transmission of serial data are briefly examined—a character-oriented protocol that treats data as blocks of ASCII-encoded characters and a bit-oriented protocol that treats data as a continuous stream of bits.

The next part of this chapter is devoted to local area networks and describes the features of some of the LANs in current use. An important aspect of LANs is the way in which the computers and peripherals are able to share the same network without apparent conflict. The final topic in this chapter is the wide area network (WAN) that connects computers together over distances longer than about a mile—WANs are used to implement the Internet.

GROWTH IN HOUSEHOLDS WITH MULTIPLE PCs

When the first edition of this text appeared, computer communications was very much a corporate affair. Only the rich communicated with each other. By the time the third edition appeared, the PC had become popular and the Internet and World Wide Web were used by people at home. Connections to the Internet were mainly via the public switched telephone network, although a lucky few had broadband connections via cable or the telephone using ASDL.

Today, high-speed connections to the Internet are commonplace and many homes have several PCs. Each member of the household may have their own PC and some may have laptop PCs with wireless networks. This means that many home users now have

their own private local area networks; by 1999 25% of US households had more than one PC and this figure was expected to reach 50% by 2005.

The growth in PC ownership is driven by several factors. More and more people are moving from being computer literate to being computer experts capable of maintaining complex systems. The cost of computing has declined in real terms and the performance of hardware has continued to increase. The market has been driven by computer games and domestic entertainment such as home theatre and the rise of the DVD, the camcorder, and the digital camera.

14.1 Background

It's expensive to construct data links between computers separated by distances ranging from the other side of town to the other side of the World. There is, however, one network that has spanned the globe for over 50 years, the *public switched telephone network* (PSTN). Some even refer to the PSTN by the acronym POTS (plain old telephone system). The telephone network doesn't provide an ideal solution to the linking of computers, because it was not originally designed to handle high-speed digital data.

During the 1980s a considerable change in the way computers were used took place. The flood of low-cost microcomputers generated a corresponding increase in the number of peripherals capable of being controlled by a computer. It is now commonplace to connect together many different computers and peripherals on one site (e.g. a factory), enabling data to be shared, control centralized, and efficiency improved. Such a network is called a *local area network* (LAN).

When the PC became popular, low-cost hardware and software were used to link PCs to the global network, the Internet. By the late 1990s networks were no longer the province of the factory or university—any school child

with a PC at home could access NASA's database to see pictures of the latest space shots before they got on the evening news. Moreover, the child didn't need to know anything about computer science other than how to operate a mouse.

Figure 14.1 illustrates the concept of a computer network with two interconnected *local area networks*. A network performs the same function as a telephone exchange and routes data from one computer to another. The LANs in Fig. 14.1 might be used to share data in, for example, a university environment. The local area networks are themselves connected to the telephone system via hardware called a *modem*. Figure 14.1 also demonstrates that a single computer can be connected to the other networks via the PSTN.

A LAN let's you communicate with a mainframe on a distant site or with one of the many microprocessors and peripherals on your own site. The local area network has made possible the paperless office in which people pass memos to each other via the network.

Figure 14.2 describes the type of network that you might now see in a school, a small office, or a home. A wireless *gateway* is connected to a PC via a cable. The gateway has a connection to a cable modem that provides a high-speed link to the Internet via a cable network. The gateway uses wireless

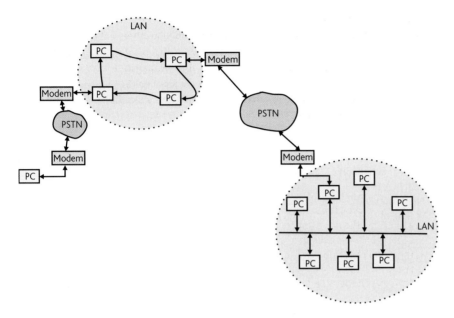

Figure 14.1 The network.

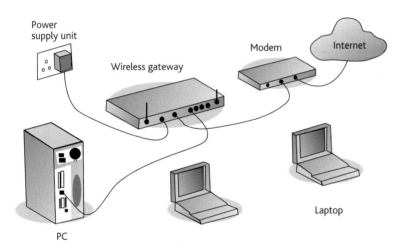

Figure 14.2 The modern small-office network.

extending over a relatively large area such as a number of separate sites or even part of a city.

A LAN is private A LAN belongs to the owner of the site on which it is operated and does not use public data transmission equipment such as the telephone network. Therefore, the owner of the LAN doesn't have to comply with the very complex legal restrictions and obligations associated with a public network. A LAN on one site can be connected to a LAN on another site by means of the PSTN. The interface between the LAN and the PSTN is called a *gateway*. A gateway is an interconnection between two or more separate networks.

A LAN offers a high data rate The rate at which information can be transmitted across a physical channel depends on the length and the electrical properties of the transmission path. LANs have relatively short transmission paths and often use coaxial cable or a twisted pair, permitting data rates up to 100 Mbits/s. This data rate is very much greater than the 9600 to 56 kbits/s supported by telephone channels.

A LAN is reliable Most LANs are relatively simple systems with a coaxial cable connecting the various nodes of the network. There are no complex switching systems like those associated with telephone networks. LANs are reliable because they link systems over short distances and aren't subject to the types of interference that plague the long-haul transmission paths of the telephone network. Furthermore, the LAN does not employ the fault- and noise-prone mechanical or electronic message-switching techniques associated with the telephone system. A well-designed LAN should offer a very long MTBF (mean time between failure) and a short MTTR (mean time to repair) if it does fail. A repair may involve little more than replacing one of the nodes that has failed. LANs are designed so that the failure of a single node has no effect on the performance of the system.

A LAN is cheap LANs have been devised to connect low-cost systems and therefore the use of expensive technology or transmission media can't be tolerated. LANs are not only cheap, but require little labor in their installation. One of the most clearly defined trends to emerge from the microprocessor

technology to connect one or more laptop computers to the base machine and the Internet.

14.1.1 Local area networks

Local area networks have changed the face of modern computing. The high performance and low cost of today's LAN makes it feasible for even the smallest organizations to link together all their computers and allied digital equipment. Some of the key features of a LAN are as follows.

A LAN is local The term *local* implies a single site—even if the site is very large. The site may be a laboratory, a factory, or an entire complex of factories. The term MAN (*metropolitan area network*) has been coined to indicate a network

---

COMMUNICATIONS HARDWARE

A few years ago, most computer users employed only one piece of communications equipment; the *modem*, which links computers to the telephone network. The modem itself was invariably an external device that connected to a PC via its serial RSC32C interface.

Today, modems are often internal devices that plug into a PC's motherboard. Indeed, many modem laptops come with an internal modem as standard.

Today's PCs are designed to connect to local area networks. The computer uses *a network interface card* (NIC), to connect to a bus called an Ethernet. Each NIC has its own unique fixed internal address created at the time of the card's manufacture. This is a physical address that identifies the computer within the network, but it is not the address by which the computer is known externally.

Some modern network interface cards use wireless communications, Wi-Fi, to allow computers, laptops, and even printers to operate over a range of between 10 m and 100 m.

Large networks require devices to amplify signals on them. The *repeater* is a device that simply links two segments of a large network together. The router simply passes information unchanged from one segment to another.

Some organizations might have multiple networks. A *bridge* is a device that links two different networks. If a computer on a network sends data to another device on the same network, the bridge takes no part in the communication. If, however, the message is intended for a device on another network, the bridge passes the message between the networks. The address examined by a bridge is the unique *media access address* given to each physical node in a network. The bridge operates at the data link layer level of a network.

The *router* is an even more sophisticated network device because it can link different types of network that may be separated by a communications path. The bridge simply detects information whose destination is on another network and passes it on, whereas a router has to be able to communicate with different types of network with different protocols. A router operates at the network level and can connect networks with different data link level protocols. Routers are able to reformat packets of information before transmitting then to another network.

---

world is the tendency for the price of anything associated with microprocessors to fall dramatically as time passes. If low-cost microprocessor systems are to be linked, the local area network chosen to do this must be cost effective.

A LAN is fair to the users A LAN should offer all its nodes full connectivity, which means that any given node should be able to communicate with any other node. Equally, each node should have the same access rights to the transmission medium, so that all nodes have the same probability that their message will be delivered across the network.[1]

The nodes of a LAN should be equal When we say that all nodes should be equal we mean that they should have the same software and the same hardware. A corollary of this statement is that it should be possible to add a new node to an existing system without modifying the software at all the other nodes.

14.1.2 **LAN network topology**

The topology of a network describes the way in which the individual users of the network are linked together. There are four basic topologies suitable for use in a LAN: the unconstrained topology, the star network, the bus, and the ring. These topologies are the same topologies used to implement the multiprocessor systems we introduced in Chapter 8.

The unconstrained network

The most general topology is the *unconstrained* network of Fig. 14.3 where individual nodes are connected together in an

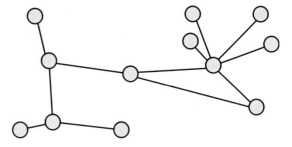

Figure 14.3 The unconstrained topology.

arbitrary fashion. Additional links can be provided to reduce bottlenecks where heavy traffic passes between groups of nodes. Further nodes and links can readily be added without disturbing the existing hardware. The road network of most countries is an unconstrained topology, with new roads being added when and where necessary.

The disadvantage of the unconstrained topology is that a decision must be made at each node on the best way to route a message to its destination. In terms of the analogy with the road system, the driver must have a road map to enable them to drive from one place to another. A message cannot just be transmitted from one node to each other node to which it is connected, as this would lead to the message being multiplied at each node and propagated round the network forever.

---

[1] The fairness criterion exists only at levels 1 and 2 of the ISO model for OSI. A higher level may limit the scope of a particular node's access rights. We discuss the ISO model for OSI later.

Instead, each node must have its own road map and make a decision on which link the message is to be transmitted on the way to its destination.

Calculating the best route through the network for each message has the computational overhead of working out routing algorithms. Furthermore, whenever a new link or node is added to the network, the routing information must be changed at each node. Figure 14.4 shows how a message may be routed through an unconstrained topology. We will return to the topic of routing.

The star network

Figure 14.5 shows how the star network routes all messages from source to destination via one central node and eliminates the need for nodes to make routing decisions. The star has a simple topology and has advantages when the network's physical topology matches its logical topology. Clearly, there are circumstances where the nodes are distributed in such a way that the links between some of the nodes and the central node are economically unviable.

The star network has two obvious disadvantages. As all messages pass through the central node, the loss of the central node brings down the network. Other networks may offer degraded but useful service if part of the network fails. Furthermore, because all traffic passes through the central node, it must be capable of working at a sufficiently high speed to handle all nodes to which it is connected.

The bus

The bus topology is illustrated in Fig. 14.6. Both the bus and the ring are attempts to minimize the complexity of a network by both removing a special-purpose central node and the need for individual nodes to make routing decisions.

In a bus all nodes are connected to a common data highway. The bus may be a single path linking all nodes. A more general form of bus consists of several interlinked buses and is called an *unrooted tree*. When a message is put on the bus by a node, it flows outwards in all directions and eventually reaches every point in the network. The bus has one topological and one practical restriction. Only one path may exist between any two points, otherwise there would be nothing to stop a message flowing round a loop forever. The practical limitation is that the bus cannot exceed some maximum distance from end to end.

The principal problem faced by the designers of a bus is how to deal with a number of nodes wanting to use the bus at the same time. This is called *bus contention* and is dealt with later.

The ring

Figure 14.7 illustrates the ring topology, in which the nodes are connected together in the form of a ring. Like the bus, this topology provides a decentralized structure, because no central node is needed to control the ring. Each node simply receives a message from one neighbor and passes it on to

its other neighbor. Messages flow in one direction round the ring.

The only routing requirement placed on each node is that it must be able to recognize a message intended for itself. The ring does not suffer from contention like the bus topology.

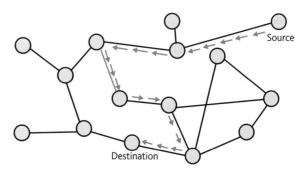

Figure 14.4 Routing a message through an unconstrained topology.

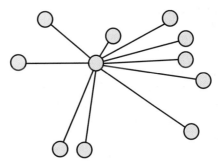

Figure 14.5 The star topology.

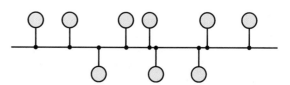

Figure 14.6 The bus topology.

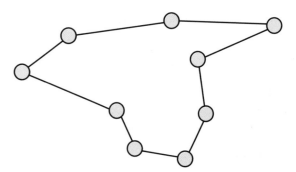

Figure 14.7 The ring topology.

However, a node on the ring has the problem of how to inject a new message into the existing traffic flow.

A ring is prone to failure because a broken link makes it impossible to pass messages all the way round the ring. Some networks employ a *double ring* structure with two links between each node. If one of the links is broken it is possible for the ring to reconfigure itself and bypass the failure.

14.1.3 History of computer communications

Before we describe computer networks, it's instructive to take a short look at the history of data transmission. Some think that electronics began in the 1960s or even later. Telecommunications predates the electronic digital computer by over a century and its history is just as exciting as the space race of the 1960s. Key players were engineers every bit as great as Newton or Einstein.

At the beginning of the nineteenth century, King Maximilian in Bavaria had seen how the French visual semaphore system helped Napoleon's military campaigns. In 1809 Maximilian asked the Bavarian Academy of Sciences to look for a way to communicate over long distances. As a result, Samuil T. von Sömmering designed a crude telegraph that used a conductor (one for each character) that required 35 parallel wires. How was information transmitted in a pre-electronic age? If you pass electricity through water containing a little acid the electric current breaks down the water into oxygen and hydrogen. Sömmering's telegraph worked by detecting the bubbles that appeared in a glass tube containing acidified water when electricity was passed through it. Sömmering's telegraph wasn't exactly suited to high-speed transmission—but it was a start.

Hans C. Oersted made the greatest leap forward in electrical engineering in 1819 when he discovered that an electric current creates a magnetic field round a conductor. Conversely, a moving magnetic field induces an electric current in a conductor.

A major driving force behind early telecommunications systems was the growth of the rail network. A system was required to warn stations down the line that a train was arriving. Charles Wheatstone and Charles William Cooke invented a telegraph in 1828 that used the magnetic field round a wire to deflect a compass needle. By 1840 a 40-mile stretch between Slough and Paddington in London had been linked using the Wheatstone and Cooke telegraph.

Figure 14.8 illustrates the operation of a different type of telegraph that produces a sound rather than the deflection of compass needles. When the key is depressed, a current flows in the circuit magnetizes the iron core inside the coil, and energizes the solenoid. The magnetized core attracts a small iron plate that produces an audible click as it strikes the core. Information is transmitted to this type of telegraph in the form of the Morse code.

Samuel Morse constructed his code from four symbols: the dot, the dash (whose duration is equal to three dots), the space between dots and dashes, and the space between words. Unlike simple codes, the Morse code is a variable length code. The original Morse key didn't send a 'bleep'—a dot was the interval between two closely spaced clicks and a dash the interval between two more widely spaced clicks. In other words, the operator had to listen to the space between clicks.

In 1843 Morse sent his assistant Alfred Vail to the printer's to count the relative frequencies of the letters they were using to set up their press. Morse gave frequently occurring letters short codes and infrequently occurring letters were given long symbols; for example, the code for E is • and Q is — —•—. It's interesting to note that the Morse code is relatively close to the optimum *Huffman* code for the English language.

The very first long-distance telecommunications networks were designed to transmit digital information from point to point (i.e. on–off telegraph signals). Information was transmitted in binary form using two signal levels (current = mark, no current = space). The transmitter was the Morse key and the receiver was the Morse telegraph.

The first long-distance data links

We take wires and cables for granted. In the early nineteenth century, plastics hadn't been invented and the only materials available for insulation and waterproofing were things like asphaltum. In 1843 a form of rubber called gutta percha was discovered and was used to insulate the signal-carrying path in cables. The Atlantic Telegraph Company created an insulated cable for underwater use containing a single copper

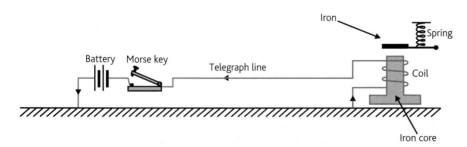

Figure 14.8 The telegraph.

conductor made of seven twisted strands, surrounded by gutta percha insulation. This cable was protected by 18 surrounding iron wires coated with hemp and tar.

Submarine cable telegraphy began with a cable crossing the English Channel to France in 1850. Alas the cable failed after only a few messages had been exchanged. A more successful attempt was made the following year.

Transatlantic cable laying from Ireland began in 1857 but was abandoned when the strain of the cable descending to the ocean bottom caused it to snap under its own weight. The Atlantic Telegraph Company tried again in 1858. Again, the cable broke after only 3 miles but the two cable-laying ships managed to splice the two ends. After several more breaks and storm damage, the cable reached Newfoundland in August 1857.

It soon became clear that this cable wasn't going to be a commercial success because the signal was too weak to detect reliably (the receiver used the magnetic field from current in the cable to deflect a magnetized needle). The original voltage used to drive a current down the cable was approximately 600 V. So, they raised the voltage to about 2000 V to drive more current along the cable. Such a high voltage burned through the primitive insulation, shorted the cable, and destroyed the first transatlantic telegraph link after about 700 messages had been transmitted in 3 months.

In England, the Telegraph Construction and Maintenance Company developed a new 2300-mile-long cable weighing 9000 tons, which was three times the diameter of the failed 1858 cable. Laying this cable required the largest ship in the world. After a failed attempt in 1865 a transatlantic link was established in 1866.

During the nineteenth century the length of cables increased as technology advanced. It soon became apparent that signals suffer distortion during transmission. The 1866 transatlantic telegraph cable could transmit only eight words per minute. By the way, it cost $100 in gold to transmit 20 words (including the address) across the first transatlantic cable.

A sharply rising pulse at the transmitter end of a cable is received at the far end as a highly distorted pulse with long rise and fall times. The sponsors of the transatlantic cable project were worried by the effect of this distortion and the problem was eventually handed to William Thomson at the University of Glasgow.

Thomson was one of the nineteenth century's greatest scientists who published more than 600 papers. He developed the second law of thermodynamics and created the absolute temperature scale. The unit of temperature with absolute zero at 0 K is called the kelvin in his honor—Thomson later became Lord Kelvin. Thomson worked on the dynamical theory of heat and carried out fundamental work in hydrodynamics. His mathematical analysis of electricity and magnetism covered the basic ideas for the electromagnetic

theory of light. I'm not certain what he did in his spare time. One of Thomson's most quoted statements that still applies today was:

I often say when you can measure what you are speaking about and express it in numbers, you know something about it, but when you cannot measure it, when you cannot express it in numbers, your knowledge of it is of a meager and unsatisfactory kind.

In 1855 Thomson presented a paper to the Royal Society analyzing the effect of pulse distortion, which became the cornerstone of what is now called transmission line theory. The cause of the problems investigated by Thomson lies in the physical properties of electrical conductors and insulators. At its simplest, the effect of a transmission line is to reduce the speed at which signals can change state. Thomson's theories enabled engineers to construct data links with much lower levels of distortion.

Origins of the telephone network

In 1872 Alexander Graham Bell who had recently emigrated to the USA started work on a method of transmitting several signals simultaneously over a single line. Bell's project was called the *harmonic telegraph*. This project failed, but it did lead to the development of the telephone in 1876. Note that development of the telephone is a complex story and Bell is no longer recognized as the sole inventor of the telephone.

A network designed to transmit intelligible speech (as opposed to hi-fi) must transmit analog signals in the frequency range 300 to about 3300 Hz (i.e. the so-called voice-band). Consequently, the telephone network now linking millions of subscribers across the World can't be used to directly transmit digital data that requires a bandwidth extending to zero frequency (i.e. d.c.). If the computer had been invented before the telephone, we wouldn't have had this problem. Transmission paths that transmit or pass signals with frequency components from d.c. to some upper limit are called *baseband channels*. Transmission paths that transmit frequencies between a lower and an upper frequency are called *bandpass channels*.

Digital information from computers or peripherals must be converted into analog form before it is transmitted across a bandpass channel such as the PSTN. At the receiving end of the network, this analog signal is reconverted into digital form. The device that converts between digital and analog signals over a data link is called a modem (i.e. modulator–demodulator). Ironically enough, all the long-haul links on modern telephone networks now transmit digital data, which means that the analog signal derived from the digital data must be converted to digital form before transmission over these links. It is probable that the PSTN will become entirely digital and speech will be converted to digital form within the subscriber's own telephone. Indeed, the only analog link in many telephone systems is just the

---

BANDWIDTH AND COMMUNICATION

If a signal conveys information, it must change over time. The minimum amount of information carried by a signal is the *bit*, which has two values, true and false or 1 and 0. When we change the state or level of the signal, we transmit a new value. *Transmission speed* is defined by both the number of *changes* in signal level we transmit per second and the number of *different signal levels* used to represent data. We can use signals with more that two valid levels. Consider the following example.

```
1 0 1 1 1 0 1 0 0 0   binary signal (two levels 0 and 1)
A C B B A D A D D C   four-level signal (four levels A = 00, B = 01, C = 10, and D = 11)
```

In the second case, each of the symbols A, B, C, D carries two bits of information because the symbol is one out of four, rather than one out of two. If symbols are transmitted at the same rate in each case, the four-level signal transmits information at twice the rate of a single level system.

Data rate is defined as the number of times a signal can be switched per second multiplied by the number of bits needed to encode all the levels that the signal can assume. Suppose a signal can have 16 different values or levels and is transmitted as 2400 symbols (values) per second, the data rate is $2400 \times 4 = 9600$ bits per second. Note that the switching rate (2400 in this case) is called the *Baud rate* after the French communications pioneer.

---

connection between the subscriber and the local exchange. This link is sometimes called the *last mile*.

Although the first telegraph systems operated from point to point, the introduction of the telephone led to the development of switching centers, or telephone exchanges. The first-generation of switches employed a telephone operator who manually plugged a subscriber's line into a line connected to the next switching center in the link. By the end of the nineteenth century, the infrastructure of the computer networks was already in place.

In 1897 an undertaker called Almon Strowger invented the automatic telephone exchange that used electromechanical devices to route calls between exchanges. When a number was dialed, a series of pulses were sent down the line to a rotary switch. If you dialed, for example 5, the five pulses would move a switch five steps to connect you to line number five, which routed your call to the next switching center. Consequently, when you called someone the number you dialed depended on the route though the system. A system was developed where each user could be called with the same number from anywhere and the exchange would automatically translate this number to the specific numbers required to perform the routing. Mechanical switching was gradually replaced by electronic switching and the pulse dialing that actually operated the switches gave way to the use of tones (i.e. messages to the switching computers).

By the time the telegraph was well established, radio was being developed. James Clerk Maxwell predicted radio waves in 1864 following his study of light and electromagnetic waves. Heinrich Hertz demonstrated the existence of radio waves in 1887 and Guglielmo Marconi is credited with being the first to use radio to span the Atlantic in 1901.

In 1906 Lee deForest invented the vacuum tube amplifier. Without a vacuum tube (or transistor) to amplify weak signals, modern electronics would have been impossible (although primitive computers using electromechanical devices could have been built without electronics).

The telegraph, telephone, and vacuum tube were all steps on the path to the development of computer networks. As each of these practical steps was taken, there was a corresponding development in the accompanying theory (in the case of radio, the theory came before the discovery). Table 14.1 provides a list of some of the most significant dates in the early development of long-distance communications systems.

Computer communications is a complex branch for computing because it covers so many areas. A programmer drags an icon from one place to another on a screen. This action causes the applications program to send a message to the operating system that might begin a sequence of transactions resulting in data being retrieved from a computer half way around the World. Data sent from one place to another has to be *encapsulated*, given an address, and sent on its way. Its progress has to be monitored and its receipt acknowledged. It has to be formatted in the way appropriate to the transmission path. All these actions have to take place over many different communications channels (telephone, radio, satellite, and fiber optic cable). Moreover, all the hardware and software components from different suppliers and constructed with different technologies have to communicate with each other.

The only way we can get such complex systems to work is to create rules or *protocols* that define how the various components communicate with each other. In the next section we look at these rules and the bodies that define them.

14.2 Protocols and computer communications

Communication between two computers is possible provided that they employ standard hardware and software conforming to agreed standards. Much of computer

1837	Charles Wheatstone patents the electric telegraph.
1844	Samuel Morse demonstrates a Baltimore to Washington, DC, telegraph link.
1847	An inelastic latex called gutta percha is discovered. It serves as a reliable insulator in water.
1850	Morse patents his telegraph.
1858	First transatlantic telegraph.
1861	First USA transcontinental telegraph cable begins service.
1864	James C. Maxwell predicts electromagnetic radiation.
1868	First successful transatlantic telegraph cable completed between UK and Canada.
1874	Jean-Maurice-Emile Baudot invents a division multiplexing scheme for telegraphs.
1875	Typewriter invented.
1876	Alexander Graham Bell patents the telephone.
1887	Heinrich Hertz discovers radio waves and verifies Maxwell's theory.
1906	Lee deForest invents the vacuum tube triode (an amplifier).
1915	USA transcontinental telephone service begins between New York and San Francisco.
1920s	Catalina Island telephone service to mainland via radio system.
1921	Radio telephone calls between England and Norway implemented.
1927	First commercial transatlantic radio telephone service begins.
1945	Arthur C. Clarke proposes using Earth-orbiting satellite as a communications relay.
1947	The transistor invented at Bell laboratories.
1948	Claude Shannon publishes his work on information theory (related to channel capacity).
1949	High-performance submarine cable developed by AT&T using polyethylene and butyl rubber dielectric.
1956	First transatlantic telephone cables. A total of 102 repeater (vacuum tube) amplifiers were used.
1957	USSR launches first satellite, Sputnik 1.
1962	First television satellite launched, Telstar 1.
1965	First commercial communications satellite launched, Early Bird (INTELSAT 1).
1966	Fiber optics first proposed.
1971	First large-scale computer network, ARPANET, comes into service.
1970s	ALOHA local area network developed for the Hawaiian islands.
1973	Bob Metcalfe develops the Ethernet.
1980	OSI 7-layer reference model (for networks) adopted.
1980	Bell Systems develop fiber optic cables.
1988	First fiber optic transatlantic cable.
1993	IPv4 + (Internet protocol version 4) developed as the backbone of the Internet.
1990s	By the end of the 1990s, 56K bps modems were widely available for use over the PTSN.
1997	The introduction of WiFi and the IEEE 802.11 standard.

Table 14.1 Key dates in the early developments in telecommunications.

communications is concerned with how computers go about exchanging data, rather than with just the mechanisms used to transmit data. Therefore, the standards used in computer communications relate not only to the hardware parts of a communication system (i.e. the plugs and sockets connecting a computer to a transmission path, the transmission path itself, the nature of the signals flowing along the transmission path), but to the procedures or *protocols* followed in transmitting the information.

Most readers will have some idea of what is meant by a *standard*, but they may not have come across the term *protocol* as it is used in computer communications. When any two parties communicate with each other (be they people or machines), they must both agree to abide by a set of unambiguous rules. For example, they must speak the same language and one may start speaking only when the other indicates a readiness to listen.

Suppose you have a bank overdraft and send a check to cover it. If after a few days you receive a threatening letter from the manager, what do you conclude? Was your check received after the manager's letter was sent? Has one of your debits reached your account and increased the overdraft? Was the check lost in the post? This confusion demonstrates that the blind transmission of information can lead to unclear and ill-defined situations. It is necessary for both parties to know exactly what messages each has, and has not, received. We need a set of rules to govern the interchange of letters.

Such a set of rules is called a protocol and, in the case of people, is learned as a child. When computers communicate with each other, the protocol must be laid down more formally. If many different computers are to communicate with each other, it is necessary that they adhere to standard protocols that have been promulgated by national and international standards organizations, trade organizations, and other related bodies.

In the 1970s and 1980s the number of computers and the volume of data to be exchanged between computers increased dramatically. Manufacturers were slow to agree on and to adopt standard protocols for the exchange of data, which led to incompatibility between computers. To add insult to injury, it was often difficult to transfer data between computers that were nominally similar. Computers frequently employed different dialects of the same high-level language and formatted data in different ways, encoded it in different ways, and transmitted it in different ways. Even the builders of the Tower of Babel had only to contend with different languages. The development of standard protocols has much improved the situation.

The issue of standardization arises not only in the world of computer communications. Standardization is an important part of all aspects of information technology. For example, the lack of suitable standards or the non-compliance with existing standards has a dampening effect on the progress of information technology. Independent manufacturers do not wish to enter a chaotic market that demands a large number of versions of each product or service produced to cater for all the various non-standard implementations. Similarly, users do not want to buy non-standard equipment or services that do not integrate with their existing systems.

14.2.1 Standards bodies

If a computer user in Middlesbrough, England accesses a computer in Phoenix, Arizona the two computers must cooperate. The commands and data sent by one computer must be recognized and complied with by the other computer. The protocols governing the communications process are formalized in a document called a *standard*. All aspects of the communications system must be standardized—from the communications protocol to the nature of the signals on the communications path to the plugs and sockets that connects the computer to the network.

How do the components of a network get standardized? There are two types of standards. One is the *de facto* or industrial standard that's imposed by a manufacturer. Microsoft's Windows operating system is an example of an industrial standard. The success of Windows has encouraged its adoption as a standard by most PC manufacturers and software houses.

The other type of standard is a national or international standard that has been promulgated by a recognized body. There are international standards for the binary representation of numbers. When the decimal number nine is transmitted over a network, it is represented by its universally agreed international standard, the binary pattern 00111001.

The world of standards involves lots of different parties with vested interests at local, national, and international levels. A standard begins life in a working party in a professional organization such as the Institute of Electrical and Electronic Engineers (IEEE) or the Electronic Industries Association (EIA). The standard generated by a professional body is forwarded to the appropriate national standards body (e.g. the American National Standards Institute (ANSI) in the USA, the British Standards Institute (BSI) in the UK, or DIN in Germany). The standard may reach the International Standards Organization (ISO) made up of members from the World's national standards organizations.

14.2.2 Open systems and standards

The International Standards Organization (ISO) has constructed a *framework* for the identification and design of protocols for existing or for future communications systems. This framework enables engineers to identify and to relate together different areas of standardization. The OSI framework doesn't imply any particular technology or method of implementing systems.

This framework is called the *Reference Model* for *Open Systems Interconnection* (ISO model for OSI) and refers to an *open system*, which, in the ISO context, is defined as

a set of one or more computers together with the software, peripherals, terminals, human operators, physical processes and means of data transfer that go with them, which make up a single information processing unit.

The expression *open system* means a system that is open to communication with other open systems. A system is open only if it employs agreed protocols when it communicates with the outside world. It does not have to employ standard protocols for communications within the system itself. An analogy with an open system is a television receiver because it is open to the reception of sound and pictures from transmitters using the agreed protocol (e.g. 525 lines/frame, 60 fields/s, NTSC color in the USA or 625 lines/frame, 50 fields/s, PAL color in the UK). A pocket calculator is a closed system because it is unable to receive inputs from other systems.

The ISO reference mode *isolates* the specific functions performed by the communications system from all other aspects of the system. Once these functions have been isolated, you can devise standards for them. In this way, any manufacturer can produce equipment or software that performs a particular function. If designers use hardware and software conforming to well-defined standards, they can create an information transmission system by putting together all the necessary parts. These parts may be obtained from more than one source. As long as their functions are clearly defined and the way in which they interact with other parts is explicitly stated, they can be used as the building blocks of a system.

Figure 14.9 illustrates the structure of the ISO reference model for OSI, where two parties, A and B, are in communication with each other. The ISO model divides the task of communicating between two points between seven layers of protocol. Each layer carries out an action or service required by the layer above it. The actions performed by any given layer of the reference model are precisely defined by the service for that layer and require an appropriate protocol for the layer between the two points that are communicating. This view conforms to current thinking about software and is strongly related to the concept of modularity.

In everyday terms, consider an engineer in one factory who wishes to communicate with an engineer in another factory.

The engineer in the first factory describes to an assistant the nature of some work that is to be done. The assistant then dictates a letter to a secretary who, in turn, types the letter and hands it to a courier. Here, the original task (i.e. communicating the needs of one engineer to another) is broken down into subtasks, each of which is performed by a different person. The engineer doesn't have to know about the actions carried out by other people involved in the exchange of data. Indeed, it does not matter to the engineer how the information is conveyed to their counterpart.

In the ISO model, communication between layers within a system takes place between a layer and the layers immediately above and below it. Layer X in System A communicates only with layers $X + 1$ and $X - 1$ in System A (see Fig. 14.9). Layer 1 is an exception, because there's no layer below it. Layer 1 communicates only with layer 2 in A and with the corresponding layer 1 in B at the other end of the communications link. In terms of the previous analogy, the secretary who types the letter communicates only with the assistant who dictates it and with the courier who transports it. Fig. 14.10 illustrates this example in terms of ISO layers, although this rather simple example doesn't correspond exactly to the ISO model. In particular, layers 3 to 6 are represented by the single layer called *assistant*.

Another characteristic of the ISO model is the apparent or *virtual* link between corresponding layers at each end of the communication channel (this link is also called *peer to peer*). Two corresponding layers at two points in a network are called *peer subsystems* and communicate using layer protocols. Therefore, a message sent by layer X at one end of the link is in the form required by the corresponding layer X at the other end. It appears that these two layers are in direct communication with each other, as they are using identical protocols. In fact, layer X at one end of the link is using the layers below it to transmit the message across the link. At the other end, layer 1 and higher layers process the message until it reaches layer X in the form it left layer X at the other end of the link. Returning to our analogy, the secretary at one factory appears to communicate directly with the secretary at the other factory, because the language used in the letter is appropriate to the task being performed by the two secretaries.

We now look at the functions performed by the seven layers of the ISO reference model for open systems interconnection, starting with the uppermost layer, the application layer.

The application layer

The highest layer of the ISO reference model is the *application layer*, which is concerned with protocols for applications programs (e.g. file transfer, electronic mail). This layer represents the interface with the end user. Strictly speaking, the OSI reference model is concerned only with communications and does not represent the way in which the end user employs the

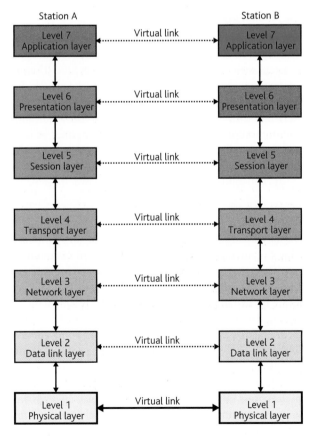

Figure 14.9 The basic reference model for open systems interconnection.

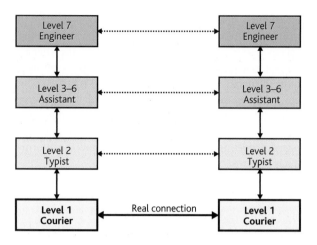

Figure 14.10 Illustrating the concept of layered protocols.

information. The protocol observed by the two users in the application layer is determined entirely by the nature of the application. Consider the communication between two lawyers when they are using the telephone. The protocol used by the lawyers is concerned with the semantics of legal jargon. Although one lawyer appears to be speaking directly to another, they are using another medium involving other protocols to transport the data. In other words, there is no real person-to-person connection but a virtual person-to-person connection built upon the telephone network.

Another example of an application process is the operation of an automatic teller at a bank. The operator is in communication with the bank and is blissfully ignorant of all the technicalities involved in the transaction. The bank asks the user what transaction they wish to make and the user indicates the nature of the transaction by pushing the appropriate button. The bank may be 10 m or 1000 km away from the user. The details involved in the communication process are entirely hidden from the user; in the reference model the user is operating at the applications level.

The presentation layer

The application layer in one system passes information to the presentation layer below it and receives information back from this layer. Recall that a layer at one end of a network can't communicate directly with the corresponding layer at the other end. Each layer except one communicates with only the layer above it and with the layer below it. At one end of the communications system the presentation layer translates data between the local format required by the application layer above it and the format used for transfer. At the other end, the format for transfer is translated into the local format of data for the application layer. By *format* we mean the way in which the computer represents information such as characters and numbers.

Consider another analogy. A Russian diplomat can phone a Chinese diplomat at the UN, even though neither speaks the other's language. Suppose the Russian diplomat speaks to a Russian-to-English interpreter who speaks to an English-to-Chinese interpreter at the other end of a telephone link, who, in turn, speaks to the Chinese diplomat. The diplomats represent the applications layer process and talk to each other about political problems. They don't speak to each other directly and use a presentation layer to format the data before it is transmitted between them. The Chinese-to-English and English-to-Russian translators represent the presentation layer.

This analogy illustrates an important characteristic of the OSI reference model. The English-to-Chinese translator may be a human or a machine. Replacing one with the other has no effect on the application layer above it or on the information transfer layers below it. All that is needed is a mechanism that translates English to Chinese, subject to specified performance criteria.

The presentation layer's principal function is the translation of data from one representation to another. This layer performs other important functions such as data encryption and text compression.

The session layer

Below the presentation layer sits the session layer. The session layer organizes the dialogue between two presentation layers. It establishes, manages, and synchronizes the channel between two application processes. This layer provides dialogue control of the type, 'Roger, over', in radio communications, and the mechanisms used to synchronize application communications (but synchronization actions must be initiated at the application layer). The session layer resolves collisions between synchronization requests. An example is '. . . did you follow that? . . .', '. . . then I'll go over it again.'

The transport layer

The four layers below the session layer are responsible for carrying the message between the two parties in communication. The transport layer isolates the session and higher layers from the network itself. It may seem surprising that four layers are needed to perform such an apparently simple task as moving data from one point in a network to another point. We are talking about establishing and maintaining connections across interlinked LANs and wide area networks with, possibly, major differences in technology and performance—not just communications over a simple wire. The reference model covers both LANs and WANs that may involve communication paths across continents and include several different communications systems. Figure 14.11 shows how the ISO model for OSI caters for communications systems with intermediate nodes.

The transport layer is responsible for the reliable transmission of messages between two application nodes of a network and for ensuring that the messages are received in the order in which they were sent. The transport layer isolates higher layers from the characteristics of the real networks by providing the reliable economic transmission required by an application independent of the characteristics of the underlying facilities (for example, error detection/correction, multiplexing to reduce cost, splitting to improve throughput, and message reordering). The transport layer doesn't have to know anything about how the network is organized.

Packet switching networks divide information into units called *packets* and then send them across a complex network of circuits. Some packets take one route through the network and others take another. Consequently, it is possible for packets to arrive at their destination out of sequence. The transport layer must assemble packets in the correct order, which involves storing the received out-of-sequence packets until the system is ready for them.

The network layer

The network layer serves the transport layer above it by conveying data between the *local* transport layer and the *remote* transport layer. The network layer is *system dependent* unlike the layers above it. Complex communications systems may have many paths between two points. The network layer chooses the optimum path for a message to cross the network or for the establishment of a virtual connection. As an analogy, consider the postal system. Mail sent to a nearby sorting office might be directed to a more distant sorting office if the local office is congested and cannot cope with the volume of traffic. Similarly, in a data transmission network, transmission paths are chosen to minimize the transit time of packets and the cost of transmission.

The data link layer

The data link layer establishes an error-free (to a given probability) connection between two adjacent points in a network. Information may be transmitted from one end of a network to the other end directly or via intermediate nodes in a series of hops. The data link layer at one node receives a message from the network layer above it and sends it via the physical layer below it to the data link layer at the adjacent node.

The data link layer also detects faulty messages and automatically asks for their retransmission. Protocols for the data link layer and the physical layer below it were the first protocols to be developed and are now widely adopted. Data link

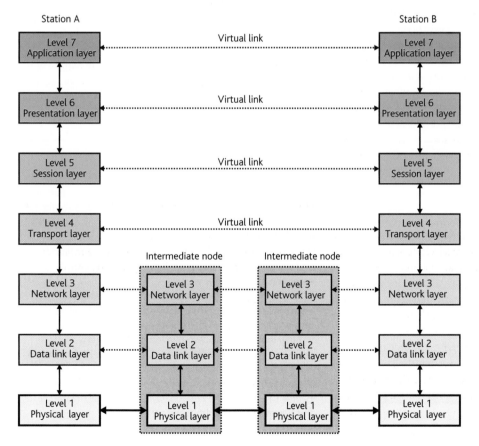

Figure 14.11 Networks with intermediate nodes between end stations.

layer protocols cover many different technologies: LANs (for example Ethernet-type networks using CMSA/CD) and WANs (for example X.25). Systems often divide this layer into two parts, a higher level *logical link control* (LLC) and a lower level *medium access control* (MAC).

The physical layer

The lowest layer, the *physical layer*, is unique because it provides the only physical connection between any two points in a network. The physical layer is responsible for receiving the individual bits of a message from the data link layer and for transmitting them over some physical medium to the adjacent physical layer, which detects the bits and passes them to the data link layer above it. The physical layer ensures that bits are received in the order they are transmitted.

The physical layer handles the physical medium (e.g. wire, radio, and optical fiber) and ensures that a stream of bits gets from one place to another. The physical layer also implements the connection strategy. There are three fundamental connection strategies. *Circuit switching* establishes a permanent connection between two parties for the duration of the information transfer. *Message switching* stores a message temporarily at each node and then sends it on its way across the network. Circuit switching uses a single route through the network, whereas in message switching different messages may travel via different routes. *Packet switching* divides a message into units called packets and transmits them across the network. Packet switching doesn't maintain a permanent connection through the network and is similar to message switching.

Packet switching comes in two forms, the *datagram* and the *virtual circuit*. A datagram service transmits packets independently and they have to be reassembled at their destination (they may arrive out of order). A virtual circuit first establishes a route through the network and then sends all the packets, in order, via this route. The difference between circuit switching and a virtual circuit is that message switching requires a connection for the duration of the connection, whereas the virtual circuit can be used by other messages.

The service offered by the physical layer is a *best effort service* because it doesn't guarantee reliable delivery of messages. Information sent on the physical medium might be lost or corrupted in transit because of electrical noise interfering with the transmitted data. On radio or telephone channels the error rate may be very high (1 bit lost in 10^3 transmitted bits), whereas on fiber optic links it may be very low (1 bit lost in 10^{12}). Layers on top of the physical layer deal with imperfections in this layer. The physical communication path may be copper wires, optical fibers, microwave links, or satellite links.

Remember that the ISO reference model permits modifications to one layer without changing the whole of a network. For example, the physical layer between two nodes can be switched from a coaxial cable to a fiber optic link without any alterations whatsoever taking place at any other level. After all, the data link layer is interested only in giving bits to, or receiving them from, the physical layer. It's not interested in how the physical layer goes about its work.

Standards and the ISO reference model for OSI

Figure 14.12 shows how actual standards for the layers of the reference model have grown. This figure is hourglass shaped. The bottom is broad to cater for the many low-level protocols

---

MESSAGE ENCAPSULATION

How do layered protocols deal with messages? In short, a higher layer wraps up a message from a lower layer in its own data structure.

The figure demonstrates how information is transported across a network by means of a system using layered protocols. In (a) we have the application-level data that is to

Data

(a) Data at the applications layer

Transport layer header	Data	Trailer

(b) Data at the transport layer

Network layer header	Transport layer header	Data	Trailer

(c) Data at the network layer

be transmitted from one computer to another. For the sake of simplicity, we'll assume that there aren't any presentation or session layers. The applications layer passes the data to the transport layer, which puts a header in front of the data and a trailer after it. The data has now been encapsulated in the same way that we put a letter into an envelope. The header and trailer include the address of the sender and the receiver.

The packet from the transport layer is handed to the network layer which, in turn, adds its own header and trailer. This process continues all the way down to the physical layer.

Now look at the process in reverse. When a network later receives a packet from the data link layer below it, the network layer strips off the network layer header and trailer and uses them to check for errors in transmission and to decide how to handle this packet. The network layer then hands the packet to the transport later about it, and so on.

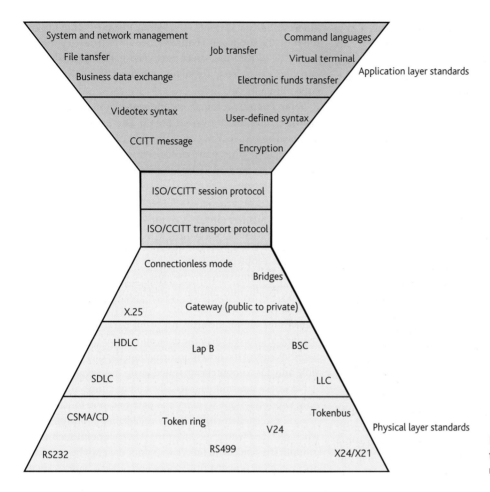

Figure 14.12 Standards for the layers of the basic reference model.

introduced to deal with diverse types of channel, technology, and network, whereas the middle is narrow because it's desirable to have as few protocols as possible to move information around a network. The top is wide because it reflects the great range of applications of LANs.

The ISO reference model for OSI isn't quite as popular today as it was in the 1980s. It was anticipated that most standards for networks would fit within the OSI framework. That hasn't happened. Many of today's standards are *propriety* (*ad hoc* or industrial) and don't conform closely to the OSI model. Some of the current standards such as the Internet TCP/IP protocol are layered even if the layers don't correspond exactly to the seven layers we've just described. Figure 14.13 shows the Internet protocol stack alongside the ISO reference model.

Because this text is devoted to the hardware aspects of computers, we look more closely at the bottom two layers of the reference model—the physical layer and the data link layer.

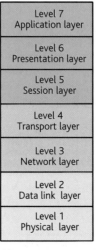

(a) ISO protocol stack.

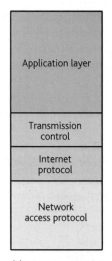

(b) Internet protocol stack.

Figure 14.13 ISO and Internet layers.

14.3 The physical layer

Figure 14.14 illustrates the physical links connecting together two stations, User A and User B. A station is a point in a network that communicates with another point in the network. Alternative words for station are node, receiver, transmitter, or host. Before we can consider the factors influencing the design of a physical channel, it's necessary to look at the function it performs.

A *physical channel* is the actual transmission path connecting two stations and may be a wire link, a radio link, or any other suitable medium. A *logical channel* is an apparent transmission path linking two stations but which may not actually exist. Of course, a logical channel is made up of one or more physical channels operating in tandem. However, the characteristics of a logical channel may be very different from those of the physical channels of which it is composed.

We can describe a physical channel under three headings:

- the signal path itself
- the mechanical interface to the signal path
- the functionality of the channel.

The signal path is concerned with the way in which data is to be transmitted electronically over a channel and the nature of the signal flowing across the channel must be defined; for example, we must ask what signal levels constitute logical 1s and logical 0s.

A second and less obvious consideration concerns the mechanical arrangement of the link. What type of plugs and sockets does it use to connect the node with the transmission path? Standard connectors are as vital as standard signal levels, if the equipment at the end of a link is to be readily interchangeable with equipment from several different manufacturers.

The third aspect of a physical layer link of importance is its functionality. In other words, what does the channel do apart from transmit data? The telephone channel, for example, not only permits voice signals to be sent from one subscriber to

another, but also transmits the dialing pulses or tones needed to set up the connection between the subscribers. In the same way, a serial data link must normally include provision for carrying supervisory signals or messages that take part in controlling the data link.

Some describe a fourth component of the physical layer that they call the *procedural aspect*. The procedural aspect governs the sequence of events that take place when a channel is set up, maintained, and closed. We include the procedural element of a standard in the functional element.

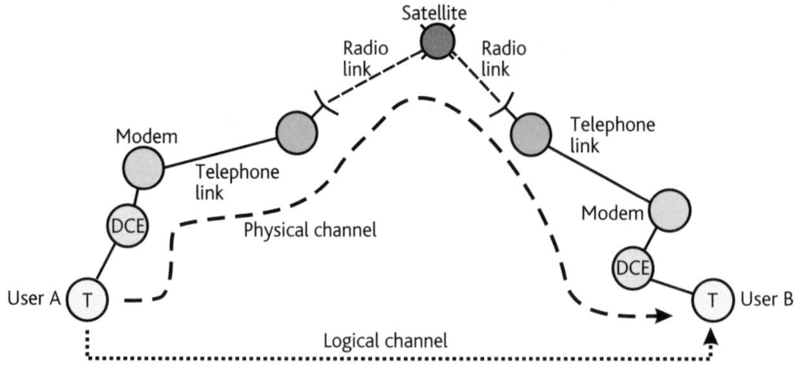

14.3.1 Serial data transmission

Although we introduced serial data transmission when we covered computer interfaces, we have included a short section on serial transmission here because we are interested in other aspects. Ideally, information should be moved from one computer to another a word at a time, with all the *m* bits of a word transmitted simultaneously. An *m*-bit parallel data highway requires *m* wires to carry the data, and two or three additional wires to control the flow of information. Parallel links are feasible only for computers separated by up to several meters.

Networks transmit data serially a bit at a time and require only two lines—one to carry the data and one to act as the ground return. Remember that a voltage has a meaning only when specified with respect to some reference point such as the ground. If a single path links two points, data can be moved in only one direction at a time. Fiber optic links require a single fiber, whereas radio links don't need a physical connection.

Multiplexing signals

A problem facing those who wish to transmit information over long distances is the cost of the physical transmission path. Whether it's the cost of constructing a line of telegraph poles from coast to coast in the nineteenth century or the cost of launching a satellite today, long-distance communications channels don't come cheap. Consequently, engineers have done everything they can to squeeze the last drop of capacity out of a communications channel.

The information-carrying capacity of a channel is determined by two parameters—its *bandwidth* and the level of noise (i.e. unwanted signals) on the channel. If you have a channel that's transporting less data than its maximum capacity permits, you are not using it fully.

The efficient use of a communications channel can be increased by a technique called *multiplexing* in which two or more streams of information share the same channel. Figure 14.15(a)

Figure 14.14 The physical channel.

HALF- AND FULL-DUPLEX CHANNELS

There are three types of transmission paths between stations. The most basic transmission path is called *simplex* and permits the transmission of information in one direction only; that is, there's a single transmitter at one end of the transmission path and a single receiver at the other end with no reverse flow of information. The other two arrangements are more interesting and are called *half duplex* and *full duplex*, respectively and are illustrated below. A half-duplex data link transmits information in only one direction at a time (i.e. from A to B or from B to A). Two-way transmission is achieved by turning round the channel.

The radio in a taxi represents a half-duplex system. Either the driver speaks to the base station or the base station speaks to the driver. They can't have a simultaneous two-way conversation. When the driver has finished speaking, they say 'over' and switch the radio from transmit mode to receive mode. On hearing 'over', the base station is switched from receive mode to transmit mode.

A full-duplex data link permits simultaneous transmission in both directions. The telephone channel is an example of a full-duplex system, because you can both speak and listen at the same time. Some data transmission systems use the telephone network in a half-duplex mode.

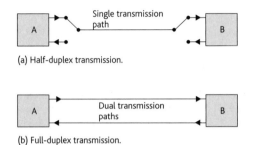

(a) Half-duplex transmission.

(b) Full-duplex transmission.

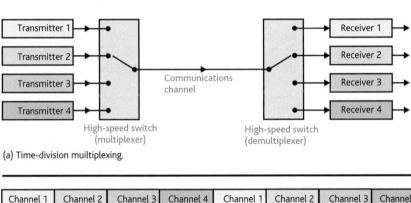

(a) Time-division muiltiplexing.

(b) A time-division multiplexed signal consists of a sequence of time slots.

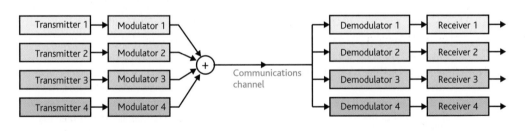

(c) Frequency-division multiplexing.

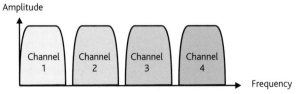

(d) A frequency-division multiplexed signal consists a series of frequency bands.

Figure 14.15 Time- and frequency-division multiplexing.

demonstrates *time division multiplexing* (TDM) in which the output of several transmitters are fed to a communications channel sequentially. In this example, the channel carries a burst of data from transmitter 1 followed by a burst of data from transmitter 2, and so on. At the receiving end of the link, a switch routes the data to receiver 1, receiver 2, . . . , in order.

If the capacity of the channel is at least four times that of each of the transmitters, all four transmitters can share the same channel. All that's needed is a means of synchronizing the switches at both ends of the data link.

A simple TDM system gives each transmitter (i.e. channel) the same amount of time whether it needs it or not. Such an arrangement leads to an inefficient use of the available bandwidth. Statistical time division multiplexing allocates time slots only to those channels that have data to transmit. Each time slot requires a channel number to identify it, because channels aren't transmitted sequentially. Statistical multiplexing is very effective.

Figure 14.15(c) demonstrates an alternative form of multiplexing called *frequency division multiplexing*, FDM. In this case the bandwidth of the channel is divided between the four transmitters. Unlike in TDM each transmitter has continuous Half- and Full-duplex Channels access to the channel but it has access to only one-quarter of the channel's bandwidth.

We're already familiar with frequency division multiplexing. All a radio station does is to change the frequency range of speech and music signals to a range that can be transmitted over the airwaves. A radio receiver filters out one range of frequencies from all the other frequencies and then converts them back to their original range.

Suppose that the bandwidth of the data from each transmitter extends from 0 to 20 kHz and the communications link has a bandwidth of 80 kHz. The output of the first transmitter is mapped onto 0 to 20 kHz (no change), the output of the second transmitter is mapped onto 20 to 40 kHz, the output of the third transmitter is mapped onto 60 to 60 kHz, and so on. A device that maps one range of frequencies onto another range of frequencies is called a modulator (we will have more to say about modulators when we introduce the modem later in this chapter).

At the receiver end of the link, filters separate the incoming signal into four bands and the signals in each of these bands are converted back to their original ranges of 0 to 20 kHz. In practice it is necessary to leave gaps between the frequency bands because filters aren't perfect. Moreover, a bandpass channel doesn't usually start from a zero frequency. A typical FDM channel might be from, say, 600 MHz to 620 MHz in 400 slices of 50 kHz each.

SYNCHRONIZING SIGNALS

Serial data transmission begs an obvious question. How is the stream of data divided up into individual bits and the bits divided into separate words? The division of the data stream into bits and words is handled in one of two ways: *asynchronously* and *synchronously*.

We met asynchronous serial systems when we described the ACIA. In an asynchronous serial transmission system the clocks at the transmitter and receiver responsible for dividing the data stream into bits are not synchronized. When the transmitter wishes to transmit a word, it places the line in a space state for one bit period. When the receiver sees this start bit, it knows that a character is about to follow. The incoming data stream can then be divided into seven bit periods and the data sampled at the center of each bit. The receiver's clock is not synchronized with the transmitter's clock and the bits are not sampled exactly in the center. If the receiver's clock is within approximately 4% or so of the transmitter's clock, the system works well.

If the duration of a single bit is T seconds, the length of a character is given by the start bit plus seven data bits plus the parity bit plus the stop bit = $10T$. Asynchronous transmission is clearly inefficient, because it requires 10 data bits to transmit 7 bits of useful information. Several formats for asynchronous data transmission are in common use; for example, eight data bits, no parity, one stop bit.

Two problems face the designer of a synchronous serial system. One is how to divide the incoming data stream into individual bits and the other is how to divide the data bits into meaningful groups. We briefly look at the division of serial data into bits and return to the division of serial data into blocks when we introduce bit-oriented protocols.

If the data stream is phase encoded, a separate clock can be derived from the received signal and the data extracted. The diagram shows a phase-encoded signal in which the data signal changes state in the center of each bit cell. A low-to-high transition signifies a 1 and a high-to-low transition signifies a 0.

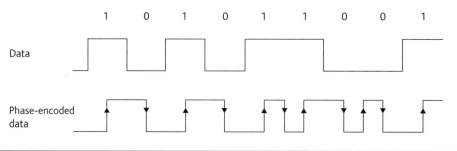

14.4 The PSTN

The most widely used transmission path for wide area digital data networks is the telephone system—often called the *public switched telephone network* (PSTN) to distinguish it from private networks. We first discuss some of the characteristics of the telephone network and then describe the modem used to interface digital equipment to the network.

14.4.1 Channel characteristics

One way of characterizing a telephone channel is to apply a sine wave (Fig. 14.16) to the transmitter end of a telephone link and then to measure its amplitude at the receiver. The *gain* of the telephone channel is expressed as a logarithm; that is, $10\log_{10}(P_o/P_i)$, where P_i is the transmitted power level and P_o the received power level. The unit of gain is the decibel (in honor of Bell) and is positive if the signal is amplified (i.e. $P_o > P_i$) and negative if the signal is attenuated (i.e. $P_o < P_i$). In a system without amplifiers, the gain is always less than 1.

By varying the frequency of the sine wave and recording the gain of the channel for each frequency, the relationship between the gain of the channel and the transmitted frequency can be derived. Such a graph is called the *amplitude–frequency distortion characteristic* of the channel

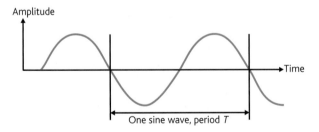

Figure 14.16 The sine wave.

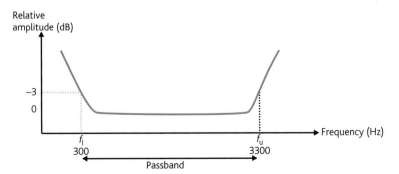

Figure 14.17 Characteristics of the telephone network.

(see Fig. 14.17). The frequency axis is invariably plotted on a logarithmic scale. An ideal channel has a flat frequency response over all the frequencies of interest; that is, the gain should not vary with frequency. A similar type of graph is used to characterize hi-fi equipment. Figure 14.17 describes the frequency response of a hypothetical ideal telephone channel. The attenuation of the channel in its passband is referred to as a 0 dB level (i.e. a gain of unity) and attenuation at other frequencies is measured with respect to this value.

Figure 14.17 demonstrates that some frequencies are transmitted with little attenuation but that frequencies below the lower cut-off point f_l and above the upper cut-off point f_u are severely attenuated. Most telephone channels are not as well behaved as the ideal channel of Fig. 14.17. The passband between f_l and f_u is not usually flat and the passband may sometimes be very much less than 300 Hz to 3300 Hz. Although most of the energy in human speech is below 3300 Hz, certain sounds have significant energy components above this frequency; for example, a cut-off point of 3300 Hz makes it very difficult to distinguish between the sibilant sounds 'f' and 's'.

Figure 14.17 doesn't tell the whole story. Signals suffer not only from amplitude–frequency distortion but also from *phase distortion*. Any signal can be decomposed into a series of sine waves and cosine waves of different frequencies. Phase distortion is related to the time delay experienced by the various sine and cosine waves making up a particular digital sequence. When a pulse sequence travels along a cable, its component sine and cosine waves suffer different delays. These signals at the receiving end of the network add up to produce a waveform with a different shape to the one that was originally transmitted. The phase distortion introduced by a telephone channel distorts the shape of transmitted pulses, making it difficult to distinguish between signals representing 0s and 1s. A device called an *equalizer* can be used to overcome some of the effects of the amplitude and phase distortion introduced by a telephone channel.

Figure 14.18 defines the limits of acceptance of attenuation–frequency distortion for a telephone channel between a single transmitter and receiver. The shaded area represents the forbidden region of unacceptable attenuation. If a real telephone channel has an amplitude–frequency distortion characteristic that falls outside the envelope of Fig. 14.18, the telephone company should try to correct the faulty line or equipment.

You might think that any signal can be transmitted across a telephone channel, as long as its frequency components fall within the envelope described by Fig. 14.18. In practice, there are restrictions on the nature of a transmitted signal because the channel is used to carry more than user

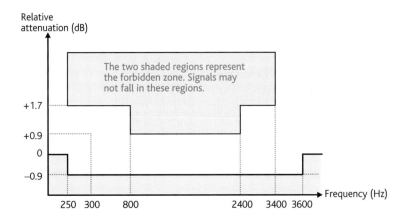

Figure 14.18 Limits of acceptance for attenuation–frequency distortion.

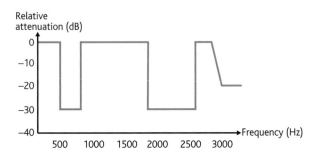

Figure 14.19 Restriction on energy content of transmitted signals.

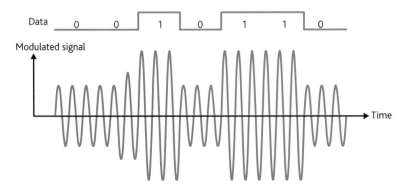

Figure 14.20 Amplitude modulation.

Because analog channels can transmit more than one signal simultaneously, the PTTs have allocated certain parts of the telephone channel's bandwidth to signaling purposes. Human speech doesn't contain appreciable energy within these signaling bands and a normal telephone conversation doesn't affect the switching and control equipment using these frequencies.

A consequence of the use of certain frequencies for signaling purposes is that data transmission systems mustn't generate signals falling within specified bands. Figure 14.19 shows the internationally agreed restriction on signals transmitted by equipment connected to the PSTN.

Any signals transmitted in the ranges 500 to 800 Hz and 1800 to 2600 Hz must have levels 38 dB below the maximum in-band signal level.

14.4.2 Modulation and data transmission

We are now going to look at a topic called *modulation*, the means of modifying signals to make them suitable for transmission over a particular channel.

Signals and modulation

A telephone channel can transmit signals within its pass band but can't transmit digital pulses that are composed of sine waves with an infinite range of frequencies. If a sequence of binary signals were presented to one end of a telephone network, some of the sine waves making up the binary pulses would be attenuated. Because the telephone network does not attenuate each frequency component equally, the sine waves at the receiving end of the network would not add up to produce the same waveform that was presented to the transmitting end. The digital signals would be so severely distorted that they would be unrecognizable at the receiving end of the circuit.

Because the telephone network can transmit voice-band signals in the range 300 to 3300 Hz, various ways of converting digital information into speech-like signals have been investigated. Figure 14.20 shows how the digital data can be used to change, or *modulate*, the amplitude of a sine wave in sympathy with a digital signal. This technique is known as *amplitude modulation* or AM. The equipment needed to generate such a signal is called a modulator, and that required to extract the digital data from the resulting signal is called a demodulator.

data. The analog channel provided by the PSTN is a linear channel in the sense that its output is the sum of all the inputs to the channel. This means that you can transmit two signals in different parts of the channel's bandwidth and then separate them at the receiver. Digital systems don't have this property—it's not generally possible to add two digital signals together at one end of a channel and then separate them at the other end.

The interface between a computer and a telephone system is called a modem (*modulator-demo*dulator). Because AM is more sensitive to noise than other modulation techniques, it is not widely used in data transmission.

Instead of modulating a sine wave by changing its amplitude, it's possible to change its frequency in sympathy with the digital data. In a binary system, one frequency represents one binary value and a different frequency represents the other. Figure 14.21 shows a frequency modulated (FM) signal. FM is widely used because it has a better tolerance to noise than AM (i.e. it is less affected by various forms of interference). As two frequencies are used to represent the two binary states, frequency modulation is sometimes referred to as frequency shift keying (FSK).

Figure 14.22 illustrates phase modulation (PM), where the phase of the sine wave is changed in sympathy with the digital signal. PM is widely used and has fairly similar characteristics to FM. If the phase change corresponding to a logical 1 is 180°, and 0° (no change) corresponds to a logical 0, 1 bit of information can be transmitted in each time slot (Fig. 14.22). If, however, the phase is shifted by multiples of 90°, 2 bits at a time can be transmitted (Fig. 14.23).

High-speed modems

Modems operate over a wide range of bit rates. Until the mid 1990s most modems operated between 300 bps to 9600 bps. Low bit rates were associated with the switched telephone network where some lines were very poor and signal impairments reduced the data rate to 2400 bps or below. The higher rates of 4800 bps and 9600 bps were generally found on privately leased lines where the telephone company offered a higher grade of service.

The growth of the Internet provided a mass market for high-speed modems. Improved modulation techniques and better signal-processing technology has had a massive impact on modem design. By the mid-1990s, low-cost modems operated at 14.4 kbaud or 28.8 kbaud. By 1998, modems capable of operating at 56 kbaud over conventional telephone lines were

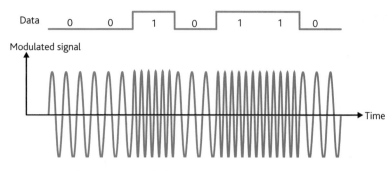

Figure 14.21 Frequency modulation.

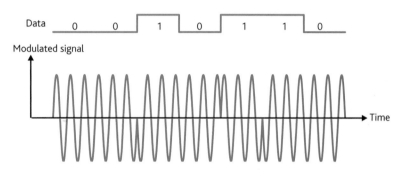

Figure 14.22 Phase modulation.

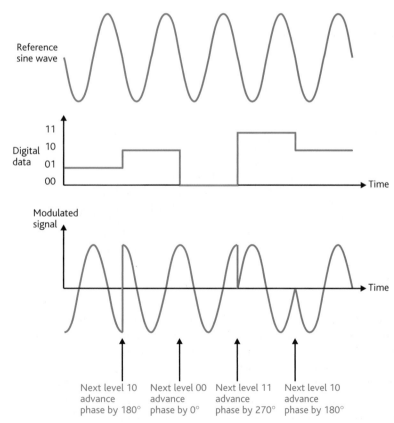

Figure 14.23 Differential phase modulation.

NOISE

Noise is the generic term for unwanted signals that are added to the received signal. One source of noise, called *thermal noise*, is caused by the random motion of electrons in matter. Thermal noise appears as the background hiss on telephone, radio, and TV circuits, and is called Gaussian noise because of its statistical properties. The amount of thermal noise depends on the temperature of the system and its bandwidth. Only by cooling the system or by reducing its bandwidth can we reduce the effects of thermal noise. Receivers that pick up the weak signals from distant space vehicles are cooled in liquid nitrogen to minimize the effects of thermal noise. In general, the contribution of thermal noise to all other forms of noise is not usually the limiting factor in terrestrial switched telephone networks.

Another source of noise is *cross-talk* picked up from other circuits due to electrical, capacitive, or magnetic coupling. We can think of cross-talk as crossed lines. Careful shielding of cables and isolation of circuits can reduce cross-talk. Impulsive noise produces the clicks and crackles on telephone circuits and is caused by transients when heavy loads such as elevator motors are switched near telephone circuits, lightning, and dirty and intermittent electrical connections. Impulsive noise accounts for the majority of transmission errors in telephone networks. The diagram illustrates impulsive noise.

When the transmitted signal reaches the receiver, some of its energy is echoed back to the transmitter. Echo cancellers at the ends of a telephone channel remove this unwanted signal. If they are poorly adjusted, the receiver gets the transmitted signal plus a time-delay and distortion of the data.

The signal-to-noise ratio of a channel is defined as $10\log_{10}(S/N)$, where S is the signal power and N the noise power. Because the signal-to-noise ratio is a logarithmic value, adding 10 dB means that the ratio increases by a factor of 10. Signal-to-noise ratio determines the error rate over the channel.

These noises are *additive* because they are added to the received signal. *Multiplicative* noise is caused by multiplying the received signal by a noise signal. The most common multiplicative noise is *phase jitter* caused by random errors in the phase of the clock used to sample the received signal. All these sources of noise make it harder to distinguish between signal levels in a digital system.

CHANNEL CAPACITY

A channel has a finite bandwidth that limits its switching speed. The maximum data rate is given by $2B \cdot \log_2 L$, where B is the channel's bandwidth and L is the number of signal levels. If the bandwidth is 3000 Hz and you are using a signal with 1024 discrete signal levels, the maximum data rate is $2 \times 3000 \times \log_2 1024 = 6000 \times 10 = 60$ kbps. This figure relates the capacity of a noiseless channel to its bandwidth.

You can increase a channel's capacity by using more signal levels. Claude Shannon investigated the theoretical capacity of a noisy channel in the late 1940s and showed that its capacity is limited by both its bandwidth and the noise level. Shannon proved that the theoretical capacity of a communications channel is given by $B \cdot \log_2(1 + S/N)$, where B is the bandwidth, S is the signal power, and N is the noise power. A telephone line with a bandwidth of 3000 Hz and a signal-to-noise ratio of 30 dB has a maximum capacity of $3000 \times \log_2(1 + 1000) = 29\,900$ bps.

Shannon's theorem provides an absolute limit that can't be bettered. Modern modems can apparently do better than theory suggests by compressing data before transmission. Moreover, the noise on telephone lines tends to be impulsive or bursty, whereas the theoretical calculations relating channel capacity to noise assume that the noise is white noise (e.g. thermal noise). By requesting the retransmission of data blocks containing errors due to noise bursts, you can increase the average data rate.

available for the price of a 1200 bps modem only a decade earlier.

High-speed modems operate by simultaneously changing the amplitude and phase of a signal. This modulation technique is called *quadrature amplitude modulation* (QAM). A QAM signal can be represented mathematically by the expression $S \cdot \sin(\omega t) + C \cdot (\omega t)$, where S and C are two constants. The term *quadrature* is used because a sine wave and a cosine wave of the same frequency and amplitude are almost identical. The only difference is that a sine wave and a cosine wave are

90° out of phase (90° represents ¼ of 360°—hence quadrature). Figure 14.24 demonstrates a 32-point QAM constellation in which each point represents one of 32 discrete signals. A signal element encodes a 5-bit value, which means a modem with a signaling speed of 2400 baud can transmit at 12 000 bps.

Figure 14.25 demonstrates that the points in a QAM constellation are spaced equally. Each circle includes the space that is closer to one of the signal elements than to any other element. When a signal element is received, the values of S and C are calculated and the value of the signal element

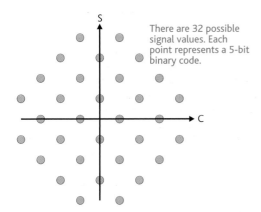

There are 32 possible signal values. Each point represents a 5-bit binary code.

Figure 14.24 The 32-point QAM constellation.

By changing the amplitude and phase of a sine wave and a cosine wave by fixed amounts, their sum generates 32 discrete points, each of which represents a 5-bit binary value.

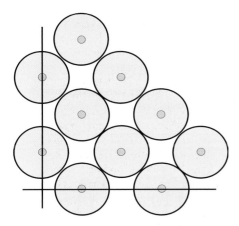

Figure 14.25 The packing of points in a QAM constellation.

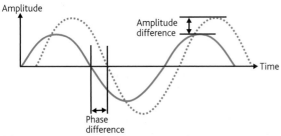

(a) Phase and amplitude difference.

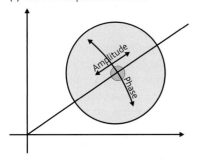

(b) Effect of phase ad amplitude errors on a QAM signal.

Figure 14.26 Effect of errors on a QAM point.

determined. If noise or other impairments cause a point to be shifted (i.e. there are errors in the received values of constants S and C), an error doesn't occur unless the values of S and C move the received point outside a circle. Figure 14.26 shows how amplitude and phase errors modify the position of a point in the QAM constellation.

14.4.3 High-speed transmission over the PSTN

The backbone of the POTS (plain old telephone system) is anything but plain. Data can be transmitted across the World via satellite, terrestrial microwave links, and fiber optic links at very high rates. The limitation on the rate at which data can be transmitted is known as *the last mile*; that is, the connection between your phone and the global network at your local switching center.

ISDN

A technology called *integrated services digital network* (ISDN) was developed in the 1980s to help overcome the bandwidth limitations imposed by the last mile. ISDN was intended for professional and business applications and is now available to anyone with a PC. There are two variants of ISDN—basic rate services and primary rate services. The basic rate service is intended for small businesses and provides three fully duplex channels. Two of these so-called B channels can carry voice or data and the third D channel is used to carry control information. B channels operate at 64 kbps and the D channel at 16 kbps.

ISDN's early popularity was due to its relatively low cost and the high quality of service it offers over the telephone line. You can combine the two B channels to achieve a data rate of 128 kbps. You can even use the D channel simultaneously to provides an auxiliary channel at 9.6 kbps. Note that ISDN can handle both voice and data transmission simultaneously.

Several protocols have been designed to control ISDN systems. V.110 and V.120 are used to connect an ISDN communications devices to high-speed ISDN lines. ISDN took a long time from its first implementation to its adoption by many businesses. However, newer technologies plus cable networks have been devised to overcome the last mile problem and ISDN did not become as commonplace as some had anticipated.

ADSL

If there's one thing you can guarantee in the computing world, it's that yesterday's state-of-the-art technology will the current standard and a new state-of-the-art technology will emerge. Just as ISDN was becoming popular in the late 1990s,

MODEM STANDARDS

In the USA, modem standards were dominated by the Bell System's *de facto* standards. Outside the USA, modem standards were determined by the International Consultative Committee on Telegraphy and Telephony (CCITT). Over time, CCITT standards became dominant when high-speed modems were introduced.

Early modems operated at data rates of 75, 300, 600, 1200, 2400, 4800, and 9600 baud. Modern modem rates are 14 400, 19 200, 28 800, 36 600, and 56 000 baud. Modem standards define the following.

- **Modulation method** Low-and medium speed modems use frequency modulation. High-speed modems employ phase modulation and QAM (quadrature amplitude modulation).

- **Channel type** Some modems operate in a *half-duplex* mode, permitting a communication path in only one direction at a time. Others support *full-duplex* operation with simultaneous, two-way communication. Some systems permit a high data rate in one direction and a low data rate in the other, or reverse, direction.

- **Originate/answer** The *originating* modem is at the end of the channel that carried out the dialing and set up the channel. The *answer* modem is at the end of the channel that receives the call. Many modems can both originate calls and answer calls, but some modems are answer-only and cannot originate a call. Originate and answer modems employ different frequencies to represent 1 s and 0 s.

- **Asynchronous/synchronous** An asynchronous data transmission system transmits information as, typically, 8-bit characters with periods of inactivity between characters. A synchronous system transmits a continuous stream of bits without pauses, even when the bits are carrying no user information.

Examples of modem standards

- CCITT V.32 2400 baud, 4800 or 9600 bps, QAM

- CCITT V.33 2400 baud, 14 400 bps, QAM

- CCITT V.34 2400 baud, 28 800 bps, QAM

- CCITT V.90 56 000 bps (this standard uses analog transmission in one direction and digital in the other)

a system called *asymmetric digital subscriber line* (ADSL) was being developed as a new high-speed *last mile* system.

As we've said, telephone lines have a bandwidth of 3000 Hz, which limits the maximum rate at which data can be transmitted. In fact, the twisted wire pair between your home and the telephone company has a much higher bandwidth. The bandwidth of a typical twisted pair less than about 3 miles is over 1 MHz.

Asymmetric digital subscriber line technology exploits the available bandwidth of the local connection. The bandwidth of the telephone link is divided into a number of 4 kHz slices as Fig. 14.27 demonstrates. The first slice from 0 to 4 kHz represents the conventional telephone bandwidth. Frequencies between 4 kHz and 24 kHz aren't used in order to provide a guard band to stop the higher frequencies interfering with conventional telephone equipment.

The spectrum between 24 kHz and 1.1 MHz is divided into 249 separate 4 kHz channels in the same way as the FM band is divided into slots for broadcasting stations. A data signal is assigned one of these slices and its spectrum tailored to fit its allocated 4 kHz slot. At the other end of the link, the signal in that 4 kHz slot is converted back into the data signal. Until recently it was very difficult to perform these operations. The advent of low-cost digital signal processing has made it much easier to process signals (i.e. to shift their range of frequencies from one band to another).

The characteristics of these slots vary with frequency; for example, there is a greater attenuation of signals in slots close to 1.1 MHz. The terminal equipment is able to use the better

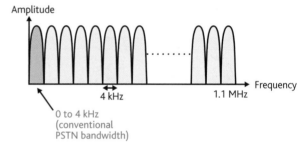

Figure 14.27 Dividing a 1.1 MHz bandwidth into 4 kHz slots.

channels to carry high data rates and to allocate the higher frequency channels to slower bit rates.

14.5 Copper cable

The majority of transmission paths are composed of twisted pairs, coaxial cable, radio links, or fiber optic links. A *twisted pair* is nothing more than two insulated wires that are twisted around each other. Why are the wires twisted? A wire acts as an antenna and picks up signals (i.e. interference). If two wires are intertwined, a signal induced in one wire is cancelled by the signal induced in the other wire. Twisted pairs are used to transport signals over relatively short distances; for example, a twisted pair connects a telephone to its local exchange. Twisted pairs, using RJ-45 telephone-style connectors, are used in some LANs.

RS232C PHYSICAL LAYER PROTOCOL

The first universal standard for the physical layer was published in 1969 by the Electronic Industry Association (EIA) and is known as RS232C (Recommended Standard 232 version C). This standard was intended for links between modems and computers but was adapted to suit devices such as printers.

RS232 specifies the plug and socket at the modem and the digital equipment (i.e. their mechanics), the nature of the transmission path, and the signals required to control the operation of the modem (i.e. the functionality of the data link).

In the standard, the modem is known as *data communications equipment* (DCE) and the digital equipment to be connected to the modem is known as *data terminal equipment* (DTE).

The following control signals implement most of the important functions of an R232 DTE to DCE link.

Request to send (RTS) is a signal from the DTE to the DCE. When asserted, RTS indicates to the DCE that the DTE wishes to transmit data to it.

Clear to send (CTS) is a signal from the DCE to the DTE and, when asserted, indicates that the DCE is ready to receive data from the DTE.

Data set ready (DSR) is a signal from the DCE to the DTE that indicates the readiness of the DCE. When this signal is asserted, the DCE is able to receive from the DTE. DSR indicates that the DCE (usually a modem) is switched on and is in its normal functioning mode (as opposed to its self-test mode).

Data terminal ready (DTR) is a signal from the DTE to the DCE. When asserted, DTR indicates that the DTE is ready to accept data from the DCE. In systems with a modem, it maintains the connection and keeps the channel open. If DTR is negated, the communication path is broken. In everyday terms, negating DTR is the same as hanging up a phone.

Because RS232 was intended for DTE to DCE links, its functions are very largely those needed to control a modem.

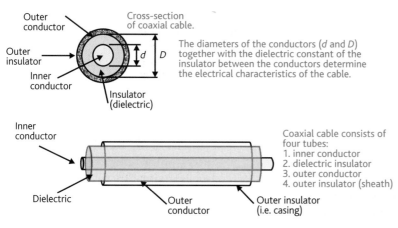

Figure 14.28 Coaxial cable.

Coaxial cable consists of an inner conductor entirely surrounded by an outer conductor and is the type of cable used to connect televisions to antennas. Between the two conductors lies an insulating material called a *dielectric*. Sometimes the outer conductor is braided or woven from fine copper wire and sometimes it's a solid conductor. Figure 14.28 illustrates the structure of coaxial cable (often abbreviated to co-ax), whose thickness may vary between 5 and 25 mm. Coaxial cables can operate at high data rates over 100 Mbits/s and are used over short to medium distances. Coaxial cable can

transmit voice-band telephone signals (permitting up to 10 000 channels per cable), cable television signals and digital signals in many local area networks. Transmission over distances greater than 1 km is achieved by feeding the signal into an amplifier (called a repeater) and regenerating it before sending it on its way down the coaxial cable.

14.5.1 Ethernet

The Ethernet was proposed by Robert Metcalfe in the early 1970s. Metcalfe joined the Xerox Corporation and developed the Ethernet (the name comes from the *ether*, a medium that was once thought to fill all space). Xerox formed a consortium with DEC and Intel who approached the IEEE and proposed the Ethernet as a standard.

The physical layer of the Ethernet was originally used a baseband coaxial cable with phase-encoded data at 10 Mbits/s. All nodes are connected to the bus, subject to two conditions. There is a restriction on the length of the bus and a loop must not exist between any two points on the bus. Figure 14.29 describes the Ethernet's topology. Ethernet data is transmitted is discrete packets or bursts of data.

STANDARDS AND CABLES

During the late 1970s it became apparent that the introduction of a large number of *ad hoc* protocols for LANs would have a bad effect on the computer industry. In 1980 the IEEE established its Standards Project 802 to provide a framework for LAN standards. The 802 committee set itself the goal of designing a standard for the new LANs that would take account of existing and prospective technology, and the needs of LAN users. The 802 committee didn't intend to produce standards for all seven layers of the ISO reference model, but limited themselves to standards for the physical and data link layers.

While the IEEE was organizing its 802 project, the Ethernet LAN was rapidly becoming a *de facto* standard for contention buses and therefore the IEEE had to incorporate it in their work. At the same time, engineers were involved in a vigorous debate about the relative merits of buses and rings as LAN topologies. The IEEE 802 committee reflected the nature of the real world, so they devised a set of standards that took account of both bus and ring topologies. They wanted the greatest happiness for the greatest number of people. The IEEE 802 draft standard includes standards for an Ethernet bus, a token ring, and a token bus. The diagram illustrates the scope of the 802 standards.

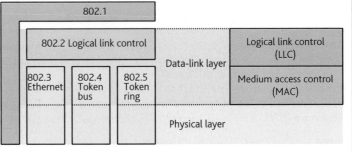

The Ethernet's 10 Mbps data rate is low by today's standards. A new standard, IEEE 802.3u, operating at 100 Mbps was ratified in 1995, and work began on a Gigabit Ethernet in the late 1990s. In March 1996, the IEEE 802.3 committee approved the 802.3z Gigabit Ethernet Standardization project.

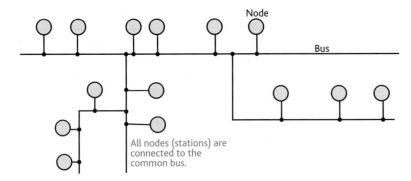

All nodes (stations) are connected to the common bus.

Figure 14.29 The bus.

Such a bus network introduces the problem of *contention*. No two nodes can access the same channel simultaneously without their messages interfering destructively with each other. When two messages overlap in time, the event is called a *collision* and both messages are lost.

The simplest solution to bus contention is for a node to go ahead and transmit a message when it wants. This approach assumes that the bus is only occasionally busy. If another node is transmitting at the same time or joins in before the message is finished, both messages are lost. If the node that sent the message doesn't receive an acknowledgement within a timeout period, it assumes that its message has been corrupted in transmission.

When a message from a node collides with a message from another node, both messages are lost. If the duration of a message is T seconds and two messages just collide, the total time lost is up to $2T$ seconds. Assuming that the probability of a station wanting to transmit a packet has a *Poisson distribution*, it can be shown that the maximum throughput of this system approaches 18% of the maximum channel capacity. A Poisson distribution is a statistical model of events such as the rate at which people use the telephone.

The simplest form of contention control is to let the transmitters retransmit their messages. Unfortunately, such a scheme wouldn't work, because the competing nodes would keep retransmitting the messages and these would keep getting scrambled. The problem of collisions in a bus network is identical to that of two people approaching the same revolving door together—they can't both get in, they step back, and advance together causing a collision, so they step back again, advance together, collide, ...

A better strategy on detecting a collision is to *back off* or wait a random time before trying to retransmit the frame. It is unlikely that the competing nodes would reschedule the transmissions for the same time. Networks operating under this form of contention control are well suited to bursty traffic; that is, the arrangement works as long as the average traffic density is very low (much less than the maximum capacity of the bus). If the amount of traffic rises, there comes a point where collisions generate repeat messages that generate further collisions and further repeats, and the system eventually collapses.

The contention control mechanism can be improved by forcing a node to listen to the bus before trying to send its frame. Obviously, if one node is already in the process of sending a message, other nodes are not going to attempt to transmit. A collision will occur only if two nodes attempt to transmit at nearly the same instant. Once a node has started transmitting and its signal has propagated throughout the network, no other node can interrupt. For almost all systems this danger zone, the propagation time of a message from one end of the network to the other, is very small and is only a tiny fraction of the duration of a message.

The contention mechanism adopted by Ethernet is called *Carrier Sense Multiple Access with Collision Detect* (CSMA/CD). When an Ethernet station wishes to transmit a packet, it listens to the state of the bus. If the bus is in use, it waits for the bus to become free. In Ethernet terminology this

is called *deference*. Once a station has started transmitting it acquires the channel, and after a delay equal to the end-to-end round trip propagation time of the network, a successful transmission without collision is guaranteed.

14.6 Fiber optic links

The very first signaling systems used optical technology—the signal fire, the smoke signal and later the semaphore. Such transmission systems were limited to line-of-sight operation and couldn't be used in fog. From the middle of the nineteenth century onward, electrical links have made it possible to communicate over long distances independently of weather conditions.

Today, the confluence of different technologies has, once again, made it possible to use light to transmit messages. Semiconductor technology has given us the laser and light-emitting diode (LED), which directly convert pulses of electricity into pulses of light in both the visible and infrared parts of the spectrum. Similarly, semiconductor electronics has created devices that can turn light directly into electricity so that we can detect the pulses of light from a laser or LED. The relatively new science of materials technology has given us the ability to create a fine thread of transparent material called an *optical fiber*. The optical fiber can pipe light from its source to its detector just as the coaxial cable pipes electronic signals from one point to another.

Seemingly, light must be transmitted in a straight line and therefore can't be used for transmission over paths that turn corners or go round bends. Fortunately, one of the properties of matter (i.e. the speed of light in a given medium) makes it possible to transmit light down a long thin cylinder of material like an optical fiber. Figures 14.30(a) and (b) demonstrate the effect of a light beam striking the surface of an optically dense material in a less dense medium such as air. Light rays striking the surface at nearly right angles to the surface pass from the material into the surrounding air after being bent or *refracted* as Fig. 14.30(a) demonstrates. The relationship between the angle of incidence θ_2 and the angle of refraction θ_1 is $\cos(\theta_2)/\cos(\theta_1) =$ index of refraction.

> **CABLE TERMINOLOGY**
>
> The physical dimensions, the electrical or optical characteristics, and the connectors of the cables used to implement the physical medium of an Ethernet connection have been standardized. Some of the common standards are as follows.
>
> | | |
> |---|---|
> | 10Base2 | 10 Mbps thin Ethernet cable (similar to TV antenna cable). |
> | 10BaseT | 10 Mbps switched Ethernet cable. Used with Ethernet routers and hubs. The cable is similar to telephone cable with the same RJ45 jack plug. |
> | 100BaseT | 100 Mbps Ethernet cable using twisted pair cable (similar to 10BaseT). |
> | 100BaseF | 100 Mbps fiber Ethernet cable. |

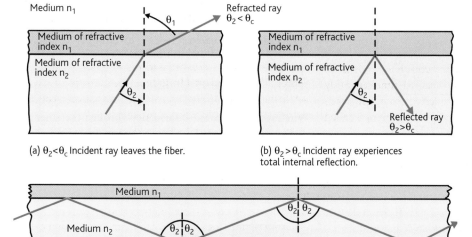

(a) $\theta_2 < \theta_c$ Incident ray leaves the fiber.

(b) $\theta_2 > \theta_c$ Incident ray experiences total internal reflection.

(c) Propagation of a ray along a fiber by repeated total internal reflection.

Figure 14.30 Total internal reflection.

Light rays striking the surface at a shallow angle suffer *total internal reflection* and are reflected just as if the surface (i.e. the boundary between the optically dense material and the air) were a mirror. The critical angle, θ_C, at which total internal reflection occurs, is a function of the refractive index of the material through which the light is propagated and the surface material at which the reflection occurs. The same phenomenon takes place when a diver looks upward. Total internal reflection at the surface of the water makes the surface look like a mirror. Figure 14.30(c) demonstrates how light is propagated along the fiber by internal reflections from the sides.

By drawing out a single long thread of a transparent material such as plastic or glass, we can create an optical fiber as illustrated in Fig. 14.31. The optical fiber consists of three parts:

- the core itself that transmits the light
- a cladding that has a different index of reflection to the core and hence causes total internal reflection at its interface with the core
- a sheath that provides the optical fiber with protection and mechanical strength.

The diameter of the optical fiber is very small indeed—often less than 100 μm. Sometimes there is an abrupt junction between the core and cladding (a step-index fiber) and sometimes the refractive index of the material varies continuously from the core to the cladding (a graded index fiber). Graded index fibers are difficult to produce and therefore more expensive than step-index fibers, but they offer lower attenuation and a higher bandwidth.

Fiber optic links can be created from many materials but a fiber drawn from high-quality fused quartz has the least attenuation and the greatest bandwidth (e.g. the attenuation can be less than 1 db/km). The bandwidth of fiber optic links can range from 200 MHz to over 10 GHz (10^9 Hz) which represents very high data rates indeed.

There are several types of optical fiber, each with its own special properties (e.g. attenuation per km, bandwidth, and cost). Two generic classes of optical fiber are the multimode and single-mode fibers. Multimode fibers operate as described by bouncing the light from side to side as it travels down the fiber. Because a light beam can take many paths down the cable, the transit time of the beam is spread out and a single pulse of light is received as a considerably broadened pulse. Consequently, a multimode fiber cannot be used at very high pulse rates.

A single-mode fiber has a diameter only a few times that of the wavelength of the light being transmitted (a typical diameter is only 5 μm). As a single-mode fiber does not support more than one optical path through the fiber, the transmitted pulse is not spread out in time and a very much greater bandwidth can be achieved.

The advantages of a fiber optic link (Fig. 14.32), over copper cable and radio technologies are as follows.

Bandwidth The bandwidth offered by the best fiber optic links is approximately 1000-fold greater than that offered by coaxial cable or microwave radio links.

Attenuation High-quality optical fibers have a lower attenuation than coaxial cables and therefore fewer repeaters are required over long links such as undersea cables.

Mechanics The optical fiber itself is truly tiny and therefore lightweight. All that is needed is a suitable sheath to protect it from mechanical damage or corrosion. It is therefore cheaper to lay fiber optic links than coaxial links.

Interference Fiber optic links are not affected by electromagnetic interference and therefore they do not suffer the effect of noise induced by anything from nearby lightening strikes to cross-talk from adjacent cables. Furthermore, because they do not use electronic signals to convey information, there's no signal leakage from an optical fiber and therefore it's much harder for unauthorized persons to eavesdrop.

14.7 Wireless links

Wireless links transmit information through the ether and don't require a physical medium to be laid down between the transmitter and receiver. Wireless links are characterized by

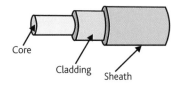

Figure 14.31 The optical fiber.

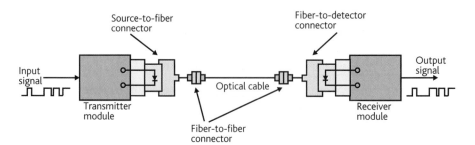

Figure 14.32 The fiber optic link.

the frequency of the radio signals used to transport data and whether or not they are terrestrial or satellite links. Table 14.2 illustrates a portion of the electromagnetic spectrum used to transmit information.

Signals in the frequency range 100 kHz to about 1000 MHz (i.e. 1 GHz) are used for terrestrial radio and television broadcasting. Frequencies above 1 GHz are called *microwaves* and are used for applications ranging from radar to information transmission to heating. Microwaves have two important properties: they travel in straight lines and they can carry high data rates.

Because microwaves travel in straight lines, the Earth's curvature limits direct links to about 100 km or so (depending on the terrain and the height of the transmitter and receiver dishes). Longer communication paths require repeaters—microwaves are picked up by an antenna on a tower, amplified, and transmitted to the next tower in the chain. Few industrial cities are without some tall landmark festooned with microwave dishes.

Since the late 1960s satellite microwave links have become increasingly more important. A satellite placed in geostationary orbit 35 700 km above the equator takes 24 hours to orbit the Earth. Because the Earth itself rotates once every 24 hours, a satellite in a geostationary orbit appears to hang motionless in space and remain over the same spot. Such a satellite can be used to transmit messages from one point on the Earth's surface to another point up to approximately 12 000 km away, as illustrated in Fig. 14.33.

Theoretically three satellites each separated by 120° could completely cover a band around the Earth. However, receivers at extreme limits of reception would have their dishes pointing along the ground at a tangent to the surface of the Earth. As the minimum practical angle of elevation is about 5°, satellites should not be more than about 110° apart for reliable operation. Data is transmitted up to the satellite on the uplink frequency, regenerated, and transmitted down again at the downlink frequency (the uplink frequency is higher than the downlink frequency). Table 14.3 describes some of the frequency bands used by satellites. Suitable microwave or coaxial links transmit data from a local source to and from the national satellite terminals.

Satellites are used to transmit television signals, telephone traffic, and data signals. Data signals can be transmitted at rates greater than 50 Mbps, which is many times faster than that offered by the public switched telephone network but rather less than that offered by the fiber optic link (and much less than that offered by the super data highways). Satellite links can be replaced by fiber optic links. The advantage of the satellite is its ability to broadcast from one transmitter to many receivers.

Satellite systems are very reliable. The sheer size of the investment in the satellite and its transport vehicle means that engineers have spent much time and energy in designing reliable satellites. Unfortunately, a satellite doesn't have an infinite life span. Its solar power panels gradually degrade due to the effects of the powerful radiation fields experienced in space, and it eventually runs out of the fuel required by its rocket jets to keep it pointing accurately at the surface of the Earth.

Satellites operate mostly in the 1 to 10 GHz band. Frequencies below 1 GHz are subject to interference from terrestrial sources of noise and the atmosphere attenuates frequencies above 10 GHz. Satellite users have to take account of a problem imposed by the length of the transmission path (about 70 000 km). Microwaves traveling at the speed of light (300 000 km/s) take approximately 250 ms to travel from the source to their destination. Consequently it is impossible to receive a reply from a transmission in under 0.5 s. Data transmission modes using half duplex become difficult to operate due to the long transit delay and the large turnaround time. Satellite data links are better suited to full-duplex operation.

High geosynchronous orbits are not the only option available. Figure 14.34 shows that satellites can be placed in one of three types of orbit. Satellites in low and medium Earth orbits

Frequency band	Name		Typical applications
3 to 30 kHz	Very low frequency	(VLF)	Long-range navigation, submarine communications
30 to 300 kHz	Low frequency	(LF)	Navigational aids and radio beacons
300 to 3000 kHz	Medium frequency	(MF)	Maritime radio, direction finding, commercial AM radio
3 to 30 MHz	High frequency	(HF)	Short-wave broadcasting, transoceanic ship and aircraft communication, telegraph, facsimile
30 to 300 MHz	Very high frequency	(VHF)	FM radio, air traffic control, police, taxi, and utilities
0.3 to 3 GHz	Ultra-high frequency	(UHF)	UHF television, navigational aids, cell phones
3 to 30 GHz	Super-high frequency	(SHF)	Microwave links, radar, satellite communications
30 to 300 GHz	Extra-high frequency	(EHF)	

Note: kHz = kilohertz = 10^3 Hz, MHz = megahertz = 10^6 Hz, GHz = gigahertz = 10^9 Hz.

Table 14.2 The radio frequency spectrum.

(a) Organization of a satellite link.

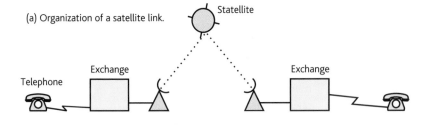

(b) The geostationary orbit.

(c) The time delay in sending a message between two ground stations.

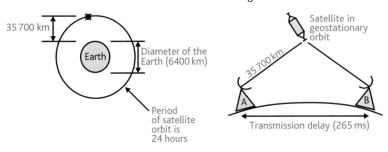

(d) The satellite's field of view is approximately one-third of the Earth's surface.

Figure 14.33 The satellite link.

Band	Frequency range	Characteristics
L-band	1.53 to 2.7 GHz	Signals penetrate buildings and structures. Low power transmitters required
Ku-band	11.7 to 17.8 GHz	Signals penetrate some structures. High data rates possible
Ka-band	18 to 31 GHz	There is a lot of available unallocated spectrum and very high data rates are possible. The signals have little penetrating power and are attenuated by rain

Table 14.3 Frequencies used in satellite communications.

appear to move across the sky, which means that when your satellite drops below the horizon you have to switch the link to another satellite. Low Earth orbits require lots of satellites for reliable communications, but the latency is very low. Fewer satellites are required to cover the World from medium Earth orbits and the latency is about 0.05 to 0.14 s.

14.7.1 Spread spectrum technology

Although a radio signal is transmitted at a specific frequency, the signal does, in fact, occupy a range of frequencies because of the modulation process. For example, an AM signal transmitted at frequency f_c, occupies the frequency range $f_c - f_m$ to $f_c + f_m$, where f_m is the maximum modulating frequency.

A problem with transmitting on a single frequency is the vulnerability of the radio link; the signal can be easily observed and it can be jammed. In the Second World War attempts were made to control torpedoes by radio links. It was clear that using a single frequency would not be a good idea because it could be jammed by transmitting another signal at the same frequency. A solution to the problem of jamming was suggested by Hedy Lamarr and George Antheil; they proposed changing the frequency of the transmitter and receiver in synchrony to avoid transmitting on a single frequency. A clockwork-driven frequency selector could be used in both the transmitter and receiver to change frequency every few seconds.

Antheil and Lamar's proposal was not put into practice until the early 1960s when the US military implemented it to provide

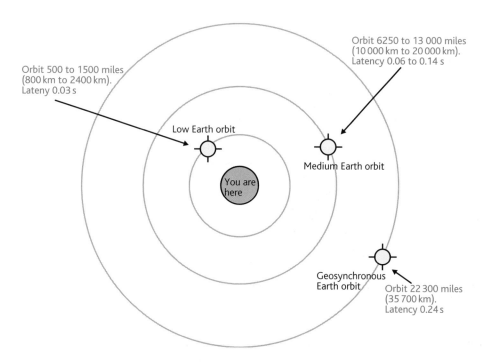

Orbit 500 to 1500 miles
(800 km to 2400 km).
Lateny 0.03 s

Orbit 6250 to 13 000 miles
(10 000 km to 20 000 km).
Latency 0.06 to 0.14 s

Low Earth orbit

You are here

Medium Earth orbit

Geosynchronous
Earth orbit

Orbit 22 300 miles
(35 700 km).
Latency 0.24 s

Figure 14.34 Satellite orbits.

secure radio links. The frequency changes (or *hops*) were made as a random sequence using electronics rather than mechanical switching. Because the frequency of the transmitted signal rapidly varies over a finite range within a band, the signal energy is distributed throughout the band. Consequently, the system is often called *spread spectrum technology*.

An advantage of spread spectrum technology is that the wireless link is less susceptible to interference. If an interfering signal is at a constant frequency, it will affect the received signal only when the interfering and data signal frequencies coincide. Moreover, if you have several spread spectrum frequencies occupying the same band at the same time, interference will take place only when the two or more frequencies are the same at the same time.

The frequency 2.4 GHz has now been allocated to spread spectrum signals[2] and IEEE standard 802.11 was developed to provide a short-range data commutations facility for laptops and similar devices. The standard uses the same type of collision control mechanism as the Ethernet.

Fourteen channels in the 2.4 GHz band are reserved for the 802.11 systems. Each channel is separated by 5 MHz. However, these channels indicate only the center frequency used by a transmitter–receiver pair. An actual wireless link uses a bandwidth of 30 MHz and, therefore, takes up five channels.

14.8 The data link layer

Now that we've looked at some of the ways in which bits are moved from one point to another by the physical layer, the next step is to show how the data link layer handles entire messages and overcomes imperfections in the physical layer. We are going to look at two popular protocols for the data link layer—a bit-oriented protocol and a protocol used by the Internet.

14.8.1 Bit-oriented protocols

A bit-oriented protocol handles *pure* binary data (i.e. strings of 1s and 0s or arbitrary length). Binary data can be a core dump, a jpeg image, a program in binary form, a floating point number, and so on. When the data is stored in a pure binary form it's apparently impossible to choose any particular data sequence as a reserved marker or flag, because that sequence may also appear as valid data. We explain how the *high-level data link control* protocol (HDLC) delivers any pattern of bits between two nodes in a data link by means of a technique called *bit stuffing*.

The key to understanding the HDLC protocol is the *HDLC frame*, the smallest unit of data that can be sent across a network by the data link layer. Frames are indivisible in the sense that they cannot be subdivided into smaller frames, just as an atom can't be divided into other atoms. However, a frame is composed of several distinct parts just as an atom is made up of neutrons, protons and electrons. Figure 14.35 illustrates the HDLC format of a single frame.

---

[2] The 2.4 GHz band is shared by other users such a Bluetooth, baby monitors, and cordless phones.

HISTORY OF WI-FI

1997 IEEE Standard 802.11 specifies a wireless LAN using 2.4 GHz with data rates of 1 and 2 MHz. Apple computer provides the first operating system to support Wi-Fi (called AirPort).

  1999 Standard 802.11b with a data rate of 11 Mbits/s is finalized. The maximum actual data rate is approximately 5 Mbits/s. This was the first Wi-Fi standard to become widely accepted and it paved the way for low-cost wireless networks.

  1999 The 802.11a standard operates at 5 GHz and provides a maximum raw data rate of 54 MHz, corresponding to a practical user data rate of about 20 Mbits/s. Radio waves at 5 GHz

are more readily absorbed than those at 2.4 GHz and 802.11a-based systems have not achieved the same success at 802.11b.

  2002 Intel's Centrino chipset had a remarkable effect on the wireless LAN market. Centrino consists of a low-power CPU, an interface chip, and an 802.11b chip. This chipset was used in countless laptops to provide portability with low-power consumption on Wi-Fi LAN connectivity.

  2003 Standard 802.11g combines the lower frequency advantage of 802.11b and the modulation rate of 802.11a to provide a raw bit rate of 54 Mbits/s in the 2.4 MHz band. Equally importantly, it is backward compatible with 802.11b. By the end of 2003, companies were producing tri-mode Wi-Fi adaptors capable of accessing 802.11a/b/g networks.

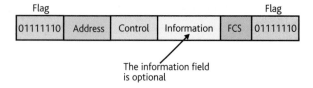

The information field is optional

Figure 14.35 The HDLC frame format.

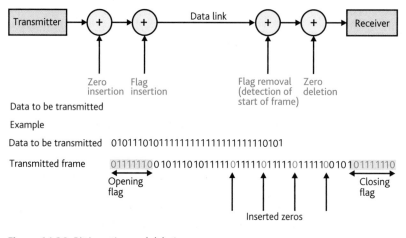

Figure 14.36 Bit insertion and deletion.

Each frame begins and ends with a unique 8-bit flag, 01111110. Whenever a receiver detects the sequence 01111110, it knows that it has located the start or the end of a frame. An error in transmission may generate a spurious flag by converting (say) the sequence 01101110 into 01111110. In such cases, the receiver will lose the current frame. Due to the unique nature of the flag, the receiver will automatically resynchronize when the next opening flag is detected.

HDLC puts no restrictions whatsoever on the nature of the data carried across the link. Consequently, higher levels of the reference model can transmit any bit sequence they wish without affecting the operation of the data link layer. The

only binary sequence that may not appear in a stream of HCLD data is the frame opening or closing flag 01111110.

A simple scheme called *zero insertion and deletion* or *bit stuffing* ensures that HDCL data is transparent. Figure 14.36 shows how bit stuffing operates. Data from the block marked transmitter is passed to an encoder marked zero insertion that operates according to a simple algorithm. A bit at its input is passed unchanged to its output unless the five preceding bits have all been 1s. In the latter case, two bits are passed to the output: a 0 followed by the input bit. As an example consider the sequence 010111111011 containing the forbidden flag sequence. If the first bit is the leftmost bit, the output of the encoder is 0101111**10**1011.

The bit-insertion mechanism guarantees that any binary sequence can appear in the input data but a flag sequence can't occur in the output data stream because five 1s are always terminated by 0. Flags intended as frame delimiters are appended to the data stream *after* the encoding block.

At the receiving end of the link, opening and closing flags are detected and removed from the data stream by the flag removal circuit. The data stream is then passed to the block marked zero deletion for decoding, which operates in the reverse way to zero insertion: if five 1s are received in succession, the next bit (which must be a 0) is deleted. For example, the received sequence 010111110101111**000** is decoded as 01011111101111100.

Now that we've described how a data stream is divided into individual bits and the bits into frames, the next step is to look at the HDLC frame. Figure 14.35 demonstrates that the HDLC frame is divided into five logical fields: an address field, a control field, an optional information field, and a frame check sequence (FCS).

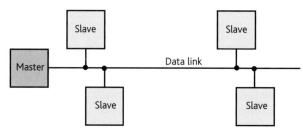

All communication is between a slave and the master.
Direct slave-to-slave communication is not permitted.

Figure 14.37 Master–slave transmission with HDLC.

Address field

The data link layer protocol may operate in one of several modes. Figure 14.37 illustrates the *master–slave* mode, where one station is the *master* station and all the other stations connected to the master are called *slaves*. In the master–slave mode only the master may send messages when it wishes. A slave is not permitted to transmit until it is invited to do so by the master.

The HDLC's address field provides the address of the slave. The master doesn't need an address because there's a unique master. When a master sends a frame, the address field identifies the slave for which the frame is intended. If the slave is transmitting a frame, the address is its own, identifying itself to the master.

Any slave receiving a frame whose address doesn't match its own address ignores the message. Unlike humans, computers don't listen to third-party traffic.

The address field is 8 bits wide permitting 127 slaves to be directly identified. If the least-significant bit of the address field bit is a logical 0, the following byte is an extension of the address field. If the least-significant bit of the extension address is also a 0, the following byte is a further extension of the address. This arrangement permits an infinitely extendable address field.

Two special-purpose addresses are defined. The address 11111111 is a global address indicating that the frame is a broadcast intended for all stations on the network. The null address 00000000 causes the frame to be ignored by all stations! A null address is included for test purposes.

Control field

The 8-bit control field determines the type of the frame being transmitted and controls the flow of messages across the data link layer. Table 14.4 defines the three types of control field used by an HDLC frame. We have numbered the control field bits 1 to 8 (bit 1 is the least-significant bit) with the least-significant bit on the left to conform to the HDLC standard.

The two least-significant bits of a C-field define one of three types of frame: I-frame, S-frame or U-frame.

THE MAC

The MAC or *media access control* is the address of a physical node in a computer network. In a PC the MAC is the address of the NIC (network interface card) or the wireless card. This address is unique and defines that particular card (no other card in the World has the same MAC).

A MAC is a 12-digit hexadecimal number (i.e. 48 bits giving 2^{48} possible unique addresses). MAC addresses are often printed on the back of a NIC, for example, 00:50:BA:BD:12:C9 belongs to one of my interface cards. The first half of the MAC address defines the node's manufacturer, which is D-Link in this case.

The MAC address is used by the data link layer to access nodes connected to the physical network. This is not to be confused with the IP (Internet protocol) address, which is a logical address identifying nodes across the entire Internet.

Frame type	1	2	3	4	5	6	7	8
I frame	0		N(S)		P/F		N(R)	
S frame	1	0	S	S	P/F		N(R)	
U frame	1	1	M	M	P/F	M	M	M

N(S)	= send sequence number
N(R)	= receive sequence number
P/F	= poll/final bit
SS	= two supervisory bits
MMMMM	= five modifier bits

Table 14.4 The format of the HDLC control field.

An I-frame or *information frame* contains an information field and is used to transport data from a higher level layer than the data link layer.

The S-frame or supervisory frame controls the flow of information on the link. Typical functions include acknowledging I-frames or requesting the retransmission of frames lost during transmission. There are four types of S-frame, the type is indicated by the two bits labeled 'S' in Table 14.4. We shall look more closely at the S-frame later.

The unnumbered frame (U-frame) provides control functions not available with the I- or C-frames. U-frames perform functions like setting up or changing the operating mode of the data link layer and connecting or disconnecting two stations.

All three types of control field have a dual-purpose *poll/final* (P/F) bit. When transmitted by a master station, this is called a *poll* bit (P-bit) and indicates that the master is asking the secondary station for a response. Recall that in the master–slave mode, the secondary station cannot transmit until it is invited to do so by the master. A control field with P/F = 1 sent by the master indicates such an invitation.

When a control field is sent by a secondary station, the P/F bit is defined as a *final* bit and, when set, indicates that the current field is the last frame of the series. In other words, a slave sets P/F to 1 when it has no more frames to send.

The state variables N(S) and N(R) in the control field are 3-bit numbers in the range 0 to 7 that define the state of the system at any instant. N(S) is called the *send sequence number* and N(R) is called the *receive sequence number*.

Only I-frames contain a send sequence number to label the current information frame; for example, if N(S) = 101 the frame is numbered 5. When this frame is received the value of N(S) is examined and compared with the previous value. If the previous value was 4, the message is received in sequence. But if the value was not 4, an error has occurred. The sequence count is modulo 8, so that it goes 67012345670 . . . . . . Consequently, if eight messages are lost, the next value of N(S) will apparently be correct.

The receive sequence number, N(R), is available in both S and I control fields. N(R) indicates the number of the *next* I-frame that the receiver *expects to see*; that is, N(R) acknowledges I-frames up to and including N(R) − 1. Suppose station A is sending an I frame to B with N(S) = 3 and N(R) = 6. This means that frame A is sending frame number 3 and has safely received frames up to 5 from B. A expects to see an information frame from B with the value of N(S) equal to 6.

By means of the N(R) and N(S) state variables, it's impossible to lose a frame without noticing it, as long as there are not more than seven outstanding I-frames that have not been acknowledged. If eight or more frames are sent, it is impossible to tell whether a value of N(R) = i refers to frame i or to frame i − 8. It is up to the system designer to ensure that this situation never happens. We will soon look at how N(S) and N(R) are used in more detail.

FCS field

Recall that the data link layer is built on top of an imperfect physical layer. Bits transmitted across a physical medium may become corrupted by noise with a 1 being transformed to a 0 or vice versa. The error rate over point-to-point links in a local area network may be of the order of 1 bit lost in every 10^{12} bits. Error rates over other channels may be much worse than this.

HDLC provides a powerful error-detection mechanism. At the receiver, the bits of the address field, control field, and I-field are treated as the coefficients of a long polynomial, which is divided by a polynomial called a *generator*. The HDLC protocol uses the CCITT generator 10001000000100001 or $x^{16} + x^{12} + x^5 + 1$. The result of the division yields a quotient (which is thrown away) and a 16-bit remainder, which is the 16-bit FCS appended to the frame.

At the receiver, the message bits forming the A-, C-, and I-fields are also divided by the generator polynomial to yield a locally calculated remainder. The calculated remainder is compared with the received remainder in the FCS field. If they match, the frame is assumed to be valid. Otherwise the frame is rejected.

You may wonder how the FCS is detected, because the I-field may be of any length and no information is sent to indicate its length directly. In fact, the FCS field cannot be detected. The receiver assembles data until the closing flag has been located and then works backward to identify the FCS and the I-field.

HDLC message exchange

The HDLC protocol supports several configurations. Here we consider only the unbalanced master–slave mode (NRM) where a slave may initiate transmission only as a result of receiving explicit permission from the master.

Before we continue, it's necessary to define the four messages associated with a supervisory frame. Table 14.5 shows how the four S-frames are encoded.

The RR (*receiver ready*) frame indicates that the station sending it is ready to receive information frames and is equivalent to saying, 'I'm ready.' The REJ (*reject*) frame indicates an error condition and usually implies that one or more frames have been lost in transmission. The REJ frame rejects all frames, starting with the frame numbered N(R). Whenever a station receives an REJ frame, it must go back and retransmit all messages after N(R) − 1. Sending all these messages is sometimes inefficient, because not all frames in a sequence may have been lost.

The RNR (*receiver not ready*) frame indicates that the station is temporarily unable to receive information frames. RNR is normally used to indicate a busy condition (e.g. the receiver's buffers may all be full). The busy condition is cleared by the transmission of an RR, REJ, or SREJ frame. An I-frame sent with the P/F bit set also clears the busy condition.

The selective reject (SREJ) frame rejects the single frame numbered N(R) and is equivalent to 'Please retransmit frame number N(R)'. The use of SREJ is more efficient than REJ, because the latter requests the retransmission of all frames after N(R) as well as N(R).

Control bit								S-frame type	
1	2	3	4	5	6	7	8		
1	0	0	0	P/F	←	N(R)	→	RR	receiver ready
1	0	0	1	P/F	←	N(R)	→	REJ	reject
1	0	1	0	P/F	←	N(R)	→	RNR	receiver not ready
1	0	1	1	P/F	←	N(R)	→	SREJ	selective reject

Table 14.5 The format of the S-frame.

Figure 14.38 demonstrates a sequence of HDLC frame exchanges between A (the master) and B (the slave) in a half-duplex mode. Each frame is denoted by type, N(S),N(R), P/F, where type is I, RR, REJ, RNR, or SREJ. Typical HDLC frames are

Type	N(S), N(R)P/F

I, 5, 0   I-frame, N(S) = 5, N(R) = 0,
I, 5, 0, P I-frame, N(S) = 5, N(R) = 0, poll bit set by master
REJ,, 4, F S-frame, N(S) = 4, reject, final bit set by slave

Note that a double comma indicates the absence of an N(S) field.

Initially in Fig. 14.38, the master station sends three I-frames. The poll bit in the third frame is set to force a response from the slave. The slave replies by sending two I-frames that are terminated by setting the F bit of the C-field. If the slave had no I-frames to send, it would have responded with RR,,3,F. The values of N(S) and N(R) are determined by the sender of the frame.

The master sends two more I-frames, terminated by a poll bit. The first frame (I,3,2) is corrupted by noise and rejected by the receiver. When the slave responds to the poll from the master, it sends a supervisory frame, REJ,,3,F, rejecting the I-frame numbered 3 and all succeeding frames. This causes the master station to repeat the two frames numbered N(S) = 3 and N(S) = 4.

When the master station sends an I-frame numbered I,5,2,P, it also is corrupted in transmission and rejected by the receiver. The secondary station cannot respond to this polled request. When the master sends a message with P = 1, it starts a timer. If a response is not received within a certain period, the *timeout*, the master station takes action. In this case, it sends a supervisory frame (RR,,2,P) to force a response. The secondary station replies with another supervisory frame (REJ,,5,F) and the master then repeats the lost message.

A selective reject frame, SREJ,,N(R), rejects only the message whose send sequence count is N(R). Therefore, SREJ,,N(R) is equivalent to 'Please repeat your message with N(S) = N(R).' If a sequence of messages are lost, it is better to use REJ,,N(R) and have N(R) and all messages following N(R) repeated.

Figure 14.39 shows the operation of an HDLC system operating in full-duplex mode, permitting the simultaneous exchange of messages in both directions.

We have explained only part of the HDLC data link layer protocol. Unnumbered fields are used to perform operations related to the setting up or establishing of the data link layer channel and the eventually clearing down of the channel.

14.8.2 The Ethernet data link layer

Figure 14.40 describe an *Ethernet* packet that consists of six fields. The 8-byte preamble is a synchronizing pattern used to detect the start of a frame and to derive a clock signal from it. The preamble consists of 7 bytes of alternating 1s and 0s followed by the pattern 10101011. Two address fields are provided, one for the source and one for the destination. A 6-byte (48-bit) address allows sufficient address space for each Ethernet node to have a unique address.

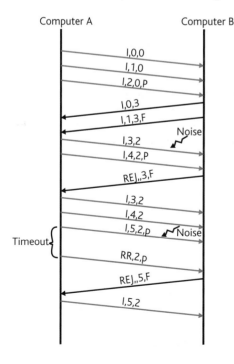

A message is denoted by type,N(S),N(R),P/F. For example, I,3,0,P indicates an information frame numbered 3, with an N(R) count of 0, and the poll bit set indicating that a response is required. Note that message 3 from A (i.e. I,3,2) is lost. Therefore, when A sends the message I,4,2,P with the poll bit set, B responds with REJ,,3,F. This indicates that B is rejecting all messages from A numbered 3 and above. The F bit is set denoting that B has no more messages to send to A.

Figure 14.38 An example of an HDLC message exchange sequence.

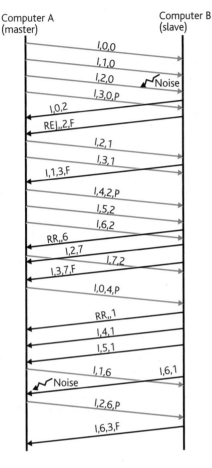

Computer A
(master)

Computer B
(slave)

- A sends a frame I,0,0 (information frame numbered 0, A is expecting a frame from B numbered 0).
- A sends frame I,1,0 (information frame numbered 1, A is still expecting a frame from B numbered 0).
- A sends frame I,2,0. This frame is corrupted by noise and is not correctly received by B.
- B sends frame I,0,2 (information frame numbered 0, B is expecting a frame from A numbered (2). Note that because A's frame I,2,0 has been lost, B is still expecting to see a frame from B labeled with N(S) = 2.
- A sends I,3,0,P (information frame numbered 3, A is expecting a frame numbered 0 from B). A is also polling B for a response. At this point A does not know that its previous message has been lost, and A has not yet received B's last message.
- B sends a reply to A's poll. This is REJ,,2,F indicating that all A's messages numbered 2 and above have been rejected. The final bit, F, is set indicating that B has nothing more to send at the moment.
- A now sends I,2,1 (information frame 2, and A is expecting to see a frame from B numbered 1). This frame is a repeat of A's information frame numbered 2, which was lost earlier.

Figure 14.39 HDLC full-duplex transmission.

Preamble (8 bytes)	Destination address (6 bytes)	Source address (6 bytes)	Type (2 bytes)	Data (variable)	CRC (4 bytes)

Figure 14.40 Ethernet packet format.

Preamble (7 bytes)	STD (1 byte)	Destination address (6 bytes)	Source address (6 bytes)	Type (2 bytes)	Data (variable)	CRC (4 bytes)

Figure 14.41 IEEE 802.3 packet format.

The type field is reserved for use by higher level layers to specify the protocol. The data field has a variable length, although the size of an Ethernet packet must be at least 64 bytes. The data field must be between 46 and 1500 bytes. The final field is a 4-byte cyclic redundancy checksum (CRC) that provides a very powerful error-detecting mechanism.

Figure 14.41 describes the format of a packet conforming to the IEEE's 802.3 standard, which is very similar to the original Ethernet packet. The preamble and start-of-frame delimiter are identical to the corresponding Ethernet preamble. The principle difference is that the 802.3 packet has a field that indicates the length of the data portion of the frame.

The 802.3 protocol covers layer 1 of the OSI reference model (the physical layer) and part of the data link layer

called the *medium access control* (MAC). The IEEE 802 standards divide the data link layer into a medium access layer and a *logical link control* (LLC).

14.9 Routing techniques

How does a message get from one point in a network to its destination? Routing in a network is analogous to routing in everyday life. The analogy between network and computer routing is close in at least one sense—the shortest route isn't always the best. Drivers avoid highly congested highways. Similarly, a network strives to avoid sending packets along a link that is either congested or costly.

CHARACTER-ORIENTED PROTOCOLS

Character-oriented protocols belong to the early days of data communication. They transmit data as ASCII characters using special 7-bit characters for formatting and flow control. For example, the string 'Alan' is sent as a sequence of four 7-bit characters 1000001001101110000110111011. This string of bits is read from left to right, with the leftmost bit representing the least-significant bit of the 'A'. We need a method of identifying the beginning of a message. Once this has been done, the bits can be divided into groups of seven (or eight if a parity bit is used) for the duration of the message. The ASCII *synchronous idle* character SYN (0010110_2) denotes the beginning of a message. The receiver reads the incoming bits and ignores them until it sees a SYN character. The following demonstrates the use of the SYN character.

Character-oriented protocols provide point-to-point communication between two stations. Like all data link layer protocols, they both control the flow of information (message sequencing and error recovery) and they set up and maintain the transmission path.

A consequence of reserving special characters for control functions is that the transmitted data stream must not contain certain combinations of bits, as these will be interpreted as control characters. Fortunately, there are ways of getting round this problem by using an escape character that modifies the meaning of following characters.

The diagram below shows the format of a BiSync frame, a protocol originally devised by IBM. The SOH, STX, and ETC characters denote start of header, start of text, and end of text, respectively.

	Character sequence	Bit sequence
Case 1	0101100 **0010110** 0100111	0101100**0010110**0100111
Case 2	0100010 1101101 0100111	010001011011010100111
Case 3	0101100 0010110 0010110	010110000101100010110

On the left we have provided three consecutive characters with spaces between successive characters. On the right we've removed spaces to show the bit stream. Case 1 shows how the SYN is detected.

This simple scheme is flawed because the end of one character plus the start of the next may look like a SYN character. Case 2 shows how a spurious SYN might be detected. To avoid this problem, two SYN characters are transmitted sequentially. If the receiver does detect a SYN, it reads the next character. If this is also a SYN the start of a message is assumed to have been located, otherwise a false synchronization is assumed and the search for a valid SYN character continued (case 3).

A BiSync frame header keeps track of the data by giving it a sequence number and providing a means of sequencing and acknowledging frames.

Figure 14.42 describes a hypothetical network consisting of six nodes A to F and 10 data links. Suppose you wish to route a message from F to C. Some of the available routings are as follows.

F–A–C
F–A–B–C
F–A–D–C
F–E–C
F–E–D–C
F–E–D–A–C
F–E–D–A–B–C
F–E–B–C
F–E–B–A–C
F–E–B–A–D–C

One of the simplest and least efficient ways of implementing routing involves a crude technique called *flooding*. When a node wishes to send a message, it sends the message on each of its links to adjacent nodes. Each node receiving the

POINT-TO-POINT PROTOCOL (PPP)

The HDLC link layer level protocol was created long before WANs and the Internet became popular. The PPP protocol has superseded HDLC in some applications. A PPP frame is like an HDLC frame. However, a PPP frame includes a 2-byte field that defines the protocol of the data it is transporting. The variable-length data field contains the datagram in the protocol defined by the protocol field.

message copies the message to all its outgoing links (apart from the link to the node on which the message was received).

You can now see where the term *flooding* came from—a message is replicated at each junction and it soon becomes a flood or avalanche. Because messages multiply at each node, you have to provide a means of stopping the process. Messages are stamped with a *best-before-date* and deleted by nodes if they exceed it. Although flooding is the simplest possible routing strategy it is inefficient because it wastes

FLOW CONTROL MECHANISMS IN RINGS

A ring network connects all nodes to each other in the form of a continuous loop. Unlike the nodes of a bus network that listen passively to data on the bus unless it is meant for them, the nodes of the ring take on an active part in all data transfers. When receiving incoming data, a node must test the packet and decide whether to keep it for itself or to pass it on to its next neighbor.

Token rings pass a special bit pattern (the *token*) round the ring from station to station. The station currently holding the token can transmit data if it so wishes. If it does not wish to take the opportunity to send data itself, it passes the token on round the ring. For example, suppose the token has the special pattern 11111111, with zero stuffing used to keep the pattern unique. A station on the ring wishing to transmit monitors its incoming traffic. When it has detected seven 1s it inverts the last bit of the token and passes it on. Thus, a pattern called a *connector* (11111110) passes on down the ring. The connector

is created to avoid sending the eighth '1', thereby passing on the token. The station holding the token may now transmit its data. After it has transmitted its data, it sends a new token down the ring. As there is only one token, contention cannot arise on the ring unless, of course, a station becomes antisocial and sends out a second token. In practice, a practical system is rather more complex, because arrangements must be included for dealing with lost tokens.

The IEEE has created a standard for the token ring LAN called 802.5. Two types of frame are supported—a three-octet frame and a variable-length frame. Each frame begins and ends with a starting and ending delimiter, which mark the frame's boundaries. The second octet provides access control (i.e. a token bit, a monitor bit, and priority bits). The short three-octet frame format is used to pass the control token round the ring from one node to the next. The IEEE 802.5 standard provides for prioritization. When a station wishes to transmit data it waits for a free token whose priority is less than its own.

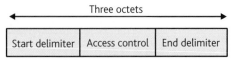

(a) Token format.

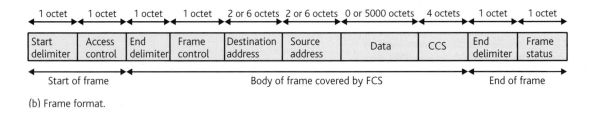

(b) Frame format.

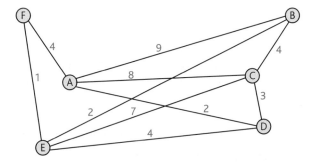

Figure 14.42 Cost of routing in a network.

Route	Cost per segment	Total cost
F–A–C	4 + 8	12
F–A–B–C	4 + 9 + 4	17
F–A–D–C	4 + 2 + 3	9
F–E–C	1 + 7	8
F–E–D–C	1 + 4 + 3	8
F–E–D–A–C	1 + 4 + 2 + 8	15
F–E–D–A–B–C	1 + 4 + 2 + 9 + 4	20
F–E–B–C	1 + 2 + 4	7
F–E–B–A–C	1 + 2 + 9 + 8	20
F–E–B–A–D–C	1 + 2 + 9 + 2 + 3	17

Table 14.6 The cost of routing a message from node F to C in Fig. 14.42.

bandwidth. Flooding is not normally used by today's networks.

Suppose now we apply a cost to each of the routings. This cost is a figure-of-merit that might be determined by the reliability of a link, its latency (i.e. delay), or its actual cost (it might be rented). We have provided a number against each link in Fig. 14.42 to indicate its cost. If we now apply these costs to the routines, we get the figure shown in Table 14.6.

Table 14.6 indicates that the cheapest route is F to E to B to C, which is slightly cheaper than the more direct route F to E to C.

How do you find the cheapest route though the network and what happens if the cost of a link changes (if every node attempts to use the same link its performance will fall and increase its cost)? Much research has been carried out into the routing of messages around complex networks. Here we can only mention some of the basic concepts of routing.

14.9.1 Centralized routing

A network with *centralized routing* used a master station with a knowledge of the whole network and the best routes between all nodes. The master station broadcasts the routing information to the other nodes. Let's see how this applies to the example of Fig. 14.42. Table 14.7 provides routing tables for nodes A to F. In each case we have calculated the cheapest route and the next node. Table 14.8 summarizes the information in Table 14.7 and gives the next node for any destination.

Consider the routing of a message from node A to B. At node A the router looks up the next destination for a message consigned to B and sends the packet to node F. Node F receives this packet and looks up the next node for a packet bound for B, which is E. At node E the packet is sent on the best route to D which is direct to B. The packet reaches B having followed the optimum route A to F to E to B.

14.9.2 Distributed routing

Getting a complete knowledge of a complex network is not easy. Another way of dealing with routing is to allow each node to build up its own database for the rest of the network. Initially each node knows only about its immediate neighbors and the cost to reach them. After a time, a node can request information from its immediate neighbors about their neighbors, and so on. Eventually, a complete picture of the network can be constructed.

The optimum route between any two points in a network isn't necessarily constant because the network itself is constantly changing. Nodes are added and removed. Links can be broken or become hopelessly congested. Maintaining a fixed table of optimum routes (called static routing) is less efficient than constantly updating routing information to cope best with the current conditions. This strategy is called adaptive routing.

14.9.3 IP (Internet protocol)

Although networks were originally developed for highly specialized applications such as reliable military communications systems and academic research tools, it's the Internet that's caught people's attention because of its impact on everyday life. The Internet began as a development of the US Defense Advanced Research Projects Agency, (DARPA) in the 1960s. This project created and developed a small experimental network using packet switching called ARPANET (the 'D' for *defense* has been dropped from the acronym). Research into the ARPANET was carried out at many universities and this network gradually evolved into what we now call the Internet.

Node A			Node B		
Destination	Next node	Cost	Destination	Next node	Cost
B	F	7	A	E	7
C	D	5	C	C	4
D	D	2	D	E	6
E	F	5	E	E	2
F	F	4	F	E	3

Node C			Node D		
Destination	Next node	Cost	Destination	Next node	Cost
A	D	8	A	A	2
B	B	4	B	E	6
D	D	3	C	C	3
E	B	6	E	E	4
F	B	7	F	E	5

Node E			Node F		
Destination	Next node	Cost	Destination	Next node	Cost
A	F	5	A	A	4
B	B	2	B	E	3
C	B	6	C	E	7
D	D	4	D	E	5
F	F	1	E	E	1

Table 14.7 Routing tables for nodes A to F.

Source node	Destination node					
	A	B	C	D	E	F
A		F	D	D	F	F
B	E		C	E	E	C
C	D	B		D	B	B
D	A	E	C		E	E
E	F	B	B	D		F
F	A	E	E	E	E	

Table 14.8 Routing matrix (next node table).

The protocol used for ARPANET's transport layer forms the basis of Internet's transmission control protocol (TCP).

The Internet links together millions of networks and individual users. In order to access the Internet, a node must use the TCP/IP protocol (*transmission control protocol/Internet protocol*), which corresponds to layers 4 and 3 of the OSI reference model, respectively. Some of the higher level protocols that make use of TCP/IP are TELNET (a remote login service that allows you to access a computer across the Internet), FTP (file transfer protocol), which allows you to

Version	Header length	Service type	Datagram length	
Identification			Flags	Fragment offset
Time to live		Protocol	Header checksum	
Source IP address				
Destination IP address				
Options			Padding	
Data (up to 64K octets total in IP packet)				

Figure 14.43 Structure of the IP layer packet.

exchange files across the Internet, and SMTM (simple mail transfer protocol), which provides electronic mail facilities. Here we provide only an overview of the TCP/IP layers.

Internet's network layer protocol, IP, routes a packet between nodes in a network. The packets used by the IP are *datagrams* and are handled by appropriate data link layer protocols—typically Ethernet protocols on LANs and X.25 protocols across public data networks (i.e. the telephone system). Figure 14.43 describes the format of an IP packet (or frame) that is received from the data link layer below it and passed to the TCP transport layer above it.

IP's version field defines the version of the Internet protocol that created the current packet. This facility allows room for growth because improvements can be added as the state of the art improves while still permitting older systems to access the network. The IP version widely used in the late 1990s was IPv4, and IPv6 was developed to deal with some of the problems created by the Internet's increasing size and to provide for time-critical services such as real-time video and speech.

The header length defines the size of the header in multiples of 32-bit words (i.e. all fields preceding the data). The minimum length is five. Because the header must be a multiple of 32 bits, IP's padding field is used to supply 0 to 3 octets to force the header to fit a 32-bit boundary. The datagram length is a 16-bit value that specifies the length of the entire IP packet, which limits the maximum size of a packet to 64K octets. In practice, typical IP packets are below 1 kbyte.

The service type field tells the transport layer how the packet is to be handled; that is, priority, delay, throughput, and reliability. The service request allows the transport layer to choose between, for example, a link with a low delay or a link that is known to be highly reliable.

The flags and fragment offset fields are used to deal with *fragmentation*. Suppose a higher level layer uses larger packets than the IP layer. A packet has to be split up (i.e. fragmented) and transmitted in chunks by the IP. The fragmentation flags indicate that an IP packet is part of a larger unit that has to be re-assembled and the fragment offset indicates where the current fragment fits (remember that IP packets can be received out of order).

The *time-to-live* field corresponds to the packet's *best-before date* and is used to specify the longest time that the packet can remain on the Internet. When a packet is created, it is given a finite life. Each time the packet passes a node, the time-to-live count is decremented. If the count reaches zero, the packet is discarded. This facility prevents packets circulating round the Internet endlessly.

The protocol field specifies the higher level protocol that is using the current packet; for example, the TCP protocol has the value 6. This facility enables the destination node to pass the IP packet to the appropriate service.

The header checksum detects errors in the header. Error checking in the data is performed by a higher level protocol. The checksum is the one's complement of the sum of all 16-bit integers in the header. When a packet is received the checksum is calculated and compared with the transmitted value. A checksum is a very crude means of providing error protection (it's not in the same league as the FCS) but it is very fast to compute.

The source and destination IP address fields provide the address of where the packet is coming from and where it's going. We will return to IP addressing later. The *options field* is optional and allows the packet to request certain facilities. For example, you can request that the packet's route through the Internet be recorded or you can request a particular route though the network. Finally, the data field contains the information required by the next highest protocol.

IP routing

Both the IP source and destination addresses are 32 bits in version 4 of the Internet protocol. Version 6 will provide 128-bit addresses (that's probably enough to give each of the Earth's molecules its own Internet address).

An IPv4 address is unique and permits 2^{32} (over 4000 million) different addresses. When specifying an Internet address it's usual to divide the 32 bits into four 8-bit fields and convert each 8-bit field into a decimal number delimited by a period; for example, the IP address 11000111 10000000 01100000 00000000 corresponds to 199.128.96.0.

Although an IP address provides 2^{32} unique values, it doesn't allow up to 4000 million nodes (or users) to exist on the Internet, because not all addresses are available. An IP address is a hierarchical structure designed to facilitate the routing of a packet through the Internet and is divided into four categories as Fig. 14.44 demonstrates.

Internet addresses have two fields—a network address and a node address. Class A Internet protocol addresses use a 7-bit network identifier and then divide each network into 2^{24} different nodes. Class B addresses can access one of $2^{14} = 16K$ networks each with 64K nodes, and class C addresses select one of $2^{12} = 4096$ networks with 254 nodes.

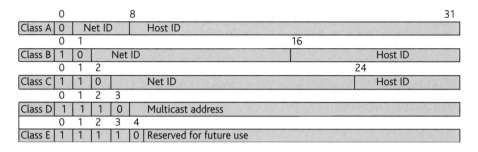

Figure 14.44 Structure of an IP address.

Source port		Destination port	
Sequence number			
Acknowledgement number			
Data offset	Reserved	Flags	Window
Checksum		Urgent pointer	
Options			Padding
Data			

Figure 14.45 Structure of TCP header.

You can easily see how inefficient this arrangement is. Although only 128 networks can use a class A address, each network gets 16 million node addresses whether they are needed or not. Class A and B addresses have long since been allocated (removing large numbers of unique addresses from the pool). This leaves only a rapidly diminishing pool of class C addresses (until the IPv6 protocol becomes more widely used).

The end user doesn't directly make use of a numeric Internet address. Logical Internet addresses are written in the form user@host.department.institution.domain. The way in which these logical addresses are mapped onto physical addresses is beyond the scope of this chapter.

Transmission control protocol

TCP performs a level-4 transport layer function by interfacing to the user and host's applications processes at each end of the net. The TCP is rather like an operating system because it carries out functions such as opening, maintaining, and closing the channel. The TCP takes data from the user at one end of the net and hands it to the IP layer below for transmission. At the other end of the net, the TCP takes data from the IP layer and passes it to the user. Figure 14.45 describes the transport header.

The source and destination port addresses provide application addresses. Each node (host) might have several application programs running on it and each application is associated with a port. This means you can run several applications, each using the Internet, on a computer at any instant.

The sequence number ensures that messages can be assembled in sequence because it contains the byte number of the first byte in the data. The acknowledgement number indicates the byte sequence number the receiving TCP node expects to receive and, therefore, acknowledges the receipt of all previous bytes. This arrangement is analogous to the HDLC protocol used by layer two protocols.

The offset defines the size of the TCP header and, therefore, the start of the data field. The *flags* field contains 6 bits

that control the operation of the TCP; for example, by indicating the last data segment or by breaking the link. The window field tells the receiving node how many data bytes the sending node can accept in return. The checksum provides basic error correction for the transport layer. The options field defines TCP options. The padding field ensures that the header fits into a 32-bit boundary.

The urgent pointer field is used in conjunction with the URG flag bit. If the URG bit is set, the urgent pointer provides a 16-bit offset from the sequence number in the current TCP header. This provides the sequence number of the last byte in urgent data (a facility used to provide a sort of interrupt facility across the Internet). The host receiving a message with its URG bit set should pass it to the higher layers ahead of any currently buffered data.

Although the TCP protocol forms the backbone of the Internet, it is rather old and has its origin in the days of the ARPANET. In particular, the TCP's error-detecting checksum is almost worthless because it isn't as powerful as the data link layer's FCS error-detecting mechanism. TCP plus IP headers are 40 bytes or more and these add a significant overhead to short data segments.

■ SUMMARY

In this chapter we have provided an overview of some of the aspects of interest to those involved with computer communications networks. Computer networks is a subject that is advancing as rapidly as any other branch of computer science, because it increases the power of computer systems and exploits many of today's growing technologies. It is all too easy to think of computer communications as a hardware-oriented discipline centered almost exclusively on the transmission of signals from point A to point B. Modern computer communications networks have software components that far outweigh their hardware components in terms of complexity and sometimes even cost. In this chapter we have introduced the ideas behind the seven layers of the ISO basic reference model for open systems intercon-nection and have described protocols for the bottom two layers.

■ PROBLEMS

14.1 If the cost of a computer and all its peripherals is so low today, why is the field of computer communications expanding so rapidly?

14.2 What is the meaning of a *protocol* and why are protocols so important in the world of communications?

14.3 What is the difference between a WAN and a LAN?

14.4 What is an *open system*?

14.5 Why has the ISO model for OSI proved so important in the development of computer communications?

14.6 What are the differences between the transport and net-work layers of the ISO reference model?

14.7 Why is the physical layer of the OSI model different from all the other layers?

14.8 What is a *virtual connection*?

14.9 What are the differences between half-duplex and full-duplex transmission modes? How is it possible to make a half-duplex system look like a full-duplex system?

14.10 What is the difference between phase and frequency modulation?

14.11 What are the types of noise that affect a data link? Which types of noise are artificial and which are natural? If you were comparing a satellite link and a telephone link, what do you think are the effect, type, and consequences of noise on each link?

14.12 What determines the maximum rate at which informa-tion can be transmitted over a data link?

14.13 Why cannot users transmit any type of signal they wish (i.e. amplitude, frequency characteristics) over the PSTN?

14.14 What is the difference between DTE and DCE?

14.15 What are the advantages and disadvantages of the fol-lowing communications media: fibre optic link, twisted pair, and satellite link?

14.16 Why is a SYN character required by character-oriented data link, and why is a SYN character not required by a bit-oriented data link?

14.17 What is *bit stuffing* and how is it used to ensure transparency?

14.18 What are the advantages and disadvantages of LANs based on the ring and bus topologies?

14.19 What is the meaning of CSMA/CS in the context of a mechanism for handling collisions on a LAN?

14.20 The maximum range of a line-of-sight microwave link, d, is given by the formula $d^2 = 2r \cdot h + h^2$, where r is the radius of the Earth and h is the height of the antenna above the Earth's surface. This formula assumes that one antenna is at surface level and the other at height h. Show that this formula is correct. Hint: it's a simple matter of trigonometry.

14.21 For each of the following bit rates determine the period of 1 bit in the units stated.

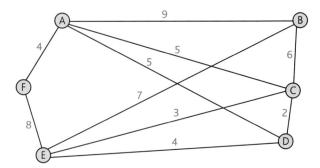

Figure 14.46 Routing in a network.

Bit rate	Unit
(a) 100 bps	ms
(b) 1 kbps	ms
(c) 56 kbps	μs
(d) 100 Mbps	ns

14.22 Each of the following time values represents 1 bit. For each value give the corresponding bit rate expressed in the units stated.

Duration	Unit of bit rate
(a) 1 s	bps
(b) 10 μs	kbps
(c) 10 μs	Mbps
(d) 15 ns	Gbps

14.23 For each of the following systems calculate the bit rate.

(a) 300 baud	2-level signal
(b) 600 baud	4-level signal
(c) 9600 baud	256-level signal

14.24 The ISO reference model has seven layers. Is that too many, too few, or just right?

14.25 Define an open system and provide three examples of open systems?

14.26 What are the relative advantages and disadvantages of satellite links in comparison with fiber optic cables?

14.17 If a signal has a signal-to-noise ratio of 50 dB and the power of the signal is 1 mW, what is the power of the noise component?

14.28 For the network of Fig. 14.46 calculate the lowest cost route between any pairs of nodes.

14.29 Suppose the network of Fig. 14.46 used flooding to route its packets. Show what would happen if a packet were to be sent from node F to node C.

14.30 A network has a bandwidth of 3400 Hz and a signal-to-noise ratio of 40 dB. What is the maximum theoretical data rate that the channel can support?

14.31 Shannon's work on the capacity of a channel relates to so-called white Gaussian noise (e.g. thermal noise). Many tele-phone channels suffer from impulse noise (switching transients that appear as clicks). Do you think that (for the same noise power) such a channel would have a better information-carrying capacity than predicted by Shannon?

14.32 Why is a checksum error detector so much worse than a cyclic redundancy code?

APPENDIX: THE 68000 INSTRUCTION SET

This appendix provides details of the 68000's most important instructions (we have omitted some of the instructions that are not relevant to this book).

In each case, we have given the definition and assembly language format of the instruction. We have also provided its size (byte, word, or longword) and the addressing modes it takes for both source and destination operands.

Finally, we have included the effect of the instruction on the 68000's condition code register. Each instruction either sets/clears a flag bit, leaves it unchanged, or has an 'undefined' effect, which is indicated by the symbols *, -, and U, respectively. A 0 in the CCR indicates that the corresponding bit is always cleared.

ADD	Add binary
Operation:	`[destination]←[source]+[destination]`
Syntax:	`ADD <ea>,`**`Dn`**
	`ADD Dn,`**`<ea>`**
Attributes:	Size=byte, word, longword
Description:	Add the source operand to the destination operand and store the result in the destination location.
Condition codes:	`X N Z V C`
	`* * * * *`

Source operand addressing modes

Dn	An	(An)	(An)+	–(An)	(d,An)	(d,An,Xi)	ABS.W	ABS.L	(d,PC)	(d,PC,Xn)	imm
✔	✔	✔	✔	✔	✔	✔	✔	✔	✔	✔	✔

Destination operand addressing modes

Dn	An	(An)	(An)+	–(An)	(d,An)	(d,An,Xi)	ABS.W	ABS.L	(d,PC)	(d,PC,Xn)	imm
✔		✔	✔	✔	✔	✔	✔	✔			

ADDA	Add address
Operation:	`[destination]←[source]+[destination]`
Syntax:	`ADDA <ea>,`**`An`**
Attributes:	Size=word, longword
Description:	Add the source operand to the destination address register and store the result in the destination address register. The source is sign-extended before it is added to the destination; e.g. if we execute `ADDA.W D3,`**`A4`** where $A4=00000100_{16}$ and $D3.W=8002_{16}$, the contents of D3 are first

sign-extended to FFFF8002$_{16}$ and added to 00000100$_{16}$ to give FFFF8102$_{16}$, which is stored in A4.

Application: To add to the contents of an address register and without updating the CCR. Note that `ADDA.W D0,A0` is the same as `LEA (A0,D0.W),A0`.

Condition codes:
```
X N Z V C
- - - - -
```
An `ADDA` operation does not affect the state of the CCR.

Source operand addressing modes

Dn	An	(An)	(An)+	–(An)	(d,An)	(d,An,Xi)	ABS.W	ABS.L	(d,PC)	(d,PC,Xn)	imm
✔	✔	✔	✔	✔	✔	✔	✔	✔	✔	✔	✔

ADDI   **Add immediate**

Operation: `[destination]←<literal>+[destination]`

Syntax: `ADDI #<data>,<ea>`

Attributes: Size=byte, word, longword

Description: Add immediate data to the destination operand. Store the result in the destination operand. `ADDI` can be used to add a literal directly to a memory location. For example, `ADDI.W #$1234,$2000` has the effect $[2000_{16}] \leftarrow [2000_{16}] + 1234_{16}$.

Condition codes:
```
X N Z V C
* * * * *
```

Destination operand addressing modes

Dn	An	(An)	(An)+	–(An)	(d,An)	(d,An,Xi)	ABS.W	ABS.L	(d,PC)	(d,PC,Xn)	imm
✔		✔	✔	✔	✔	✔	✔	✔			

ADDQ   **Add quick**

Operation: `[destination]←<literal>+[destination]`

Syntax: `ADDQ #<data>,<ea>`

Sample syntax: `ADDQ #6,D3`

Attributes: Size=byte, word, longword

Description: Add the immediate data to the contents of the destination operand. The immediate data must be in the range 1 to 8. Word and longword operations on address registers do not affect condition codes and a word operation on an address register affects all bits of the register.

Application: `ADDQ` is used to add a small constant to the operand at the effective address. Some assemblers permit you to write `ADD` and then choose `ADDQ` **automatically** if the constant is in the range 1 to 8.

Condition codes:
```
X N Z V C
* * * * *
```
The CCR is not updated if the destination operand is an address register.

Destination operand addressing modes

Dn	An	(An)	(An)+	–(An)	(d,An)	(d,An,Xi)	ABS.W	ABS.L	(d,PC)	(d,PC,Xn)	imm
✔	✔	✔	✔	✔	✔	✔	✔	✔			

ADDX	Add extended

Operation: [destination] ← [source] + [destination] + [X]

Syntax: ADDX Dy, **Dx**

             ADDX −(Ay), **−(Ax)**

Attributes: Size=byte, word, longword

Description: Add the source operand to the destination operand along with the extend bit, and store the result in the destination location. The only legal addressing modes are data register direct and memory to memory with address register indirect using predecrementing.

Application: The ADDX instruction is used in chain arithmetic to add together strings of bytes (words or longwords). Consider the addition of two 128-bit numbers, each of which is stored as four consecutive longwords.

```
         LEA      Number1,A0      A0 points at the first number
         LEA      Number2,A1      A1 points at the second number
         MOVE     #3,D0           Four longwords to add
         MOVE     #$00,CCR        Clear the X-bit and Z-bit of the CCR
LOOP     ADDX     −(A0),−(A1)     Add a pair of numbers
         DBRA     D0,LOOP         Repeat until all added
```

Condition codes: X N Z V C

                             * * * * *

The Z-bit is cleared if the result is non-zero, and left unchanged otherwise. The Z-bit can be used to test for zero after a chain of multiple precision operations.

AND	AND logical

Operation: [destination] ← [source] · [destination]

Syntax: AND $<ea>$, **Dn**

             AND Dn, **$<ea>$**

Attributes: Size=byte, word, longword

Description: AND the source operand to the destination operand and store the result in the destination location.

Application: AND is used to mask bits. If you wish to clear bits 3 to 6 of data register D7, you can execute AND #%10000111,D7. Unfortunately, the AND operation cannot be used with an address register as either a source or a destination operand. If you wish to perform a logical operation on an address register, you have to copy the address to a data register and then perform the operation there.

Condition codes: X N Z V C

                             - * * 0 0

Source operand addressing modes

Dn	An	(An)	(An)+	−(An)	(d,An)	(d,An,Xi)	ABS.W	ABS.L	(d,PC)	(d,PC,Xn)	imm
✔		✔	✔	✔	✔	✔	✔	✔	✔	✔	✔

Destination operand addressing modes

Dn	An	(An)	(An)+	−(An)	(d,An)	(d,An,Xi)	ABS.W	ABS.L	(d,PC)	(d,PC,Xn)	imm
✔		✔	✔	✔	✔	✔	✔	✔			

ANDI	AND immediate
Operation:	[destination]←<literal>·[destination]
Syntax:	ANDI #<data>,<ea>
Attributes:	Size=byte, word, longword
Description:	AND the immediate data to the destination operand. The ANDI instruction permits a literal operand to be ANDed with a destination other than a data register. For example, ANDI #$FE00,$1234 or ANDI.B #$F0,(A2)+.
Condition codes:	X N Z V C
	- * * 0 0

Destination operand addressing modes

Dn	An	(An)	(An)+	–(An)	(d,An)	(d,An,Xi)	ABS.W	ABS.L	(d,PC)	(d,PC,Xn)	imm
✔		✔	✔	✔	✔	✔	✔	✔			

ANDI to CCR	AND immediate to CCR
Operation:	[CCR]←<data>·[CCR]
Syntax:	ANDI #<data>,CCR
Attributes:	Size=byte
Description:	AND the immediate data to the condition code register (i.e. the least-significant byte of the status register).
Application:	ANDI is used to clear selected bits of the CCR. For example, ANDI #$FA,CCR clears the Z- and C-bits, i.e. XNZVC=X N 0 V 0.
Condition codes:	X N Z V C
	* * * * *

X: cleared if bit 4 of data is zero
N: cleared if bit 3 of data is zero
Z: cleared if bit 2 of data is zero
V: cleared if bit 1 of data is zero
C: cleared if bit 0 of data is zero

ANDI to SR	AND immediate to status register
Operation:	IF [S]=1
	THEN
	[SR]←<literal>·[SR]
	ELSE TRAP
Syntax:	ANDI #<data>,SR
Attributes:	Size=word
Description:	AND the immediate data to the status register and store the result in the status register. All bits of the SR are affected.
Application:	This instruction is used to clear the interrupt mask, the S-bit, and the T-bit of the SR. ANDI #<data>,SR affects both the status byte of the SR and the CCR. For example, ANDI #$7FFF,SR clears the trace bit of the status register, whereas ANDI #$7FFE, SR clears the trace bit and also clears the carry bit of the CCR.
Condition codes:	X N Z V C
	* * * * *

ASL, ASR	Arithmetic shift left /right
Operation:	[destination]←[destination] shifted by <count>
Syntax:	ASL Dx,**Dy**
	ASR Dx,**Dy**
	ASL #<data>,**Dy**
	ASR #<data>,**Dy**
	ASL <ea>
	ASR <ea>
Attributes:	Size=byte, word, longword

Description:

Arithmetically shift the bits of the operand in the specified direction (i.e. left or right). The shift count may be specified in one of three ways. The count may be a literal, the contents of a data register, or the value 1. An immediate (i.e. literal) count permits a shift of 1 to 8 places. If the count is in a register, the value is modulo 64 (i.e. 0 to 63). If no count is specified, one shift is made (i.e. ASL <ea> shifts the contents of the **word** at the effective address one place left).

An arithmetic shift left shifts a zero into the least-significant bit position and shifts the most-significant bit out into both the X- and the C-bits of the CCR. The overflow bit of the CCR is set if a sign change occurs during shifting (i.e. if the most-significant bit changes value during shifting).

The effect of an arithmetic shift right is to shift the least-significant bit into both the X- and C-bits of the CCR. The most-significant bit (i.e. the sign bit) is **replicated** to preserve the sign of the number.

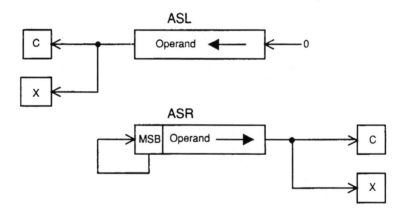

Application:

ASL multiplies a two's complement number by 2. ASL is almost identical to the corresponding logical shift, LSR. The only difference between ASL and LSL is that ASL sets the V-bit of the CCR if overflow occurs, whereas LSL clears the V-bit to zero. An ASR divides a two's complement number by 2. When applied to the contents of a memory location, all 68000 shift operations operate on a word.

Condition codes:

```
X N Z V C
* * * * *
```

The X-bit and the C-bit are set according to the last bit shifted out of the operand. If the shift count is zero, the C-bit is cleared. The V-bit is set if the most-significant bit is changed at any time during the shift operation and cleared otherwise.

Destination operand addressing modes

Dn	An	(An)	(An)+	–(An)	(d,An)	(d,An,Xi)	ABS.W	ABS.L	(d,PC)	(d,PC,Xn)	imm
✔		✔	✔	✔	✔	✔	✔	✔			

Bcc	Branch on condition cc
Operation:	If cc=1 THEN [PC]←[PC]+d
Syntax:	Bcc <label>
Sample syntax:	BEQ Loop_4
	BVC *+8
Attributes:	BEQ takes an 8-bit or a 16-bit offset (i.e. displacement).
Description:	If the specified logical condition is met, program execution continues at location [PC]+displacement, d. The displacement is a two's complement value. The value in the PC corresponds to the current location plus two. The range of the branch is -126 to $+128$ bytes with an 8-bit offset, and -32 kbyte to $+32$ kbyte with a 16-bit offset. A short branch to the next instruction is impossible, since the branch code 0 indicates a long branch with a 16-bit offset.

BCC	branch on carry clear	$\overline{C}$
BCS	branch on carry set	C
BEQ	branch on equal	Z
BGE	branch on greater than or equal	$N \cdot V + \overline{N} \cdot \overline{V}$
BGT	branch on greater than	$N \cdot V \cdot \overline{Z} + \overline{N} \cdot \overline{V} \cdot \overline{Z}$
BHI	branch on higher than	$\overline{C} \cdot \overline{Z}$
BLE	branch on less than or equal	$Z + N \cdot \overline{V} + \overline{N} \cdot V$
BLS	branch on lower than or same	$C + Z$
BLT	branch on less than	$N \cdot \overline{V} + \overline{N} \cdot V$
BMI	branch on minus (i.e. negative)	N
BNE	branch on not equal	$\overline{Z}$
BPL	branch on plus (i.e. positive)	$\overline{N}$
BVC	branch on overflow clear	$\overline{V}$
BVS	branch on overflow set	V

There are two types of conditional branch instruction: those that branch on an unsigned condition and those that branch on a signed condition; e.g. $FF is greater than $10 when the numbers are unsigned (i.e. 255 is greater than 16). However, if the numbers are signed, $FF is less than $10 (i.e. -1 is less than 16).

The signed comparisons are:

BGE	branch on greater than or equal
BGT	branch on greater than
BLE	branch on lower than or equal
BLT	branch on less than

The unsigned comparisons are:

BHS	BCC	branch on higher than or same
BHI		branch on higher than
BLS		branch on lower than or same
BLO	BCS	branch on less than

The official mnemonics BCC (branch on carry clear) and BCS (branch on carry set) can be renamed as BHS (branch on higher than or same) and BLO (branch on less than), respectively. Many 68000 assemblers support these alternative mnemonics.

Condition codes:	X N Z V C
	- - - - -

BCLR	Test a bit and clear
Operation:	[Z]←$\overline{\text{<bit number> OF [destination]}}$
	<bit number> OF [destination]←0
Syntax:	BCLR Dn,<**ea**>
	BCLR #<data>,<**ea**>

Attributes:	Size=byte, longword
Description:	A bit in the destination operand is tested and the state of the specified bit is reflected in the condition of the Z-bit in the condition code. After the test, the state of the specified bit is cleared in the destination. If a data register is the destination, the bit numbering is modulo 32, allowing bit manipulation of all bits in a data register. If a memory location is the destination, a byte is read from that location, the bit operation performed using the bit number modulo 8, and the byte written back to the location. Bit zero refers to the least-significant bit. The bit number for this operation may be specified either by an immediate value or dynamically by the contents of a data register.
Application:	Suppose that the contents of memory location \$1234 are 11111010_2, and the operation BCLR #4, **\$1234** is carried out. This instruction tests bit 4. It is a 1 and therefore the Z-bit of the CCR is set to 0. Bit 4 of the destination operand is cleared and the new contents of \$1234 are: 11101010_2.
Condition codes:	X N Z V C
	- - * - -

Z: set if the bit tested is zero, cleared otherwise.

Destination operand addressing modes

Dn	An	(An)	(An)+	−(An)	(d,An)	(d,An,Xi)	ABS.W	ABS.L	(d,PC)	(d,PC,Xn)	imm
✔		✔	✔	✔	✔	✔	✔	✔			

Data register direct addressing, Dn, uses a longword operand. Other modes use a byte operand.

BRA	**Branch always**
Operation:	[PC]←[PC]+d
Syntax:	BRA <label>
	BRA <literal>
Attributes:	Size=byte, word
Description:	Program execution continues at location [PC]+d. The displacement, d, is a two's complement value (8 bits for a short branch and 16 bits for a long branch). The value in the PC corresponds to the current location plus two. A short branch to the next instruction is impossible, since the branch code 0 is used to indicate a long branch with a 16-bit offset.
Application:	A BRA is an unconditional relative jump (or goto). You use a BRA instruction to write position independent code, because the destination address (branch target address) is specified with respect to the current value of the PC. A JMP instruction does not produce position-independent code.
Condition codes:	X N Z V C
	- - - - -

BSET	**Test a bit and set**
Operation:	[Z]← <bit number> OF [destination]
	<bit number> OF [destination]←0
Syntax:	BSET Dn,<ea>
	BSET #<data>,<ea>
Attributes:	Size=byte, longword
Description:	A bit in the destination operand is tested and the state of the specified bit is reflected in the condition of the Z-bit of the condition code. After the test, the specified bit is set in the destination. If a data register is the destination then the bit numbering is modulo 32, allowing bit manipulation of all bits in a data register. If a memory location is the destination, a byte is read from that location, the bit operation performed using bit number modulo 8, and the byte written back to the location. Bit zero refers to the least-significant bit. The bit number for this operation may be specified either by an immediate value or dynamically by the contents of a data register.

Condition codes: X N Z V C

- - * - -

Z: set if the bit tested is zero, cleared otherwise.

Destination operand addressing mode for BSET Dn, <**ea**> form

Dn	An	(An)	(An)+	–(An)	(d,An)	(d,An,Xi)	ABS.W	ABS.L	(d,PC)	(d,PC,Xn)	imm
✔		✔	✔	✔	✔	✔	✔	✔			

BSR   Branch to subroutine

Operation: [SP]←[SP]−4; [[SP]]←[PC]; [PC]←[PC]+d
Syntax: BSR <label>
                    BSR <literal>
Attributes: Size=byte, word
Description: The longword address of the instruction immediately following the BSR instruction is pushed
                    on to the system stack pointed at by A7. Program execution then continues at location [PC]+
                    displacement, *d*. The displacement is an 8-bit two's complement value for a short branch, or a
                    16-bit two's complement value for a long branch. The value in the PC corresponds to the cur-
                    rent location plus two. Note that a short branch to the next instruction is impossible, since the
                    branch code 0 is used to indicate a long branch with a 16-bit offset.
Applicaton: BSR is used to call a procedure or a subroutine. It provides relative addressing (and therefore
                    position-independent code) and its use is preferable to JSR.
Condition codes: X N Z V C

- - - - -

BTST   Test a bit

Operation: [Z]←<bit number> OF [destination]
Syntax: BTST Dn, <**ea**>
                    BTST #<data>, <**ea**>
Attributes: Size=byte, longword
Description: A bit in the destination operand is tested and the state of the specified bit is reflected in the con-
                    dition of the Z-bit in the CCR. The destination is not modified by a BTST instruction. If a data
                    register is the destination, then the bit numbering is modulo 32, allowing bit manipulation of all
                    bits in a data register. If a memory location is the destination, a byte is read from that location
                    and the bit operation performed. Bit 0 refers to the least-significant bit. The bit number for this
                    operation may be specified either statically by an immediate value or dynamically by the con-
                    tents of a data register.
Condition codes: X N Z V C

- - * - -

Z: set if the bit tested is zero, cleared otherwise.

Destination operand addressing modes for BTST Dn, <ea> form

Dn	An	(An)	(An)+	–(An)	(d,An)	(d,An,Xi)	ABS.W	ABS.L	(d,PC)	(d,PC,Xn)	imm
✔		✔	✔	✔	✔	✔	✔	✔			

CLR	Clear an operand
Operation:	[destination]←0
Syntax:	CLR <ea>
Sample syntax:	CLR (A4)+
Attributes:	Size=byte, word, longword
Description:	The destination is cleared by loading with all zeros. The CLR instruction can't be used to clear an address register. You can use SUBA.L A0, **A0** to clear A0.
Condition codes:	X N Z V C
	- 0 1 0 0

Source operand addressing modes

Dn	An	(An)	(An)+	–(An)	(d,An)	(d,An,Xi)	ABS.W	ABS.L	(d,PC)	(d,PC,Xn)	imm
✔		✔	✔	✔	✔	✔	✔	✔			

CMP	Compare
Operation:	[destination]-[source]
Syntax:	CMP <ea>,**Dn**
Sample syntax:	CMP (Test,A6,D3.W),**D2**
Attributes:	Size=byte, word, longword
Description:	Subtract the source operand from the destination operand and set the condition codes accordingly. The destination must be a data register. The destination is not modified by this instruction.
Condition codes:	X N Z V C
	- * * * *

Source operand addressing modes

Dn	An	(An)	(An)+	–(An)	(d,An)	(d,An,Xi)	ABS.W	ABS.L	(d,PC)	(d,PC,Xn)	imm
✔	✔	✔	✔	✔	✔	✔	✔	✔	✔	✔	✔

CMPA	Compare address
Operation:	[destination]-[source]
Syntax:	CMPA <ea>,**An**
Sample syntax:	CMPA.L #$1000,**A4**
	CMPA.W (A2)+,**A6**
	CMPA.L D5,**A2**
Attributes:	Size=word, longword
Description:	Subtract the source operand from the destination address register and set the condition codes accordingly. The address register is not modified. The size of the operation may be specified as word or longword. Word length operands are sign-extended to 32 bits before the comparison is carried out.
Condition codes:	X N Z V C
	- * * * *

Source operand addressing modes

Dn	An	(An)	(An)+	–(An)	(d,An)	(d,An,Xi)	ABS.W	ABS.L	(d,PC)	(d,PC,Xn)	imm
✔	✔	✔	✔	✔	✔	✔	✔	✔	✔	✔	✔

CMPI	Compare immediate
Operation:	[destination]-<immediate data>
Syntax:	CMPI #<data>,<**ea**>
Attributes:	Size=byte, word, longword
Description:	Subtract the immediate data from the destination operand and set the condition codes accordingly—the destination is not modified. CMPI permits the comparison of a literal with memory.
Condition codes:	X N Z V C - * * * *

Destination operand addressing modes

Dn	An	(An)	(An)+	–(An)	(d,An)	(d,An,Xi)	ABS.W	ABS.L	(d,PC)	(d,PC,Xn)	imm
✔		✔	✔	✔	✔	✔	✔	✔			

CMPM	Compare memory with memory
Operation:	[destination]-[source]
Syntax:	CMPM (Ay)+,(**Ax**)+
Attributes:	Size=byte, word, longword
Sample syntax:	CMPM.B (A3)+,(**A4**)+
Description:	Subtract the source operand from the destination operand and set the condition codes accordingly. The destination is not modified by this instruction. The only permitted addressing mode is address register indirect with postincrementing for both source and destination operands.
Application:	Used to compare the contents of two blocks of memory. For example:

```
*         Compare two blocks of memory for equality

          LEA     Source,A0      A0 points to source block
          LEA     Destination,A1 A1 points to destination block
          MOVE.W  #Count-1,D0    Compare Count words
    RPT   CMPM.W  (A0)+,(A1)+    Compare pair of words
          DBNE    D0,RPT         Repeat until all done
          .
          .
```

Condition codes:	X N Z V C - * * * *

DBcc	Test condition, decrement, and branch
Operation:	IF(condition false) THEN [Dn]←[Dn]−1 {decrement loop counter} IF [Dn]=−1 THEN [PC] ←[PC]+2 {fall through to next instruction} ELSE [PC] ← [PC]+d {take branch} ELSE [PC]←[PC]+2 {fall through to next instruction}
Syntax:	DBcc Dn,<label>
Attributes:	Size=word
Description:	The DBcc instruction provides an automatic looping facility. The DBcc instruction requires three parameters: a branch condition (specified by 'cc'), a data register that serves as the loop down-counter, and a label that indicates the start of the loop. The DBcc first tests the condition 'cc', and if 'cc' is true the loop is terminated and the branch back to <label> not taken. The 14 branch conditions supported by Bcc are also supported by DBcc, as well as DBF and DBT

(F=false, and T=true). Many assemblers permit the mnemonic DBF to be expressed as DBRA (i.e. decrement and branch back).

The condition tested by the DBcc instruction works in the **opposite** sense to a Bcc. For example, BCC means branch on carry clear, whereas DBcc means continue (i.e. exit the loop) on carry clear. That is, the DBcc condition is a loop terminator. If the termination condition is not true, the low-order 16 bits of the specified data register are decremented. If the result is −1, the loop is not taken and the next instruction is executed. If the result is not −1, a branch is made to 'label'. The label is a 16-bit signed value, permitting a branch range of −32 to +32 kbyte. The loop may be executed up to 64K times.

We can use the instruction DBEQ, decrement and branch on zero, to mechanize the high-level language construct REPEAT...UNTIL.

```
LOOP   ...                    REPEAT
       ...
       ...                    [D0]:=[D0]−1
       ...
       DBEQ    D0,REPEAT      UNTIL [DO]=−1 OR [Z]=1
```

Application: Suppose we wish to input a block of 512 bytes of data (the data is returned in register D1). If the input routine returns a value zero in D1, an error has occurred and the loop must be exited.

```
        LEA      Dest,A0       Set up a pointer to the data destination
        MOVE.W   #511,D0       512 bytes to be input
AGAIN   BSR      INPUT         Get a data value in D1
        MOVE.B   D1,(A0)+      Store it
        DBEQ     D0,AGAIN      REPEAT until D1=0 OR 512 times
```

Condition codes: X N Z V C
                   - - - - -
                   Not affected.

DIVS, DIVU	Signed divide, unsigned divide

Operation: [destination]←[destination]/[source]

Syntax: DIVS <ea>,**Dn**
           DIVU <ea>,**Dn**

Attributes: Size=a longword is divided by a word to give a longword result quotient and remainder.

Description: Divide the destination operand by the source operand and store the result in the destination. The destination is a longword and the source is a 16-bit value. The result (i.e. destination register) is a 32-bit value arranged so that the quotient is the lower-order word and the remainder is the upper-order word. DIVU performs division on unsigned values and DIVS performs division on two's complement values. An attempt to divide by zero causes an exception. For DIVS, the sign of the remainder is always the same as the sign of the dividend (unless the remainder is zero).

Attempting to divide a number by zero results in a divide-by-zero exception. If overflow is detected during division, the operands are unaffected. Overflow is checked for at the start of the operation and occurs if the quotient is larger than a 16-bit signed integer. If the upper word of the dividend is greater than or equal to the divisor, the V-bit is set and the instruction terminated.

Application: The division of D0 by D1 is carried out by DIVU D1, **D0** and results in:

$$[D0_{(0:15)}] \leftarrow [D0_{(0:31)}]/[D1_{(0:15)}]$$

$$[D0_{(16:31)}] \leftarrow remainder$$

Condition codes: X N Z V C
                   - * * * 0

The X-bit is not affected by a division. The N-bit is set if the quotient is negative. The Z-bit is set if the quotient is zero. The V-bit is set if division overflow occurs (in which case the Z- and N-bits are undefined). The C-bit is always cleared.

Source operand addressing modes

Dn	An	(An)	(An)+	-(An)	(d,An)	(d,An,Xi)	ABS.W	ABS.L	(d,PC)	(d,PC,Xn)	imm
✔		✔	✔	✔	✔	✔	✔	✔	✔	✔	✔

EOR	Exclusive OR logical
Operation:	[destination]←[source]+[destination]
Syntax:	EOR Dn,<**ea**>
Sample syntax:	EOR D3,−(**A3**)
Attributes:	Size=byte, word, longword
Description:	EOR (exclusive or) the source operand with the destination operand and store the result in the destination location. The source operand must be a data register and the operation EOR <ea>,**Dn** is not permitted.
Application:	The EOR instruction is used to toggle (i.e. change the state of) selected bits in the operand. For example, if [D0]=00001111, and [D1]=10101010, the operation EOR.B D0,**D1** toggles bits 0 to 3 of D1 and results in [D1]=10100101.
Condition codes:	X N Z V C
	- * * 0 0

Destination operand addressing modes

Dn	An	(An)	(An)+	-(An)	(d,An)	(d,An,Xi)	ABS.W	ABS.L	(d,PC)	(d,PC,Xn)	imm
✔		✔	✔	✔	✔	✔	✔	✔			

EORI	EOR immediate
Operation:	[destination]←<literal>+[destination]
Syntax:	EORI #<data>,<**ea**>
Attributes:	Size=byte, word, longword
Description:	EOR the immediate data with the contents of the destination operand. Store the result in the destination operand.
Condition codes:	X N Z V C
	- * * 0 0

Destination operand addressing modes

Dn	An	(An)	(An)+	-(An)	(d,An)	(d,An,Xi)	ABS.W	ABS.L	(d,PC)	(d,PC,Xn)	imm
✔		✔	✔	✔	✔	✔	✔	✔			

EXG	Exchange registers
Operation:	[Rx]←[Ry];[Ry]←[Rx]
Syntax:	EXG Rx,**Ry**
Sample syntax:	EXG D3,**D4**
	EXG D2,**A0**
	EXG A7,**D5**
Attributes:	Size=longword

Description:	Exchange the contents of two registers. This is a longword operation because the entire 32-bit contents of two registers are exchanged. The instruction permits the exchange of address registers, data registers, and address and data registers.
Application:	One application of EXG is to load an address into a data register and then process it using instructions that act on data registers. Then the reverse operation can be used to return the result to the address register. Using EXG preserves the original contents of the data register.
Condition codes:	X N Z V C
	- - - - -

EXT	Sign-extend a data register
Operation:	[destination] ← sign-extended [destination]
Syntax:	EXT.W Dn
	EXT.L Dn
Attributes:	Size = word, longword
Description:	Extend the least-significant byte in a data register to a word, or extend the least-significant word in a data register to a longword. If the operation is word sized, bit 7 of the designated data register is copied to bits $(8:15)$. If the operation is longword sized, bit 15 is copied to bits $(16:31)$.
Application:	If $[D0] = \$12345678$, EXT.W D0 results in 12340078_{16}.
	If $[D0] = \$12345678$, EXT.L D0 results in 00005678_{16}.
Condition codes:	X N Z V C
	- * * 0 0

ILLEGAL	Illegal instruction
Operation:	[SSP] ← [SSP] − 4; [[SSP]] ← [PC];
	[SSP] ← [SSP] − 2; [[SSP]] ← [SR];
	[PC] ← Illegal instruction vector
Syntax:	ILLEGAL
Attributes:	None
Description:	The bit pattern of the illegal instruction, $4AFC_{16}$, causes the illegal instruction trap to be taken. As in all exceptions, the contents of the program counter and the processor status word are pushed on to the supervisor stack at the start of exception processing.
Application:	Any **unknown** pattern of bits read by the 68000 during an instruction read phase would cause an illegal instruction trap. The ILLEGAL instruction can be thought of as an **official** illegal instruction. It can be used to test the illegal instruction trap and will always be an illegal instruction in any future enhancement of the 68000.
Condition codes:	X N Z V C
	- - - - -

JMP	Jump (unconditionally)
Operation:	[PC] ← destination
Syntax:	JMP <ea>
Attributes:	Unsized
Description:	Program execution continues at the effective address specified by the instruction.
Application:	Apart from a simple unconditional jump to an address fixed at compile time (i.e. JMP label), the JMP instruction is useful for the calculation of **dynamic** or **computed** jumps. For example, the instruction JMP (A0,D0.L) jumps to the location pointed at by the contents of address

register A0, offset by the contents of data register D0. Note that JMP provides several addressing modes, while BRA provides a single addressing mode (i.e. PC relative).

Condition codes: X N Z V C

                      - - - - -

Source operand addressing modes

Dn	An	(An)	(An)+	−(An)	(d,An)	(d,An,Xi)	ABS.W	ABS.L	(d,PC)	(d,PC,Xn)	imm
		✔			✔	✔	✔	✔	✔	✔	

JSR	Jump to subroutine

Operation: [SP] ← [SP] − 4; [[SP]] ← [PC]
                      [PC] ← destination
Syntax: JSR <ea>
Attributes: Unsized
Description: JSR pushes the longword address of the instruction immediately following the JSR onto the system stack. Program execution then continues at the address specified in the instruction.
Application: JSR (Ai) calls the procedure pointed at by address register Ai. The instruction JSR (Ai, Dj) calls the procedure at the location [Ai] + [Dj], which permits dynamically computed addresses.
Condition codes: X N Z V C

                      - - - - -

Source operand addressing modes

Dn	An	(An)	(An)+	−(An)	(d,An)	(d,An,Xi)	ABS.W	ABS.L	(d,PC)	(d,PC,Xn)	imm
		✔			✔	✔	✔	✔	✔	✔	

LEA	Load effective address

Operation: [An] ← <ea>
Syntax: LEA <ea>, An
Sample syntax: LEA   Table, A0
                      LEA   (Table, PC), A0
                      LEA   (−6, A0, D0.L), A6
                      LEA   (Table, PC, D0), A6
Attributes: Size = longword
Description: The effective address is computed and loaded into an address register. LEA (−6, A0, D0.W), A1 calculates the sum of address register A0 plus data register D0.W sign-extended to 32 bits minus 6, and deposits this result in address register A1. The difference between the LEA and PEA instructions is that LEA calculates an effective address and puts it in an address register, whereas PEA calculates an effective address in the same way but pushes it on the stack.
Application: LEA is a very powerful instruction used to calculate an effective address. In particular, the use of LEA facilitates the writing of **position-independent code**. For example, LEA (TABLE, PC), **A0** calculates the effective address of 'TABLE' with respect to the PC and deposits it in A0.

                      LEA   (Table, PC), A0   Compute address of Table with respect to the pc
                      MOVE (A0), D1   Pick up the first item in the table
                      .   Do something with this item

```
                 MOVE  D1,(A0)        Put it back in the table
                    .
                    .
          Table DS.W 100
```

Condition codes: X N Z V C
                          - - - - -

Source operand addressing modes

Dn	An	(An)	(An)+	−(An)	(d,An)	(d,An,Xi)	ABS.W	ABS.L	(d,PC)	(d,PC,Xn)	imm
		✔			✔	✔	✔	✔	✔	✔	

LINK	Link and allocate

Operation: $[SP] \leftarrow [SP] - 4; [[SP]] \leftarrow [An];$
                    $[An] \leftarrow [SP]; [SP] \leftarrow [SP] + d$

Syntax: LINK An, #<displacement>

Sample syntax: LINK A6, #−12

Attributes: Size=word

Description: The contents of the specified address register are first pushed onto the stack. Then, this address register is loaded with the updated stack pointer. Finally, the 16-bit sign-extended displacement, d, is added to the stack pointer. The contents of the address register occupy two words on the stack. A **negative displacement** must be used to allocate stack area to a procedure. At the end of a LINK instruction, the old value of address register An has been pushed on the stack and the new An is pointing at the base of the stack frame. The stack pointer itself has been moved up by d bytes and is pointing at the top of the stack frame. Address register An is called the **frame pointer** because it is used to reference data on the stack frame. By convention, programmers often use A6 as a frame pointer.

Application: The LINK and UNLK instructions are used to create local workspace on the top of a procedure's stack. Consider the code:

```
      Subrtn LINK A6,#−12    Create a 12-byte workspace
        .
        .
             MOVE D3,(−8,A6)  Access the stack frame via A6
        .
        .
             UNLK A6          Collapse the workspace
             RTS             Return from subroutine
```

Condition codes: X N Z V C
                          - - - - -   The LINK instruction does not affect the CCR.

LSL, LSR	Logical shift left/right

Operation: $[destination] \leftarrow [destination]$ shifted by <count>

Syntax: LSL Dx, **Dy**
                    LSR Dx, **Dy**
                    LSL #<data>, **Dy**
                    LSR #<data>, **Dy**
                    LSL <ea>
                    LSR <ea>

Attributes: Size=byte, word, longword

Description: Logically shift the bits of the operand in the specified direction (i.e. left or right). A zero is shifted into the input position and the bit shifted out is copied into both the C- and the

X-bits of the CCR. The shift count may be specified in one of three ways. The count may be a literal, the contents of a data register, or the value 1. An immediate count permits a shift of 1 to 8 places. If the count is in a register, the value is modulo 64—from 0 to 63. If no count is specified, one shift is made (e.g. LSL <ea> shifts the **word** at the effective address one position left).

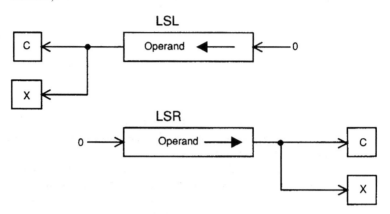

Application:	If $[D3.W] = 1100110010101110_2$, LSL.W #5, **D3** produces the result 1001010111000000_2. After the shift, the X-and C-bits of the CCR are set to 1 (since the last bit shifted out was a 1).
Condition codes:	X N Z V C * * * 0 *

The X-bit is set to the last bit shifted out of the operand and is equal to the C-bit. However, a zero shift count leaves the X-bit unaffected and the C-bit cleared.

Destination operand addressing modes

Dn	An	(An)	(An)+	-(An)	(d,An)	(d,An,Xi)	ABS.W	ABS.L	(d,PC)	(d,PC,Xn)	imm
✔		✔	✔	✔	✔	✔	✔	✔			

MOVE	Copy data from source to destination
Operation:	[destination] ← [source]
Syntax:	MOVE <ea>,<ea>

Sample syntax:	MOVE (A5),−(A2)
	MOVE −(A5),(A2)+
	MOVE #$123,(A6)+
	MOVE Temp1,Temp2

Attributes:	Size=byte, word, longword
Description:	Move the contents of the source to the destination location. The data is examined as it is moved and the condition codes set accordingly. Note that this is actually a **copy** command because the source is not affected by the move. The move instruction has the widest range of addressing modes of all the 68000's instructions.
Condition codes:	X N Z V C - * * 0 0

Source operand addressing modes

Dn	An	(An)	(An)+	-(An)	(d,An)	(d,An,Xi)	ABS.W	ABS.L	(d,PC)	(d,PC,Xn)	imm
✔	✔	✔	✔	✔	✔	✔	✔	✔	✔	✔	✔

Destination operand addressing modes

Dn	An	(An)	(An)+	−(An)	(d,An)	(d,An,Xi)	ABS.W	ABS.L	(d,PC)	(d,PC,Xn)	imm
✔		✔	✔	✔	✔	✔	✔	✔			

MOVEA	Move address
Operation:	[An] ← [source]
Syntax:	MOVEA <ea>, **An**
Attributes:	Size=word, longword
Description:	Move the contents of the source to the destination location, which is an address register. The source must be a word or longword. If it is a word, it is sign-extended to a longword. The condition codes are not affected.
Application:	The MOVEA instruction is used to load an address register (some assemblers simply employ the MOVE mnemonic for both MOVE and MOVEA). The instruction LEA can often be used to perform the same operation (e.g. MOVEA.L #$1234, **A0** is the same as LEA $1234, **A0**). Take care because the MOVEA.W #$8000, **A0** instruction sign-extends the source operand to $FFFF8000 before loading it into A0, whereas LEA $8000, **A0** loads A0 with $00008000. You should appreciate that the MOVEA and LEA instructions are not interchangeable. The operation MOVEA (Ai), An cannot be implemented by an LEA instruction, since MOVEA (Ai), **An** performs a memory access to obtain the source operand, as the following RTL demonstrates.

```
LEA    (Ai),An   =[An] ← [Ai]
MOVEA  (Ai),An   =[An] ← [M([Ai])]
```

Condition codes:	X N Z V C
	- - - - -

Source operand addressing modes

Dn	An	(An)	(An)+	−(An)	(d,An)	(d,An,Xi)	ABS.W	ABS.L	(d,PC)	(d,PC,Xn)	imm
✔	✔	✔	✔	✔	✔	✔	✔	✔	✔	✔	✔

MOVE to CCR	Copy data to CCR from source
Operation:	[CCR] ← [source]
Syntax:	MOVE <ea>, **CCR**
Attributes:	Size=word
Description:	Move the contents of the source operand to the condition code register. The source operand is a word, but only the low-order **byte** contains the condition codes. The upper byte is neglected. Note that MOVE <ea>, **CCR** is a word operation, but ANDI, ORI and EORI to CCR are all byte operations.
Application:	The move to CCR instruction permits the programmer to preset the CCR. For example, MOVE #0, **CCR** clears all the CCR's bits.
Condition codes:	X N Z V C
	- - - - -

Source operand addressing modes

Dn	An	(An)	(An)+	−(An)	(d,An)	(d,An,Xi)	ABS.W	ABS.L	(d,PC)	(d,PC,Xn)	imm
✔		✔	✔	✔	✔	✔	✔	✔	✔	✔	✔

MOVE from SR	Copy data from SR to destination
Operation:	[destination] ← [SR]
Syntax:	MOVE SR,<**ea**>
Attributes:	Size=word
Description:	Move the contents of the status register to the destination location. The source operand, the status register, is a word. This instruction is not privileged in the 68000, but is privileged in the 68010, 68020, and 68030. Executing a MOVE SR,<ea> while in the user mode on these processors results in a privilege violation trap.
Condition codes:	X N Z V C
	- - - - -

Destination operand addressing modes

Dn	An	(An)	(An)+	–(An)	(d,An)	(d,An,Xi)	ABS.W	ABS.L	(d,PC)	(d,PC,Xn)	imm
✔		✔	✔	✔	✔	✔	✔	✔			

MOVE to SR	Copy data to SR from source
Operation:	IF [S]=1
	THEN [SR] ← [source]
	ELSE TRAP
Syntax:	MOVE <ea>,**SR**
Attributes:	Size=word
Description:	Move the contents of the source operand to the status register. The source operand is a word and all bits of the status register are affected.
Application:	The MOVE to SR instruction allows the programmer to preset the contents of the status register. This instruction permits the trace mode, interrupt mask, and status bits to be modified. For example, MOVE #$2700,**SR** moves 00100111 00000000 to the status register, which clears all bits of the CCR, sets the S-bit, clears the T-bit, and sets the interrupt mask level to 7.
Condition codes:	X N Z V C
	* * * * *

Source operand addressing modes

Dn	An	(An)	(An)+	–(An)	(d,An)	(d,An,Xi)	ABS.W	ABS.L	(d,PC)	(d,PC,Xn)	imm
✔		✔	✔	✔	✔	✔	✔	✔	✔	✔	✔

MOVE USP	Copy data to or from USP
Operation 1:	IF [S]=1 {MOVE USP,An form}
	THEN [USP] ← [An]
	ELSE TRAP
Operation 2:	IF [S]=1 {MOVE An,USP form}
	THEN [An] ← [USP]
	ELSE TRAP
Syntax 1:	MOVE USP,**An**
Syntax 2:	MOVE An,**USP**
Attributes:	Size=longword

Description:	Move the contents of the user stack pointer to an address register or vice versa. This is a privileged instruction and allows the operating system running in the supervisor state either to read the contents of the user stack pointer or to set up the user stack pointer.
Condition codes:	X N Z V C
	- - - - -

MOVEM	Move multiple registers
Operation 1:	REPEAT [destination_register] ← [source] UNTIL all registers in list moved
Operation 2:	REPEAT [destination] ← [source_register] UNTIL all registers in list moved
Syntax 1:	MOVEM <ea>,<**register list**>
Syntax 2:	MOVEM <**register list**>,<**ea**>
Sample syntax:	MOVEM.L D0-D7/A0-A6,**$1234** MOVEM.L (A5),**D0-D2/D5-D7/A0-A3/A6** MOVEM.W (A7)+,**D0-D5/D7/A0-A6** MOVEM.W D0-D5/D7/A0-A6,**−(A7)**
Attributes:	Size=word, longword
Description:	The group of registers specified by <register list> is copied to or from consecutive memory locations. The starting location is provided by the effective address. Any combination of the 68000's sixteen address and data registers can be copied by a single MOVEM instruction. Note that either a word or a longword can be moved, and that a word is sign-extended to a longword when it is moved (even if the destination is a data register). When a group of registers is transferred to or from memory (using an addressing mode other than predecrementing or postincrementing), the registers are transferred starting at the specified address and up through higher addresses. The order of transfer of registers is data register D0 to D7, followed by address register A0 to A7. MOVEM.L D0-D2/D4/A5/A6,**$1234** copies registers D0,D1,D2,D4,A5,A6 to memory, starting at location $1234 (where D0 is stored) and moving to locations $1238, $123C, ... The address counter is incremented by 2 or 4 after each move according to whether the operation is moving words or longwords, respectively. If the effective address is in the predecrement mode (i.e. −(An)), only a register to memory operation is permitted. The registers are stored starting at the specified address minus two (or four for longword operands) and down through lower addresses. The order of storing is from address register A7 to address register A0, then from data register D7 to data register D0. The decremented address register is updated to contain the address of the last word stored. If the effective address is in the postincrement mode (i.e. (An)+), only a memory to register transfer is permitted. The registers are loaded starting at the specified address and up through higher addresses. The order of loading is the inverse of that used by the predecrement mode and is D0 to D7 followed by A0 to A7. The incremented address register is updated to contain the address of the last word plus two (or four for longword operands). Note that the MOVEM instruction has a side effect. An extra bus cycle occurs for memory operands, and an operand at one address higher than the last register in the list is accessed. This extra access is an 'overshoot' and has no effect as far as the programmer is concerned. However, it could cause a problem if the overshoot extended beyond the bounds of physical memory. Once again, remember that MOVEM.W sign-extends words when they are moved to data registers.

Application:	This instruction is used to save working registers on entry to a subroutine and to restore them at the end of a subroutine.
	BSR Example
	    .
	    .

```
Example MOVEM.L  D0-D5/A0-A3,-(SP)  Save registers
        .
        .
        Body of subroutine
        .
        .
        MOVEM.L (SP)+,D0-D5/A0-A3  Restore registers
        RTS                        Return
```

Condition codes: X N Z V C
                   - - - - -

Source operand addressing modes (memory to register)

Dn	An	(An)	(An)+	–(An)	(d,An)	(d,An,Xi)	ABS.W	ABS.L	(d,PC)	(d,PC,Xn)	imm
		✔	✔		✔	✔	✔	✔	✔	✔	

Destinaton operand addressing modes (register to memory)

Dn	An	(An)	(An)+	–(An)	(d,An)	(d,An,Xi)	ABS.W	ABS.L	(d,PC)	(d,PC,Xn)	imm
		✔		✔	✔	✔	✔	✔			

MOVEQ	Move quick (copy a small literal to a destination)

Operation: [destination]←<literal>
Syntax: MOVEQ #<data>,Dn
Attributes: Size = longword
Description: Move the specified literal to a data register. The literal is an eight-bit field within the MOVEQ op-code and specifies a signed value in the range −128 to +127. When the source operand is transferred, it is sign-extended to 32 bits. Consequently, although only 8 bits are moved, the MOVEQ instruction is a **longword** operation.
Application: MOVEQ is used to load small integers into a data register. Beware of its sign-extension. The two operations MOVE.B #12,**D0** and MOVEQ #12,**D0** are not equivalent. The former has the effect $[D0_{(0:7)}]\leftarrow 12$, whereas the latter has the effect $[D0_{(0:31)}] \leftarrow 12$ (with sign-extension).
Condition codes: X N Z V C
                  - * * 0 0

MULS, MULU	Signed multiply, unsigned multiply

Operation: [destination] ← [destination] * [source]
Syntax: MULS <ea>,Dn
                  MULU <ea>,Dn
Attributes: Size=word (the product is a longword)
Description: Multiply the 16-bit destination operand by the 16-bit source operand and store the result in the destination. Both the source and destination are 16-bit word values and the destination result is a 32-bit longword. The product is therefore a correct 32-bit product and is not truncated. MULU performs multiplication with unsigned values and MULS performs multiplication with two's complement values.
Application: MULU D1,**D2** multiplies the low-order words of data registers D1 and D2 and puts the 32-bit result in D2. MULU #$1234,**D3** multiplies the low-order word of D3 by the 16-bit literal $1234 and puts the 32-bit result in D3.

Condition codes:

```
X N Z V C
- * * 0 0
```

Source operand addressing modes

Dn	An	(An)	(An)+	–(An)	(d,An)	(d,An,Xi)	ABS.W	ABS.L	(d,PC)	(d,PC,Xn)	imm
✔		✔	✔	✔	✔	✔	✔	✔	✔	✔	✔

NEG — Negate

Operation: $[\text{destination}] \leftarrow 0 - [\text{destination}]$

Syntax: NEG <ea>

Attributes: Size=byte, word, longword

Description: Subtract the destination operand from 0 and store the result in the destination location. The difference between NOT and NEG is that NOT performs a bit-by-bit logical complementation, whereas NEG performs a 2's complement arithmetic subtraction. All bits of the condition code register are modified by a NEG operation; e.g. if D3.B $= 11100111_2$, the logical operation NEG.B D3 results in D3=00011001_2 (XNZVC=10001) and NOT.B D3 results in D3$=00011000_2$ (XNZVC=−0000).

Condition codes:

```
X N Z V C
* * * * *      Note that the X-bit is set to the value of the C-bit.
```

Destination operand addressing modes

Dn	An	(An)	(An)+	–(An)	(d,An)	(d,An,Xi)	ABS.W	ABS.L	(d,PC)	(d,PC,Xn)	imm
✔		✔	✔	✔	✔	✔	✔	✔			

NEGX — Negate with extend

Operation: $[\text{destination}] \leftarrow 0 - [\text{destination}] - [X]$

Syntax: NEGX <ea>

Attributes: Size=byte, word, longword

Description: The operand addressed as the destination and the extend bit are subtracted from zero. NEGX is the same as NEG except that the X-bit is also subtracted from zero.

Condition codes:

```
X N Z V C
* * * * *
```

The Z-bit is cleared if the result is non-zero and is unchanged otherwise. The X-bit is set to the same value as the C-bit.

Destination operand addressing modes

Dn	An	(An)	(An)+	–(An)	(d,An)	(d,An,Xi)	ABS.W	ABS.L	(d,PC)	(d,PC,Xn)	imm
✔		✔	✔	✔	✔	✔	✔	✔			

NOP — No operation

Operation: None

Syntax: NOP

Attributes: Unsized

Description: The no operation instruction NOP performs no **computation**. Execution continues with the instruction following the NOP instruction. The processor's state is not modified by an NOP.

Application:	NOPs can be used to introduce a **delay** in code. Some programmers use them to provide space for **patches**—two or more NOPs can later be replaced by branch or jump instructions to fix a bug. This use of the NOP is seriously frowned upon, as errors should be corrected by reassembling the code rather than by patching it.
Condition codes:	X N Z V C
	- - - - -

NOT   Logical complement

Operation:	[destination] ← [destination]
Syntax:	NOT <ea>
Attributes:	Size = byte, word, longword
Description:	Calculate the logical complement of the destination and store the result in the destination. The difference between NOT and NEG is that NOT performs a bit-by-bit logical complementation, whereas a NEG performs a two's complement arithmetic subtraction. Moreover, NEG updates all bits of the CCR, while NOT clears the V- and C-bits, updates the N- and Z-bits, and doesn't affect the X-bit.
Condition codes:	X N Z V C
	- * * 0 0

Source operand addressing modes

Dn	An	(An)	(An)+	–(An)	(d,An)	(d,An,Xi)	ABS.W	ABS.L	(d,PC)	(d,PC,Xn)	imm
✔		✔	✔	✔	✔	✔	✔	✔			

OR   OR logical

Operation:	[destination] ← [source] + [destination]
Syntax:	OR <ea>, **Dn**
	OR Dn, **<ea>**
Attributes:	Size = byte, word, longword
Description:	OR the source operand to the destination operand and store the result in the destination location.
Application:	The OR instruction is used to set selected bits of the operand. For example, we can set the four most-significant bits of a longword operand in D0 by executing:
	OR.L #$F0000000, **D0**
Condition codes:	X N Z V C
	- * * 0 0

Source operand addressing modes

Dn	An	(An)	(An)+	–(An)	(d,An)	(d,An,Xi)	ABS.W	ABS.L	(d,PC)	(d,PC,Xn)	imm
✔		✔	✔	✔	✔	✔	✔	✔	✔	✔	✔

Destination operand addressing modes

Dn	An	(An)	(An)+	–(An)	(d,An)	(d,An,Xi)	ABS.W	ABS.L	(d,PC)	(d,PC,Xn)	imm
✔		✔	✔	✔	✔	✔	✔	✔			

ORI	OR immediate
Operation:	`[destination]←<literal>+[destination]`
Syntax:	`ORI #<data>,<ea>`
Attributes:	Size=byte, word, longword
Description:	OR the immediate data with the destination operand. Store the result in the destination operand.
Condition codes:	X N Z V C - * * 0 0
Application:	ORI forms the logical OR of the immediate source with the effective address, which may be a memory location. For example, `ORI.B #%00000011,(A0)+`

Destination operand addressing modes

Dn	An	(An)	(An)+	–(An)	(d,An)	(d,An,Xi)	ABS.W	ABS.L	(d,PC)	(d,PC,Xn)	imm
✔		✔	✔	✔	✔	✔	✔	✔			

ORI to CCR	Inclusive OR immediate to CCR
Operation:	`[CCR]←<literal>+[CCR]`
Syntax:	`ORI #<data>,CCR`
Attributes:	Size=byte
Description:	OR the immediate data with the condition code register (i.e. the least-significant byte of the status register). The Z flag of the CCR can be set by `ORI #$04,CCR`.
Condition codes:	X N Z V C * * * * *

X is set if bit 4 of data=1; unchanged otherwise
N is set if bit 3 of data=1; unchanged otherwise
Z is set if bit 2 of data=1; unchanged otherwise
V is set if bit 1 of data=1; unchanged otherwise
C is set if bit 0 of data=1; unchanged otherwise

ORI to SR	Inclusive OR immediate to status register

Operation:	`IF [S]=1`
	    `THEN`
	        `[SR]←<literal>+[SR]`
	    `ELSE TRAP`

Syntax:	`ORI #<data>,SR`
Attributes:	Size=word
Description:	OR the immediate data to the status register and store the result in the status register. All bits of the status register are affected.
Application:	Used to set bits in the SR (i.e. the S, T, and interrupt mask bits). For example, `ORI #$8000,SR` sets bit 15 of the SR (i.e. the trace bit).
Condition codes:	X N Z V C * * * * *

X is set if bit 4 of data=1; unchanged otherwise
N is set if bit 3 of data=1; unchanged otherwise
Z is set if bit 2 of data=1; unchanged otherwise
V is set if bit 1 of data=1; unchanged otherwise
C is set if bit 0 of data=1; unchanged otherwise

PEA	Push effective address

Operation: `[SP] ← [SP]−4; [[SP]] ← <ea>`
Syntax: `PEA <ea>`
Attributes: Size = longword
Description: The longword effective address specified by the instruction is computed and pushed onto the stack. For example, `PEA XYZ` would push the address of 'XYZ' on to the stack. The difference between `PEA` and `LEA` is that `LEA` calculates an effective address and puts it in an address register, whereas `PEA` calculates an effective address in the same way but pushes it on the stack.

Application: `PEA` calculates an effective address to be used later in address register indirect addressing. In particular, it facilitates the writing of position-independent code. For example, `PEA (TABLE, PC)` calculates the address of `TABLE` with respect to the PC and pushes it on the stack. This address can be read by a procedure and then used to access the data to which it points. Consider the example:

```
PEA     Wednesday     Push the parameter address on the stack
BSR     Subroutine    Call the procedure
LEA     (4,SP),SP     Remove space occupied by the parameter
```
Subroutine:
```
MOVEA.L (4,SP),A0  A0 points to parameter under return address
MOVE.W  (A0),D2    Access the actual parameter - Wednesday
.
RTS
```

Condition codes:
```
X N Z V C
- - - - -
```

Source operand addressing modes

Dn	An	(An)	(An)+	−(An)	(d,An)	(d,An,Xi)	ABS.W	ABS.L	(d,PC)	(d,PC,Xn)	imm
		✔			✔	✔	✔	✔	✔	✔	

ROL, ROR	Rotate left/right (without extend)

Operation: `[destination] ← [destination] rotated by <count>`
Syntax:
```
ROL  Dx,Dy
ROR  Dx,Dy
ROL  #<data>,Dy
ROR  #<data>,Dy
ROL  <ea>
ROR  <ea>
```
Attributes: Size=byte, word, longword
Description: Rotate the bits of the operand in the direction indicated. The extend bit, X, is not included in the operation. A rotate operation is circular in the sense that the bit shifted out at one end is shifted into the other end. That is, no bit is lost or destroyed by a rotate operation. The bit shifted out is also copied into the C-bit of the CCR, but not into the X-bit. The shift count may be specified in one of three ways: the count may be a literal, the contents of a data register, or the value 1. An immediate count permits a shift of 1 to 8 places. If the count is in a register, the value is modulo 64, allowing a range of 0 to 63. If no count is specified, the **word** at the effective address is rotated by one place (e.g. `ROL <ea>`).

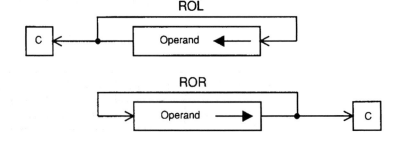

Condition codes:

X N Z V C
- * * 0 *

The X-bit is not affected and the C-bit is set to the last bit rotated out of the operand (C is set to zero if the shift count is 0).

Destination operand addressing modes

Dn	An	(An)	(An)+	–(An)	(d,An)	(d,An,Xi)	ABS.W	ABS.L	(d,PC)	(d,PC,Xn)	imm
✔		✔	✔	✔	✔	✔	✔	✔			

ROXL, ROXR	Rotate left/right with extend
Operation:	[destination] ← [destination] rotated by <count>
Syntax:	ROXL Dx, **Dy**
	ROXR Dx, **Dy**
	ROXL #<data>, **Dy**
	ROXR #<data>, **Dy**
	ROXL <ea>
	ROXR <ea>
Attributes:	Size=byte, word, longword
Description:	Rotate the bits of the operand in the direction indicated. The extend bit of the CCR is included in the rotation. A rotate operation is circular in the sense that the bit shifted out at one end is shifted into the other end. That is, no bit is lost or destroyed by a rotate operation. Since the X-bit is included in the rotate, the rotation is performed over 9 bits (.B), 17 bits (.W), or 33 bits (.L). The bit shifted out is also copied into the C-bit of the CCR as well as the X-bit. The shift count may be specified in one of three ways: the count may be a literal, the contents of a data register, or the value 1. An immediate count permits a shift of 1 to 8 places. If the count is in a register, the value is modulo 64 and the range is from 0 to 63. If no count is specified, the word at the specified effective address is rotated by one place (i.e. ROXL <ea>).

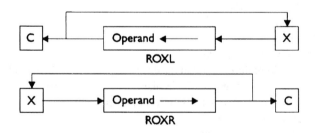

Condition codes:

X N Z V C
* * * 0 *

The X- and the C-bit are set to the last bit rotated out of the operand. If the rotate count is zero, the X-bit is unaffected and the C-bit is set to the X-bit.

Destination operand addressing modes

Dn	An	(An)	(An)+	–(An)	(d,An)	(d,An,Xi)	ABS.W	ABS.L	(d,PC)	(d,PC,Xn)	imm
✔		✔	✔	✔	✔	✔	✔	✔			

RTE	**Return from exception**

Operation:	IF [S]=1 THEN
	       [SR] ← [[SP]]; [SP] ← [SP]+2
	       [PC] ← [[SP]]; [SP] ← [SP]+4
	         ELSE TRAP

Syntax:	RTE
Attributes:	Unsized
Description:	The status register and program counter are pulled from the stack. The previous values of the SR and PC are lost. The RTE is used to terminate an exception handler. Note that the behavior of the RTE instruction depends on the nature of both the exception and processor type. The 68010 and later models push more information on the stack following an exception than the 68000. The processor determines how much to remove from the stack.
Condition codes:	X N Z V C * * * * *
	The CCR is restored to its pre-exception state.

RTS	**Return from subroutine**
Operation:	[PC] ← [[SP]]; [SP] ← [SP]+4
Syntax:	RTS
Attributes:	Unsized
Description:	The program counter is pulled from the stack and the previous value of the PC is lost. RTS is used to terminate a subroutine.
Condition codes:	X N Z V C - - - - -

STOP	**Load status register and stop**

Operation:	IF [S]=1 THEN
	        [SR] ← <data>
	        STOP
	       ELSE TRAP

Syntax:	STOP #<data>
Sample syntax:	STOP #$2700 STOP #SetUp
Attributes:	Unsized
Description:	The immediate operand is copied into the entire status register (i.e. both status byte and CCR are modified), and the program counter advanced to point to the next instruction to be executed. The processor then suspends all further processing and halts. That is, the privileged STOP instruction stops the 68000. The execution of instructions resumes when a trace, an interrupt, or a reset exception occurs. A trace exception will occur if the trace bit is set when the STOP instruction is encountered. If an interrupt request arrives whose priority is higher than the current processor priority, an interrupt exception occurs, otherwise the interrupt request has no effect. If the bit of the immediate data corresponding to the S-bit is clear (i.e. user mode selected), execution of the STOP instruction will cause a privilege violation. An external reset will always initiate reset exception processing.
Condition codes:	X N Z V C * * * * * Set according to the literal.

SUB	Subtract binary
Operation:	[destination] ← [destination] − [source]
Syntax:	SUB <ea>,**Dn**
	SUB Dn,**<ea>**
Attributes:	Size=byte, word, longword
Description:	Subtract the source operand from the destination operand and store the result in the destination location.
Condition codes:	X N Z V C
	* * * * *

Source operand addressing modes

Dn	An	(An)	(An)+	−(An)	(d,An)	(d,An,Xi)	ABS.W	ABS.L	(d,PC)	(d,PC,Xn)	imm
✔	✔	✔	✔	✔	✔	✔	✔	✔	✔	✔	✔

Destination operand addressing modes

Dn	An	(An)	(An)+	−(An)	(d,An)	(d,An,Xi)	ABS.W	ABS.L	(d,PC)	(d,PC,Xn)	imm
✔		✔	✔	✔	✔	✔	✔	✔			

SUBA	Subtract address
Operation:	[destination] ← [destination] − [source]
Syntax:	SUBA <ea>,**An**
Attributes:	Size=word, longword
Description:	Subtract the source operand from the destination operand and store the result in the destination address register. Word operations are sign-extended to 32 bits prior to subtraction.
Condition codes:	X N Z V C
	- - - - -

Source operand addressing modes

Dn	An	(An)	(An)+	−(An)	(d,An)	(d,An,Xi)	ABS.W	ABS.L	(d,PC)	(d,PC,Xn)	imm
✔	✔	✔	✔	✔	✔	✔	✔	✔	✔	✔	✔

SUBI	Subtract immediate
Operation:	[destination] ← [destination] − [source]
Syntax:	SUBI #<data>,**<ea>**
Attributes:	Size=byte, word, longword
Description:	Subtract the immediate data from the destination operand. Store the result in the destination operand.
Condition codes:	X N Z V C
	* * * * *

Destination operand addressing modes

Dn	An	(An)	(An)+	−(An)	(d,An)	(d,An,Xi)	ABS.W	ABS.L	(d,PC)	(d,PC,Xn)	imm
✔		✔	✔	✔	✔	✔	✔	✔			

SUBQ	Subtract quick
Operation:	`[destination] ← [destination] − [source]`
Syntax:	`SUBQ #<data>,<`**ea**`>`
Attributes:	Size=byte, word, longword
Description:	Subtract the immediate data from the destination operand. The immediate data must be in the range 1 to 8. Word and longword operations on address registers do not affect condition codes. A word operation on an address register affects the entire 32-bit address.
Condition codes:	X N Z V C * * * * *

Destination operand addressing modes

Dn	An	(An)	(An)+	−(An)	(d,An)	(d,An,Xi)	ABS.W	ABS.L	(d,PC)	(d,PC,Xn)	imm
✔	✔	✔	✔	✔	✔	✔	✔	✔			

SUBX	Subtract extended
Operation:	`[destination] ← [destination] − [source] − [x]`
Syntax:	`SUBX Dx,`**Dy** `SUBX −(Ax),−`**(Ay)**
Attributes:	Size=byte, word, longword
Description:	Subtract the source operand from the destination operand along with the extend bit, and store the result in the destination location. The only legal addressing modes are data register direct and memory to memory with address register indirect using auto-decrementing.
Condition codes:	X N Z V C * * * * *

Z: Cleared if the result is non-zero, unchanged otherwise. The Z-bit can be used to test for zero after a chain of multiple precision operations.

SWAP	Swap register halves
Operation:	$[Register_{(16:31)}] ← [Register_{(0:15)}];$ $[Register_{(0:15)}] ← [Register_{(16:31)}]$
Syntax:	`SWAP Dn`
Attributes:	Size=word
Description:	Exchange the upper and lower 16-bit words of a data register.
Application:	The `SWAP  Dn` instruction enables the higher-order word in a register to take part in word operations by moving it into the lower-order position. `SWAP  Dn` is effectively equivalent to `ROR.L Di,`**Dn**, where [Di]=16. However, `SWAP` clears the C-bit of the CCR, whereas `ROR` sets it according to the last bit to be shifted into the carry bit.
Condition codes:	X N Z V C - * * 0 0

The N-bit is set if most-significant bit of the 32-bit result is set and cleared otherwise. The Z-bit is set if 32-bit result is zero and cleared otherwise.

TRAP	Trap

Operation:	`s ← 1;`
	`[SSP] ← [SSP] −4; [[SSP]] ← [PC];`
	`[SSP] ← [SSP] −2; [[SSP]] ← [SR];`
	`[PC] ←vector`

Syntax:	`Trap #<vector>`

Attributes:	Unsized
Description:	This instruction forces the processor to initiate exception processing. The vector number used by the TRAP instruction is in the range 0 to 15 and, therefore, supports 16 traps (i.e. TRAP #0 to TRAP #15).
Application:	The TRAP instruction is used to perform operating system calls and is system independent. That is, the effect of the call depends on the particular operating environment. For example, the University of Teesside 68000 simulator uses TRAP #15 to perform I/O. The ASCII character in D1.B is displayed by the following sequence.

```
MOVE.B #6,D0  Set up to display a character parameter in D0
TRAP   #15    Now call the operating system
```

Condition codes:	X N Z V C
	- - - - -

TST	Test an operand

Operation:	[CCR] ← tested ([operand])
	i.e. [operand] − 0; update CCR
Syntax:	TST <ea>
Attributes:	Size=byte, word, longword
Description:	The operand is compared with zero. No results is saved, but the contents of the CCR are set according to the results. The effect of TST <ea> is the same as CMPI #0,<ea> except that the CMPI instruction also sets/clears the V- and C-bits of the CCR.
Condition codes:	X N Z V C
	- * * 0 0

Source operand addressing modes

Dn	An	(An)	(An)+	−(An)	(d,An)	(d,An,Xi)	ABS.W	ABS.L	(d,PC)	(d,PC,Xn)	imm
✔		✔	✔	✔	✔	✔	✔	✔	✔	✔	

UNLK	Unlink

Operation:	[SP] ← [An]; [An] ← [[SP]]; [SP] ← [SP]+4
Syntax:	UNLK An
Attributes:	Unsized
Description:	The stack pointer is loaded from the specified address register and the old contents of the pointer are lost (this has the effect of collapsing the stack frame). The address register is then loaded with the longword pulled off the stack.
Application:	The UNLK instruction is used in conjuction with the LINK instruction. The LINK creates a stack frame at the start of a procedure, and the UNLK collapses the stack frame prior to a return from the procedure.
Condition codes:	X N Z V C
	- - - - -

BIBLIOGRAPHY

Logic, Computers Architecture, Computer Organization

Buchanan, William & Wilson, Austin. (2001) *Advanced PC Architecture*. Addison-Wesley.

Carpinelli, John, D. (2001) *Computer Systems Organization & Architecture*. Addison-Wesley.

Clements, Alan. (1997). *Microprocessor Systems Design (3rd edition)*. International Thomson Publishing.

Dowd, Kevin. (1993). *High Performance Computing*. O'Reilly & Associates Inc., Sebastopol, CA.

Furber, Steve. (1996). *ARM System Architecture*. Addison-Wesley, Harlow.

Hamacher, Carl V., Vranesic, Zvonko G., & Zaky, Safwat G. (2002). *Computer Organization (5th edition)*. McGraw-Hill.

Hayes, John P. (1998). *Computer Architecture and Organization (3rd edition)*. McGraw-Hill.

Heuring, Vincent P., Jordan, Harry E. (2004). *Computer Systems Design and Architecture* (Second edition). Prentice Hall.

Karp Alan H. & Flatt, Horace P. (1990). Measuring Parallel Processor Performance. *Communications of the ACM*, Vol. 33, No. 1, May 1990, pp539–543.

Mano, Morris M. & Kime, Charles R. (2000). *Logic and Computer Design Fundamentals*. Prentice Hall.

Null, Linda & Lobur, Julia. (2003). *The Essentials of Computer Organization and Architecture*. Jones and Bartlett Computer Science.

Patterson, David A. & Hennessy, John L. (2005). *Computer Organization & Design (3nd edition)*. Morgan Kaufmann Publishers, San Francisco.

Roth, Charles H. (1992). *Fundamentals of Logic Design (4th edition)*. West Publishing Company.

Sima, Dezso, Fountain, Terence & Kacsuk, Peter. (1997). *Advanced Computer Architectures—A Design Space approach*. Addison-Wesley.

Skahill, Kevin. (1996). *VHDL for Programmable Logic*. Addison-Wesley.

Sloss, Andrew N., Symes, Dominic & Wright, Chris. (2004). *ARM System Developer's Guide*. Elsevier.

Stallings, William. (2006). *Computer Organization and Architecture* (Seventh edition). Prentice Hall.

Tanenbaum, Andrew S. (2006). *Structured Computer Organization (Fifth edition)*. Prentice-Hall International.

Wakerly, John F. (2000). *Digital Design (3rd edition)*. Prentice Hall International Inc.

Warford, Stanley J. (1999). *Computer Systems*. Jones and Bartlett Publishers, Sudbury, MA.

Wilkinson, Barry. (1996). *Computer Architecture (2nd edition)*. Prentice Hall Europe.

Yarbrough, John M. (1997). *Digital Logic Applications and Design*. West Publishing Company.

Operating Systems

Bryant, Randal E. & O'Hallaron, David. (2003). *Computer Systems—a programmer's perspective*. Prentice Hall.

Cooling, Jim E. (1997). *Real-time Software Systems*. International Thomson Publishing.

Flynn, Ida M. & McIver McHoes, Ann, (1997). *Understanding Operating Systems (2nd edition)*. International Thomson Publishing.

Rajkumar, Davis. (2001). *Operating Systems—a systematic view*. Addison-Wesley.

Stallings, William. (2002). *Operating Systems—Internals and Design Principles (4th edition)*. Prentice-Hall International.

Williams, Rob. (2001). *Computer Systems Architecture—a networking approach*. Addison-Wesley.

Wolf, Wayne. (2001) *Computers as Components*. Morgan Kaufmann.

Memory Systems.

Bell, Alan E. (1996). *Next-Generation Compact Discs*. Scientific American, July 1996, pp28–37.

Burger, Doug & Goodman, James, R. (1997). *Billion-Transistor Architectures*. Computer, September 1997, pp46–48.

Gemmell, James D. et al. (1994). *Delay-Sensitive Multimedia on Disks*. IEEE Multimedia, Fall, 1994, pp56–66.

Hewlett-Packard. (1997). *Digital Modulation in Communications Systems—an Introduction*. Application Note 1298, Hewlett-Packard Company.

Hill, Mark D. (1988). *A Case for Direct-Mapped Caches*. Computer, December 1988, pp25–39.

Lubell, Peter D. (1995). *The Gathering Storm in High-Density Compact Disks*. IEEE Spectrum, August 1995, pp32–37.

Pohlmann, Ken C. (1992). *The Compact Disc Handbook*. Oxford University Press, Cambridge.

Prince, Betty (1999). *High Performance Memories (Revised edition)*. John Wiley & Sons, Ltd., Chichester.

Smith, Alan Jay (1983). *Cache Memories*. Computing Surveys, Vol. 14, No. 3, September 1982, pp473–530.

Williams, E. W. (1996). *The CD-ROM and Optical Disc Recording Systems*. Oxford University Press, Oxford.

I/O techniques, Peripherals.

Johnson, Barry W. (1987). *A Course on the Design of Reliable Digital Systems*. IEEE Transactions on Education, Vol. E-30, No. 1, February 1987, pp27–36.

Kuc, Roman (1999). *The Information Age*. Thomson learning.

Marven, Craig & Ewers, Gillian. (1996). *A Simple Approach to Digital Signal Processing*. John Wiley & Sons, Ltd., Chichester.

Morrison, T. P. (1997). *The Art of Computerized Measurement*. Oxford University Press, Oxford.

Schultz, Jerome S. (1991). *Biosensors*. Scientific American, August 1991, pp64–69.

Communications

Comer, Douglas E. (2003). *Computer Networks and Internets (4th Edition)*. Prentice Hall.

Halsall, Fred (1995). *Data Communications, Computer Networks and Open Systems (4th edition)*. Addison-Wesley.

Shay, William A. (1995). *Understanding Data Communications Systems*. International Thomson Publishing.

Stallings, William (2003). *Data and Computer Communications, (Seventh Edition)*. Prentice Hall.

Tanenbaum, Andrew S. (2002). *Computer Networks (Fourth edition)*. Prentice Hall.

Index

The Software Contained on the CD

The enclosed CD contains four major items of software, all of which run on IBM PCs and their clones. I have tested the software on several PCs under Windows 98 for the third edition and under Windows XP for this fourth edition. One item runs only under DOS.

• A 68000 processor DOS-based cross-assembler and simulator
• A 68000 processor Windows-based editor, cross-assembler and simulator
• A digital logic simulator
• A simulator for the ARM microprocessor
• Documentation for the 68000 processor family

These items are in separate directories and have appropriate readme files. You also need Adobe Acrobat Reader to view some of the information such as the Motorola and ARM's user manuals. The CD also contains copies of the Adobe Acrobat Reader that you can install if you do not already have it.

IT IS IMPORTANT THAT YOU APPRECIATE THAT NONE OF THE SOFTWARE IS OWNED BY OXFORD UNIVERSITY PRESS. ALL THE SOFTWARE WAS KINDLY SUPPLIED BY THIRD PARTIES FOR USE BY THE READERS OF THIS BOOK.

THIS SOFTWARE IS SUBJECT TO THE INDIVIDUAL CONDITIONS STATED BY THE APPROPRIATE COPYRIGHT HOLDERS.

THE SOFTWARE HAS BEEN SUPPLIED TO OUP ON THE CONDITION THAT IT IS NOT SUPPORTED.

ONE ITEM OF SOFTWARE ON THE CD, WINZIP, IS SUPPLIED AS A DEMONSTRATION COPY AND MAY NOT BE USED FOR MORE THAN 21 DAYS WITHOUT PAYMENT. This software is required only if you cannot unzip the ARM development software.

The four directories on the CD containing the above items are
• 68Ksim
• Digital
• ArmSim
• 68Kdocs
• Easy68K_4ed

I suggest that you copy 68Kdocs and 68Ksim to your hard disk. The DOS-based 68K simulator software simply has to be copied to your system and does not require any installation procedure. You simply run the appropriate X68K.EXE or E68K.EXE file from your DOS prompt. The Windows-based 68K simulator has to be installed.

NOTE When I tested the DOS-based 68K simulator I found that some of the demonstration files had become "read-only" in the transfer to the CD. This means that you will get an error message when you try and assemble them or run them. You can solve their problem by changing the attribute from read-only to read/write. this problem affected only the demonstration/test files.

NOTE The ARM software also includes a substantial amount of documentation including the ARM Reference Manual in the subdirectory PDF. Note also that I have already unzipped the ARM software on the CD and you will be able to find the documentation in ArmSim\ARM202U\PDF. The documentation goes well beyond the level of this text and has been included to allow readers to delve more deeply into the ARM's architecture.

The digital logic simulator, Digital Works, must be installed on your system. Similarly, you must unzip the ARM logic simulator files and install them on your hard disk.

The following is the testing schedule that was used to test this CD. Further information about the packages can be found in the CD's files and in the body of the text.

OUP have set up an online resource centre to support this book. Its URL is: www.oxfordtextbooks.co.uk/orc/clements4e

I can be contacted by email at a.clements@tees.ac.uk

CD Testing Schedule

This "testing schedule" has been devised to allow my "pre-release testers" to examine the software on this disk before it is released with *Principles of Computer Hardware*. It should also help other readers to get the software going. This software contains third-party utilities, simulators, and documentation (in Adobe's Portable Document Format).

1. Read the Readme.txt file in the root directory.

2. Install Adobe Acrobat Reader. The CD contains AdbeRdr70_enu_full.exe that will install Version 7 on a PC with Windows XP.

   You can also install Version 4 Adobe Acrobat Reader (for compatibility with the 3rd edition of the book) of using one of the two files ar40eng.exe or rs40eng.exe. The former is a Windows 95 version and the latter a Windows 98 version.

3. If you have Adobe acrobat Reader already installed or have just installed it, open the 68Kdocs directory and click on the 68Kprm.pdf file. This should enable you to read Motorola's definitive document on the 68000 family.

4. Test the 68K simulator. Open directory 68Ksim and click on the pdf document sim.pdf. This will open the guide to the use of the simulator software in Adobe Acrobat Reader.

5. Examine the other .txt files in directory 68Ksim.

6. Use an ASCII text editor to create a file, for example, TEST.X68 that contains a minimal 68K assembly language program. (You can use one of the 'demo' files provided on the CD.) Go into the DOS command-line mode on your PC and assemble the program with the command line X68K TEST -L.

   Note that you MUST not provide the extension .X68 or the assembly with fail. The extension, -L, is used to generate a listing file. That is, X68K TEST -L will generate TEST.BIN (if assembly is successful) and TEST.LIS.

If assembly succeeds (i.e. there are no errors in your source code), invoke the simulator from the DOS command line with the command E68K TEST.

You can test the simulator (if you have read the documentation) and then exit by using the Q (quit) command. This takes you back to the DOS command level. If you run a program that puts you in an infinite loop, you can get out by hitting the escape key.

NOTE that this directory contains several test files (i.e. Demo1.bin and Demo2.x68). You can assemble Demo1.x68 with the command X68K DEMO1 -L. You can then run the binary file with E68K DEOM1. To execute a program in the simulator type GO followed by a carriage return (i.e., the "enter" key).

7. Test Digital Works. Open the directory Digital and double click on dw20_95.exe to install Digital Works into the directory of your choice. If you change to the directory where Digital Works is located, double clicking on Digital.exe will run Digital Works. Note that Digital Works also puts a command on the Windows 98 Start/Programs menu.

The simplest way of testing Digital Works is to select a gate my moving the cursor to it and then clicking on that gate's icon. Then move the cursor to the work area and then click again. A copy of the gate should be moved to the work area.

8. Test the ARM simulator. This is the most complex software on the CD and, for the purpose of *The Principles of Computer Hardware* you will be using only a fraction of its capabilities. Note that the package includes considerable documentation in Adobe's PDF format.

You must first install the ARM software. I have provided 202u_w32_v1.zip which is the package I downloaded from ARM's university web site. The directory ARM202U was created by unzipping 202u_w32_v1.zip.

When I tested this package, I first unzipped the files to C:\ which created the directory 'C:\ARM202U' containing the unzipped files and subdirectories. I then changed the name of the directory to 'C:\ARM200' to suit the software's initial default paths to its \BIN and \LIB directories.

The following provides an introduction to testing this software:

a. Put the file clements.s (the test program written by me and located in directory ARMsim) in C:\ARM200\BIN.

b. Run the simulator package from Windows by clicking on Apm.exe in the \BIN directory.

c. Use the Project pull-down menu and select 'New Project'

d. Give the project a name and save the project in the C:\ARM200\BIN directory. This will create an 'Edit Project' window that asks for files to include.

e. If you have created a source file with the extension .S (e.g. CLEMENTS.S) add it to the project and click OK.

I have created CLEMENTS.S for you to test. You should have copied this to the \BIN directory.

f. Note that the system needs to know where the compiler, etc., is. Click on 'Options' and select 'Directories'. You will probably have to give the path of the compiler, etc. on your own system if you have not used the path C:\ARM200\BIN.

g. From the Project pull-down menu select 'Build name.APJ', where 'name' is the name of the project. You should get a 'Build complete' message if your source code had no errors.

h. From the Project pull-down menu select 'Debug name.APJ' to enter the debugger/simulator mode.

i. In the debugger you can use the 'View' pull-down menu to see registers, etc. Select the 'User registers' menu. This system loads the program at 8080 hexadecimal. Change the PC to 8080 by clicking on it.

j. You can now run the code line-by-line with the step into command (one of the icons on the debugger toolbar).

k. Note—from the "Project" pull-down menu you can edit your source code.

9. Test the 68K Windows-based simulator. This is a system created by a team led by Chuck Kelly. The software is available in the public domain and I would suggest that you obtain the latest version from the Internet at www.monroeccc.edu/ckelly/easy68k.htm. The version in this CD has been included to ensure that all readers have a copy of this software.

a. Click on SetupEASy68K/exe to install EASy68K. Installation puts the software in a sub-directory EASy68k (we've created this directory on the CD).

b. The sub-directory EASy68k contains several files including EDIT68k.exe and SIM68k.exe. If you double-click on EDIT68k.exe, you will invoke a text editor that uses a template for a 68K assembly language program. You can type your 68K assembly language into this template and save it. The EDIT68k program is intuitive to use and has a 'Help' function.

c. You can assemble a program from within the editor. Select the 'Project' tab in the editor window to get the 'Assemble source' option. Left-click on this and your program will be assembled. If you make any errors, you will have to re-edit the source. If there are no errors, you can select the 'Close' button and exit, or the 'Execute' button to enter the simulator.

d. If you select the 'Execute' button, the 68K simulator is invoked. Now you can run the code to its completion or execute it line-by-line. The simulator displays the 68K's register and you can also open memory or stack windows. The F7 function key can be used to execute code an instruction at a time.

Last modified on 14 July 2005

CD-ROM conditions of use and copyrights

Please read these terms before proceeding with the CD installation. By installing the CD you agree to be bound by these terms, including the terms applicable to the software described below.

The enclosed CD contains four major items of software, all of which run on IBM PCs and their clones. One item runs only under DOS.

- A 68000 cross-assembler and simulator
- A digital logic simulator
- A simulator the ARM microprocessor
- Documentation for the 68000 family

These items are in separate directories and have appropriate "readme" files. You also need Adobe Acrobat Reader to view some of the information such as Motorola and ARM's user manuals. The CD also contains a copy of the Adobe Acrobat Reader that you can install if you do not already have it.

The materials contained on this CD-ROM have been supplied by the author of the book. Whilst every effort has been made to check the software routines and the text, there is always the possibility of error and users are advised to confirm the information in this product through independent sources.

Alan Clements and/or his licensors grant you a non-exclusive licence to use this CD to search, view and display the contents of this CD on a single computer at a single location and to print off multiple screens from the CD for your own private use or study. All rights not expressly granted to you are reserved to Alan Clements and/or his licensors, and you shall not adapt, modify, translate, reverse engineer, decompile or disassemble any part of the software on this CD, except to the extent permitted by law.

These terms shall be subject to English laws and the English courts shall have jurisdiction.

THIS CD-ROM IS PROVIDED 'AS IS' WITHOUT WARRANTY OF ANY KIND, EXPRESS OR IMPLIED, INCLUDING BUT NOT LIMITED TO IMPLIED WARRANTIES OF SATISFACTORY QUALITY OR FITNESS FOR A PARTICULAR PURPOSE. IN NO EVENT SHALL ANYONE ASSOCIATED WITH THIS PRODUCT BE LIABLE FOR ANY DIRECT, INDIRECT, SPECIAL, CONSEQUENTIAL, OR INCIDENTAL DAMAGES RESULTING FROM ITS USE.

THIS SOFTWARE IS SUBJECT TO THE INDIVIDUAL CONDITIONS STATED BY THE APPROPRIATE COPYRIGHT HOLDERS WHICH ARE GIVEN BELOW AND ON THE CD WALLET COVER.

THE SOFTWARE IS NOT SUPPORTED.

ONE ITEM OF SOFTWARE ON THE CD, WINZIP, IS SUPPLIED AS A DEMONSTRATION COPY AND MAY NOT BE USED FOR MORE THAN 21 DAYS WITHOUT PAYMENT. This software is required only if you cannot unzip the ARM development software.

DIGITAL WORKS 95 VERSION 2.04 is © John Barker 2000. TERMS OF USE: Digital Works 95 version 2.04 (The Product) shall only be used by the individual who purchased this book. The Product may not be used for profit or commercial gain. The Product shall only be installed on a single machine at any one time. No part of the Product shall be made available over a Wide Area Network or the internet. The title and copyright in all parts of the Product remain the property of David John Baker. The Product and elements of the Product may not be reverse engineered, sold, lent, displayed, hired out or copied. It shall only be installed on a single machine at any one time.
M6800PM/AD—MOTOROLA M68000 FAMILY PROGRAMMERS REFERENCE MANUAL Copyright of Motorola. Used by permission.

Schedule 2

Shrinkwrap Agreement

End User Licence Agreement for the ARM Software Development Toolkit 2.02u Version 2

IMPORTANT READ CAREFULLY PRIOR TO ANY INSTALLATION OR USE OF THE SOFTWARE

You are in possession of certain software ("Software") identified in the attached Schedule 1. The Software is owned by ARM Limited ("ARM") or its licensors and is protected by copyright laws and international copyright treaties as well as other intellectual property laws and treaties. The Software is licensed not sold. You were advised, at the time that the Software was provided to you, that any use, by you, of the Software will be regulated by the terms and conditions of this Agreement ("Agreement").

ACCEPTANCE

If you agree with and accept the terms and conditions of this Agreement it shall become a legally binding agreement between you and ARM Limited and you may proceed to install, copy and use the Software in accordance with the terms and conditions of the Agreement.

REJECTION AND RIGHT TO A REFUND

If you do not agree with or do not wish to be bound by the terms and conditions of this Agreement you may NOT install, copy or use the Software.

TERMS AND CONDITIONS

1. Software Licence Grant

ARM hereby grants to you, subject to the terms and conditions of this Agreement, a non-exclusive, non-transferable, worldwide licence, solely for non-commercial purposes, to;

- use and copy the Software identified in Schedule 1 Part A and Schedule 1 Part B;
- incorporate into software application programs that you develop, the Software identified in Schedule 1 Part B; and
- use the documentation identified in Schedule 1 Part C.

2. Restrictions on Use of the Software

Except for the making of one additional copy of the Software for backup purposes only, copying of the Software by you is limited to the extent necessary for; (a) use of the Software on a single computer; and (b) incorporation into software application programs developed by you as permitted under the terms of this Agreement.

Except to the extent that such activity is permitted by applicable law you shall not reverse engineer, decompile or disassemble any of the Software identified in Schedule 1 Part A. If the Software was provided to you in Europe you shall not reverse engineer, decompile or disassemble any of the Software identified in Schedule 1 Part A for the purposes of error correction.

You shall only use the Software on a single computer connected to a single monitor at any one time except that you may use the Software from a common disc running on a server and shared by multiple computers provided that one authorised copy of the Software has been licensed for each computer concurrently using the Software.

You shall not make copies of the documentation identified in Schedule 1 Part B.

You acquire no rights to the Software other than as expressly provided by this Agreement.

You shall not remove from the Software any copyright notice or other notice and shall ensure that any such notice is reproduced in any copies of the whole or any part of the Software made by you.

3. No Support

For the avoidance of doubt, this license to use the Software does not provide you with any right to receive any support and maintenance in respect of the Software.

4. Restrictions on Transfer of Licensed Rights

The rights granted to you under this agreement may not be assigned, sublicensed or otherwise transferred by you to any third party without the prior written consent of ARM. You shall not rent or lease the Software.

5. Limitation of Liability

THE SOFTWARE IS LICENSED "AS IS". ARM EXPRESSLY DISCLAIMS ALL REPRESENTATIONS, WARRANTIES, CONDITIONS OR OTHER TERMS, EXPRESS OR IMPLIED, INCLUDING WITHOUT LIMITATION THE IMPLIED WARRANTIES OF NON-INFRINGEMENT, SATISFACTORY QUALITY AND FITNESS FOR A PARTICULAR PURPOSE.

TO THE MAXIMUM EXTENT PERMITTED BY APPLICABLE LAW, IN NO EVENT SHALL ARM BE LIABLE FOR ANY INDIRECT, SPECIAL, INCIDENTAL OR CONSEQUENTIAL DAMAGES (INCLUDING LOSS OF PROFITS) ARISING OUT OF THE USE OR INABILITY TO USE THE SOFTWARE WHETHER BASED ON A CLAIM UNDER CONTACT, TORT OR OTHER LEGAL THEORY, EVEN IF ARM WAS ADVISED OF THE POSSIBILITY OF SUCH DAMAGES. ARM does not seek to limit or exclude liability for death or personal injury arising from ARM's negligence and because some jurisdictions do not permit the exclusion or limitation of liability for consequential or incidental damages the above limitation relating to liability for consequential damages may not apply to you.

6. Term and Termination

This Agreement shall remain in force until terminated by you or by ARM.

Without prejudice to any of its other rights if you are in breach of any of the terms and conditions of this Agreement then ARM may terminate the Agreement immediately upon giving written notice to you.

You may terminate this Agreement at any time.

Upon termination of this Agreement by you or by ARM you shall stop using the Software and destroy all copies of the Software in your possession together with all documentation and related materials.

The provisions of Clauses 5, 6 and 7 shall survive termination of the Agreement.

7. General

This Agreement is governed by English Law.

This is the only agreement between you and ARM relating to the Software and it may only be modified by written agreement between you and ARM. This Agreement may not be modified by purchase orders, advertising or other representation by any person.

If any Clause in this Agreement is held by a court of law to be illegal or unenforceable the remaining provisions of the Agreement shall not be affected thereby.

The failure by ARM to enforce any of the provisions of this Agreement, unless waived in writing, shall not constitute a waiver of ARM's rights to enforce such provision or any other provision of the Agreement in the future.

Use, copying or disclosure by the US Government is subject to the restrictions set out in subparagraph (c)(1)(ii) of the Rights in Technical Data and Computer Software clause at DFARS 252.227 7013 or subparagraphs (c)(1) and (2) of the Commercial Computer Software – Restricted Rights at 48 CFR 52.227-19, as applicable.

You agree that you will not export or re-export the Software to any country, person or entity or end user subject to U.S.A. export restrictions. Restricted countries currently include, but are not necessarily limited to, Cuba, Iran, Iraq, Libya, North Korea, Syria and the Federal Republic of Yugoslavia (Serbia and Montenegro, U.N. Protected Areas and areas of Bosnia and Herzegovina under the control of Bosnian Serb forces).